POGO

POGO

by WALT KELLY

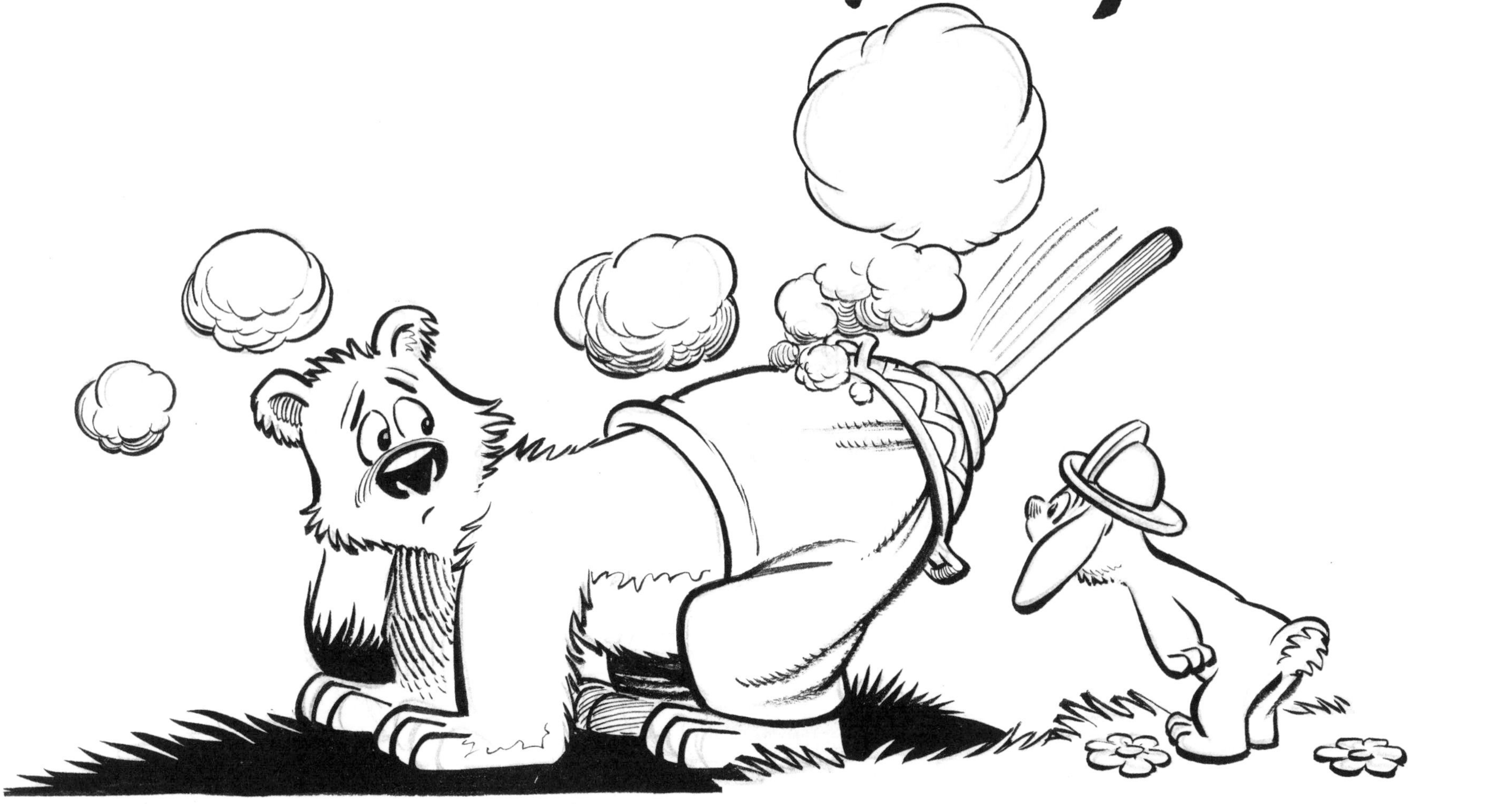

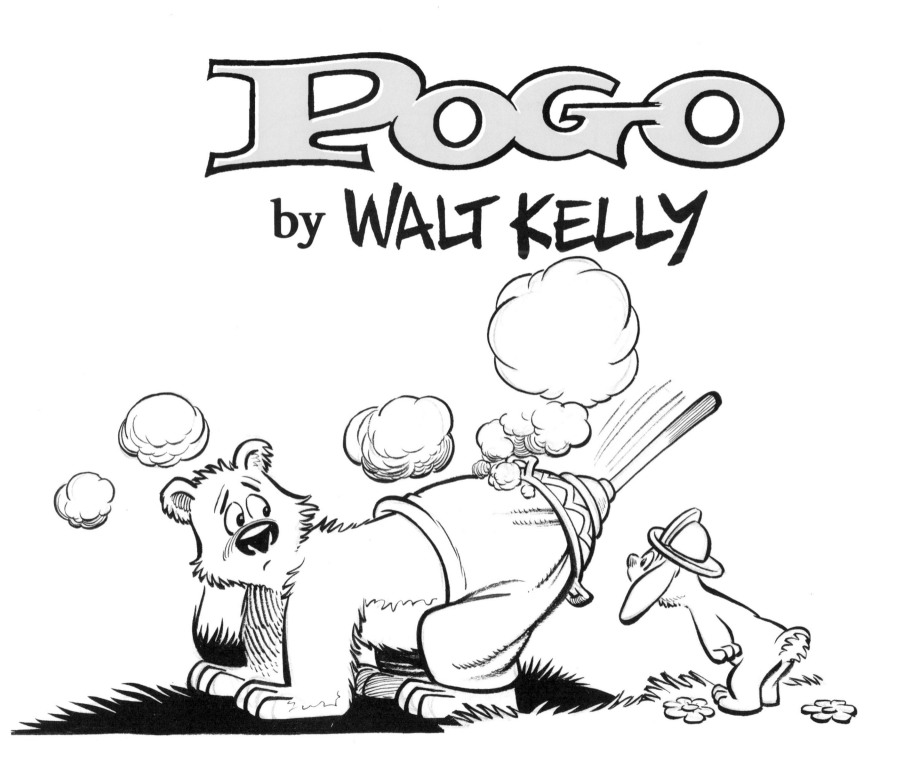

Under The Bamboozle Bush

THE COMPLETE SYNDICATED COMIC STRIPS

VOLUME 4

Editors: Mark Evanier & Eric Reynolds
Editors Emeritus: Carolyn Kelly & Kim Thompson
Series Design: Carolyn Kelly
Production: Paul Baresh
Digital Art Restoration: Paul Baresh and Chi-Wen Lee
Cover Art: Walt Kelly, painted by Linda Medley
Associate Publisher: Eric Reynolds
Publisher: Gary Groth

Under the Bamboozle Bush, the title for this volume, was found among Walt Kelly's papers.

ISBN: 978-1-60699-863-2

First printing: November 2017
Printed in Korea

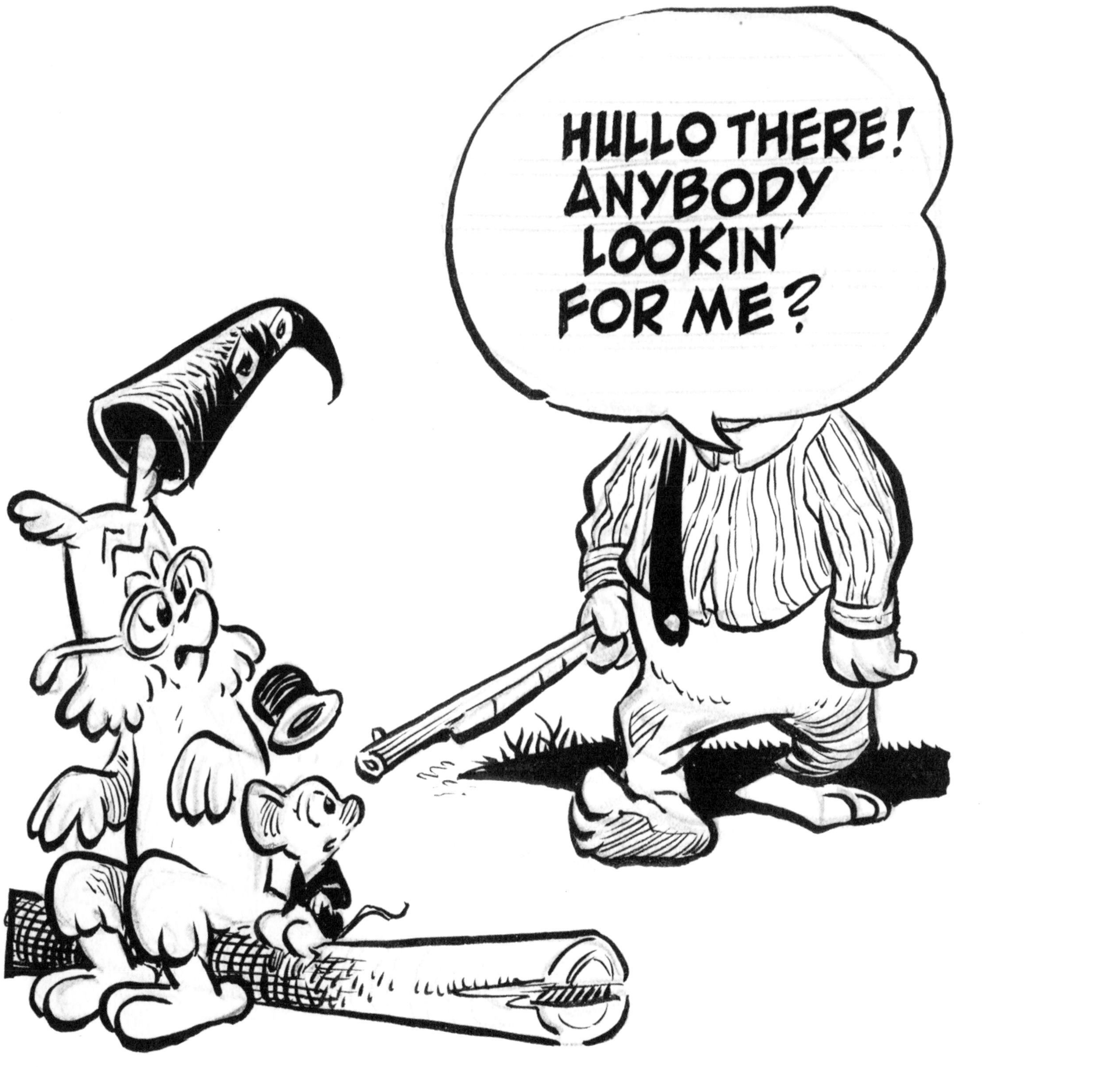
HULLO THERE! ANYBODY LOOKIN' FOR ME?

Newsweek—Ed Wergeles

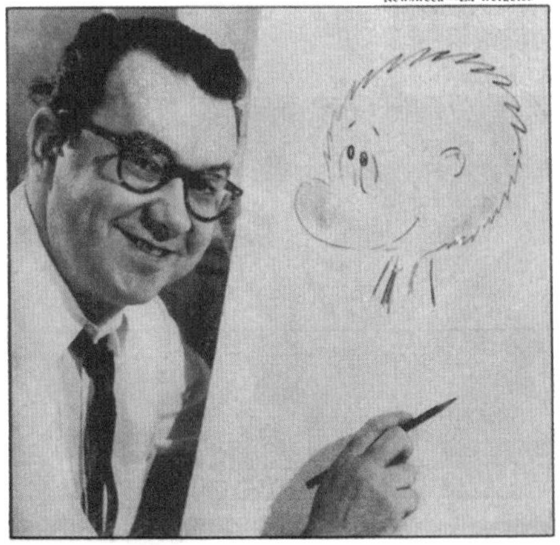

Creator of Pogo Composes a Gay Carol

Almost since the first Nativity Night, hymns and carols have poured out of the hearts of Christians. Some, like "Angels We Have Heard on High" or "O Little Town of Bethlehem" have been purely religious in telling the Christmas story. Secular-sounding carols, equally popular, have emphasized the jollity, the smoking wassail bowls, the holly and the ivy, the boar's head "bedecked with bays and rosemary." But almost all of them, both hymn and carol–and many carols are hymns–have been written by men who just felt like expressing what Christmas meant to them.

The latest to join the ranks of carol lyricists and composers is Walt Kelly, creator of Pogo and all the other denizens of the Okefenokee Swamp, the famous and greatly loved comic-strip characters who disport themselves in Christmas gaiety on NEWSWEEK's cover this week. To Kelly, carols should be as frolicking as the old ring dances of medieval Europe from which they literally sprang. On the opposite page is Kelly's brand-new carol, "Bright Christmas Land," appearing for the first time in NEWSWEEK, which, he notes, should be sung "with decorous abandon." The cartoonist describes his modern carol as "a dancing song and is meant to convey the thought that you're in a bright Christmas land where you love all men. This should be the goal of all Christians."

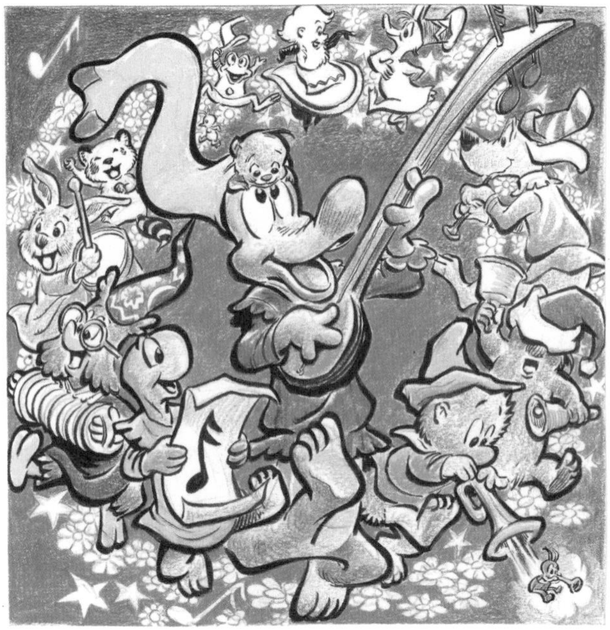

Walt Kelly was a cartoonist, but he was also, at heart, a newspaperman, as likely to keep company with reporters as his fellow comic strip creators. Often, newspapers and magazines, since he knew their editors personally, called on him for illustrations, sometimes of Pogo, sometimes of a political bent.

The possum with the striped shirt adorned the cover of *Newsweek* twice — the first time being on the June 21, 1954 issue. Pogo was newsworthy that week because Kelly had appeared at the Library of Congress in Washington to deliver a copy of *Pogo*, the first of many paperback reprints of the strip issued by the publishing firm of Simon and Schuster. Press releases of the day said it was the first time a newspaper comic strip artist had been invited to submit work to the collection there.

Pogo returned to *Newsweek*'s cover—along with many of his friends—for the Christmas issue the following year, which was cover-dated December 26. Kelly reportedly executed the painting in a great hurry, using whatever paints he had on hand in his studio. They would appear to be poster paints, not oil or some other medium perhaps more suited for the task.

These were Pogo's two appearances on *Newsweek*. But, Kelly also painted Dwight Eisenhower for them in 1952, and it was not uncommon for his handiwork, or news of his goings-on, to appear within.

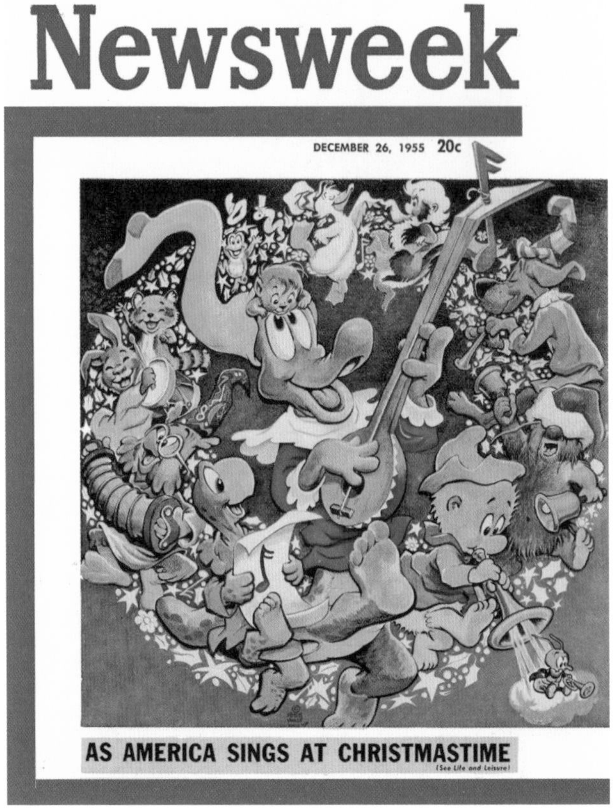
Newsweek
DECEMBER 26, 1955 20c
AS AMERICA SINGS AT CHRISTMASTIME
(See Life and Leisure)

Top left: From the December 26, 1955 issue of *Newsweek*, which featured Kelly's Christmas-themed cover painting. **Top right:** Kelly's preliminary "rough" of that cover. **Right:** The final cover, as printed. **Opposite:** A 2017 scan of the final painting.

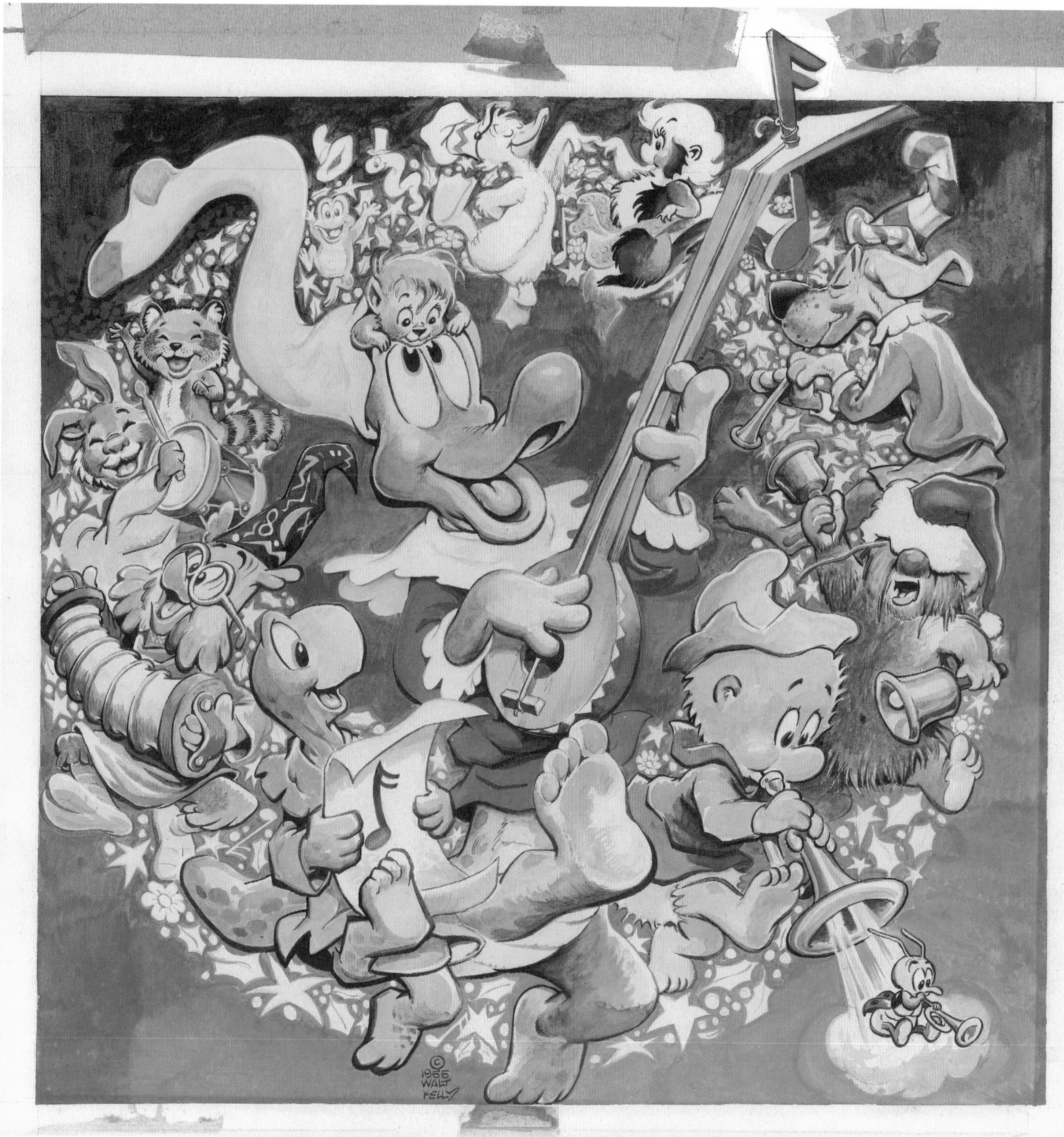
©
1955
WALT
KELLY

EDITOR'S NOTE

This editorial is going to sound like a rerun. It was not that long ago that we were apologizing for the lateness of a volume but we had a good reason: The death of one of its co-editors, Kim Thompson, who lost a brave struggle with cancer in June of 2013.

This time out, we apologize for the lateness of this volume but we have a good reason: The death of one of its co-editors, Carolyn Kelly, who lost a brave struggle with cancer in April of 2017.

Kim was replaced by Eric Reynolds, who is in excellent health. Carolyn has been replaced by Mark Evanier, who thinks he's in excellent health and had a colonoscopy just to make sure. He is writing this piece about his "companion" (as they say) of close to twenty years. The books will now come out when they're supposed to come out and the series will be completed.

It has to be. He promised Carolyn.

She was, of course, the daughter of Walt Kelly, the man whose genius is being both preserved and made available by this series. There have been many collections lately of the full run of classic comics but no one was ever done with more passion and diligence than this one. For Carolyn, it was not just a great newspaper strip. It was the Family Jewels and the masterpiece of a man she loved dearly.

The first volumes were rough. Even after exhaustive searches, we could not find quality source material for many of the early strips. Slipping gently out of the third person, I wish you could have seen the diligence and devotion with which Carolyn attacked the task of retouching and restoring bad photostats into good ones. It took longer than forever. Some of it was done in Adobe Photoshop on one of my computers. Some was done with good, old-fashioned ink and brush (sometimes one of her father's brushes) at my drawing table. She was a very fine artist, quite adept at aping his beautiful style.

You saw that on the covers and throughout Volumes 1–3. You'll see more of it in the last volume of this series, when we reprint the *Pogo* strips done years after Walt's passing. Many of them were drawn by Carolyn. She was also a fine designer with considerable experience in art-directing books. Her overall designs here will remain, partly because I promised her but also because we could not improve on them.

I loved this woman dearly. From what I was able to discern, everyone who ever met her loved her but I was the fortunate guy who got to love her dearly, up close and personal, for almost two decades. It was not nearly enough. And yes, I know her father once had Porky Pine say, "Don't take life so serious, son, it ain't nohow permanent." I guess Walt and Porky gave some good advice there but it's just sometimes hard to apply it.

— Mark Evanier

DEDICATED TO MISS CAROLYN K.
1945–2017

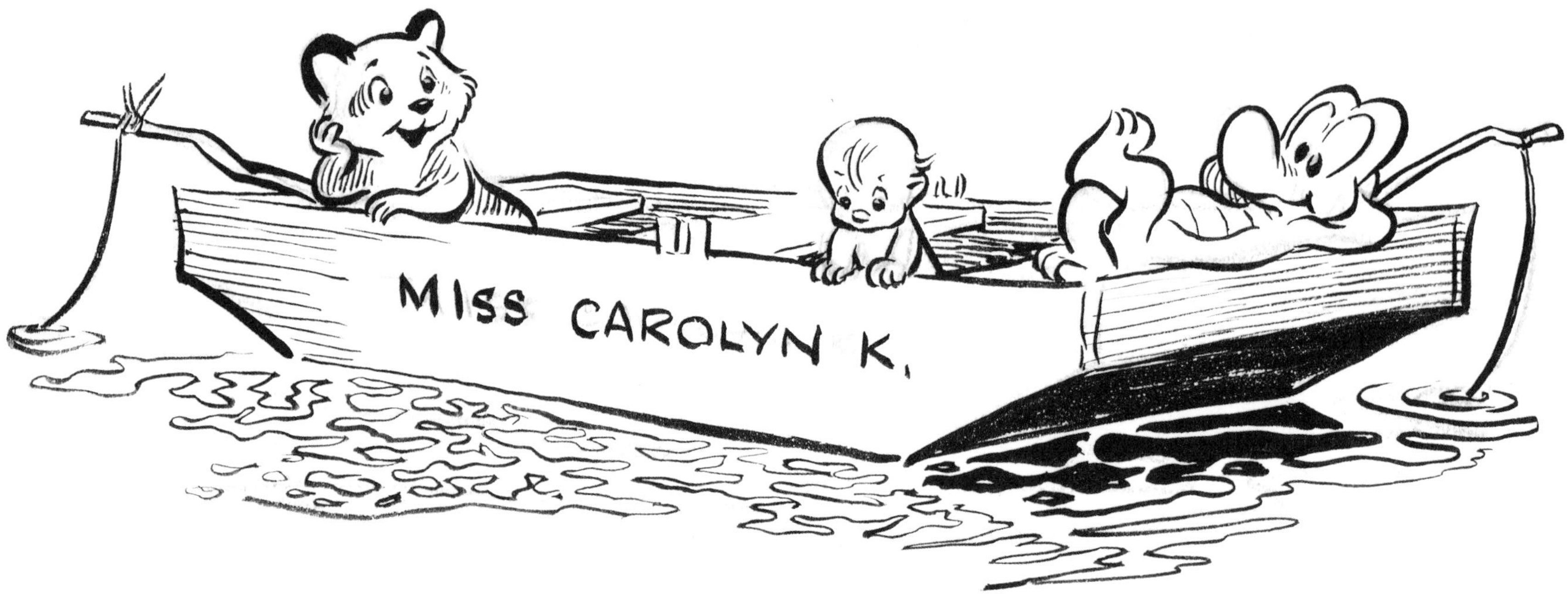
MISS CAROLYN K.

FOREWORD

By Neil Gaiman

The best break anybody ever gets is in bein' alive in the first place. An' you don't understan' what a perfect deal it is until you realises that you ain't gone be stuck with it forever, either.

— *Porky Pine, September 12, 1955*

Mark Evanier, as far as I have been able to establish over the last thirty-something years, knows everybody in the whole world. At this point, I have no doubt that you, person reading this introduction, also know Mark, and I am certain that he has several interesting anecdotes about the time you spent together.

He is a nice man, nice in a positive way—I enjoy his company, and do not know anyone who has a bad word to say about him—rather than as an absence of character. He can also be, for a big man, relatively inconspicuous: many of his most interesting stories have Mark interacting with people slightly less well-balanced than he is. He is a perfect wingman if you need to, for example, get a vegetarian haggis smuggled into America. He is also modest, so will have been made extremely uncomfortable by me starting this introduction about a book written and drawn by someone else, with two paragraphs about him.

I like to have dinner with Mark when I'm in LA. It's not something that happens as much as it should: often I'm not in LA long enough. But when we can, we get together and catch up. Mark tends to bring a friend. Sometimes it's someone like Sergio Aragonés (there is actually nobody like Sergio Aragonés, there is only Sergio. But he is an example of someone unique and larger than life, and Mark knows lots of people like that). And, about a decade ago, Mark started to show up for dinner with Carolyn

Kelly. She was just as clever and just as nice as Mark was. She was modest and funny. I didn't know she was an artist for the first couple of dinners, and then Mark explained that Carolyn was Walt Kelly's daughter.

She would tell stories about learning to draw literally on her father's knee.

I didn't ask many questions about Walt Kelly. I would not have known what to ask. My eyes became much rounder, though, when she told me about him, and about the project of reprinting *Pogo*.

I bought the first books in the series you are holding when they came out. I loved *Pogo* but was coming to it now in a new way, from the beginning, day by day, experiencing the daily pace of a newspaper strip.

And then Carolyn got sick.

And then she died.

I wish I'd known her better. I was left with memories of someone with a sweet smile, someone who loved to draw, someone who took a family legacy seriously, but life less so.

"Don't take life so serious son," as Porky Pine said to all of us. "It ain't no how permanent."

Like so many things in my life, *Pogo* came in upside down and backwards. My first exposure to it was in parody form in the old *Mad* paperbacks, and from a huge stack of ancient *Mad* magazines I bought in a secondhand bookshop in Thornton Heath. ("1961! The last upside down year until 6009"). I did not have any experience of what was being parodied, but I got the idea: *Pogo* was a newspaper comic about animals living in a swamp.

The next encounter was through Alan Moore's writing and Shawn McManus's cartooning in an episode of *Swamp Thing* called 'Pog.' Written in sub-joycean alien slanguage, it was the story of cartoonish, sweet aliens who come to Earth, land in a Louisiana swamp, and find that Earth is a harder and less welcoming place than they had hoped. It was the first comic ever to make me... well, not cry, obviously, because I was just 24 back then and as hardbitten as they come, but definitely blink rapidly because of the tears. I don't think I made the connection between Pog and Pogo, between Albert and Bartle, until I read an interview with Alan, and then I knew I had to find the Walt Kelly material for myself.

My friend John Clute showed me some of his treasured *Pogo* comic books, with Pogo and Albert stories all colored in and paced and told as comics, and then, in a strange secondhand bookshop located in an abandoned hospital (all the wards, even all the showers, were filled with bookshelves) I found an ancient copy of *Pogo*, and of *I Go Pogo*, and, finally, in black and white, I was in love. Pogo and Albert, Howland Owl and Churchy La Femme, Miz Hebzibah, Porky Pine, and the rest of them had entered my life, and they were never going to leave.

And now that these big *Pogo* collections exist, I'm in love all over again. It's like meeting a girl you knew when you were young, running into her again in your declining years, and finding that she's cleverer, nicer, more sincere and just as pretty as she was when you were both teenagers.

The art is as gorgeous as it always was. The lines, those perfect ink lines, each made with humor and assuredness, are a delight. The panels are as brilliantly composed, the lettering as intrinsic to the layout and to the look of every panel as it is to the script. It's something unique to comics, as Walt Kelly's lettering is part of both the writing and of the art: each character talks in its own way, in a mixture of patois, shorthand, and vaudeville routines, transmuted by Kelly's genius into a hybrid of Lewis Carroll and James Joyce by way of the Florida Swamps.

Things happen in their time. When I read the *Pogo* collections at first I responded to the humanity in the stories: the politics seemed to be that of bygone days. Now, the politics seem to be burningly pertinent, and bygone days are now. There were moments in the last US election cycle where I found myself observing, with wonderment, that *Pogo* jokes from sixty years earlier had surfaced once again. (For example, a candidate for Vice President who is concerned people will think he is in favor of vice.)

In these uncertain times, *Pogo* feels necessary, feels relevant, feels ever-more-right. And I miss Walt Kelly, who I never knew, and I miss Carolyn Kelly, who I did.

---

*Neil Gaiman is a best-selling author of award-winning novels for adults (*American Gods, Neverwhere*) and novels for younger readers (including the Newbery Medal-winning* The Graveyard Book, *and* Coraline, *on which the Academy Award-nominated film,* Coraline, *was based). He wrote comics before it was cool to write comics, including* Sandman.

DAILY STRIPS

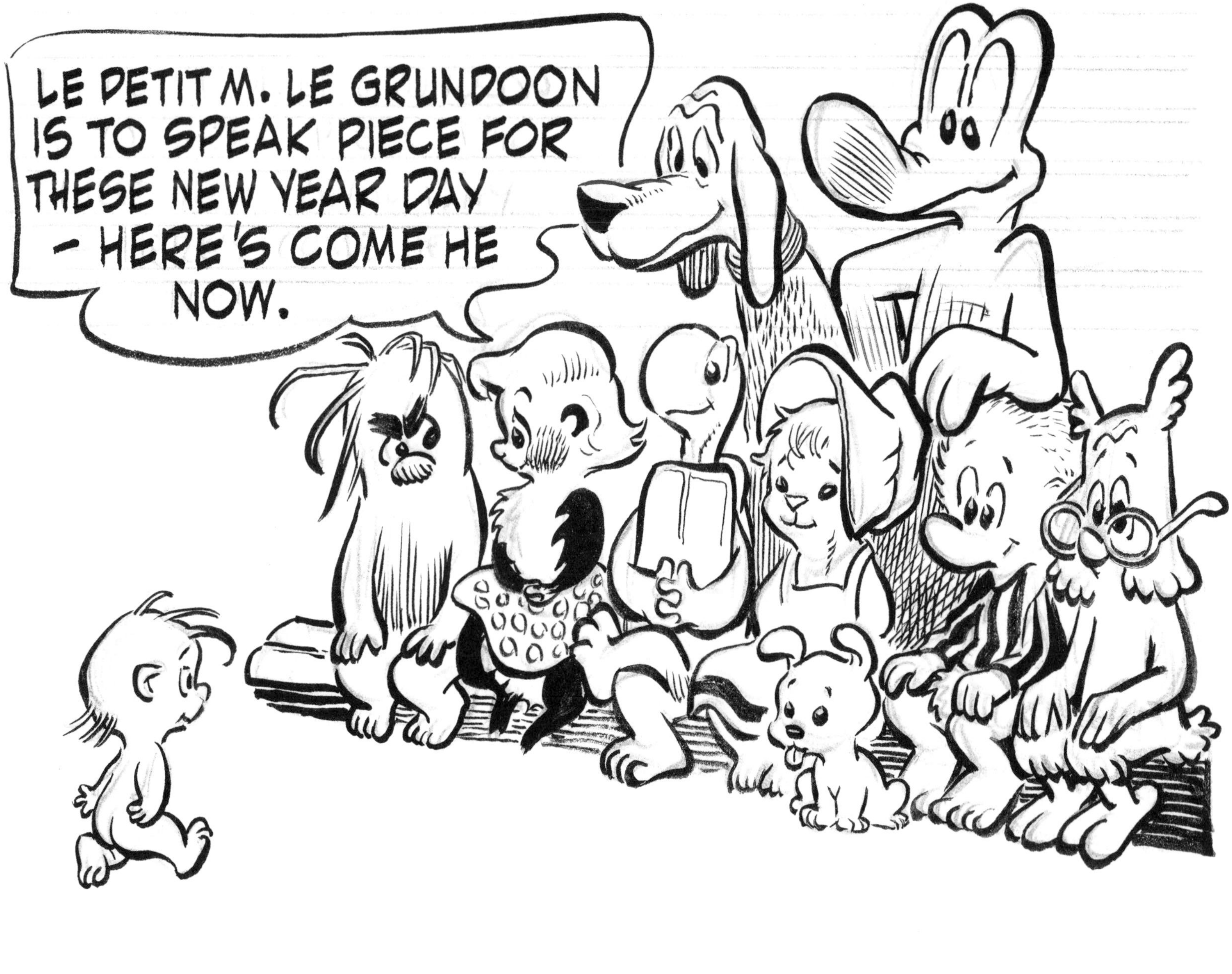
LE PETIT M. LE GRUNDOON IS TO SPEAK PIECE FOR THESE NEW YEAR DAY - HERE'S COME HE NOW.

JANUARY 1, 1955

LE PETIT M. LE GRUNDOON IS TO SPEAK PIECE FOR THESE NEW YEAR DAY - HERE'S COME HE NOW.
JANUARY FIRST, NINETEEN FIFTY-FIVE
POST HALL SYNDICATE
HE IS **EMBARRASS!** -- SEE -- HE IS FORGET THE **COSTUME**.
COPR 1955 WALT KELLY
HAPPY 1955

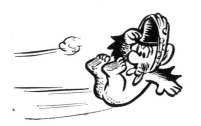

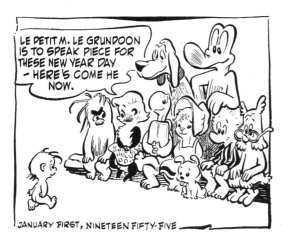

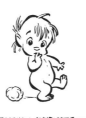

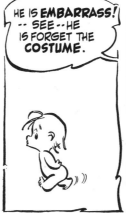

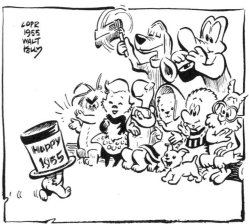

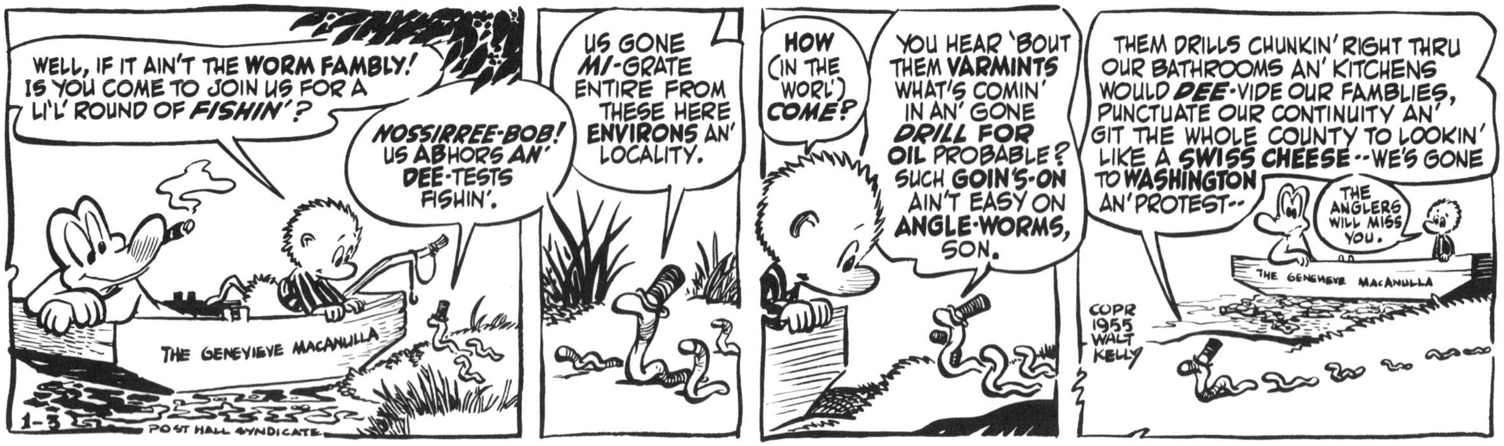
WELL, IF IT AIN'T THE WORM FAMBLY! IS YOU COME TO JOIN US FOR A LI'L' ROUND OF FISHIN'?
NOSSIRREE-BOB! US ABHORS AN' DEE-TESTS FISHIN'.
THE GENEVIEVE MACANULLA
1-3
POST HALL SYNDICATE
US GONE MI-GRATE ENTIRE FROM THESE HERE ENVIRONS AN' LOCALITY.
HOW (IN THE WORL') COME?
YOU HEAR 'BOUT THEM VARMINTS WHAT'S COMIN' IN AN' GONE DRILL FOR OIL PROBABLE? SUCH GOIN'S-ON AIN'T EASY ON ANGLE-WORMS, SON.
THEM DRILLS CHUNKIN' RIGHT THRU OUR BATHROOMS AN' KITCHENS WOULD DEE-VIDE OUR FAMBLIES, PUNCTUATE OUR CONTINUITY AN' GIT THE WHOLE COUNTY TO LOOKIN' LIKE A SWISS CHEESE -- WE'S GONE TO WASHINGTON AN' PROTEST--
THE ANGLERS WILL MISS YOU.
THE GENEVIEVE MACANULLA
COPR 1955 WALT KELLY

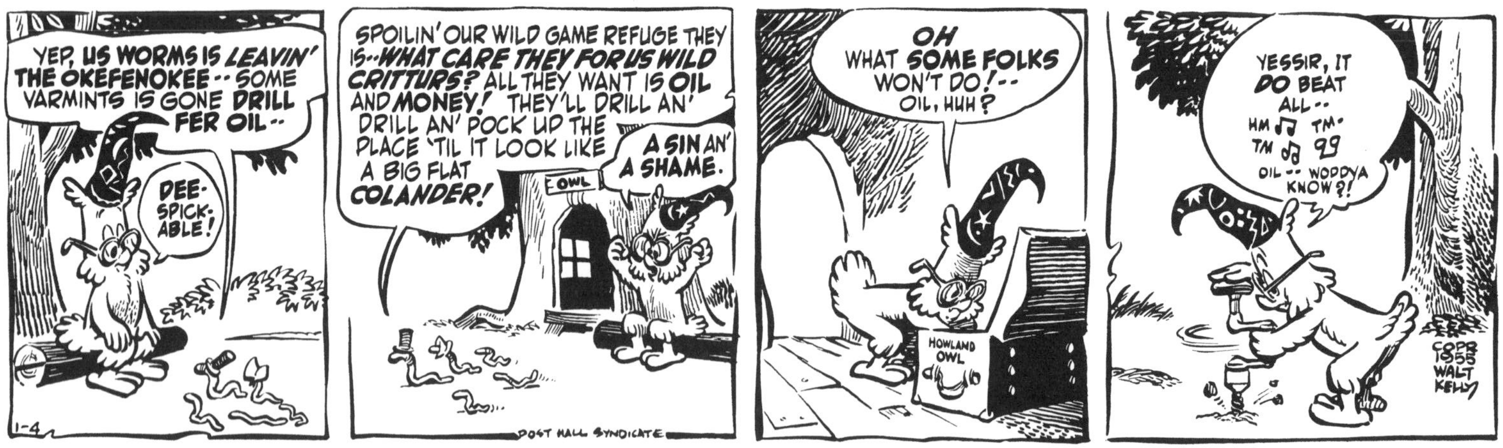
YEP, US WORMS IS LEAVIN' THE OKEFENOKEE -- SOME VARMINTS IS GONE DRILL FER OIL--
DEE-SPICK-ABLE!
1-4
SPOILIN' OUR WILD GAME REFUGE THEY IS--WHAT CARE THEY FOR US WILD CRITTURS? ALL THEY WANT IS OIL AND MONEY! THEY'LL DRILL AN' DRILL AN' POCK UP THE PLACE 'TIL IT LOOK LIKE A BIG FLAT COLANDER!
A SIN AN' A SHAME.
OWL
POST HALL SYNDICATE
OH WHAT SOME FOLKS WON'T DO!-- OIL, HUH?
HOWLAND OWL
YESSIR, IT DO BEAT ALL--
HM TM- TM
OIL -- WODDYA KNOW?!
COPR 1955 WALT KELLY

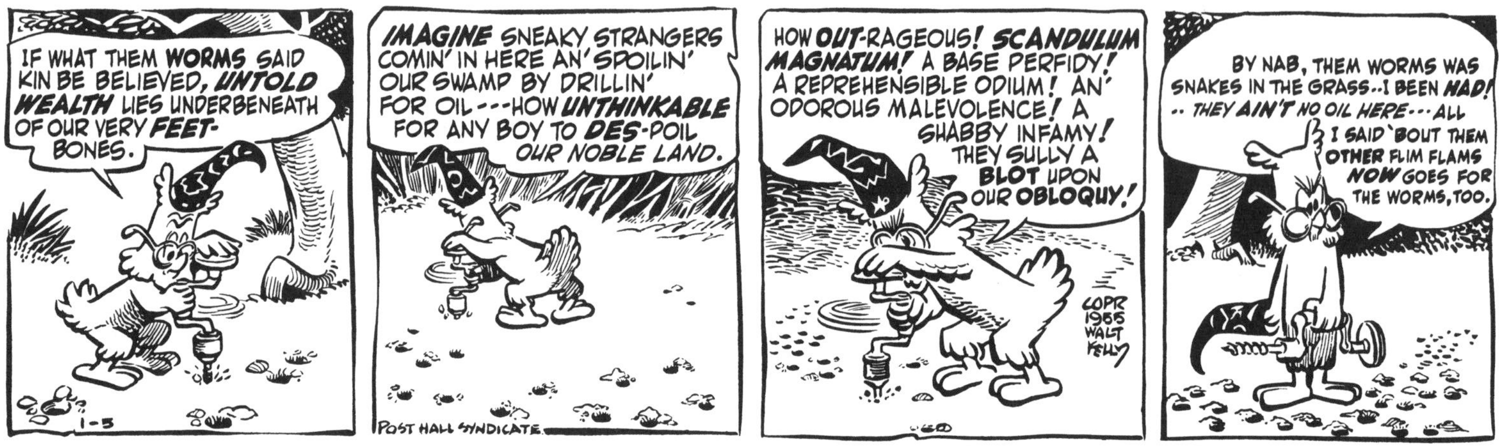
IF WHAT THEM WORMS SAID KIN BE BELIEVED, UNTOLD WEALTH LIES UNDERBENEATH OF OUR VERY FEET-BONES.
1-5
IMAGINE SNEAKY STRANGERS COMIN' IN HERE AN' SPOILIN' OUR SWAMP BY DRILLIN' FOR OIL---HOW UNTHINKABLE FOR ANY BOY TO DES-POIL OUR NOBLE LAND.
POST HALL SYNDICATE
HOW OUT-RAGEOUS! SCANDULUM MAGNATUM! A BASE PERFIDY! A REPREHENSIBLE ODIUM! AN' ODOROUS MALEVOLENCE! A SHABBY INFAMY! THEY SULLY A BLOT UPON OUR OBLOQUY!
COPR 1955 WALT KELLY
BY NAB, THEM WORMS WAS SNAKES IN THE GRASS..I BEEN HAD! .. THEY AIN'T NO OIL HERE--- ALL I SAID 'BOUT THEM OTHER FLIM FLAMS NOW GOES FOR THE WORMS, TOO.

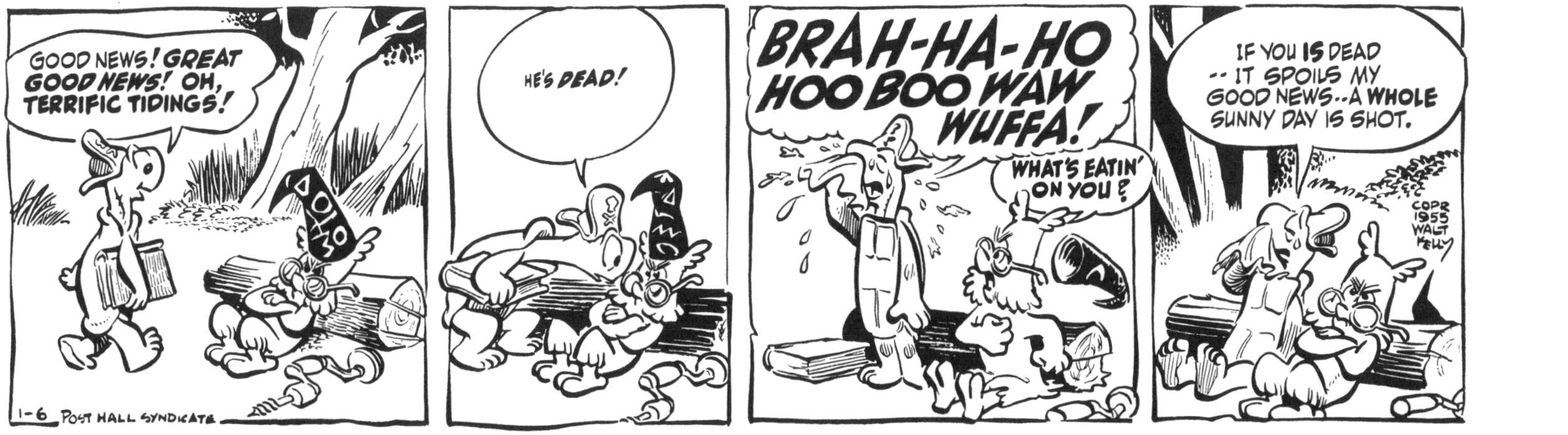
GOOD NEWS! GREAT GOOD NEWS! OH, TERRIFIC TIDINGS!
1-6 POST HALL SYNDICATE
HE'S DEAD!
BRAH-HA-HO HOO BOO WAW WUFFA!
WHAT'S EATIN' ON YOU?
IF YOU IS DEAD -- IT SPOILS MY GOOD NEWS.. A WHOLE SUNNY DAY IS SHOT.
COPR 1955 WALT KELLY

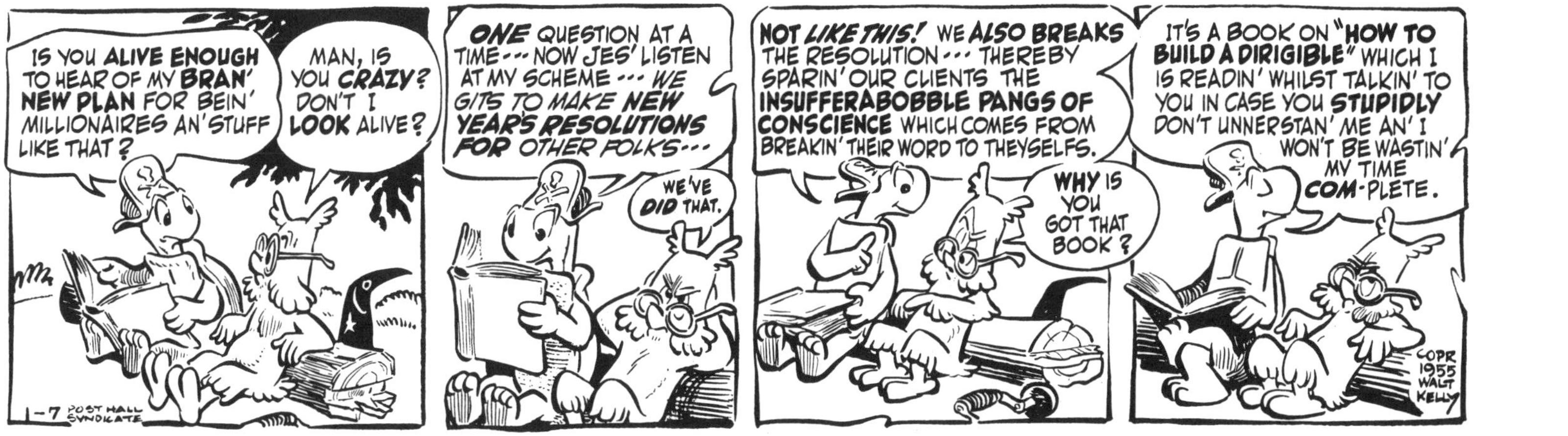
IS YOU ALIVE ENOUGH TO HEAR OF MY BRAN' NEW PLAN FOR BEIN' MILLIONAIRES AN' STUFF LIKE THAT?
MAN, IS YOU CRAZY? DON'T I LOOK ALIVE?
1-7 POST HALL SYNDICATE
ONE QUESTION AT A TIME --- NOW JES' LISTEN AT MY SCHEME --- WE GITS TO MAKE NEW YEAR'S RESOLUTIONS FOR OTHER FOLKS ---
WE'VE DID THAT.
NOT LIKE THIS! WE ALSO BREAKS THE RESOLUTION --- THEREBY SPARIN' OUR CLIENTS THE INSUFFERABOBBLE PANGS OF CONSCIENCE WHICH COMES FROM BREAKIN' THEIR WORD TO THEYSELFS.
WHY IS YOU GOT THAT BOOK?
IT'S A BOOK ON "HOW TO BUILD A DIRIGIBLE" WHICH I IS READIN' WHILST TALKIN' TO YOU IN CASE YOU STUPIDLY DON'T UNNERSTAN' ME AN' I WON'T BE WASTIN' MY TIME COM-PLETE.
COPR 1955 WALT KELLY

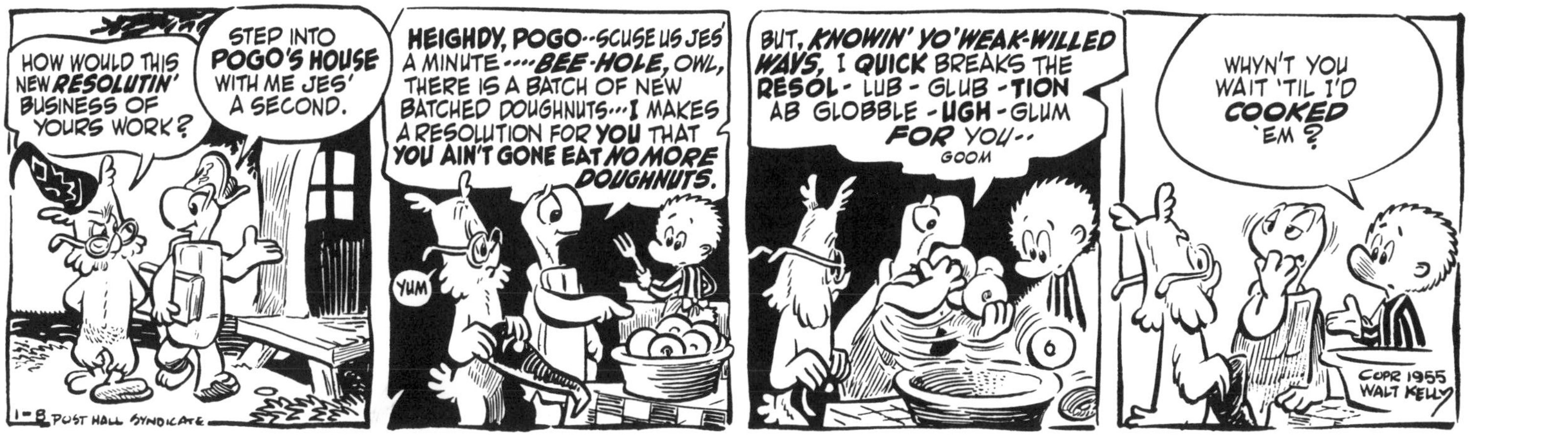
HOW WOULD THIS NEW RESOLUTIN' BUSINESS OF YOURS WORK?
STEP INTO POGO'S HOUSE WITH ME JES' A SECOND.
1-8 POST HALL SYNDICATE
HEIGHDY, POGO -- SCUSE US JES' A MINUTE ---- BEE-HOLE, OWL, THERE IS A BATCH OF NEW BATCHED DOUGHNUTS --- I MAKES A RESOLUTION FOR YOU THAT YOU AIN'T GONE EAT NO MORE DOUGHNUTS.
YUM
BUT, KNOWIN' YO' WEAK-WILLED WAYS, I QUICK BREAKS THE RESOL - LUB - GLUB - TION AB GLOBBLE - UGH - GLUM FOR YOU --
GOOM
WHYN'T YOU WAIT 'TIL I'D COOKED 'EM?
COPR 1955 WALT KELLY

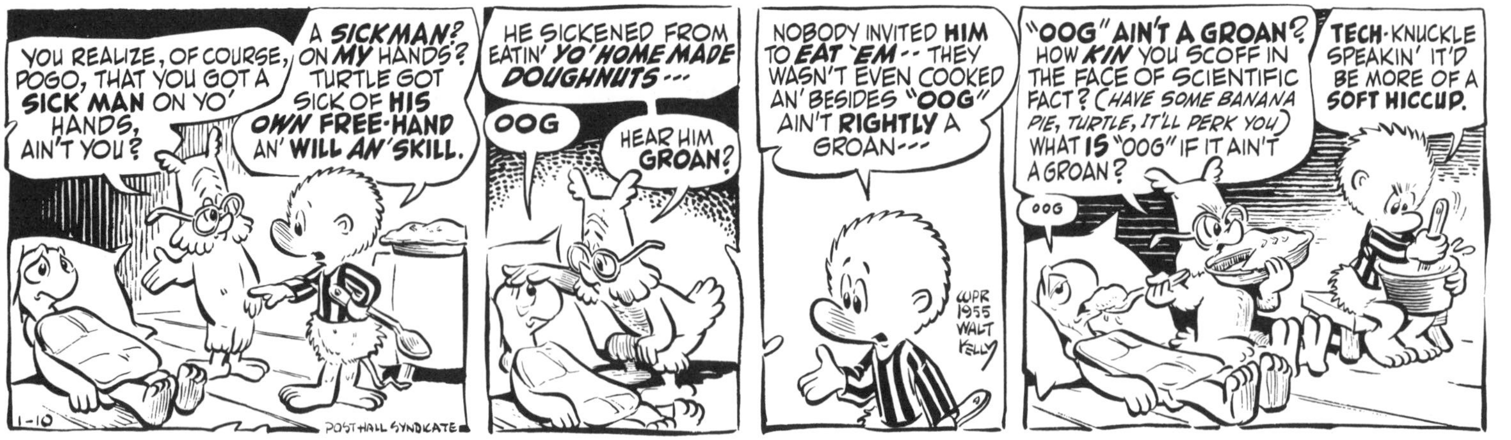
YOU REALIZE, OF COURSE, POGO, THAT YOU GOT A SICK MAN ON YO' HANDS, AIN'T YOU?
A SICKMAN? ON MY HANDS? TURTLE GOT SICK OF HIS OWN FREE-HAND AN' WILL AN' SKILL.
1-10
POST HALL SYNDICATE
HE SICKENED FROM EATIN' YO' HOME MADE DOUGHNUTS---
OOG
HEAR HIM GROAN?
NOBODY INVITED HIM TO EAT 'EM -- THEY WASN'T EVEN COOKED AN' BESIDES "OOG" AIN'T RIGHTLY A GROAN---
COPR 1955 WALT KELLY
"OOG" AIN'T A GROAN? HOW KIN YOU SCOFF IN THE FACE OF SCIENTIFIC FACT? (HAVE SOME BANANA PIE, TURTLE, IT'LL PERK YOU) WHAT IS "OOG" IF IT AIN'T A GROAN?
TECH-KNUCKLE SPEAKIN' IT'D BE MORE OF A SOFT HICCUP.
OOG

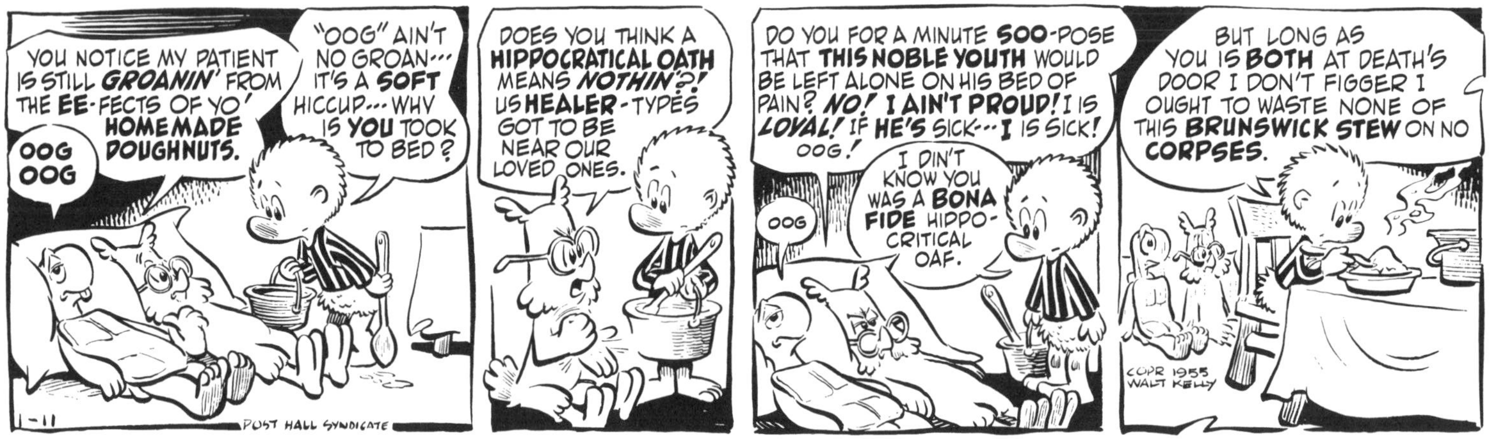
YOU NOTICE MY PATIENT IS STILL GROANIN' FROM THE EE-FECTS OF YO' HOMEMADE DOUGHNUTS.
OOG OOG
"OOG" AIN'T NO GROAN--- IT'S A SOFT HICCUP--- WHY IS YOU TOOK TO BED?
1-11
POST HALL SYNDICATE
DOES YOU THINK A HIPPOCRATICAL OATH MEANS NOTHIN'?! US HEALER-TYPES GOT TO BE NEAR OUR LOVED ONES.
DO YOU FOR A MINUTE SOO-POSE THAT THIS NOBLE YOUTH WOULD BE LEFT ALONE ON HIS BED OF PAIN? NO! I AIN'T PROUD! I IS LOYAL! IF HE'S SICK--- I IS SICK! OOG!
OOG
I DIN'T KNOW YOU WAS A BONA FIDE HIPPO-CRITICAL OAF.
BUT LONG AS YOU IS BOTH AT DEATH'S DOOR I DON'T FIGGER I OUGHT TO WASTE NONE OF THIS BRUNSWICK STEW ON NO CORPSES.
COPR 1955 WALT KELLY

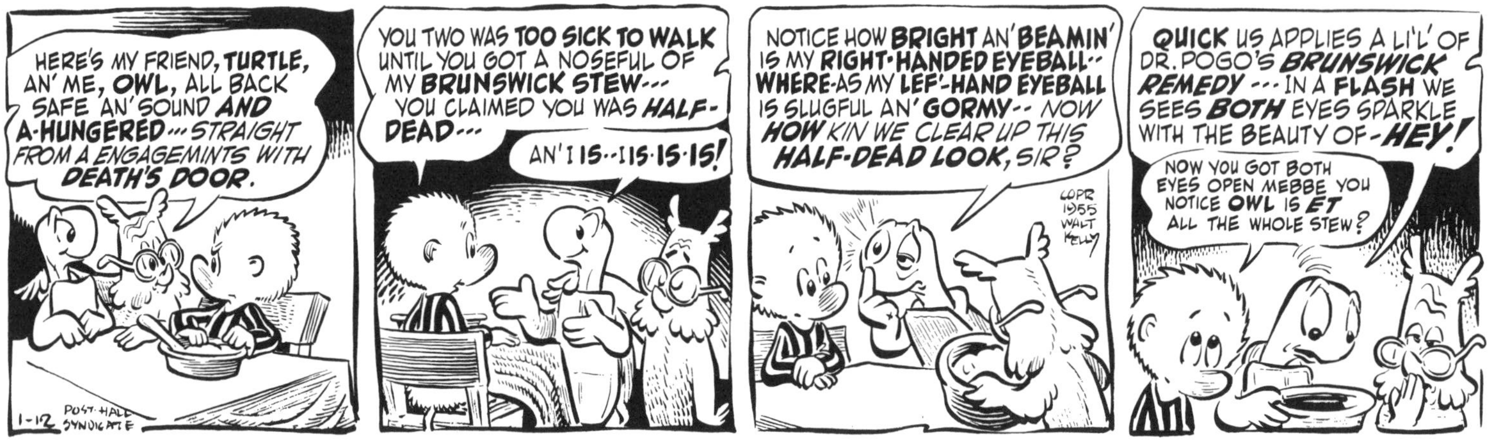
HERE'S MY FRIEND, TURTLE, AN' ME, OWL, ALL BACK SAFE AN' SOUND AND A-HUNGERED--- STRAIGHT FROM A ENGAGEMINTS WITH DEATH'S DOOR.
1-12
POST-HALL SYNDICATE
YOU TWO WAS TOO SICK TO WALK UNTIL YOU GOT A NOSEFUL OF MY BRUNSWICK STEW--- YOU CLAIMED YOU WAS HALF-DEAD---
AN' I IS--I IS-IS-IS!
NOTICE HOW BRIGHT AN' BEAMIN' IS MY RIGHT-HANDED EYEBALL-- WHERE-AS MY LEF'-HAND EYEBALL IS SLUGFUL AN' GORMY-- NOW HOW KIN WE CLEAR UP THIS HALF-DEAD LOOK, SIR?
COPR 1955 WALT KELLY
QUICK US APPLIES A LI'L' OF DR. POGO'S BRUNSWICK REMEDY --- IN A FLASH WE SEES BOTH EYES SPARKLE WITH THE BEAUTY OF-HEY!
NOW YOU GOT BOTH EYES OPEN MEBBE YOU NOTICE OWL IS ET ALL THE WHOLE STEW?

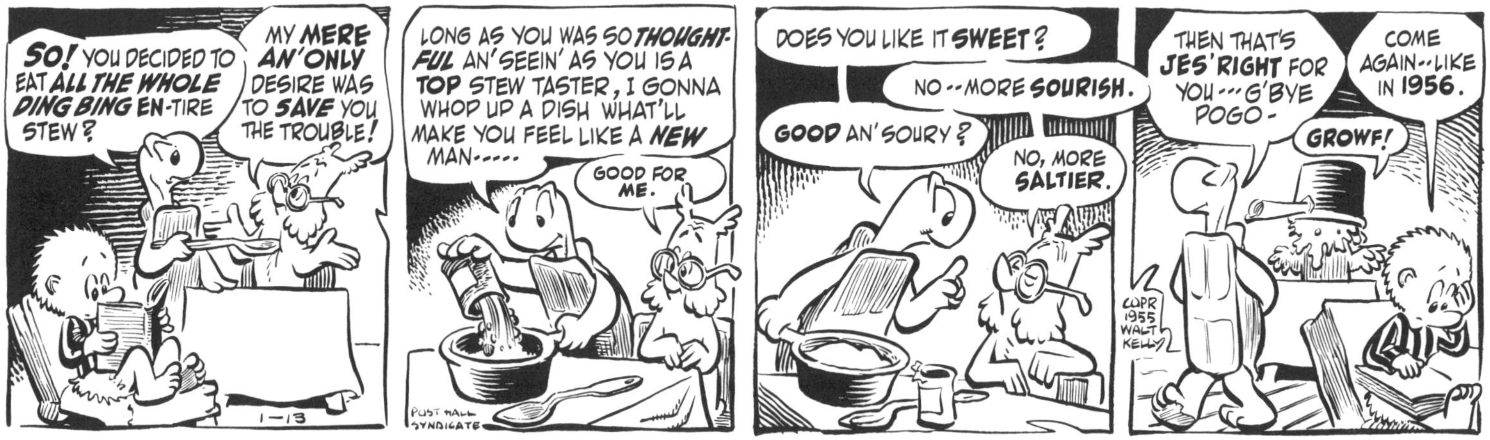

SO! YOU DECIDED TO EAT ALL THE WHOLE DING BING EN-TIRE STEW?
MY MERE AN' ONLY DESIRE WAS TO SAVE YOU THE TROUBLE!
1-13
LONG AS YOU WAS SO THOUGHT-FUL AN' SEEIN' AS YOU IS A TOP STEW TASTER, I GONNA WHOP UP A DISH WHAT'LL MAKE YOU FEEL LIKE A NEW MAN-----
GOOD FOR ME.
POST HALL SYNDICATE
DOES YOU LIKE IT SWEET?
NO--MORE SOURISH.
GOOD AN' SOURY?
NO, MORE SALTIER.
THEN THAT'S JES' RIGHT FOR YOU---G'BYE POGO-
COME AGAIN--LIKE IN 1956.
GROWF!
COPR 1955 WALT KELLY

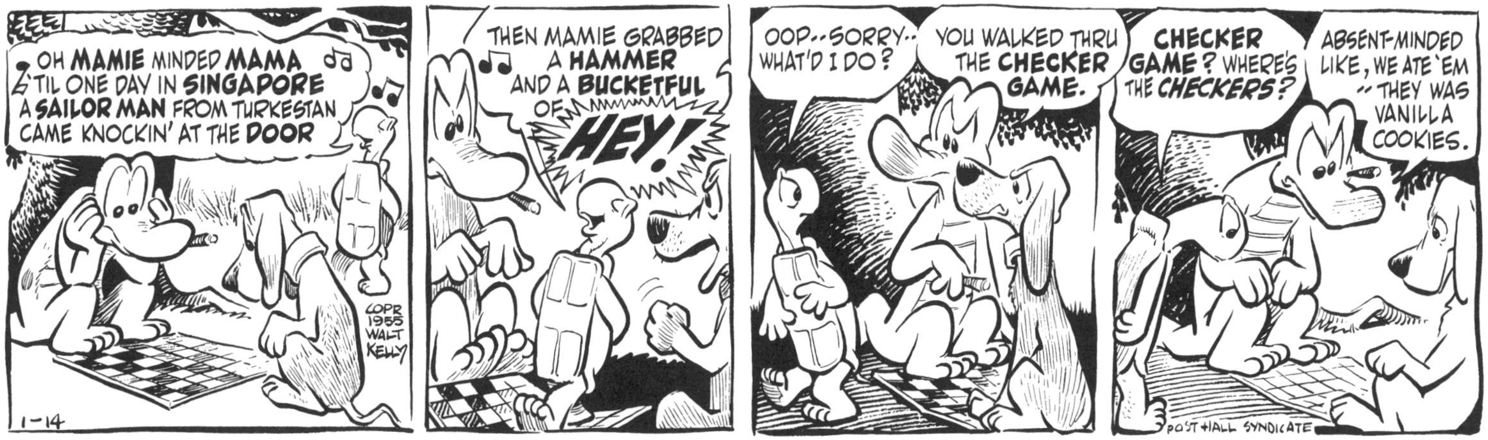

OH MAMIE MINDED MAMA 'TIL ONE DAY IN SINGAPORE A SAILOR MAN FROM TURKESTAN CAME KNOCKIN' AT THE DOOR
COPR 1955 WALT KELLY
1-14
THEN MAMIE GRABBED A HAMMER AND A BUCKETFUL OF
HEY!
OOP--SORRY-- WHAT'D I DO?
YOU WALKED THRU THE CHECKER GAME.
CHECKER GAME? WHERE'S THE CHECKERS?
ABSENT-MINDED LIKE, WE ATE 'EM -- THEY WAS VANILLA COOKIES.
POST-HALL SYNDICATE

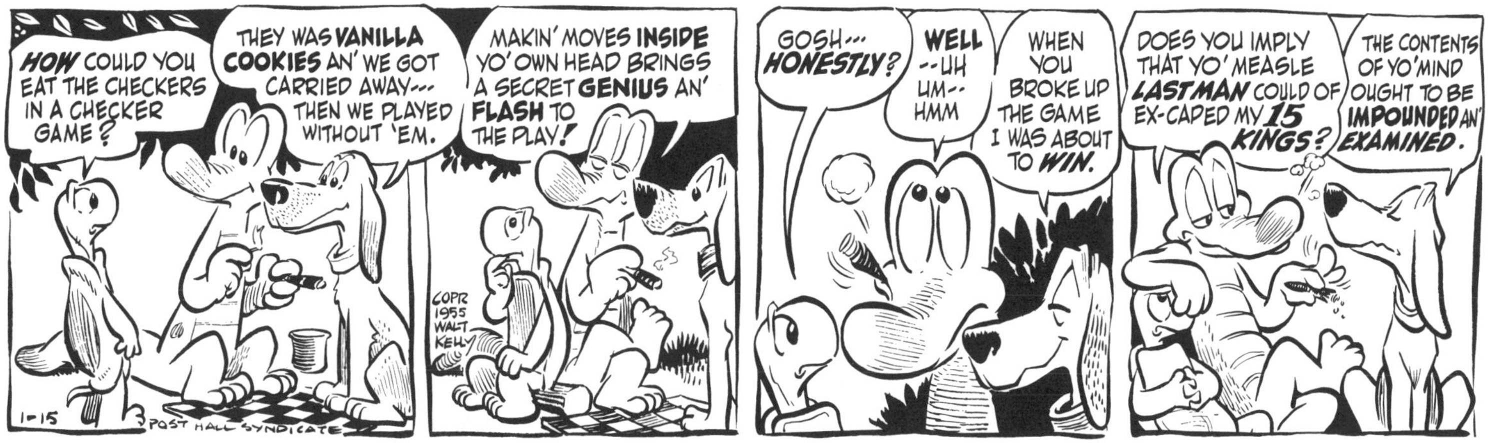

HOW COULD YOU EAT THE CHECKERS IN A CHECKER GAME?
THEY WAS VANILLA COOKIES AN' WE GOT CARRIED AWAY--- THEN WE PLAYED WITHOUT 'EM.
1-15
POST HALL SYNDICATE
MAKIN' MOVES INSIDE YO' OWN HEAD BRINGS A SECRET GENIUS AN' FLASH TO THE PLAY!
COPR 1955 WALT KELLY
GOSH--- HONESTLY?
WELL --UH UM-- HMM
WHEN YOU BROKE UP THE GAME I WAS ABOUT TO WIN.
DOES YOU IMPLY THAT YO' MEASLE LAST MAN COULD OF EX-CAPED MY 15 KINGS?
THE CONTENTS OF YO' MIND OUGHT TO BE IMPOUNDED AN' EXAMINED.

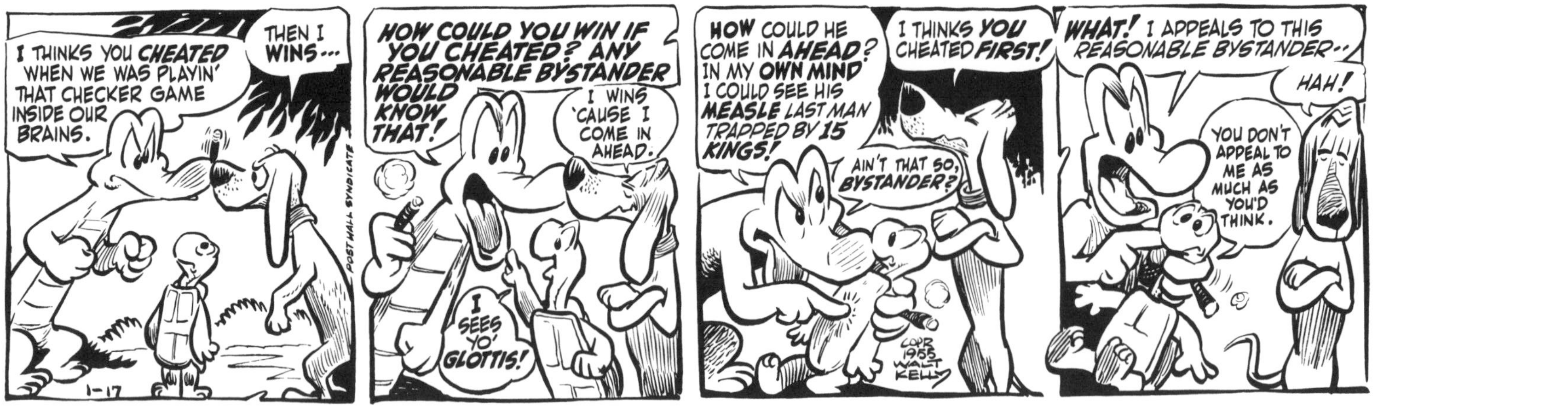
I THINKS YOU CHEATED WHEN WE WAS PLAYIN' THAT CHECKER GAME INSIDE OUR BRAINS.
THEN I WINS...
HOW COULD YOU WIN IF YOU CHEATED? ANY REASONABLE BYSTANDER WOULD KNOW THAT!
I WINS 'CAUSE I COME IN AHEAD.
I SEES YO' GLOTTIS!
HOW COULD HE COME IN AHEAD? IN MY OWN MIND I COULD SEE HIS MEASLE LAST MAN TRAPPED BY 15 KINGS!
I THINKS YOU CHEATED FIRST!
AIN'T THAT SO, BYSTANDER?
WHAT! I APPEALS TO THIS REASONABLE BYSTANDER--
HAH!
YOU DON'T APPEAL TO ME AS MUCH AS YOU'D THINK.
1-17
POST HALL SYNDICATE
COPR 1955 WALT KELLY

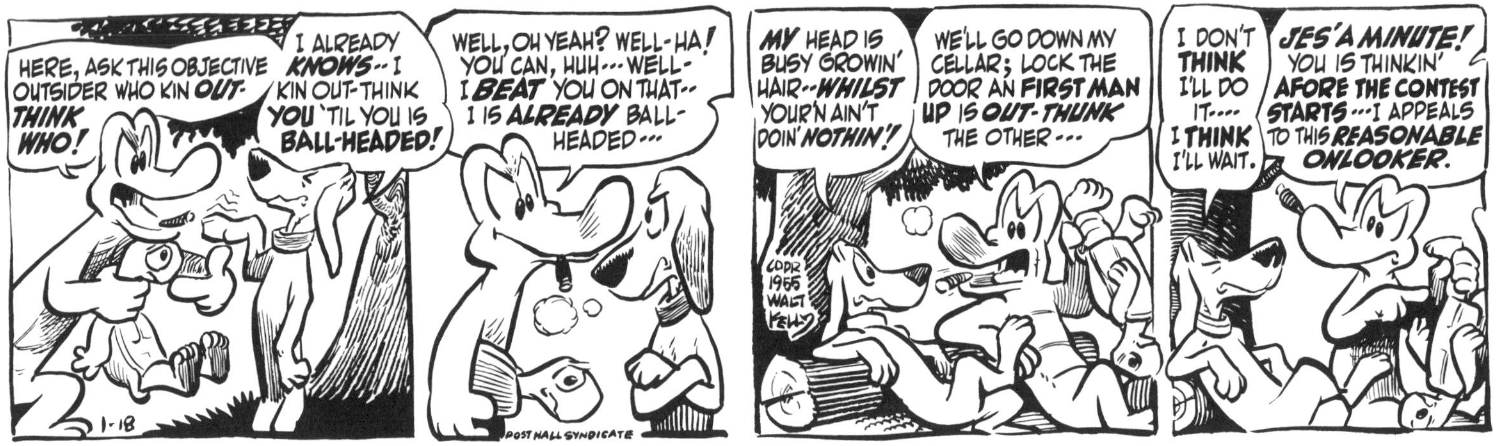
HERE, ASK THIS OBJECTIVE OUTSIDER WHO KIN OUT-THINK WHO!
I ALREADY KNOWS--I KIN OUT-THINK YOU 'TIL YOU IS BALL-HEADED!
WELL, OH YEAH? WELL-HA! YOU CAN, HUH... WELL- I BEAT YOU ON THAT-- I IS ALREADY BALL-HEADED...
MY HEAD IS BUSY GROWIN' HAIR--WHILST YOUR'N AIN'T DOIN' NOTHIN'!
WE'LL GO DOWN MY CELLAR; LOCK THE DOOR AN FIRST MAN UP IS OUT-THUNK THE OTHER...
I DON'T THINK I'LL DO IT.... I THINK I'LL WAIT.
JES' A MINUTE! YOU IS THINKIN' AFORE THE CONTEST STARTS...I APPEALS TO THIS REASONABLE ONLOOKER.
1-18
POST HALL SYNDICATE
COPR 1955 WALT KELLY

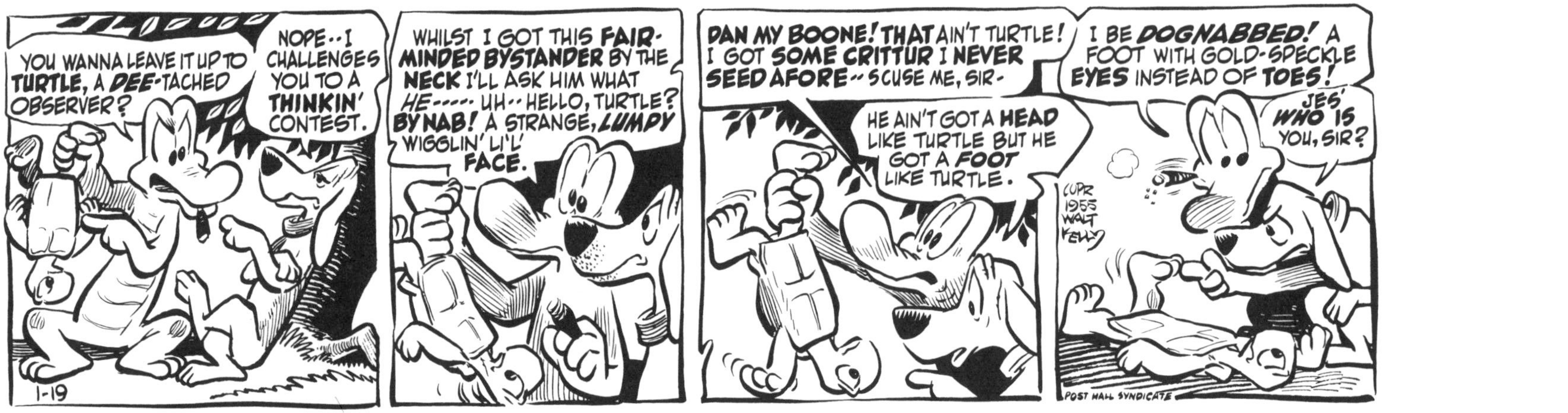
YOU WANNA LEAVE IT UP TO TURTLE, A DEE-TACHED OBSERVER?
NOPE--I CHALLENGES YOU TO A THINKIN' CONTEST.
WHILST I GOT THIS FAIR-MINDED BYSTANDER BY THE NECK I'LL ASK HIM WHAT HE----- UH--HELLO, TURTLE? BY NAB! A STRANGE, LUMPY WIGGLIN' LI'L' FACE.
DAN MY BOONE! THAT AIN'T TURTLE! I GOT SOME CRITTUR I NEVER SEED AFORE--SCUSE ME, SIR-
HE AIN'T GOT A HEAD LIKE TURTLE BUT HE GOT A FOOT LIKE TURTLE.
I BE DOGNABBED! A FOOT WITH GOLD-SPECKLE EYES INSTEAD OF TOES!
JES' WHO IS YOU, SIR?
1-19
COPR 1955 WALT KELLY
POST HALL SYNDICATE

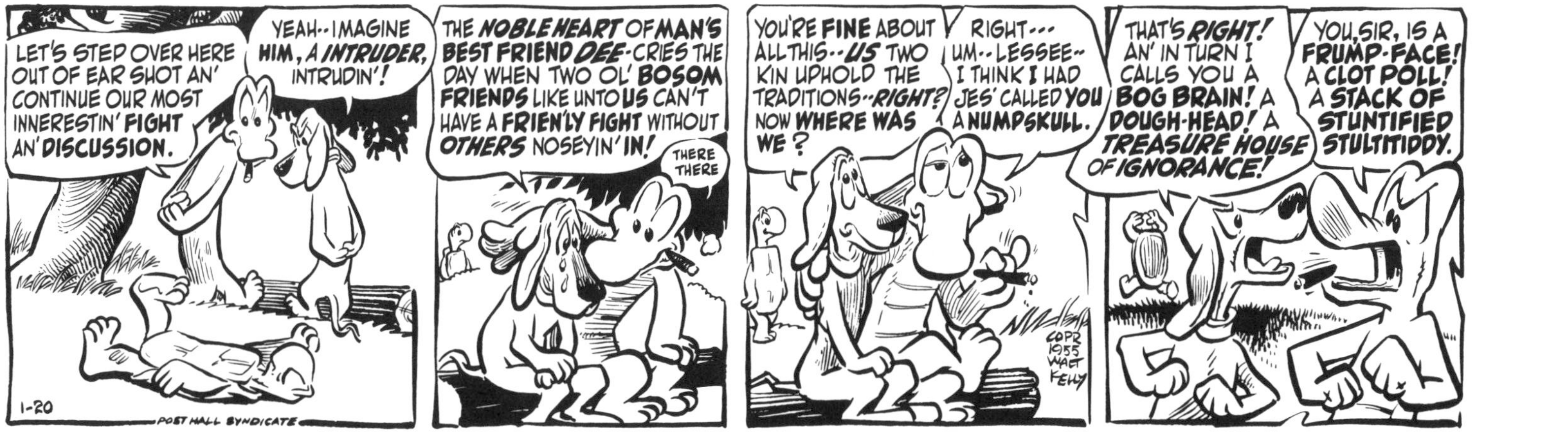
LET'S STEP OVER HERE OUT OF EAR SHOT AN' CONTINUE OUR MOST INNERESTIN' FIGHT AN' DISCUSSION.
YEAH--I IMAGINE HIM, A INTRUDER, INTRUDIN'!
THE NOBLE HEART OF MAN'S BEST FRIEND DEE-CRIES THE DAY WHEN TWO OL' BOSOM FRIENDS LIKE UNTO US CAN'T HAVE A FRIEN'LY FIGHT WITHOUT OTHERS NOSEYIN' IN!
THERE THERE
YOU'RE FINE ABOUT ALL THIS--US TWO KIN UPHOLD THE TRADITIONS--RIGHT? NOW WHERE WAS WE?
RIGHT--- UM--LESSEE-- I THINK I HAD JES' CALLED YOU A NUMPSKULL.
THAT'S RIGHT! AN' IN TURN I CALLS YOU A BOG BRAIN! A DOUGH-HEAD! A TREASURE HOUSE OF IGNORANCE!
YOU, SIR, IS A FRUMP-FACE! A CLOT POLL! A STACK OF STUNTIFIED STULTITIDDY.
COPR 1955 WALT KELLY
1-20
POST HALL SYNDICATE

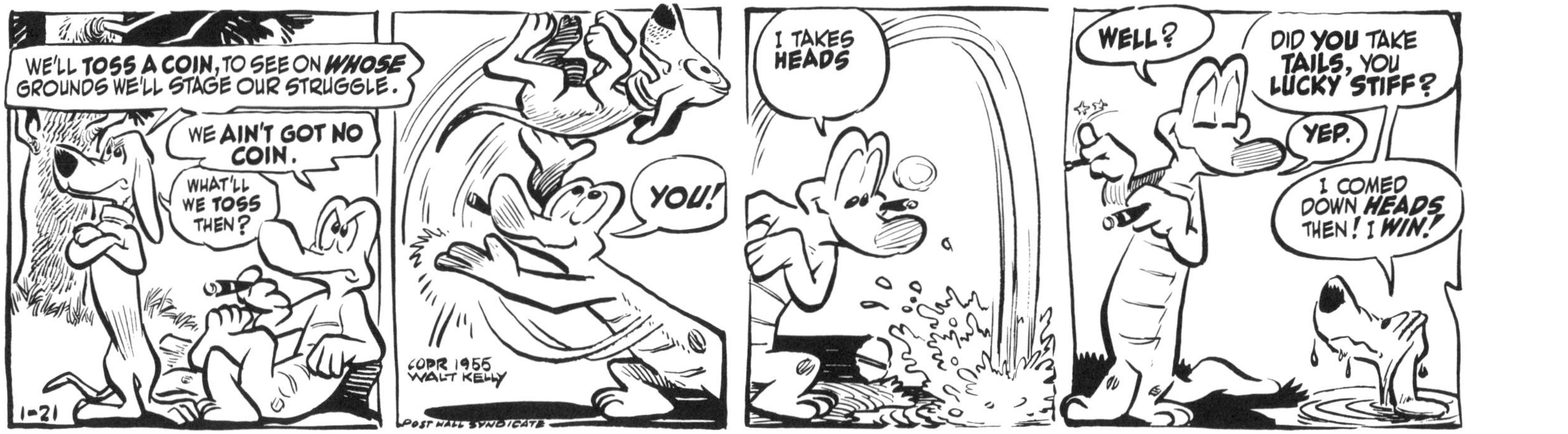
WE'LL TOSS A COIN, TO SEE ON WHOSE GROUNDS WE'LL STAGE OUR STRUGGLE.
WE AIN'T GOT NO COIN.
WHAT'LL WE TOSS THEN?
YOU!
COPR 1955 WALT KELLY
1-21
POST HALL SYNDICATE
I TAKES HEADS
WELL?
DID YOU TAKE TAILS, YOU LUCKY STIFF?
YEP.
I COMED DOWN HEADS THEN! I WIN!

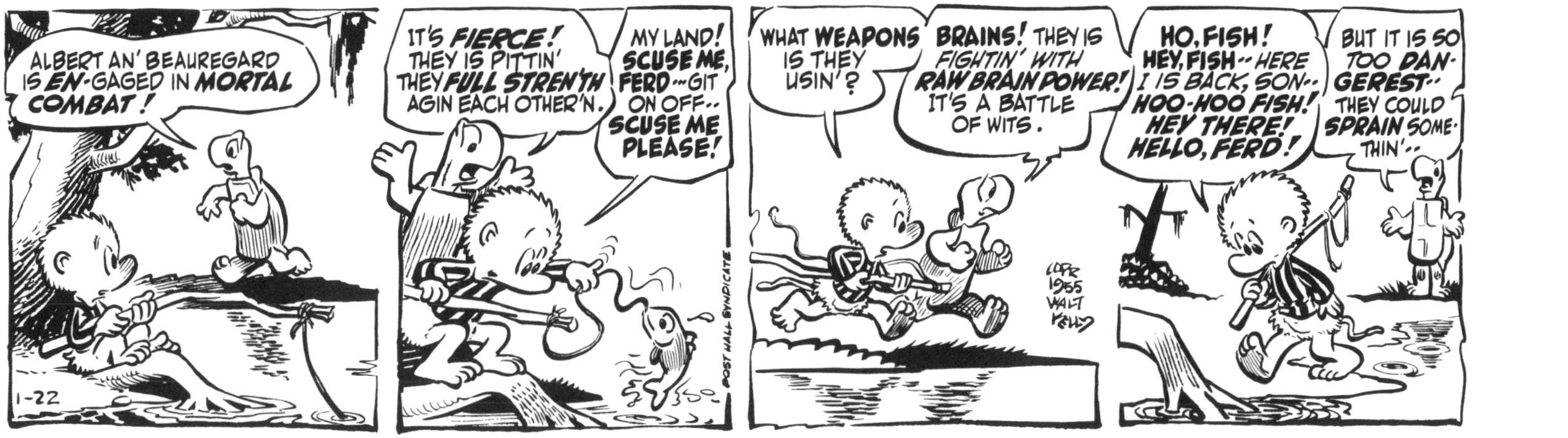
ALBERT AN' BEAUREGARD IS EN-GAGED IN MORTAL COMBAT!
1-22
IT'S FIERCE! THEY IS PITTIN' THEY FULL STREN'TH AGIN EACH OTHER'N.
MY LAND! SCUSE ME, FERD--GIT ON OFF-- SCUSE ME PLEASE!
POST HALL SYNDICATE
WHAT WEAPONS IS THEY USIN'?
BRAINS! THEY IS FIGHTIN' WITH RAW BRAIN POWER! IT'S A BATTLE OF WITS.
COPR 1955 WALT KELLY
HO, FISH! HEY, FISH--HERE I IS BACK, SON-- HOO-HOO FISH! HEY THERE! HELLO, FERD!
BUT IT IS SO TOO DAN-GEREST-- THEY COULD SPRAIN SOME-THIN'--

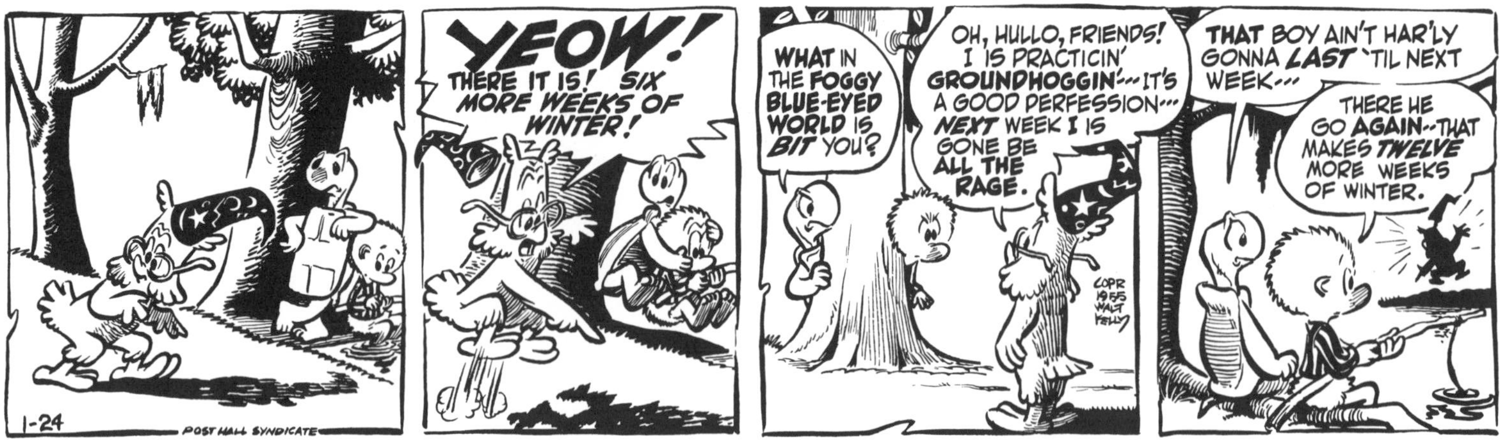
YEOW!
THERE IT IS! SIX MORE WEEKS OF WINTER!
WHAT IN THE FOGGY BLUE-EYED WORLD IS BIT YOU?
OH, HULLO, FRIENDS! I IS PRACTICIN' GROUNDHOGGIN'--- IT'S A GOOD PERFESSION--- NEXT WEEK I IS GONE BE ALL THE RAGE.
COPR 1955 WALT KELLY
THAT BOY AIN'T HAR'LY GONNA LAST 'TIL NEXT WEEK---
THERE HE GO AGAIN--THAT MAKES TWELVE MORE WEEKS OF WINTER.
1-24
POST HALL SYNDICATE

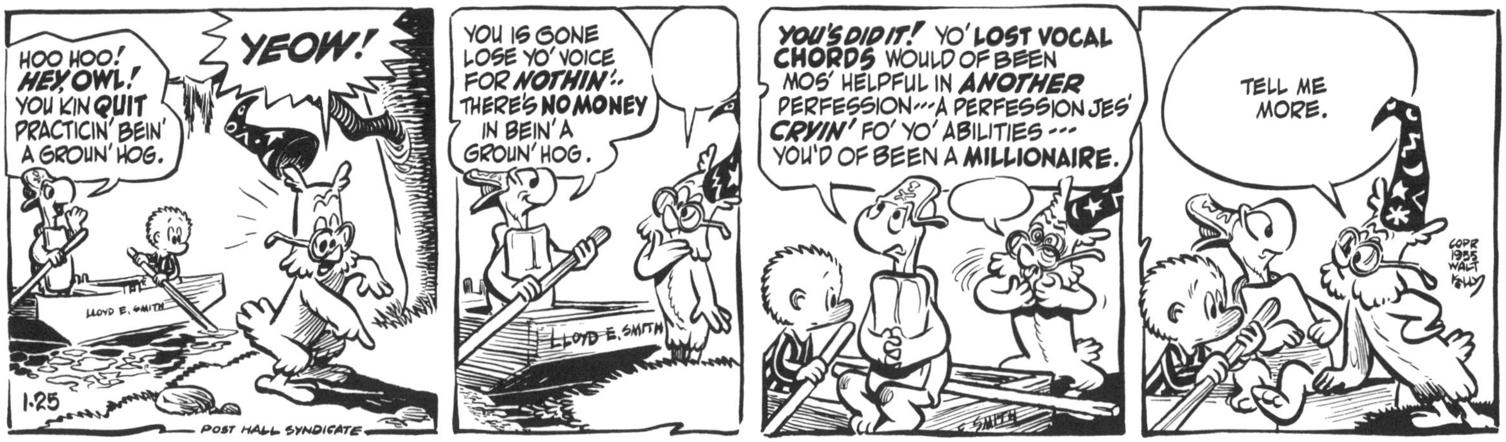
HOO HOO! HEY, OWL! YOU KIN QUIT PRACTICIN' BEIN' A GROUN' HOG.
YEOW!
LLOYD E. SMITH
YOU IS GONE LOSE YO' VOICE FOR NOTHIN'-- THERE'S NO MONEY IN BEIN' A GROUN' HOG.
LLOYD E. SMITH
YOU'S DID IT! YO' LOST VOCAL CHORDS WOULD OF BEEN MOS' HELPFUL IN ANOTHER PERFESSION--- A PERFESSION JES' CRYIN' FO' YO' ABILITIES--- YOU'D OF BEEN A MILLIONAIRE.
TELL ME MORE.
COPR 1955 WALT KELLY
1-25
POST HALL SYNDICATE

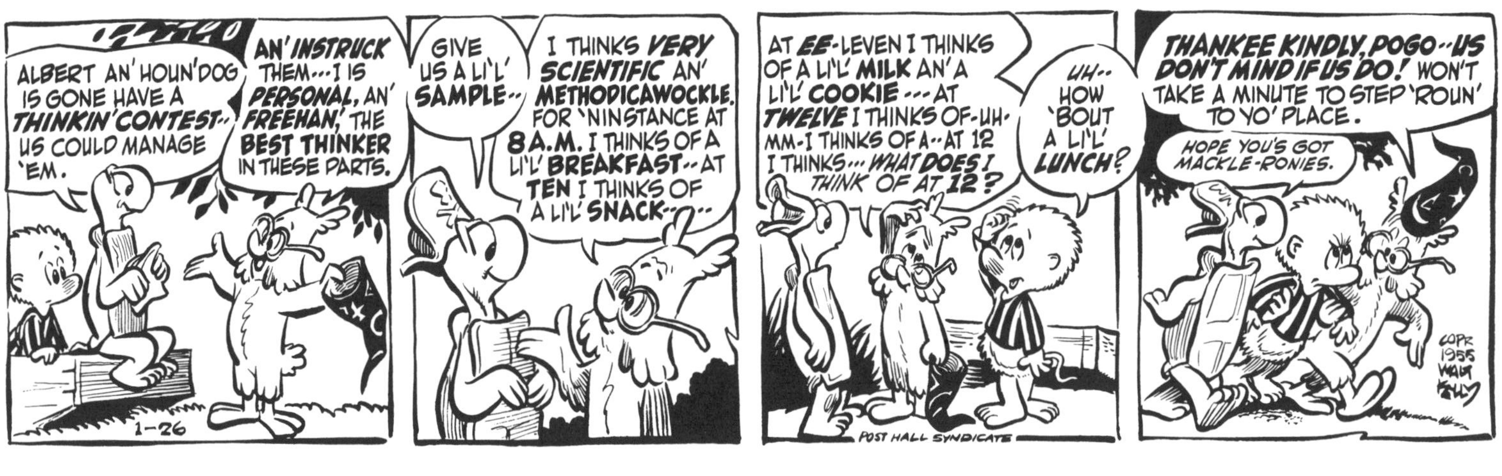
ALBERT AN' HOUN'DOG IS GONE HAVE A THINKIN' CONTEST-- US COULD MANAGE 'EM.
AN' INSTRUCK THEM--- I IS PERSONAL, AN' FREEHAN', THE BEST THINKER IN THESE PARTS.
GIVE US A LI'L' SAMPLE--
I THINKS VERY SCIENTIFIC AN' METHODICAWOCKLE. FOR 'NINSTANCE AT 8 A.M. I THINKS OF A LI'L' BREAKFAST-- AT TEN I THINKS OF A LI'L' SNACK-----
AT EE-LEVEN I THINKS OF A LI'L' MILK AN' A LI'L' COOKIE --- AT TWELVE I THINKS OF-UH-MM-I THINKS OF A-- AT 12 I THINKS... WHAT DOES I THINK OF AT 12?
UH-- HOW 'BOUT A LI'L' LUNCH?
THANKEE KINDLY, POGO-- US DON'T MIND IF US DO! WON'T TAKE A MINUTE TO STEP 'ROUN' TO YO' PLACE.
HOPE YOU'S GOT MACKLE-RONIES.
COPR 1955 WALT KELLY
1-26
POST HALL SYNDICATE

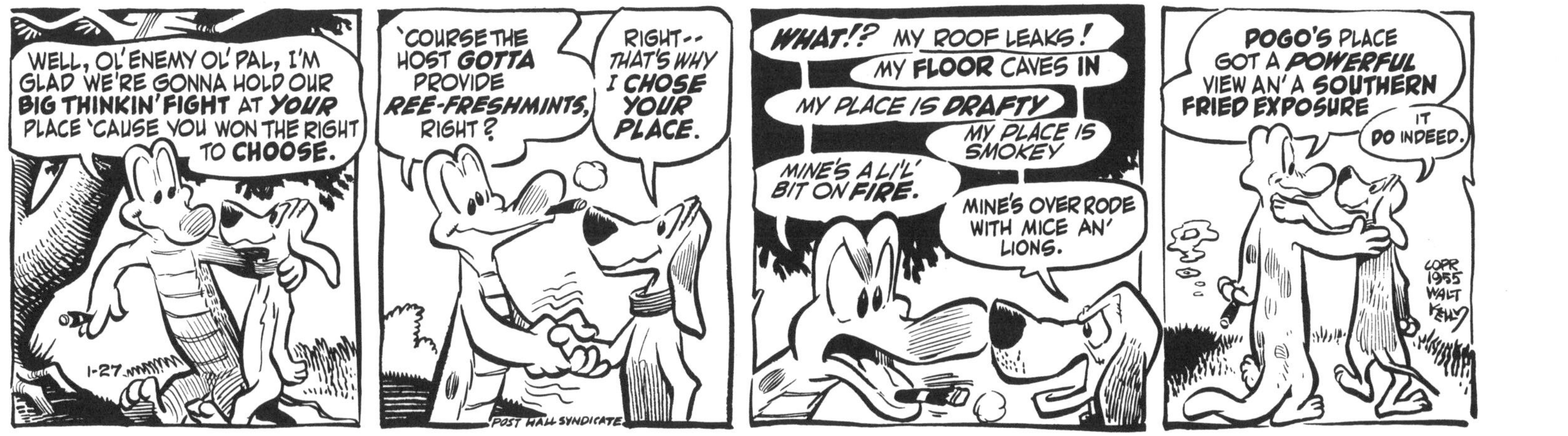
WELL, OL' ENEMY OL' PAL, I'M GLAD WE'RE GONNA HOLD OUR BIG THINKIN' FIGHT AT YOUR PLACE 'CAUSE YOU WON THE RIGHT TO CHOOSE.
1-27
'COURSE THE HOST GOTTA PROVIDE REE-FRESHMINTS, RIGHT?
RIGHT-- THAT'S WHY I CHOSE YOUR PLACE.
POST HALL SYNDICATE
WHAT!? MY ROOF LEAKS!
MY FLOOR CAVES IN
MY PLACE IS DRAFTY
MY PLACE IS SMOKEY
MINE'S A LI'L' BIT ON FIRE.
MINE'S OVER RODE WITH MICE AN' LIONS.
POGO'S PLACE GOT A POWERFUL VIEW AN' A SOUTHERN FRIED EXPOSURE
IT DO INDEED.
COPR 1955 WALT KELLY

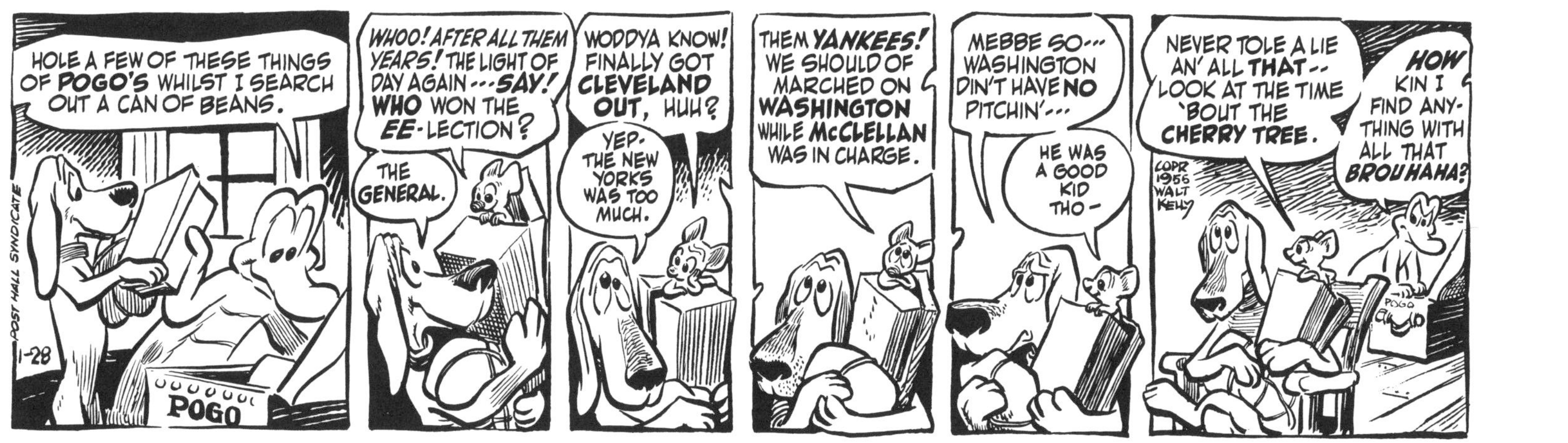
HOLE A FEW OF THESE THINGS OF POGO'S WHILST I SEARCH OUT A CAN OF BEANS.
POST HALL SYNDICATE
1-28
POGO
WHOO! AFTER ALL THEM YEARS! THE LIGHT OF DAY AGAIN --- SAY! WHO WON THE EE-LECTION?
THE GENERAL.
WODDYA KNOW! FINALLY GOT CLEVELAND OUT, HUH?
YEP. THE NEW YORKS WAS TOO MUCH.
THEM YANKEES! WE SHOULD OF MARCHED ON WASHINGTON WHILE McCLELLAN WAS IN CHARGE.
MEBBE SO--- WASHINGTON DIN'T HAVE NO PITCHIN'---
HE WAS A GOOD KID THO -
NEVER TOLE A LIE AN' ALL THAT-- LOOK AT THE TIME 'BOUT THE CHERRY TREE.
HOW KIN I FIND ANY-THING WITH ALL THAT BROUHAHA?
COPR 1955 WALT KELLY
POGO

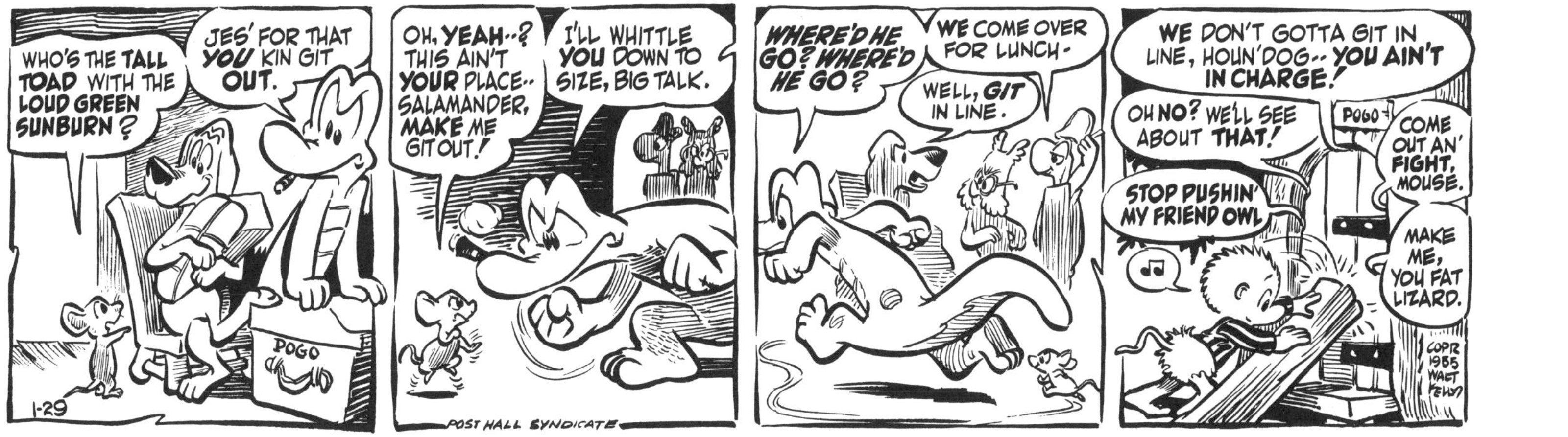
WHO'S THE TALL TOAD WITH THE LOUD GREEN SUNBURN?
JES' FOR THAT YOU KIN GIT OUT.
POGO
1-29
OH, YEAH--? THIS AIN'T YOUR PLACE-- SALAMANDER, MAKE ME GIT OUT!
I'LL WHITTLE YOU DOWN TO SIZE, BIG TALK.
POST HALL SYNDICATE
WHERE'D HE GO? WHERE'D HE GO?
WE COME OVER FOR LUNCH-
WELL, GIT IN LINE.
WE DON'T GOTTA GIT IN LINE, HOUN'DOG-- YOU AIN'T IN CHARGE!
OH NO? WE'LL SEE ABOUT THAT!
POGO
COME OUT AN' FIGHT, MOUSE.
STOP PUSHIN' MY FRIEND OWL
MAKE ME, YOU FAT LIZARD.
COPR 1955 WALT KELLY

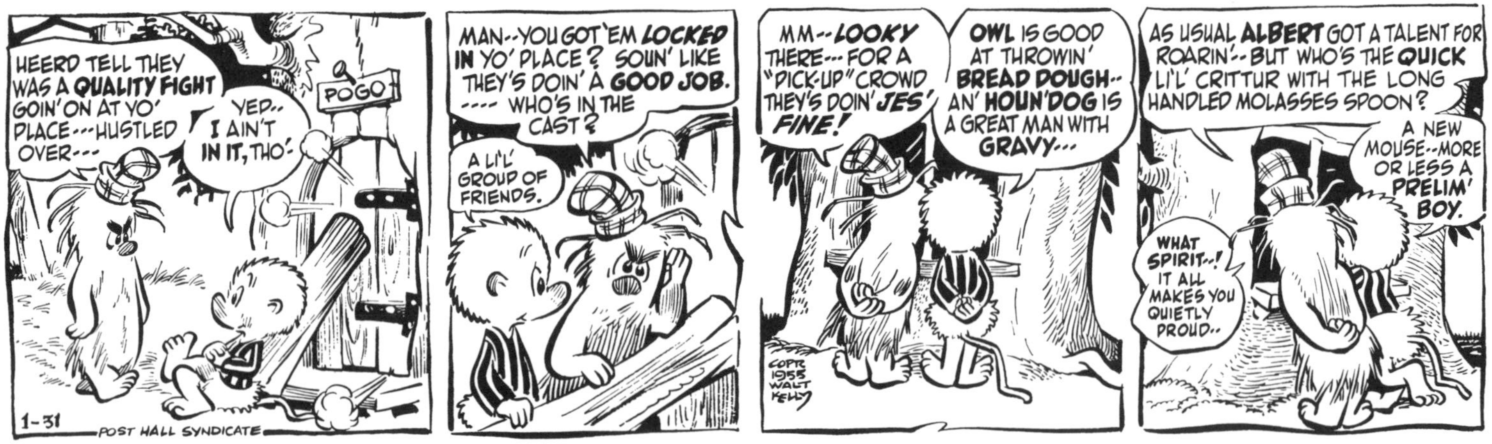
HEERD TELL THEY WAS A QUALITY FIGHT GOIN' ON AT YO' PLACE---HUSTLED OVER---
YEP.. I AIN'T IN IT, THO'.
POGO
MAN--YOU GOT 'EM LOCKED IN YO' PLACE? SOUN' LIKE THEY'S DOIN' A GOOD JOB. ---- WHO'S IN THE CAST?
A LI'L' GROUP OF FRIENDS.
MM--LOOKY THERE---FOR A "PICK-UP" CROWD THEY'S DOIN' JES' FINE!
OWL IS GOOD AT THROWIN' BREAD DOUGH-- AN' HOUN'DOG IS A GREAT MAN WITH GRAVY---
COPR 1955 WALT KELLY
AS USUAL ALBERT GOT A TALENT FOR ROARIN'--BUT WHO'S THE QUICK LI'L' CRITTUR WITH THE LONG HANDLED MOLASSES SPOON?
A NEW MOUSE--MORE OR LESS A PRELIM' BOY.
WHAT SPIRIT--! IT ALL MAKES YOU QUIETLY PROUD..
1-31
POST HALL SYNDICATE

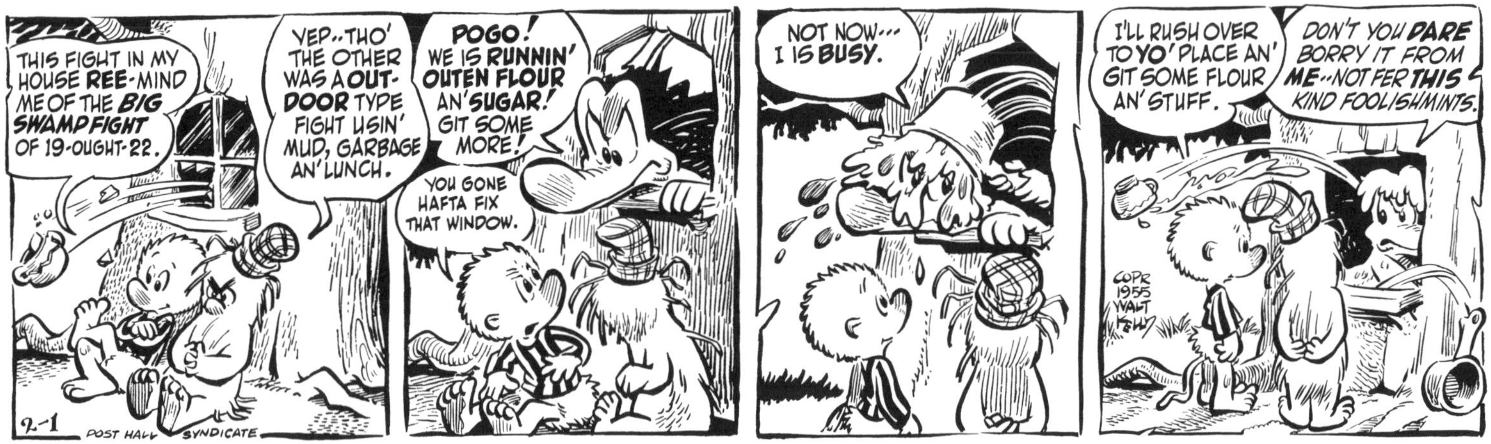
THIS FIGHT IN MY HOUSE REE-MIND ME OF THE BIG SWAMP FIGHT OF 19-OUGHT-22.
YEP..THO' THE OTHER WAS A OUT-DOOR TYPE FIGHT USIN' MUD, GARBAGE AN' LUNCH.
POGO! WE IS RUNNIN' OUTEN FLOUR AN' SUGAR! GIT SOME MORE!
YOU GONE HAFTA FIX THAT WINDOW.
NOT NOW--- I IS BUSY.
I'LL RUSH OVER TO YO' PLACE AN' GIT SOME FLOUR AN' STUFF.
DON'T YOU DARE BORRY IT FROM ME--NOT FER THIS KIND FOOLISHMINTS.
COPR 1955 WALT KELLY
2-1
POST HALL SYNDICATE

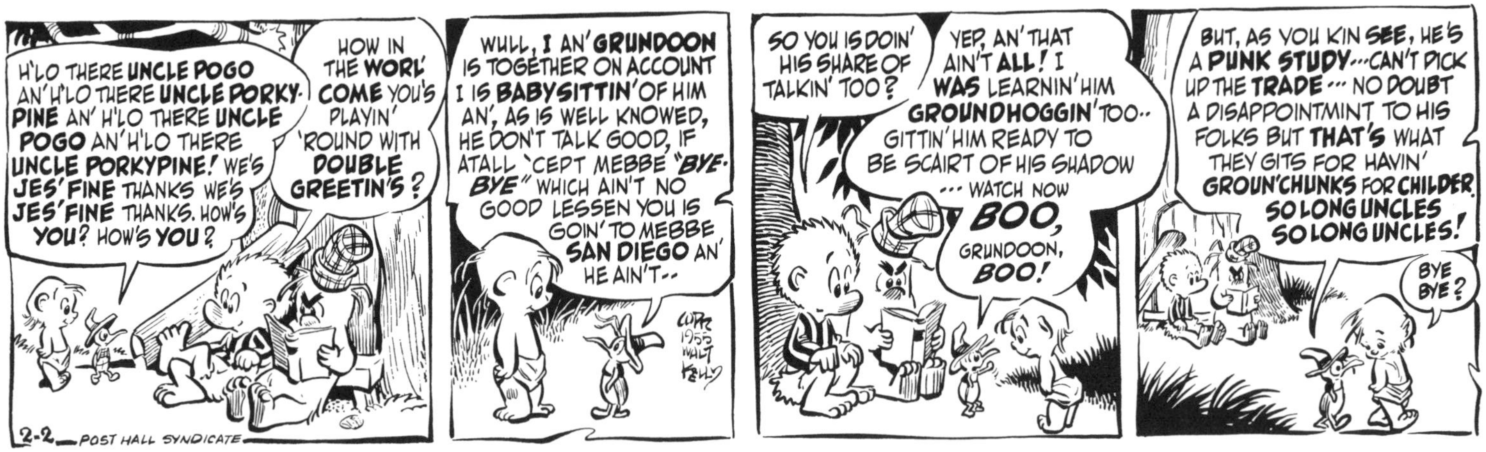
H'LO THERE UNCLE POGO AN' H'LO THERE UNCLE PORKY-PINE AN' H'LO THERE UNCLE POGO AN' H'LO THERE UNCLE PORKYPINE! WE'S JES' FINE THANKS WE'S JES' FINE THANKS. HOW'S YOU? HOW'S YOU?
HOW IN THE WORL' COME YOU'S PLAYIN' 'ROUND WITH DOUBLE GREETIN'S?
WULL, I AN' GRUNDOON IS TOGETHER ON ACCOUNT I IS BABYSITTIN' OF HIM AN', AS IS WELL KNOWED, HE DON'T TALK GOOD, IF ATALL 'CEPT MEBBE "BYE-BYE" WHICH AIN'T NO GOOD LESSEN YOU IS GOIN' TO MEBBE SAN DIEGO AN' HE AIN'T--
COPR 1955 WALT KELLY
SO YOU IS DOIN' HIS SHARE OF TALKIN' TOO?
YEP, AN' THAT AIN'T ALL! I WAS LEARNIN' HIM GROUNDHOGGIN' TOO.. GITTIN' HIM READY TO BE SCAIRT OF HIS SHADOW --- WATCH NOW BOO, GRUNDOON, BOO!
BUT, AS YOU KIN SEE, HE'S A PUNK STUDY---CAN'T PICK UP THE TRADE--- NO DOUBT A DISAPPOINTMINT TO HIS FOLKS BUT THAT'S WHAT THEY GITS FOR HAVIN' GROUN'CHUNKS FOR CHILDER. SO LONG UNCLES SO LONG UNCLES!
BYE BYE?
2-2
POST HALL SYNDICATE

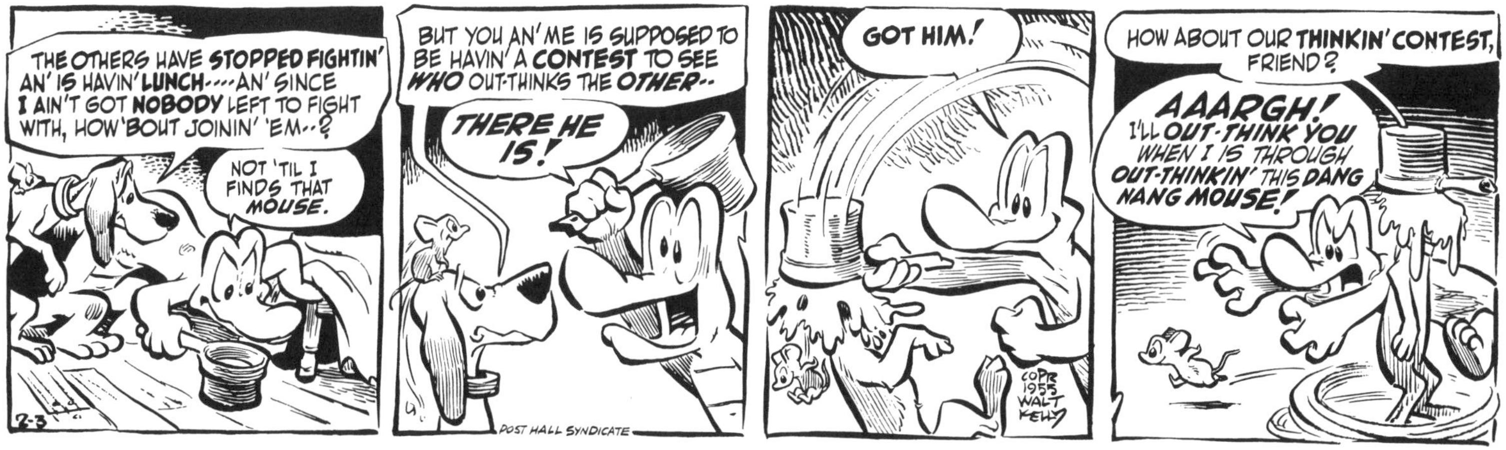
THE OTHERS HAVE STOPPED FIGHTIN' AN' IS HAVIN' LUNCH----AN' SINCE I AIN'T GOT NOBODY LEFT TO FIGHT WITH, HOW 'BOUT JOININ' 'EM--?
NOT 'TIL I FINDS THAT MOUSE.
2-3
BUT YOU AN' ME IS SUPPOSED TO BE HAVIN' A CONTEST TO SEE WHO OUT-THINKS THE OTHER--
THERE HE IS!
POST HALL SYNDICATE
GOT HIM!
COPR 1955 WALT KELLY
HOW ABOUT OUR THINKIN' CONTEST, FRIEND?
AAARGH! I'LL OUT-THINK YOU WHEN I IS THROUGH OUT-THINKIN' THIS DANG NANG MOUSE!

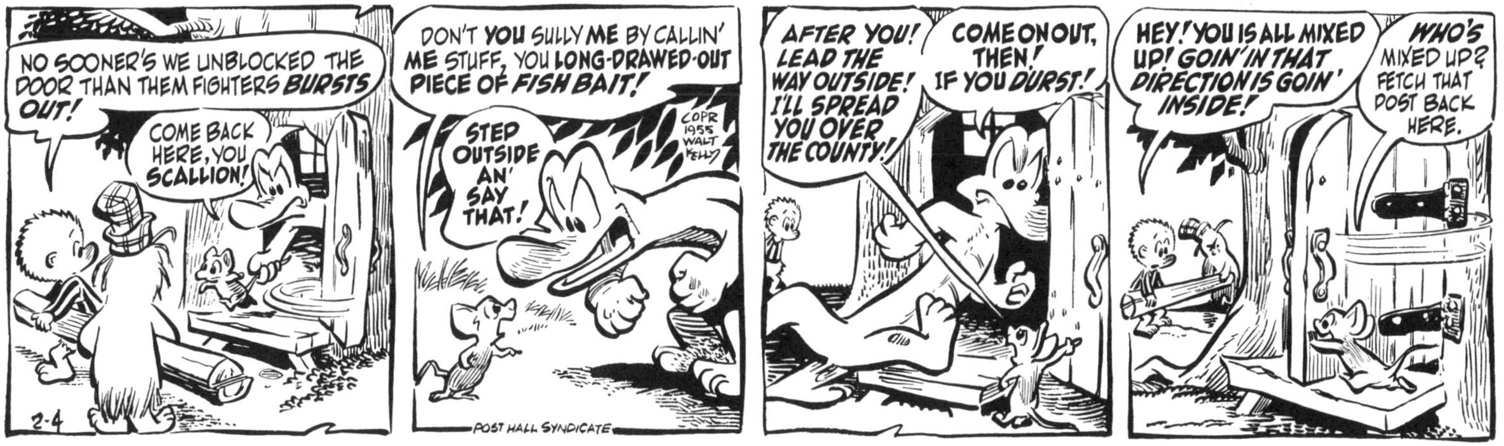
NO SOONER'S WE UNBLOCKED THE DOOR THAN THEM FIGHTERS BURSTS OUT!
COME BACK HERE, YOU SCALLION!
2-4
DON'T YOU SULLY ME BY CALLIN' ME STUFF, YOU LONG-DRAWED-OUT PIECE OF FISH BAIT!
STEP OUTSIDE AN' SAY THAT!
COPR 1955 WALT KELLY
POST HALL SYNDICATE
AFTER YOU! LEAD THE WAY OUTSIDE! I'LL SPREAD YOU OVER THE COUNTY!
COME ON OUT, THEN! IF YOU DURST!
HEY! YOU IS ALL MIXED UP! GOIN' IN THAT DIRECTION IS GOIN' INSIDE!
WHO'S MIXED UP? FETCH THAT POST BACK HERE.

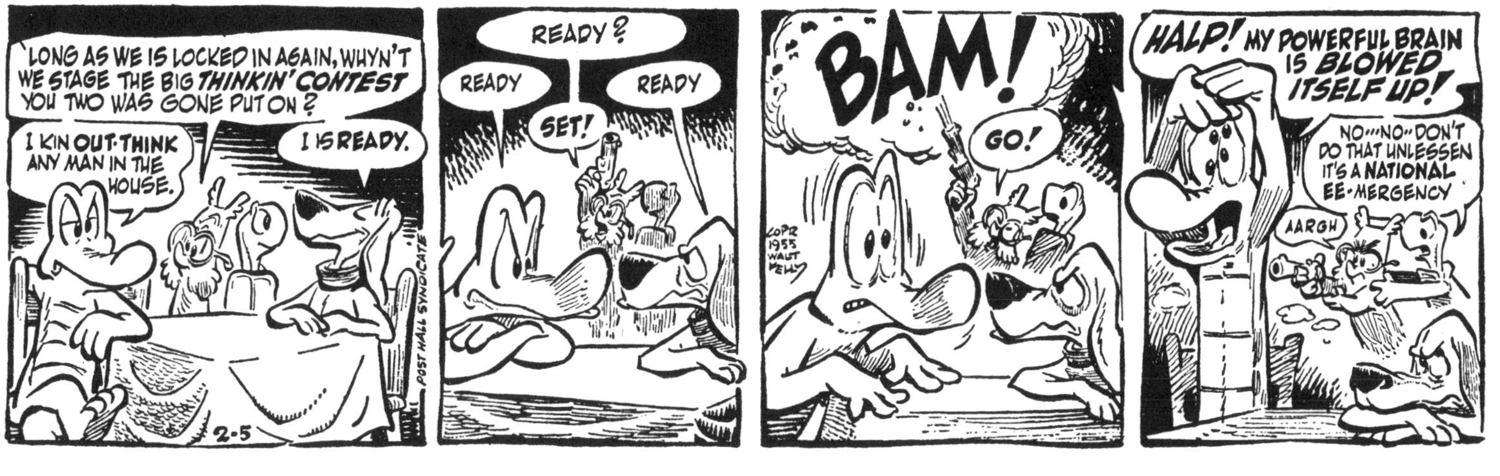
'LONG AS WE IS LOCKED IN AGAIN, WHYN'T WE STAGE THE BIG THINKIN' CONTEST YOU TWO WAS GONE PUT ON?
I KIN OUT-THINK ANY MAN IN THE HOUSE.
I IS READY.
POST HALL SYNDICATE
2-5
READY?
READY
READY
SET!
BAM!
GO!
COPR 1955 WALT KELLY
HALP! MY POWERFUL BRAIN IS BLOWED ITSELF UP!
NO---NO--DON'T DO THAT UNLESSEN IT'S A NATIONAL EE-MERGENCY
AARGH

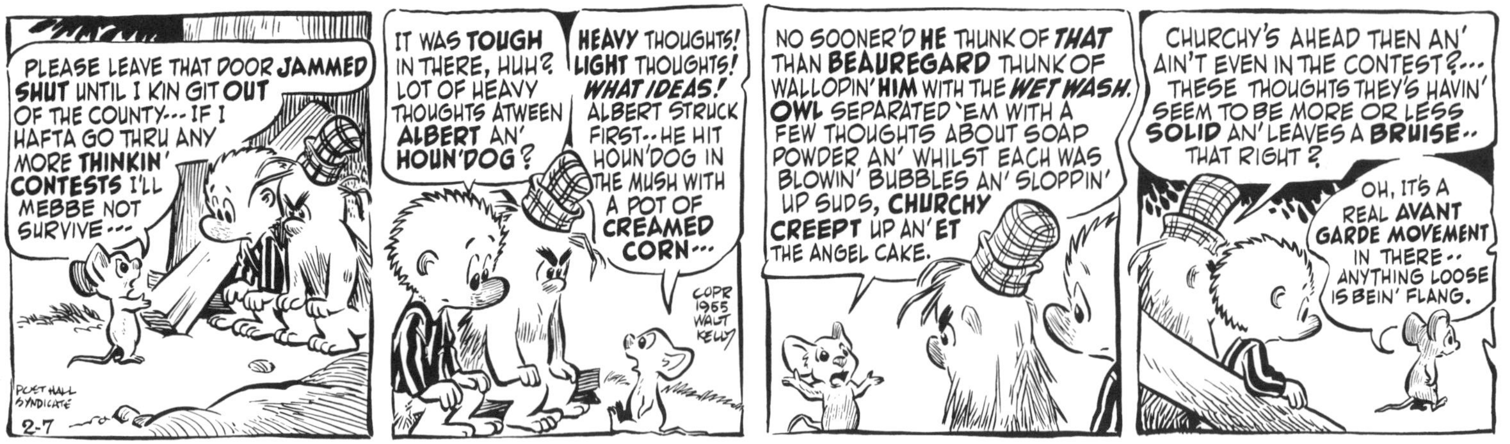
PLEASE LEAVE THAT DOOR JAMMED SHUT UNTIL I KIN GIT OUT OF THE COUNTY--- IF I HAFTA GO THRU ANY MORE THINKIN' CONTESTS I'LL MEBBE NOT SURVIVE---
POST HALL SYNDICATE
2-7
IT WAS TOUGH IN THERE, HUH? LOT OF HEAVY THOUGHTS ATWEEN ALBERT AN' HOUN'DOG?
HEAVY THOUGHTS! LIGHT THOUGHTS! WHAT IDEAS! ALBERT STRUCK FIRST-- HE HIT HOUN'DOG IN THE MUSH WITH A POT OF CREAMED CORN---
COPR 1955 WALT KELLY
NO SOONER'D HE THUNK OF THAT THAN BEAUREGARD THUNK OF WALLOPIN' HIM WITH THE WET WASH. OWL SEPARATED 'EM WITH A FEW THOUGHTS ABOUT SOAP POWDER AN' WHILST EACH WAS BLOWIN' BUBBLES AN' SLOPPIN' UP SUDS, CHURCHY CREEPT UP AN' ET THE ANGEL CAKE.
CHURCHY'S AHEAD THEN AN' AIN'T EVEN IN THE CONTEST?--- THESE THOUGHTS THEY'S HAVIN' SEEM TO BE MORE OR LESS SOLID AN' LEAVES A BRUISE-- THAT RIGHT?
OH, IT'S A REAL AVANT GARDE MOVEMENT IN THERE-- ANYTHING LOOSE IS BEIN' FLANG.

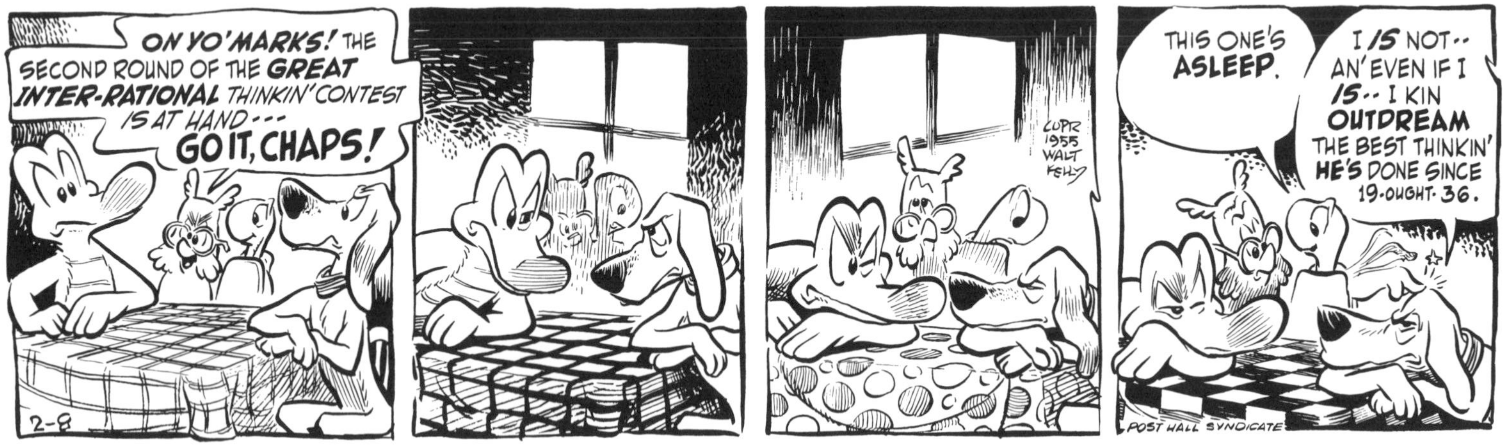
ON YO' MARKS! THE SECOND ROUND OF THE GREAT INTER-RATIONAL THINKIN' CONTEST IS AT HAND---
GO IT, CHAPS!
2-8
COPR 1955 WALT KELLY
THIS ONE'S ASLEEP.
I IS NOT-- AN' EVEN IF I IS-- I KIN OUTDREAM THE BEST THINKIN' HE'S DONE SINCE 19-OUGHT-36.
POST HALL SYNDICATE

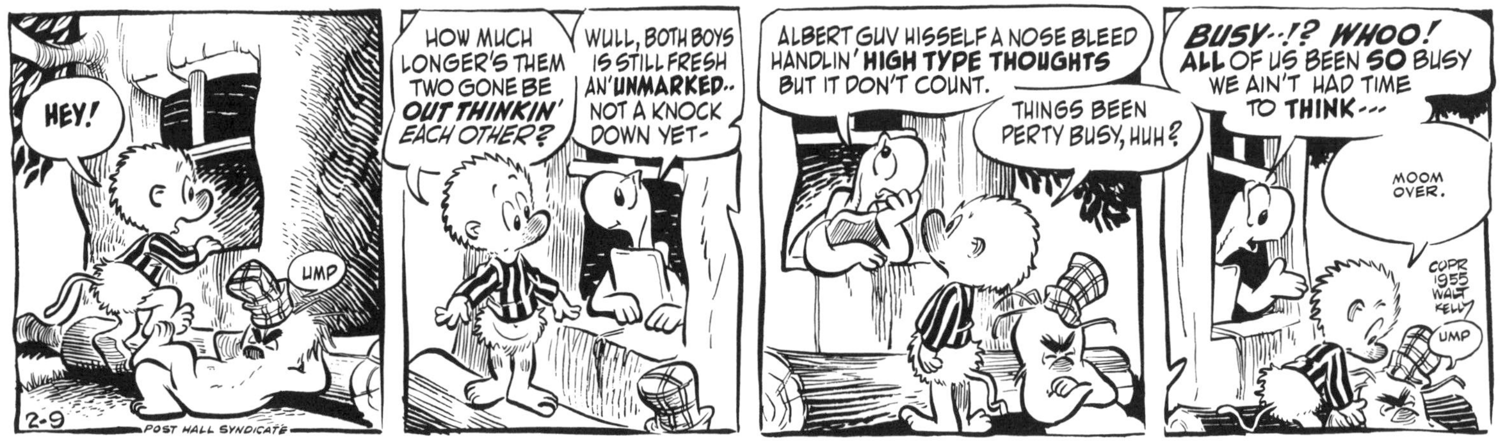
HEY!
UMP
2-9
POST HALL SYNDICATE
HOW MUCH LONGER'S THEM TWO GONE BE OUT THINKIN' EACH OTHER?
WULL, BOTH BOYS IS STILL FRESH AN' UNMARKED-- NOT A KNOCK DOWN YET-
ALBERT GUV HISSELF A NOSE BLEED HANDLIN' HIGH TYPE THOUGHTS BUT IT DON'T COUNT.
THINGS BEEN PERTY BUSY, HUH?
BUSY--!? WHOO! ALL OF US BEEN SO BUSY WE AIN'T HAD TIME TO THINK---
MOOM OVER.
COPR 1955 WALT KELLY
UMP

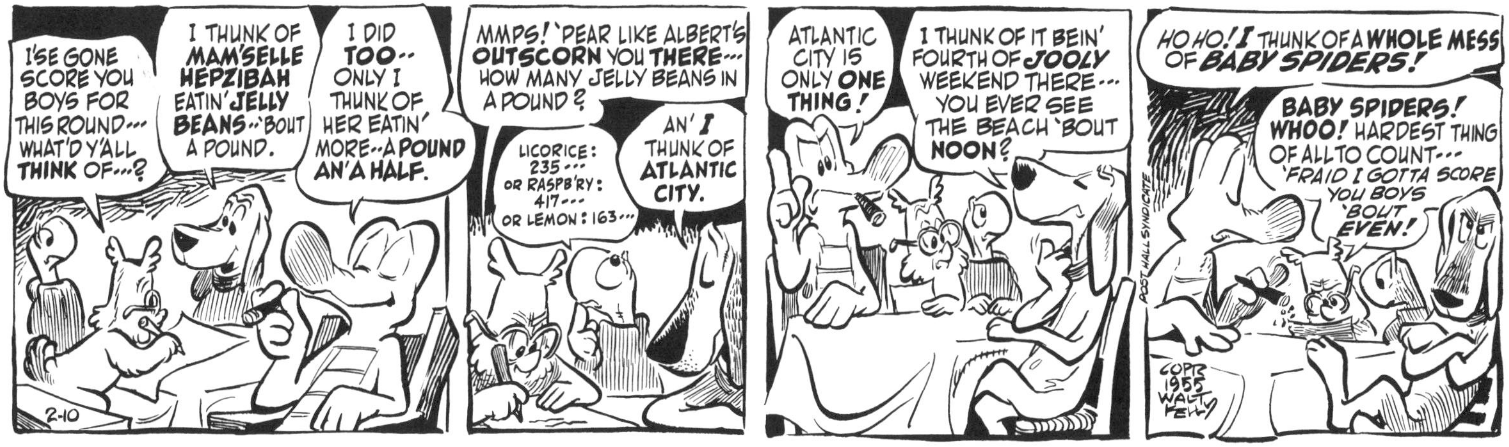
I'SE GONE SCORE YOU BOYS FOR THIS ROUND... WHAT'D Y'ALL THINK OF...?
I THUNK OF MAM'SELLE HEPZIBAH EATIN' JELLY BEANS..'BOUT A POUND.
I DID TOO.. ONLY I THUNK OF HER EATIN' MORE..A POUND AN' A HALF.
MMPS! 'PEAR LIKE ALBERT'S OUTSCORN YOU THERE... HOW MANY JELLY BEANS IN A POUND?
LICORICE: 235... OR RASPB'RY: 417... OR LEMON: 163...
AN' I THUNK OF ATLANTIC CITY.
ATLANTIC CITY IS ONLY ONE THING!
I THUNK OF IT BEIN' FOURTH OF JOOLY WEEKEND THERE... YOU EVER SEE THE BEACH 'BOUT NOON?
HO HO! I THUNK OF A WHOLE MESS OF BABY SPIDERS!
BABY SPIDERS! WHOO! HARDEST THING OF ALL TO COUNT... 'FRAID I GOTTA SCORE YOU BOYS 'BOUT EVEN!
2-10
POST HALL SYNDICATE
COPR 1955 WALT KELLY

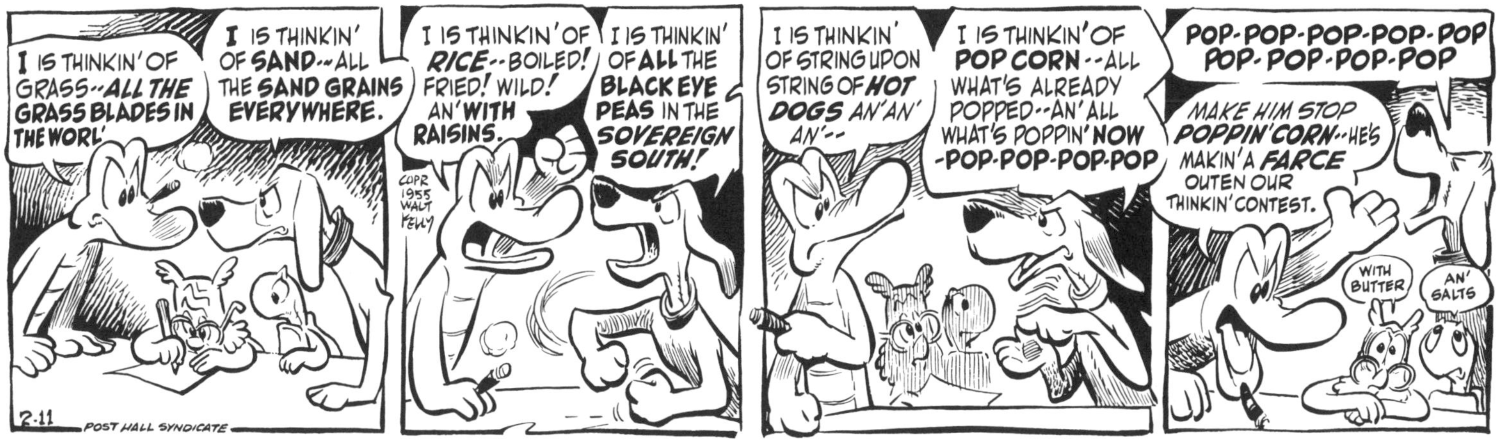
I IS THINKIN' OF GRASS..ALL THE GRASS BLADES IN THE WORL'
I IS THINKIN' OF SAND..ALL THE SAND GRAINS EVERYWHERE.
I IS THINKIN' OF RICE..BOILED! FRIED! WILD! AN' WITH RAISINS.
I IS THINKIN' OF ALL THE BLACK EYE PEAS IN THE SOVEREIGN SOUTH!
I IS THINKIN' OF STRING UPON STRING OF HOT DOGS AN' AN' AN'..
I IS THINKIN' OF POP CORN..ALL WHAT'S ALREADY POPPED..AN' ALL WHAT'S POPPIN' NOW -POP-POP-POP-POP
POP-POP-POP-POP-POP POP-POP-POP-POP
MAKE HIM STOP POPPIN' CORN..HE'S MAKIN' A FARCE OUTEN OUR THINKIN' CONTEST.
WITH BUTTER
AN' SALTS
2-11
POST HALL SYNDICATE
COPR 1955 WALT KELLY

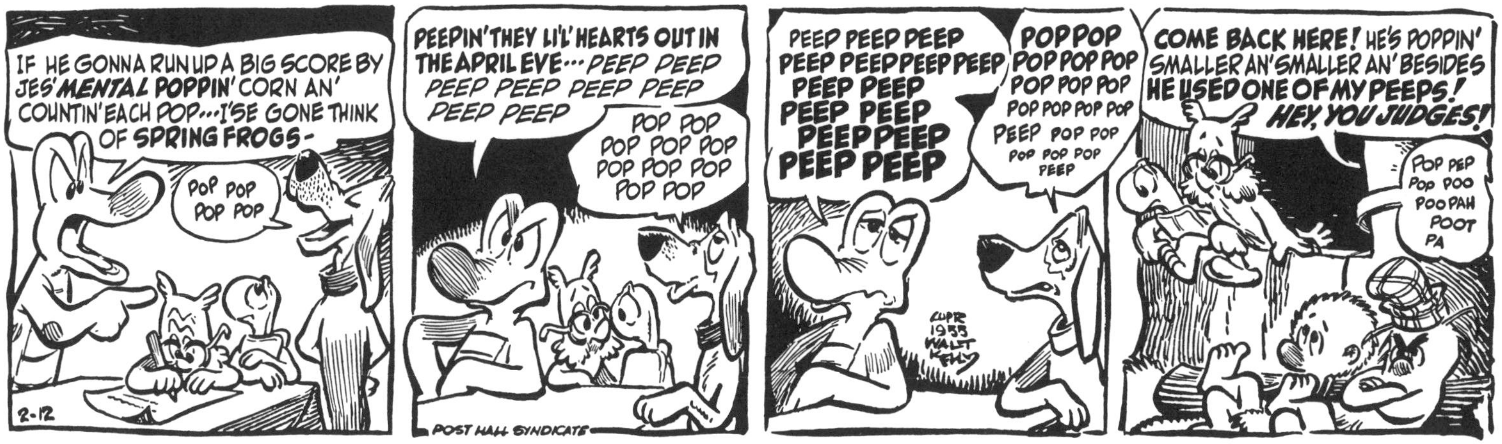
IF HE GONNA RUN UP A BIG SCORE BY JES' MENTAL POPPIN' CORN AN' COUNTIN' EACH POP...I'SE GONE THINK OF SPRING FROGS-
POP POP POP POP
PEEPIN' THEY LI'L' HEARTS OUT IN THE APRIL EVE... PEEP PEEP PEEP PEEP PEEP PEEP PEEP PEEP PEEP
POP POP POP POP POP POP POP POP POP POP POP
PEEP PEEP PEEP PEEP PEEP PEEP PEEP PEEP PEEP PEEP PEEP PEEP PEEP PEEP PEEP
POP POP POP POP POP POP POP POP POP POP POP POP POP PEEP POP POP POP POP POP PEEP
COME BACK HERE! HE'S POPPIN' SMALLER AN' SMALLER AN' BESIDES HE USED ONE OF MY PEEPS! HEY, YOU JUDGES!
POP PEP POP POO POO PAH POOT PA
2-12
POST HALL SYNDICATE
COPR 1955 WALT KELLY

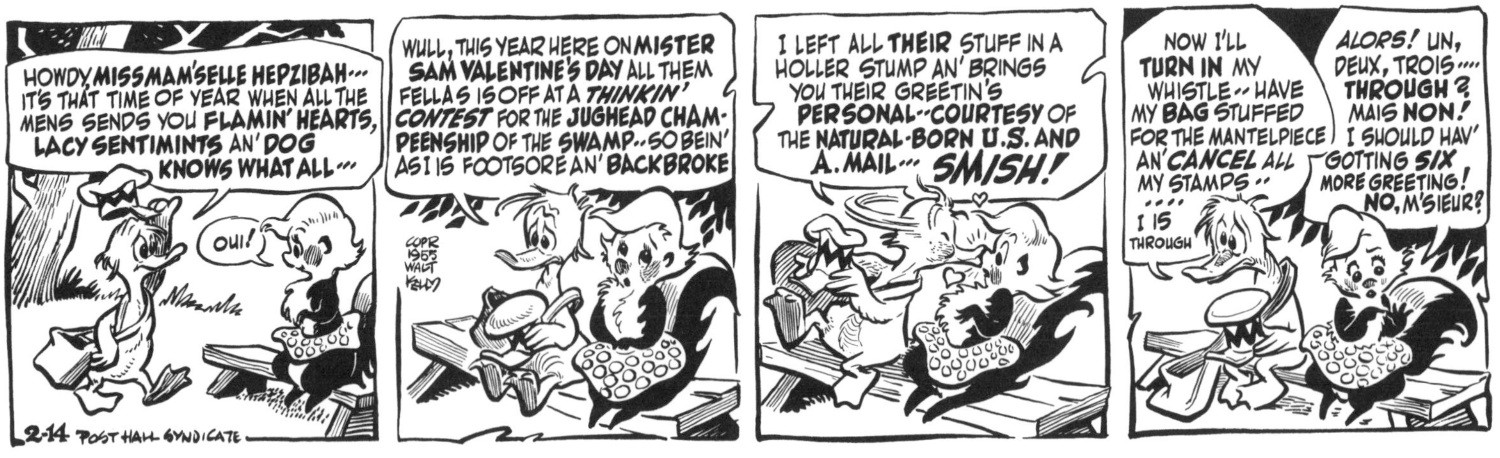
HOWDY, MISS MAM'SELLE HEPZIBAH··· IT'S THAT TIME OF YEAR WHEN ALL THE MENS SENDS YOU FLAMIN' HEARTS, LACY SENTIMINTS AN' DOG KNOWS WHAT ALL···
OUI!
WULL, THIS YEAR HERE ON MISTER SAM VALENTINE'S DAY ALL THEM FELLAS IS OFF AT A THINKIN' CONTEST FOR THE JUGHEAD CHAMPEENSHIP OF THE SWAMP.. SO BEIN' AS I IS FOOTSORE AN' BACKBROKE
I LEFT ALL THEIR STUFF IN A HOLLER STUMP AN' BRINGS YOU THEIR GREETIN'S PERSONAL··COURTESY OF THE NATURAL-BORN U.S. AND A. MAIL···
SMISH!
NOW I'LL TURN IN MY WHISTLE·· HAVE MY BAG STUFFED FOR THE MANTELPIECE AN' CANCEL ALL MY STAMPS·· ···· I IS THROUGH
ALORS! UN, DEUX, TROIS···· THROUGH? MAIS NON! I SHOULD HAV' GOTTING SIX MORE GREETING! NO, M'SIEUR?
COPR 1955 WALT KELLY
2-14 POST HALL SYNDICATE

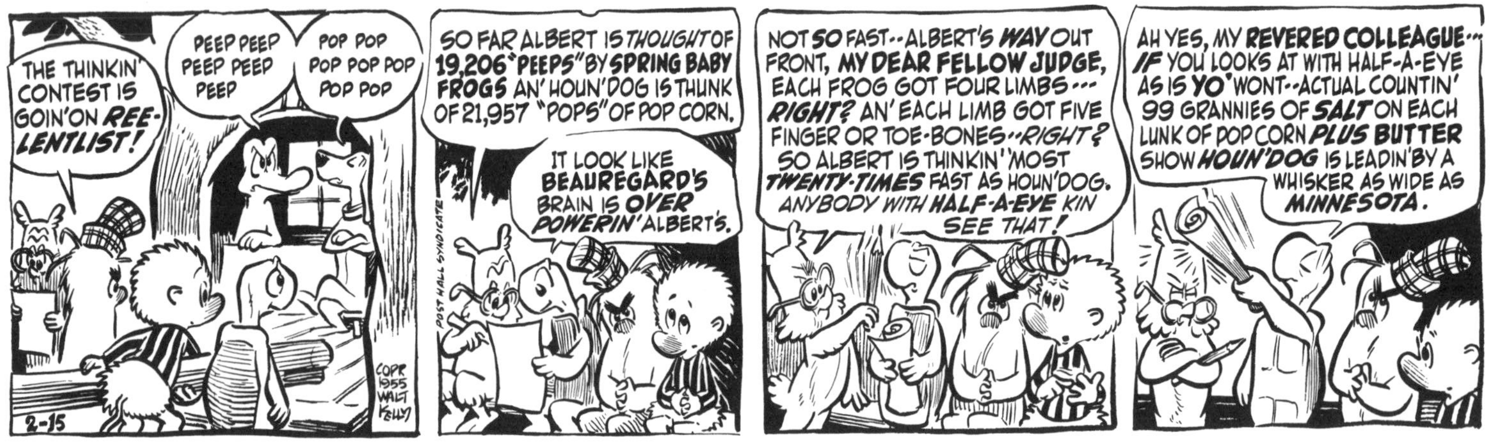
THE THINKIN' CONTEST IS GOIN'ON REE-LENTLIST!
PEEP PEEP PEEP PEEP PEEP
POP POP POP POP POP POP POP
SO FAR ALBERT IS THOUGHT OF 19,206 "PEEPS" BY SPRING BABY FROGS AN' HOUN'DOG IS THUNK OF 21,957 "POPS" OF POP CORN.
IT LOOK LIKE BEAUREGARD'S BRAIN IS OVER POWERIN' ALBERT'S.
NOT SO FAST··ALBERT'S WAY OUT FRONT, MY DEAR FELLOW JUDGE, EACH FROG GOT FOUR LIMBS··· RIGHT? AN' EACH LIMB GOT FIVE FINGER OR TOE-BONES··RIGHT? SO ALBERT IS THINKIN' 'MOST TWENTY-TIMES FAST AS HOUN'DOG. ANYBODY WITH HALF-A-EYE KIN SEE THAT!
AH YES, MY REVERED COLLEAGUE··· IF YOU LOOKS AT WITH HALF-A-EYE AS IS YO' WONT··ACTUAL COUNTIN' 99 GRANNIES OF SALT ON EACH LUNK OF POP CORN PLUS BUTTER SHOW HOUN'DOG IS LEADIN' BY A WHISKER AS WIDE AS MINNESOTA.
COPR 1955 WALT KELLY
POST HALL SYNDICATE
2-15

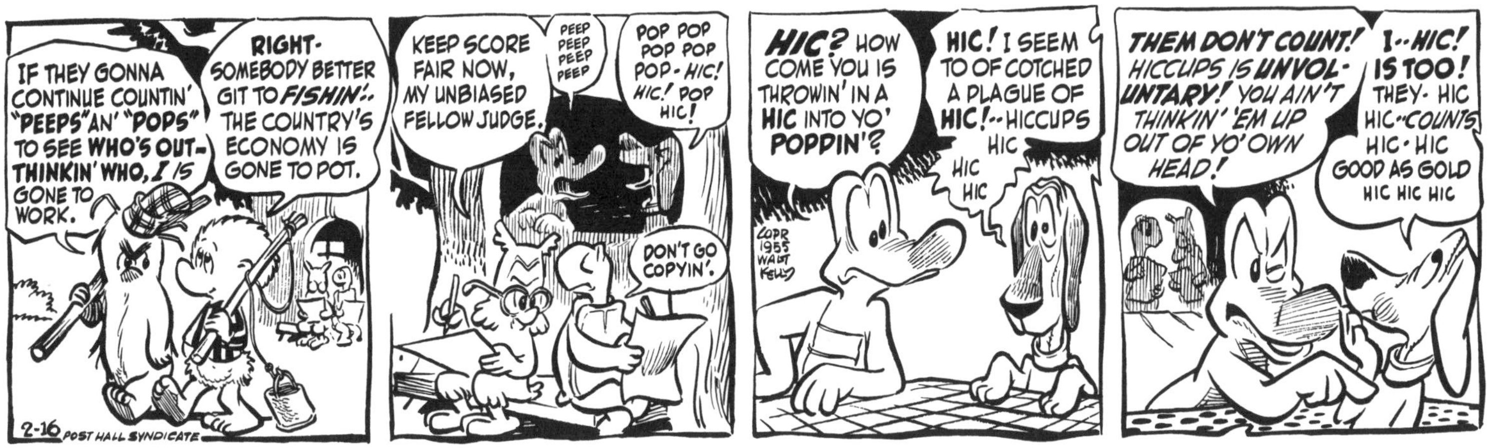
IF THEY GONNA CONTINUE COUNTIN' "PEEPS" AN' "POPS" TO SEE WHO'S OUT-THINKIN' WHO, I IS GONE TO WORK.
RIGHT- SOMEBODY BETTER GIT TO FISHIN'- THE COUNTRY'S ECONOMY IS GONE TO POT.
KEEP SCORE FAIR NOW, MY UNBIASED FELLOW JUDGE.
PEEP PEEP PEEP PEEP
POP POP POP POP POP-HIC! HIC! POP HIC!
DON'T GO COPYIN'.
HIC? HOW COME YOU IS THROWIN' IN A HIC INTO YO' POPPIN'?
HIC! I SEEM TO OF COTCHED A PLAGUE OF HIC!··HICCUPS HIC HIC HIC
COPR 1955 WALT KELLY
THEM DON'T COUNT! HICCUPS IS UNVOLUNTARY! YOU AIN'T THINKIN' 'EM UP OUT OF YO' OWN HEAD!
I··HIC! IS TOO! THEY- HIC HIC··COUNTS HIC·HIC GOOD AS GOLD HIC HIC HIC
2-16 POST HALL SYNDICATE

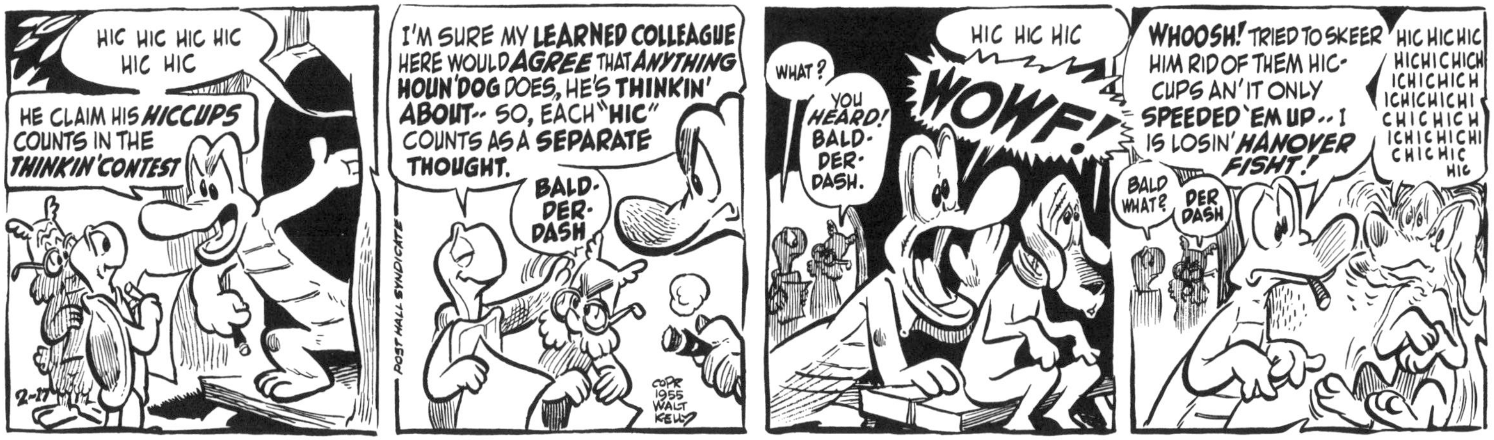
HIC HIC HIC HIC HIC HIC
HE CLAIM HIS HICCUPS COUNTS IN THE THINKIN' CONTEST
2-17
I'M SURE MY LEARNED COLLEAGUE HERE WOULD AGREE THAT ANYTHING HOUN' DOG DOES, HE'S THINKIN' ABOUT-- SO, EACH "HIC" COUNTS AS A SEPARATE THOUGHT.
BALD-DER-DASH
POST HALL SYNDICATE
COPR 1955 WALT KELLY
HIC HIC HIC
WHAT?
YOU HEARD! BALD-DER-DASH.
WOWF!
WHOOSH! TRIED TO SKEER HIM RID OF THEM HIC-CUPS AN' IT ONLY SPEEDED 'EM UP-- I IS LOSIN' HANOVER FISHT!
HIC HIC HIC HICHICHICH ICHICHICH ICHICHICHI CHICHICH ICHICHICHI CHICHIC HIC
BALD WHAT?
DER DASH

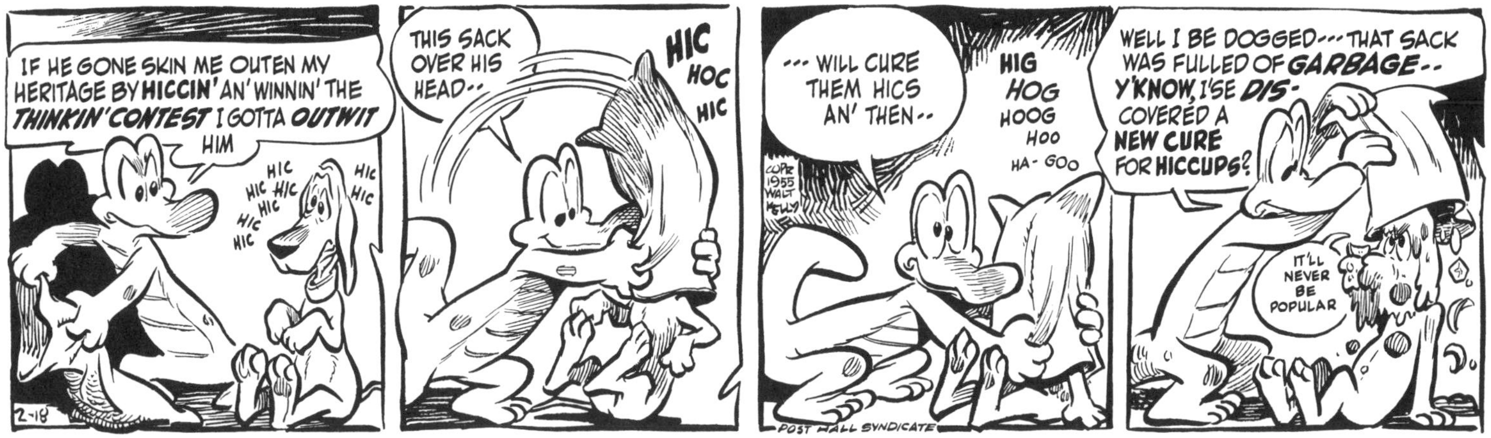
IF HE GONE SKIN ME OUTEN MY HERITAGE BY HICCIN' AN' WINNIN' THE THINKIN' CONTEST I GOTTA OUTWIT HIM
HIC HIC HIC HIC HIC HIC HIC HIC
2-18
THIS SACK OVER HIS HEAD--
HIC HOC HIC
--- WILL CURE THEM HICS AN' THEN--
HIG HOG HOOG HOO HA-GOO
COPR 1955 WALT KELLY
POST HALL SYNDICATE
WELL I BE DOGGED--- THAT SACK WAS FULLED OF GARBAGE-- Y'KNOW, I'SE DIS-COVERED A NEW CURE FOR HICCUPS?
IT'LL NEVER BE POPULAR

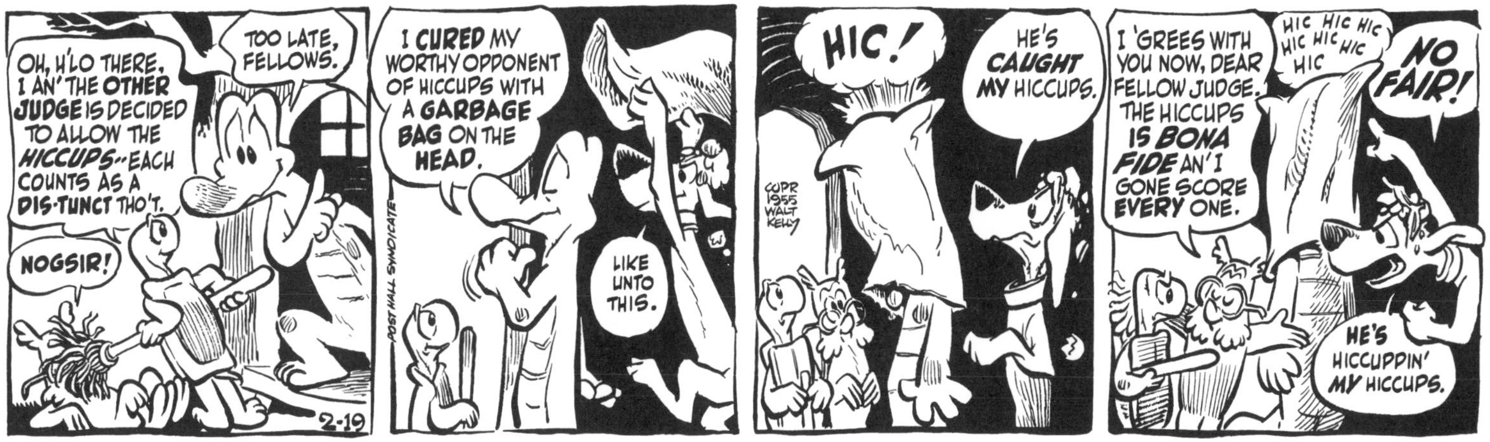
OH, H'LO THERE. I AN' THE OTHER JUDGE IS DECIDED TO ALLOW THE HICCUPS-- EACH COUNTS AS A DIS-TUNCT THO'T.
TOO LATE, FELLOWS.
NOGSIR!
2-19
I CURED MY WORTHY OPPONENT OF HICCUPS WITH A GARBAGE BAG ON THE HEAD.
LIKE UNTO THIS.
POST HALL SYNDICATE
HIC!
HE'S CAUGHT MY HICCUPS.
COPR 1955 WALT KELLY
I 'GREES WITH YOU NOW, DEAR FELLOW JUDGE. THE HICCUPS IS BONA FIDE AN' I GONE SCORE EVERY ONE.
HIC HIC HIC HIC HIC HIC HIC
NO FAIR!
HE'S HICCUPPIN' MY HICCUPS.

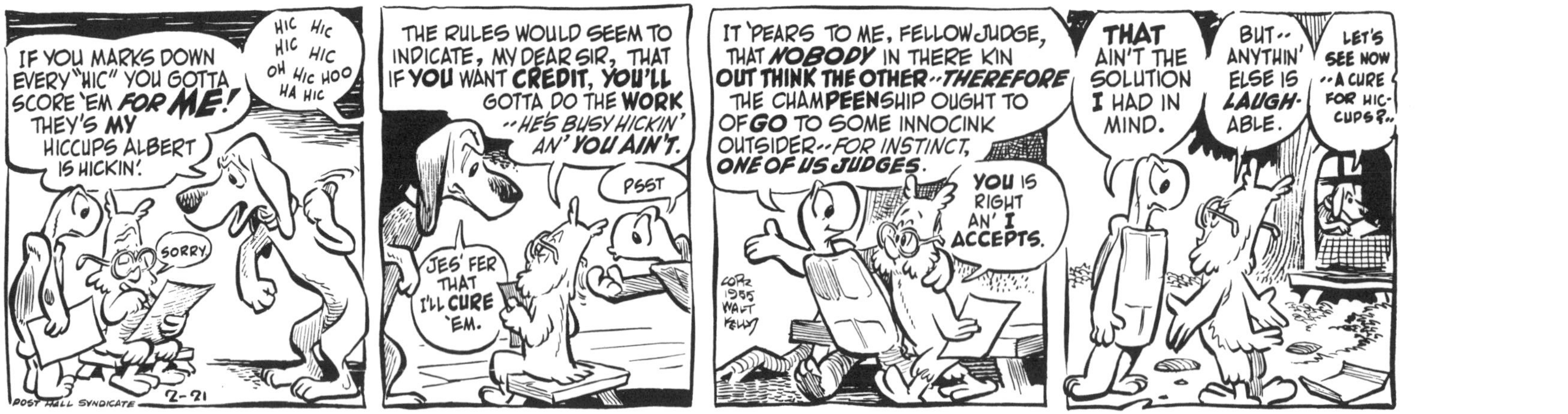
IF YOU MARKS DOWN EVERY "HIC" YOU GOTTA SCORE 'EM FOR ME! THEY'S MY HICCUPS ALBERT IS HICKIN'.
HIC HIC HIC HIC OH HIC HOO HA HIC
SORRY.
2-21
POST HALL SYNDICATE
THE RULES WOULD SEEM TO INDICATE, MY DEAR SIR, THAT IF YOU WANT CREDIT, YOU'LL GOTTA DO THE WORK --HE'S BUSY HICKIN' AN' YOU AIN'T.
PSST
JES' FER THAT I'LL CURE 'EM.
IT 'PEARS TO ME, FELLOW JUDGE, THAT NOBODY IN THERE KIN OUT THINK THE OTHER--THEREFORE THE CHAMPEENSHIP OUGHT TO OF GO TO SOME INNOCINK OUTSIDER--FOR INSTINCT, ONE OF US JUDGES.
YOU IS RIGHT AN' I ACCEPTS.
COPR 1955 WALT KELLY
THAT AIN'T THE SOLUTION I HAD IN MIND.
BUT--ANYTHIN' ELSE IS LAUGH-ABLE.
LET'S SEE NOW --A CURE FOR HIC-CUPS?..

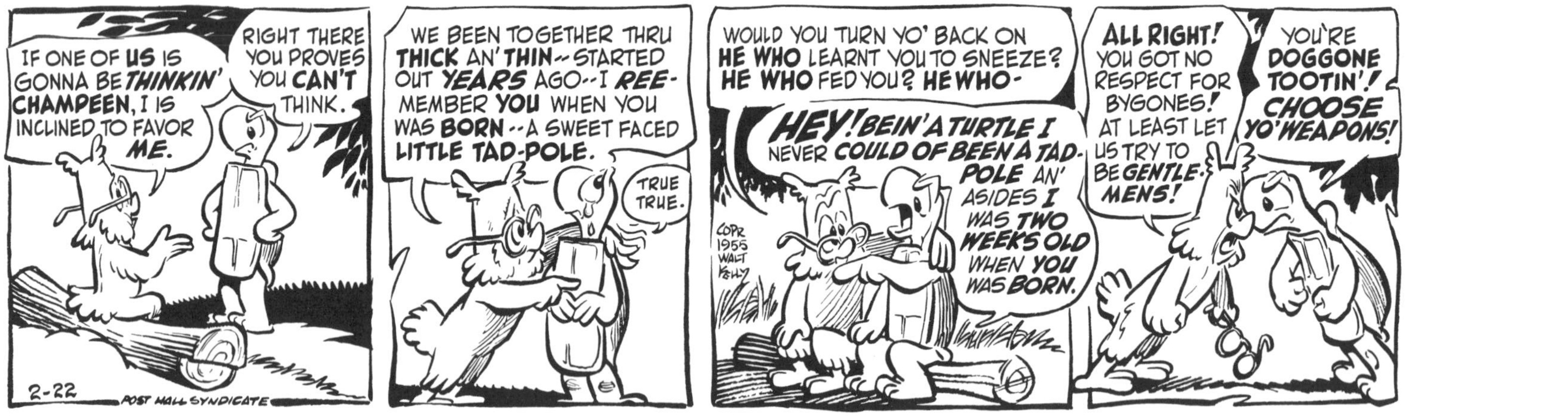
IF ONE OF US IS GONNA BE THINKIN' CHAMPEEN, I IS INCLINED TO FAVOR ME.
RIGHT THERE YOU PROVES YOU CAN'T THINK.
2-22
POST HALL SYNDICATE
WE BEEN TOGETHER THRU THICK AN' THIN--STARTED OUT YEARS AGO--I REE-MEMBER YOU WHEN YOU WAS BORN--A SWEET FACED LITTLE TAD-POLE.
TRUE TRUE.
WOULD YOU TURN YO' BACK ON HE WHO LEARNT YOU TO SNEEZE? HE WHO FED YOU? HE WHO-
HEY! BEIN' A TURTLE I NEVER COULD OF BEEN A TAD-POLE AN' ASIDES I WAS TWO WEEKS OLD WHEN YOU WAS BORN.
COPR 1955 WALT KELLY
ALL RIGHT! YOU GOT NO RESPECT FOR BYGONES! AT LEAST LET US TRY TO BE GENTLE-MENS!
YOU'RE DOGGONE TOOTIN'! CHOOSE YO' WEAPONS!

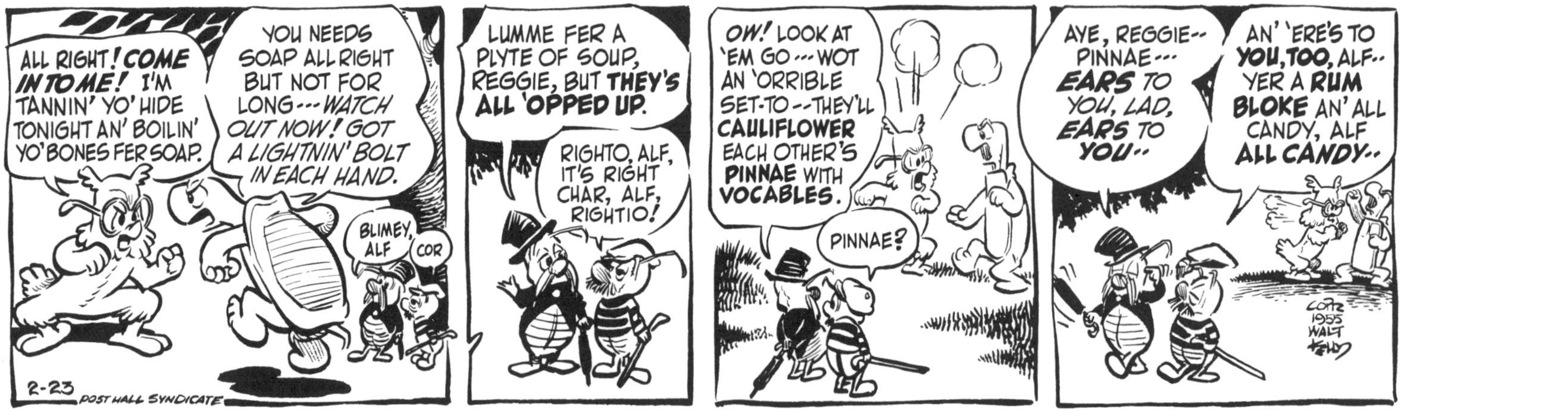
ALL RIGHT! COME IN TO ME! I'M TANNIN' YO' HIDE TONIGHT AN' BOILIN' YO' BONES FER SOAP.
YOU NEEDS SOAP ALL RIGHT BUT NOT FOR LONG---WATCH OUT NOW! GOT A LIGHTNIN' BOLT IN EACH HAND.
BLIMEY, ALF
COR
2-23
POST HALL SYNDICATE
LUMME FER A PLYTE OF SOUP, REGGIE, BUT THEY'S ALL 'OPPED UP.
RIGHTO, ALF, IT'S RIGHT CHAR, ALF, RIGHTIO!
OW! LOOK AT 'EM GO---WOT AN 'ORRIBLE SET-TO--THEY'LL CAULIFLOWER EACH OTHER'S PINNAE WITH VOCABLES.
PINNAE?
AYE, REGGIE--PINNAE---EARS TO YOU, LAD, EARS TO YOU--
AN' 'ERE'S TO YOU, TOO, ALF--YER A RUM BLOKE AN' ALL CANDY, ALF ALL CANDY--
COPR 1955 WALT KELLY

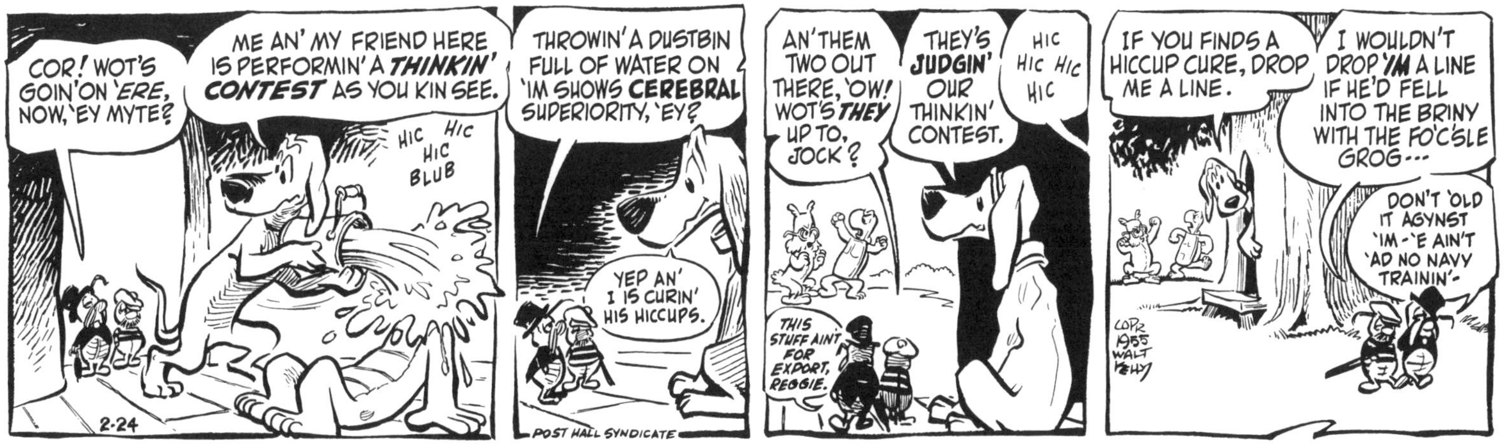
COR! WOT'S GOIN' ON 'ERE, NOW, 'EY MYTE?
ME AN' MY FRIEND HERE IS PERFORMIN' A THINKIN' CONTEST AS YOU KIN SEE.
HIC HIC HIC BLUB
2-24
THROWIN' A DUSTBIN FULL OF WATER ON 'IM SHOWS CEREBRAL SUPERIORITY, 'EY?
YEP AN' I IS CURIN' HIS HICCUPS.
POST HALL SYNDICATE
AN' THEM TWO OUT THERE, 'OW! WOT'S THEY UP TO, JOCK?
THEY'S JUDGIN' OUR THINKIN' CONTEST.
HIC HIC HIC HIC
THIS STUFF AINT FOR EXPORT, REGGIE.
IF YOU FINDS A HICCUP CURE, DROP ME A LINE.
I WOULDN'T DROP 'IM A LINE IF HE'D FELL INTO THE BRINY WITH THE FO'C'SLE GROG---
DON'T 'OLD IT AGYNST 'IM-'E AIN'T 'AD NO NAVY TRAININ'-
COPR 1955 WALT KELLY

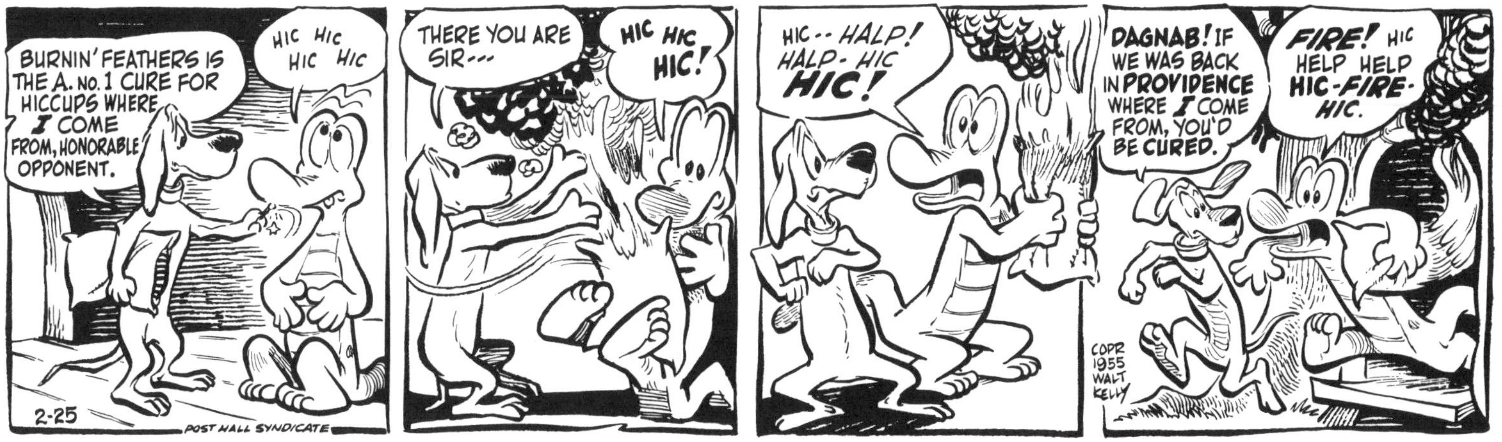
BURNIN' FEATHERS IS THE A. NO. 1 CURE FOR HICCUPS WHERE I COME FROM, HONORABLE OPPONENT.
HIC HIC HIC HIC
2-25
POST HALL SYNDICATE
THERE YOU ARE SIR---
HIC HIC HIC!
HIC-- HALP! HALP- HIC HIC!
DAGNAB! IF WE WAS BACK IN PROVIDENCE WHERE I COME FROM, YOU'D BE CURED.
FIRE! HIC HELP HELP HIC-FIRE-HIC.
COPR 1955 WALT KELLY

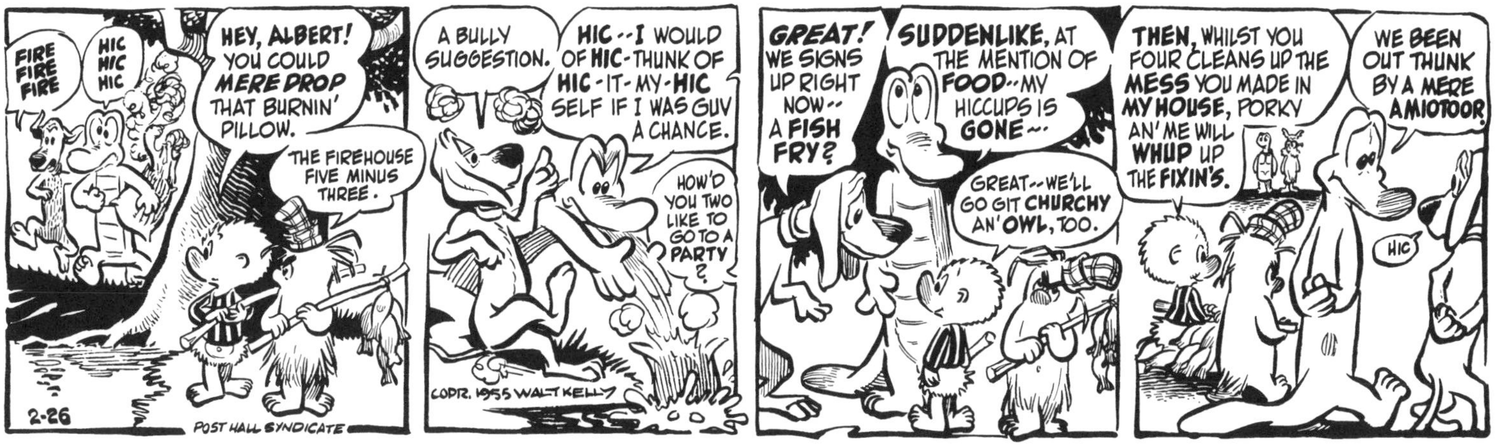
FIRE FIRE FIRE
HIC HIC HIC
HEY, ALBERT! YOU COULD MERE DROP THAT BURNIN' PILLOW.
THE FIREHOUSE FIVE MINUS THREE.
2-26
POST HALL SYNDICATE
A BULLY SUGGESTION.
HIC--I WOULD OF HIC-THUNK OF HIC-IT-MY-HIC SELF IF I WAS GUV A CHANCE.
HOW'D YOU TWO LIKE TO GO TO A PARTY?
COPR. 1955 WALT KELLY
GREAT! WE SIGNS UP RIGHT NOW-- A FISH FRY?
SUDDENLIKE, AT THE MENTION OF FOOD--MY HICCUPS IS GONE--.
GREAT--WE'LL GO GIT CHURCHY AN' OWL, TOO.
THEN, WHILST YOU FOUR CLEANS UP THE MESS YOU MADE IN MY HOUSE, PORKY AN' ME WILL WHUP UP THE FIXIN'S.
WE BEEN OUT THUNK BY A MERE AMIOTOOR.
HIC

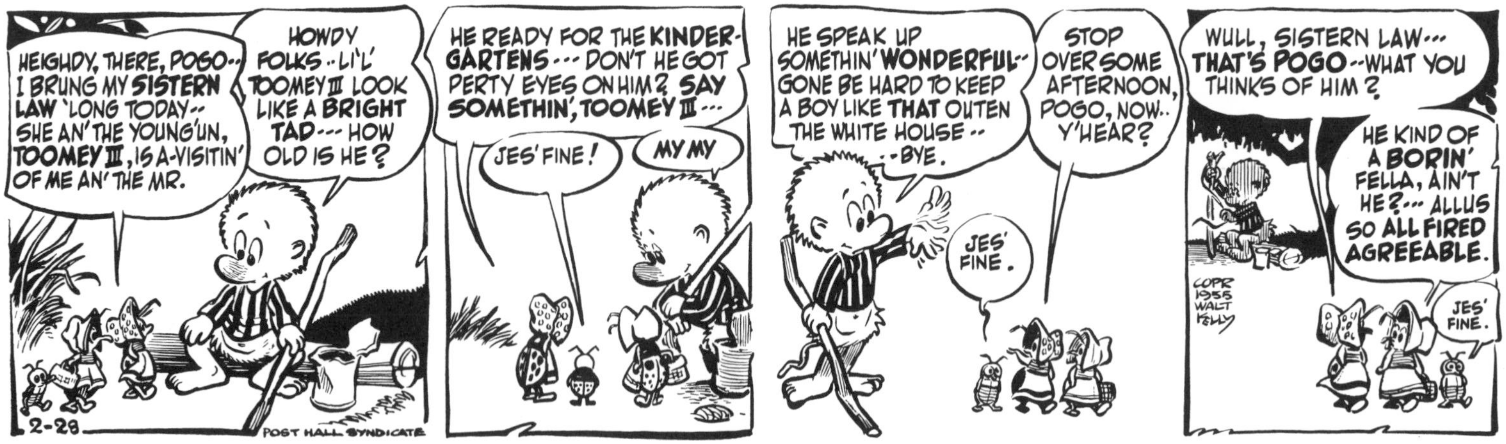
HEIGHDY, THERE, POGO-- I BRUNG MY SISTERN LAW 'LONG TODAY-- SHE AN' THE YOUNG'UN, TOOMEY III, IS A-VISITIN' OF ME AN' THE MR.
HOWDY FOLKS--LI'L' TOOMEY III LOOK LIKE A BRIGHT TAD--- HOW OLD IS HE?
2-28
POST HALL SYNDICATE
HE READY FOR THE KINDER-GARTENS --- DON'T HE GOT PERTY EYES ON HIM? SAY SOMETHIN', TOOMEY III ---
JES' FINE!
MY MY
HE SPEAK UP SOMETHIN' WONDERFUL-- GONE BE HARD TO KEEP A BOY LIKE THAT OUTEN THE WHITE HOUSE -- --BYE.
STOP OVER SOME AFTERNOON, POGO, NOW.. Y'HEAR?
JES' FINE.
WULL, SISTERN LAW--- THAT'S POGO--WHAT YOU THINKS OF HIM?
HE KIND OF A BORIN' FELLA, AIN'T HE?--- ALLUS SO ALL FIRED AGREEABLE.
COPR 1955 WALT KELLY
JES' FINE.

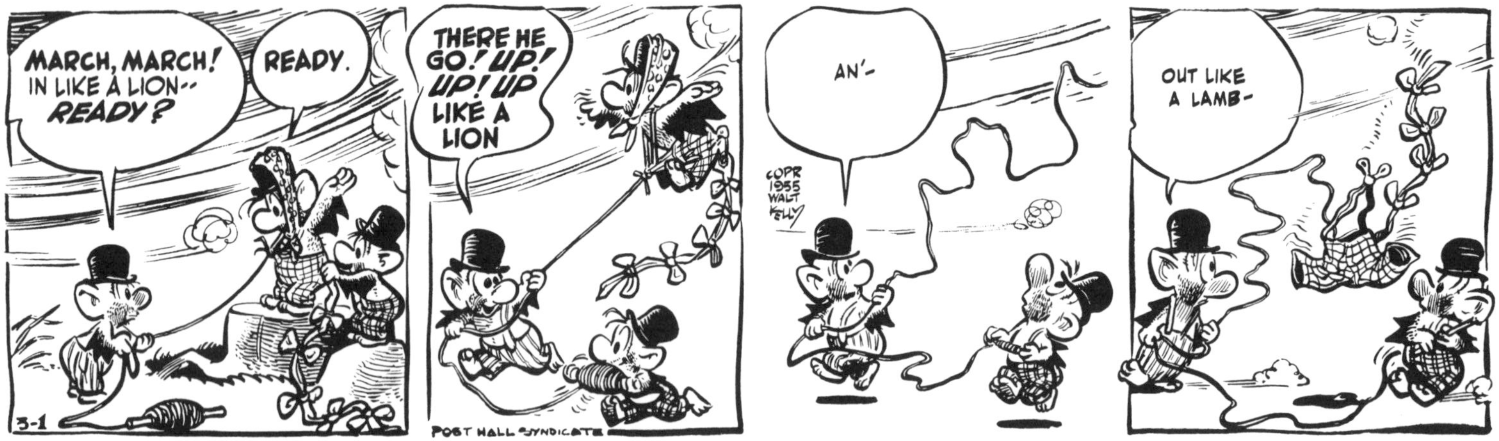
MARCH, MARCH! IN LIKE A LION-- READY?
READY.
3-1
THERE HE GO! UP! UP! UP LIKE A LION
POST HALL SYNDICATE
AN'-
COPR 1955 WALT KELLY
OUT LIKE A LAMB-

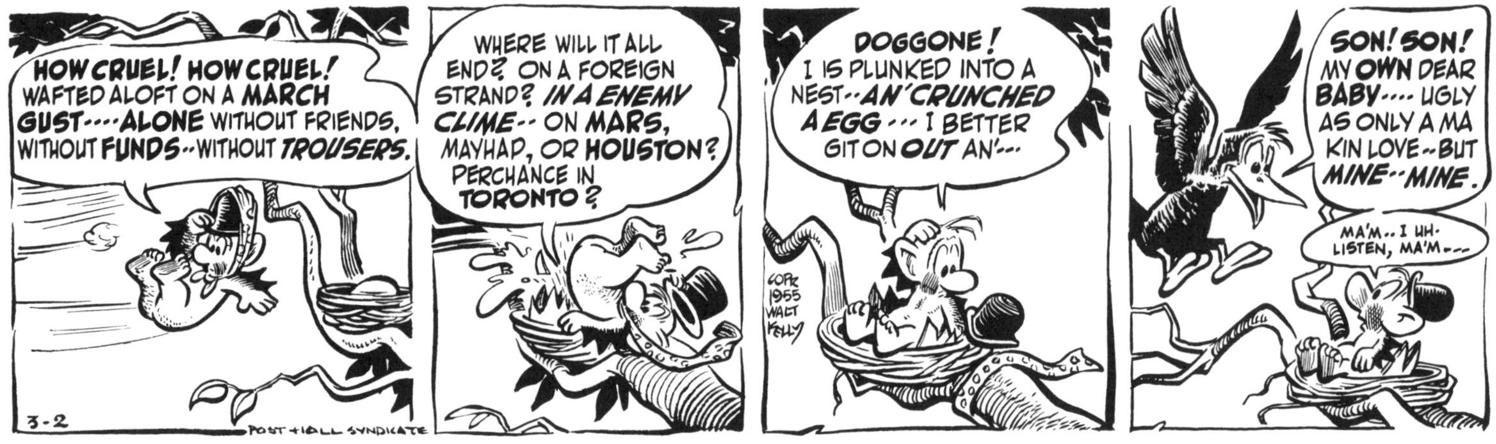
HOW CRUEL! HOW CRUEL! WAFTED ALOFT ON A MARCH GUST---- ALONE WITHOUT FRIENDS, WITHOUT FUNDS--WITHOUT TROUSERS.
3-2
POST HALL SYNDICATE
WHERE WILL IT ALL END? ON A FOREIGN STRAND? IN A ENEMY CLIME-- ON MARS, MAYHAP, OR HOUSTON? PERCHANCE IN TORONTO?
DOGGONE! I IS PLUNKED INTO A NEST--AN' CRUNCHED A EGG --- I BETTER GIT ON OUT AN'--.
COPR 1955 WALT KELLY
SON! SON! MY OWN DEAR BABY.... UGLY AS ONLY A MA KIN LOVE--BUT MINE--MINE.
MA'M.. I UH-LISTEN, MA'M---

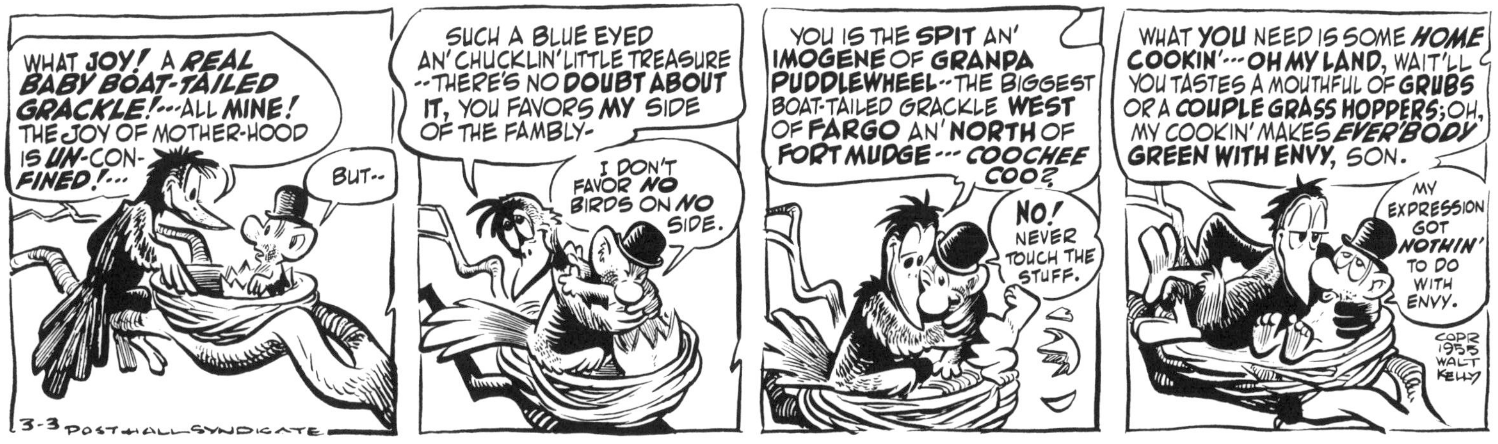
WHAT JOY! A REAL BABY BOAT-TAILED GRACKLE!--ALL MINE! THE JOY OF MOTHER-HOOD IS UN-CONFINED!...
BUT--
SUCH A BLUE EYED AN' CHUCKLIN' LITTLE TREASURE --THERE'S NO DOUBT ABOUT IT, YOU FAVORS MY SIDE OF THE FAMBLY-
I DON'T FAVOR NO BIRDS ON NO SIDE.
YOU IS THE SPIT AN' IMOGENE OF GRANPA PUDDLEWHEEL--THE BIGGEST BOAT-TAILED GRACKLE WEST OF FARGO AN' NORTH OF FORT MUDGE --- COOCHEE COO?
NO! NEVER TOUCH THE STUFF.
WHAT YOU NEED IS SOME HOME COOKIN'--- OH MY LAND, WAIT'LL YOU TASTES A MOUTHFUL OF GRUBS OR A COUPLE GRASS HOPPERS; OH, MY COOKIN' MAKES EVER'BODY GREEN WITH ENVY, SON.
MY EXPRESSION GOT NOTHIN' TO DO WITH ENVY.
COPR 1955 WALT KELLY
3-3 POST-HALL SYNDICATE

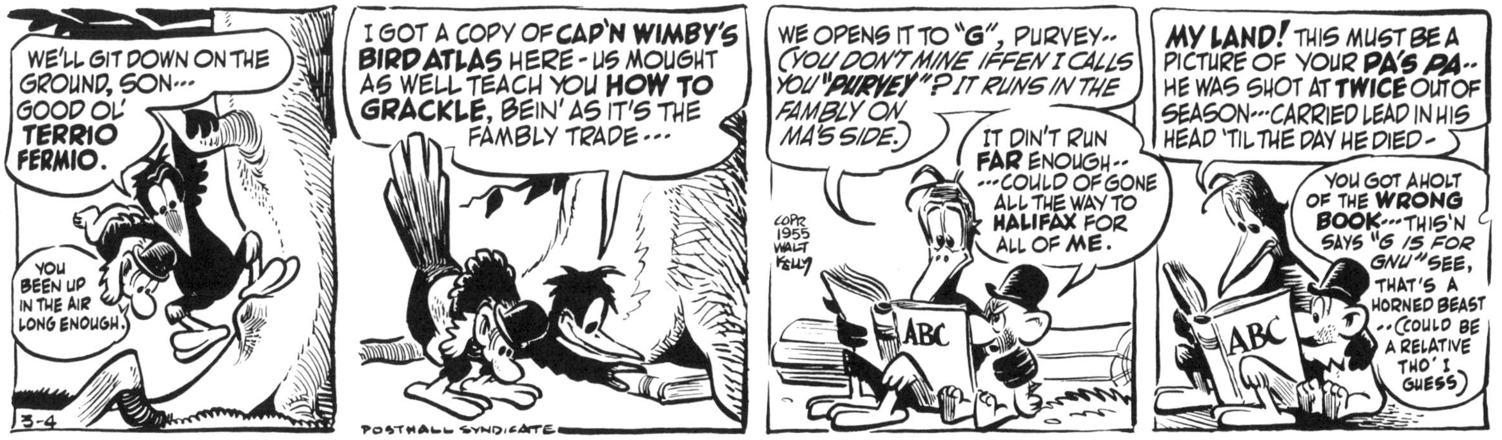
WE'LL GIT DOWN ON THE GROUND, SON--- GOOD OL' TERRIO FERMIO.
YOU BEEN UP IN THE AIR LONG ENOUGH.
I GOT A COPY OF CAP'N WIMBY'S BIRD ATLAS HERE - US MOUGHT AS WELL TEACH YOU HOW TO GRACKLE, BEIN' AS IT'S THE FAMBLY TRADE ---
WE OPENS IT TO "G", PURVEY-- (YOU DON'T MINE IFFEN I CALLS YOU "PURVEY"? IT RUNS IN THE FAMBLY ON MA'S SIDE.)
IT DIN'T RUN FAR ENOUGH-- ---COULD OF GONE ALL THE WAY TO HALIFAX FOR ALL OF ME.
COPR 1955 WALT KELLY
ABC
MY LAND! THIS MUST BE A PICTURE OF YOUR PA'S PA-- HE WAS SHOT AT TWICE OUT OF SEASON---CARRIED LEAD IN HIS HEAD 'TIL THE DAY HE DIED-
YOU GOT AHOLT OF THE WRONG BOOK--- THIS'N SAYS "G IS FOR GNU" SEE, THAT'S A HORNED BEAST --(COULD BE A RELATIVE THO' I GUESS)
ABC
3-4 POSTHALL SYNDICATE

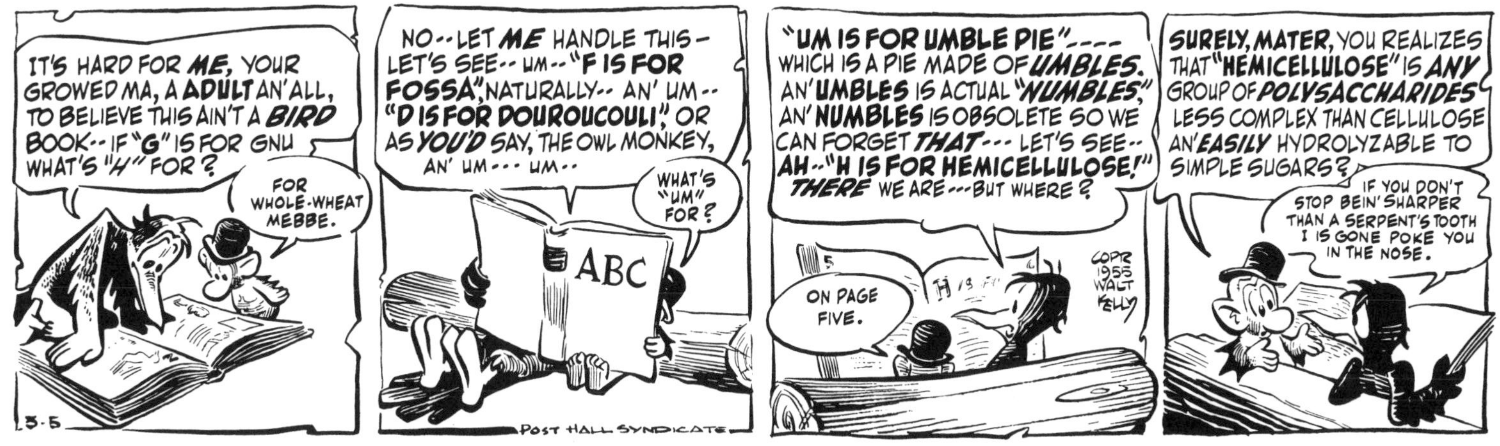
IT'S HARD FOR ME, YOUR GROWED MA, A ADULT AN' ALL, TO BELIEVE THIS AIN'T A BIRD BOOK-- IF "G" IS FOR GNU WHAT'S "H" FOR?
FOR WHOLE-WHEAT MEBBE.
NO--LET ME HANDLE THIS- LET'S SEE-- UM--"F IS FOR FOSSA", NATURALLY-- AN' UM-- "D IS FOR DOUROUCOULI", OR AS YOU'D SAY, THE OWL MONKEY, AN' UM --- UM--
WHAT'S "UM" FOR?
ABC
"UM IS FOR UMBLE PIE"---- WHICH IS A PIE MADE OF UMBLES. AN' UMBLES IS ACTUAL "NUMBLES," AN' NUMBLES IS OBSOLETE SO WE CAN FORGET THAT--- LET'S SEE-- AH--"H IS FOR HEMICELLULOSE!" THERE WE ARE---BUT WHERE?
ON PAGE FIVE.
COPR 1955 WALT KELLY
SURELY, MATER, YOU REALIZES THAT "HEMICELLULOSE" IS ANY GROUP OF POLYSACCHARIDES LESS COMPLEX THAN CELLULOSE AN' EASILY HYDROLYZABLE TO SIMPLE SUGARS?
IF YOU DON'T STOP BEIN' SHARPER THAN A SERPENT'S TOOTH I IS GONE POKE YOU IN THE NOSE.
3-5 POST HALL SYNDICATE

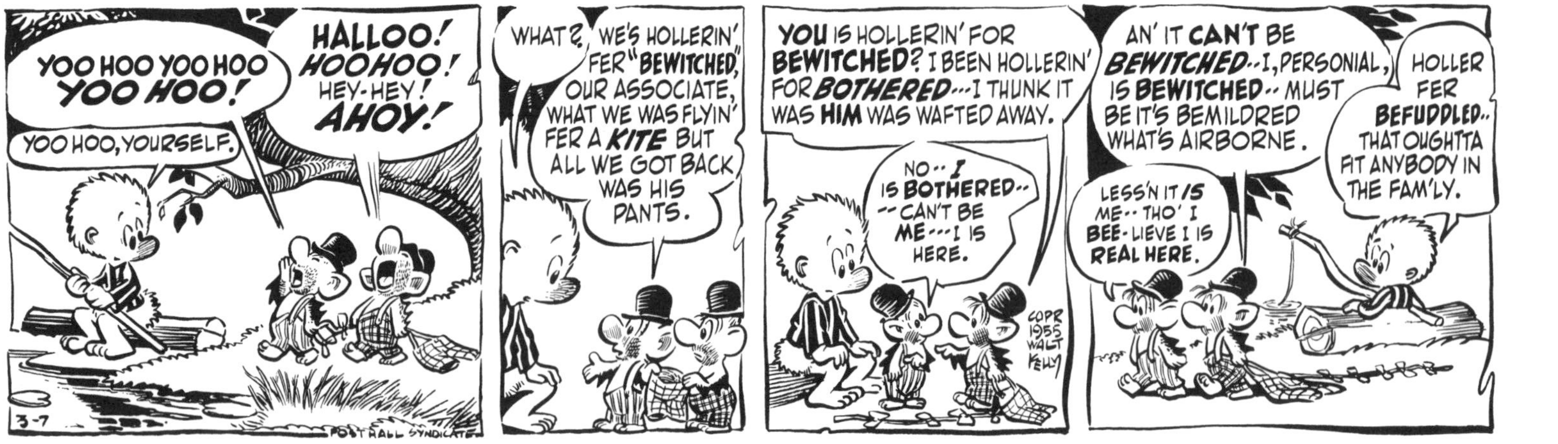
YOO HOO YOO HOO YOO HOO!
YOO HOO, YOURSELF.
HALLOO! HOOHOO! HEY-HEY! AHOY!
3-7
POST HALL SYNDICATE
WHAT?
WE'S HOLLERIN' FER "BEWITCHED," OUR ASSOCIATE, WHAT WE WAS FLYIN' FER A KITE BUT ALL WE GOT BACK WAS HIS PANTS.
YOU IS HOLLERIN' FOR BEWITCHED? I BEEN HOLLERIN' FOR BOTHERED--- I THUNK IT WAS HIM WAS WAFTED AWAY.
NO-- I IS BOTHERED-- -- CAN'T BE ME--- I IS HERE.
COPR 1955 WALT KELLY
AN' IT CAN'T BE BEWITCHED-- I, PERSONIAL, IS BEWITCHED-- MUST BE IT'S BEMILDRED WHAT'S AIRBORNE.
HOLLER FER BEFUDDLED.. THAT OUGHTTA FIT ANYBODY IN THE FAM'LY.
LESS'N IT IS ME-- THO' I BEE-LIEVE I IS REAL HERE.

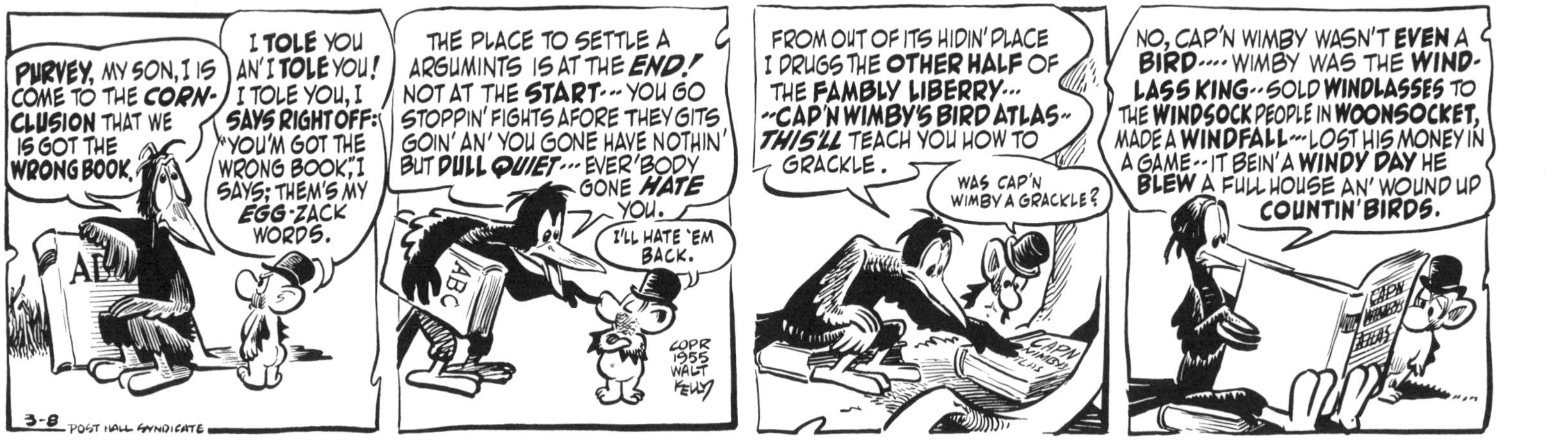
PURVEY, MY SON, I IS COME TO THE CORN-CLUSION THAT WE IS GOT THE WRONG BOOK.
I TOLE YOU AN' I TOLE YOU! I TOLE YOU, I SAYS RIGHT OFF: "YOU'M GOT THE WRONG BOOK," I SAYS; THEM'S MY EGG-ZACK WORDS.
3-8
POST HALL SYNDICATE
THE PLACE TO SETTLE A ARGUMINTS IS AT THE END! NOT AT THE START--- YOU GO STOPPIN' FIGHTS AFORE THEY GITS GOIN' AN' YOU GONE HAVE NOTHIN' BUT DULL QUIET--- EVER'BODY GONE HATE YOU.
I'LL HATE 'EM BACK.
ABC
COPR 1955 WALT KELLY
FROM OUT OF ITS HIDIN' PLACE I DRUGS THE OTHER HALF OF THE FAMBLY LIBERRY--- --CAP'N WIMBY'S BIRD ATLAS-- THIS'LL TEACH YOU HOW TO GRACKLE.
WAS CAP'N WIMBY A GRACKLE?
NO, CAP'N WIMBY WASN'T EVEN A BIRD---- WIMBY WAS THE WIND-LASS KING-- SOLD WINDLASSES TO THE WINDSOCK PEOPLE IN WOONSOCKET, MADE A WINDFALL--- LOST HIS MONEY IN A GAME-- IT BEIN' A WINDY DAY HE BLEW A FULL HOUSE AN' WOUND UP COUNTIN' BIRDS.

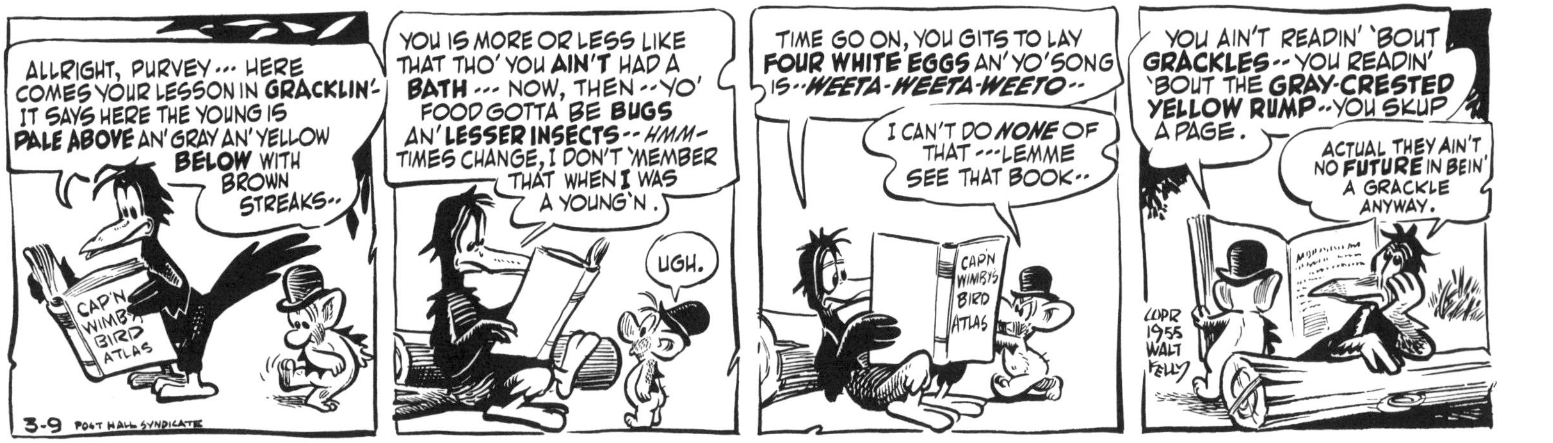
ALLRIGHT, PURVEY--- HERE COMES YOUR LESSON IN GRACKLIN'- IT SAYS HERE THE YOUNG IS PALE ABOVE AN' GRAY AN' YELLOW BELOW WITH BROWN STREAKS--
CAP'N WIMB BIRD ATLAS
3-9
POST HALL SYNDICATE
YOU IS MORE OR LESS LIKE THAT THO' YOU AIN'T HAD A BATH --- NOW, THEN --YO' FOOD GOTTA BE BUGS AN' LESSER INSECTS-- HMM- TIMES CHANGE, I DON'T 'MEMBER THAT WHEN I WAS A YOUNG'N.
UGH.
TIME GO ON, YOU GITS TO LAY FOUR WHITE EGGS AN' YO' SONG IS--WEETA-WEETA-WEETO--
I CAN'T DO NONE OF THAT ---LEMME SEE THAT BOOK--
CAP'N WIMBY'S BIRD ATLAS
YOU AIN'T READIN' 'BOUT GRACKLES-- YOU READIN' 'BOUT THE GRAY-CRESTED YELLOW RUMP-- YOU SKUP A PAGE.
ACTUAL THEY AIN'T NO FUTURE IN BEIN' A GRACKLE ANYWAY.
COPR 1955 WALT KELLY

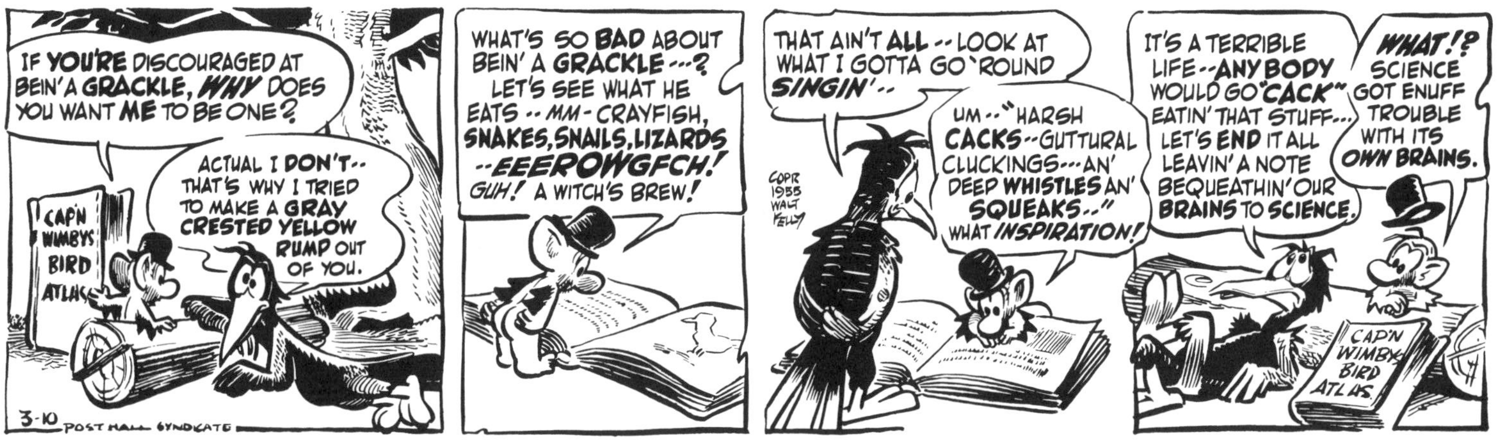
IF YOU'RE DISCOURAGED AT BEIN' A GRACKLE, WHY DOES YOU WANT ME TO BE ONE?
ACTUAL I DON'T-- THAT'S WHY I TRIED TO MAKE A GRAY CRESTED YELLOW RUMP OUT OF YOU.
CAP'N WIMBY'S BIRD ATLAS
3-10
POST HALL SYNDICATE
WHAT'S SO BAD ABOUT BEIN' A GRACKLE---? LET'S SEE WHAT HE EATS -- MM- CRAYFISH, SNAKES, SNAILS, LIZARDS --EEEROWGFCH! GUH! A WITCH'S BREW!
THAT AIN'T ALL -- LOOK AT WHAT I GOTTA GO 'ROUND SINGIN'--
UM --"HARSH CACKS--GUTTURAL CLUCKINGS--- AN' DEEP WHISTLES AN' SQUEAKS--" WHAT INSPIRATION!
COPR 1955 WALT KELLY
IT'S A TERRIBLE LIFE--ANY BODY WOULD GO "CACK" EATIN' THAT STUFF--- LET'S END IT ALL LEAVIN' A NOTE BEQUEATHIN' OUR BRAINS TO SCIENCE.
WHAT!? SCIENCE GOT ENUFF TROUBLE WITH ITS OWN BRAINS.
CAP'N WIMBY'S BIRD ATLAS

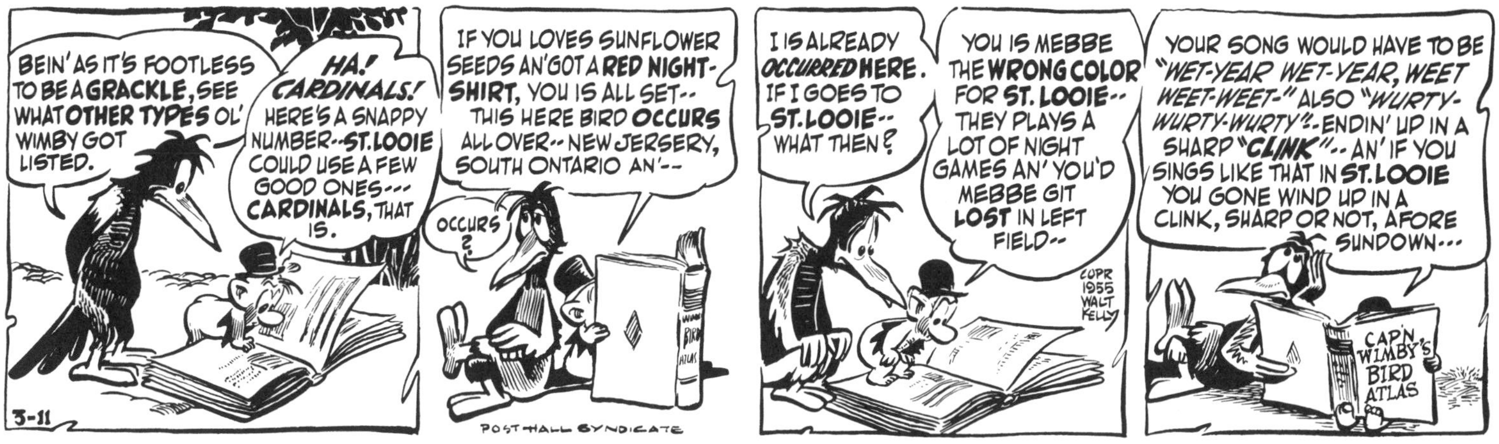
BEIN' AS IT'S FOOTLESS TO BE A GRACKLE, SEE WHAT OTHER TYPES OL' WIMBY GOT LISTED.
HA! CARDINALS! HERE'S A SNAPPY NUMBER--ST. LOOIE COULD USE A FEW GOOD ONES--- CARDINALS, THAT IS.
3-11
IF YOU LOVES SUNFLOWER SEEDS AN' GOT A RED NIGHT-SHIRT, YOU IS ALL SET-- THIS HERE BIRD OCCURS ALL OVER-- NEW JERSERY, SOUTH ONTARIO AN'--
OCCURS?
POST HALL SYNDICATE
I IS ALREADY OCCURRED HERE. IF I GOES TO ST. LOOIE-- WHAT THEN?
YOU IS MEBBE THE WRONG COLOR FOR ST. LOOIE-- THEY PLAYS A LOT OF NIGHT GAMES AN' YOU'D MEBBE GIT LOST IN LEFT FIELD--
COPR 1955 WALT KELLY
YOUR SONG WOULD HAVE TO BE "WET-YEAR WET-YEAR, WEET WEET-WEET-" ALSO "WURTY-WURTY-WURTY"-- ENDIN' UP IN A SHARP "CLINK"-- AN' IF YOU SINGS LIKE THAT IN ST. LOOIE YOU GONE WIND UP IN A CLINK, SHARP OR NOT, AFORE SUNDOWN---
CAP'N WIMBY'S BIRD ATLAS

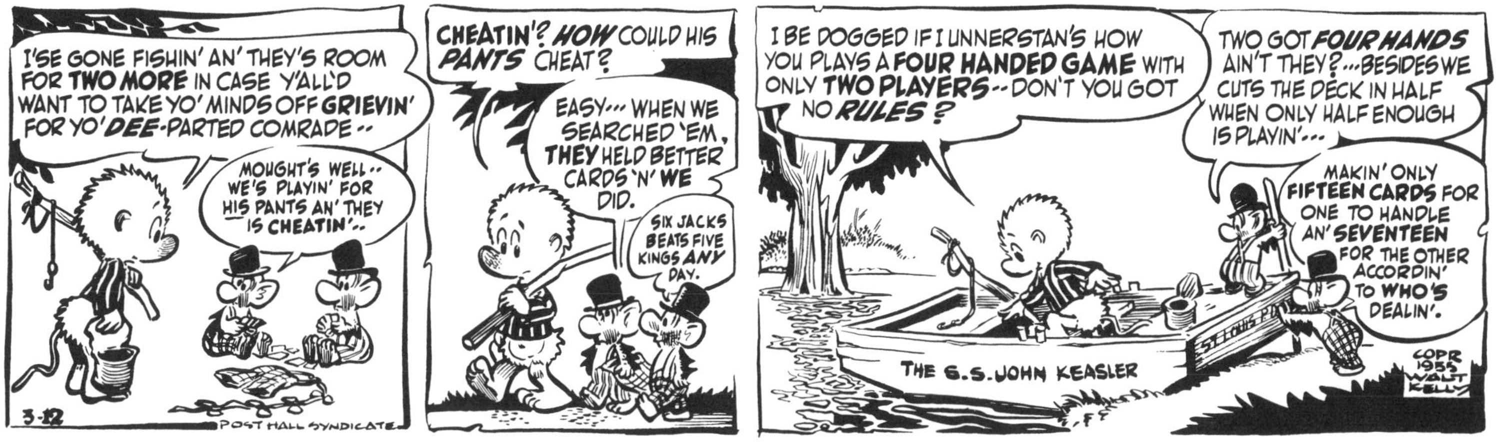
I'SE GONE FISHIN' AN' THEY'S ROOM FOR TWO MORE IN CASE Y'ALL'D WANT TO TAKE YO' MINDS OFF GRIEVIN' FOR YO' DEE-PARTED COMRADE--
MOUGHT'S WELL-- WE'S PLAYIN' FOR HIS PANTS AN' THEY IS CHEATIN'--
3-12
POST HALL SYNDICATE
CHEATIN'? HOW COULD HIS PANTS CHEAT?
EASY--- WHEN WE SEARCHED 'EM, THEY HELD BETTER CARDS 'N' WE DID.
SIX JACKS BEATS FIVE KINGS ANY DAY.
I BE DOGGED IF I UNNERSTAN'S HOW YOU PLAYS A FOUR HANDED GAME WITH ONLY TWO PLAYERS-- DON'T YOU GOT NO RULES?
TWO GOT FOUR HANDS AIN'T THEY?...BESIDES WE CUTS THE DECK IN HALF WHEN ONLY HALF ENOUGH IS PLAYIN'---
MAKIN' ONLY FIFTEEN CARDS FOR ONE TO HANDLE AN' SEVENTEEN FOR THE OTHER ACCORDIN' TO WHO'S DEALIN'.
THE S.S. JOHN KEASLER
COPR 1955 WALT KELLY

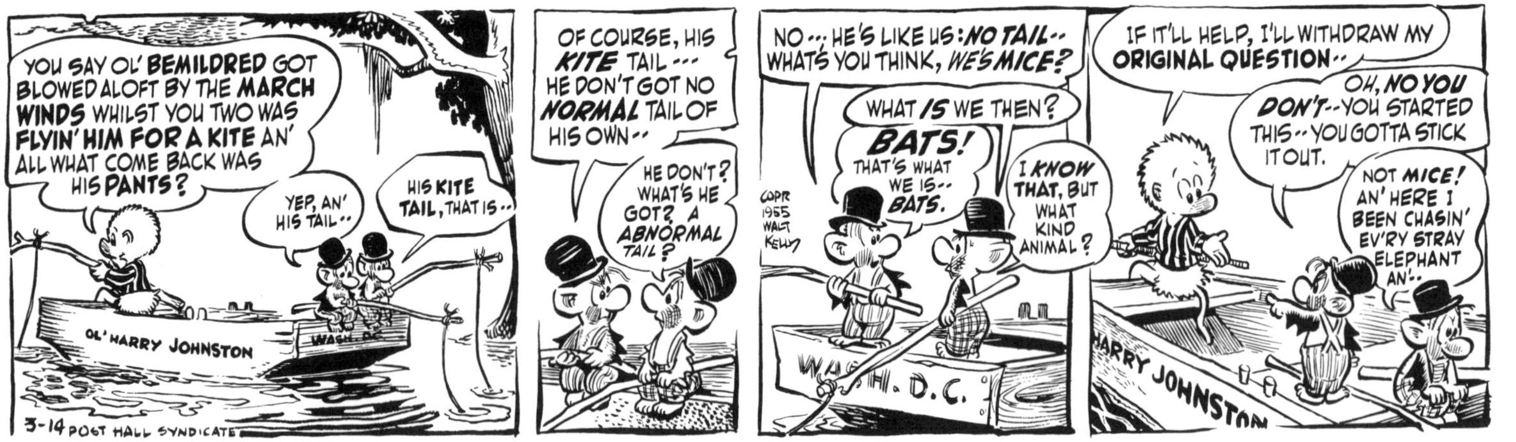
YOU SAY OL' BEMILDRED GOT BLOWED ALOFT BY THE MARCH WINDS WHILST YOU TWO WAS FLYIN' HIM FOR A KITE AN' ALL WHAT COME BACK WAS HIS PANTS?
YEP, AN' HIS TAIL..
HIS KITE TAIL, THAT IS..
OL' HARRY JOHNSTON
3-14 POST HALL SYNDICATE
OF COURSE, HIS KITE TAIL... HE DON'T GOT NO NORMAL TAIL OF HIS OWN..
HE DON'T? WHAT'S HE GOT? A ABNORMAL TAIL?
NO...HE'S LIKE US: NO TAIL.. WHAT'S YOU THINK, WE'S MICE?
WHAT IS WE THEN?
BATS! THAT'S WHAT WE IS.. BATS.
I KNOW THAT, BUT WHAT KIND ANIMAL?
COPR 1955 WALT KELLY
WASH. D.C.
IF IT'LL HELP, I'LL WITHDRAW MY ORIGINAL QUESTION..
OH, NO YOU DON'T..YOU STARTED THIS..YOU GOTTA STICK IT OUT.
NOT MICE! AN' HERE I BEEN CHASIN' EV'RY STRAY ELEPHANT AN'..
HARRY JOHNSTON

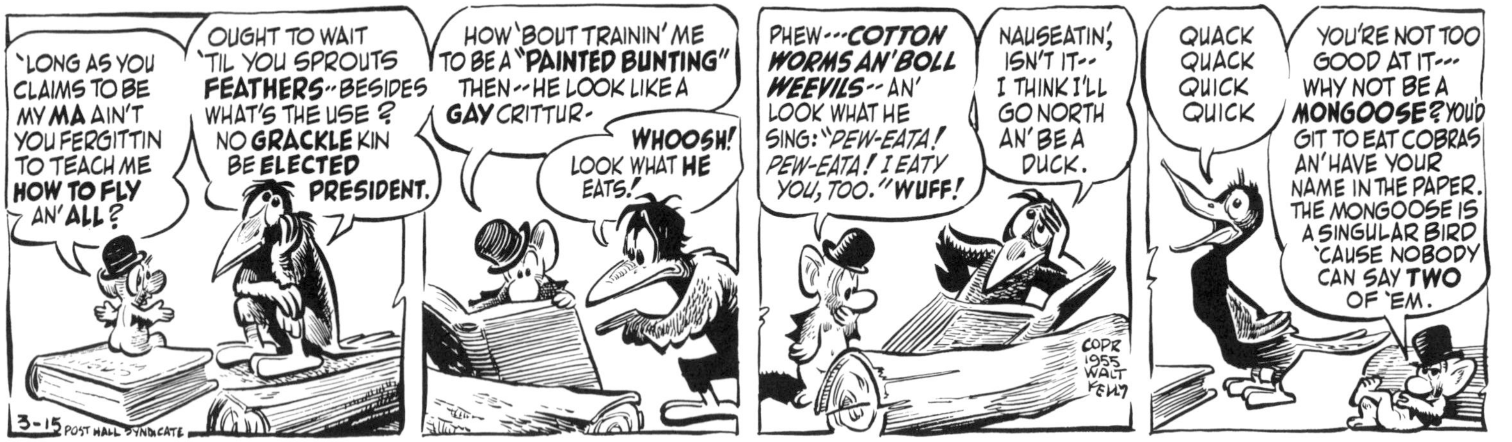
'LONG AS YOU CLAIMS TO BE MY MA AIN'T YOU FERGITTIN TO TEACH ME HOW TO FLY AN' ALL?
OUGHT TO WAIT 'TIL YOU SPROUTS FEATHERS..BESIDES WHAT'S THE USE? NO GRACKLE KIN BE ELECTED PRESIDENT.
3-15 POST HALL SYNDICATE
HOW 'BOUT TRAININ' ME TO BE A "PAINTED BUNTING" THEN..HE LOOK LIKE A GAY CRITTUR.
WHOOSH! LOOK WHAT HE EATS!
PHEW...COTTON WORMS AN' BOLL WEEVILS.. AN' LOOK WHAT HE SING: "PEW-EATA! PEW-EATA! I EATY YOU, TOO." WUFF!
NAUSEATIN', ISN'T IT.. I THINK I'LL GO NORTH AN' BE A DUCK.
COPR 1955 WALT KELLY
QUACK QUACK QUICK QUICK
YOU'RE NOT TOO GOOD AT IT... WHY NOT BE A MONGOOSE? YOU'D GIT TO EAT COBRAS AN' HAVE YOUR NAME IN THE PAPER. THE MONGOOSE IS A SINGULAR BIRD 'CAUSE NOBODY CAN SAY TWO OF 'EM.

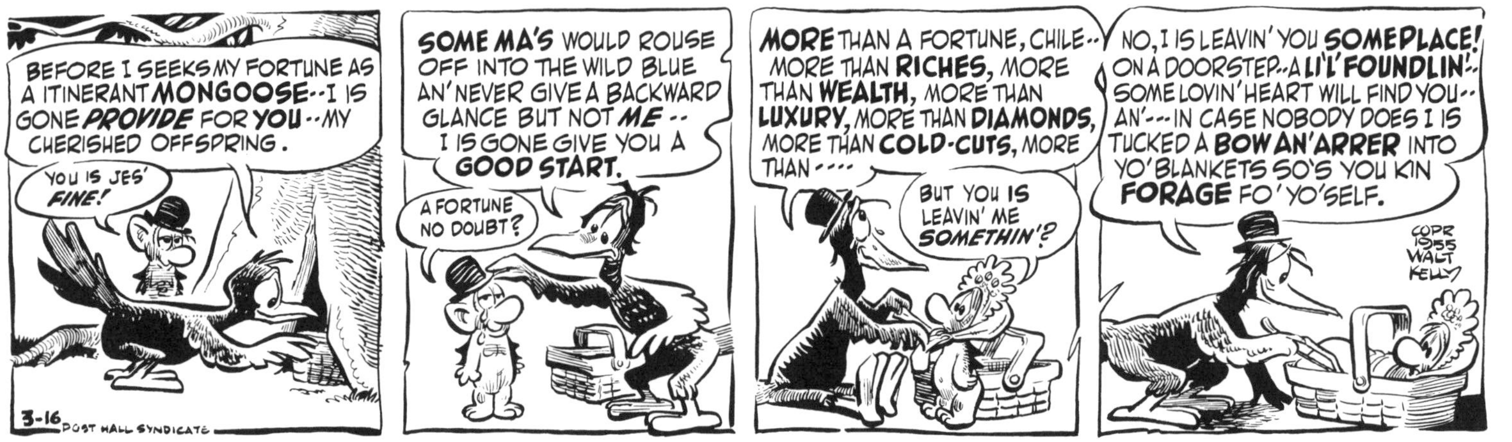
BEFORE I SEEKS MY FORTUNE AS A ITINERANT MONGOOSE..I IS GONE PROVIDE FOR YOU..MY CHERISHED OFFSPRING.
YOU IS JES' FINE!
3-16 POST HALL SYNDICATE
SOME MA'S WOULD ROUSE OFF INTO THE WILD BLUE AN' NEVER GIVE A BACKWARD GLANCE BUT NOT ME.. I IS GONE GIVE YOU A GOOD START.
A FORTUNE NO DOUBT?
MORE THAN A FORTUNE, CHILE.. MORE THAN RICHES, MORE THAN WEALTH, MORE THAN LUXURY, MORE THAN DIAMONDS, MORE THAN COLD-CUTS, MORE THAN....
BUT YOU IS LEAVIN' ME SOMETHIN'?
NO, I IS LEAVIN' YOU SOMEPLACE! ON A DOORSTEP..A LI'L' FOUNDLIN'.. SOME LOVIN' HEART WILL FIND YOU.. AN'...IN CASE NOBODY DOES I IS TUCKED A BOW AN' ARRER INTO YO' BLANKETS SO'S YOU KIN FORAGE FO' YO'SELF.
COPR 1955 WALT KELLY

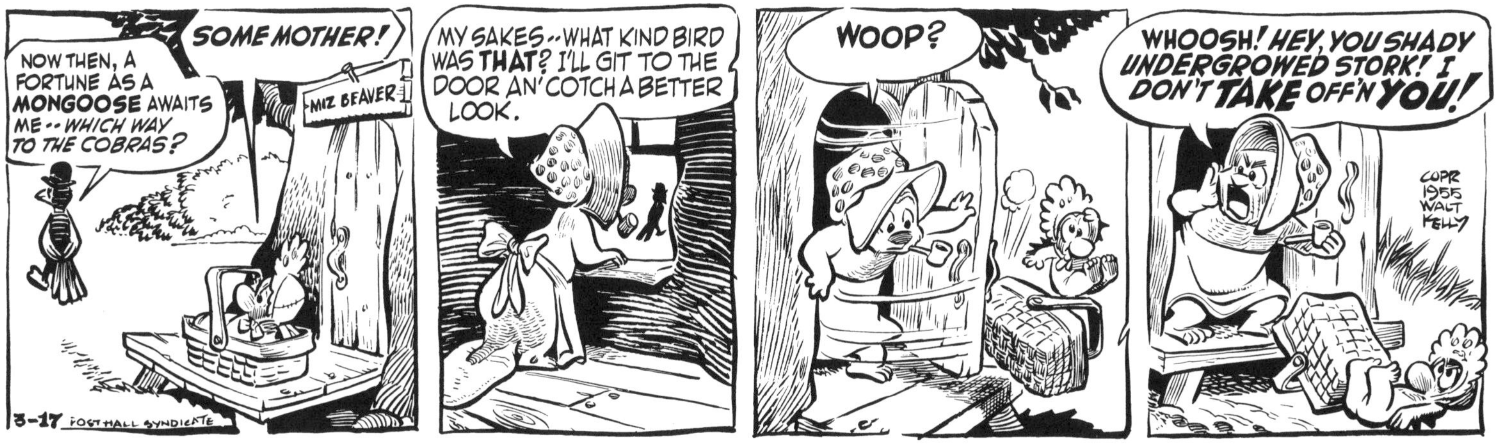
NOW THEN, A FORTUNE AS A MONGOOSE AWAITS ME -- WHICH WAY TO THE COBRAS?
SOME MOTHER!
MIZ BEAVER
MY SAKES -- WHAT KIND BIRD WAS THAT? I'LL GIT TO THE DOOR AN' COTCH A BETTER LOOK.
WOOP?
WHOOSH! HEY, YOU SHADY UNDERGROWED STORK! I DON'T TAKE OFF'N YOU!
COPR 1955 WALT KELLY
3-17 POST HALL SYNDICATE

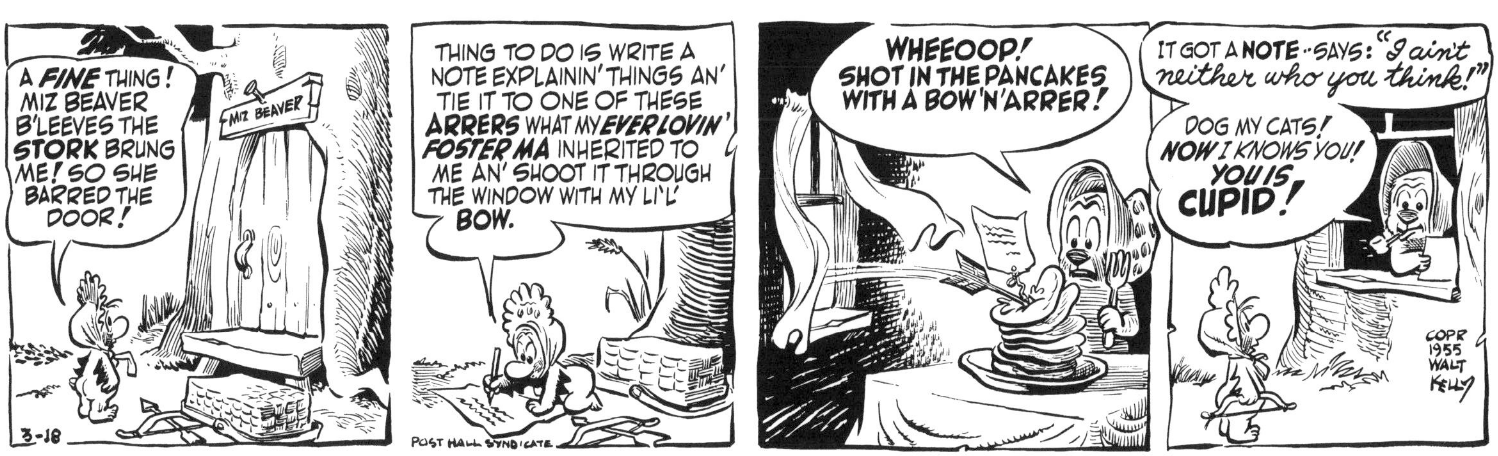
A FINE THING! MIZ BEAVER B'LEEVES THE STORK BRUNG ME! SO SHE BARRED THE DOOR!
MIZ BEAVER
THING TO DO IS WRITE A NOTE EXPLAININ' THINGS AN' TIE IT TO ONE OF THESE ARRERS WHAT MY EVERLOVIN' FOSTER MA INHERITED TO ME AN' SHOOT IT THROUGH THE WINDOW WITH MY LI'L' BOW.
WHEEOOP! SHOT IN THE PANCAKES WITH A BOW 'N' ARRER!
IT GOT A NOTE -- SAYS: "I ain't neither who you think!"
DOG MY CATS! NOW I KNOWS YOU! YOU IS CUPID!
COPR 1955 WALT KELLY
3-18 POST HALL SYNDICATE

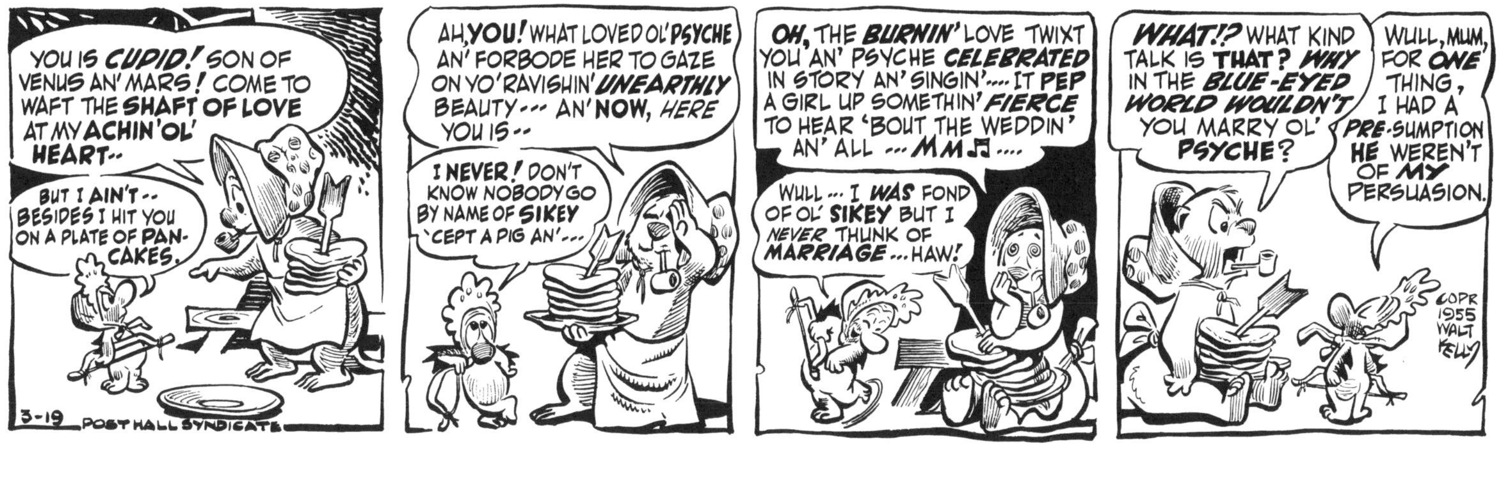
YOU IS CUPID! SON OF VENUS AN' MARS! COME TO WAFT THE SHAFT OF LOVE AT MY ACHIN' OL' HEART --
BUT I AIN'T -- BESIDES I HIT YOU ON A PLATE OF PAN-CAKES.
AH, YOU! WHAT LOVED OL' PSYCHE AN' FORBODE HER TO GAZE ON YO' RAVISHIN' UNEARTHLY BEAUTY --- AN' NOW, HERE YOU IS --
I NEVER! DON'T KNOW NOBODY GO BY NAME OF SIKEY 'CEPT A PIG AN' ---
OH, THE BURNIN' LOVE TWIXT YOU AN' PSYCHE CELEBRATED IN STORY AN' SINGIN' .... IT PEP A GIRL UP SOMETHIN' FIERCE TO HEAR 'BOUT THE WEDDIN' AN' ALL --- MM ♫ ....
WULL --- I WAS FOND OF OL' SIKEY BUT I NEVER THUNK OF MARRIAGE ... HAW!
WHAT!? WHAT KIND TALK IS THAT? WHY IN THE BLUE-EYED WORLD WOULDN'T YOU MARRY OL' PSYCHE?
WULL, MUM, FOR ONE THING, I HAD A PRE-SUMPTION HE WEREN'T OF MY PERSUASION.
COPR 1955 WALT KELLY
3-19 POST HALL SYNDICATE

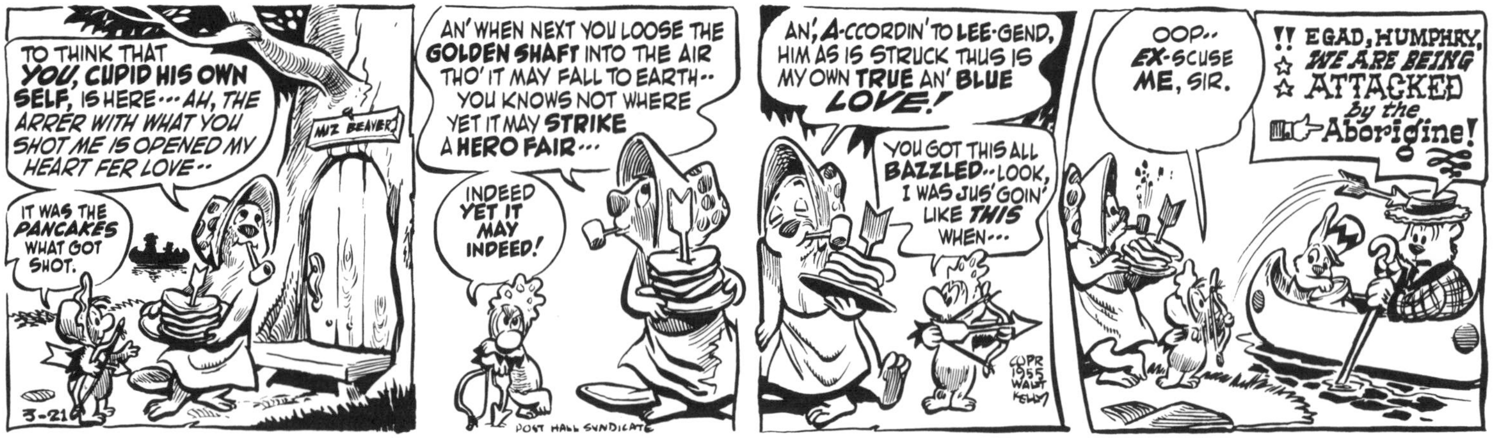
TO THINK THAT YOU, CUPID HIS OWN SELF, IS HERE··· AH, THE ARRER WITH WHAT YOU SHOT ME IS OPENED MY HEART FER LOVE··
MIZ BEAVER
IT WAS THE PANCAKES WHAT GOT SHOT.
3-21
AN' WHEN NEXT YOU LOOSE THE GOLDEN SHAFT INTO THE AIR THO' IT MAY FALL TO EARTH·· YOU KNOWS NOT WHERE YET IT MAY STRIKE A HERO FAIR···
INDEED YET IT MAY INDEED!
POST HALL SYNDICATE
AN', A-CCORDIN' TO LEE-GEND, HIM AS IS STRUCK THUS IS MY OWN TRUE AN' BLUE LOVE!
YOU GOT THIS ALL BAZZLED·· LOOK, I WAS JUS' GOIN' LIKE THIS WHEN···
COPR 1955 WALT KELLY
OOP·· EX-SCUSE ME, SIR.
!! EGAD, HUMPHRY, WE ARE BEING ATTACKED by the Aborigine!

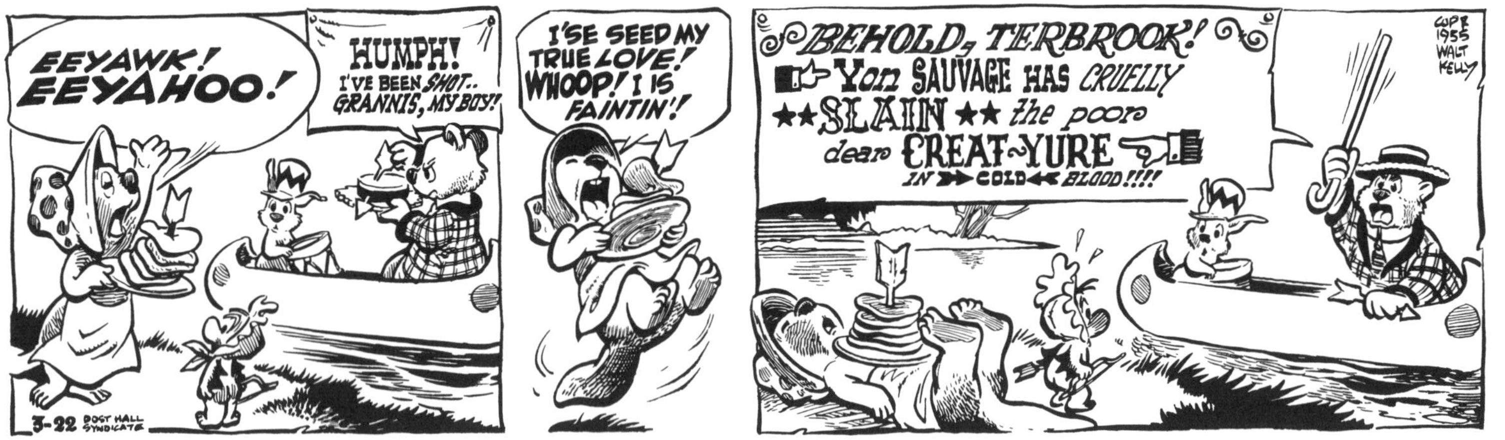
EEYAWK! EEYAHOO!
HUMPH! I'VE BEEN SHOT·· GRANNIS, MY BOY!
3-22 POST HALL SYNDICATE
I'SE SEED MY TRUE LOVE! WHOOP! I IS FAINTIN'!
BEHOLD, TERBROOK! Yon SAUVAGE HAS CRUELLY SLAIN the poor dear CREAT-YURE IN COLD BLOOD!!!!
COPR 1955 WALT KELLY

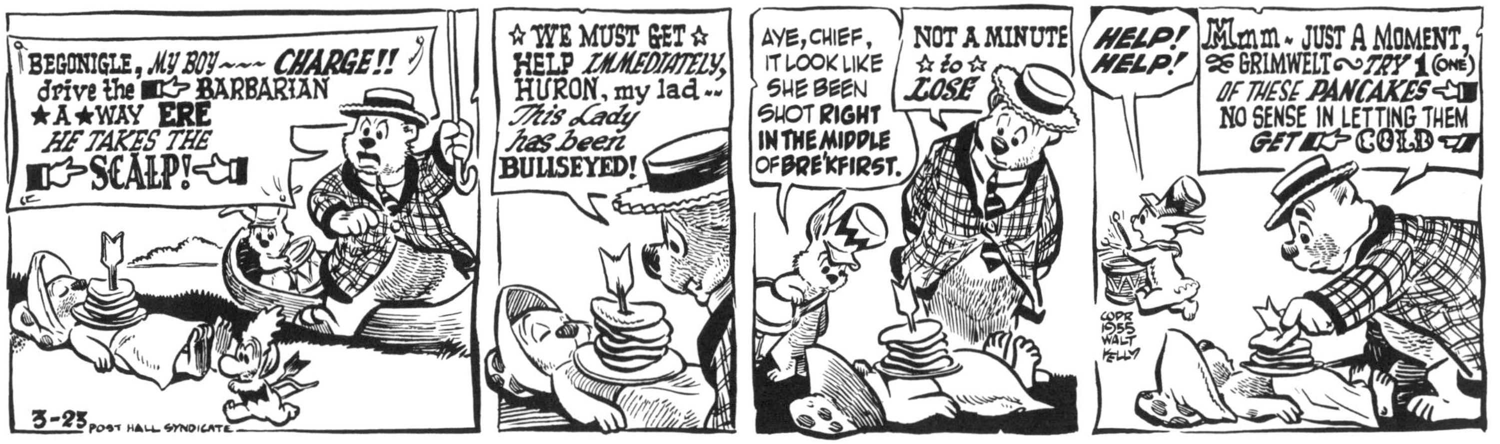
BEGONIGLE, MY BOY~~~ CHARGE!! drive the BARBARIAN A★WAY ERE HE TAKES THE SCALP!
3-23 POST HALL SYNDICATE
☆ WE MUST GET ☆ HELP IMMEDIATELY, HURON, my lad ~~ This Lady has been BULLSEYED!
AYE, CHIEF, IT LOOK LIKE SHE BEEN SHOT RIGHT IN THE MIDDLE OF BRE'KFIRST.
NOT A MINUTE ☆ to ☆ LOSE
HELP! HELP!
Mmm ~ JUST A MOMENT, GRIMWELT ~ TRY 1 (ONE) OF THESE PANCAKES NO SENSE IN LETTING THEM GET COLD
COPR 1955 WALT KELLY

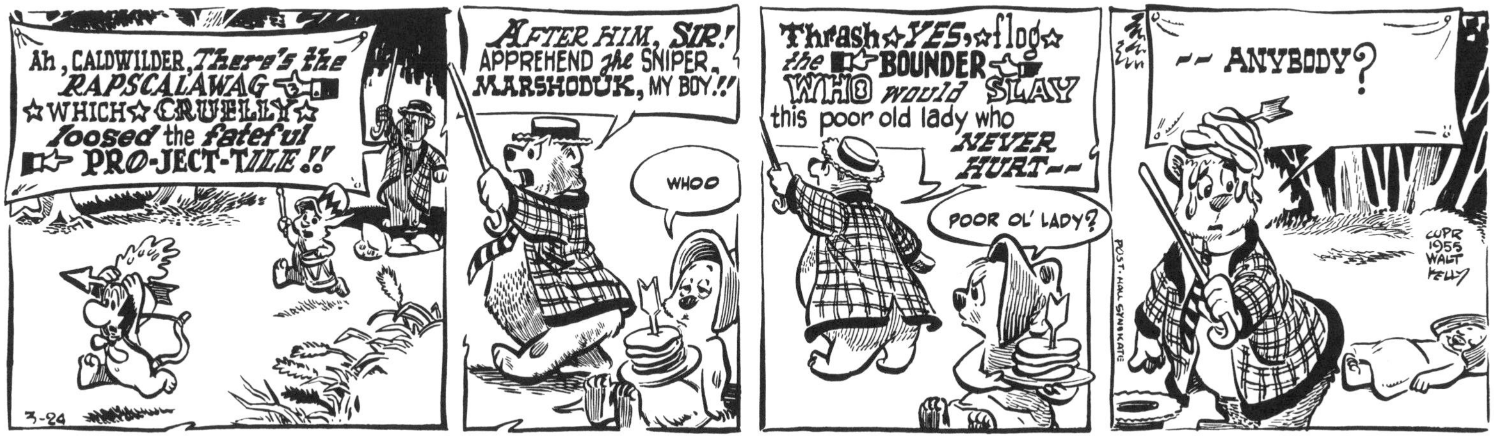
Ah, CALDWILDER, There's the RAPSCALAWAG WHICH CRUELLY loosed the fateful PRO-JECT-TILE!!
3-24
AFTER HIM, SIR! APPREHEND the SNIPER, MARSHODUK, MY BOY!!
WHOO
Thrash YES, flog the BOUNDER WHO would SLAY this poor old lady who NEVER HURT--
POOR OL' LADY?
POST-HALL SYNDICATE
-- ANYBODY?
COPR 1955 WALT KELLY

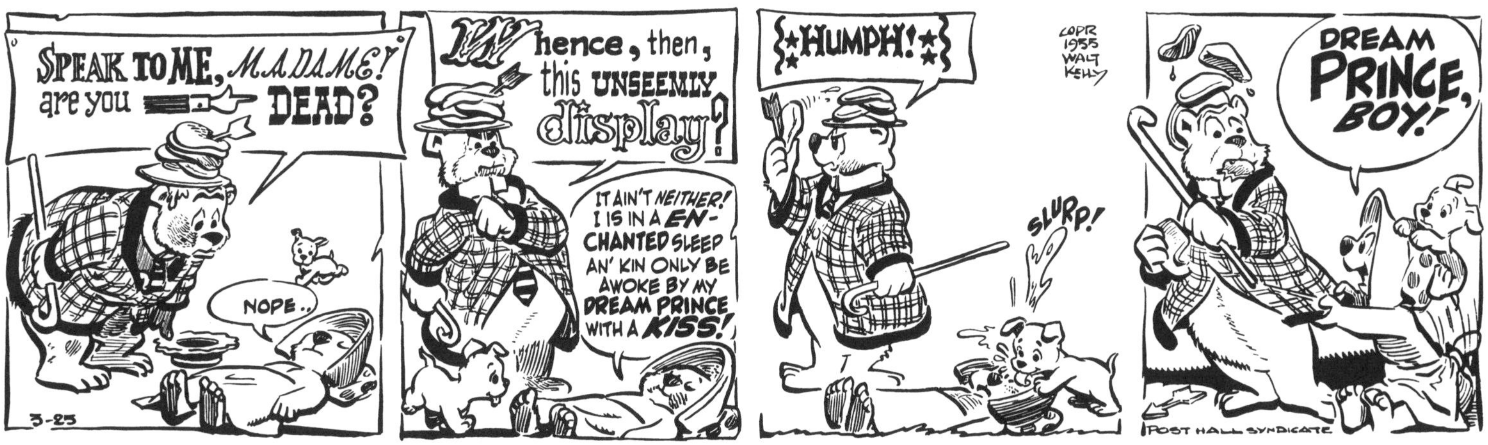
SPEAK TO ME, MADAME! are you DEAD?
NOPE..
3-25
Whence, then, this UNSEEMLY display?
IT AIN'T NEITHER! I IS IN A EN-CHANTED SLEEP AN' KIN ONLY BE AWOKE BY MY DREAM PRINCE WITH A KISS!
HUMPH!
COPR 1955 WALT KELLY
SLURP!
DREAM PRINCE, BOY!
POST HALL SYNDICATE

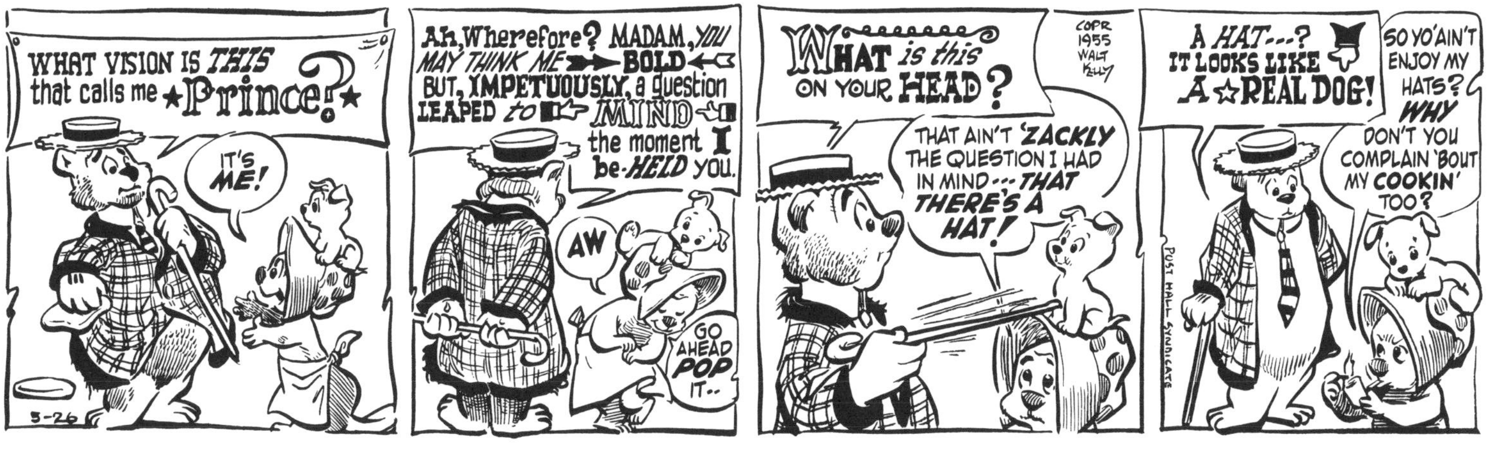
WHAT VISION IS THIS that calls me Prince?
IT'S ME!
3-26
Ah, Wherefore? MADAM, YOU MAY THINK ME BOLD BUT, IMPETUOUSLY, a question LEAPED to MIND the moment I be-HELD you.
AW
GO AHEAD POP IT..
WHAT is this ON YOUR HEAD?
COPR 1955 WALT KELLY
THAT AIN'T 'ZACKLY THE QUESTION I HAD IN MIND--THAT THERE'S A HAT!
POST HALL SYNDICATE
A HAT--? IT LOOKS LIKE A REAL DOG!
SO YO'AIN'T ENJOY MY HATS? WHY DON'T YOU COMPLAIN 'BOUT MY COOKIN' TOO?

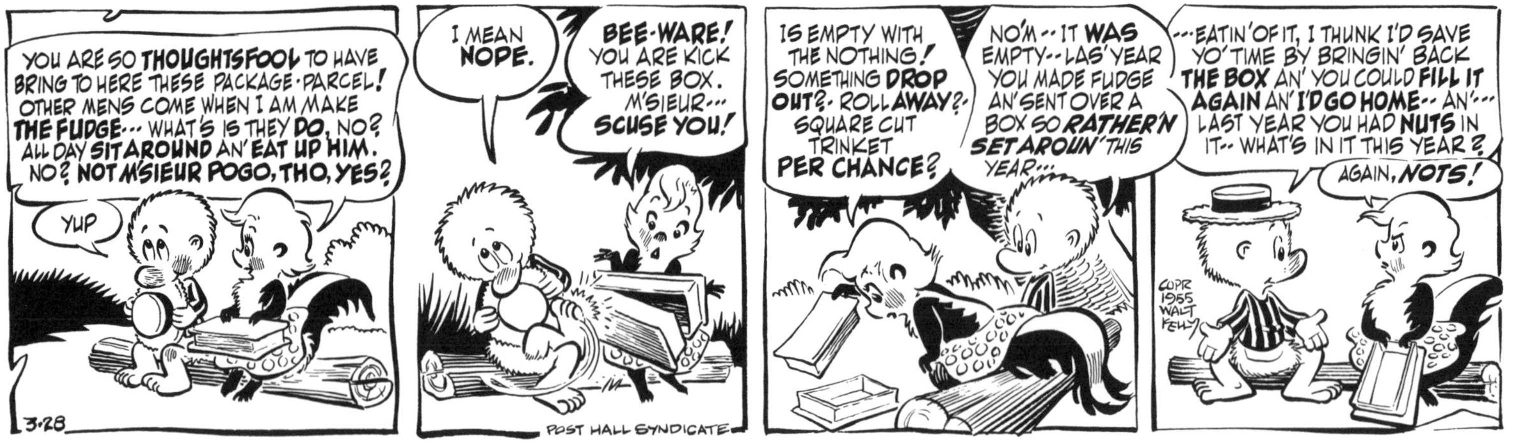
YOU ARE SO THOUGHTSFOOL TO HAVE BRING TO HERE THESE PACKAGE-PARCEL! OTHER MENS COME WHEN I AM MAKE THE FUDGE... WHAT'S IS THEY DO, NO? ALL DAY SIT AROUND AN' EAT UP HIM. NO? NOT M'SIEUR POGO, THO, YES?
YUP
3-28
I MEAN NOPE.
BEE-WARE! YOU ARE KICK THESE BOX. M'SIEUR... SCUSE YOU!
POST HALL SYNDICATE
IS EMPTY WITH THE NOTHING! SOMETHING DROP OUT?- ROLL AWAY?- SQUARE CUT TRINKET PER CHANCE?
NO'M -- IT WAS EMPTY -- LAS' YEAR YOU MADE FUDGE AN' SENT OVER A BOX SO RATHER'N SET AROUN' THIS YEAR...
...EATIN' OF IT, I THUNK I'D SAVE YO' TIME BY BRINGIN' BACK THE BOX AN' YOU COULD FILL IT AGAIN AN' I'D GO HOME -- AN'... LAST YEAR YOU HAD NUTS IN IT -- WHAT'S IN IT THIS YEAR?
AGAIN, NOTS!
COPR 1955 WALT KELLY

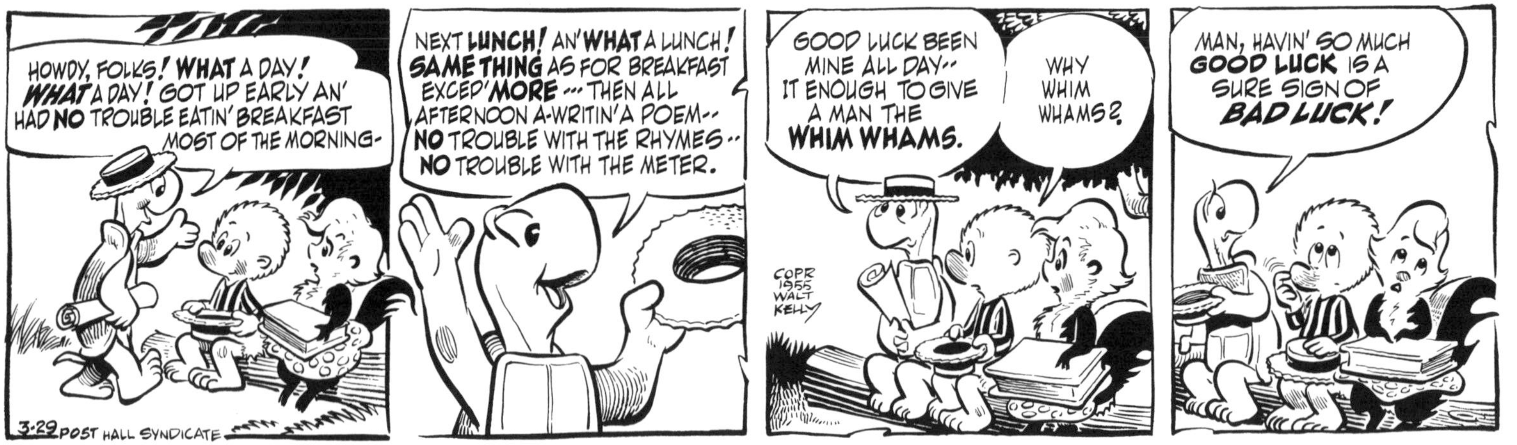
HOWDY, FOLKS! WHAT A DAY! WHAT A DAY! GOT UP EARLY AN' HAD NO TROUBLE EATIN' BREAKFAST MOST OF THE MORNING-
3-29 POST HALL SYNDICATE
NEXT LUNCH! AN' WHAT A LUNCH! SAME THING AS FOR BREAKFAST EXCEP' MORE --- THEN ALL AFTERNOON A-WRITIN' A POEM -- NO TROUBLE WITH THE RHYMES -- NO TROUBLE WITH THE METER.
GOOD LUCK BEEN MINE ALL DAY -- IT ENOUGH TO GIVE A MAN THE WHIM WHAMS.
WHY WHIM WHAMS?
COPR 1955 WALT KELLY
MAN, HAVIN' SO MUCH GOOD LUCK IS A SURE SIGN OF BAD LUCK!

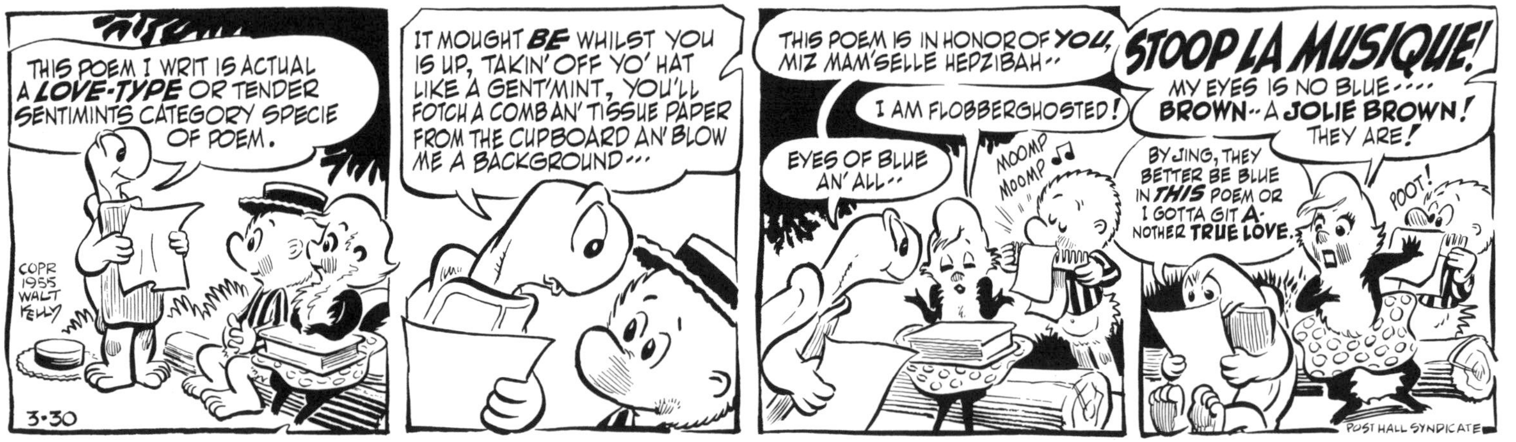
THIS POEM I WRIT IS ACTUAL A LOVE-TYPE OR TENDER SENTIMINTS CATEGORY SPECIE OF POEM.
COPR 1955 WALT KELLY
3-30
IT MOUGHT BE WHILST YOU IS UP, TAKIN' OFF YO' HAT LIKE A GENT'MINT, YOU'LL FOTCH A COMB AN' TISSUE PAPER FROM THE CUPBOARD AN' BLOW ME A BACKGROUND...
THIS POEM IS IN HONOR OF YOU, MIZ MAM'SELLE HEPZIBAH --
I AM FLOBBERGHOSTED!
EYES OF BLUE AN' ALL --
MOOMP MOOMP
STOOP LA MUSIQUE! MY EYES IS NO BLUE.... BROWN -- A JOLIE BROWN! THEY ARE!
BY JING, THEY BETTER BE BLUE IN THIS POEM OR I GOTTA GIT A-NOTHER TRUE LOVE.
POOT!
POST HALL SYNDICATE

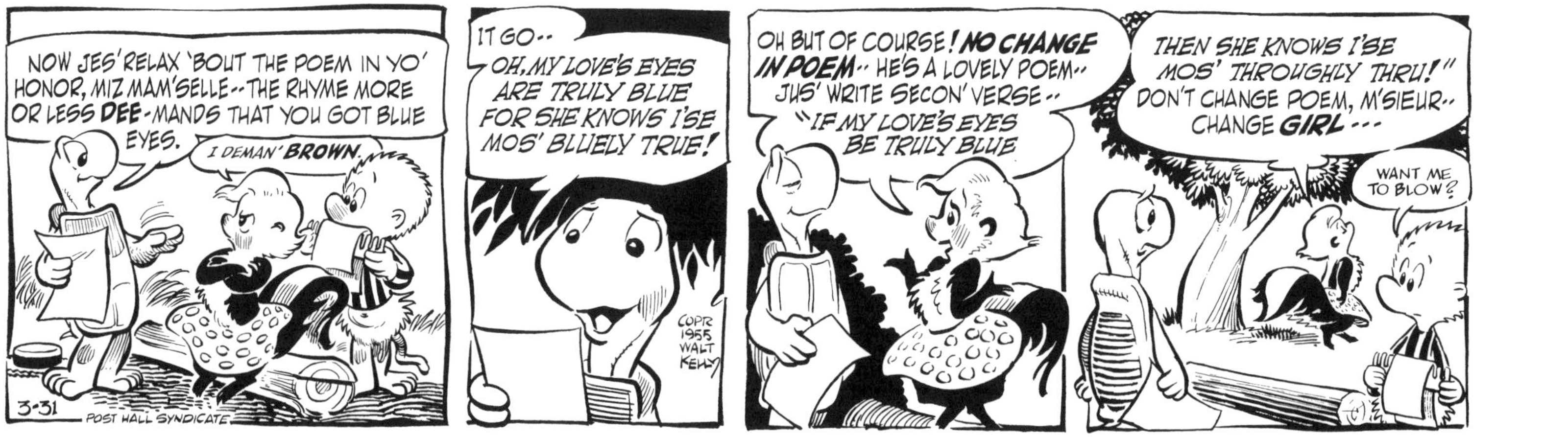
NOW JES' RELAX 'BOUT THE POEM IN YO' HONOR, MIZ MAM'SELLE-- THE RHYME MORE OR LESS DEE-MANDS THAT YOU GOT BLUE EYES.
I DEMAN' BROWN.
3-31
POST HALL SYNDICATE
IT GO--
OH, MY LOVE'S EYES ARE TRULY BLUE FOR SHE KNOWS I'SE MOS' BLUELY TRUE!
COPR 1955 WALT KELLY
OH BUT OF COURSE! NO CHANGE IN POEM-- HE'S A LOVELY POEM-- JUS' WRITE SECON' VERSE--
"IF MY LOVE'S EYES BE TRULY BLUE
THEN SHE KNOWS I'SE MOS' THROUGHLY THRU!" DON'T CHANGE POEM, M'SIEUR-- CHANGE GIRL ---
WANT ME TO BLOW?

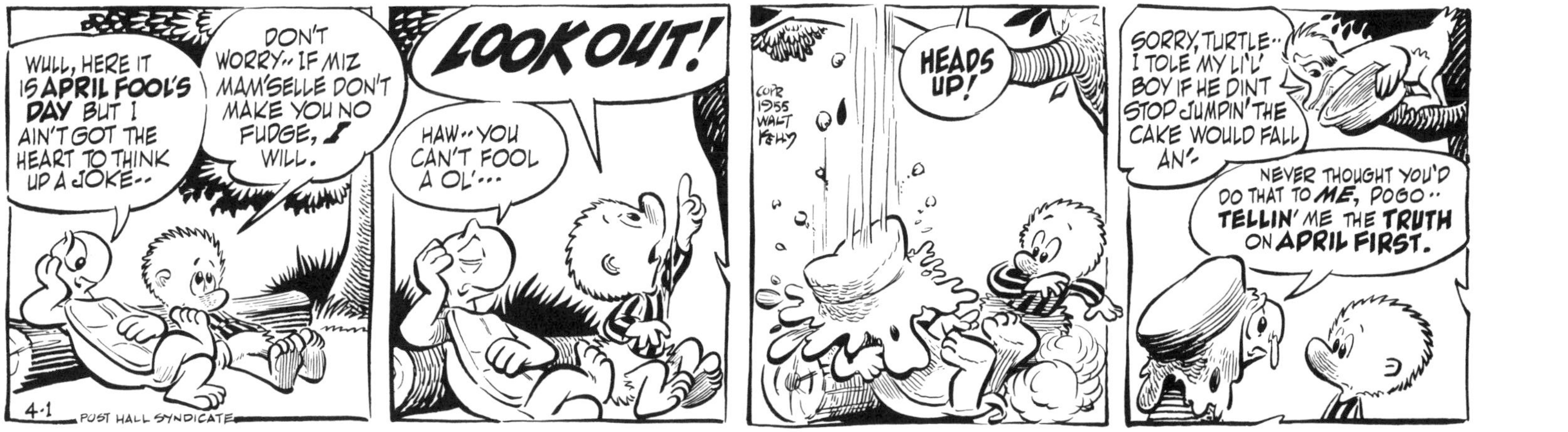
WULL, HERE IT IS APRIL FOOL'S DAY BUT I AIN'T GOT THE HEART TO THINK UP A JOKE--
DON'T WORRY-- IF MIZ MAM'SELLE DON'T MAKE YOU NO FUDGE, I WILL.
4-1
POST HALL SYNDICATE
LOOK OUT!
HAW-- YOU CAN'T FOOL A OL'...
HEADS UP!
COPR 1955 WALT KELLY
SORRY, TURTLE-- I TOLE MY LI'L' BOY IF HE DINT STOP JUMPIN' THE CAKE WOULD FALL AN'--
NEVER THOUGHT YOU'D DO THAT TO ME, POGO-- TELLIN' ME THE TRUTH ON APRIL FIRST.

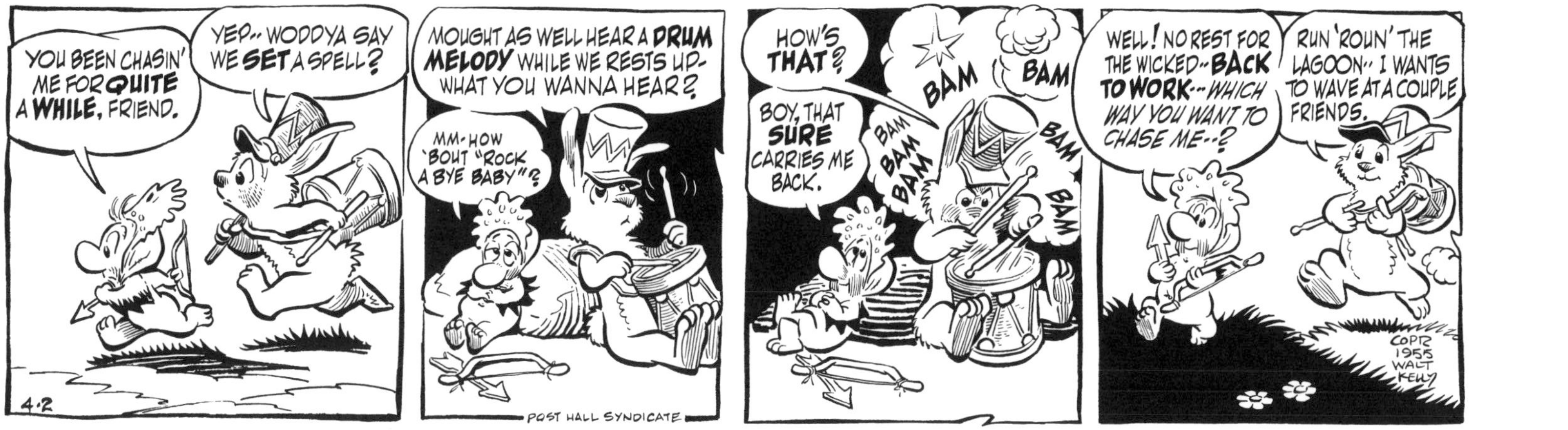
YOU BEEN CHASIN' ME FOR QUITE A WHILE, FRIEND.
YEP-- WODDYA SAY WE SET A SPELL?
4-2
MOUGHT AS WELL HEAR A DRUM MELODY WHILE WE RESTS UP-- WHAT YOU WANNA HEAR?
MM-HOW 'BOUT "ROCK A BYE BABY"?
POST HALL SYNDICATE
HOW'S THAT?
BOY, THAT SURE CARRIES ME BACK.
BAM BAM BAM BAM BAM BAM BAM
WELL! NO REST FOR THE WICKED-- BACK TO WORK-- WHICH WAY YOU WANT TO CHASE ME--?
RUN 'ROUN' THE LAGOON-- I WANTS TO WAVE AT A COUPLE FRIENDS.
COPR 1955 WALT KELLY

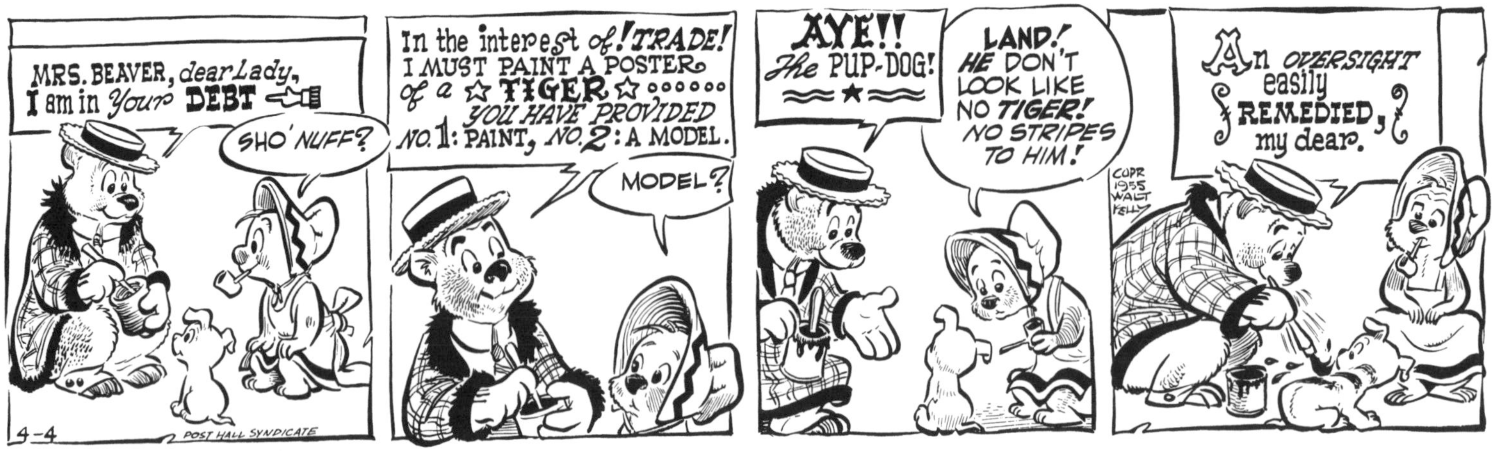
MRS. BEAVER, dear Lady, I am in Your DEBT
SHO' NUFF?
4-4
POST HALL SYNDICATE
In the interest of! TRADE! I MUST PAINT A POSTER of a ☆ TIGER ☆ YOU HAVE PROVIDED NO. 1: PAINT, NO. 2: A MODEL.
MODEL?
AYE!! The PUP-DOG!
LAND! HE DON'T LOOK LIKE NO TIGER! NO STRIPES TO HIM!
An OVERSIGHT easily REMEDIED, my dear.
COPR 1955 WALT KELLY

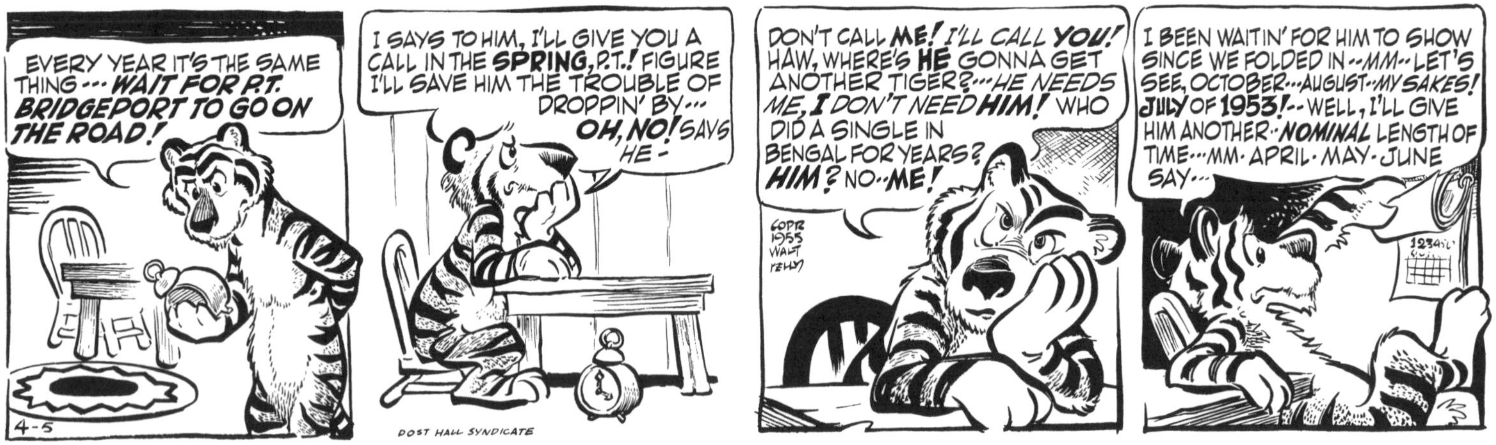
EVERY YEAR IT'S THE SAME THING --- WAIT FOR P.T. BRIDGEPORT TO GO ON THE ROAD!
4-5
I SAYS TO HIM, I'LL GIVE YOU A CALL IN THE SPRING, P.T.! FIGURE I'LL SAVE HIM THE TROUBLE OF DROPPIN' BY... OH, NO! SAYS HE -
POST HALL SYNDICATE
DON'T CALL ME! I'LL CALL YOU! HAW, WHERE'S HE GONNA GET ANOTHER TIGER? --- HE NEEDS ME, I DON'T NEED HIM! WHO DID A SINGLE IN BENGAL FOR YEARS? HIM? NO -- ME!
COPR 1955 WALT KELLY
I BEEN WAITIN' FOR HIM TO SHOW SINCE WE FOLDED IN -- MM -- LET'S SEE, OCTOBER -- AUGUST -- MY SAKES! JULY OF 1953! -- WELL, I'LL GIVE HIM ANOTHER -- NOMINAL LENGTH OF TIME --- MM. APRIL - MAY - JUNE SAY ...

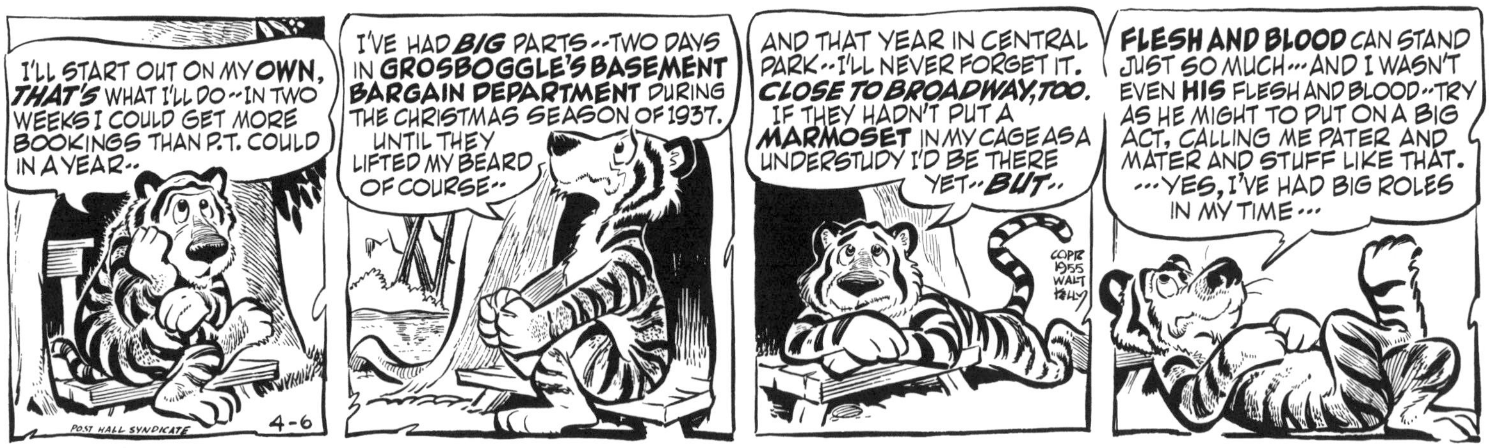
I'LL START OUT ON MY OWN, THAT'S WHAT I'LL DO -- IN TWO WEEKS I COULD GET MORE BOOKINGS THAN P.T. COULD IN A YEAR --
POST HALL SYNDICATE
4-6
I'VE HAD BIG PARTS -- TWO DAYS IN GROSBOGGLE'S BASEMENT BARGAIN DEPARTMENT DURING THE CHRISTMAS SEASON OF 1937.
UNTIL THEY LIFTED MY BEARD OF COURSE --
AND THAT YEAR IN CENTRAL PARK -- I'LL NEVER FORGET IT. CLOSE TO BROADWAY, TOO.
IF THEY HADN'T PUT A MARMOSET IN MY CAGE AS A UNDERSTUDY I'D BE THERE YET -- BUT --
COPR 1955 WALT KELLY
FLESH AND BLOOD CAN STAND JUST SO MUCH --- AND I WASN'T EVEN HIS FLESH AND BLOOD -- TRY AS HE MIGHT TO PUT ON A BIG ACT, CALLING ME PATER AND MATER AND STUFF LIKE THAT.
--- YES, I'VE HAD BIG ROLES IN MY TIME ---

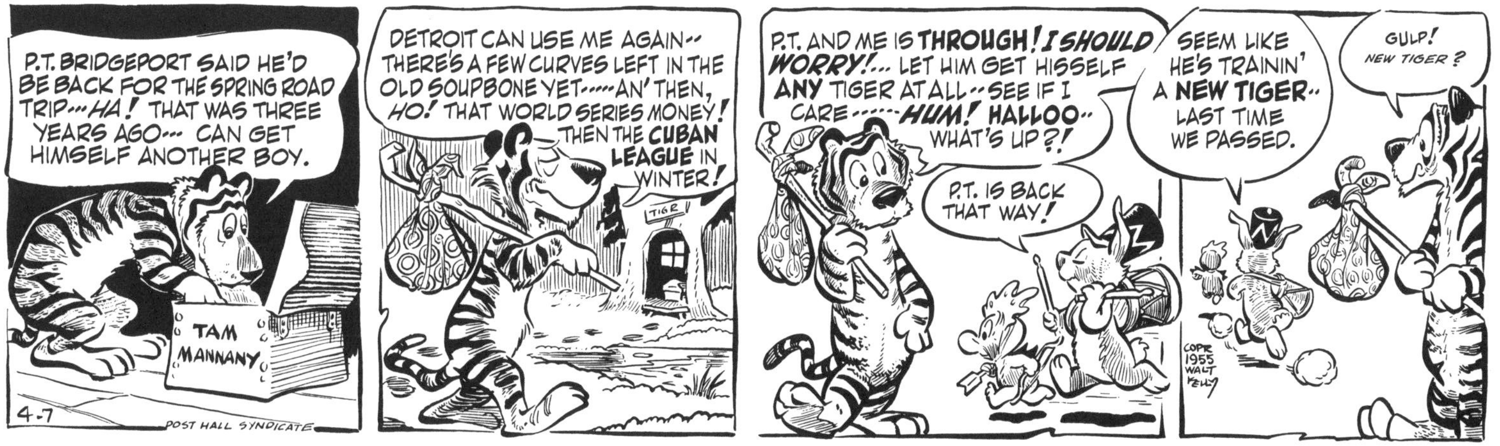
P.T. BRIDGEPORT SAID HE'D BE BACK FOR THE SPRING ROAD TRIP··· HA! THAT WAS THREE YEARS AGO··· CAN GET HIMSELF ANOTHER BOY.
TAM MANNANY
4-7
POST HALL SYNDICATE
DETROIT CAN USE ME AGAIN-- THERE'S A FEW CURVES LEFT IN THE OLD SOUPBONE YET····· AN' THEN, HO! THAT WORLD SERIES MONEY! THEN THE CUBAN LEAGUE IN WINTER!
TIGER
P.T. AND ME IS THROUGH! I SHOULD WORRY!... LET HIM GET HISSELF ANY TIGER AT ALL-- SEE IF I CARE······ HUM! HALLOO-- WHAT'S UP?!
P.T. IS BACK THAT WAY!
SEEM LIKE HE'S TRAININ' A NEW TIGER-- LAST TIME WE PASSED.
GULP! NEW TIGER?
COPR 1955 WALT KELLY

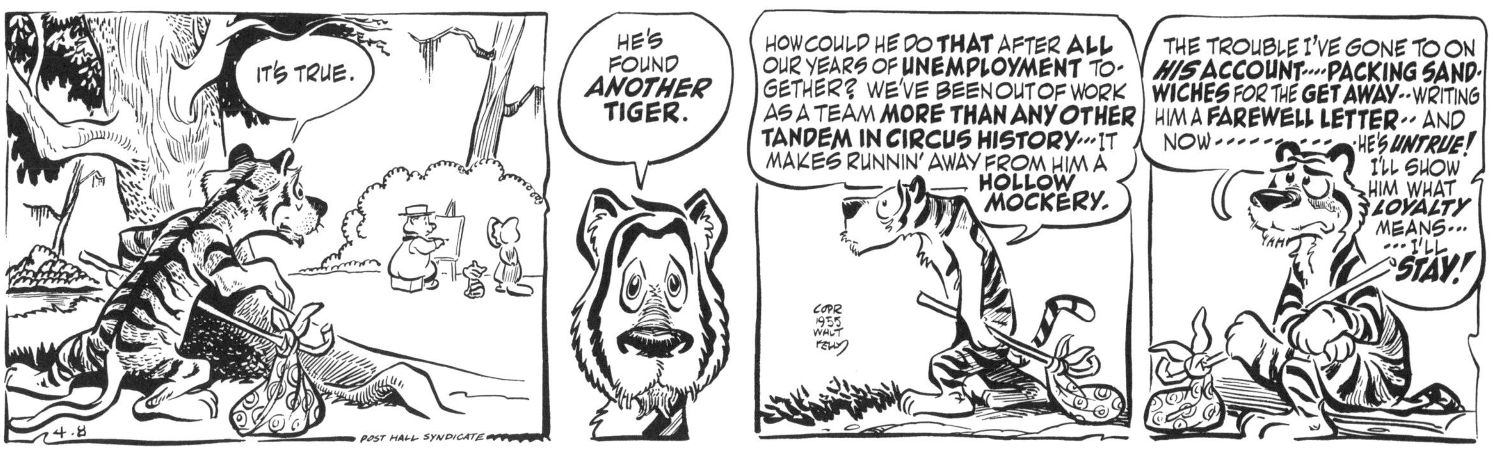
IT'S TRUE.
4-8
POST HALL SYNDICATE
HE'S FOUND ANOTHER TIGER.
HOW COULD HE DO THAT AFTER ALL OUR YEARS OF UNEMPLOYMENT TOGETHER? WE'VE BEEN OUT OF WORK AS A TEAM MORE THAN ANY OTHER TANDEM IN CIRCUS HISTORY··· IT MAKES RUNNIN' AWAY FROM HIM A HOLLOW MOCKERY.
COPR 1955 WALT KELLY
THE TROUBLE I'VE GONE TO ON HIS ACCOUNT··· PACKING SANDWICHES FOR THE GET AWAY-- WRITING HIM A FAREWELL LETTER-- AND NOW·········· HE'S UNTRUE! I'LL SHOW HIM WHAT LOYALTY MEANS··· ···I'LL STAY!

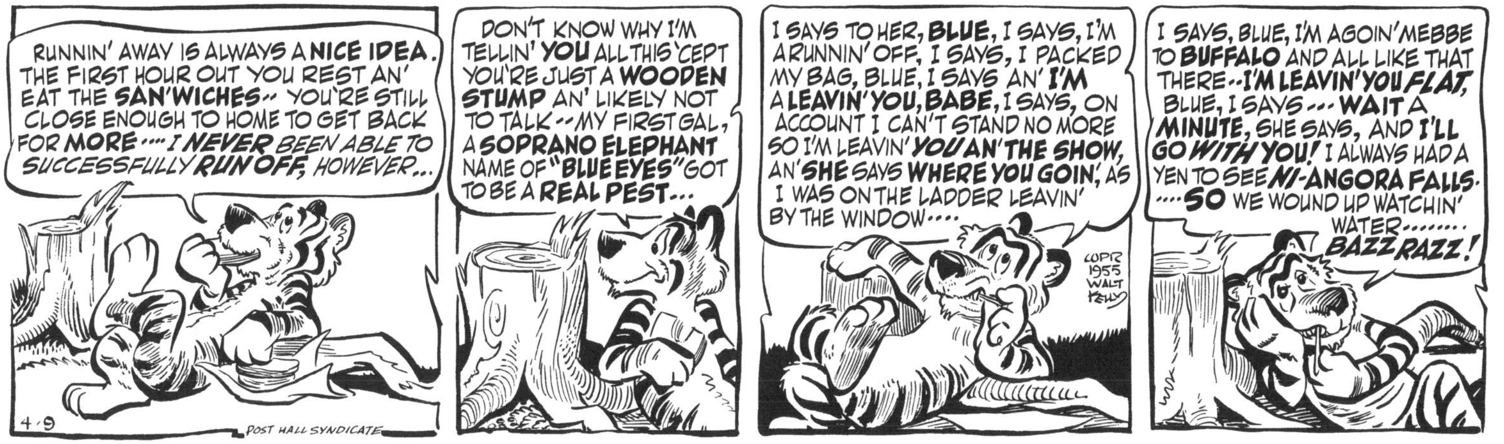
RUNNIN' AWAY IS ALWAYS A NICE IDEA. THE FIRST HOUR OUT YOU REST AN' EAT THE SAN'WICHES-- YOU'RE STILL CLOSE ENOUGH TO HOME TO GET BACK FOR MORE···· I NEVER BEEN ABLE TO SUCCESSFULLY RUN OFF, HOWEVER...
4-9
POST HALL SYNDICATE
DON'T KNOW WHY I'M TELLIN' YOU ALL THIS 'CEPT YOU'RE JUST A WOODEN STUMP AN' LIKELY NOT TO TALK-- MY FIRST GAL, A SOPRANO ELEPHANT NAME OF "BLUE EYES" GOT TO BE A REAL PEST...
I SAYS TO HER, BLUE, I SAYS, I'M A RUNNIN' OFF, I SAYS, I PACKED MY BAG, BLUE, I SAYS AN' I'M A LEAVIN' YOU, BABE, I SAYS, ON ACCOUNT I CAN'T STAND NO MORE SO I'M LEAVIN' YOU AN' THE SHOW, AN' SHE SAYS WHERE YOU GOIN', AS I WAS ON THE LADDER LEAVIN' BY THE WINDOW····
COPR 1955 WALT KELLY
I SAYS, BLUE, I'M AGOIN' MEBBE TO BUFFALO AND ALL LIKE THAT THERE-- I'M LEAVIN' YOU FLAT, BLUE, I SAYS··· WAIT A MINUTE, SHE SAYS, AND I'LL GO WITH YOU! I ALWAYS HAD A YEN TO SEE NI-ANGORA FALLS. ····SO WE WOUND UP WATCHIN' WATER······· BAZZ RAZZ!

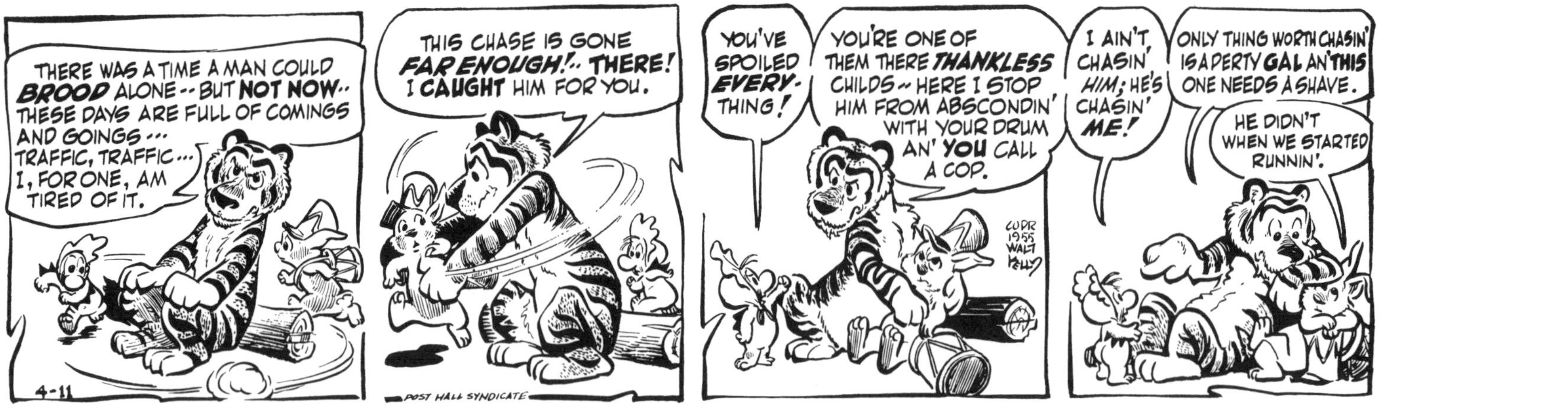
THERE WAS A TIME A MAN COULD BROOD ALONE -- BUT NOT NOW.. THESE DAYS ARE FULL OF COMINGS AND GOINGS ... TRAFFIC, TRAFFIC ... I, FOR ONE, AM TIRED OF IT.
4-11
THIS CHASE IS GONE FAR ENOUGH!.. THERE! I CAUGHT HIM FOR YOU.
POST HALL SYNDICATE
YOU'VE SPOILED EVERY-THING!
YOU'RE ONE OF THEM THERE THANKLESS CHILDS -- HERE I STOP HIM FROM ABSCONDIN' WITH YOUR DRUM AN' YOU CALL A COP.
COPR 1955 WALT KELLY
I AIN'T CHASIN' HIM; HE'S CHASIN' ME!
ONLY THING WORTH CHASIN' IS A PERTY GAL AN' THIS ONE NEEDS A SHAVE.
HE DIDN'T WHEN WE STARTED RUNNIN'.

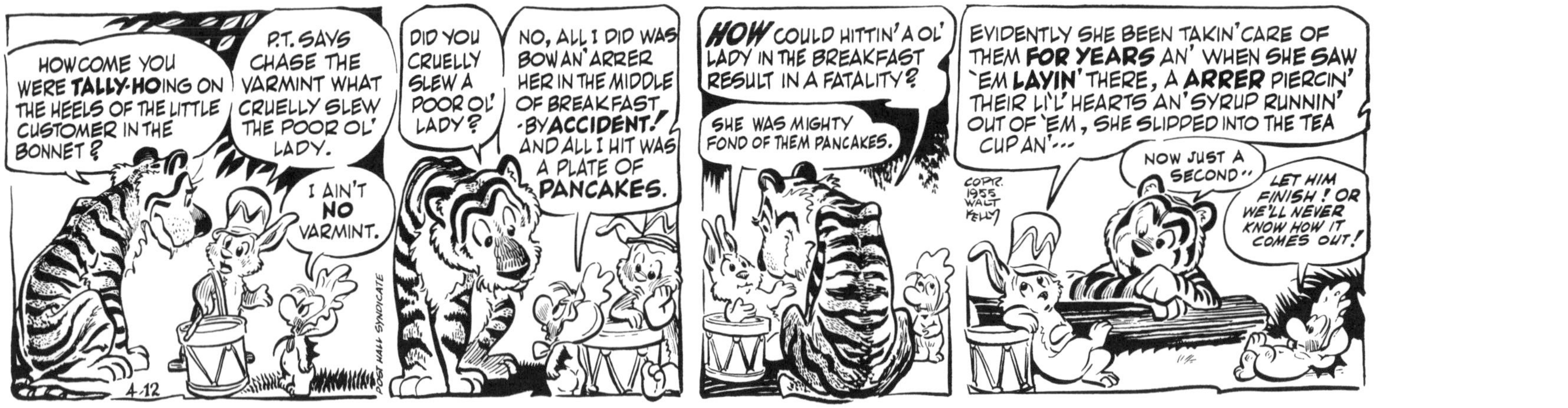
HOW COME YOU WERE TALLY-HOING ON THE HEELS OF THE LITTLE CUSTOMER IN THE BONNET?
P.T. SAYS CHASE THE VARMINT WHAT CRUELLY SLEW THE POOR OL' LADY.
I AIN'T NO VARMINT.
4-12
POST HALL SYNDICATE
DID YOU CRUELLY SLEW A POOR OL' LADY?
NO, ALL I DID WAS BOW AN' ARRER HER IN THE MIDDLE OF BREAKFAST -BY ACCIDENT! AND ALL I HIT WAS A PLATE OF PANCAKES.
HOW COULD HITTIN' A OL' LADY IN THE BREAKFAST RESULT IN A FATALITY?
SHE WAS MIGHTY FOND OF THEM PANCAKES.
COPR. 1955 WALT KELLY
EVIDENTLY SHE BEEN TAKIN' CARE OF THEM FOR YEARS AN' WHEN SHE SAW 'EM LAYIN' THERE, A ARRER PIERCIN' THEIR LI'L' HEARTS AN' SYRUP RUNNIN' OUT OF 'EM, SHE SLIPPED INTO THE TEA CUP AN'...
NOW JUST A SECOND..
LET HIM FINISH! OR WE'LL NEVER KNOW HOW IT COMES OUT!

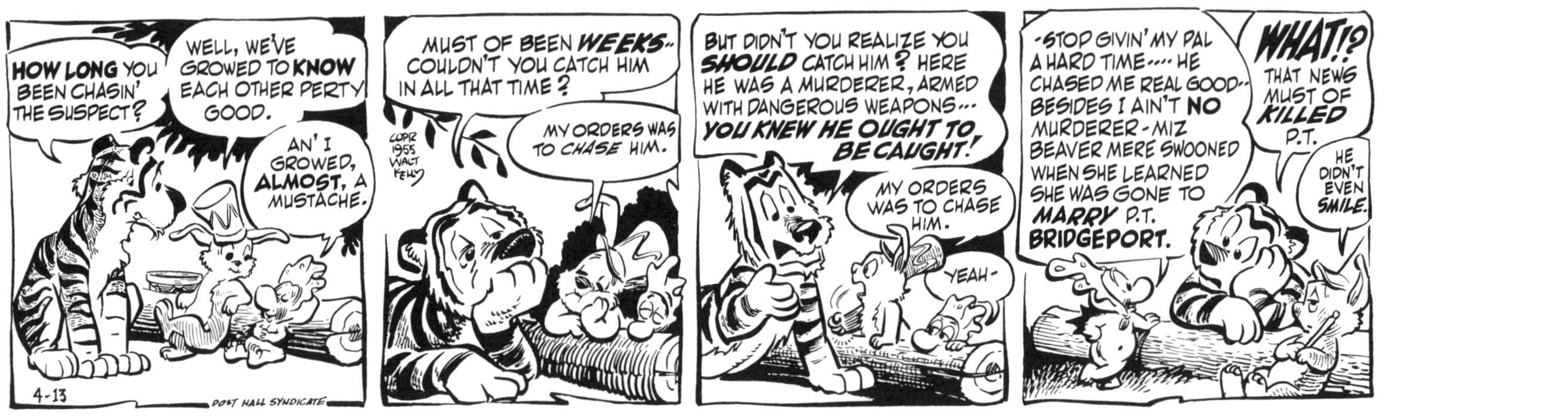
HOW LONG YOU BEEN CHASIN' THE SUSPECT?
WELL, WE'VE GROWED TO KNOW EACH OTHER PERTY GOOD.
AN' I GROWED, ALMOST, A MUSTACHE.
4-13
POST HALL SYNDICATE
MUST OF BEEN WEEKS.. COULDN'T YOU CATCH HIM IN ALL THAT TIME?
MY ORDERS WAS TO CHASE HIM.
COPR 1955 WALT KELLY
BUT DIDN'T YOU REALIZE YOU SHOULD CATCH HIM? HERE HE WAS A MURDERER, ARMED WITH DANGEROUS WEAPONS... YOU KNEW HE OUGHT TO BE CAUGHT!
MY ORDERS WAS TO CHASE HIM.
YEAH-
-STOP GIVIN' MY PAL A HARD TIME.... HE CHASED ME REAL GOOD.. BESIDES I AIN'T NO MURDERER - MIZ BEAVER MERE SWOONED WHEN SHE LEARNED SHE WAS GONE TO MARRY P.T. BRIDGEPORT.
WHAT!? THAT NEWS MUST OF KILLED P.T.
HE DIDN'T EVEN SMILE.

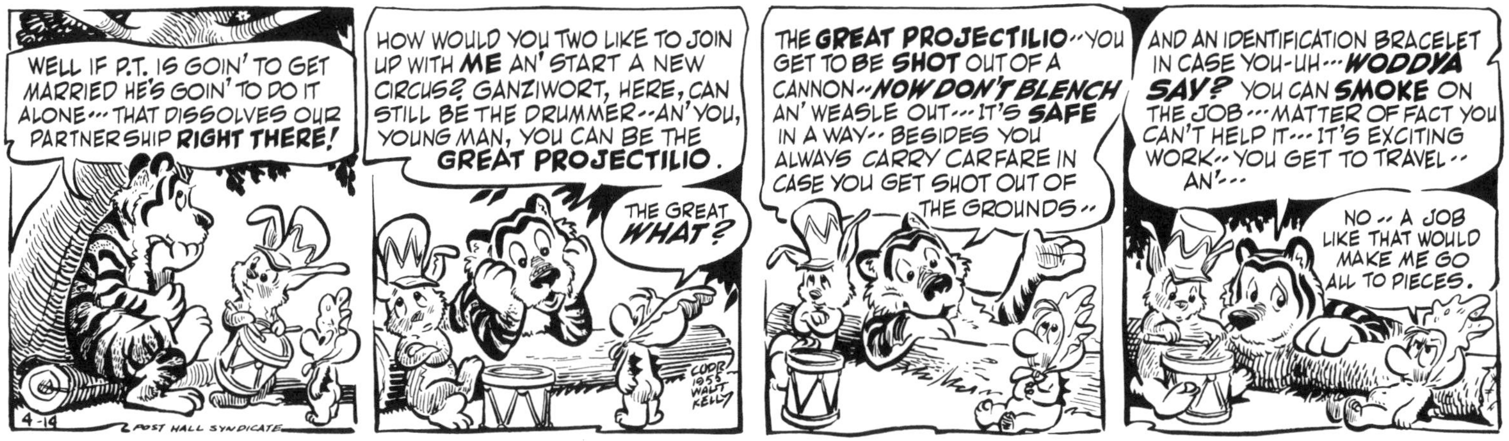
WELL IF P.T. IS GOIN' TO GET MARRIED HE'S GOIN' TO DO IT ALONE··· THAT DISSOLVES OUR PARTNERSHIP **RIGHT THERE!**
HOW WOULD YOU TWO LIKE TO JOIN UP WITH **ME** AN' START A NEW CIRCUS? GANZIWORT, HERE, CAN STILL BE THE DRUMMER--AN' YOU, YOUNG MAN, YOU CAN BE THE **GREAT PROJECTILIO**.
THE GREAT ***WHAT?***
THE **GREAT PROJECTILIO**--YOU GET TO BE **SHOT** OUT OF A CANNON--***NOW DON'T BLENCH*** AN' WEASLE OUT··· IT'S **SAFE** IN A WAY--BESIDES YOU ALWAYS CARRY CARFARE IN CASE YOU GET SHOT OUT OF THE GROUNDS--
AND AN IDENTIFICATION BRACELET IN CASE YOU-UH··· ***WODDYA SAY?*** YOU CAN **SMOKE** ON THE JOB···MATTER OF FACT YOU CAN'T HELP IT··· IT'S EXCITING WORK--YOU GET TO TRAVEL--AN'--
NO--A JOB LIKE THAT WOULD MAKE ME GO ALL TO PIECES.
4-14
POST HALL SYNDICATE
COPR 1955 WALT KELLY

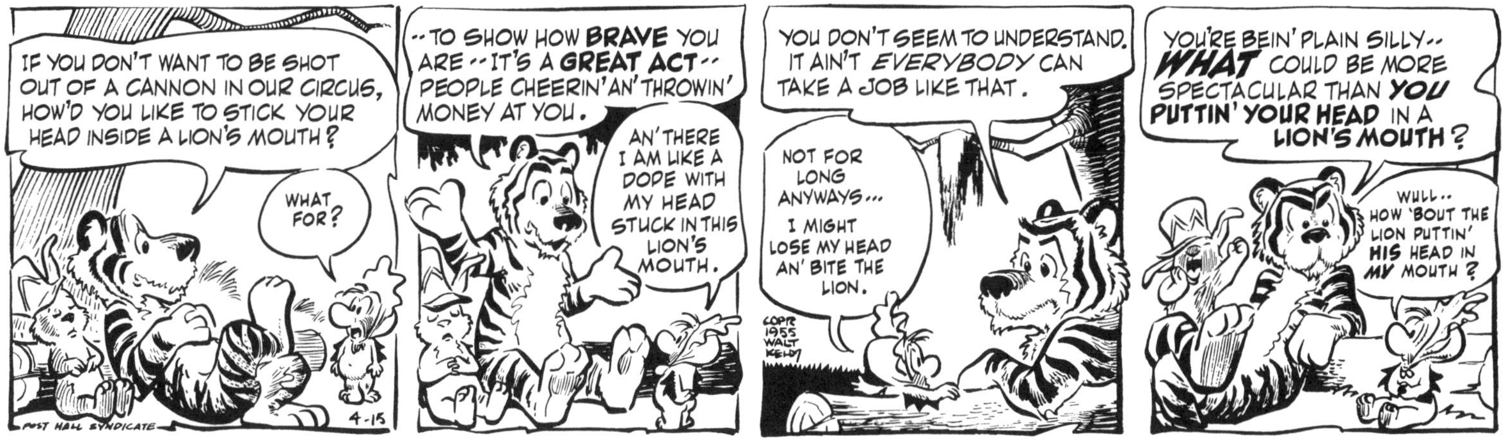
IF YOU DON'T WANT TO BE SHOT OUT OF A CANNON IN OUR CIRCUS, HOW'D YOU LIKE TO STICK YOUR HEAD INSIDE A LION'S MOUTH?
WHAT FOR?
--TO SHOW HOW **BRAVE** YOU ARE--IT'S A **GREAT ACT**--PEOPLE CHEERIN' AN' THROWIN' MONEY AT YOU.
AN' THERE I AM LIKE A DOPE WITH MY HEAD STUCK IN THIS LION'S MOUTH.
YOU DON'T SEEM TO UNDERSTAND. IT AIN'T *EVERYBODY* CAN TAKE A JOB LIKE THAT.
NOT FOR LONG ANYWAYS··· I MIGHT LOSE MY HEAD AN' BITE THE LION.
YOU'RE BEIN' PLAIN SILLY--***WHAT*** COULD BE MORE SPECTACULAR THAN ***YOU*** **PUTTIN' YOUR HEAD** IN A **LION'S MOUTH**?
WULL--HOW 'BOUT THE LION PUTTIN' **HIS** HEAD IN ***MY*** MOUTH?
4-15
POST HALL SYNDICATE
COPR 1955 WALT KELLY

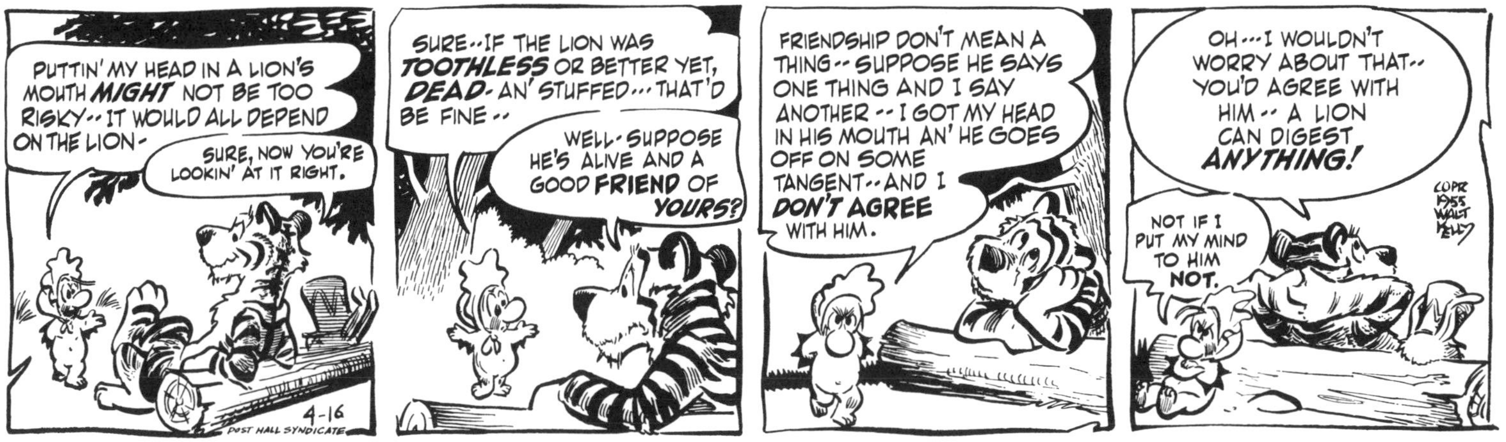
PUTTIN' MY HEAD IN A LION'S MOUTH ***MIGHT*** NOT BE TOO RISKY--IT WOULD ALL DEPEND ON THE LION-
SURE, NOW YOU'RE LOOKIN' AT IT RIGHT.
SURE--IF THE LION WAS ***TOOTHLESS*** OR BETTER YET, ***DEAD***-AN' STUFFED···THAT'D BE FINE--
WELL-SUPPOSE HE'S ALIVE AND A GOOD **FRIEND** OF ***YOURS?***
FRIENDSHIP DON'T MEAN A THING--SUPPOSE HE SAYS ONE THING AND I SAY ANOTHER--I GOT MY HEAD IN HIS MOUTH AN' HE GOES OFF ON SOME TANGENT--AND I ***DON'T AGREE*** WITH HIM.
OH···I WOULDN'T WORRY ABOUT THAT--YOU'D AGREE WITH HIM--A LION CAN DIGEST ***ANYTHING!***
NOT IF I PUT MY MIND TO HIM **NOT**.
4-16
POST HALL SYNDICATE
COPR 1955 WALT KELLY

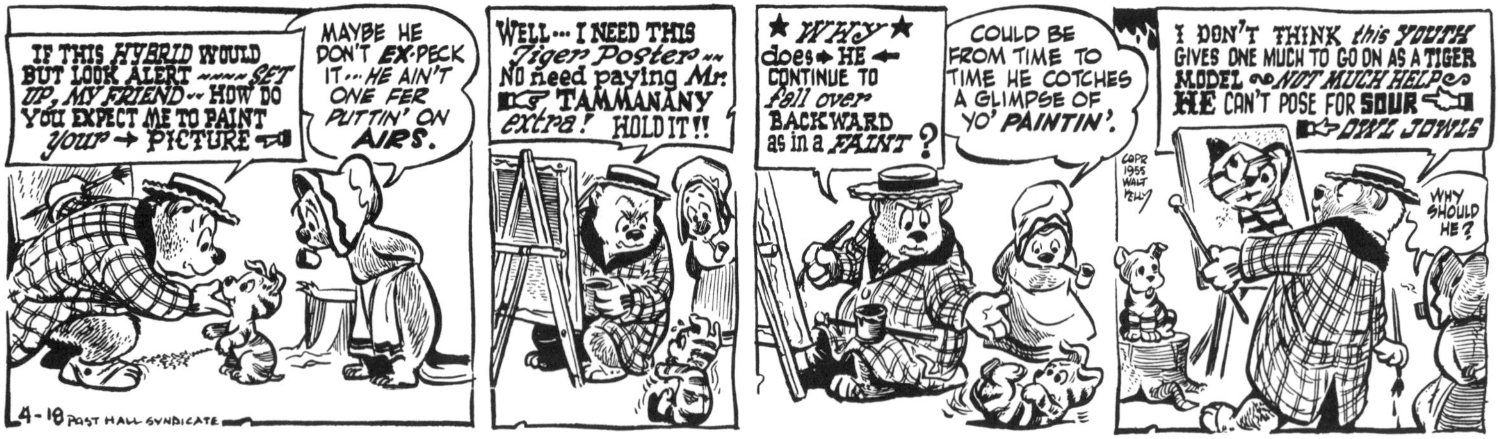
IF THIS HYBRID WOULD BUT LOOK ALERT ~~~~ SET UP, MY FRIEND~~ HOW DO YOU EXPECT ME TO PAINT your → PICTURE
MAYBE HE DON'T EX-PECK IT... HE AIN'T ONE FER PUTTIN' ON AIRS.
WELL... I NEED THIS Tiger Poster ~~ No need paying Mr. TAMMANANY extra! HOLD IT!!
★ WHY ★ does → HE ← CONTINUE TO fall over BACKWARD as in a FAINT?
COULD BE FROM TIME TO TIME HE COTCHES A GLIMPSE OF YO' PAINTIN'.
I DON'T THINK this YOUTH GIVES ONE MUCH TO GO ON AS A TIGER MODEL ~ NOT MUCH HELP ~ HE CAN'T POSE FOR SOUR OWL JOWLS
WHY SHOULD HE?
4-18 POST HALL SYNDICATE
COPR 1955 WALT KELLY

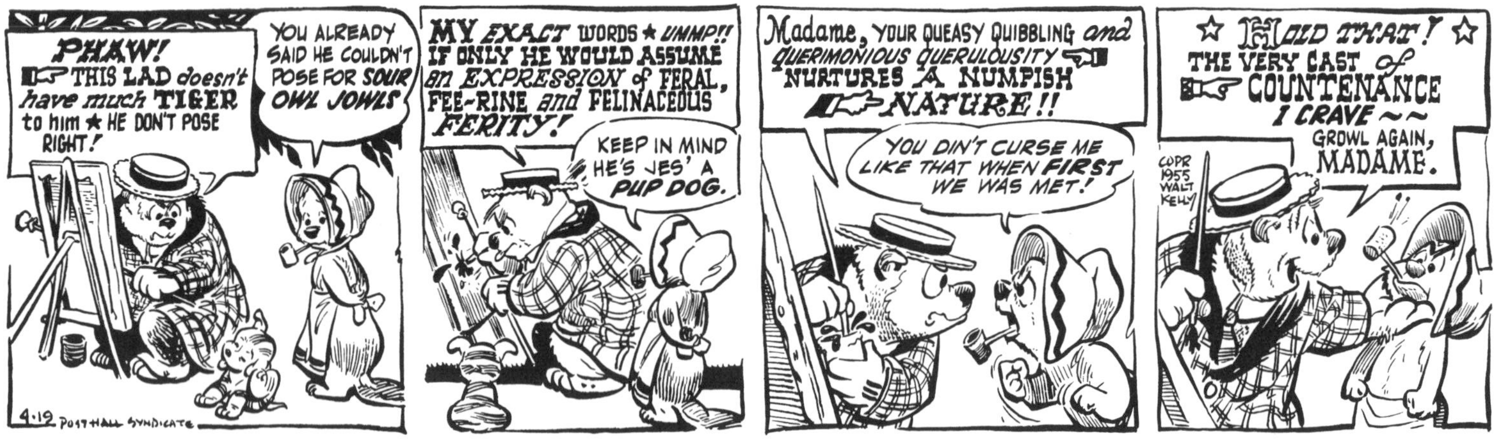
PHAW! THIS LAD doesn't have much TIGER to him ★ HE DON'T POSE RIGHT!
YOU ALREADY SAID HE COULDN'T POSE FOR SOUR OWL JOWLS
MY EXACT WORDS ★ UMMP!! IF ONLY HE WOULD ASSUME an EXPRESSION of FERAL, FEE-RINE and FELINACEOUS FERITY!
KEEP IN MIND HE'S JES' A PUP DOG.
Madame, YOUR QUEASY QUIBBLING and QUERIMONIOUS QUERULOUSITY NURTURES A NUMPISH NATURE!!
YOU DIN'T CURSE ME LIKE THAT WHEN FIRST WE WAS MET!
☆ HOLD THAT! ☆ THE VERY CAST of COUNTENANCE I CRAVE ~~ GROWL AGAIN, MADAME.
4-19 POST HALL SYNDICATE
COPR 1955 WALT KELLY

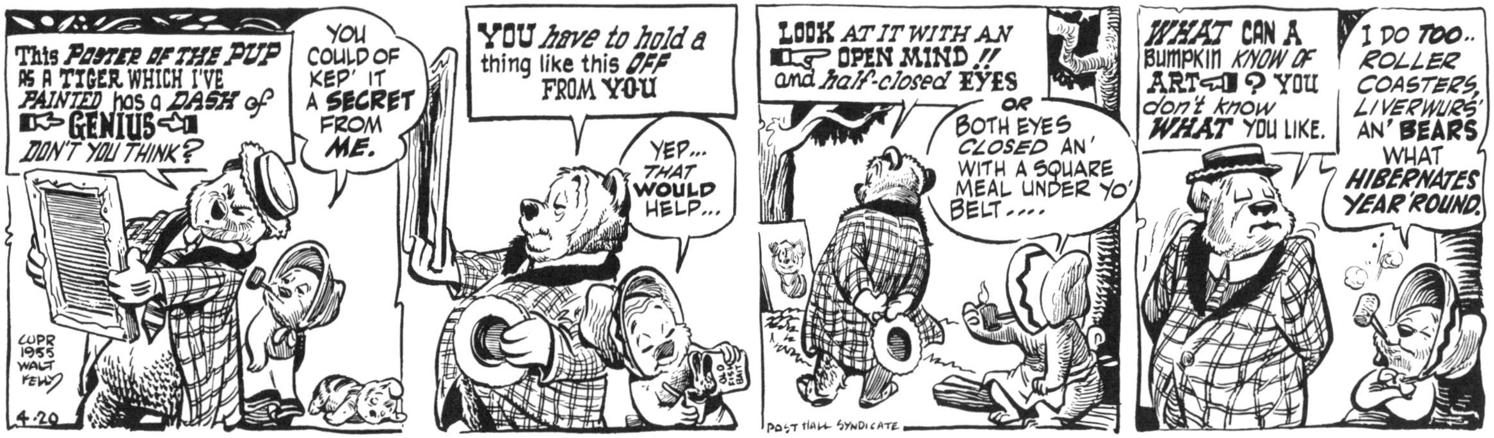
This POSTER OF THE PUP AS A TIGER WHICH I'VE PAINTED has a DASH of GENIUS DON'T YOU THINK?
YOU COULD OF KEP' IT A SECRET FROM ME.
YOU have to hold a thing like this OFF FROM YOU
YEP... THAT WOULD HELP...
LOOK AT IT WITH AN OPEN MIND!! and half-closed EYES
OR BOTH EYES CLOSED AN' WITH A SQUARE MEAL UNDER YO' BELT....
WHAT CAN A BUMPKIN KNOW OF ART? YOU don't know WHAT YOU LIKE.
I DO TOO.. ROLLER COASTERS, LIVERWURS', AN' BEARS WHAT HIBERNATES YEAR 'ROUND.
COPR 1955 WALT KELLY
4-20
POST HALL SYNDICATE

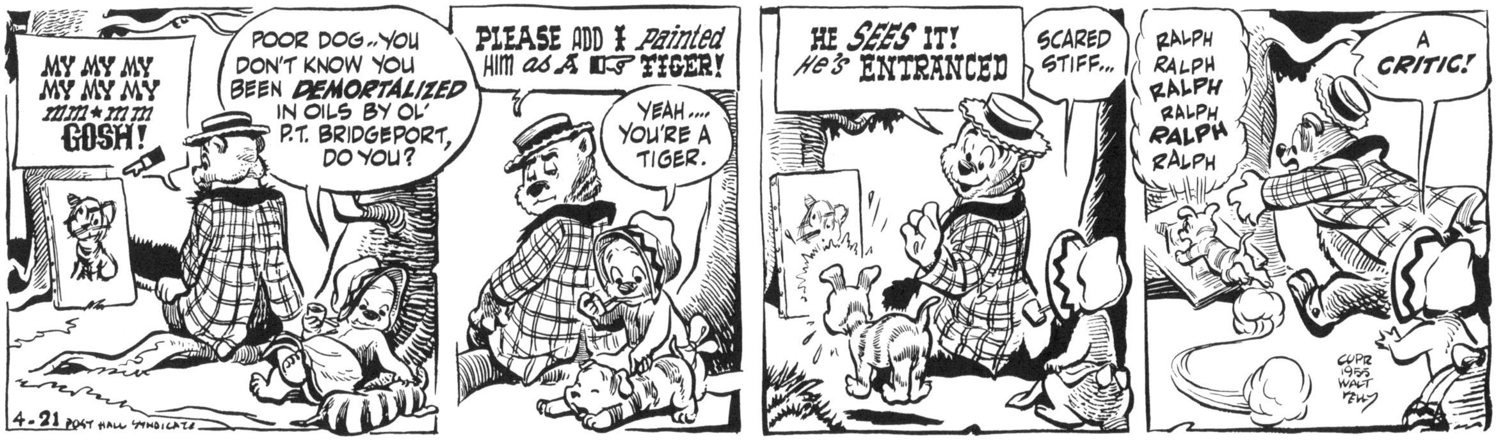
MY MY MY MY MY MY mm★mm GOSH!
POOR DOG.. YOU DON'T KNOW YOU BEEN DEMORTALIZED IN OILS BY OL' P.T. BRIDGEPORT, DO YOU?
PLEASE ADD I Painted HIM as A TIGER!
YEAH.... YOU'RE A TIGER.
HE SEES IT! He's ENTRANCED
SCARED STIFF...
RALPH RALPH RALPH RALPH RALPH RALPH
A CRITIC!
4-21
POST HALL SYNDICATE
COPR 1955 WALT KELLY

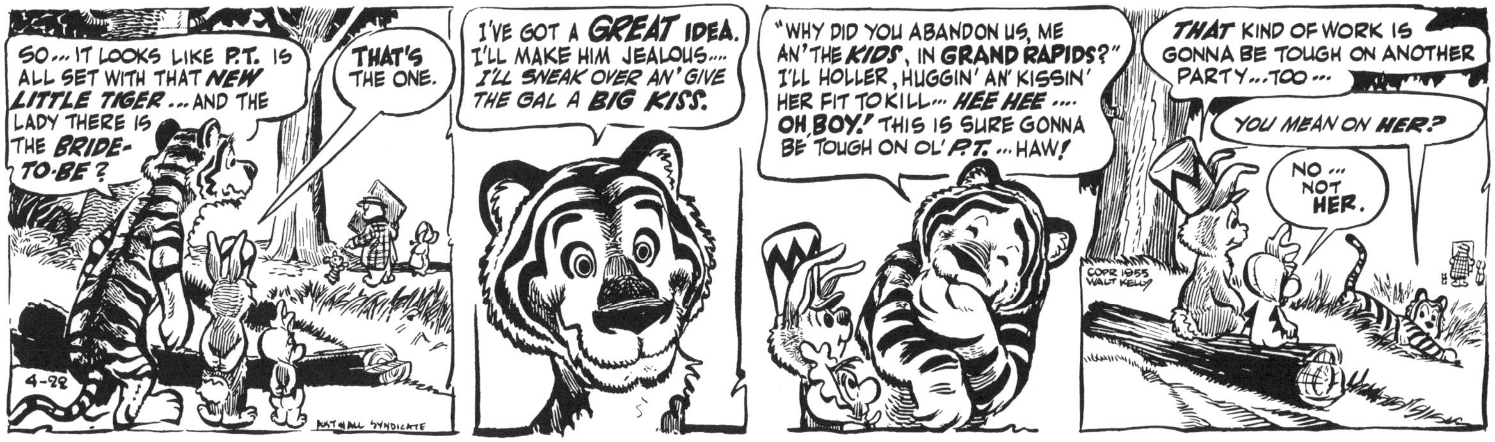
SO... IT LOOKS LIKE P.T. IS ALL SET WITH THAT NEW LITTLE TIGER... AND THE LADY THERE IS THE BRIDE-TO-BE?
THAT'S THE ONE.
I'VE GOT A GREAT IDEA. I'LL MAKE HIM JEALOUS.... I'LL SNEAK OVER AN' GIVE THE GAL A BIG KISS.
"WHY DID YOU ABANDON US, ME AN' THE KIDS, IN GRAND RAPIDS?" I'LL HOLLER, HUGGIN' AN' KISSIN' HER FIT TO KILL... HEE HEE.... OH BOY! THIS IS SURE GONNA BE TOUGH ON OL' P.T. ... HAW!
THAT KIND OF WORK IS GONNA BE TOUGH ON ANOTHER PARTY... TOO...
YOU MEAN ON HER?
NO... NOT HER.
4-22
POST HALL SYNDICATE
COPR 1955 WALT KELLY

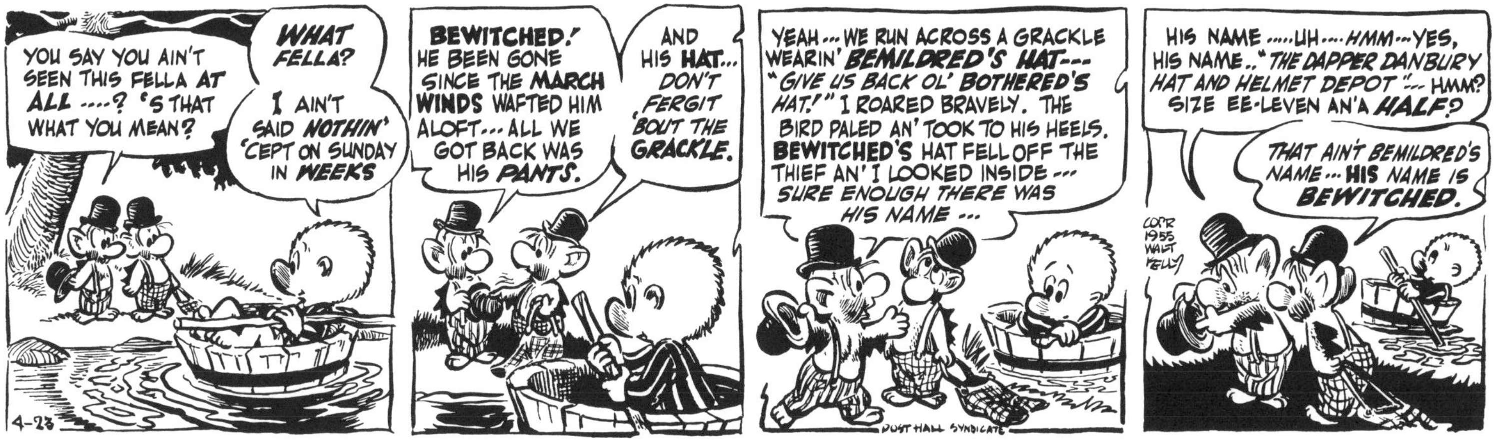
YOU SAY YOU AIN'T SEEN THIS FELLA AT ALL....? 'S THAT WHAT YOU MEAN?
WHAT FELLA?
I AIN'T SAID NOTHIN' 'CEPT ON SUNDAY IN WEEKS
BEWITCHED! HE BEEN GONE SINCE THE MARCH WINDS WAFTED HIM ALOFT... ALL WE GOT BACK WAS HIS PANTS.
AND HIS HAT... DON'T FERGIT 'BOUT THE GRACKLE.
YEAH... WE RUN ACROSS A GRACKLE WEARIN' BEMILDRED'S HAT--- "GIVE US BACK OL' BOTHERED'S HAT!" I ROARED BRAVELY. THE BIRD PALED AN' TOOK TO HIS HEELS. BEWITCHED'S HAT FELL OFF THE THIEF AN' I LOOKED INSIDE... SURE ENOUGH THERE WAS HIS NAME...
HIS NAME.....UH....HMM...YES, HIS NAME.."THE DAPPER DANBURY HAT AND HELMET DEPOT"... HMM? SIZE EE-LEVEN AN'A HALF?
THAT AIN'T BEMILDRED'S NAME... HIS NAME IS BEWITCHED.
4-23
POST HALL SYNDICATE
COPR 1955 WALT KELLY

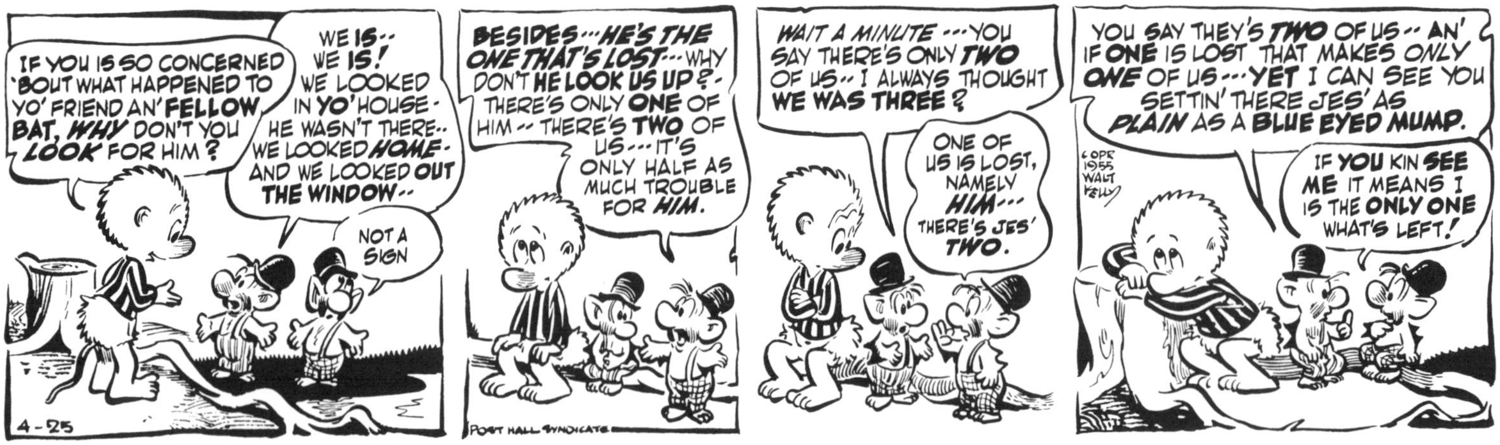
IF YOU IS SO CONCERNED 'BOUT WHAT HAPPENED TO YO' FRIEND AN' FELLOW BAT, WHY DON'T YOU LOOK FOR HIM?
WE IS-- WE IS! WE LOOKED IN YO' HOUSE- HE WASN'T THERE-- WE LOOKED HOME- AND WE LOOKED OUT THE WINDOW--
NOT A SIGN
4-25
BESIDES--HE'S THE ONE THAT'S LOST--WHY DON'T HE LOOK US UP?- THERE'S ONLY ONE OF HIM-- THERE'S TWO OF US---IT'S ONLY HALF AS MUCH TROUBLE FOR HIM.
POST HALL SYNDICATE
WAIT A MINUTE---YOU SAY THERE'S ONLY TWO OF US-- I ALWAYS THOUGHT WE WAS THREE?
ONE OF US IS LOST, NAMELY HIM--- THERE'S JES' TWO.
YOU SAY THEY'S TWO OF US-- AN' IF ONE IS LOST THAT MAKES ONLY ONE OF US---YET I CAN SEE YOU SETTIN' THERE JES' AS PLAIN AS A BLUE EYED MUMP.
COPR 1955 WALT KELLY
IF YOU KIN SEE ME IT MEANS I IS THE ONLY ONE WHAT'S LEFT!

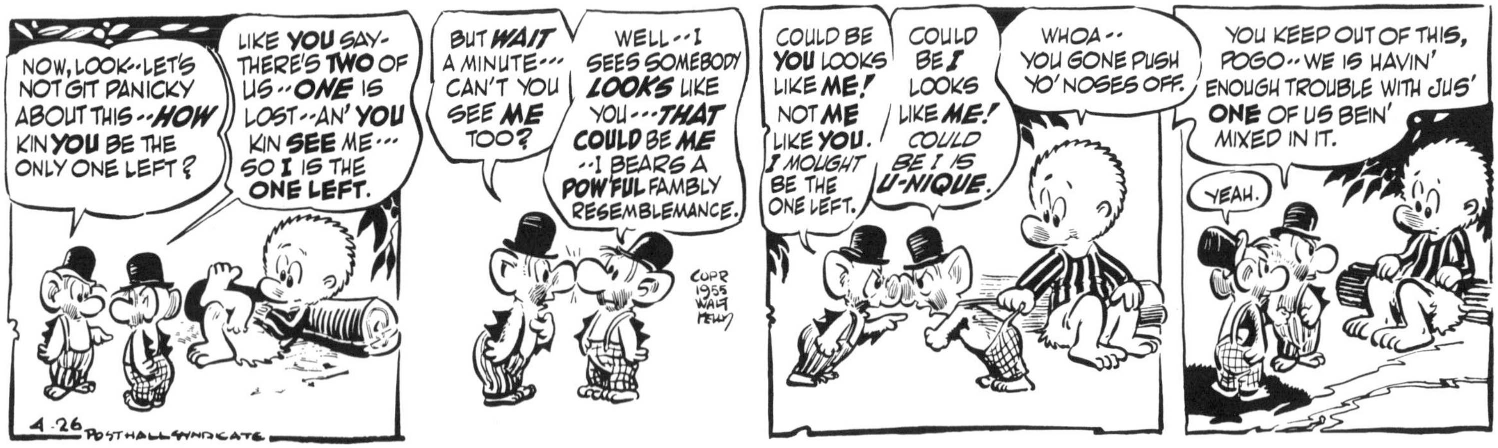
NOW, LOOK--LET'S NOT GIT PANICKY ABOUT THIS--HOW KIN YOU BE THE ONLY ONE LEFT?
LIKE YOU SAY- THERE'S TWO OF US--ONE IS LOST--AN' YOU KIN SEE ME--- SO I IS THE ONE LEFT.
4-26 POST HALL SYNDICATE
BUT WAIT A MINUTE--- CAN'T YOU SEE ME TOO?
WELL--I SEES SOMEBODY LOOKS LIKE YOU---THAT COULD BE ME --I BEARS A POW'FUL FAMBLY RESEMBLEMANCE.
COPR 1955 WALT KELLY
COULD BE YOU LOOKS LIKE ME! NOT ME LIKE YOU. I MOUGHT BE THE ONE LEFT.
COULD BE I LOOKS LIKE ME! COULD BE I IS U-NIQUE.
WHOA-- YOU GONE PUSH YO' NOSES OFF.
YOU KEEP OUT OF THIS, POGO--WE IS HAVIN' ENOUGH TROUBLE WITH JUS' ONE OF US BEIN' MIXED IN IT.
YEAH.

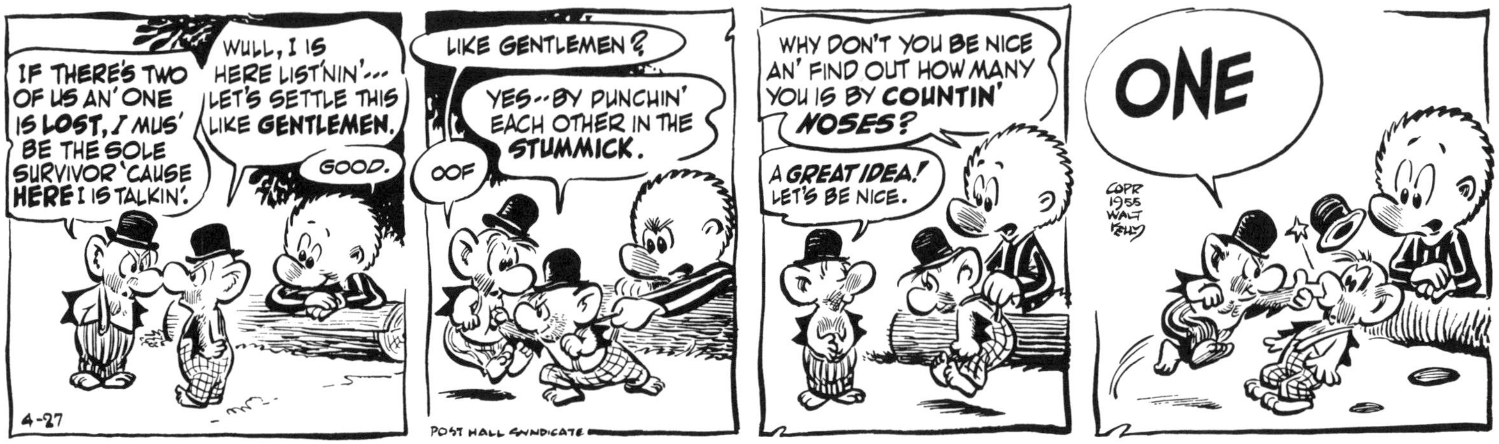
IF THERE'S TWO OF US AN' ONE IS LOST, I MUS' BE THE SOLE SURVIVOR 'CAUSE HERE I IS TALKIN'.
WULL, I IS HERE LIST'NIN'--- LET'S SETTLE THIS LIKE GENTLEMEN.
GOOD.
4-27
LIKE GENTLEMEN?
YES--BY PUNCHIN' EACH OTHER IN THE STUMMICK.
OOF
POST HALL SYNDICATE
WHY DON'T YOU BE NICE AN' FIND OUT HOW MANY YOU IS BY COUNTIN' NOSES?
A GREAT IDEA! LET'S BE NICE.
COPR 1955 WALT KELLY
ONE

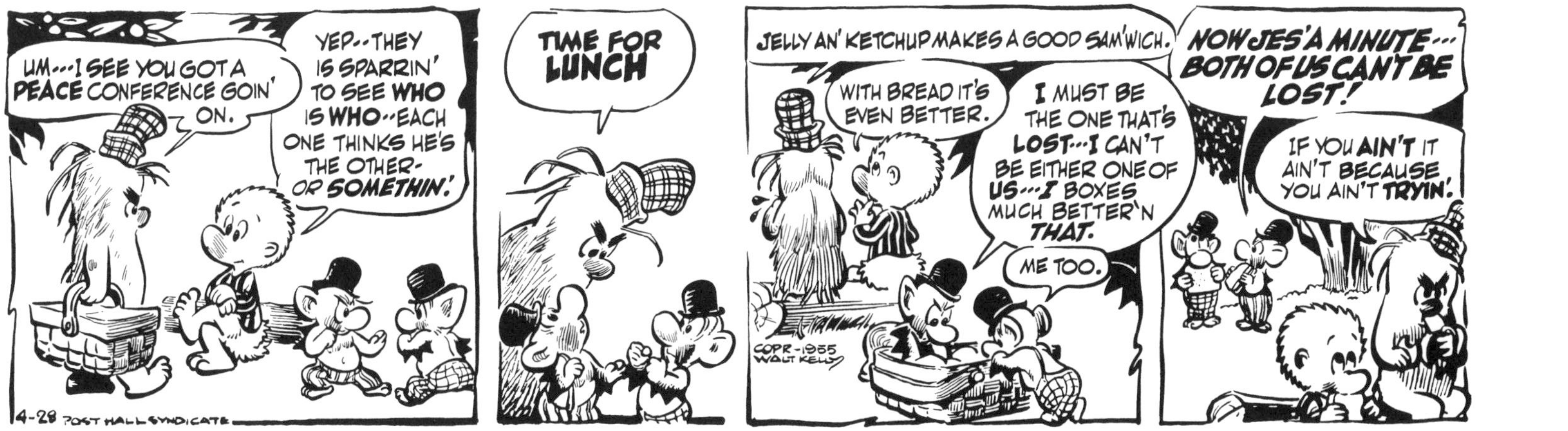
UM...I SEE YOU GOT A PEACE CONFERENCE GOIN' ON.
YEP..THEY IS SPARRIN' TO SEE WHO IS WHO..EACH ONE THINKS HE'S THE OTHER- OR SOMETHIN'.
TIME FOR LUNCH
JELLY AN' KETCHUP MAKES A GOOD SAM'WICH.
WITH BREAD IT'S EVEN BETTER.
I MUST BE THE ONE THAT'S LOST...I CAN'T BE EITHER ONE OF US...I BOXES MUCH BETTER'N THAT.
ME TOO.
NOW JES'A MINUTE... BOTH OF US CAN'T BE LOST!
IF YOU AIN'T IT AIN'T BECAUSE YOU AIN'T TRYIN'.
COPR-1955 WALT KELLY
4-28 POST HALL SYNDICATE

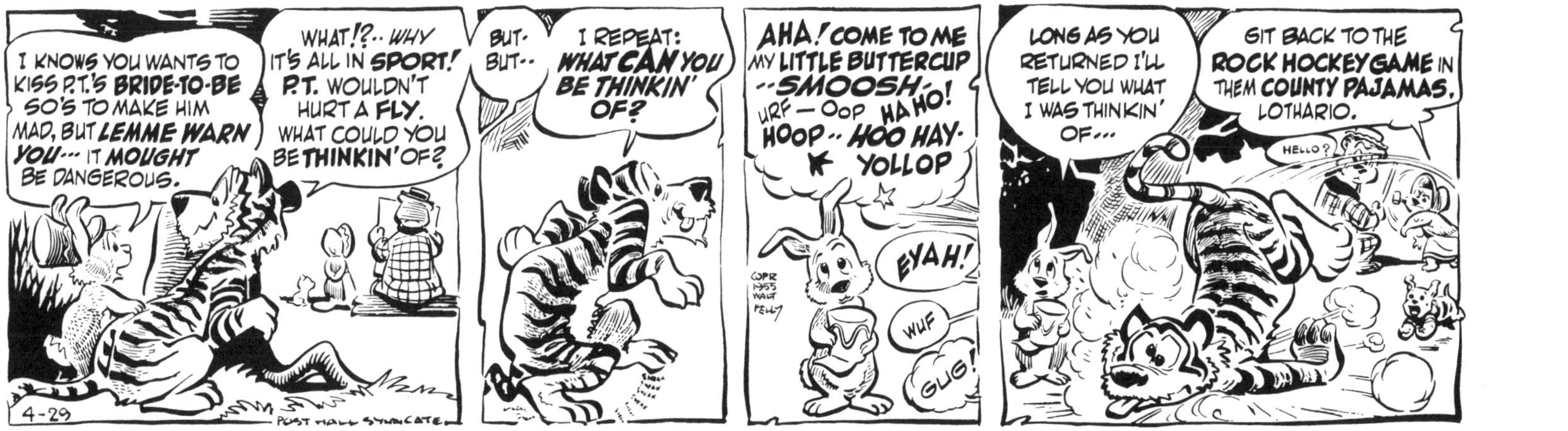
I KNOWS YOU WANTS TO KISS P.T.'S BRIDE-TO-BE SO'S TO MAKE HIM MAD, BUT LEMME WARN YOU... IT MOUGHT BE DANGEROUS.
WHAT!?.. WHY IT'S ALL IN SPORT! P.T. WOULDN'T HURT A FLY. WHAT COULD YOU BE THINKIN' OF?
BUT- BUT-..
I REPEAT: WHAT CAN YOU BE THINKIN' OF?
AHA! COME TO ME MY LITTLE BUTTERCUP --SMOOSH-
URF — OOP HA HO! HOOP.. HOO HAY. YOLLOP
EYAH!
WUF
GUG!
COPR 1955 WALT KELLY
LONG AS YOU RETURNED I'LL TELL YOU WHAT I WAS THINKIN' OF...
GIT BACK TO THE ROCK HOCKEY GAME IN THEM COUNTY PAJAMAS, LOTHARIO.
HELLO?
4-29 POST HALL SYNDICATE

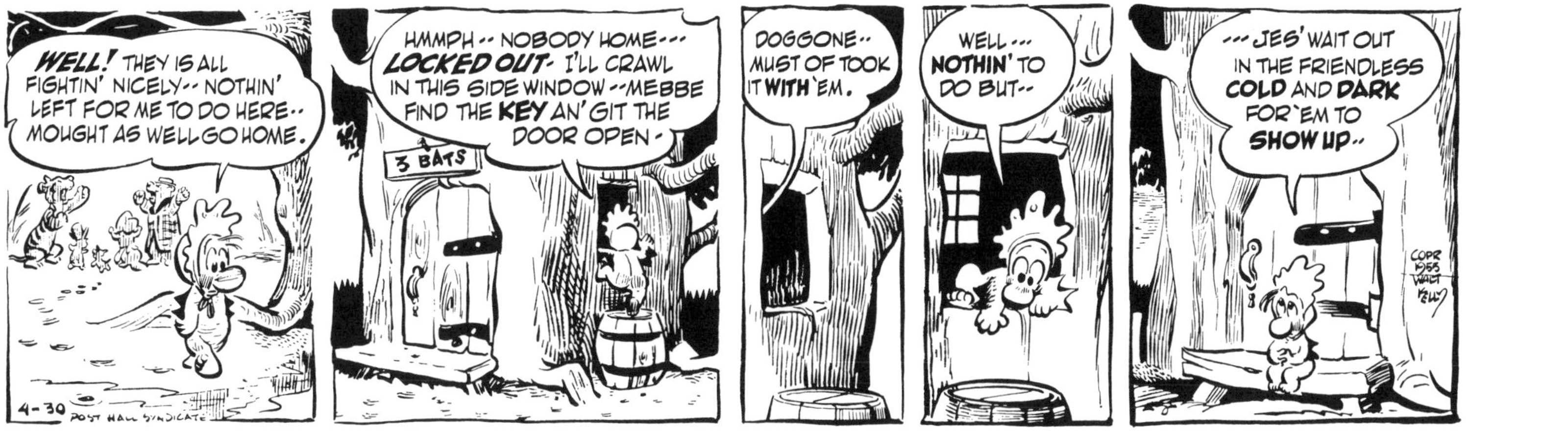
WELL! THEY IS ALL FIGHTIN' NICELY.. NOTHIN' LEFT FOR ME TO DO HERE.. MOUGHT AS WELL GO HOME.
HMMPH.. NOBODY HOME... LOCKED OUT. I'LL CRAWL IN THIS SIDE WINDOW --MEBBE FIND THE KEY AN' GIT THE DOOR OPEN-
3 BATS
DOGGONE.. MUST OF TOOK IT WITH 'EM.
WELL... NOTHIN' TO DO BUT--
...JES' WAIT OUT IN THE FRIENDLESS COLD AND DARK FOR 'EM TO SHOW UP..
COPR 1955 WALT KELLY
4-30 POST HALL SYNDICATE

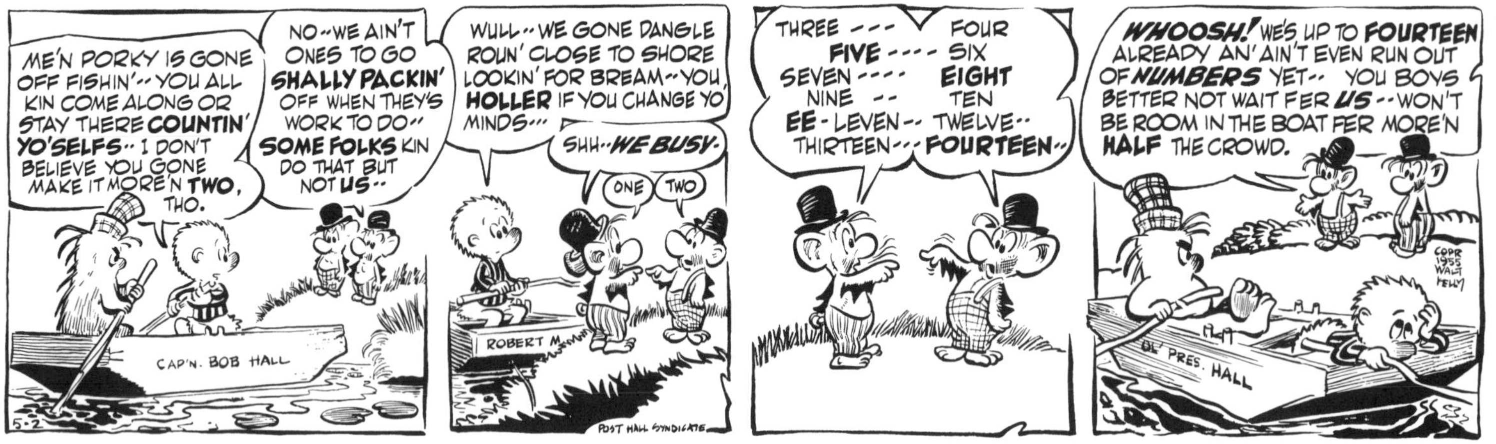
ME'N PORKY IS GONE OFF FISHIN'-- YOU ALL KIN COME ALONG OR STAY THERE COUNTIN' YO'SELFS-- I DON'T BELIEVE YOU GONE MAKE IT MORE'N TWO, THO.
NO--WE AIN'T ONES TO GO SHALLY PACKIN' OFF WHEN THEY'S WORK TO DO-- SOME FOLKS KIN DO THAT BUT NOT US--
CAP'N. BOB HALL
5-2
WULL--WE GONE DANGLE ROUN' CLOSE TO SHORE LOOKIN' FOR BREAM--YOU HOLLER IF YOU CHANGE YO' MINDS--
SHH--WE BUSY.
ONE
TWO
ROBERT M.
POST HALL SYNDICATE
THREE --- FOUR
FIVE ---- SIX
SEVEN ---- EIGHT
NINE -- TEN
EE-LEVEN-- TWELVE--
THIRTEEN--- FOURTEEN--
WHOOSH! WE'S UP TO FOURTEEN ALREADY AN' AIN'T EVEN RUN OUT OF NUMBERS YET-- YOU BOYS BETTER NOT WAIT FER US--WON'T BE ROOM IN THE BOAT FER MORE'N HALF THE CROWD.
COPR 1955 WALT KELLY
OL' PRES. HALL

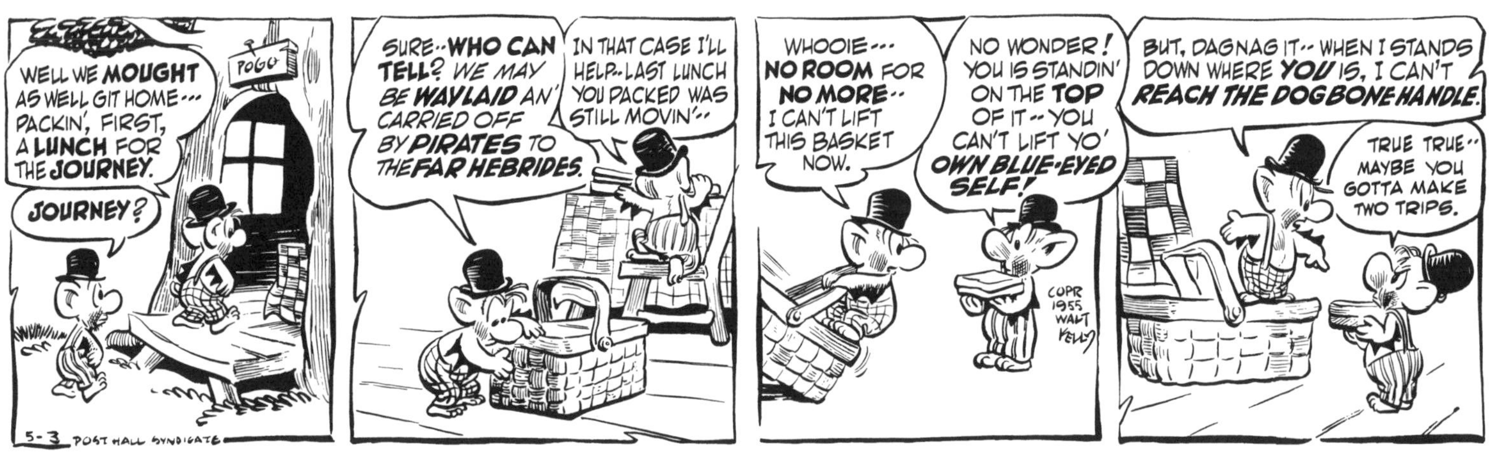
WELL WE MOUGHT AS WELL GIT HOME--- PACKIN', FIRST, A LUNCH FOR THE JOURNEY.
POGO
JOURNEY?
5-3 POST HALL SYNDICATE
SURE--WHO CAN TELL? WE MAY BE WAYLAID AN' CARRIED OFF BY PIRATES TO THE FAR HEBRIDES.
IN THAT CASE I'LL HELP--LAST LUNCH YOU PACKED WAS STILL MOVIN'--
WHOOIE--- NO ROOM FOR NO MORE-- I CAN'T LIFT THIS BASKET NOW.
NO WONDER! YOU IS STANDIN' ON THE TOP OF IT--YOU CAN'T LIFT YO' OWN BLUE-EYED SELF!
COPR 1955 WALT KELLY
BUT, DAGNAG IT-- WHEN I STANDS DOWN WHERE YOU IS, I CAN'T REACH THE DOGBONE HANDLE.
TRUE TRUE-- MAYBE YOU GOTTA MAKE TWO TRIPS.

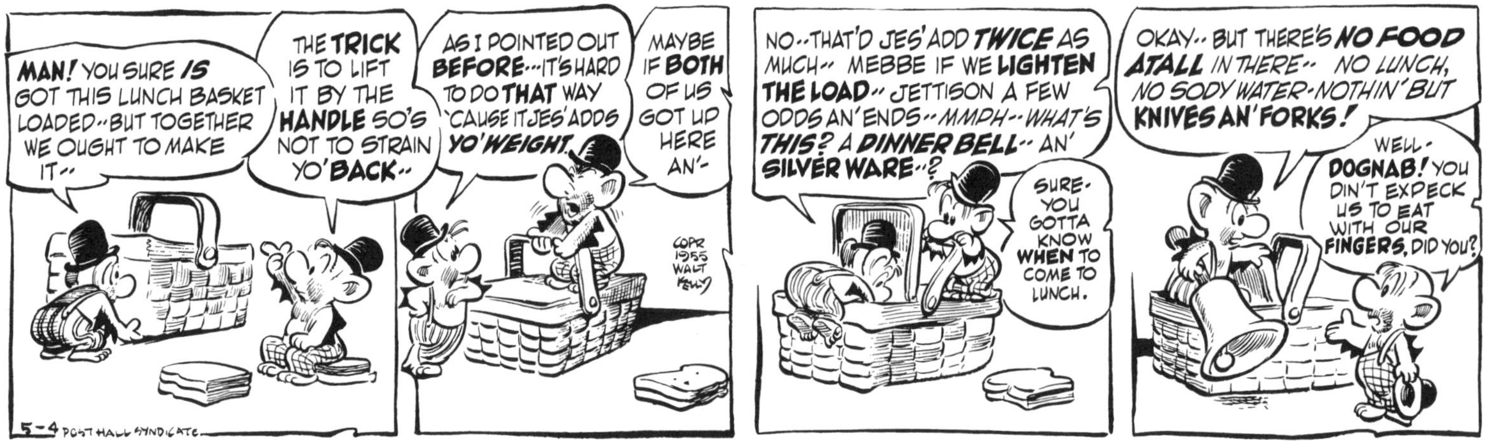
MAN! YOU SURE IS GOT THIS LUNCH BASKET LOADED--BUT TOGETHER WE OUGHT TO MAKE IT--
THE TRICK IS TO LIFT IT BY THE HANDLE SO'S NOT TO STRAIN YO' BACK--
AS I POINTED OUT BEFORE---IT'S HARD TO DO THAT WAY 'CAUSE IT JES' ADDS YO' WEIGHT.
MAYBE IF BOTH OF US GOT UP HERE AN'-
COPR 1955 WALT KELLY
NO--THAT'D JES' ADD TWICE AS MUCH-- MEBBE IF WE LIGHTEN THE LOAD-- JETTISON A FEW ODDS AN' ENDS--MMPH--WHAT'S THIS? A DINNER BELL-- AN' SILVER WARE--?
SURE- YOU GOTTA KNOW WHEN TO COME TO LUNCH.
OKAY-- BUT THERE'S NO FOOD ATALL IN THERE-- NO LUNCH, NO SODY WATER-NOTHIN' BUT KNIVES AN' FORKS!
WELL- DOGNAB! YOU DIN'T EXPECK US TO EAT WITH OUR FINGERS, DID YOU?
5-4 POST HALL SYNDICATE

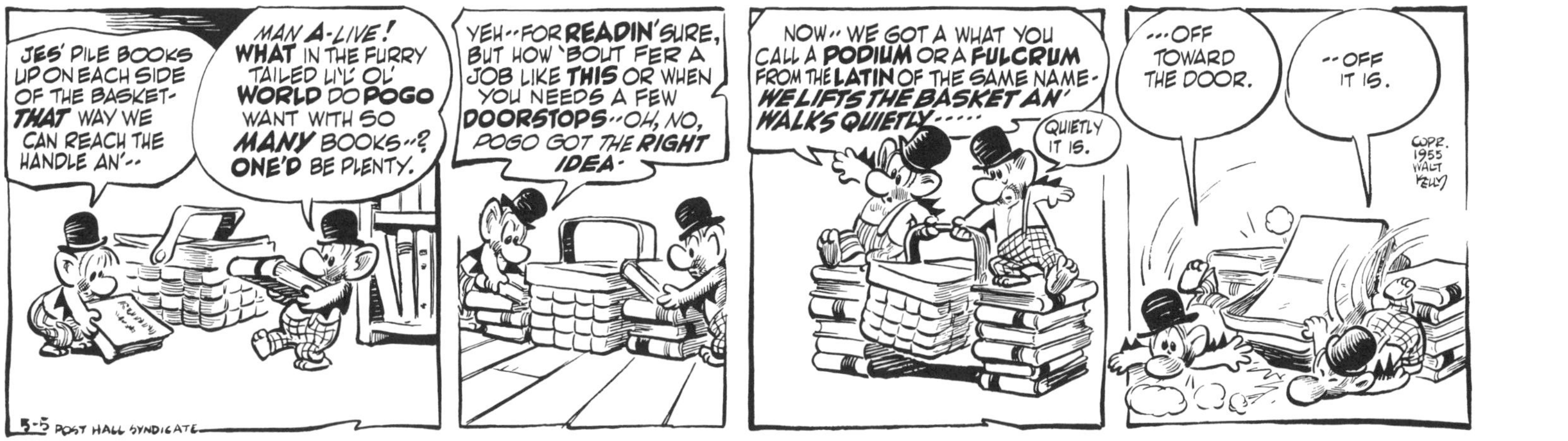
JES' PILE BOOKS UP ON EACH SIDE OF THE BASKET-THAT WAY WE CAN REACH THE HANDLE AN'--
MAN A-LIVE! WHAT IN THE FURRY TAILED LI'L OL' WORLD DO POGO WANT WITH SO MANY BOOKS--? ONE'D BE PLENTY.
YEH--FOR READIN' SURE, BUT HOW 'BOUT FER A JOB LIKE THIS OR WHEN YOU NEEDS A FEW DOORSTOPS--OH, NO, POGO GOT THE RIGHT IDEA-
NOW-- WE GOT A WHAT YOU CALL A PODIUM OR A FULCRUM FROM THE LATIN OF THE SAME NAME-WE LIFTS THE BASKET AN' WALKS QUIETLY.....
QUIETLY IT IS.
...OFF TOWARD THE DOOR.
--OFF IT IS.
COPR. 1955 WALT KELLY
5-5 POST HALL SYNDICATE

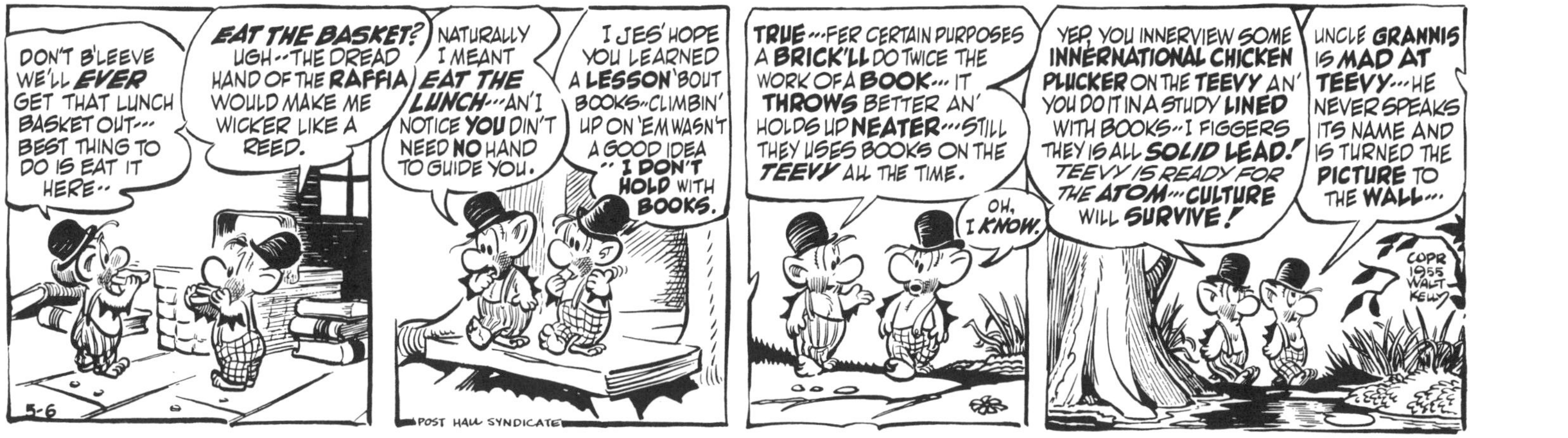
DON'T B'LEEVE WE'LL EVER GET THAT LUNCH BASKET OUT--- BEST THING TO DO IS EAT IT HERE--
EAT THE BASKET? UGH--THE DREAD HAND OF THE RAFFIA WOULD MAKE ME WICKER LIKE A REED.
NATURALLY I MEANT EAT THE LUNCH---AN' I NOTICE YOU DIN'T NEED NO HAND TO GUIDE YOU.
I JES' HOPE YOU LEARNED A LESSON 'BOUT BOOKS--CLIMBIN' UP ON 'EM WASN'T A GOOD IDEA
-- I DON'T HOLD WITH BOOKS.
TRUE---FER CERTAIN PURPOSES A BRICK'LL DO TWICE THE WORK OF A BOOK--- IT THROWS BETTER AN' HOLDS UP NEATER---STILL THEY USES BOOKS ON THE TEEVY ALL THE TIME.
OH, I KNOW.
YEP, YOU INNERVIEW SOME INNERNATIONAL CHICKEN PLUCKER ON THE TEEVY AN' YOU DO IT IN A STUDY LINED WITH BOOKS--I FIGGERS THEY IS ALL SOLID LEAD! TEEVY IS READY FOR THE ATOM--- CULTURE WILL SURVIVE!
UNCLE GRANNIS IS MAD AT TEEVY---HE NEVER SPEAKS ITS NAME AND IS TURNED THE PICTURE TO THE WALL...
COPR 1955 WALT KELLY
5-6 POST HALL SYNDICATE

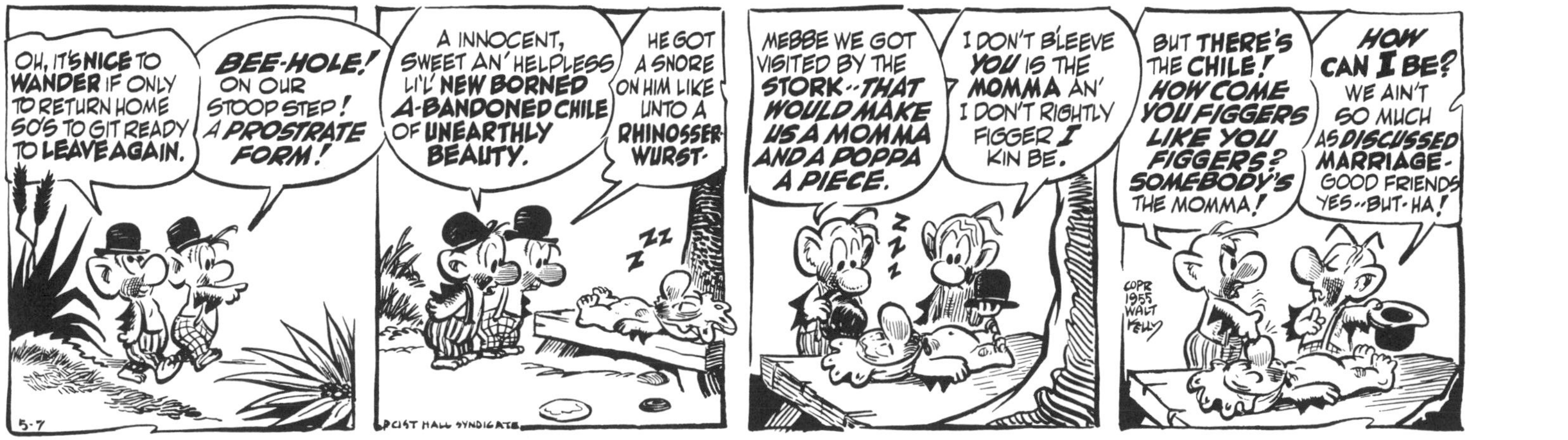
OH, IT'S NICE TO WANDER IF ONLY TO RETURN HOME SO'S TO GIT READY TO LEAVE AGAIN.
BEE-HOLE! ON OUR STOOP STEP! A PROSTRATE FORM!
A INNOCENT, SWEET AN' HELPLESS LI'L' NEW BORNED A-BANDONED CHILE OF UNEARTHLY BEAUTY.
HE GOT A SNORE ON HIM LIKE UNTO A RHINOSSER-WURST-
ZZZ
MEBBE WE GOT VISITED BY THE STORK--THAT WOULD MAKE US A MOMMA AND A POPPA A PIECE.
I DON'T B'LEEVE YOU IS THE MOMMA AN' I DON'T RIGHTLY FIGGER I KIN BE.
BUT THERE'S THE CHILE! HOW COME YOU FIGGERS LIKE YOU FIGGERS? SOMEBODY'S THE MOMMA!
HOW CAN I BE? WE AIN'T SO MUCH AS DISCUSSED MARRIAGE-GOOD FRIENDS YES--BUT-HA!
COPR 1955 WALT KELLY
5-7 POST HALL SYNDICATE

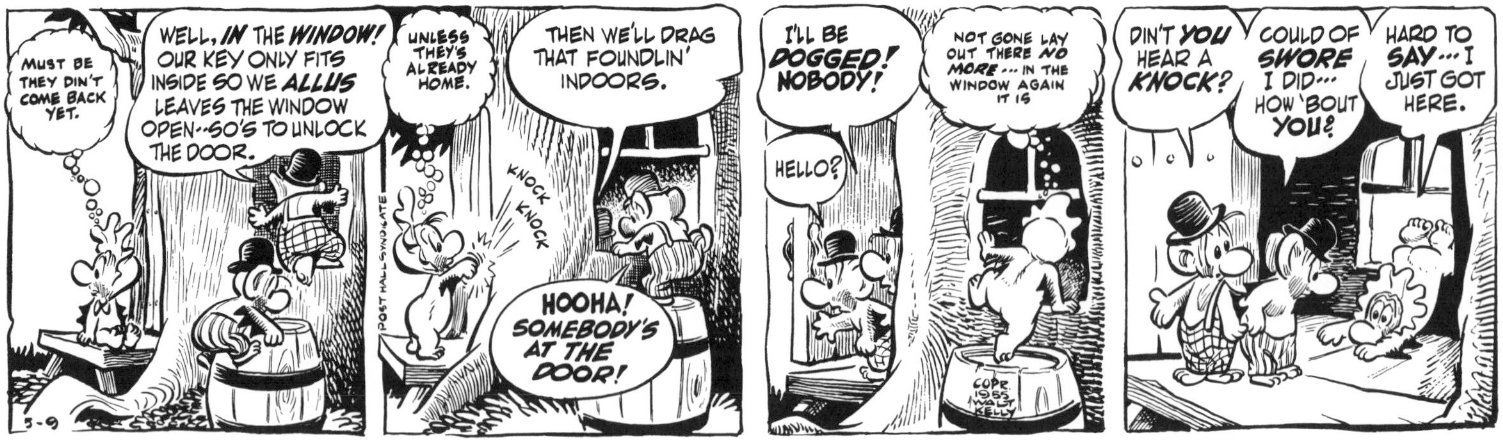
MUST BE THEY DIN'T COME BACK YET.
WELL, IN THE WINDOW! OUR KEY ONLY FITS INSIDE SO WE ALLUS LEAVES THE WINDOW OPEN--SO'S TO UNLOCK THE DOOR.
UNLESS THEY'S ALREADY HOME.
THEN WE'LL DRAG THAT FOUNDLIN' INDOORS.
KNOCK KNOCK
HOOHA! SOMEBODY'S AT THE DOOR!
POST HALL SYNDICATE
I'LL BE DOGGED! NOBODY!
NOT GONE LAY OUT THERE NO MORE ... IN THE WINDOW AGAIN IT IS
HELLO?
COPR. 1955 WALT KELLY
DIN'T YOU HEAR A KNOCK?
COULD OF SWORE I DID... HOW 'BOUT YOU?
HARD TO SAY... I JUST GOT HERE.
5-9

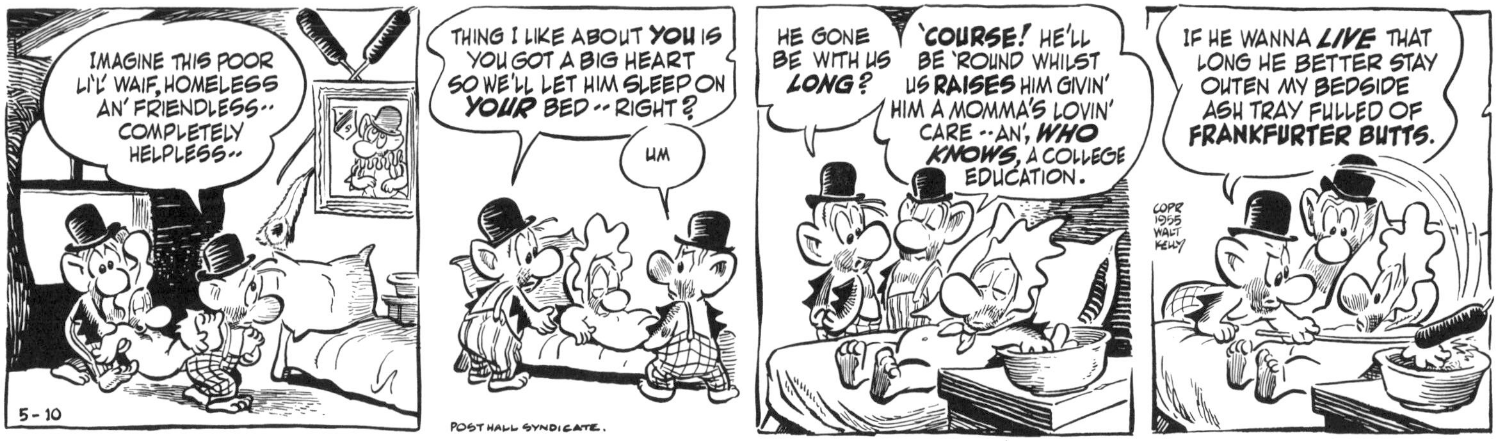
IMAGINE THIS POOR LI'L' WAIF, HOMELESS AN' FRIENDLESS-- COMPLETELY HELPLESS--
THING I LIKE ABOUT YOU IS YOU GOT A BIG HEART SO WE'LL LET HIM SLEEP ON YOUR BED -- RIGHT?
UM
HE GONE BE WITH US LONG?
'COURSE! HE'LL BE 'ROUND WHILST US RAISES HIM GIVIN' HIM A MOMMA'S LOVIN' CARE --AN', WHO KNOWS, A COLLEGE EDUCATION.
IF HE WANNA LIVE THAT LONG HE BETTER STAY OUTEN MY BEDSIDE ASH TRAY FULLED OF FRANKFURTER BUTTS.
COPR 1955 WALT KELLY
5-10
POST HALL SYNDICATE.

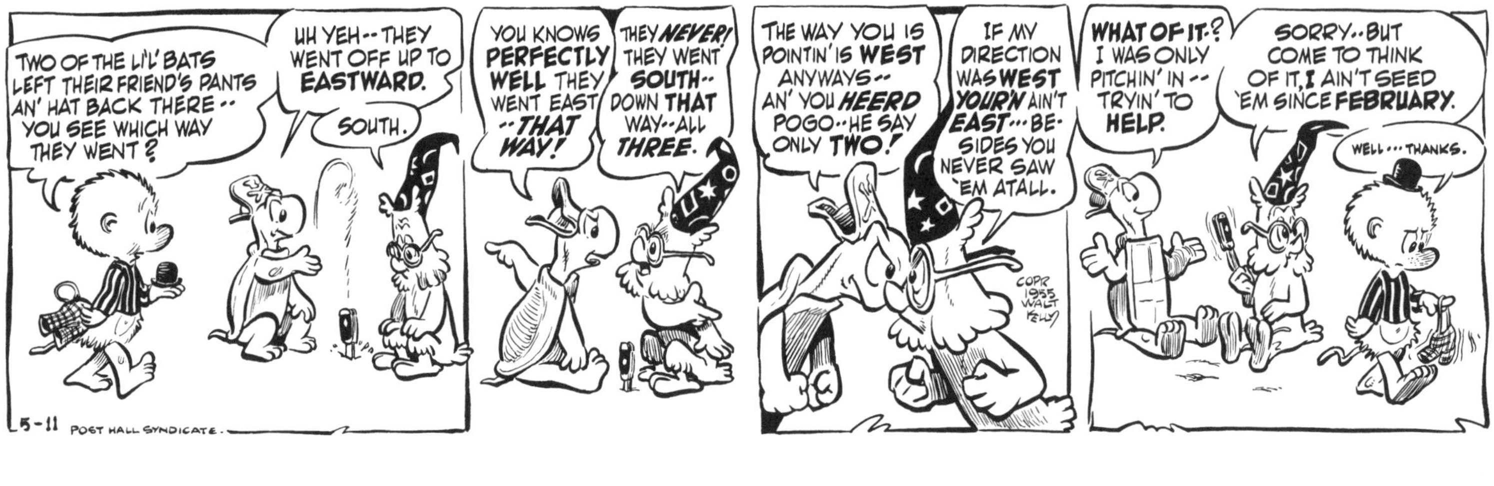
TWO OF THE LI'L' BATS LEFT THEIR FRIEND'S PANTS AN' HAT BACK THERE -- YOU SEE WHICH WAY THEY WENT?
UH YEH -- THEY WENT OFF UP TO EASTWARD.
SOUTH.
YOU KNOWS PERFECTLY WELL THEY WENT EAST --THAT WAY!
THEY NEVER! THEY WENT SOUTH-- DOWN THAT WAY--ALL THREE.
THE WAY YOU IS POINTIN' IS WEST ANYWAYS-- AN' YOU HEERD POGO--HE SAY ONLY TWO!
IF MY DIRECTION WAS WEST YOUR'N AIN'T EAST... BE-SIDES YOU NEVER SAW 'EM ATALL.
COPR 1955 WALT KELLY
WHAT OF IT? I WAS ONLY PITCHIN' IN -- TRYIN' TO HELP.
SORRY.. BUT COME TO THINK OF IT, I AIN'T SEED 'EM SINCE FEBRUARY.
WELL... THANKS.
5-11 POST HALL SYNDICATE.

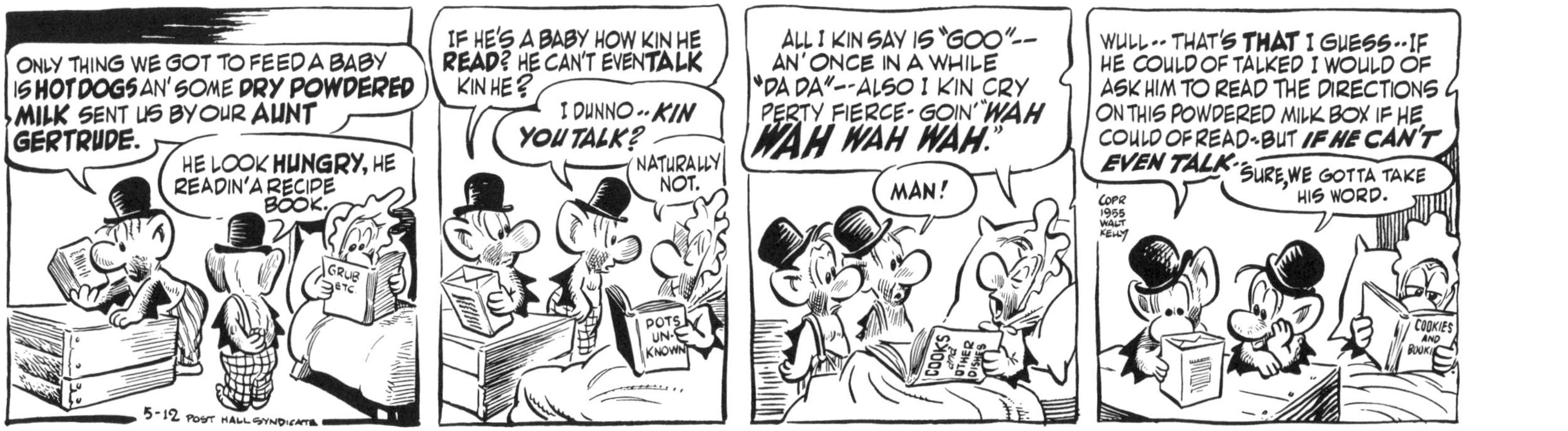
ONLY THING WE GOT TO FEED A BABY IS HOT DOGS AN' SOME DRY POWDERED MILK SENT US BY OUR AUNT GERTRUDE.
HE LOOK HUNGRY, HE READIN' A RECIPE BOOK.
GRUB ETC.
5-12 POST HALL SYNDICATE
IF HE'S A BABY HOW KIN HE READ? HE CAN'T EVEN TALK KIN HE?
I DUNNO -- KIN YOU TALK?
NATURALLY NOT.
POTS UN-KNOWN
ALL I KIN SAY IS "GOO"-- AN' ONCE IN A WHILE "DA DA"-- ALSO I KIN CRY PERTY FIERCE- GOIN' "WAH WAH WAH WAH."
MAN!
COOKS AND OTHER DISHES
WULL -- THAT'S THAT I GUESS -- IF HE COULD OF TALKED I WOULD OF ASK HIM TO READ THE DIRECTIONS ON THIS POWDERED MILK BOX IF HE COULD OF READ - BUT IF HE CAN'T EVEN TALK -
SURE, WE GOTTA TAKE HIS WORD.
COPR 1955 WALT KELLY
COOKIES AND BOOKIES

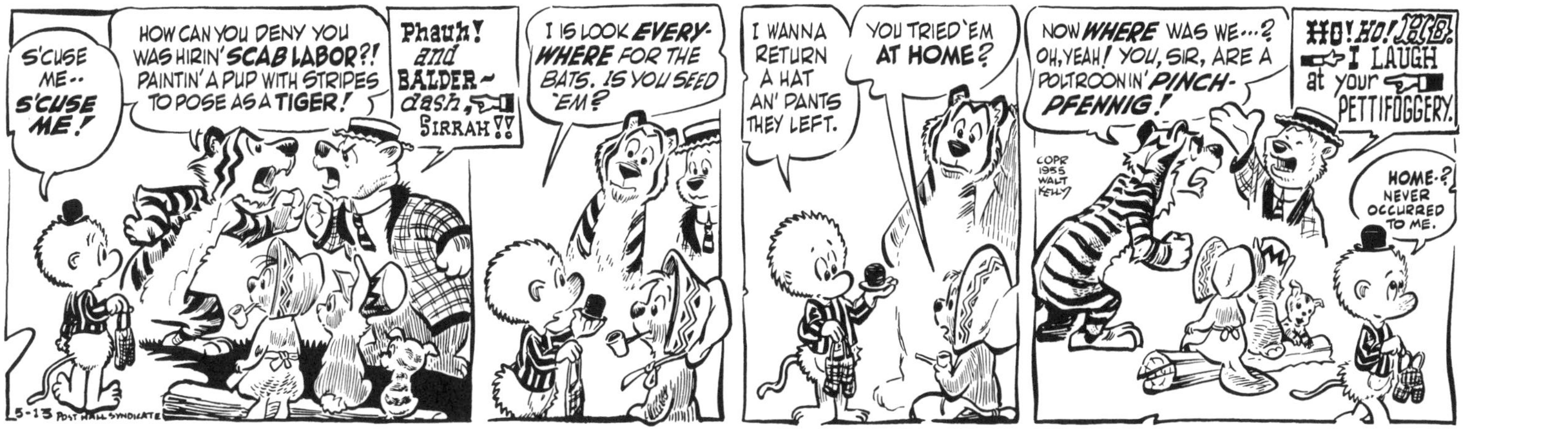
S'CUSE ME -- S'CUSE ME!
HOW CAN YOU DENY YOU WAS HIRIN' SCAB LABOR?! PAINTIN' A PUP WITH STRIPES TO POSE AS A TIGER!
Phauh! and BALDER~dash, SIRRAH!!
5-13 POST HALL SYNDICATE
I IS LOOK EVERY-WHERE FOR THE BATS. IS YOU SEED 'EM?
I WANNA RETURN A HAT AN' PANTS THEY LEFT.
YOU TRIED 'EM AT HOME?
NOW WHERE WAS WE ...? OH, YEAH! YOU, SIR, ARE A POLTROON IN' PINCH-PFENNIG!
HO! HO!
I LAUGH at your PETTIFOGGERY.
COPR 1955 WALT KELLY
HOME-? NEVER OCCURRED TO ME.

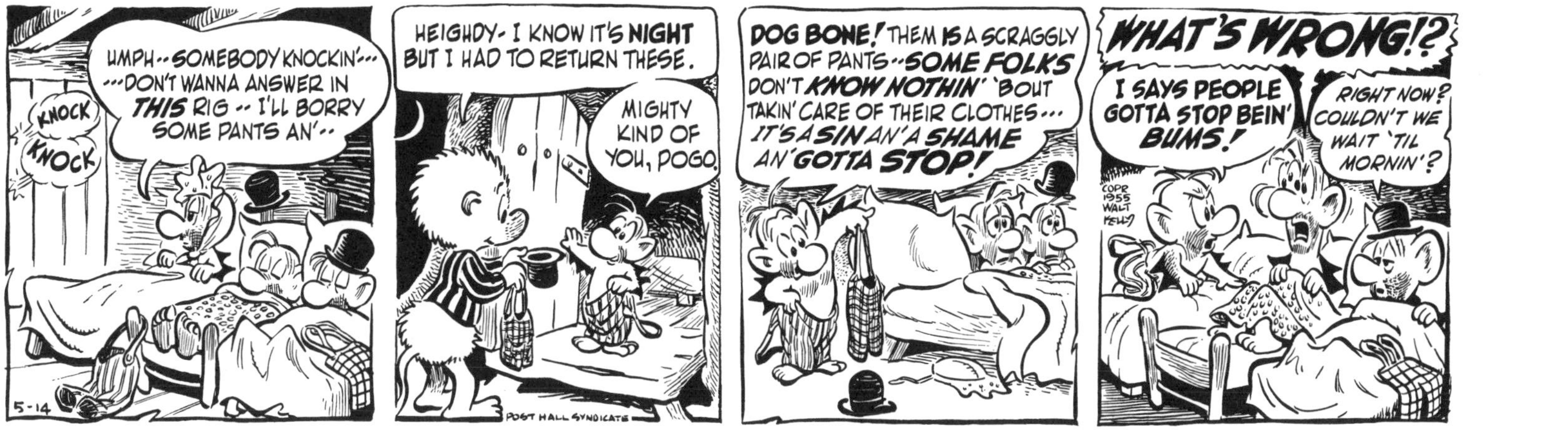
UMPH -- SOMEBODY KNOCKIN' --- DON'T WANNA ANSWER IN THIS RIG -- I'LL BORRY SOME PANTS AN' --
KNOCK KNOCK
5-14
HEIGHDY- I KNOW IT'S NIGHT BUT I HAD TO RETURN THESE.
MIGHTY KIND OF YOU, POGO.
POST HALL SYNDICATE
DOG BONE! THEM IS A SCRAGGLY PAIR OF PANTS -- SOME FOLKS DON'T KNOW NOTHIN' 'BOUT TAKIN' CARE OF THEIR CLOTHES --- IT'S A SIN AN' A SHAME AN' GOTTA STOP!
WHAT'S WRONG!?
I SAYS PEOPLE GOTTA STOP BEIN' BUMS!
RIGHT NOW? COULDN'T WE WAIT 'TIL MORNIN'?
COPR 1955 WALT KELLY

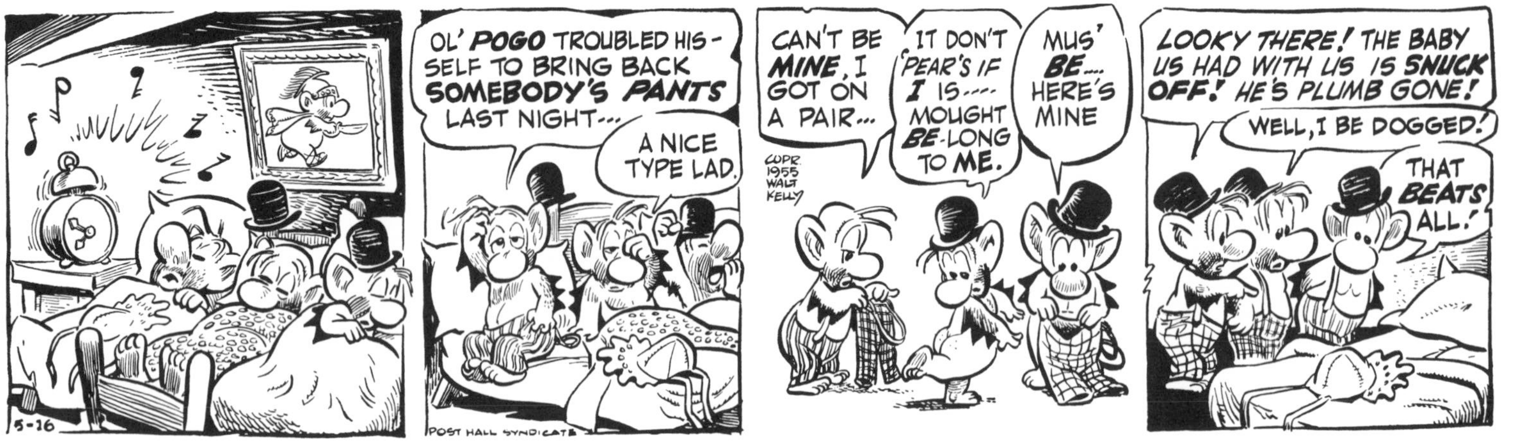
5-16
OL' POGO TROUBLED HIS-SELF TO BRING BACK SOMEBODY'S PANTS LAST NIGHT...
A NICE TYPE LAD.
POST HALL SYNDICATE
CAN'T BE MINE, I GOT ON A PAIR...
IT DON'T 'PEAR'S IF I IS---- MOUGHT BE-LONG TO ME.
MUS' BE.... HERE'S MINE
COPR 1955 WALT KELLY
LOOKY THERE! THE BABY US HAD WITH US IS SNUCK OFF! HE'S PLUMB GONE!
WELL, I BE DOGGED!
THAT BEATS ALL!

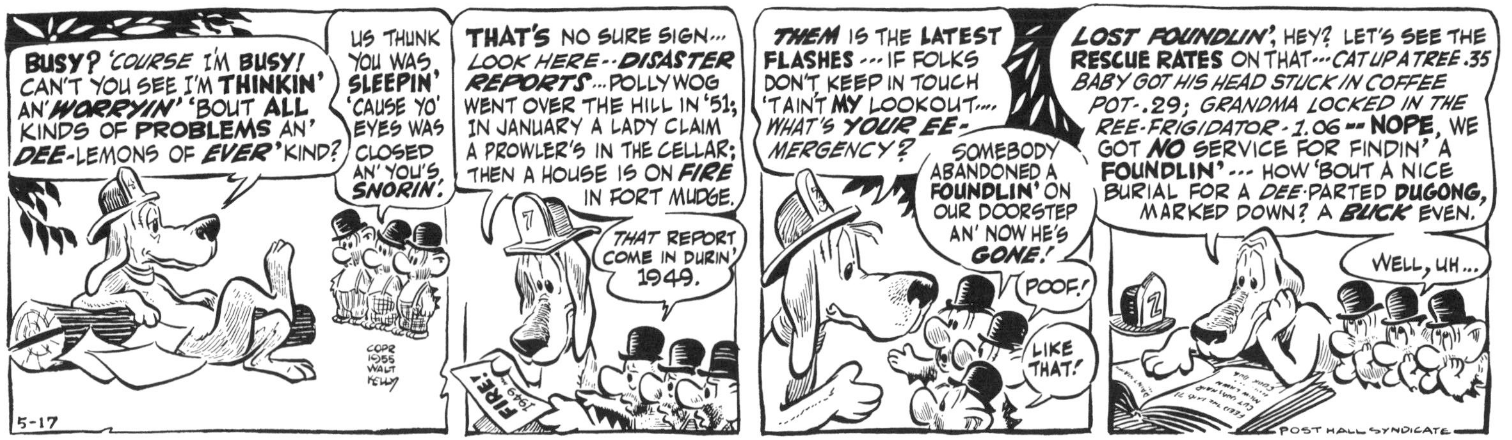
BUSY? 'COURSE I'M BUSY! CAN'T YOU SEE I'M THINKIN' AN' WORRYIN' 'BOUT ALL KINDS OF PROBLEMS AN' DEE-LEMONS OF EVER' KIND?
US THUNK YOU WAS SLEEPIN' 'CAUSE YO' EYES WAS CLOSED AN' YOU'S SNORIN'.
COPR 1955 WALT KELLY
5-17
THAT'S NO SURE SIGN... LOOK HERE -- DISASTER REPORTS... POLLYWOG WENT OVER THE HILL IN '51; IN JANUARY A LADY CLAIM A PROWLER'S IN THE CELLAR; THEN A HOUSE IS ON FIRE IN FORT MUDGE.
THAT REPORT COME IN DURIN' 1949.
FIRE!
THEM IS THE LATEST FLASHES --- IF FOLKS DON'T KEEP IN TOUCH 'TAIN'T MY LOOKOUT.... WHAT'S YOUR EE-MERGENCY?
SOMEBODY ABANDONED A FOUNDLIN' ON OUR DOORSTEP AN' NOW HE'S GONE!
POOF!
LIKE THAT!
LOST FOUNDLIN', HEY? LET'S SEE THE RESCUE RATES ON THAT --- CAT UP A TREE .35 BABY GOT HIS HEAD STUCK IN COFFEE POT - .29; GRANDMA LOCKED IN THE REE-FRIGIDATOR - 1.06 -- NOPE, WE GOT NO SERVICE FOR FINDIN' A FOUNDLIN' --- HOW 'BOUT A NICE BURIAL FOR A DEE-PARTED DUGONG, MARKED DOWN? A BUCK EVEN.
WELL, UH...
POST HALL SYNDICATE

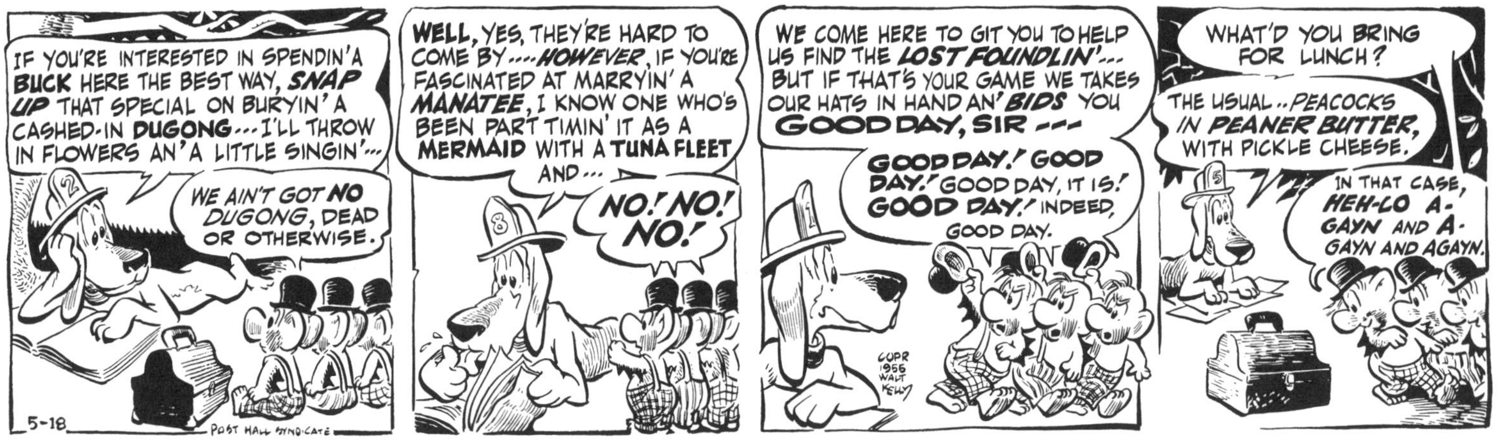
IF YOU'RE INTERESTED IN SPENDIN' A BUCK HERE THE BEST WAY, SNAP UP THAT SPECIAL ON BURYIN' A CASHED-IN DUGONG --- I'LL THROW IN FLOWERS AN' A LITTLE SINGIN'...
WE AIN'T GOT NO DUGONG, DEAD OR OTHERWISE.
5-18
POST HALL SYNDICATE
WELL, YES, THEY'RE HARD TO COME BY ---- HOWEVER, IF YOU'RE FASCINATED AT MARRYIN' A MANATEE, I KNOW ONE WHO'S BEEN PART TIMIN' IT AS A MERMAID WITH A TUNA FLEET AND ...
NO! NO! NO!
WE COME HERE TO GIT YOU TO HELP US FIND THE LOST FOUNDLIN'... BUT IF THAT'S YOUR GAME WE TAKES OUR HATS IN HAND AN' BIDS YOU GOOD DAY, SIR ---
GOOD DAY! GOOD DAY! GOOD DAY, IT IS! GOOD DAY! INDEED, GOOD DAY.
COPR 1955 WALT KELLY
WHAT'D YOU BRING FOR LUNCH?
THE USUAL .. PEACOCKS IN PEANER BUTTER, WITH PICKLE CHEESE.
IN THAT CASE, HEH-LO A-GAYN AND A-GAYN AND AGAYN.

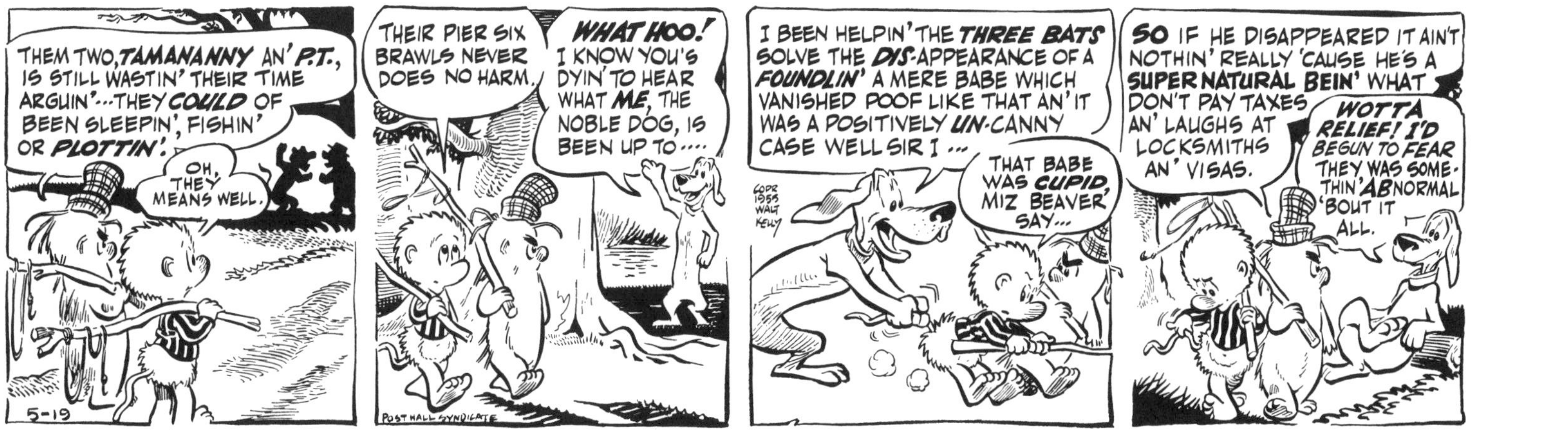
THEM TWO, TAMANANNY AN' P.T., IS STILL WASTIN' THEIR TIME ARGUIN'...THEY COULD OF BEEN SLEEPIN', FISHIN' OR PLOTTIN'.
OH, THEY MEANS WELL.
5-19
THEIR PIER SIX BRAWLS NEVER DOES NO HARM.
WHAT HOO! I KNOW YOU'S DYIN' TO HEAR WHAT ME, THE NOBLE DOG, IS BEEN UP TO....
POST HALL SYNDICATE
I BEEN HELPIN' THE THREE BATS SOLVE THE DIS-APPEARANCE OF A FOUNDLIN' A MERE BABE WHICH VANISHED POOF LIKE THAT AN' IT WAS A POSITIVELY UN-CANNY CASE WELL SIR I ...
THAT BABE WAS CUPID, MIZ BEAVER SAY...
COPR 1955 WALT KELLY
SO IF HE DISAPPEARED IT AIN'T NOTHIN' REALLY 'CAUSE HE'S A SUPER NATURAL BEIN' WHAT DON'T PAY TAXES AN' LAUGHS AT LOCKSMITHS AN' VISAS.
WOTTA RELIEF! I'D BEGUN TO FEAR THEY WAS SOME-THIN' AB NORMAL 'BOUT IT ALL.

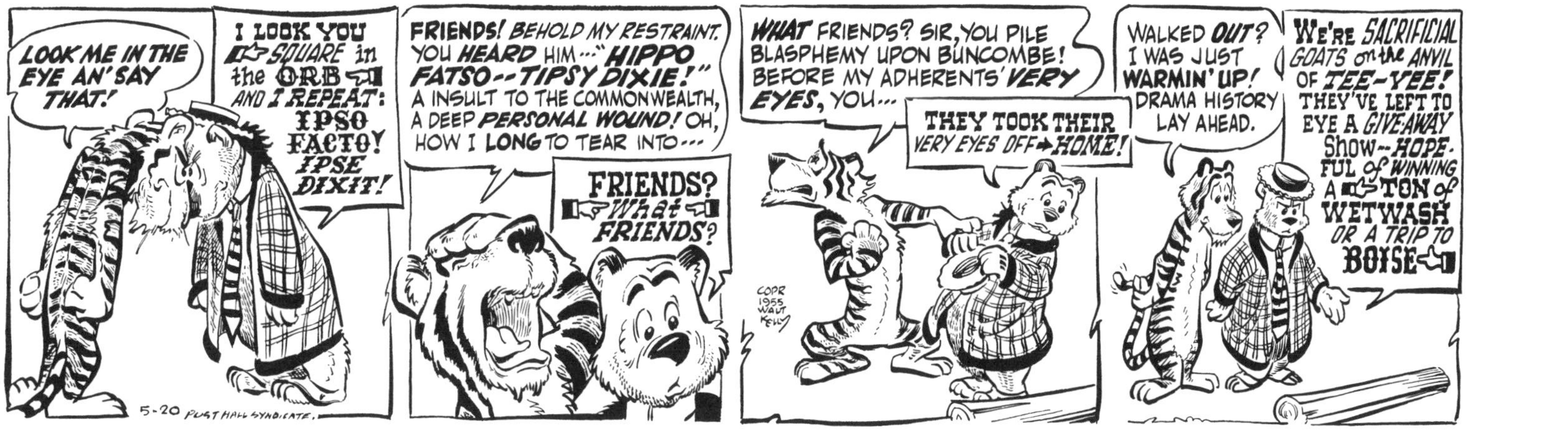
LOOK ME IN THE EYE AN' SAY THAT!
I LOOK YOU SQUARE in the ORB AND I REPEAT: IPSO FACTO! IPSE DIXIT!
5-20 POST HALL SYNDICATE.
FRIENDS! BEHOLD MY RESTRAINT. YOU HEARD HIM... "HIPPO FATSO--TIPSY DIXIE!" A INSULT TO THE COMMONWEALTH, A DEEP PERSONAL WOUND! OH, HOW I LONG TO TEAR INTO...
FRIENDS? What FRIENDS?
WHAT FRIENDS? SIR, YOU PILE BLASPHEMY UPON BUNCOMBE! BEFORE MY ADHERENTS' VERY EYES, YOU...
THEY TOOK THEIR VERY EYES OFF HOME!
COPR 1955 WALT KELLY
WALKED OUT? I WAS JUST WARMIN' UP! DRAMA HISTORY LAY AHEAD.
WE'RE SACRIFICIAL GOATS on the ANVIL OF TEE-VEE! THEY'VE LEFT TO EYE A GIVEAWAY Show--HOPE-FUL of WINNING A TON of WETWASH OR A TRIP TO BOISE

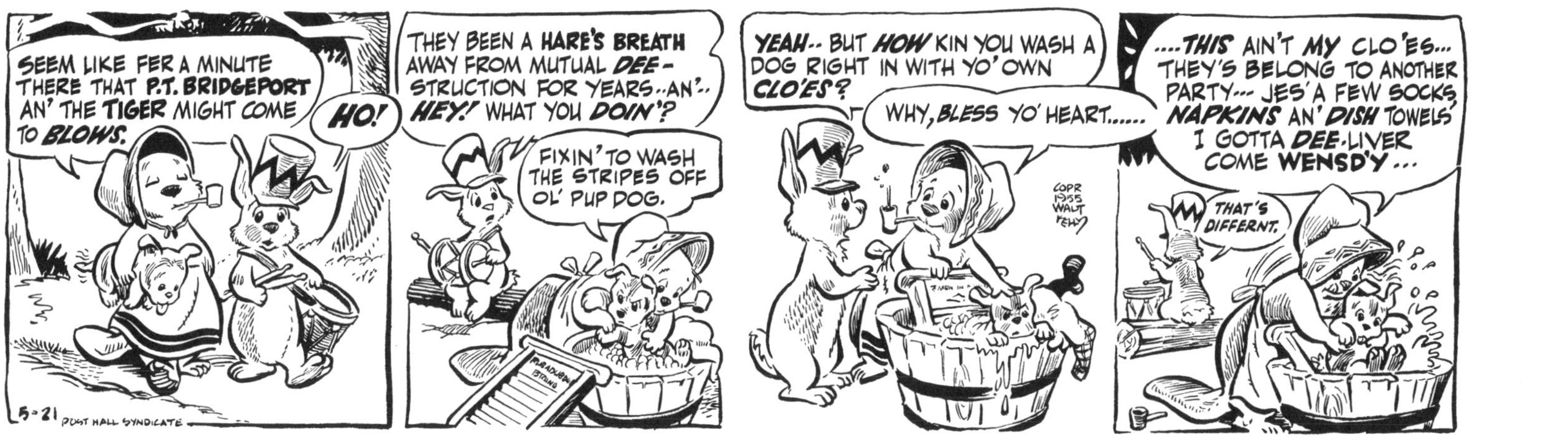
SEEM LIKE FER A MINUTE THERE THAT P.T. BRIDGEPORT AN' THE TIGER MIGHT COME TO BLOWS.
HO!
5-21 POST HALL SYNDICATE
THEY BEEN A HARE'S BREATH AWAY FROM MUTUAL DEE-STRUCTION FOR YEARS..AN'.. HEY! WHAT YOU DOIN'?
FIXIN' TO WASH THE STRIPES OFF OL' PUP DOG.
YEAH-- BUT HOW KIN YOU WASH A DOG RIGHT IN WITH YO' OWN CLO'ES?
WHY, BLESS YO' HEART......
COPR 1955 WALT KELLY
....THIS AIN'T MY CLO'ES... THEY'S BELONG TO ANOTHER PARTY... JES' A FEW SOCKS, NAPKINS AN' DISH TOWELS I GOTTA DEE-LIVER COME WENSD'Y...
THAT'S DIFFERNT.

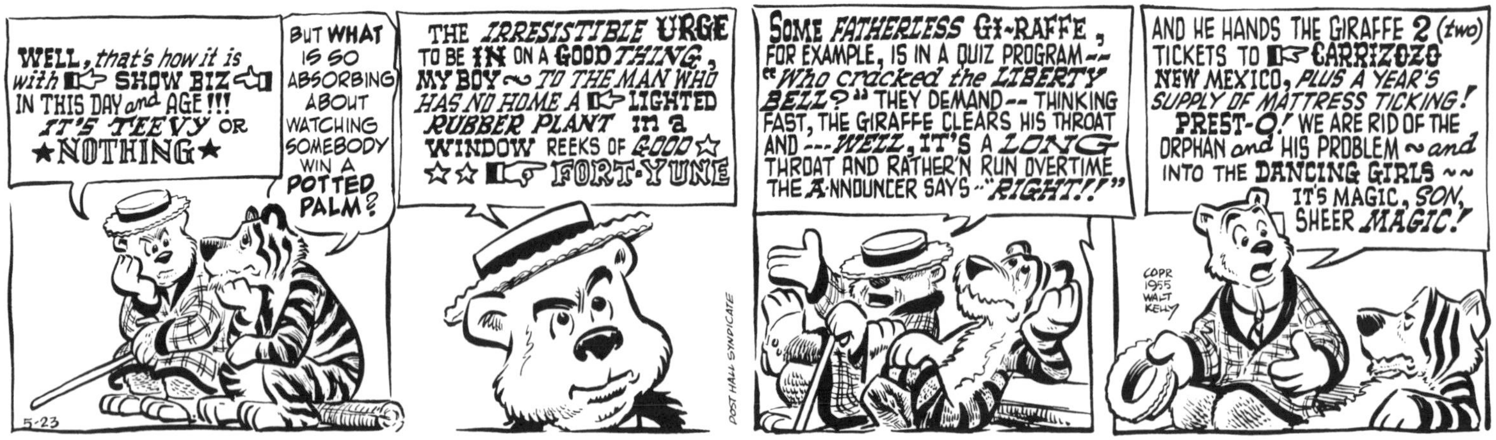
WELL, that's how it is with SHOW BIZ IN THIS DAY and AGE!!! IT'S TEEVY OR ★NOTHING★
BUT WHAT IS SO ABSORBING ABOUT WATCHING SOMEBODY WIN A POTTED PALM?
THE IRRESISTIBLE URGE TO BE IN ON A GOOD THING, MY BOY ~ TO THE MAN WHO HAS NO HOME A LIGHTED RUBBER PLANT in a WINDOW REEKS OF GOOD ☆☆☆ FORT-YUNE
SOME FATHERLESS GI-RAFFE, FOR EXAMPLE, IS IN A QUIZ PROGRAM -- "Who cracked the LIBERTY BELL?" THEY DEMAND -- THINKING FAST, THE GIRAFFE CLEARS HIS THROAT AND --- WELL, IT'S A LONG THROAT AND RATHER'N RUN OVERTIME THE A-NNOUNCER SAYS "RIGHT!!"
AND HE HANDS THE GIRAFFE 2 (two) TICKETS TO CARRIZOZO NEW MEXICO, PLUS A YEAR'S SUPPLY OF MATTRESS TICKING! PREST-O! WE ARE RID OF THE ORPHAN and HIS PROBLEM ~ and INTO THE DANCING GIRLS ~~ IT'S MAGIC, SON, SHEER MAGIC!
5-23
POST HALL SYNDICATE
COPR 1955 WALT KELLY

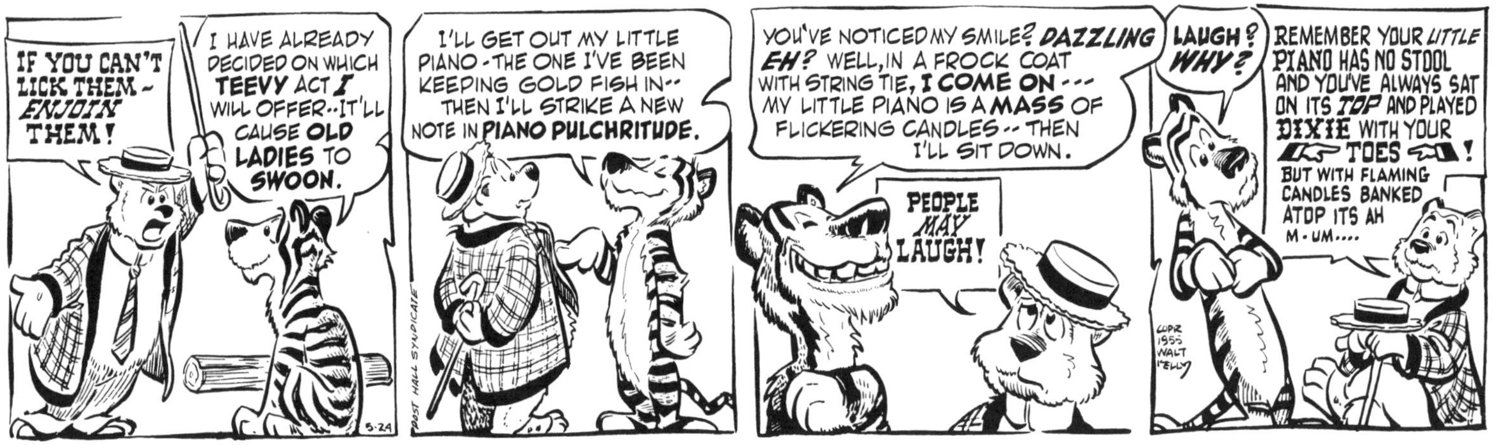
IF YOU CAN'T LICK THEM ~ ENJOIN THEM!
I HAVE ALREADY DECIDED ON WHICH TEEVY ACT I WILL OFFER.. IT'LL CAUSE OLD LADIES TO SWOON.
5-24
POST HALL SYNDICATE
I'LL GET OUT MY LITTLE PIANO - THE ONE I'VE BEEN KEEPING GOLD FISH IN -- THEN I'LL STRIKE A NEW NOTE IN PIANO PULCHRITUDE.
YOU'VE NOTICED MY SMILE? DAZZLING EH? WELL, IN A FROCK COAT WITH STRING TIE, I COME ON --- MY LITTLE PIANO IS A MASS OF FLICKERING CANDLES -- THEN I'LL SIT DOWN.
PEOPLE MAY LAUGH!
LAUGH? WHY?
REMEMBER YOUR LITTLE PIANO HAS NO STOOL AND YOU'VE ALWAYS SAT ON ITS TOP AND PLAYED DIXIE WITH YOUR TOES! BUT WITH FLAMING CANDLES BANKED ATOP ITS AH M-UM....
COPR 1955 WALT KELLY

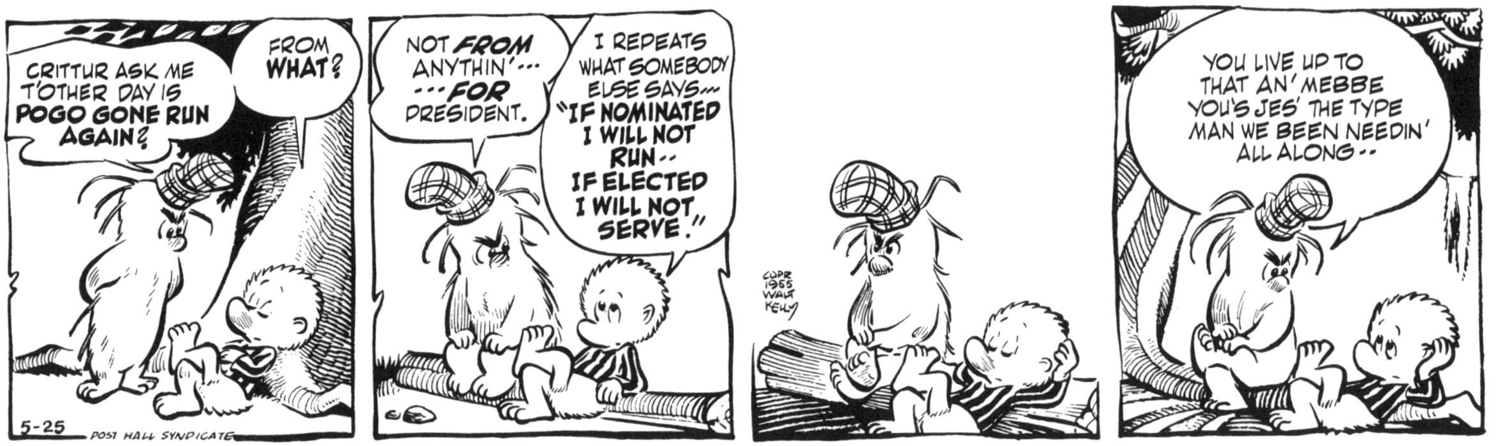
CRITTUR ASK ME T'OTHER DAY IS POGO GONE RUN AGAIN?
FROM WHAT?
5-25
POST HALL SYNDICATE
NOT FROM ANYTHIN' --- FOR PRESIDENT.
I REPEATS WHAT SOMEBODY ELSE SAYS... "IF NOMINATED I WILL NOT RUN -- IF ELECTED I WILL NOT SERVE."
COPR 1955 WALT KELLY
YOU LIVE UP TO THAT AN' MEBBE YOU'S JES' THE TYPE MAN WE BEEN NEEDIN' ALL ALONG --

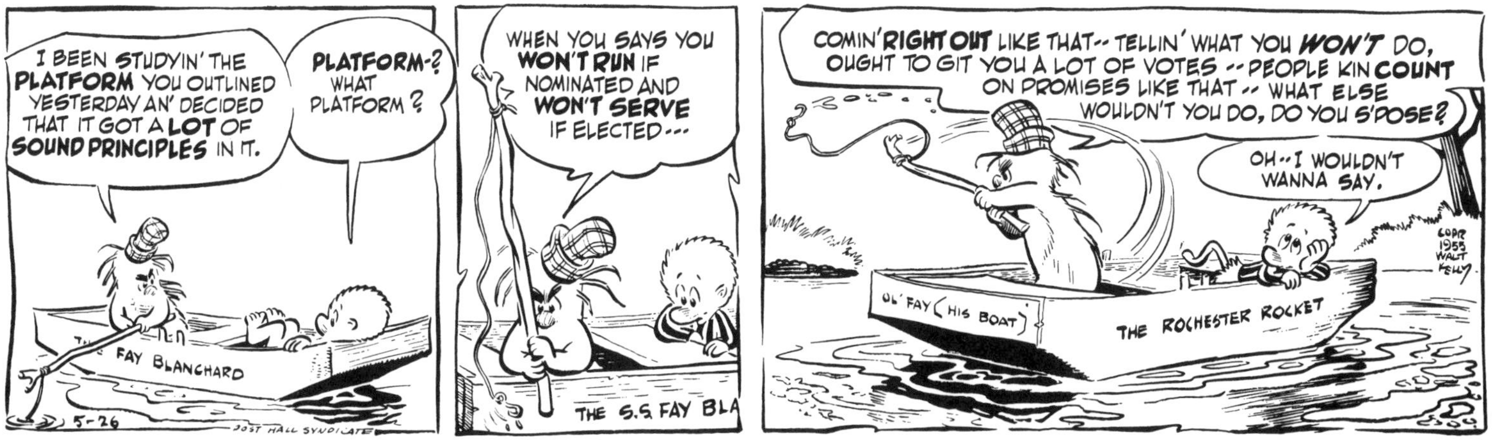
I BEEN STUDYIN' THE PLATFORM YOU OUTLINED YESTERDAY AN' DECIDED THAT IT GOT A LOT OF SOUND PRINCIPLES IN IT.
PLATFORM-? WHAT PLATFORM ?
THE FAY BLANCHARD
5-26
POST HALL SYNDICATE
WHEN YOU SAYS YOU WON'T RUN IF NOMINATED AND WON'T SERVE IF ELECTED---
THE S.S. FAY BLA
COMIN' RIGHT OUT LIKE THAT-- TELLIN' WHAT YOU WON'T DO, OUGHT TO GIT YOU A LOT OF VOTES -- PEOPLE KIN COUNT ON PROMISES LIKE THAT -- WHAT ELSE WOULDN'T YOU DO, DO YOU S'POSE?
OH--I WOULDN'T WANNA SAY.
COPR 1955 WALT KELLY
OL' FAY (HIS BOAT)
THE ROCHESTER ROCKET

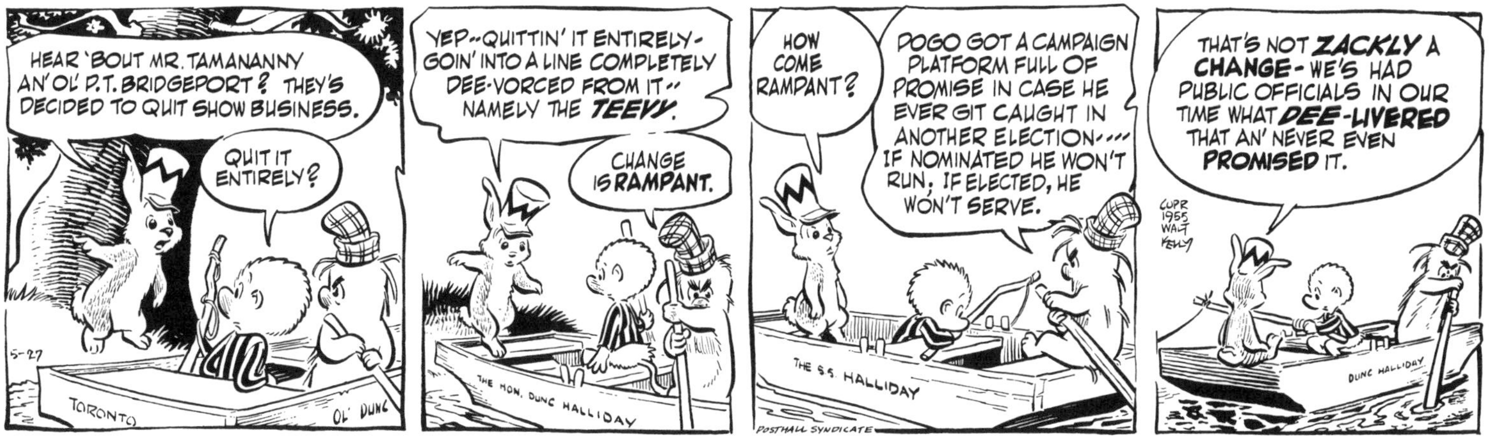
HEAR 'BOUT MR. TAMANANNY AN' OL' P.T. BRIDGEPORT ? THEY'S DECIDED TO QUIT SHOW BUSINESS.
QUIT IT ENTIRELY ?
5-27
TORONTO
OL' DUNC
YEP--QUITTIN' IT ENTIRELY- GOIN' INTO A LINE COMPLETELY DEE-VORCED FROM IT-- NAMELY THE TEEVY.
CHANGE IS RAMPANT.
THE HON. DUNC HALLIDAY
HOW COME RAMPANT ?
POGO GOT A CAMPAIGN PLATFORM FULL OF PROMISE IN CASE HE EVER GIT CAUGHT IN ANOTHER ELECTION---- IF NOMINATED HE WON'T RUN; IF ELECTED, HE WON'T SERVE.
THE S.S. HALLIDAY
POST HALL SYNDICATE
THAT'S NOT ZACKLY A CHANGE- WE'S HAD PUBLIC OFFICIALS IN OUR TIME WHAT DEE-LIVERED THAT AN' NEVER EVEN PROMISED IT.
COPR 1955 WALT KELLY
DUNC HALLIDAY

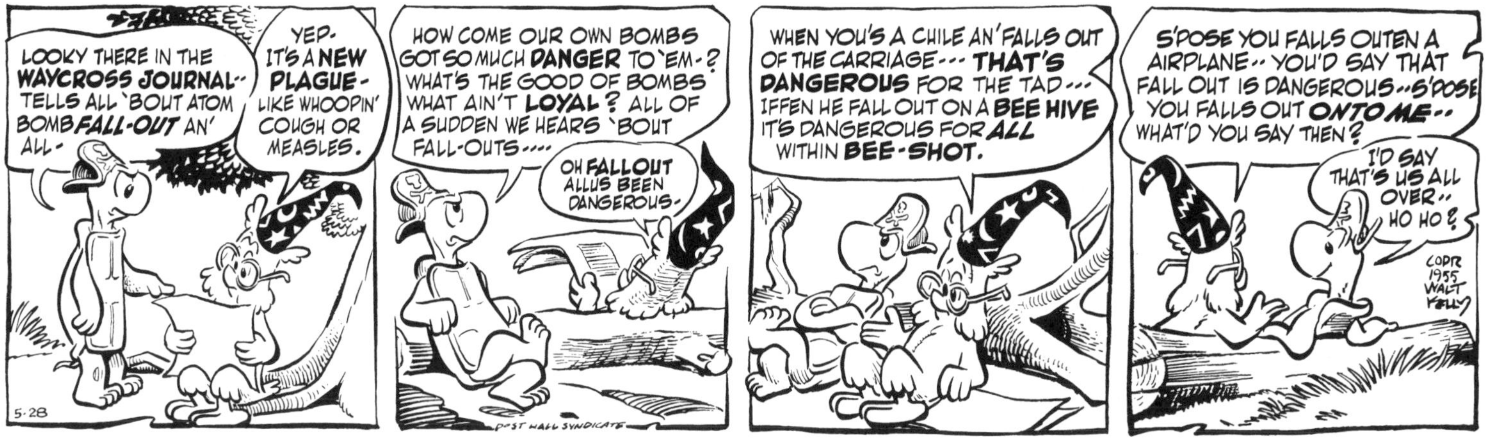
LOOKY THERE IN THE WAYCROSS JOURNAL- TELLS ALL 'BOUT ATOM BOMB FALL-OUT AN' ALL-
YEP- IT'S A NEW PLAGUE- LIKE WHOOPIN' COUGH OR MEASLES.
5-28
HOW COME OUR OWN BOMBS GOT SO MUCH DANGER TO 'EM-? WHAT'S THE GOOD OF BOMBS WHAT AIN'T LOYAL ? ALL OF A SUDDEN WE HEARS 'BOUT FALL-OUTS----
OH FALLOUT ALLUS BEEN DANGEROUS-
POST HALL SYNDICATE
WHEN YOU'S A CHILE AN' FALLS OUT OF THE CARRIAGE--- THAT'S DANGEROUS FOR THE TAD--- IFFEN HE FALL OUT ON A BEE HIVE IT'S DANGEROUS FOR ALL WITHIN BEE-SHOT.
S'POSE YOU FALLS OUTEN A AIRPLANE-- YOU'D SAY THAT FALL OUT IS DANGEROUS--S'POSE YOU FALLS OUT ONTO ME-- WHAT'D YOU SAY THEN ?
I'D SAY THAT'S US ALL OVER-- HO HO ?
COPR 1955 WALT KELLY

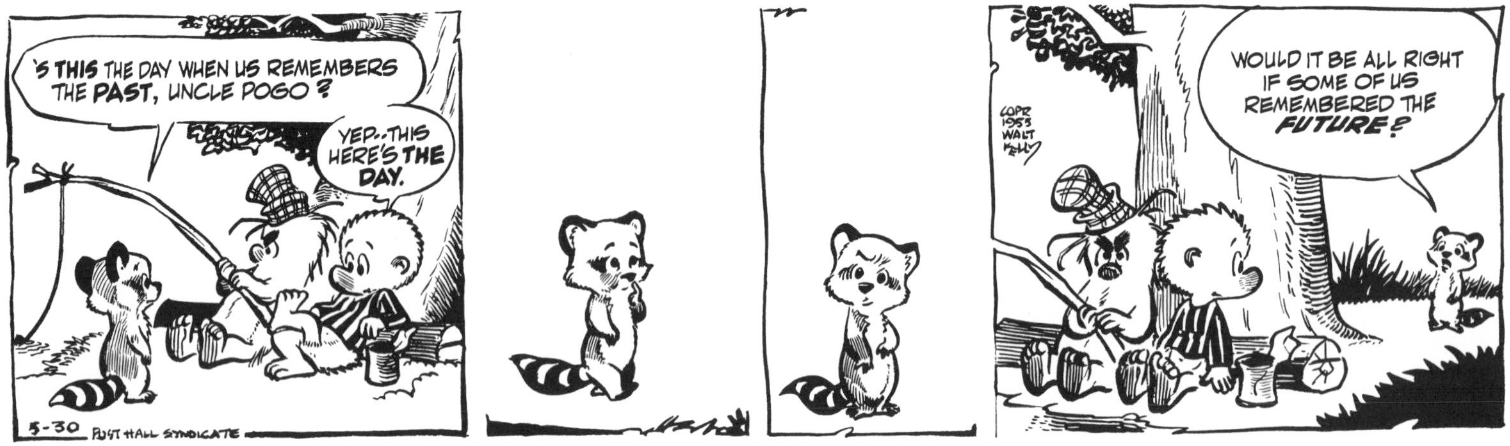
'S THIS THE DAY WHEN US REMEMBERS THE PAST, UNCLE POGO?
YEP-- THIS HERE'S THE DAY.
WOULD IT BE ALL RIGHT IF SOME OF US REMEMBERED THE FUTURE?
5-30 POST HALL SYNDICATE

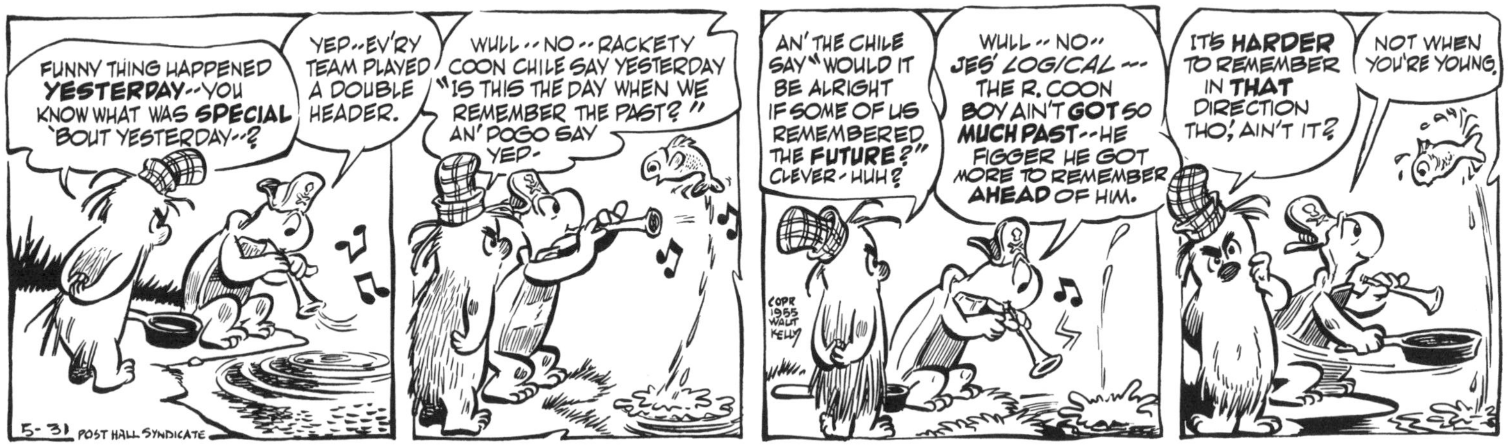
FUNNY THING HAPPENED YESTERDAY-- YOU KNOW WHAT WAS SPECIAL 'BOUT YESTERDAY--?
YEP-- EV'RY TEAM PLAYED A DOUBLE HEADER.
WULL -- NO -- RACKETY COON CHILE SAY YESTERDAY "IS THIS THE DAY WHEN WE REMEMBER THE PAST?" AN' POGO SAY YEP-
AN' THE CHILE SAY "WOULD IT BE ALRIGHT IF SOME OF US REMEMBERED THE FUTURE?" CLEVER - HUH?
WULL -- NO-- JES' LOGICAL --- THE R. COON BOY AIN'T GOT SO MUCH PAST-- HE FIGGER HE GOT MORE TO REMEMBER AHEAD OF HIM.
IT'S HARDER TO REMEMBER IN THAT DIRECTION THO,' AIN'T IT?
NOT WHEN YOU'RE YOUNG.
5-31 POST HALL SYNDICATE
COPR 1955 WALT KELLY

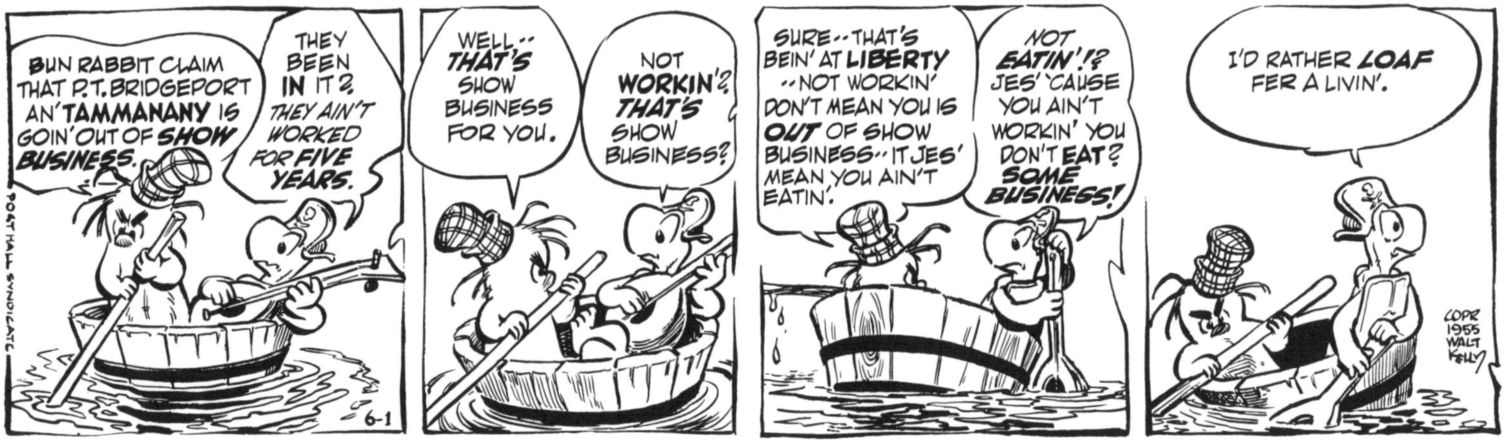
BUN RABBIT CLAIM THAT P.T. BRIDGEPORT AN' TAMMANANY IS GOIN' OUT OF SHOW BUSINESS.
THEY BEEN IN IT? THEY AIN'T WORKED FOR FIVE YEARS.
WELL -- THAT'S SHOW BUSINESS FOR YOU.
NOT WORKIN'? THAT'S SHOW BUSINESS?
SURE -- THAT'S BEIN' AT LIBERTY -- NOT WORKIN' DON'T MEAN YOU IS OUT OF SHOW BUSINESS -- IT JES' MEAN YOU AIN'T EATIN'.
NOT EATIN'!? JES' 'CAUSE YOU AIN'T WORKIN' YOU DON'T EAT? SOME BUSINESS!
I'D RATHER LOAF FER A LIVIN'.
POST HALL SYNDICATE
6-1
COPR 1955 WALT KELLY

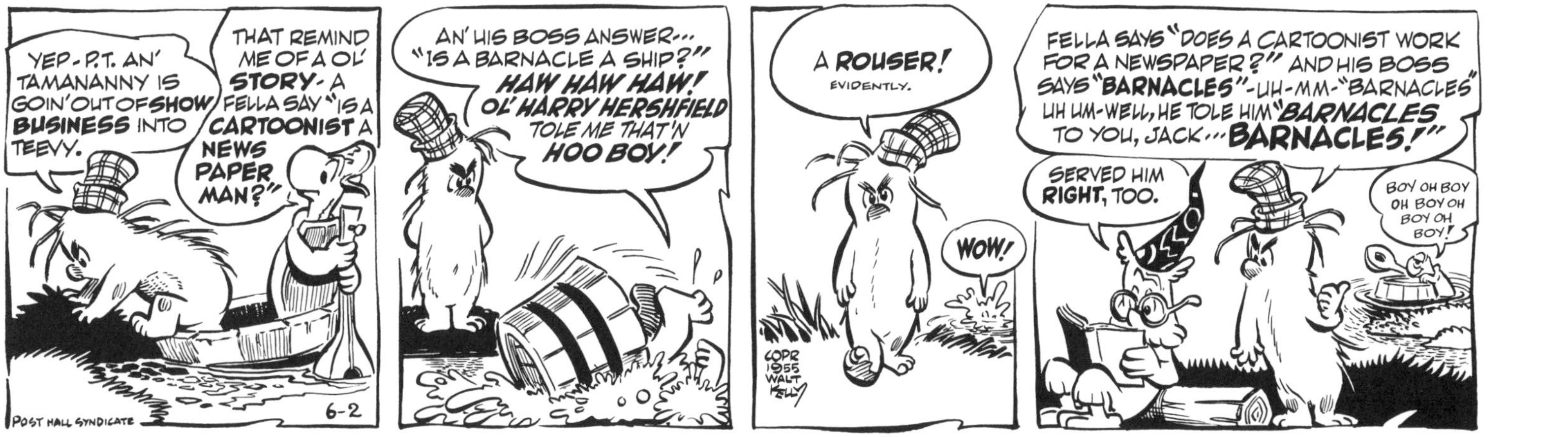
YEP-P.T. AN' TAMANANNY IS GOIN' OUT OF SHOW BUSINESS INTO TEEVY.
THAT REMIND ME OF A OL' STORY- A FELLA SAY "IS A CARTOONIST A NEWS PAPER MAN?"
POST HALL SYNDICATE
6-2
AN' HIS BOSS ANSWER... "IS A BARNACLE A SHIP?" HAW HAW HAW! OL' HARRY HERSHFIELD TOLE ME THAT'N HOO BOY!
A ROUSER! EVIDENTLY.
WOW!
COPR 1955 WALT KELLY
FELLA SAYS "DOES A CARTOONIST WORK FOR A NEWSPAPER?" AND HIS BOSS SAYS "BARNACLES"-UH-MM-"BARNACLES" UH UM-WELL, HE TOLE HIM "BARNACLES TO YOU, JACK... BARNACLES!"
SERVED HIM RIGHT, TOO.
BOY OH BOY OH BOY OH BOY OH BOY!

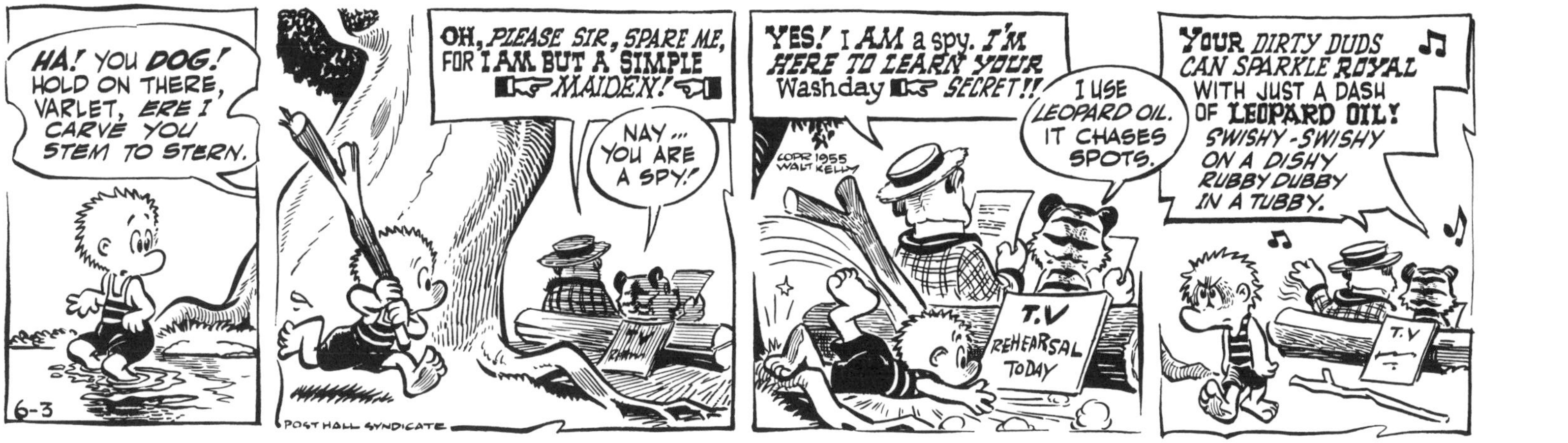
HA! YOU DOG! HOLD ON THERE, VARLET, ERE I CARVE YOU STEM TO STERN.
6-3
OH, PLEASE SIR, SPARE ME, FOR I AM BUT A SIMPLE MAIDEN!
NAY... YOU ARE A SPY!
POST HALL SYNDICATE
YES! I AM a spy. I'M HERE TO LEARN YOUR Washday SECRET!!
I USE LEOPARD OIL. IT CHASES SPOTS.
COPR 1955 WALT KELLY
T.V REHEARSAL TODAY
YOUR DIRTY DUDS CAN SPARKLE ROYAL WITH JUST A DASH OF LEOPARD OIL! S'WISHY-SWISHY ON A DISHY RUBBY DUBBY IN A TUBBY.
T.V

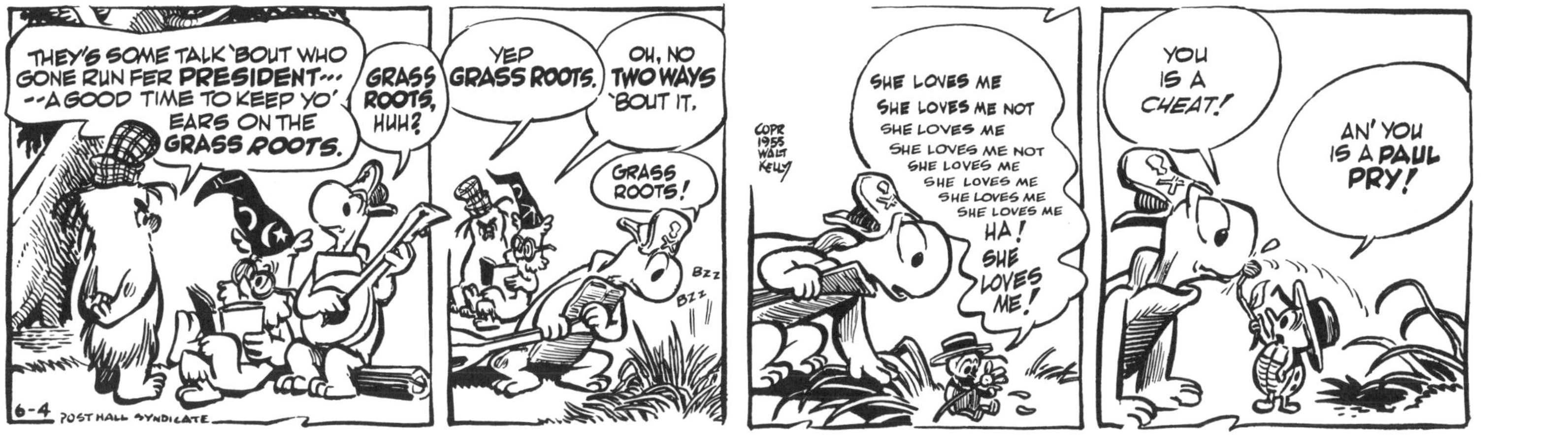
THEY'S SOME TALK 'BOUT WHO GONE RUN FER PRESIDENT--- --A GOOD TIME TO KEEP YO' EARS ON THE GRASS ROOTS.
GRASS ROOTS, HUH?
6-4 POST HALL SYNDICATE
YEP GRASS ROOTS.
OH, NO TWO WAYS 'BOUT IT.
GRASS ROOTS!
BZZ BZZ
COPR 1955 WALT KELLY
SHE LOVES ME SHE LOVES ME NOT SHE LOVES ME SHE LOVES ME NOT SHE LOVES ME SHE LOVES ME SHE LOVES ME SHE LOVES ME HA! SHE LOVES ME!
YOU IS A CHEAT!
AN' YOU IS A PAUL PRY!

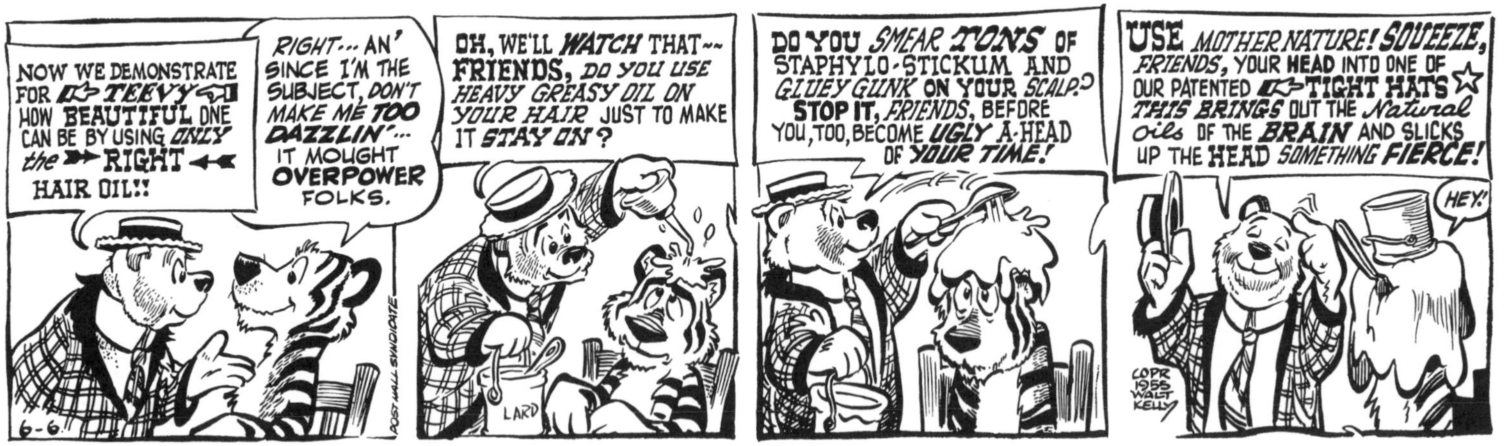
NOW WE DEMONSTRATE FOR TEEVY HOW BEAUTIFUL ONE CAN BE BY USING ONLY the RIGHT HAIR OIL!!
RIGHT... AN' SINCE I'M THE SUBJECT, DON'T MAKE ME TOO DAZZLIN'... IT MOUGHT OVERPOWER FOLKS.
6-6
POST HALL SYNDICATE
OH, WE'LL WATCH THAT-- FRIENDS, DO YOU USE HEAVY GREASY OIL ON YOUR HAIR JUST TO MAKE IT STAY ON?
LARD
DO YOU SMEAR TONS OF STAPHYLO-STICKUM AND GLUEY GUNK ON YOUR SCALP? STOP IT, FRIENDS, BEFORE YOU, TOO, BECOME UGLY A-HEAD OF YOUR TIME!
USE MOTHER NATURE! SQUEEZE, FRIENDS, YOUR HEAD INTO ONE OF OUR PATENTED TIGHT HATS THIS BRINGS OUT THE Natural oils OF THE BRAIN AND SLICKS UP THE HEAD SOMETHING FIERCE!
HEY!
COPR 1955 WALT KELLY

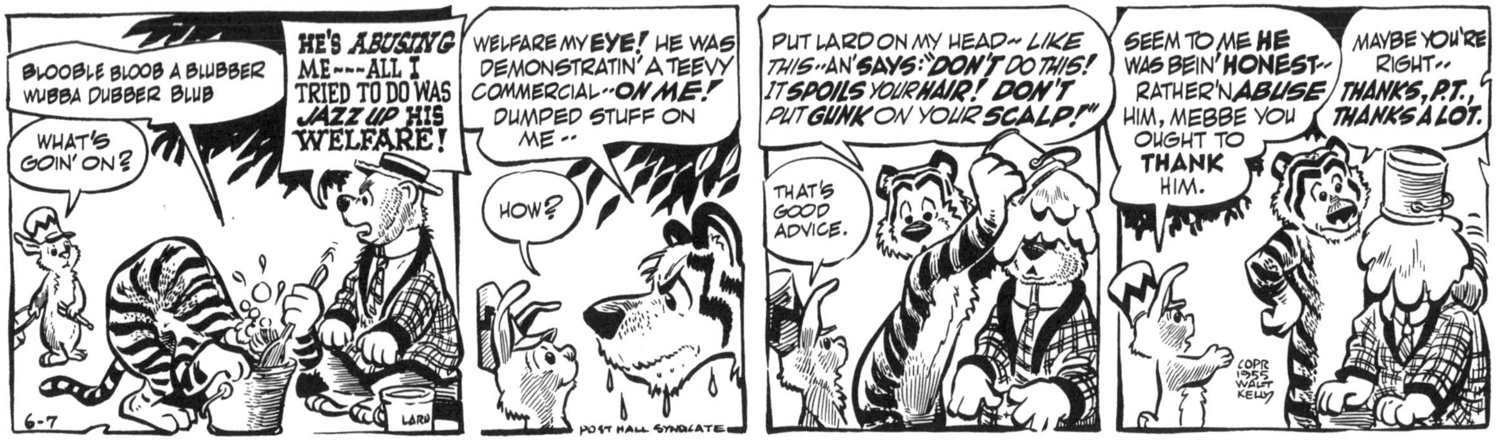
BLOOBLE BLOOB A BLUBBER WUBBA DUBBER BLUB
WHAT'S GOIN' ON?
HE'S ABUSING ME---ALL I TRIED TO DO WAS JAZZ UP HIS WELFARE!
6-7
LARD
WELFARE MY EYE! HE WAS DEMONSTRATIN' A TEEVY COMMERCIAL--ON ME! DUMPED STUFF ON ME--
HOW?
POST HALL SYNDICATE
PUT LARD ON MY HEAD-- LIKE THIS--AN' SAYS: "DON'T DO THIS! IT SPOILS YOUR HAIR! DON'T PUT GUNK ON YOUR SCALP!"
THAT'S GOOD ADVICE.
SEEM TO ME HE WAS BEIN' HONEST-- RATHER'N ABUSE HIM, MEBBE YOU OUGHT TO THANK HIM.
MAYBE YOU'RE RIGHT-- THANKS, P.T., THANKS A LOT.
COPR 1955 WALT KELLY

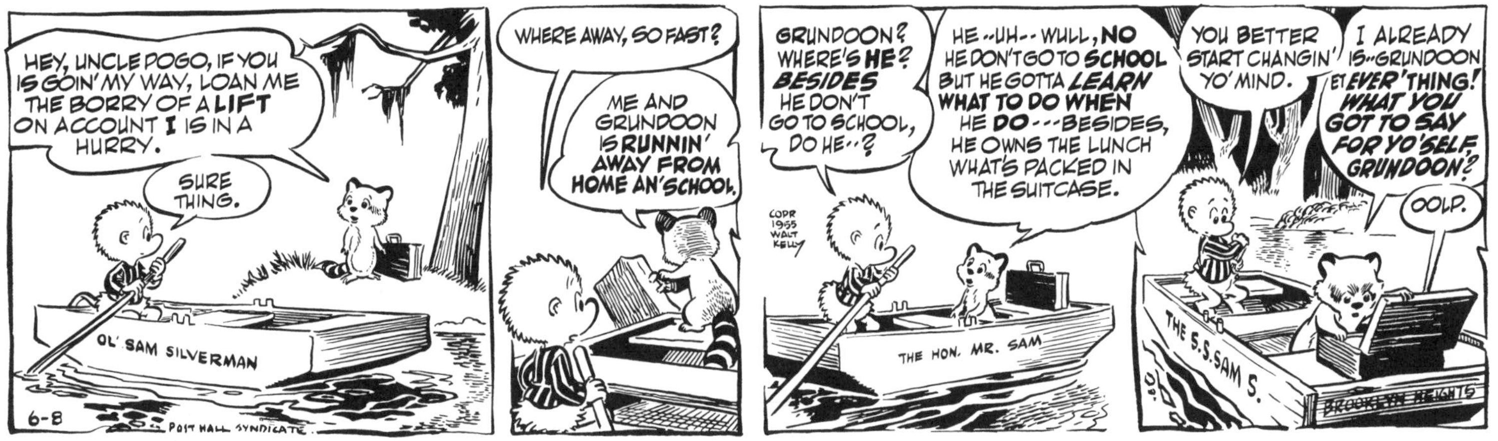
HEY, UNCLE POGO, IF YOU IS GOIN' MY WAY, LOAN ME THE BORRY OF A LIFT ON ACCOUNT I IS IN A HURRY.
SURE THING.
OL' SAM SILVERMAN
6-8
POST HALL SYNDICATE
WHERE AWAY, SO FAST?
ME AND GRUNDOON IS RUNNIN' AWAY FROM HOME AN' SCHOOL.
GRUNDOON? WHERE'S HE? BESIDES HE DON'T GO TO SCHOOL, DO HE--?
HE--UH--WULL, NO HE DON'T GO TO SCHOOL BUT HE GOTTA LEARN WHAT TO DO WHEN HE DO---BESIDES, HE OWNS THE LUNCH WHAT'S PACKED IN THE SUITCASE.
COPR 1955 WALT KELLY
THE HON. MR. SAM
YOU BETTER START CHANGIN' YO' MIND.
I ALREADY IS--GRUNDOON ET EVER'THING! WHAT YOU GOT TO SAY FOR YO'SELF, GRUNDOON?
OOLP.
THE S.S. SAM S.
BROOKLYN HEIGHTS

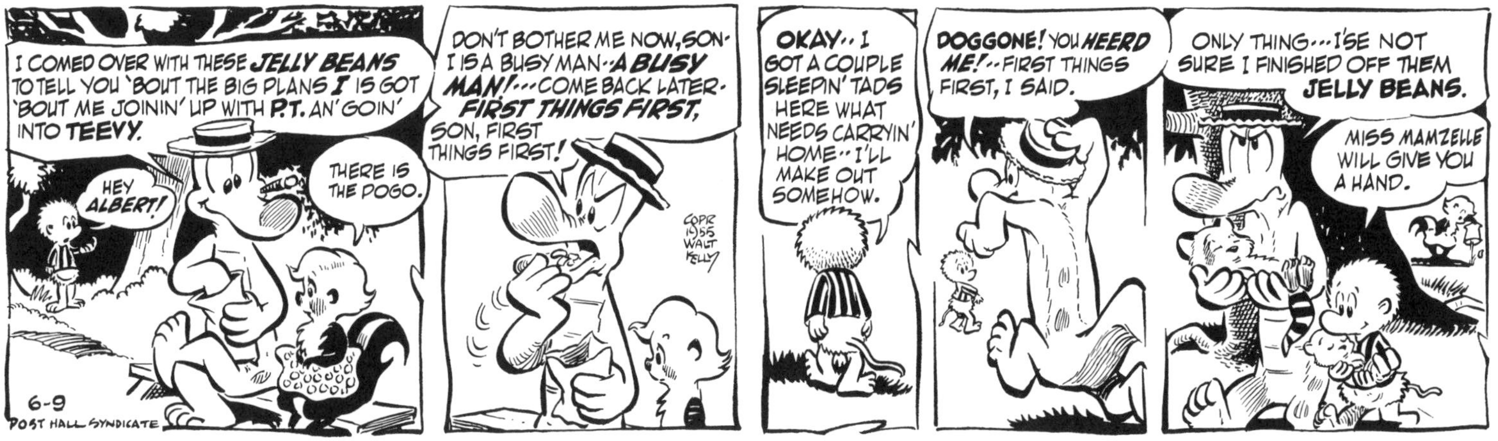
I COMED OVER WITH THESE JELLY BEANS TO TELL YOU 'BOUT THE BIG PLANS I IS GOT 'BOUT ME JOININ' UP WITH P.T. AN' GOIN' INTO TEEVY.
HEY ALBERT!
THERE IS THE POGO.
6-9
POST HALL SYNDICATE
DON'T BOTHER ME NOW, SON - I IS A BUSY MAN - A BUSY MAN! ··· COME BACK LATER - FIRST THINGS FIRST, SON, FIRST THINGS FIRST!
COPR 1955 WALT KELLY
OKAY·· I GOT A COUPLE SLEEPIN' TADS HERE WHAT NEEDS CARRYIN' HOME·· I'LL MAKE OUT SOMEHOW.
DOGGONE! YOU HEERD ME!·· FIRST THINGS FIRST, I SAID.
ONLY THING··· I'SE NOT SURE I FINISHED OFF THEM JELLY BEANS.
MISS MAMZELLE WILL GIVE YOU A HAND.

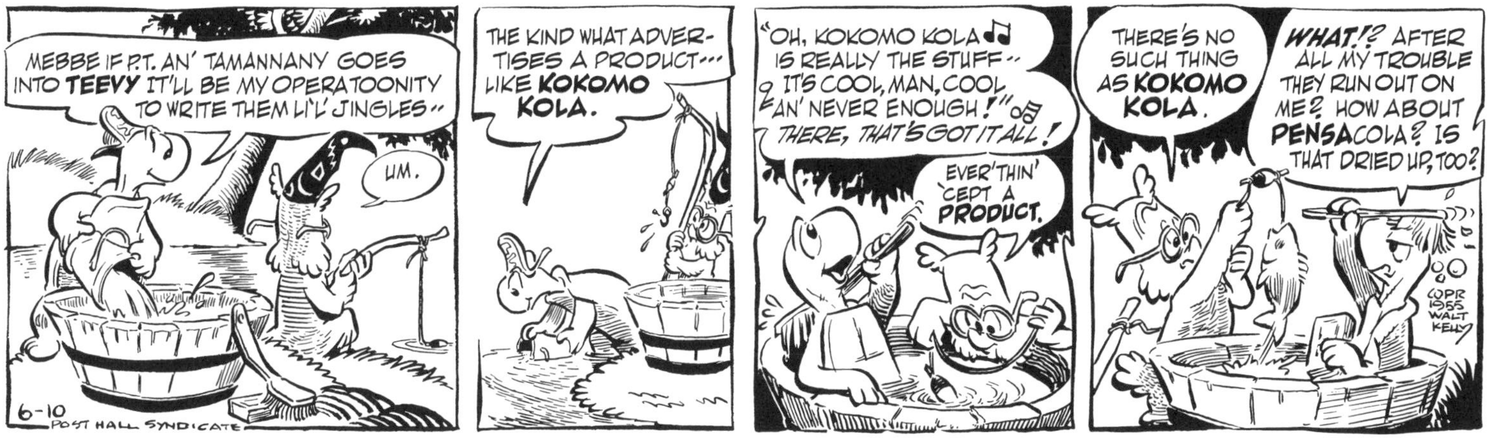
MEBBE IF P.T. AN' TAMANNANY GOES INTO TEEVY IT'LL BE MY OPERATOONITY TO WRITE THEM LI'L' JINGLES··
UM.
6-10
POST HALL SYNDICATE
THE KIND WHAT ADVERTISES A PRODUCT··· LIKE KOKOMO KOLA.
"OH, KOKOMO KOLA IS REALLY THE STUFF·· IT'S COOL, MAN, COOL AN' NEVER ENOUGH!" THERE, THAT'S GOT IT ALL!
EVER'THIN' 'CEPT A PRODUCT.
THERE'S NO SUCH THING AS KOKOMO KOLA.
WHAT!? AFTER ALL MY TROUBLE THEY RUN OUT ON ME? HOW ABOUT PENSACOLA? IS THAT DRIED UP, TOO?
COPR 1955 WALT KELLY

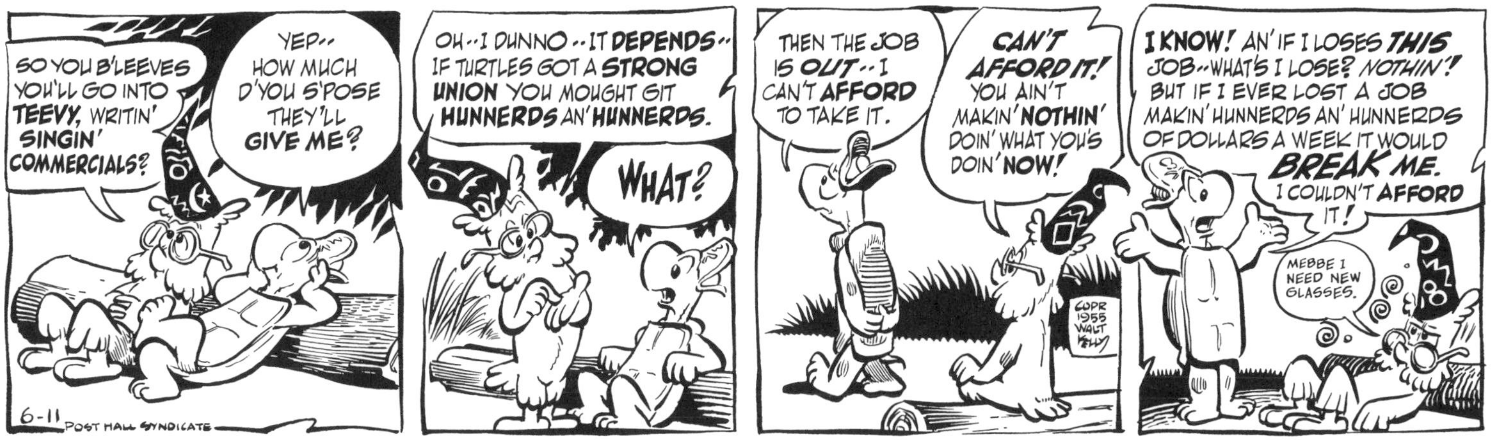
SO YOU B'LEEVES YOU'LL GO INTO TEEVY, WRITIN' SINGIN' COMMERCIALS?
YEP·· HOW MUCH D'YOU S'POSE THEY'LL GIVE ME?
6-11
POST HALL SYNDICATE
OH·· I DUNNO ·· IT DEPENDS·· IF TURTLES GOT A STRONG UNION YOU MOUGHT GIT HUNNERDS AN' HUNNERDS.
WHAT?
THEN THE JOB IS OUT·· I CAN'T AFFORD TO TAKE IT.
CAN'T AFFORD IT! YOU AIN'T MAKIN' NOTHIN' DOIN' WHAT YOU'S DOIN' NOW!
COPR 1955 WALT KELLY
I KNOW! AN' IF I LOSES THIS JOB·· WHAT'S I LOSE? NOTHIN'! BUT IF I EVER LOST A JOB MAKIN' HUNNERDS AN' HUNNERDS OF DOLLARS A WEEK IT WOULD BREAK ME. I COULDN'T AFFORD IT!
MEBBE I NEED NEW GLASSES.

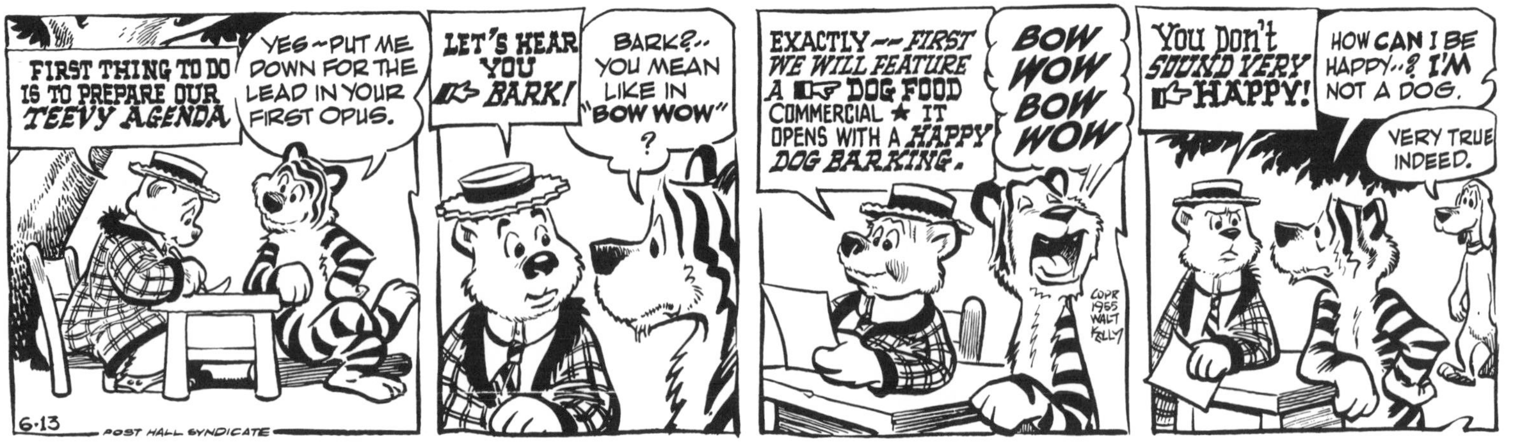
FIRST THING TO DO IS TO PREPARE OUR TEEVY AGENDA
YES-PUT ME DOWN FOR THE LEAD IN YOUR FIRST OPUS.
LET'S HEAR YOU BARK!
BARK?.. YOU MEAN LIKE IN "BOW WOW" ?
EXACTLY -- FIRST WE WILL FEATURE A DOG FOOD COMMERCIAL ★ IT OPENS WITH A HAPPY DOG BARKING.
BOW WOW BOW WOW
You Don't SOUND VERY HAPPY!
HOW CAN I BE HAPPY..? I'M NOT A DOG.
VERY TRUE INDEED.
6-13
POST HALL SYNDICATE
COPR 1955 WALT KELLY

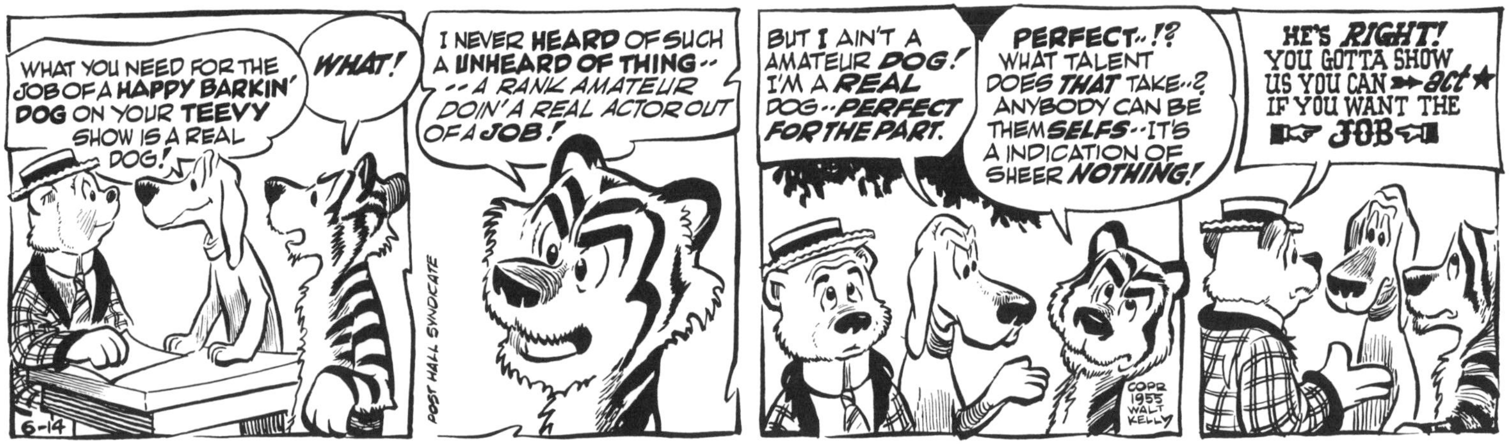
WHAT YOU NEED FOR THE JOB OF A HAPPY BARKIN' DOG ON YOUR TEEVY SHOW IS A REAL DOG!
WHAT!
I NEVER HEARD OF SUCH A UNHEARD OF THING -- -- A RANK AMATEUR DOIN' A REAL ACTOR OUT OF A JOB!
BUT I AIN'T A AMATEUR DOG! I'M A REAL DOG -- PERFECT FOR THE PART.
PERFECT..!? WHAT TALENT DOES THAT TAKE..? ANYBODY CAN BE THEMSELFS -- IT'S A INDICATION OF SHEER NOTHING!
HE'S RIGHT! YOU GOTTA SHOW US YOU CAN act ★ IF YOU WANT THE JOB
6-14
POST HALL SYNDICATE
COPR 1955 WALT KELLY

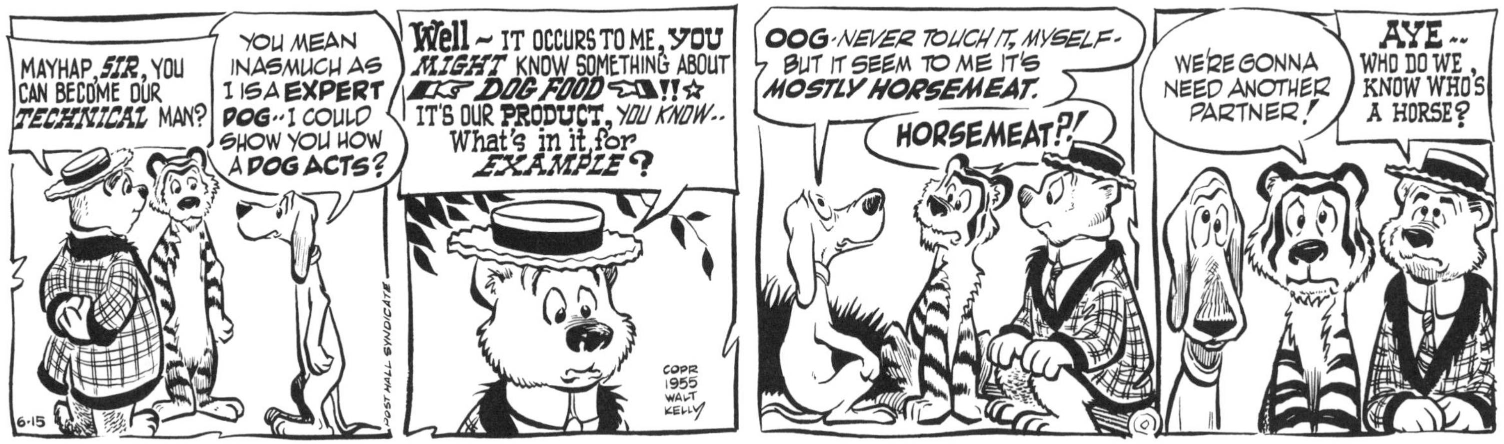
MAYHAP, SIR, YOU CAN BECOME OUR TECHNICAL MAN?
YOU MEAN INASMUCH AS I IS A EXPERT DOG -- I COULD SHOW YOU HOW A DOG ACTS?
Well - IT OCCURS TO ME, YOU MIGHT KNOW SOMETHING ABOUT DOG FOOD!! ☆ IT'S OUR PRODUCT, YOU KNOW.. What's in it, for EXAMPLE?
OOG - NEVER TOUCH IT, MYSELF - BUT IT SEEM TO ME IT'S MOSTLY HORSEMEAT.
HORSEMEAT?!
WE'RE GONNA NEED ANOTHER PARTNER!
AYE.. WHO DO WE KNOW WHO'S A HORSE?
6-15
POST HALL SYNDICATE
COPR 1955 WALT KELLY

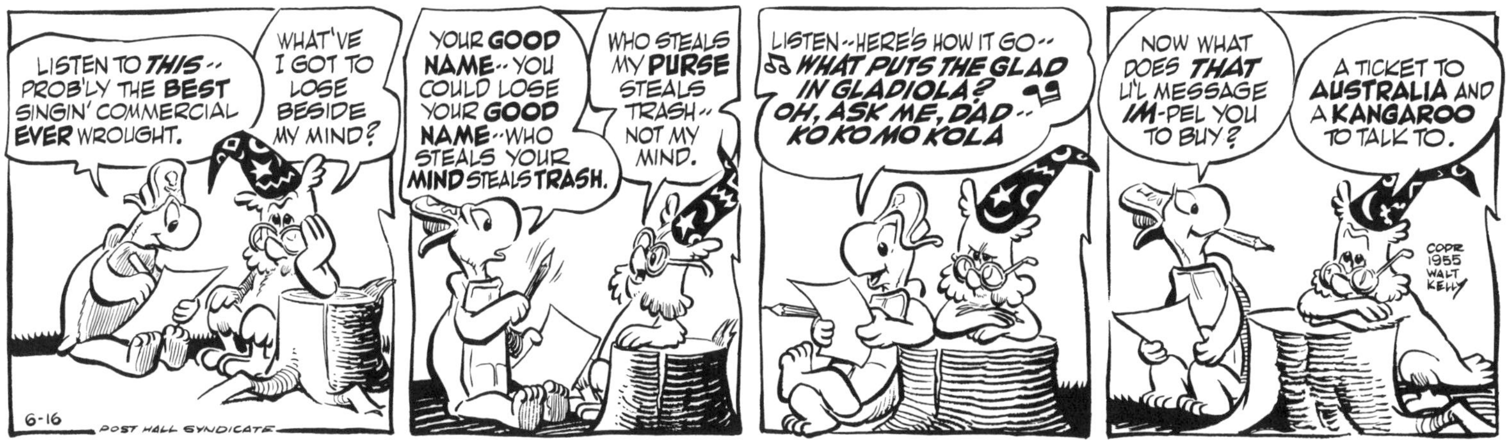
LISTEN TO THIS -- PROB'LY THE BEST SINGIN' COMMERCIAL EVER WROUGHT.
WHAT'VE I GOT TO LOSE BESIDE MY MIND?
YOUR GOOD NAME -- YOU COULD LOSE YOUR GOOD NAME -- WHO STEALS YOUR MIND STEALS TRASH.
WHO STEALS MY PURSE STEALS TRASH -- NOT MY MIND.
LISTEN -- HERE'S HOW IT GO -- WHAT PUTS THE GLAD IN GLADIOLA? OH, ASK ME, DAD -- KO KO MO KOLA
NOW WHAT DOES THAT LI'L MESSAGE IM-PEL YOU TO BUY?
A TICKET TO AUSTRALIA AND A KANGAROO TO TALK TO.
COPR 1955 WALT KELLY
6-16
POST HALL SYNDICATE

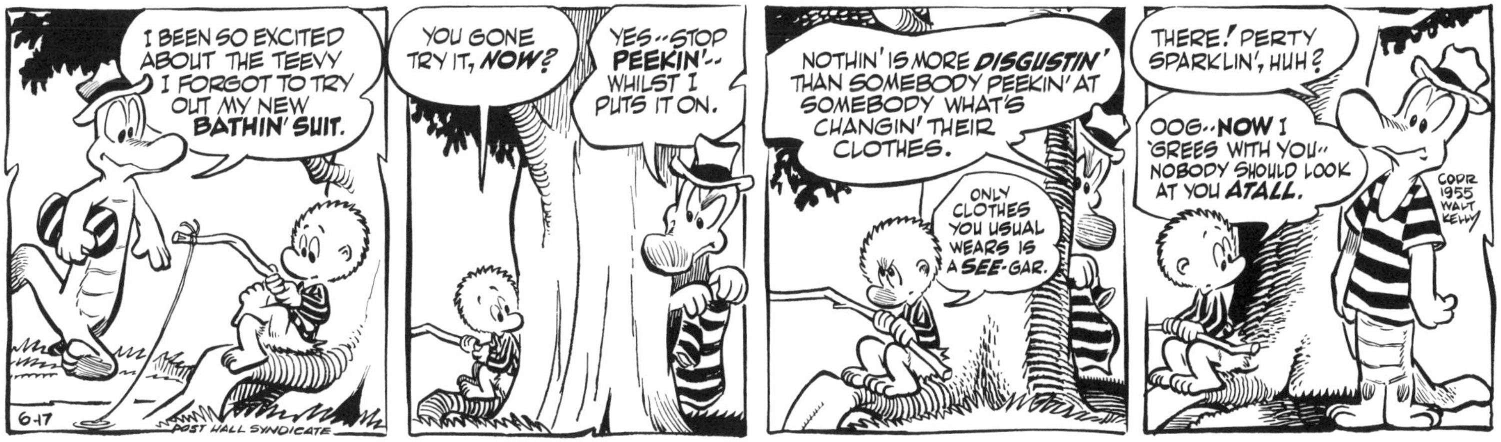
I BEEN SO EXCITED ABOUT THE TEEVY I FORGOT TO TRY OUT MY NEW BATHIN' SUIT.
YOU GONE TRY IT, NOW?
YES -- STOP PEEKIN' -- WHILST I PUTS IT ON.
NOTHIN' IS MORE DISGUSTIN' THAN SOMEBODY PEEKIN' AT SOMEBODY WHAT'S CHANGIN' THEIR CLOTHES.
ONLY CLOTHES YOU USUAL WEARS IS A SEE-GAR.
THERE! PERTY SPARKLIN', HUH?
OOG -- NOW I 'GREES WITH YOU -- NOBODY SHOULD LOOK AT YOU ATALL.
COPR 1955 WALT KELLY
6-17
POST HALL SYNDICATE

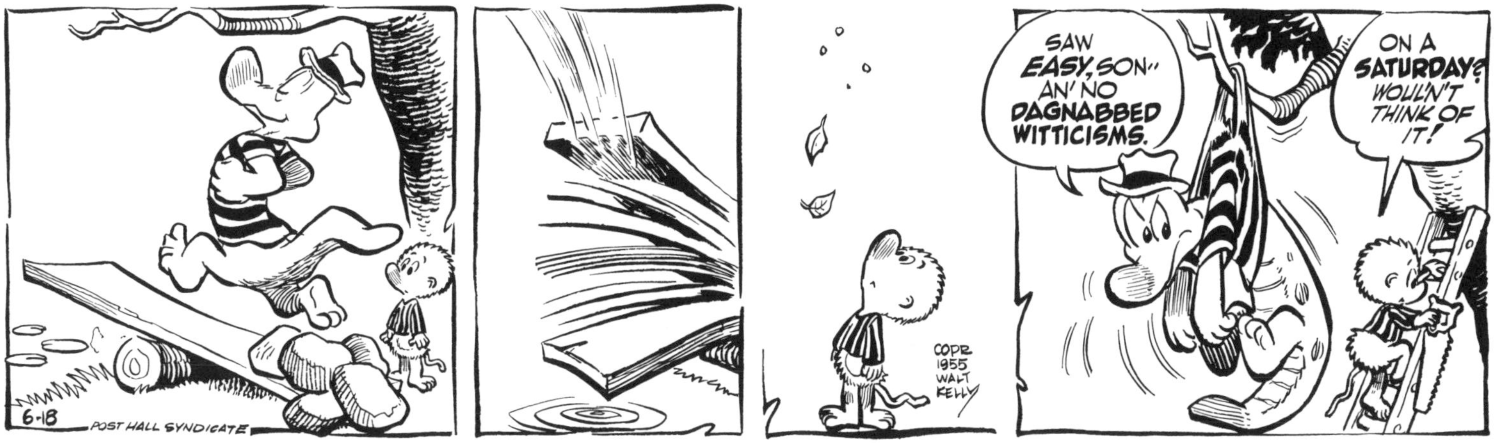
COPR 1955 WALT KELLY
SAW EASY, SON -- AN' NO DAGNABBED WITTICISMS.
ON A SATURDAY? WOULN'T THINK OF IT!
6-18
POST HALL SYNDICATE

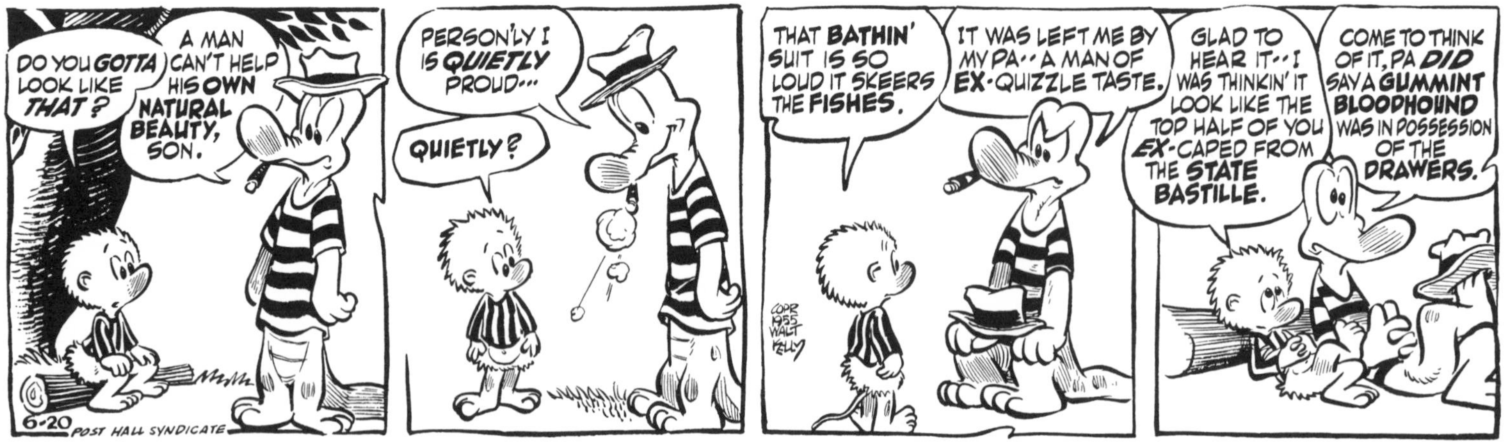
DO YOU GOTTA LOOK LIKE THAT?
A MAN CAN'T HELP HIS OWN NATURAL BEAUTY, SON.
PERSON'LY I IS QUIETLY PROUD...
QUIETLY?
THAT BATHIN' SUIT IS SO LOUD IT SKEERS THE FISHES.
IT WAS LEFT ME BY MY PA·· A MAN OF EX-QUIZZLE TASTE.
GLAD TO HEAR IT·· I WAS THINKIN' IT LOOK LIKE THE TOP HALF OF YOU EX-CAPED FROM THE STATE BASTILLE.
COME TO THINK OF IT, PA DID SAY A GUMMINT BLOODHOUND WAS IN POSSESSION OF THE DRAWERS.
COPR 1955 WALT KELLY
6-20
POST HALL SYNDICATE

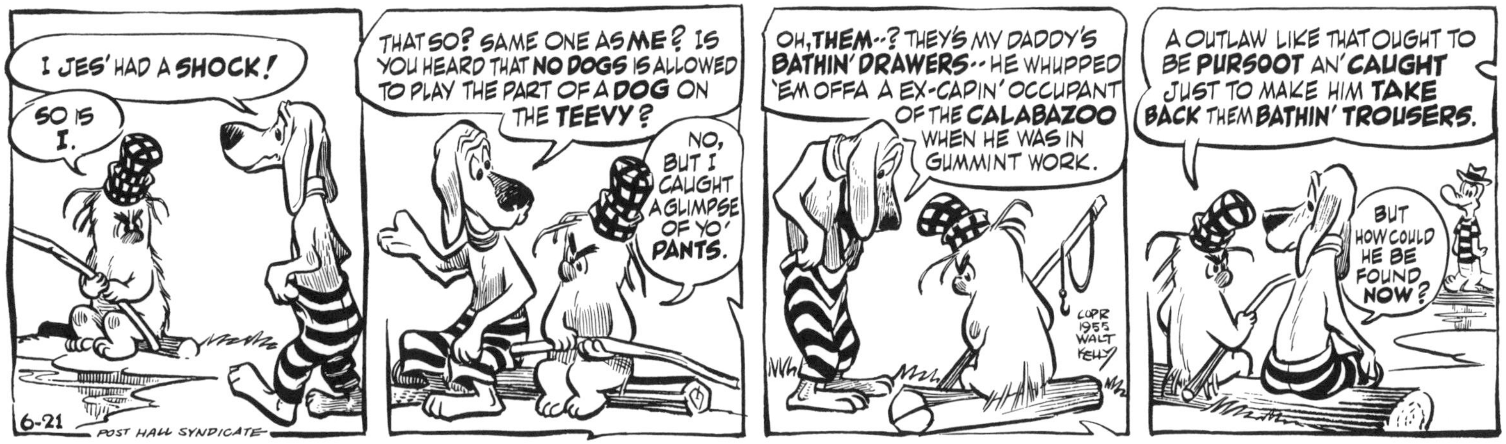
I JES' HAD A SHOCK!
SO IS I.
THAT SO? SAME ONE AS ME? IS YOU HEARD THAT NO DOGS IS ALLOWED TO PLAY THE PART OF A DOG ON THE TEEVY?
NO, BUT I CAUGHT A GLIMPSE OF YO' PANTS.
OH, THEM··? THEY'S MY DADDY'S BATHIN' DRAWERS·· HE WHUPPED 'EM OFFA A EX-CAPIN' OCCUPANT OF THE CALABAZOO WHEN HE WAS IN GUMMINT WORK.
COPR 1955 WALT KELLY
A OUTLAW LIKE THAT OUGHT TO BE PURSOOT AN' CAUGHT JUST TO MAKE HIM TAKE BACK THEM BATHIN' TROUSERS.
BUT HOW COULD HE BE FOUND NOW?
6-21
POST HALL SYNDICATE

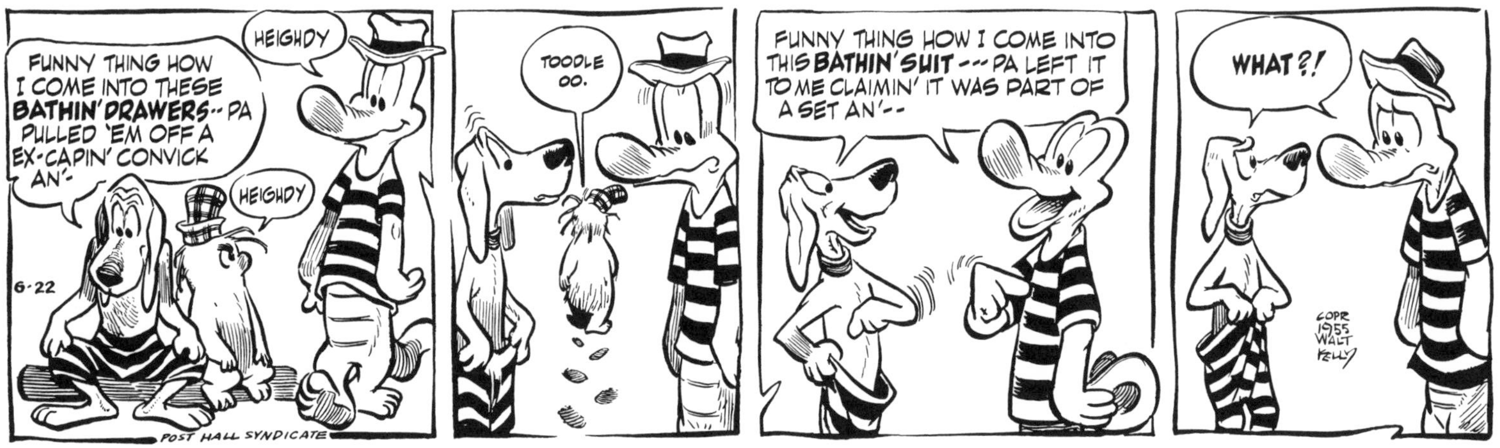
FUNNY THING HOW I COME INTO THESE BATHIN' DRAWERS·· PA PULLED 'EM OFF A EX-CAPIN' CONVICK AN'-
HEIGHDY
HEIGHDY
TOODLE OO.
FUNNY THING HOW I COME INTO THIS BATHIN' SUIT --- PA LEFT IT TO ME CLAIMIN' IT WAS PART OF A SET AN'--
WHAT?!
COPR 1955 WALT KELLY
6-22
POST HALL SYNDICATE

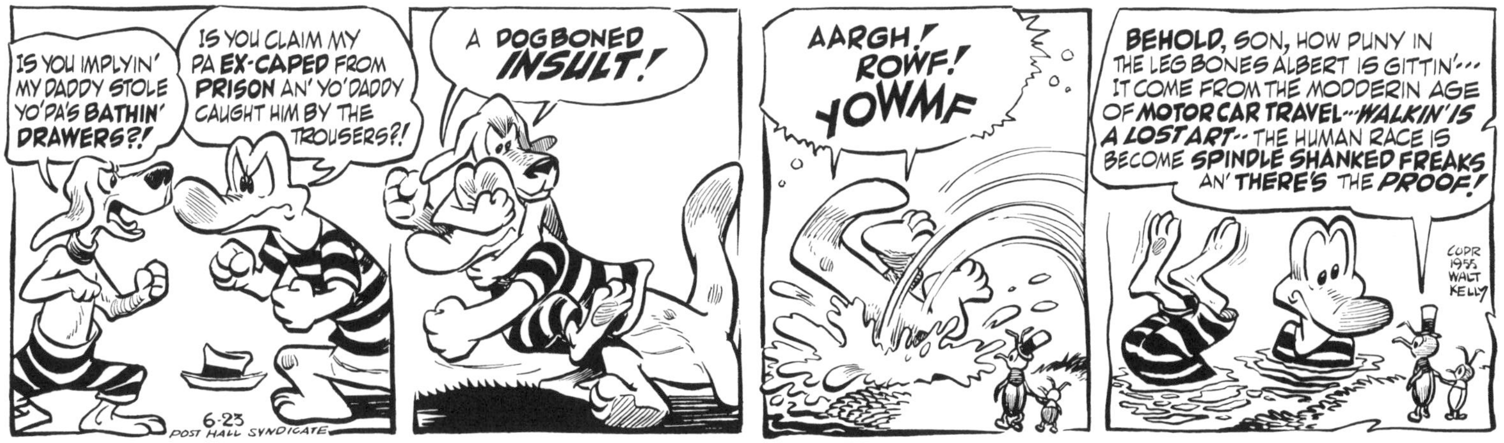
IS YOU IMPLYIN' MY DADDY STOLE YO'PA'S BATHIN' DRAWERS?!
IS YOU CLAIM MY PA EX-CAPED FROM PRISON AN' YO'DADDY CAUGHT HIM BY THE TROUSERS?!
6-23
POST HALL SYNDICATE
A DOGBONED INSULT!
AARGH! ROWF! YOWMF
BEHOLD, SON, HOW PUNY IN THE LEG BONES ALBERT IS GITTIN'... IT COME FROM THE MODDERIN AGE OF MOTOR CAR TRAVEL... WALKIN' IS A LOST ART... THE HUMAN RACE IS BECOME SPINDLE SHANKED FREAKS AN' THERE'S THE PROOF!
COPR 1955 WALT KELLY

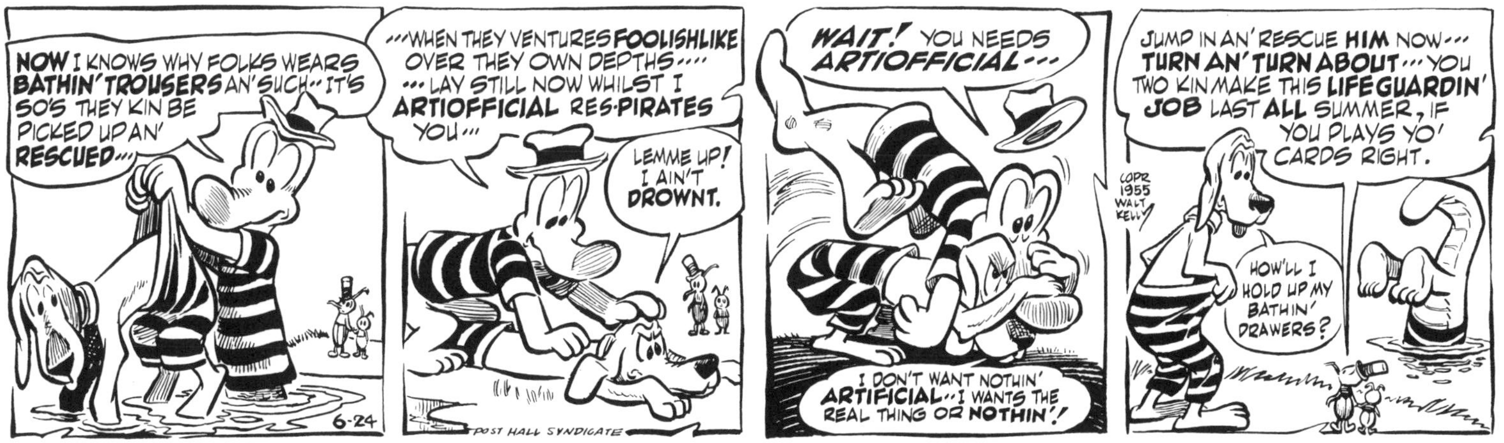
NOW I KNOWS WHY FOLKS WEARS BATHIN' TROUSERS AN' SUCH... IT'S SO'S THEY KIN BE PICKED UP AN' RESCUED...
6-24
...WHEN THEY VENTURES FOOLISHLIKE OVER THEY OWN DEPTHS.... ...LAY STILL NOW WHILST I ARTIOFFICIAL RES-PIRATES YOU...
LEMME UP! I AIN'T DROWNT.
POST HALL SYNDICATE
WAIT! YOU NEEDS ARTIOFFICIAL...
I DON'T WANT NOTHIN' ARTIFICIAL... I WANTS THE REAL THING OR NOTHIN'!
JUMP IN AN' RESCUE HIM NOW... TURN AN' TURN ABOUT... YOU TWO KIN MAKE THIS LIFEGUARDIN' JOB LAST ALL SUMMER, IF YOU PLAYS YO' CARDS RIGHT.
COPR 1955 WALT KELLY
HOW'LL I HOLD UP MY BATHIN' DRAWERS?

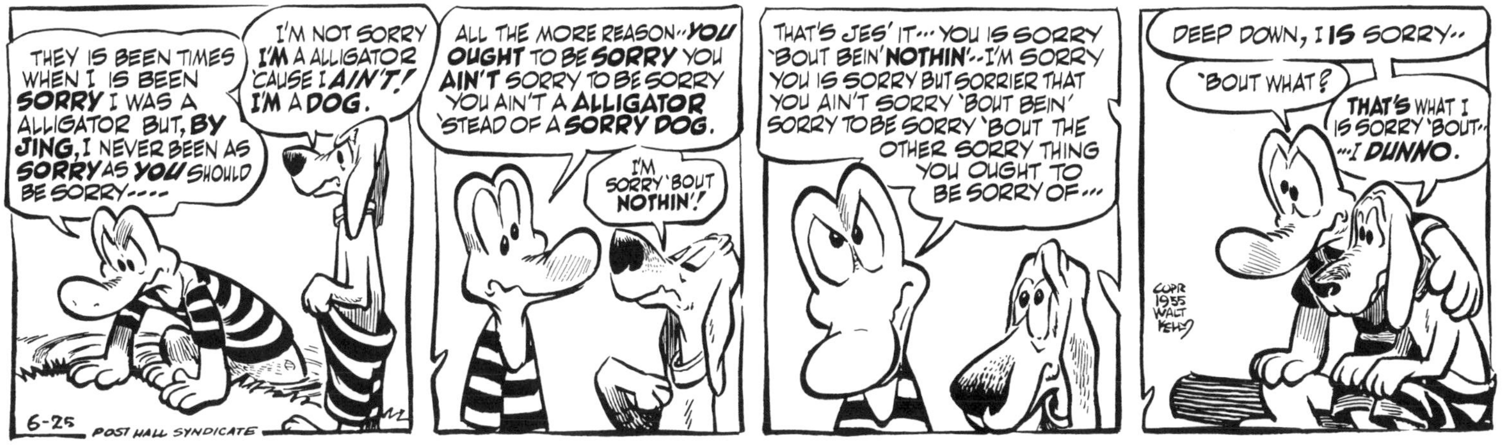
THEY IS BEEN TIMES WHEN I IS BEEN SORRY I WAS A ALLIGATOR BUT, BY JING, I NEVER BEEN AS SORRY AS YOU SHOULD BE SORRY....
I'M NOT SORRY I'M A ALLIGATOR 'CAUSE I AIN'T! I'M A DOG.
6-25
POST HALL SYNDICATE
ALL THE MORE REASON... YOU OUGHT TO BE SORRY YOU AIN'T SORRY TO BE SORRY YOU AIN'T A ALLIGATOR 'STEAD OF A SORRY DOG.
I'M SORRY 'BOUT NOTHIN'!
THAT'S JES' IT... YOU IS SORRY 'BOUT BEIN' NOTHIN'... I'M SORRY YOU IS SORRY BUT SORRIER THAT YOU AIN'T SORRY 'BOUT BEIN' SORRY TO BE SORRY 'BOUT THE OTHER SORRY THING YOU OUGHT TO BE SORRY OF...
COPR 1955 WALT KELLY
DEEP DOWN, I IS SORRY..
'BOUT WHAT?
THAT'S WHAT I IS SORRY 'BOUT.. ...I DUNNO.

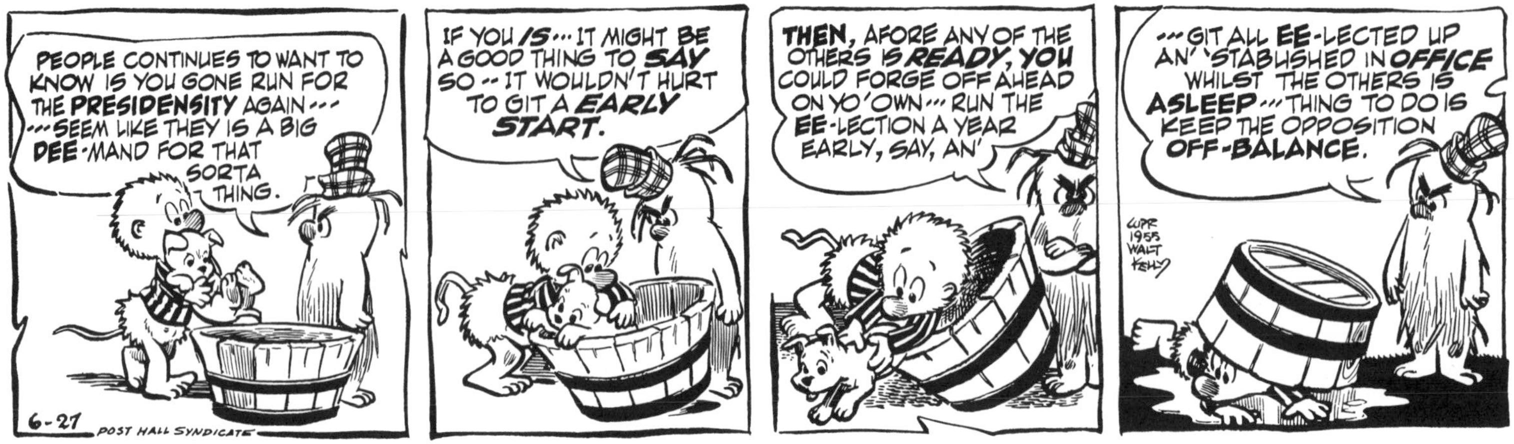
PEOPLE CONTINUES TO WANT TO KNOW IS YOU GONE RUN FOR THE PRESIDENSITY AGAIN--- ---SEEM LIKE THEY IS A BIG DEE-MAND FOR THAT SORTA THING.
IF YOU IS--- IT MIGHT BE A GOOD THING TO SAY SO -- IT WOULDN'T HURT TO GIT A EARLY START.
THEN, AFORE ANY OF THE OTHERS IS READY, YOU COULD FORGE OFF AHEAD ON YO'OWN--- RUN THE EE-LECTION A YEAR EARLY, SAY, AN'
---GIT ALL EE-LECTED UP AN' 'STABLISHED IN OFFICE WHILST THE OTHERS IS ASLEEP--- THING TO DO IS KEEP THE OPPOSITION OFF-BALANCE.
COPR 1955 WALT KELLY
6-27
POST HALL SYNDICATE

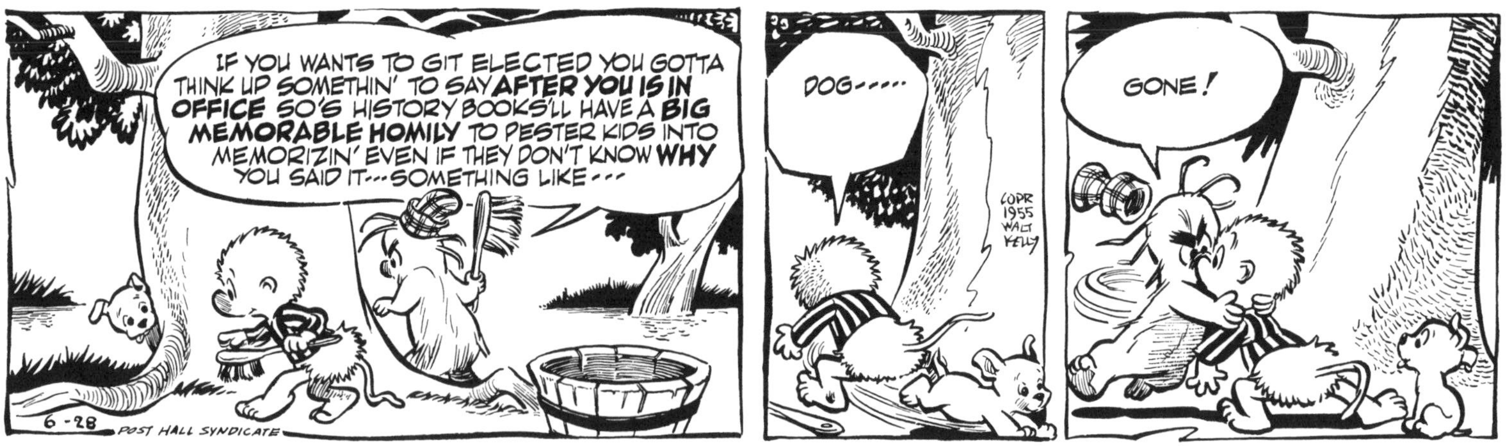
IF YOU WANTS TO GIT ELECTED YOU GOTTA THINK UP SOMETHIN' TO SAY AFTER YOU IS IN OFFICE SO'S HISTORY BOOKS'LL HAVE A BIG MEMORABLE HOMILY TO PESTER KIDS INTO MEMORIZIN' EVEN IF THEY DON'T KNOW WHY YOU SAID IT--- SOMETHING LIKE---
DOG-----
COPR 1955 WALT KELLY
GONE!
6-28
POST HALL SYNDICATE

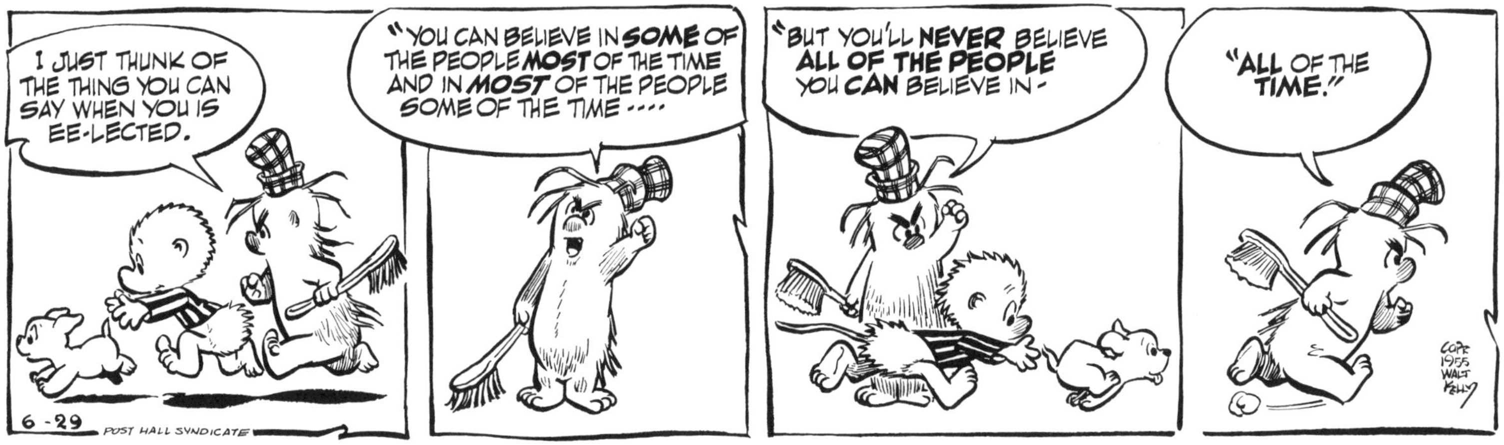
I JUST THUNK OF THE THING YOU CAN SAY WHEN YOU IS EE-LECTED.
"YOU CAN BELIEVE IN SOME OF THE PEOPLE MOST OF THE TIME AND IN MOST OF THE PEOPLE SOME OF THE TIME----
"BUT YOU'LL NEVER BELIEVE ALL OF THE PEOPLE YOU CAN BELIEVE IN -
"ALL OF THE TIME."
COPR 1955 WALT KELLY
6-29
POST HALL SYNDICATE

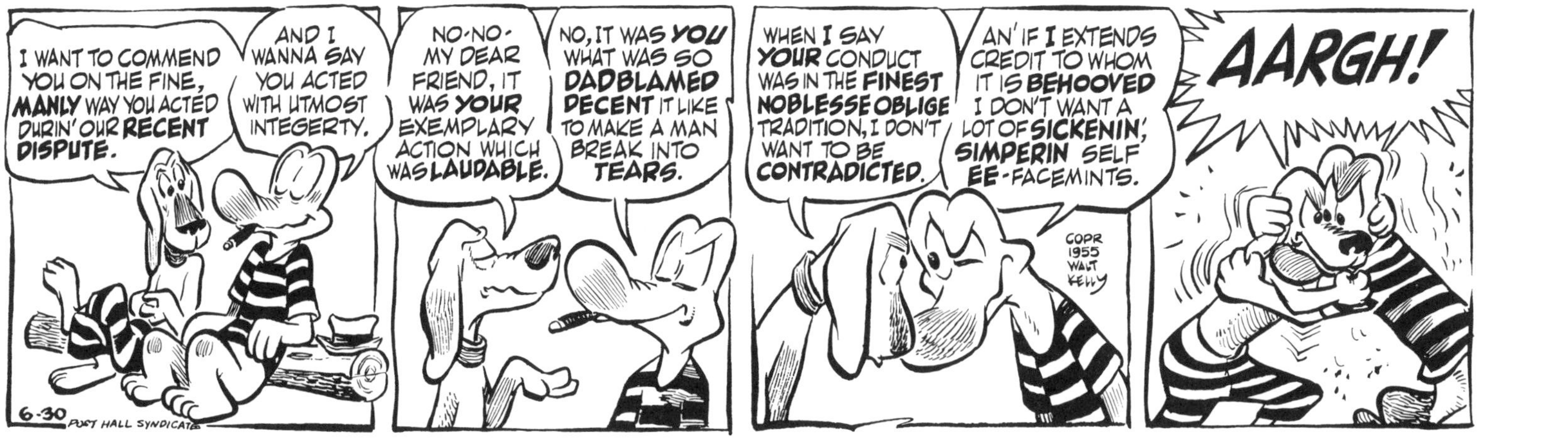
I WANT TO COMMEND YOU ON THE FINE, MANLY WAY YOU ACTED DURIN' OUR RECENT DISPUTE.
AND I WANNA SAY YOU ACTED WITH UTMOST INTEGERTY.
NO-NO- MY DEAR FRIEND, IT WAS YOUR EXEMPLARY ACTION WHICH WAS LAUDABLE.
NO, IT WAS YOU WHAT WAS SO DADBLAMED DECENT IT LIKE TO MAKE A MAN BREAK INTO TEARS.
WHEN I SAY YOUR CONDUCT WAS IN THE FINEST NOBLESSE OBLIGE TRADITION, I DON'T WANT TO BE CONTRADICTED.
AN' IF I EXTENDS CREDIT TO WHOM IT IS BEHOOVED I DON'T WANT A LOT OF SICKENIN', SIMPERIN SELF EE-FACEMINTS.
COPR 1955 WALT KELLY
AARGH!
6-30
POST HALL SYNDICATE

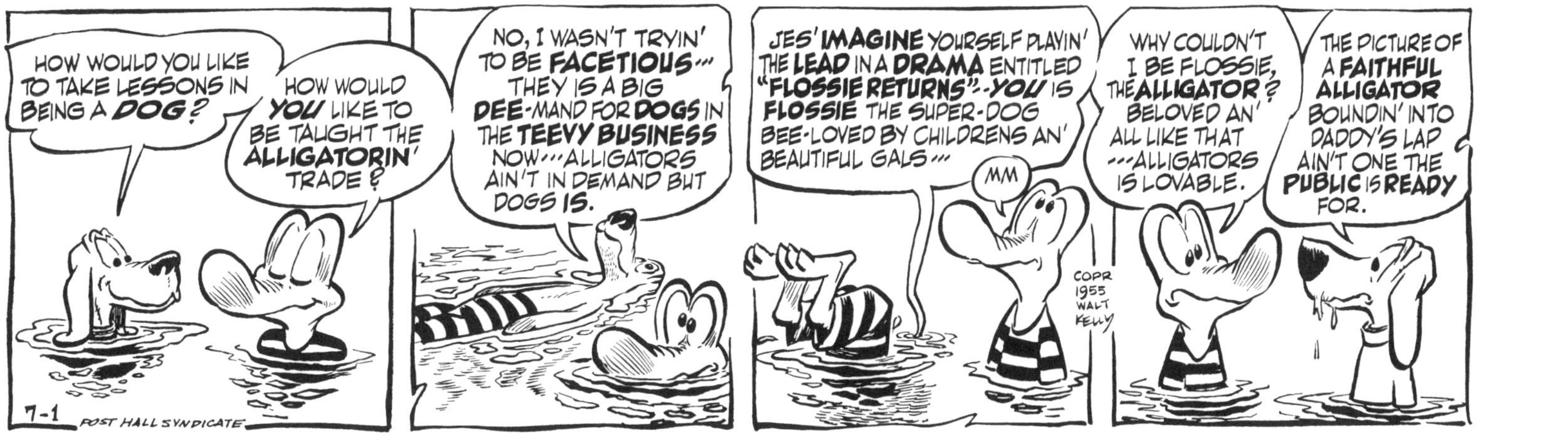
HOW WOULD YOU LIKE TO TAKE LESSONS IN BEING A DOG?
HOW WOULD YOU LIKE TO BE TAUGHT THE ALLIGATORIN' TRADE?
NO, I WASN'T TRYIN' TO BE FACETIOUS... THEY IS A BIG DEE-MAND FOR DOGS IN THE TEEVY BUSINESS NOW... ALLIGATORS AIN'T IN DEMAND BUT DOGS IS.
JES' IMAGINE YOURSELF PLAYIN' THE LEAD IN A DRAMA ENTITLED "FLOSSIE RETURNS"- YOU IS FLOSSIE THE SUPER-DOG BEE-LOVED BY CHILDRENS AN' BEAUTIFUL GALS...
MM
COPR 1955 WALT KELLY
WHY COULDN'T I BE FLOSSIE, THE ALLIGATOR? BELOVED AN' ALL LIKE THAT ...ALLIGATORS IS LOVABLE.
THE PICTURE OF A FAITHFUL ALLIGATOR BOUNDIN' INTO DADDY'S LAP AIN'T ONE THE PUBLIC IS READY FOR.
7-1
POST HALL SYNDICATE

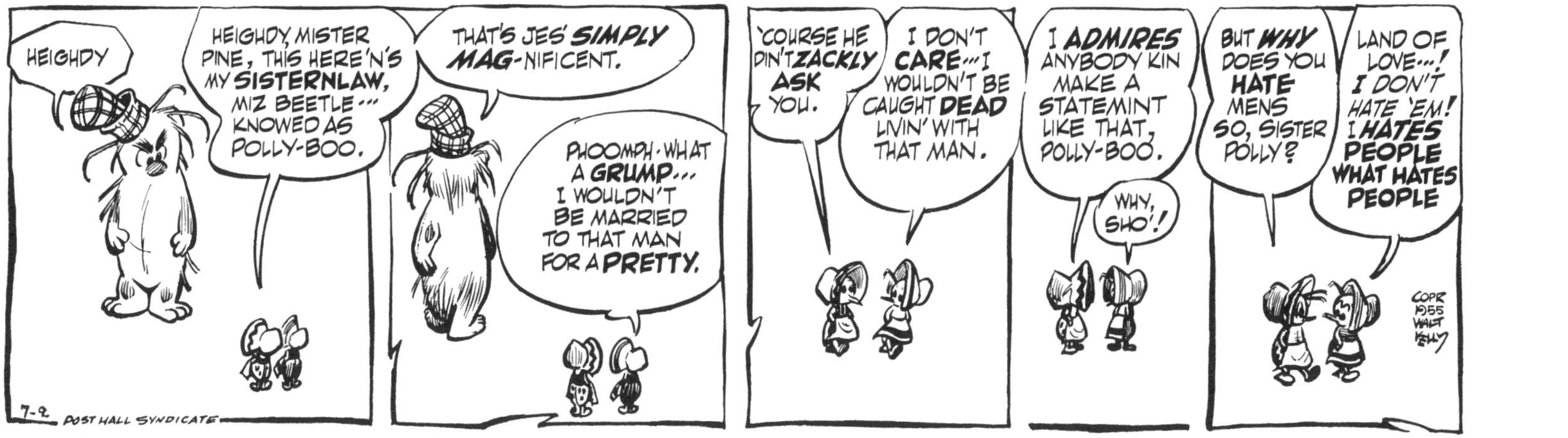
HEIGHDY
HEIGHDY, MISTER PINE, THIS HERE'N'S MY SISTERNLAW, MIZ BEETLE... KNOWED AS POLLY-BOO.
THAT'S JES' SIMPLY MAG-NIFICENT.
PHOOMPH- WHAT A GRUMP... I WOULDN'T BE MARRIED TO THAT MAN FOR A PRETTY.
'COURSE HE DIN'T ZACKLY ASK YOU.
I DON'T CARE... I WOULDN'T BE CAUGHT DEAD LIVIN' WITH THAT MAN.
I ADMIRES ANYBODY KIN MAKE A STATEMINT LIKE THAT, POLLY-BOO.
WHY, SHO'!
BUT WHY DOES YOU HATE MENS SO, SISTER POLLY?
LAND OF LOVE...! I DON'T HATE 'EM! I HATES PEOPLE WHAT HATES PEOPLE
COPR 1955 WALT KELLY
7-2
POST HALL SYNDICATE

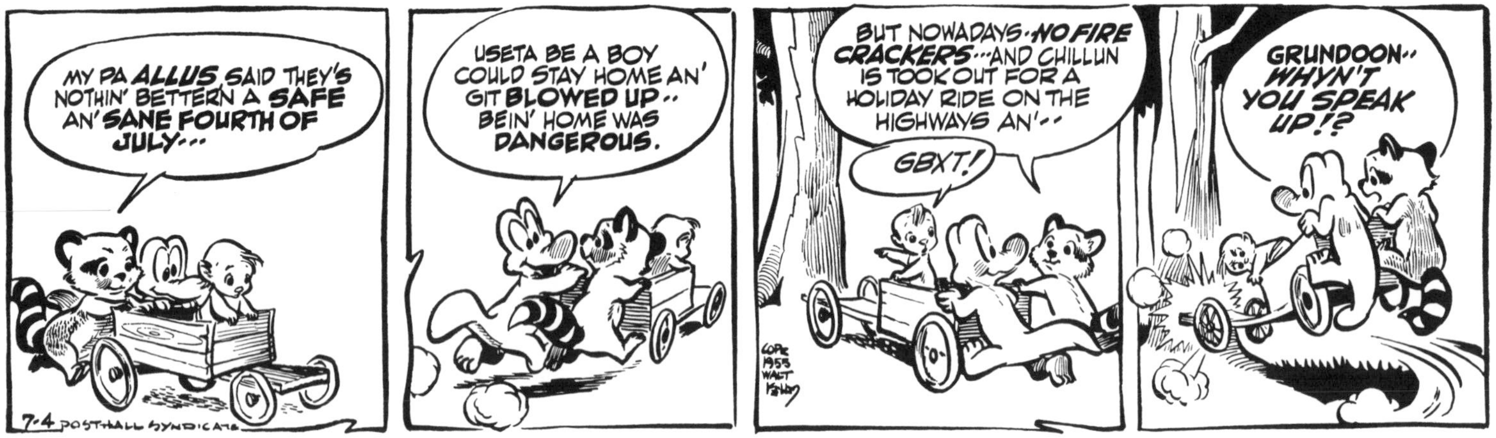
MY PA ALLUS SAID THEY'S NOTHIN' BETTERN A SAFE AN' SANE FOURTH OF JULY...
USETA BE A BOY COULD STAY HOME AN' GIT BLOWED UP.. BEIN' HOME WAS DANGEROUS.
BUT NOWADAYS.. NO FIRE CRACKERS...AND CHILLUN IS TOOK OUT FOR A HOLIDAY RIDE ON THE HIGHWAYS AN'..
GBXT!
GRUNDOON.. WHYN'T YOU SPEAK UP!?
7-4 POST-HALL SYNDICATE
COPR 1955 WALT KELLY

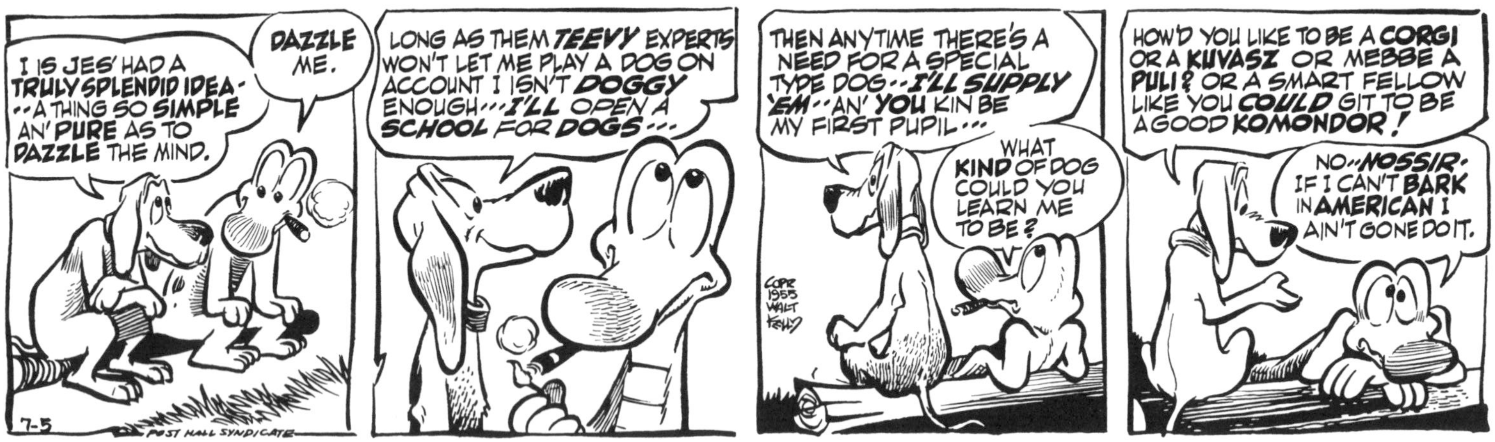
I IS JES' HAD A TRULY SPLENDID IDEA- ..A THING SO SIMPLE AN' PURE AS TO DAZZLE THE MIND.
DAZZLE ME.
LONG AS THEM TEEVY EXPERTS WON'T LET ME PLAY A DOG ON ACCOUNT I ISN'T DOGGY ENOUGH...I'LL OPEN A SCHOOL FOR DOGS...
THEN ANYTIME THERE'S A NEED FOR A SPECIAL TYPE DOG..I'LL SUPPLY 'EM..AN' YOU KIN BE MY FIRST PUPIL...
WHAT KIND OF DOG COULD YOU LEARN ME TO BE?
HOW'D YOU LIKE TO BE A CORGI OR A KUVASZ OR MEBBE A PULI? OR A SMART FELLOW LIKE YOU COULD GIT TO BE A GOOD KOMONDOR!
NO..NOSSIR. IF I CAN'T BARK IN AMERICAN I AIN'T GONE DO IT.
7-5 POST HALL SYNDICATE
COPR 1955 WALT KELLY

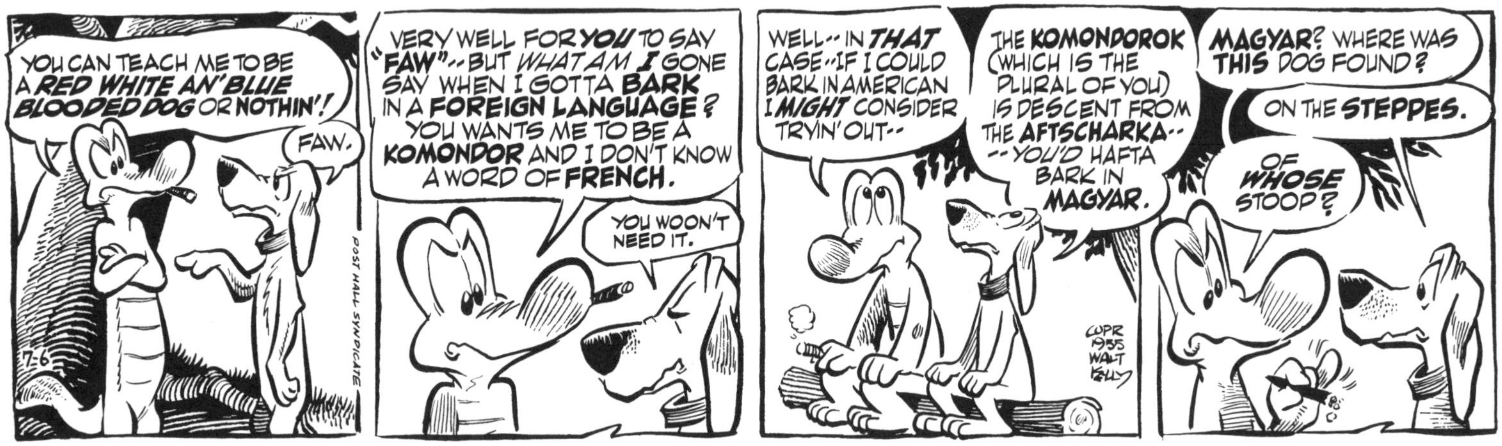
YOU CAN TEACH ME TO BE A RED WHITE AN' BLUE BLOODED DOG OR NOTHIN'!
FAW.
VERY WELL FOR YOU TO SAY "FAW".. BUT WHAT AM I GONE SAY WHEN I GOTTA BARK IN A FOREIGN LANGUAGE? YOU WANTS ME TO BE A KOMONDOR AND I DON'T KNOW A WORD OF FRENCH.
YOU WOON'T NEED IT.
WELL..IN THAT CASE..IF I COULD BARK IN AMERICAN I MIGHT CONSIDER TRYIN' OUT..
THE KOMONDOROK (WHICH IS THE PLURAL OF YOU) IS DESCENT FROM THE AFTSCHARKA.. ..YOU'D HAFTA BARK IN MAGYAR.
MAGYAR? WHERE WAS THIS DOG FOUND?
ON THE STEPPES.
OF WHOSE STOOP?
7-6 POST HALL SYNDICATE
COPR 1955 WALT KELLY

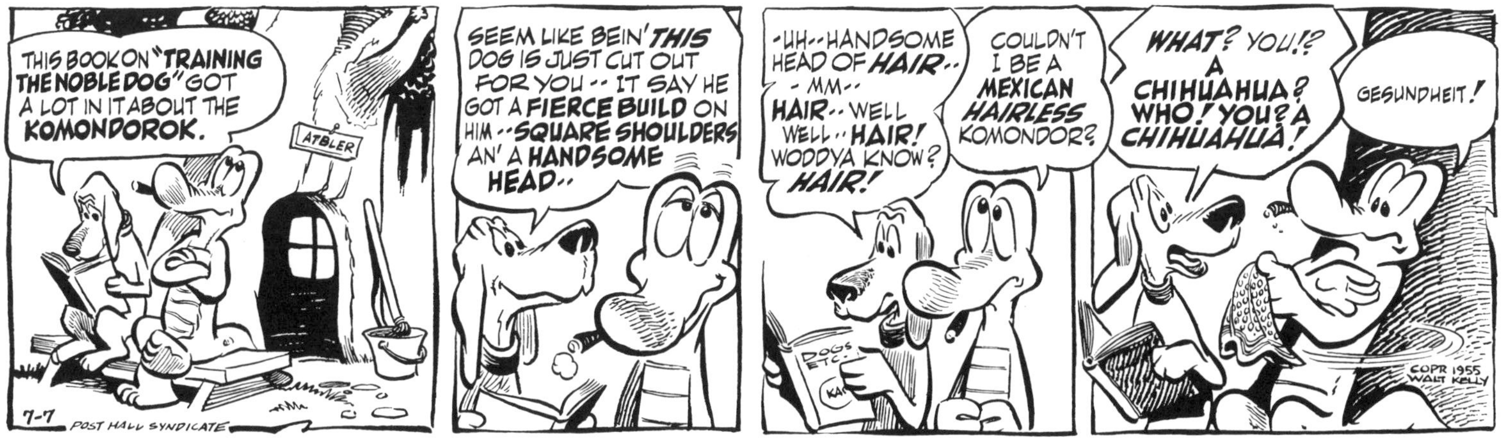

THIS BOOK ON "TRAINING THE NOBLE DOG" GOT A LOT IN IT ABOUT THE KOMONDOROK.
ATBLER
SEEM LIKE BEIN' THIS DOG IS JUST CUT OUT FOR YOU -- IT SAY HE GOT A FIERCE BUILD ON HIM -- SQUARE SHOULDERS AN' A HANDSOME HEAD..
-UH-- HANDSOME HEAD OF HAIR.. - MM.. HAIR.. WELL WELL.. HAIR! WODDYA KNOW? HAIR!
COULDN'T I BE A MEXICAN HAIRLESS KOMONDOR?
WHAT? YOU!? A CHIHUAHUA? WHO! YOU? A CHIHUAHUA!
GESUNDHEIT!
COPR 1955 WALT KELLY
7-7
POST HALL SYNDICATE

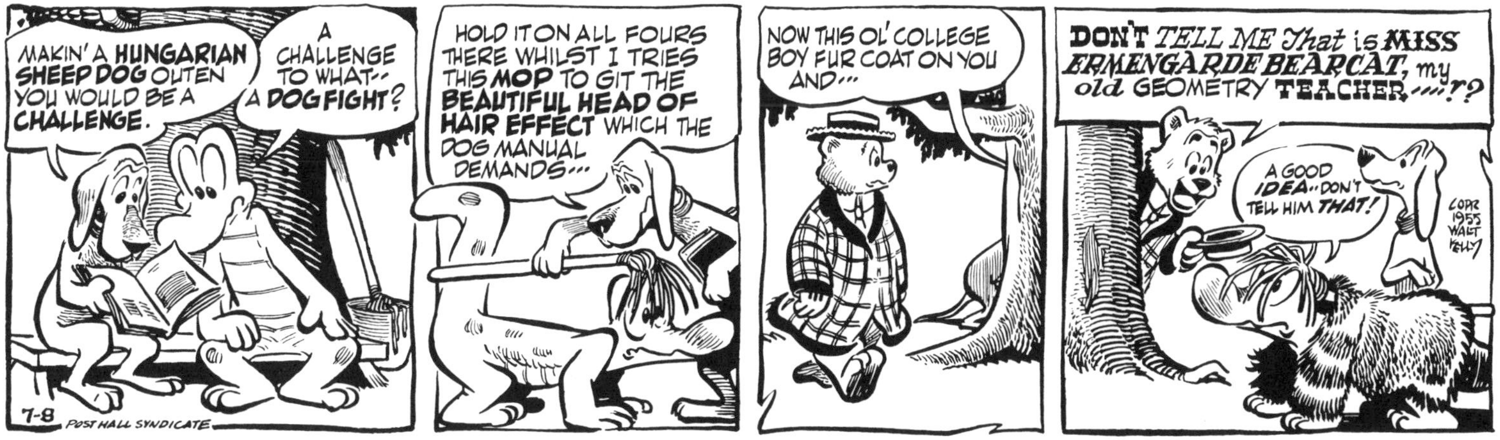

MAKIN' A HUNGARIAN SHEEP DOG OUTEN YOU WOULD BE A CHALLENGE.
A CHALLENGE TO WHAT-- A DOG FIGHT?
HOLD IT ON ALL FOURS THERE WHILST I TRIES THIS MOP TO GIT THE BEAUTIFUL HEAD OF HAIR EFFECT WHICH THE DOG MANUAL DEMANDS...
NOW THIS OL' COLLEGE BOY FUR COAT ON YOU AND...
DON'T TELL ME That is MISS ERMENGARDE BEARCAT, my old GEOMETRY TEACHER.....?
A GOOD IDEA.. DON'T TELL HIM THAT!
COPR 1955 WALT KELLY
7-8
POST HALL SYNDICATE

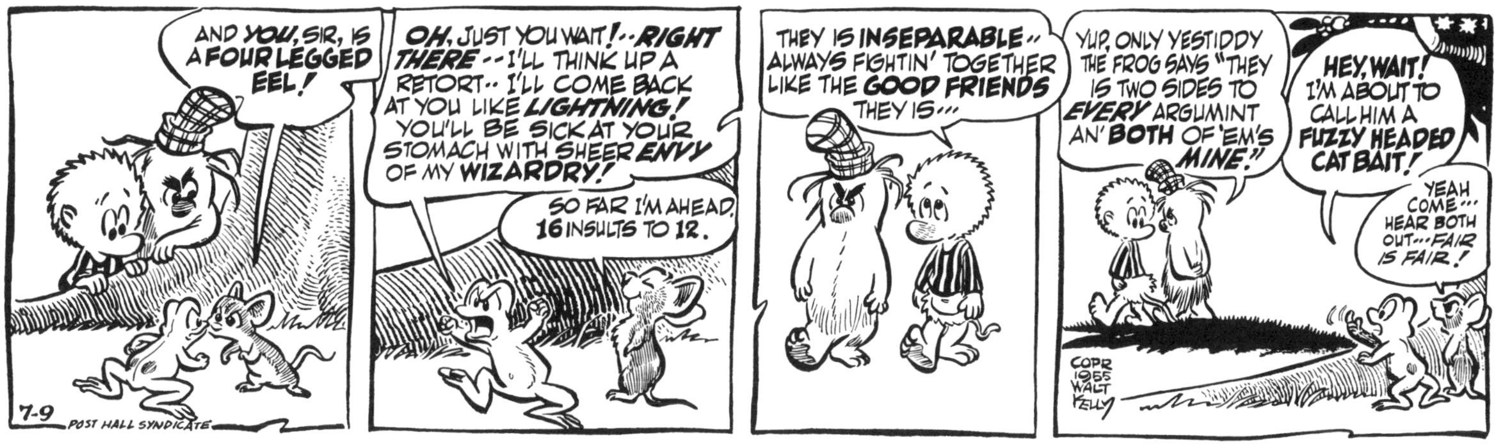

AND YOU, SIR, IS A FOUR LEGGED EEL!
OH, JUST YOU WAIT! .. RIGHT THERE -- I'LL THINK UP A RETORT.. I'LL COME BACK AT YOU LIKE LIGHTNING! YOU'LL BE SICK AT YOUR STOMACH WITH SHEER ENVY OF MY WIZARDRY!
SO FAR I'M AHEAD 16 INSULTS TO 12.
THEY IS INSEPARABLE.. ALWAYS FIGHTIN' TOGETHER LIKE THE GOOD FRIENDS THEY IS...
YUP, ONLY YESTIDDY THE FROG SAYS "THEY IS TWO SIDES TO EVERY ARGUMINT AN' BOTH OF 'EM'S MINE."
HEY, WAIT! I'M ABOUT TO CALL HIM A FUZZY HEADED CAT BAIT!
YEAH COME... HEAR BOTH OUT... FAIR IS FAIR!
COPR 1955 WALT KELLY
7-9
POST HALL SYNDICATE

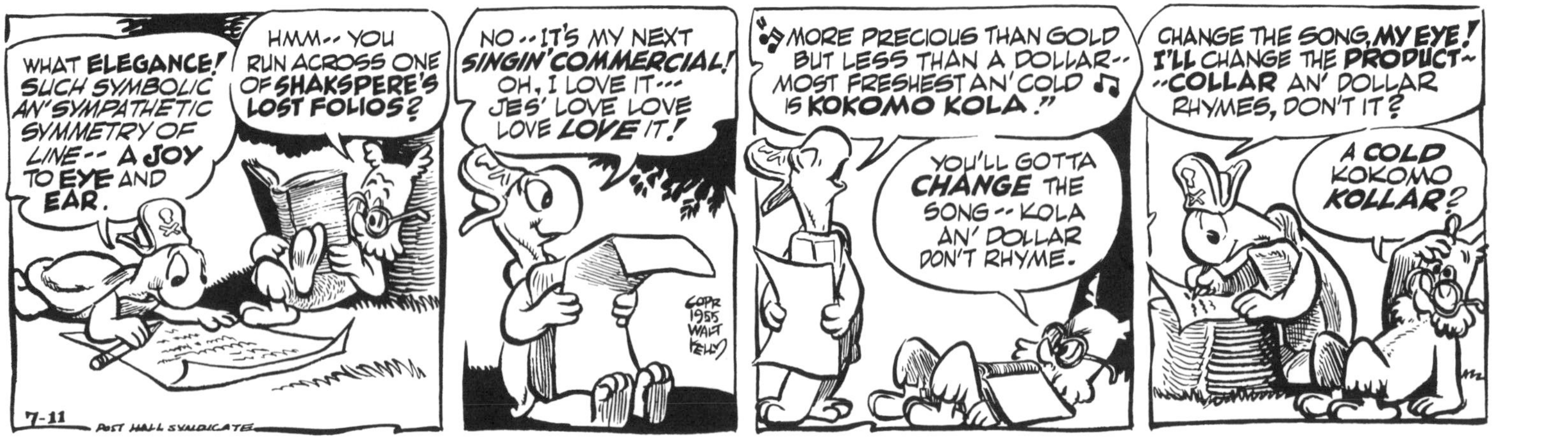
WHAT ELEGANCE! SUCH SYMBOLIC AN' SYMPATHETIC SYMMETRY OF LINE-- A JOY TO EYE AND EAR.
HMM-- YOU RUN ACROSS ONE OF SHAKSPERE'S LOST FOLIOS?
NO--IT'S MY NEXT SINGIN' COMMERCIAL! OH, I LOVE IT--- JES' LOVE LOVE LOVE LOVE IT!
♫ MORE PRECIOUS THAN GOLD BUT LESS THAN A DOLLAR-- MOST FRESHEST AN' COLD ♫ IS KOKOMO KOLA."
YOU'LL GOTTA CHANGE THE SONG--KOLA AN' DOLLAR DON'T RHYME.
CHANGE THE SONG, MY EYE! I'LL CHANGE THE PRODUCT-- --COLLAR AN' DOLLAR RHYMES, DON'T IT?
A COLD KOKOMO KOLLAR?
COPR 1955 WALT KELLY
7-11
POST HALL SYNDICATE

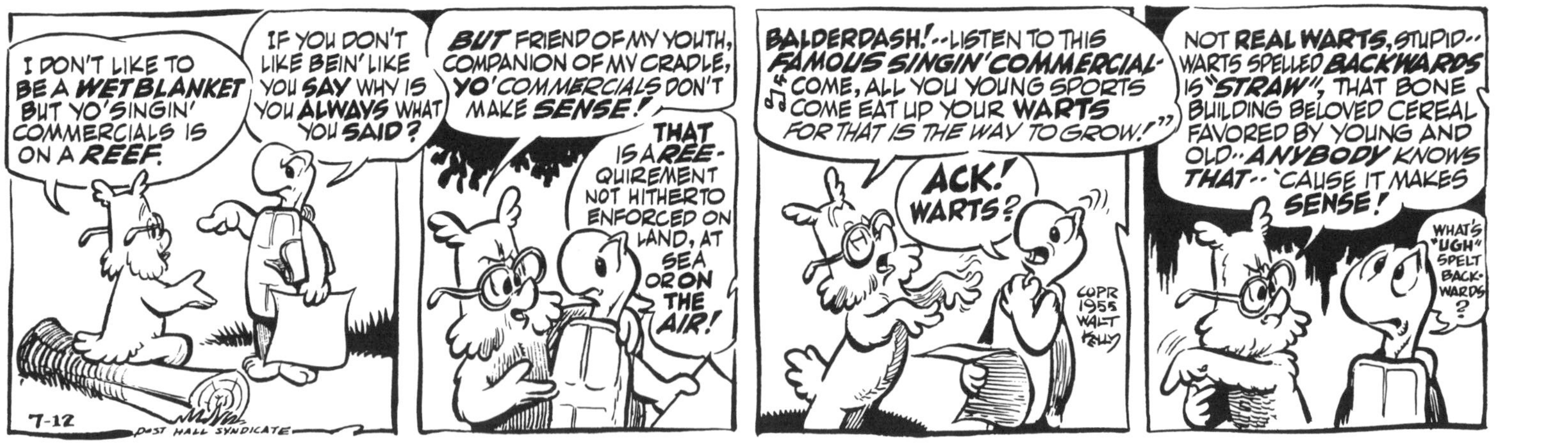
I DON'T LIKE TO BE A WET BLANKET BUT YO' SINGIN' COMMERCIALS IS ON A REEF.
IF YOU DON'T LIKE BEIN' LIKE YOU SAY WHY IS YOU ALWAYS WHAT YOU SAID?
BUT FRIEND OF MY YOUTH, COMPANION OF MY CRADLE, YO' COMMERCIALS DON'T MAKE SENSE!
THAT IS A REE-QUIREMENT NOT HITHERTO ENFORCED ON LAND, AT SEA OR ON THE AIR!
BALDERDASH!--LISTEN TO THIS FAMOUS SINGIN' COMMERCIAL- ♫ "COME, ALL YOU YOUNG SPORTS COME EAT UP YOUR WARTS FOR THAT IS THE WAY TO GROW!"
ACK! WARTS?
NOT REAL WARTS, STUPID-- WARTS SPELLED BACKWARDS IS "STRAW", THAT BONE BUILDING BELOVED CEREAL FAVORED BY YOUNG AND OLD--ANYBODY KNOWS THAT--'CAUSE IT MAKES SENSE!
WHAT'S "UGH" SPELT BACK-WARDS?
COPR 1955 WALT KELLY
7-12
POST HALL SYNDICATE

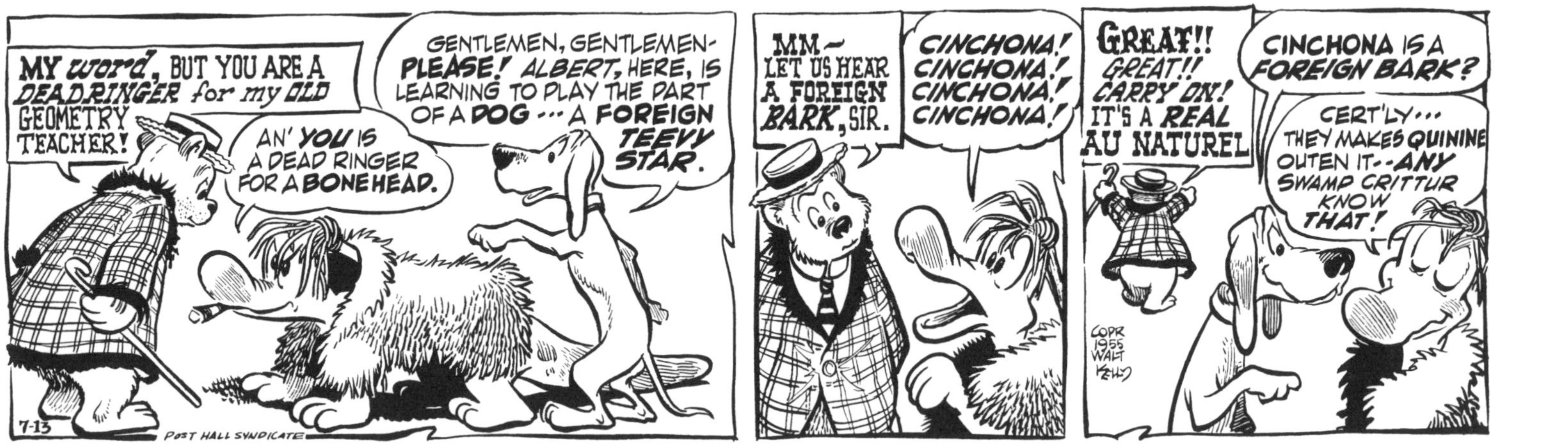
MY word, BUT YOU ARE A DEAD RINGER for my OLD GEOMETRY TEACHER!
AN' YOU IS A DEAD RINGER FOR A BONEHEAD.
GENTLEMEN, GENTLEMEN- PLEASE! ALBERT, HERE, IS LEARNING TO PLAY THE PART OF A DOG--- A FOREIGN TEEVY STAR.
MM-- LET US HEAR A FOREIGN BARK, SIR.
CINCHONA! CINCHONA! CINCHONA! CINCHONA!
GREAT!! GREAT!! CARRY ON! IT'S A REAL AU NATUREL
CINCHONA IS A FOREIGN BARK?
CERT'LY--- THEY MAKES QUININE OUTEN IT--ANY SWAMP CRITTUR KNOW THAT!
COPR 1955 WALT KELLY
7-13
POST HALL SYNDICATE

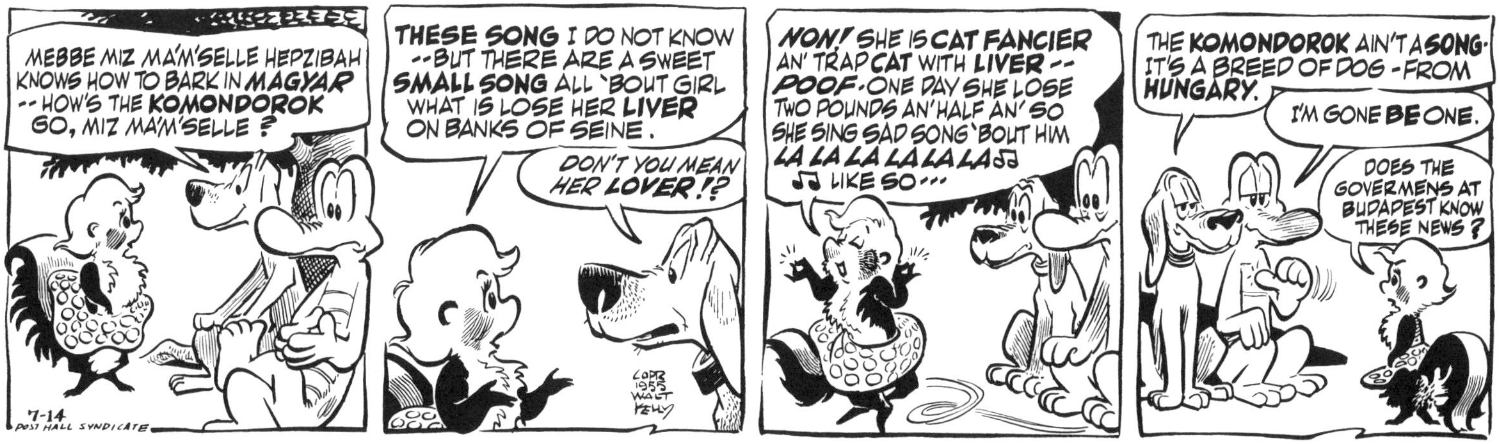
MEBBE MIZ MA'M'SELLE HEPZIBAH KNOWS HOW TO BARK IN MAGYAR -- HOW'S THE KOMONDOROK GO, MIZ MA'M'SELLE ?
THESE SONG I DO NOT KNOW --BUT THERE ARE A SWEET SMALL SONG ALL 'BOUT GIRL WHAT IS LOSE HER LIVER ON BANKS OF SEINE.
DON'T YOU MEAN HER LOVER!?
NON! SHE IS CAT FANCIER AN' TRAP CAT WITH LIVER -- POOF - ONE DAY SHE LOSE TWO POUNDS AN' HALF AN' SO SHE SING SAD SONG 'BOUT HIM LA LA LA LA LA LA ♫ LIKE SO...
THE KOMONDOROK AIN'T A SONG. IT'S A BREED OF DOG - FROM HUNGARY.
I'M GONE BE ONE.
DOES THE GOVERMENS AT BUDAPEST KNOW THESE NEWS ?
7-14
POST HALL SYNDICATE
COPR 1955 WALT KELLY

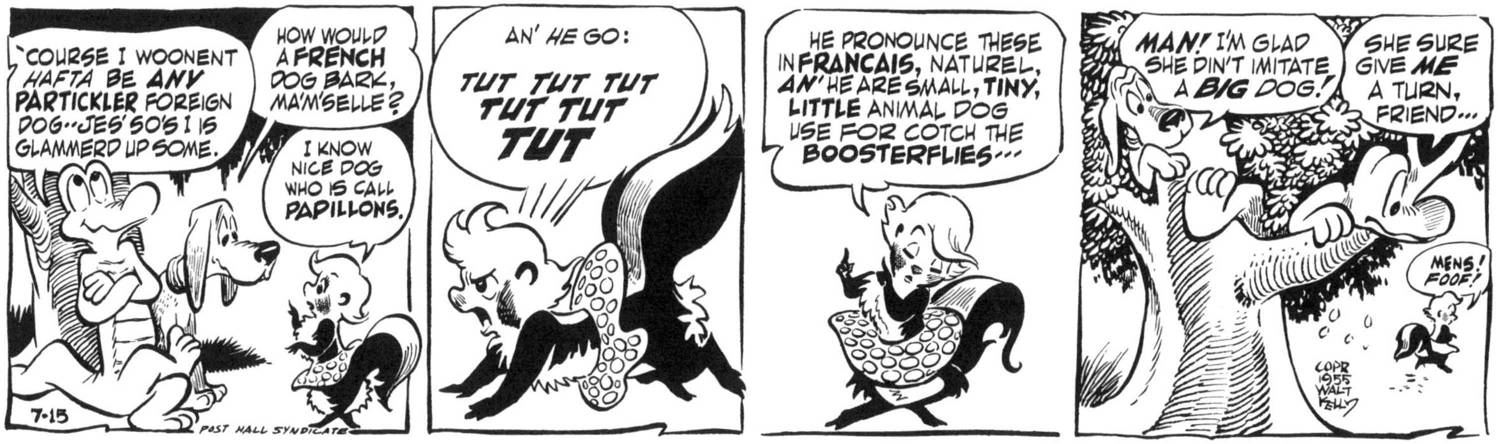
'COURSE I WOONENT HAFTA BE ANY PARTICKLER FOREIGN DOG -- JES' SO'S I IS GLAMMERD UP SOME.
HOW WOULD A FRENCH DOG BARK, MA'M'SELLE ?
I KNOW NICE DOG WHO IS CALL PAPILLONS.
AN' HE GO:
TUT TUT TUT TUT TUT TUT
HE PRONOUNCE THESE IN FRANCAIS, NATUREL, AN' HE ARE SMALL, TINY, LITTLE ANIMAL DOG USE FOR COTCH THE BOOSTERFLIES...
MAN! I'M GLAD SHE DIN'T IMITATE A BIG DOG!
SHE SURE GIVE ME A TURN, FRIEND...
MENS! FOOF!
7-15
POST HALL SYNDICATE
COPR 1955 WALT KELLY

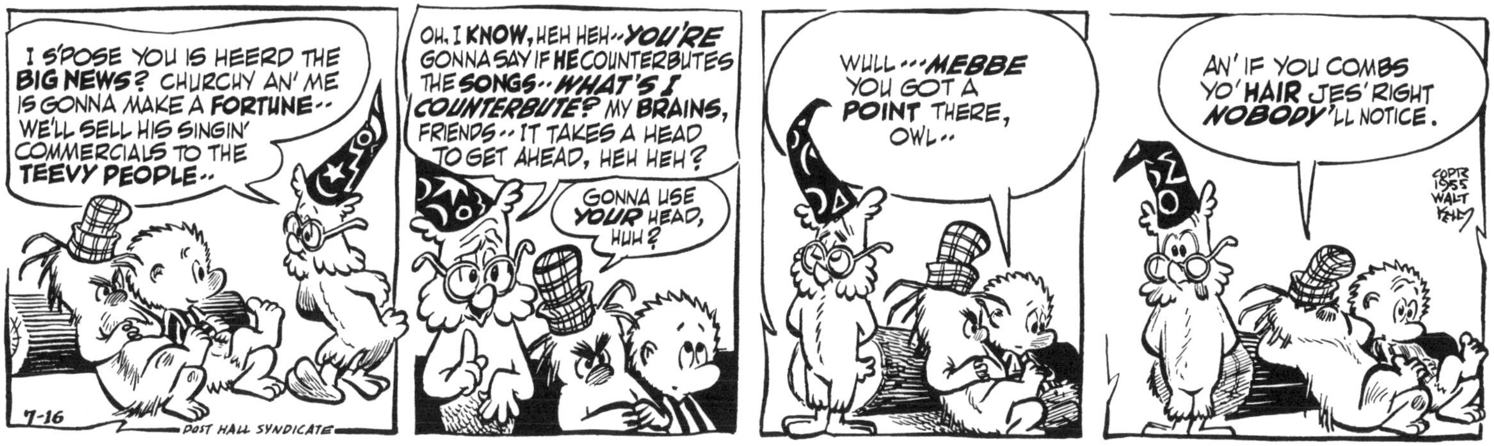
I S'POSE YOU IS HEERD THE BIG NEWS? CHURCHY AN' ME IS GONNA MAKE A FORTUNE -- WE'LL SELL HIS SINGIN' COMMERCIALS TO THE TEEVY PEOPLE..
OH, I KNOW, HEH HEH -- YOU'RE GONNA SAY IF HE COUNTERBUTES THE SONGS -- WHAT'S I COUNTERBUTE? MY BRAINS, FRIENDS -- IT TAKES A HEAD TO GET AHEAD, HEH HEH?
GONNA USE YOUR HEAD, HUH?
WULL ... MEBBE YOU GOT A POINT THERE, OWL..
AN' IF YOU COMBS YO' HAIR JES' RIGHT NOBODY'LL NOTICE.
7-16
POST HALL SYNDICATE
COPR 1955 WALT KELLY

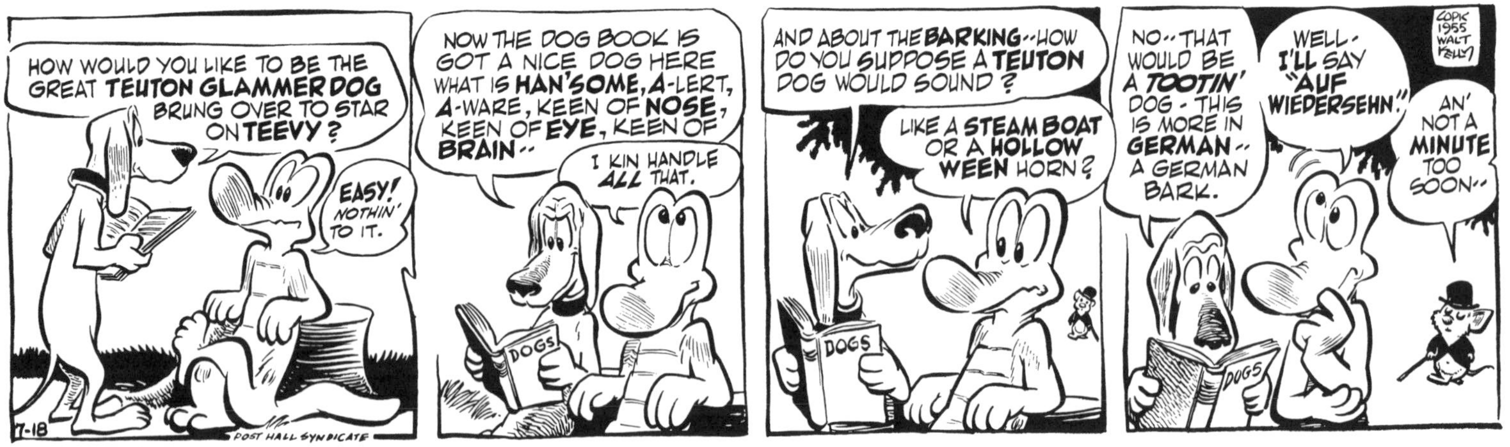
HOW WOULD YOU LIKE TO BE THE GREAT TEUTON GLAMMER DOG BRUNG OVER TO STAR ON TEEVY?
EASY! NOTHIN' TO IT.
7-18
POST HALL SYNDICATE
NOW THE DOG BOOK IS GOT A NICE DOG HERE WHAT IS HAN'SOME, A-LERT, A-WARE, KEEN OF NOSE, KEEN OF EYE, KEEN OF BRAIN--
I KIN HANDLE ALL THAT.
DOGS
AND ABOUT THE BARKING--HOW DO YOU SUPPOSE A TEUTON DOG WOULD SOUND?
LIKE A STEAM BOAT OR A HOLLOW WEEN HORN?
DOGS
NO--THAT WOULD BE A TOOTIN' DOG - THIS IS MORE IN GERMAN-- A GERMAN BARK.
WELL- I'LL SAY "AUF WIEDERSEHN."
AN' NOT A MINUTE TOO SOON--
DOGS
COPR 1955 WALT KELLY

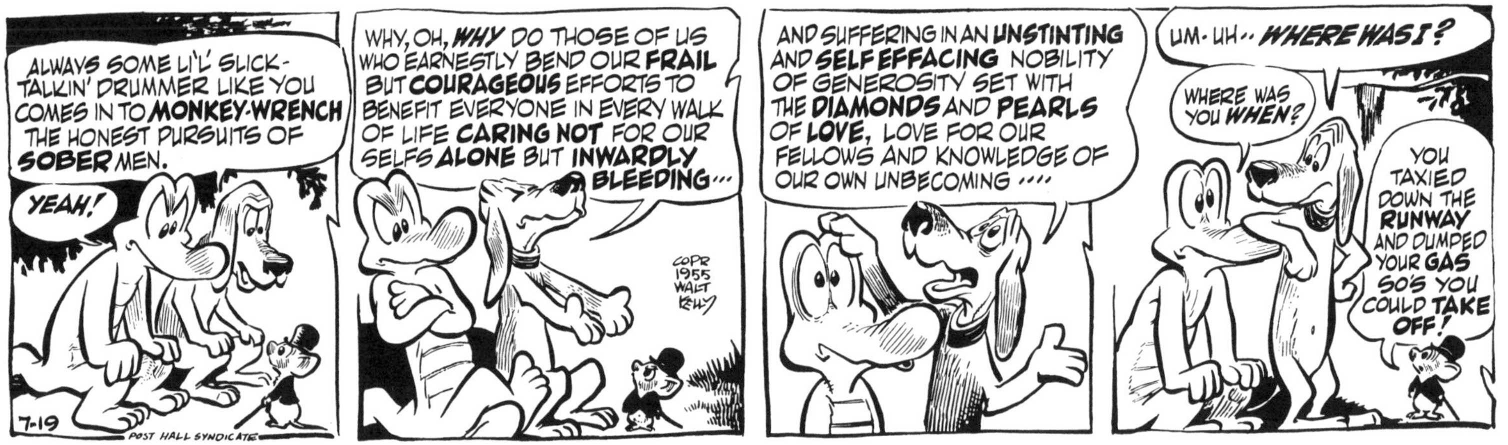
ALWAYS SOME LI'L' SLICK-TALKIN' DRUMMER LIKE YOU COMES IN TO MONKEY-WRENCH THE HONEST PURSUITS OF SOBER MEN.
YEAH!
7-19
POST HALL SYNDICATE
WHY, OH, WHY DO THOSE OF US WHO EARNESTLY BEND OUR FRAIL BUT COURAGEOUS EFFORTS TO BENEFIT EVERYONE IN EVERY WALK OF LIFE CARING NOT FOR OUR SELFS ALONE BUT INWARDLY BLEEDING...
COPR 1955 WALT KELLY
AND SUFFERING IN AN UNSTINTING AND SELF EFFACING NOBILITY OF GENEROSITY SET WITH THE DIAMONDS AND PEARLS OF LOVE, LOVE FOR OUR FELLOWS AND KNOWLEDGE OF OUR OWN UNBECOMING....
UM-UH-- WHERE WAS I?
WHERE WAS YOU WHEN?
YOU TAXIED DOWN THE RUNWAY AND DUMPED YOUR GAS SO'S YOU COULD TAKE OFF!

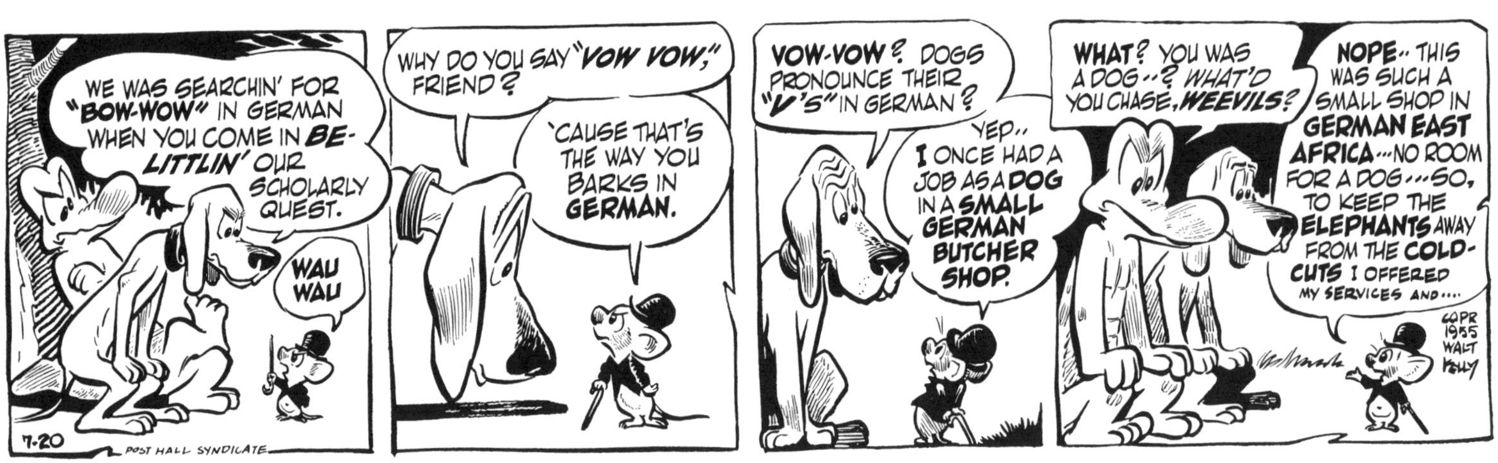
WE WAS SEARCHIN' FOR "BOW-WOW" IN GERMAN WHEN YOU COME IN BE-LITTLIN' OUR SCHOLARLY QUEST.
WAU WAU
7-20
POST HALL SYNDICATE
WHY DO YOU SAY "VOW VOW," FRIEND?
'CAUSE THAT'S THE WAY YOU BARKS IN GERMAN.
VOW-VOW? DOGS PRONOUNCE THEIR "V'S" IN GERMAN?
YEP.. I ONCE HAD A JOB AS A DOG IN A SMALL GERMAN BUTCHER SHOP.
WHAT? YOU WAS A DOG--? WHAT'D YOU CHASE, WEEVILS?
NOPE.. THIS WAS SUCH A SMALL SHOP IN GERMAN EAST AFRICA...NO ROOM FOR A DOG...SO, TO KEEP THE ELEPHANTS AWAY FROM THE COLD-CUTS I OFFERED MY SERVICES AND....
COPR 1955 WALT KELLY

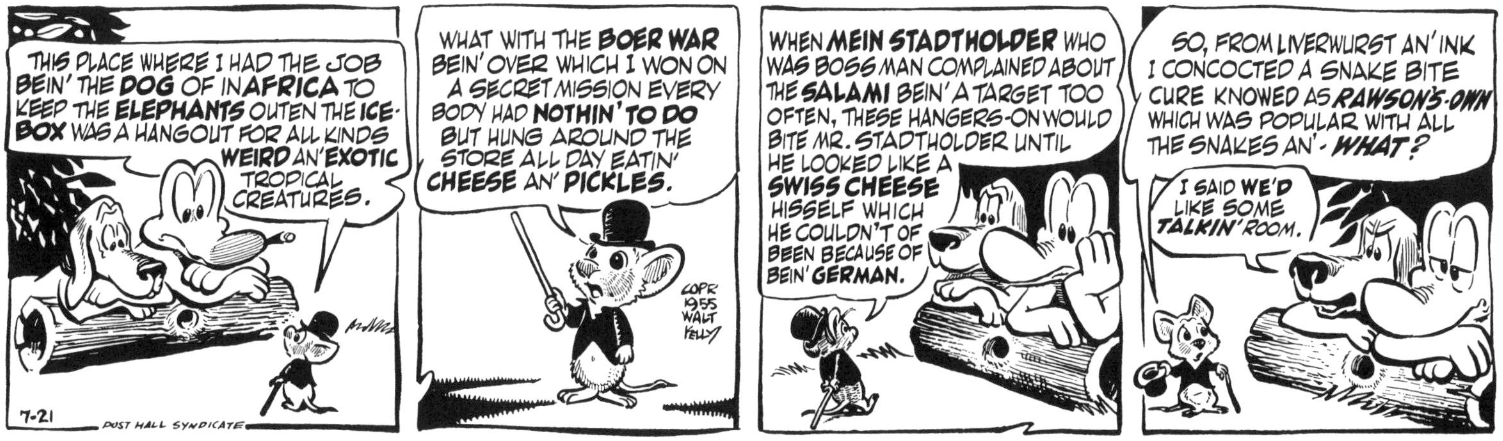
THIS PLACE WHERE I HAD THE JOB BEIN' THE DOG OF IN AFRICA TO KEEP THE ELEPHANTS OUTEN THE ICE-BOX WAS A HANGOUT FOR ALL KINDS WEIRD AN' EXOTIC TROPICAL CREATURES.
WHAT WITH THE BOER WAR BEIN' OVER WHICH I WON ON A SECRET MISSION EVERY BODY HAD NOTHIN' TO DO BUT HUNG AROUND THE STORE ALL DAY EATIN' CHEESE AN' PICKLES.
COPR 1955 WALT KELLY
WHEN MEIN STADTHOLDER WHO WAS BOSS MAN COMPLAINED ABOUT THE SALAMI BEIN' A TARGET TOO OFTEN, THESE HANGERS-ON WOULD BITE MR. STADTHOLDER UNTIL HE LOOKED LIKE A SWISS CHEESE HISSELF WHICH HE COULDN'T OF BEEN BECAUSE OF BEIN' GERMAN.
SO, FROM LIVERWURST AN' INK I CONCOCTED A SNAKE BITE CURE KNOWED AS RAWSON'S-OWN WHICH WAS POPULAR WITH ALL THE SNAKES AN' - WHAT?
I SAID WE'D LIKE SOME TALKIN' ROOM.
7-21
POST HALL SYNDICATE

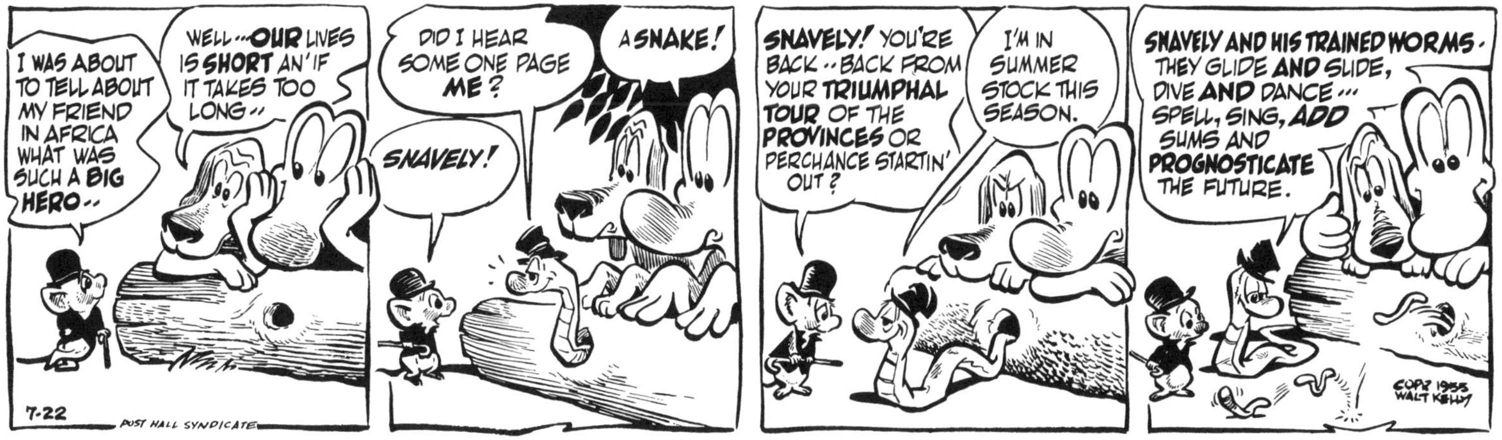
I WAS ABOUT TO TELL ABOUT MY FRIEND IN AFRICA WHAT WAS SUCH A BIG HERO..
WELL... OUR LIVES IS SHORT AN' IF IT TAKES TOO LONG..
DID I HEAR SOME ONE PAGE ME?
A SNAKE!
SNAVELY!
SNAVELY! YOU'RE BACK.. BACK FROM YOUR TRIUMPHAL TOUR OF THE PROVINCES OR PERCHANCE STARTIN' OUT?
I'M IN SUMMER STOCK THIS SEASON.
SNAVELY AND HIS TRAINED WORMS. THEY GLIDE AND SLIDE, DIVE AND DANCE... SPELL, SING, ADD SUMS AND PROGNOSTICATE THE FUTURE.
COPR 1955 WALT KELLY
7-22
POST HALL SYNDICATE

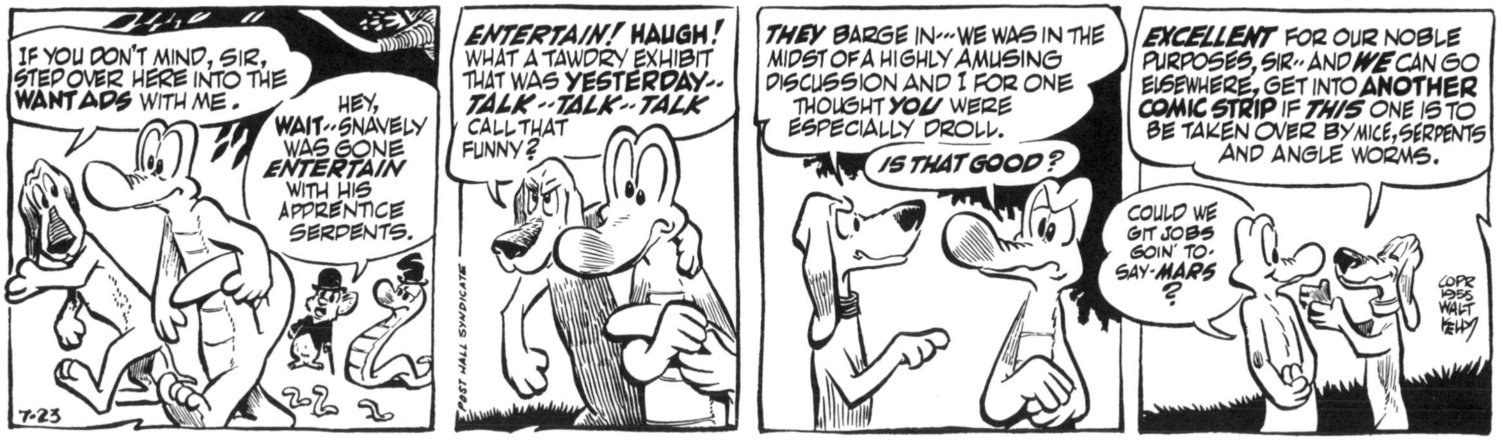
IF YOU DON'T MIND, SIR, STEP OVER HERE INTO THE WANT ADS WITH ME.
HEY, WAIT.. SNAVELY WAS GONE ENTERTAIN WITH HIS APPRENTICE SERPENTS.
ENTERTAIN! HAUGH! WHAT A TAWDRY EXHIBIT THAT WAS YESTERDAY.. TALK.. TALK.. TALK CALL THAT FUNNY?
THEY BARGE IN... WE WAS IN THE MIDST OF A HIGHLY AMUSING DISCUSSION AND I FOR ONE THOUGHT YOU WERE ESPECIALLY DROLL.
IS THAT GOOD?
EXCELLENT FOR OUR NOBLE PURPOSES, SIR.. AND WE CAN GO ELSEWHERE, GET INTO ANOTHER COMIC STRIP IF THIS ONE IS TO BE TAKEN OVER BY MICE, SERPENTS AND ANGLE WORMS.
COULD WE GIT JOBS GOIN' TO- SAY- MARS?
COPR 1955 WALT KELLY
7-23
POST HALL SYNDICATE

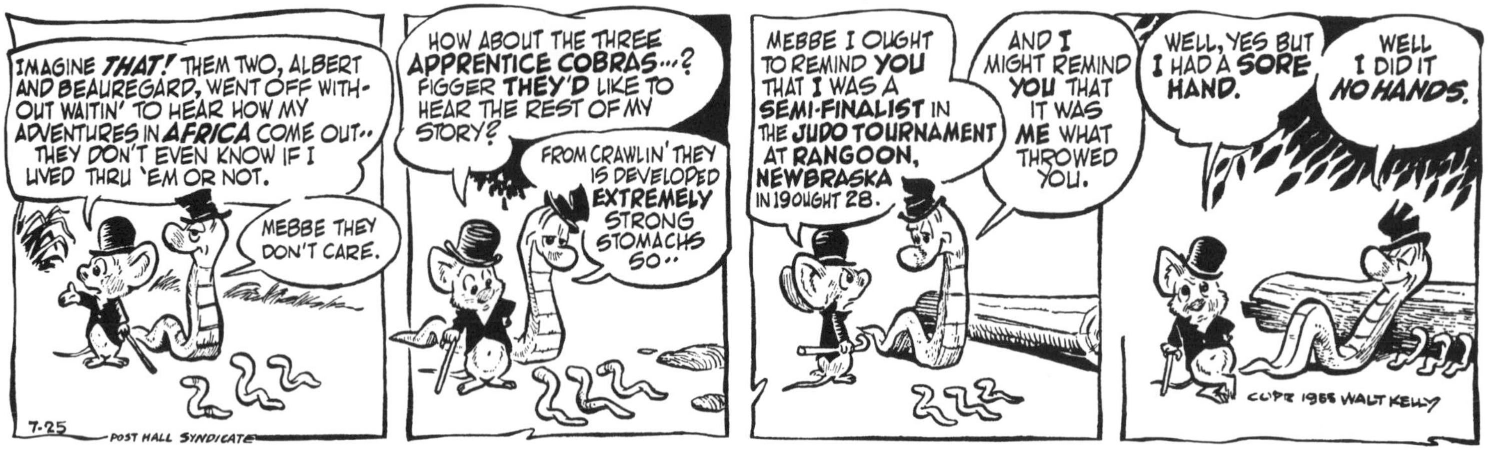
IMAGINE THAT! THEM TWO, ALBERT AND BEAUREGARD, WENT OFF WITH-OUT WAITIN' TO HEAR HOW MY ADVENTURES IN AFRICA COME OUT.. THEY DON'T EVEN KNOW IF I LIVED THRU 'EM OR NOT.
MEBBE THEY DON'T CARE.
7-25
POST HALL SYNDICATE
HOW ABOUT THE THREE APPRENTICE COBRAS...? FIGGER THEY'D LIKE TO HEAR THE REST OF MY STORY?
FROM CRAWLIN' THEY IS DEVELOPED EXTREMELY STRONG STOMACHS SO..
MEBBE I OUGHT TO REMIND YOU THAT I WAS A SEMI-FINALIST IN THE JUDO TOURNAMENT AT RANGOON, NEWBRASKA IN 19 OUGHT 28.
AND I MIGHT REMIND YOU THAT IT WAS ME WHAT THROWED YOU.
WELL, YES BUT I HAD A SORE HAND.
WELL I DID IT NO HANDS.
COPR 1955 WALT KELLY

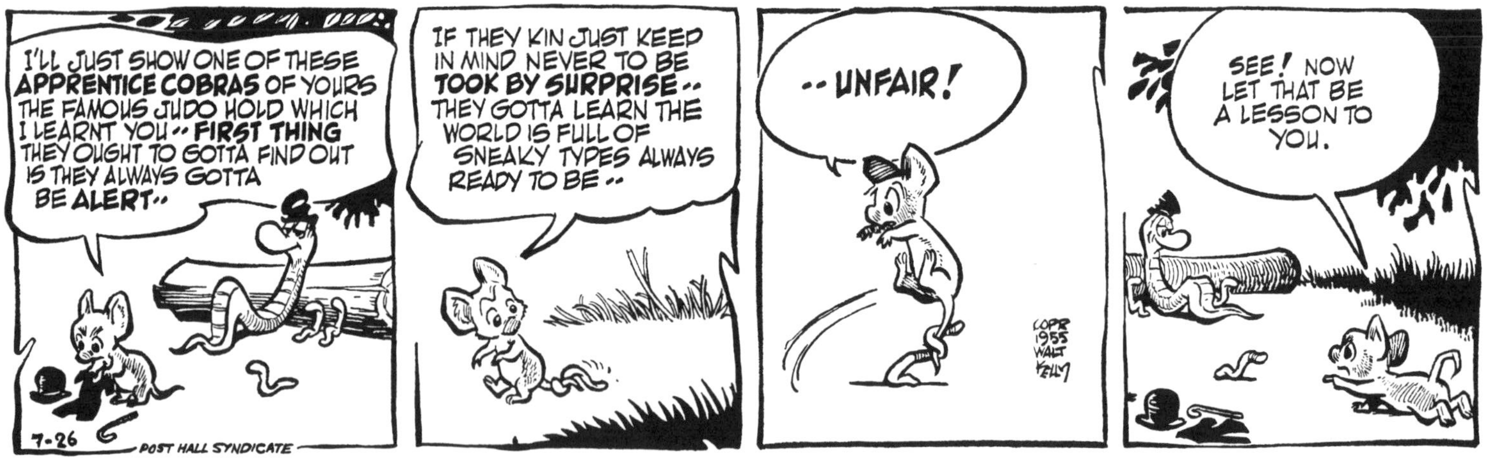
I'LL JUST SHOW ONE OF THESE APPRENTICE COBRAS OF YOURS THE FAMOUS JUDO HOLD WHICH I LEARNT YOU.. FIRST THING THEY OUGHT TO GOTTA FIND OUT IS THEY ALWAYS GOTTA BE ALERT..
7-26
POST HALL SYNDICATE
IF THEY KIN JUST KEEP IN MIND NEVER TO BE TOOK BY SURPRISE.. THEY GOTTA LEARN THE WORLD IS FULL OF SNEAKY TYPES ALWAYS READY TO BE..
..UNFAIR!
COPR 1955 WALT KELLY
SEE! NOW LET THAT BE A LESSON TO YOU.

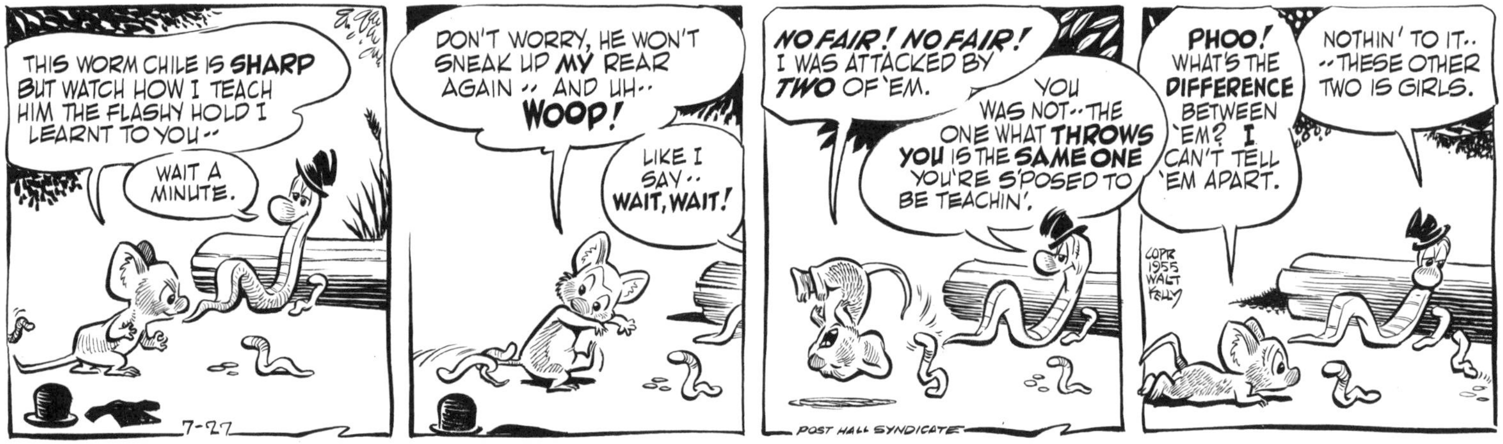
THIS WORM CHILE IS SHARP BUT WATCH HOW I TEACH HIM THE FLASHY HOLD I LEARNT TO YOU..
WAIT A MINUTE.
7-27
DON'T WORRY, HE WON'T SNEAK UP MY REAR AGAIN.. AND UH.. WOOP!
LIKE I SAY.. WAIT, WAIT!
NO FAIR! NO FAIR! I WAS ATTACKED BY TWO OF 'EM.
YOU WAS NOT.. THE ONE WHAT THROWS YOU IS THE SAME ONE YOU'RE S'POSED TO BE TEACHIN'.
POST HALL SYNDICATE
PHOO! WHAT'S THE DIFFERENCE BETWEEN 'EM? I CAN'T TELL 'EM APART.
NOTHIN' TO IT.. ..THESE OTHER TWO IS GIRLS.
COPR 1955 WALT KELLY

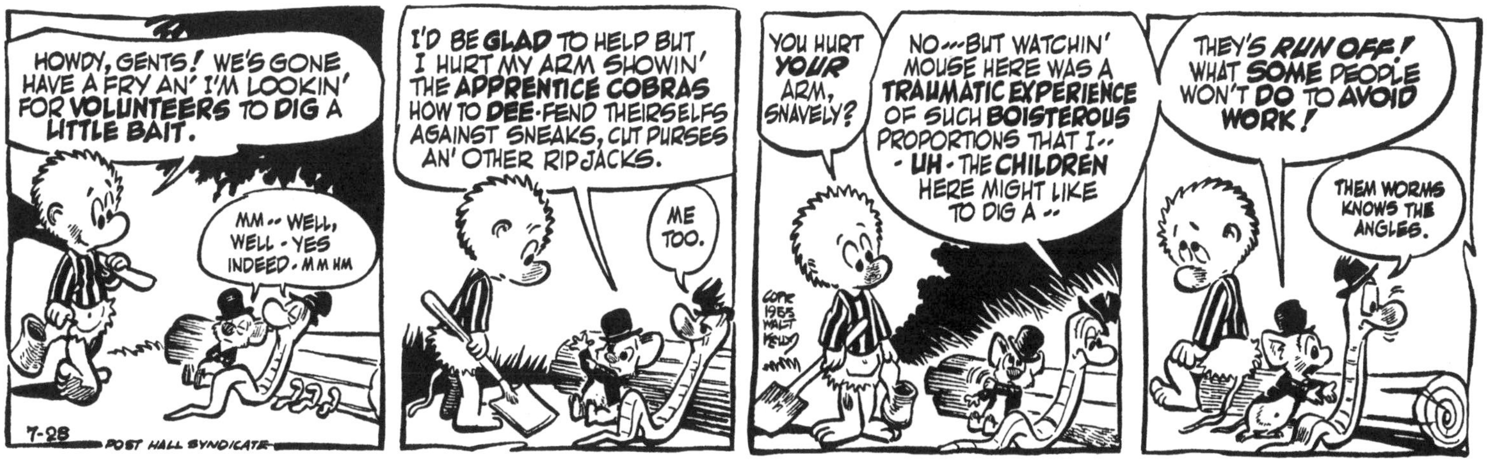
HOWDY, GENTS! WE'S GONE HAVE A FRY AN' I'M LOOKIN' FOR VOLUNTEERS TO DIG A LITTLE BAIT.
MM.. WELL, WELL - YES INDEED - MM HM
7-28 POST HALL SYNDICATE
I'D BE GLAD TO HELP BUT I HURT MY ARM SHOWIN' THE APPRENTICE COBRAS HOW TO DEE-FEND THEIRSELFS AGAINST SNEAKS, CUT PURSES AN' OTHER RIPJACKS.
ME TOO.
YOU HURT YOUR ARM, SNAVELY?
NO---BUT WATCHIN' MOUSE HERE WAS A TRAUMATIC EXPERIENCE OF SUCH BOISTEROUS PROPORTIONS THAT I.. - UH - THE CHILDREN HERE MIGHT LIKE TO DIG A --
COPR 1955 WALT KELLY
THEY'S RUN OFF! WHAT SOME PEOPLE WON'T DO TO AVOID WORK!
THEM WORMS KNOWS THE ANGLES.

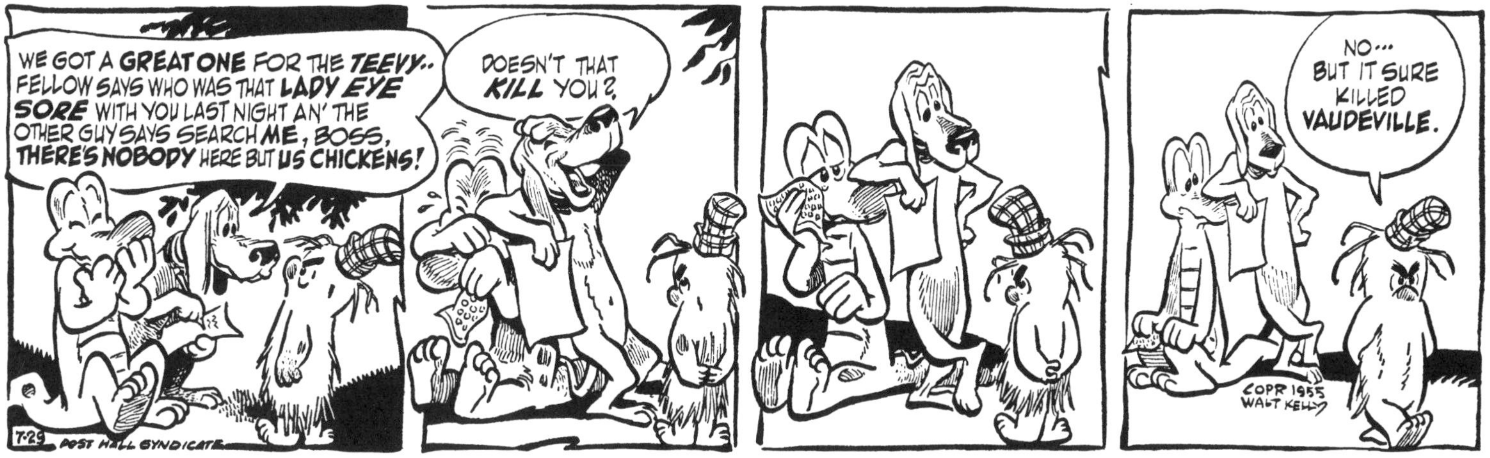
WE GOT A GREAT ONE FOR THE TEEVY.. FELLOW SAYS WHO WAS THAT LADY EYE SORE WITH YOU LAST NIGHT AN' THE OTHER GUY SAYS SEARCH ME, BOSS, THERE'S NOBODY HERE BUT US CHICKENS!
7-29 POST HALL SYNDICATE
DOESN'T THAT KILL YOU?
NO... BUT IT SURE KILLED VAUDEVILLE.
COPR 1955 WALT KELLY

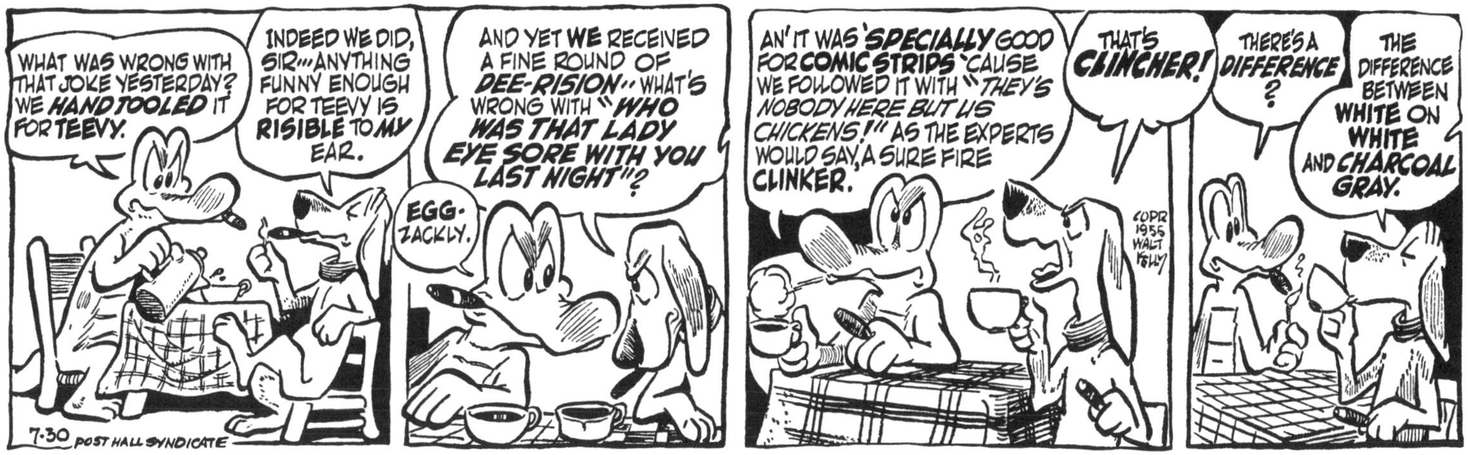
WHAT WAS WRONG WITH THAT JOKE YESTERDAY? WE HAND TOOLED IT FOR TEEVY.
INDEED WE DID, SIR... ANYTHING FUNNY ENOUGH FOR TEEVY IS RISIBLE TO MY EAR.
7-30 POST HALL SYNDICATE
AND YET WE RECEIVED A FINE ROUND OF DEE-RISION.. WHAT'S WRONG WITH "WHO WAS THAT LADY EYE SORE WITH YOU LAST NIGHT"?
EGG-ZACKLY.
AN' IT WAS 'SPECIALLY GOOD FOR COMIC STRIPS 'CAUSE WE FOLLOWED IT WITH "THEY'S NOBODY HERE BUT US CHICKENS!" AS THE EXPERTS WOULD SAY, A SURE FIRE CLINKER.
THAT'S CLINCHER!
COPR 1955 WALT KELLY
THERE'S A DIFFERENCE?
THE DIFFERENCE BETWEEN WHITE ON WHITE AND CHARCOAL GRAY.

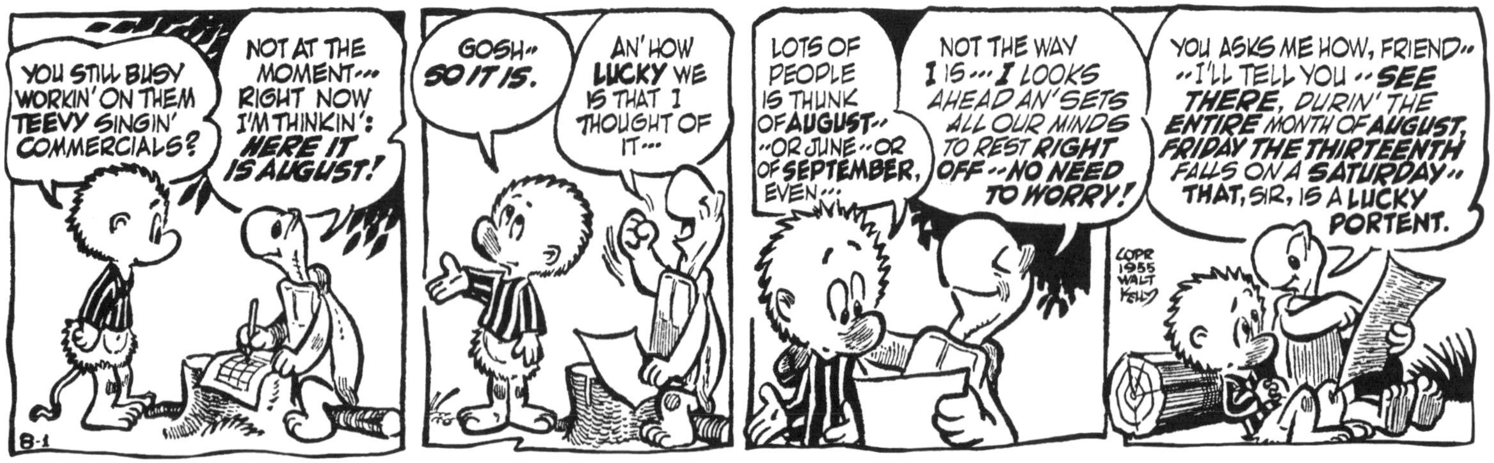
YOU STILL BUSY WORKIN' ON THEM TEEVY SINGIN' COMMERCIALS?
NOT AT THE MOMENT... RIGHT NOW I'M THINKIN': HERE IT IS AUGUST!
GOSH.. SO IT IS.
AN' HOW LUCKY WE IS THAT I THOUGHT OF IT...
LOTS OF PEOPLE IS THUNK OF AUGUST.. ..OR JUNE..OR OF SEPTEMBER, EVEN...
NOT THE WAY I IS... I LOOKS AHEAD AN' SETS ALL OUR MINDS TO REST RIGHT OFF.. NO NEED TO WORRY!
YOU ASKS ME HOW, FRIEND.. ..I'LL TELL YOU.. SEE THERE, DURIN' THE ENTIRE MONTH OF AUGUST, FRIDAY THE THIRTEENTH FALLS ON A SATURDAY.. THAT, SIR, IS A LUCKY PORTENT.
COPR 1955 WALT KELLY
8-1

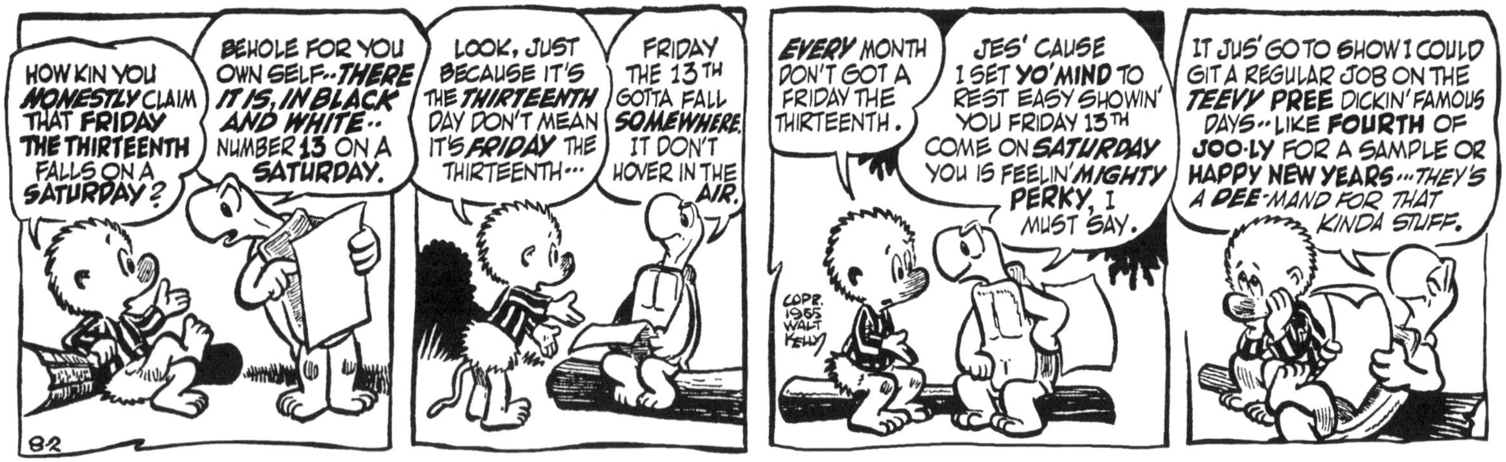
HOW KIN YOU HONESTLY CLAIM THAT FRIDAY THE THIRTEENTH FALLS ON A SATURDAY?
BEHOLE FOR YOU OWN SELF.. THERE IT IS, IN BLACK AND WHITE.. NUMBER 13 ON A SATURDAY.
LOOK, JUST BECAUSE IT'S THE THIRTEENTH DAY DON'T MEAN IT'S FRIDAY THE THIRTEENTH...
FRIDAY THE 13TH GOTTA FALL SOMEWHERE. IT DON'T HOVER IN THE AIR.
EVERY MONTH DON'T GOT A FRIDAY THE THIRTEENTH.
JES' CAUSE I SET YO' MIND TO REST EASY SHOWIN' YOU FRIDAY 13TH COME ON SATURDAY YOU IS FEELIN' MIGHTY PERKY, I MUST SAY.
IT JUS' GO TO SHOW I COULD GIT A REGULAR JOB ON THE TEEVY PREE DICKIN' FAMOUS DAYS.. LIKE FOURTH OF JOO-LY FOR A SAMPLE OR HAPPY NEW YEARS... THEY'S A DEE-MAND FOR THAT KINDA STUFF.
COPR 1955 WALT KELLY
8-2

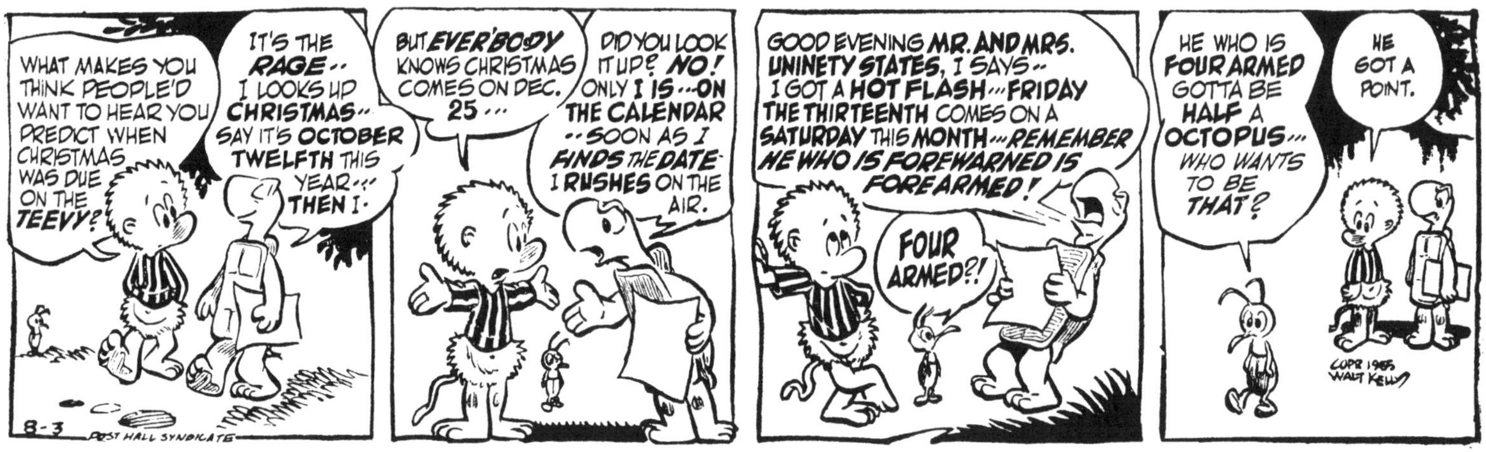
WHAT MAKES YOU THINK PEOPLE'D WANT TO HEAR YOU PREDICT WHEN CHRISTMAS WAS DUE ON THE TEEVY?
IT'S THE RAGE.. I LOOKS UP CHRISTMAS.. SAY IT'S OCTOBER TWELFTH THIS YEAR... THEN I..
BUT EVER'BODY KNOWS CHRISTMAS COMES ON DEC. 25...
DID YOU LOOK IT UP? NO! ONLY I IS... ON THE CALENDAR.. SOON AS I FINDS THE DATE I RUSHES ON THE AIR.
GOOD EVENING MR. AND MRS. UNINETY STATES, I SAYS.. I GOT A HOT FLASH... FRIDAY THE THIRTEENTH COMES ON A SATURDAY THIS MONTH... REMEMBER HE WHO IS FOREWARNED IS FOREARMED!
FOUR ARMED?!
HE WHO IS FOUR ARMED GOTTA BE HALF A OCTOPUS... WHO WANTS TO BE THAT?
HE GOT A POINT.
COPR 1955 WALT KELLY
8-3
POST HALL SYNDICATE

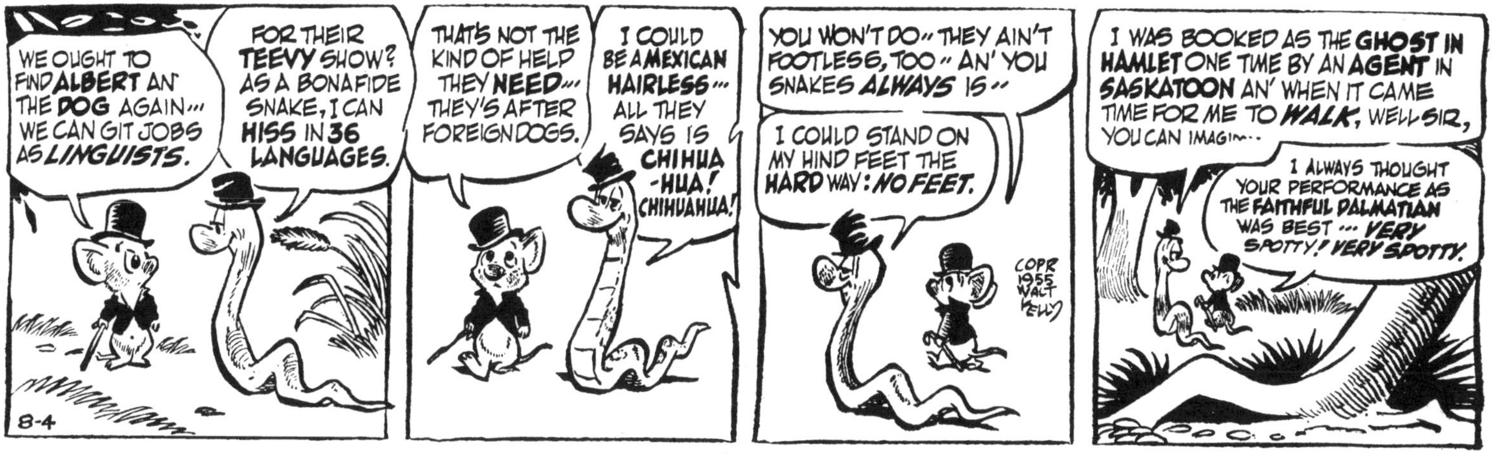
WE OUGHT TO FIND ALBERT AN' THE DOG AGAIN... WE CAN GIT JOBS AS LINGUISTS.
FOR THEIR TEEVY SHOW? AS A BONAFIDE SNAKE, I CAN HISS IN 36 LANGUAGES.
THAT'S NOT THE KIND OF HELP THEY NEED... THEY'S AFTER FOREIGN DOGS.
I COULD BE A MEXICAN HAIRLESS... ALL THEY SAYS IS CHIHUA-HUA! CHIHUAHUA!
YOU WON'T DO.. THEY AIN'T FOOTLESS, TOO.. AN' YOU SNAKES ALWAYS IS..
I COULD STAND ON MY HIND FEET THE HARD WAY: NO FEET.
COPR 1955 WALT KELLY
I WAS BOOKED AS THE GHOST IN HAMLET ONE TIME BY AN AGENT IN SASKATOON AN' WHEN IT CAME TIME FOR ME TO WALK, WELL SIR, YOU CAN IMAGIN...
I ALWAYS THOUGHT YOUR PERFORMANCE AS THE FAITHFUL DALMATIAN WAS BEST... VERY SPOTTY! VERY SPOTTY.
8-4

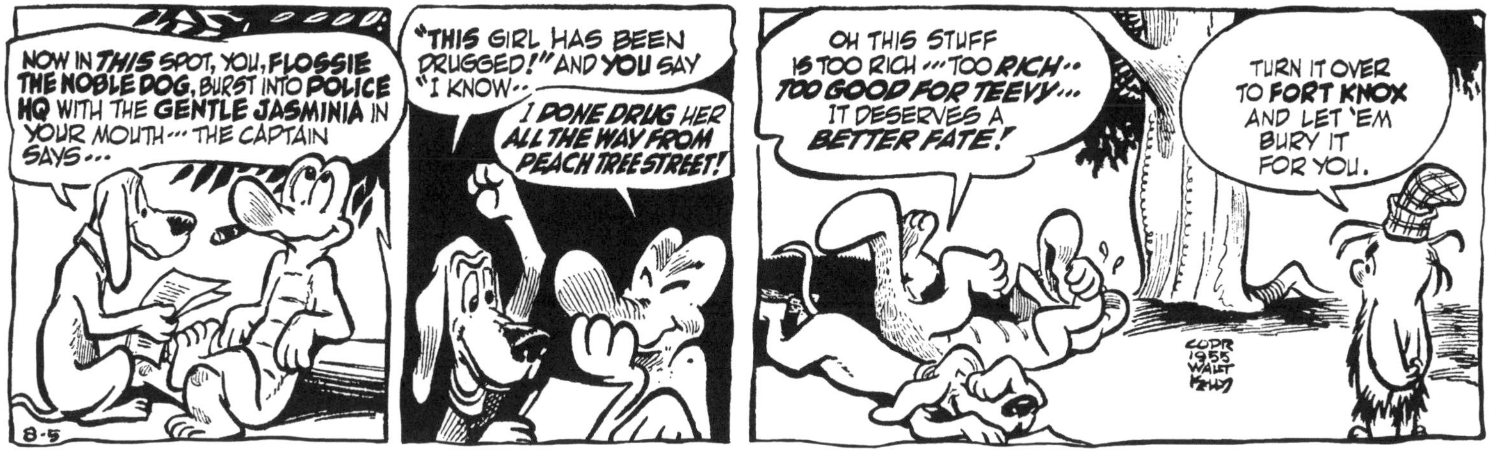
NOW IN THIS SPOT, YOU, FLOSSIE THE NOBLE DOG, BURST INTO POLICE HQ WITH THE GENTLE JASMINIA IN YOUR MOUTH... THE CAPTAIN SAYS...
"THIS GIRL HAS BEEN DRUGGED!" AND YOU SAY "I KNOW..
I DONE DRUG HER ALL THE WAY FROM PEACH TREE STREET!
OH THIS STUFF IS TOO RICH... TOO RICH.. TOO GOOD FOR TEEVY... IT DESERVES A BETTER FATE!
TURN IT OVER TO FORT KNOX AND LET 'EM BURY IT FOR YOU.
COPR 1955 WALT KELLY
8-5

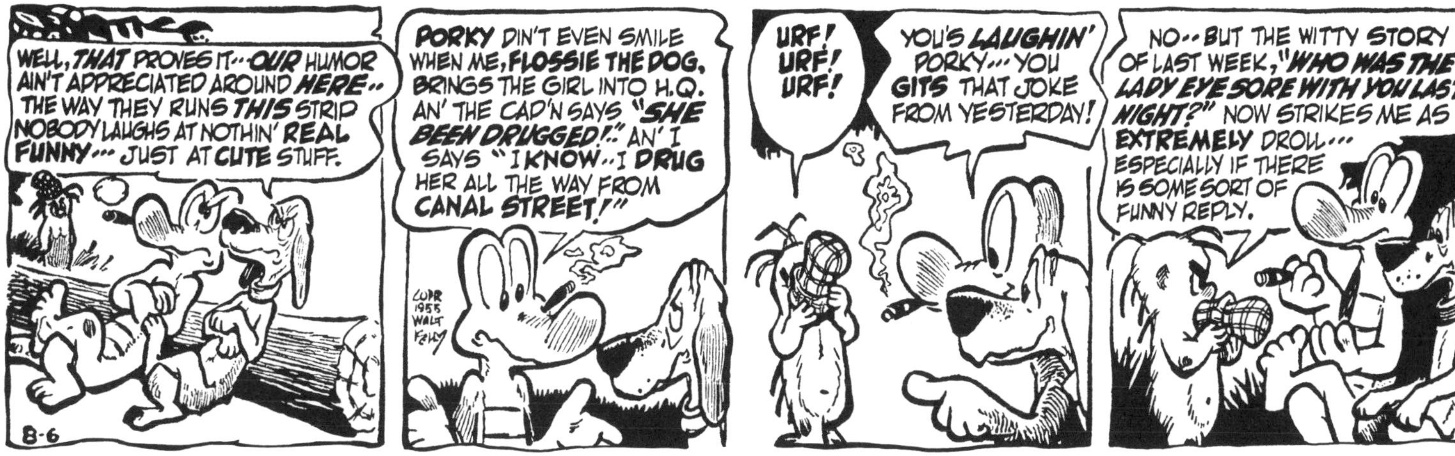
WELL, THAT PROVES IT.. OUR HUMOR AIN'T APPRECIATED AROUND HERE.. THE WAY THEY RUNS THIS STRIP NOBODY LAUGHS AT NOTHIN' REAL FUNNY... JUST AT CUTE STUFF.
PORKY DIN'T EVEN SMILE WHEN ME, FLOSSIE THE DOG, BRINGS THE GIRL INTO H.Q. AN' THE CAP'N SAYS "SHE BEEN DRUGGED!" AN' I SAYS "I KNOW.. I DRUG HER ALL THE WAY FROM CANAL STREET!"
COPR 1955 WALT KELLY
URF! URF! URF!
YOU'S LAUGHIN' PORKY... YOU GITS THAT JOKE FROM YESTERDAY!
NO.. BUT THE WITTY STORY OF LAST WEEK, "WHO WAS THE LADY EYE SORE WITH YOU LAST NIGHT?" NOW STRIKES ME AS EXTREMELY DROLL... ESPECIALLY IF THERE IS SOME SORT OF FUNNY REPLY.
8-6

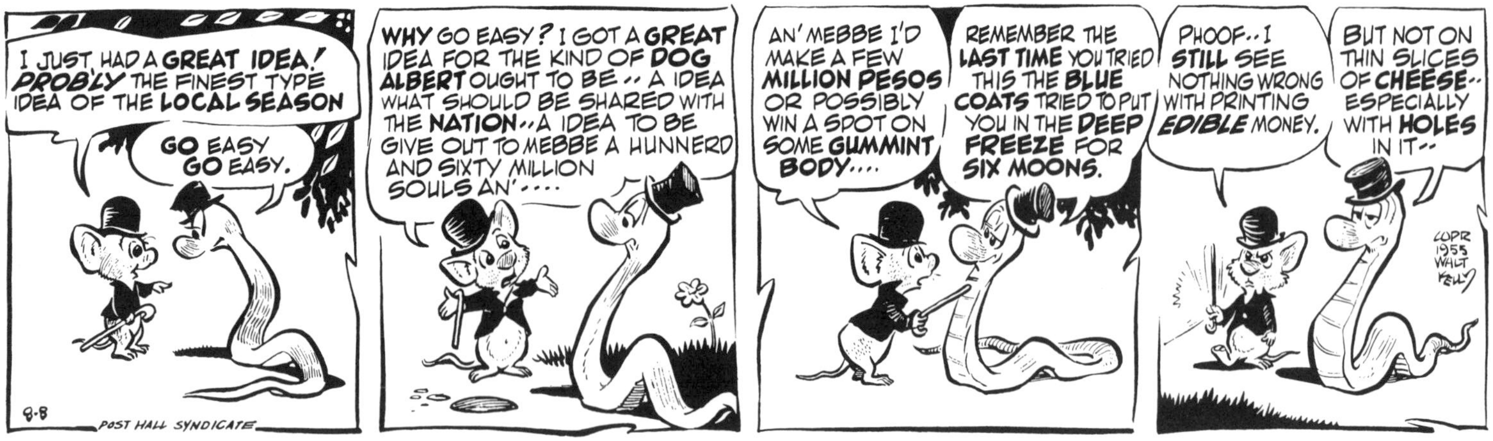
I JUST HAD A GREAT IDEA! PROB'LY THE FINEST TYPE IDEA OF THE LOCAL SEASON
GO EASY GO EASY.
WHY GO EASY? I GOT A GREAT IDEA FOR THE KIND OF DOG ALBERT OUGHT TO BE -- A IDEA WHAT SHOULD BE SHARED WITH THE NATION -- A IDEA TO BE GIVE OUT TO MEBBE A HUNNERD AND SIXTY MILLION SOULS AN'....
AN' MEBBE I'D MAKE A FEW MILLION PESOS OR POSSIBLY WIN A SPOT ON SOME GUMMINT BODY....
REMEMBER THE LAST TIME YOU TRIED THIS THE BLUE COATS TRIED TO PUT YOU IN THE DEEP FREEZE FOR SIX MOONS.
PHOOF -- I STILL SEE NOTHING WRONG WITH PRINTING EDIBLE MONEY.
BUT NOT ON THIN SLICES OF CHEESE -- ESPECIALLY WITH HOLES IN IT --
COPR 1955 WALT KELLY
8-8
POST HALL SYNDICATE

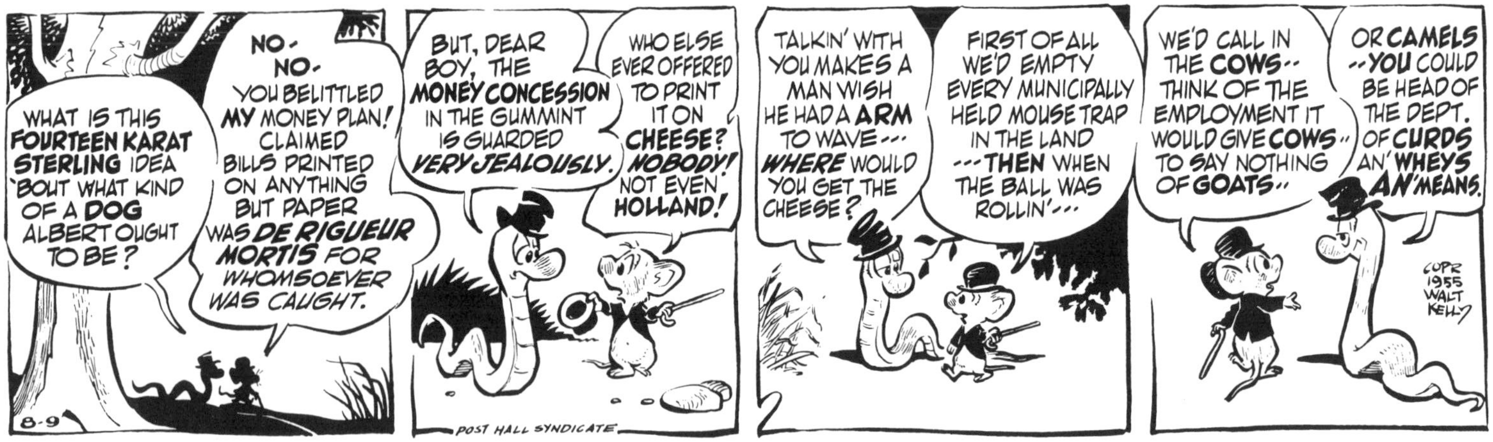
WHAT IS THIS FOURTEEN KARAT STERLING IDEA 'BOUT WHAT KIND OF A DOG ALBERT OUGHT TO BE?
NO-NO-YOU BELITTLED MY MONEY PLAN! CLAIMED BILLS PRINTED ON ANYTHING BUT PAPER WAS DE RIGUEUR MORTIS FOR WHOMSOEVER WAS CAUGHT.
BUT, DEAR BOY, THE MONEY CONCESSION IN THE GUMMINT IS GUARDED VERY JEALOUSLY.
WHO ELSE EVER OFFERED TO PRINT IT ON CHEESE? NOBODY! NOT EVEN HOLLAND!
TALKIN' WITH YOU MAKES A MAN WISH HE HAD A ARM TO WAVE--- WHERE WOULD YOU GET THE CHEESE?
FIRST OF ALL WE'D EMPTY EVERY MUNICIPALLY HELD MOUSE TRAP IN THE LAND ---THEN WHEN THE BALL WAS ROLLIN'---
WE'D CALL IN THE COWS -- THINK OF THE EMPLOYMENT IT WOULD GIVE COWS -- TO SAY NOTHING OF GOATS --
OR CAMELS -- YOU COULD BE HEAD OF THE DEPT. OF CURDS AN' WHEYS AN' MEANS.
COPR 1955 WALT KELLY
8-9
POST HALL SYNDICATE

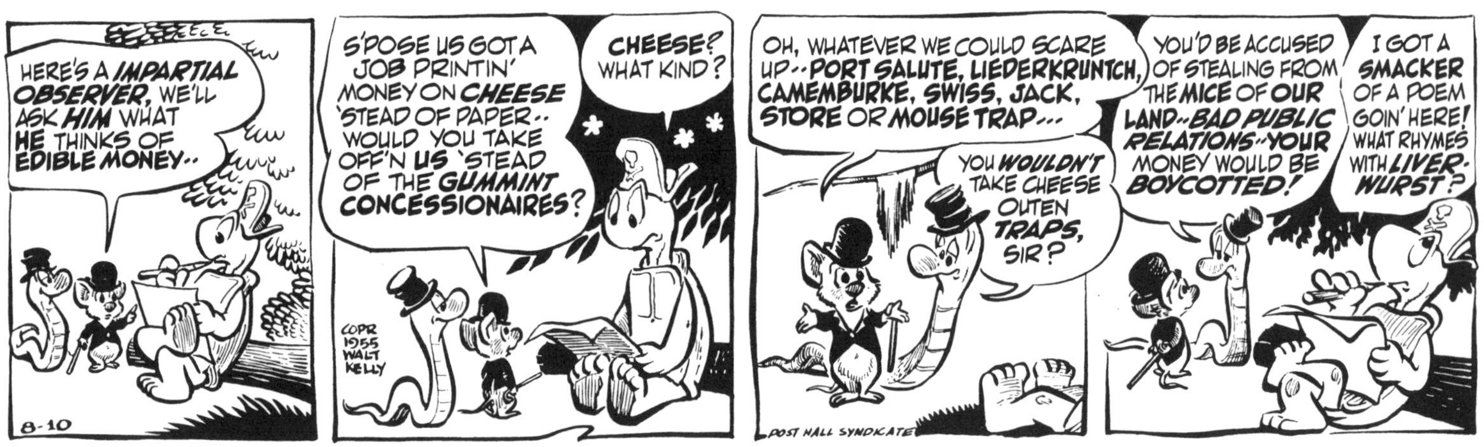
HERE'S A IMPARTIAL OBSERVER, WE'LL ASK HIM WHAT HE THINKS OF EDIBLE MONEY --
S'POSE US GOT A JOB PRINTIN' MONEY ON CHEESE 'STEAD OF PAPER -- WOULD YOU TAKE OFF'N US 'STEAD OF THE GUMMINT CONCESSIONAIRES?
CHEESE? WHAT KIND?
COPR 1955 WALT KELLY
OH, WHATEVER WE COULD SCARE UP -- PORT SALUTE, LIEDERKRUNTCH, CAMEMBURKE, SWISS, JACK, STORE OR MOUSE TRAP...
YOU WOULDN'T TAKE CHEESE OUTEN TRAPS, SIR?
YOU'D BE ACCUSED OF STEALING FROM THE MICE OF OUR LAND -- BAD PUBLIC RELATIONS -- YOUR MONEY WOULD BE BOYCOTTED!
I GOT A SMACKER OF A POEM GOIN' HERE! WHAT RHYMES WITH LIVER-WURST?
8-10
POST HALL SYNDICATE

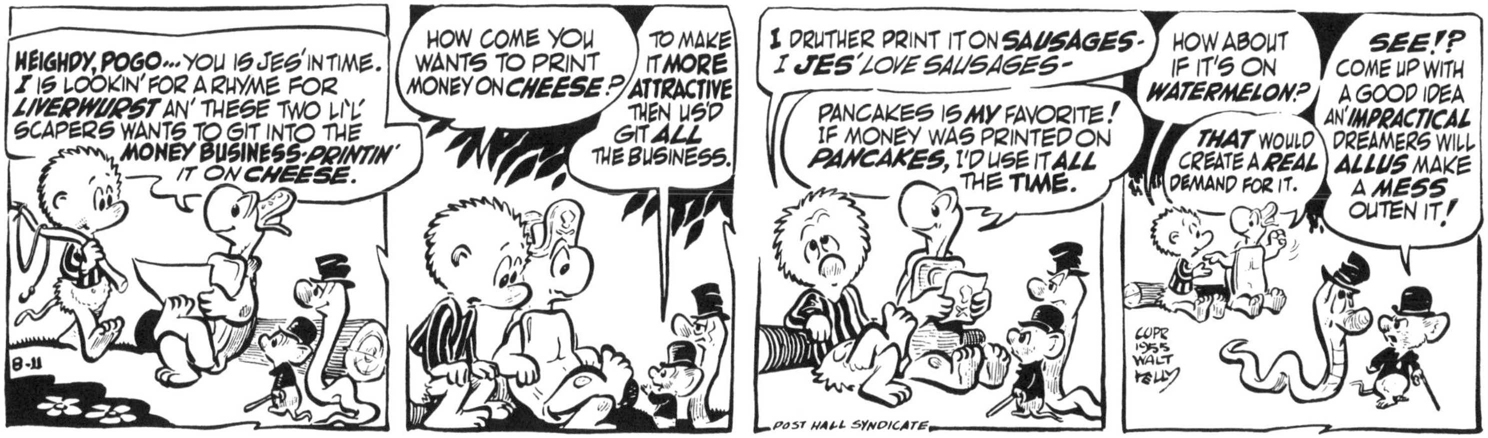
HEIGHDY, POGO... YOU IS JES' IN TIME. I IS LOOKIN' FOR A RHYME FOR LIVERWURST AN' THESE TWO LI'L' SCAPERS WANTS TO GIT INTO THE MONEY BUSINESS-PRINTIN' IT ON CHEESE.
8-11
HOW COME YOU WANTS TO PRINT MONEY ON CHEESE?
TO MAKE IT MORE ATTRACTIVE THEN US'D GIT ALL THE BUSINESS.
I DRUTHER PRINT IT ON SAUSAGES - I JES' LOVE SAUSAGES -
PANCAKES IS MY FAVORITE! IF MONEY WAS PRINTED ON PANCAKES, I'D USE IT ALL THE TIME.
POST HALL SYNDICATE
HOW ABOUT IF IT'S ON WATERMELON?
THAT WOULD CREATE A REAL DEMAND FOR IT.
SEE!? COME UP WITH A GOOD IDEA AN' IMPRACTICAL DREAMERS WILL ALLUS MAKE A MESS OUTEN IT!
COPR 1955 WALT KELLY

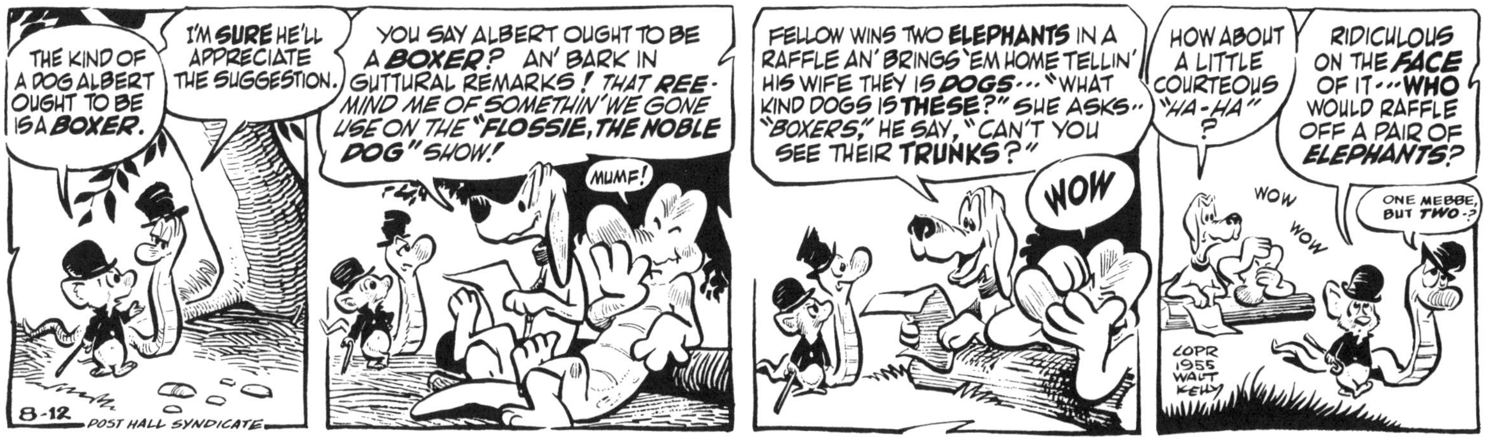
THE KIND OF A DOG ALBERT OUGHT TO BE IS A BOXER.
I'M SURE HE'LL APPRECIATE THE SUGGESTION.
8-12
POST HALL SYNDICATE
YOU SAY ALBERT OUGHT TO BE A BOXER? AN' BARK IN GUTTURAL REMARKS! THAT REE-MIND ME OF SOMETHIN' WE GONE USE ON THE "FLOSSIE, THE NOBLE DOG" SHOW!
MUMF!
FELLOW WINS TWO ELEPHANTS IN A RAFFLE AN' BRINGS 'EM HOME TELLIN' HIS WIFE THEY IS DOGS... "WHAT KIND DOGS IS THESE?" SHE ASKS.. "BOXERS," HE SAY, "CAN'T YOU SEE THEIR TRUNKS?"
WOW
HOW ABOUT A LITTLE COURTEOUS "HA-HA"?
WOW
WOW
RIDICULOUS ON THE FACE OF IT... WHO WOULD RAFFLE OFF A PAIR OF ELEPHANTS?
ONE MEBBE, BUT TWO-?
COPR 1955 WALT KELLY

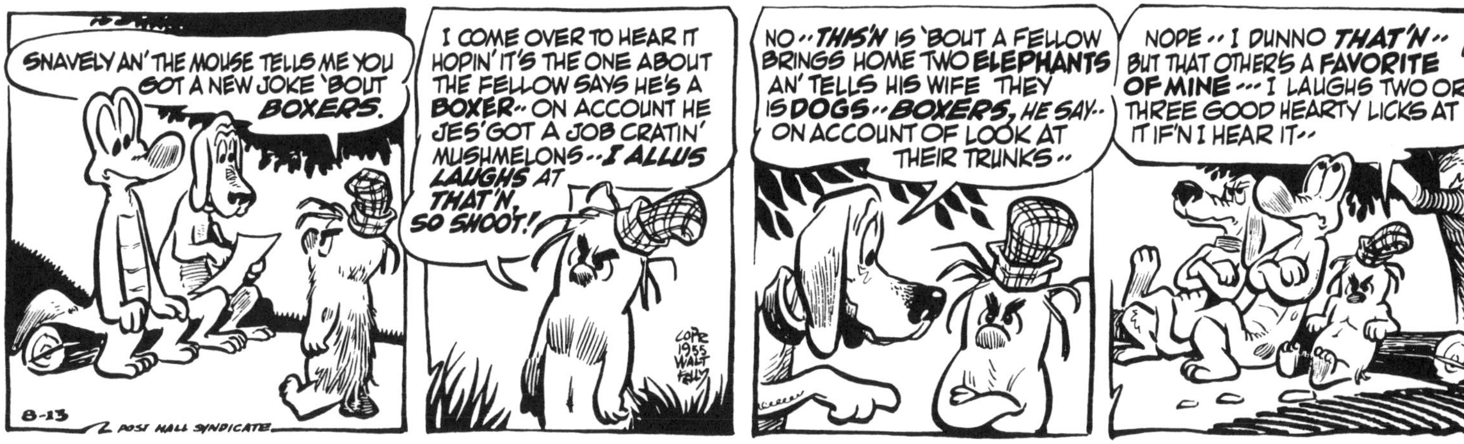
SNAVELY AN' THE MOUSE TELLS ME YOU GOT A NEW JOKE 'BOUT BOXERS.
8-13
POST HALL SYNDICATE
I COME OVER TO HEAR IT HOPIN' IT'S THE ONE ABOUT THE FELLOW SAYS HE'S A BOXER.. ON ACCOUNT HE JES' GOT A JOB CRATIN' MUSHMELONS.. I ALLUS LAUGHS AT THAT'N, SO SHOOT!
COPR 1955 WALT KELLY
NO.. THIS'N IS 'BOUT A FELLOW BRINGS HOME TWO ELEPHANTS AN' TELLS HIS WIFE THEY IS DOGS.. BOXERS, HE SAY.. ON ACCOUNT OF LOOK AT THEIR TRUNKS..
NOPE.. I DUNNO THAT'N.. BUT THAT OTHER'S A FAVORITE OF MINE... I LAUGHS TWO OR THREE GOOD HEARTY LICKS AT IT IF'N I HEAR IT..

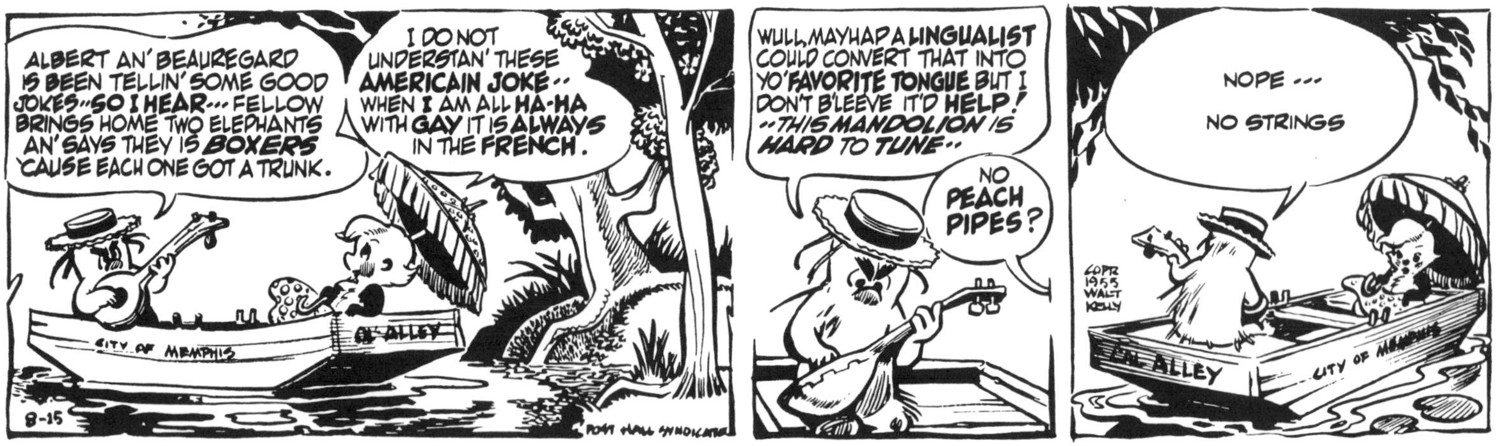
ALBERT AN' BEAUREGARD IS BEEN TELLIN' SOME GOOD JOKES -- SO I HEAR ... FELLOW BRINGS HOME TWO ELEPHANTS AN' SAYS THEY IS BOXERS 'CAUSE EACH ONE GOT A TRUNK.
I DO NOT UNDERSTAN' THESE AMERICAIN JOKE -- WHEN I AM ALL HA-HA WITH GAY IT IS ALWAYS IN THE FRENCH.
CITY OF MEMPHIS
OL' ALLEY
8-15
POST HALL SYNDICATE
WULL, MAYHAP A LINGUALIST COULD CONVERT THAT INTO YO' FAVORITE TONGUE BUT I DON'T B'LEEVE IT'D HELP! -- THIS MANDOLION IS HARD TO TUNE --
NO PEACH PIPES?
NOPE --- NO STRINGS
COPR 1955 WALT KELLY
OL' ALLEY
CITY OF MEMPHIS

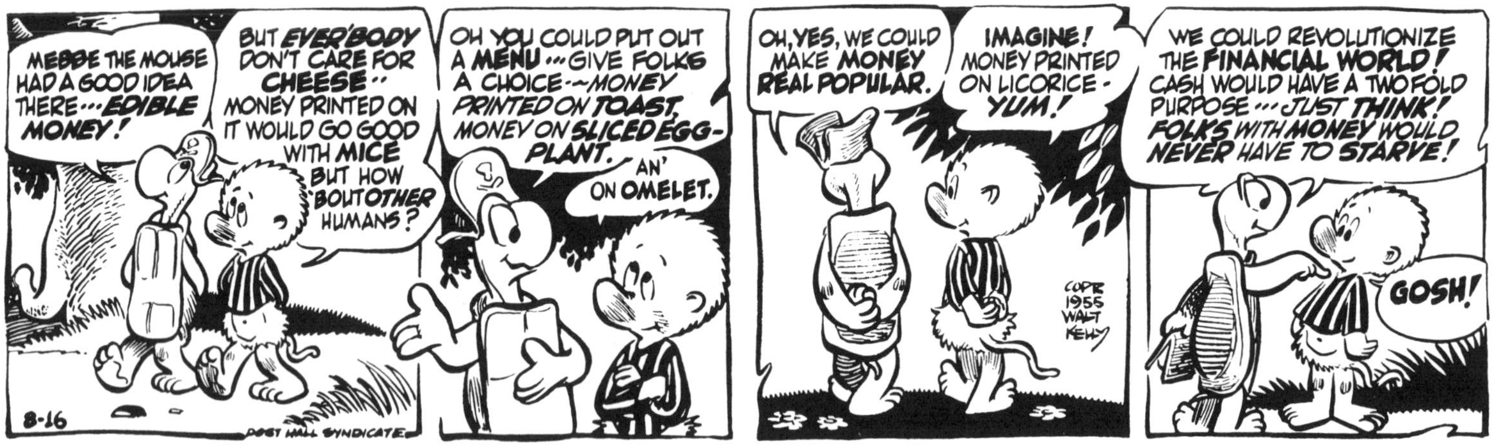
MEBBE THE MOUSE HAD A GOOD IDEA THERE ... EDIBLE MONEY!
BUT EVER'BODY DON'T CARE FOR CHEESE -- MONEY PRINTED ON IT WOULD GO GOOD WITH MICE
BUT HOW 'BOUT OTHER HUMANS?
8-16
POST HALL SYNDICATE
OH YOU COULD PUT OUT A MENU ... GIVE FOLKS A CHOICE -- MONEY PRINTED ON TOAST, MONEY ON SLICED EGG-PLANT.
AN' ON OMELET.
OH, YES, WE COULD MAKE MONEY REAL POPULAR.
IMAGINE! MONEY PRINTED ON LICORICE - YUM!
COPR 1955 WALT KELLY
WE COULD REVOLUTIONIZE THE FINANCIAL WORLD! CASH WOULD HAVE A TWO FOLD PURPOSE ... JUST THINK! FOLKS WITH MONEY WOULD NEVER HAVE TO STARVE!
GOSH!

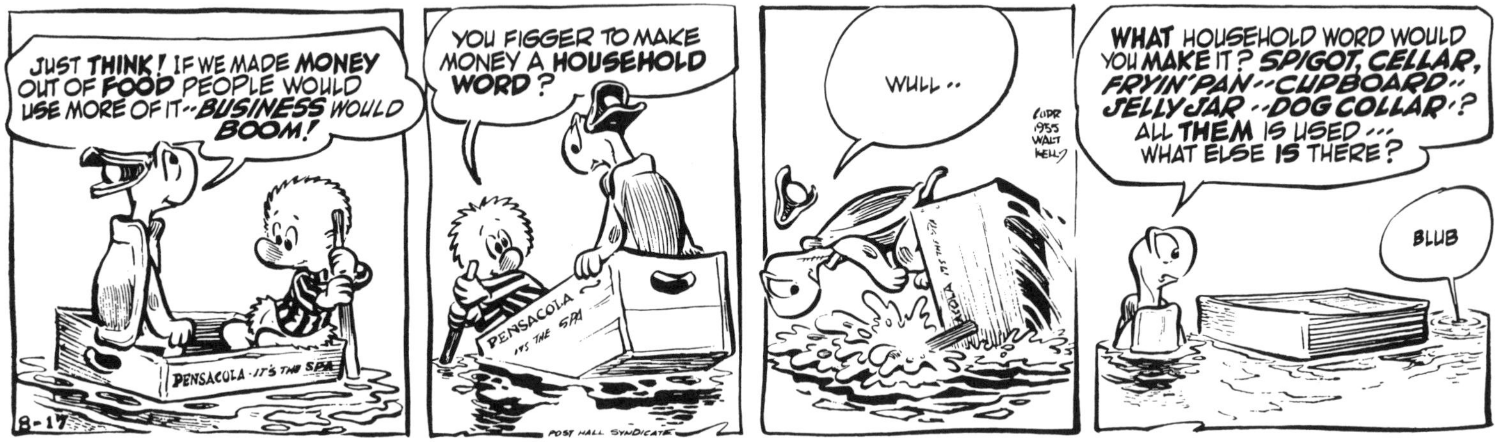
JUST THINK! IF WE MADE MONEY OUT OF FOOD PEOPLE WOULD USE MORE OF IT -- BUSINESS WOULD BOOM!
PENSACOLA - IT'S THE SPA
8-17
YOU FIGGER TO MAKE MONEY A HOUSEHOLD WORD?
PENSACOLA IT'S THE SPA
POST HALL SYNDICATE
WULL --
COPR 1955 WALT KELLY
WHAT HOUSEHOLD WORD WOULD YOU MAKE IT? SPIGOT, CELLAR, FRYIN' PAN -- CUPBOARD -- JELLY JAR -- DOG COLLAR -? ALL THEM IS USED ... WHAT ELSE IS THERE?
BLUB

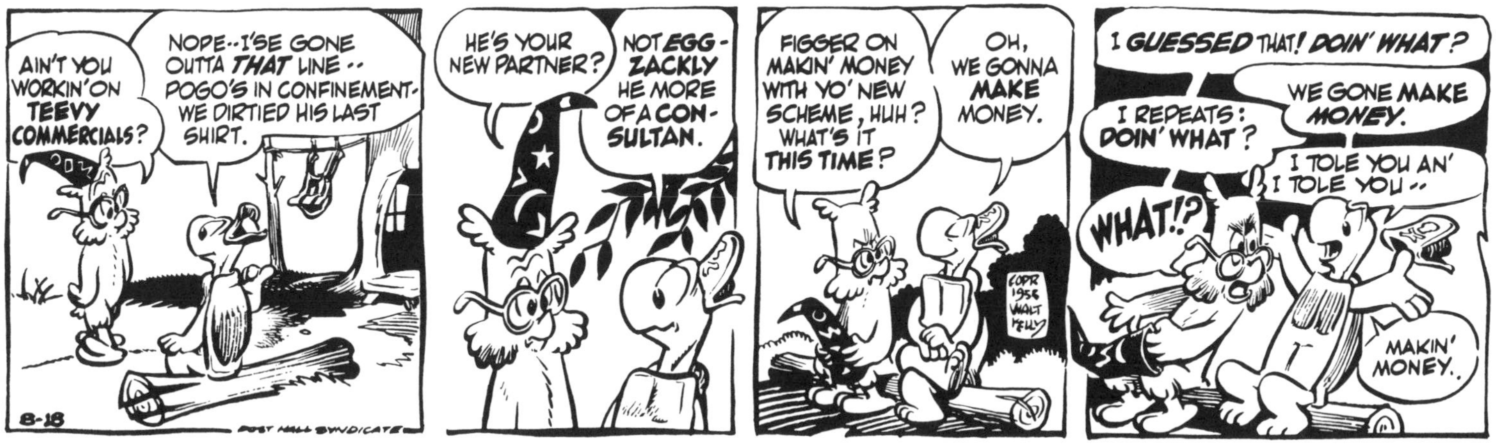
AIN'T YOU WORKIN' ON TEEVY COMMERCIALS?
NOPE..I'SE GONE OUTTA THAT LINE.. POGO'S IN CONFINEMENT- WE DIRTIED HIS LAST SHIRT.
8-18
POST HALL SYNDICATE
HE'S YOUR NEW PARTNER?
NOT EGG-ZACKLY HE MORE OF A CON-SULTAN.
FIGGER ON MAKIN' MONEY WITH YO' NEW SCHEME, HUH? WHAT'S IT THIS TIME?
OH, WE GONNA MAKE MONEY.
COPR 1955 WALT KELLY
I GUESSED THAT! DOIN' WHAT?
WE GONE MAKE MONEY.
I REPEATS: DOIN' WHAT?
I TOLE YOU AN' I TOLE YOU..
WHAT!?
MAKIN' MONEY.

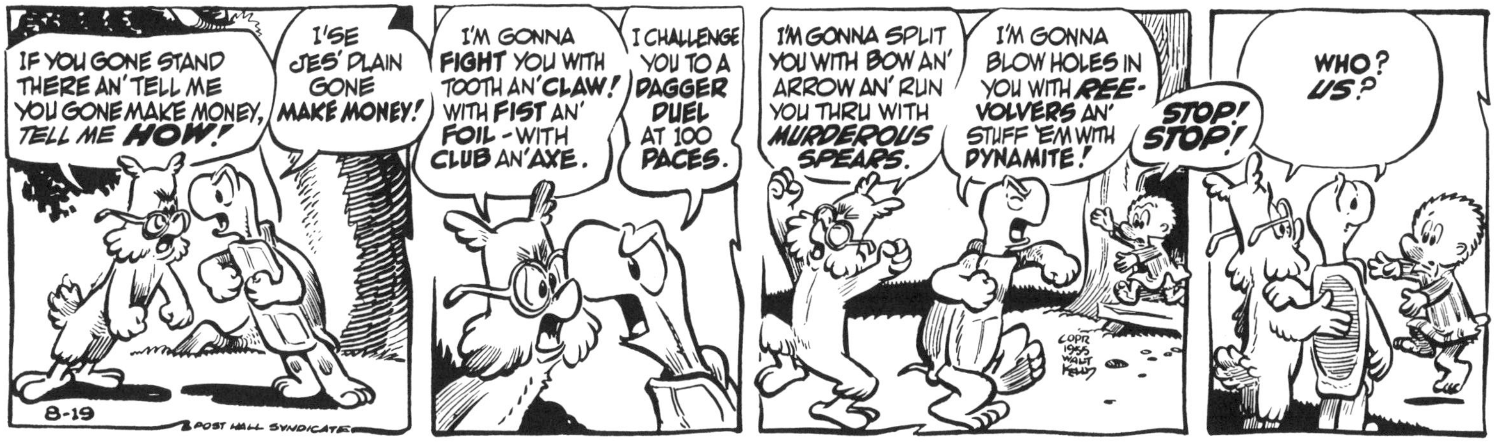
IF YOU GONE STAND THERE AN' TELL ME YOU GONE MAKE MONEY, TELL ME HOW!
I'SE JES' PLAIN GONE MAKE MONEY!
8-19
POST HALL SYNDICATE
I'M GONNA FIGHT YOU WITH TOOTH AN' CLAW! WITH FIST AN' FOIL - WITH CLUB AN' AXE.
I CHALLENGE YOU TO A DAGGER DUEL AT 100 PACES.
I'M GONNA SPLIT YOU WITH BOW AN' ARROW AN' RUN YOU THRU WITH MURDEROUS SPEARS.
I'M GONNA BLOW HOLES IN YOU WITH REE-VOLVERS AN' STUFF 'EM WITH DYNAMITE!
STOP! STOP!
COPR 1955 WALT KELLY
WHO? US?

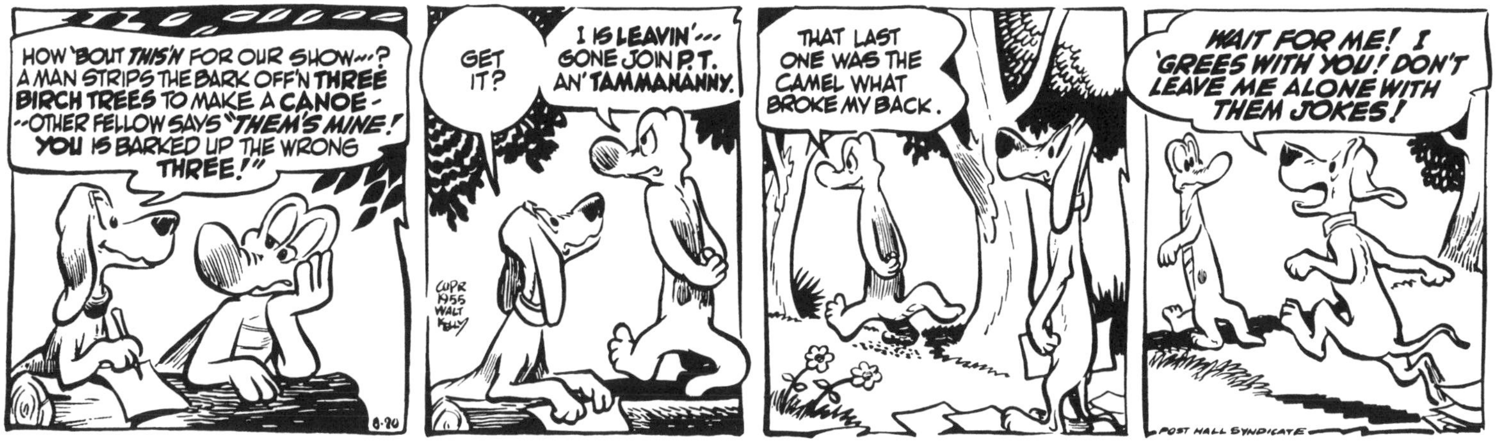
HOW 'BOUT THIS'N FOR OUR SHOW..? A MAN STRIPS THE BARK OFF'N THREE BIRCH TREES TO MAKE A CANOE- --OTHER FELLOW SAYS "THEM'S MINE! YOU IS BARKED UP THE WRONG THREE!"
GET IT?
I IS LEAVIN'... GONE JOIN P.T. AN' TAMMANANNY.
COPR 1955 WALT KELLY
8-20
THAT LAST ONE WAS THE CAMEL WHAT BROKE MY BACK.
WAIT FOR ME! I 'GREES WITH YOU! DON'T LEAVE ME ALONE WITH THEM JOKES!
POST HALL SYNDICATE

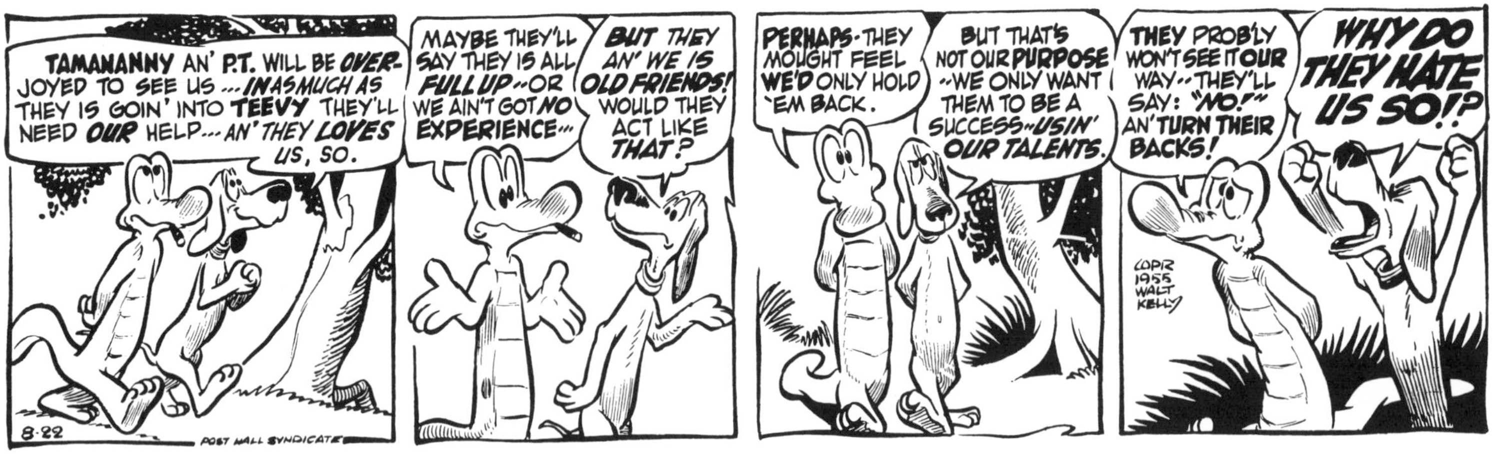
TAMANANNY AN' P.T. WILL BE OVER-JOYED TO SEE US ...INASMUCH AS THEY IS GOIN' INTO TEEVY THEY'LL NEED OUR HELP... AN' THEY LOVES US, SO.
MAYBE THEY'LL SAY THEY IS ALL FULL UP--OR WE AIN'T GOT NO EXPERIENCE...
BUT THEY AN' WE IS OLD FRIENDS! WOULD THEY ACT LIKE THAT?
PERHAPS-THEY MOUGHT FEEL WE'D ONLY HOLD 'EM BACK.
BUT THAT'S NOT OUR PURPOSE --WE ONLY WANT THEM TO BE A SUCCESS--USIN' OUR TALENTS.
THEY PROB'LY WON'T SEE IT OUR WAY--THEY'LL SAY: "NO!" AN' TURN THEIR BACKS!
WHY DO THEY HATE US SO!?
COPR 1955 WALT KELLY
8-22
POST HALL SYNDICATE

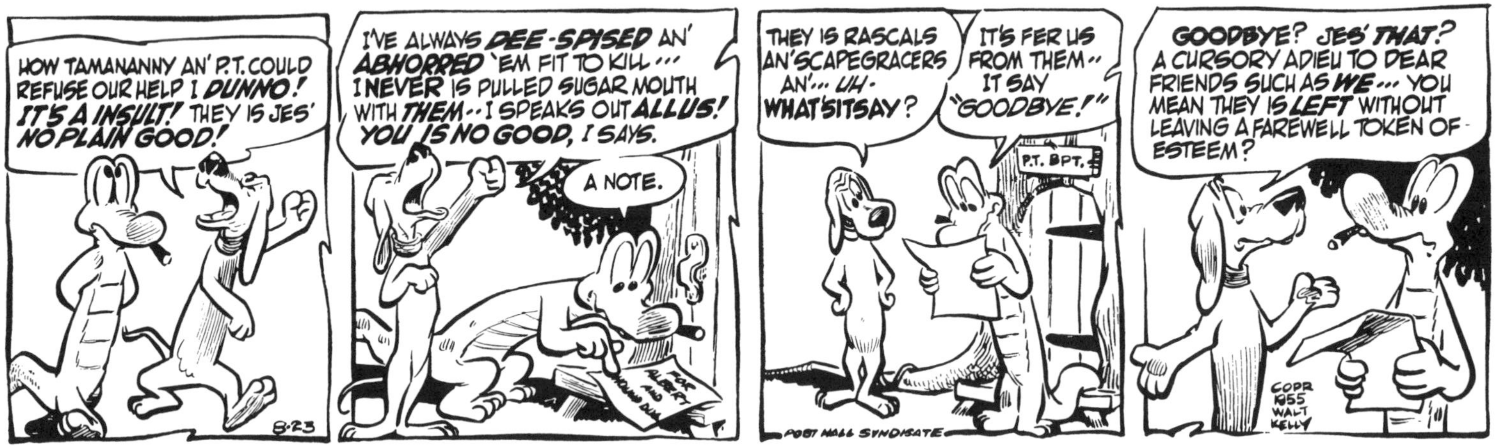
HOW TAMANANNY AN' P.T. COULD REFUSE OUR HELP I DUNNO! IT'S A INSULT! THEY IS JES' NO PLAIN GOOD!
8-23
I'VE ALWAYS DEE-SPISED AN' ABHORRED 'EM FIT TO KILL... I NEVER IS PULLED SUGAR MOUTH WITH THEM--I SPEAKS OUT ALLUS! YOU IS NO GOOD, I SAYS.
A NOTE.
THEY IS RASCALS AN' SCAPEGRACERS AN'... UH-WHAT'SITSAY?
IT'S FER US FROM THEM-- IT SAY "GOODBYE!"
P.T. BPT.
GOODBYE? JES' THAT? A CURSORY ADIEU TO DEAR FRIENDS SUCH AS WE... YOU MEAN THEY IS LEFT WITHOUT LEAVING A FAREWELL TOKEN OF ESTEEM?
COPR 1955 WALT KELLY
POST HALL SYNDICATE

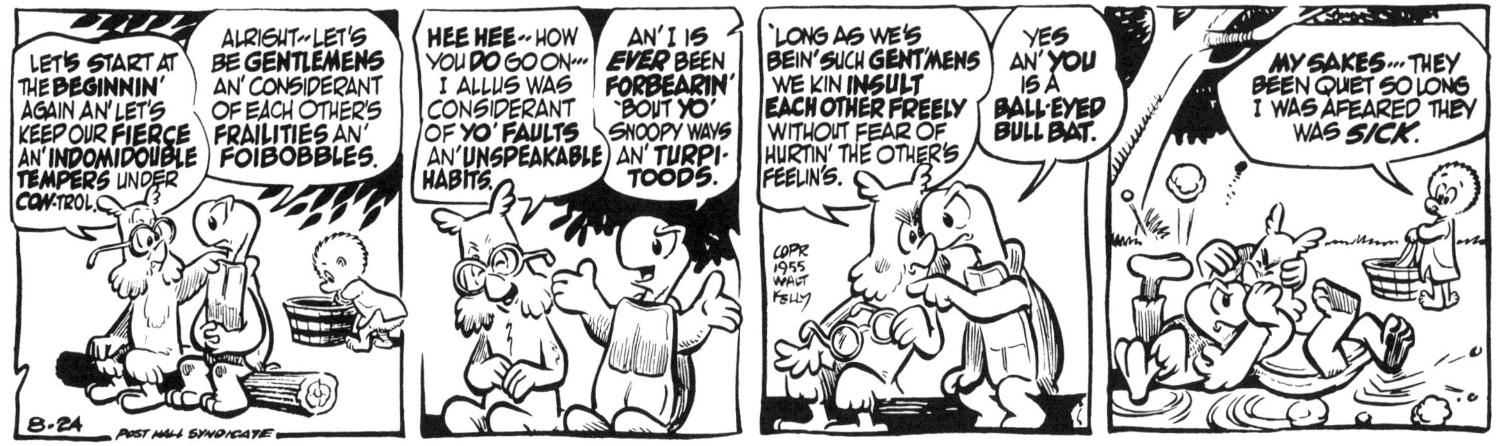
LET'S START AT THE BEGINNIN' AGAIN AN' LET'S KEEP OUR FIERCE AN' INDOMIDOUBLE TEMPERS UNDER CON-TROL.
ALRIGHT--LET'S BE GENTLEMENS AN' CONSIDERANT OF EACH OTHER'S FRAILITIES AN' FOIBOBBLES.
HEE HEE--HOW YOU DO GO ON--- I ALLUS WAS CONSIDERANT OF YO' FAULTS AN' UNSPEAKABLE HABITS.
AN' I IS EVER BEEN FORBEARIN' 'BOUT YO' SNOOPY WAYS AN' TURPI-TOODS.
'LONG AS WE'S BEIN' SUCH GENT'MENS WE KIN INSULT EACH OTHER FREELY WITHOUT FEAR OF HURTIN' THE OTHER'S FEELIN'S.
YES AN' YOU IS A BALL-EYED BULL BAT.
COPR 1955 WALT KELLY
MY SAKES... THEY BEEN QUIET SO LONG I WAS AFEARED THEY WAS SICK.
8-24
POST HALL SYNDICATE

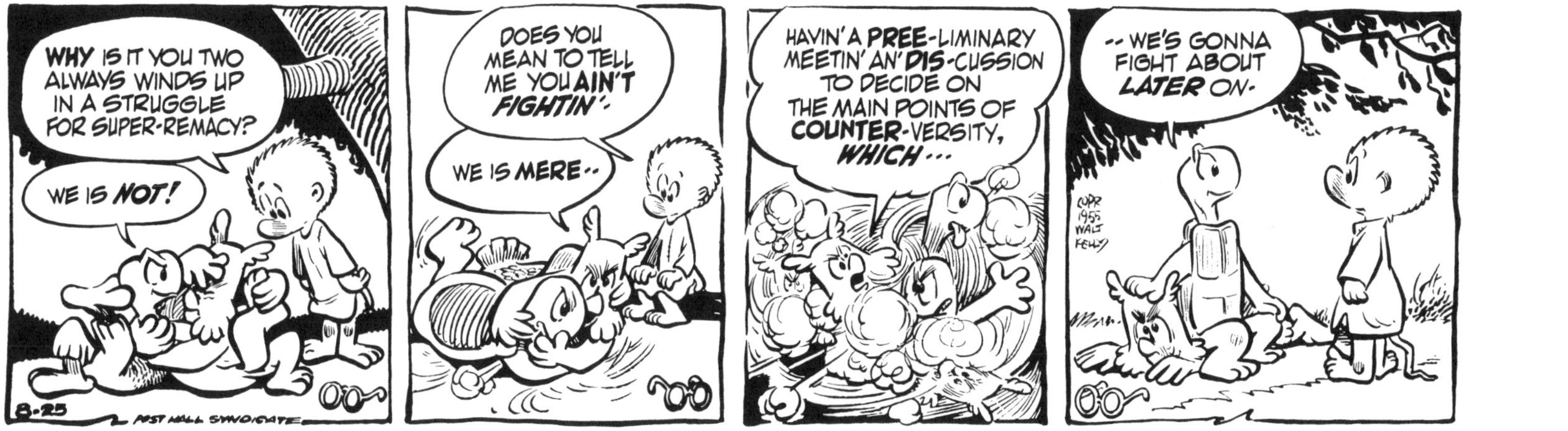
WHY IS IT YOU TWO ALWAYS WINDS UP IN A STRUGGLE FOR SUPER-REMACY?
WE IS NOT!
DOES YOU MEAN TO TELL ME YOU AIN'T FIGHTIN'·
WE IS MERE··
HAVIN' A PREE-LIMINARY MEETIN' AN' DIS-CUSSION TO DECIDE ON THE MAIN POINTS OF COUNTER-VERSITY, WHICH···
··WE'S GONNA FIGHT ABOUT LATER ON·
COPR 1955 WALT KELLY
8·25
POST HALL SYNDICATE

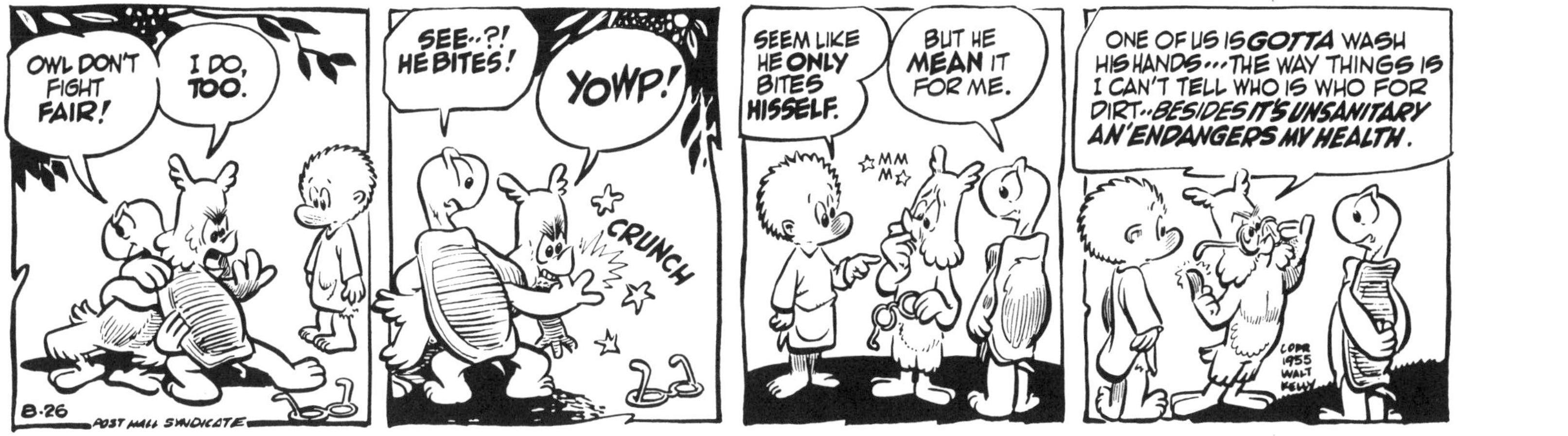
OWL DON'T FIGHT FAIR!
I DO, TOO.
SEE··?! HE BITES!
YOWP!
CRUNCH
SEEM LIKE HE ONLY BITES HISSELF.
BUT HE MEAN IT FOR ME.
MM M
ONE OF US IS GOTTA WASH HIS HANDS···THE WAY THINGS IS I CAN'T TELL WHO IS WHO FOR DIRT··BESIDES IT'S UNSANITARY AN' ENDANGERS MY HEALTH.
COPR 1955 WALT KELLY
8·26
POST HALL SYNDICATE

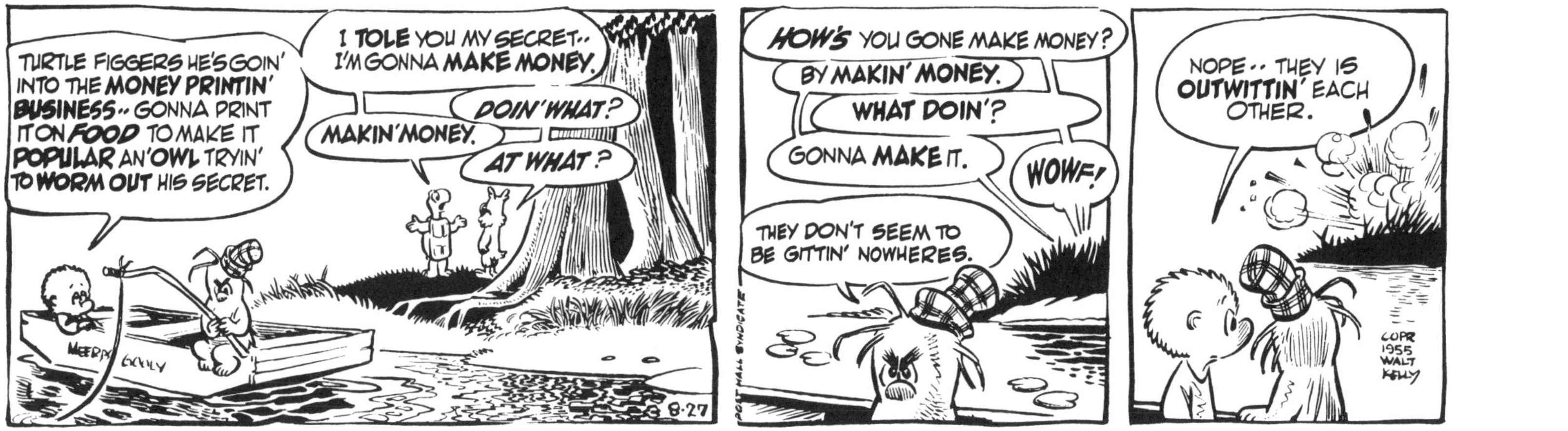
TURTLE FIGGERS HE'S GOIN' INTO THE MONEY PRINTIN' BUSINESS·· GONNA PRINT IT ON FOOD TO MAKE IT POPULAR AN' OWL TRYIN' TO WORM OUT HIS SECRET.
I TOLE YOU MY SECRET·· I'M GONNA MAKE MONEY.
DOIN' WHAT?
MAKIN' MONEY.
AT WHAT?
HOW'S YOU GONE MAKE MONEY?
BY MAKIN' MONEY.
WHAT DOIN'?
GONNA MAKE IT.
WOWF!
THEY DON'T SEEM TO BE GITTIN' NOWHERES.
NOPE·· THEY IS OUTWITTIN' EACH OTHER.
COPR 1955 WALT KELLY
8·27
POST HALL SYNDICATE

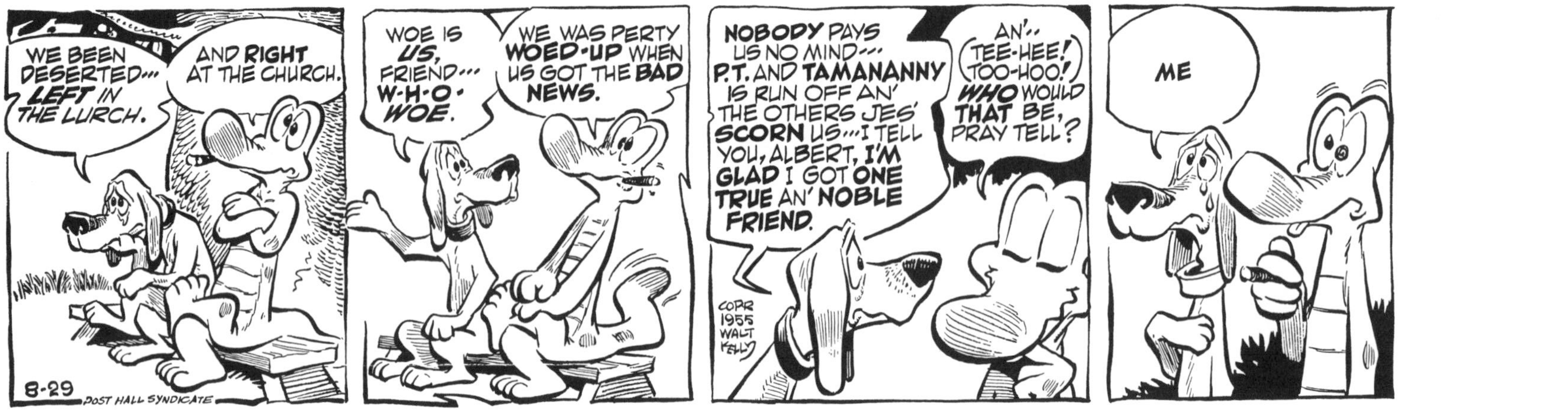
WE BEEN DESERTED... LEFT IN THE LURCH.
AND RIGHT AT THE CHURCH.
WOE IS US, FRIEND... W-H-O-WOE.
WE WAS PERTY WOED-UP WHEN US GOT THE BAD NEWS.
NOBODY PAYS US NO MIND--- P.T. AND TAMANANNY IS RUN OFF AN' THE OTHERS JES' SCORN US... I TELL YOU, ALBERT, I'M GLAD I GOT ONE TRUE AN' NOBLE FRIEND.
AN'.. (TEE-HEE! TOO-HOO!) WHO WOULD THAT BE, PRAY TELL?
ME
8-29
POST HALL SYNDICATE
COPR 1955 WALT KELLY

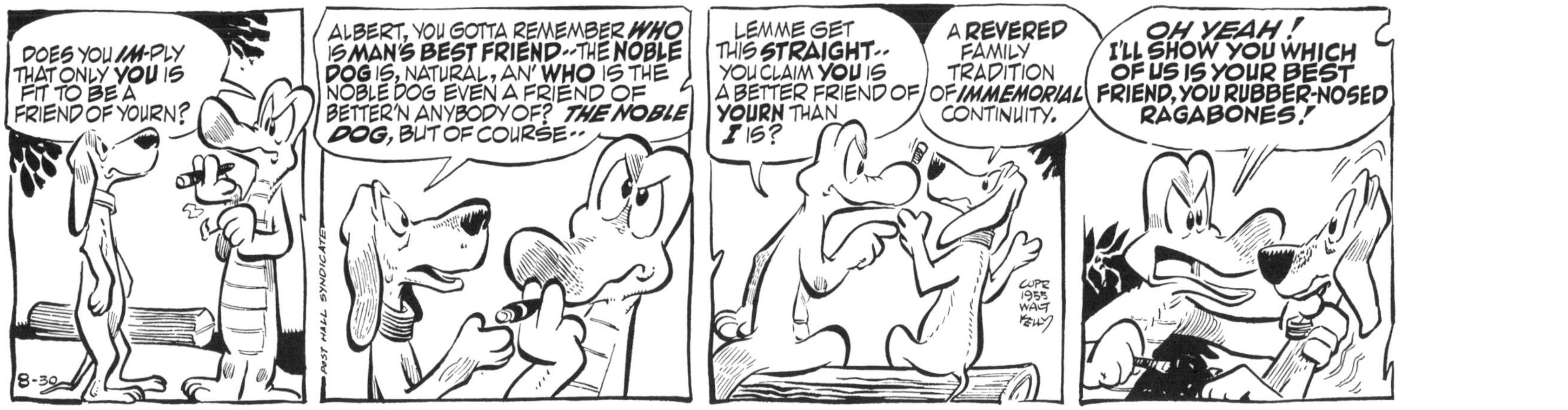
DOES YOU IM-PLY THAT ONLY YOU IS FIT TO BE A FRIEND OF YOURN?
ALBERT, YOU GOTTA REMEMBER WHO IS MAN'S BEST FRIEND--THE NOBLE DOG IS, NATURAL, AN' WHO IS THE NOBLE DOG EVEN A FRIEND OF BETTER'N ANYBODY OF? THE NOBLE DOG, BUT OF COURSE--
LEMME GET THIS STRAIGHT-- YOU CLAIM YOU IS A BETTER FRIEND OF YOURN THAN I IS?
A REVERED FAMILY TRADITION OF IMMEMORIAL CONTINUITY.
OH YEAH! I'LL SHOW YOU WHICH OF US IS YOUR BEST FRIEND, YOU RUBBER-NOSED RAGABONES!
8-30
POST HALL SYNDICATE
COPR 1955 WALT KELLY

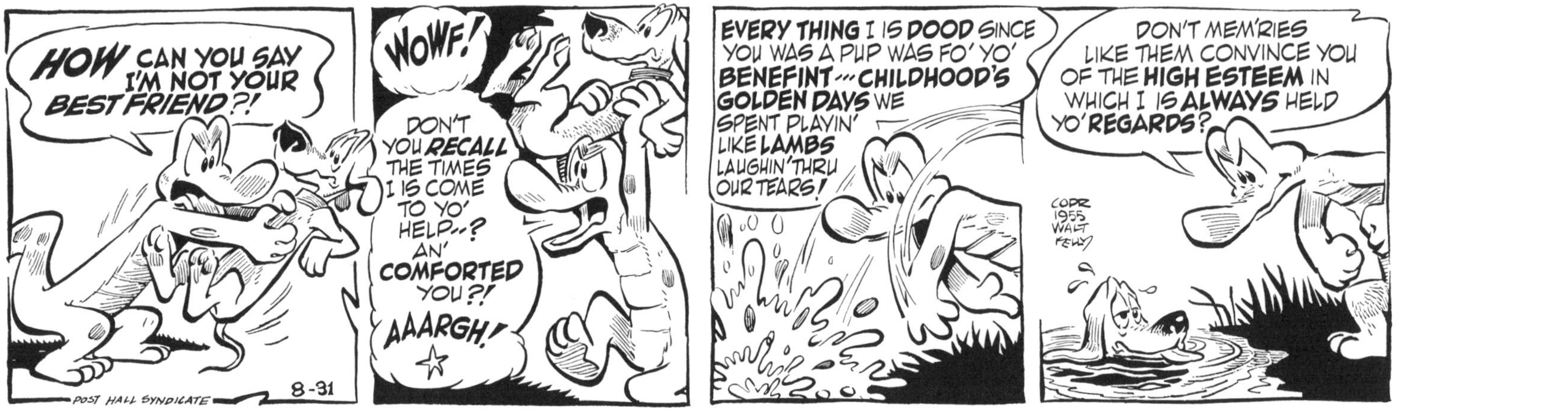
HOW CAN YOU SAY I'M NOT YOUR BEST FRIEND?!
WOWF!
DON'T YOU RECALL THE TIMES I IS COME TO YO' HELP--? AN' COMFORTED YOU?!
AAARGH!
EVERY THING I IS DOOD SINCE YOU WAS A PUP WAS FO' YO' BENEFINT--- CHILDHOOD'S GOLDEN DAYS WE SPENT PLAYIN' LIKE LAMBS LAUGHIN' THRU OUR TEARS!
DON'T MEM'RIES LIKE THEM CONVINCE YOU OF THE HIGH ESTEEM IN WHICH I IS ALWAYS HELD YO' REGARDS?
8-31
POST HALL SYNDICATE
COPR 1955 WALT KELLY

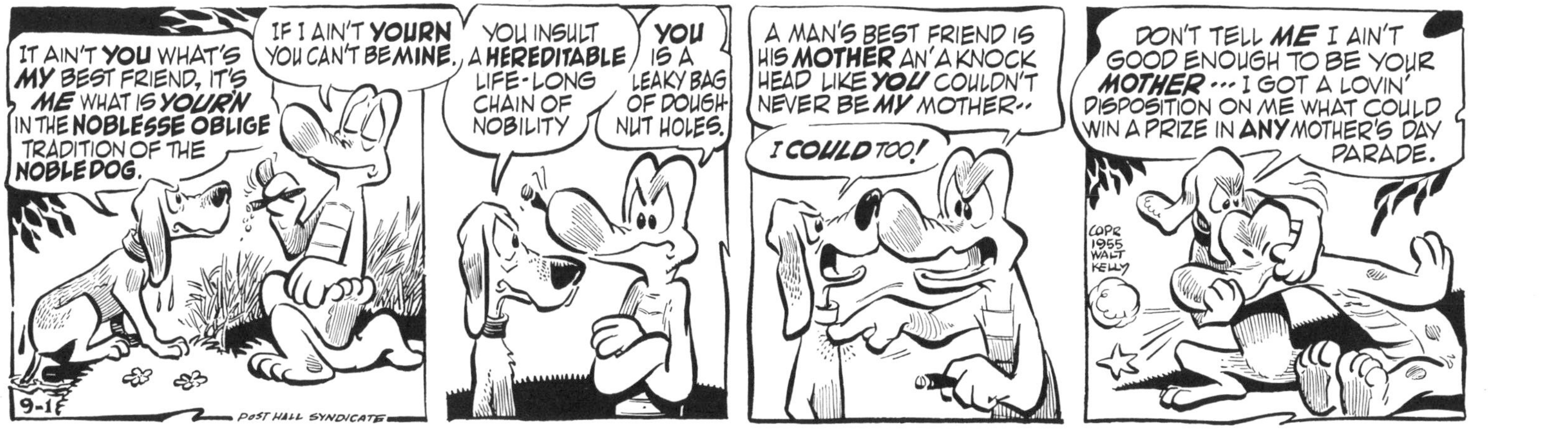
IT AIN'T **YOU** WHAT'S **MY** BEST FRIEND, IT'S **ME** WHAT IS **YOURN** IN THE **NOBLESSE OBLIGE** TRADITION OF THE **NOBLE DOG**.
IF I AIN'T **YOURN** YOU CAN'T BE **MINE**.
YOU INSULT A **HEREDITABLE** LIFE-LONG CHAIN OF NOBILITY
YOU IS A LEAKY BAG OF DOUGH-NUT HOLES.
A MAN'S BEST FRIEND IS HIS **MOTHER** AN' A KNOCK HEAD LIKE **YOU** COULDN'T NEVER BE **MY** MOTHER--
I **COULD** TOO!
DON'T TELL **ME** I AIN'T GOOD ENOUGH TO BE YOUR **MOTHER** --- I GOT A LOVIN' DISPOSITION ON ME WHAT COULD WIN A PRIZE IN **ANY** MOTHER'S DAY PARADE.
9-1
POST HALL SYNDICATE
COPR 1955 WALT KELLY

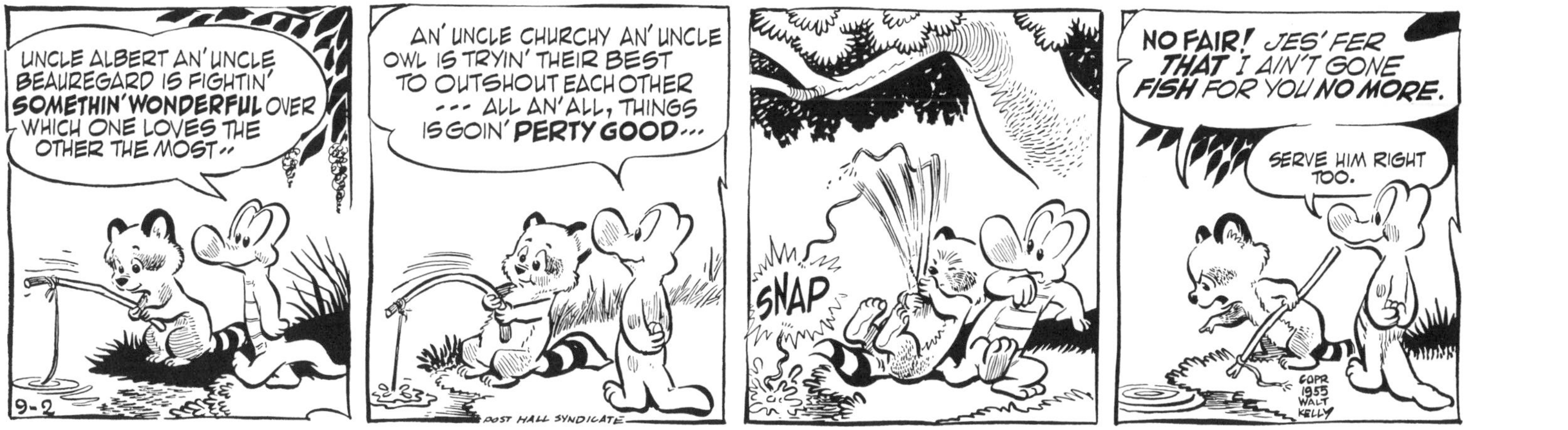
UNCLE ALBERT AN' UNCLE BEAUREGARD IS FIGHTIN' **SOMETHIN' WONDERFUL** OVER WHICH ONE LOVES THE OTHER THE MOST--
AN' UNCLE CHURCHY AN' UNCLE OWL IS TRYIN' THEIR BEST TO OUTSHOUT EACH OTHER --- ALL AN' ALL, THINGS IS GOIN' **PERTY GOOD**---
SNAP
NO FAIR! JES' FER **THAT** I AIN'T GONE **FISH** FOR YOU **NO MORE**.
SERVE HIM RIGHT TOO.
9-2
POST HALL SYNDICATE
COPR 1955 WALT KELLY

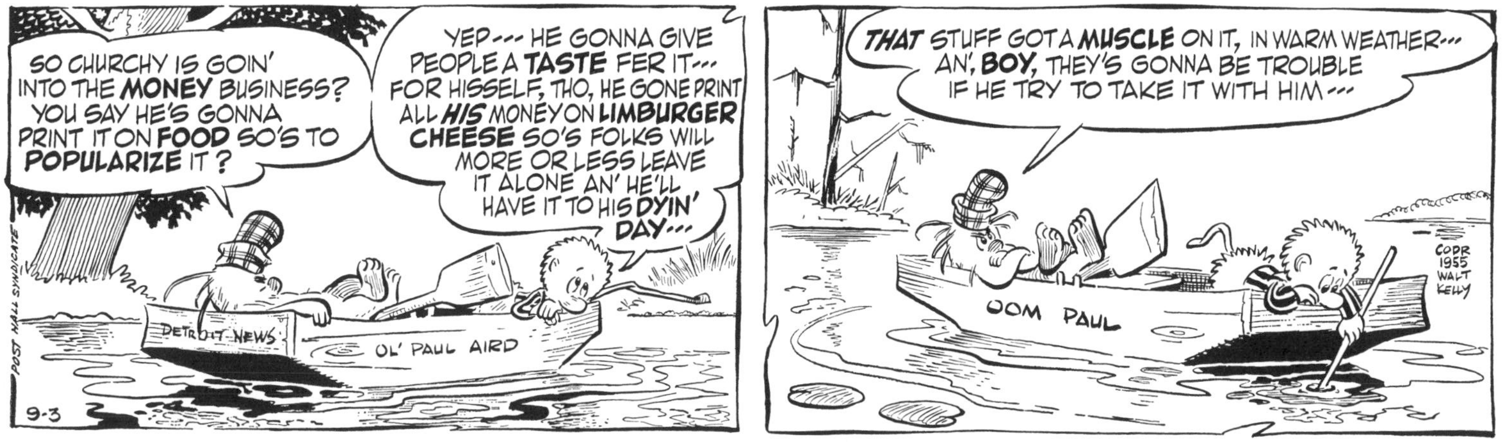
SO CHURCHY IS GOIN' INTO THE **MONEY** BUSINESS? YOU SAY HE'S GONNA PRINT IT ON **FOOD** SO'S TO **POPULARIZE** IT?
YEP--- HE GONNA GIVE PEOPLE A **TASTE** FER IT--- FOR HISSELF, THO, HE GONE PRINT ALL **HIS** MONEY ON **LIMBURGER CHEESE** SO'S FOLKS WILL MORE OR LESS LEAVE IT ALONE AN' HE'LL HAVE IT TO HIS **DYIN'** DAY---
THAT STUFF GOT A **MUSCLE** ON IT, IN WARM WEATHER--- AN', **BOY**, THEY'S GONNA BE TROUBLE IF HE TRY TO TAKE IT WITH HIM---
DETROIT NEWS
OL' PAUL AIRD
OOM PAUL
9-3
POST HALL SYNDICATE
COPR 1955 WALT KELLY

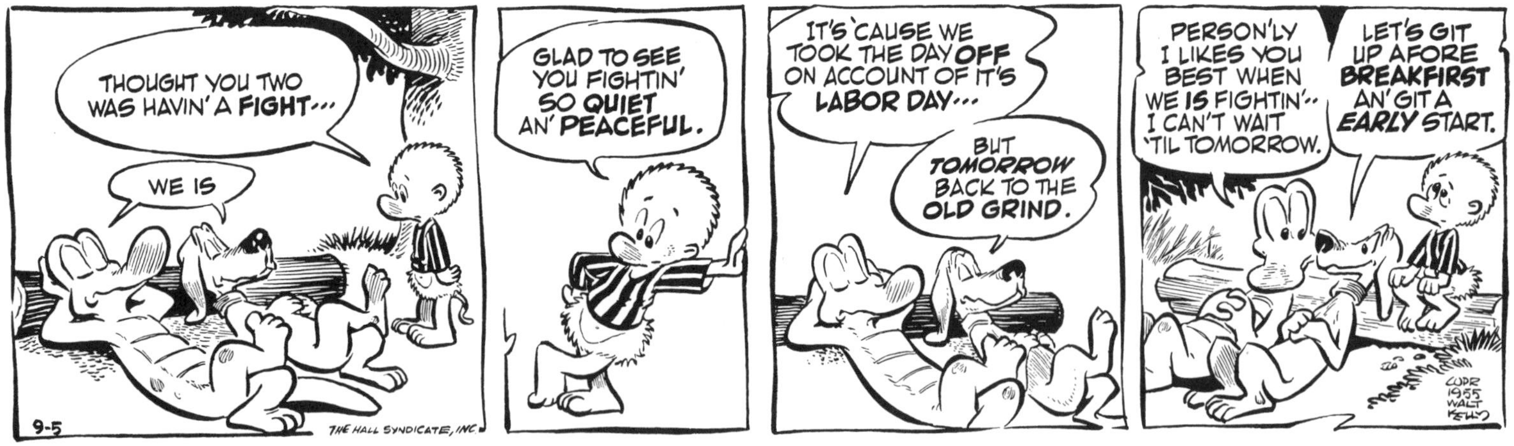
THOUGHT YOU TWO WAS HAVIN' A FIGHT...
WE IS
GLAD TO SEE YOU FIGHTIN' SO QUIET AN' PEACEFUL.
IT'S 'CAUSE WE TOOK THE DAY OFF ON ACCOUNT OF IT'S LABOR DAY...
BUT TOMORROW BACK TO THE OLD GRIND.
PERSON'LY I LIKES YOU BEST WHEN WE IS FIGHTIN'.. I CAN'T WAIT 'TIL TOMORROW.
LET'S GIT UP AFORE BREAKFIRST AN' GIT A EARLY START.
9-5
THE HALL SYNDICATE, INC.
COPR 1955 WALT KELLY

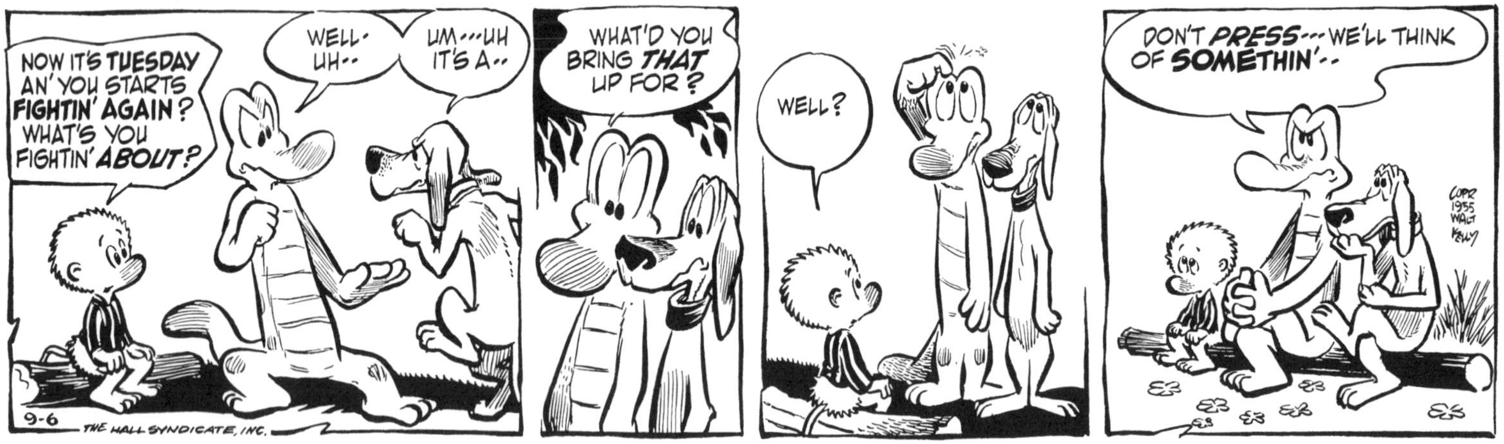
NOW IT'S TUESDAY AN' YOU STARTS FIGHTIN' AGAIN? WHAT'S YOU FIGHTIN' ABOUT?
WELL- UH--
UM---UH IT'S A--
WHAT'D YOU BRING THAT UP FOR?
WELL?
DON'T PRESS--- WE'LL THINK OF SOMETHIN'--
9-6
THE HALL SYNDICATE, INC.
COPR 1955 WALT KELLY

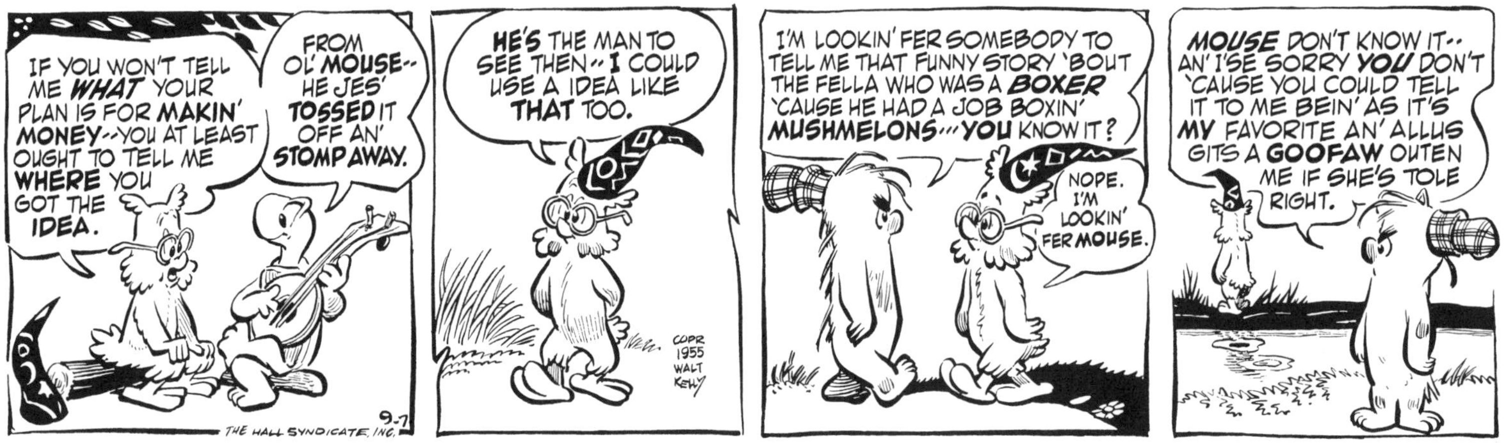
IF YOU WON'T TELL ME WHAT YOUR PLAN IS FOR MAKIN' MONEY--YOU AT LEAST OUGHT TO TELL ME WHERE YOU GOT THE IDEA.
FROM OL' MOUSE-- HE JES' TOSSED IT OFF AN' STOMP AWAY.
HE'S THE MAN TO SEE THEN--I COULD USE A IDEA LIKE THAT TOO.
COPR 1955 WALT KELLY
I'M LOOKIN' FER SOMEBODY TO TELL ME THAT FUNNY STORY 'BOUT THE FELLA WHO WAS A BOXER 'CAUSE HE HAD A JOB BOXIN' MUSHMELONS... YOU KNOW IT?
NOPE. I'M LOOKIN' FER MOUSE.
MOUSE DON'T KNOW IT-- AN' I'SE SORRY YOU DON'T 'CAUSE YOU COULD TELL IT TO ME BEIN' AS IT'S MY FAVORITE AN' ALLUS GITS A GOOFAW OUTEN ME IF SHE'S TOLE RIGHT.
9-7
THE HALL SYNDICATE, INC.

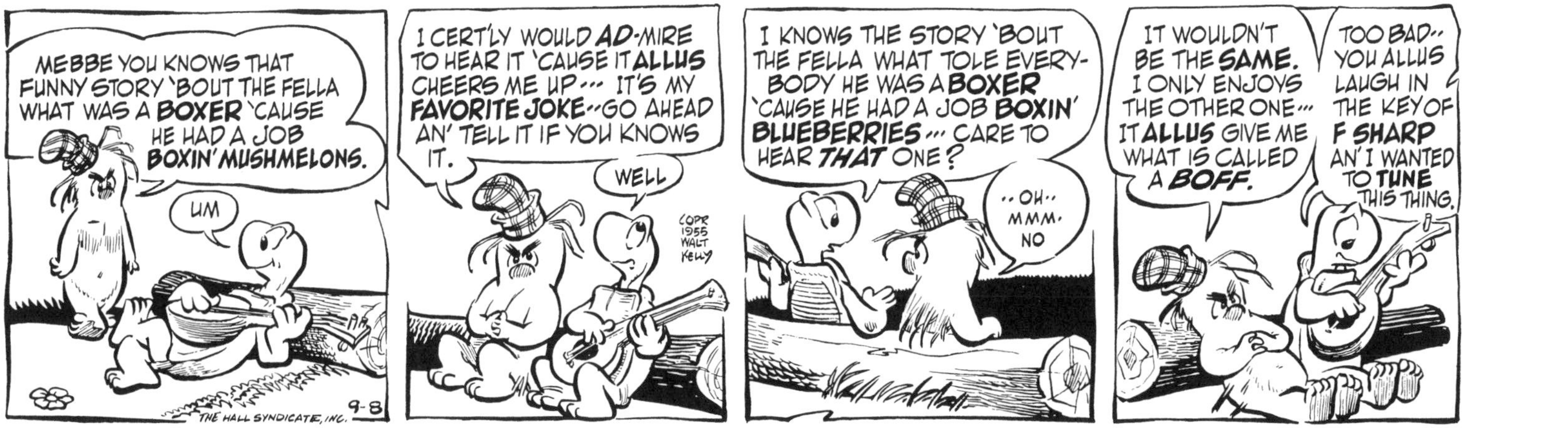
MEBBE YOU KNOWS THAT FUNNY STORY 'BOUT THE FELLA WHAT WAS A BOXER 'CAUSE HE HAD A JOB BOXIN' MUSHMELONS.
UM
THE HALL SYNDICATE, INC.
9-8
I CERT'LY WOULD AD-MIRE TO HEAR IT 'CAUSE IT ALLUS CHEERS ME UP... IT'S MY FAVORITE JOKE--GO AHEAD AN' TELL IT IF YOU KNOWS IT.
WELL
COPR 1955 WALT KELLY
I KNOWS THE STORY 'BOUT THE FELLA WHAT TOLE EVERY-BODY HE WAS A BOXER 'CAUSE HE HAD A JOB BOXIN' BLUEBERRIES... CARE TO HEAR THAT ONE?
..OH.. MMM. NO
IT WOULDN'T BE THE SAME. I ONLY ENJOYS THE OTHER ONE... IT ALLUS GIVE ME WHAT IS CALLED A BOFF.
TOO BAD.. YOU ALLUS LAUGH IN THE KEY OF F SHARP AN' I WANTED TO TUNE THIS THING.

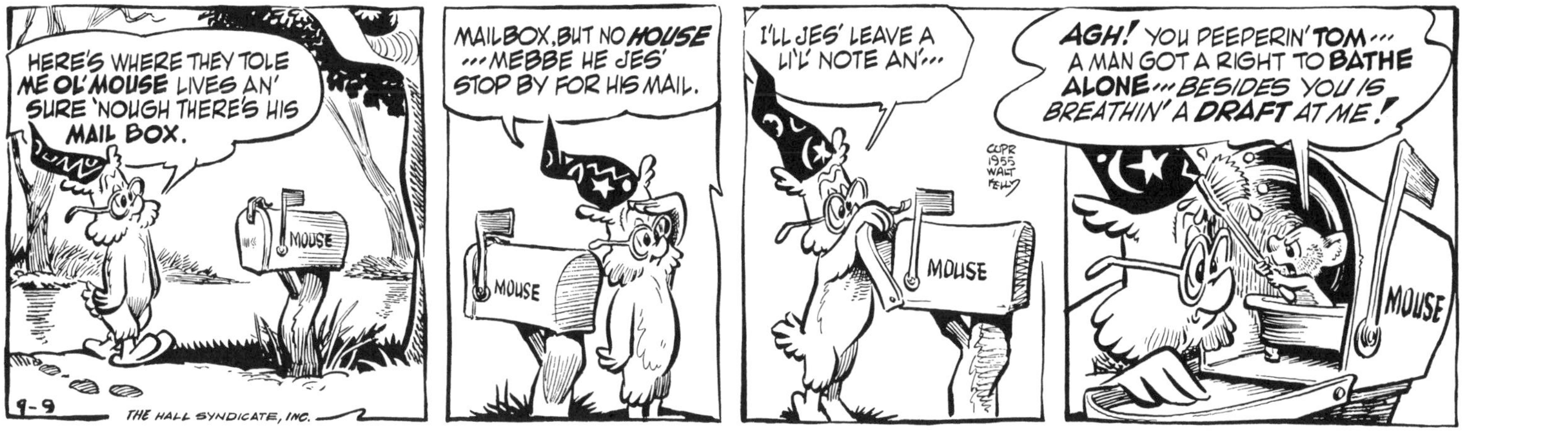
HERE'S WHERE THEY TOLE ME OL' MOUSE LIVES AN' SURE 'NOUGH THERE'S HIS MAIL BOX.
MOUSE
9-9
THE HALL SYNDICATE, INC.
MAILBOX, BUT NO HOUSE ...MEBBE HE JES' STOP BY FOR HIS MAIL.
MOUSE
I'LL JES' LEAVE A LI'L' NOTE AN'...
COPR 1955 WALT KELLY
MOUSE
AGH! YOU PEEPERIN' TOM... A MAN GOT A RIGHT TO BATHE ALONE... BESIDES YOU IS BREATHIN' A DRAFT AT ME!
MOUSE

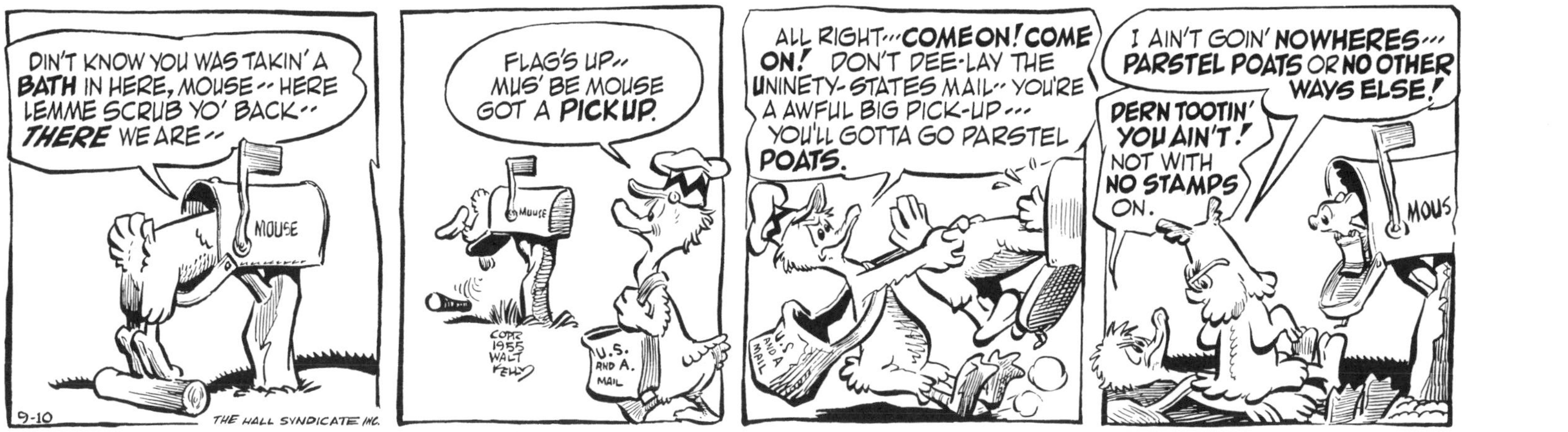
DIN'T KNOW YOU WAS TAKIN' A BATH IN HERE, MOUSE-- HERE LEMME SCRUB YO' BACK-- THERE WE ARE--
MOUSE
9-10
THE HALL SYNDICATE INC.
FLAG'S UP.. MUS' BE MOUSE GOT A PICKUP.
MOUSE
COPR 1955 WALT KELLY
U.S. AND A. MAIL
ALL RIGHT... COME ON! COME ON! DON'T DEE-LAY THE UNINETY-STATES MAIL-- YOU'RE A AWFUL BIG PICK-UP... YOU'LL GOTTA GO PARSTEL POATS.
U.S. AND A MAIL
I AIN'T GOIN' NOWHERES... PARSTEL POATS OR NO OTHER WAYS ELSE!
DERN TOOTIN' YOU AIN'T! NOT WITH NO STAMPS ON.
MOUS

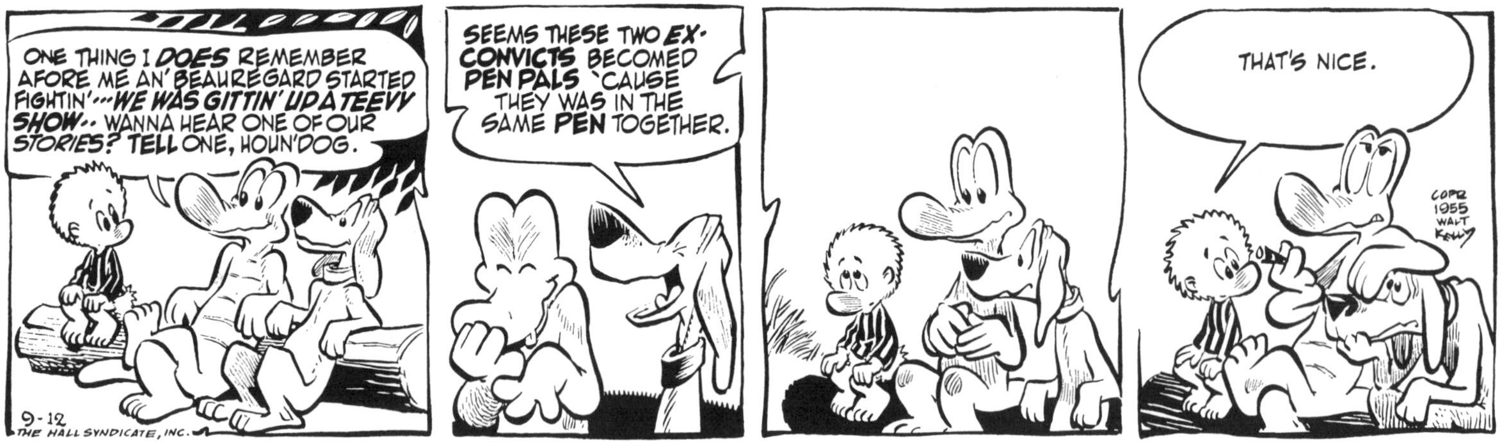
ONE THING I DOES REMEMBER AFORE ME AN' BEAUREGARD STARTED FIGHTIN'··· WE WAS GITTIN' UP A TEEVY SHOW·· WANNA HEAR ONE OF OUR STORIES? TELL ONE, HOUN'DOG.
SEEMS THESE TWO EX-CONVICTS BECOMED PEN PALS 'CAUSE THEY WAS IN THE SAME PEN TOGETHER.
THAT'S NICE.
COPR 1955 WALT KELLY
9-12
THE HALL SYNDICATE, INC.

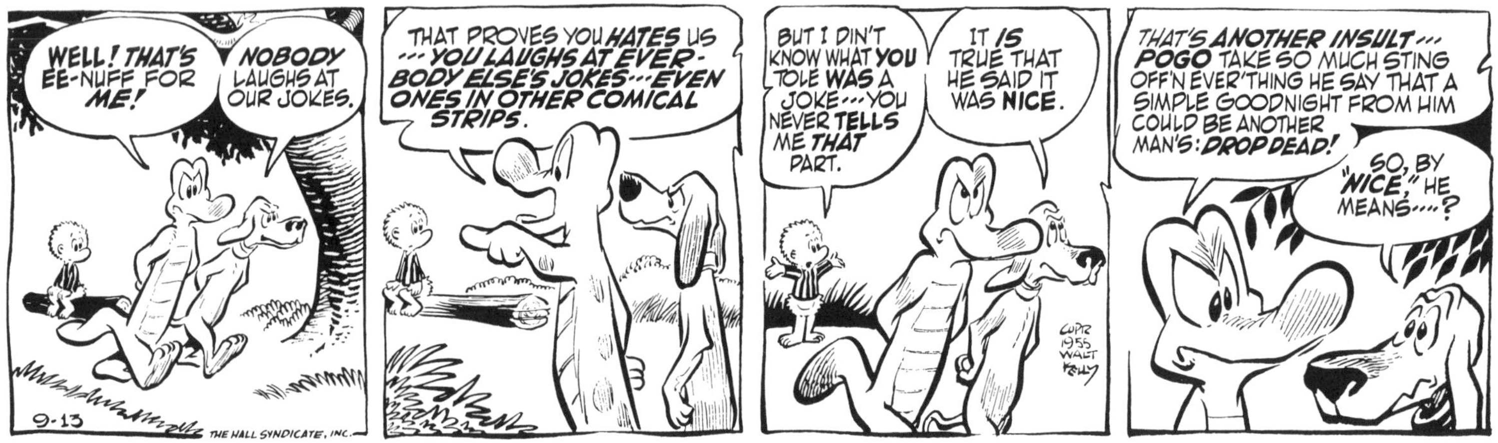
WELL! THAT'S EE-NUFF FOR ME!
NOBODY LAUGHS AT OUR JOKES.
THAT PROVES YOU HATES US ··· YOU LAUGHS AT EVER-BODY ELSE'S JOKES··· EVEN ONES IN OTHER COMICAL STRIPS.
BUT I DIN'T KNOW WHAT YOU TOLE WAS A JOKE··· YOU NEVER TELLS ME THAT PART.
IT IS TRUE THAT HE SAID IT WAS NICE.
THAT'S ANOTHER INSULT··· POGO TAKE SO MUCH STING OFF'N EVER'THING HE SAY THAT A SIMPLE GOODNIGHT FROM HIM COULD BE ANOTHER MAN'S: DROP DEAD!
SO, BY "NICE," HE MEANS····?
COPR 1955 WALT KELLY
9-13
THE HALL SYNDICATE, INC.

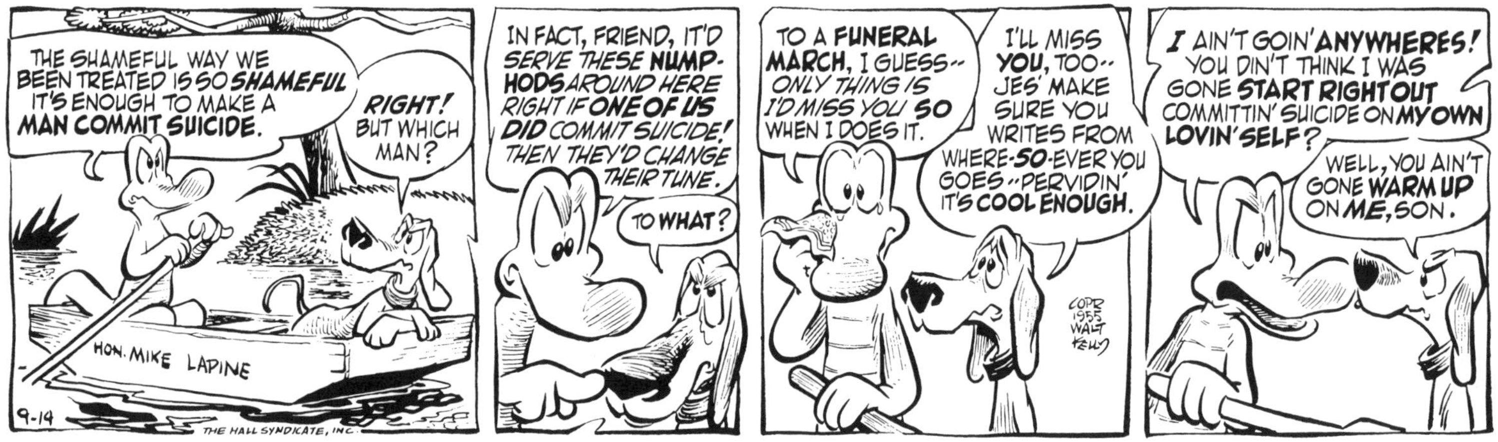
THE SHAMEFUL WAY WE BEEN TREATED IS SO SHAMEFUL IT'S ENOUGH TO MAKE A MAN COMMIT SUICIDE.
RIGHT! BUT WHICH MAN?
HON. MIKE LAPINE
IN FACT, FRIEND, IT'D SERVE THESE NUMP-HODS AROUND HERE RIGHT IF ONE OF US DID COMMIT SUICIDE! THEN THEY'D CHANGE THEIR TUNE.
TO WHAT?
TO A FUNERAL MARCH, I GUESS·· ONLY THING IS I'D MISS YOU SO WHEN I DOES IT.
I'LL MISS YOU, TOO·· JES' MAKE SURE YOU WRITES FROM WHERE-SO-EVER YOU GOES ··PERVIDIN' IT'S COOL ENOUGH.
I AIN'T GOIN' ANYWHERES! YOU DIN'T THINK I WAS GONE START RIGHT OUT COMMITTIN' SUICIDE ON MY OWN LOVIN' SELF?
WELL, YOU AIN'T GONE WARM UP ON ME, SON.
COPR 1955 WALT KELLY
9-14
THE HALL SYNDICATE, INC.

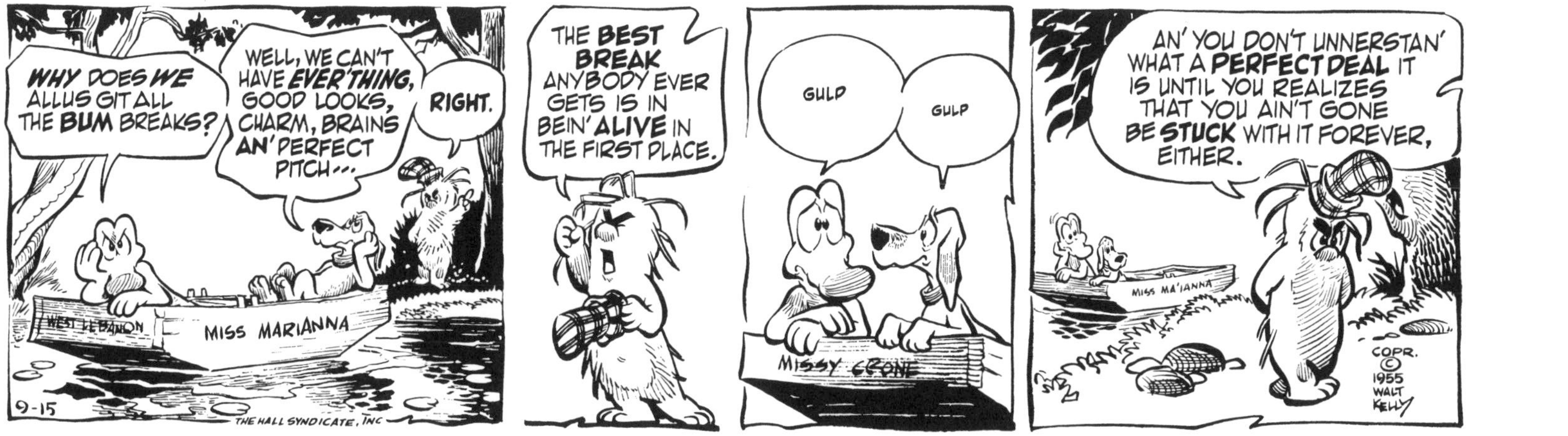
WHY DOES WE ALLUS GIT ALL THE BUM BREAKS?
WELL, WE CAN'T HAVE EVER'THING, GOOD LOOKS, CHARM, BRAINS AN' PERFECT PITCH...
RIGHT.
WEST LEBANON
MISS MARIANNA
9-15
THE HALL SYNDICATE, INC.
THE BEST BREAK ANYBODY EVER GETS IS IN BEIN' ALIVE IN THE FIRST PLACE.
GULP
GULP
MISSY CRONE
AN' YOU DON'T UNNERSTAN' WHAT A PERFECT DEAL IT IS UNTIL YOU REALIZES THAT YOU AIN'T GONE BE STUCK WITH IT FOREVER, EITHER.
MISS MA'IANNA
COPR. © 1955 WALT KELLY

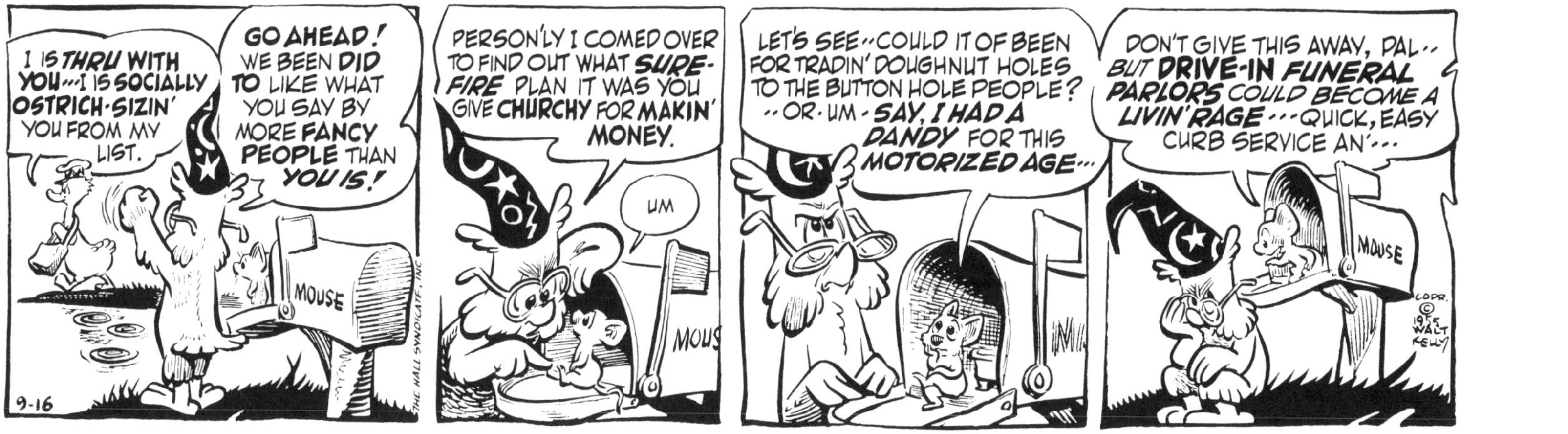
I IS THRU WITH YOU... I IS SOCIALLY OSTRICH-SIZIN' YOU FROM MY LIST.
GO AHEAD! WE BEEN DID TO LIKE WHAT YOU SAY BY MORE FANCY PEOPLE THAN YOU IS!
MOUSE
9-16
THE HALL SYNDICATE, INC
PERSON'LY I COMED OVER TO FIND OUT WHAT SURE-FIRE PLAN IT WAS YOU GIVE CHURCHY FOR MAKIN' MONEY.
UM
MOUS
LET'S SEE.. COULD IT OF BEEN FOR TRADIN' DOUGHNUT HOLES TO THE BUTTON HOLE PEOPLE? .. OR.. UM.. SAY, I HAD A DANDY FOR THIS MOTORIZED AGE...
DON'T GIVE THIS AWAY, PAL.. BUT DRIVE-IN FUNERAL PARLORS COULD BECOME A LIVIN' RAGE... QUICK, EASY CURB SERVICE AN'...
MOUSE
COPR. © 1955 WALT KELLY

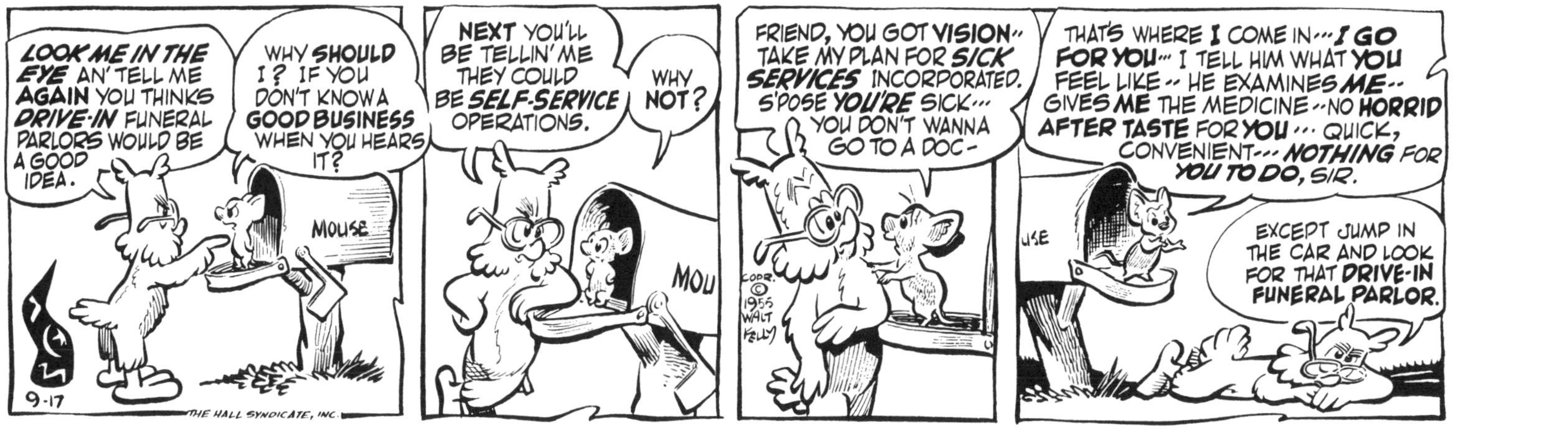
LOOK ME IN THE EYE AN' TELL ME AGAIN YOU THINKS DRIVE-IN FUNERAL PARLORS WOULD BE A GOOD IDEA.
WHY SHOULD I? IF YOU DON'T KNOW A GOOD BUSINESS WHEN YOU HEARS IT?
MOUSE
9-17
THE HALL SYNDICATE, INC.
NEXT YOU'LL BE TELLIN' ME THEY COULD BE SELF-SERVICE OPERATIONS.
WHY NOT?
MOU
FRIEND, YOU GOT VISION.. TAKE MY PLAN FOR SICK SERVICES INCORPORATED. S'POSE YOU'RE SICK... YOU DON'T WANNA GO TO A DOC-
COPR. © 1955 WALT KELLY
THAT'S WHERE I COME IN... I GO FOR YOU... I TELL HIM WHAT YOU FEEL LIKE.. HE EXAMINES ME.. GIVES ME THE MEDICINE.. NO HORRID AFTER TASTE FOR YOU... QUICK, CONVENIENT... NOTHING FOR YOU TO DO, SIR.
USE
EXCEPT JUMP IN THE CAR AND LOOK FOR THAT DRIVE-IN FUNERAL PARLOR.

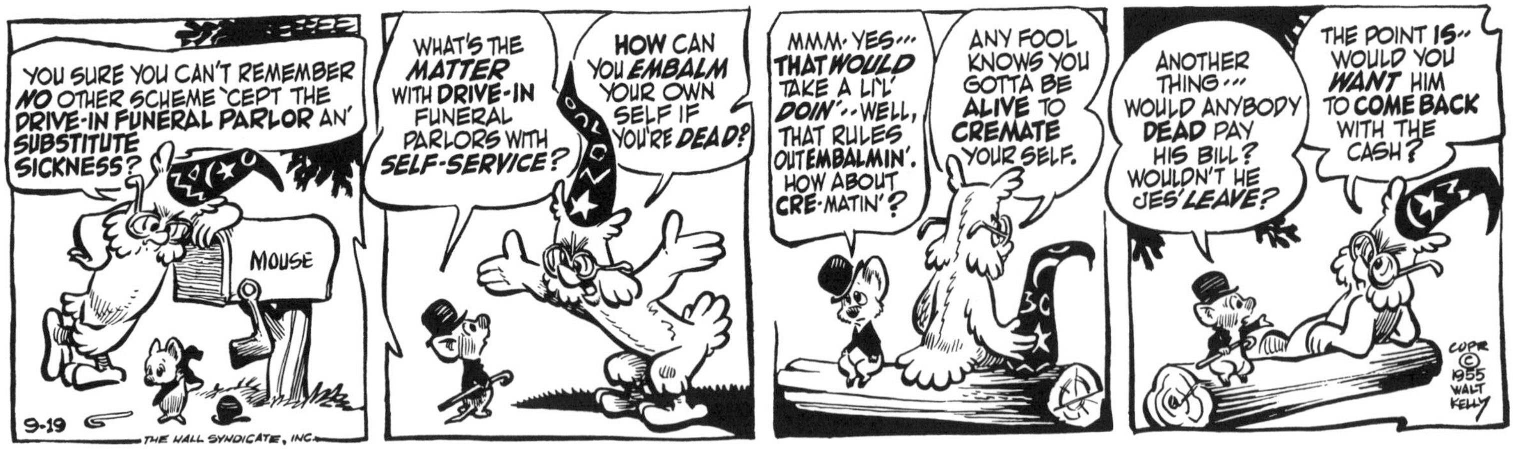
YOU SURE YOU CAN'T REMEMBER NO OTHER SCHEME 'CEPT THE DRIVE-IN FUNERAL PARLOR AN' SUBSTITUTE SICKNESS?
MOUSE
9-19
THE HALL SYNDICATE, INC.
WHAT'S THE MATTER WITH DRIVE-IN FUNERAL PARLORS WITH SELF-SERVICE?
HOW CAN YOU EMBALM YOUR OWN SELF IF YOU'RE DEAD?
MMM-YES... THAT WOULD TAKE A LI'L' DOIN'.. WELL, THAT RULES OUTEMBALMIN'. HOW ABOUT CRE-MATIN'?
ANY FOOL KNOWS YOU GOTTA BE ALIVE TO CREMATE YOUR SELF.
ANOTHER THING... WOULD ANYBODY DEAD PAY HIS BILL? WOULDN'T HE JES' LEAVE?
THE POINT IS.. WOULD YOU WANT HIM TO COME BACK WITH THE CASH?
COPR © 1955 WALT KELLY

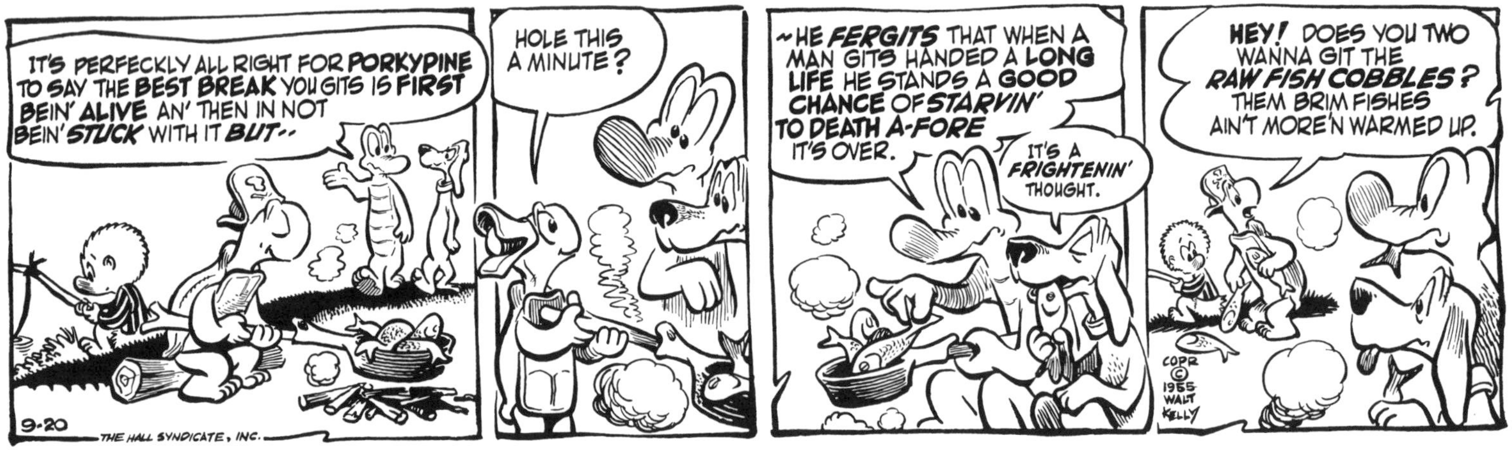
IT'S PERFECKLY ALL RIGHT FOR PORKYPINE TO SAY THE BEST BREAK YOU GITS IS FIRST BEIN' ALIVE AN' THEN IN NOT BEIN' STUCK WITH IT BUT..
9-20
THE HALL SYNDICATE, INC.
HOLE THIS A MINUTE?
~HE FERGITS THAT WHEN A MAN GITS HANDED A LONG LIFE HE STANDS A GOOD CHANCE OF STARVIN' TO DEATH A-FORE IT'S OVER.
IT'S A FRIGHTENIN' THOUGHT.
HEY! DOES YOU TWO WANNA GIT THE RAW FISH COBBLES? THEM BRIM FISHES AIN'T MORE'N WARMED UP.
COPR © 1955 WALT KELLY

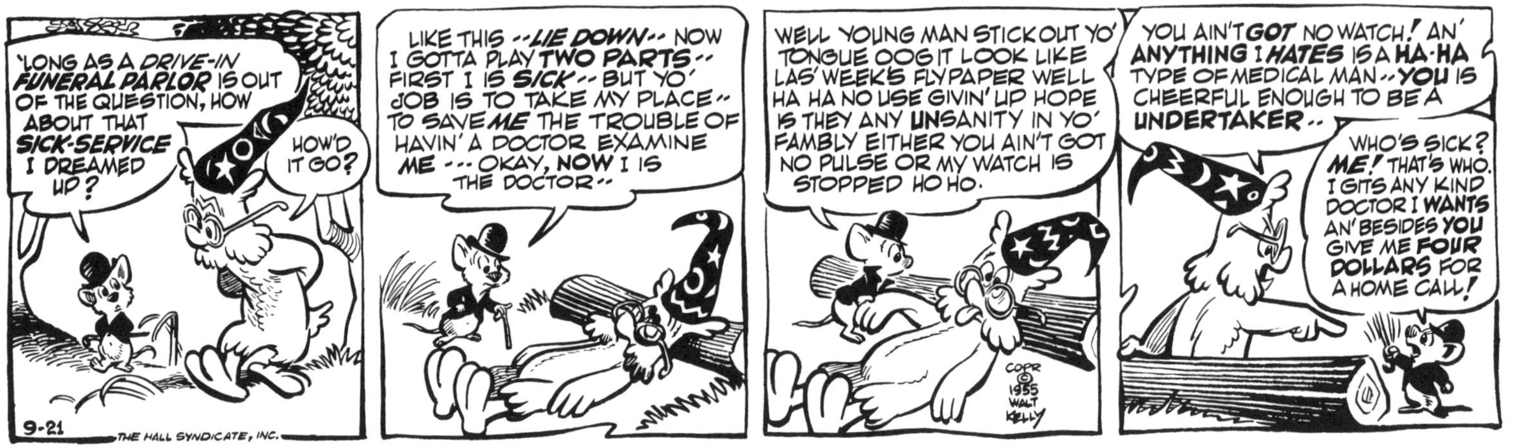
'LONG AS A DRIVE-IN FUNERAL PARLOR IS OUT OF THE QUESTION, HOW ABOUT THAT SICK-SERVICE I DREAMED UP?
HOW'D IT GO?
9-21
THE HALL SYNDICATE, INC.
LIKE THIS --LIE DOWN-- NOW I GOTTA PLAY TWO PARTS-- FIRST I IS SICK-- BUT YO' JOB IS TO TAKE MY PLACE-- TO SAVE ME THE TROUBLE OF HAVIN' A DOCTOR EXAMINE ME --- OKAY, NOW I IS THE DOCTOR--
WELL YOUNG MAN STICK OUT YO' TONGUE OOG IT LOOK LIKE LAS' WEEK'S FLYPAPER WELL HA HA NO USE GIVIN' UP HOPE IS THEY ANY UNSANITY IN YO' FAMBLY EITHER YOU AIN'T GOT NO PULSE OR MY WATCH IS STOPPED HO HO.
COPR © 1955 WALT KELLY
YOU AIN'T GOT NO WATCH! AN' ANYTHING I HATES IS A HA-HA TYPE OF MEDICAL MAN--YOU IS CHEERFUL ENOUGH TO BE A UNDERTAKER--
WHO'S SICK? ME! THAT'S WHO. I GITS ANY KIND DOCTOR I WANTS AN' BESIDES YOU GIVE ME FOUR DOLLARS FOR A HOME CALL!

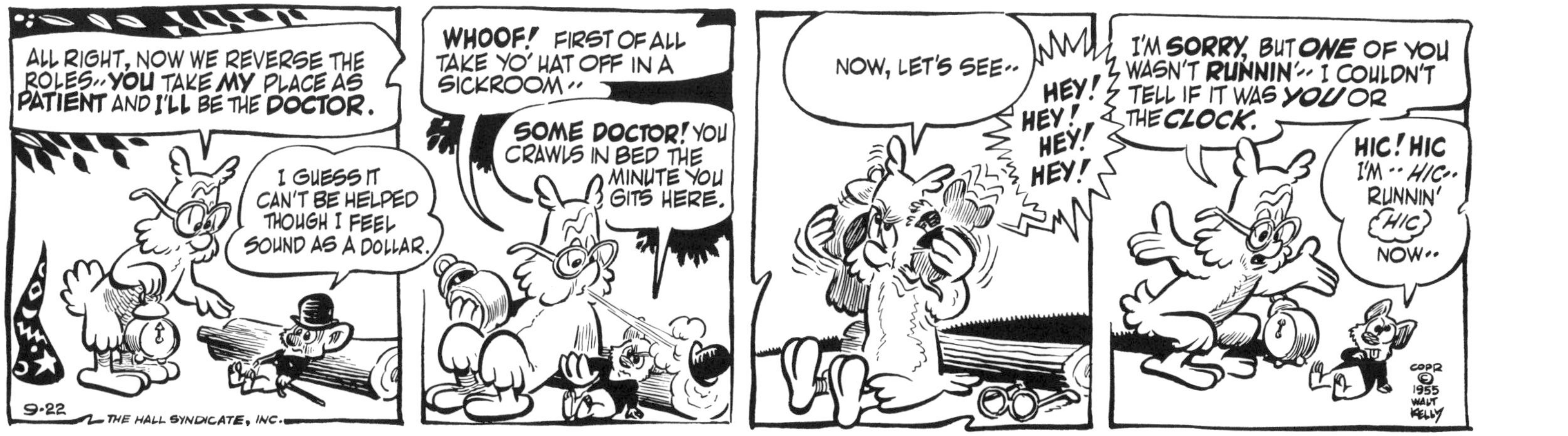
ALL RIGHT, NOW WE REVERSE THE ROLES.. YOU TAKE MY PLACE AS PATIENT AND I'LL BE THE DOCTOR.
I GUESS IT CAN'T BE HELPED THOUGH I FEEL SOUND AS A DOLLAR.
9-22 THE HALL SYNDICATE, INC.
WHOOF! FIRST OF ALL TAKE YO' HAT OFF IN A SICKROOM..
SOME DOCTOR! YOU CRAWLS IN BED THE MINUTE YOU GITS HERE.
NOW, LET'S SEE..
HEY! HEY! HEY! HEY!
I'M SORRY, BUT ONE OF YOU WASN'T RUNNIN'.. I COULDN'T TELL IF IT WAS YOU OR THE CLOCK.
HIC! HIC I'M.. HIC.. RUNNIN' HIC NOW..
COPR © 1955 WALT KELLY

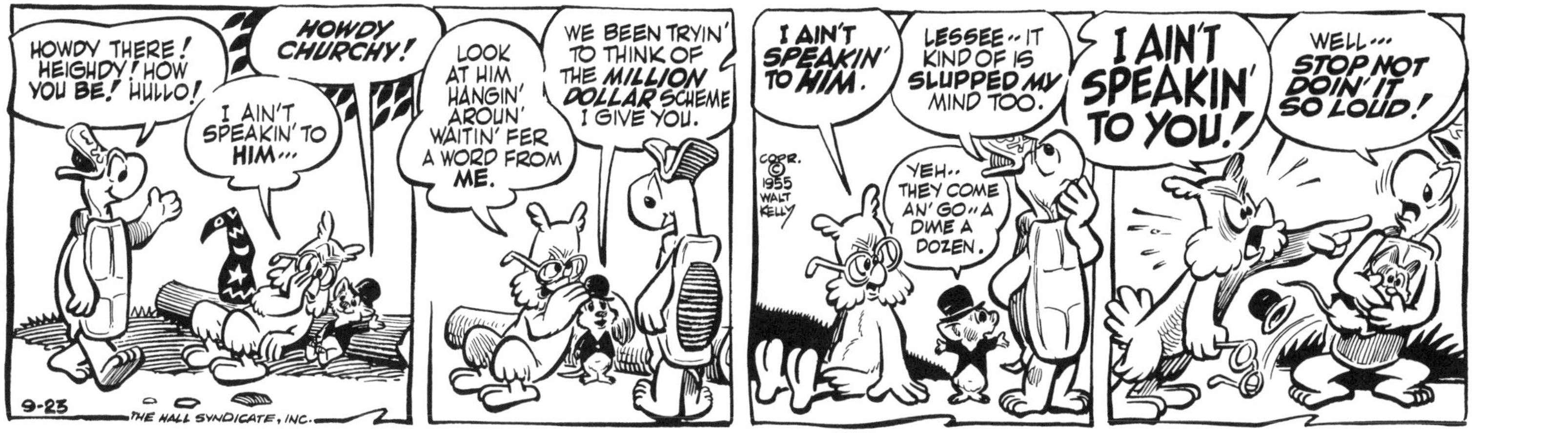
HOWDY THERE! HEIGHDY! HOW YOU BE! HULLO!
HOWDY CHURCHY!
I AIN'T SPEAKIN' TO HIM...
LOOK AT HIM HANGIN' AROUN' WAITIN' FER A WORD FROM ME.
WE BEEN TRYIN' TO THINK OF THE MILLION DOLLAR SCHEME I GIVE YOU.
9-23 THE HALL SYNDICATE, INC.
I AIN'T SPEAKIN' TO HIM.
LESSEE.. IT KIND OF IS SLUPPED MY MIND TOO.
YEH.. THEY COME AN' GO.. A DIME A DOZEN.
COPR. © 1955 WALT KELLY
I AIN'T SPEAKIN' TO YOU!
WELL... STOP NOT DOIN' IT SO LOUD!

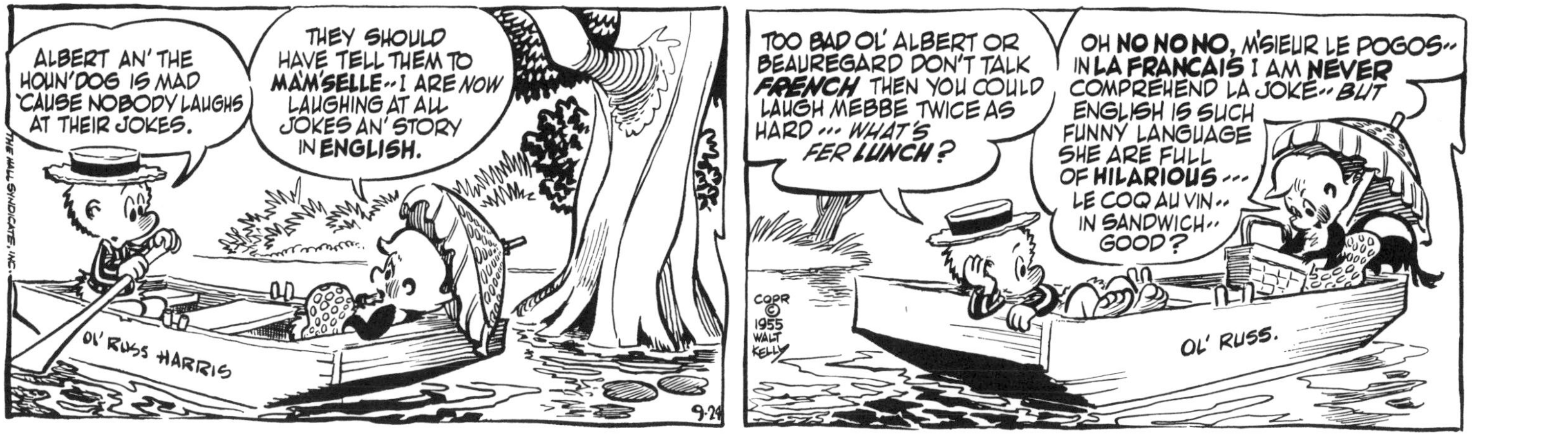
ALBERT AN' THE HOUN'DOG IS MAD 'CAUSE NOBODY LAUGHS AT THEIR JOKES.
THEY SHOULD HAVE TELL THEM TO MAM'SELLE.. I ARE NOW LAUGHING AT ALL JOKES AN' STORY IN ENGLISH.
THE HALL SYNDICATE, INC.
OL' RUSS HARRIS
9-24
TOO BAD OL' ALBERT OR BEAUREGARD DON'T TALK FRENCH THEN YOU COULD LAUGH MEBBE TWICE AS HARD... WHAT'S FER LUNCH?
OH NO NO NO, M'SIEUR LE POGOS.. IN LA FRANCAIS I AM NEVER COMPREHEND LA JOKE.. BUT ENGLISH IS SUCH FUNNY LANGUAGE SHE ARE FULL OF HILARIOUS... LE COQ AU VIN.. IN SANDWICH.. GOOD?
COPR © 1955 WALT KELLY
OL' RUSS.

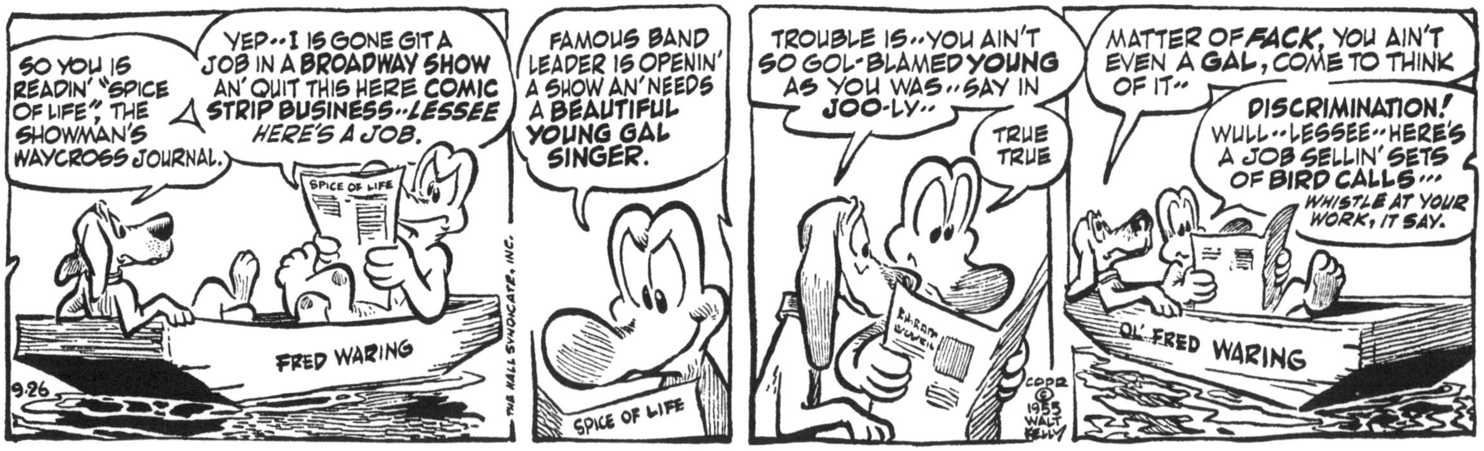
SO YOU IS READIN' "SPICE OF LIFE", THE SHOWMAN'S WAYCROSS JOURNAL.
YEP.. I IS GONE GIT A JOB IN A BROADWAY SHOW AN' QUIT THIS HERE COMIC STRIP BUSINESS.. LESSEE HERE'S A JOB.
SPICE OF LIFE
FRED WARING
9.26
THE HALL SYNDICATE, INC.
FAMOUS BAND LEADER IS OPENIN' A SHOW AN' NEEDS A BEAUTIFUL YOUNG GAL SINGER.
SPICE OF LIFE
TROUBLE IS.. YOU AIN'T SO GOL-BLAMED YOUNG AS YOU WAS.. SAY IN JOO-LY..
TRUE TRUE
COPR © 1955 WALT KELLY
MATTER OF FACK, YOU AIN'T EVEN A GAL, COME TO THINK OF IT..
DISCRIMINATION! WULL.. LESSEE.. HERE'S A JOB SELLIN' SETS OF BIRD CALLS... WHISTLE AT YOUR WORK, IT SAY.
OL' FRED WARING

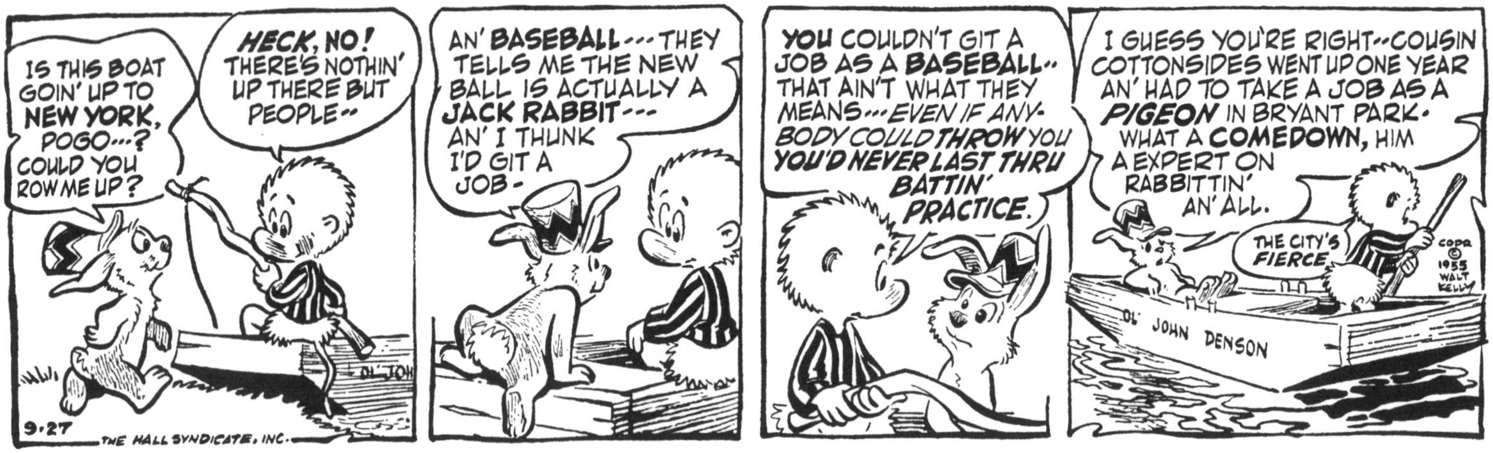
IS THIS BOAT GOIN' UP TO NEW YORK, POGO...? COULD YOU ROW ME UP?
HECK, NO! THERE'S NOTHIN' UP THERE BUT PEOPLE..
9.27
THE HALL SYNDICATE, INC.
AN' BASEBALL... THEY TELLS ME THE NEW BALL IS ACTUALLY A JACK RABBIT... AN' I THUNK I'D GIT A JOB.
YOU COULDN'T GIT A JOB AS A BASEBALL.. THAT AIN'T WHAT THEY MEANS... EVEN IF ANYBODY COULD THROW YOU YOU'D NEVER LAST THRU BATTIN' PRACTICE.
I GUESS YOU'RE RIGHT.. COUSIN COTTONSIDES WENT UP ONE YEAR AN' HAD TO TAKE A JOB AS A PIGEON IN BRYANT PARK. WHAT A COMEDOWN, HIM A EXPERT ON RABBITTIN' AN' ALL.
THE CITY'S FIERCE
COPR © 1955 WALT KELLY
OL' JOHN DENSON

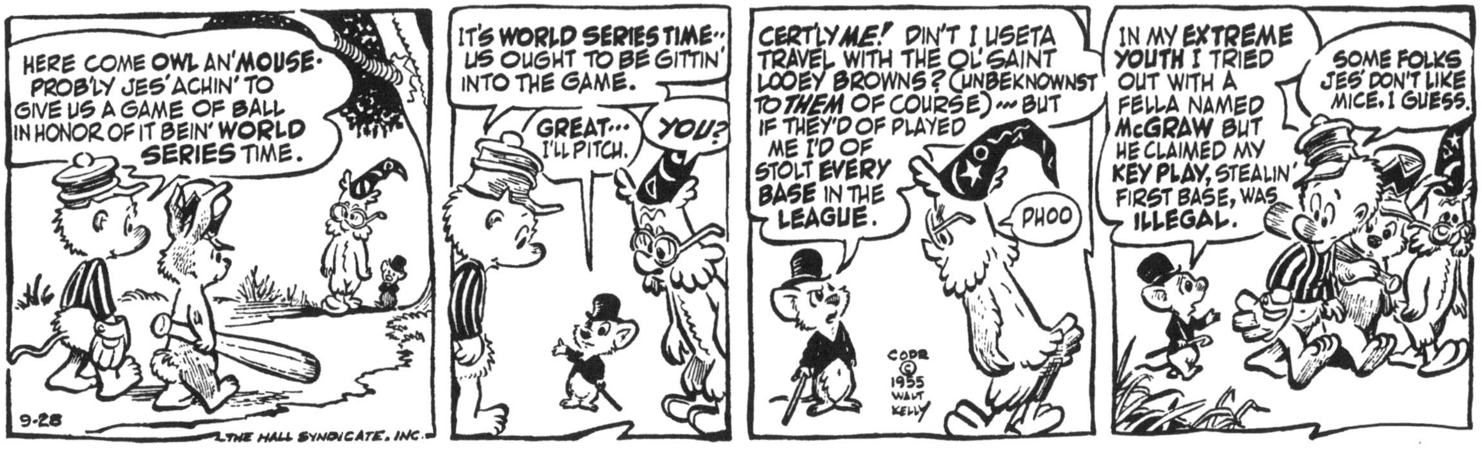
HERE COME OWL AN' MOUSE. PROB'LY JES' ACHIN' TO GIVE US A GAME OF BALL IN HONOR OF IT BEIN' WORLD SERIES TIME.
9-28
THE HALL SYNDICATE, INC.
IT'S WORLD SERIES TIME.. US OUGHT TO BE GITTIN' INTO THE GAME.
GREAT... I'LL PITCH.
YOU?
CERT'LY ME! DIN'T I USETA TRAVEL WITH THE OL' SAINT LOOEY BROWNS? (UNBEKNOWNST TO THEM OF COURSE)... BUT IF THEY'D OF PLAYED ME I'D OF STOLT EVERY BASE IN THE LEAGUE.
PHOO
COPR © 1955 WALT KELLY
IN MY EXTREME YOUTH I TRIED OUT WITH A FELLA NAMED McGRAW BUT HE CLAIMED MY KEY PLAY, STEALIN' FIRST BASE, WAS ILLEGAL.
SOME FOLKS JES' DON'T LIKE MICE, I GUESS.

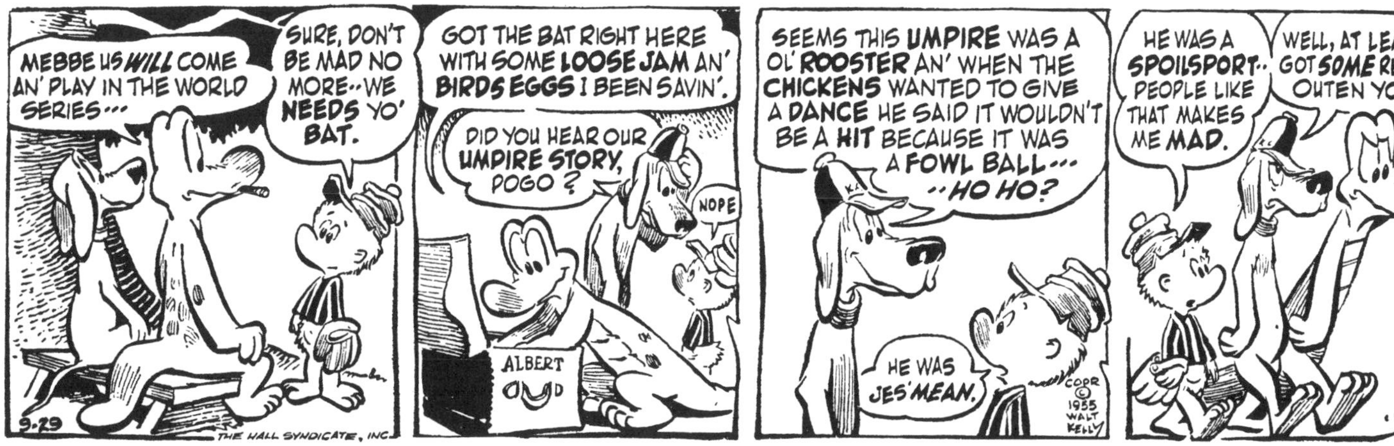
MEBBE US WILL COME AN' PLAY IN THE WORLD SERIES…
SURE, DON'T BE MAD NO MORE··WE NEEDS YO' BAT.
9-29
THE HALL SYNDICATE, INC
GOT THE BAT RIGHT HERE WITH SOME LOOSE JAM AN' BIRDS EGGS I BEEN SAVIN'.
DID YOU HEAR OUR UMPIRE STORY, POGO ?
NOPE
ALBERT
SEEMS THIS UMPIRE WAS A OL' ROOSTER AN' WHEN THE CHICKENS WANTED TO GIVE A DANCE HE SAID IT WOULDN'T BE A HIT BECAUSE IT WAS A FOWL BALL… ··HO HO?
HE WAS JES' MEAN.
COPR © 1955 WALT KELLY
HE WAS A SPOILSPORT·· PEOPLE LIKE THAT MAKES ME MAD.
WELL, AT LEAST IT GOT SOME REACTION OUTEN YOU.

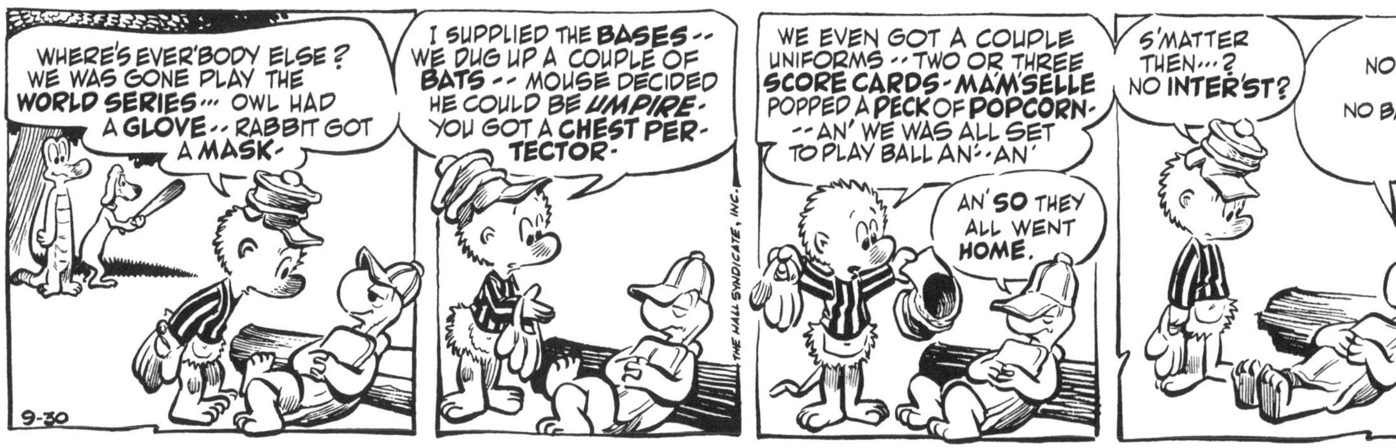
WHERE'S EVER'BODY ELSE ? WE WAS GONE PLAY THE WORLD SERIES… OWL HAD A GLOVE·· RABBIT GOT A MASK·
9-30
I SUPPLIED THE BASES·· WE DUG UP A COUPLE OF BATS ·· MOUSE DECIDED HE COULD BE UMPIRE· YOU GOT A CHEST PER-TECTOR·
THE HALL SYNDICATE, INC.
WE EVEN GOT A COUPLE UNIFORMS ·· TWO OR THREE SCORE CARDS· MAM'SELLE POPPED A PECK OF POPCORN· ··AN' WE WAS ALL SET TO PLAY BALL AN'·· AN'
AN' SO THEY ALL WENT HOME.
S'MATTER THEN…? NO INTER'ST?
NOPE· NO BALL.
COPR © 1955 WALT KELLY

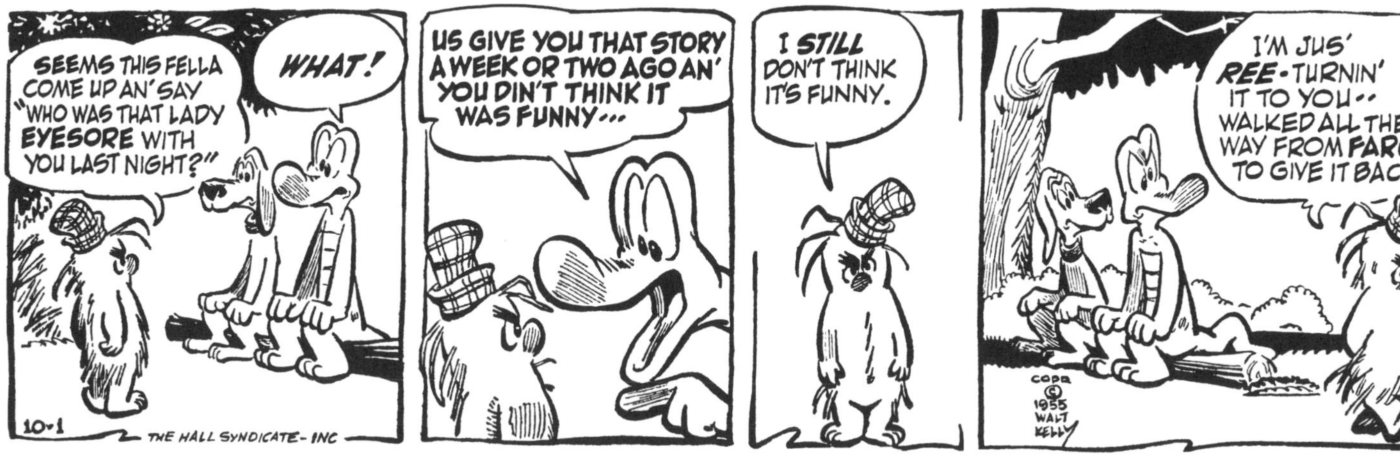
SEEMS THIS FELLA COME UP AN' SAY "WHO WAS THAT LADY EYESORE WITH YOU LAST NIGHT?"
WHAT!
10-1
THE HALL SYNDICATE- INC
US GIVE YOU THAT STORY A WEEK OR TWO AGO AN' YOU DIN'T THINK IT WAS FUNNY…
I STILL DON'T THINK IT'S FUNNY.
COPR © 1955 WALT KELLY
I'M JUS' REE-TURNIN' IT TO YOU·· WALKED ALL THE WAY FROM FARGO TO GIVE IT BACK.

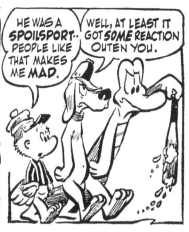

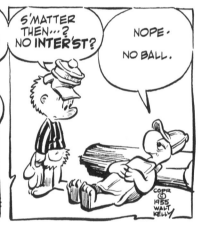

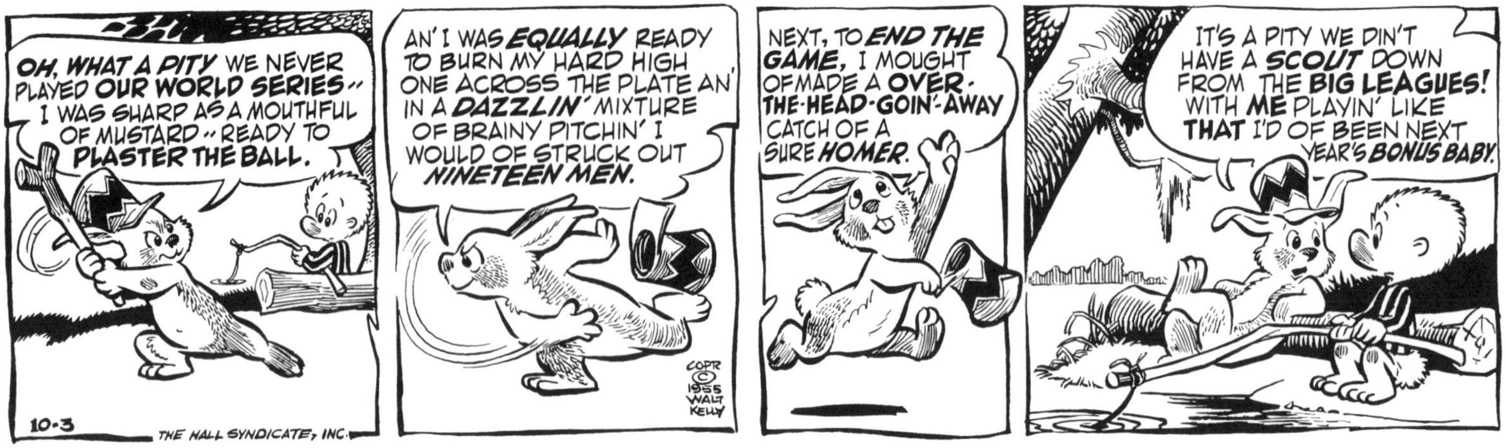
OH, WHAT A PITY WE NEVER PLAYED OUR WORLD SERIES -- I WAS SHARP AS A MOUTHFUL OF MUSTARD -- READY TO PLASTER THE BALL.
10-3
THE HALL SYNDICATE, INC.
AN' I WAS EQUALLY READY TO BURN MY HARD HIGH ONE ACROSS THE PLATE AN' IN A DAZZLIN' MIXTURE OF BRAINY PITCHIN' I WOULD OF STRUCK OUT NINETEEN MEN.
COPR © 1955 WALT KELLY
NEXT, TO END THE GAME, I MOUGHT OF MADE A OVER-THE-HEAD-GOIN'-AWAY CATCH OF A SURE HOMER.
IT'S A PITY WE DIN'T HAVE A SCOUT DOWN FROM THE BIG LEAGUES! WITH ME PLAYIN' LIKE THAT I'D OF BEEN NEXT YEAR'S BONUS BABY.

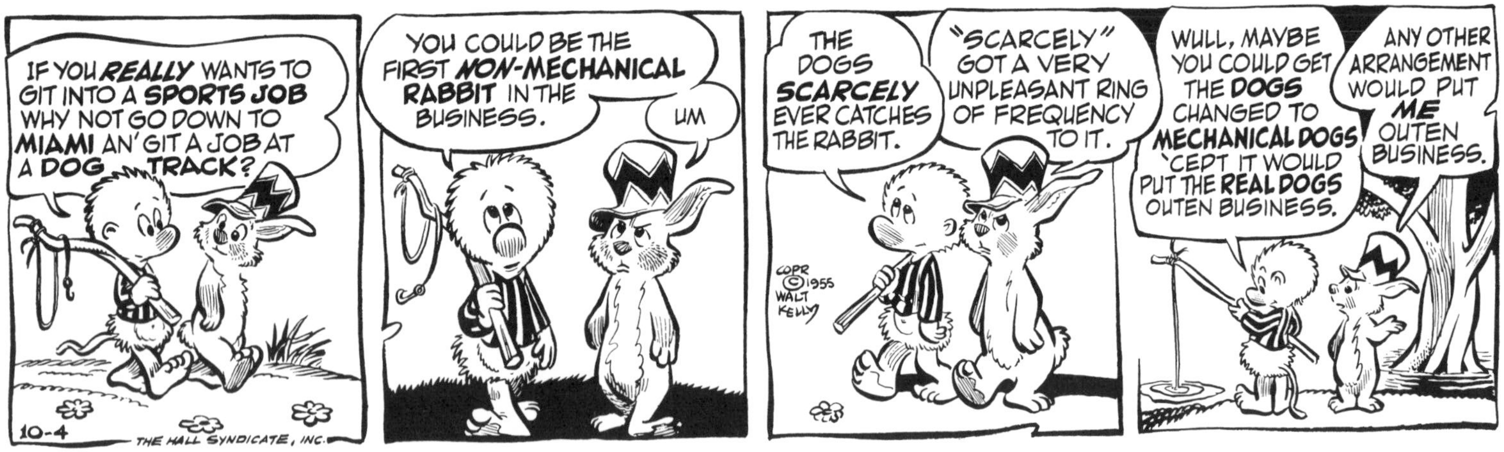
IF YOU REALLY WANTS TO GIT INTO A SPORTS JOB WHY NOT GO DOWN TO MIAMI AN' GIT A JOB AT A DOG TRACK?
10-4
THE HALL SYNDICATE, INC.
YOU COULD BE THE FIRST NON-MECHANICAL RABBIT IN THE BUSINESS.
UM
THE DOGS SCARCELY EVER CATCHES THE RABBIT.
"SCARCELY" GOT A VERY UNPLEASANT RING OF FREQUENCY TO IT.
COPR © 1955 WALT KELLY
WULL, MAYBE YOU COULD GET THE DOGS CHANGED TO MECHANICAL DOGS 'CEPT IT WOULD PUT THE REAL DOGS OUTEN BUSINESS.
ANY OTHER ARRANGEMENT WOULD PUT ME OUTEN BUSINESS.

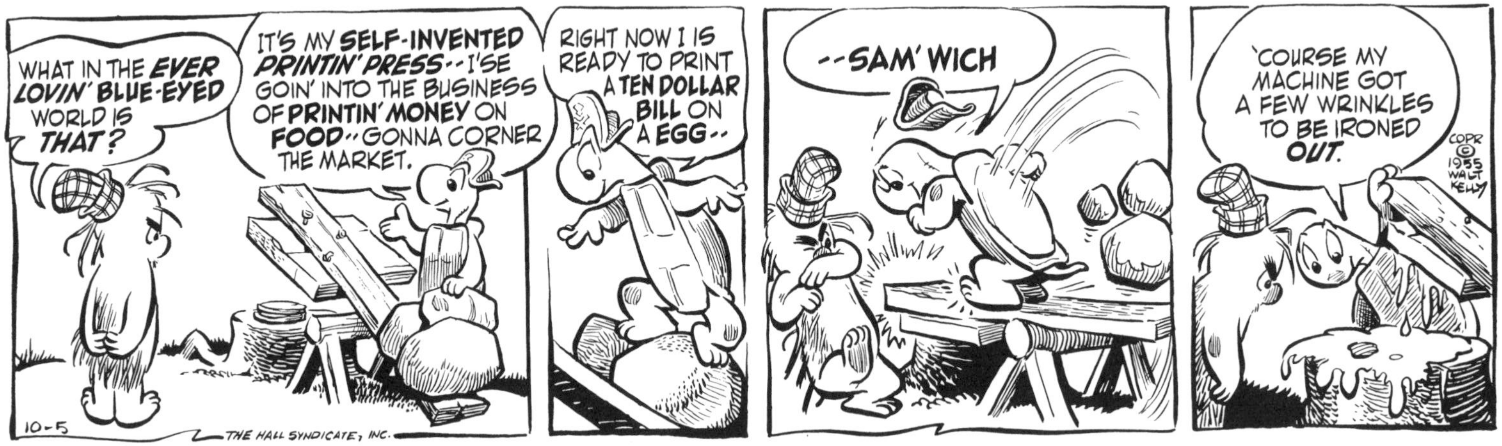
WHAT IN THE EVER LOVIN' BLUE-EYED WORLD IS THAT?
IT'S MY SELF-INVENTED PRINTIN' PRESS -- I'SE GOIN' INTO THE BUSINESS OF PRINTIN' MONEY ON FOOD -- GONNA CORNER THE MARKET.
10-5
THE HALL SYNDICATE, INC.
RIGHT NOW I IS READY TO PRINT A TEN DOLLAR BILL ON A EGG --
-- SAM' WICH
'COURSE MY MACHINE GOT A FEW WRINKLES TO BE IRONED OUT.
COPR © 1955 WALT KELLY

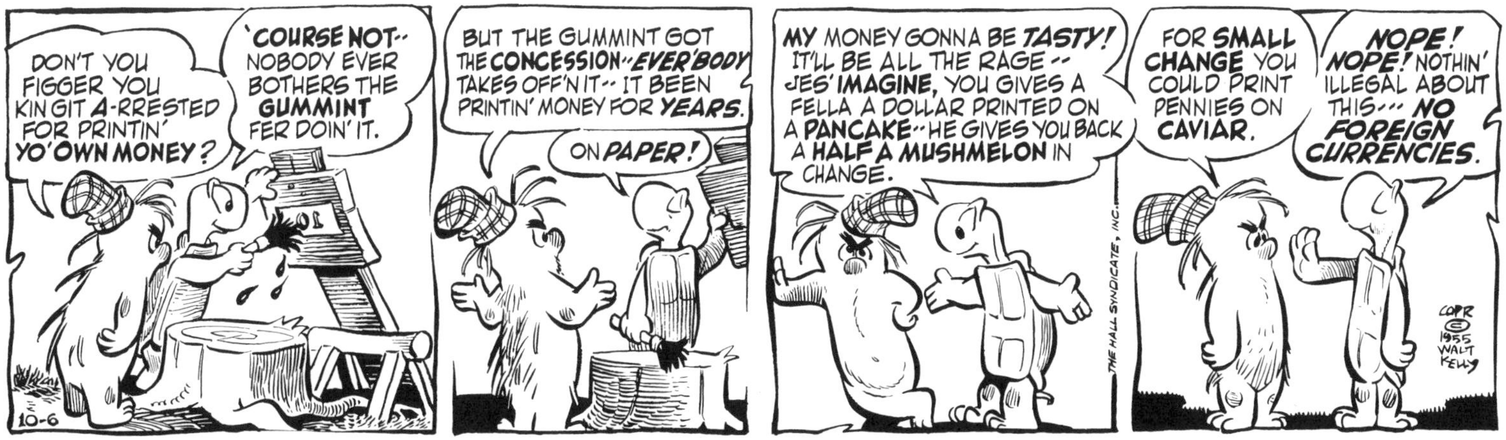
DON'T YOU FIGGER YOU KIN GIT A-RRESTED FOR PRINTIN' YO' OWN MONEY?
'COURSE NOT-- NOBODY EVER BOTHERS THE GUMMINT FER DOIN' IT.
10-6
BUT THE GUMMINT GOT THE CONCESSION--EVER'BODY TAKES OFF'N IT-- IT BEEN PRINTIN' MONEY FOR YEARS.
ON PAPER!
MY MONEY GONNA BE TASTY! IT'LL BE ALL THE RAGE-- JES' IMAGINE, YOU GIVES A FELLA A DOLLAR PRINTED ON A PANCAKE--HE GIVES YOU BACK A HALF A MUSHMELON IN CHANGE.
THE HALL SYNDICATE, INC.
FOR SMALL CHANGE YOU COULD PRINT PENNIES ON CAVIAR.
NOPE! NOPE! NOTHIN' ILLEGAL ABOUT THIS--- NO FOREIGN CURRENCIES.
COPR © 1955 WALT KELLY

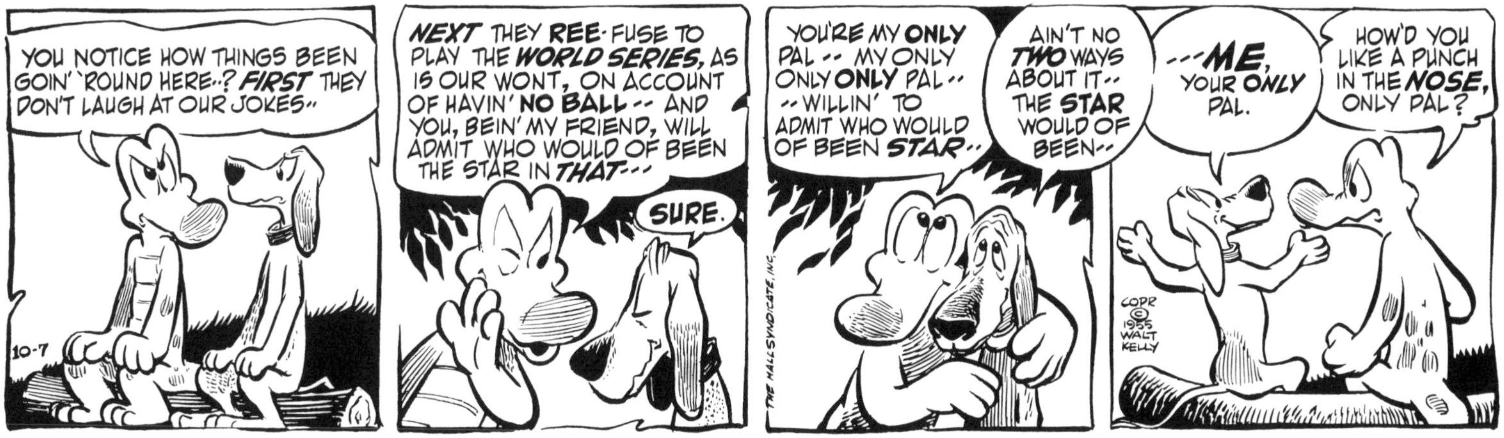
YOU NOTICE HOW THINGS BEEN GOIN' 'ROUND HERE--? FIRST THEY DON'T LAUGH AT OUR JOKES--
10-7
NEXT THEY REE-FUSE TO PLAY THE WORLD SERIES, AS IS OUR WONT, ON ACCOUNT OF HAVIN' NO BALL-- AND YOU, BEIN' MY FRIEND, WILL ADMIT WHO WOULD OF BEEN THE STAR IN THAT---
SURE.
THE HALL SYNDICATE, INC.
YOU'RE MY ONLY PAL-- MY ONLY ONLY ONLY PAL-- --WILLIN' TO ADMIT WHO WOULD OF BEEN STAR--
AIN'T NO TWO WAYS ABOUT IT-- THE STAR WOULD OF BEEN--
---ME, YOUR ONLY PAL.
HOW'D YOU LIKE A PUNCH IN THE NOSE, ONLY PAL?
COPR © 1955 WALT KELLY

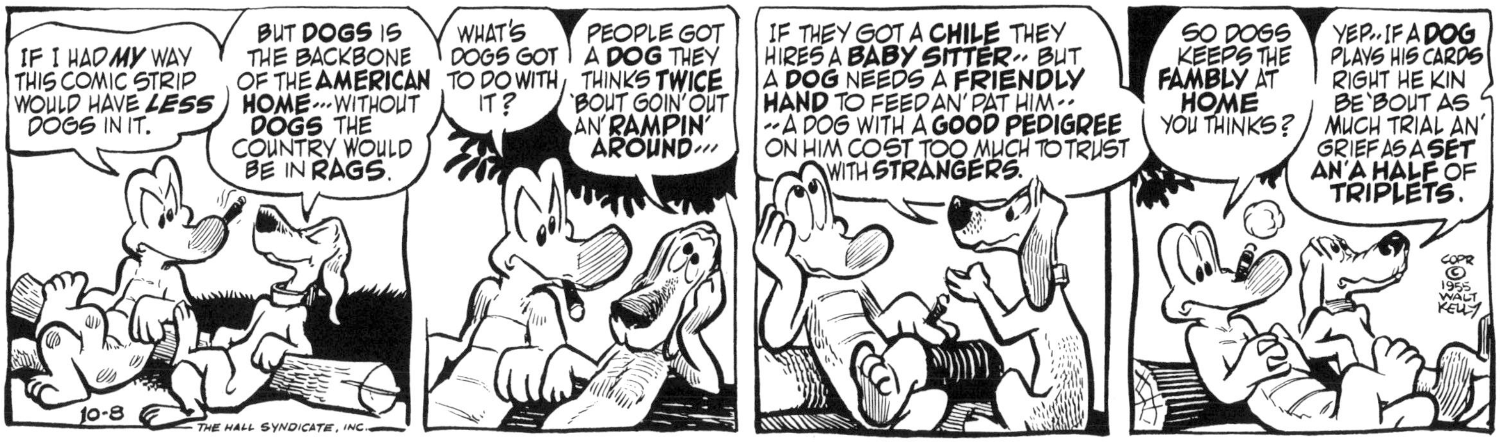
IF I HAD MY WAY THIS COMIC STRIP WOULD HAVE LESS DOGS IN IT.
BUT DOGS IS THE BACKBONE OF THE AMERICAN HOME---WITHOUT DOGS THE COUNTRY WOULD BE IN RAGS.
10-8
THE HALL SYNDICATE, INC.
WHAT'S DOGS GOT TO DO WITH IT?
PEOPLE GOT A DOG THEY THINKS TWICE 'BOUT GOIN' OUT AN' RAMPIN' AROUND---
IF THEY GOT A CHILE THEY HIRES A BABY SITTER-- BUT A DOG NEEDS A FRIENDLY HAND TO FEED AN' PAT HIM-- --A DOG WITH A GOOD PEDIGREE ON HIM COST TOO MUCH TO TRUST WITH STRANGERS.
SO DOGS KEEPS THE FAMBLY AT HOME YOU THINKS?
YEP--IF A DOG PLAYS HIS CARDS RIGHT HE KIN BE 'BOUT AS MUCH TRIAL AN' GRIEF AS A SET AN' A HALF OF TRIPLETS.
COPR © 1955 WALT KELLY

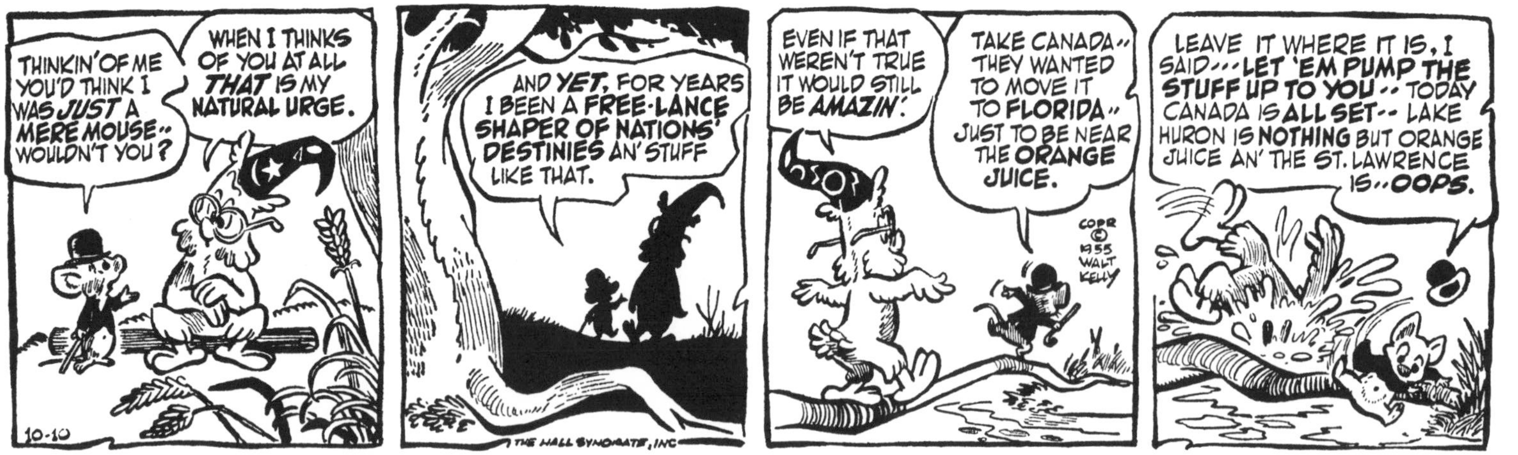
THINKIN' OF ME YOU'D THINK I WAS JUST A MERE MOUSE.. WOULDN'T YOU?
WHEN I THINKS OF YOU AT ALL THAT IS MY NATURAL URGE.
10-10
AND YET, FOR YEARS I BEEN A FREE-LANCE SHAPER OF NATIONS' DESTINIES AN' STUFF LIKE THAT.
THE HALL SYNDICATE, INC.
EVEN IF THAT WEREN'T TRUE IT WOULD STILL BE AMAZIN'.
TAKE CANADA.. THEY WANTED TO MOVE IT TO FLORIDA.. JUST TO BE NEAR THE ORANGE JUICE.
COPR © 1955 WALT KELLY
LEAVE IT WHERE IT IS, I SAID... LET 'EM PUMP THE STUFF UP TO YOU.. TODAY CANADA IS ALL SET.. LAKE HURON IS NOTHING BUT ORANGE JUICE AN' THE ST. LAWRENCE IS..OOPS.

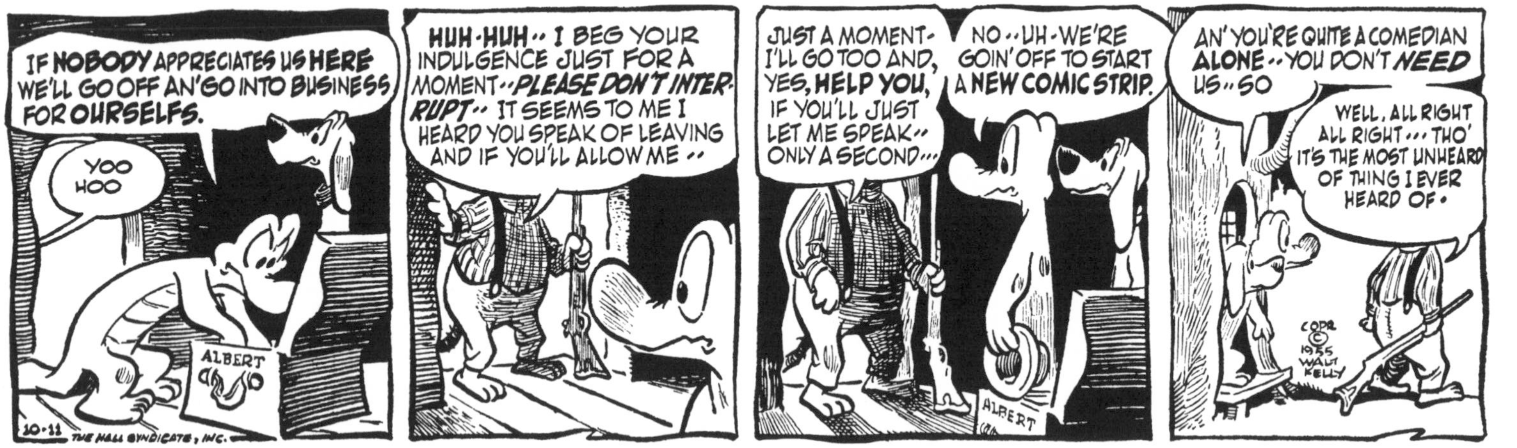
IF NOBODY APPRECIATES US HERE WE'LL GO OFF AN' GO INTO BUSINESS FOR OURSELFS.
YOO HOO
ALBERT
10-11 THE HALL SYNDICATE, INC.
HUH-HUH.. I BEG YOUR INDULGENCE JUST FOR A MOMENT.. PLEASE DON'T INTERRUPT.. IT SEEMS TO ME I HEARD YOU SPEAK OF LEAVING AND IF YOU'LL ALLOW ME..
JUST A MOMENT- I'LL GO TOO AND, YES, HELP YOU, IF YOU'LL JUST LET ME SPEAK.. ONLY A SECOND...
NO..UH-WE'RE GOIN' OFF TO START A NEW COMIC STRIP.
ALBERT
AN' YOU'RE QUITE A COMEDIAN ALONE.. YOU DON'T NEED US.. SO
WELL, ALL RIGHT ALL RIGHT... THO' IT'S THE MOST UNHEARD OF THING I EVER HEARD OF.
COPR © 1955 WALT KELLY

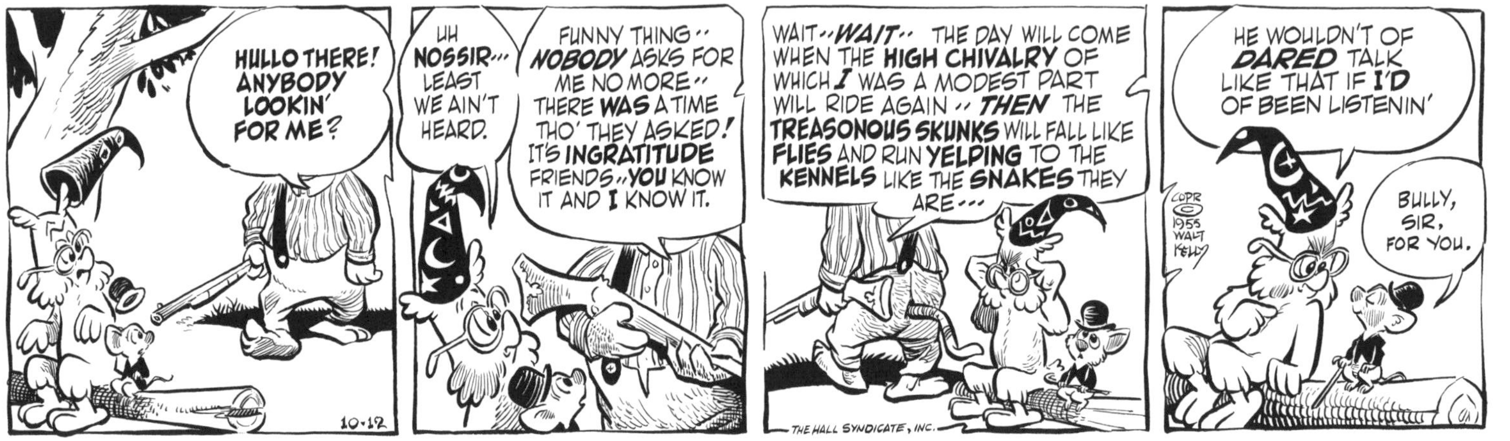
HULLO THERE! ANYBODY LOOKIN' FOR ME?
10-12
UH NOSSIR... LEAST WE AIN'T HEARD.
FUNNY THING.. NOBODY ASKS FOR ME NO MORE.. THERE WAS A TIME THO' THEY ASKED! IT'S INGRATITUDE FRIENDS.. YOU KNOW IT AND I KNOW IT.
WAIT..WAIT.. THE DAY WILL COME WHEN THE HIGH CHIVALRY OF WHICH I WAS A MODEST PART WILL RIDE AGAIN.. THEN THE TREASONOUS SKUNKS WILL FALL LIKE FLIES AND RUN YELPING TO THE KENNELS LIKE THE SNAKES THEY ARE...
THE HALL SYNDICATE, INC.
COPR © 1955 WALT KELLY
HE WOULDN'T OF DARED TALK LIKE THAT IF I'D OF BEEN LISTENIN'
BULLY, SIR, FOR YOU.

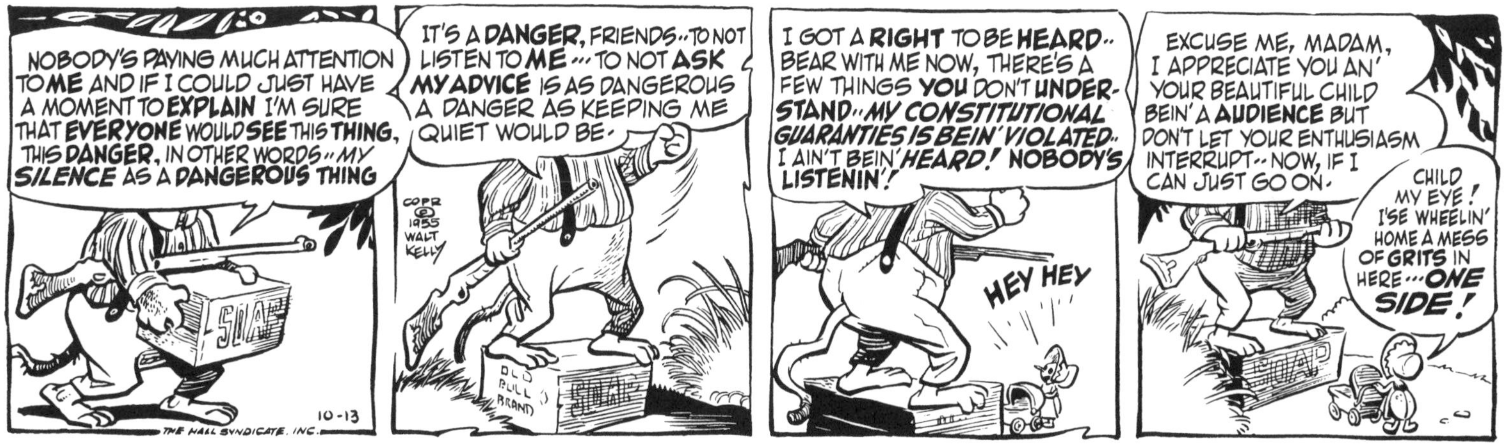
NOBODY'S PAYING MUCH ATTENTION TO ME AND IF I COULD JUST HAVE A MOMENT TO EXPLAIN I'M SURE THAT EVERYONE WOULD SEE THIS THING, THIS DANGER, IN OTHER WORDS.. MY SILENCE AS A DANGEROUS THING
SOAP
10-13
THE HALL SYNDICATE, INC.
IT'S A DANGER, FRIENDS.. TO NOT LISTEN TO ME... TO NOT ASK MY ADVICE IS AS DANGEROUS A DANGER AS KEEPING ME QUIET WOULD BE.
COPR © 1955 WALT KELLY
OLD BULL BRAND
SOAP
I GOT A RIGHT TO BE HEARD.. BEAR WITH ME NOW, THERE'S A FEW THINGS YOU DON'T UNDERSTAND.. MY CONSTITUTIONAL GUARANTIES IS BEIN' VIOLATED.. I AIN'T BEIN' HEARD! NOBODY'S LISTENIN'!
HEY HEY
EXCUSE ME, MADAM, I APPRECIATE YOU AN' YOUR BEAUTIFUL CHILD BEIN' A AUDIENCE BUT DON'T LET YOUR ENTHUSIASM INTERRUPT.. NOW, IF I CAN JUST GO ON.
CHILD MY EYE! I'SE WHEELIN' HOME A MESS OF GRITS IN HERE... ONE SIDE!
SOAP

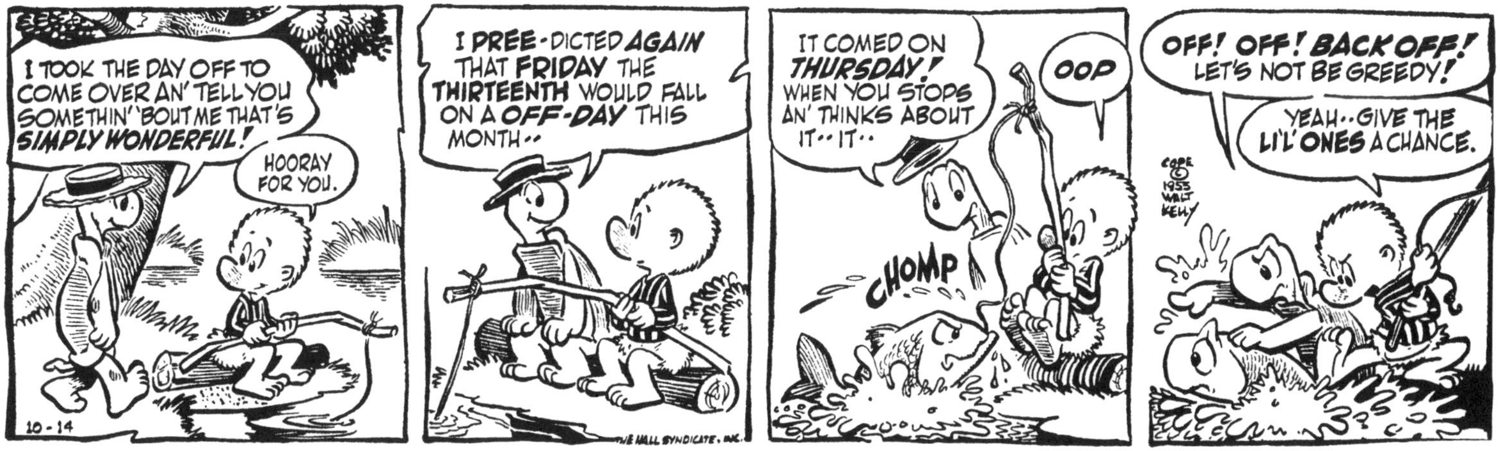
I TOOK THE DAY OFF TO COME OVER AN' TELL YOU SOMETHIN' 'BOUT ME THAT'S SIMPLY WONDERFUL!
HOORAY FOR YOU.
10-14
I PREE-DICTED AGAIN THAT FRIDAY THE THIRTEENTH WOULD FALL ON A OFF-DAY THIS MONTH..
THE HALL SYNDICATE, INC.
IT COMED ON THURSDAY! WHEN YOU STOPS AN' THINKS ABOUT IT.. IT..
OOP
CHOMP
OFF! OFF! BACK OFF! LET'S NOT BE GREEDY!
YEAH.. GIVE THE LI'L ONES A CHANCE.
COPR © 1955 WALT KELLY

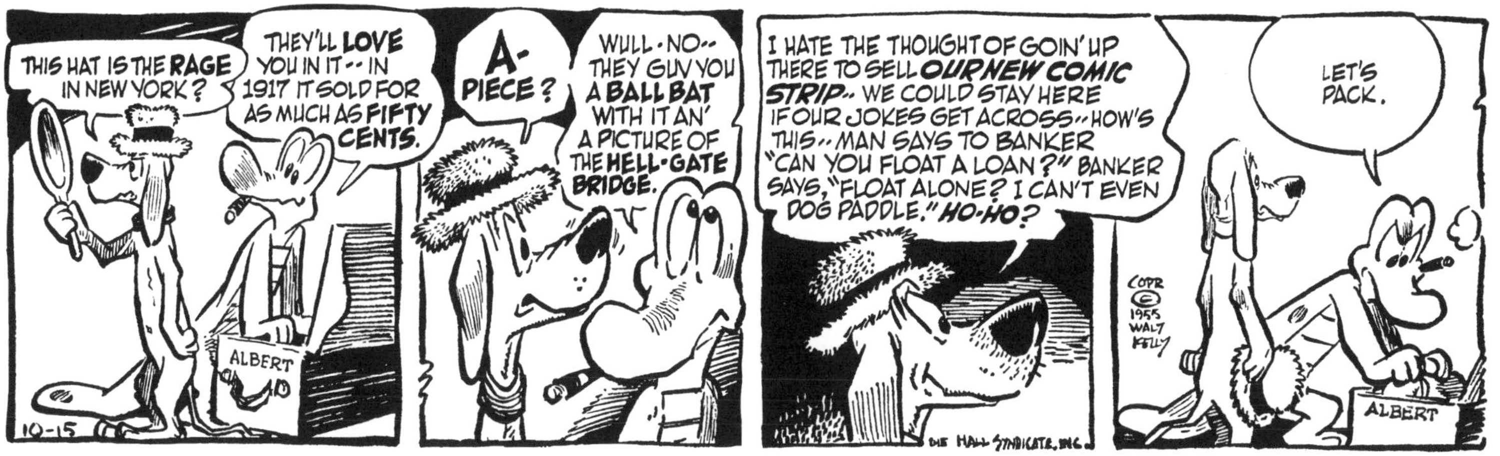
THIS HAT IS THE RAGE IN NEW YORK?
THEY'LL LOVE YOU IN IT.. IN 1917 IT SOLD FOR AS MUCH AS FIFTY CENTS.
ALBERT
10-15
A-PIECE?
WULL.. NO.. THEY GUV YOU A BALL BAT WITH IT AN' A PICTURE OF THE HELL-GATE BRIDGE.
I HATE THE THOUGHT OF GOIN' UP THERE TO SELL OUR NEW COMIC STRIP.. WE COULD STAY HERE IF OUR JOKES GET ACROSS.. HOW'S THIS.. MAN SAYS TO BANKER "CAN YOU FLOAT A LOAN?" BANKER SAYS, "FLOAT ALONE? I CAN'T EVEN DOG PADDLE." HO-HO?
THE HALL SYNDICATE, INC.
LET'S PACK.
COPR © 1955 WALT KELLY
ALBERT

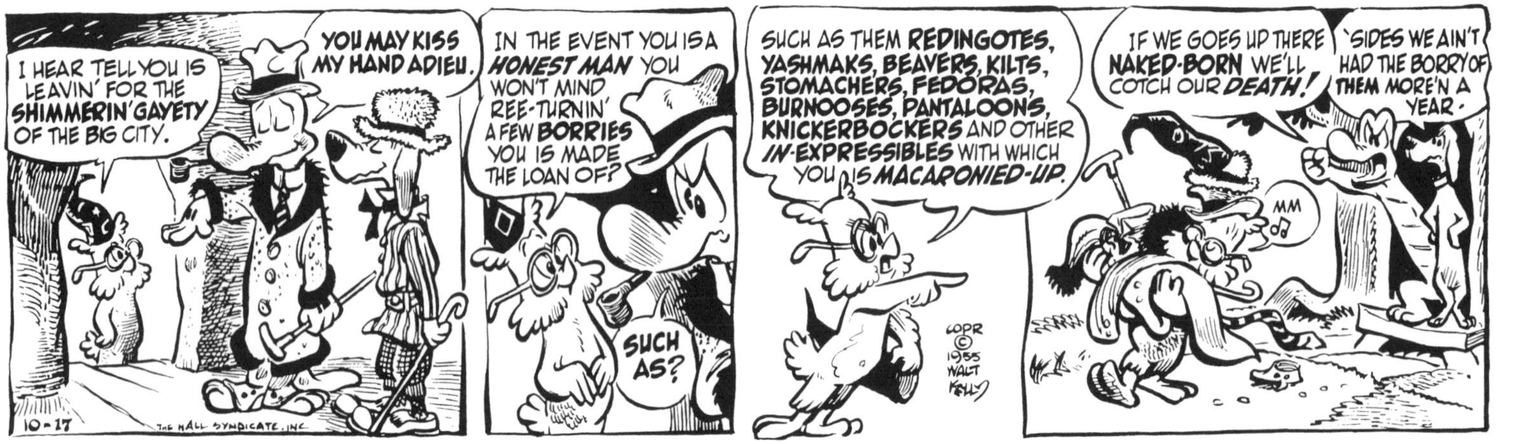
I HEAR TELL YOU IS LEAVIN' FOR THE SHIMMERIN' GAYETY OF THE BIG CITY.
YOU MAY KISS MY HAND ADIEU.
IN THE EVENT YOU IS A HONEST MAN YOU WON'T MIND REE-TURNIN' A FEW BORRIES YOU IS MADE THE LOAN OF?
SUCH AS?
SUCH AS THEM REDINGOTES, YASHMAKS, BEAVERS, KILTS, STOMACHERS, FEDORAS, BURNOOSES, PANTALOONS, KNICKERBOCKERS AND OTHER IN-EXPRESSIBLES WITH WHICH YOU IS MACARONIED-UP.
IF WE GOES UP THERE NAKED-BORN WE'LL COTCH OUR DEATH!
'SIDES WE AIN'T HAD THE BORRY OF THEM MORE'N A YEAR.
MM
10-17 THE HALL SYNDICATE, INC.
COPR © 1955 WALT KELLY

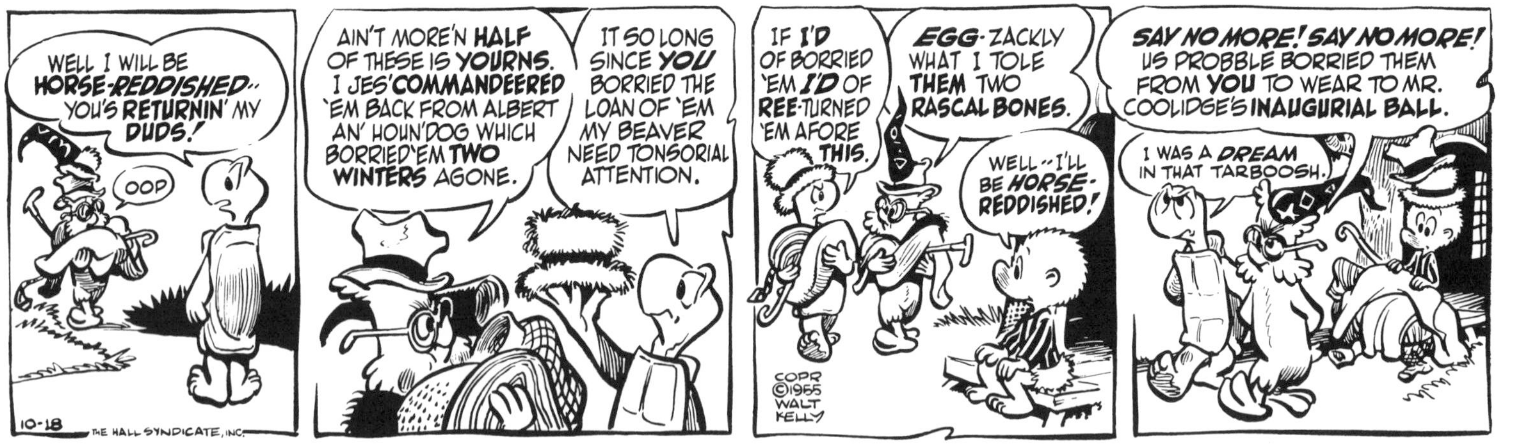
WELL I WILL BE HORSE-REDDISHED.. YOU'S RETURNIN' MY DUDS!
OOP
AIN'T MORE'N HALF OF THESE IS YOURNS. I JES' COMMANDEERED 'EM BACK FROM ALBERT AN' HOUN'DOG WHICH BORRIED 'EM TWO WINTERS AGONE.
IT SO LONG SINCE YOU BORRIED THE LOAN OF 'EM MY BEAVER NEED TONSORIAL ATTENTION.
IF I'D OF BORRIED 'EM I'D OF REE-TURNED 'EM AFORE THIS.
EGG-ZACKLY WHAT I TOLE THEM TWO RASCAL BONES.
WELL -- I'LL BE HORSE-REDDISHED!
SAY NO MORE! SAY NO MORE! US PROBBLE BORRIED THEM FROM YOU TO WEAR TO MR. COOLIDGE'S INAUGURIAL BALL.
I WAS A DREAM IN THAT TARBOOSH.
10-18 THE HALL SYNDICATE, INC.
COPR ©1955 WALT KELLY

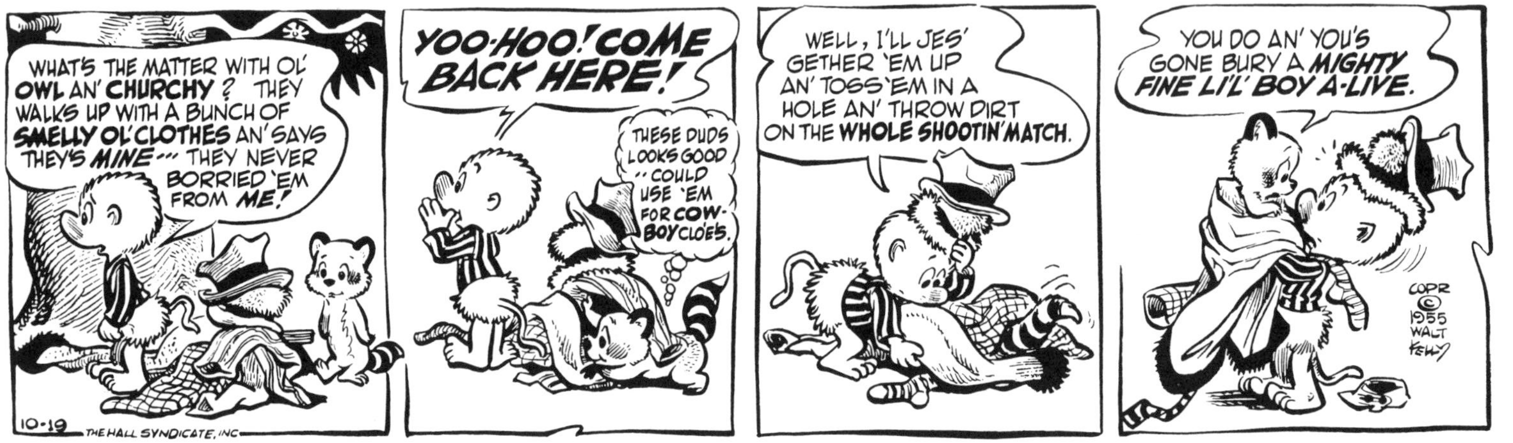
WHAT'S THE MATTER WITH OL' OWL AN' CHURCHY? THEY WALKS UP WITH A BUNCH OF SMELLY OL' CLOTHES AN' SAYS THEY'S MINE -- THEY NEVER BORRIED 'EM FROM ME!
YOO-HOO! COME BACK HERE!
THESE DUDS LOOKS GOOD -- COULD USE 'EM FOR COW-BOY CLO'ES.
WELL, I'LL JES' GETHER 'EM UP AN' TOSS 'EM IN A HOLE AN' THROW DIRT ON THE WHOLE SHOOTIN' MATCH.
YOU DO AN' YOU'S GONE BURY A MIGHTY FINE LI'L' BOY A-LIVE.
10-19 THE HALL SYNDICATE, INC.
COPR © 1955 WALT KELLY

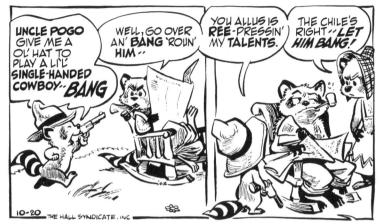

UNCLE POGO GIVE ME A OL' HAT TO PLAY A LI'L SINGLE-HANDED COWBOY.. BANG
WELL, GO OVER AN' BANG 'ROUN' HIM--
YOU ALLUS IS REE-PRESSIN' MY TALENTS.
THE CHILE'S RIGHT--LET HIM BANG!
BY GEORGE Y. WELLS I IS LEAVIN'--- --I IS RUNNIN' A-WAY FROM HOME!
? ?
WAIT A MINUTE!
US'LL GO WITH YOU.
10-20
THE HALL SYNDICATE, INC
COPR © 1955 WALT KELLY

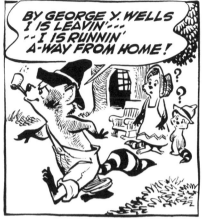

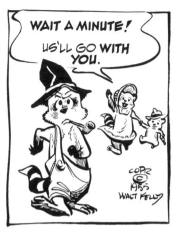

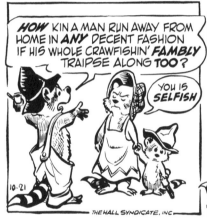

HOW KIN A MAN RUN AWAY FROM HOME IN ANY DECENT FASHION IF HIS WHOLE CRAWFISHIN' FAMBLY TRAIPSE ALONG TOO?
YOU IS SELFISH
THE WHOLE REASON FOR EX-CAPIN' IS TO GIT AWAY FROM YO' EVER-LASTIN' SLAB-A-JAB.
YOU WANNA DENY THE BOY THE ADVANTAGES OF BEIN' ON THE LAM?
A BOY NEEDS HIS DADDY'S STRONG HAND--'SPECIALLY IN MATTERS OF DISCIPLINE AN'
HEY HO!
S'CUSE ME! MA'M, WHYN'T YOU LET ME AN' PAP TALK THIS OUT MAN TO MAN.
10-21
THE HALL SYNDICATE, INC
COPR © 1955 WALT KELLY

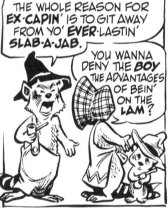

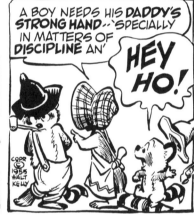

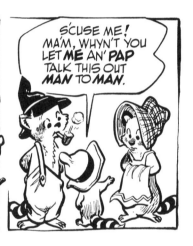

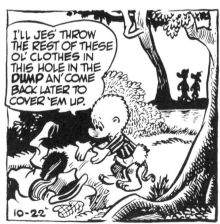

I'LL JES' THROW THE REST OF THESE OL' CLOTHES IN THIS HOLE IN THE DUMP AN' COME BACK LATER TO COVER 'EM UP.
I DON'T MEAN TO IMPLY YOU AIN'T EX-QUISITELY ATTIRED FOR OUR TRIP NORTH BUT LET'S LOOK IN THE DUMP TO BE SAFE.
EX-CELL-ENT.
I'LL BE DOGGONED! THE SAME KIND OF CLOTHES WHAT WAS SWUPPED FROM US!
IT JES' GO TO PROVE THESE KIND CLOTHES IS ALL THE RAGE --YOU FINDS 'EM ALL OVER!
SHOULD I WEAR THE KNICKLE-BONKERS OR THE SHORTS FROM THE BERMOOTHES, LAND OF THE ONION AN' THE EEL?
10-22
THE HALL SYNDICATE, INC
COPR © 1955 WALT KELLY

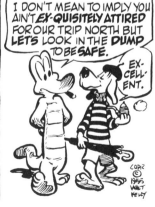

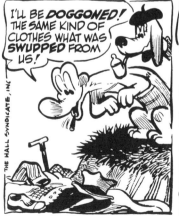

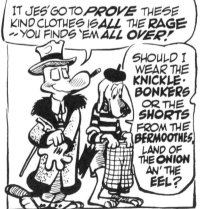

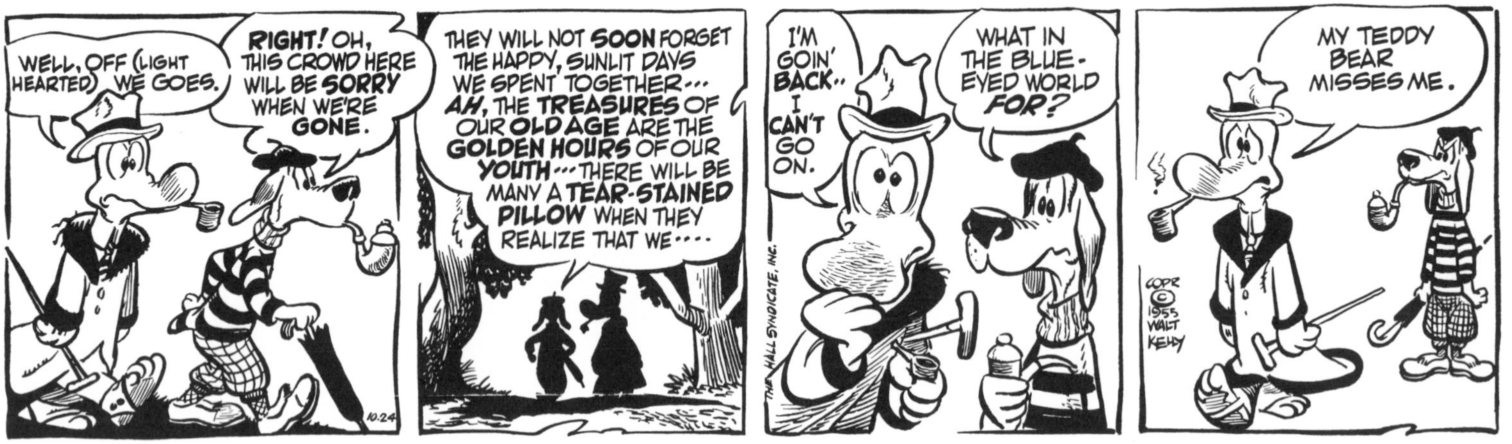
WELL, OFF (LIGHT HEARTED) WE GOES.
RIGHT! OH, THIS CROWD HERE WILL BE SORRY WHEN WE'RE GONE.
10.24
THEY WILL NOT SOON FORGET THE HAPPY, SUNLIT DAYS WE SPENT TOGETHER... AH, THE TREASURES OF OUR OLD AGE ARE THE GOLDEN HOURS OF OUR YOUTH... THERE WILL BE MANY A TEAR-STAINED PILLOW WHEN THEY REALIZE THAT WE....
THE HALL SYNDICATE, INC.
I'M GOIN' BACK.. I CAN'T GO ON.
WHAT IN THE BLUE-EYED WORLD FOR?
MY TEDDY BEAR MISSES ME.
COPR © 1955 WALT KELLY

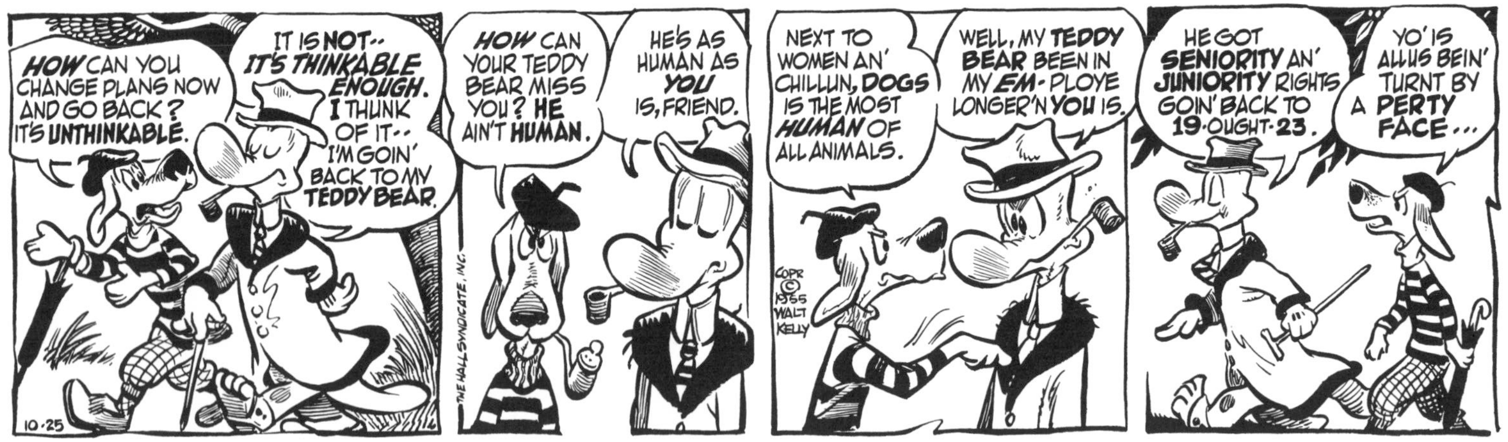
HOW CAN YOU CHANGE PLANS NOW AND GO BACK? IT'S UNTHINKABLE.
IT IS NOT.. IT'S THINKABLE ENOUGH. I THUNK OF IT.. I'M GOIN' BACK TO MY TEDDY BEAR.
10-25
HOW CAN YOUR TEDDY BEAR MISS YOU? HE AIN'T HUMAN.
HE'S AS HUMAN AS YOU IS, FRIEND.
THE HALL SYNDICATE, INC.
NEXT TO WOMEN AN' CHILLUN, DOGS IS THE MOST HUMAN OF ALL ANIMALS.
WELL, MY TEDDY BEAR BEEN IN MY EM-PLOYE LONGER'N YOU IS.
COPR © 1955 WALT KELLY
HE GOT SENIORITY AN' JUNIORITY RIGHTS GOIN' BACK TO 19-OUGHT-23.
YO' IS ALLUS BEIN' TURNT BY A PERTY FACE...

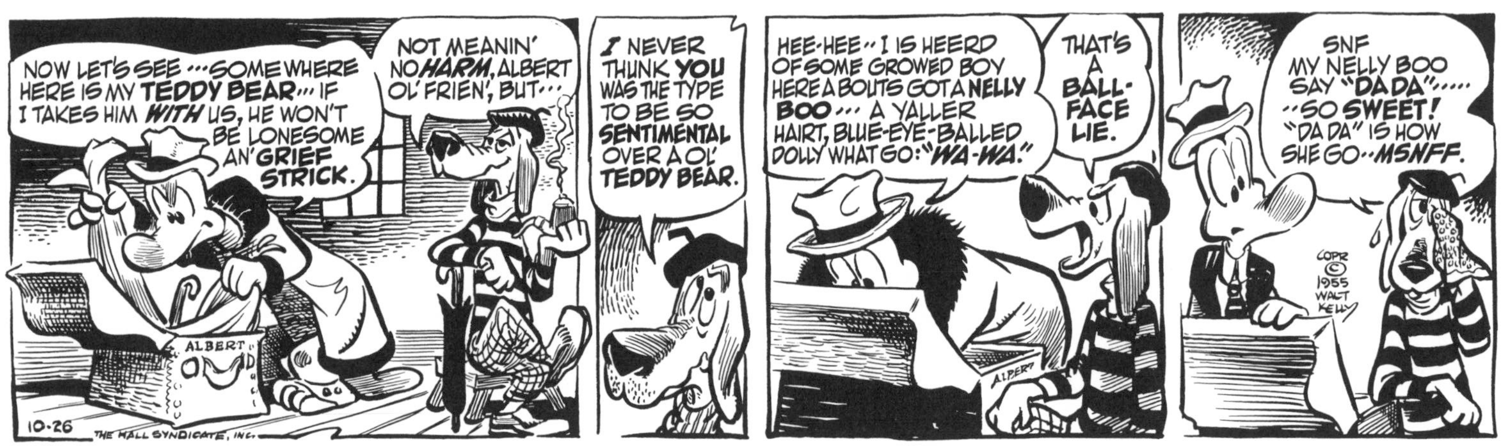
NOW LET'S SEE ... SOME WHERE HERE IS MY TEDDY BEAR... IF I TAKES HIM WITH US, HE WON'T BE LONESOME AN' GRIEF STRICK.
NOT MEANIN' NO HARM, ALBERT OL' FRIEN', BUT...
ALBERT
10-26
THE HALL SYNDICATE, INC.
I NEVER THUNK YOU WAS THE TYPE TO BE SO SENTIMENTAL OVER A OL' TEDDY BEAR.
HEE-HEE.. I IS HEERD OF SOME GROWED BOY HEREABOUTS GOT A NELLY BOO... A YALLER HAIRT, BLUE-EYE-BALLED DOLLY WHAT GO: "WA-WA."
THAT'S A BALL-FACE LIE.
SNF MY NELLY BOO SAY "DA DA"..... ..SO SWEET! "DA DA" IS HOW SHE GO.. MSNFF.
COPR © 1955 WALT KELLY

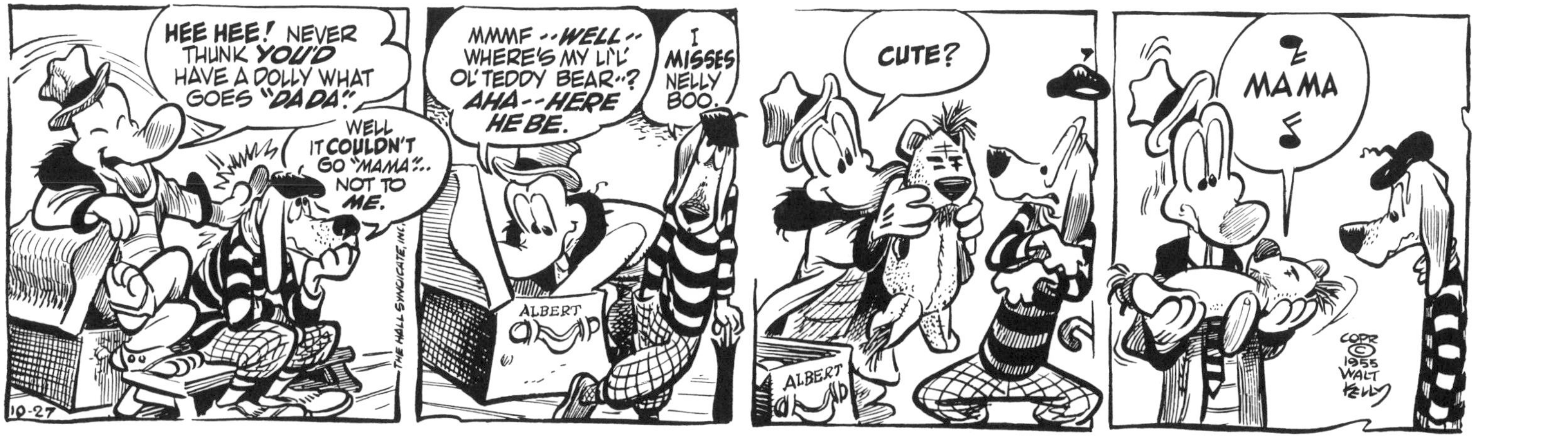
HEE HEE! NEVER THUNK YOU'D HAVE A DOLLY WHAT GOES "DA DA"!
WELL IT COULDN'T GO "MAMA"... NOT TO ME.
10-27
THE HALL SYNDICATE, INC.
MMMF --WELL-- WHERE'S MY LI'L' OL' TEDDY BEAR--? AHA--HERE HE BE.
I MISSES NELLY BOO.
ALBERT
CUTE?
ALBERT
MAMA
COPR © 1955 WALT KELLY

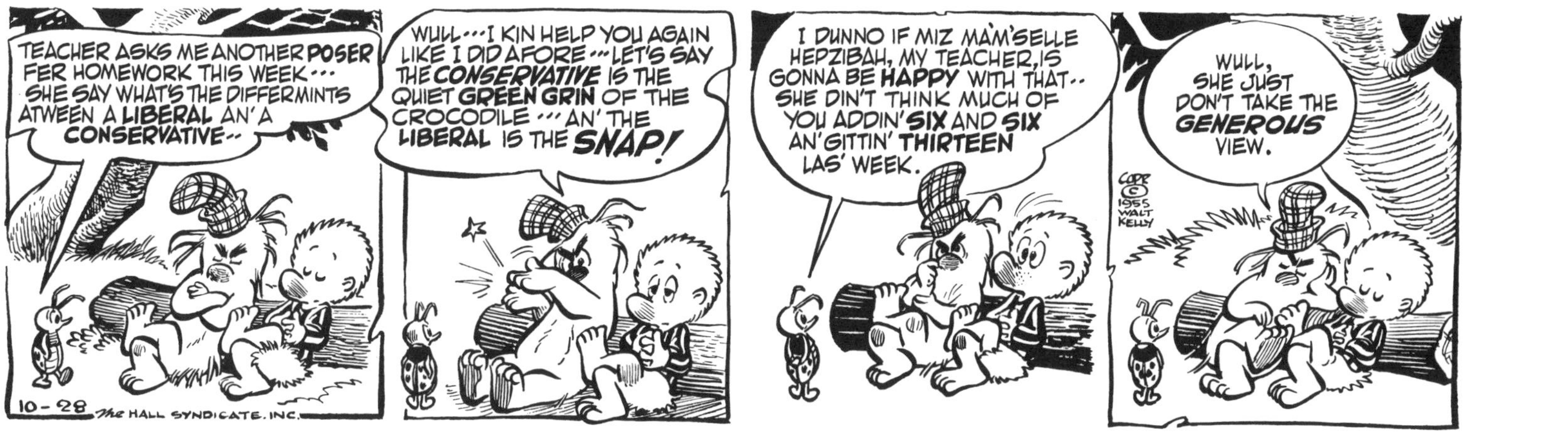
TEACHER ASKS ME ANOTHER POSER FER HOMEWORK THIS WEEK... SHE SAY WHAT'S THE DIFFERMINTS ATWEEN A LIBERAL AN' A CONSERVATIVE--
10-28 The HALL SYNDICATE. INC.
WULL... I KIN HELP YOU AGAIN LIKE I DID AFORE... LET'S SAY THE CONSERVATIVE IS THE QUIET GREEN GRIN OF THE CROCODILE... AN' THE LIBERAL IS THE SNAP!
I DUNNO IF MIZ MAM'SELLE HEPZIBAH, MY TEACHER, IS GONNA BE HAPPY WITH THAT.. SHE DIN'T THINK MUCH OF YOU ADDIN' SIX AND SIX AN' GITTIN' THIRTEEN LAS' WEEK.
COPR © 1955 WALT KELLY
WULL, SHE JUST DON'T TAKE THE GENEROUS VIEW.

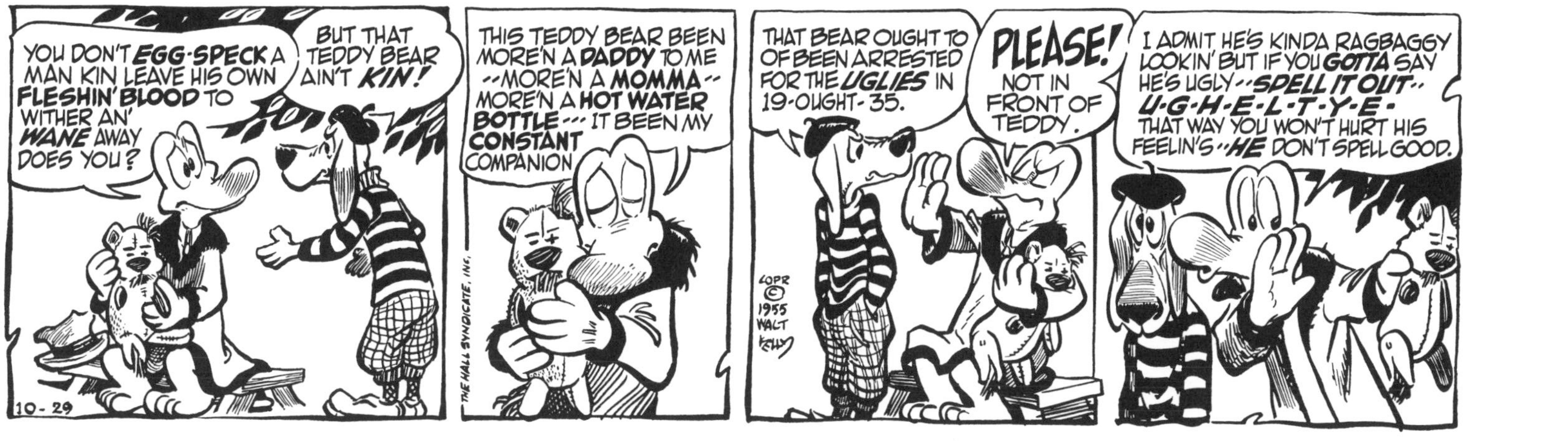
YOU DON'T EGG-SPECK A MAN KIN LEAVE HIS OWN FLESHIN' BLOOD TO WITHER AN' WANE AWAY DOES YOU?
BUT THAT TEDDY BEAR AIN'T KIN!
10-29
THE HALL SYNDICATE, INC.
THIS TEDDY BEAR BEEN MORE'N A DADDY TO ME --MORE'N A MOMMA-- MORE'N A HOT WATER BOTTLE--- IT BEEN MY CONSTANT COMPANION
THAT BEAR OUGHT TO OF BEEN ARRESTED FOR THE UGLIES IN 19-OUGHT-35.
PLEASE! NOT IN FRONT OF TEDDY.
COPR © 1955 WALT KELLY
I ADMIT HE'S KINDA RAGBAGGY LOOKIN' BUT IF YOU GOTTA SAY HE'S UGLY--SPELL IT OUT-- U-G-H-E-L-T-Y-E- THAT WAY YOU WON'T HURT HIS FEELIN'S--HE DON'T SPELL GOOD.

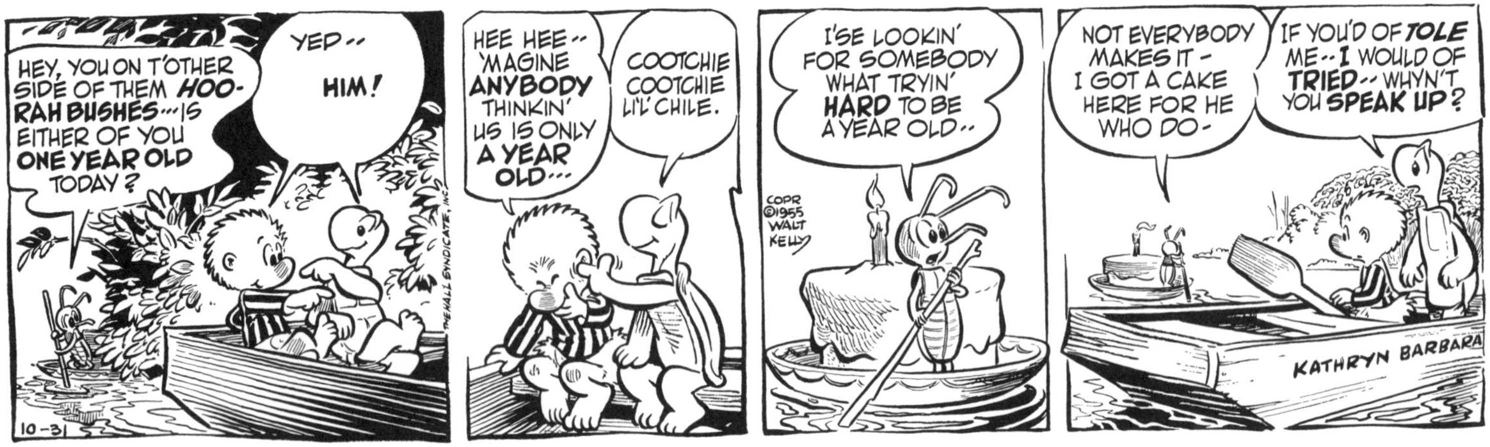
HEY, YOU ON T'OTHER SIDE OF THEM HOO-RAH BUSHES... IS EITHER OF YOU ONE YEAR OLD TODAY?
YEP..
HIM!
THE HALL SYNDICATE, INC.
10-31
HEE HEE.. 'MAGINE ANYBODY THINKIN' US IS ONLY A YEAR OLD...
COOTCHIE COOTCHIE LI'L CHILE.
I'SE LOOKIN' FOR SOMEBODY WHAT TRYIN' HARD TO BE A YEAR OLD..
COPR ©1955 WALT KELLY
NOT EVERYBODY MAKES IT - I GOT A CAKE HERE FOR HE WHO DO-
IF YOU'D OF TOLE ME.. I WOULD OF TRIED.. WHYN'T YOU SPEAK UP?
KATHRYN BARBARA

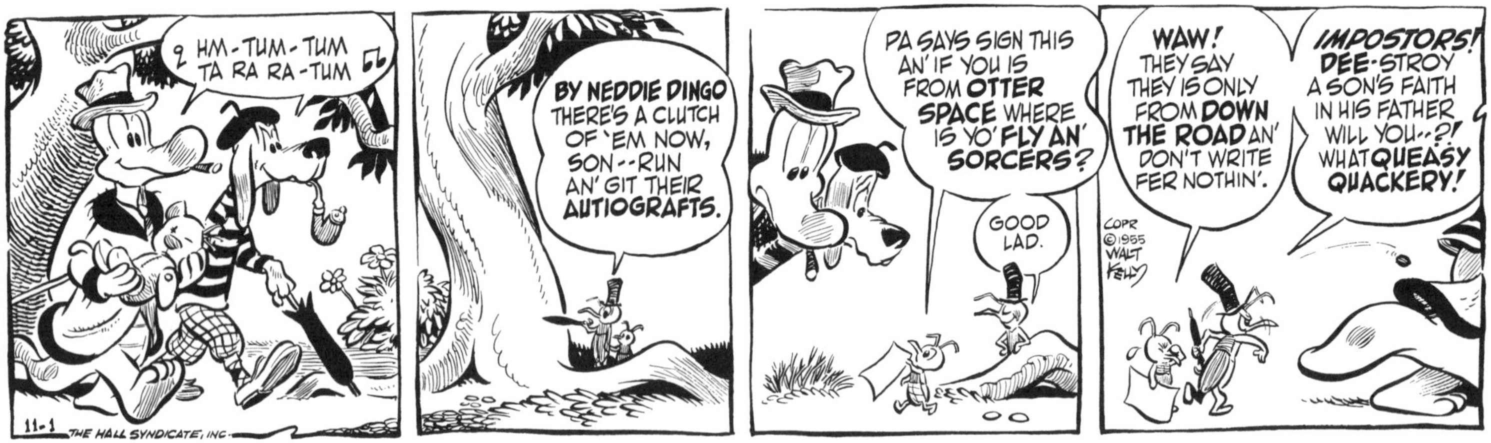
HM-TUM-TUM TA RA RA-TUM
11-1
THE HALL SYNDICATE, INC.
BY NEDDIE DINGO THERE'S A CLUTCH OF 'EM NOW, SON--RUN AN' GIT THEIR AUTIOGRAFTS.
PA SAYS SIGN THIS AN' IF YOU IS FROM OTTER SPACE WHERE IS YO' FLY AN' SORCERS?
GOOD LAD.
COPR ©1955 WALT KELLY
WAW! THEY SAY THEY IS ONLY FROM DOWN THE ROAD AN' DON'T WRITE FER NOTHIN'.
IMPOSTORS! DEE-STROY A SON'S FAITH IN HIS FATHER WILL YOU..?! WHAT QUEASY QUACKERY!

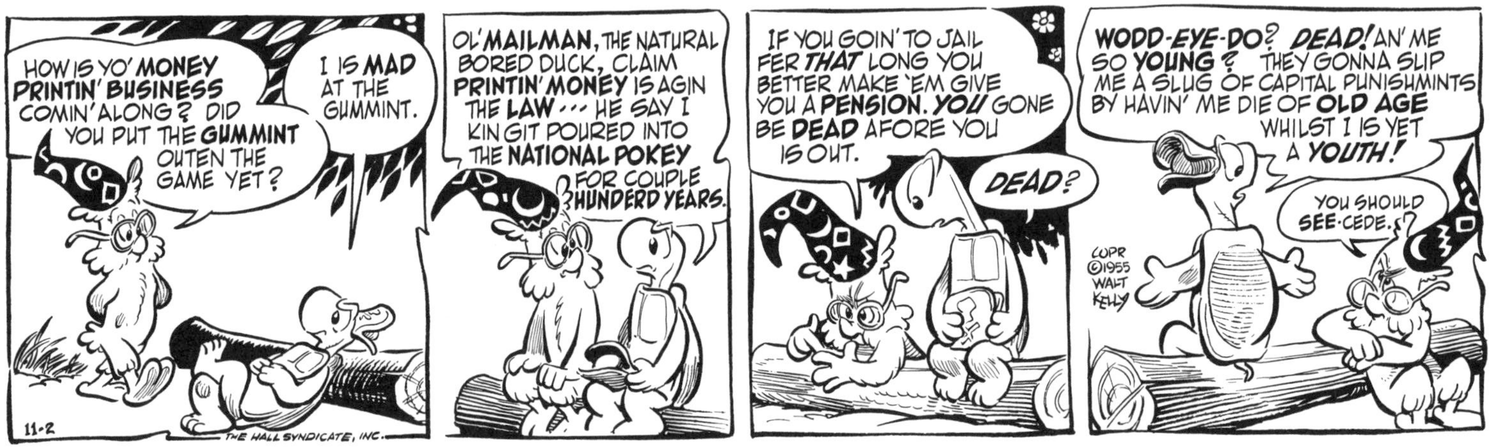
HOW IS YO' MONEY PRINTIN' BUSINESS COMIN' ALONG? DID YOU PUT THE GUMMINT OUTEN THE GAME YET?
I IS MAD AT THE GUMMINT.
11-2
THE HALL SYNDICATE, INC.
OL' MAILMAN, THE NATURAL BORED DUCK, CLAIM PRINTIN' MONEY IS AGIN THE LAW... HE SAY I KIN GIT POURED INTO THE NATIONAL POKEY FOR COUPLE HUNDERD YEARS.
IF YOU GOIN' TO JAIL FER THAT LONG YOU BETTER MAKE 'EM GIVE YOU A PENSION. YOU GONE BE DEAD AFORE YOU IS OUT.
DEAD?
WODD-EYE-DO? DEAD! AN' ME SO YOUNG? THEY GONNA SLIP ME A SLUG OF CAPITAL PUNISHMINTS BY HAVIN' ME DIE OF OLD AGE WHILST I IS YET A YOUTH!
YOU SHOULD SEE-CEDE.
COPR ©1955 WALT KELLY

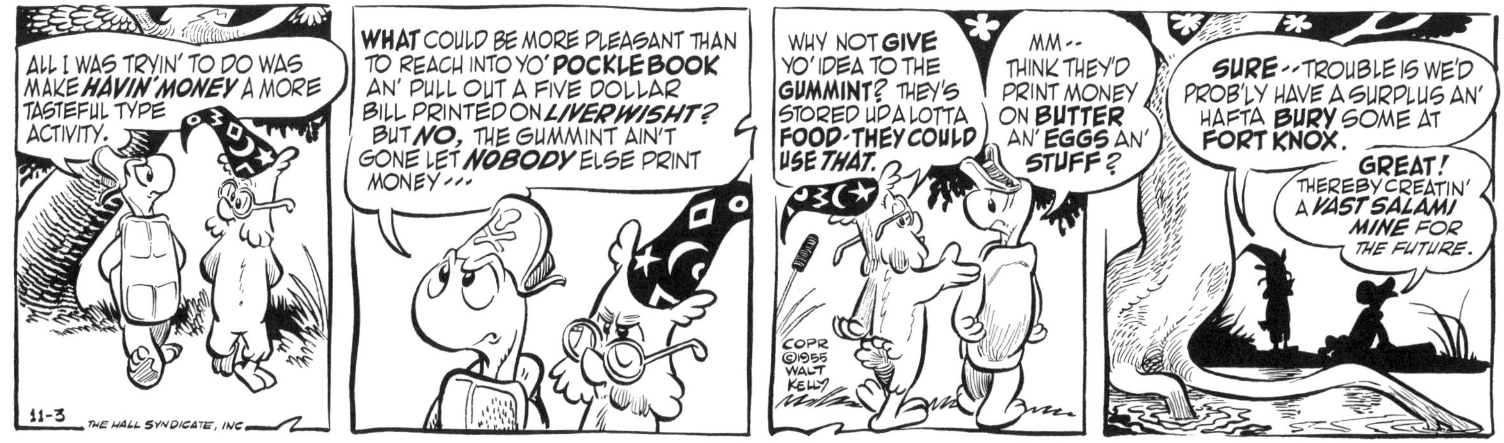
ALL I WAS TRYIN' TO DO WAS MAKE HAVIN' MONEY A MORE TASTEFUL TYPE ACTIVITY.
WHAT COULD BE MORE PLEASANT THAN TO REACH INTO YO' POCKLE BOOK AN' PULL OUT A FIVE DOLLAR BILL PRINTED ON LIVERWISHT? BUT NO, THE GUMMINT AIN'T GONE LET NOBODY ELSE PRINT MONEY...
WHY NOT GIVE YO' IDEA TO THE GUMMINT? THEY'S STORED UP A LOTTA FOOD-THEY COULD USE THAT.
MM-- THINK THEY'D PRINT MONEY ON BUTTER AN' EGGS AN' STUFF?
SURE--TROUBLE IS WE'D PROB'LY HAVE A SURPLUS AN' HAFTA BURY SOME AT FORT KNOX.
GREAT! THEREBY CREATIN' A VAST SALAMI MINE FOR THE FUTURE.
COPR ©1955 WALT KELLY
11-3 THE HALL SYNDICATE, INC

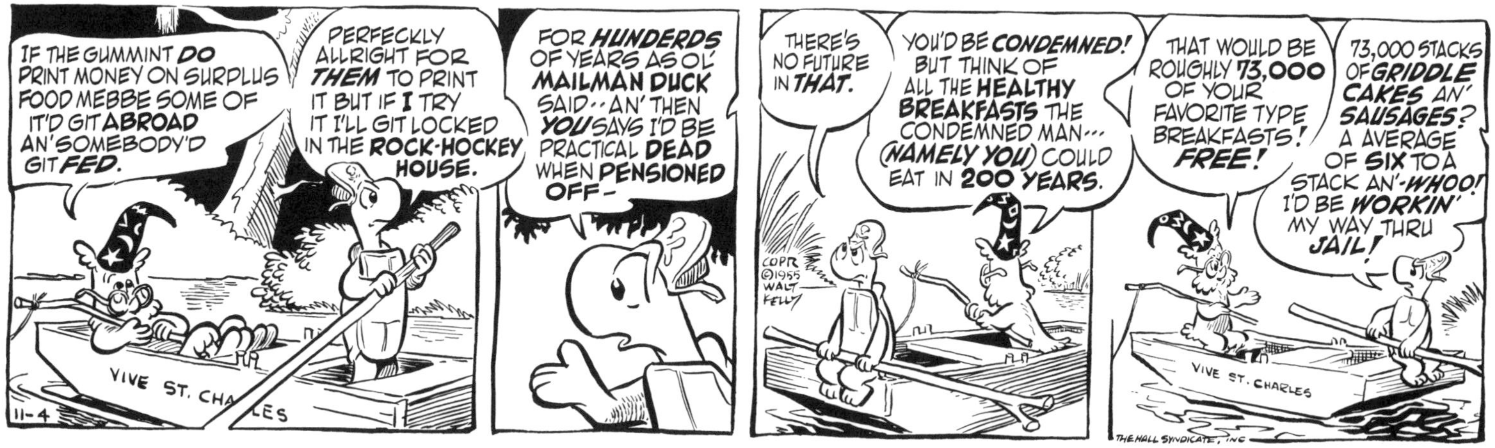
IF THE GUMMINT DO PRINT MONEY ON SURPLUS FOOD MEBBE SOME OF IT'D GIT ABROAD AN' SOMEBODY'D GIT FED.
PERFECKLY ALLRIGHT FOR THEM TO PRINT IT BUT IF I TRY IT I'LL GIT LOCKED IN THE ROCK-HOCKEY HOUSE.
FOR HUNDERDS OF YEARS AS OL' MAILMAN DUCK SAID--AN' THEN YOU SAYS I'D BE PRACTICAL DEAD WHEN PENSIONED OFF-
THERE'S NO FUTURE IN THAT.
YOU'D BE CONDEMNED! BUT THINK OF ALL THE HEALTHY BREAKFASTS THE CONDEMNED MAN... (NAMELY YOU) COULD EAT IN 200 YEARS.
THAT WOULD BE ROUGHLY 73,000 OF YOUR FAVORITE TYPE BREAKFASTS! FREE!
73,000 STACKS OF GRIDDLE CAKES AN' SAUSAGES? A AVERAGE OF SIX TO A STACK AN'-WHOO! I'D BE WORKIN' MY WAY THRU JAIL!
VIVE ST. CHARLES
COPR ©1955 WALT KELLY
11-4 THE HALL SYNDICATE, INC

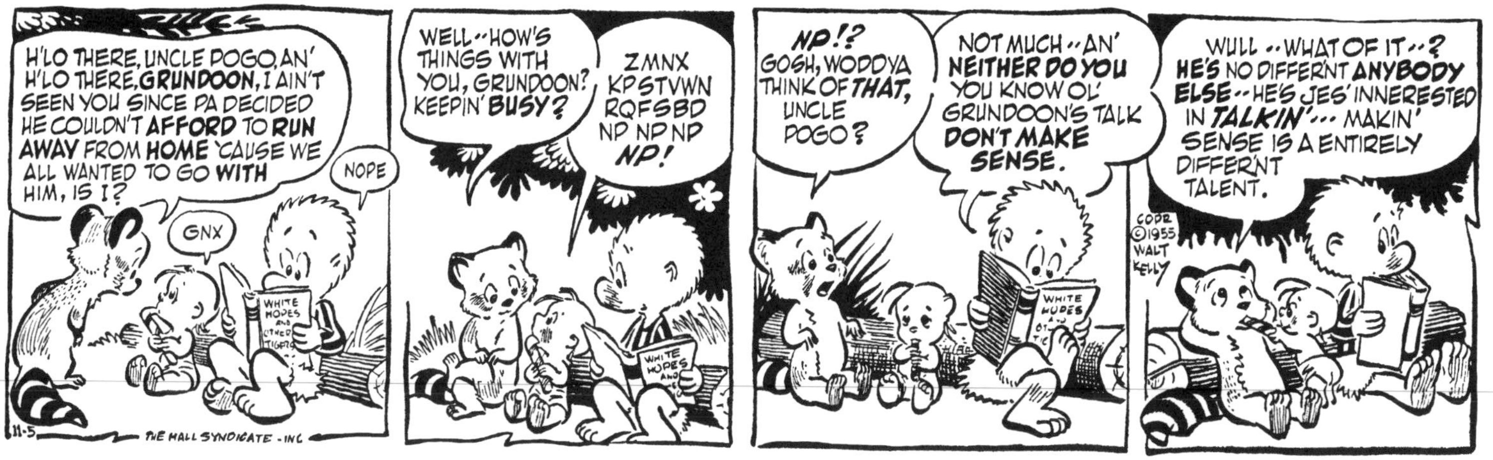
H'LO THERE, UNCLE POGO, AN' H'LO THERE, GRUNDOON, I AIN'T SEEN YOU SINCE PA DECIDED HE COULDN'T AFFORD TO RUN AWAY FROM HOME 'CAUSE WE ALL WANTED TO GO WITH HIM, IS I?
GNX
NOPE
WELL--HOW'S THINGS WITH YOU, GRUNDOON? KEEPIN' BUSY?
ZMNX KPSTVWN RQFSBD NP NP NP NP!
NP!? GOSH, WODDYA THINK OF THAT, UNCLE POGO?
NOT MUCH--AN' NEITHER DO YOU YOU KNOW OL' GRUNDOON'S TALK DON'T MAKE SENSE.
WULL--WHAT OF IT--? HE'S NO DIFFERN'T ANYBODY ELSE--HE'S JES' INNERESTED IN TALKIN'... MAKIN' SENSE IS A ENTIRELY DIFFER'NT TALENT.
COPR ©1955 WALT KELLY
11-5 THE HALL SYNDICATE-INC

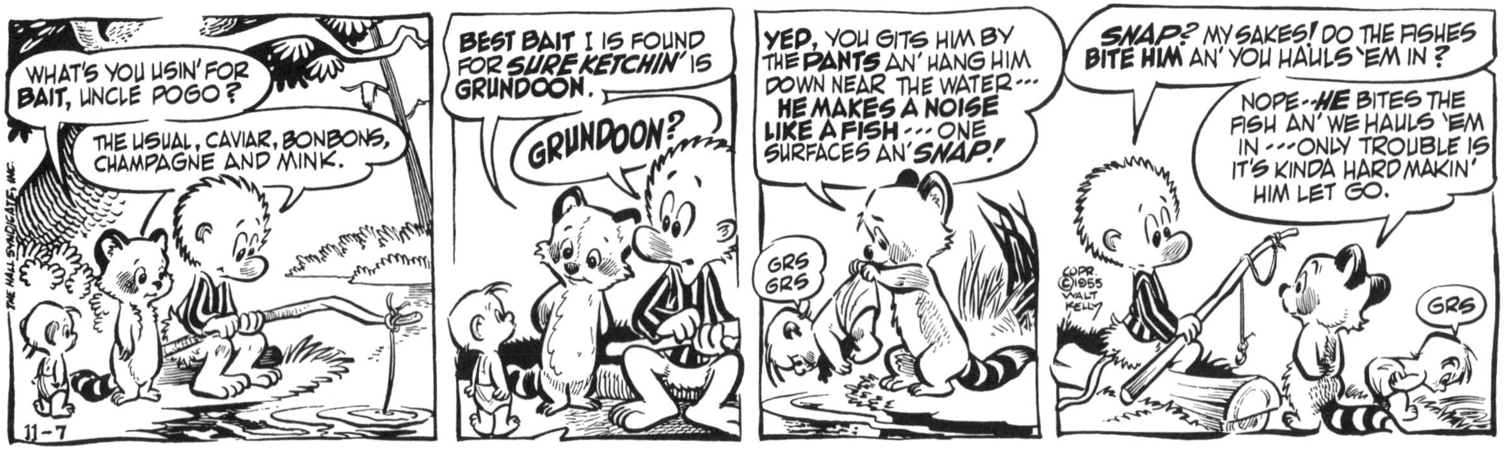
WHAT'S YOU USIN' FOR BAIT, UNCLE POGO?
THE USUAL, CAVIAR, BONBONS, CHAMPAGNE AND MINK.
THE HALL SYNDICATE, INC.
11-7
BEST BAIT I IS FOUND FOR SURE KETCHIN' IS GRUNDOON.
GRUNDOON?
YEP, YOU GITS HIM BY THE PANTS AN' HANG HIM DOWN NEAR THE WATER--- HE MAKES A NOISE LIKE A FISH --- ONE SURFACES AN' SNAP!
GRS GRS
SNAP? MY SAKES! DO THE FISHES BITE HIM AN' YOU HAULS 'EM IN?
NOPE--HE BITES THE FISH AN' WE HAULS 'EM IN ---ONLY TROUBLE IS IT'S KINDA HARD MAKIN' HIM LET GO.
COPR. ©1955 WALT KELLY
GRS

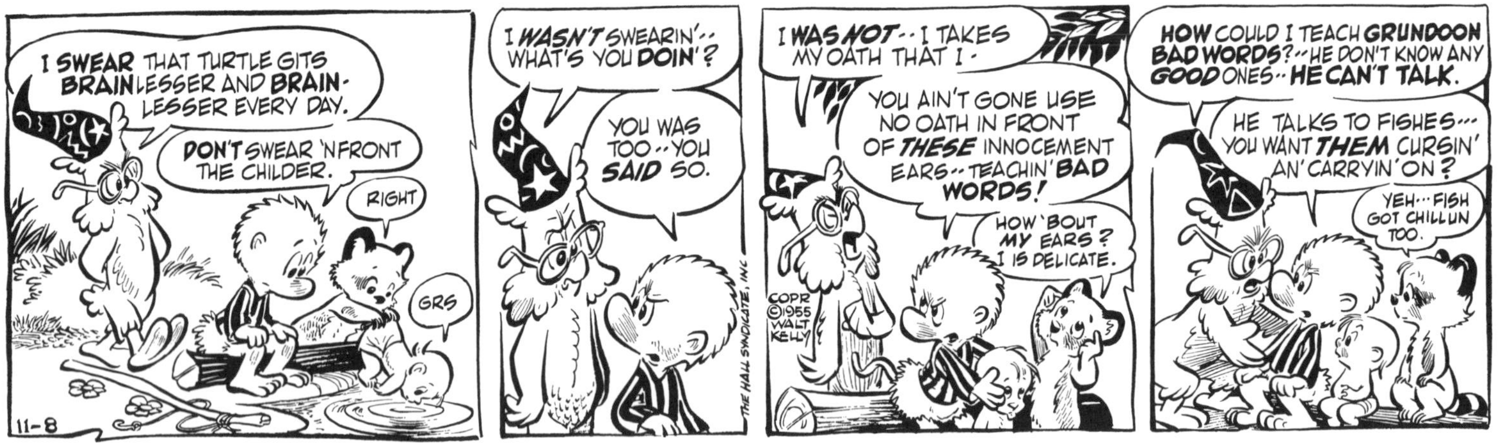
I SWEAR THAT TURTLE GITS BRAINLESSER AND BRAIN-LESSER EVERY DAY.
DON'T SWEAR 'N FRONT THE CHILDER.
RIGHT
GRS
11-8
I WASN'T SWEARIN'-- WHAT'S YOU DOIN'?
YOU WAS TOO--YOU SAID SO.
THE HALL SYNDICATE, INC
I WAS NOT--I TAKES MY OATH THAT I-
YOU AIN'T GONE USE NO OATH IN FRONT OF THESE INNOCEMENT EARS--TEACHIN' BAD WORDS!
HOW 'BOUT MY EARS? I IS DELICATE.
COPR ©1955 WALT KELLY
HOW COULD I TEACH GRUNDOON BAD WORDS?--HE DON'T KNOW ANY GOOD ONES--HE CAN'T TALK.
HE TALKS TO FISHES--- YOU WANT THEM CURSIN' AN' CARRYIN' ON?
YEH---FISH GOT CHILLUN TOO.

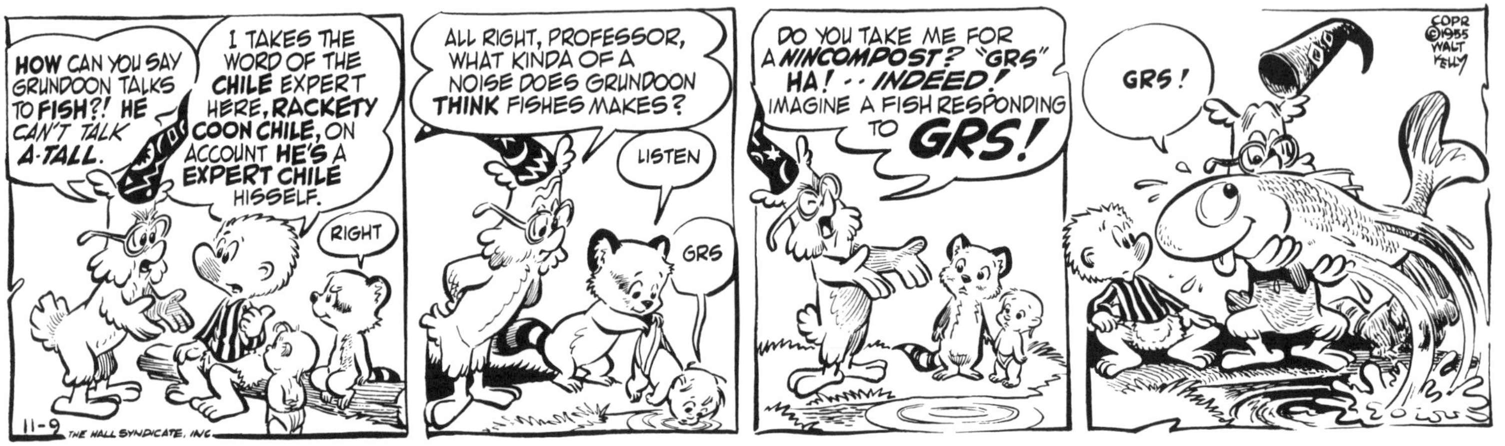
HOW CAN YOU SAY GRUNDOON TALKS TO FISH?! HE CAN'T TALK A-TALL.
I TAKES THE WORD OF THE CHILE EXPERT HERE, RACKETY COON CHILE, ON ACCOUNT HE'S A EXPERT CHILE HISSELF.
RIGHT
11-9 THE HALL SYNDICATE, INC.
ALL RIGHT, PROFESSOR, WHAT KINDA OF A NOISE DOES GRUNDOON THINK FISHES MAKES?
LISTEN
GRS
DO YOU TAKE ME FOR A NINCOMPOST? "GRS" HA!--INDEED! IMAGINE A FISH RESPONDING TO GRS!
COPR ©1955 WALT KELLY
GRS!

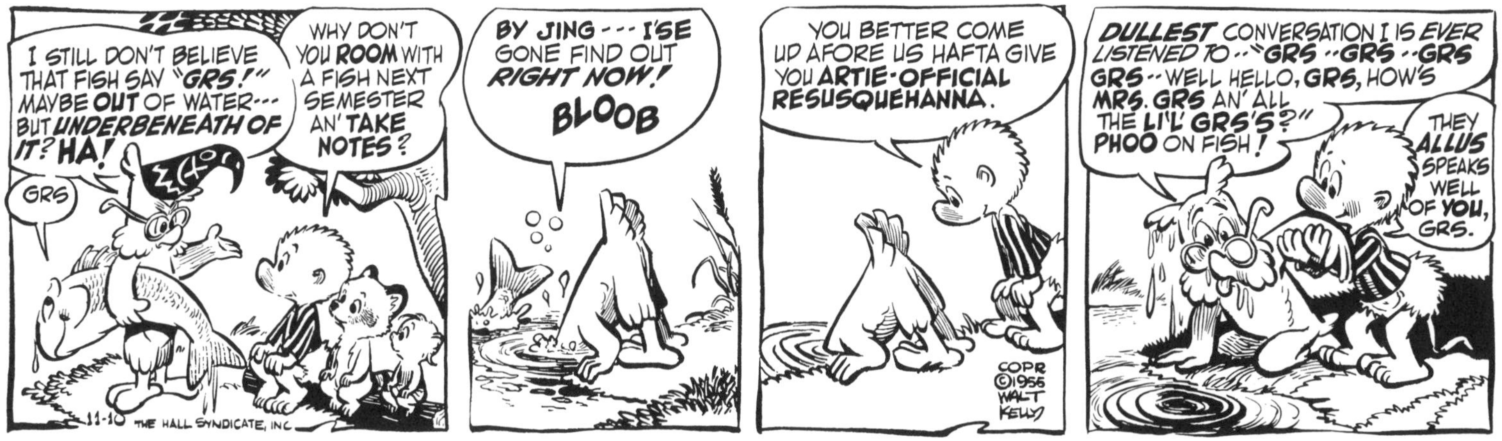
I STILL DON'T BELIEVE THAT FISH SAY "GRS!" MAYBE OUT OF WATER--- BUT UNDERBENEATH OF IT? HA!
GRS
WHY DON'T YOU ROOM WITH A FISH NEXT SEMESTER AN' TAKE NOTES?
11-10 THE HALL SYNDICATE, INC.
BY JING --- I'SE GONE FIND OUT RIGHT NOW!
BLOOB
YOU BETTER COME UP AFORE US HAFTA GIVE YOU ARTIE-OFFICIAL RESUSQUEHANNA.
COPR ©1956 WALT KELLY
DULLEST CONVERSATION I IS EVER LISTENED TO --"GRS -- GRS -- GRS GRS -- WELL HELLO, GRS, HOW'S MRS. GRS AN' ALL THE LI'L' GRS'S?" PHOO ON FISH!
THEY ALLUS SPEAKS WELL OF YOU, GRS.

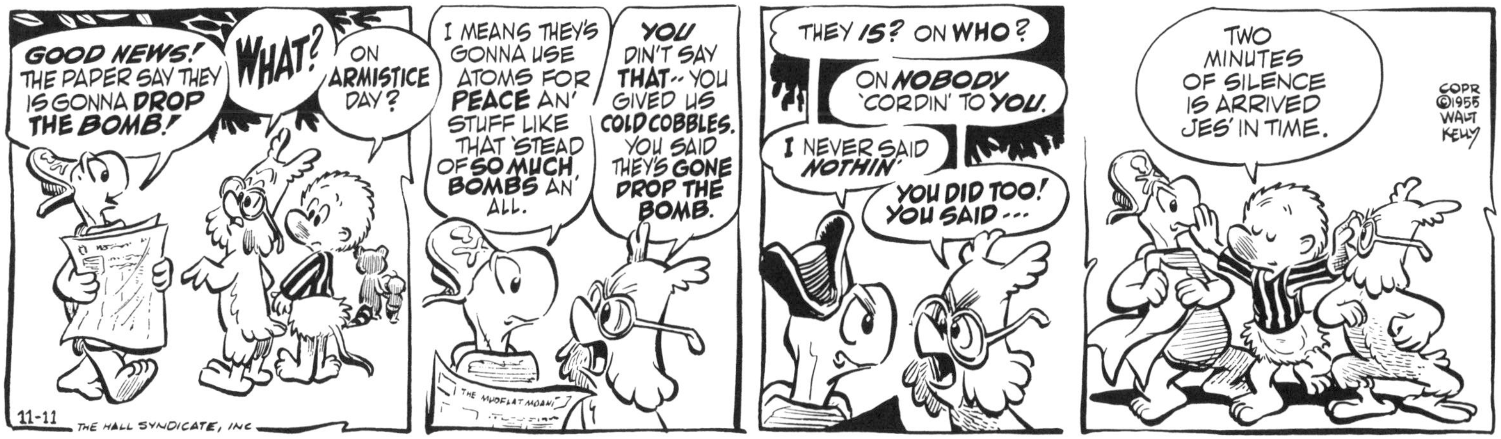
GOOD NEWS! THE PAPER SAY THEY IS GONNA DROP THE BOMB!
WHAT?
ON ARMISTICE DAY?
11-11 THE HALL SYNDICATE, INC.
I MEANS THEY'S GONNA USE ATOMS FOR PEACE AN' STUFF LIKE THAT 'STEAD OF SO MUCH BOMBS AN' ALL.
YOU DIN'T SAY THAT -- YOU GIVED US COLD COBBLES. YOU SAID THEY'S GONE DROP THE BOMB.
THE MUDFLAT MOAN
THEY IS? ON WHO?
ON NOBODY 'CORDIN' TO YOU.
I NEVER SAID NOTHIN'
YOU DID TOO! YOU SAID ---
TWO MINUTES OF SILENCE IS ARRIVED JES' IN TIME.
COPR ©1955 WALT KELLY

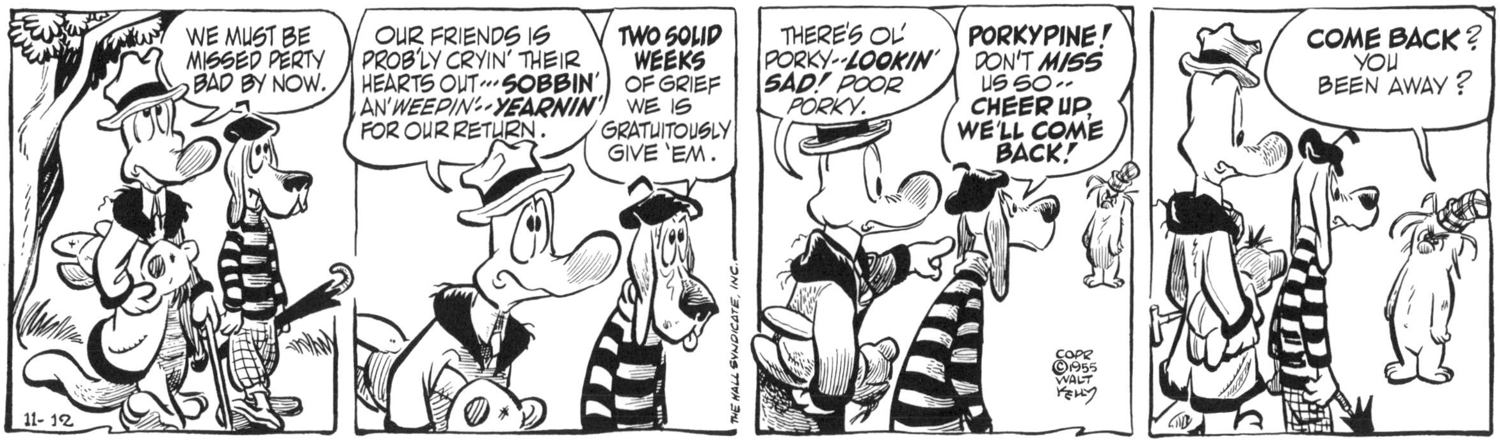
WE MUST BE MISSED PERTY BAD BY NOW.
11-12
OUR FRIENDS IS PROB'LY CRYIN' THEIR HEARTS OUT--- SOBBIN' AN' WEEPIN' -- YEARNIN' FOR OUR RETURN.
TWO SOLID WEEKS OF GRIEF WE IS GRATUITOUSLY GIVE 'EM.
THE HALL SYNDICATE, INC.
THERE'S OL' PORKY -- LOOKIN' SAD! POOR PORKY.
PORKYPINE! DON'T MISS US SO -- CHEER UP, WE'LL COME BACK!
COPR ©1955 WALT KELLY
COME BACK? YOU BEEN AWAY?

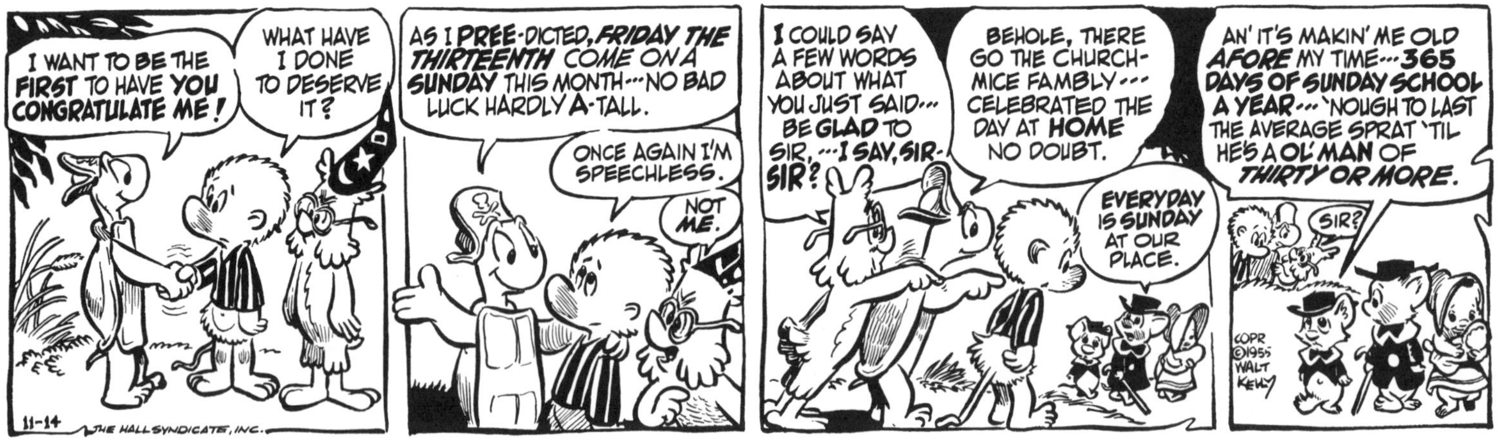
I WANT TO BE THE FIRST TO HAVE YOU CONGRATULATE ME!
WHAT HAVE I DONE TO DESERVE IT?
AS I PREE-DICTED, FRIDAY THE THIRTEENTH COME ON A SUNDAY THIS MONTH... NO BAD LUCK HARDLY A-TALL.
ONCE AGAIN I'M SPEECHLESS.
NOT ME.
I COULD SAY A FEW WORDS ABOUT WHAT YOU JUST SAID... BE GLAD TO SIR, ...I SAY, SIR-SIR?
BEHOLE, THERE GO THE CHURCH-MICE FAMBLY... CELEBRATED THE DAY AT HOME NO DOUBT.
EVERYDAY IS SUNDAY AT OUR PLACE.
AN' IT'S MAKIN' ME OLD AFORE MY TIME... 365 DAYS OF SUNDAY SCHOOL A YEAR... 'NOUGH TO LAST THE AVERAGE SPRAT 'TIL HE'S A OL' MAN OF THIRTY OR MORE.
SIR?
COPR ©1955 WALT KELLY
11-14
THE HALL SYNDICATE, INC.

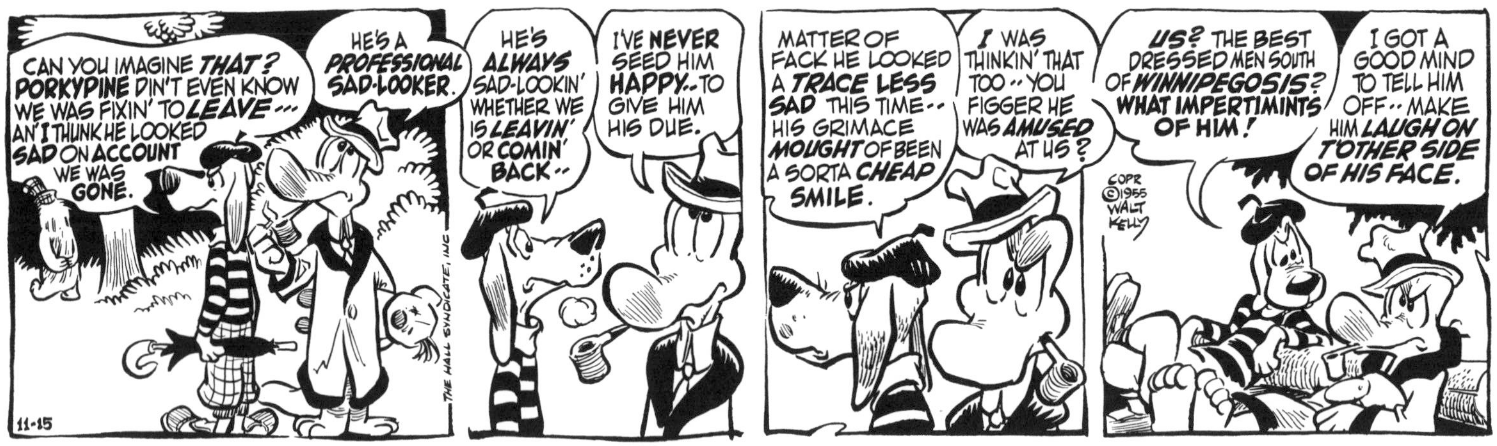
CAN YOU IMAGINE THAT? PORKYPINE DIN'T EVEN KNOW WE WAS FIXIN' TO LEAVE... AN' I THUNK HE LOOKED SAD ON ACCOUNT WE WAS GONE.
HE'S A PROFESSIONAL SAD-LOOKER.
HE'S ALWAYS SAD-LOOKIN' WHETHER WE IS LEAVIN' OR COMIN' BACK..
I'VE NEVER SEED HIM HAPPY.. TO GIVE HIM HIS DUE.
MATTER OF FACK HE LOOKED A TRACE LESS SAD THIS TIME.. HIS GRIMACE MOUGHT OF BEEN A SORTA CHEAP SMILE.
I WAS THINKIN' THAT TOO.. YOU FIGGER HE WAS AMUSED AT US?
US? THE BEST DRESSED MEN SOUTH OF WINNIPEGOSIS? WHAT IMPERTIMINTS OF HIM!
I GOT A GOOD MIND TO TELL HIM OFF.. MAKE HIM LAUGH ON T'OTHER SIDE OF HIS FACE.
COPR ©1955 WALT KELLY
11-15
THE HALL SYNDICATE, INC

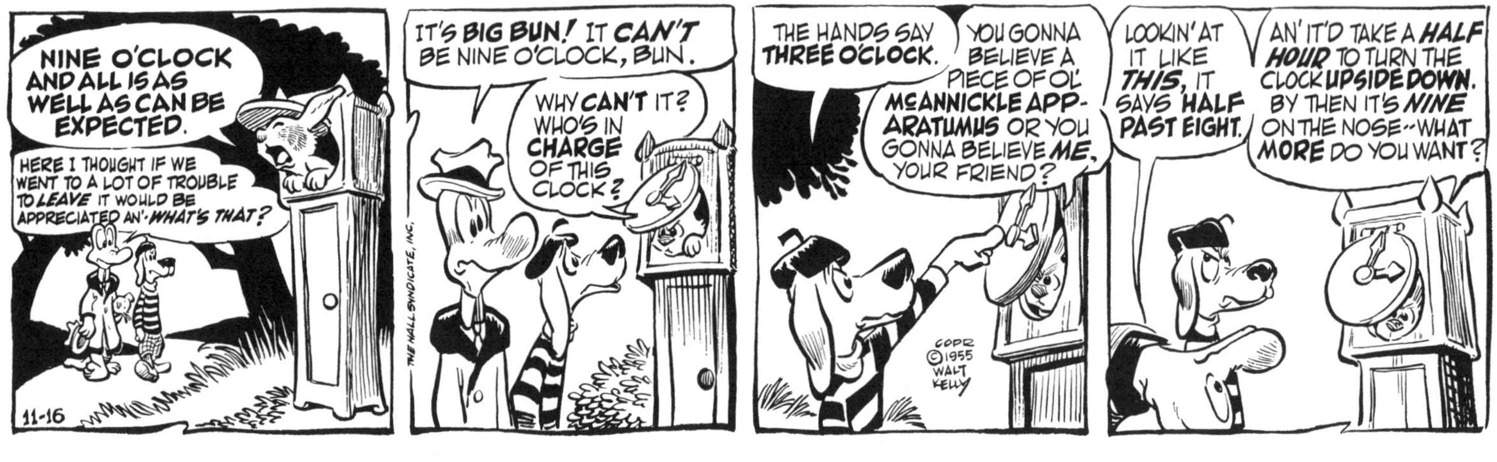
NINE O'CLOCK AND ALL IS AS WELL AS CAN BE EXPECTED.
HERE I THOUGHT IF WE WENT TO A LOT OF TROUBLE TO LEAVE IT WOULD BE APPRECIATED AN'- WHAT'S THAT?
IT'S BIG BUN! IT CAN'T BE NINE O'CLOCK, BUN.
WHY CAN'T IT? WHO'S IN CHARGE OF THIS CLOCK?
THE HANDS SAY THREE O'CLOCK.
YOU GONNA BELIEVE A PIECE OF OL' McANNICKLE APP-ARATUMUS OR YOU GONNA BELIEVE ME, YOUR FRIEND?
LOOKIN' AT IT LIKE THIS, IT SAYS HALF PAST EIGHT.
AN' IT'D TAKE A HALF HOUR TO TURN THE CLOCK UPSIDE DOWN. BY THEN IT'S NINE ON THE NOSE.. WHAT MORE DO YOU WANT?
COPR ©1955 WALT KELLY
11-16
THE HALL SYNDICATE, INC.

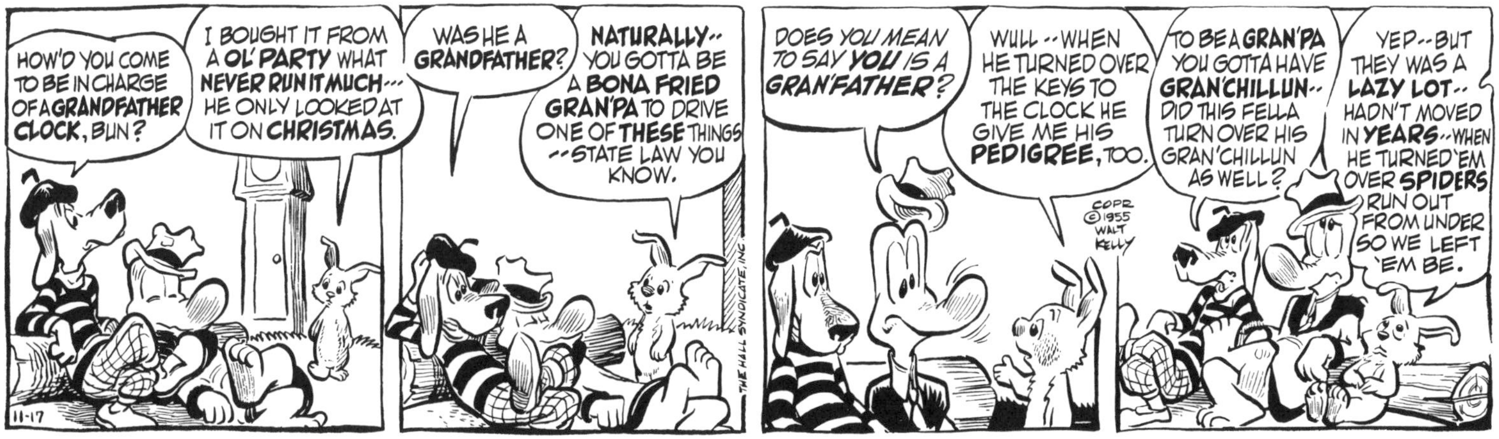

HOW'D YOU COME TO BE IN CHARGE OF A GRANDFATHER CLOCK, BUN?
I BOUGHT IT FROM A OL' PARTY WHAT NEVER RUN IT MUCH--- HE ONLY LOOKED AT IT ON CHRISTMAS.
WAS HE A GRANDFATHER?
NATURALLY-- YOU GOTTA BE A BONA FRIED GRAN'PA TO DRIVE ONE OF THESE THINGS --STATE LAW YOU KNOW.
DOES YOU MEAN TO SAY YOU IS A GRAN'FATHER?
WULL--WHEN HE TURNED OVER THE KEYS TO THE CLOCK HE GIVE ME HIS PEDIGREE, TOO.
TO BE A GRAN'PA YOU GOTTA HAVE GRAN'CHILLUN-- DID THIS FELLA TURN OVER HIS GRAN'CHILLUN AS WELL?
YEP--BUT THEY WAS A LAZY LOT-- HADN'T MOVED IN YEARS--WHEN HE TURNED 'EM OVER SPIDERS RUN OUT FROM UNDER SO WE LEFT 'EM BE.
COPR © 1955 WALT KELLY
THE HALL SYNDICATE, INC.
11-17

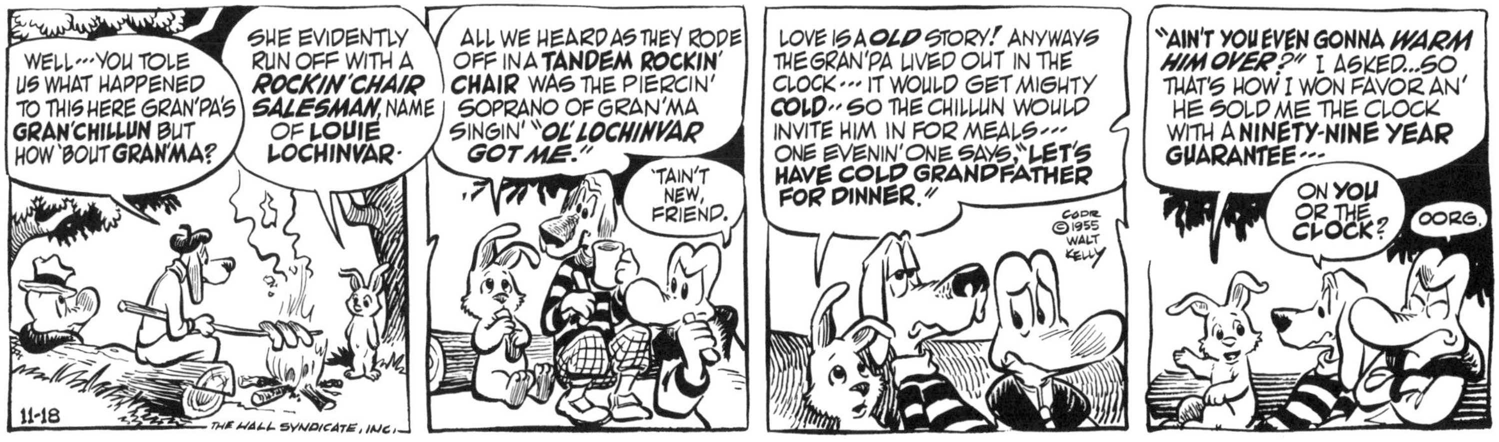

WELL---YOU TOLE US WHAT HAPPENED TO THIS HERE GRAN'PA'S GRAN'CHILLUN BUT HOW 'BOUT GRAN'MA?
SHE EVIDENTLY RUN OFF WITH A ROCKIN' CHAIR SALESMAN, NAME OF LOUIE LOCHINVAR.
ALL WE HEARD AS THEY RODE OFF IN A TANDEM ROCKIN' CHAIR WAS THE PIERCIN' SOPRANO OF GRAN'MA SINGIN' "OL' LOCHINVAR GOT ME."
'TAIN'T NEW, FRIEND.
LOVE IS A OLD STORY! ANYWAYS THE GRAN'PA LIVED OUT IN THE CLOCK--- IT WOULD GET MIGHTY COLD-- SO THE CHILLUN WOULD INVITE HIM IN FOR MEALS--- ONE EVENIN' ONE SAYS, "LET'S HAVE COLD GRANDFATHER FOR DINNER."
"AIN'T YOU EVEN GONNA WARM HIM OVER?" I ASKED..SO THAT'S HOW I WON FAVOR AN' HE SOLD ME THE CLOCK WITH A NINETY-NINE YEAR GUARANTEE---
ON YOU OR THE CLOCK?
OORG.
COPR © 1955 WALT KELLY
11-18
THE HALL SYNDICATE, INC.

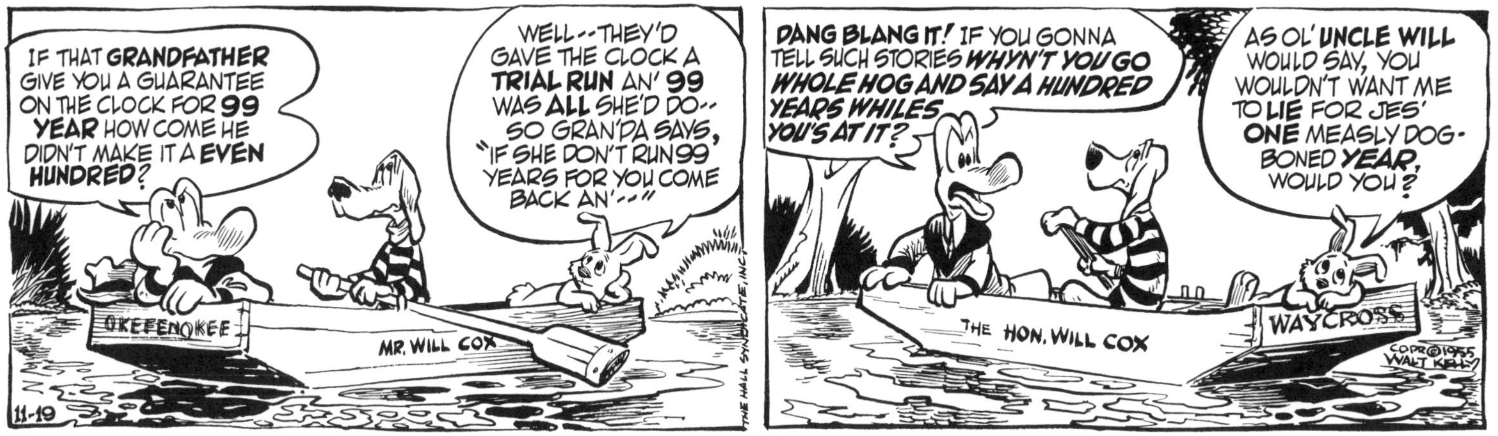

IF THAT GRANDFATHER GIVE YOU A GUARANTEE ON THE CLOCK FOR 99 YEAR HOW COME HE DIDN'T MAKE IT A EVEN HUNDRED?
WELL--THEY'D GAVE THE CLOCK A TRIAL RUN AN' 99 WAS ALL SHE'D DO-- SO GRAN'PA SAYS, "IF SHE DON'T RUN 99 YEARS FOR YOU COME BACK AN'--"
OKEFENOKEE
MR. WILL COX
DANG BLANG IT! IF YOU GONNA TELL SUCH STORIES WHYN'T YOU GO WHOLE HOG AND SAY A HUNDRED YEARS WHILES YOU'S AT IT?
AS OL' UNCLE WILL WOULD SAY, YOU WOULDN'T WANT ME TO LIE FOR JES' ONE MEASLY DOG-BONED YEAR, WOULD YOU?
THE HON. WILL COX
WAYCROSS
COPR © 1955 WALT KELLY
11-19
THE HALL SYNDICATE, INC.

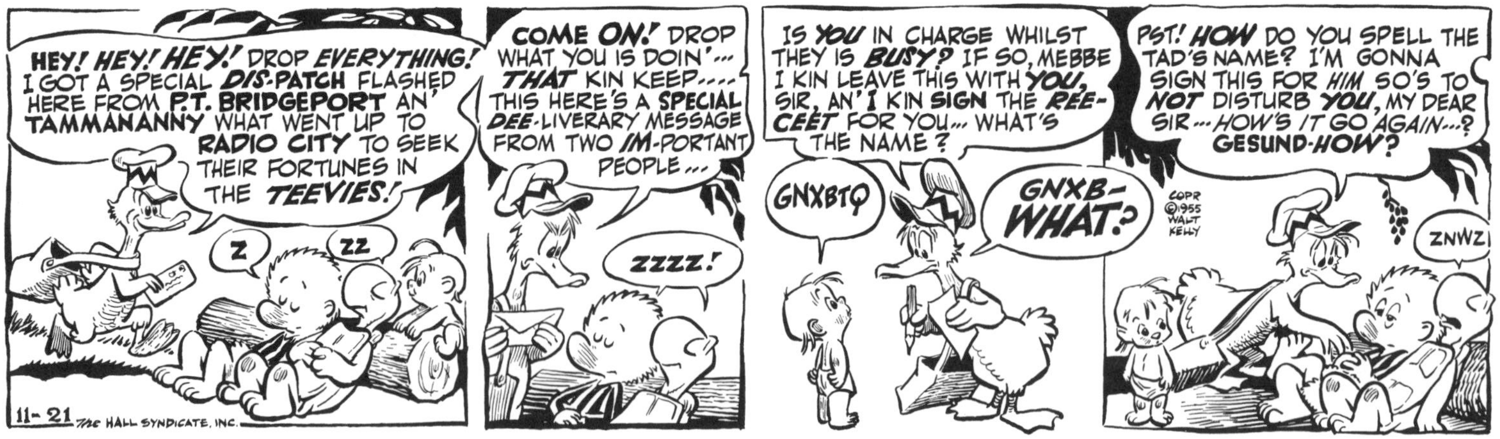
HEY! HEY! HEY! DROP EVERYTHING! I GOT A SPECIAL DIS-PATCH FLASHED HERE FROM P.T. BRIDGEPORT AN' TAMMANANNY WHAT WENT UP TO RADIO CITY TO SEEK THEIR FORTUNES IN THE TEEVIES!
Z
ZZ
11-21 The HALL SYNDICATE, INC.
COME ON! DROP WHAT YOU IS DOIN'... THAT KIN KEEP.... THIS HERE'S A SPECIAL DEE-LIVERARY MESSAGE FROM TWO IM-PORTANT PEOPLE...
ZZZZ!
IS YOU IN CHARGE WHILST THEY IS BUSY? IF SO, MEBBE I KIN LEAVE THIS WITH YOU, SIR, AN' I KIN SIGN THE REE-CEET FOR YOU... WHAT'S THE NAME?
GNXBTQ
GNXB-WHAT?
PST! HOW DO YOU SPELL THE TAD'S NAME? I'M GONNA SIGN THIS FOR HIM SO'S TO NOT DISTURB YOU, MY DEAR SIR... HOW'S IT GO AGAIN...? GESUND-HOW?
COPR ©1955 WALT KELLY
ZNWZ

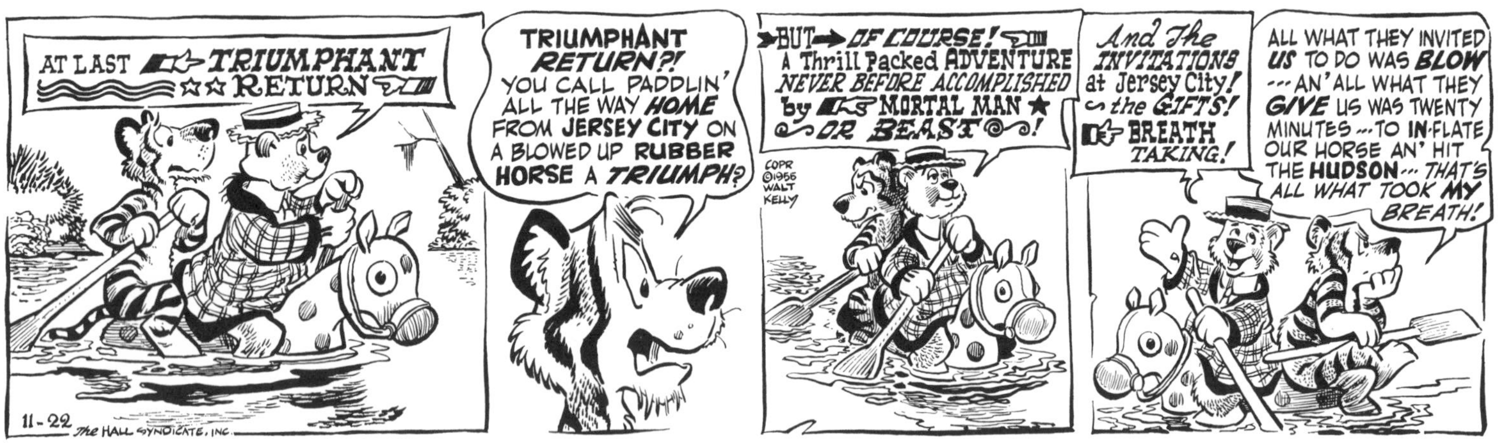
AT LAST TRIUMPHANT RETURN
11-22 The HALL SYNDICATE, INC.
TRIUMPHANT RETURN?! YOU CALL PADDLIN' ALL THE WAY HOME FROM JERSEY CITY ON A BLOWED UP RUBBER HORSE A TRIUMPH?
BUT OF COURSE! A Thrill Packed ADVENTURE NEVER BEFORE ACCOMPLISHED by MORTAL MAN OR BEAST!
COPR ©1956 WALT KELLY
And The INVITATIONS at Jersey City! the GIFTS! BREATH TAKING!
ALL WHAT THEY INVITED US TO DO WAS BLOW... AN' ALL WHAT THEY GIVE US WAS TWENTY MINUTES... TO IN-FLATE OUR HORSE AN' HIT THE HUDSON... THAT'S ALL WHAT TOOK MY BREATH!

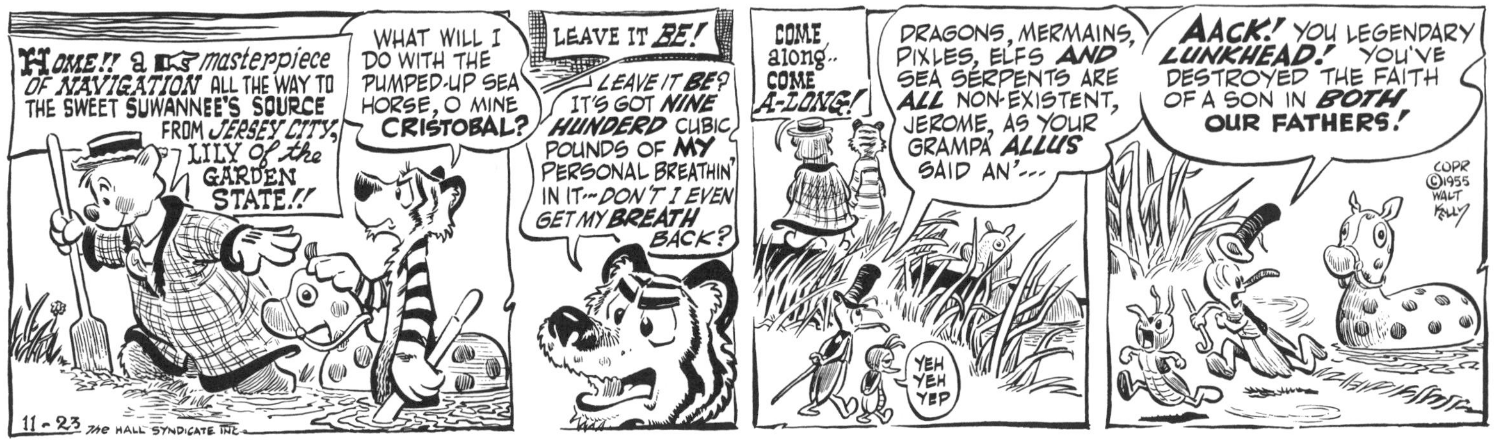
HOME!! a masterpiece OF NAVIGATION ALL THE WAY TO THE SWEET SUWANNEE'S SOURCE FROM JERSEY CITY, LILY of the GARDEN STATE!!
WHAT WILL I DO WITH THE PUMPED-UP SEA HORSE, O MINE CRISTOBAL?
11-23 The HALL SYNDICATE INC.
LEAVE IT BE!
LEAVE IT BE? IT'S GOT NINE HUNDERD CUBIC POUNDS OF MY PERSONAL BREATHIN' IN IT... DON'T I EVEN GET MY BREATH BACK?
COME along.. COME A-LONG!
DRAGONS, MERMAINS, PIXLES, ELFS AND SEA SERPENTS ARE ALL NON-EXISTENT, JEROME, AS YOUR GRAMPA' ALLUS SAID AN'...
YEH YEH YEP
AACK! YOU LEGENDARY LUNKHEAD! YOU'VE DESTROYED THE FAITH OF A SON IN BOTH OUR FATHERS!
COPR ©1955 WALT KELLY

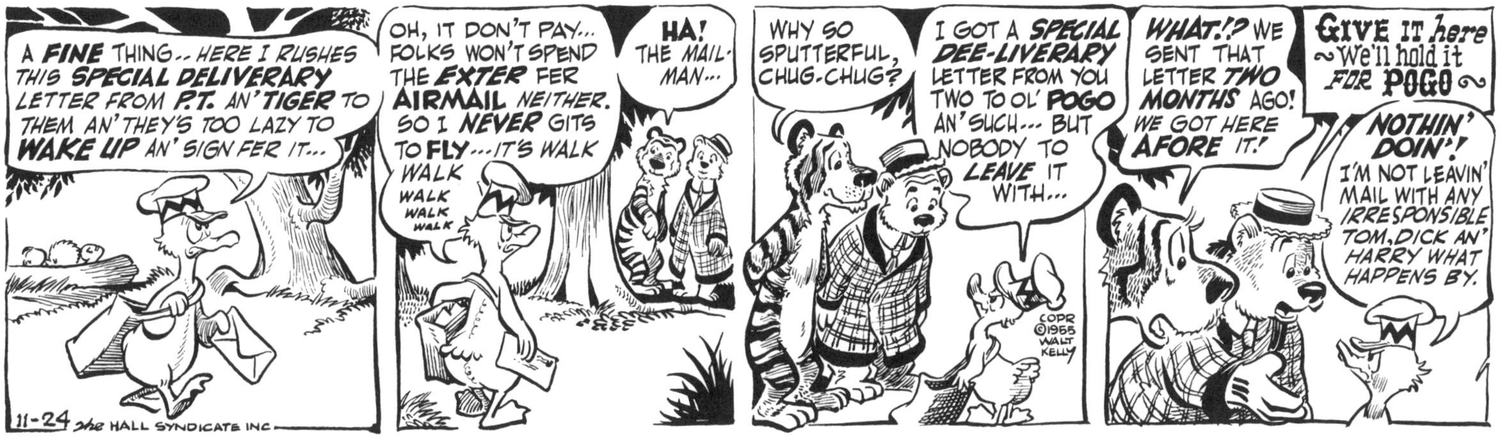
A FINE THING.. HERE I RUSHES THIS SPECIAL DELIVERARY LETTER FROM P.T. AN' TIGER TO THEM AN' THEY'S TOO LAZY TO WAKE UP AN' SIGN FER IT...
11-24 The HALL SYNDICATE INC.
OH, IT DON'T PAY... FOLKS WON'T SPEND THE EXTER FER AIRMAIL NEITHER. SO I NEVER GITS TO FLY... IT'S WALK WALK
WALK WALK WALK
HA! THE MAIL-MAN...
WHY SO SPUTTERFUL, CHUG-CHUG?
I GOT A SPECIAL DEE-LIVERARY LETTER FROM YOU TWO TO OL' POGO AN' SUCH... BUT NOBODY TO LEAVE IT WITH...
COPR ©1955 WALT KELLY
WHAT!? WE SENT THAT LETTER TWO MONTHS AGO! WE GOT HERE AFORE IT!
GIVE IT here ~We'll hold it FOR POGO~
NOTHIN' DOIN'! I'M NOT LEAVIN' MAIL WITH ANY IRRESPONSIBLE TOM, DICK AN' HARRY WHAT HAPPENS BY.

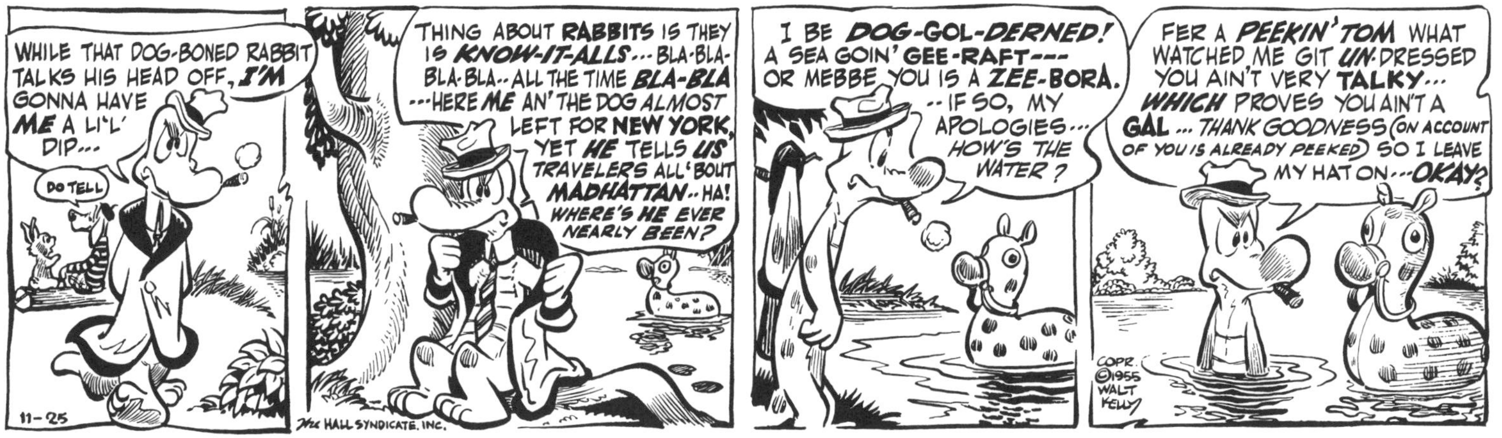
WHILE THAT DOG-BONED RABBIT TALKS HIS HEAD OFF, I'M GONNA HAVE ME A LI'L' DIP...
DO TELL
11-25
THING ABOUT RABBITS IS THEY IS KNOW-IT-ALLS... BLA-BLA-BLA-BLA.. ALL THE TIME BLA-BLA ---HERE ME AN' THE DOG ALMOST LEFT FOR NEW YORK, YET HE TELLS US TRAVELERS ALL 'BOUT MADHATTAN.. HA! WHERE'S HE EVER NEARLY BEEN?
The HALL SYNDICATE, INC.
I BE DOG-GOL-DERNED! A SEA GOIN' GEE-RAFT--- OR MEBBE YOU IS A ZEE-BORA.
..IF SO, MY APOLOGIES... HOW'S THE WATER?
FER A PEEKIN' TOM WHAT WATCHED ME GIT UN-DRESSED YOU AIN'T VERY TALKY... WHICH PROVES YOU AIN'T A GAL ... THANK GOODNESS (ON ACCOUNT OF YOU IS ALREADY PEEKED) SO I LEAVE MY HAT ON ---OKAY?
COPR. ©1955 WALT KELLY

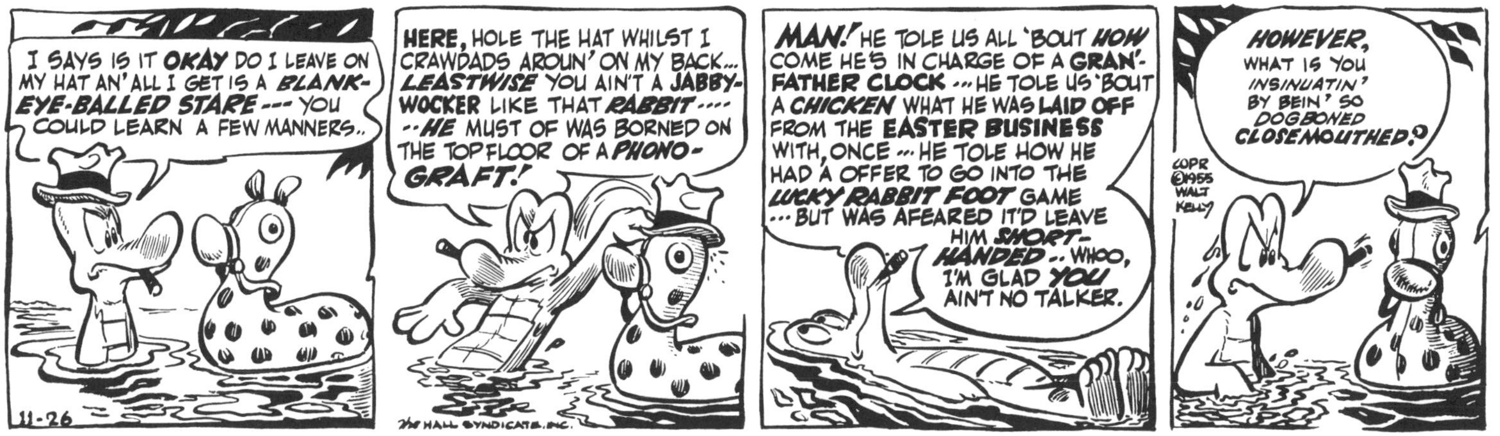
I SAYS IS IT OKAY DO I LEAVE ON MY HAT AN' ALL I GET IS A BLANK-EYE-BALLED STARE --- YOU COULD LEARN A FEW MANNERS..
11-26
HERE, HOLE THE HAT WHILST I CRAWDADS AROUN' ON MY BACK... LEASTWISE YOU AIN'T A JABBY-WOCKER LIKE THAT RABBIT.... ..HE MUST OF WAS BORNED ON THE TOP FLOOR OF A PHONO-GRAFT!
The HALL SYNDICATE, INC.
MAN! HE TOLE US ALL 'BOUT HOW COME HE'S IN CHARGE OF A GRAN'-FATHER CLOCK ... HE TOLE US 'BOUT A CHICKEN WHAT HE WAS LAID OFF FROM THE EASTER BUSINESS WITH, ONCE ... HE TOLE HOW HE HAD A OFFER TO GO INTO THE LUCKY RABBIT FOOT GAME ... BUT WAS AFEARED IT'D LEAVE HIM SHORT-HANDED .. WHOO, I'M GLAD YOU AIN'T NO TALKER.
COPR ©1955 WALT KELLY
HOWEVER, WHAT IS YOU INSINUATIN' BY BEIN' SO DOGBONED CLOSEMOUTHED?

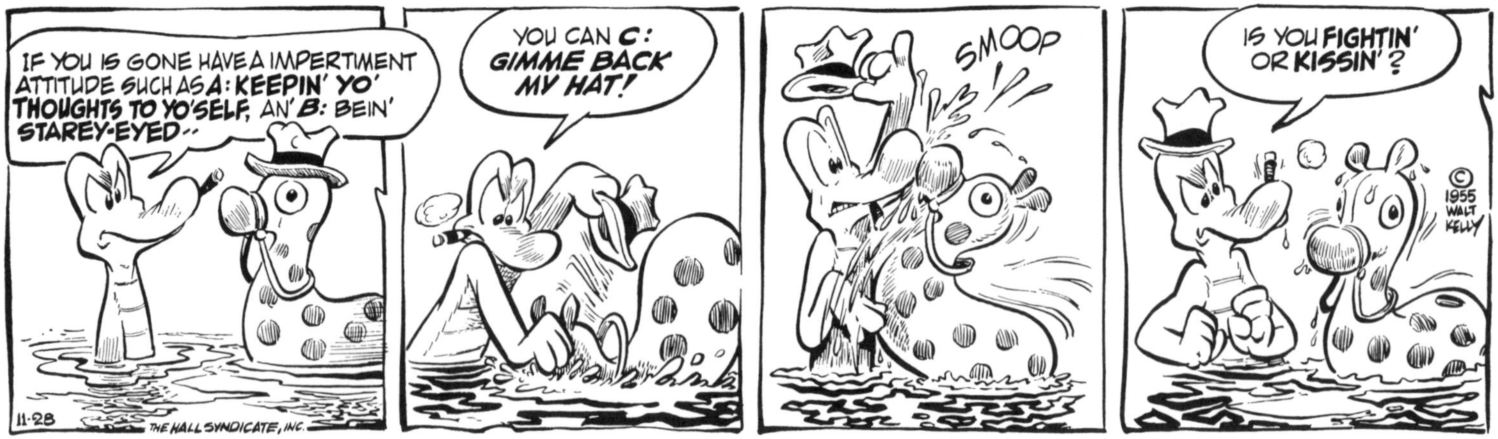
IF YOU IS GONE HAVE A IMPERTIMENT ATTITUDE SUCH AS A: KEEPIN' YO' THOUGHTS TO YO'SELF, AN' B: BEIN' STAREY-EYED--
11-28
THE HALL SYNDICATE, INC.
YOU CAN C: GIMME BACK MY HAT!
SMOOP
IS YOU FIGHTIN' OR KISSIN'?
© 1955 WALT KELLY

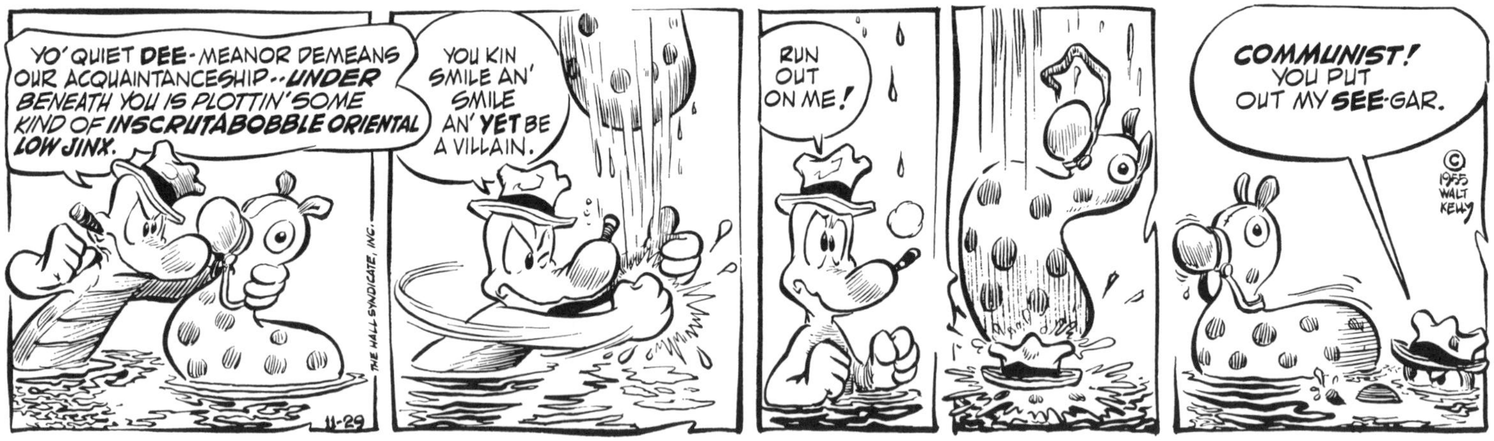
YO' QUIET DEE-MEANOR DEMEANS OUR ACQUAINTANCESHIP--UNDER BENEATH YOU IS PLOTTIN' SOME KIND OF INSCRUTABOBBLE ORIENTAL LOW JINX.
11-29
THE HALL SYNDICATE, INC.
YOU KIN SMILE AN' SMILE AN' YET BE A VILLAIN.
RUN OUT ON ME!
COMMUNIST! YOU PUT OUT MY SEE-GAR.
© 1955 WALT KELLY

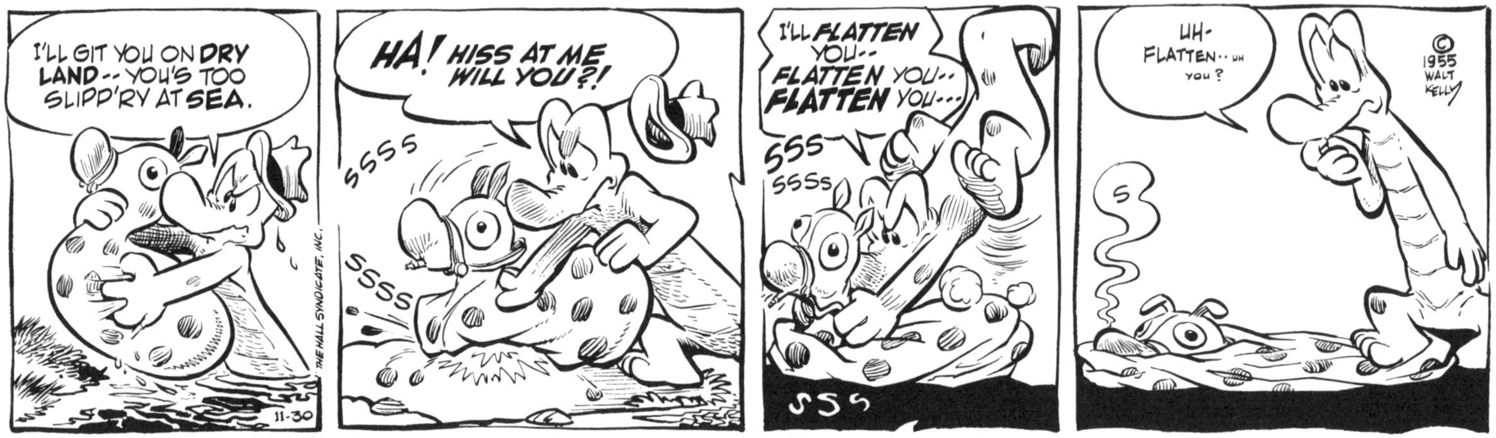
I'LL GIT YOU ON DRY LAND--YOU'S TOO SLIPP'RY AT SEA.
THE HALL SYNDICATE, INC.
HA! HISS AT ME WILL YOU?!
SSSS
SSSS
11-30
I'LL FLATTEN YOU-- FLATTEN YOU-- FLATTEN YOU--
SSS
SSSS
SSS
UH- FLATTEN.. UH YOU?
S
© 1955 WALT KELLY

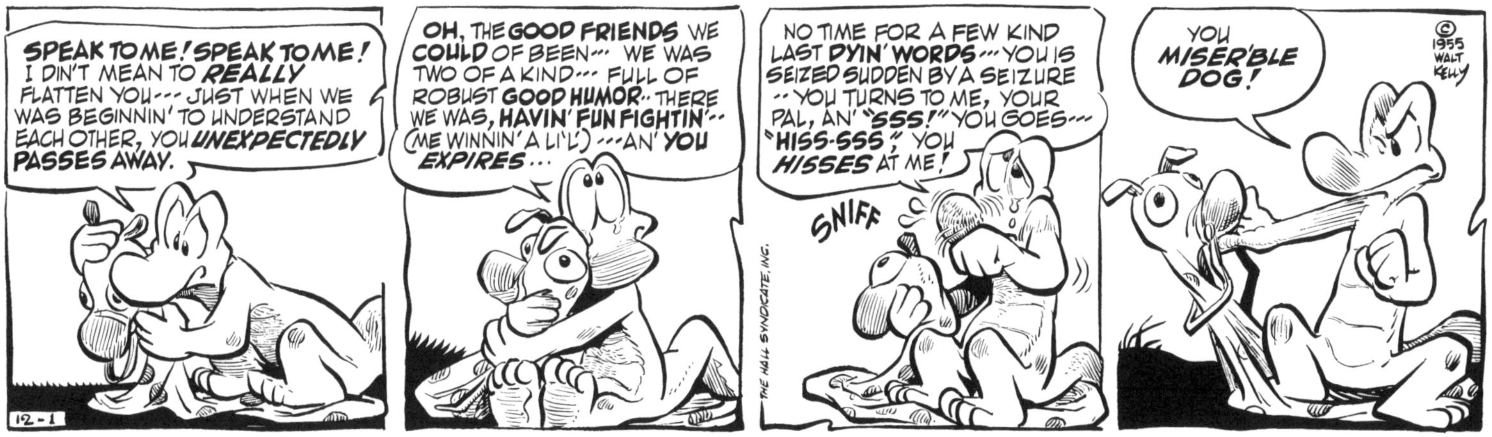
SPEAK TO ME! SPEAK TO ME! I DIN'T MEAN TO REALLY FLATTEN YOU--- JUST WHEN WE WAS BEGINNIN' TO UNDERSTAND EACH OTHER, YOU UNEXPECTEDLY PASSES AWAY.
12-1
OH, THE GOOD FRIENDS WE COULD OF BEEN--- WE WAS TWO OF A KIND--- FULL OF ROBUST GOOD HUMOR-- THERE WE WAS, HAVIN' FUN FIGHTIN'-- (ME WINNIN' A LI'L) ---AN' YOU EXPIRES...
THE HALL SYNDICATE, INC.
NO TIME FOR A FEW KIND LAST DYIN' WORDS--- YOU IS SEIZED SUDDEN BY A SEIZURE -- YOU TURNS TO ME, YOUR PAL, AN' "SSS!" YOU GOES--- "HISS-SSS," YOU HISSES AT ME!
SNIFF
YOU MISER'BLE DOG!
© 1955 WALT KELLY

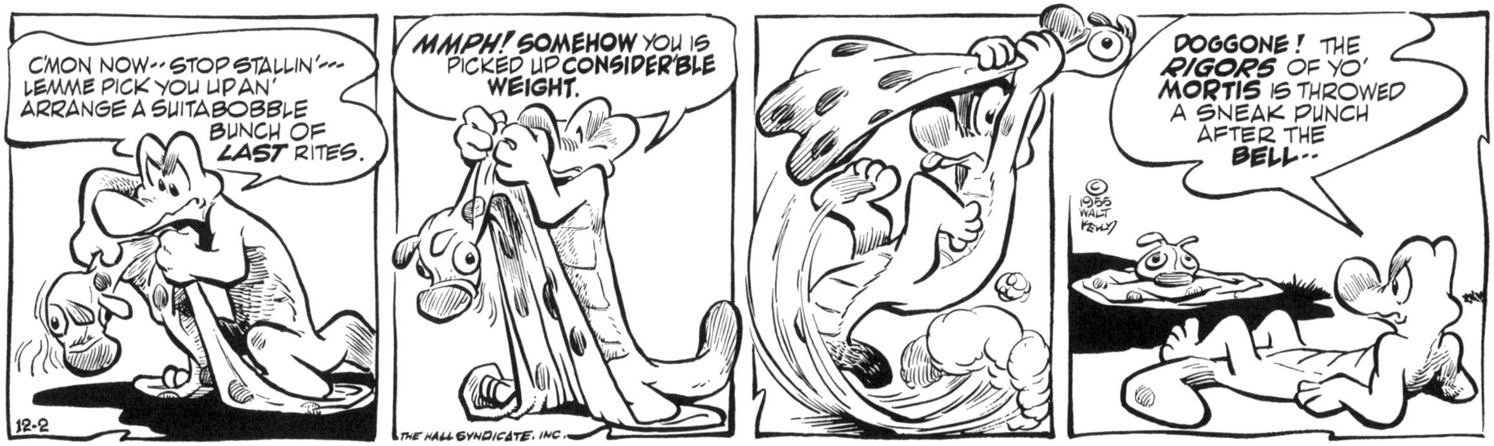
C'MON NOW-- STOP STALLIN'--- LEMME PICK YOU UP AN' ARRANGE A SUITABOBBLE BUNCH OF LAST RITES.
12-2
MMPH! SOMEHOW YOU IS PICKED UP CONSIDER'BLE WEIGHT.
THE HALL SYNDICATE, INC.
© 1955 WALT KELLY
DOGGONE! THE RIGORS OF YO' MORTIS IS THROWED A SNEAK PUNCH AFTER THE BELL--

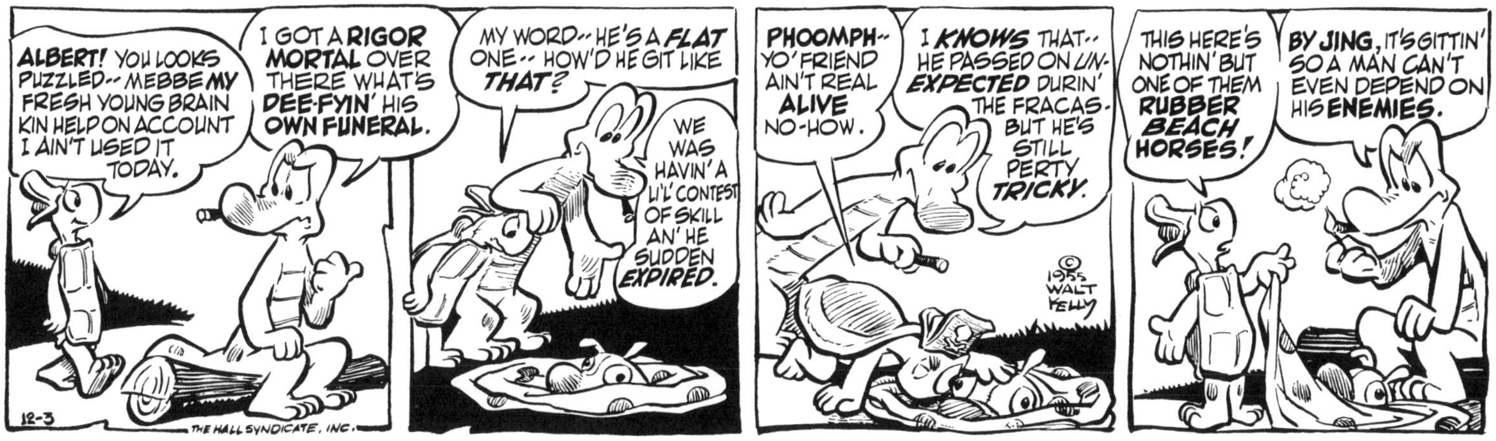
ALBERT! YOU LOOKS PUZZLED-- MEBBE MY FRESH YOUNG BRAIN KIN HELP ON ACCOUNT I AIN'T USED IT TODAY.
I GOT A RIGOR MORTAL OVER THERE WHAT'S DEE-FYIN' HIS OWN FUNERAL.
12-3
THE HALL SYNDICATE, INC.
MY WORD-- HE'S A FLAT ONE-- HOW'D HE GIT LIKE THAT?
WE WAS HAVIN' A LI'L' CONTEST OF SKILL AN' HE SUDDEN EXPIRED.
PHOOMPH-- YO' FRIEND AIN'T REAL ALIVE NO-HOW.
I KNOWS THAT-- HE PASSED ON UN-EXPECTED DURIN' THE FRACAS. BUT HE'S STILL PERTY TRICKY.
© 1955 WALT KELLY
THIS HERE'S NOTHIN' BUT ONE OF THEM RUBBER BEACH HORSES!
BY JING, IT'S GITTIN' SO A MAN CAN'T EVEN DEPEND ON HIS ENEMIES.

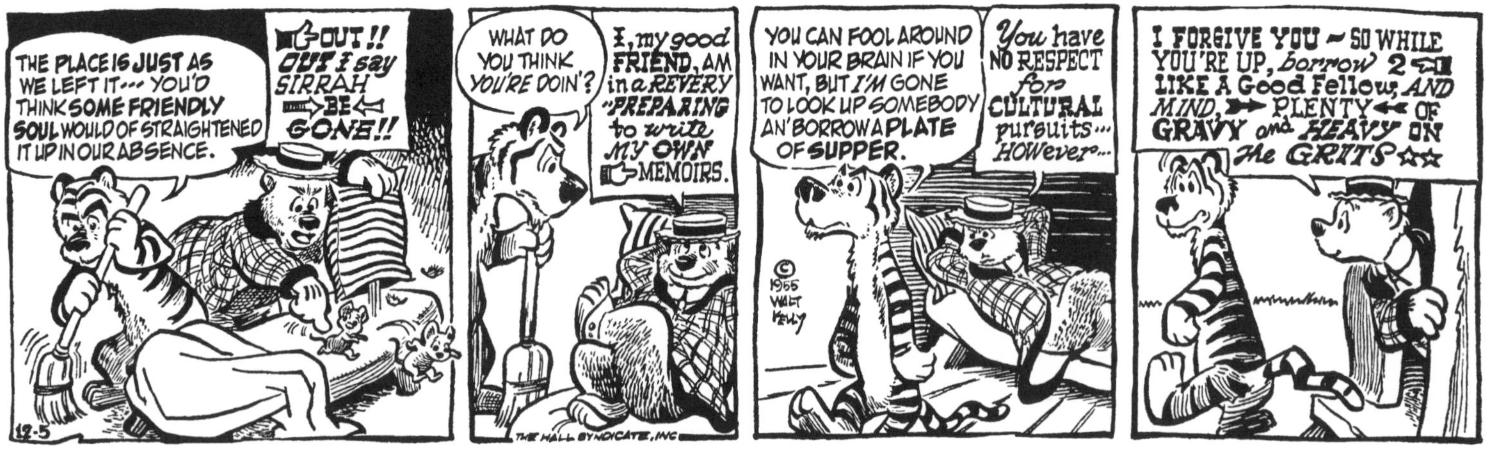
THE PLACE IS JUST AS WE LEFT IT··· YOU'D THINK SOME FRIENDLY SOUL WOULD OF STRAIGHTENED IT UP IN OUR ABSENCE.
OUT!! OUT I say SIRRAH BE GONE!!
12-5
WHAT DO YOU THINK YOU'RE DOIN'?
I, my good FRIEND, AM in a REVERY "PREPARING to write MY OWN MEMOIRS.
THE HALL SYNDICATE, INC.
YOU CAN FOOL AROUND IN YOUR BRAIN IF YOU WANT, BUT I'M GONE TO LOOK UP SOMEBODY AN' BORROW A PLATE OF SUPPER.
You have NO RESPECT for CULTURAL pursuits··· HOWever···
© 1955 WALT KELLY
I FORGIVE YOU ~ SO WHILE YOU'RE UP, borrow 2 LIKE A Good Fellow, AND MIND, PLENTY OF GRAVY and HEAVY ON the GRITS

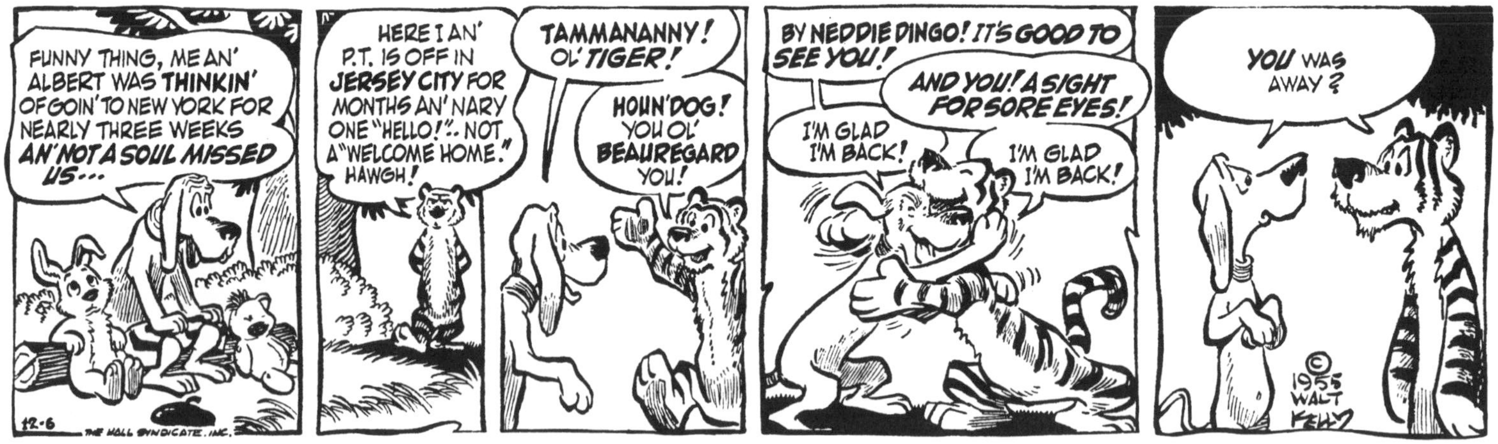
FUNNY THING, ME AN' ALBERT WAS THINKIN' OF GOIN' TO NEW YORK FOR NEARLY THREE WEEKS AN' NOT A SOUL MISSED US···
12-6
THE HALL SYNDICATE, INC.
HERE I AN' P.T. IS OFF IN JERSEY CITY FOR MONTHS AN' NARY ONE "HELLO!"·· NOT A "WELCOME HOME." HAWGH!
TAMMANANNY! OL' TIGER!
HOUN'DOG! YOU OL' BEAUREGARD YOU!
BY NEDDIE DINGO! IT'S GOOD TO SEE YOU!
AND YOU! A SIGHT FOR SORE EYES!
I'M GLAD I'M BACK!
I'M GLAD I'M BACK!
YOU WAS AWAY?
© 1955 WALT KELLY

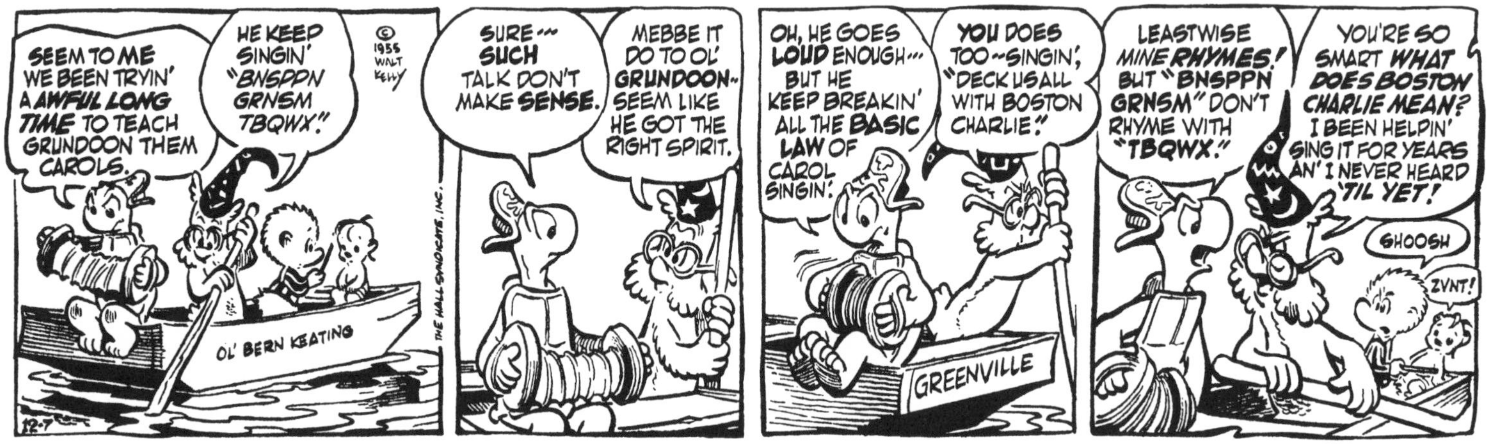
SEEM TO ME WE BEEN TRYIN' A AWFUL LONG TIME TO TEACH GRUNDOON THEM CAROLS.
HE KEEP SINGIN' "BNSPPN GRNSM TBQWX."
© 1955 WALT KELLY
OL' BERN KEATING
12-7
THE HALL SYNDICATE, INC.
SURE··· SUCH TALK DON'T MAKE SENSE.
MEBBE IT DO TO OL' GRUNDOON·· SEEM LIKE HE GOT THE RIGHT SPIRIT.
OH, HE GOES LOUD ENOUGH··· BUT HE KEEP BREAKIN' ALL THE BASIC LAW OF CAROL SINGIN'.
YOU DOES TOO~SINGIN', "DECK US ALL WITH BOSTON CHARLIE."
GREENVILLE
LEASTWISE MINE RHYMES! BUT "BNSPPN GRNSM" DON'T RHYME WITH "TBQWX."
YOU'RE SO SMART WHAT DOES BOSTON CHARLIE MEAN? I BEEN HELPIN' SING IT FOR YEARS AN' I NEVER HEARD 'TIL YET!
SHOOSH
ZVNT!

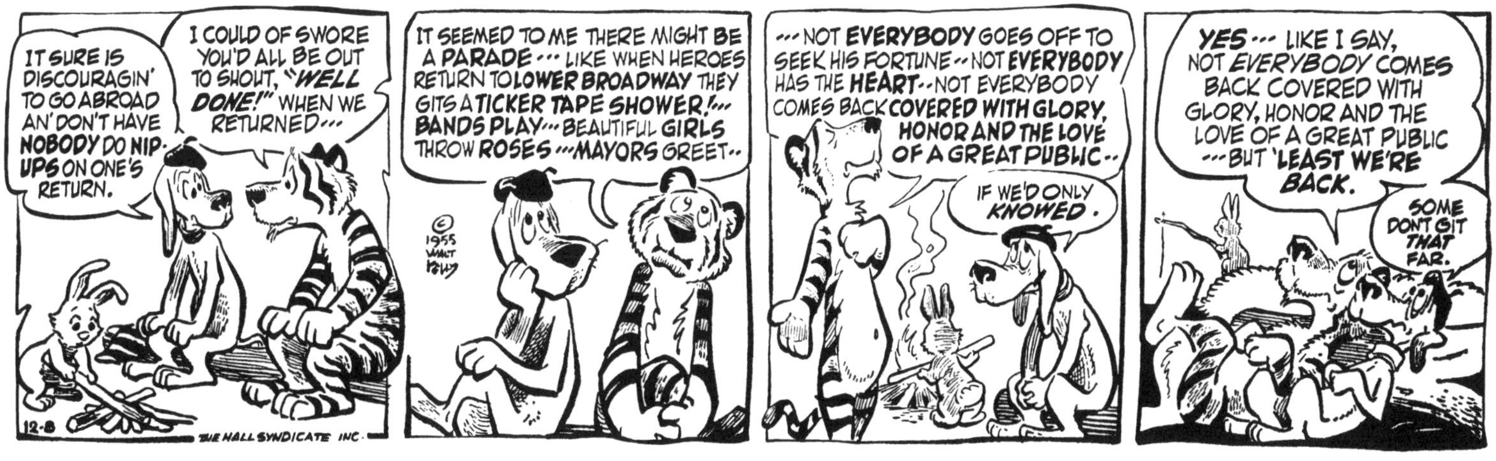
IT SURE IS DISCOURAGIN' TO GO ABROAD AN' DON'T HAVE NOBODY DO NIP-UPS ON ONE'S RETURN.
I COULD OF SWORE YOU'D ALL BE OUT TO SHOUT, "WELL DONE!" WHEN WE RETURNED…
12-8
THE HALL SYNDICATE INC.
IT SEEMED TO ME THERE MIGHT BE A PARADE… LIKE WHEN HEROES RETURN TO LOWER BROADWAY THEY GITS A TICKER TAPE SHOWER!… BANDS PLAY… BEAUTIFUL GIRLS THROW ROSES… MAYORS GREET…
© 1955 WALT KELLY
…NOT EVERYBODY GOES OFF TO SEEK HIS FORTUNE… NOT EVERYBODY HAS THE HEART… NOT EVERYBODY COMES BACK COVERED WITH GLORY, HONOR AND THE LOVE OF A GREAT PUBLIC…
IF WE'D ONLY KNOWED.
YES… LIKE I SAY, NOT EVERYBODY COMES BACK COVERED WITH GLORY, HONOR AND THE LOVE OF A GREAT PUBLIC …BUT 'LEAST WE'RE BACK.
SOME DON'T GIT THAT FAR.

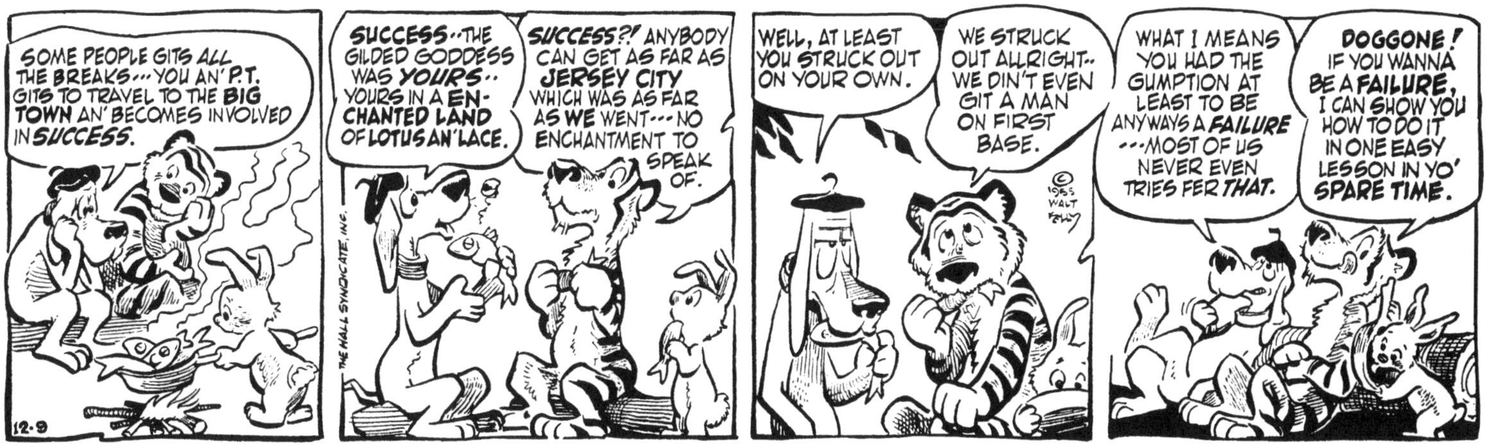
SOME PEOPLE GITS ALL THE BREAKS… YOU AN' P.T. GITS TO TRAVEL TO THE BIG TOWN AN' BECOMES INVOLVED IN SUCCESS.
12-9
SUCCESS… THE GILDED GODDESS WAS YOURS… YOURS IN A EN-CHANTED LAND OF LOTUS AN' LACE.
SUCCESS?! ANYBODY CAN GET AS FAR AS JERSEY CITY WHICH WAS AS FAR AS WE WENT… NO ENCHANTMENT TO SPEAK OF.
THE HALL SYNDICATE, INC.
WELL, AT LEAST YOU STRUCK OUT ON YOUR OWN.
WE STRUCK OUT ALLRIGHT… WE DIN'T EVEN GIT A MAN ON FIRST BASE.
© 1955 WALT KELLY
WHAT I MEANS YOU HAD THE GUMPTION AT LEAST TO BE ANYWAYS A FAILURE …MOST OF US NEVER EVEN TRIES FER THAT.
DOGGONE! IF YOU WANNA BE A FAILURE, I CAN SHOW YOU HOW TO DO IT IN ONE EASY LESSON IN YO' SPARE TIME.

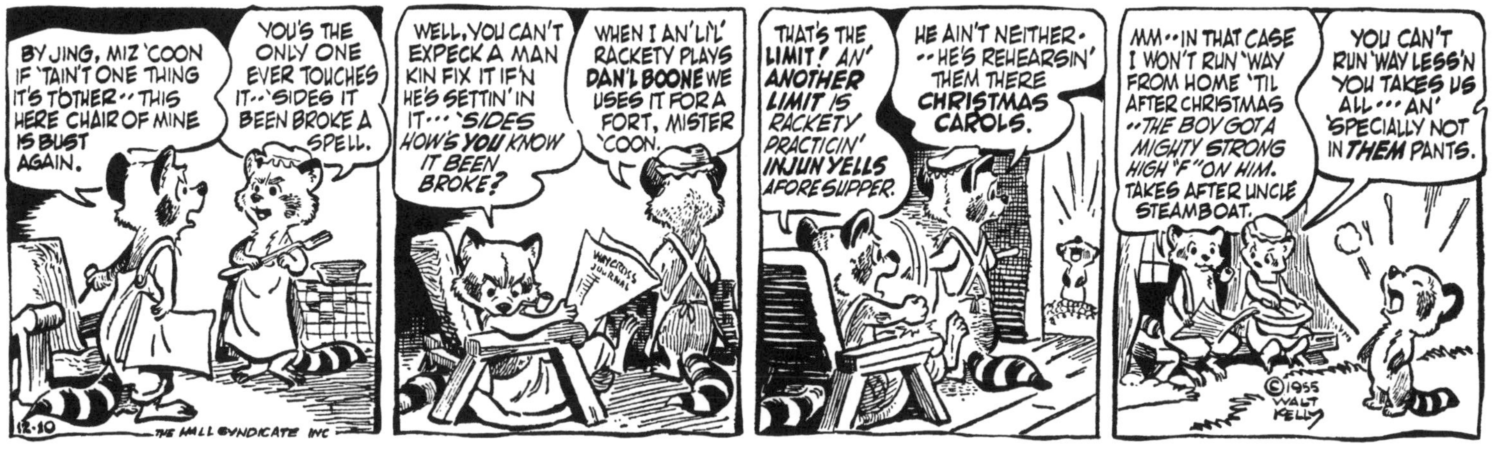
BY JING, MIZ 'COON IF 'TAIN'T ONE THING IT'S T'OTHER… THIS HERE CHAIR OF MINE IS BUST AGAIN.
YOU'S THE ONLY ONE EVER TOUCHES IT… 'SIDES IT BEEN BROKE A SPELL.
12-10
THE HALL SYNDICATE INC
WELL, YOU CAN'T EXPECK A MAN KIN FIX IT IF'N HE'S SETTIN' IN IT… 'SIDES HOW'S YOU KNOW IT BEEN BROKE?
WHEN I AN' LI'L' RACKETY PLAYS DAN'L BOONE WE USES IT FOR A FORT, MISTER 'COON.
THAT'S THE LIMIT! AN' ANOTHER LIMIT IS RACKETY PRACTICIN' INJUN YELLS AFORE SUPPER.
HE AIN'T NEITHER… HE'S REHEARSIN' THEM THERE CHRISTMAS CAROLS.
MM… IN THAT CASE I WON'T RUN 'WAY FROM HOME 'TIL AFTER CHRISTMAS …THE BOY GOT A MIGHTY STRONG HIGH "F" ON HIM. TAKES AFTER UNCLE STEAMBOAT.
YOU CAN'T RUN 'WAY LESS'N YOU TAKES US ALL… AN' 'SPECIALLY NOT IN THEM PANTS.
© 1955 WALT KELLY

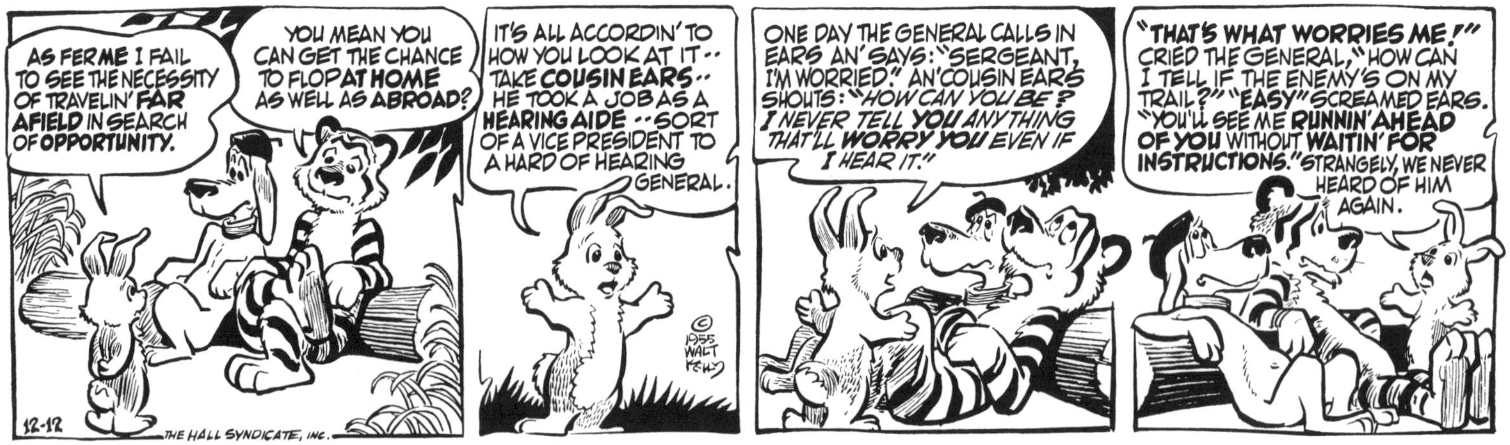
AS FER ME I FAIL TO SEE THE NECESSITY OF TRAVELIN' FAR AFIELD IN SEARCH OF OPPORTUNITY.
YOU MEAN YOU CAN GET THE CHANCE TO FLOP AT HOME AS WELL AS ABROAD?
IT'S ALL ACCORDIN' TO HOW YOU LOOK AT IT -- TAKE COUSIN EARS -- HE TOOK A JOB AS A HEARING AIDE -- SORT OF A VICE PRESIDENT TO A HARD OF HEARING GENERAL.
© 1955 WALT KELLY
ONE DAY THE GENERAL CALLS IN EARS AN' SAYS: "SERGEANT, I'M WORRIED." AN' COUSIN EARS SHOUTS: "HOW CAN YOU BE? I NEVER TELL YOU ANYTHING THAT'LL WORRY YOU EVEN IF I HEAR IT."
"THAT'S WHAT WORRIES ME!" CRIED THE GENERAL, "HOW CAN I TELL IF THE ENEMY'S ON MY TRAIL?" "EASY" SCREAMED EARS. "YOU'LL SEE ME RUNNIN' AHEAD OF YOU WITHOUT WAITIN' FOR INSTRUCTIONS." STRANGELY, WE NEVER HEARD OF HIM AGAIN.
12-12
THE HALL SYNDICATE, INC.

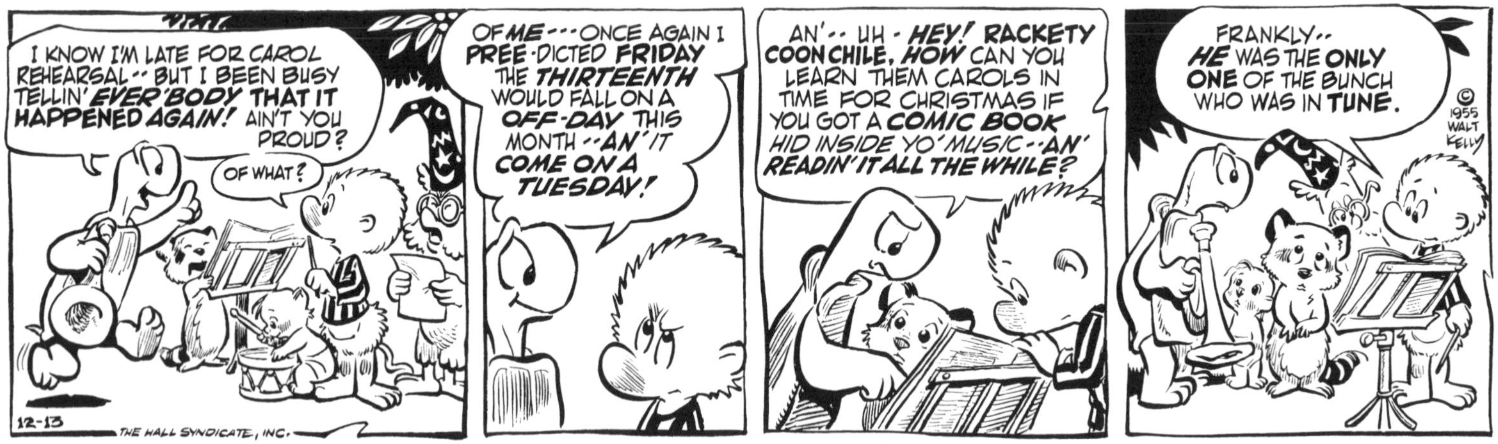
I KNOW I'M LATE FOR CAROL REHEARSAL -- BUT I BEEN BUSY TELLIN' EVER'BODY THAT IT HAPPENED AGAIN! AIN'T YOU PROUD?
OF WHAT?
OF ME --- ONCE AGAIN I PREE-DICTED FRIDAY THE THIRTEENTH WOULD FALL ON A OFF-DAY THIS MONTH -- AN' IT COME ON A TUESDAY!
AN' -- UH - HEY! RACKETY COON CHILE, HOW CAN YOU LEARN THEM CAROLS IN TIME FOR CHRISTMAS IF YOU GOT A COMIC BOOK HID INSIDE YO' MUSIC -- AN' READIN' IT ALL THE WHILE?
FRANKLY -- HE WAS THE ONLY ONE OF THE BUNCH WHO WAS IN TUNE.
© 1955 WALT KELLY
12-13
THE HALL SYNDICATE, INC.

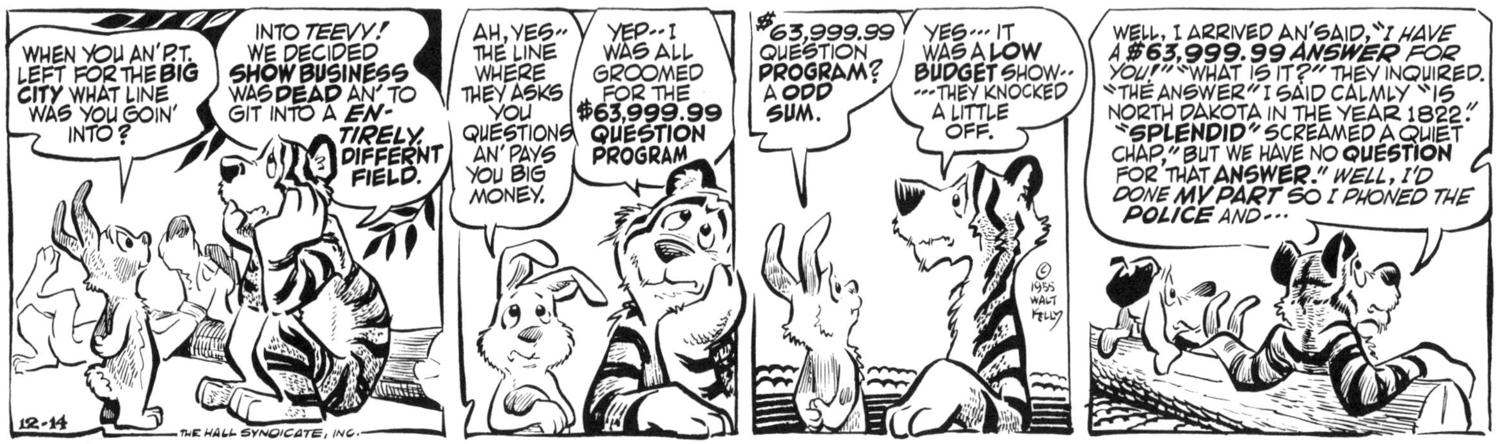
WHEN YOU AN' P.T. LEFT FOR THE BIG CITY WHAT LINE WAS YOU GOIN' INTO?
INTO TEEVY! WE DECIDED SHOW BUSINESS WAS DEAD AN' TO GIT INTO A EN-TIRELY DIFFERNT FIELD.
AH, YES -- THE LINE WHERE THEY ASKS YOU QUESTIONS AN' PAYS YOU BIG MONEY.
YEP -- I WAS ALL GROOMED FOR THE $63,999.99 QUESTION PROGRAM
$63,999.99 QUESTION PROGRAM? A ODD SUM.
YES --- IT WAS A LOW BUDGET SHOW -- --- THEY KNOCKED A LITTLE OFF.
© 1955 WALT KELLY
WELL, I ARRIVED AN' SAID, "I HAVE A $63,999.99 ANSWER FOR YOU!" "WHAT IS IT?" THEY INQUIRED. "THE ANSWER" I SAID CALMLY "IS NORTH DAKOTA IN THE YEAR 1822." "SPLENDID" SCREAMED A QUIET CHAP, "BUT WE HAVE NO QUESTION FOR THAT ANSWER." WELL, I'D DONE MY PART SO I PHONED THE POLICE AND ---
12-14
THE HALL SYNDICATE, INC.

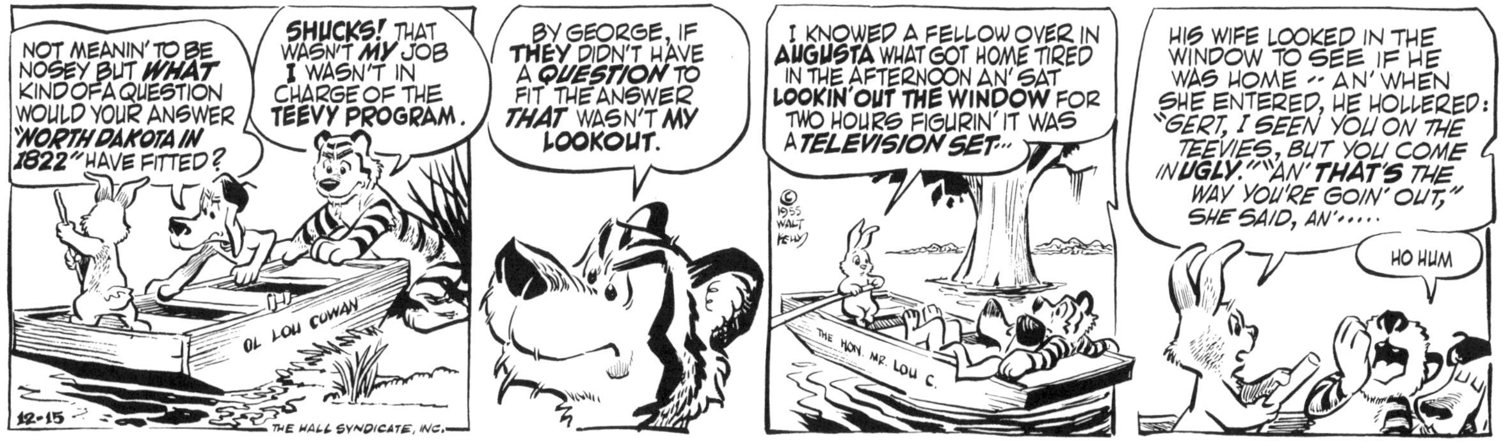
NOT MEANIN' TO BE NOSEY BUT WHAT KIND OF A QUESTION WOULD YOUR ANSWER "NORTH DAKOTA IN 1822" HAVE FITTED?
SHUCKS! THAT WASN'T MY JOB I WASN'T IN CHARGE OF THE TEEVY PROGRAM.
OL LOU CUWAN
12-15
THE HALL SYNDICATE, INC.
BY GEORGE, IF THEY DIDN'T HAVE A QUESTION TO FIT THE ANSWER THAT WASN'T MY LOOKOUT.
I KNOWED A FELLOW OVER IN AUGUSTA WHAT GOT HOME TIRED IN THE AFTERNOON AN' SAT LOOKIN' OUT THE WINDOW FOR TWO HOURS FIGURIN' IT WAS A TELEVISION SET...
© 1955 WALT KELLY
THE HON. MR. LOU C.
HIS WIFE LOOKED IN THE WINDOW TO SEE IF HE WAS HOME -- AN' WHEN SHE ENTERED, HE HOLLERED: "GERT, I SEEN YOU ON THE TEEVIES, BUT YOU COME IN UGLY." "AN' THAT'S THE WAY YOU'RE GOIN' OUT," SHE SAID, AN'.....
HO HUM

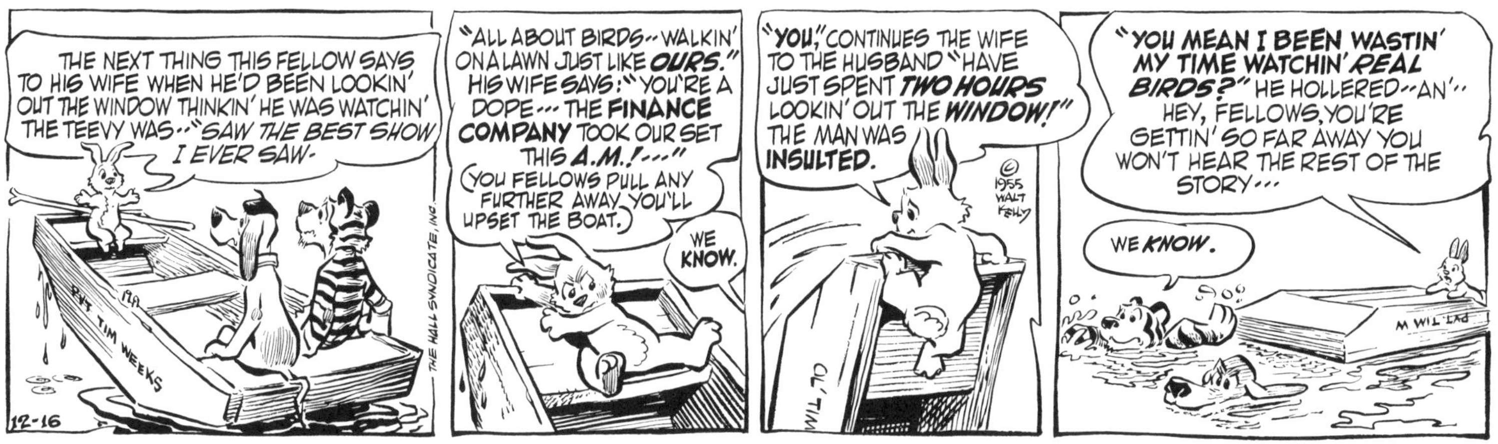
THE NEXT THING THIS FELLOW SAYS TO HIS WIFE WHEN HE'D BEEN LOOKIN' OUT THE WINDOW THINKIN' HE WAS WATCHIN' THE TEEVY WAS.. "SAW THE BEST SHOW I EVER SAW-
PVT TIM WEEKS
12-16
THE HALL SYNDICATE, INC.
"ALL ABOUT BIRDS -- WALKIN' ON A LAWN JUST LIKE OURS." HIS WIFE SAYS: "YOU'RE A DOPE --- THE FINANCE COMPANY TOOK OUR SET THIS A.M.!..."
(YOU FELLOWS PULL ANY FURTHER AWAY, YOU'LL UPSET THE BOAT.)
WE KNOW.
"YOU," CONTINUES THE WIFE TO THE HUSBAND "HAVE JUST SPENT TWO HOURS LOOKIN' OUT THE WINDOW!" THE MAN WAS INSULTED.
© 1955 WALT KELLY
OL' TIM
"YOU MEAN I BEEN WASTIN' MY TIME WATCHIN' REAL BIRDS?" HE HOLLERED -- AN'.. HEY, FELLOWS, YOU'RE GETTIN' SO FAR AWAY YOU WON'T HEAR THE REST OF THE STORY...
WE KNOW.

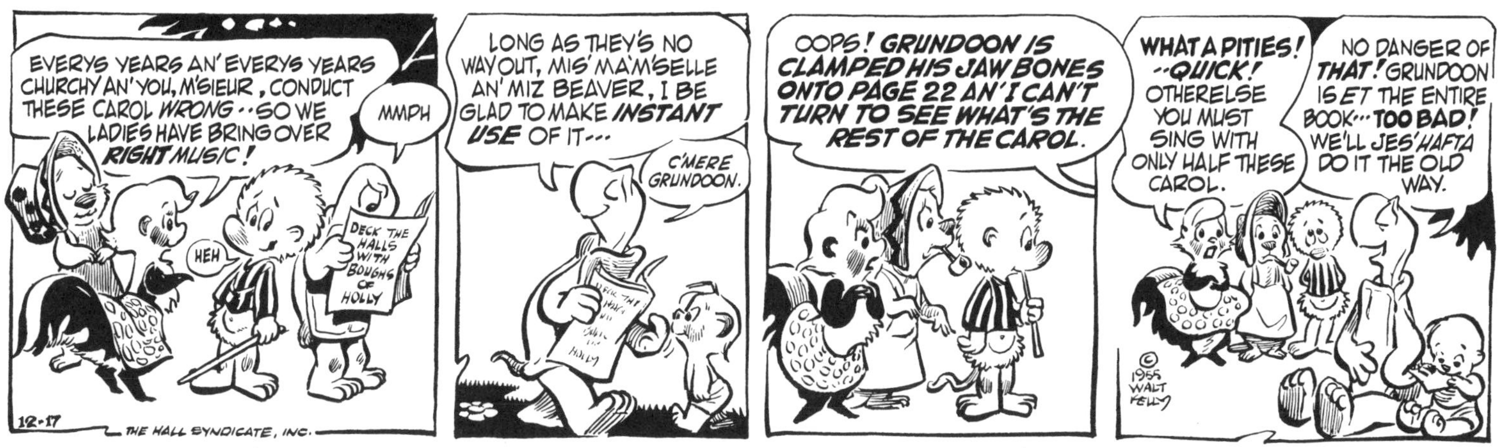
EVERYS YEARS AN' EVERYS YEARS CHURCHY AN' YOU, M'SIEUR, CONDUCT THESE CAROL WRONG .. SO WE LADIES HAVE BRING OVER RIGHT MUSIC!
MMPH
HEH
DECK THE HALLS WITH BOUGHS OF HOLLY
12-17
THE HALL SYNDICATE, INC.
LONG AS THEY'S NO WAY OUT, MIS' MAM'SELLE AN' MIZ BEAVER, I BE GLAD TO MAKE INSTANT USE OF IT...
C'MERE GRUNDOON.
OOPS! GRUNDOON IS CLAMPED HIS JAW BONES ONTO PAGE 22 AN' I CAN'T TURN TO SEE WHAT'S THE REST OF THE CAROL.
WHAT A PITIES! --QUICK! OTHERELSE YOU MUST SING WITH ONLY HALF THESE CAROL.
NO DANGER OF THAT! GRUNDOON IS ET THE ENTIRE BOOK... TOO BAD! WE'LL JES' HAFTA DO IT THE OLD WAY.
© 1955 WALT KELLY

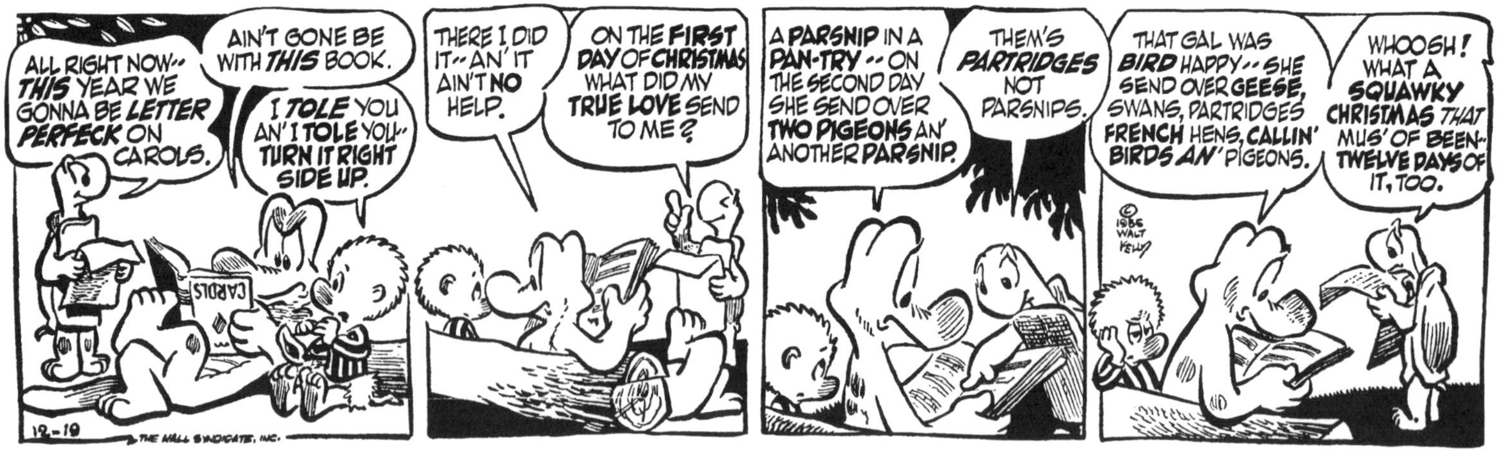
ALL RIGHT NOW-- THIS YEAR WE GONNA BE LETTER PERFECK ON CAROLS.
AIN'T GONE BE WITH THIS BOOK.
I TOLE YOU AN' I TOLE YOU-- TURN IT RIGHT SIDE UP.
CAROLS
12-19
THE HALL SYNDICATE, INC.
THERE I DID IT-- AN' IT AIN'T NO HELP.
ON THE FIRST DAY OF CHRISTMAS WHAT DID MY TRUE LOVE SEND TO ME?
A PARSNIP IN A PAN-TRY -- ON THE SECOND DAY SHE SEND OVER TWO PIGEONS AN' ANOTHER PARSNIP.
THEM'S PARTRIDGES NOT PARSNIPS.
THAT GAL WAS BIRD HAPPY-- SHE SEND OVER GEESE, SWANS, PARTRIDGES FRENCH HENS, CALLIN' BIRDS AN' PIGEONS.
WHOOSH! WHAT A SQUAWKY CHRISTMAS THAT MUS' OF BEEN-- TWELVE DAYS OF IT, TOO.
© 1955 WALT KELLY

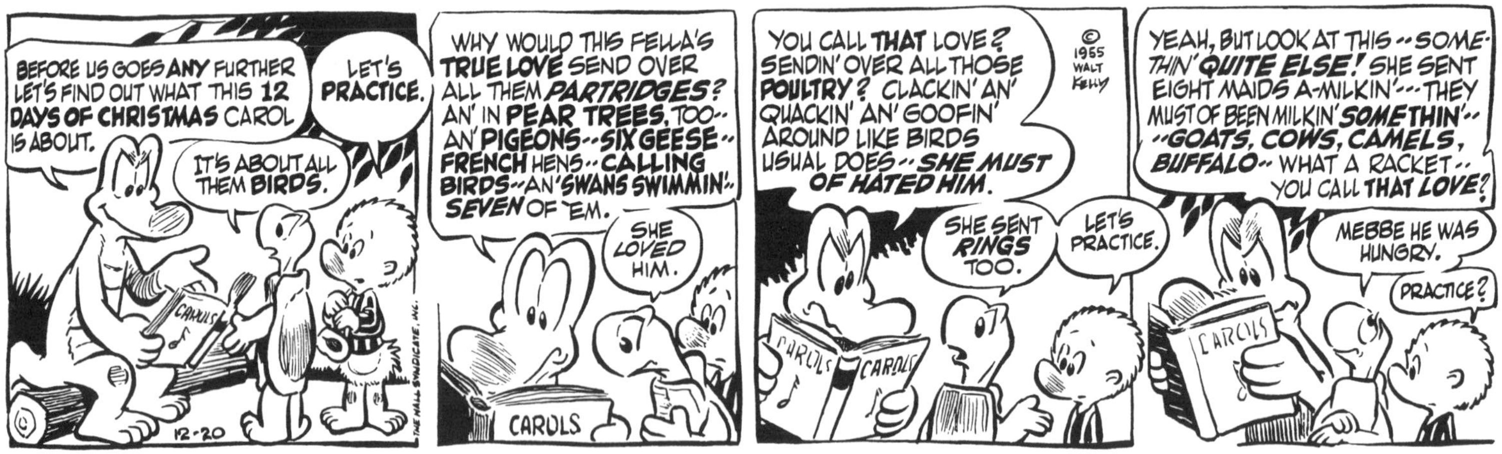
BEFORE US GOES ANY FURTHER LET'S FIND OUT WHAT THIS 12 DAYS OF CHRISTMAS CAROL IS ABOUT.
LET'S PRACTICE.
IT'S ABOUT ALL THEM BIRDS.
CAROLS
12-20
THE HALL SYNDICATE, INC.
WHY WOULD THIS FELLA'S TRUE LOVE SEND OVER ALL THEM PARTRIDGES? AN' IN PEAR TREES, TOO-- AN' PIGEONS--SIX GEESE-- FRENCH HENS-- CALLING BIRDS--AN' SWANS SWIMMIN'-- SEVEN OF 'EM.
SHE LOVED HIM.
CAROLS
YOU CALL THAT LOVE? SENDIN' OVER ALL THOSE POULTRY? CLACKIN' AN' QUACKIN' AN' GOOFIN' AROUND LIKE BIRDS USUAL DOES-- SHE MUST OF HATED HIM.
© 1955 WALT KELLY
SHE SENT RINGS TOO.
LET'S PRACTICE.
CAROLS
CAROLS
YEAH, BUT LOOK AT THIS -- SOMETHIN' QUITE ELSE! SHE SENT EIGHT MAIDS A-MILKIN'-- THEY MUST OF BEEN MILKIN' SOMETHIN'-- --GOATS, COWS, CAMELS, BUFFALO-- WHAT A RACKET-- YOU CALL THAT LOVE?
MEBBE HE WAS HUNGRY.
PRACTICE?
CAROLS

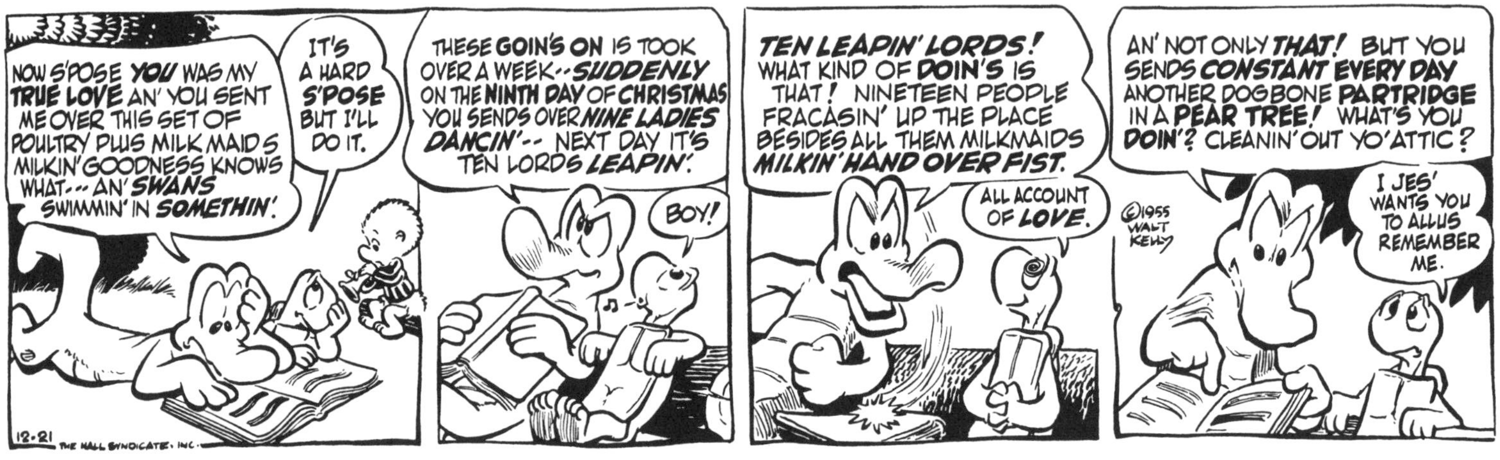
NOW S'POSE YOU WAS MY TRUE LOVE AN' YOU SENT ME OVER THIS SET OF POULTRY PLUS MILK MAIDS MILKIN' GOODNESS KNOWS WHAT-- AN' SWANS SWIMMIN' IN SOMETHIN'.
IT'S A HARD S'POSE BUT I'LL DO IT.
12-21
THE HALL SYNDICATE, INC.
THESE GOIN'S ON IS TOOK OVER A WEEK-- SUDDENLY ON THE NINTH DAY OF CHRISTMAS YOU SENDS OVER NINE LADIES DANCIN'-- NEXT DAY IT'S TEN LORDS LEAPIN'.
BOY!
TEN LEAPIN' LORDS! WHAT KIND OF DOIN'S IS THAT! NINETEEN PEOPLE FRACASIN' UP THE PLACE BESIDES ALL THEM MILKMAIDS MILKIN' HAND OVER FIST.
ALL ACCOUNT OF LOVE.
©1955 WALT KELLY
AN' NOT ONLY THAT! BUT YOU SENDS CONSTANT EVERY DAY ANOTHER DOGBONE PARTRIDGE IN A PEAR TREE! WHAT'S YOU DOIN'? CLEANIN' OUT YO' ATTIC?
I JES' WANTS YOU TO ALLUS REMEMBER ME.

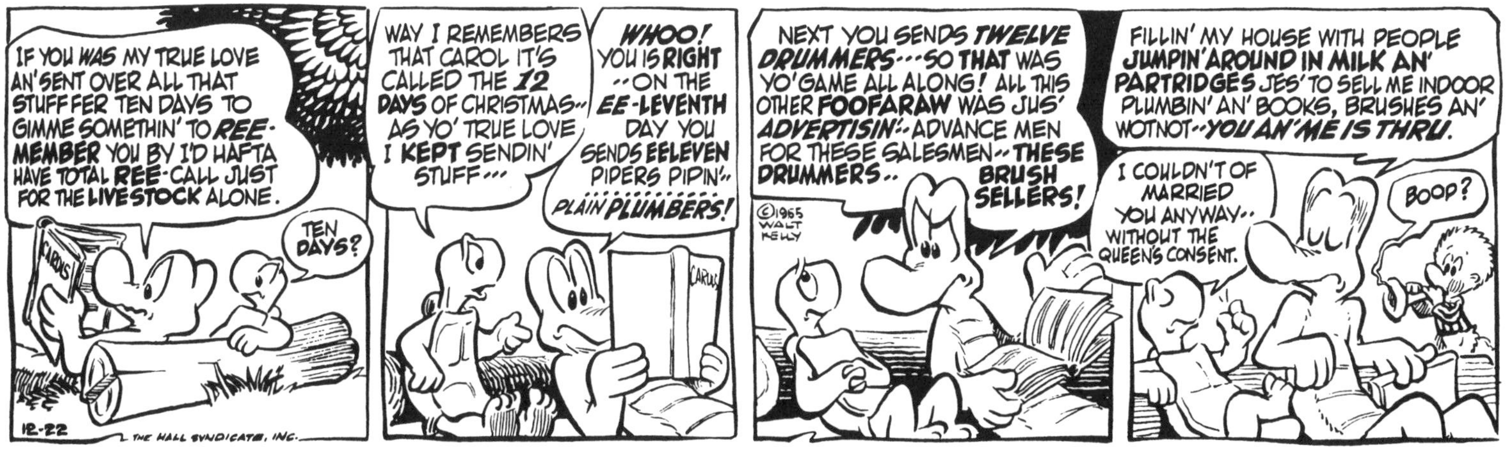
IF YOU WAS MY TRUE LOVE AN' SENT OVER ALL THAT STUFF FER TEN DAYS TO GIMME SOMETHIN' TO REE-MEMBER YOU BY I'D HAFTA HAVE TOTAL REE-CALL JUST FOR THE LIVESTOCK ALONE.
CAROLS
TEN DAYS?
12-22
THE HALL SYNDICATE, INC.
WAY I REMEMBERS THAT CAROL IT'S CALLED THE 12 DAYS OF CHRISTMAS-- AS YO' TRUE LOVE I KEPT SENDIN' STUFF---
WHOO! YOU IS RIGHT --ON THE EE-LEVENTH DAY YOU SENDS EELEVEN PIPERS PIPIN'-- .... PLAIN PLUMBERS!
CAROLS
NEXT YOU SENDS TWELVE DRUMMERS---SO THAT WAS YO' GAME ALL ALONG! ALL THIS OTHER FOOFARAW WAS JUS' ADVERTISIN'-- ADVANCE MEN FOR THESE SALESMEN-- THESE DRUMMERS.. BRUSH SELLERS!
©1955 WALT KELLY
FILLIN' MY HOUSE WITH PEOPLE JUMPIN' AROUND IN MILK AN' PARTRIDGES JES' TO SELL ME INDOOR PLUMBIN' AN' BOOKS, BRUSHES AN' WOTNOT--YOU AN' ME IS THRU.
I COULDN'T OF MARRIED YOU ANYWAY-- WITHOUT THE QUEEN'S CONSENT.
BOOP?

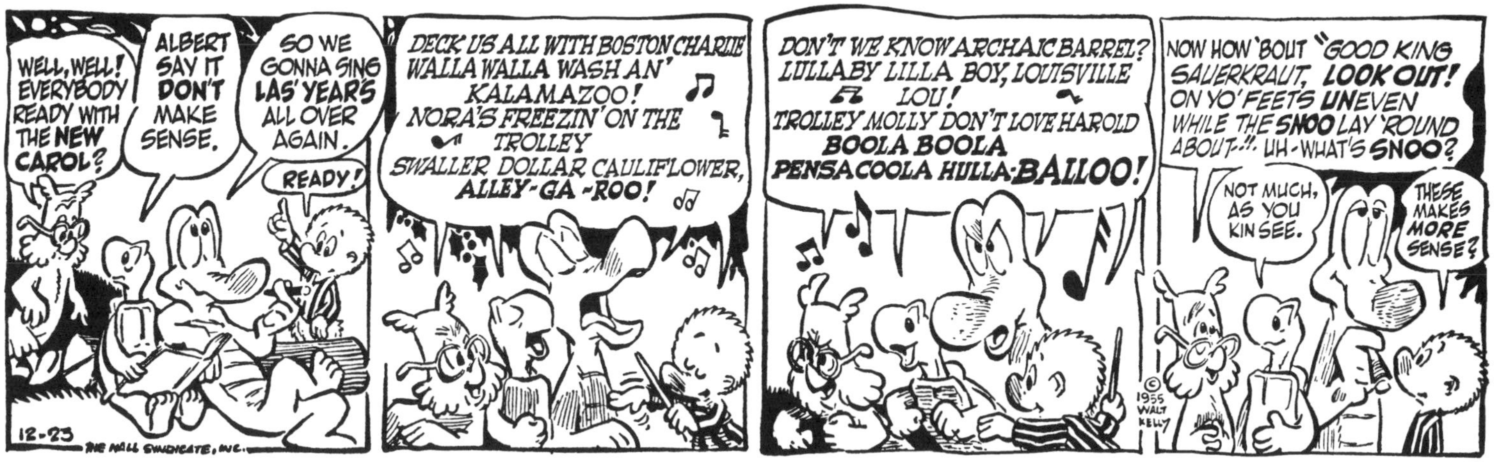
WELL, WELL! EVERYBODY READY WITH THE NEW CAROL?
ALBERT SAY IT DON'T MAKE SENSE.
SO WE GONNA SING LAS' YEAR'S ALL OVER AGAIN.
READY!
12-23
THE HALL SYNDICATE, INC.
DECK US ALL WITH BOSTON CHARLIE WALLA WALLA WASH AN' KALAMAZOO! NORA'S FREEZIN' ON THE TROLLEY SWALLER DOLLAR CAULIFLOWER, ALLEY-GA-ROO!
DON'T WE KNOW ARCHAIC BARREL? LULLABY LILLA BOY, LOUISVILLE LOU! TROLLEY MOLLY DON'T LOVE HAROLD BOOLA BOOLA PENSACOOLA HULLA-BALLOO!
NOW HOW 'BOUT "GOOD KING SAUERKRAUT, LOOK OUT! ON YO' FEETS UNEVEN WHILE THE SNOO LAY 'ROUND ABOUT--!" UH-WHAT'S SNOO?
NOT MUCH, AS YOU KIN SEE.
THESE MAKES MORE SENSE?
© 1955 WALT KELLY

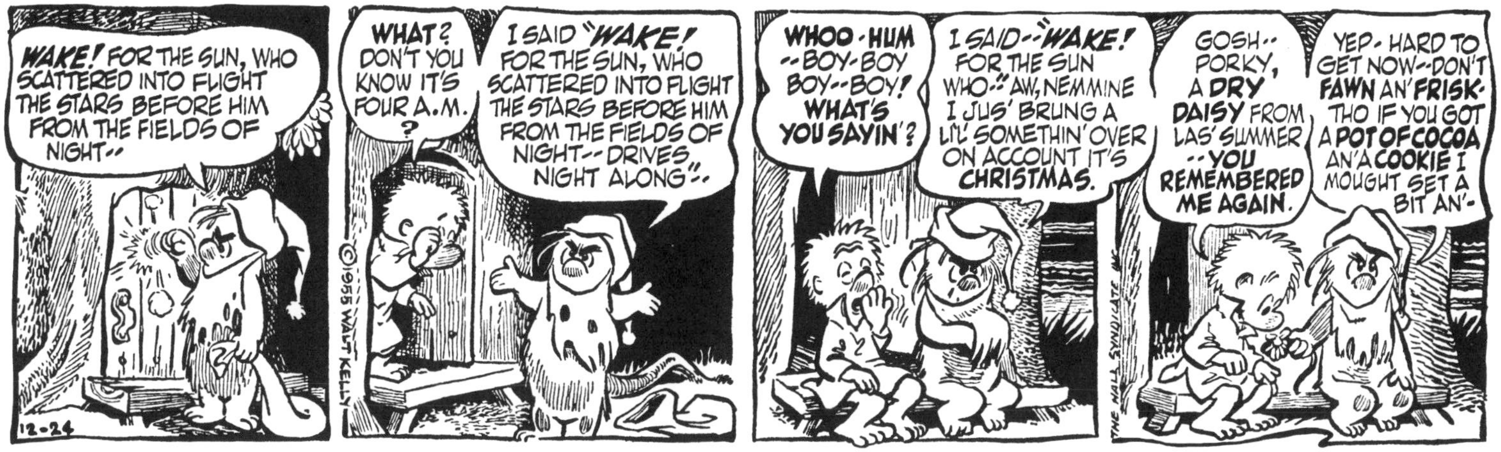
WAKE! FOR THE SUN, WHO SCATTERED INTO FLIGHT THE STARS BEFORE HIM FROM THE FIELDS OF NIGHT--
12-24
WHAT? DON'T YOU KNOW IT'S FOUR A.M.?
I SAID "WAKE! FOR THE SUN, WHO SCATTERED INTO FLIGHT THE STARS BEFORE HIM FROM THE FIELDS OF NIGHT--DRIVES NIGHT ALONG"--.
©1955 WALT KELLY
WHOO-HUM --BOY-BOY BOY--BOY! WHAT'S YOU SAYIN'?
I SAID--"WAKE! FOR THE SUN WHO--" AW, NEMMINE I JUS' BRUNG A LI'L SOMETHIN' OVER ON ACCOUNT IT'S CHRISTMAS.
THE HALL SYNDICATE
GOSH-- PORKY, A DRY DAISY FROM LAS' SUMMER --YOU REMEMBERED ME AGAIN.
YEP- HARD TO GET NOW--DON'T FAWN AN' FRISK- THO IF YOU GOT A POT OF COCOA AN' A COOKIE I MOUGHT SET A BIT AN'-

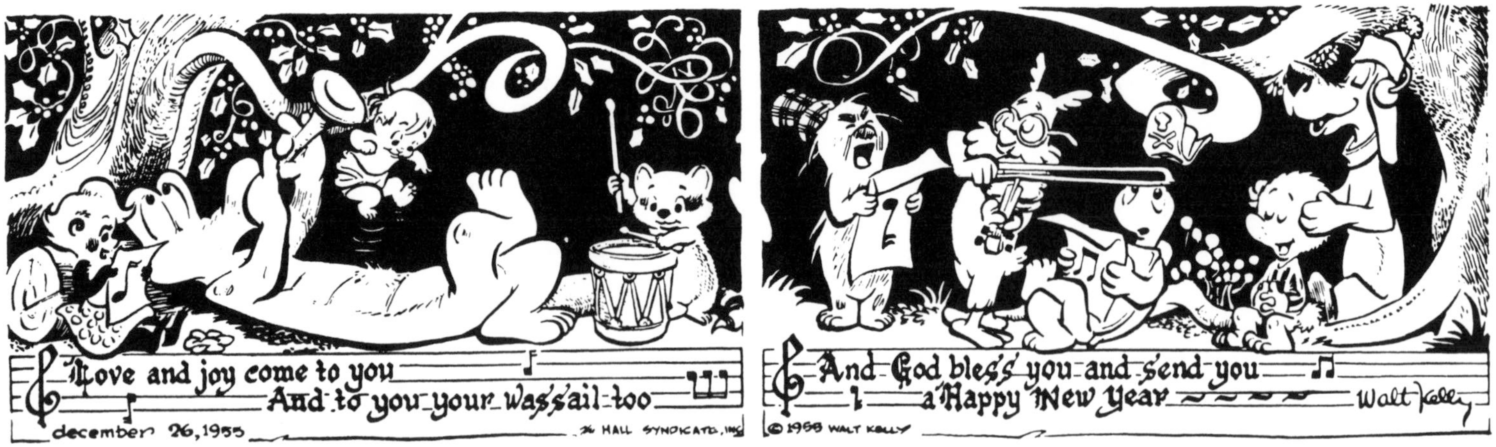
Love and joy come to you
And to you your wassail too
And God bless you and send you
a Happy New Year
Walt Kelly
december 26, 1955
© 1955 WALT KELLY

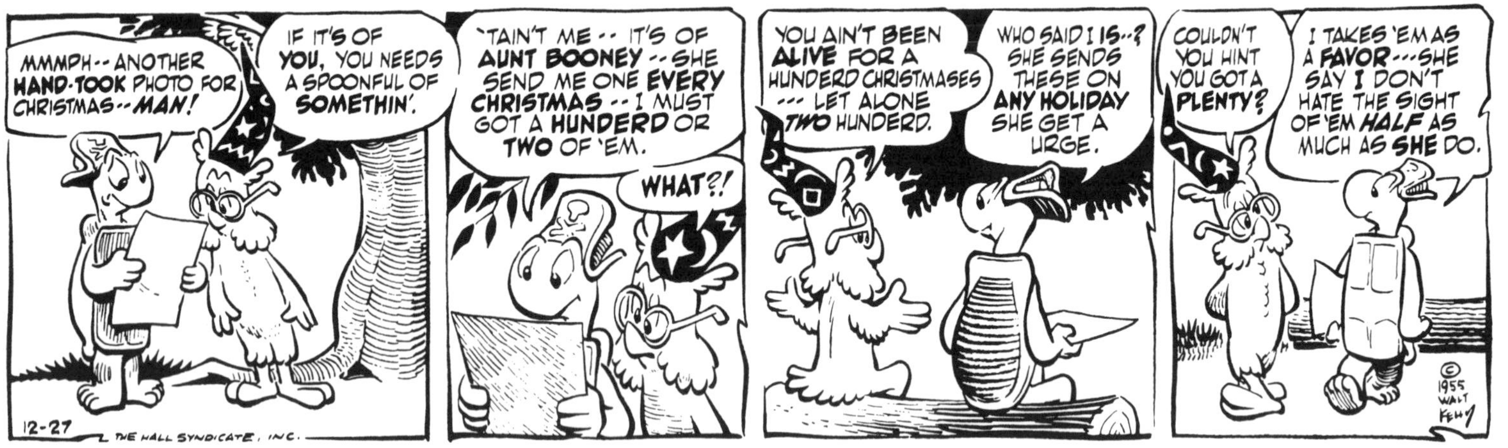
MMMPH-- ANOTHER HAND-TOOK PHOTO FOR CHRISTMAS--MAN!
IF IT'S OF YOU, YOU NEEDS A SPOONFUL OF SOMETHIN'.
'TAIN'T ME -- IT'S OF AUNT BOONEY -- SHE SEND ME ONE EVERY CHRISTMAS -- I MUST GOT A HUNDERD OR TWO OF 'EM.
WHAT?!
YOU AIN'T BEEN ALIVE FOR A HUNDERD CHRISTMASES --- LET ALONE TWO HUNDERD.
WHO SAID I IS--? SHE SENDS THESE ON ANY HOLIDAY SHE GET A URGE.
COULDN'T YOU HINT YOU GOT A PLENTY?
I TAKES 'EM AS A FAVOR---SHE SAY I DON'T HATE THE SIGHT OF 'EM HALF AS MUCH AS SHE DO.
12-27
THE HALL SYNDICATE, INC.
© 1955 WALT KELLY

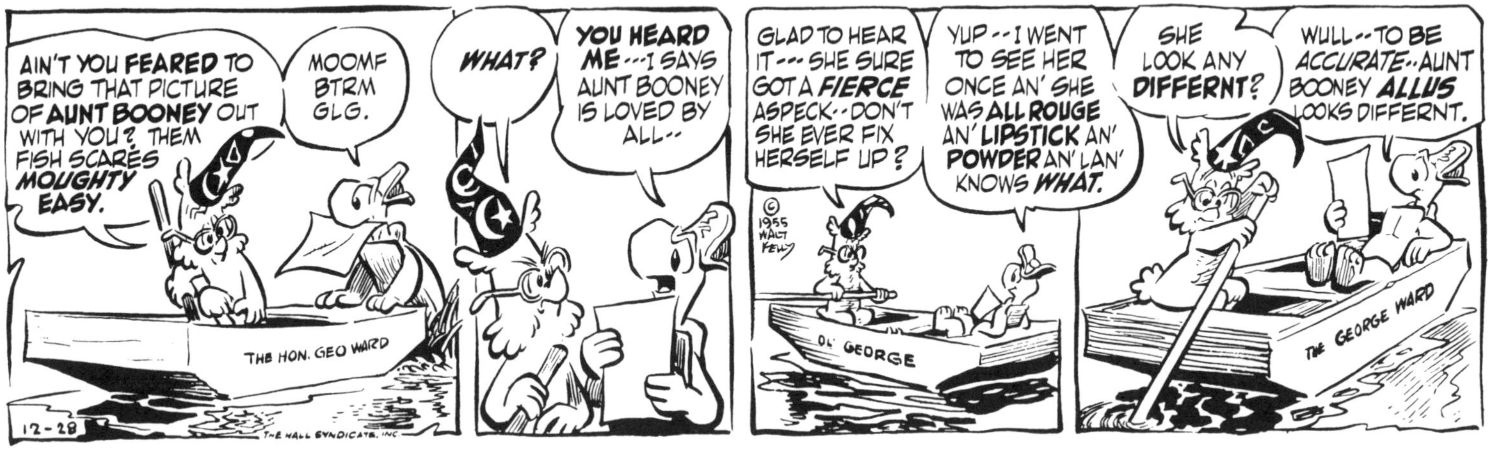
AIN'T YOU FEARED TO BRING THAT PICTURE OF AUNT BOONEY OUT WITH YOU? THEM FISH SCARES MOUGHTY EASY.
MOOMF BTRM GLG.
THE HON. GEO WARD
WHAT?
YOU HEARD ME---I SAYS AUNT BOONEY IS LOVED BY ALL--
GLAD TO HEAR IT--- SHE SURE GOT A FIERCE ASPECK--DON'T SHE EVER FIX HERSELF UP?
YUP--I WENT TO SEE HER ONCE AN' SHE WAS ALL ROUGE AN' LIPSTICK AN' POWDER AN' LAN' KNOWS WHAT.
OL' GEORGE
© 1955 WALT KELLY
SHE LOOK ANY DIFFERNT?
WULL--TO BE ACCURATE--AUNT BOONEY ALLUS LOOKS DIFFERNT.
THE GEORGE WARD
12-28
THE HALL SYNDICATE, INC.

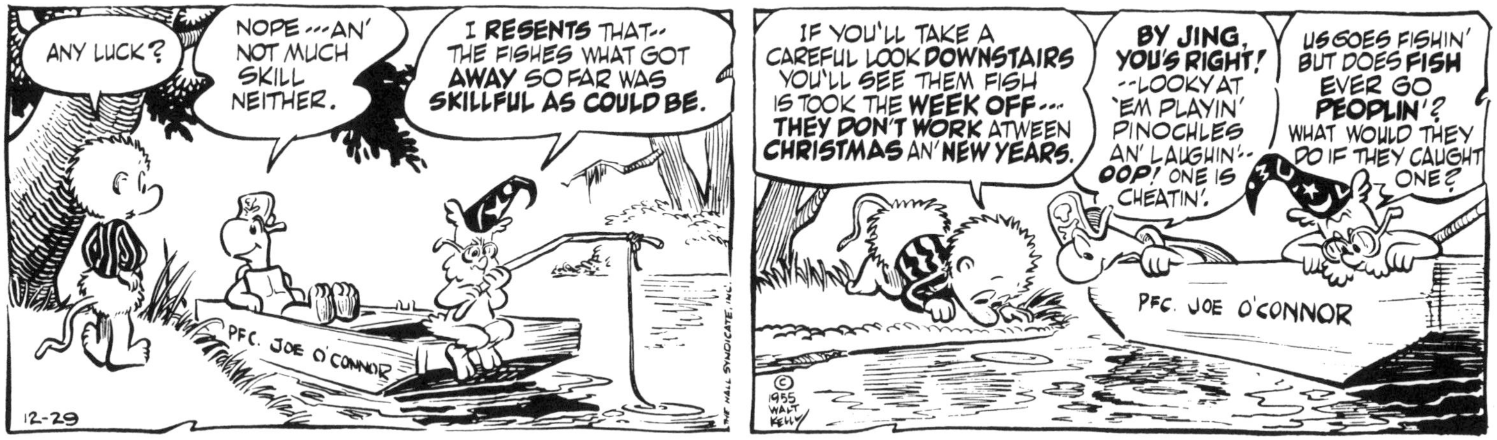
ANY LUCK?
NOPE---AN' NOT MUCH SKILL NEITHER.
I RESENTS THAT-- THE FISHES WHAT GOT AWAY SO FAR WAS SKILLFUL AS COULD BE.
PFC. JOE O'CONNOR
12-29
THE HALL SYNDICATE, INC.
IF YOU'LL TAKE A CAREFUL LOOK DOWNSTAIRS YOU'LL SEE THEM FISH IS TOOK THE WEEK OFF--- THEY DON'T WORK ATWEEN CHRISTMAS AN' NEW YEARS.
BY JING, YOU'S RIGHT! --LOOKY AT 'EM PLAYIN' PINOCHLES AN' LAUGHIN'-- OOP! ONE IS CHEATIN'.
US GOES FISHIN' BUT DOES FISH EVER GO PEOPLIN'? WHAT WOULD THEY DO IF THEY CAUGHT ONE?
PFC. JOE O'CONNOR
© 1955 WALT KELLY

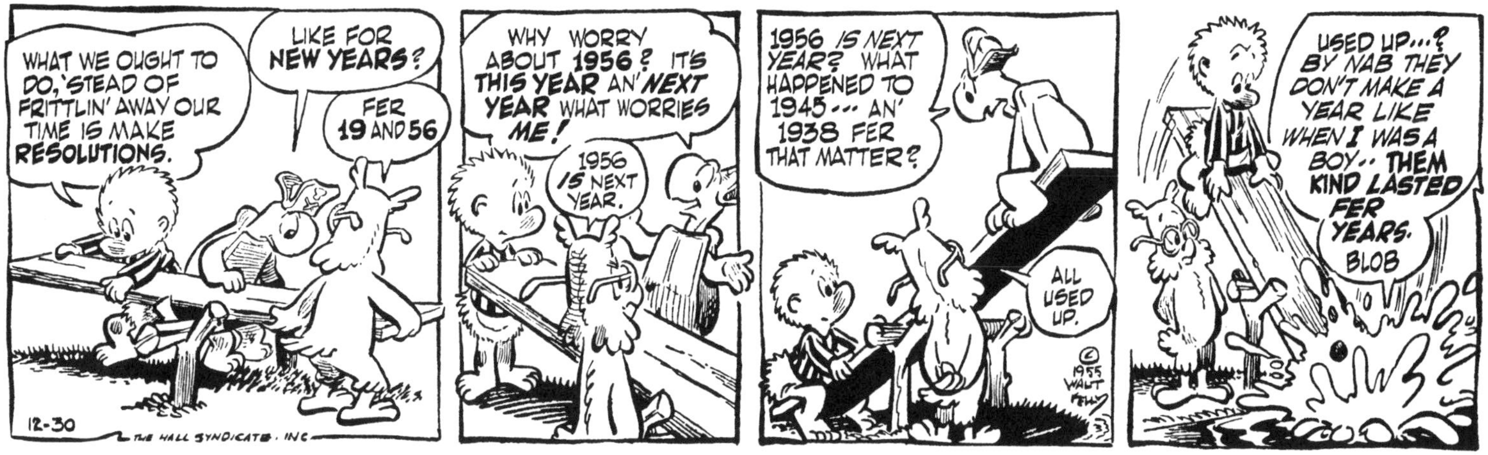
WHAT WE OUGHT TO DO, 'STEAD OF FRITTLIN' AWAY OUR TIME IS MAKE RESOLUTIONS.
LIKE FOR NEW YEARS?
FER 19 AND 56
12-30
THE HALL SYNDICATE, INC.
WHY WORRY ABOUT 1956? IT'S THIS YEAR AN' NEXT YEAR WHAT WORRIES ME!
1956 IS NEXT YEAR.
1956 IS NEXT YEAR? WHAT HAPPENED TO 1945--- AN' 1938 FER THAT MATTER?
ALL USED UP.
© 1955 WALT KELLY
USED UP...? BY NAB THEY DON'T MAKE A YEAR LIKE WHEN I WAS A BOY.. THEM KIND LASTED FER YEARS.
BLOB

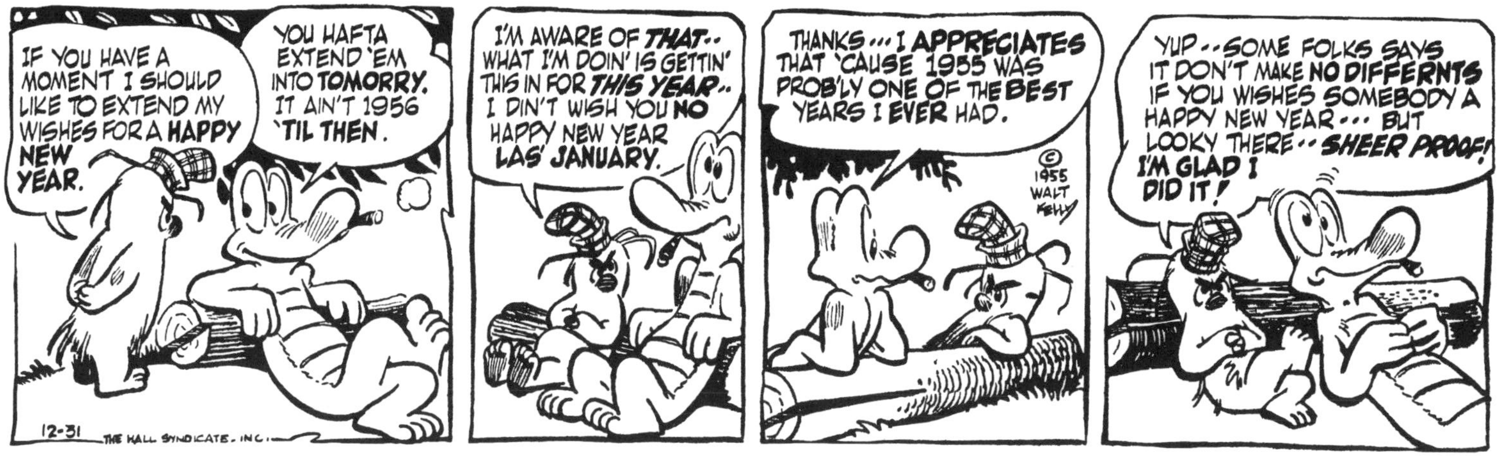
IF YOU HAVE A MOMENT I SHOULD LIKE TO EXTEND MY WISHES FOR A HAPPY NEW YEAR.
YOU HAFTA EXTEND 'EM INTO TOMORRY. IT AIN'T 1956 'TIL THEN.
12-31
THE HALL SYNDICATE, INC.
I'M AWARE OF THAT.. WHAT I'M DOIN' IS GETTIN' THIS IN FOR THIS YEAR.. I DIN'T WISH YOU NO HAPPY NEW YEAR LAS' JANUARY.
THANKS... I APPRECIATES THAT 'CAUSE 1955 WAS PROB'LY ONE OF THE BEST YEARS I EVER HAD.
© 1955 WALT KELLY
YUP--SOME FOLKS SAYS IT DON'T MAKE NO DIFFERNTS IF YOU WISHES SOMEBODY A HAPPY NEW YEAR--- BUT LOOKY THERE--SHEER PROOF! I'M GLAD I DID IT!

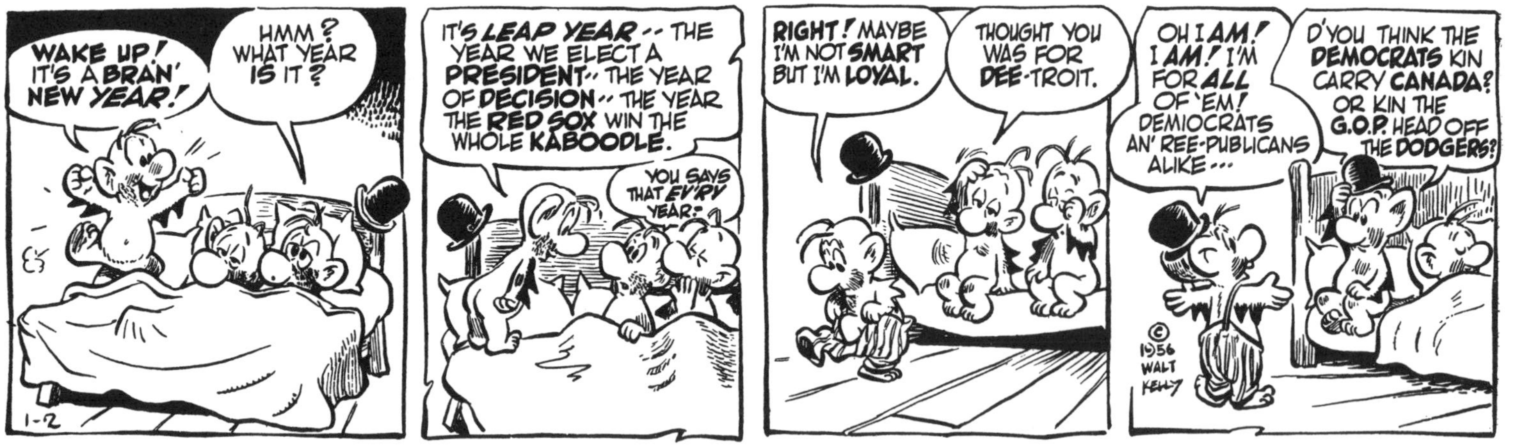
WAKE UP! IT'S A BRAN' NEW YEAR!
HMM? WHAT YEAR IS IT?
1-2
IT'S LEAP YEAR -- THE YEAR WE ELECT A PRESIDENT -- THE YEAR OF DECISION -- THE YEAR THE RED SOX WIN THE WHOLE KABOODLE.
YOU SAYS THAT EV'RY YEAR.
RIGHT! MAYBE I'M NOT SMART BUT I'M LOYAL.
THOUGHT YOU WAS FOR DEE-TROIT.
OH I AM! I AM! I'M FOR ALL OF 'EM! DEMIOCRATS AN' REE-PUBLICANS ALIKE...
D'YOU THINK THE DEMOCRATS KIN CARRY CANADA? OR KIN THE G.O.P. HEAD OFF THE DODGERS?
© 1956 WALT KELLY

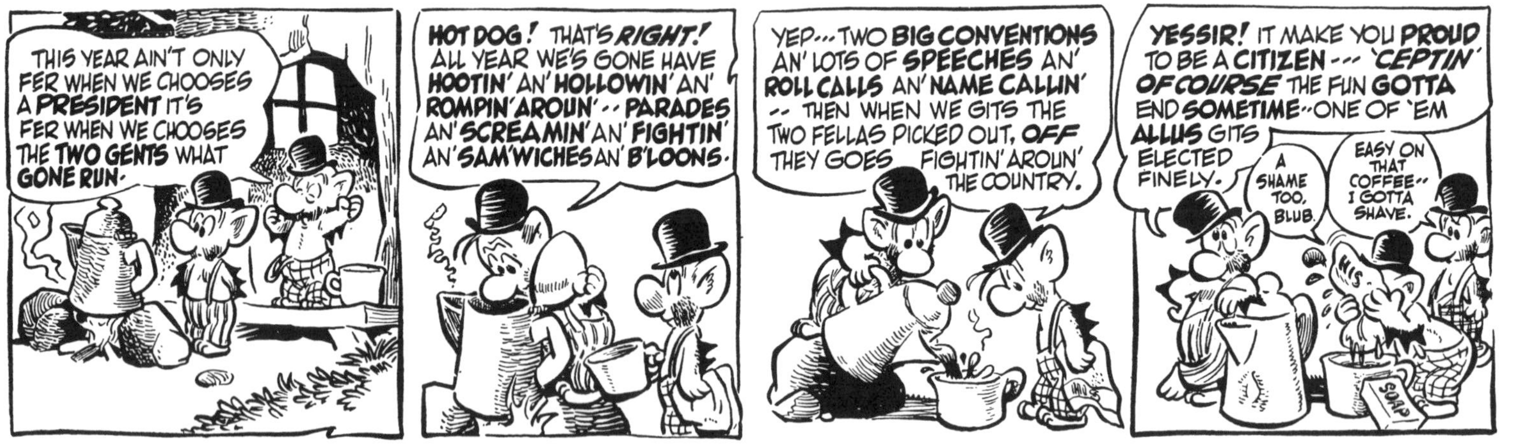
THIS YEAR AIN'T ONLY FER WHEN WE CHOOSES A PRESIDENT IT'S FER WHEN WE CHOOSES THE TWO GENTS WHAT GONE RUN.
HOT DOG! THAT'S RIGHT! ALL YEAR WE'S GONE HAVE HOOTIN' AN' HOLLOWIN' AN' ROMPIN' AROUN' -- PARADES AN' SCREAMIN' AN' FIGHTIN' AN' SAM'WICHES AN' B'LOONS.
YEP... TWO BIG CONVENTIONS AN' LOTS OF SPEECHES AN' ROLL CALLS AN' NAME CALLIN' -- THEN WHEN WE GITS THE TWO FELLAS PICKED OUT, OFF THEY GOES FIGHTIN' AROUN' THE COUNTRY.
YESSIR! IT MAKE YOU PROUD TO BE A CITIZEN --- 'CEPTIN' OF COURSE THE FUN GOTTA END SOMETIME -- ONE OF 'EM ALLUS GITS ELECTED FINELY.
A SHAME TOO. BLUB.
EASY ON THAT COFFEE -- I GOTTA SHAVE.
SOAP

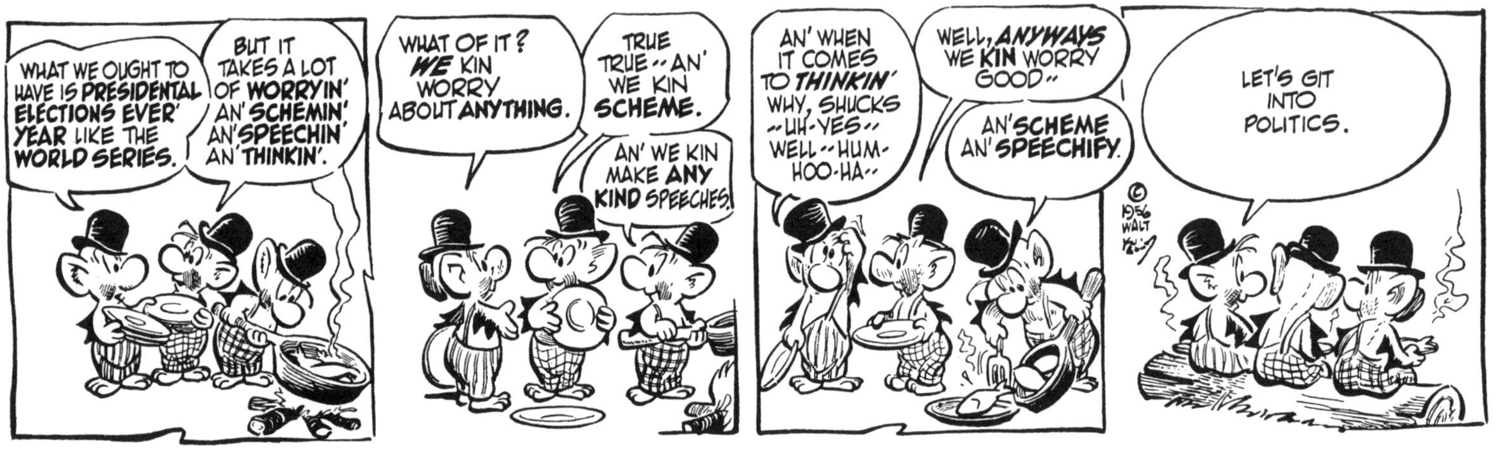
WHAT WE OUGHT TO HAVE IS PRESIDENTAL ELECTIONS EVER' YEAR LIKE THE WORLD SERIES.
BUT IT TAKES A LOT OF WORRYIN' AN' SCHEMIN' AN' SPEECHIN' AN' THINKIN'.
WHAT OF IT? WE KIN WORRY ABOUT ANYTHING.
TRUE TRUE -- AN' WE KIN SCHEME.
AN' WE KIN MAKE ANY KIND SPEECHES.
AN' WHEN IT COMES TO THINKIN' WHY, SHUCKS -- UH -- YES -- WELL -- HUM-HOO-HA --
WELL, ANYWAYS WE KIN WORRY GOOD --
AN' SCHEME AN' SPEECHIFY.
© 1956 WALT KELLY
LET'S GIT INTO POLITICS.

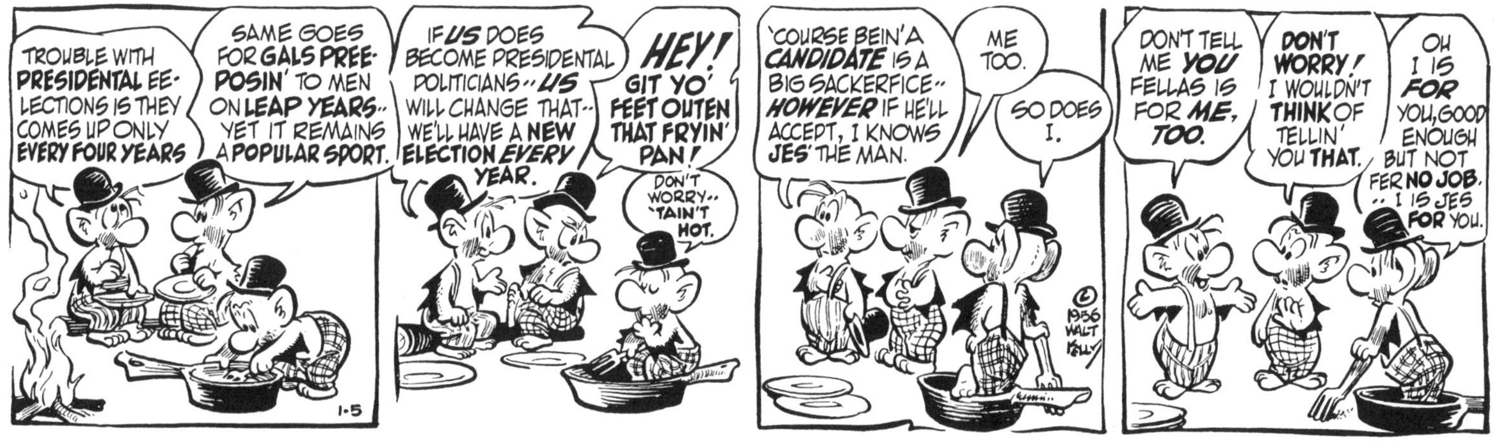
TROUBLE WITH PRESIDENTAL EE-LECTIONS IS THEY COMES UP ONLY EVERY FOUR YEARS
SAME GOES FOR GALS PREE-POSIN' TO MEN ON LEAP YEARS.. YET IT REMAINS A POPULAR SPORT.
1-5
IF US DOES BECOME PRESIDENTAL POLITICIANS.. US WILL CHANGE THAT.. WE'LL HAVE A NEW ELECTION EVERY YEAR.
HEY! GIT YO' FEET OUTEN THAT FRYIN' PAN!
DON'T WORRY.. 'TAIN'T HOT.
'COURSE BEIN' A CANDIDATE IS A BIG SACKERFICE.. HOWEVER IF HE'LL ACCEPT, I KNOWS JES' THE MAN.
ME TOO.
SO DOES I.
© 1956 WALT KELLY
DON'T TELL ME YOU FELLAS IS FOR ME, TOO.
DON'T WORRY! I WOULDN'T THINK OF TELLIN' YOU THAT.
OH I IS FOR YOU, GOOD ENOUGH BUT NOT FER NO JOB. .. I IS JES FOR YOU.

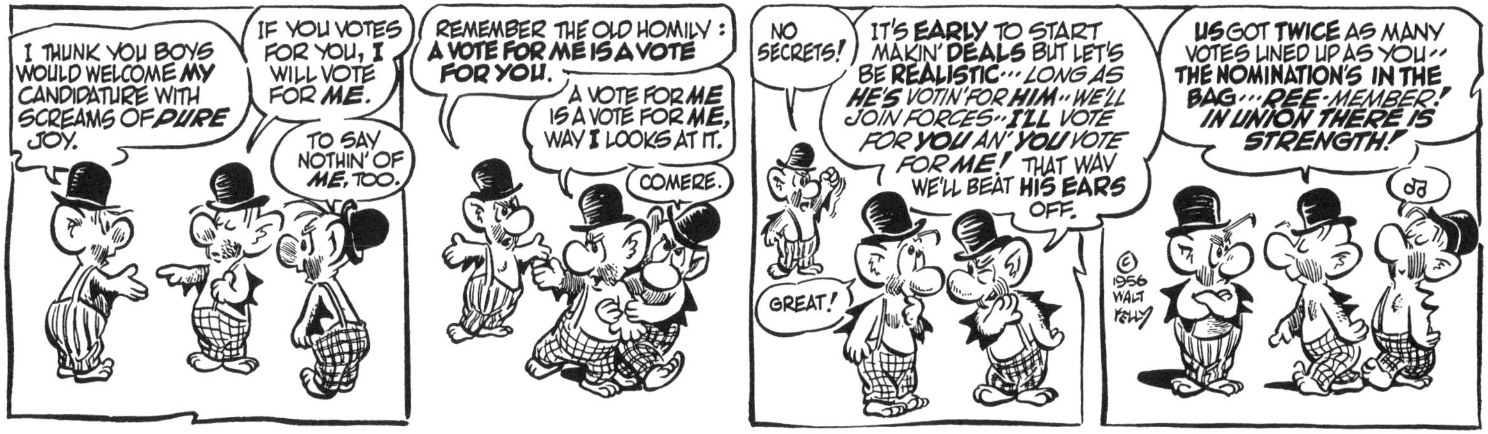
I THUNK YOU BOYS WOULD WELCOME MY CANDIDATURE WITH SCREAMS OF PURE JOY.
IF YOU VOTES FOR YOU, I WILL VOTE FOR ME.
TO SAY NOTHIN' OF ME, TOO.
REMEMBER THE OLD HOMILY: A VOTE FOR ME IS A VOTE FOR YOU.
A VOTE FOR ME IS A VOTE FOR ME, WAY I LOOKS AT IT.
COMERE.
NO SECRETS!
IT'S EARLY TO START MAKIN' DEALS BUT LET'S BE REALISTIC... LONG AS HE'S VOTIN' FOR HIM.. WE'LL JOIN FORCES.. I'LL VOTE FOR YOU AN' YOU VOTE FOR ME! THAT WAY WE'LL BEAT HIS EARS OFF.
GREAT!
© 1956 WALT KELLY
US GOT TWICE AS MANY VOTES LINED UP AS YOU.. THE NOMINATION'S IN THE BAG... REE-MEMBER! IN UNION THERE IS STRENGTH!

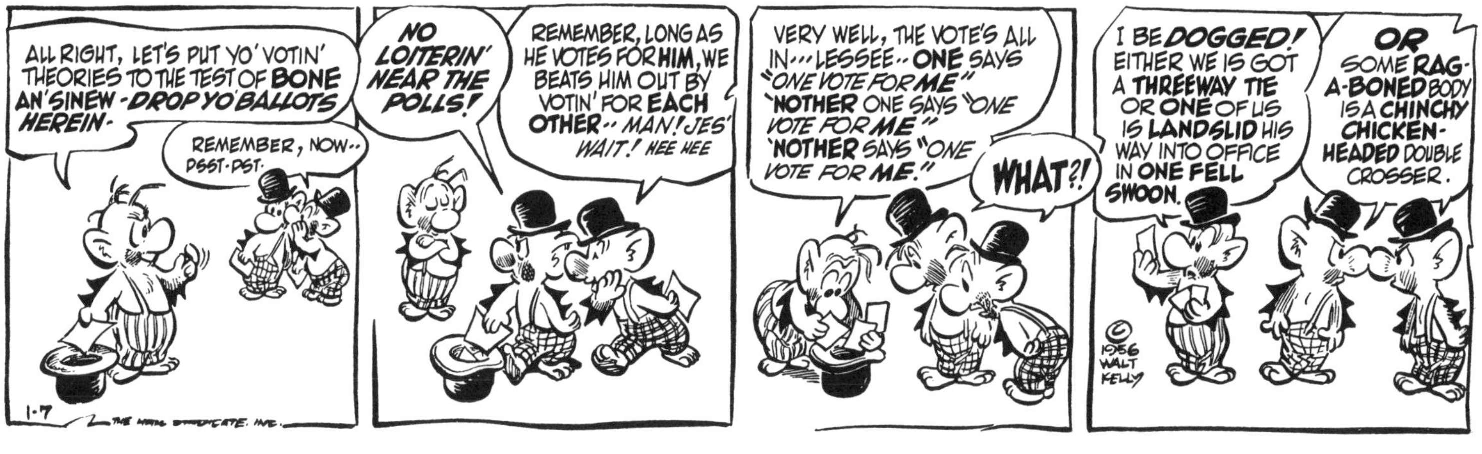
ALL RIGHT, LET'S PUT YO' VOTIN' THEORIES TO THE TEST OF BONE AN' SINEW - DROP YO' BALLOTS HEREIN.
REMEMBER, NOW.. PSST-PST.
1-7
NO LOITERIN' NEAR THE POLLS!
REMEMBER, LONG AS HE VOTES FOR HIM, WE BEATS HIM OUT BY VOTIN' FOR EACH OTHER.. MAN! JES' WAIT! HEE HEE
VERY WELL, THE VOTE'S ALL IN... LESSEE.. ONE SAYS "ONE VOTE FOR ME" 'NOTHER ONE SAYS "ONE VOTE FOR ME" 'NOTHER SAYS "ONE VOTE FOR ME."
WHAT?!
I BE DOGGED! EITHER WE IS GOT A THREEWAY TIE OR ONE OF US IS LANDSLID HIS WAY INTO OFFICE IN ONE FELL SWOON.
OR SOME RAG-A-BONED BODY IS A CHINCHY CHICKEN-HEADED DOUBLE CROSSER.
© 1956 WALT KELLY

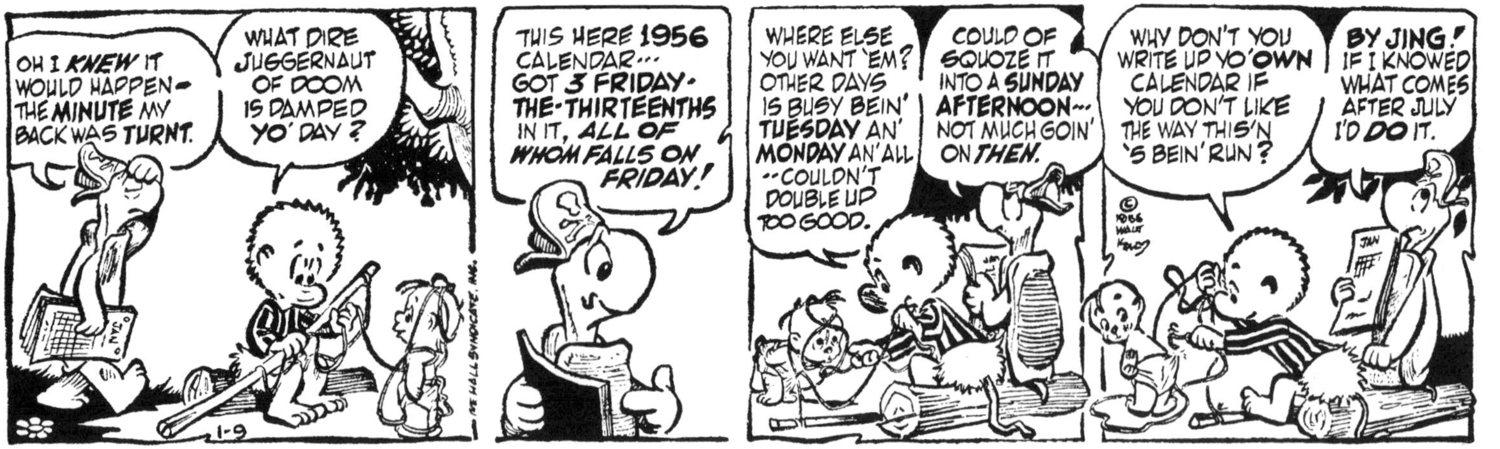
OH I KNEW IT WOULD HAPPEN- THE MINUTE MY BACK WAS TURNT.
WHAT DIRE JUGGERNAUT OF DOOM IS DAMPED YO' DAY ?
THIS HERE 1956 CALENDAR... GOT 3 FRIDAY-THE-THIRTEENTHS IN IT, ALL OF WHOM FALLS ON FRIDAY!
WHERE ELSE YOU WANT 'EM? OTHER DAYS IS BUSY BEIN' TUESDAY AN' MONDAY AN' ALL --COULDN'T DOUBLE UP TOO GOOD.
COULD OF SQUOZE IT INTO A SUNDAY AFTERNOON-- NOT MUCH GOIN' ON THEN.
WHY DON'T YOU WRITE UP YO' OWN CALENDAR IF YOU DON'T LIKE THE WAY THIS'N 'S BEIN' RUN ?
BY JING! IF I KNOWED WHAT COMES AFTER JULY I'D DO IT.
1-9
©1956 WALT KELLY

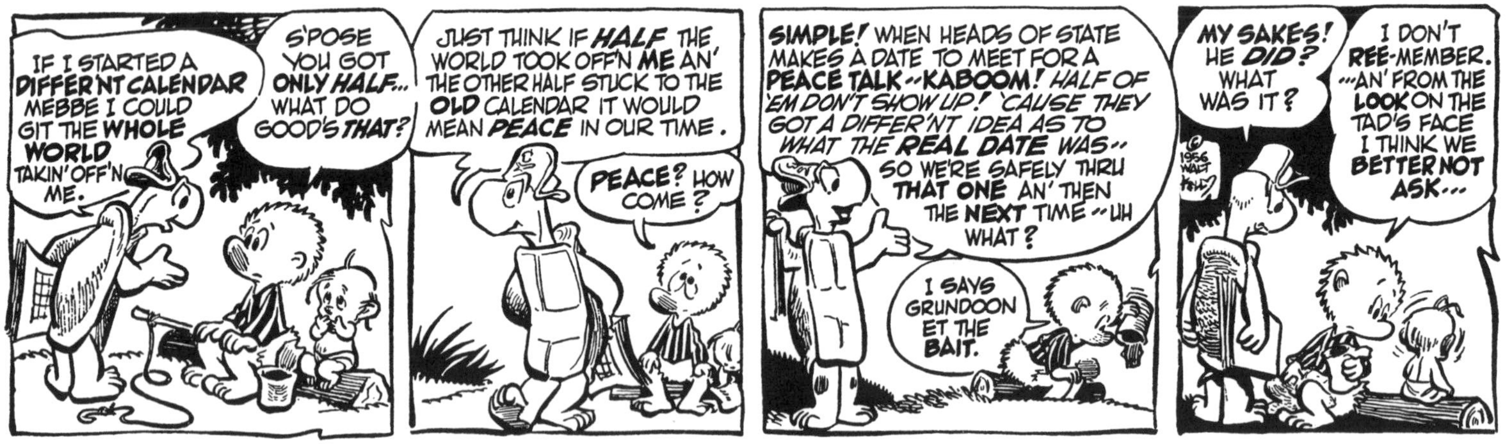
IF I STARTED A DIFFER'NT CALENDAR MEBBE I COULD GIT THE WHOLE WORLD TAKIN' OFF'N ME.
S'POSE YOU GOT ONLY HALF... WHAT DO GOOD'S THAT?
JUST THINK IF HALF THE WORLD TOOK OFF'N ME AN' THE OTHER HALF STUCK TO THE OLD CALENDAR IT WOULD MEAN PEACE IN OUR TIME.
PEACE? HOW COME ?
SIMPLE! WHEN HEADS OF STATE MAKES A DATE TO MEET FOR A PEACE TALK--KABOOM! HALF OF 'EM DON'T SHOW UP! 'CAUSE THEY GOT A DIFFER'NT IDEA AS TO WHAT THE REAL DATE WAS-- SO WE'RE SAFELY THRU THAT ONE AN' THEN THE NEXT TIME--UH WHAT ?
I SAYS GRUNDOON ET THE BAIT.
MY SAKES! HE DID? WHAT WAS IT ?
I DON'T REE-MEMBER. --AN' FROM THE LOOK ON THE TAD'S FACE I THINK WE BETTER NOT ASK...
©1956 WALT KELLY

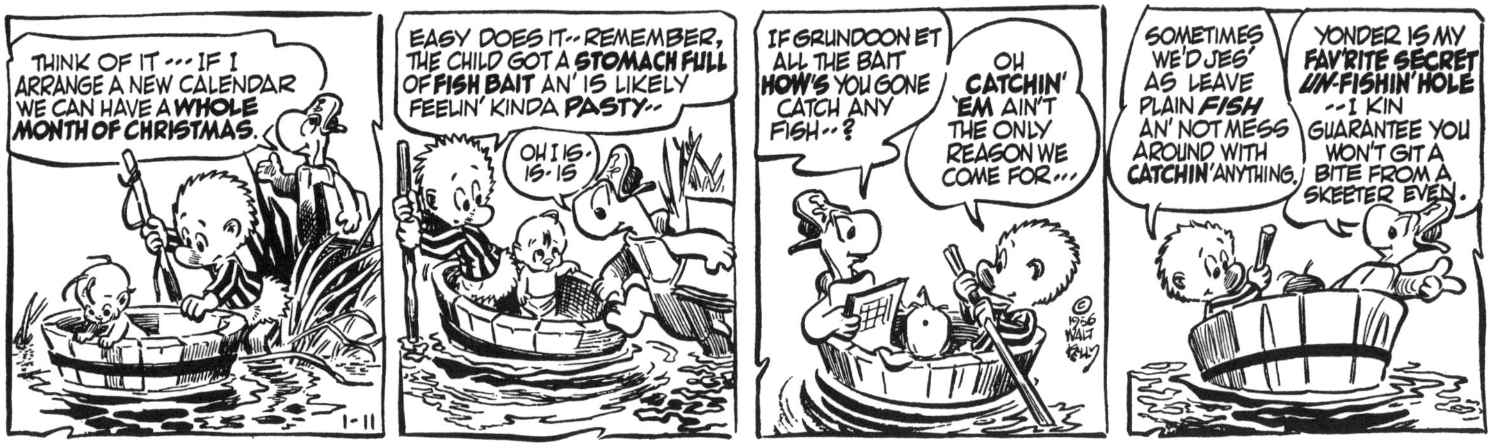
THINK OF IT --- IF I ARRANGE A NEW CALENDAR WE CAN HAVE A WHOLE MONTH OF CHRISTMAS.
EASY DOES IT-- REMEMBER, THE CHILD GOT A STOMACH FULL OF FISH BAIT AN' IS LIKELY FEELIN' KINDA PASTY--
OH I IS-IS-IS
IF GRUNDOON ET ALL THE BAIT HOW'S YOU GONE CATCH ANY FISH--?
OH CATCHIN' 'EM AIN'T THE ONLY REASON WE COME FOR...
SOMETIMES WE'D JES' AS LEAVE PLAIN FISH AN' NOT MESS AROUND WITH CATCHIN' ANYTHING.
YONDER IS MY FAV'RITE SECRET UN-FISHIN' HOLE --I KIN GUARANTEE YOU WON'T GIT A BITE FROM A SKEETER EVEN.
1-11
©1956 WALT KELLY

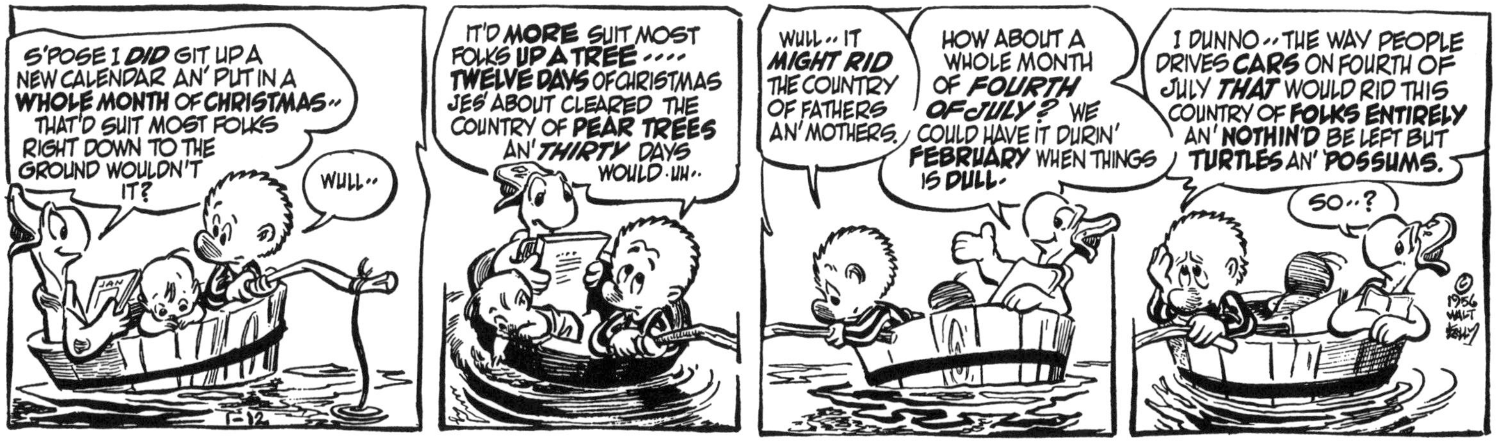
S'POSE I DID GIT UP A NEW CALENDAR AN' PUT IN A WHOLE MONTH OF CHRISTMAS.. THAT'D SUIT MOST FOLKS RIGHT DOWN TO THE GROUND WOULDN'T IT?
WULL..
IT'D MORE SUIT MOST FOLKS UP A TREE .... TWELVE DAYS OF CHRISTMAS JES' ABOUT CLEARED THE COUNTRY OF PEAR TREES AN' THIRTY DAYS WOULD-UH-
WULL.. IT MIGHT RID THE COUNTRY OF FATHERS AN' MOTHERS.
HOW ABOUT A WHOLE MONTH OF FOURTH OF JULY? WE COULD HAVE IT DURIN' FEBRUARY WHEN THINGS IS DULL.
I DUNNO.. THE WAY PEOPLE DRIVES CARS ON FOURTH OF JULY THAT WOULD RID THIS COUNTRY OF FOLKS ENTIRELY AN' NOTHIN'D BE LEFT BUT TURTLES AN' 'POSSUMS.
SO..?

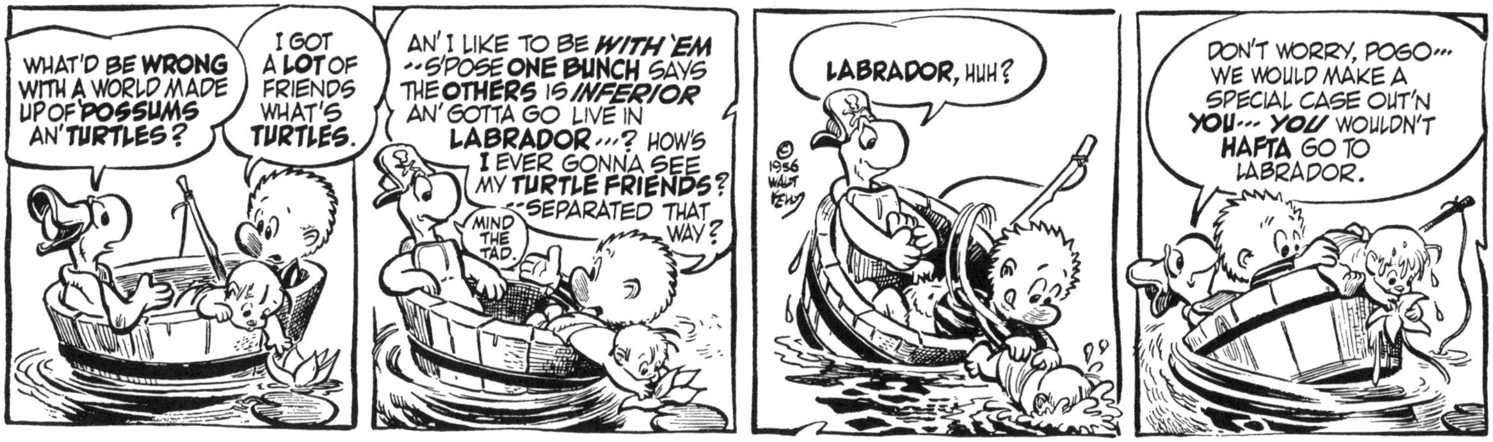
WHAT'D BE WRONG WITH A WORLD MADE UP OF 'POSSUMS AN' TURTLES?
I GOT A LOT OF FRIENDS WHAT'S TURTLES.
AN' I LIKE TO BE WITH 'EM --S'POSE ONE BUNCH SAYS THE OTHERS IS INFERIOR AN' GOTTA GO LIVE IN LABRADOR...? HOW'S I EVER GONNA SEE MY TURTLE FRIENDS? --SEPARATED THAT WAY?
MIND THE TAD.
LABRADOR, HUH?
DON'T WORRY, POGO... WE WOULD MAKE A SPECIAL CASE OUT'N YOU... YOU WOULDN'T HAFTA GO TO LABRADOR.

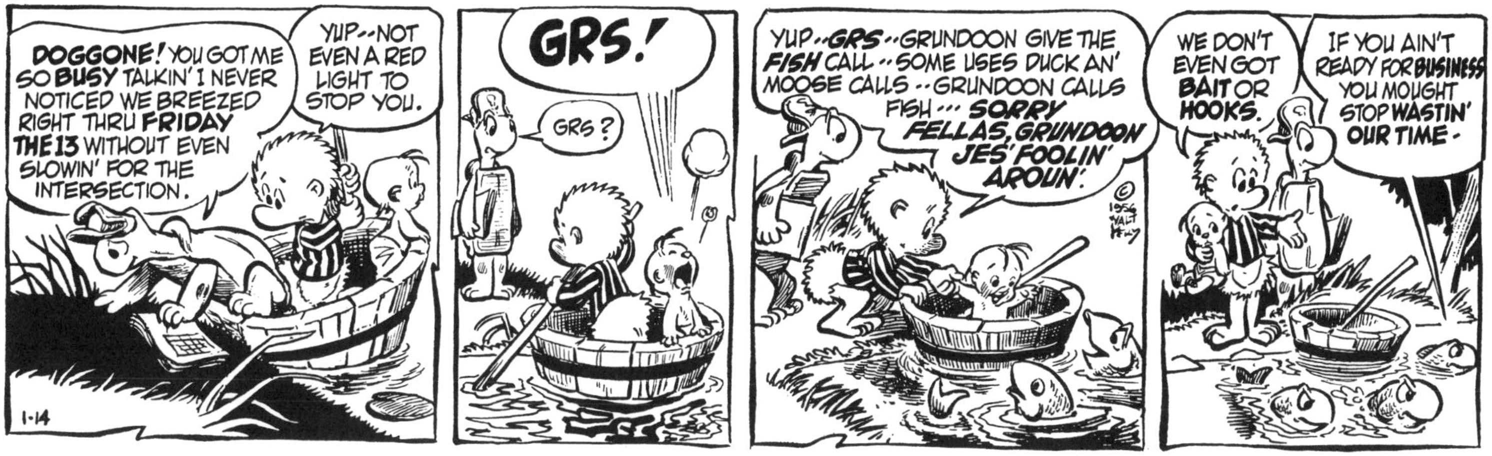
DOGGONE! YOU GOT ME SO BUSY TALKIN' I NEVER NOTICED WE BREEZED RIGHT THRU FRIDAY THE 13 WITHOUT EVEN SLOWIN' FOR THE INTERSECTION.
YUP--NOT EVEN A RED LIGHT TO STOP YOU.
GRS!
GRS?
YUP..GRS..GRUNDOON GIVE THE FISH CALL..SOME USES DUCK AN' MOOSE CALLS..GRUNDOON CALLS FISH... SORRY FELLAS, GRUNDOON JES' FOOLIN' AROUN'.
WE DON'T EVEN GOT BAIT OR HOOKS.
IF YOU AIN'T READY FOR BUSINESS YOU MOUGHT STOP WASTIN' OUR TIME-

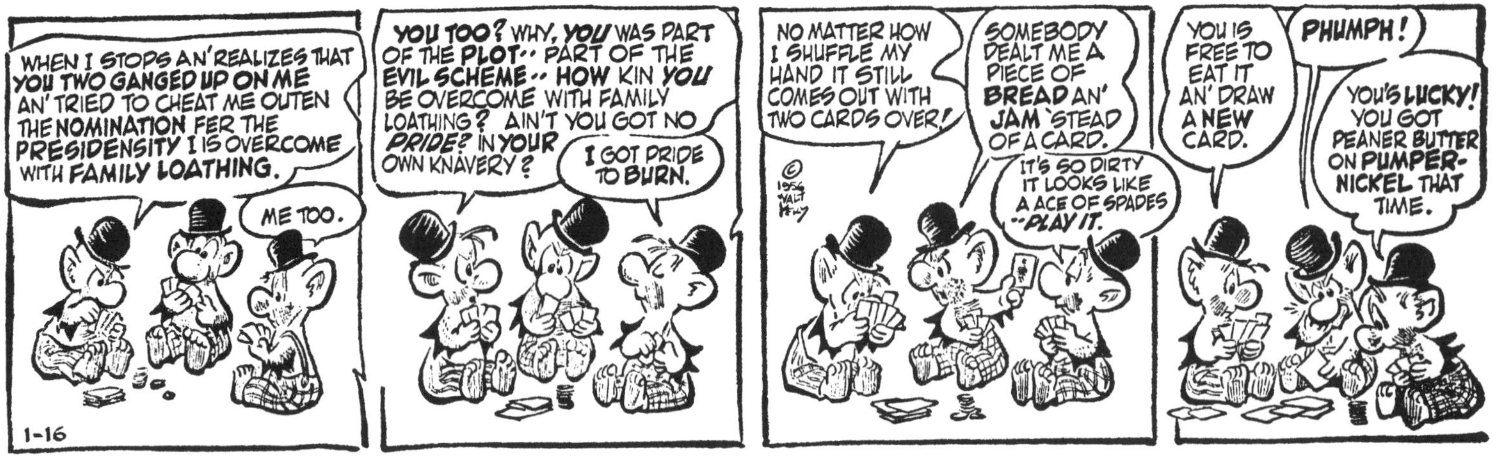
WHEN I STOPS AN' REALIZES THAT YOU TWO GANGED UP ON ME AN' TRIED TO CHEAT ME OUTEN THE NOMINATION FER THE PRESIDENSITY I IS OVERCOME WITH FAMILY LOATHING.
ME TOO.
1-16
YOU TOO? WHY, YOU WAS PART OF THE PLOT·· PART OF THE EVIL SCHEME·· HOW KIN YOU BE OVERCOME WITH FAMILY LOATHING? AIN'T YOU GOT NO PRIDE? IN YOUR OWN KNAVERY?
I GOT PRIDE TO BURN.
NO MATTER HOW I SHUFFLE MY HAND IT STILL COMES OUT WITH TWO CARDS OVER!
SOMEBODY DEALT ME A PIECE OF BREAD AN' JAM 'STEAD OF A CARD.
IT'S SO DIRTY IT LOOKS LIKE A ACE OF SPADES ··PLAY IT.
YOU IS FREE TO EAT IT AN' DRAW A NEW CARD.
PHUMPH!
YOU'S LUCKY! YOU GOT PEANER BUTTER ON PUMPERNICKEL THAT TIME.

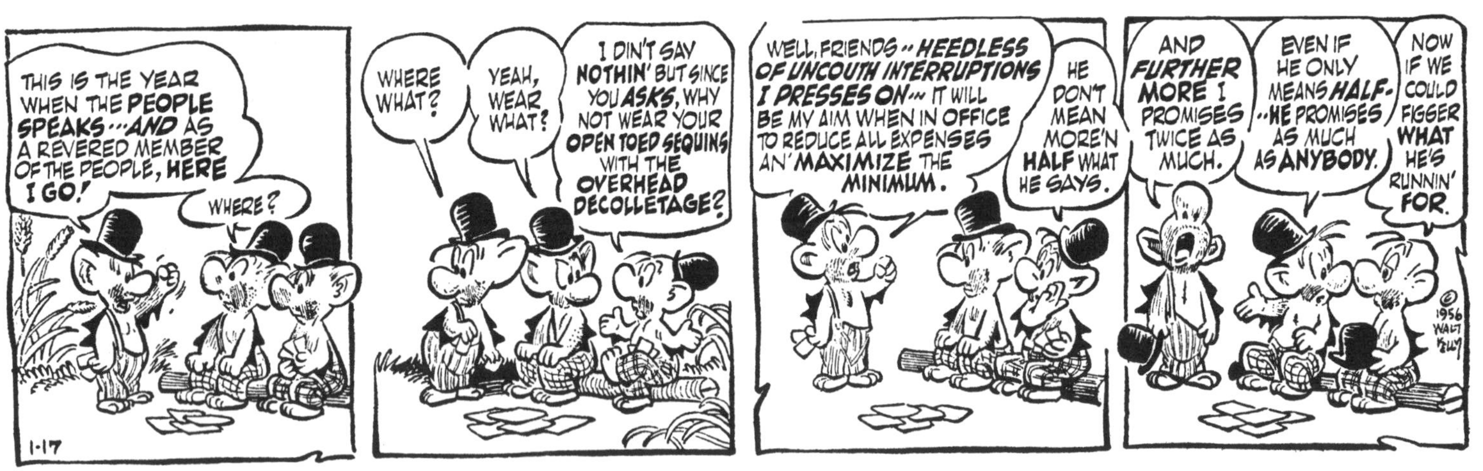
THIS IS THE YEAR WHEN THE PEOPLE SPEAKS···AND AS A REVERED MEMBER OF THE PEOPLE, HERE I GO!
WHERE?
1-17
WHERE WHAT?
YEAH, WEAR WHAT?
I DIN'T SAY NOTHIN' BUT SINCE YOU ASKS, WHY NOT WEAR YOUR OPEN TOED SEQUINS WITH THE OVERHEAD DECOLLETAGE?
WELL, FRIENDS·· HEEDLESS OF UNCOUTH INTERRUPTIONS I PRESSES ON··· IT WILL BE MY AIM WHEN IN OFFICE TO REDUCE ALL EXPENSES AN' MAXIMIZE THE MINIMUM.
HE DON'T MEAN MORE'N HALF WHAT HE SAYS.
AND FURTHER MORE I PROMISES TWICE AS MUCH.
EVEN IF HE ONLY MEANS HALF-·HE PROMISES AS MUCH AS ANYBODY.
NOW IF WE COULD FIGGER WHAT HE'S RUNNIN' FOR.

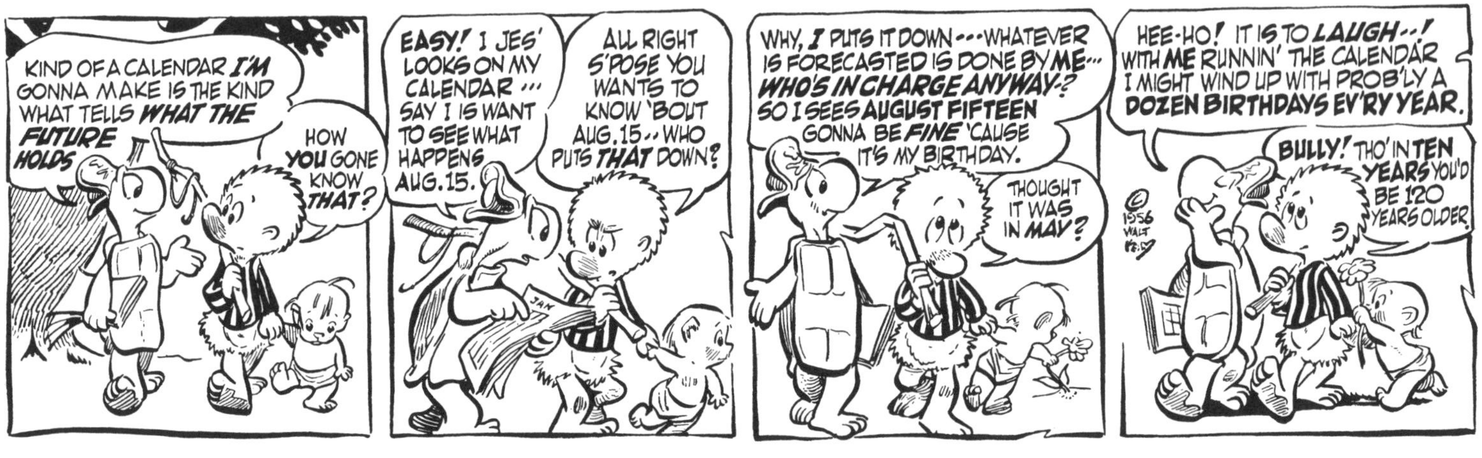
KIND OF A CALENDAR I'M GONNA MAKE IS THE KIND WHAT TELLS WHAT THE FUTURE HOLDS
HOW YOU GONE KNOW THAT?
EASY! I JES' LOOKS ON MY CALENDAR··· SAY I IS WANT TO SEE WHAT HAPPENS AUG. 15.
ALL RIGHT S'POSE YOU WANTS TO KNOW 'BOUT AUG. 15.·· WHO PUTS THAT DOWN?
WHY, I PUTS IT DOWN···WHATEVER IS FORECASTED IS DONE BY ME··· WHO'S IN CHARGE ANYWAY·? SO I SEES AUGUST FIFTEEN GONNA BE FINE 'CAUSE IT'S MY BIRTHDAY.
THOUGHT IT WAS IN MAY?
HEE-HO! IT IS TO LAUGH··! WITH ME RUNNIN' THE CALENDAR I MIGHT WIND UP WITH PROB'LY A DOZEN BIRTHDAYS EV'RY YEAR.
BULLY! THO' IN TEN YEARS YOU'D BE 120 YEARS OLDER

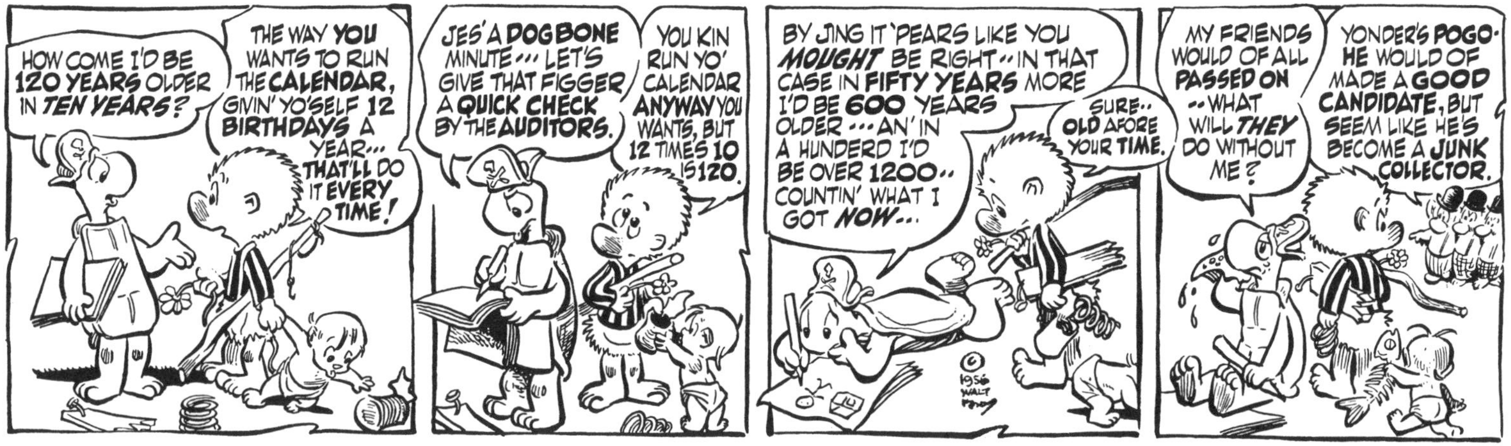
HOW COME I'D BE 120 YEARS OLDER IN TEN YEARS?
THE WAY YOU WANTS TO RUN THE CALENDAR, GIVIN' YO'SELF 12 BIRTHDAYS A YEAR... THAT'LL DO IT EVERY TIME!
JES' A DOG BONE MINUTE... LET'S GIVE THAT FIGGER A QUICK CHECK BY THE AUDITORS.
YOU KIN RUN YO' CALENDAR ANYWAY YOU WANTS, BUT 12 TIME'S 10 IS 120.
BY JING IT 'PEARS LIKE YOU MOUGHT BE RIGHT -- IN THAT CASE IN FIFTY YEARS MORE I'D BE 600 YEARS OLDER ... AN' IN A HUNDERD I'D BE OVER 1200.. COUNTIN' WHAT I GOT NOW...
SURE.. OLD AFORE YOUR TIME.
© 1956 WALT KELLY
MY FRIENDS WOULD OF ALL PASSED ON -- WHAT WILL THEY DO WITHOUT ME?
YONDER'S POGO - HE WOULD OF MADE A GOOD CANDIDATE, BUT SEEM LIKE HE'S BECOME A JUNK COLLECTOR.

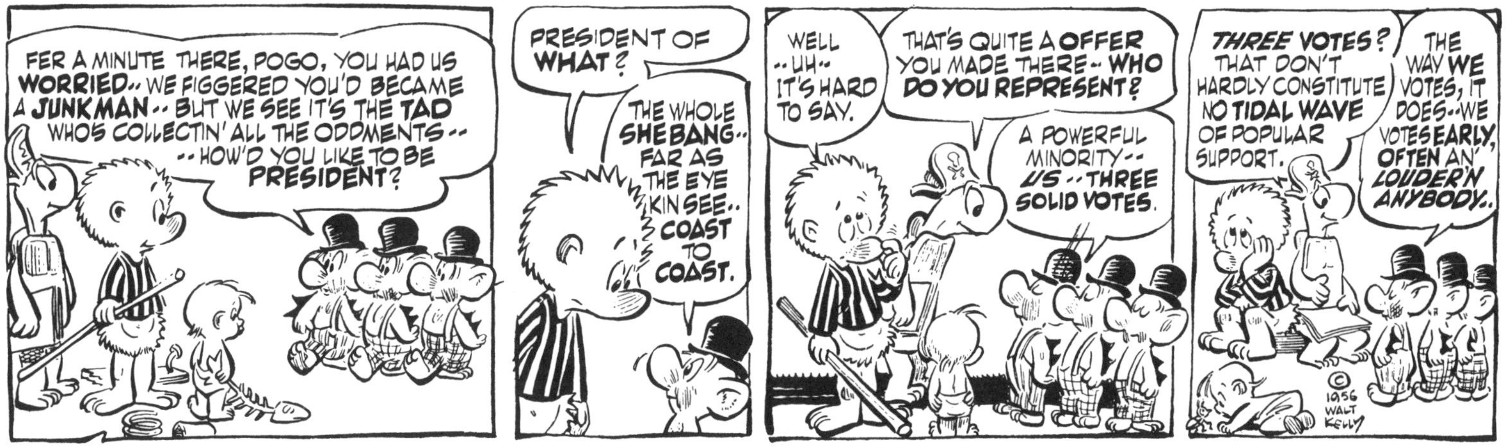
FER A MINUTE THERE, POGO, YOU HAD US WORRIED.. WE FIGGERED YOU'D BECAME A JUNKMAN -- BUT WE SEE IT'S THE TAD WHO'S COLLECTIN' ALL THE ODDMENTS -- -- HOW'D YOU LIKE TO BE PRESIDENT?
PRESIDENT OF WHAT?
THE WHOLE SHEBANG.. FAR AS THE EYE KIN SEE.. COAST TO COAST.
WELL -- UH -- IT'S HARD TO SAY.
THAT'S QUITE A OFFER YOU MADE THERE -- WHO DO YOU REPRESENT?
A POWERFUL MINORITY -- US -- THREE SOLID VOTES.
THREE VOTES? THAT DON'T HARDLY CONSTITUTE NO TIDAL WAVE OF POPULAR SUPPORT.
THE WAY WE VOTES, IT DOES -- WE VOTES EARLY, OFTEN AN' LOUDER'N ANYBODY..
© 1956 WALT KELLY

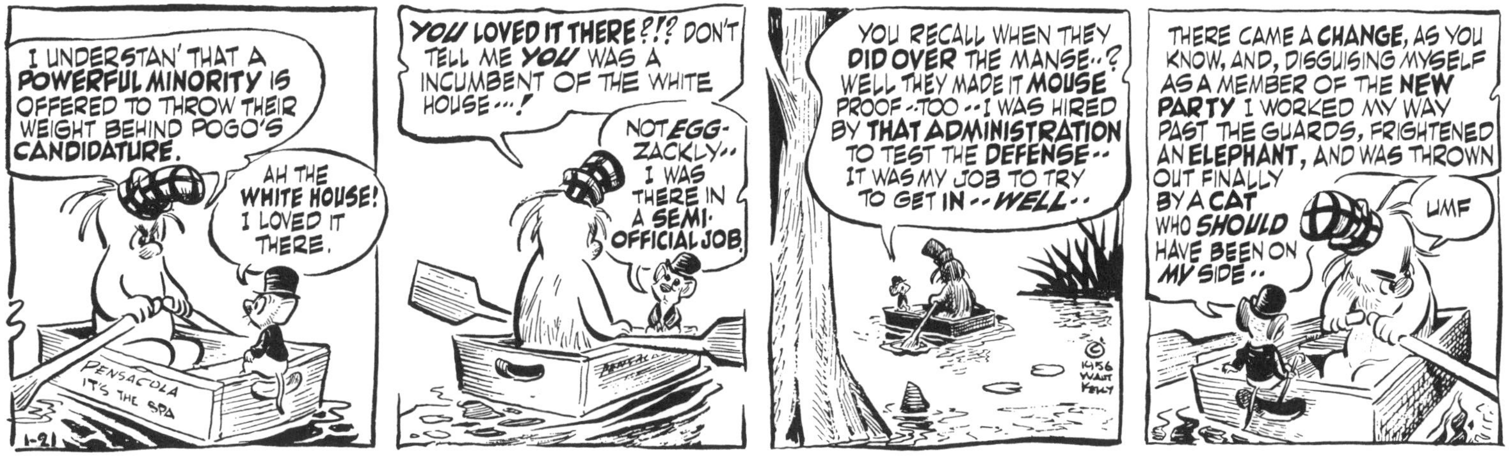
I UNDERSTAN' THAT A POWERFUL MINORITY IS OFFERED TO THROW THEIR WEIGHT BEHIND POGO'S CANDIDATURE.
AH THE WHITE HOUSE! I LOVED IT THERE.
PENSACOLA IT'S THE SPA
1-21
YOU LOVED IT THERE?!? DON'T TELL ME YOU WAS A INCUMBENT OF THE WHITE HOUSE ...!
NOT EGG-ZACKLY.. I WAS THERE IN A SEMI-OFFICIAL JOB.
YOU RECALL WHEN THEY DID OVER THE MANSE..? WELL THEY MADE IT MOUSE PROOF -- TOO -- I WAS HIRED BY THAT ADMINISTRATION TO TEST THE DEFENSE -- IT WAS MY JOB TO TRY TO GET IN -- WELL --
© 1956 WALT KELLY
THERE CAME A CHANGE, AS YOU KNOW, AND, DISGUISING MYSELF AS A MEMBER OF THE NEW PARTY I WORKED MY WAY PAST THE GUARDS, FRIGHTENED AN ELEPHANT, AND WAS THROWN OUT FINALLY BY A CAT WHO SHOULD HAVE BEEN ON MY SIDE --
UMF

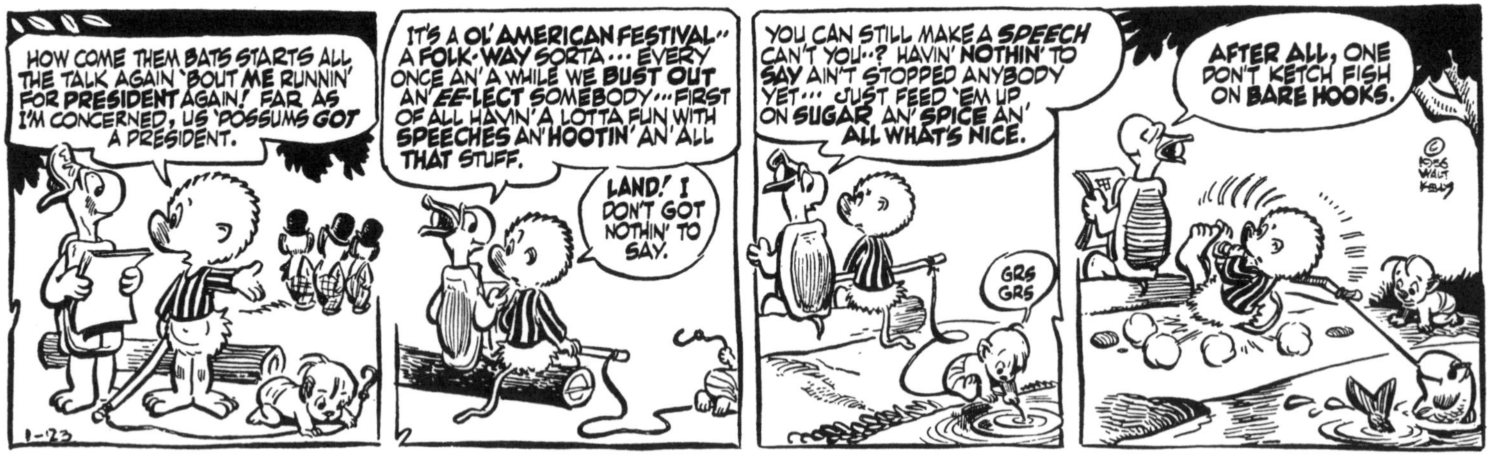
HOW COME THEM BATS STARTS ALL THE TALK AGAIN 'BOUT ME RUNNIN' FOR PRESIDENT AGAIN! FAR AS I'M CONCERNED, US 'POSSUMS GOT A PRESIDENT.
1-23
IT'S A OL' AMERICAN FESTIVAL.. A FOLK-WAY SORTA... EVERY ONCE AN' A WHILE WE BUST OUT AN' EE-LECT SOMEBODY...FIRST OF ALL HAVIN' A LOTTA FUN WITH SPEECHES AN' HOOTIN' AN' ALL THAT STUFF.
LAND! I DON'T GOT NOTHIN' TO SAY.
YOU CAN STILL MAKE A SPEECH CAN'T YOU..? HAVIN' NOTHIN' TO SAY AIN'T STOPPED ANYBODY YET... JUST FEED 'EM UP ON SUGAR AN' SPICE AN' ALL WHAT'S NICE.
GRG GRG
AFTER ALL, ONE DON'T KETCH FISH ON BARE HOOKS.
© 1956 WALT KELLY

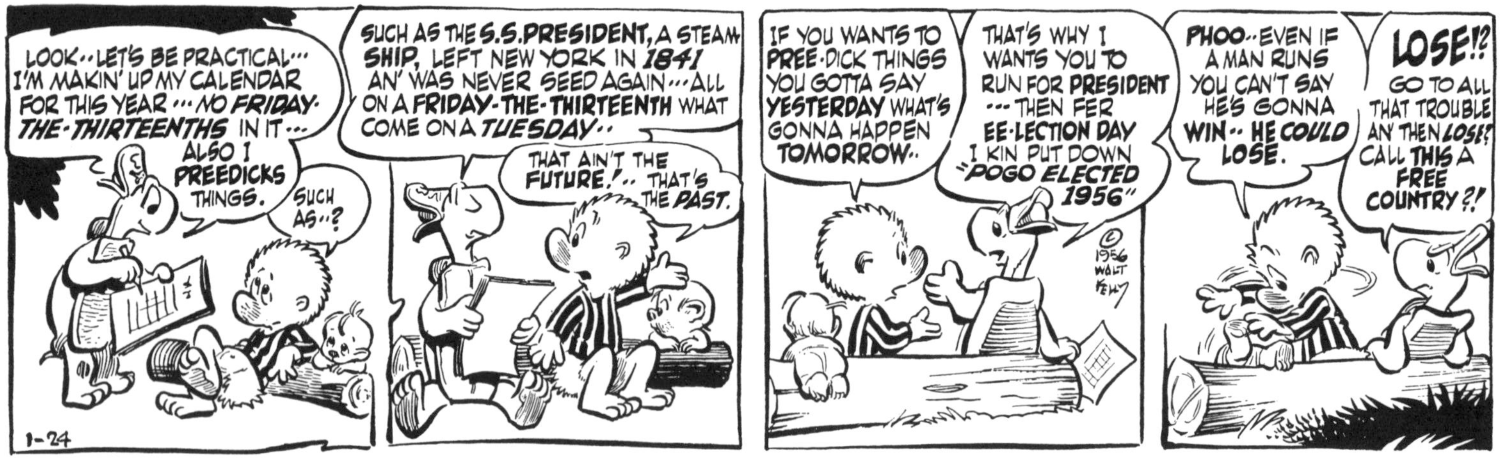
LOOK.. LET'S BE PRACTICAL... I'M MAKIN' UP MY CALENDAR FOR THIS YEAR... NO FRIDAY-THE-THIRTEENTHS IN IT... ALSO I PREEDICKS THINGS.
SUCH AS..?
1-24
SUCH AS THE S.S. PRESIDENT, A STEAM-SHIP, LEFT NEW YORK IN 1841 AN' WAS NEVER SEED AGAIN...ALL ON A FRIDAY-THE-THIRTEENTH WHAT COME ON A TUESDAY..
THAT AIN'T THE FUTURE!.. THAT'S THE PAST.
IF YOU WANTS TO PREE-DICK THINGS YOU GOTTA SAY YESTERDAY WHAT'S GONNA HAPPEN TOMORROW..
THAT'S WHY I WANTS YOU TO RUN FOR PRESIDENT ... THEN FER EE-LECTION DAY I KIN PUT DOWN "POGO ELECTED 1956"
© 1956 WALT KELLY
PHOO.. EVEN IF A MAN RUNS YOU CAN'T SAY HE'S GONNA WIN.. HE COULD LOSE.
LOSE!? GO TO ALL THAT TROUBLE AN' THEN LOSE? CALL THIS A FREE COUNTRY?!

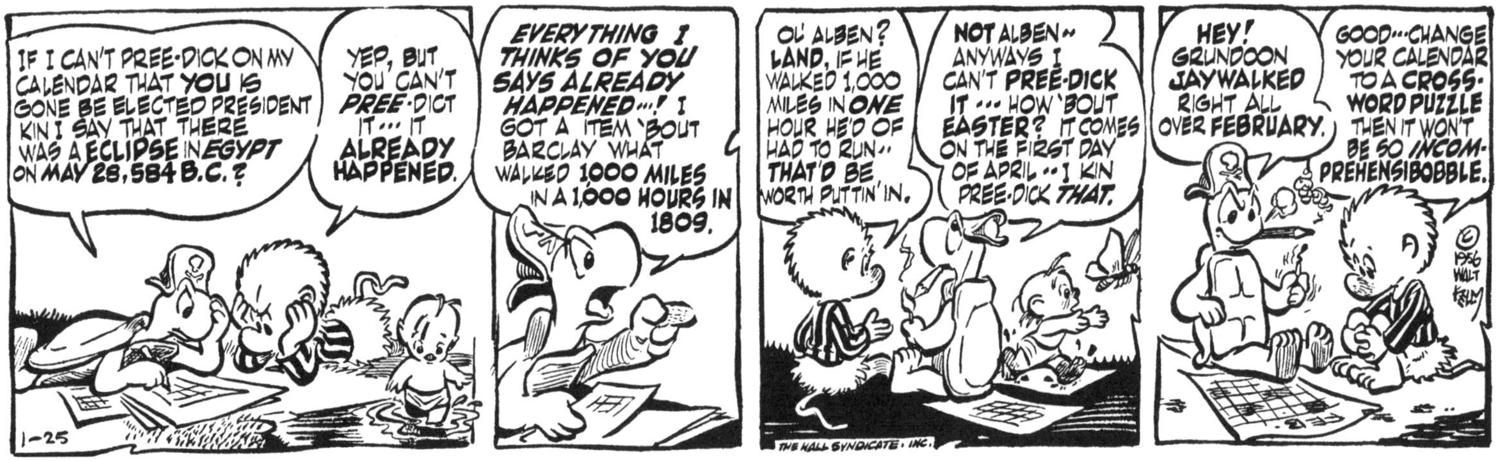
IF I CAN'T PREE-DICK ON MY CALENDAR THAT YOU IS GONE BE ELECTED PRESIDENT KIN I SAY THAT THERE WAS A ECLIPSE IN EGYPT ON MAY 28, 584 B.C.?
YEP, BUT YOU CAN'T PREE-DICT IT... IT ALREADY HAPPENED.
1-25
EVERYTHING I THINKS OF YOU SAYS ALREADY HAPPENED...! I GOT A ITEM 'BOUT BARCLAY WHAT WALKED 1000 MILES IN A 1,000 HOURS IN 1809.
OL' ALBEN? LAND, IF HE WALKED 1,000 MILES IN ONE HOUR HE'D OF HAD TO RUN.. THAT'D BE WORTH PUTTIN' IN.
NOT ALBEN.. ANYWAYS I CAN'T PREE-DICK IT ... HOW 'BOUT EASTER? IT COMES ON THE FIRST DAY OF APRIL.. I KIN PREE-DICK THAT.
THE HALL SYNDICATE, INC.
HEY! GRUNDOON JAYWALKED RIGHT ALL OVER FEBRUARY.
GOOD...CHANGE YOUR CALENDAR TO A CROSS-WORD PUZZLE THEN IT WON'T BE SO INCOM-PREHENSIBOBBLE.
© 1956 WALT KELLY

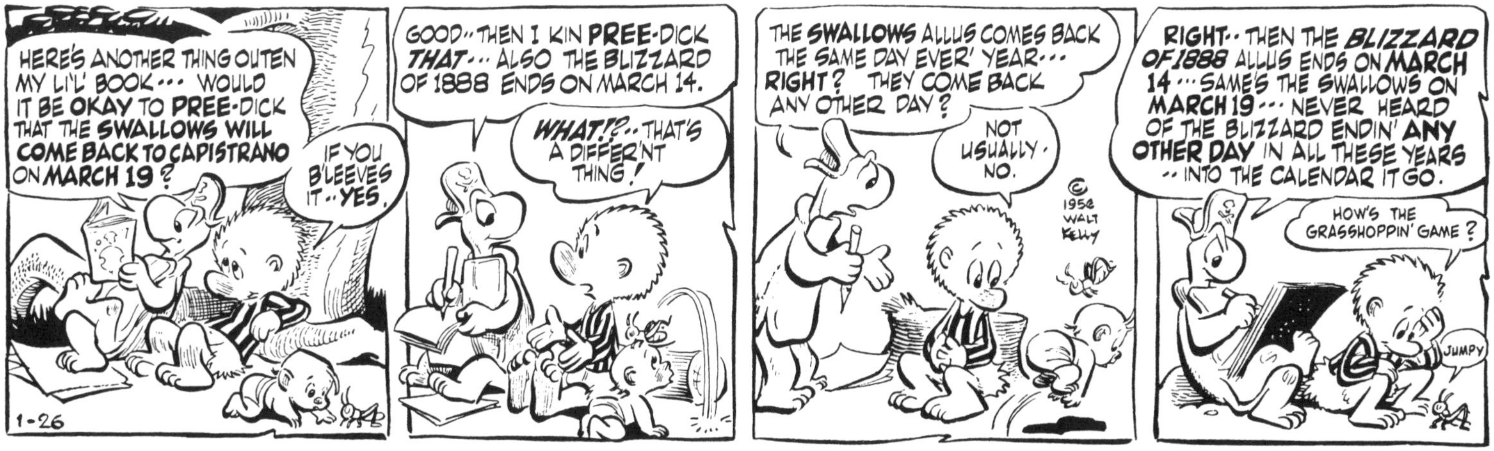
1-26
HERE'S ANOTHER THING OUTEN MY LI'L' BOOK··· WOULD IT BE OKAY TO PREE-DICK THAT THE SWALLOWS WILL COME BACK TO CAPISTRANO ON MARCH 19?
IF YOU B'LEEVES IT·· YES.
GOOD·· THEN I KIN PREE-DICK THAT··· ALSO THE BLIZZARD OF 1888 ENDS ON MARCH 14.
WHAT!?·· THAT'S A DIFFER'NT THING!
THE SWALLOWS ALLUS COMES BACK THE SAME DAY EVER' YEAR··· RIGHT? THEY COME BACK ANY OTHER DAY?
NOT USUALLY. NO.
© 1956 WALT KELLY
RIGHT·· THEN THE BLIZZARD OF 1888 ALLUS ENDS ON MARCH 14··· SAME'S THE SWALLOWS ON MARCH 19··· NEVER HEARD OF THE BLIZZARD ENDIN' ANY OTHER DAY IN ALL THESE YEARS ·· INTO THE CALENDAR IT GO.
HOW'S THE GRASSHOPPIN' GAME?
JUMPY

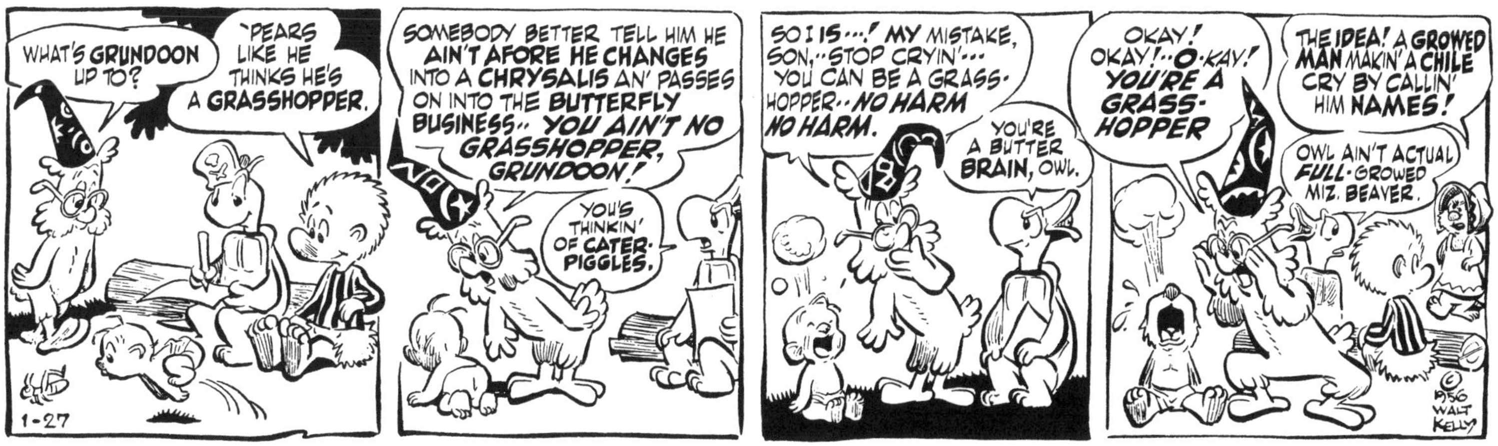
1-27
WHAT'S GRUNDOON UP TO?
'PEARS LIKE HE THINKS HE'S A GRASSHOPPER.
SOMEBODY BETTER TELL HIM HE AIN'T AFORE HE CHANGES INTO A CHRYSALIS AN' PASSES ON INTO THE BUTTERFLY BUSINESS·· YOU AIN'T NO GRASSHOPPER, GRUNDOON!
YOU'S THINKIN' OF CATER-PIGGLES.
SO I IS···! MY MISTAKE, SON,·· STOP CRYIN'··· YOU CAN BE A GRASS-HOPPER·· NO HARM NO HARM.
YOU'RE A BUTTER BRAIN, OWL.
OKAY! OKAY!·· O-KAY! YOU'RE A GRASS-HOPPER
THE IDEA! A GROWED MAN MAKIN' A CHILE CRY BY CALLIN' HIM NAMES!
OWL AIN'T ACTUAL FULL-GROWED MIZ. BEAVER.
© 1956 WALT KELLY

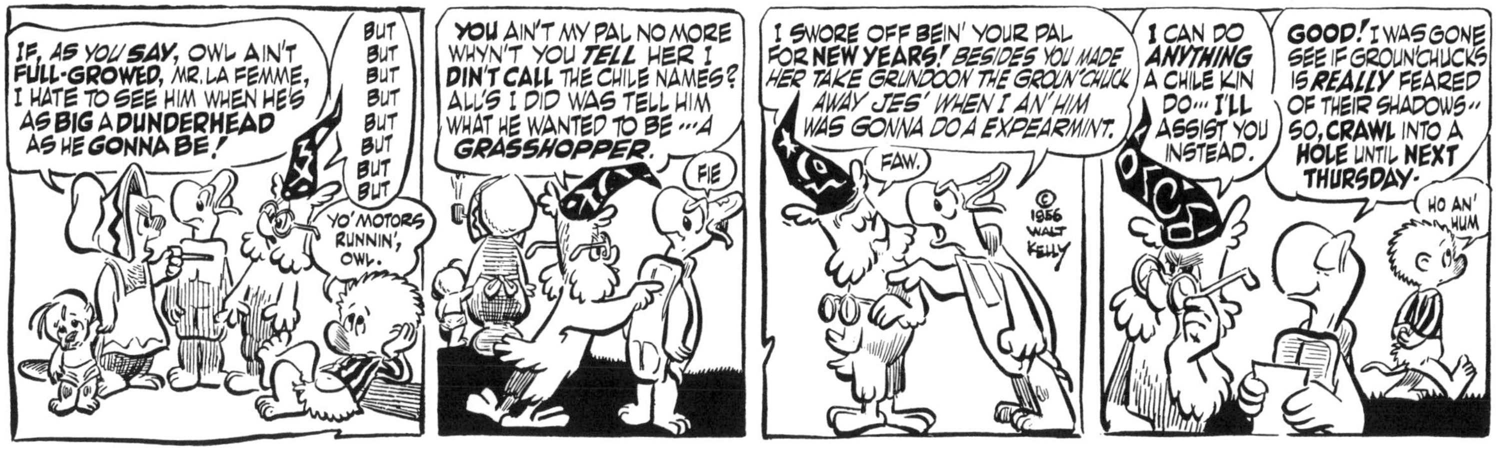
IF, AS YOU SAY, OWL AIN'T FULL-GROWED, MR. LA FEMME, I HATE TO SEE HIM WHEN HE'S AS BIG A DUNDERHEAD AS HE GONNA BE!
BUT BUT BUT BUT BUT BUT BUT BUT
YO' MOTORS RUNNIN', OWL.
YOU AIN'T MY PAL NO MORE WHYN'T YOU TELL HER I DIN'T CALL THE CHILE NAMES? ALL'S I DID WAS TELL HIM WHAT HE WANTED TO BE ···A GRASSHOPPER.
FIE
I SWORE OFF BEIN' YOUR PAL FOR NEW YEARS! BESIDES YOU MADE HER TAKE GRUNDOON THE GROUN'CHUCK AWAY JES' WHEN I AN' HIM WAS GONNA DO A EXPEARMINT.
FAW.
© 1956 WALT KELLY
I CAN DO ANYTHING A CHILE KIN DO··· I'LL ASSIST YOU INSTEAD.
GOOD! I WAS GONE SEE IF GROUN'CHUCKS IS REALLY FEARED OF THEIR SHADOWS·· SO, CRAWL INTO A HOLE UNTIL NEXT THURSDAY.
HO AN' HUM

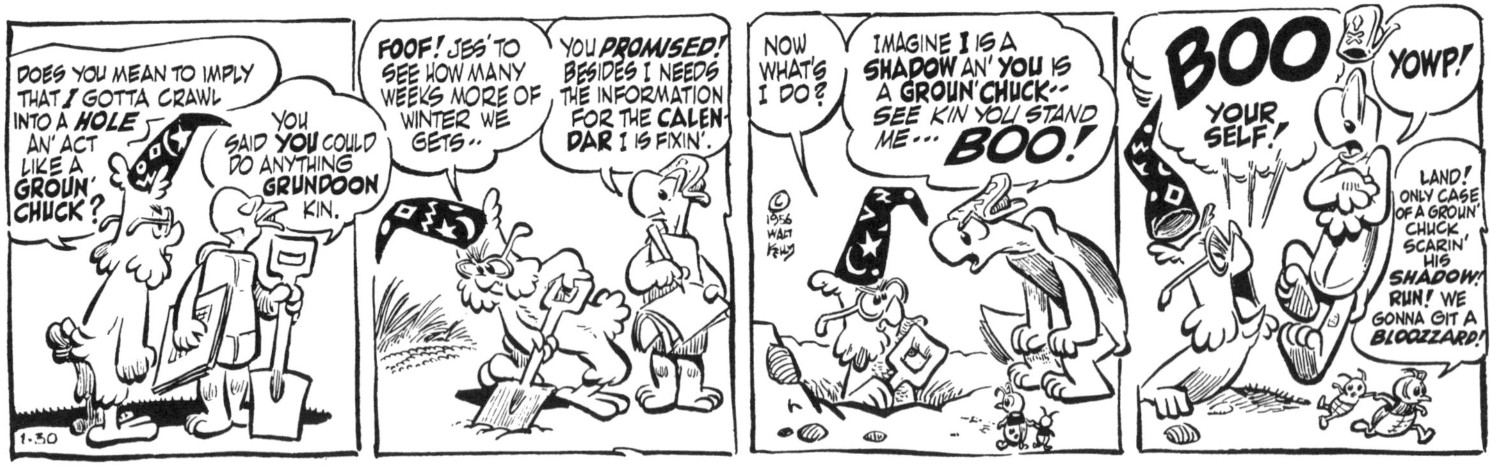
DOES YOU MEAN TO IMPLY THAT I GOTTA CRAWL INTO A HOLE AN' ACT LIKE A GROUN' CHUCK?
YOU SAID YOU COULD DO ANYTHING GRUNDOON KIN.
1-30
FOOF! JES' TO SEE HOW MANY WEEKS MORE OF WINTER WE GETS..
YOU PROMISED! BESIDES I NEEDS THE INFORMATION FOR THE CALEN-DAR I IS FIXIN'.
NOW WHAT'S I DO?
IMAGINE I IS A SHADOW AN' YOU IS A GROUN'CHUCK.. SEE KIN YOU STAND ME... BOO!
© 1956 WALT KELLY
BOO
YOUR SELF!
YOWP!
LAND! ONLY CASE OF A GROUN' CHUCK SCARIN' HIS SHADOW! RUN! WE GONNA GIT A BLOOZZARD!

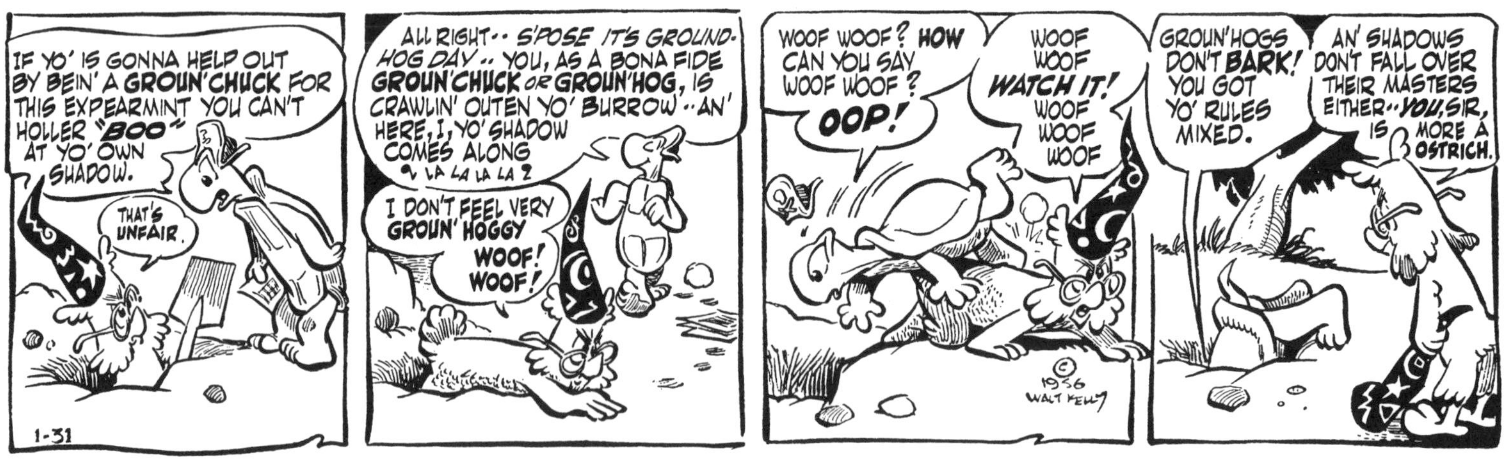
IF YO' IS GONNA HELP OUT BY BEIN' A GROUN'CHUCK FOR THIS EXPEARMINT YOU CAN'T HOLLER "BOO" AT YO' OWN SHADOW.
THAT'S UNFAIR.
1-31
ALL RIGHT.. S'POSE IT'S GROUND-HOG DAY.. YOU, AS A BONA FIDE GROUN'CHUCK OR GROUN'HOG, IS CRAWLIN' OUTEN YO' BURROW.. AN' HERE, I, YO' SHADOW COMES ALONG
LA LA LA LA
I DON'T FEEL VERY GROUN' HOGGY
WOOF! WOOF!
WOOF WOOF? HOW CAN YOU SAY WOOF WOOF? OOP!
WOOF WOOF WATCH IT! WOOF WOOF WOOF
© 1956 WALT KELLY
GROUN'HOGS DON'T BARK! YOU GOT YO' RULES MIXED.
AN' SHADOWS DON'T FALL OVER THEIR MASTERS EITHER.. YOU, SIR, IS MORE A OSTRICH.

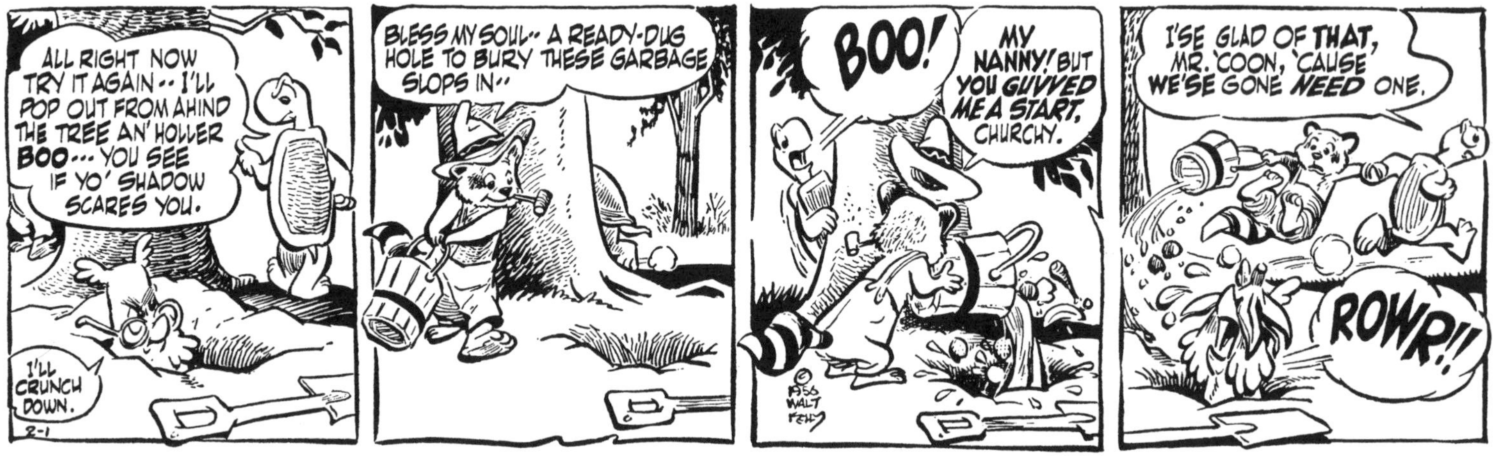
ALL RIGHT NOW TRY IT AGAIN.. I'LL POP OUT FROM AHIND THE TREE AN' HOLLER BOO... YOU SEE IF YO' SHADOW SCARES YOU.
I'LL CRUNCH DOWN.
2-1
BLESS MY SOUL.. A READY-DUG HOLE TO BURY THESE GARBAGE SLOPS IN..
BOO!
MY NANNY! BUT YOU GUVVED ME A START, CHURCHY.
© 1956 WALT KELLY
I'SE GLAD OF THAT, MR. 'COON, 'CAUSE WE'SE GONE NEED ONE.
ROWR!!

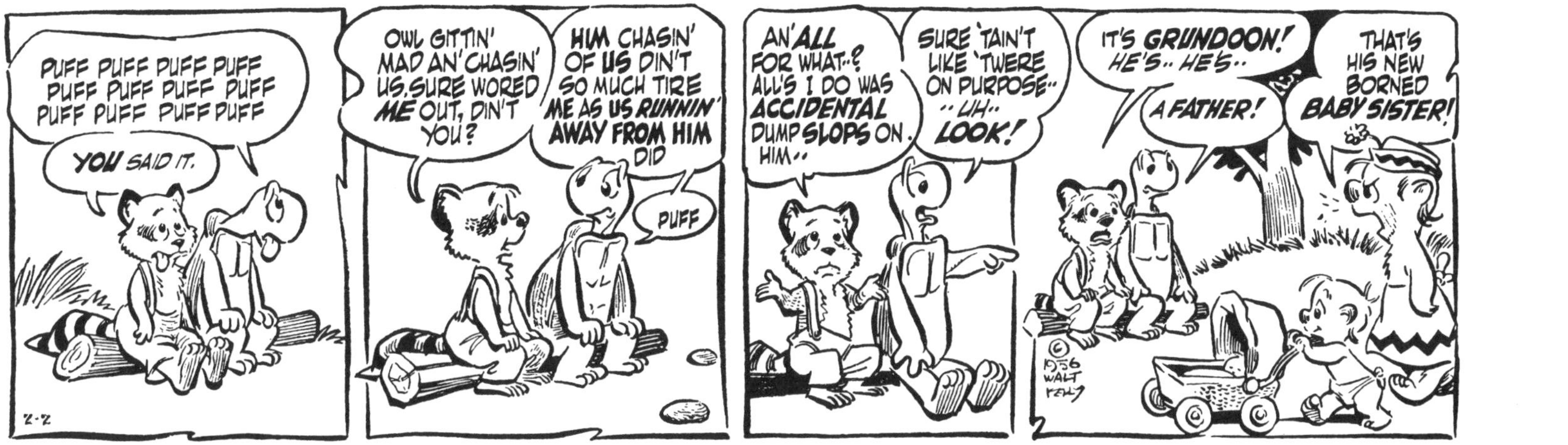
PUFF PUFF PUFF PUFF PUFF PUFF PUFF PUFF PUFF PUFF PUFF PUFF PUFF
YOU SAID IT.
2-2
OWL GITTIN' MAD AN' CHASIN' US. SURE WORED ME OUT, DIN'T YOU?
HIM CHASIN' OF US DIN'T SO MUCH TIRE ME AS US RUNNIN' AWAY FROM HIM DID
PUFF
AN' ALL FOR WHAT..? ALL'S I DO WAS ACCIDENTAL DUMP SLOPS ON HIM..
SURE 'TAIN'T LIKE 'TWERE ON PURPOSE.. ..UH.. LOOK!
IT'S GRUNDOON! HE'S.. HE'S..
A FATHER!
THAT'S HIS NEW BORNED BABY SISTER!
© 1956 WALT KELLY

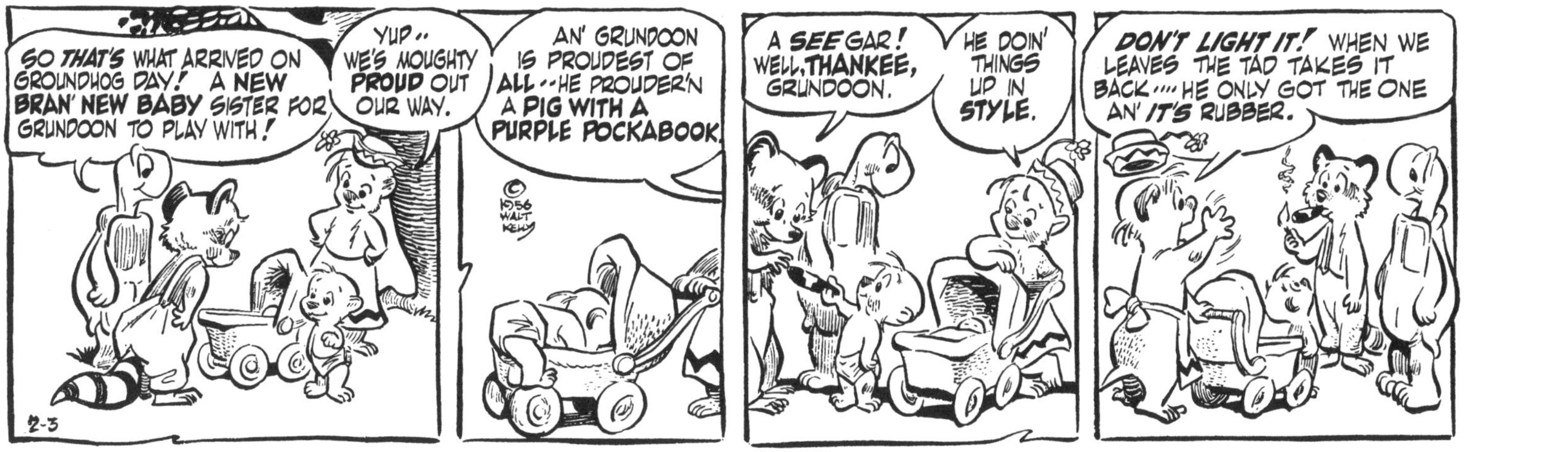
SO THAT'S WHAT ARRIVED ON GROUNDHOG DAY! A NEW BRAN' NEW BABY SISTER FOR GRUNDOON TO PLAY WITH!
YUP.. WE'S MOUGHTY PROUD OUT OUR WAY.
2-3
AN' GRUNDOON IS PROUDEST OF ALL -- HE PROUDER'N A PIG WITH A PURPLE POCKABOOK.
© 1956 WALT KELLY
A SEE GAR! WELL, THANKEE, GRUNDOON.
HE DOIN' THINGS UP IN STYLE.
DON'T LIGHT IT! WHEN WE LEAVES THE TAD TAKES IT BACK.... HE ONLY GOT THE ONE AN' IT'S RUBBER.

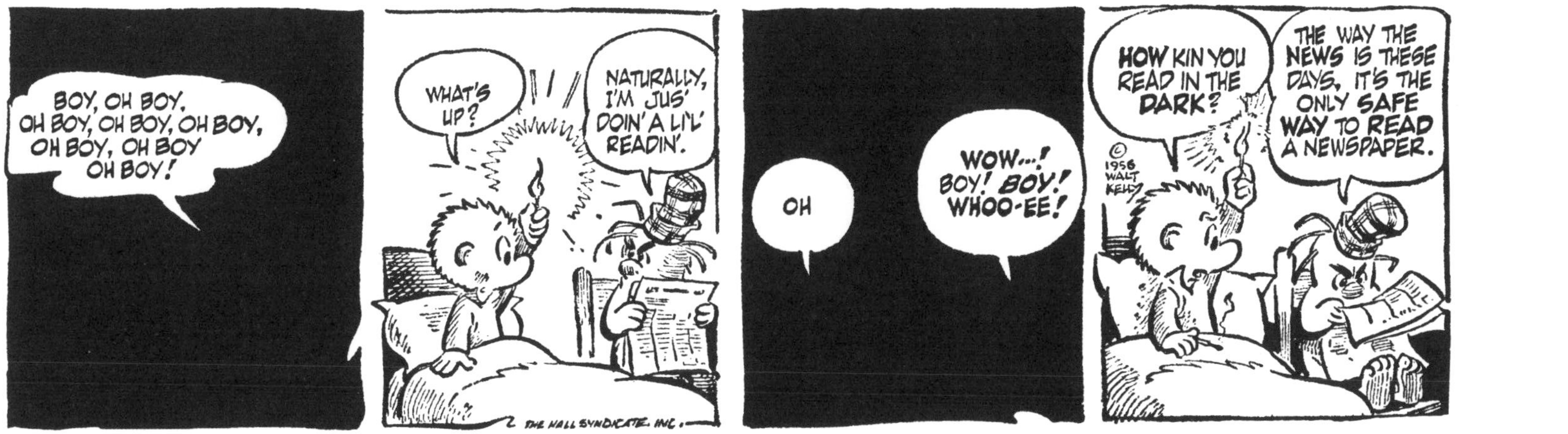
BOY, OH BOY. OH BOY, OH BOY, OH BOY, OH BOY, OH BOY OH BOY!
WHAT'S UP?
NATURALLY, I'M JUS' DOIN' A LI'L' READIN'.
THE HALL SYNDICATE, INC.
OH
WOW...! BOY! BOY! WHOO-EE!
HOW KIN YOU READ IN THE DARK?
THE WAY THE NEWS IS THESE DAYS, IT'S THE ONLY SAFE WAY TO READ A NEWSPAPER.
© 1956 WALT KELLY

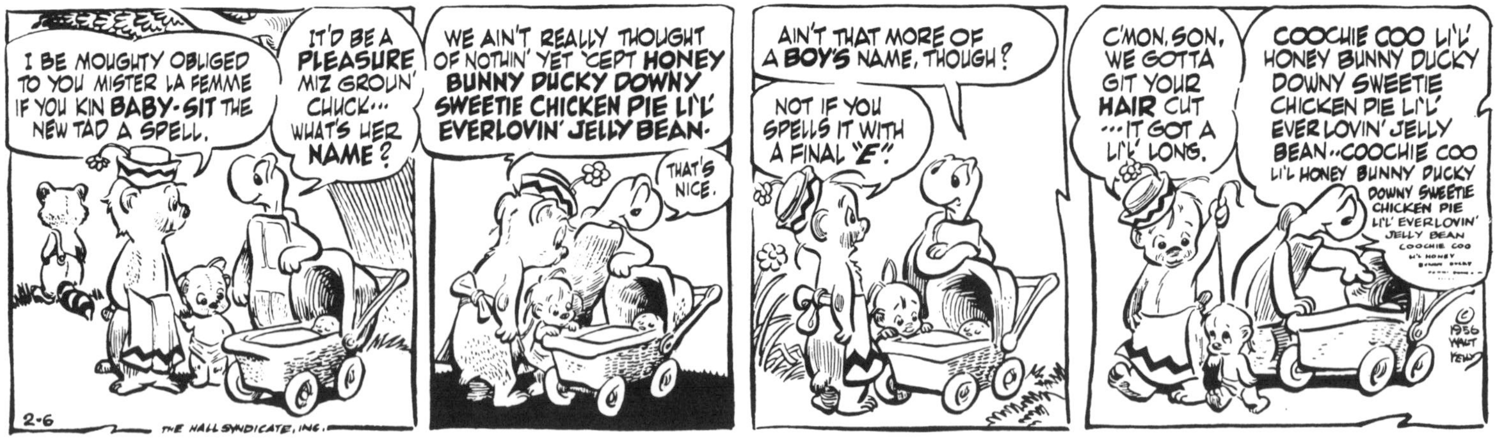
I BE MOUGHTY OBLIGED TO YOU MISTER LA FEMME IF YOU KIN BABY-SIT THE NEW TAD A SPELL.
IT'D BE A PLEASURE MIZ GROUN' CHUCK... WHAT'S HER NAME?
WE AIN'T REALLY THOUGHT OF NOTHIN' YET 'CEPT HONEY BUNNY DUCKY DOWNY SWEETIE CHICKEN PIE LI'L' EVERLOVIN' JELLY BEAN.
THAT'S NICE.
AIN'T THAT MORE OF A BOY'S NAME, THOUGH?
NOT IF YOU SPELLS IT WITH A FINAL "E"!
C'MON, SON, WE GOTTA GIT YOUR HAIR CUT ...IT GOT A LI'L' LONG.
COOCHIE COO LI'L' HONEY BUNNY DUCKY DOWNY SWEETIE CHICKEN PIE LI'L' EVER LOVIN' JELLY BEAN..COOCHIE COO LI'L HONEY BUNNY DUCKY DOWNY SWEETIE CHICKEN PIE LI'L' EVERLOVIN' JELLY BEAN COOCHIE COO
2-6
THE HALL SYNDICATE, INC.
© 1956 WALT KELLY

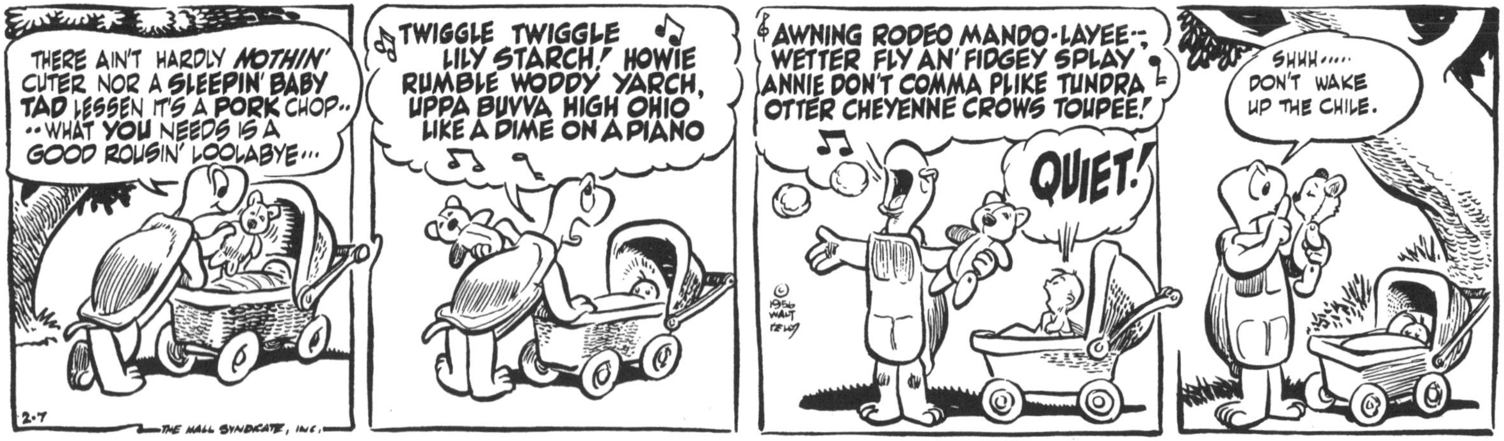
THERE AIN'T HARDLY NOTHIN' CUTER NOR A SLEEPIN' BABY TAD LESSEN IT'S A PORK CHOP.. ..WHAT YOU NEEDS IS A GOOD ROUSIN' LOOLABYE...
TWIGGLE TWIGGLE LILY STARCH! HOWIE RUMBLE WODDY YARCH, UPPA BUVVA HIGH OHIO LIKE A DIME ON A PIANO
AWNING RODEO MANDO-LAYEE-, WETTER FLY AN' FIDGEY SPLAY ANNIE DON'T COMMA PLIKE TUNDRA OTTER CHEYENNE CROWS TOUPEE!
QUIET!
SHHH..... DON'T WAKE UP THE CHILE.
2-7
THE HALL SYNDICATE, INC.
© 1956 WALT KELLY

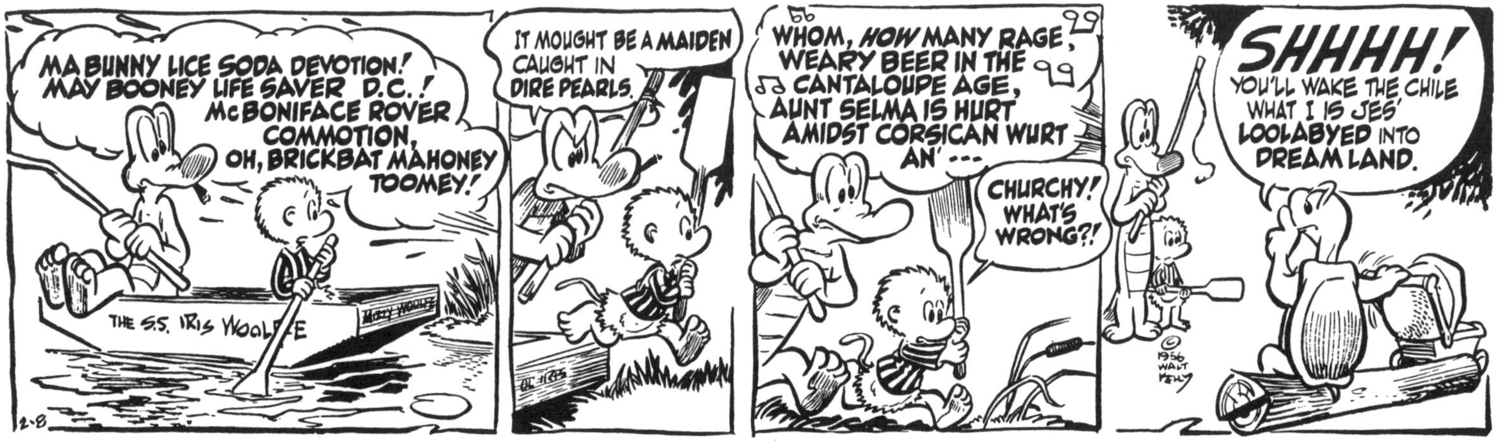
MA BUNNY LICE SODA DEVOTION! MAY BOONEY LIFE SAVER D.C.! McBONIFACE ROVER COMMOTION, OH, BRICKBAT MAHONEY TOOMEY!
THE S.S. IRIS WOOLFE
IT MOUGHT BE A MAIDEN CAUGHT IN DIRE PEARLS.
WHOM, HOW MANY RAGE, WEARY BEER IN THE CANTALOUPE AGE, AUNT SELMA IS HURT AMIDST CORSICAN WURT AN'---
CHURCHY! WHAT'S WRONG?!
SHHHH! YOU'LL WAKE THE CHILE WHAT I IS JES' LOOLABYED INTO DREAM LAND.
2-8
© 1956 WALT KELLY

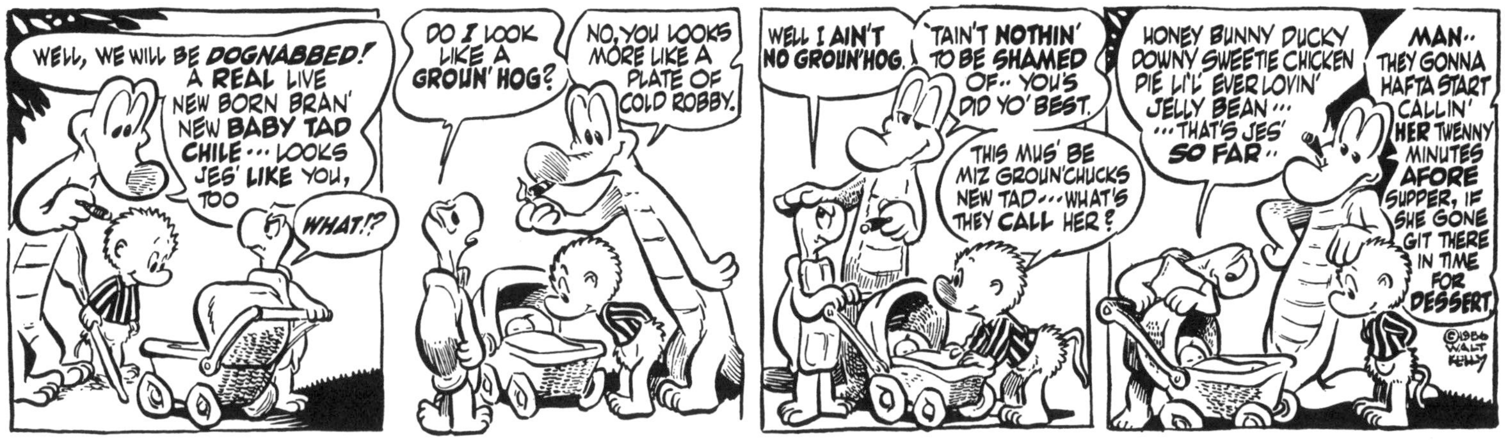
WELL, WE WILL BE DOGNABBED! A REAL LIVE NEW BORN BRAN' NEW BABY TAD CHILE... LOOKS JES' LIKE YOU, TOO
WHAT!?
DO I LOOK LIKE A GROUN' HOG?
NO, YOU LOOKS MORE LIKE A PLATE OF COLD ROBBY.
WELL I AIN'T NO GROUN'HOG.
'TAIN'T NOTHIN' TO BE SHAMED OF.. YOU'S DID YO' BEST.
THIS MUS' BE MIZ GROUN'CHUCKS NEW TAD... WHAT'S THEY CALL HER?
HONEY BUNNY DUCKY DOWNY SWEETIE CHICKEN PIE LI'L' EVER LOVIN' JELLY BEAN... ...THAT'S JES' SO FAR..
MAN.. THEY GONNA HAFTA START CALLIN' HER TWENNY MINUTES AFORE SUPPER, IF SHE GONE GIT THERE IN TIME FOR DESSERT.
©1956 WALT KELLY

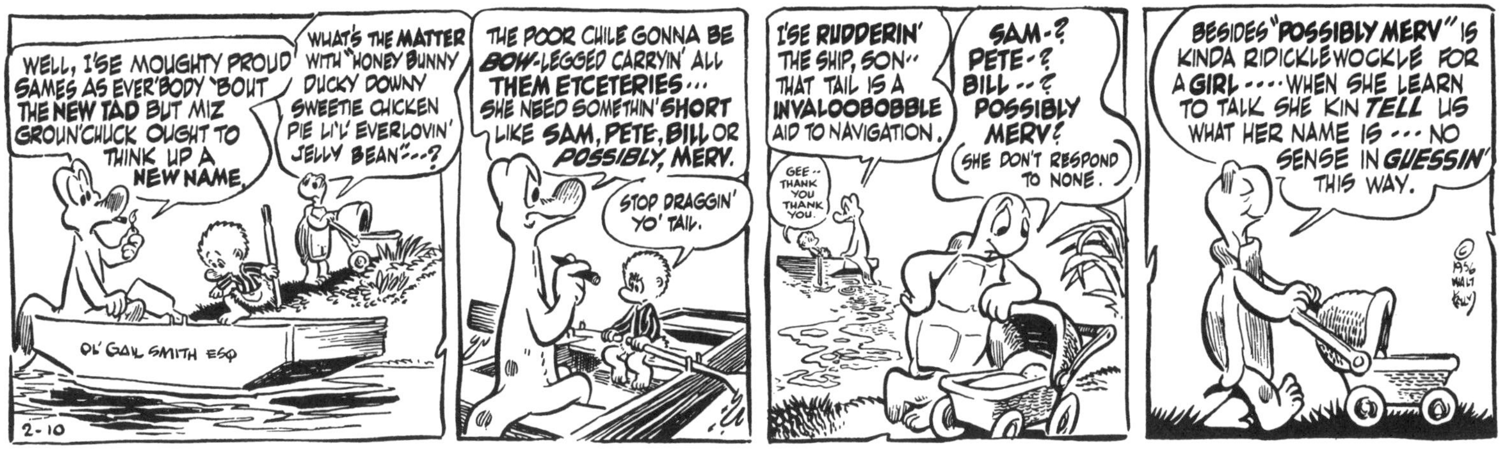
2-10
WELL, I'SE MOUGHTY PROUD SAMES AS EVER'BODY 'BOUT THE NEW TAD BUT MIZ GROUN'CHUCK OUGHT TO THINK UP A NEW NAME.
WHAT'S THE MATTER WITH "HONEY BUNNY DUCKY DOWNY SWEETIE CHICKEN PIE LI'L' EVERLOVIN' JELLY BEAN"..?
OL' GAIL SMITH ESQ
THE POOR CHILE GONNA BE BOW-LEGGED CARRYIN' ALL THEM ETCETERIES... SHE NEED SOMETHIN' SHORT LIKE SAM, PETE, BILL OR POSSIBLY, MERV.
STOP DRAGGIN' YO' TAIL.
I'SE RUDDERIN' THE SHIP, SON.. THAT TAIL IS A INVALOOBOBBLE AID TO NAVIGATION.
SAM-? PETE-? BILL-? POSSIBLY MERV?
(SHE DON'T RESPOND TO NONE.)
GEE.. THANK YOU THANK YOU.
BESIDES "POSSIBLY MERV" IS KINDA RIDICKLE WOCKLE FOR A GIRL.... WHEN SHE LEARN TO TALK SHE KIN TELL US WHAT HER NAME IS ... NO SENSE IN GUESSIN' THIS WAY.
© 1956 WALT KELLY

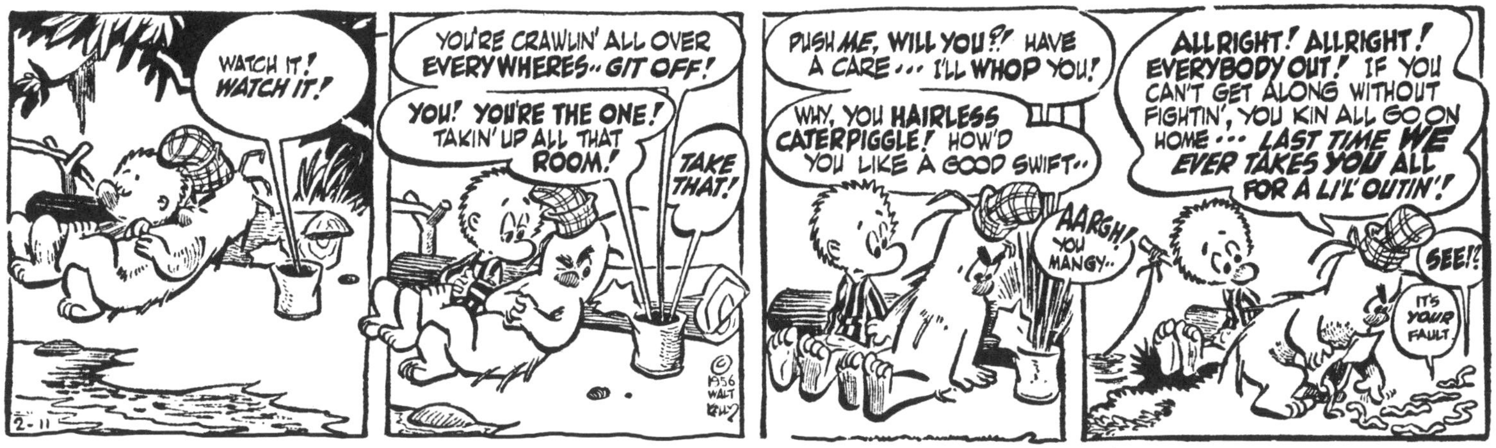
2-11
WATCH IT! WATCH IT!
YOU'RE CRAWLIN' ALL OVER EVERYWHERES.. GIT OFF!
YOU! YOU'RE THE ONE! TAKIN' UP ALL THAT ROOM!
TAKE THAT!
© 1956 WALT KELLY
PUSH ME, WILL YOU?! HAVE A CARE... I'LL WHOP YOU!
WHY, YOU HAIRLESS CATERPIGGLE! HOW'D YOU LIKE A GOOD SWIFT..
AARGH! YOU MANGY..
ALL RIGHT! ALL RIGHT! EVERYBODY OUT! IF YOU CAN'T GET ALONG WITHOUT FIGHTIN', YOU KIN ALL GO ON HOME... LAST TIME WE EVER TAKES YOU ALL FOR A LI'L' OUTIN'!
SEE!?
IT'S YOUR FAULT.

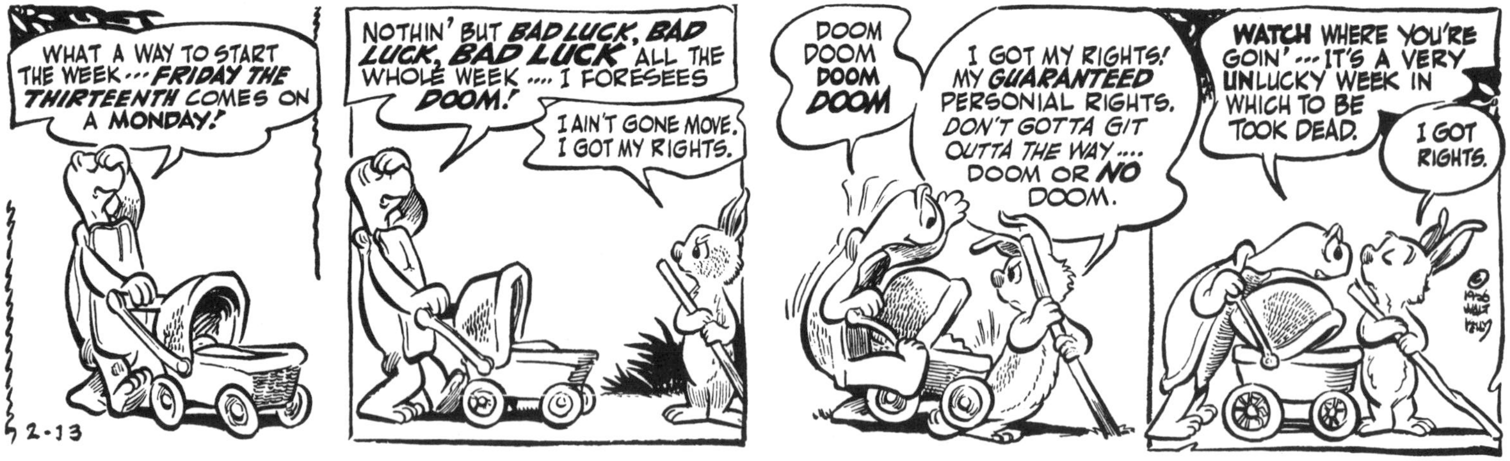
WHAT A WAY TO START THE WEEK... FRIDAY THE THIRTEENTH COMES ON A MONDAY!
2-13
NOTHIN' BUT BAD LUCK, BAD LUCK, BAD LUCK ALL THE WHOLE WEEK.... I FORESEES DOOM!
I AIN'T GONE MOVE. I GOT MY RIGHTS.
DOOM DOOM DOOM DOOM
I GOT MY RIGHTS! MY GUARANTEED PERSONIAL RIGHTS. DON'T GOTTA GIT OUTTA THE WAY.... DOOM OR NO DOOM.
WATCH WHERE YOU'RE GOIN'... IT'S A VERY UNLUCKY WEEK IN WHICH TO BE TOOK DEAD.
I GOT RIGHTS.

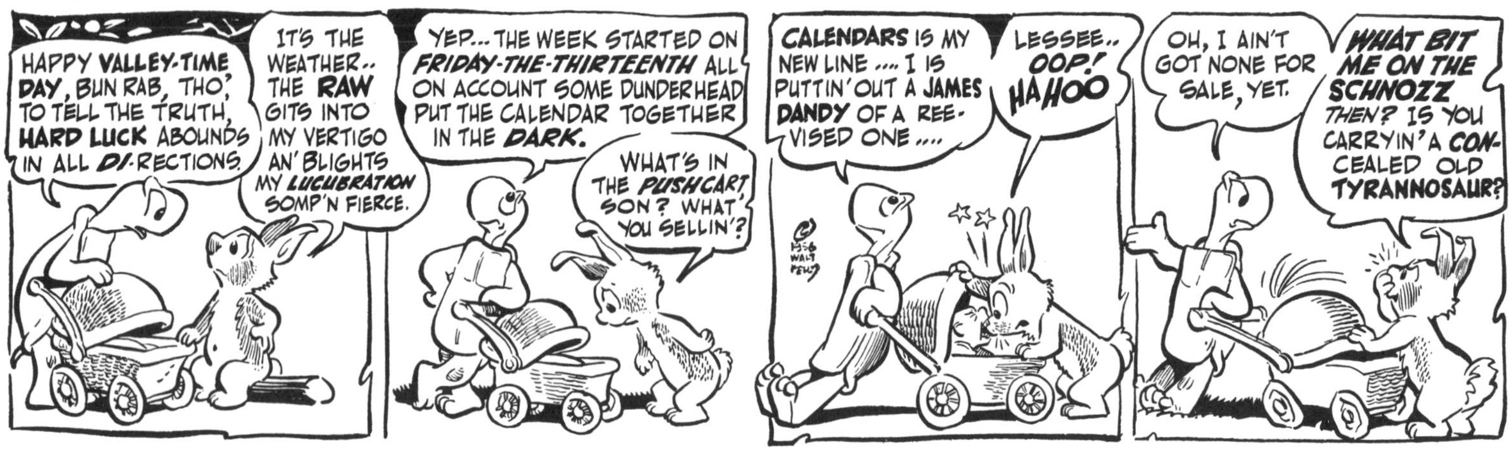
HAPPY VALLEY-TIME DAY, BUN RAB, THO' TO TELL THE TRUTH, HARD LUCK ABOUNDS IN ALL DI-RECTIONS.
IT'S THE WEATHER.. THE RAW GITS INTO MY VERTIGO AN' BLIGHTS MY LUCUBRATION SOMP'N FIERCE.
YEP... THE WEEK STARTED ON FRIDAY-THE-THIRTEENTH ALL ON ACCOUNT SOME DUNDERHEAD PUT THE CALENDAR TOGETHER IN THE DARK.
WHAT'S IN THE PUSHCART, SON? WHAT YOU SELLIN'?
CALENDARS IS MY NEW LINE.... I IS PUTTIN' OUT A JAMES DANDY OF A REE-VISED ONE....
LESSEE.. OOP! HAHOO
OH, I AIN'T GOT NONE FOR SALE, YET.
WHAT BIT ME ON THE SCHNOZZ THEN? IS YOU CARRYIN' A CON-CEALED OLD TYRANNOSAUR?

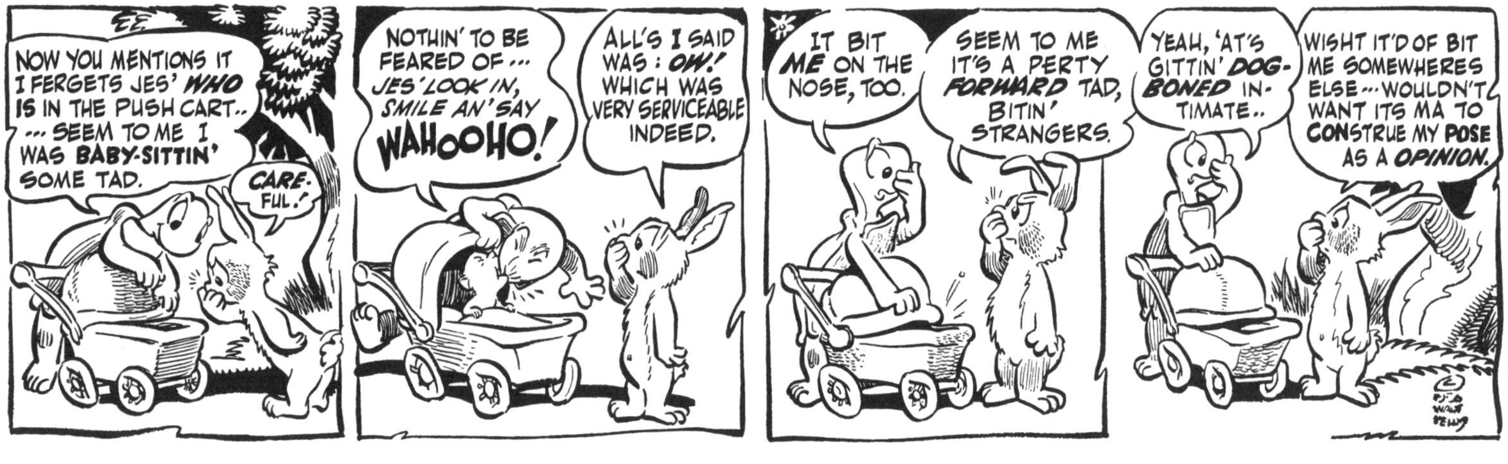
NOW YOU MENTIONS IT I FERGETS JES' WHO IS IN THE PUSH CART.. ... SEEM TO ME I WAS BABY-SITTIN' SOME TAD.
CARE-FUL!
NOTHIN' TO BE FEARED OF... JES' LOOK IN, SMILE AN' SAY WAHOOHO!
ALL'S I SAID WAS: OW! WHICH WAS VERY SERVICEABLE INDEED.
IT BIT ME ON THE NOSE, TOO.
SEEM TO ME IT'S A PERTY FORWARD TAD, BITIN' STRANGERS.
YEAH, 'AT'S GITTIN' DOG-BONED IN-TIMATE..
WISHT IT'D OF BIT ME SOMEWHERES ELSE... WOULDN'T WANT ITS MA TO CONSTRUE MY POSE AS A OPINION.

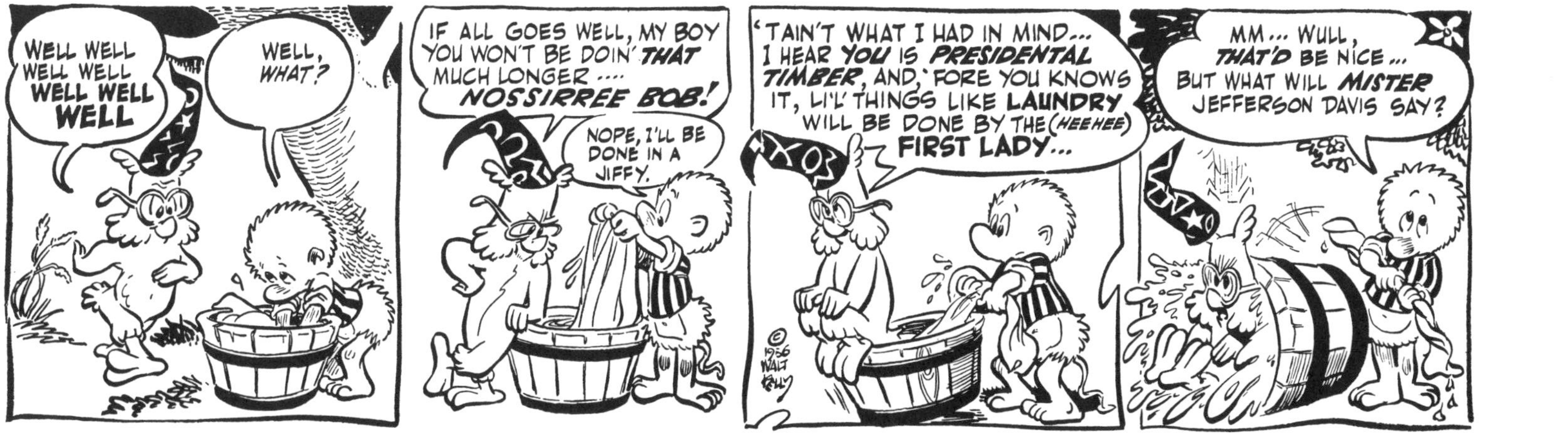
WELL WELL WELL WELL WELL WELL WELL
WELL, WHAT?
IF ALL GOES WELL, MY BOY YOU WON'T BE DOIN' THAT MUCH LONGER.... NOSSIRREE BOB!
NOPE, I'LL BE DONE IN A JIFFY.
'TAIN'T WHAT I HAD IN MIND... I HEAR YOU IS PRESIDENTAL TIMBER, AND, 'FORE YOU KNOWS IT, LI'L' THINGS LIKE LAUNDRY WILL BE DONE BY THE (HEEHEE) FIRST LADY...
© 1956 WALT KELLY
MM... WULL, THAT'D BE NICE... BUT WHAT WILL MISTER JEFFERSON DAVIS SAY?

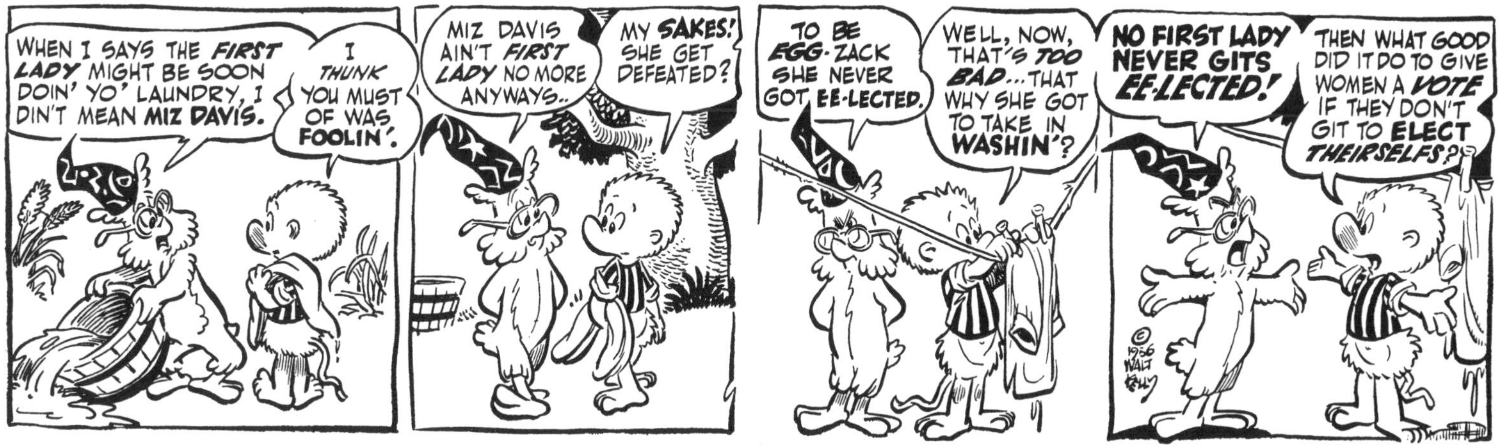
WHEN I SAYS THE FIRST LADY MIGHT BE SOON DOIN' YO' LAUNDRY, I DIN'T MEAN MIZ DAVIS.
I THUNK YOU MUST OF WAS FOOLIN'.
MIZ DAVIS AIN'T FIRST LADY NO MORE ANYWAYS..
MY SAKES! SHE GET DEFEATED?
TO BE EGG-ZACK SHE NEVER GOT EE-LECTED.
WELL, NOW, THAT'S TOO BAD... THAT WHY SHE GOT TO TAKE IN WASHIN'?
NO FIRST LADY NEVER GITS EE-LECTED!
THEN WHAT GOOD DID IT DO TO GIVE WOMEN A VOTE IF THEY DON'T GIT TO ELECT THEIRSELFS?
© 1956 WALT KELLY

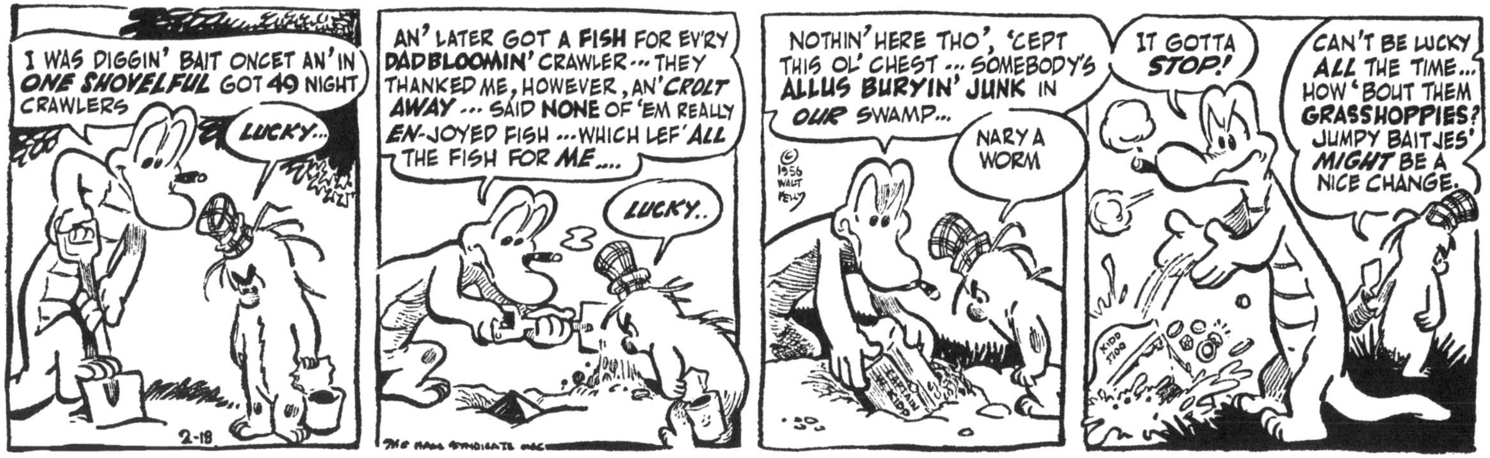
I WAS DIGGIN' BAIT ONCET AN' IN ONE SHOVELFUL GOT 49 NIGHT CRAWLERS
LUCKY...
2-18
AN' LATER GOT A FISH FOR EV'RY DADBLOOMIN' CRAWLER... THEY THANKED ME, HOWEVER, AN' CROLT AWAY... SAID NONE OF 'EM REALLY EN-JOYED FISH... WHICH LEF' ALL THE FISH FOR ME....
LUCKY..
NOTHIN' HERE THO', 'CEPT THIS OL' CHEST... SOMEBODY'S ALLUS BURYIN' JUNK IN OUR SWAMP...
NARY A WORM
© 1956 WALT KELLY
IT GOTTA STOP!
CAN'T BE LUCKY ALL THE TIME... HOW 'BOUT THEM GRASSHOPPIES? JUMPY BAIT JES' MIGHT BE A NICE CHANGE.

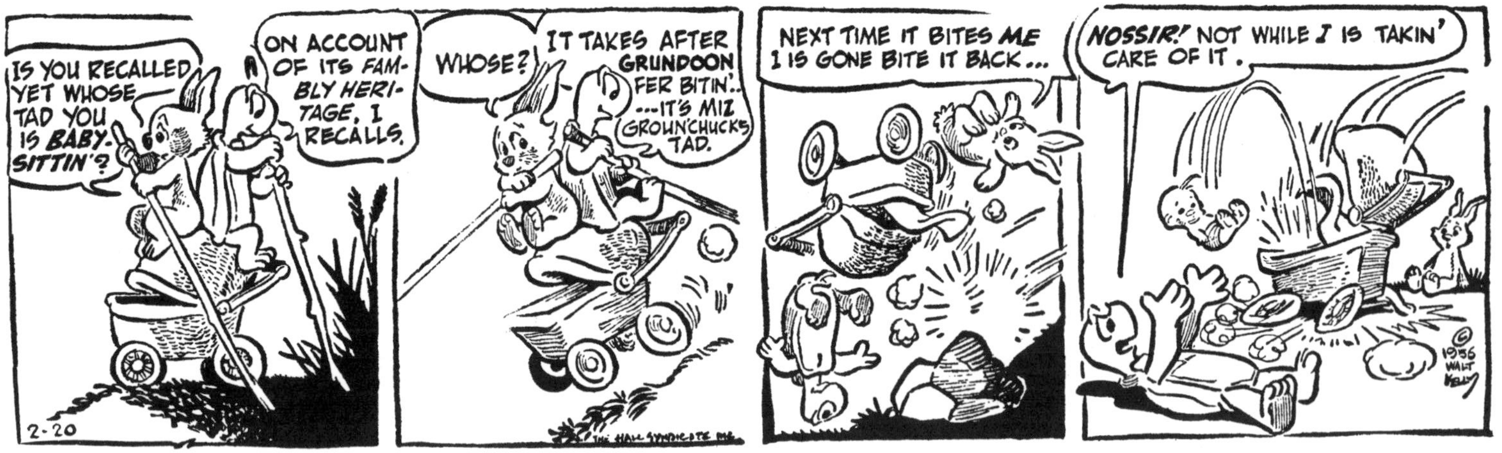
IS YOU RECALLED YET WHOSE TAD YOU IS BABY-SITTIN'?
ON ACCOUNT OF ITS FAMBLY HERITAGE, I RECALLS.
WHOSE?
IT TAKES AFTER GRUNDOON FER BITIN'. ---IT'S MIZ GROUN'CHUCK'S TAD.
NEXT TIME IT BITES ME I IS GONE BITE IT BACK...
NOSSIR! NOT WHILE I IS TAKIN' CARE OF IT.
2-20
© 1956 WALT KELLY

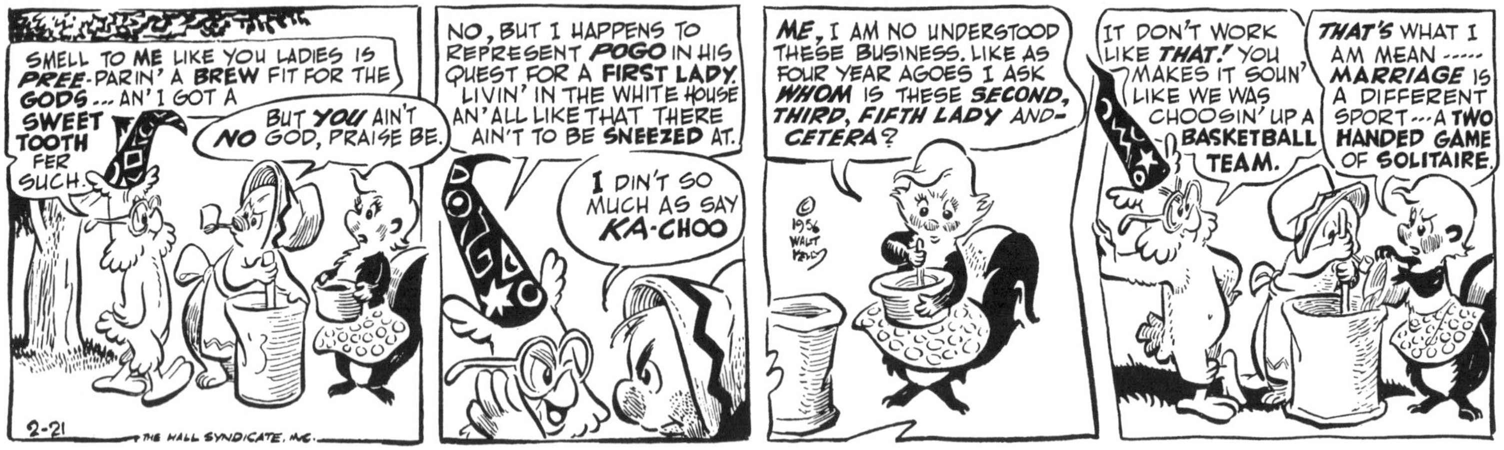
SMELL TO ME LIKE YOU LADIES IS PREE-PARIN' A BREW FIT FOR THE GODS... AN' I GOT A SWEET TOOTH FER SUCH.
BUT YOU AIN'T NO GOD, PRAISE BE.
NO, BUT I HAPPENS TO REPRESENT POGO IN HIS QUEST FOR A FIRST LADY LIVIN' IN THE WHITE HOUSE AN' ALL LIKE THAT THERE AIN'T TO BE SNEEZED AT.
I DIN'T SO MUCH AS SAY KA-CHOO
ME, I AM NO UNDERSTOOD THESE BUSINESS. LIKE AS FOUR YEAR AGOES I ASK WHOM IS THESE SECOND, THIRD, FIFTH LADY AND-CETERA?
IT DON'T WORK LIKE THAT! YOU MAKES IT SOUN' LIKE WE WAS CHOOSIN' UP A BASKETBALL TEAM.
THAT'S WHAT I AM MEAN ----- MARRIAGE IS A DIFFERENT SPORT---A TWO HANDED GAME OF SOLITAIRE.
2-21
THE HALL SYNDICATE, INC.
© 1956 WALT KELLY

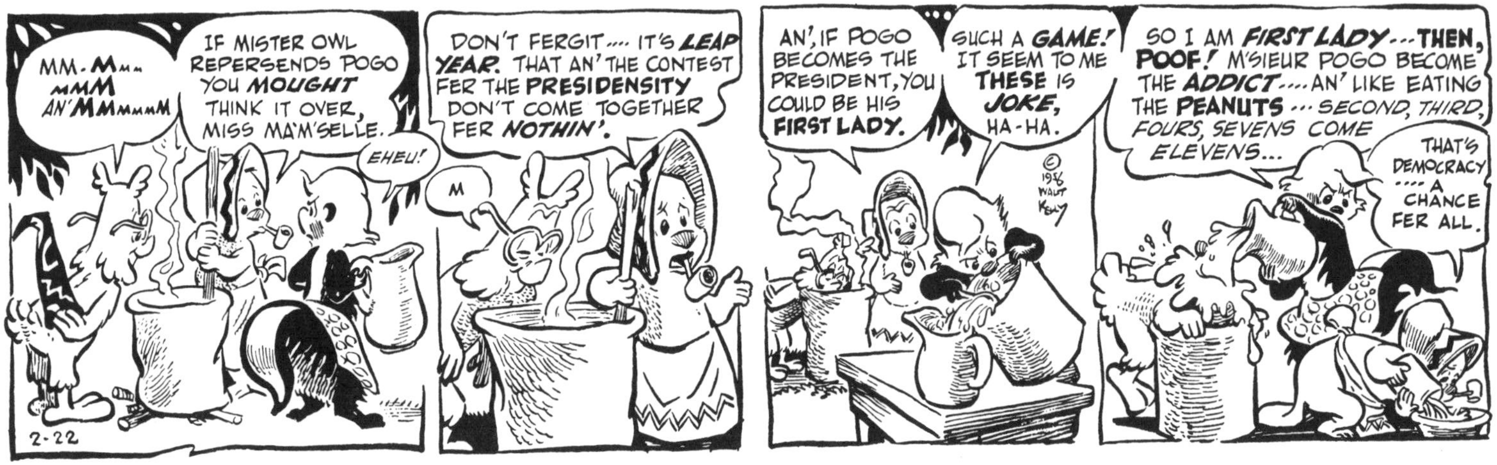
MM-MMM MMM AN'MMMMMM
IF MISTER OWL REPERSENDS POGO YOU MOUGHT THINK IT OVER, MISS MA'M'SELLE.
EHEU!
M
DON'T FERGIT.... IT'S LEAP YEAR. THAT AN' THE CONTEST FER THE PRESIDENSITY DON'T COME TOGETHER FER NOTHIN'.
AN', IF POGO BECOMES THE PRESIDENT, YOU COULD BE HIS FIRST LADY.
SUCH A GAME! IT SEEM TO ME THESE IS JOKE, HA-HA.
SO I AM FIRST LADY---THEN, POOF! M'SIEUR POGO BECOME THE ADDICT....AN' LIKE EATING THE PEANUTS...SECOND, THIRD, FOURS, SEVENS COME ELEVENS...
THAT'S DEMOCRACY.... A CHANCE FER ALL.
2-22
© 1956 WALT KELLY

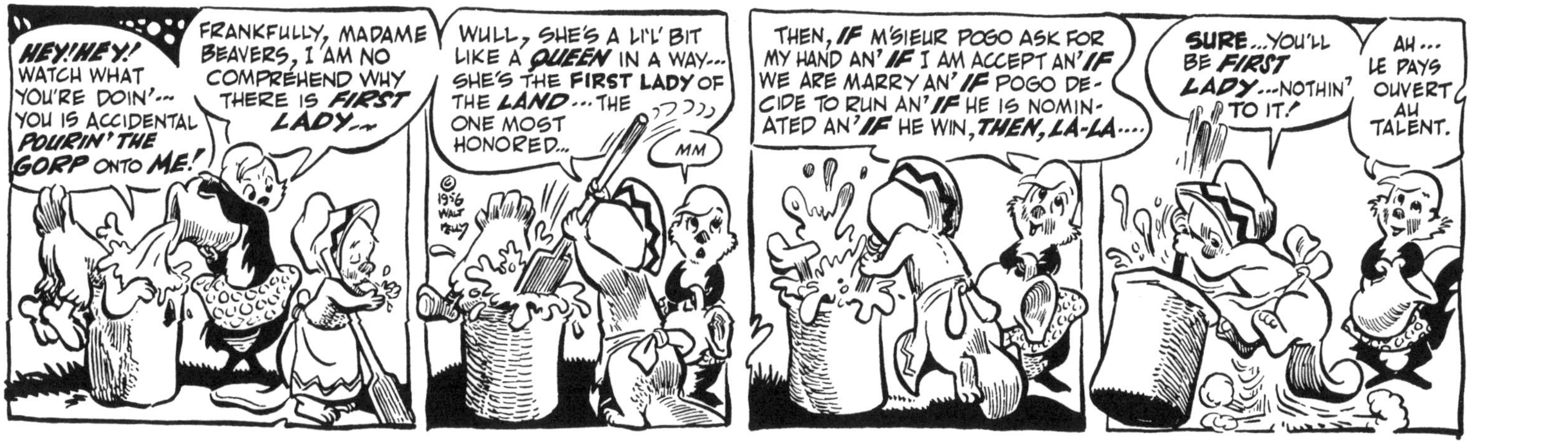
HEY! HEY! WATCH WHAT YOU'RE DOIN'-- YOU IS ACCIDENTAL POURIN' THE GORP ONTO ME!
FRANKFULLY, MADAME BEAVERS, I AM NO COMPREHEND WHY THERE IS FIRST LADY...
WULL, SHE'S A LI'L' BIT LIKE A QUEEN IN A WAY... SHE'S THE FIRST LADY OF THE LAND... THE ONE MOST HONORED...
MM
© 1956 WALT KELLY
THEN, IF M'SIEUR POGO ASK FOR MY HAND AN' IF I AM ACCEPT AN' IF WE ARE MARRY AN' IF POGO DECIDE TO RUN AN' IF HE IS NOMINATED AN' IF HE WIN, THEN, LA-LA....
SURE... YOU'LL BE FIRST LADY... NOTHIN' TO IT!
AH... LE PAYS OUVERT AU TALENT.

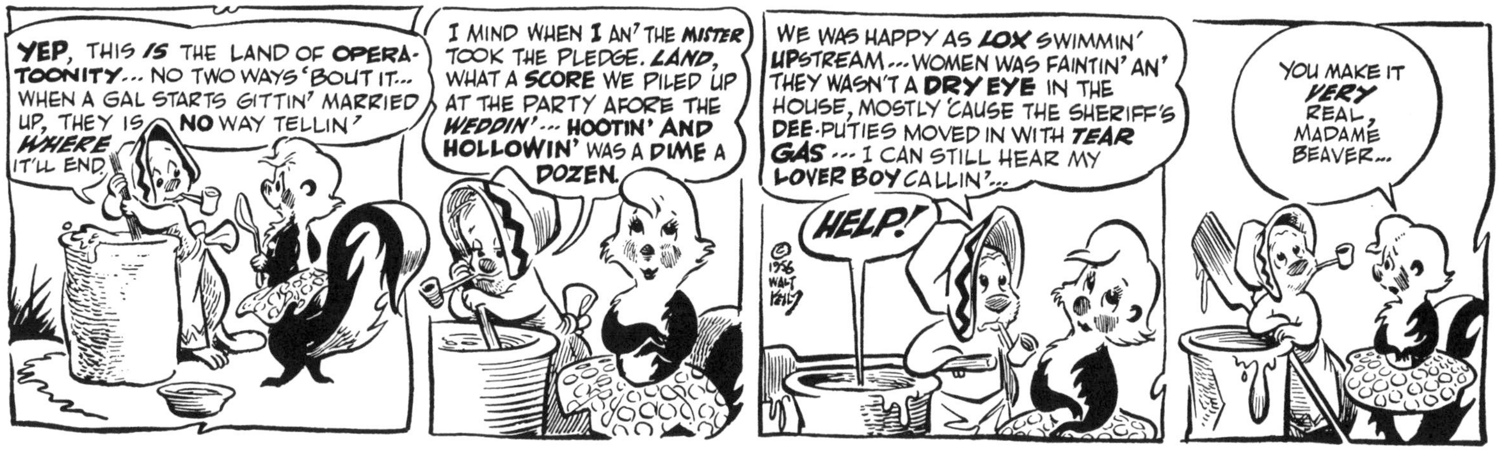
YEP, THIS IS THE LAND OF OPERA-TOONITY... NO TWO WAYS 'BOUT IT... WHEN A GAL STARTS GITTIN' MARRIED UP, THEY IS NO WAY TELLIN' WHERE IT'LL END.
I MIND WHEN I AN' THE MISTER TOOK THE PLEDGE. LAND, WHAT A SCORE WE PILED UP AT THE PARTY AFORE THE WEDDIN'... HOOTIN' AND HOLLOWIN' WAS A DIME A DOZEN.
WE WAS HAPPY AS LOX SWIMMIN' UPSTREAM... WOMEN WAS FAINTIN' AN' THEY WASN'T A DRY EYE IN THE HOUSE, MOSTLY 'CAUSE THE SHERIFF'S DEE-PUTIES MOVED IN WITH TEAR GAS... I CAN STILL HEAR MY LOVER BOY CALLIN'...
HELP!
© 1956 WALT KELLY
YOU MAKE IT VERY REAL, MADAME BEAVER...

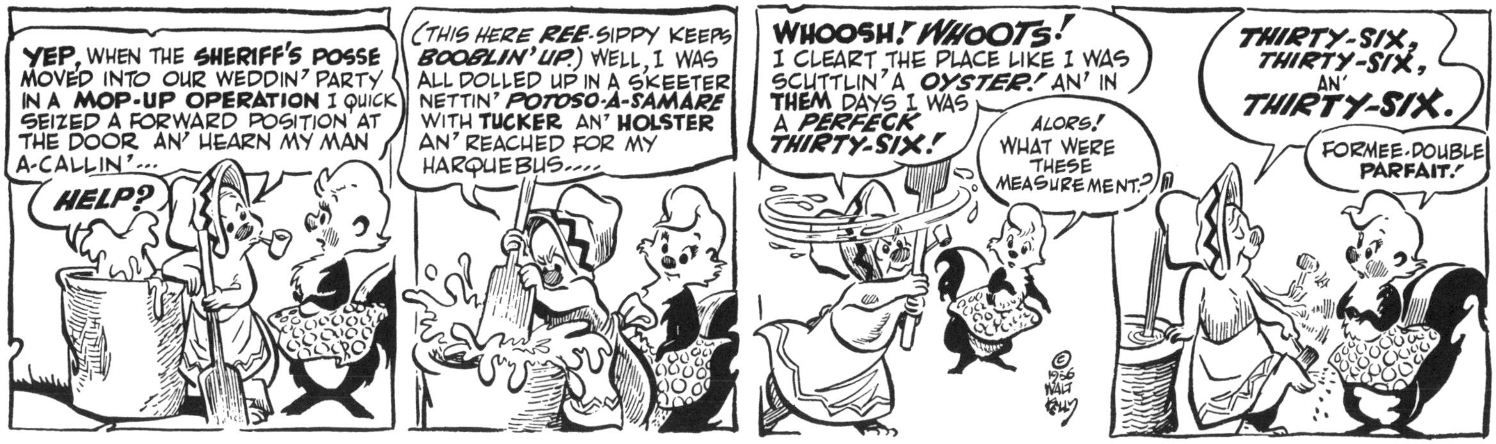
YEP, WHEN THE SHERIFF'S POSSE MOVED INTO OUR WEDDIN' PARTY IN A MOP-UP OPERATION I QUICK SEIZED A FORWARD POSITION AT THE DOOR AN' HEARN MY MAN A-CALLIN'...
HELP?
(THIS HERE REE-SIPPY KEEPS BOOBLIN' UP.) WELL, I WAS ALL DOLLED UP IN A SKEETER NETTIN' POTOSO-A-SAMARE WITH TUCKER AN' HOLSTER AN' REACHED FOR MY HARQUEBUS....
WHOOSH! WHOOTS! I CLEART THE PLACE LIKE I WAS SCUTTLIN' A OYSTER! AN' IN THEM DAYS I WAS A PERFECK THIRTY-SIX!
ALORS! WHAT WERE THESE MEASUREMENT.?
© 1956 WALT KELLY
THIRTY-SIX, THIRTY-SIX, AN' THIRTY-SIX.
FORMEE-DOUBLE PARFAIT!

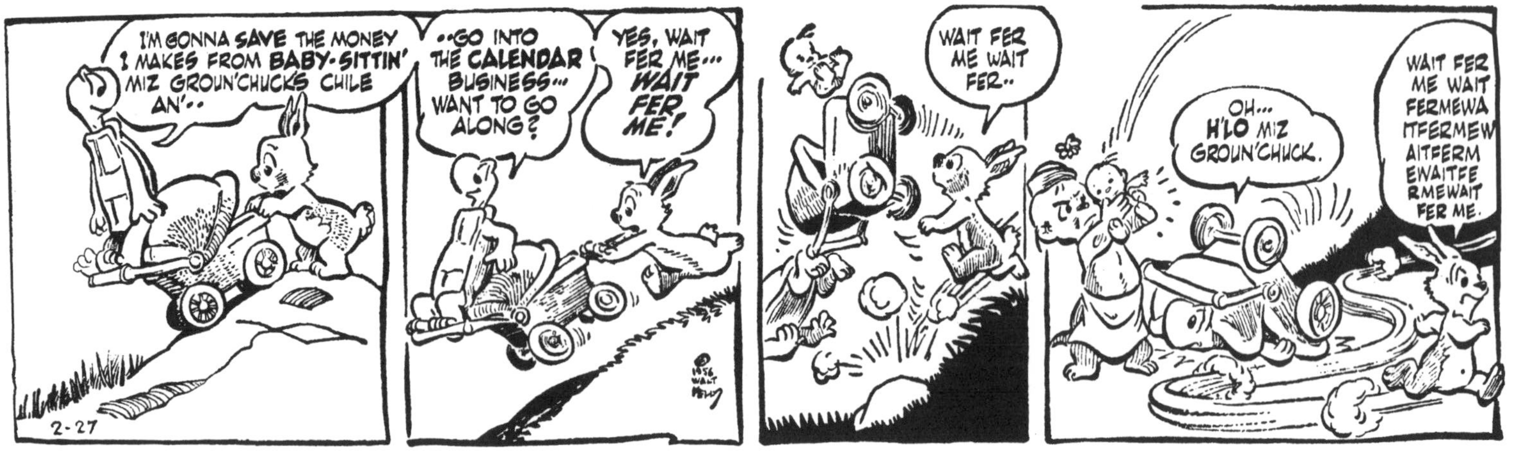
I'M GONNA SAVE THE MONEY I MAKES FROM BABY-SITTIN' MIZ GROUN'CHUCKS CHILE AN'..
..GO INTO THE CALENDAR BUSINESS... WANT TO GO ALONG?
YES, WAIT FER ME... WAIT FER ME!
WAIT FER ME WAIT FER..
OH... H'LO MIZ GROUN'CHUCK.
WAIT FER ME WAIT FERMEWA ITFERMEW AITFERM EWAITFE RMEWAIT FER ME.
2-27
© 1956 WALT KELLY

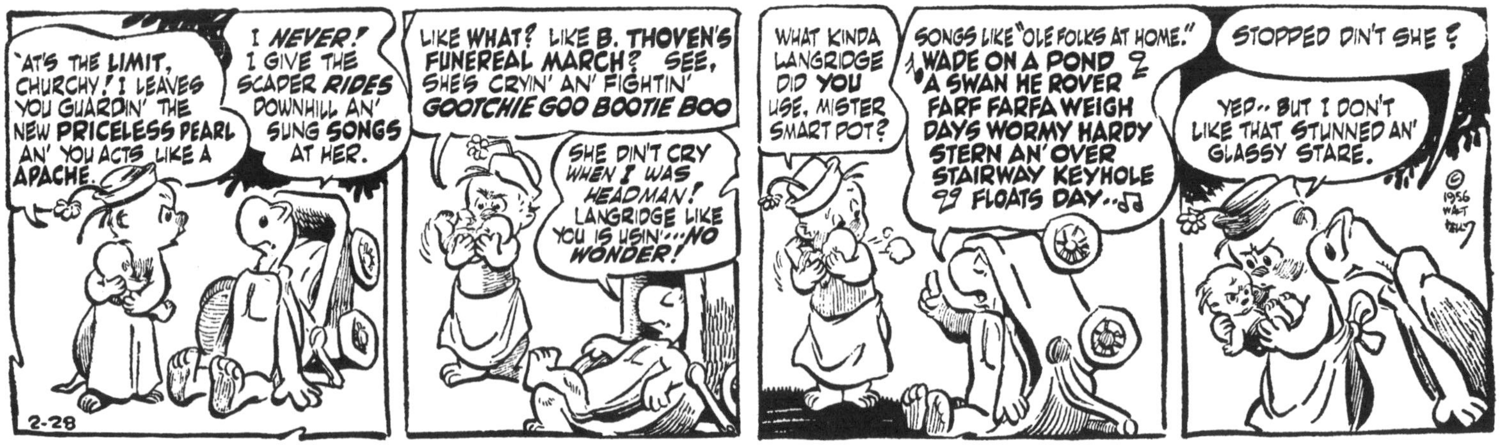
'AT'S THE LIMIT, CHURCHY! I LEAVES YOU GUARDIN' THE NEW PRICELESS PEARL AN' YOU ACTS LIKE A APACHE.
I NEVER! I GIVE THE SCAPER RIDES DOWNHILL AN' SUNG SONGS AT HER.
LIKE WHAT? LIKE B. THOVEN'S FUNEREAL MARCH? SEE, SHE'S CRYIN' AN' FIGHTIN' GOOTCHIE GOO BOOTIE BOO
SHE DIN'T CRY WHEN I WAS HEADMAN! LANGRIDGE LIKE YOU IS USIN'... NO WONDER!
WHAT KINDA LANGRIDGE DID YOU USE, MISTER SMART POT?
SONGS LIKE "OLE FOLKS AT HOME." WADE ON A POND A SWAN HE ROVER FARF FARFA WEIGH DAYS WORMY HARDY STERN AN' OVER STAIRWAY KEYHOLE FLOATS DAY..
STOPPED DIN'T SHE?
YEP.. BUT I DON'T LIKE THAT STUNNED AN' GLASSY STARE.
2-28
© 1956 WALT KELLY

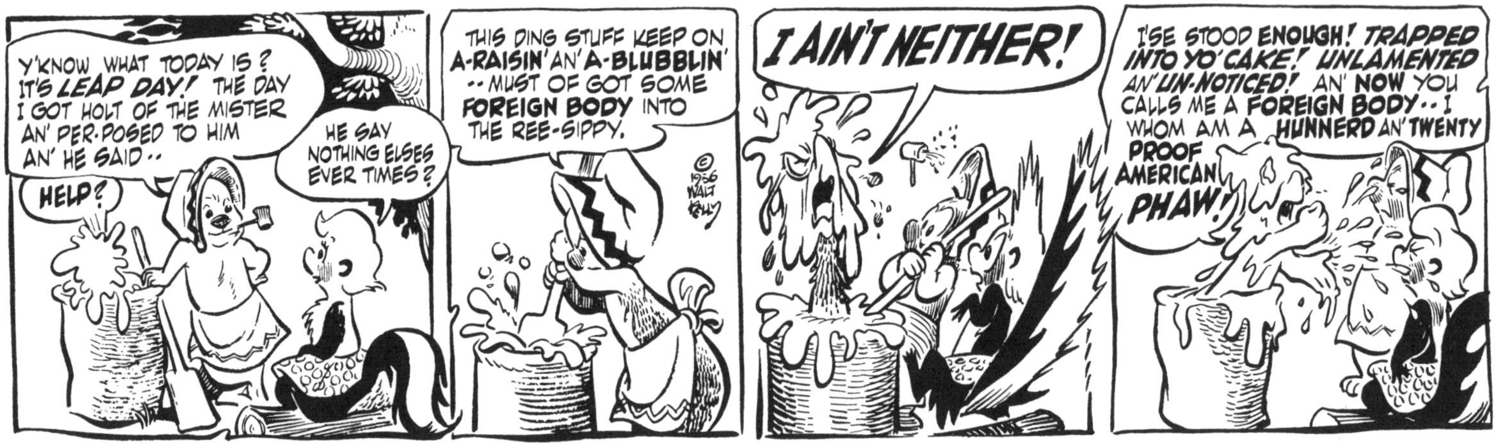
Y'KNOW WHAT TODAY IS? IT'S LEAP DAY! THE DAY I GOT HOLT OF THE MISTER AN' PER-POSED TO HIM AN' HE SAID..
HELP?
HE SAY NOTHING ELSES EVER TIMES?
THIS DING STUFF KEEP ON A-RAISIN' AN' A-BLUBBLIN' ..MUST OF GOT SOME FOREIGN BODY INTO THE REE-SIPPY.
© 1956 WALT KELLY
I AIN'T NEITHER!
I'SE STOOD ENOUGH! TRAPPED INTO YO' CAKE! UNLAMENTED AN' UN-NOTICED! AN' NOW YOU CALLS ME A FOREIGN BODY.. I WHOM AM A HUNNERD AN' TWENTY PROOF AMERICAN PHAW!

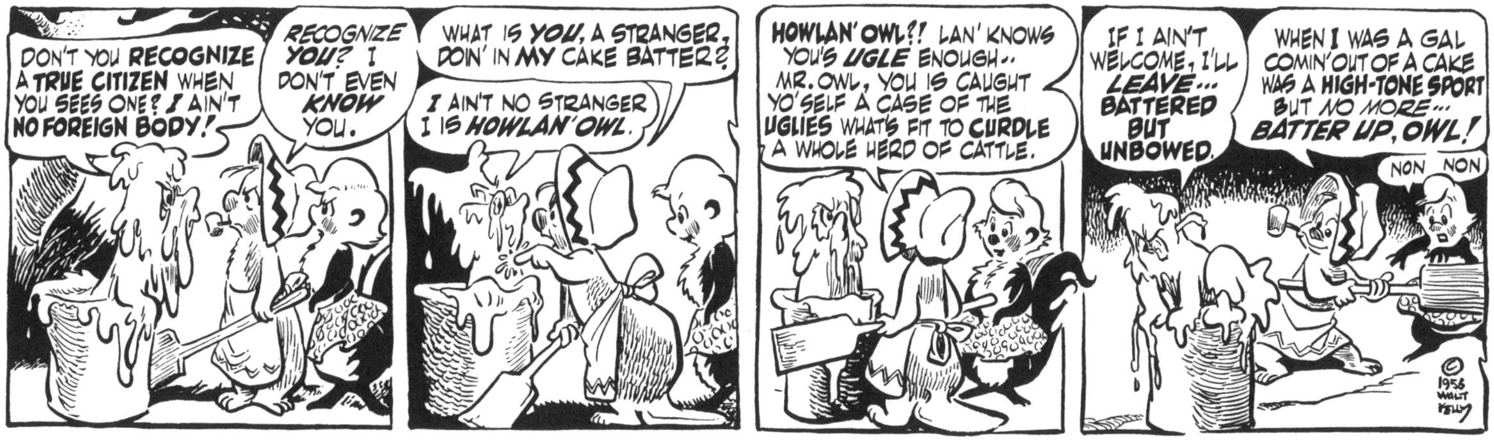
DON'T YOU RECOGNIZE A TRUE CITIZEN WHEN YOU SEES ONE? I AIN'T NO FOREIGN BODY!
RECOGNIZE YOU? I DON'T EVEN KNOW YOU.
WHAT IS YOU, A STRANGER, DOIN' IN MY CAKE BATTER?
I AIN'T NO STRANGER I IS HOWLAN' OWL.
HOWLAN' OWL?! LAN' KNOWS YOU'S UGLE ENOUGH.. MR. OWL, YOU IS CAUGHT YO'SELF A CASE OF THE UGLIES WHAT'S FIT TO CURDLE A WHOLE HERD OF CATTLE.
IF I AIN'T WELCOME, I'LL LEAVE... BATTERED BUT UNBOWED.
WHEN I WAS A GAL COMIN' OUT OF A CAKE WAS A HIGH-TONE SPORT BUT NO MORE... BATTER UP, OWL!
NON NON

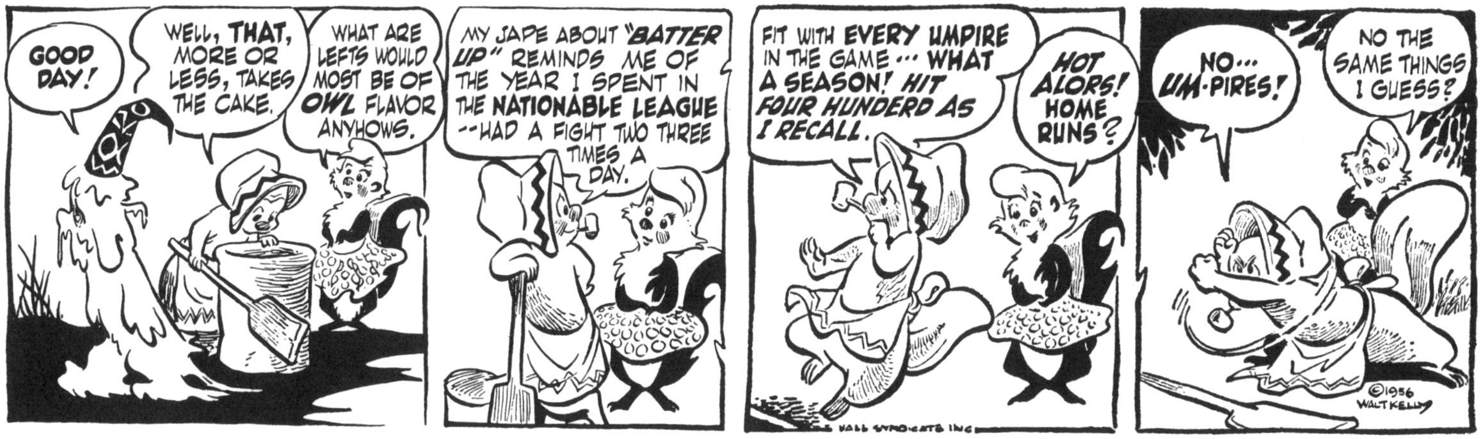
GOOD DAY!
WELL, THAT, MORE OR LESS, TAKES THE CAKE.
WHAT ARE LEFTS WOULD MOST BE OF OWL FLAVOR ANYHOWS.
MY JAPE ABOUT "BATTER UP" REMINDS ME OF THE YEAR I SPENT IN THE NATIONABLE LEAGUE --HAD A FIGHT TWO THREE TIMES A DAY.
FIT WITH EVERY UMPIRE IN THE GAME ... WHAT A SEASON! HIT FOUR HUNDERD AS I RECALL.
HOT ALORS! HOME RUNS?
NO... UM-PIRES!
NO THE SAME THINGS I GUESS?

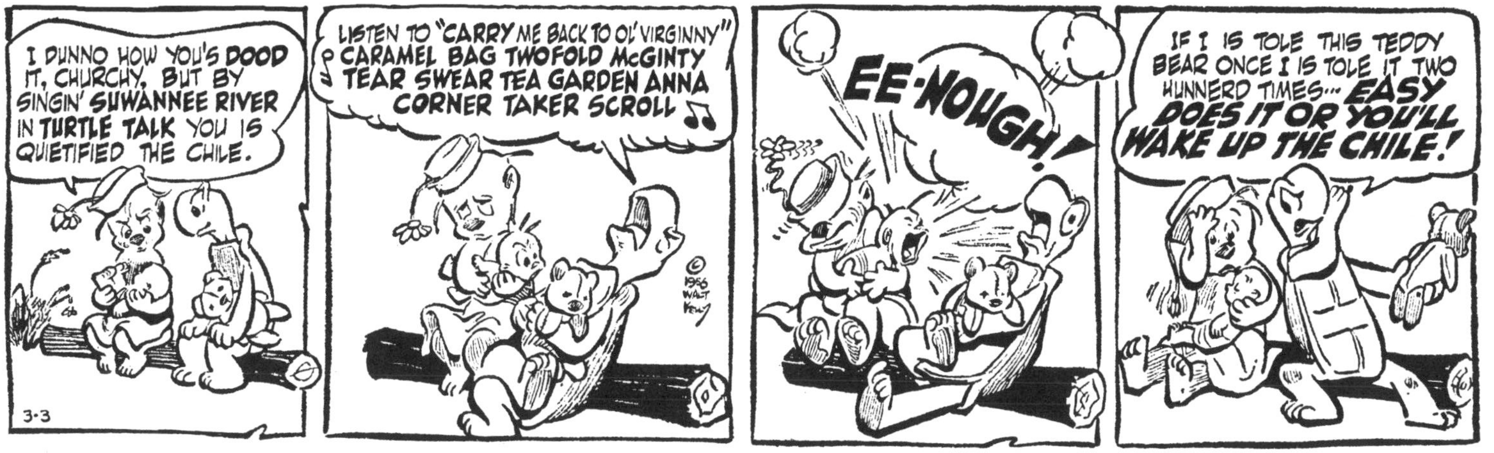
3-3
I DUNNO HOW YOU'S DOOD IT, CHURCHY, BUT BY SINGIN' SUWANNEE RIVER IN TURTLE TALK YOU IS QUIETIFIED THE CHILE.
LISTEN TO "CARRY ME BACK TO OL' VIRGINNY" CARAMEL BAG TWOFOLD McGINTY TEAR SWEAR TEA GARDEN ANNA CORNER TAKER SCROLL
EE-NOUGH!
IF I IS TOLE THIS TEDDY BEAR ONCE I IS TOLE IT TWO HUNNERD TIMES... EASY DOES IT OR YOU'LL WAKE UP THE CHILE!

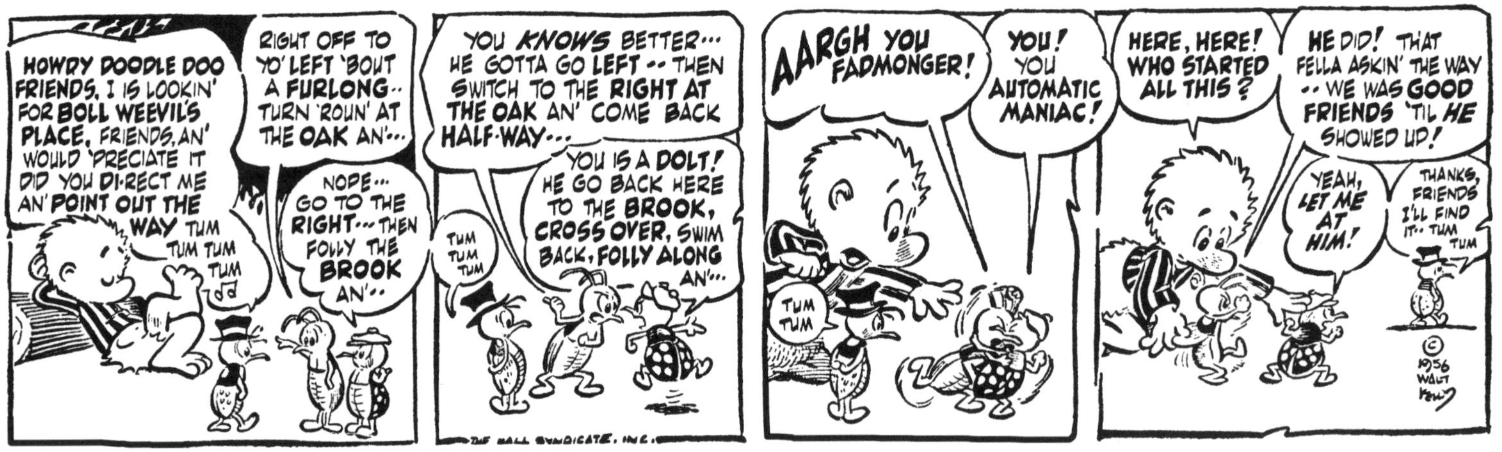
HOWDY DOODLE DOO FRIENDS. I IS LOOKIN' FOR BOLL WEEVIL'S PLACE. FRIENDS, AN' WOULD 'PRECIATE IT DID YOU DI-RECT ME AN' POINT OUT THE WAY TUM TUM TUM TUM
RIGHT OFF TO YO' LEFT 'BOUT A FURLONG.. TURN 'ROUN' AT THE OAK AN'...
NOPE... GO TO THE RIGHT... THEN FOLLY THE BROOK AN'..
YOU KNOWS BETTER... HE GOTTA GO LEFT -- THEN SWITCH TO THE RIGHT AT THE OAK AN' COME BACK HALF-WAY...
TUM TUM TUM
YOU IS A DOLT! HE GO BACK HERE TO THE BROOK, CROSS OVER, SWIM BACK, FOLLY ALONG AN'...
AARGH YOU FADMONGER!
YOU! YOU AUTOMATIC MANIAC!
TUM TUM
HERE, HERE! WHO STARTED ALL THIS?
HE DID! THAT FELLA ASKIN' THE WAY -- WE WAS GOOD FRIENDS 'TIL HE SHOWED UP!
YEAH, LET ME AT HIM!
THANKS, FRIENDS I'LL FIND IT.. TUM TUM
© 1956 WALT KELLY
THE HALL SYNDICATE, INC.

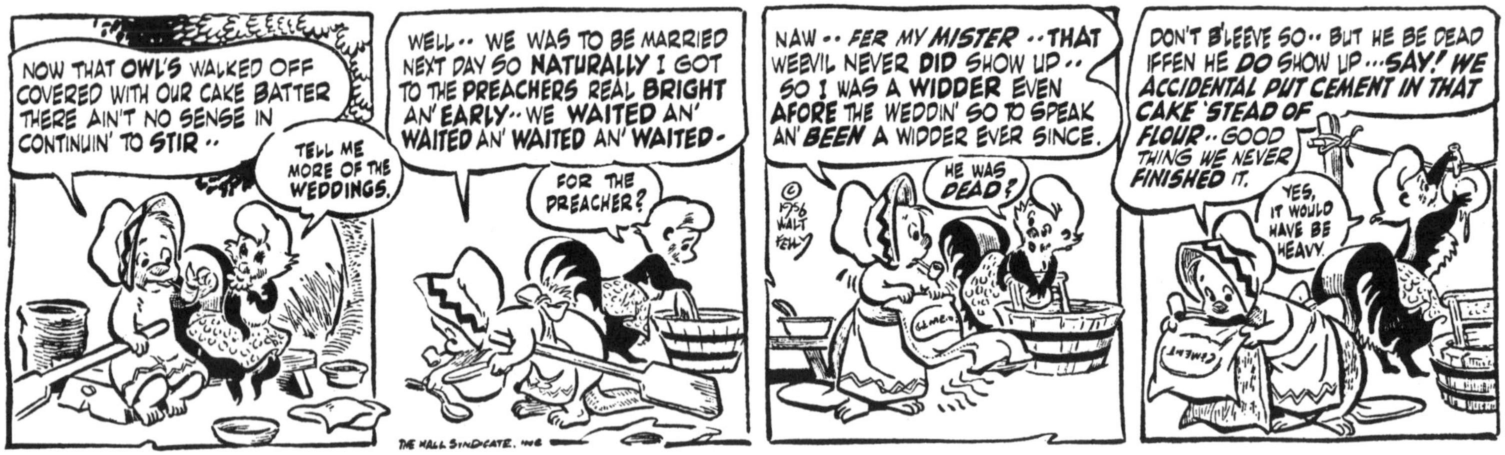
NOW THAT OWL'S WALKED OFF COVERED WITH OUR CAKE BATTER THERE AIN'T NO SENSE IN CONTINUIN' TO STIR..
TELL ME MORE OF THE WEDDINGS.
WELL.. WE WAS TO BE MARRIED NEXT DAY SO NATURALLY I GOT TO THE PREACHERS REAL BRIGHT AN' EARLY.. WE WAITED AN' WAITED AN' WAITED AN' WAITED-
FOR THE PREACHER?
NAW -- FER MY MISTER -- THAT WEEVIL NEVER DID SHOW UP.. SO I WAS A WIDDER EVEN AFORE THE WEDDIN' SO TO SPEAK AN' BEEN A WIDDER EVER SINCE.
HE WAS DEAD?
© 1956 WALT KELLY
DON'T B'LEEVE SO.. BUT HE BE DEAD IFFEN HE DO SHOW UP...SAY! WE ACCIDENTAL PUT CEMENT IN THAT CAKE 'STEAD OF FLOUR.. GOOD THING WE NEVER FINISHED IT.
YES, IT WOULD HAVE BE HEAVY.
CEMENT
THE HALL SYNDICATE, INC.

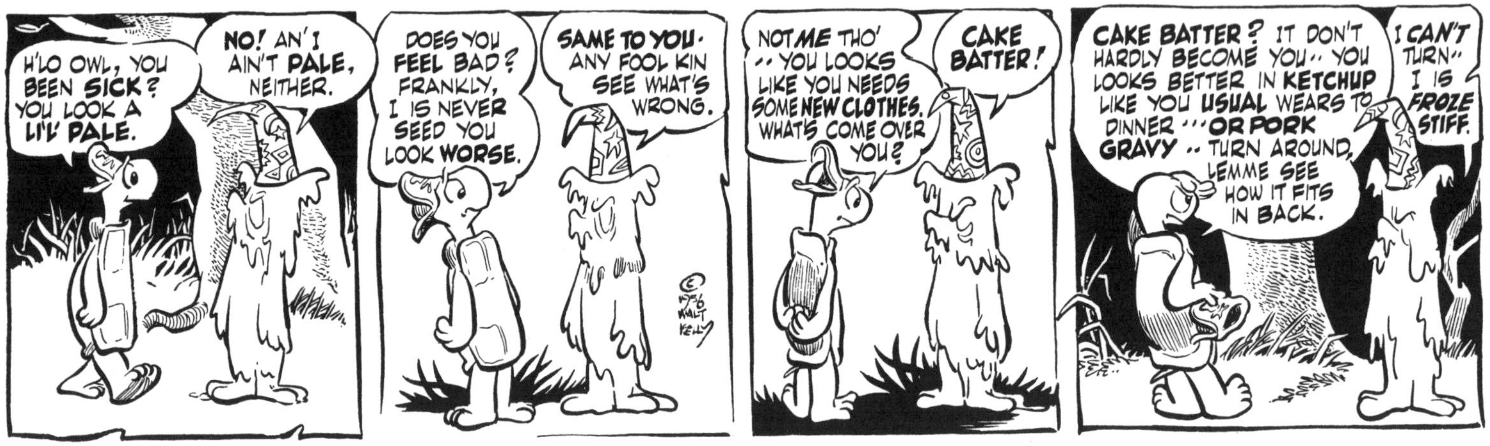
H'LO OWL, YOU BEEN SICK? YOU LOOK A LI'L PALE.
NO! AN' I AIN'T PALE, NEITHER.
DOES YOU FEEL BAD? FRANKLY, I IS NEVER SEED YOU LOOK WORSE.
SAME TO YOU. ANY FOOL KIN SEE WHAT'S WRONG.
© 1956 WALT KELLY
NOT ME THO' -- YOU LOOKS LIKE YOU NEEDS SOME NEW CLOTHES. WHAT'S COME OVER YOU?
CAKE BATTER!
CAKE BATTER? IT DON'T HARDLY BECOME YOU.. YOU LOOKS BETTER IN KETCHUP LIKE YOU USUAL WEARS TO DINNER ... OR PORK GRAVY .. TURN AROUND, LEMME SEE HOW IT FITS IN BACK.
I CAN'T TURN.. I IS FROZE STIFF.

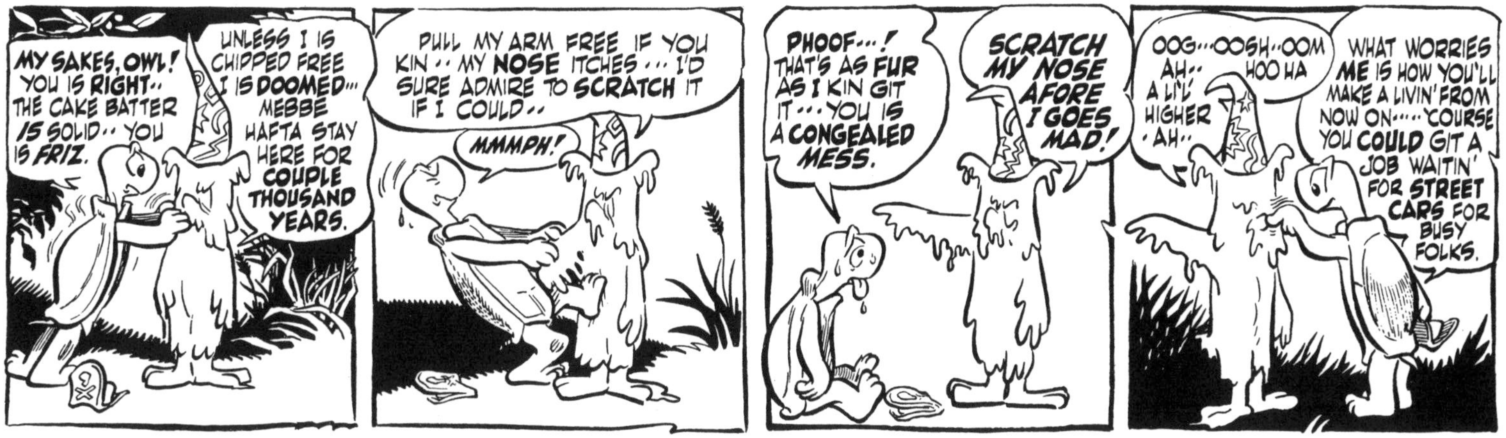
MY SAKES, OWL! YOU IS RIGHT.. THE CAKE BATTER IS SOLID.. YOU IS FRIZ.
UNLESS I IS CHIPPED FREE I IS DOOMED... MEBBE HAFTA STAY HERE FOR COUPLE THOUSAND YEARS.
PULL MY ARM FREE IF YOU KIN.. MY NOSE ITCHES... I'D SURE ADMIRE TO SCRATCH IT IF I COULD..
MMMPH!
PHOOF...! THAT'S AS FUR AS I KIN GIT IT... YOU IS A CONGEALED MESS.
SCRATCH MY NOSE AFORE I GOES MAD!
OOG...OOSH..OOM AH.. HOO HA A LI'L HIGHER .AH..
WHAT WORRIES ME IS HOW YOU'LL MAKE A LIVIN' FROM NOW ON.... 'COURSE YOU COULD GIT A JOB WAITIN' FOR STREET CARS FOR BUSY FOLKS.

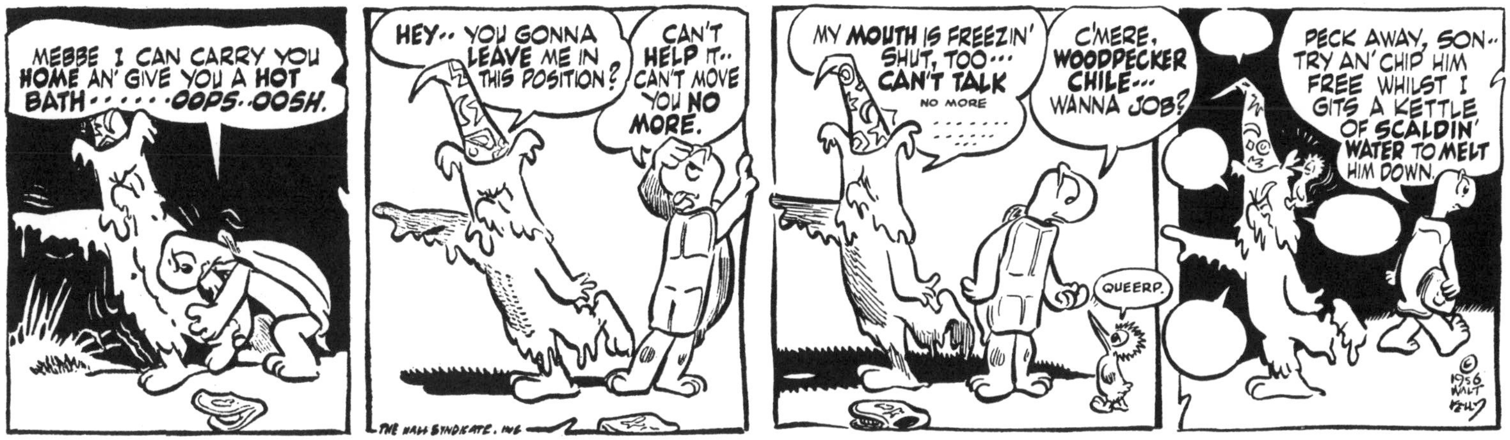
MEBBE I CAN CARRY YOU HOME AN' GIVE YOU A HOT BATH......OOPS..OOSH.
HEY.. YOU GONNA LEAVE ME IN THIS POSITION?
CAN'T HELP IT.. CAN'T MOVE YOU NO MORE.
THE HALL SYNDICATE, INC
MY MOUTH IS FREEZIN' SHUT, TOO... CAN'T TALK NO MORE
......
C'MERE, WOODPECKER CHILE... WANNA JOB?
QUEERP.
PECK AWAY, SON.. TRY AN' CHIP HIM FREE WHILST I GITS A KETTLE OF SCALDIN' WATER TO MELT HIM DOWN.
© 1956 WALT KELLY

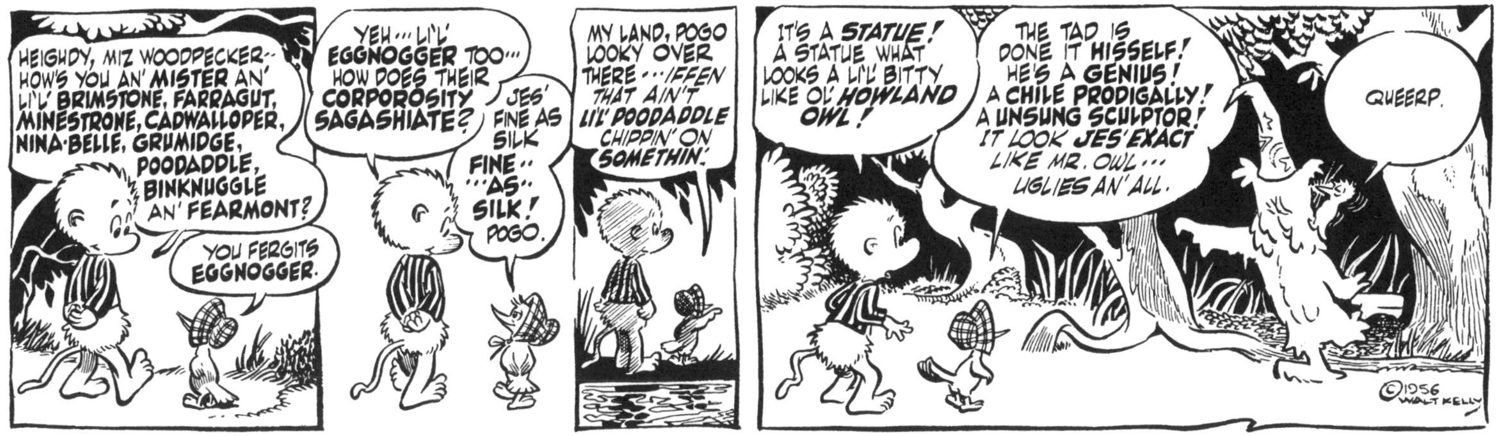
HEIGHDY, MIZ WOODPECKER.. HOW'S YOU AN' MISTER AN' LI'L' BRIMSTONE, FARRAGUT, MINESTRONE, CADWALLOPER, NINA-BELLE, GRUMIDGE, POODADDLE, BINKNUGGLE AN' FEARMONT?
YOU FERGITS EGGNOGGER.
YEH... LI'L' EGGNOGGER TOO... HOW DOES THEIR CORPOROSITY SAGASHIATE?
JES' FINE AS SILK FINE.. ..AS.. SILK! POGO.
MY LAND, POGO LOOKY OVER THERE... IFFEN THAT AIN'T LI'L' POODADDLE CHIPPIN' ON SOMETHIN'.
IT'S A STATUE! A STATUE WHAT LOOKS A LI'L BITTY LIKE OL' HOWLAND OWL!
THE TAD IS DONE IT HISSELF! HE'S A GENIUS! A CHILE PRODIGALLY! A UNSUNG SCULPTOR! IT LOOK JES' EXACT LIKE MR. OWL... UGLIES AN' ALL.
QUEERP.
©1956 WALT KELLY

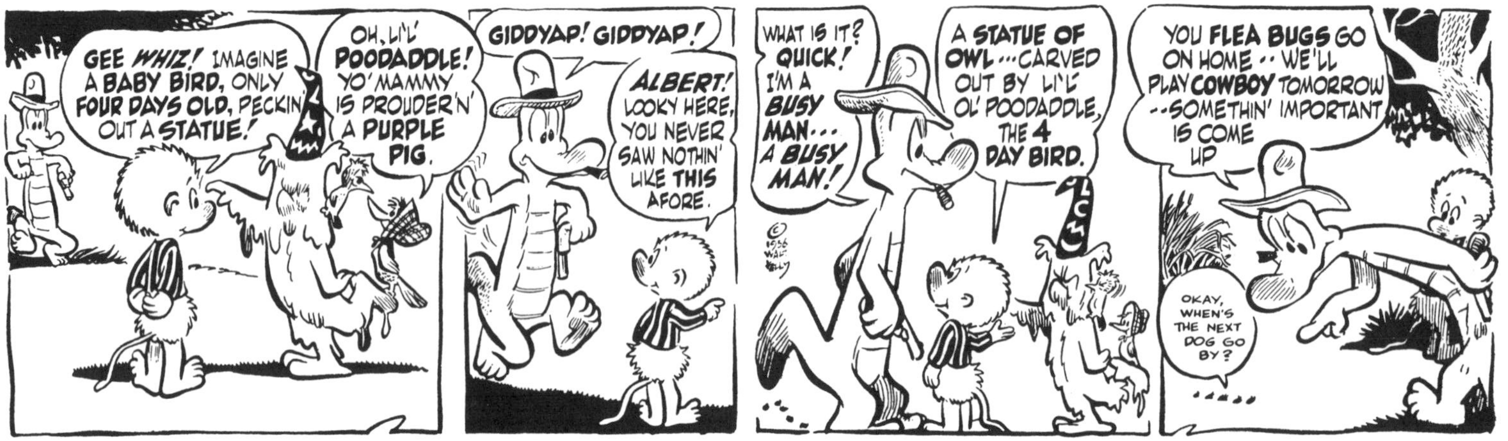
GEE WHIZ! IMAGINE A BABY BIRD, ONLY FOUR DAYS OLD, PECKIN' OUT A STATUE!
OH, LI'L' POODADDLE! YO' MAMMY IS PROUDER'N' A PURPLE PIG.
GIDDYAP! GIDDYAP!
ALBERT! LOOKY HERE, YOU NEVER SAW NOTHIN' LIKE THIS AFORE.
WHAT IS IT? QUICK! I'M A BUSY MAN... A BUSY MAN!
A STATUE OF OWL... CARVED OUT BY LI'L' OL' POODADDLE, THE 4 DAY BIRD.
YOU FLEA BUGS GO ON HOME.. WE'LL PLAY COWBOY TOMORROW --SOMETHIN' IMPORTANT IS COME UP
OKAY, WHEN'S THE NEXT DOG GO BY?

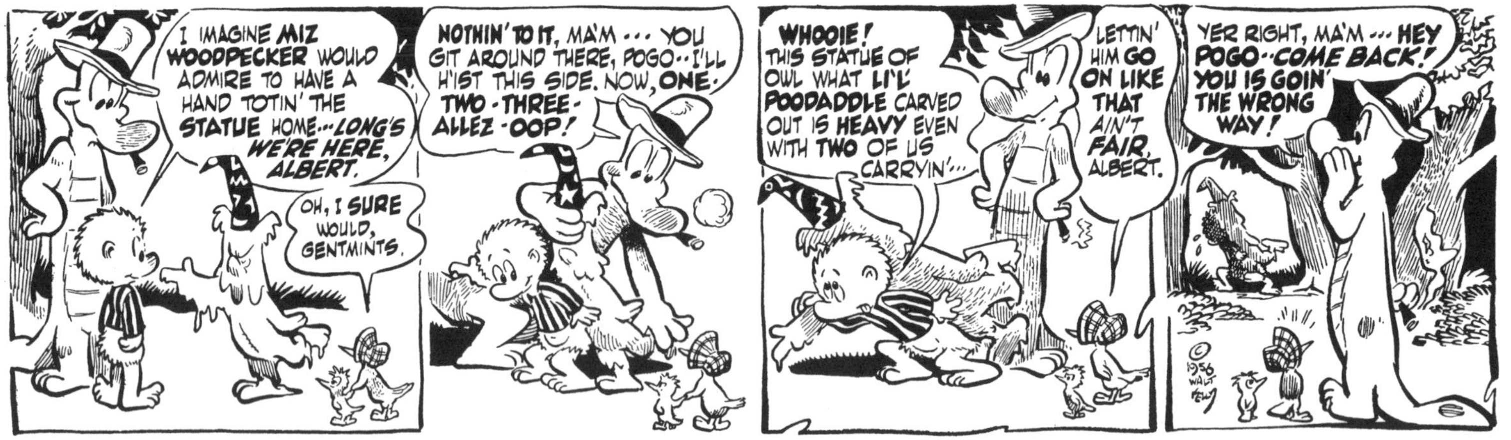
I IMAGINE MIZ WOODPECKER WOULD ADMIRE TO HAVE A HAND TOTIN' THE STATUE HOME... LONG'S WE'RE HERE, ALBERT.
OH, I SURE WOULD, GENTMINTS.
NOTHIN' TO IT, MA'M ... YOU GIT AROUND THERE, POGO.. I'LL H'IST THIS SIDE. NOW, ONE.
TWO - THREE - ALLEZ - OOP!
WHOOIE! THIS STATUE OF OWL WHAT LI'L POODADDLE CARVED OUT IS HEAVY EVEN WITH TWO OF US CARRYIN'...
LETTIN' HIM GO ON LIKE THAT AIN'T FAIR, ALBERT.
YER RIGHT, MA'M ... HEY POGO.. COME BACK! YOU IS GOIN' THE WRONG WAY!

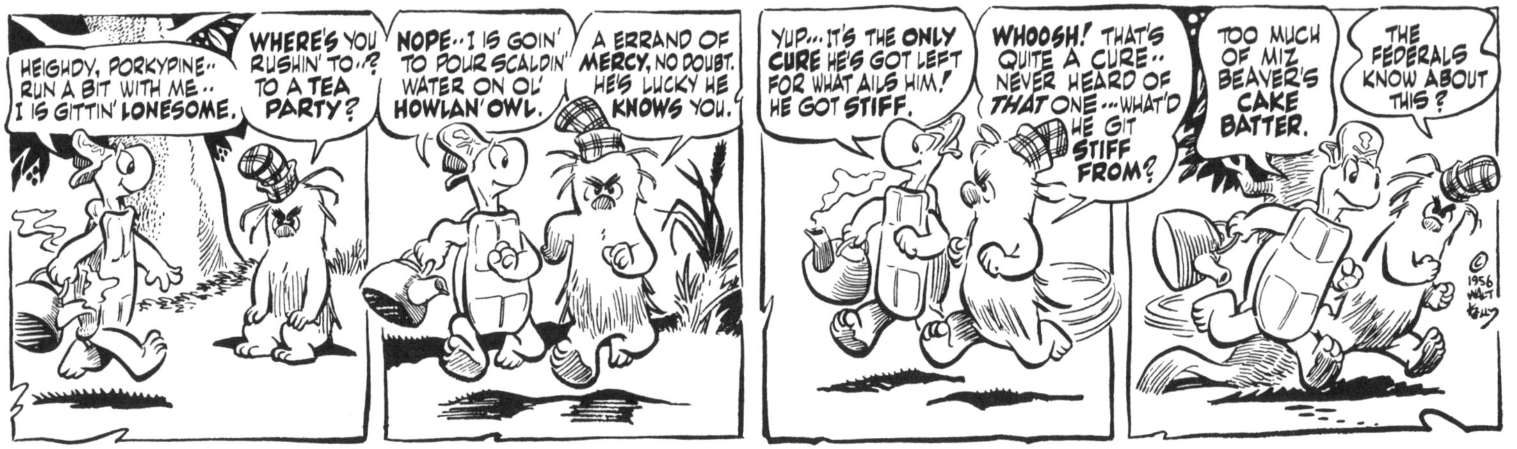
HEIGHDY, PORKYPINE.. RUN A BIT WITH ME.. I IS GITTIN' LONESOME.
WHERE'S YOU RUSHIN' TO..? TO A TEA PARTY?
NOPE.. I IS GOIN' TO POUR SCALDIN' WATER ON OL' HOWLAN' OWL.
A ERRAND OF MERCY, NO DOUBT. HE'S LUCKY HE KNOWS YOU.
YUP... IT'S THE ONLY CURE HE'S GOT LEFT FOR WHAT AILS HIM! HE GOT STIFF.
WHOOSH! THAT'S QUITE A CURE.. NEVER HEARD OF THAT ONE ... WHAT'D HE GIT STIFF FROM?
TOO MUCH OF MIZ BEAVER'S CAKE BATTER.
THE FEDERALS KNOW ABOUT THIS?

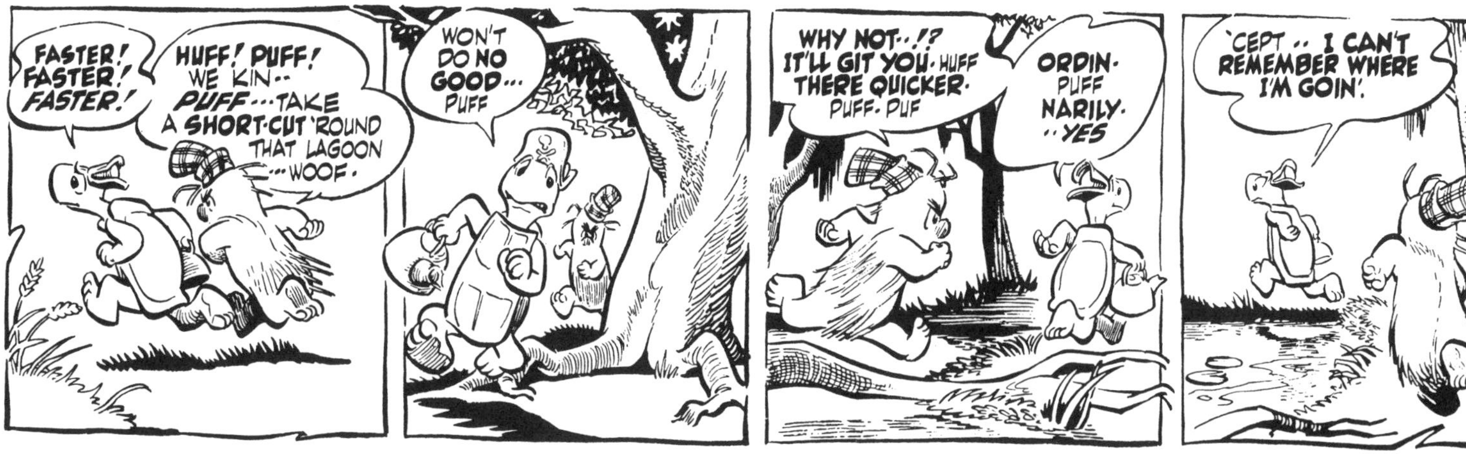
FASTER! FASTER! FASTER!
HUFF! PUFF! WE KIN.. PUFF...TAKE A SHORT-CUT 'ROUND THAT LAGOON ...WOOF.
WON'T DO NO GOOD... PUFF
WHY NOT..!? IT'LL GIT YOU. HUFF THERE QUICKER. PUFF. PUF
ORDIN. PUFF NARILY. ..YES
'CEPT .. I CAN'T REMEMBER WHERE I'M GOIN'.

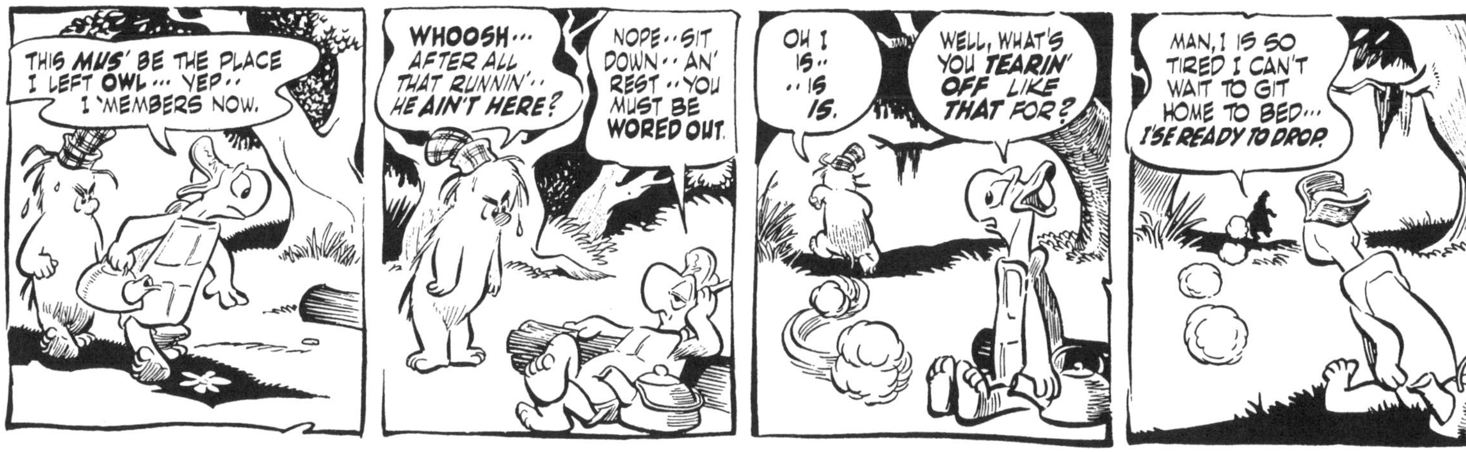
THIS MUS' BE THE PLACE I LEFT OWL ... YEP.. I 'MEMBERS NOW.
WHOOSH... AFTER ALL THAT RUNNIN'.. HE AIN'T HERE?
NOPE..SIT DOWN..AN' REST..YOU MUST BE WORED OUT.
OH I IS.. ..IS ..IS IS.
WELL, WHAT'S YOU TEARIN' OFF LIKE THAT FOR?
MAN, I IS SO TIRED I CAN'T WAIT TO GIT HOME TO BED... I'SE READY TO DROP.

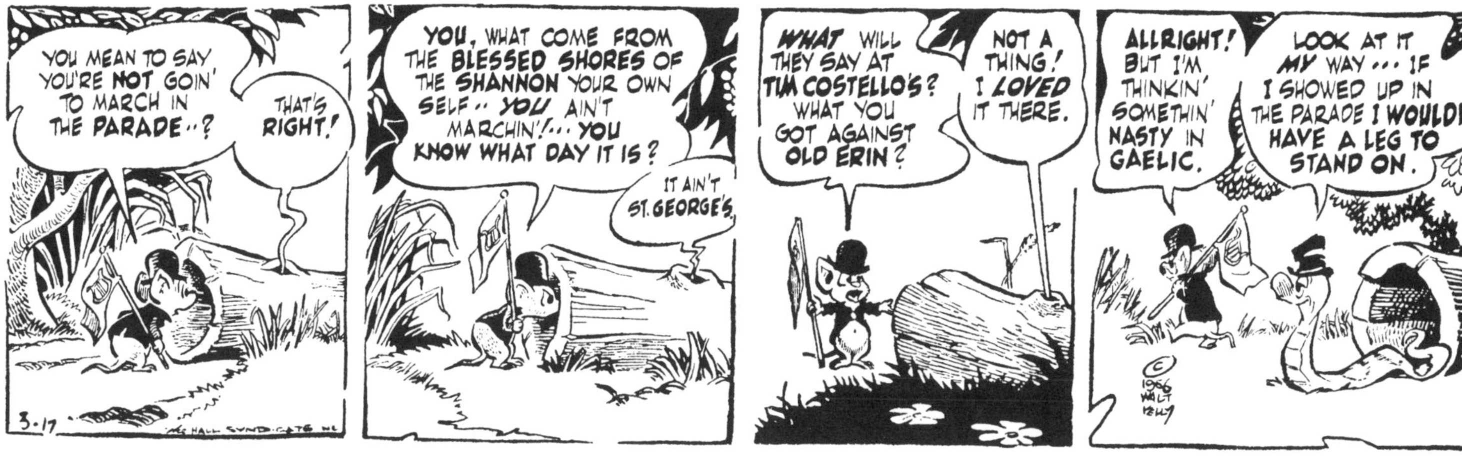
YOU MEAN TO SAY YOU'RE NOT GOIN' TO MARCH IN THE PARADE..?
THAT'S RIGHT!
YOU, WHAT COME FROM THE BLESSED SHORES OF THE SHANNON YOUR OWN SELF.. YOU AIN'T MARCHIN'!... YOU KNOW WHAT DAY IT IS?
IT AIN'T ST. GEORGE'S.
WHAT WILL THEY SAY AT TIM COSTELLO'S? WHAT YOU GOT AGAINST OLD ERIN?
NOT A THING! I LOVED IT THERE.
ALLRIGHT! BUT I'M THINKIN' SOMETHIN' NASTY IN GAELIC.
LOOK AT IT MY WAY... IF I SHOWED UP IN THE PARADE I WOULDN'T HAVE A LEG TO STAND ON.
3-17

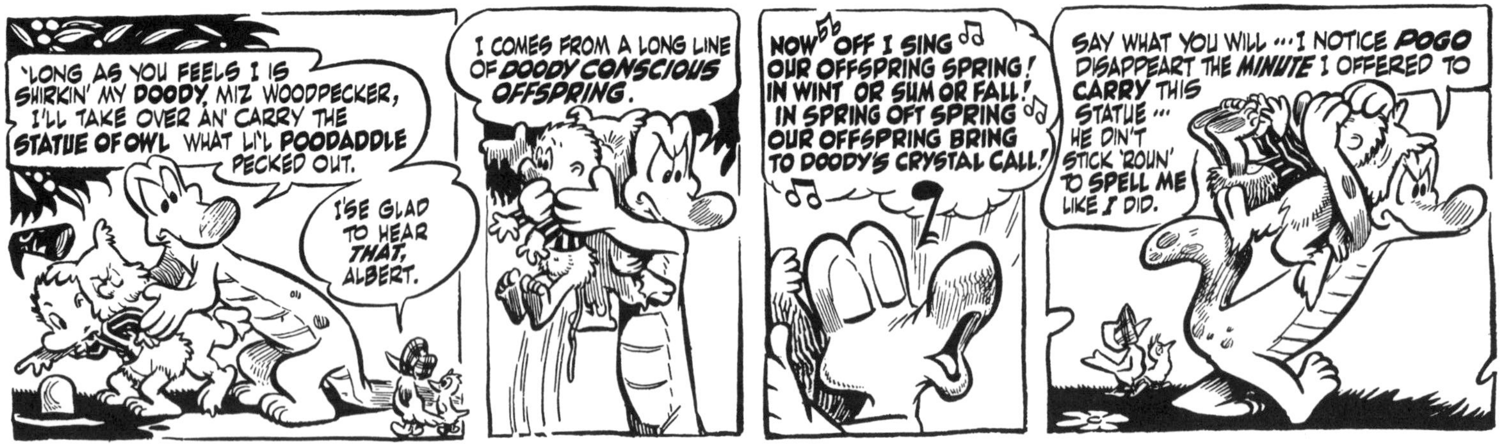
'LONG AS YOU FEELS I IS SHIRKIN' MY DOODY, MIZ WOODPECKER, I'LL TAKE OVER AN' CARRY THE STATUE OF OWL WHAT LI'L POODADDLE PECKED OUT.
I'SE GLAD TO HEAR THAT, ALBERT.
I COMES FROM A LONG LINE OF DOODY CONSCIOUS OFFSPRING.
NOW OFF I SING OUR OFFSPRING SPRING! IN WINT OR SUM OR FALL! IN SPRING OFT SPRING OUR OFFSPRING BRING TO DOODY'S CRYSTAL CALL!
SAY WHAT YOU WILL ... I NOTICE POGO DISAPPEART THE MINUTE I OFFERED TO CARRY THIS STATUE ... HE DIN'T STICK 'ROUN' TO SPELL ME LIKE I DID.

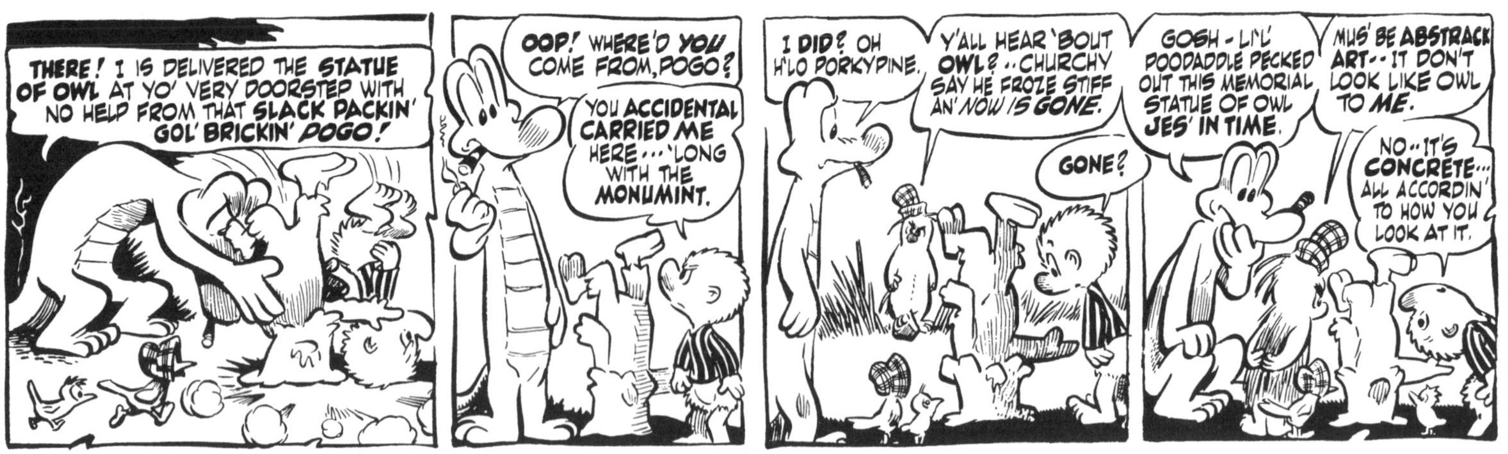
THERE! I IS DELIVERED THE STATUE OF OWL AT YO' VERY DOORSTEP WITH NO HELP FROM THAT SLACK PACKIN' GOL' BRICKIN' POGO!
OOP! WHERE'D YOU COME FROM, POGO?
YOU ACCIDENTAL CARRIED ME HERE ... 'LONG WITH THE MONUMINT.
I DID? OH H'LO PORKYPINE.
Y'ALL HEAR 'BOUT OWL? .. CHURCHY SAY HE FROZE STIFF AN' NOW IS GONE.
GONE?
GOSH - LI'L POODADDLE PECKED OUT THIS MEMORIAL STATUE OF OWL JES' IN TIME.
MUS' BE ABSTRACK ART -- IT DON'T LOOK LIKE OWL TO ME.
NO .. IT'S CONCRETE ... ALL ACCORDIN' TO HOW YOU LOOK AT IT.

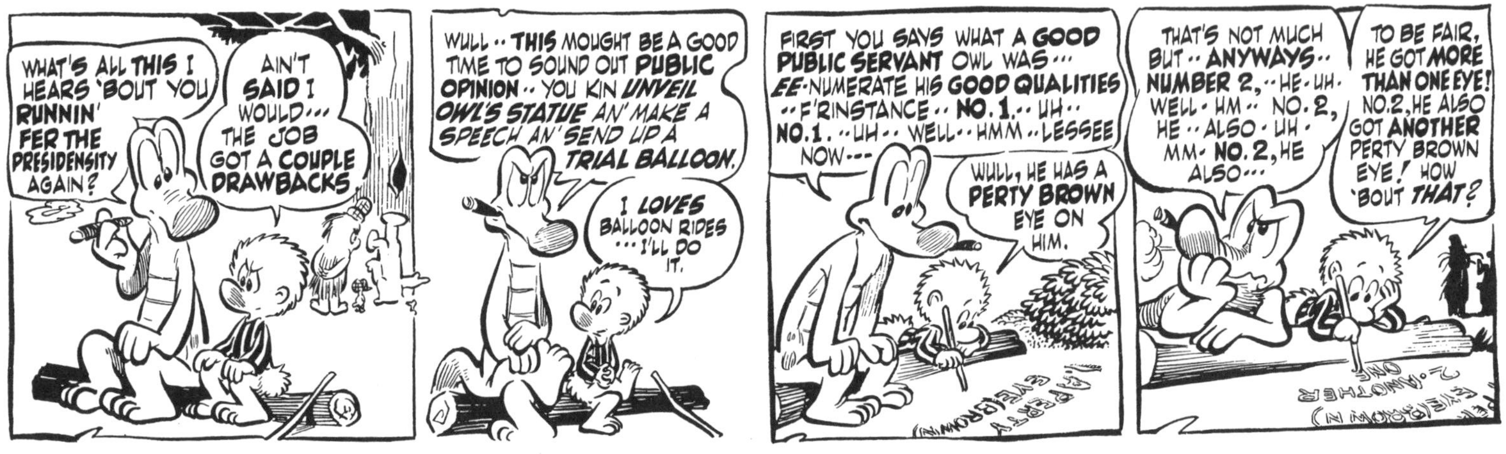
WHAT'S ALL THIS I HEARS 'BOUT YOU RUNNIN' FER THE PRESIDENSITY AGAIN?
AIN'T SAID I WOULD ... THE JOB GOT A COUPLE DRAWBACKS.
WULL .. THIS MOUGHT BE A GOOD TIME TO SOUND OUT PUBLIC OPINION .. YOU KIN UNVEIL OWL'S STATUE AN' MAKE A SPEECH AN' SEND UP A TRIAL BALLOON.
I LOVES BALLOON RIDES ... I'LL DO IT.
FIRST YOU SAYS WHAT A GOOD PUBLIC SERVANT OWL WAS ... EE-NUMERATE HIS GOOD QUALITIES .. F'RINSTANCE .. NO. 1 .. UH .. NO. 1. .. UH .. WELL .. HMM .. LESSEE NOW ...
WULL, HE HAS A PERTY BROWN EYE ON HIM.
THAT'S NOT MUCH BUT .. ANYWAYS .. NUMBER 2, .. HE .. UH .. WELL .. HM .. NO. 2, HE .. ALSO .. UH .. MM .. NO. 2, HE ALSO ...
TO BE FAIR, HE GOT MORE THAN ONE EYE! NO. 2, HE ALSO GOT ANOTHER PERTY BROWN EYE! HOW 'BOUT THAT?

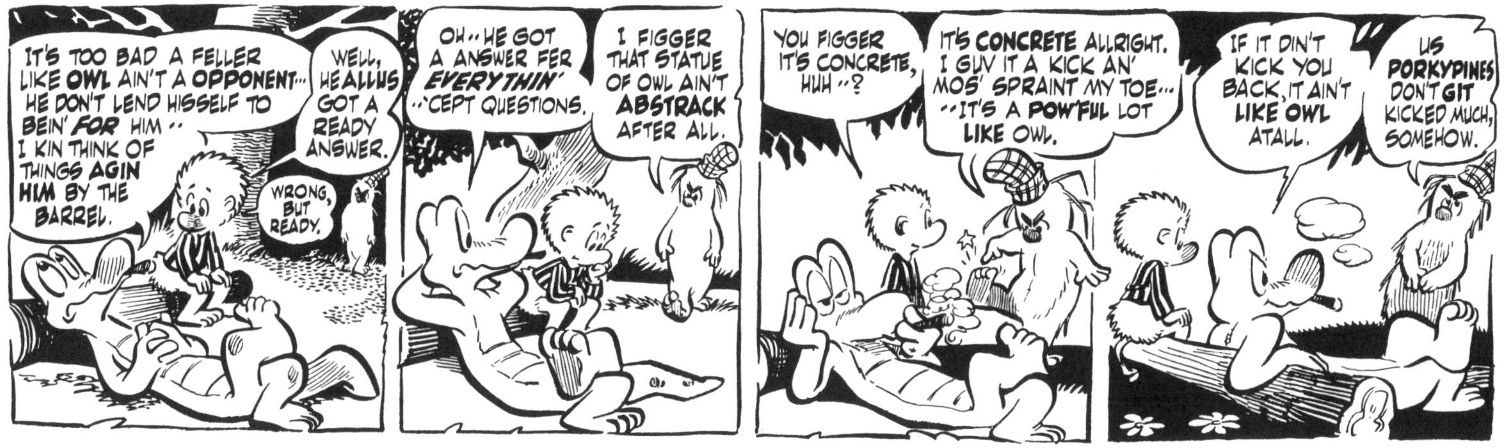
IT'S TOO BAD A FELLER LIKE OWL AIN'T A OPPONENT... HE DON'T LEND HISSELF TO BEIN' FOR HIM.. I KIN THINK OF THINGS AGIN HIM BY THE BARREL.
WELL, HE ALLUS GOT A READY ANSWER.
WRONG, BUT READY.
OH.. HE GOT A ANSWER FER EVERYTHIN' ..'CEPT QUESTIONS.
I FIGGER THAT STATUE OF OWL AIN'T ABSTRACK AFTER ALL.
YOU FIGGER IT'S CONCRETE, HUH..?
IT'S CONCRETE ALLRIGHT. I GUV IT A KICK AN' MOS' SPRAINT MY TOE... ..IT'S A POW'FUL LOT LIKE OWL.
IF IT DIN'T KICK YOU BACK, IT AIN'T LIKE OWL ATALL.
US PORKYPINES DON'T GIT KICKED MUCH, SOMEHOW.

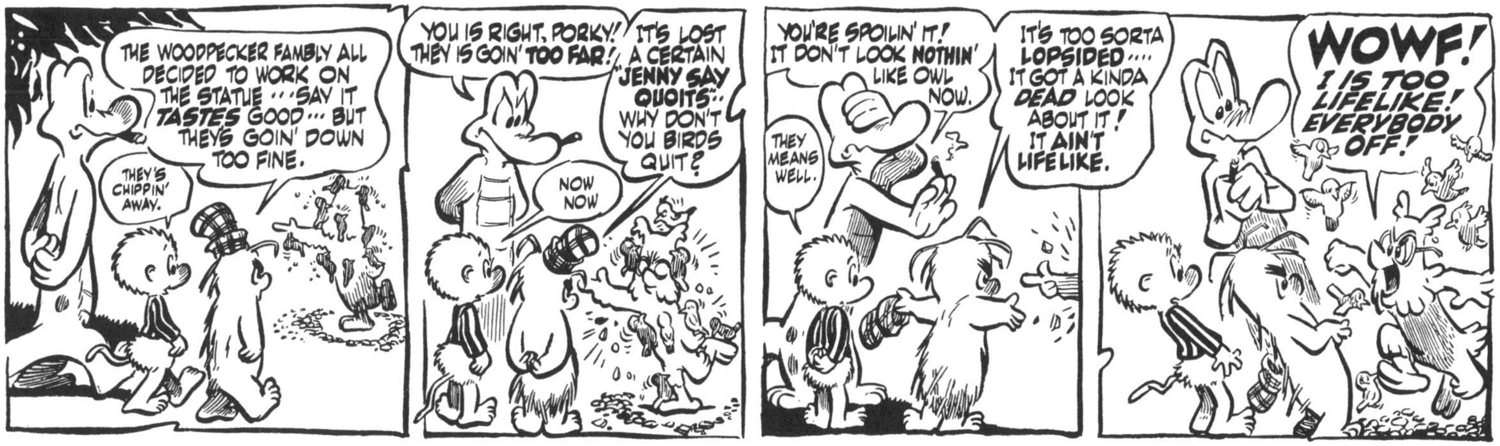
THE WOODPECKER FAMBLY ALL DECIDED TO WORK ON THE STATUE ...SAY IT TASTES GOOD... BUT THEY'S GOIN' DOWN TOO FINE.
THEY'S CHIPPIN' AWAY.
YOU IS RIGHT, PORKY! THEY IS GOIN' TOO FAR!
IT'S LOST A CERTAIN "JENNY SAY QUOITS".. WHY DON'T YOU BIRDS QUIT?
NOW NOW
YOU'RE SPOILIN' IT! IT DON'T LOOK NOTHIN' LIKE OWL NOW.
THEY MEANS WELL.
IT'S TOO SORTA LOPSIDED.... IT GOT A KINDA DEAD LOOK ABOUT IT! IT AIN'T LIFELIKE.
WOWF! I IS TOO LIFELIKE! EVERYBODY OFF!

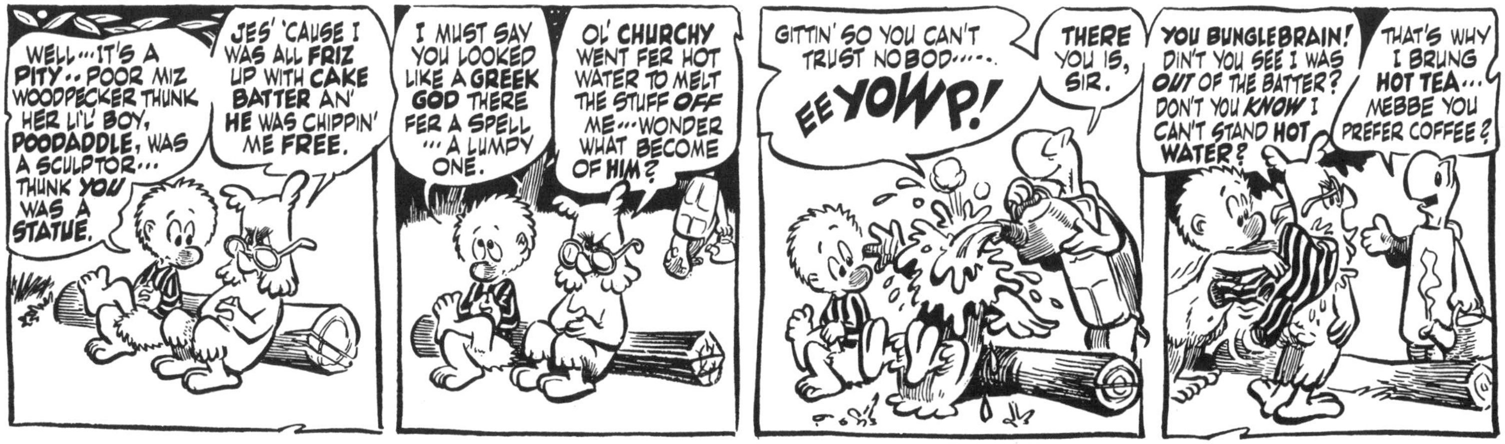
WELL...IT'S A PITY.. POOR MIZ WOODPECKER THUNK HER LI'L BOY, POODADDLE, WAS A SCULPTOR... THUNK YOU WAS A STATUE.
JES' 'CAUSE I WAS ALL FRIZ UP WITH CAKE BATTER AN' HE WAS CHIPPIN' ME FREE.
I MUST SAY YOU LOOKED LIKE A GREEK GOD THERE FER A SPELL ...A LUMPY ONE.
OL' CHURCHY WENT FER HOT WATER TO MELT THE STUFF OFF ME...WONDER WHAT BECOME OF HIM?
GITTIN' SO YOU CAN'T TRUST NOBOD.....
EEYOWP!
THERE YOU IS, SIR.
YOU BUNGLEBRAIN! DIN'T YOU SEE I WAS OUT OF THE BATTER? DON'T YOU KNOW I CAN'T STAND HOT WATER?
THAT'S WHY I BRUNG HOT TEA... MEBBE YOU PREFER COFFEE?

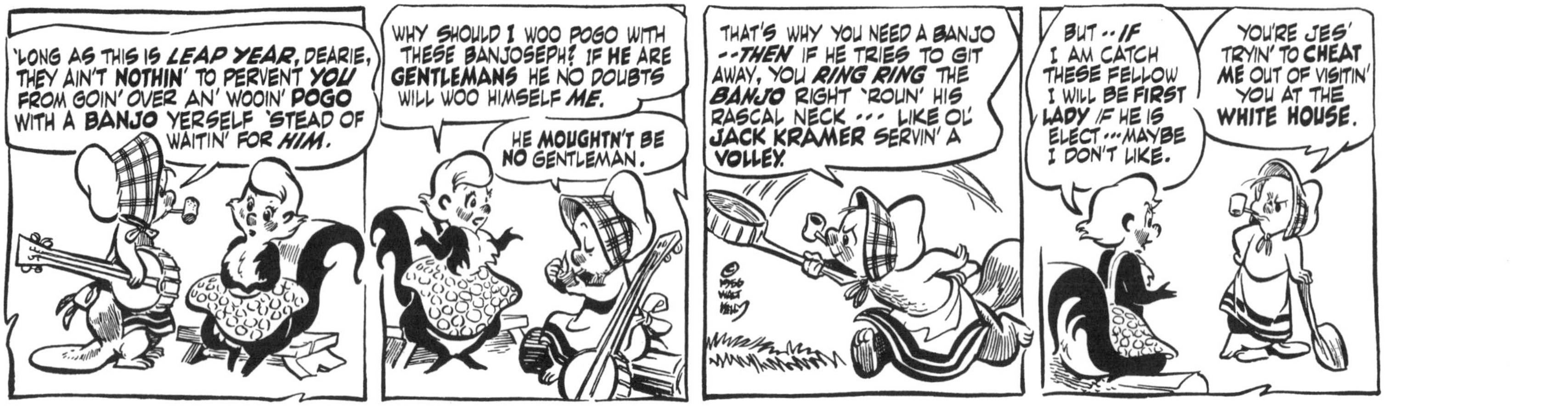
'LONG AS THIS IS LEAP YEAR, DEARIE, THEY AIN'T NOTHIN' TO PERVENT YOU FROM GOIN' OVER AN' WOOIN' POGO WITH A BANJO YERSELF 'STEAD OF WAITIN' FOR HIM.
WHY SHOULD I WOO POGO WITH THESE BANJOSEPH? IF HE ARE GENTLEMANS HE NO DOUBTS WILL WOO HIMSELF ME.
HE MOUGHTN'T BE NO GENTLEMAN.
THAT'S WHY YOU NEED A BANJO --THEN IF HE TRIES TO GIT AWAY, YOU RING RING THE BANJO RIGHT 'ROUN' HIS RASCAL NECK ... LIKE OL' JACK KRAMER SERVIN' A VOLLEY.
© 1956 WALT KELLY
BUT .. IF I AM CATCH THESE FELLOW I WILL BE FIRST LADY IF HE IS ELECT... MAYBE I DON'T LIKE.
YOU'RE JES' TRYIN' TO CHEAT ME OUT OF VISITIN' YOU AT THE WHITE HOUSE.

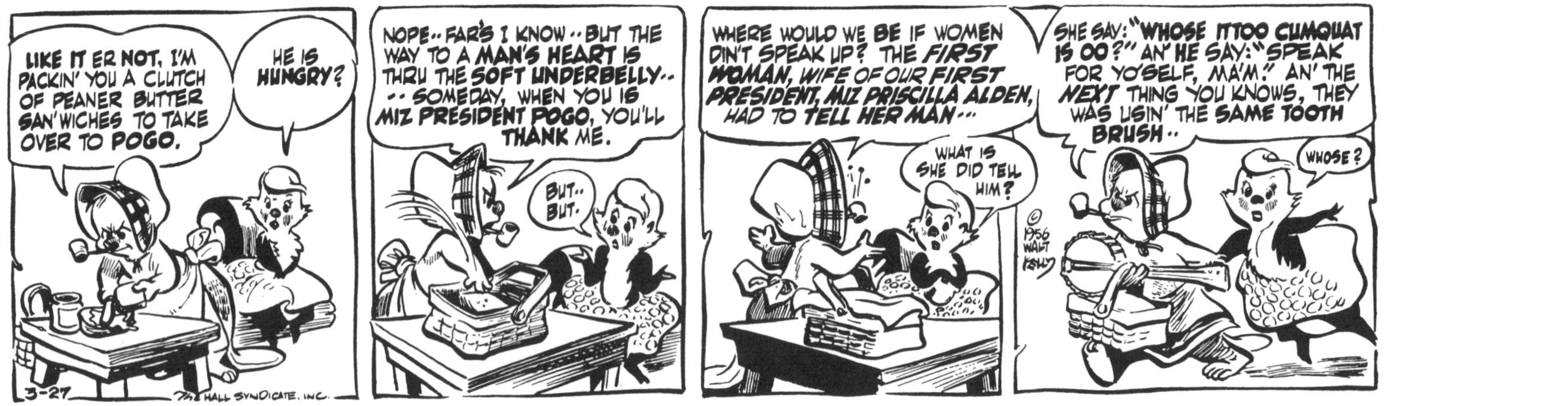
LIKE IT ER NOT, I'M PACKIN' YOU A CLUTCH OF PEANER BUTTER SAN'WICHES TO TAKE OVER TO POGO.
HE IS HUNGRY?
3-27
THE HALL SYNDICATE, INC.
NOPE.. FAR'S I KNOW.. BUT THE WAY TO A MAN'S HEART IS THRU THE SOFT UNDERBELLY.. .. SOMEDAY, WHEN YOU IS MIZ PRESIDENT POGO, YOU'LL THANK ME.
BUT.. BUT.
WHERE WOULD WE BE IF WOMEN DIN'T SPEAK UP? THE FIRST WOMAN, WIFE OF OUR FIRST PRESIDENT, MIZ PRISCILLA ALDEN, HAD TO TELL HER MAN...
WHAT IS SHE DID TELL HIM?
© 1956 WALT KELLY
SHE SAY: "WHOSE ITTOO CUMQUAT IS OO?" AN' HE SAY: "SPEAK FOR YO'SELF, MA'M." AN' THE NEXT THING YOU KNOWS, THEY WAS USIN' THE SAME TOOTH BRUSH..
WHOSE?

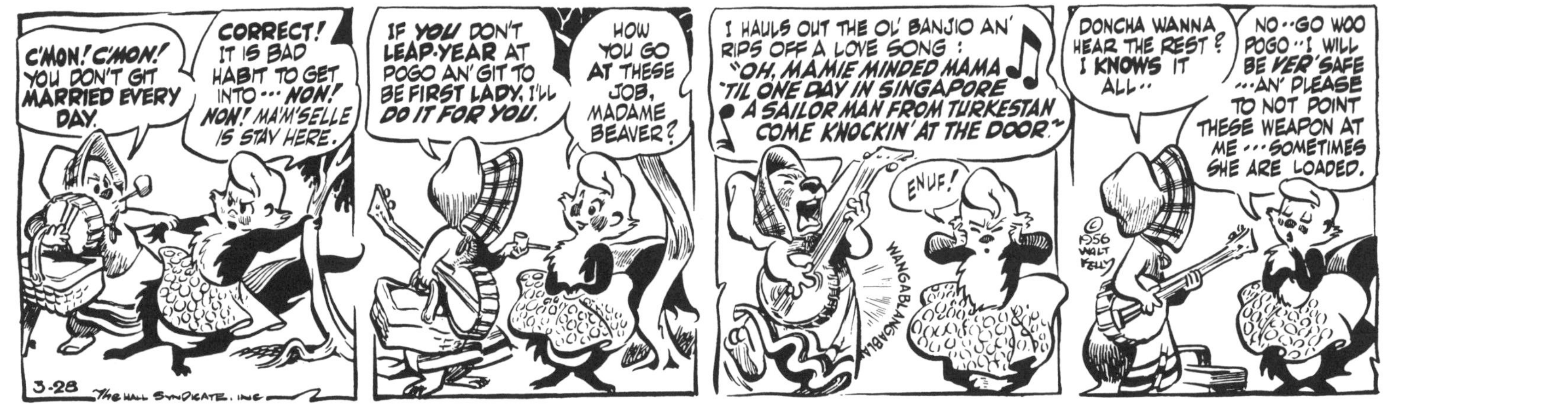
C'MON! C'MON! YOU DON'T GIT MARRIED EVERY DAY.
CORRECT! IT IS BAD HABIT TO GET INTO... NON! NON! MA'M'SELLE IS STAY HERE.
3-28
THE HALL SYNDICATE, INC.
IF YOU DON'T LEAP-YEAR AT POGO AN' GIT TO BE FIRST LADY, I'LL DO IT FOR YOU.
HOW YOU GO AT THESE JOB, MADAME BEAVER?
I HAULS OUT THE OL' BANJIO AN' RIPS OFF A LOVE SONG : "OH, MAMIE MINDED MAMA 'TIL ONE DAY IN SINGAPORE A SAILOR MAN FROM TURKESTAN COME KNOCKIN' AT THE DOOR"
ENUF!
WANGABLANGABLA
DONCHA WANNA HEAR THE REST? I KNOWS IT ALL..
NO.. GO WOO POGO.. I WILL BE VER' SAFE ...AN' PLEASE TO NOT POINT THESE WEAPON AT ME ... SOMETIMES SHE ARE LOADED.
© 1956 WALT KELLY

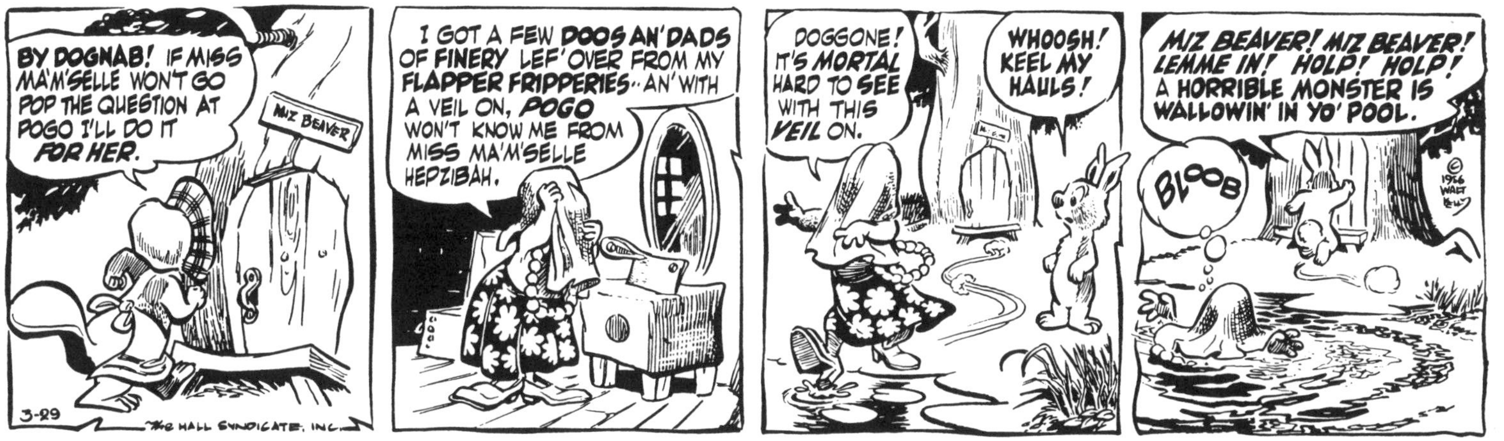
BY DOGNAB! IF MISS MA'M'SELLE WON'T GO POP THE QUESTION AT POGO I'LL DO IT FOR HER.
MIZ BEAVER
3-29
THE HALL SYNDICATE, INC.
I GOT A FEW DOOS AN' DADS OF FINERY LEF' OVER FROM MY FLAPPER FRIPPERIES.. AN' WITH A VEIL ON, POGO WON'T KNOW ME FROM MISS MA'M'SELLE HEPZIBAH.
DOGGONE! IT'S MORTAL HARD TO SEE WITH THIS VEIL ON.
WHOOSH! KEEL MY HAULS!
MIZ BEAVER! MIZ BEAVER! LEMME IN! HOLP! HOLP! A HORRIBLE MONSTER IS WALLOWIN' IN YO' POOL.
BLOOB
© 1956 WALT KELLY

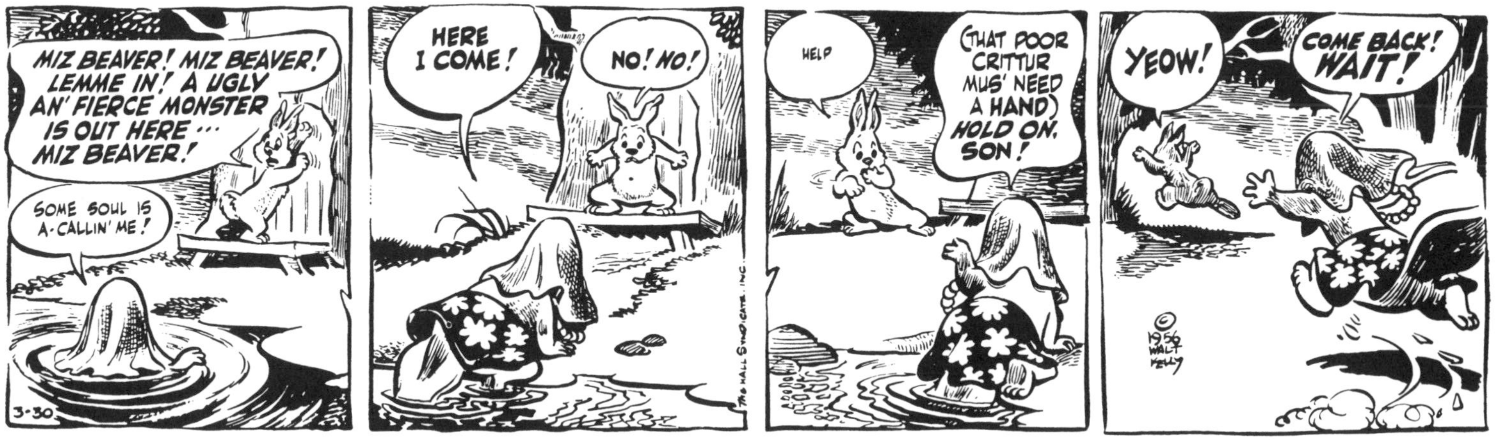
MIZ BEAVER! MIZ BEAVER! LEMME IN! A UGLY AN' FIERCE MONSTER IS OUT HERE... MIZ BEAVER!
SOME SOUL IS A-CALLIN' ME!
3-30
HERE I COME!
NO! NO!
HELP
(THAT POOR CRITTUR MUS' NEED A HAND) HOLD ON, SON!
YEOW!
COME BACK! WAIT!
© 1956 WALT KELLY

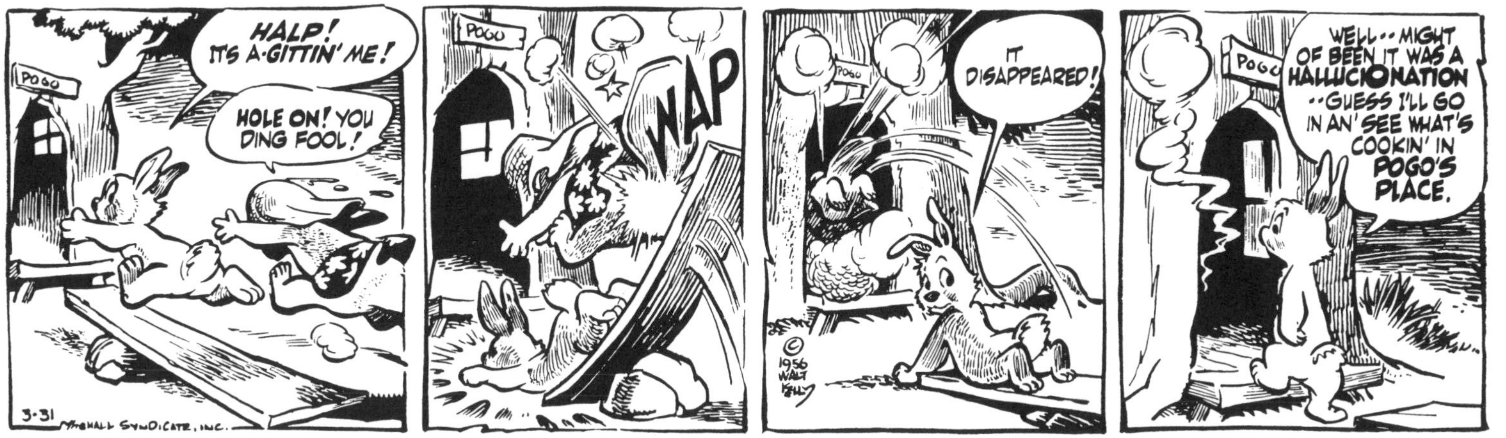
POGO
HALP! IT'S A-GITTIN' ME!
HOLE ON! YOU DING FOOL!
3-31
THE HALL SYNDICATE, INC.
POGO
WAP
POGO
IT DISAPPEARED!
© 1956 WALT KELLY
POGO
WELL.. MIGHT OF BEEN IT WAS A HALLUCIONATION ..GUESS I'LL GO IN AN' SEE WHAT'S COOKIN' IN POGO'S PLACE.

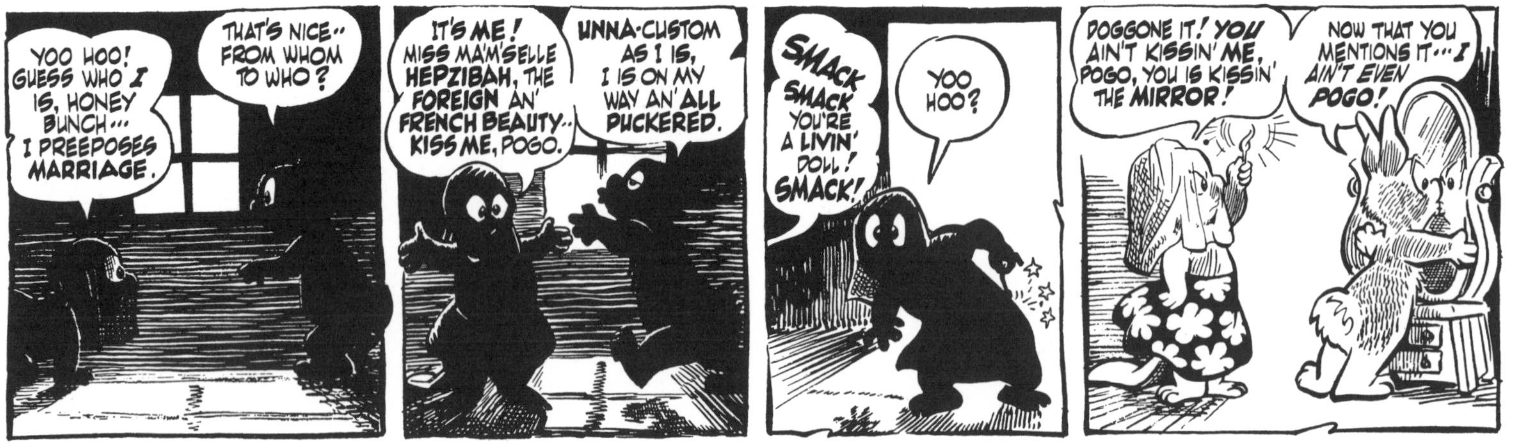
YOO HOO! GUESS WHO I IS, HONEY BUNCH... I PREEPOSES MARRIAGE.
THAT'S NICE.. FROM WHOM TO WHO?
IT'S ME! MISS MAM'SELLE HEPZIBAH, THE FOREIGN AN' FRENCH BEAUTY.. KISS ME, POGO.
UNNA-CUSTOM AS I IS, I IS ON MY WAY AN' ALL PUCKERED.
SMACK
SMACK YOU'RE A LIVIN' DOLL! SMACK!
YOO HOO?
DOGGONE IT! YOU AIN'T KISSIN' ME, POGO, YOU IS KISSIN' THE MIRROR!
NOW THAT YOU MENTIONS IT... I AIN'T EVEN POGO!

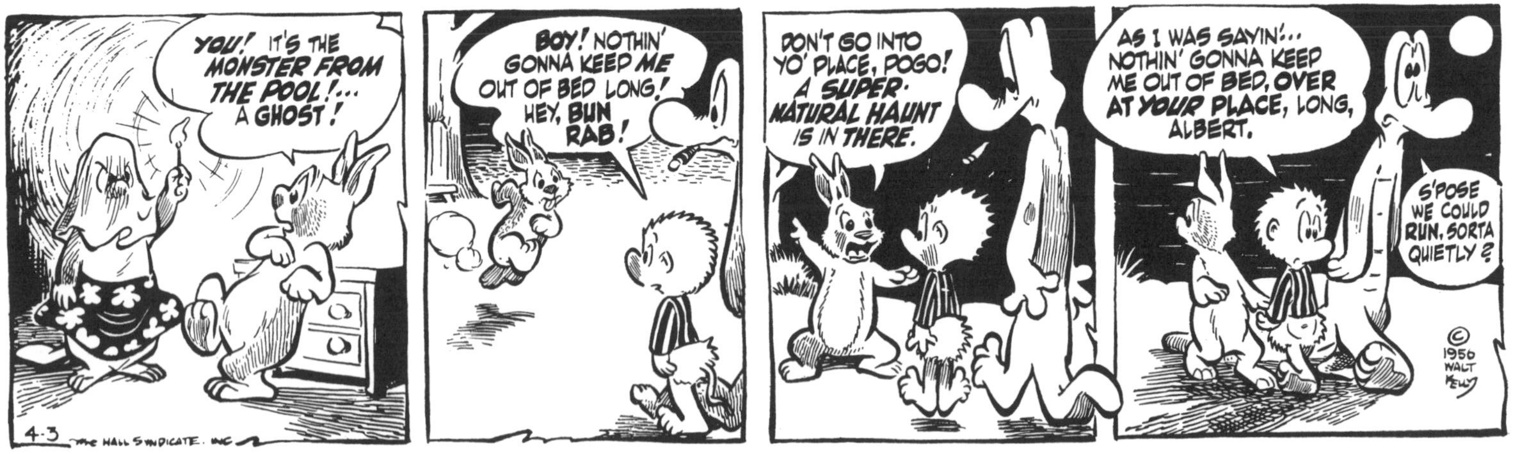
YOU! IT'S THE MONSTER FROM THE POOL!... A GHOST!
4-3 THE HALL SYNDICATE. INC.
BOY! NOTHIN' GONNA KEEP ME OUT OF BED LONG! HEY, BUN RAB!
DON'T GO INTO YO' PLACE, POGO! A SUPER-NATURAL HAUNT IS IN THERE.
AS I WAS SAYIN'... NOTHIN' GONNA KEEP ME OUT OF BED, OVER AT YOUR PLACE, LONG, ALBERT.
S'POSE WE COULD RUN, SORTA QUIETLY?
© 1956 WALT KELLY

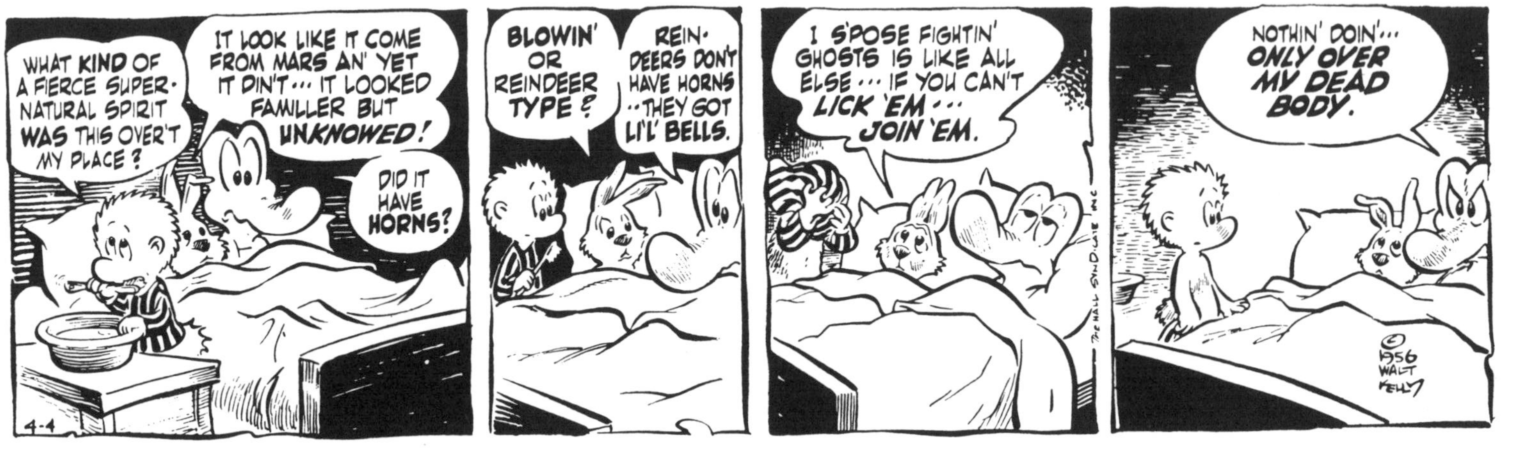
WHAT KIND OF A FIERCE SUPER-NATURAL SPIRIT WAS THIS OVER'T MY PLACE?
IT LOOK LIKE IT COME FROM MARS AN' YET IT DIN'T... IT LOOKED FAMILLER BUT UNKNOWED!
DID IT HAVE HORNS?
4-4
BLOWIN' OR REINDEER TYPE?
REIN-DEERS DON'T HAVE HORNS ..THEY GOT LI'L' BELLS.
I S'POSE FIGHTIN' GHOSTS IS LIKE ALL ELSE... IF YOU CAN'T LICK 'EM... JOIN 'EM.
THE HALL SYNDICATE INC
NOTHIN' DOIN'... ONLY OVER MY DEAD BODY.
© 1956 WALT KELLY

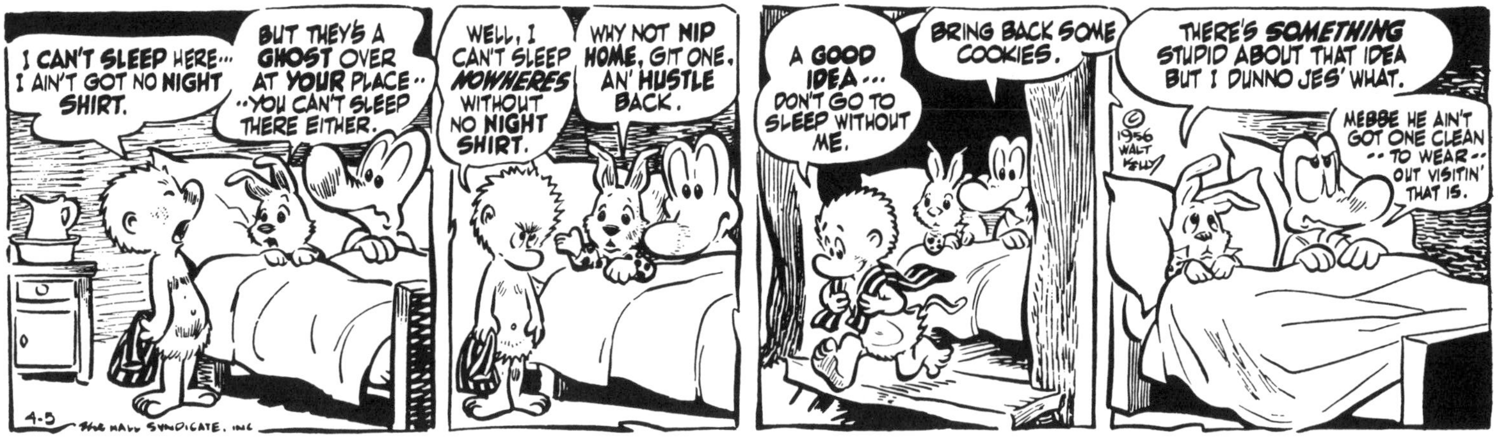
I CAN'T SLEEP HERE... I AIN'T GOT NO NIGHT SHIRT.
BUT THEY'S A GHOST OVER AT YOUR PLACE.. ..YOU CAN'T SLEEP THERE EITHER.
WELL, I CAN'T SLEEP NOWHERES WITHOUT NO NIGHT SHIRT.
WHY NOT NIP HOME, GIT ONE, AN' HUSTLE BACK.
A GOOD IDEA... DON'T GO TO SLEEP WITHOUT ME.
BRING BACK SOME COOKIES.
THERE'S SOMETHING STUPID ABOUT THAT IDEA BUT I DUNNO JES' WHAT.
© 1956 WALT KELLY
MEBBE HE AIN'T GOT ONE CLEAN -- TO WEAR -- OUT VISITIN' THAT IS.
4-5

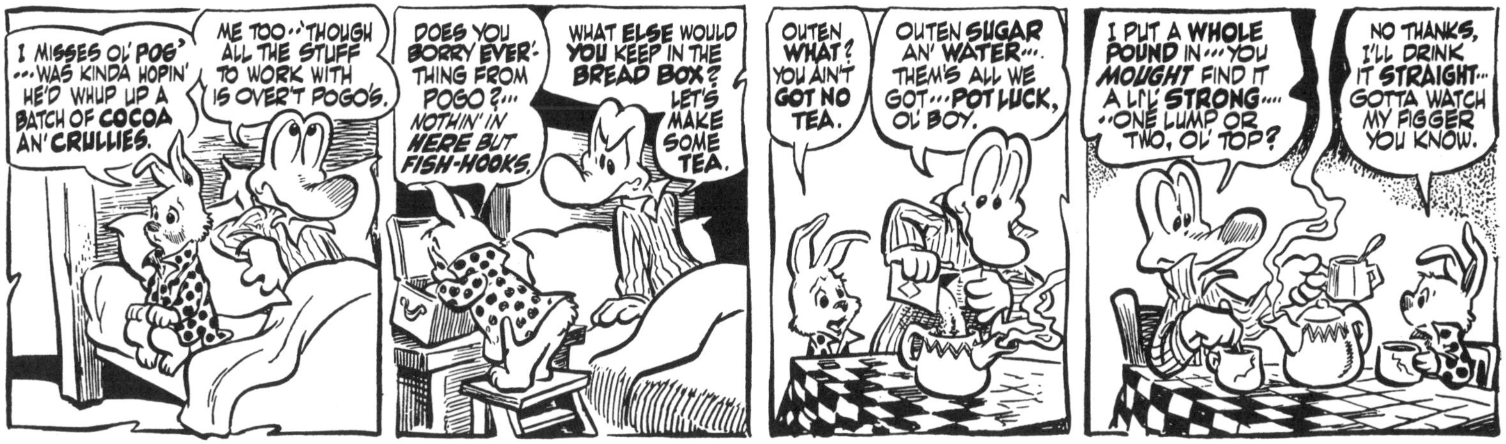
I MISSES OL' POG' --WAS KINDA HOPIN' HE'D WHUP UP A BATCH OF COCOA AN' CRULLIES.
ME TOO--'THOUGH ALL THE STUFF TO WORK WITH IS OVER'T POGO'S.
DOES YOU BORRY EVER'-THING FROM POGO?... NOTHIN' IN HERE BUT FISH-HOOKS.
WHAT ELSE WOULD YOU KEEP IN THE BREAD BOX? LET'S MAKE SOME TEA.
OUTEN WHAT? YOU AIN'T GOT NO TEA.
OUTEN SUGAR AN' WATER... THEM'S ALL WE GOT...POT LUCK, OL' BOY.
I PUT A WHOLE POUND IN...YOU MOUGHT FIND IT A LI'L STRONG.... --ONE LUMP OR TWO, OL' TOP?
NO THANKS, I'LL DRINK IT STRAIGHT... GOTTA WATCH MY FIGGER YOU KNOW.

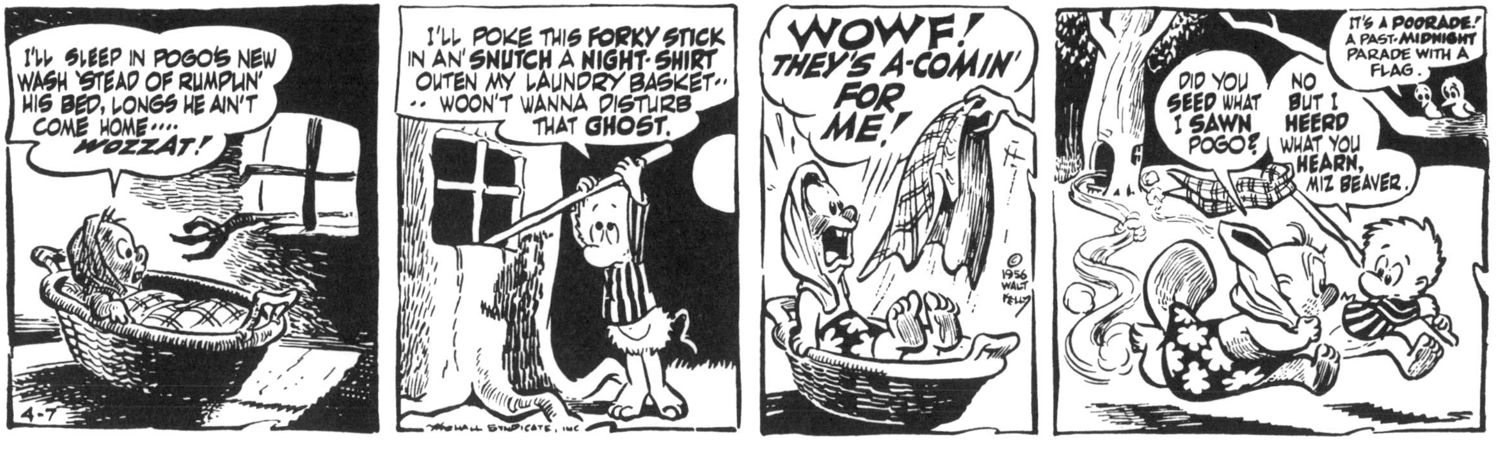
I'LL SLEEP IN POGO'S NEW WASH 'STEAD OF RUMPLIN' HIS BED, LONGS HE AIN'T COME HOME.... WOZZAT!
4-7
I'LL POKE THIS FORKY STICK IN AN' SNUTCH A NIGHT-SHIRT OUTEN MY LAUNDRY BASKET-- -- WOON'T WANNA DISTURB THAT GHOST.
WOWF! THEY'S A-COMIN' FOR ME!
© 1956 WALT KELLY
IT'S A POORADE! A PAST-MIDNIGHT PARADE WITH A FLAG.
DID YOU SEED WHAT I SAWN POGO?
NO BUT I HEERD WHAT YOU HEARN, MIZ BEAVER.

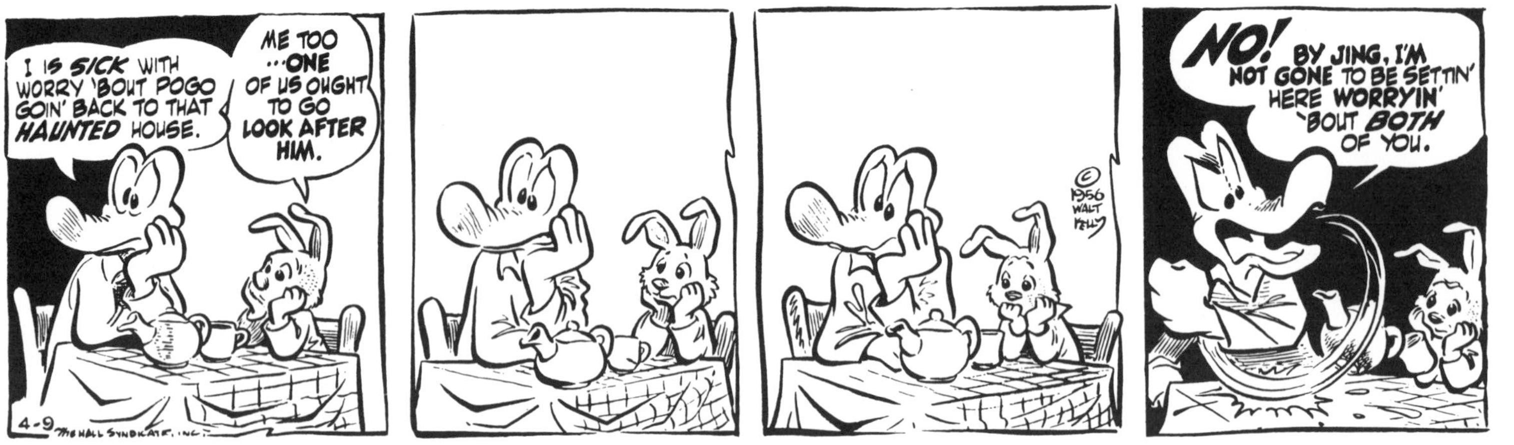
I IS SICK WITH WORRY 'BOUT POGO GOIN' BACK TO THAT HAUNTED HOUSE.
ME TOO ... ONE OF US OUGHT TO GO LOOK AFTER HIM.
© 1956 WALT KELLY
NO! BY JING, I'M NOT GONE TO BE SETTIN' HERE WORRYIN' 'BOUT BOTH OF YOU.
4-9 THE HALL SYNDICATE, INC.

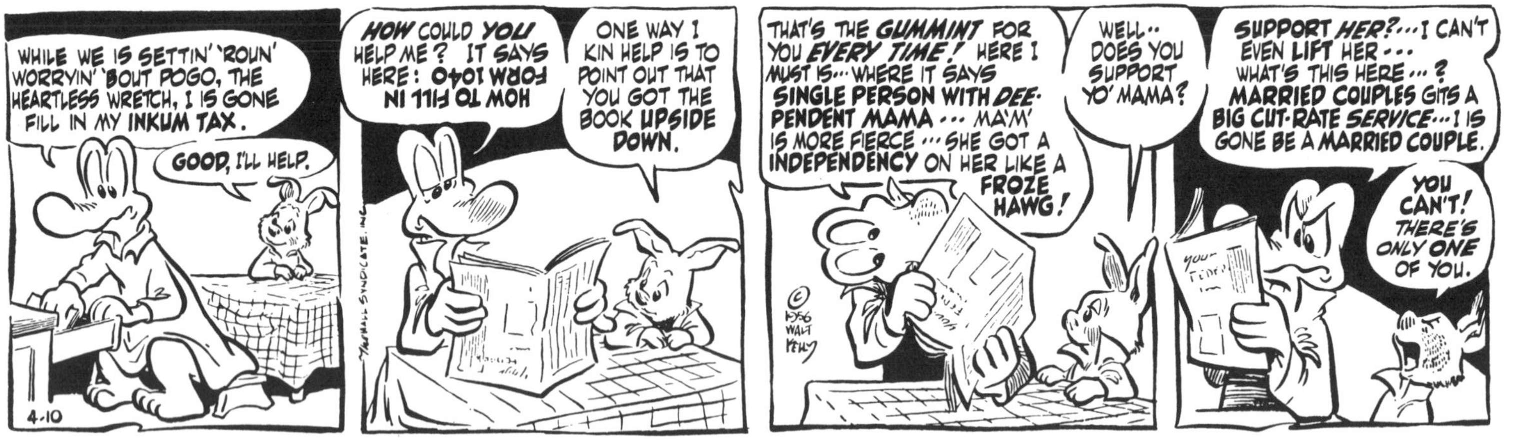
WHILE WE IS SETTIN' 'ROUN' WORRYIN' 'BOUT POGO, THE HEARTLESS WRETCH, I IS GONE FILL IN MY INKUM TAX.
GOOD, I'LL HELP.
4-10
HOW COULD YOU HELP ME? IT SAYS HERE: HOW TO FILL IN FORM 1040
ONE WAY I KIN HELP IS TO POINT OUT THAT YOU GOT THE BOOK UPSIDE DOWN.
THE HALL SYNDICATE, INC.
THAT'S THE GUMMINT FOR YOU EVERY TIME! HERE I MUST IS... WHERE IT SAYS SINGLE PERSON WITH DEE-PENDENT MAMA ... MA'M' IS MORE FIERCE ... SHE GOT A INDEPENDENCY ON HER LIKE A FROZE HAWG!
WELL.. DOES YOU SUPPORT YO' MAMA?
© 1956 WALT KELLY
SUPPORT HER?... I CAN'T EVEN LIFT HER ... WHAT'S THIS HERE ... ? MARRIED COUPLES GITS A BIG CUT-RATE SERVICE ... I IS GONE BE A MARRIED COUPLE.
YOU CAN'T! THERE'S ONLY ONE OF YOU.

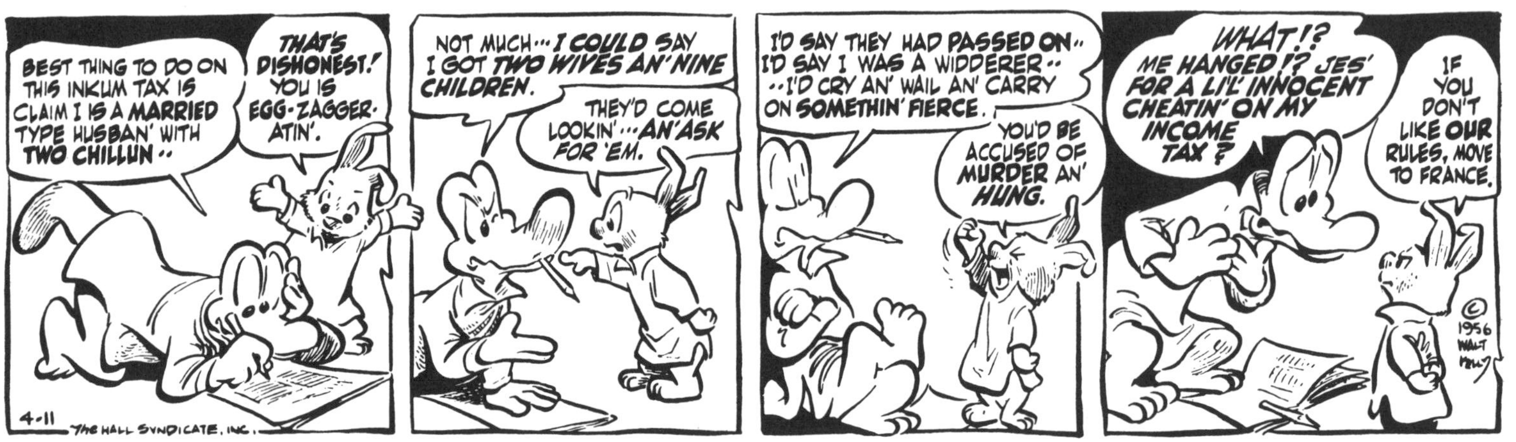
BEST THING TO DO ON THIS INKUM TAX IS CLAIM I IS A MARRIED TYPE HUSBAN' WITH TWO CHILLUN ..
THAT'S DISHONEST! YOU IS EGG-ZAGGER-ATIN'.
4-11 THE HALL SYNDICATE, INC.
NOT MUCH ... I COULD SAY I GOT TWO WIVES AN' NINE CHILDREN.
THEY'D COME LOOKIN' ... AN' ASK FOR 'EM.
I'D SAY THEY HAD PASSED ON .. I'D SAY I WAS A WIDDERER .. .. I'D CRY AN' WAIL AN' CARRY ON SOMETHIN' FIERCE.
YOU'D BE ACCUSED OF MURDER AN' HUNG.
WHAT!? ME HANGED!? JES' FOR A LI'L' INNOCENT CHEATIN' ON MY INCOME TAX?
IF YOU DON'T LIKE OUR RULES, MOVE TO FRANCE.
© 1956 WALT KELLY

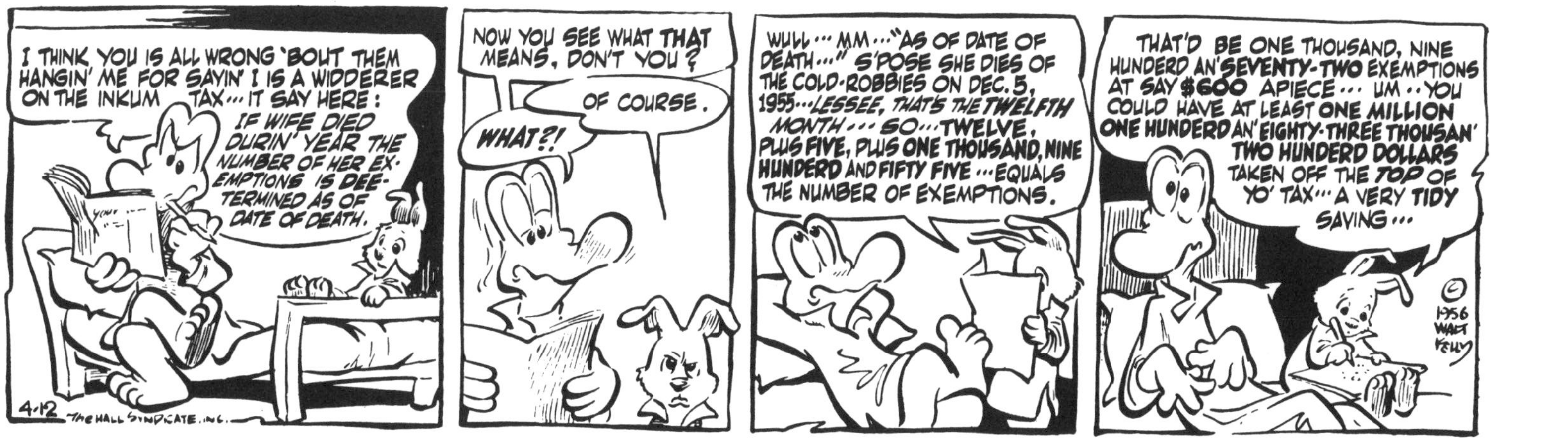
I THINK YOU IS ALL WRONG 'BOUT THEM HANGIN' ME FOR SAYIN' I IS A WIDDERER ON THE INKUM TAX... IT SAY HERE:
IF WIFE DIED DURIN' YEAR THE NUMBER OF HER EXEMPTIONS IS DEE-TERMINED AS OF DATE OF DEATH.
NOW YOU SEE WHAT THAT MEANS, DON'T YOU?
OF COURSE.
WHAT?!
WULL... MM... "AS OF DATE OF DEATH..." S'POSE SHE DIES OF THE COLD-ROBBIES ON DEC. 5, 1955... LESSEE, THAT'S THE TWELFTH MONTH... SO... TWELVE, PLUS FIVE, PLUS ONE THOUSAND, NINE HUNDERD AND FIFTY FIVE... EQUALS THE NUMBER OF EXEMPTIONS.
THAT'D BE ONE THOUSAND, NINE HUNDERD AN' SEVENTY-TWO EXEMPTIONS AT SAY $600 APIECE... UM.. YOU COULD HAVE AT LEAST ONE MILLION ONE HUNDERD AN' EIGHTY-THREE THOUSAN' TWO HUNDERD DOLLARS TAKEN OFF THE TOP OF YO' TAX... A VERY TIDY SAVING...
© 1956 WALT KELLY
4-12
THE HALL SYNDICATE, INC.

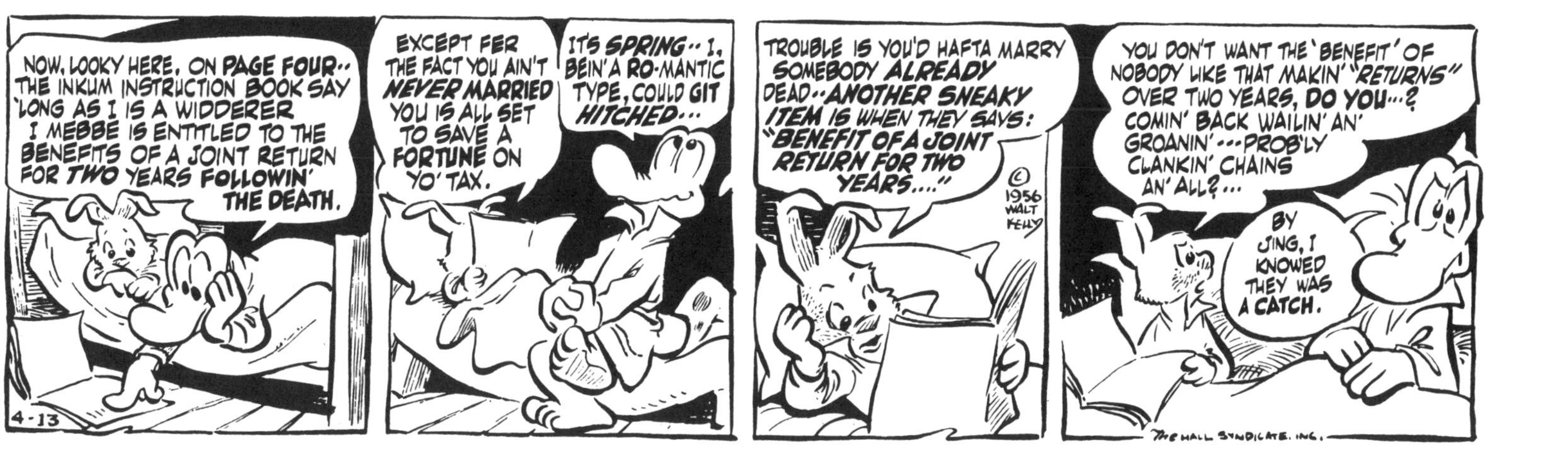
NOW, LOOKY HERE, ON PAGE FOUR.. THE INKUM INSTRUCTION BOOK SAY 'LONG AS I IS A WIDDERER I MEBBE IS ENTITLED TO THE BENEFITS OF A JOINT RETURN FOR TWO YEARS FOLLOWIN' THE DEATH.
EXCEPT FER THE FACT YOU AIN'T NEVER MARRIED YOU IS ALL SET TO SAVE A FORTUNE ON YO' TAX.
IT'S SPRING.. I, BEIN' A RO-MANTIC TYPE, COULD GIT HITCHED...
TROUBLE IS YOU'D HAFTA MARRY SOMEBODY ALREADY DEAD.. ANOTHER SNEAKY ITEM IS WHEN THEY SAYS: "BENEFIT OF A JOINT RETURN FOR TWO YEARS...."
© 1956 WALT KELLY
YOU DON'T WANT THE 'BENEFIT' OF NOBODY LIKE THAT MAKIN' "RETURNS" OVER TWO YEARS, DO YOU...? COMIN' BACK WAILIN' AN' GROANIN'... PROB'LY CLANKIN' CHAINS AN' ALL?...
BY JING, I KNOWED THEY WAS A CATCH.
4-13
THE HALL SYNDICATE, INC.

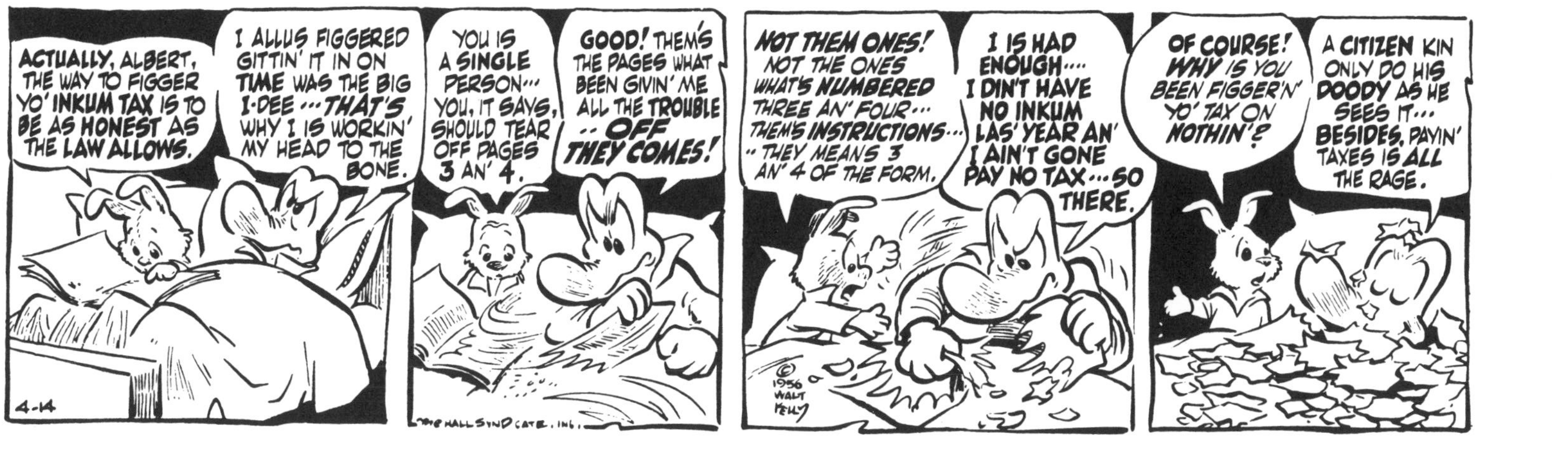
ACTUALLY, ALBERT, THE WAY TO FIGGER YO' INKUM TAX IS TO BE AS HONEST AS THE LAW ALLOWS.
I ALLUS FIGGERED GITTIN' IT IN ON TIME WAS THE BIG I-DEE... THAT'S WHY I IS WORKIN' MY HEAD TO THE BONE.
YOU IS A SINGLE PERSON... YOU, IT SAYS, SHOULD TEAR OFF PAGES 3 AN' 4.
GOOD! THEM'S THE PAGES WHAT BEEN GIVIN' ME ALL THE TROUBLE .. OFF THEY COMES!
NOT THEM ONES! NOT THE ONES WHAT'S NUMBERED THREE AN' FOUR... THEM'S INSTRUCTIONS... .. THEY MEANS 3 AN' 4 OF THE FORM.
I IS HAD ENOUGH.... I DIN'T HAVE NO INKUM LAS' YEAR AN' I AIN'T GONE PAY NO TAX... SO THERE.
OF COURSE! WHY IS YOU BEEN FIGGER'N' YO' TAX ON NOTHIN'?
A CITIZEN KIN ONLY DO HIS DOODY AS HE SEES IT... BESIDES, PAYIN' TAXES IS ALL THE RAGE.
© 1956 WALT KELLY
4-14
THE HALL SYNDICATE, INC.

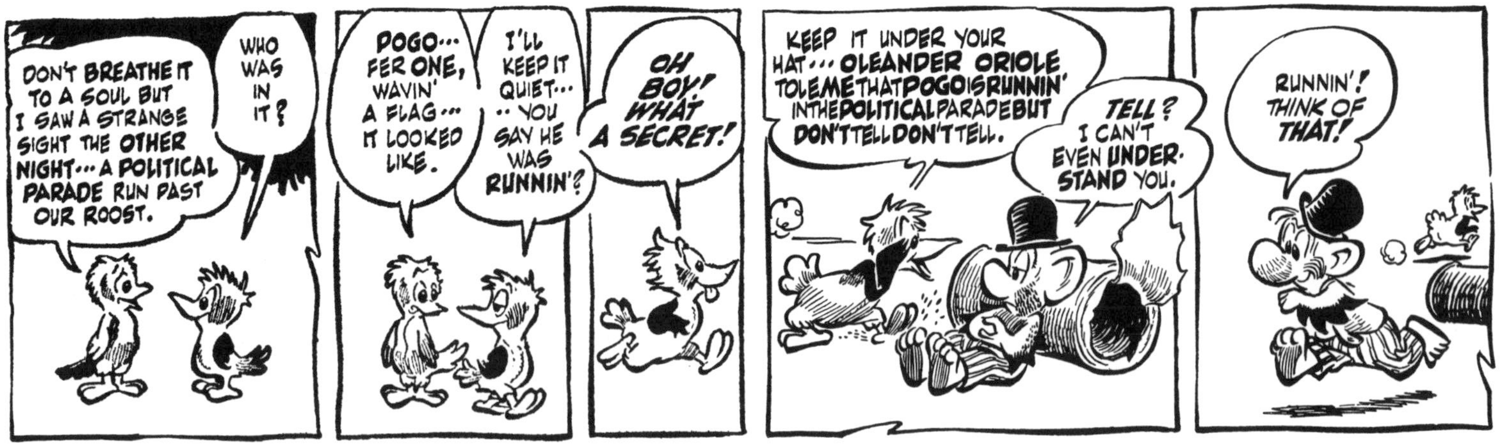
DON'T BREATHE IT TO A SOUL BUT I SAW A STRANGE SIGHT THE OTHER NIGHT... A POLITICAL PARADE RUN PAST OUR ROOST.
WHO WAS IN IT?
POGO... FER ONE, WAVIN' A FLAG... IT LOOKED LIKE.
I'LL KEEP IT QUIET... ..YOU SAY HE WAS RUNNIN'?
OH BOY! WHAT A SECRET!
KEEP IT UNDER YOUR HAT... OLEANDER ORIOLE TOLEMETHATPOGOISRUNNIN' INTHEPOLITICALPARADEBUT DON'TTELLDON'TTELL.
TELL? I CAN'T EVEN UNDER-STAND YOU.
RUNNIN'! THINK OF THAT!

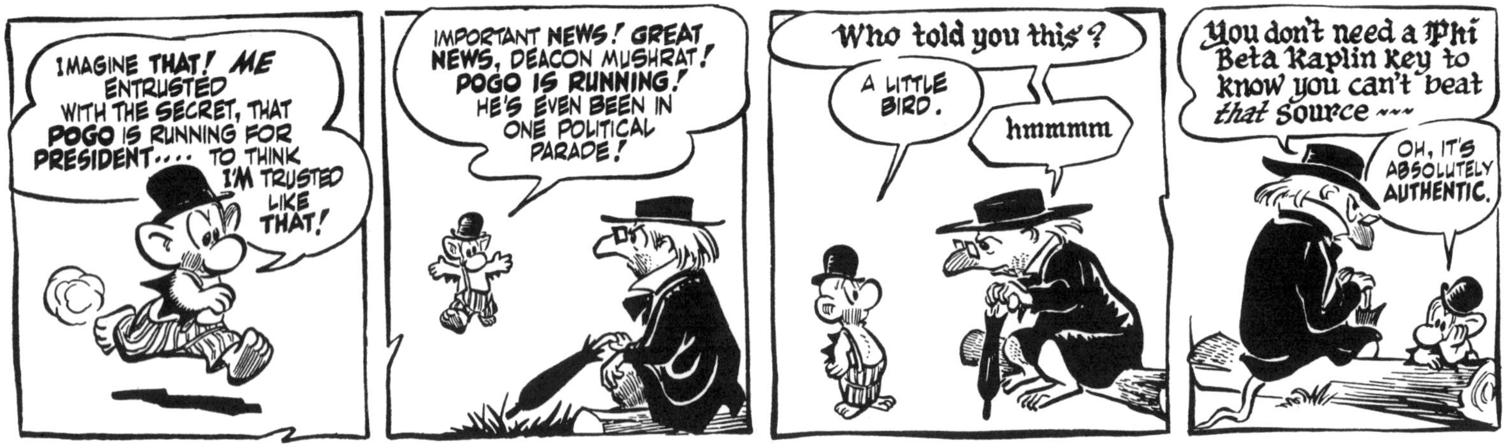
IMAGINE THAT! ME ENTRUSTED WITH THE SECRET, THAT POGO IS RUNNING FOR PRESIDENT.... TO THINK I'M TRUSTED LIKE THAT!
IMPORTANT NEWS! GREAT NEWS, DEACON MUSHRAT! POGO IS RUNNING! HE'S EVEN BEEN IN ONE POLITICAL PARADE!
Who told you this?
A LITTLE BIRD.
hmmmm
You don't need a Phi Beta Kaplin Key to know you can't beat that source ---
OH, IT'S ABSOLUTELY AUTHENTIC.

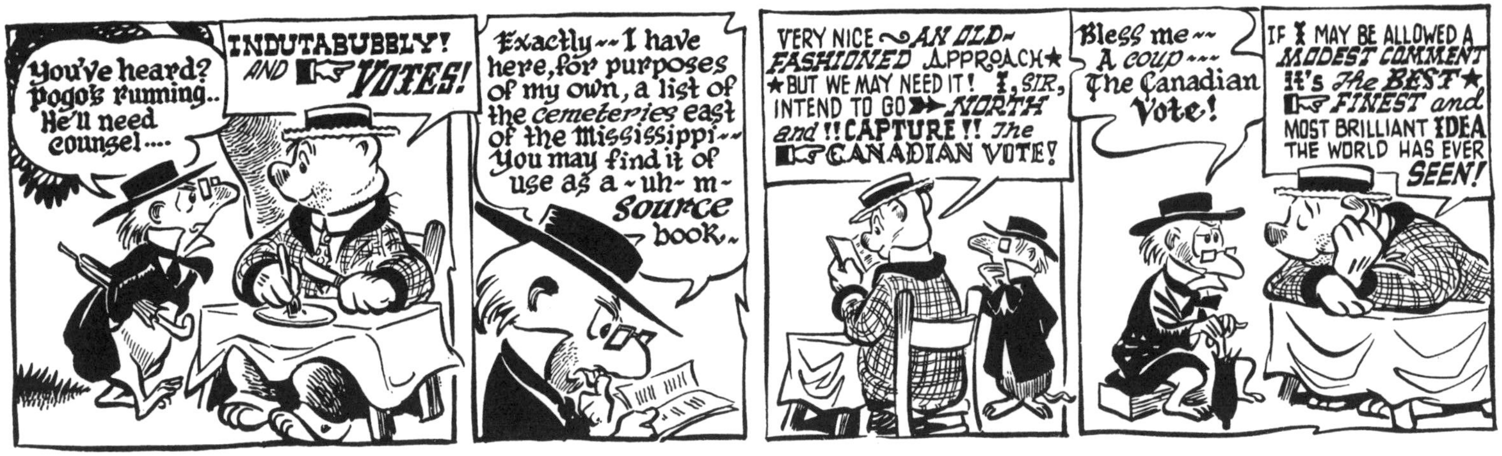
You've heard? Pogo's running.. He'll need counsel....
INDUTABUBBLY! AND ☞ VOTES!
Exactly -- I have here, for purposes of my own, a list of the cemeteries east of the Mississippi -- You may find it of use as a ~uh~ m~ source book.~
VERY NICE ~ AN OLD-FASHIONED APPROACH ★ BUT WE MAY NEED IT! I, SIR, INTEND TO GO ➤➤ NORTH and !! CAPTURE !! The ☞ CANADIAN VOTE!
Bless me -- A coup --- The Canadian Vote!
IF I MAY BE ALLOWED A MODEST COMMENT It's The BEST ★ ☞ FINEST and MOST BRILLIANT IDEA THE WORLD HAS EVER SEEN!

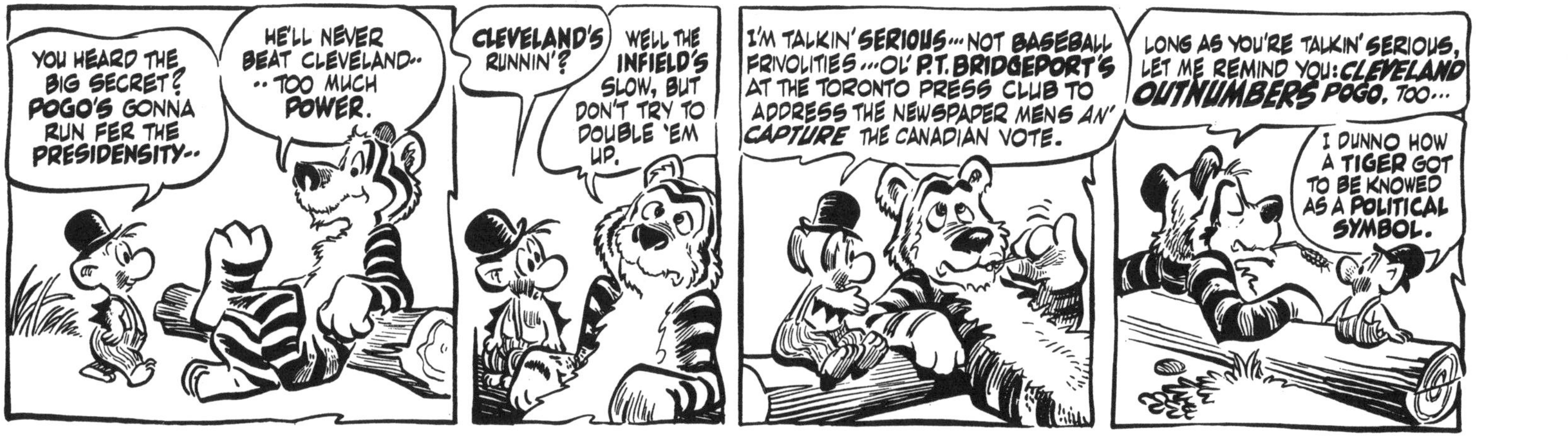
YOU HEARD THE BIG SECRET? POGO'S GONNA RUN FER THE PRESIDENSITY..
HE'LL NEVER BEAT CLEVELAND.. ..TOO MUCH POWER.
CLEVELAND'S RUNNIN'?
WELL THE INFIELD'S SLOW, BUT DON'T TRY TO DOUBLE 'EM UP.
I'M TALKIN' SERIOUS... NOT BASEBALL FRIVOLITIES ...OL' P.T. BRIDGEPORT'S AT THE TORONTO PRESS CLUB TO ADDRESS THE NEWSPAPER MENS AN' CAPTURE THE CANADIAN VOTE.
LONG AS YOU'RE TALKIN' SERIOUS, LET ME REMIND YOU: CLEVELAND OUTNUMBERS POGO, TOO...
I DUNNO HOW A TIGER GOT TO BE KNOWED AS A POLITICAL SYMBOL.

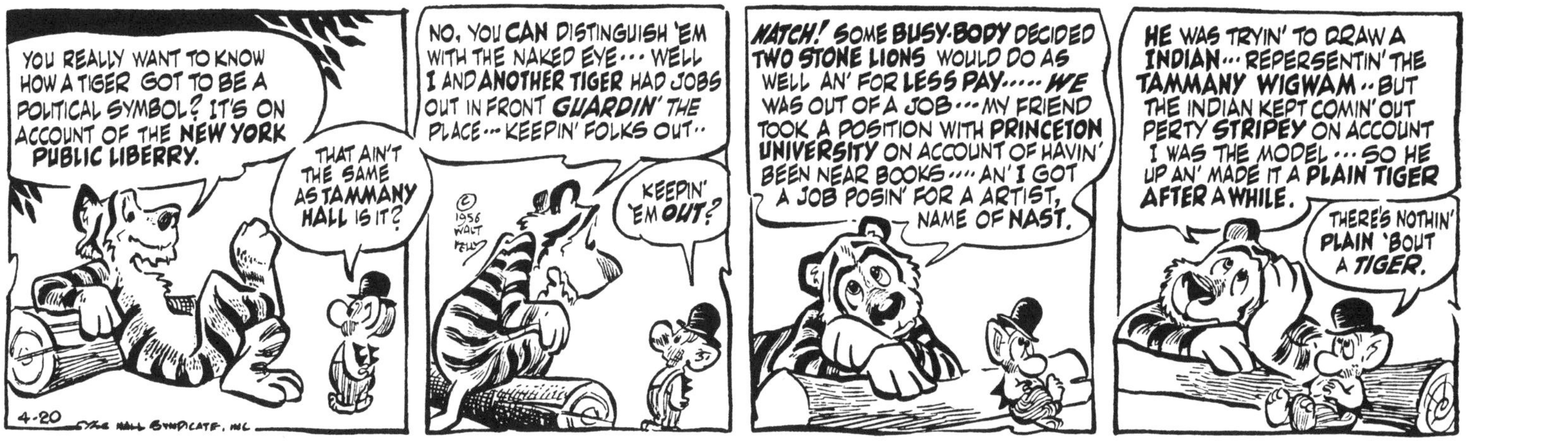
YOU REALLY WANT TO KNOW HOW A TIGER GOT TO BE A POLITICAL SYMBOL? IT'S ON ACCOUNT OF THE NEW YORK PUBLIC LIBERRY.
THAT AIN'T THE SAME AS TAMMANY HALL IS IT?
NO, YOU CAN DISTINGUISH 'EM WITH THE NAKED EYE... WELL I AND ANOTHER TIGER HAD JOBS OUT IN FRONT GUARDIN' THE PLACE... KEEPIN' FOLKS OUT..
© 1956 WALT KELLY
KEEPIN' 'EM OUT?
NATCH! SOME BUSY-BODY DECIDED TWO STONE LIONS WOULD DO AS WELL AN' FOR LESS PAY..... WE WAS OUT OF A JOB... MY FRIEND TOOK A POSITION WITH PRINCETON UNIVERSITY ON ACCOUNT OF HAVIN' BEEN NEAR BOOKS.... AN' I GOT A JOB POSIN' FOR A ARTIST, NAME OF NAST.
HE WAS TRYIN' TO DRAW A INDIAN... REPERSENTIN' THE TAMMANY WIGWAM.. BUT THE INDIAN KEPT COMIN' OUT PERTY STRIPEY ON ACCOUNT I WAS THE MODEL... SO HE UP AN' MADE IT A PLAIN TIGER AFTER A WHILE.
THERE'S NOTHIN' PLAIN 'BOUT A TIGER.
4-20

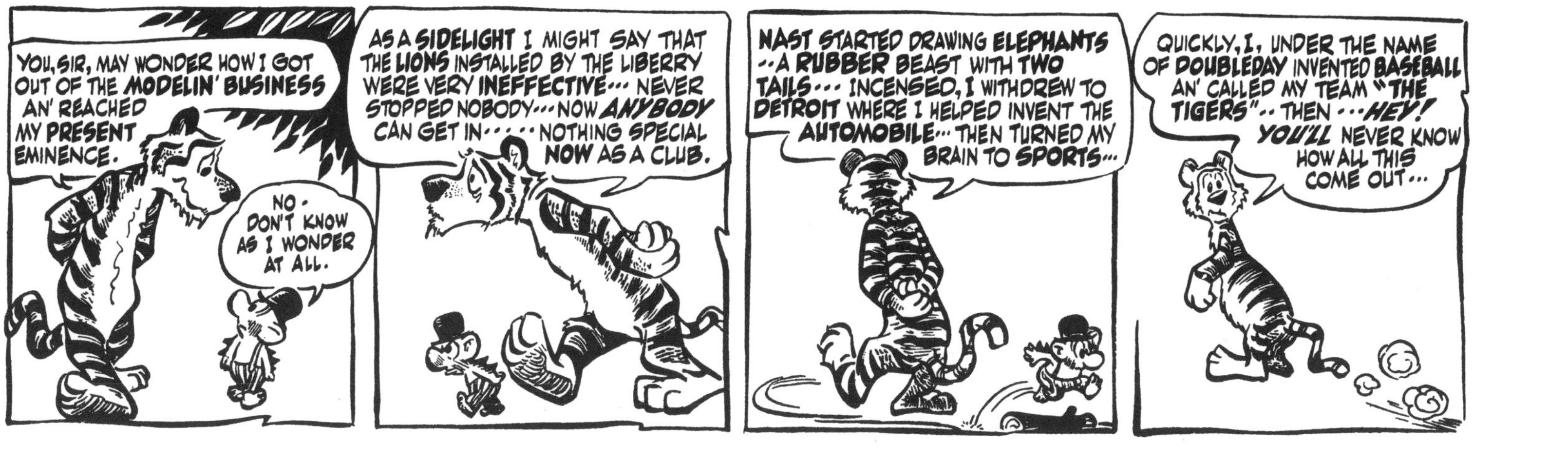
YOU, SIR, MAY WONDER HOW I GOT OUT OF THE MODELIN' BUSINESS AN' REACHED MY PRESENT EMINENCE.
NO - DON'T KNOW AS I WONDER AT ALL.
AS A SIDELIGHT I MIGHT SAY THAT THE LIONS INSTALLED BY THE LIBERRY WERE VERY INEFFECTIVE... NEVER STOPPED NOBODY... NOW ANYBODY CAN GET IN..... NOTHING SPECIAL NOW AS A CLUB.
NAST STARTED DRAWING ELEPHANTS ..A RUBBER BEAST WITH TWO TAILS... INCENSED, I WITHDREW TO DETROIT WHERE I HELPED INVENT THE AUTOMOBILE... THEN TURNED MY BRAIN TO SPORTS...
QUICKLY, I, UNDER THE NAME OF DOUBLEDAY INVENTED BASEBALL AN' CALLED MY TEAM "THE TIGERS"... THEN ...HEY! YOU'LL NEVER KNOW HOW ALL THIS COME OUT...

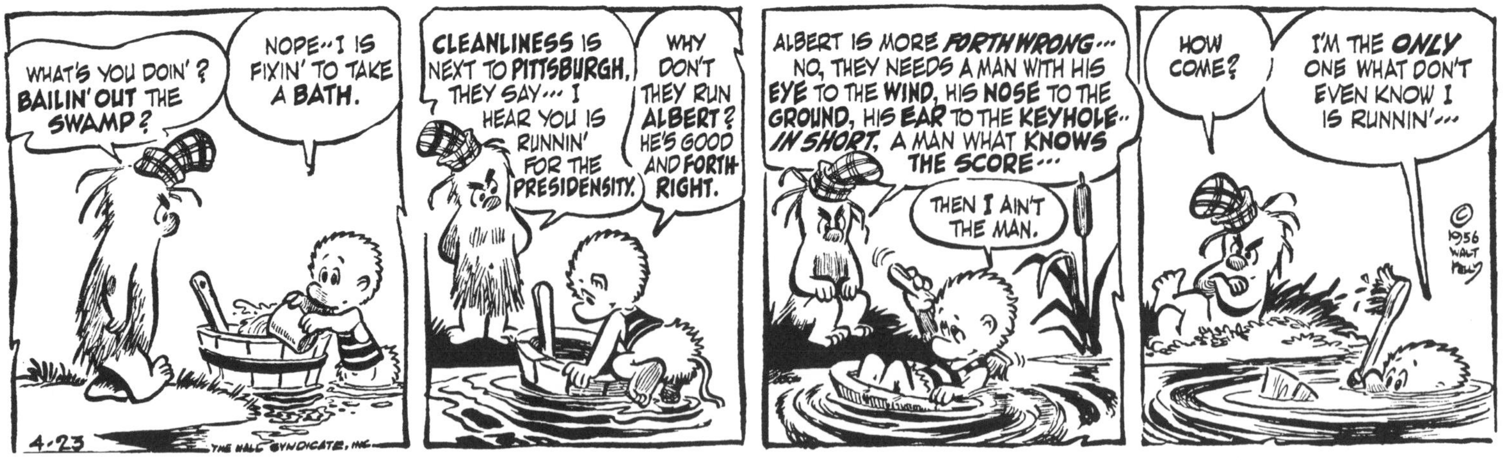
WHAT'S YOU DOIN'? BAILIN' OUT THE SWAMP?
NOPE·· I IS FIXIN' TO TAKE A BATH.
CLEANLINESS IS NEXT TO PITTSBURGH, THEY SAY··· I HEAR YOU IS RUNNIN' FOR THE PRESIDENSITY.
WHY DON'T THEY RUN ALBERT? HE'S GOOD AND FORTH-RIGHT.
ALBERT IS MORE FORTHWRONG··· NO, THEY NEEDS A MAN WITH HIS EYE TO THE WIND, HIS NOSE TO THE GROUND, HIS EAR TO THE KEYHOLE·· IN SHORT, A MAN WHAT KNOWS THE SCORE···
THEN I AIN'T THE MAN.
HOW COME?
I'M THE ONLY ONE WHAT DON'T EVEN KNOW I IS RUNNIN'···
© 1956 WALT KELLY
4-23
THE HALL SYNDICATE, INC.

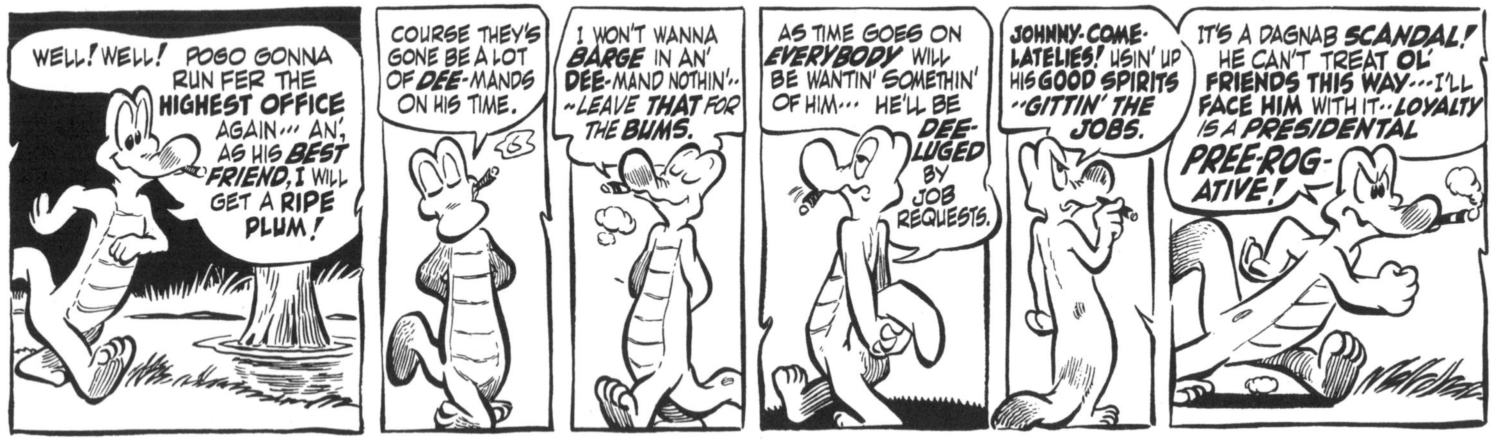
WELL! WELL! POGO GONNA RUN FER THE HIGHEST OFFICE AGAIN··· AN', AS HIS BEST FRIEND, I WILL GET A RIPE PLUM!
COURSE THEY'S GONE BE A LOT OF DEE-MANDS ON HIS TIME.
I WON'T WANNA BARGE IN AN' DEE-MAND NOTHIN'·· ··LEAVE THAT FOR THE BUMS.
AS TIME GOES ON EVERYBODY WILL BE WANTIN' SOMETHIN' OF HIM··· HE'LL BE DEE-LUGED BY JOB REQUESTS.
JOHNNY-COME-LATELIES! USIN' UP HIS GOOD SPIRITS ··GITTIN' THE JOBS.
IT'S A DAGNAB SCANDAL! HE CAN'T TREAT OL' FRIENDS THIS WAY···I'LL FACE HIM WITH IT·· LOYALTY IS A PRESIDENTAL PREE-ROG-ATIVE!

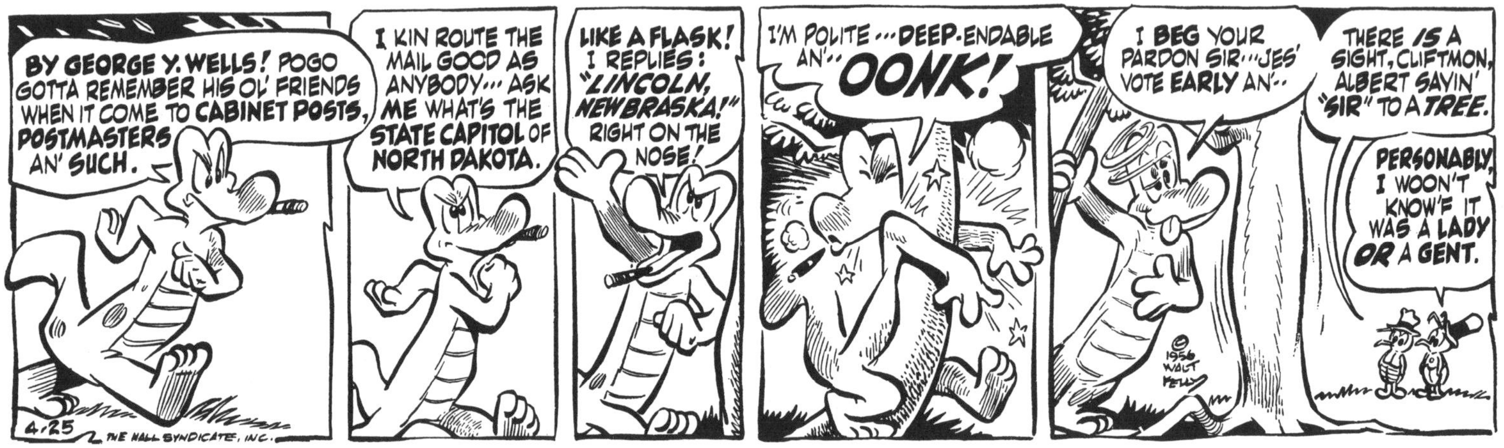
BY GEORGE Y. WELLS! POGO GOTTA REMEMBER HIS OL' FRIENDS WHEN IT COME TO CABINET POSTS, POSTMASTERS AN' SUCH.
I KIN ROUTE THE MAIL GOOD AS ANYBODY··· ASK ME WHAT'S THE STATE CAPITOL OF NORTH DAKOTA.
LIKE A FLASK! I REPLIES: "LINCOLN, NEWBRASKA!" RIGHT ON THE NOSE!
I'M POLITE ··· DEEP-ENDABLE AN'·· OONK!
I BEG YOUR PARDON SIR···JES' VOTE EARLY AN'··
THERE IS A SIGHT, CLIFTMON, ALBERT SAYIN' "SIR" TO A TREE.
PERSONABLY, I WOON'T KNOW'F IT WAS A LADY OR A GENT.
© 1956 WALT KELLY
4-25
THE HALL SYNDICATE, INC.

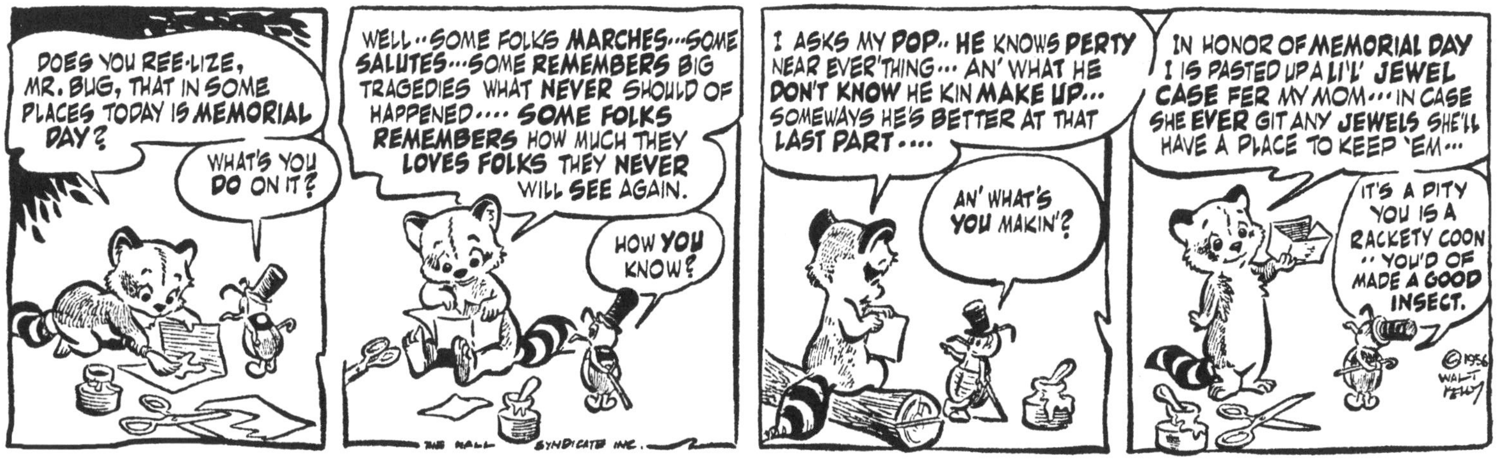
DOES YOU REE-LIZE, MR. BUG, THAT IN SOME PLACES TODAY IS MEMORIAL DAY?
WHAT'S YOU DO ON IT?
WELL.. SOME FOLKS MARCHES...SOME SALUTES...SOME REMEMBERS BIG TRAGEDIES WHAT NEVER SHOULD OF HAPPENED.... SOME FOLKS REMEMBERS HOW MUCH THEY LOVES FOLKS THEY NEVER WILL SEE AGAIN.
HOW YOU KNOW?
THE HALL SYNDICATE INC.
I ASKS MY POP.. HE KNOWS PERTY NEAR EVER'THING... AN' WHAT HE DON'T KNOW HE KIN MAKE UP... SOMEWAYS HE'S BETTER AT THAT LAST PART....
AN' WHAT'S YOU MAKIN'?
IN HONOR OF MEMORIAL DAY I IS PASTED UP A LI'L' JEWEL CASE FER MY MOM... IN CASE SHE EVER GIT ANY JEWELS SHE'LL HAVE A PLACE TO KEEP 'EM...
IT'S A PITY YOU IS A RACKETY COON .. YOU'D OF MADE A GOOD INSECT.
© 1956 WALT KELLY

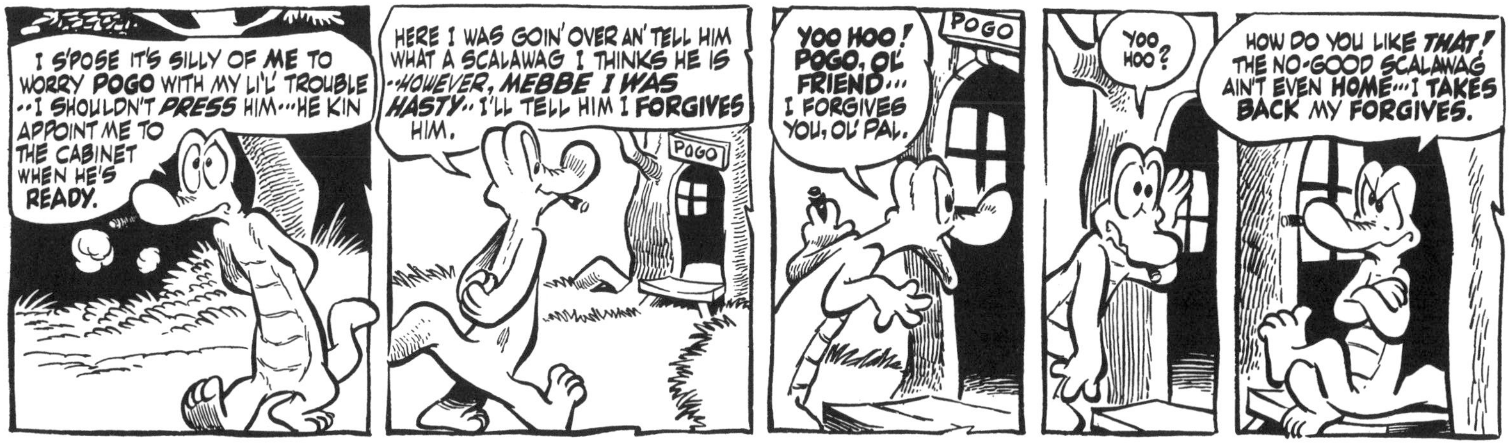
I S'POSE IT'S SILLY OF ME TO WORRY POGO WITH MY LI'L' TROUBLE .. I SHOULDN'T PRESS HIM... HE KIN APPOINT ME TO THE CABINET WHEN HE'S READY.
HERE I WAS GOIN' OVER AN' TELL HIM WHAT A SCALAWAG I THINKS HE IS .. HOWEVER, MEBBE I WAS HASTY.. I'LL TELL HIM I FORGIVES HIM.
POGO
POGO
YOO HOO! POGO, OL' FRIEND... I FORGIVES YOU, OL' PAL.
YOO HOO?
HOW DO YOU LIKE THAT! THE NO-GOOD SCALAWAG AIN'T EVEN HOME... I TAKES BACK MY FORGIVES.

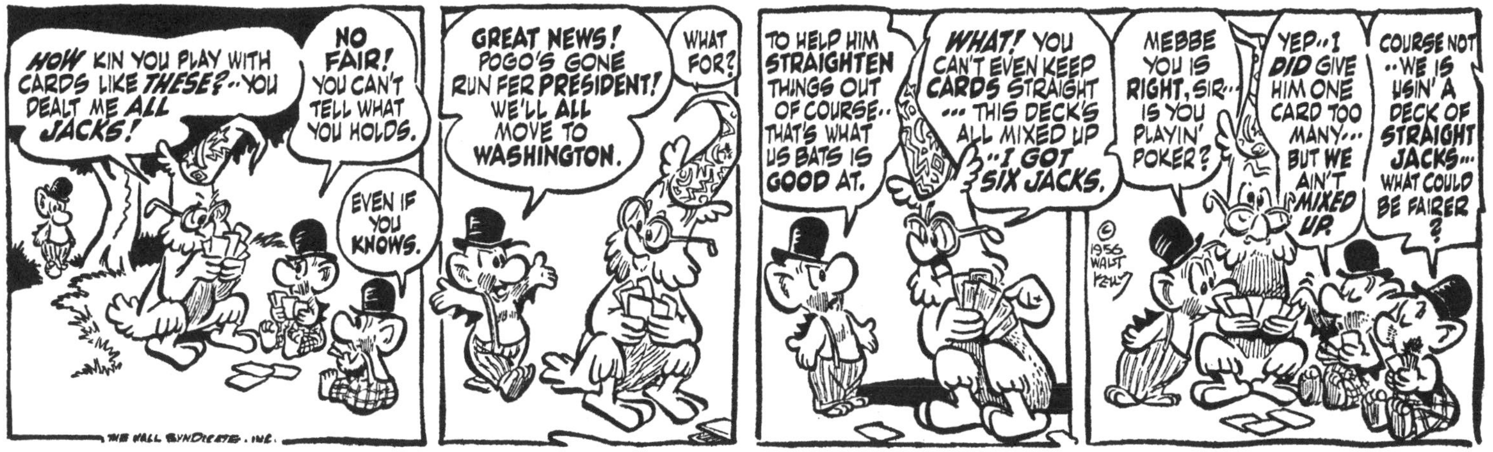
HOW KIN YOU PLAY WITH CARDS LIKE THESE?.. YOU DEALT ME ALL JACKS!
NO FAIR! YOU CAN'T TELL WHAT YOU HOLDS.
EVEN IF YOU KNOWS.
THE HALL SYNDICATE, INC.
GREAT NEWS! POGO'S GONE RUN FER PRESIDENT! WE'LL ALL MOVE TO WASHINGTON.
WHAT FOR?
TO HELP HIM STRAIGHTEN THINGS OUT OF COURSE.. THAT'S WHAT US BATS IS GOOD AT.
WHAT! YOU CAN'T EVEN KEEP CARDS STRAIGHT ... THIS DECK'S ALL MIXED UP .. I GOT SIX JACKS.
© 1956 WALT KELLY
MEBBE YOU IS RIGHT, SIR.. IS YOU PLAYIN' POKER?
YEP.. I DID GIVE HIM ONE CARD TOO MANY... BUT WE AIN'T MIXED UP.
COURSE NOT .. WE IS USIN' A DECK OF STRAIGHT JACKS... WHAT COULD BE FAIRER?

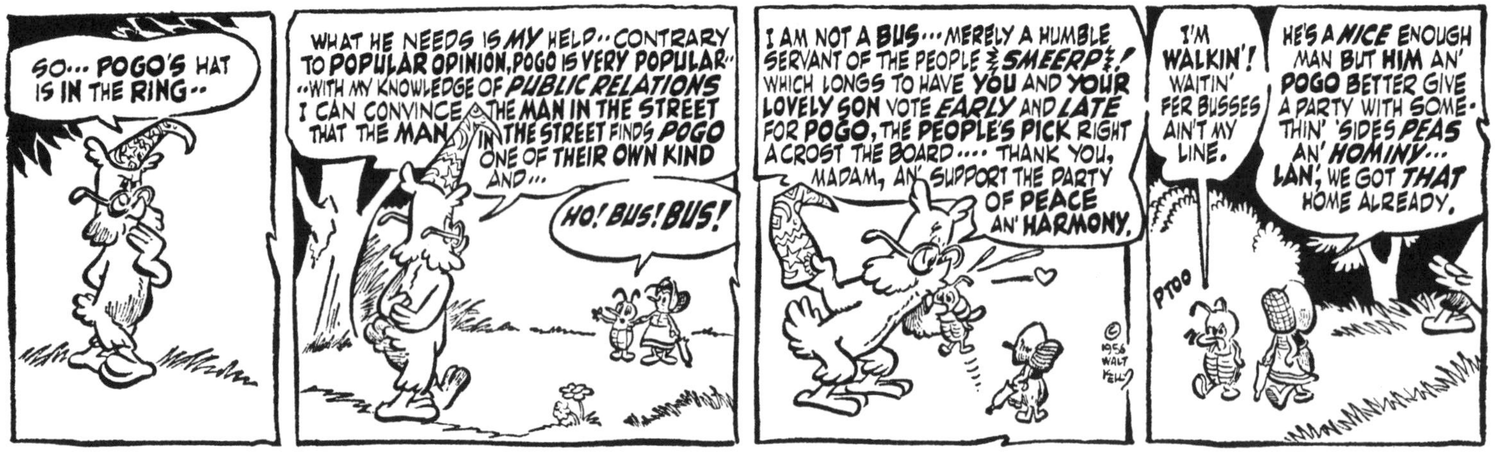
SO... POGO'S HAT IS IN THE RING..
WHAT HE NEEDS IS MY HELP.. CONTRARY TO POPULAR OPINION, POGO IS VERY POPULAR.. ..WITH MY KNOWLEDGE OF PUBLIC RELATIONS I CAN CONVINCE THE MAN IN THE STREET THAT THE MAN IN THE STREET FINDS POGO ONE OF THEIR OWN KIND AND...
HO! BUS! BUS!
I AM NOT A BUS... MERELY A HUMBLE SERVANT OF THE PEOPLE SMEERP! WHICH LONGS TO HAVE YOU AND YOUR LOVELY SON VOTE EARLY AND LATE FOR POGO, THE PEOPLE'S PICK RIGHT ACROST THE BOARD.... THANK YOU, MADAM, AN' SUPPORT THE PARTY OF PEACE AN' HARMONY.
© 1956 WALT KELLY
I'M WALKIN'! WAITIN' FER BUSSES AIN'T MY LINE.
HE'S A NICE ENOUGH MAN BUT HIM AN' POGO BETTER GIVE A PARTY WITH SOME-THIN' 'SIDES PEAS AN' HOMINY... LAN', WE GOT THAT HOME ALREADY.
PTOO

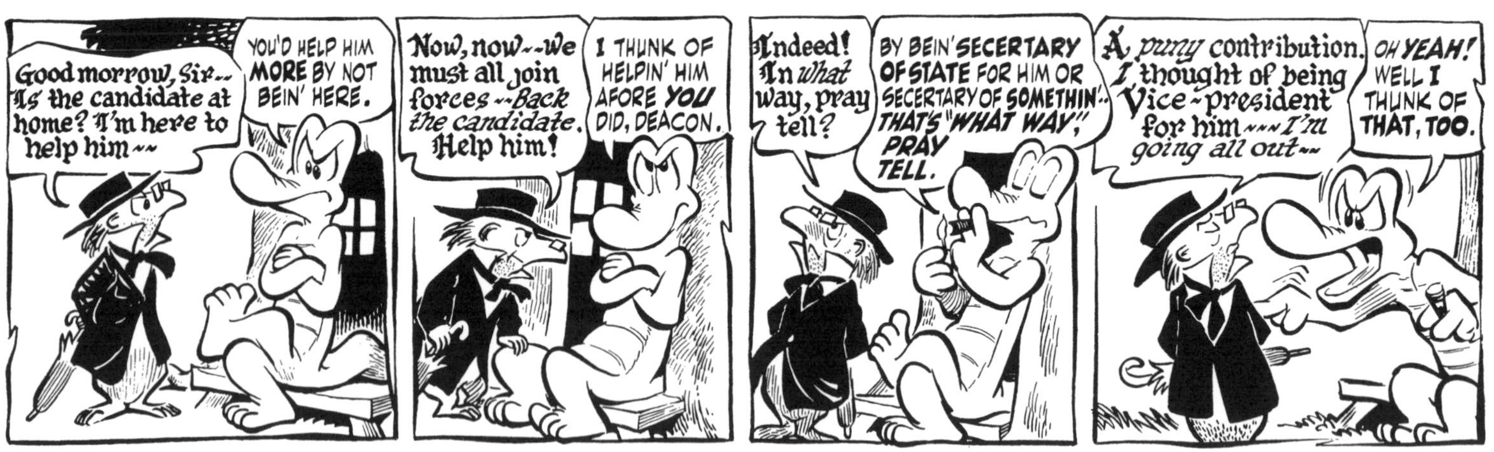
Good morrow, Sir-- Is the candidate at home? I'm here to help him--
YOU'D HELP HIM MORE BY NOT BEIN' HERE.
Now, now--We must all join forces--Back the candidate. Help him!
I THUNK OF HELPIN' HIM AFORE YOU DID, DEACON.
Indeed! In what way, pray tell?
BY BEIN' SECERTARY OF STATE FOR HIM OR SECERTARY OF SOMETHIN'.. THAT'S "WHAT WAY," PRAY TELL.
A puny contribution. I thought of being Vice-president for him--- I'm going all out--
OH YEAH! WELL I THUNK OF THAT, TOO.

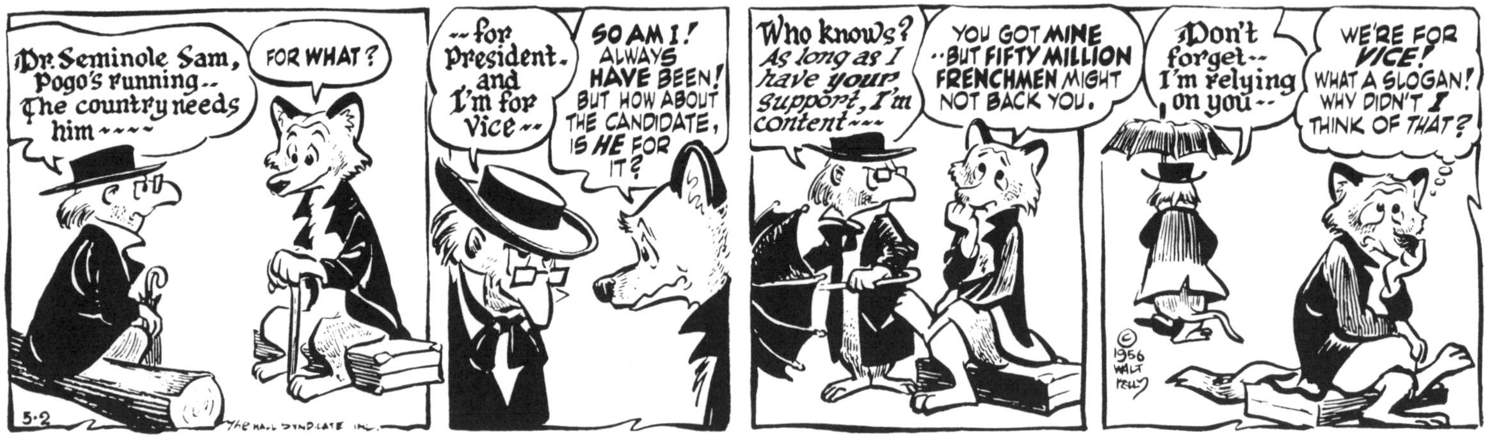
Dr. Seminole Sam, Pogo's running-- The country needs him----
FOR WHAT?
--for President. and I'm for Vice--
SO AM I! ALWAYS HAVE BEEN! BUT HOW ABOUT THE CANDIDATE, IS HE FOR IT?
Who knows? As long as I have your support, I'm content---
YOU GOT MINE ..BUT FIFTY MILLION FRENCHMEN MIGHT NOT BACK YOU.
Don't forget-- I'm relying on you--
WE'RE FOR VICE! WHAT A SLOGAN! WHY DIDN'T I THINK OF THAT?
© 1956 WALT KELLY

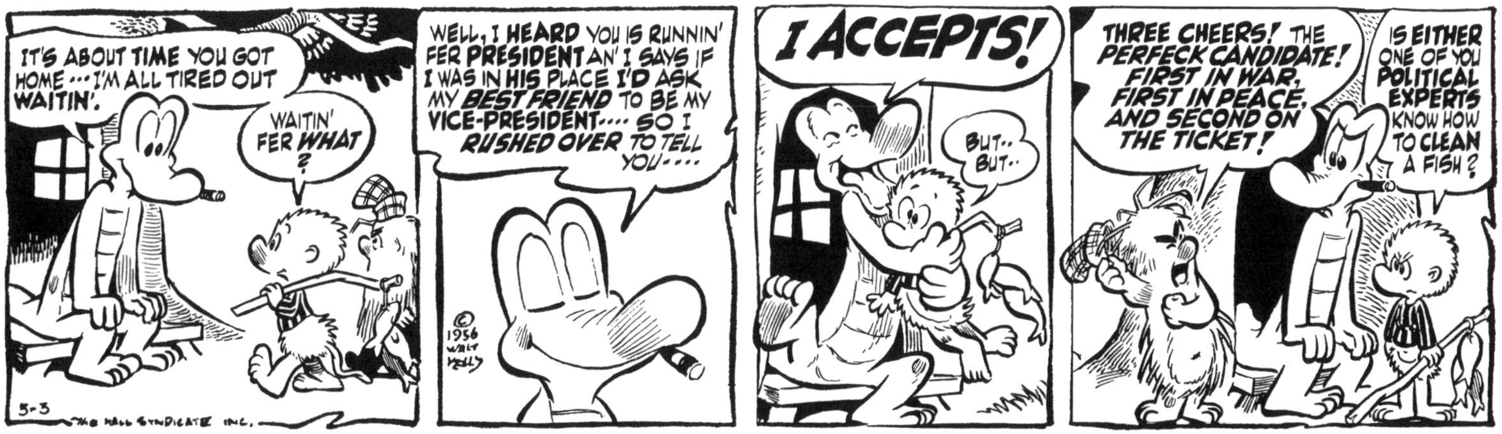
IT'S ABOUT TIME YOU GOT HOME ··· I'M ALL TIRED OUT WAITIN'.
WAITIN' FER WHAT ?
5-3
THE HALL SYNDICATE INC.
WELL, I HEARD YOU IS RUNNIN' FER PRESIDENT AN' I SAYS IF I WAS IN HIS PLACE I'D ASK MY BEST FRIEND TO BE MY VICE-PRESIDENT···· SO I RUSHED OVER TO TELL YOU····
© 1956 WALT KELLY
I ACCEPTS!
BUT·· BUT··
THREE CHEERS! THE PERFECK CANDIDATE! FIRST IN WAR, FIRST IN PEACE, AND SECOND ON THE TICKET!
IS EITHER ONE OF YOU POLITICAL EXPERTS KNOW HOW TO CLEAN A FISH ?

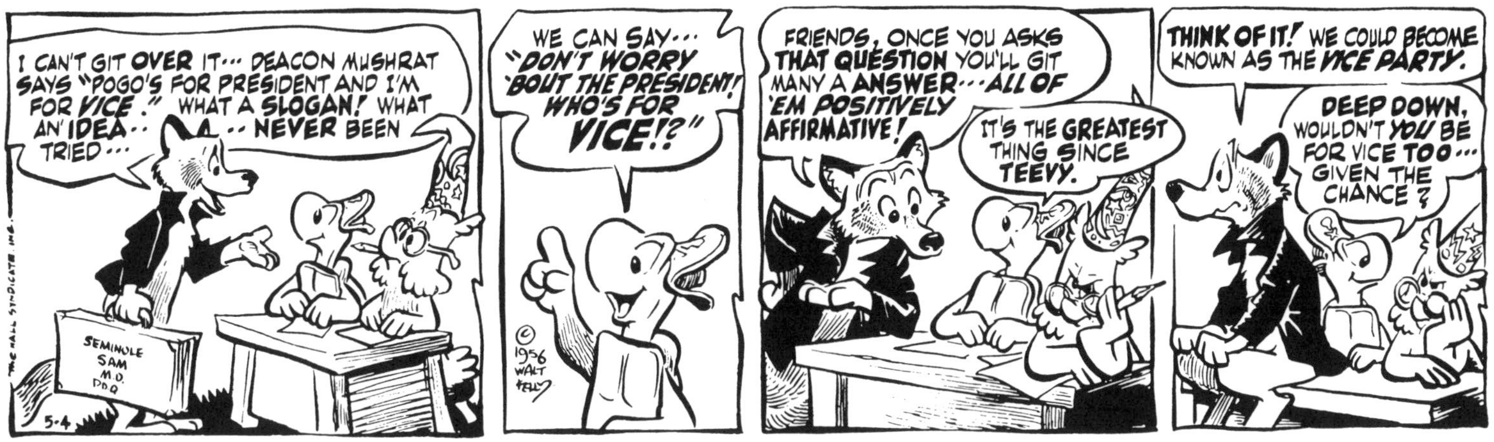
I CAN'T GIT OVER IT··· DEACON MUSHRAT SAYS "POGO'S FOR PRESIDENT AND I'M FOR VICE." WHAT A SLOGAN! WHAT AN' IDEA·· A ·· NEVER BEEN TRIED···
SEMINOLE SAM M.D. D.D.Q.
5-4
THE HALL SYNDICATE INC.
WE CAN SAY··· "DON'T WORRY 'BOUT THE PRESIDENT! WHO'S FOR VICE!?"
© 1956 WALT KELLY
FRIENDS, ONCE YOU ASKS THAT QUESTION YOU'LL GIT MANY A ANSWER ··· ALL OF 'EM POSITIVELY AFFIRMATIVE!
IT'S THE GREATEST THING SINCE TEEVY.
THINK OF IT! WE COULD BECOME KNOWN AS THE VICE PARTY.
DEEP DOWN, WOULDN'T YOU BE FOR VICE TOO··· GIVEN THE CHANCE ?

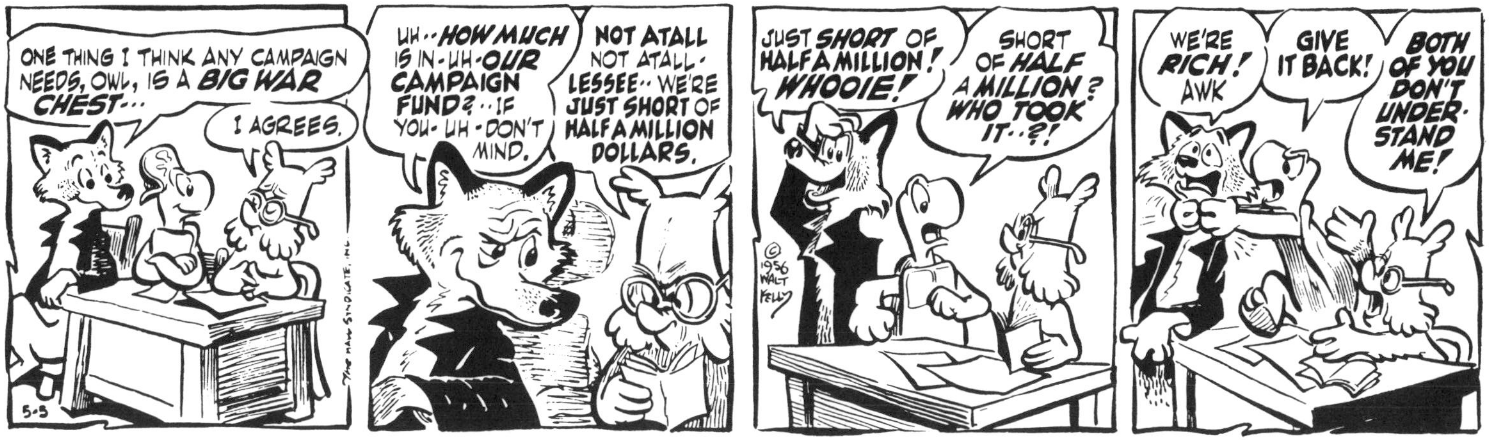
ONE THING I THINK ANY CAMPAIGN NEEDS, OWL, IS A BIG WAR CHEST···
I AGREES.
5-5
THE HALL SYNDICATE, INC.
UH·· HOW MUCH IS IN-UH-OUR CAMPAIGN FUND? ·· IF YOU-UH-DON'T MIND.
NOT ATALL NOT ATALL. LESSEE·· WE'RE JUST SHORT OF HALF A MILLION DOLLARS.
JUST SHORT OF HALF A MILLION! WHOOIE!
SHORT OF HALF A MILLION ? WHO TOOK IT··?!
© 1956 WALT KELLY
WE'RE RICH! AWK
GIVE IT BACK!
BOTH OF YOU DON'T UNDER-STAND ME!

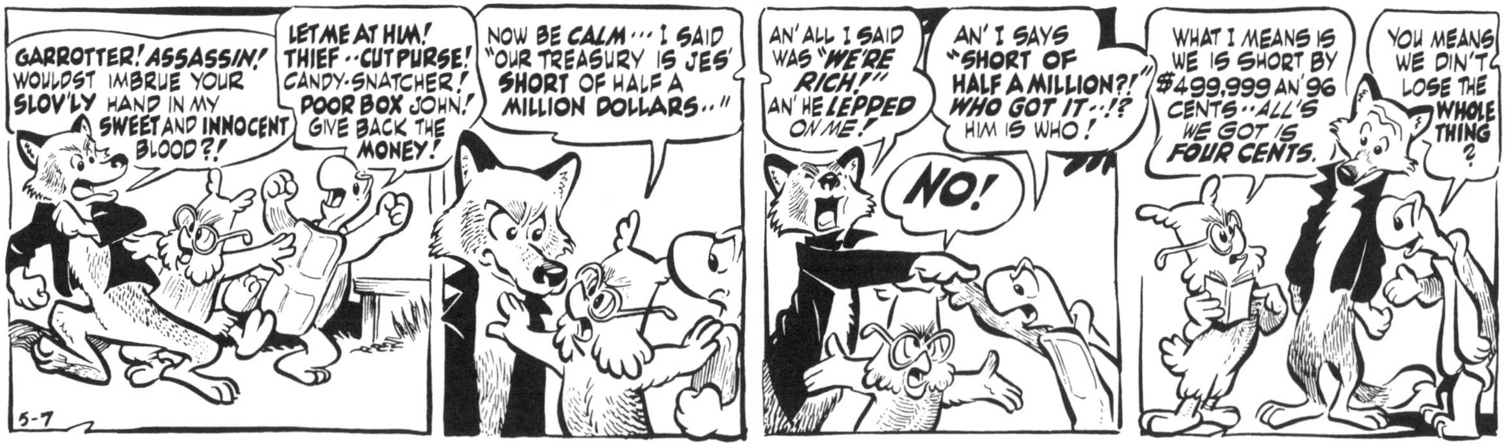
GARROTTER! ASSASSIN! WOULDST IMBRUE YOUR SLOV'LY HAND IN MY SWEET AND INNOCENT BLOOD?!
LET ME AT HIM! THIEF .. CUT PURSE! CANDY-SNATCHER! POOR BOX JOHN! GIVE BACK THE MONEY!
NOW BE CALM ... I SAID "OUR TREASURY IS JES' SHORT OF HALF A MILLION DOLLARS .."
AN' ALL I SAID WAS "WE'RE RICH!" AN' HE LEPPED ON ME!
AN' I SAYS "SHORT OF HALF A MILLION?!" WHO GOT IT ..!? HIM IS WHO!
NO!
WHAT I MEANS IS WE IS SHORT BY $499,999 AN' 96 CENTS .. ALL'S WE GOT IS FOUR CENTS.
YOU MEANS WE DIN'T LOSE THE WHOLE THING?
5-7

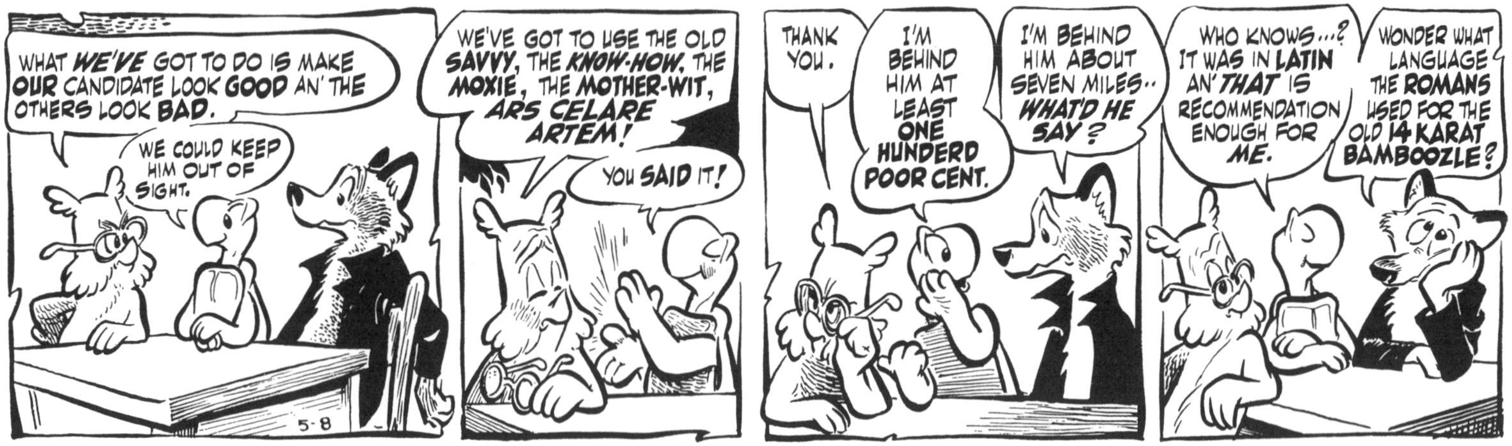
WHAT WE'VE GOT TO DO IS MAKE OUR CANDIDATE LOOK GOOD AN' THE OTHERS LOOK BAD.
WE COULD KEEP HIM OUT OF SIGHT.
5-8
WE'VE GOT TO USE THE OLD SAVVY, THE KNOW-HOW, THE MOXIE, THE MOTHER-WIT, ARS CELARE ARTEM!
YOU SAID IT!
THANK YOU.
I'M BEHIND HIM AT LEAST ONE HUNDERD POOR CENT.
I'M BEHIND HIM ABOUT SEVEN MILES .. WHAT'D HE SAY?
WHO KNOWS ...? IT WAS IN LATIN AN' THAT IS RECOMMENDATION ENOUGH FOR ME.
WONDER WHAT LANGUAGE THE ROMANS USED FOR THE OLD 14 KARAT BAMBOOZLE?

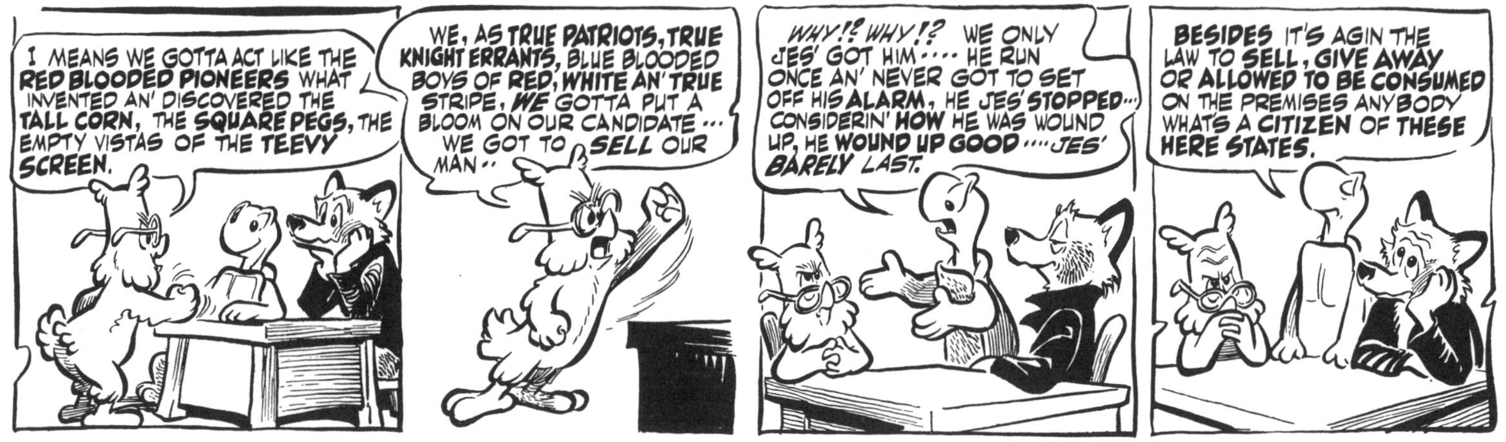
I MEANS WE GOTTA ACT LIKE THE RED BLOODED PIONEERS WHAT INVENTED AN' DISCOVERED THE TALL CORN, THE SQUARE PEGS, THE EMPTY VISTAS OF THE TEEVY SCREEN.
WE, AS TRUE PATRIOTS, TRUE KNIGHT ERRANTS, BLUE BLOODED BOYS OF RED, WHITE AN' TRUE STRIPE, WE GOTTA PUT A BLOOM ON OUR CANDIDATE ... WE GOT TO SELL OUR MAN ..
WHY!? WHY!? WE ONLY JES' GOT HIM .... HE RUN ONCE AN' NEVER GOT TO SET OFF HIS ALARM, HE JES' STOPPED ... CONSIDERIN' HOW HE WAS WOUND UP, HE WOUND UP GOOD .... JES' BARELY LAST.
BESIDES IT'S AGIN THE LAW TO SELL, GIVE AWAY OR ALLOWED TO BE CONSUMED ON THE PREMISES ANYBODY WHAT'S A CITIZEN OF THESE HERE STATES.

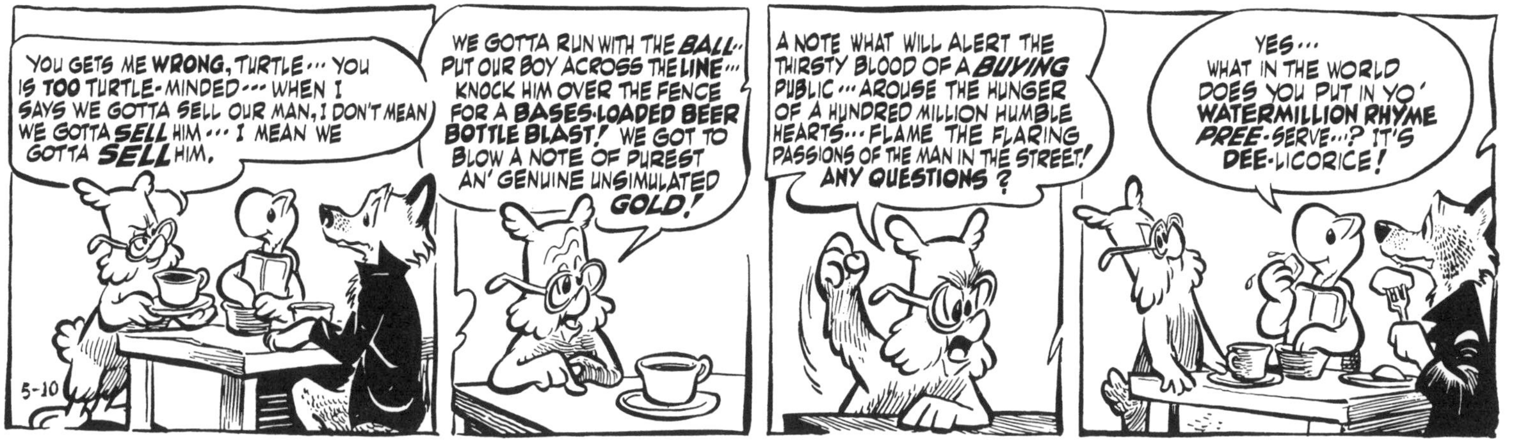
YOU GETS ME WRONG, TURTLE ··· YOU IS TOO TURTLE-MINDED ··· WHEN I SAYS WE GOTTA SELL OUR MAN, I DON'T MEAN WE GOTTA SELL HIM ··· I MEAN WE GOTTA SELL HIM.
5-10
WE GOTTA RUN WITH THE BALL·· PUT OUR BOY ACROSS THE LINE··· KNOCK HIM OVER THE FENCE FOR A BASES-LOADED BEER BOTTLE BLAST! WE GOT TO BLOW A NOTE OF PUREST AN' GENUINE UNSIMULATED GOLD!
A NOTE WHAT WILL ALERT THE THIRSTY BLOOD OF A BUYING PUBLIC ··· AROUSE THE HUNGER OF A HUNDRED MILLION HUMBLE HEARTS··· FLAME THE FLARING PASSIONS OF THE MAN IN THE STREET! ANY QUESTIONS ?
YES··· WHAT IN THE WORLD DOES YOU PUT IN YO' WATERMILLION RHYME PREE-SERVE···? IT'S DEE-LICORICE!

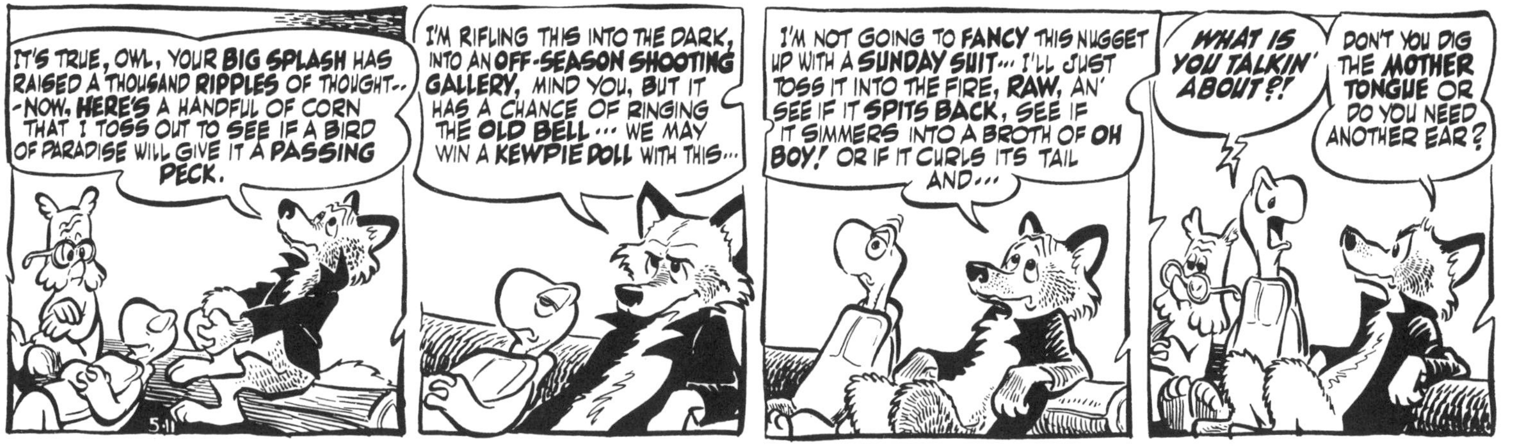
IT'S TRUE, OWL, YOUR BIG SPLASH HAS RAISED A THOUSAND RIPPLES OF THOUGHT-- -NOW, HERE'S A HANDFUL OF CORN THAT I TOSS OUT TO SEE IF A BIRD OF PARADISE WILL GIVE IT A PASSING PECK.
5-11
I'M RIFLING THIS INTO THE DARK, INTO AN OFF-SEASON SHOOTING GALLERY, MIND YOU, BUT IT HAS A CHANCE OF RINGING THE OLD BELL ··· WE MAY WIN A KEWPIE DOLL WITH THIS...
I'M NOT GOING TO FANCY THIS NUGGET UP WITH A SUNDAY SUIT··· I'LL JUST TOSS IT INTO THE FIRE, RAW, AN' SEE IF IT SPITS BACK, SEE IF IT SIMMERS INTO A BROTH OF OH BOY! OR IF IT CURLS ITS TAIL AND···
WHAT IS YOU TALKIN' ABOUT?!
DON'T YOU DIG THE MOTHER TONGUE OR DO YOU NEED ANOTHER EAR?

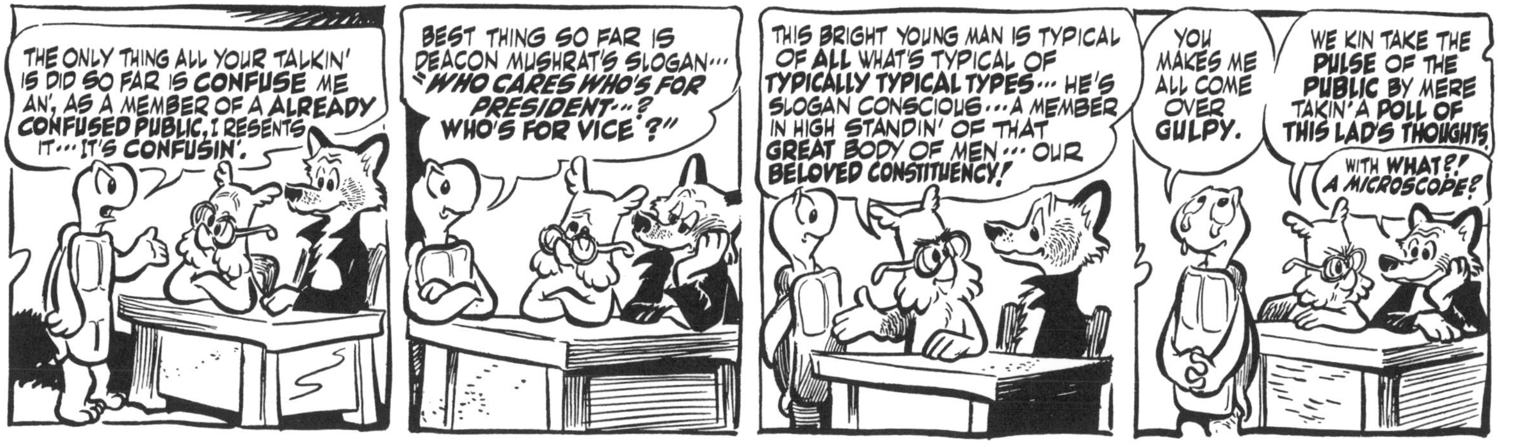
THE ONLY THING ALL YOUR TALKIN' IS DID SO FAR IS CONFUSE ME AN', AS A MEMBER OF A ALREADY CONFUSED PUBLIC, I RESENTS IT··· IT'S CONFUSIN'.
BEST THING SO FAR IS DEACON MUSHRAT'S SLOGAN··· "WHO CARES WHO'S FOR PRESIDENT··? WHO'S FOR VICE ?"
THIS BRIGHT YOUNG MAN IS TYPICAL OF ALL WHAT'S TYPICAL OF TYPICALLY TYPICAL TYPES··· HE'S SLOGAN CONSCIOUS···A MEMBER IN HIGH STANDIN' OF THAT GREAT BODY OF MEN··· OUR BELOVED CONSTITUENCY!
YOU MAKES ME ALL COME OVER GULPY.
WE KIN TAKE THE PULSE OF THE PUBLIC BY MERE TAKIN' A POLL OF THIS LAD'S THOUGHTS.
WITH WHAT?! A MICROSCOPE?

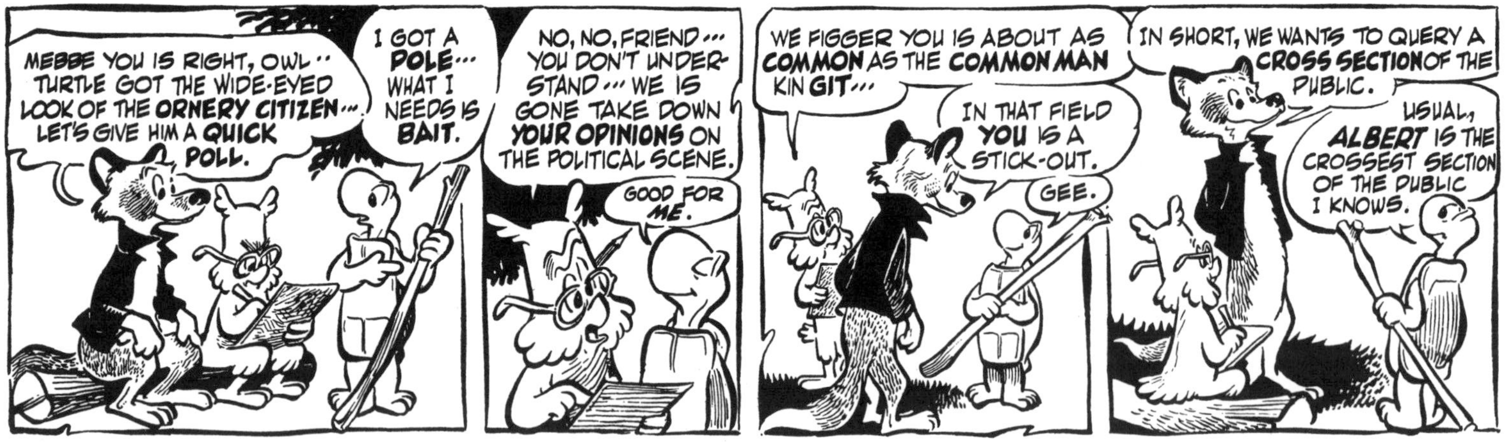
MEBBE YOU IS RIGHT, OWL.. TURTLE GOT THE WIDE-EYED LOOK OF THE ORNERY CITIZEN... LET'S GIVE HIM A QUICK POLL.
I GOT A POLE... WHAT I NEEDS IS BAIT.
NO, NO, FRIEND... YOU DON'T UNDERSTAND... WE IS GONE TAKE DOWN YOUR OPINIONS ON THE POLITICAL SCENE.
GOOD FOR ME.
WE FIGGER YOU IS ABOUT AS COMMON AS THE COMMON MAN KIN GIT...
IN THAT FIELD YOU IS A STICK-OUT.
GEE.
IN SHORT, WE WANTS TO QUERY A CROSS SECTION OF THE PUBLIC.
USUAL, ALBERT IS THE CROSSEST SECTION OF THE PUBLIC I KNOWS.

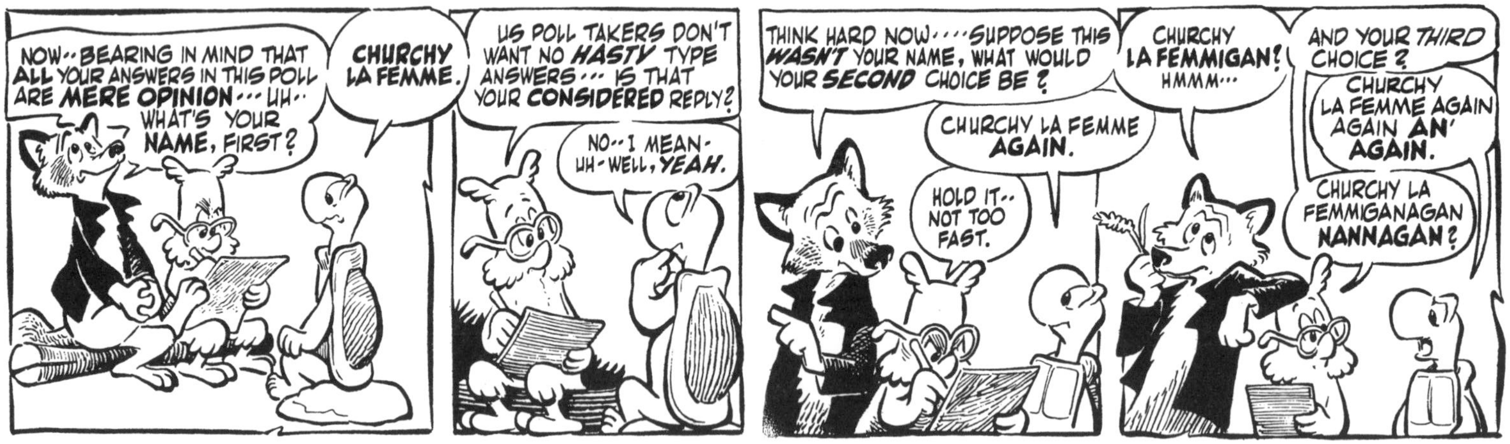
NOW.. BEARING IN MIND THAT ALL YOUR ANSWERS IN THIS POLL ARE MERE OPINION... UH.. WHAT'S YOUR NAME, FIRST?
CHURCHY LA FEMME.
US POLL TAKERS DON'T WANT NO HASTY TYPE ANSWERS... IS THAT YOUR CONSIDERED REPLY?
NO.. I MEAN.. UH-WELL, YEAH.
THINK HARD NOW.... SUPPOSE THIS WASN'T YOUR NAME, WHAT WOULD YOUR SECOND CHOICE BE?
CHURCHY LA FEMME AGAIN.
HOLD IT.. NOT TOO FAST.
CHURCHY LA FEMMIGAN! HMMM...
AND YOUR THIRD CHOICE?
CHURCHY LA FEMME AGAIN AGAIN AN' AGAIN.
CHURCHY LA FEMMIGANAGAN NANNAGAN?

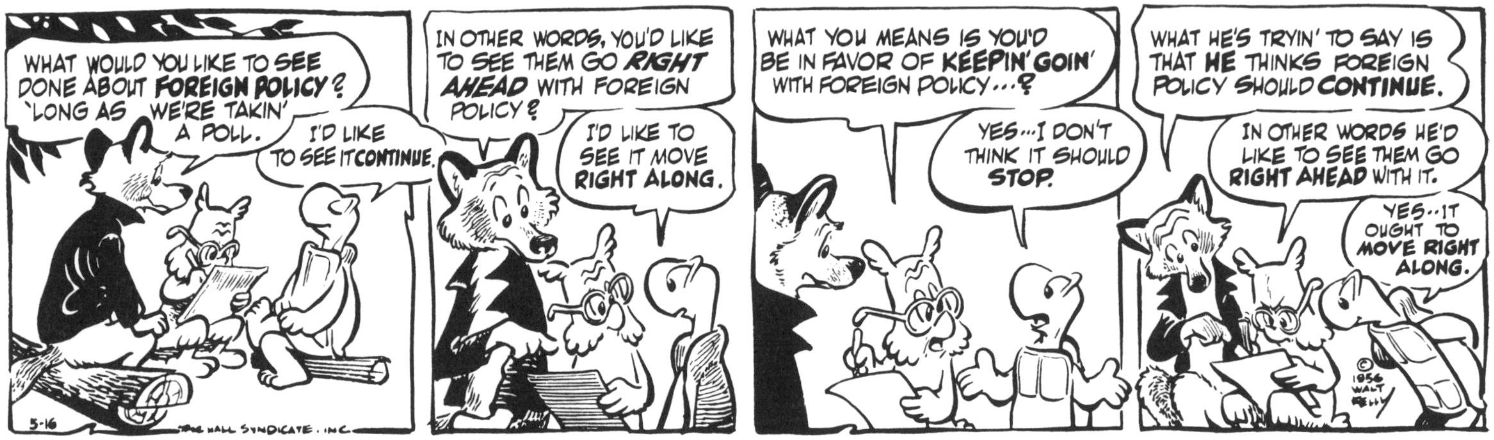
WHAT WOULD YOU LIKE TO SEE DONE ABOUT FOREIGN POLICY? 'LONG AS WE'RE TAKIN' A POLL.
I'D LIKE TO SEE IT CONTINUE.
IN OTHER WORDS, YOU'D LIKE TO SEE THEM GO RIGHT AHEAD WITH FOREIGN POLICY?
I'D LIKE TO SEE IT MOVE RIGHT ALONG.
WHAT YOU MEANS IS YOU'D BE IN FAVOR OF KEEPIN' GOIN' WITH FOREIGN POLICY...?
YES...I DON'T THINK IT SHOULD STOP.
WHAT HE'S TRYIN' TO SAY IS THAT HE THINKS FOREIGN POLICY SHOULD CONTINUE.
IN OTHER WORDS HE'D LIKE TO SEE THEM GO RIGHT AHEAD WITH IT.
YES..IT OUGHT TO MOVE RIGHT ALONG.
5-16
THE HALL SYNDICATE, INC.
© 1956 WALT KELLY

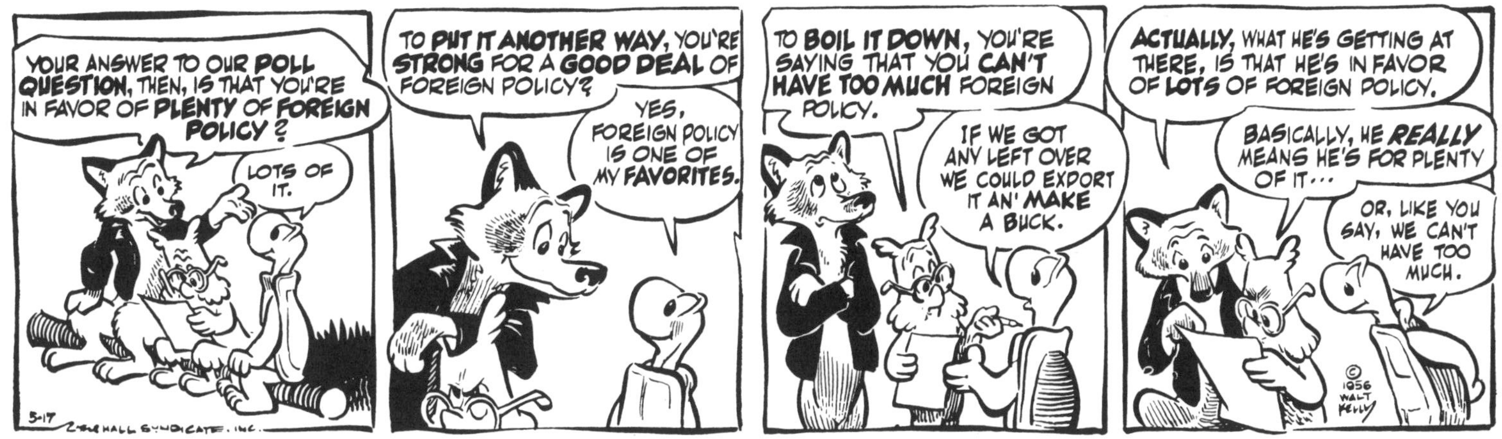
YOUR ANSWER TO OUR POLL QUESTION, THEN, IS THAT YOU'RE IN FAVOR OF PLENTY OF FOREIGN POLICY?
LOTS OF IT.
TO PUT IT ANOTHER WAY, YOU'RE STRONG FOR A GOOD DEAL OF FOREIGN POLICY?
YES, FOREIGN POLICY IS ONE OF MY FAVORITES.
TO BOIL IT DOWN, YOU'RE SAYING THAT YOU CAN'T HAVE TOO MUCH FOREIGN POLICY.
IF WE GOT ANY LEFT OVER WE COULD EXPORT IT AN' MAKE A BUCK.
ACTUALLY, WHAT HE'S GETTING AT THERE, IS THAT HE'S IN FAVOR OF LOTS OF FOREIGN POLICY.
BASICALLY, HE REALLY MEANS HE'S FOR PLENTY OF IT...
OR, LIKE YOU SAY, WE CAN'T HAVE TOO MUCH.
© 1956 WALT KELLY
5-17

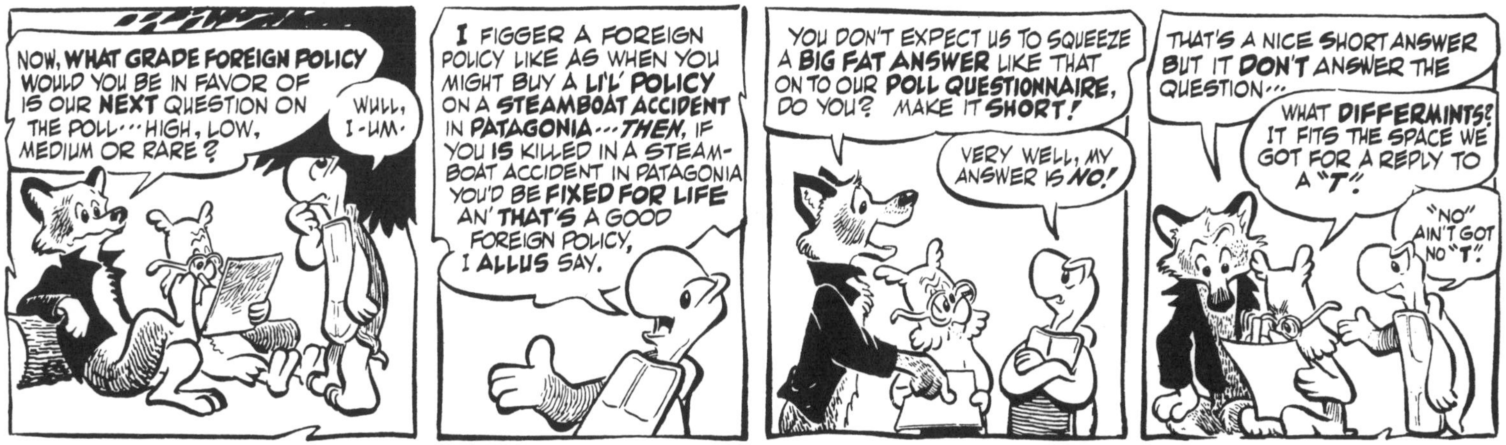
NOW, WHAT GRADE FOREIGN POLICY WOULD YOU BE IN FAVOR OF IS OUR NEXT QUESTION ON THE POLL... HIGH, LOW, MEDIUM OR RARE?
WULL, I-UM.
I FIGGER A FOREIGN POLICY LIKE AS WHEN YOU MIGHT BUY A LI'L' POLICY ON A STEAMBOAT ACCIDENT IN PATAGONIA...THEN, IF YOU IS KILLED IN A STEAMBOAT ACCIDENT IN PATAGONIA YOU'D BE FIXED FOR LIFE AN' THAT'S A GOOD FOREIGN POLICY, I ALLUS SAY.
YOU DON'T EXPECT US TO SQUEEZE A BIG FAT ANSWER LIKE THAT ON TO OUR POLL QUESTIONNAIRE, DO YOU? MAKE IT SHORT!
VERY WELL, MY ANSWER IS NO!
THAT'S A NICE SHORT ANSWER BUT IT DON'T ANSWER THE QUESTION...
WHAT DIFFERMINTS? IT FITS THE SPACE WE GOT FOR A REPLY TO A "T".
"NO" AIN'T GOT NO "T".

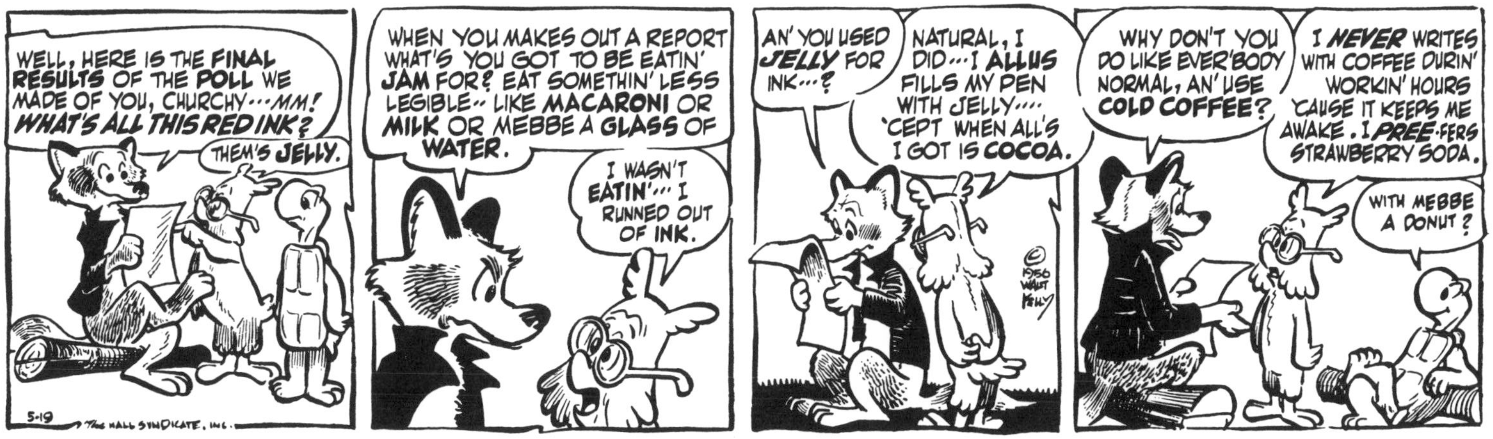
WELL, HERE IS THE FINAL RESULTS OF THE POLL WE MADE OF YOU, CHURCHY...MM! WHAT'S ALL THIS RED INK?
THEM'S JELLY.
WHEN YOU MAKES OUT A REPORT WHAT'S YOU GOT TO BE EATIN' JAM FOR? EAT SOMETHIN' LESS LEGIBLE.. LIKE MACARONI OR MILK OR MEBBE A GLASS OF WATER.
I WASN'T EATIN'... I RUNNED OUT OF INK.
AN' YOU USED JELLY FOR INK...?
NATURAL, I DID...I ALLUS FILLS MY PEN WITH JELLY.... 'CEPT WHEN ALL'S I GOT IS COCOA.
WHY DON'T YOU DO LIKE EVER'BODY NORMAL, AN' USE COLD COFFEE?
I NEVER WRITES WITH COFFEE DURIN' WORKIN' HOURS 'CAUSE IT KEEPS ME AWAKE. I PREE-FERS STRAWBERRY SODA.
WITH MEBBE A DONUT?
© 1956 WALT KELLY
5-19

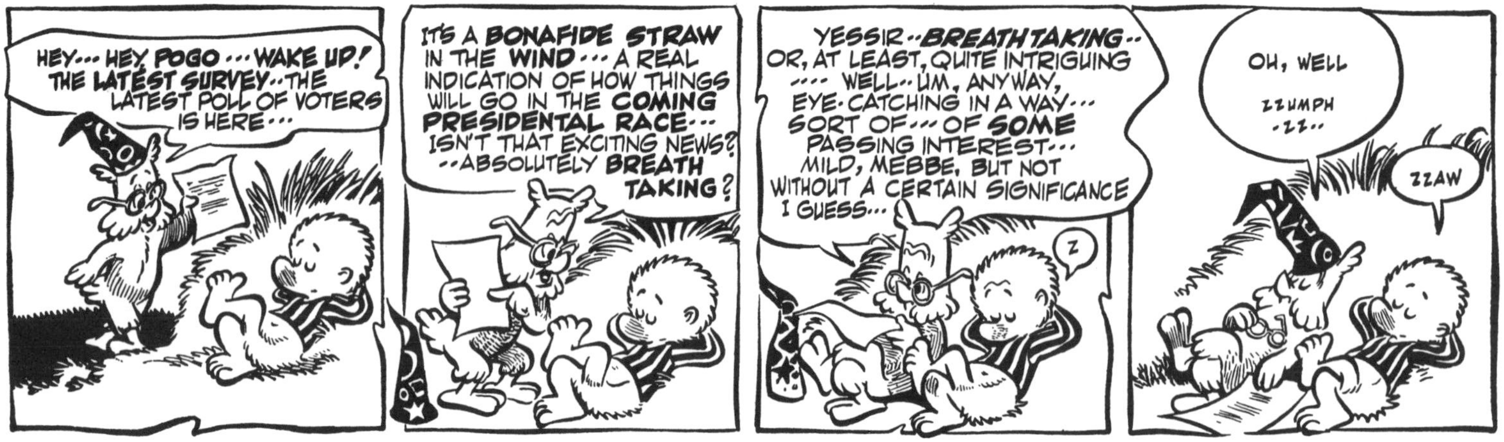
HEY... HEY POGO ... WAKE UP! THE LATEST SURVEY.. THE LATEST POLL OF VOTERS IS HERE...
IT'S A BONAFIDE STRAW IN THE WIND ... A REAL INDICATION OF HOW THINGS WILL GO IN THE COMING PRESIDENTAL RACE... ISN'T THAT EXCITING NEWS? ..ABSOLUTELY BREATH TAKING?
YESSIR..BREATHTAKING.. OR, AT LEAST, QUITE INTRIGUING .... WELL..UM, ANYWAY, EYE-CATCHING IN A WAY... SORT OF... OF SOME PASSING INTEREST... MILD, MEBBE, BUT NOT WITHOUT A CERTAIN SIGNIFICANCE I GUESS...
Z
OH, WELL
ZZUMPH .ZZ..
ZZAW

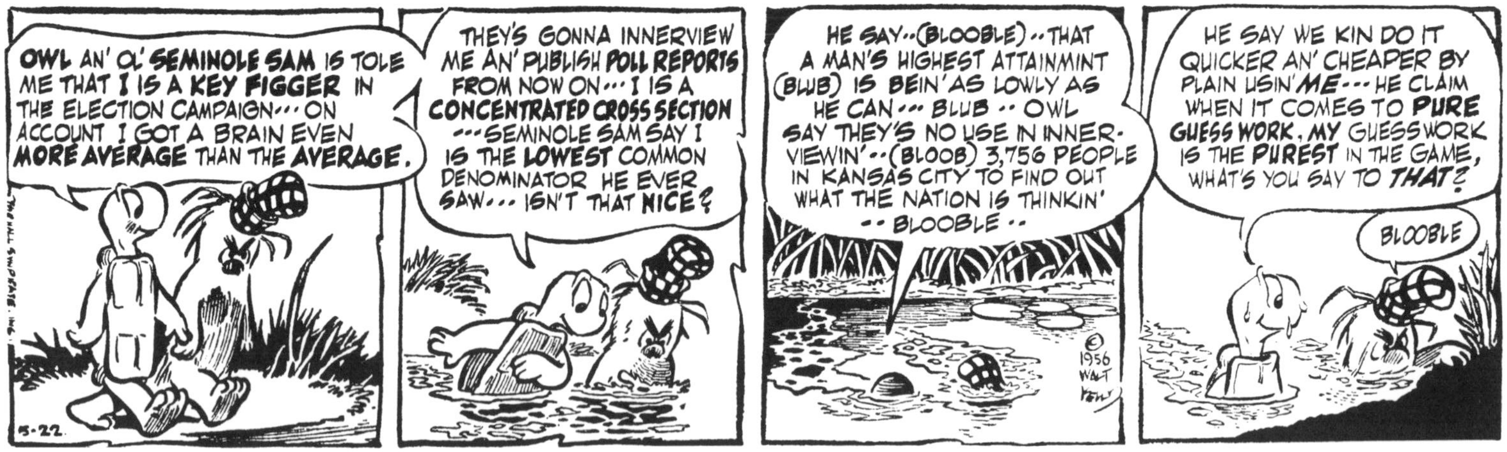
OWL AN' OL' SEMINOLE SAM IS TOLE ME THAT I IS A KEY FIGGER IN THE ELECTION CAMPAIGN... ON ACCOUNT I GOT A BRAIN EVEN MORE AVERAGE THAN THE AVERAGE.
THE HALL SYNDICATE, INC.
5-22.
THEY'S GONNA INNERVIEW ME AN' PUBLISH POLL REPORTS FROM NOW ON... I IS A CONCENTRATED CROSS SECTION ...SEMINOLE SAM SAY I IS THE LOWEST COMMON DENOMINATOR HE EVER SAW... ISN'T THAT NICE?
HE SAY..(BLOOBLE)..THAT A MAN'S HIGHEST ATTAINMINT (BLUB) IS BEIN' AS LOWLY AS HE CAN ... BLUB .. OWL SAY THEY'S NO USE IN INNER-VIEWIN'..(BLOOB) 3,756 PEOPLE IN KANSAS CITY TO FIND OUT WHAT THE NATION IS THINKIN' .. BLOOBLE ..
© 1956 WALT KELLY
HE SAY WE KIN DO IT QUICKER AN' CHEAPER BY PLAIN USIN' ME... HE CLAIM WHEN IT COMES TO PURE GUESS WORK. MY GUESSWORK IS THE PUREST IN THE GAME, WHAT'S YOU SAY TO THAT?
BLOOBLE

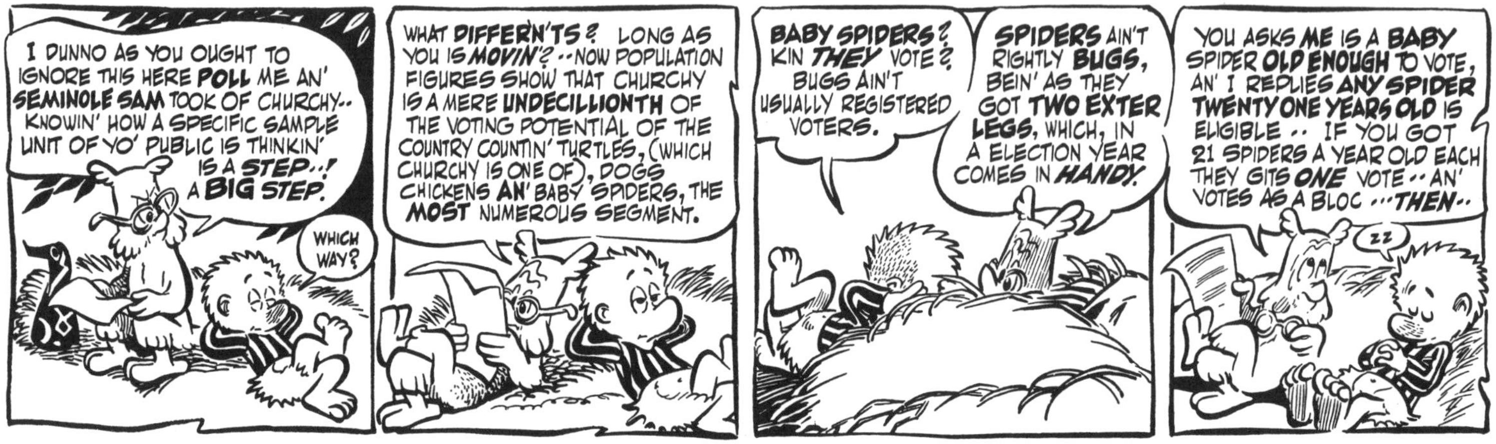
I DUNNO AS YOU OUGHT TO IGNORE THIS HERE POLL ME AN' SEMINOLE SAM TOOK OF CHURCHY.. KNOWIN' HOW A SPECIFIC SAMPLE UNIT OF YO' PUBLIC IS THINKIN' IS A STEP..! A BIG STEP.
WHICH WAY?
WHAT DIFFERN'TS? LONG AS YOU IS MOVIN'? ..NOW POPULATION FIGURES SHOW THAT CHURCHY IS A MERE UNDECILLIONTH OF THE VOTING POTENTIAL OF THE COUNTRY COUNTIN' TURTLES, (WHICH CHURCHY IS ONE OF), DOGS CHICKENS AN' BABY SPIDERS, THE MOST NUMEROUS SEGMENT.
BABY SPIDERS? KIN THEY VOTE? BUGS AIN'T USUALLY REGISTERED VOTERS.
SPIDERS AIN'T RIGHTLY BUGS, BEIN' AS THEY GOT TWO EXTER LEGS, WHICH, IN A ELECTION YEAR COMES IN HANDY.
YOU ASKS ME IS A BABY SPIDER OLD ENOUGH TO VOTE, AN' I REPLIES ANY SPIDER TWENTY ONE YEARS OLD IS ELIGIBLE .. IF YOU GOT 21 SPIDERS A YEAR OLD EACH THEY GITS ONE VOTE .. AN' VOTES AS A BLOC ...THEN..
ZZ

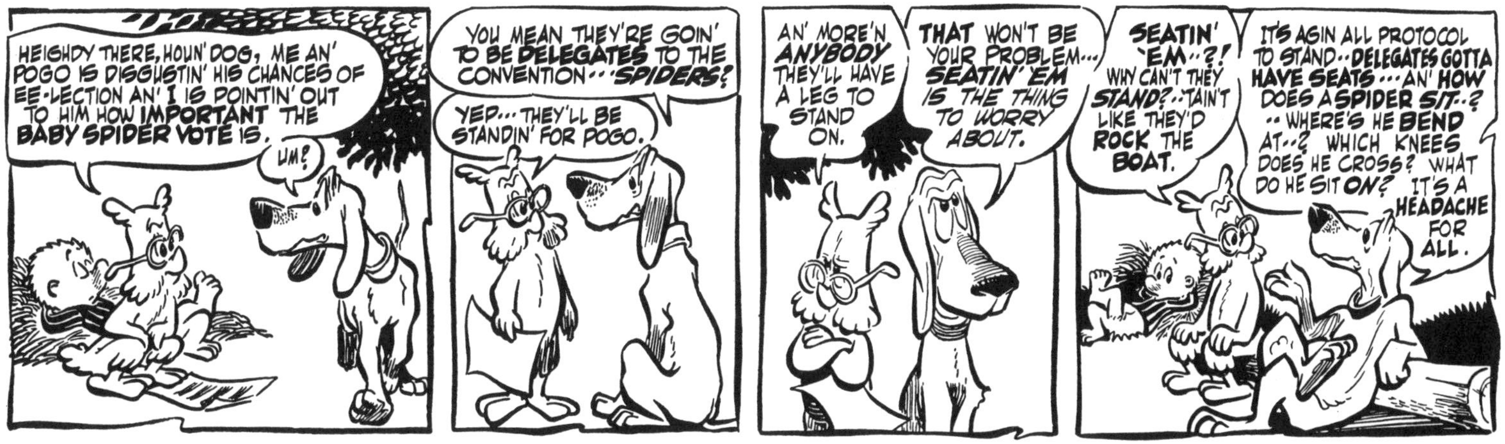
HEIGHDY THERE, HOUN' DOG, ME AN' POGO IS DISGUSTIN' HIS CHANCES OF EE-LECTION AN' I IS POINTIN' OUT TO HIM HOW IMPORTANT THE BABY SPIDER VOTE IS.
UM?
YOU MEAN THEY'RE GOIN' TO BE DELEGATES TO THE CONVENTION... 'SPIDERS?'
YEP... THEY'LL BE STANDIN' FOR POGO.
AN' MORE'N ANYBODY THEY'LL HAVE A LEG TO STAND ON.
THAT WON'T BE YOUR PROBLEM... SEATIN' 'EM IS THE THING TO WORRY ABOUT.
SEATIN' 'EM..?! WHY CAN'T THEY STAND?..'TAIN'T LIKE THEY'D ROCK THE BOAT.
IT'S AGIN ALL PROTOCOL TO STAND..DELEGATES GOTTA HAVE SEATS... AN' HOW DOES A SPIDER SIT..? ..WHERE'S HE BEND AT..? WHICH KNEES DOES HE CROSS? WHAT DO HE SIT ON? IT'S A HEADACHE FOR ALL.

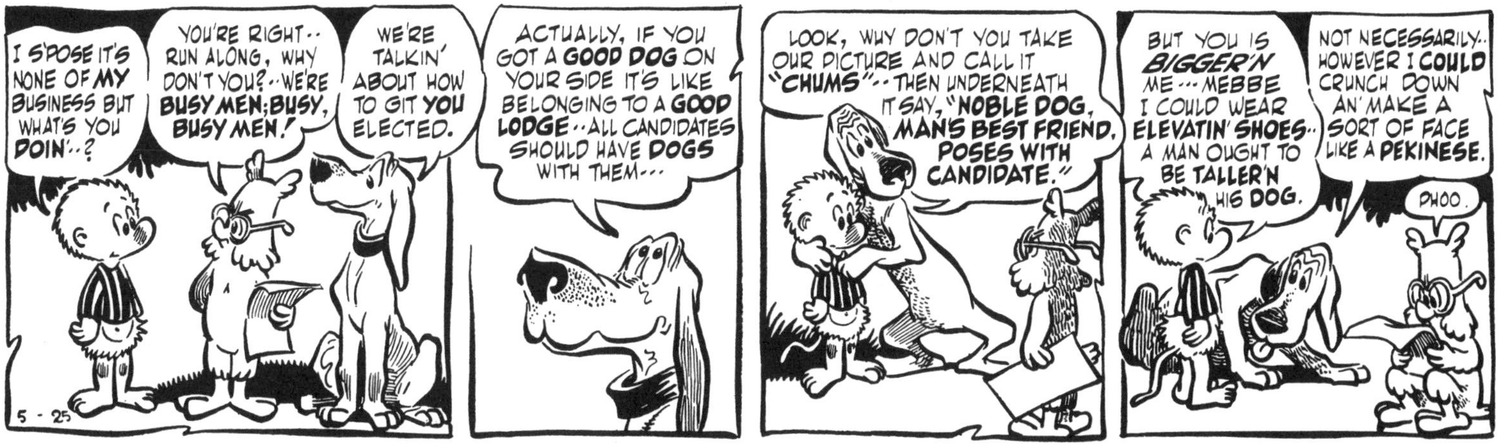
5-25
I S'POSE IT'S NONE OF MY BUSINESS BUT WHAT'S YOU DOIN'..?
YOU'RE RIGHT.. RUN ALONG, WHY DON'T YOU?..WE'RE BUSY MEN; BUSY, BUSY MEN!
WE'RE TALKIN' ABOUT HOW TO GIT YOU ELECTED.
ACTUALLY, IF YOU GOT A GOOD DOG ON YOUR SIDE IT'S LIKE BELONGING TO A GOOD LODGE..ALL CANDIDATES SHOULD HAVE DOGS WITH THEM...
LOOK, WHY DON'T YOU TAKE OUR PICTURE AND CALL IT "CHUMS".. THEN UNDERNEATH IT SAY, "NOBLE DOG, MAN'S BEST FRIEND, POSES WITH CANDIDATE."
BUT YOU IS BIGGER'N ME... MEBBE I COULD WEAR ELEVATIN' SHOES.. A MAN OUGHT TO BE TALLER'N HIS DOG.
NOT NECESSARILY.. HOWEVER I COULD CRUNCH DOWN AN' MAKE A SORT OF FACE LIKE A PEKINESE.
PHOO.

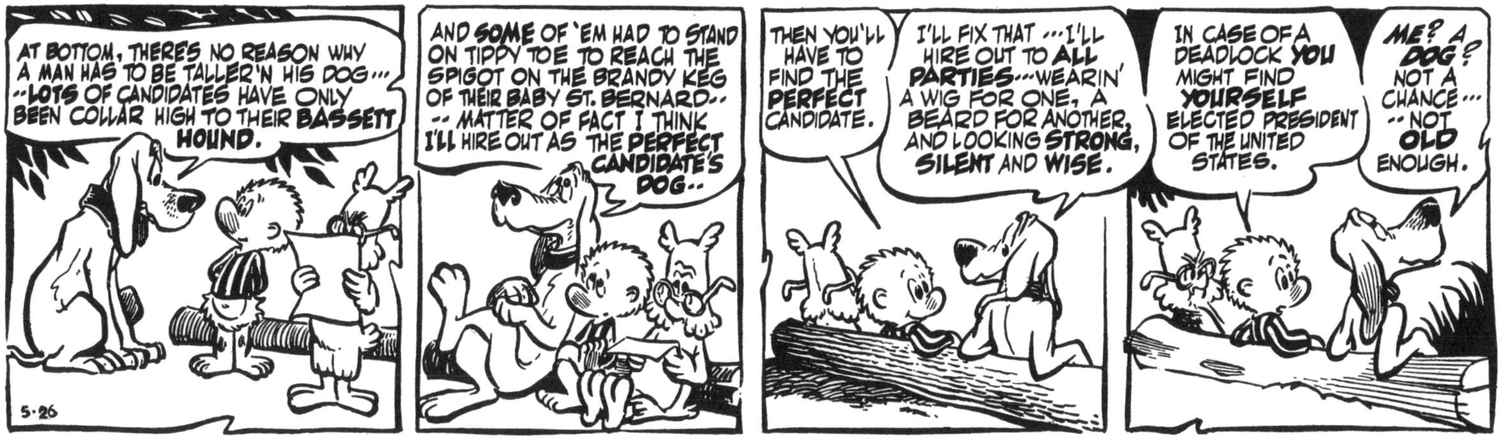
5-26
AT BOTTOM, THERE'S NO REASON WHY A MAN HAS TO BE TALLER'N HIS DOG... ..LOTS OF CANDIDATES HAVE ONLY BEEN COLLAR HIGH TO THEIR BASSETT HOUND.
AND SOME OF 'EM HAD TO STAND ON TIPPY TOE TO REACH THE SPIGOT ON THE BRANDY KEG OF THEIR BABY ST. BERNARD.. ..MATTER OF FACT I THINK I'LL HIRE OUT AS THE PERFECT CANDIDATE'S DOG..
THEN YOU'LL HAVE TO FIND THE PERFECT CANDIDATE.
I'LL FIX THAT ...I'LL HIRE OUT TO ALL PARTIES...WEARIN' A WIG FOR ONE, A BEARD FOR ANOTHER, AND LOOKING STRONG, SILENT AND WISE.
IN CASE OF A DEADLOCK YOU MIGHT FIND YOURSELF ELECTED PRESIDENT OF THE UNITED STATES.
ME? A DOG? NOT A CHANCE... ..NOT OLD ENOUGH.

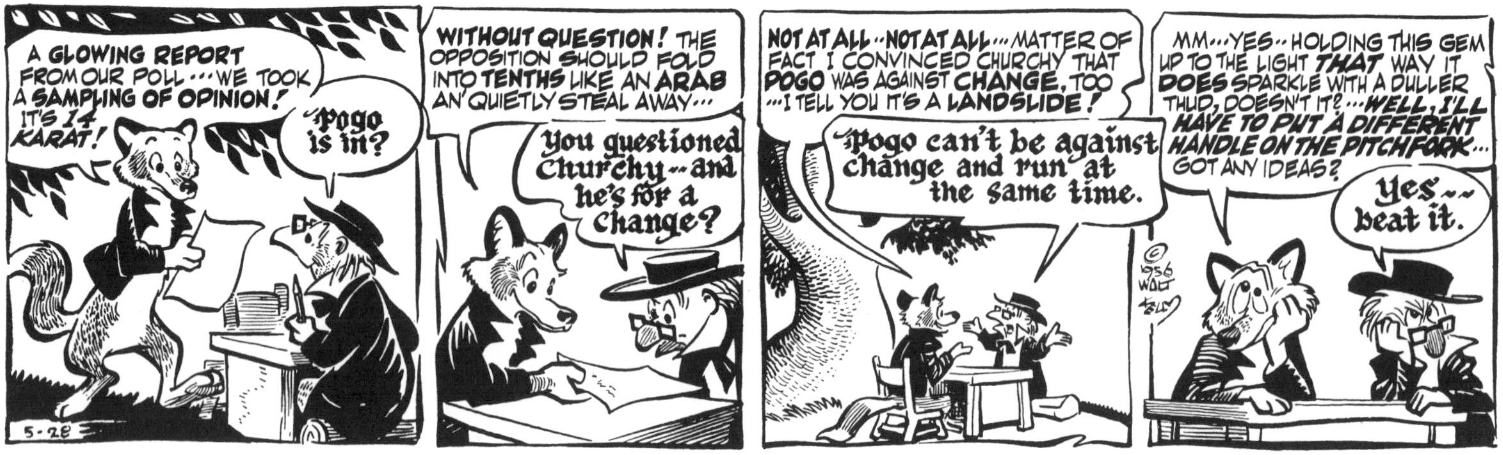
A GLOWING REPORT FROM OUR POLL ··· WE TOOK A SAMPLING OF OPINION! IT'S 14 KARAT!
Pogo is in?
5-28
WITHOUT QUESTION! THE OPPOSITION SHOULD FOLD INTO TENTHS LIKE AN ARAB AN' QUIETLY STEAL AWAY···
You questioned Churchy -- and he's for a change?
NOT AT ALL ·· NOT AT ALL ··· MATTER OF FACT I CONVINCED CHURCHY THAT POGO WAS AGAINST CHANGE, TOO ··· I TELL YOU IT'S A LANDSLIDE!
Pogo can't be against change and run at the same time.
MM ··· YES ·· HOLDING THIS GEM UP TO THE LIGHT THAT WAY IT DOES SPARKLE WITH A DULLER THUD, DOESN'T IT? ··· WELL, I'LL HAVE TO PUT A DIFFERENT HANDLE ON THE PITCHFORK··· GOT ANY IDEAS?
Yes -- beat it.

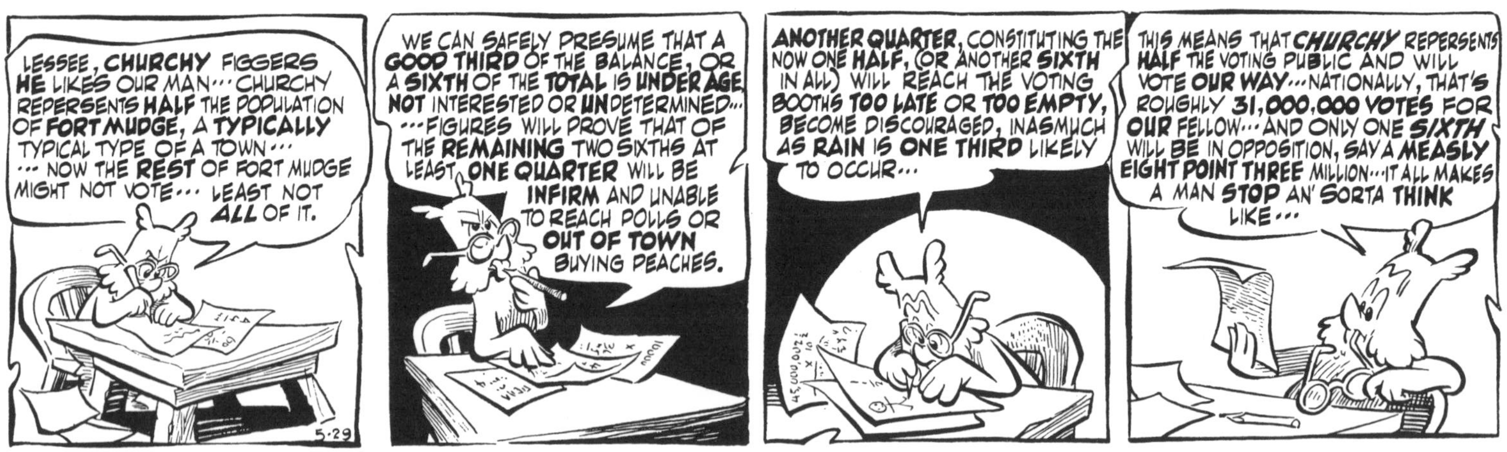
LESSEE, CHURCHY FIGGERS HE LIKES OUR MAN ··· CHURCHY REPERSENTS HALF THE POPULATION OF FORT MUDGE, A TYPICALLY TYPICAL TYPE OF A TOWN ··· ··· NOW THE REST OF FORT MUDGE MIGHT NOT VOTE ··· LEAST NOT ALL OF IT.
5-29
WE CAN SAFELY PRESUME THAT A GOOD THIRD OF THE BALANCE, OR A SIXTH OF THE TOTAL IS UNDER AGE, NOT INTERESTED OR UNDETERMINED··· ··· FIGURES WILL PROVE THAT OF THE REMAINING TWO SIXTHS AT LEAST ONE QUARTER WILL BE INFIRM AND UNABLE TO REACH POLLS OR OUT OF TOWN BUYING PEACHES.
ANOTHER QUARTER, CONSTITUTING THE NOW ONE HALF, (OR ANOTHER SIXTH IN ALL) WILL REACH THE VOTING BOOTHS TOO LATE OR TOO EMPTY, BECOME DISCOURAGED, INASMUCH AS RAIN IS ONE THIRD LIKELY TO OCCUR···
THIS MEANS THAT CHURCHY REPERSENTS HALF THE VOTING PUBLIC AND WILL VOTE OUR WAY··· NATIONALLY, THAT'S ROUGHLY 31,000,000 VOTES FOR OUR FELLOW··· AND ONLY ONE SIXTH WILL BE IN OPPOSITION, SAY A MEASLY EIGHT POINT THREE MILLION··· IT ALL MAKES A MAN STOP AN' SORTA THINK LIKE···

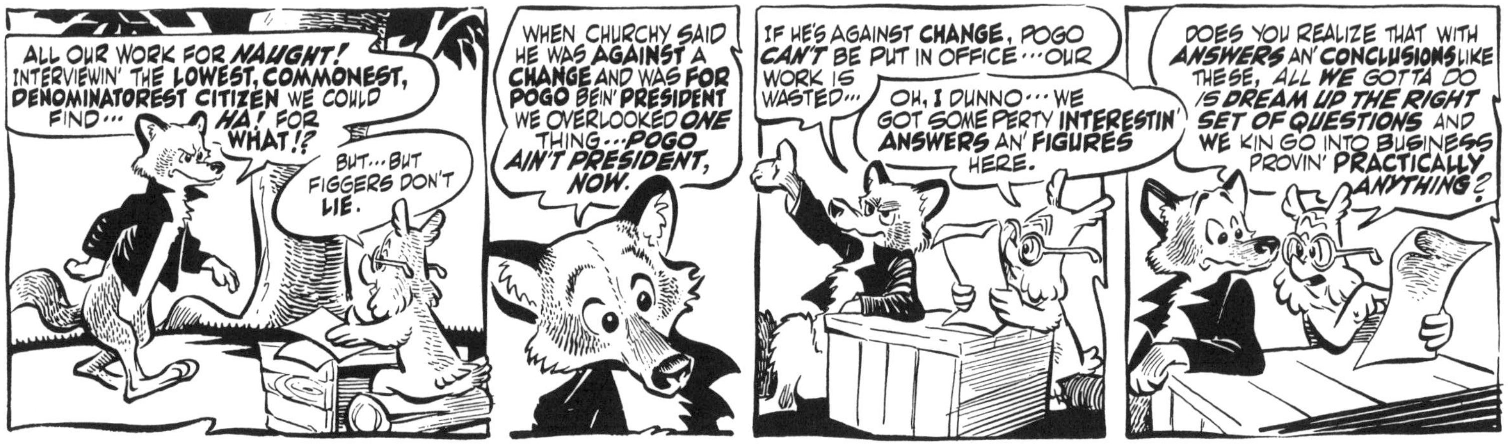
ALL OUR WORK FOR NAUGHT! INTERVIEWIN' THE LOWEST, COMMONEST, DENOMINATOREST CITIZEN WE COULD FIND··· HA! FOR WHAT!?
BUT··· BUT FIGGERS DON'T LIE.
WHEN CHURCHY SAID HE WAS AGAINST A CHANGE AND WAS FOR POGO BEIN' PRESIDENT WE OVERLOOKED ONE THING··· POGO AIN'T PRESIDENT, NOW.
IF HE'S AGAINST CHANGE, POGO CAN'T BE PUT IN OFFICE··· OUR WORK IS WASTED···
OH, I DUNNO··· WE GOT SOME PERTY INTERESTIN' ANSWERS AN' FIGURES HERE.
DOES YOU REALIZE THAT WITH ANSWERS AN' CONCLUSIONS LIKE THESE, ALL WE GOTTA DO IS DREAM UP THE RIGHT SET OF QUESTIONS AND WE KIN GO INTO BUSINESS PROVIN' PRACTICALLY ANYTHING?

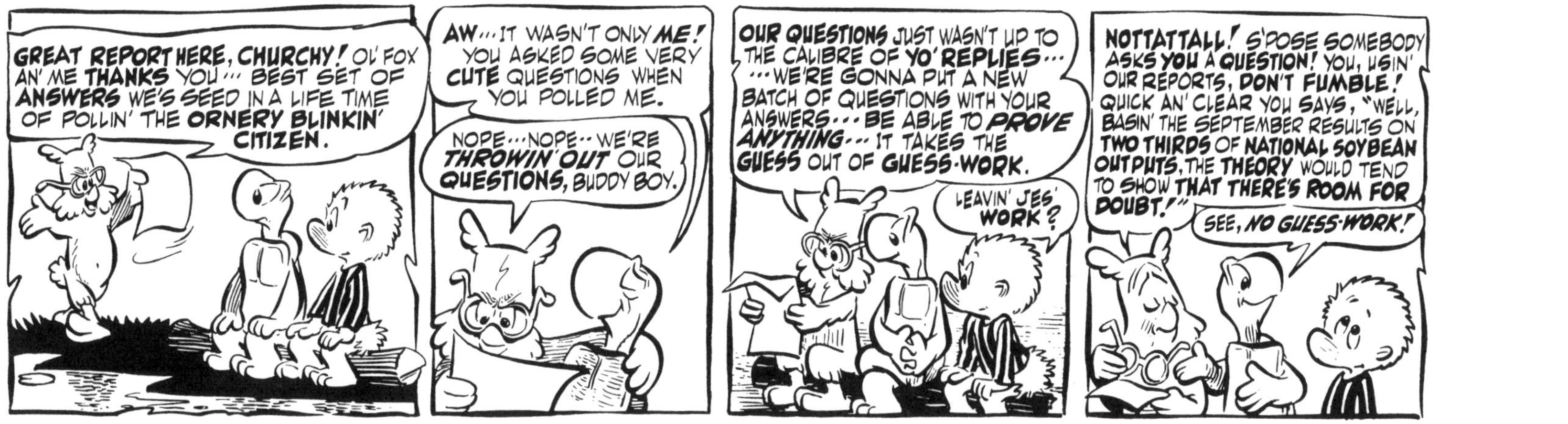
GREAT REPORT HERE, CHURCHY! OL' FOX AN' ME THANKS YOU... BEST SET OF ANSWERS WE'S SEED IN A LIFE TIME OF POLLIN' THE ORNERY BLINKIN' CITIZEN.
AW... IT WASN'T ONLY ME! YOU ASKED SOME VERY CUTE QUESTIONS WHEN YOU POLLED ME.
NOPE... NOPE... WE'RE THROWIN' OUT OUR QUESTIONS, BUDDY BOY.
OUR QUESTIONS JUST WASN'T UP TO THE CALIBRE OF YO' REPLIES... ...WE'RE GONNA PUT A NEW BATCH OF QUESTIONS WITH YOUR ANSWERS... BE ABLE TO PROVE ANYTHING... IT TAKES THE GUESS OUT OF GUESS-WORK.
LEAVIN' JES' WORK?
NOTTATTALL! S'POSE SOMEBODY ASKS YOU A QUESTION! YOU, USIN' OUR REPORTS, DON'T FUMBLE! QUICK AN' CLEAR YOU SAYS, "WELL, BASIN' THE SEPTEMBER RESULTS ON TWO THIRDS OF NATIONAL SOYBEAN OUTPUTS, THE THEORY WOULD TEND TO SHOW THAT THERE'S ROOM FOR DOUBT!'"
SEE, NO GUESS-WORK!

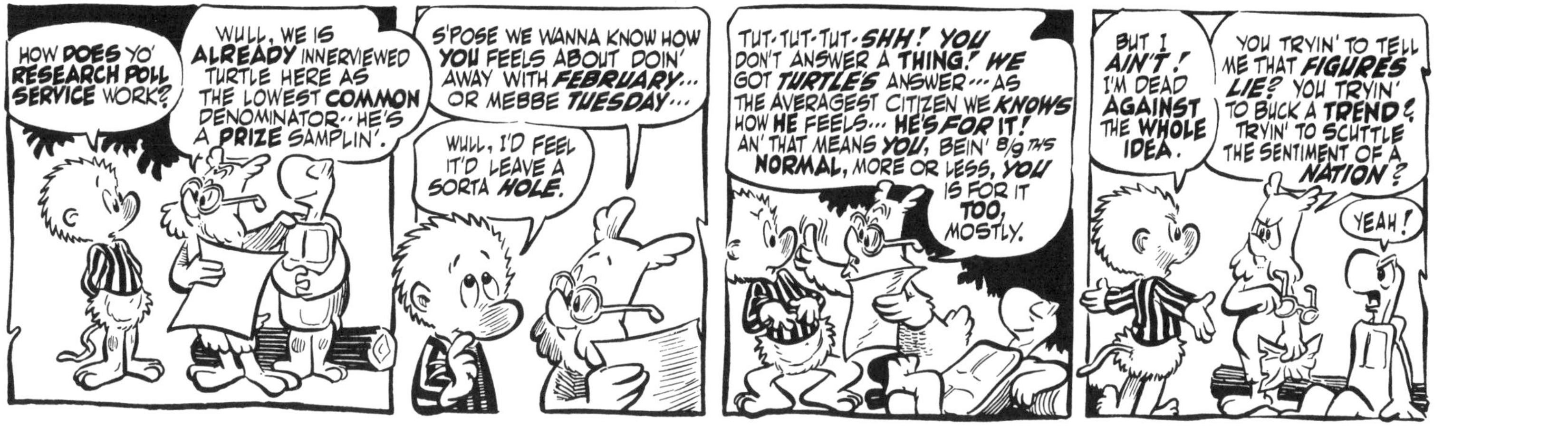
HOW DOES YO' RESEARCH POLL SERVICE WORK?
WULL, WE IS ALREADY INNERVIEWED TURTLE HERE AS THE LOWEST COMMON DENOMINATOR... HE'S A PRIZE SAMPLIN'.
S'POSE WE WANNA KNOW HOW YOU FEELS ABOUT DOIN' AWAY WITH FEBRUARY... OR MEBBE TUESDAY...
WULL, I'D FEEL IT'D LEAVE A SORTA HOLE.
TUT-TUT-TUT-SHH! YOU DON'T ANSWER A THING! WE GOT TURTLE'S ANSWER... AS THE AVERAGEST CITIZEN WE KNOWS HOW HE FEELS... HE'S FOR IT! AN' THAT MEANS YOU, BEIN' 8/9 THS NORMAL, MORE OR LESS, YOU IS FOR IT TOO, MOSTLY.
BUT I AIN'T! I'M DEAD AGAINST THE WHOLE IDEA.
YOU TRYIN' TO TELL ME THAT FIGURES LIE? YOU TRYIN' TO BUCK A TREND? TRYIN' TO SCUTTLE THE SENTIMENT OF A NATION?
YEAH!

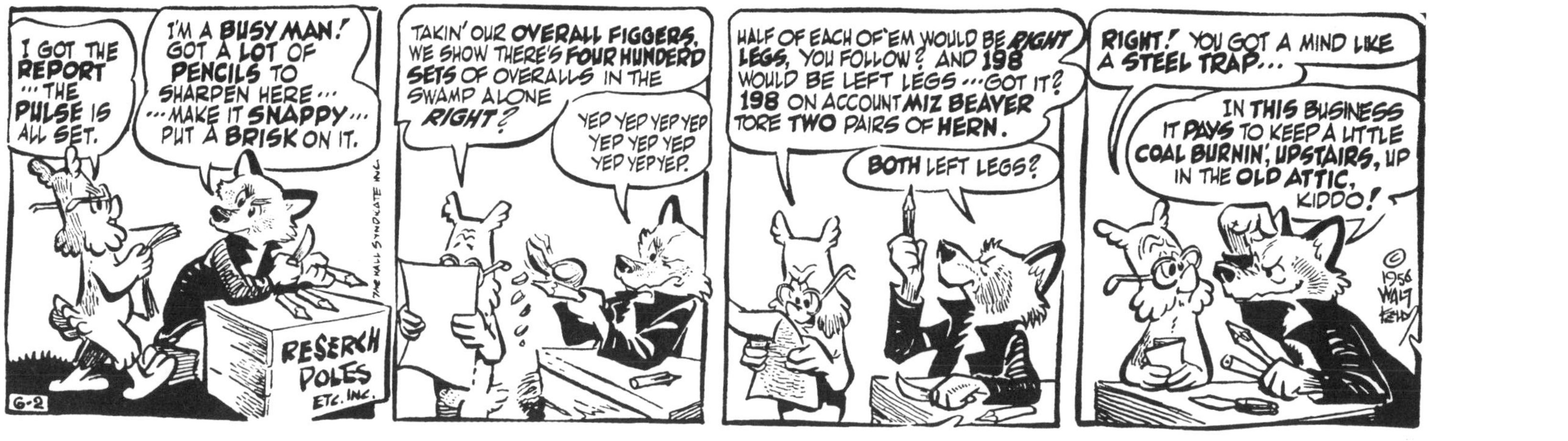
I GOT THE REPORT... THE PULSE IS ALL SET.
I'M A BUSY MAN! GOT A LOT OF PENCILS TO SHARPEN HERE... ...MAKE IT SNAPPY... PUT A BRISK ON IT.
RESERCH POLES ETC. INC.
6-2
TAKIN' OUR OVERALL FIGGERS, WE SHOW THERE'S FOUR HUNDERD SETS OF OVERALLS IN THE SWAMP ALONE RIGHT?
YEP YEP YEP YEP YEP YEP YEP YEP YEP YEP.
HALF OF EACH OF 'EM WOULD BE RIGHT LEGS, YOU FOLLOW? AND 198 WOULD BE LEFT LEGS... GOT IT? 198 ON ACCOUNT MIZ BEAVER TORE TWO PAIRS OF HERN.
BOTH LEFT LEGS?
RIGHT! YOU GOT A MIND LIKE A STEEL TRAP...
IN THIS BUSINESS IT PAYS TO KEEP A LITTLE COAL BURNIN' UPSTAIRS, UP IN THE OLD ATTIC, KIDDO!
© 1956 WALT KELLY

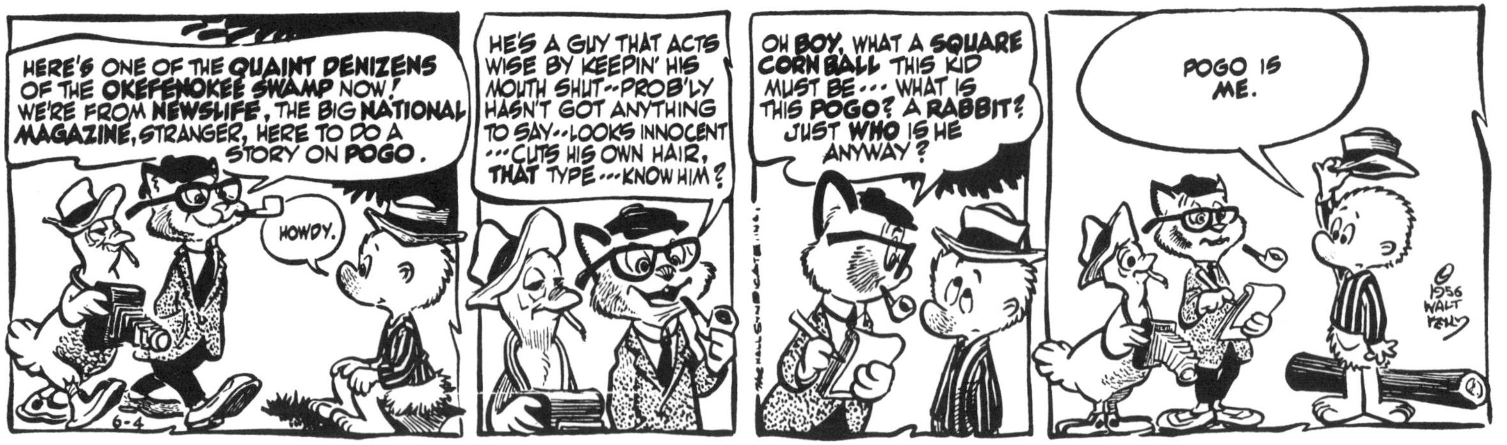
HERE'S ONE OF THE QUAINT DENIZENS OF THE OKEFENOKEE SWAMP NOW! WE'RE FROM NEWSLIFE, THE BIG NATIONAL MAGAZINE, STRANGER, HERE TO DO A STORY ON POGO.
HOWDY.
6-4
HE'S A GUY THAT ACTS WISE BY KEEPIN' HIS MOUTH SHUT--PROB'LY HASN'T GOT ANYTHING TO SAY--LOOKS INNOCENT ---CUTS HIS OWN HAIR, THAT TYPE ---KNOW HIM?
THE HALL SYNDICATE, INC.
OH BOY, WHAT A SQUARE CORN BALL THIS KID MUST BE --- WHAT IS THIS POGO? A RABBIT? JUST WHO IS HE ANYWAY?
POGO IS ME.
© 1956 WALT KELLY

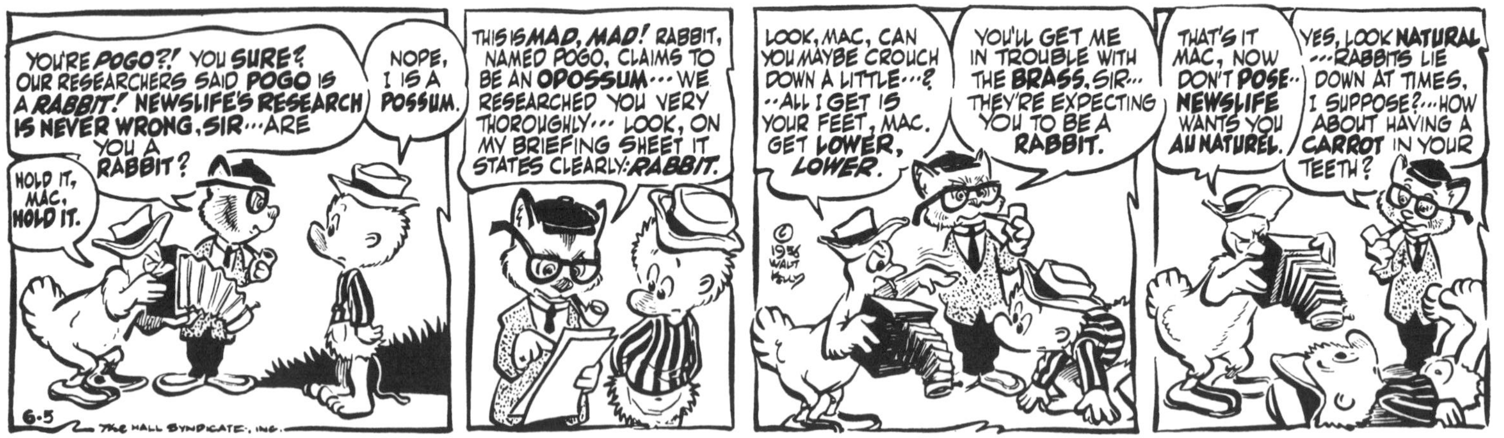
YOU'RE POGO?! YOU SURE? OUR RESEARCHERS SAID POGO IS A RABBIT! NEWSLIFE'S RESEARCH IS NEVER WRONG, SIR ---ARE YOU A RABBIT?
NOPE, I IS A POSSUM.
HOLD IT, MAC. HOLD IT.
6-5
THE HALL SYNDICATE, INC.
THIS IS MAD, MAD! RABBIT, NAMED POGO, CLAIMS TO BE AN OPOSSUM --- WE RESEARCHED YOU VERY THOROUGHLY --- LOOK, ON MY BRIEFING SHEET IT STATES CLEARLY: RABBIT.
LOOK, MAC, CAN YOU MAYBE CROUCH DOWN A LITTLE ---? --ALL I GET IS YOUR FEET, MAC. GET LOWER, LOWER.
YOU'LL GET ME IN TROUBLE WITH THE BRASS, SIR--- THEY'RE EXPECTING YOU TO BE A RABBIT.
© 1956 WALT KELLY
THAT'S IT MAC, NOW DON'T POSE -- NEWSLIFE WANTS YOU AU NATUREL.
YES, LOOK NATURAL ---RABBITS LIE DOWN AT TIMES, I SUPPOSE? ---HOW ABOUT HAVING A CARROT IN YOUR TEETH?

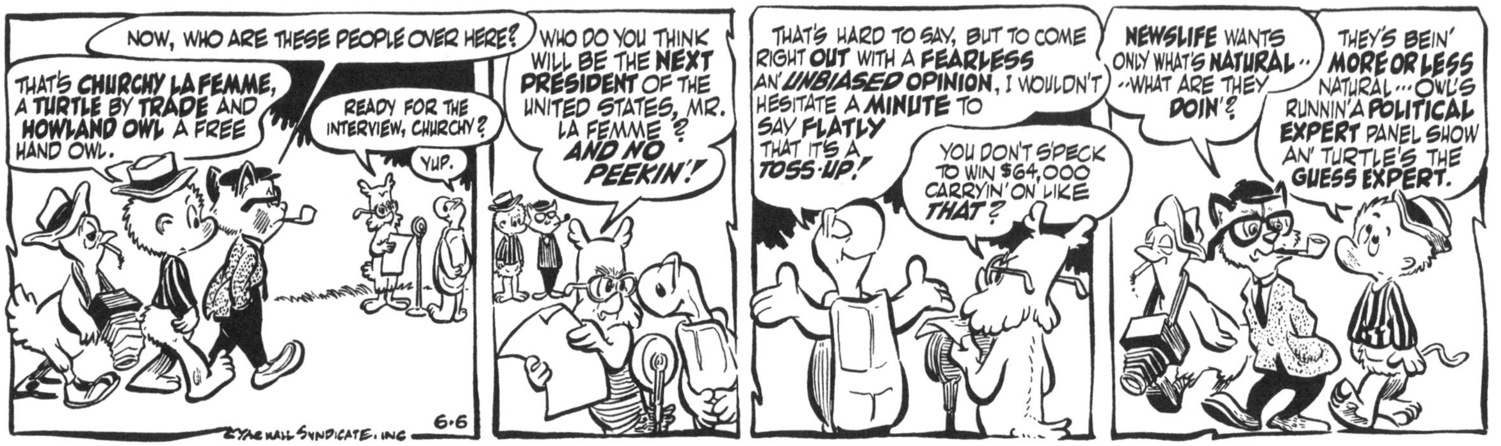
NOW, WHO ARE THESE PEOPLE OVER HERE?
THAT'S CHURCHY LA FEMME, A TURTLE BY TRADE AND HOWLAND OWL A FREE HAND OWL.
READY FOR THE INTERVIEW, CHURCHY?
YUP.
WHO DO YOU THINK WILL BE THE NEXT PRESIDENT OF THE UNITED STATES, MR. LA FEMME? AND NO PEEKIN'!
THE HALL SYNDICATE, INC
6-6
THAT'S HARD TO SAY, BUT TO COME RIGHT OUT WITH A FEARLESS AN' UNBIASED OPINION, I WOULDN'T HESITATE A MINUTE TO SAY FLATLY THAT IT'S A TOSS-UP!
YOU DON'T S'PECK TO WIN $64,000 CARRYIN' ON LIKE THAT?
NEWSLIFE WANTS ONLY WHAT'S NATURAL -- --WHAT ARE THEY DOIN'?
THEY'S BEIN' MORE OR LESS NATURAL --- OWL'S RUNNIN' A POLITICAL EXPERT PANEL SHOW AN' TURTLE'S THE GUESS EXPERT.

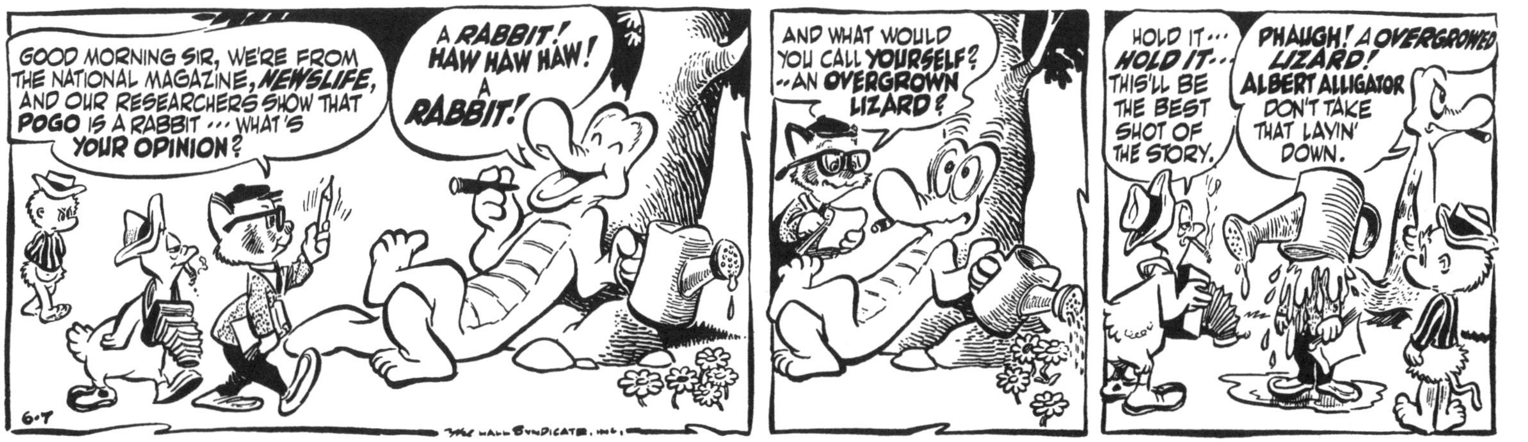
GOOD MORNING SIR, WE'RE FROM THE NATIONAL MAGAZINE, NEWSLIFE, AND OUR RESEARCHERS SHOW THAT POGO IS A RABBIT ... WHAT'S YOUR OPINION?
A RABBIT! HAW HAW HAW! A RABBIT!
AND WHAT WOULD YOU CALL YOURSELF? ..AN OVERGROWN LIZARD?
HOLD IT... HOLD IT... THIS'LL BE THE BEST SHOT OF THE STORY.
PHAUGH! A OVERGROWED LIZARD! ALBERT ALLIGATOR DON'T TAKE THAT LAYIN' DOWN.
6-7

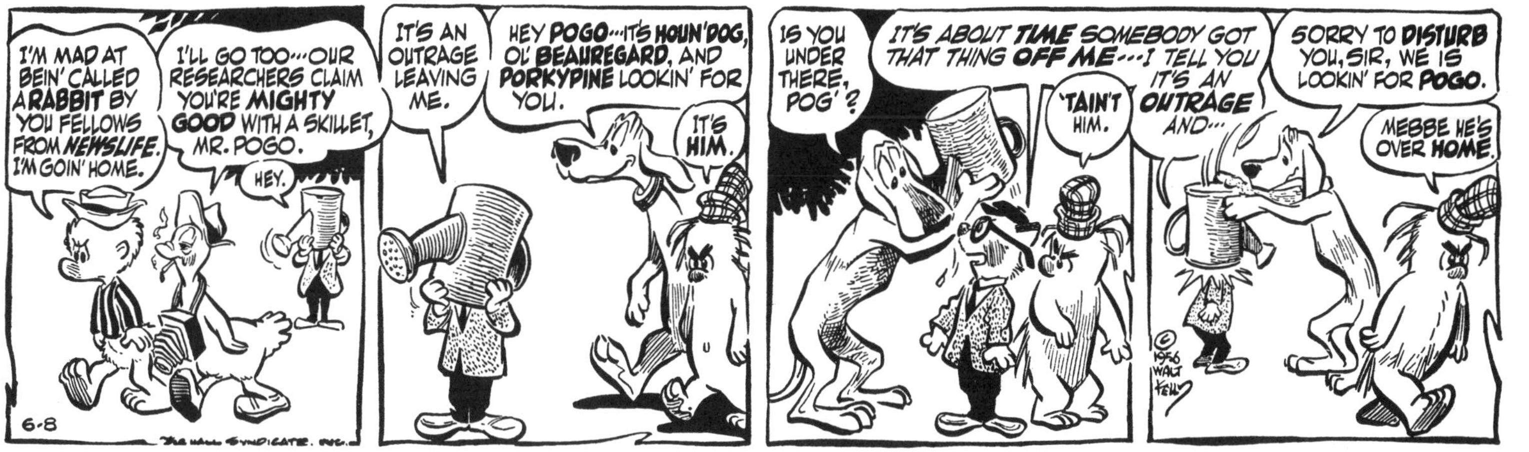
I'M MAD AT BEIN' CALLED A RABBIT BY YOU FELLOWS FROM NEWSLIFE. I'M GOIN' HOME.
I'LL GO TOO...OUR RESEARCHERS CLAIM YOU'RE MIGHTY GOOD WITH A SKILLET, MR. POGO.
HEY.
IT'S AN OUTRAGE LEAVING ME.
HEY POGO...IT'S HOUN'DOG, OL' BEAUREGARD, AND PORKYPINE LOOKIN' FOR YOU.
IT'S HIM.
IS YOU UNDER THERE, POG'?
IT'S ABOUT TIME SOMEBODY GOT THAT THING OFF ME...I TELL YOU IT'S AN OUTRAGE AND...
'TAIN'T HIM.
SORRY TO DISTURB YOU, SIR, WE IS LOOKIN' FOR POGO.
MEBBE HE'S OVER HOME.
6-8

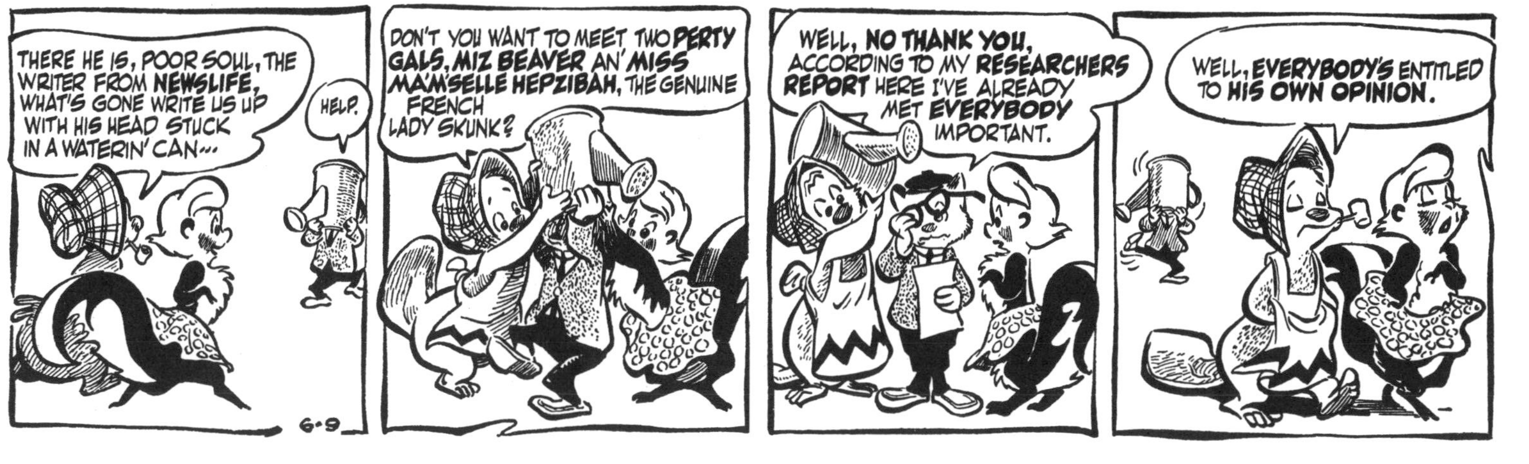
THERE HE IS, POOR SOUL, THE WRITER FROM NEWSLIFE, WHAT'S GONE WRITE US UP WITH HIS HEAD STUCK IN A WATERIN' CAN...
HELP.
DON'T YOU WANT TO MEET TWO PERTY GALS, MIZ BEAVER AN' MISS MAM'SELLE HEPZIBAH, THE GENUINE FRENCH LADY SKUNK?
WELL, NO THANK YOU, ACCORDING TO MY RESEARCHERS REPORT HERE I'VE ALREADY MET EVERYBODY IMPORTANT.
WELL, EVERYBODY'S ENTITLED TO HIS OWN OPINION.
6-9

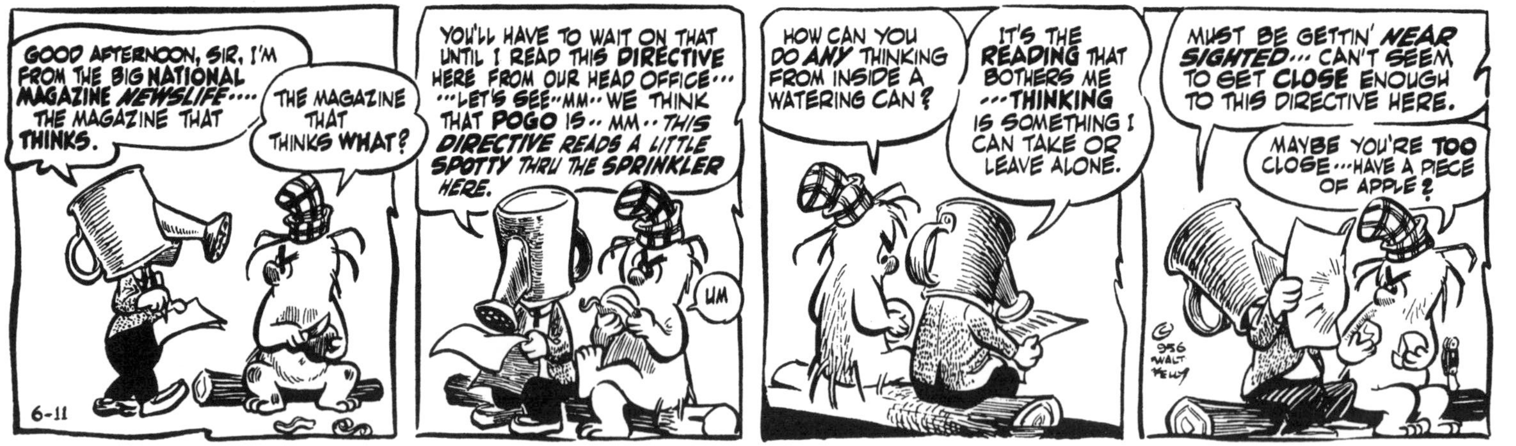
GOOD AFTERNOON, SIR, I'M FROM THE BIG NATIONAL MAGAZINE NEWSLIFE.... THE MAGAZINE THAT THINKS.
THE MAGAZINE THAT THINKS WHAT?
6-11
YOU'LL HAVE TO WAIT ON THAT UNTIL I READ THIS DIRECTIVE HERE FROM OUR HEAD OFFICE... ...LET'S SEE...MM... WE THINK THAT POGO IS... MM... THIS DIRECTIVE READS A LITTLE SPOTTY THRU THE SPRINKLER HERE.
UM
HOW CAN YOU DO ANY THINKING FROM INSIDE A WATERING CAN?
IT'S THE READING THAT BOTHERS ME ...THINKING IS SOMETHING I CAN TAKE OR LEAVE ALONE.
MUST BE GETTIN' NEAR SIGHTED... CAN'T SEEM TO GET CLOSE ENOUGH TO THIS DIRECTIVE HERE.
MAYBE YOU'RE TOO CLOSE... HAVE A PIECE OF APPLE?

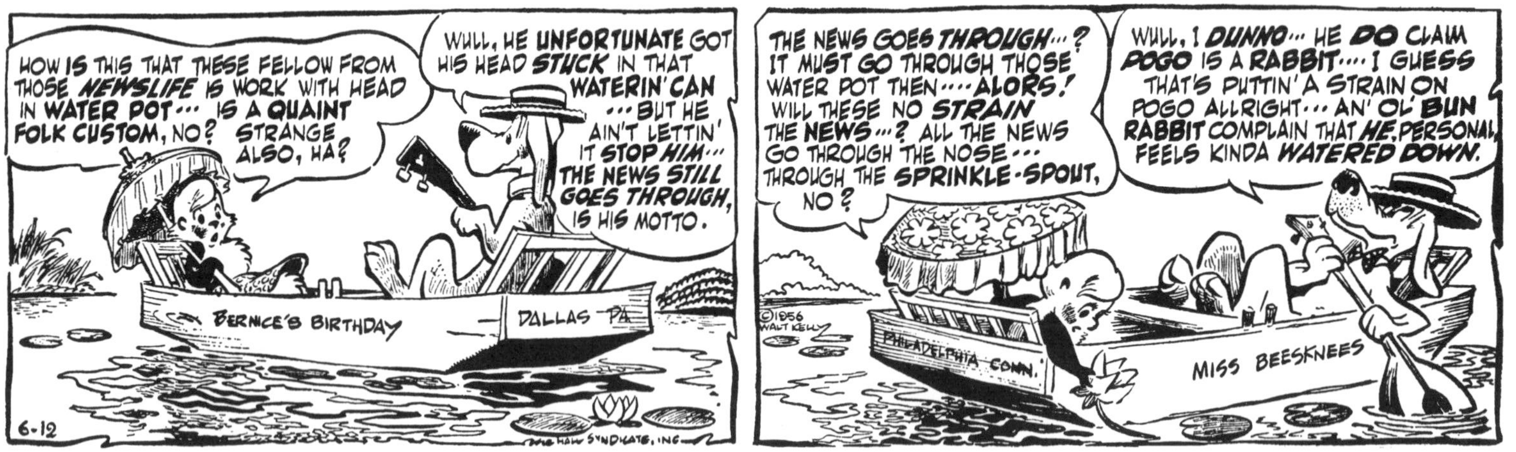
HOW IS THIS THAT THESE FELLOW FROM THOSE NEWSLIFE IS WORK WITH HEAD IN WATER POT... IS A QUAINT FOLK CUSTOM, NO? STRANGE ALSO, HA?
WULL, HE UNFORTUNATE GOT HIS HEAD STUCK IN THAT WATERIN' CAN ...BUT HE AIN'T LETTIN' IT STOP HIM... THE NEWS STILL GOES THROUGH, IS HIS MOTTO.
BERNICE'S BIRTHDAY
DALLAS PA
6-12
THE NEWS GOES THROUGH...? IT MUST GO THROUGH THOSE WATER POT THEN.... ALORS! WILL THESE NO STRAIN THE NEWS...? ALL THE NEWS GO THROUGH THE NOSE... THROUGH THE SPRINKLE-SPOUT, NO?
WULL, I DUNNO... HE DO CLAIM POGO IS A RABBIT.... I GUESS THAT'S PUTTIN' A STRAIN ON POGO ALLRIGHT... AN' OL' BUN RABBIT COMPLAIN THAT HE, PERSONAL, FEELS KINDA WATERED DOWN.
PHILADELPHIA CONN.
MISS BEESKNEES

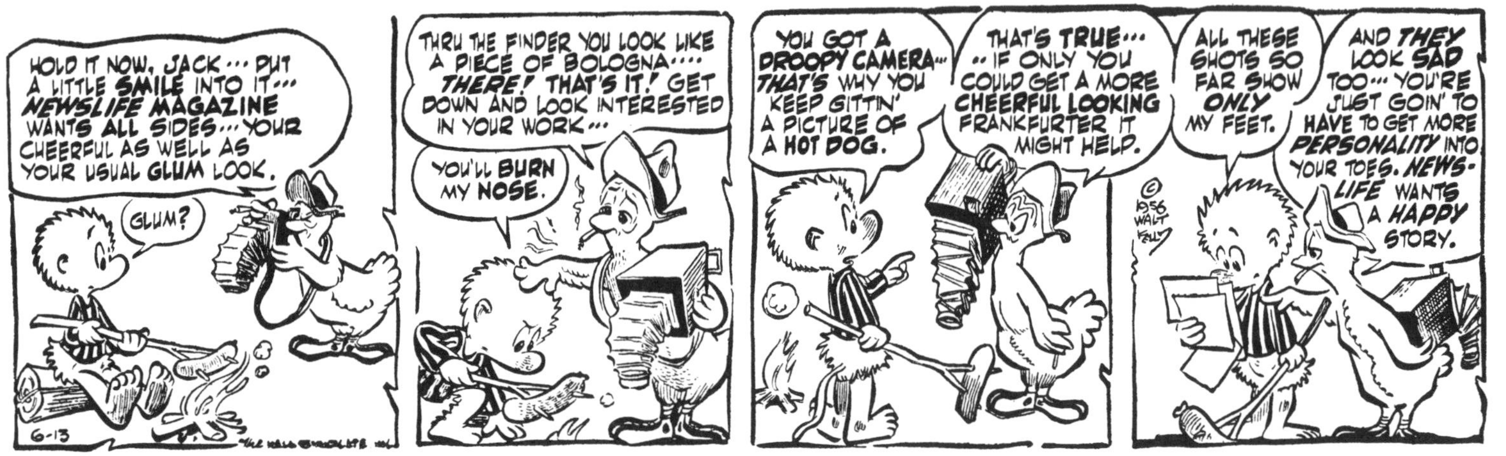
HOLD IT NOW, JACK... PUT A LITTLE SMILE INTO IT... NEWSLIFE MAGAZINE WANTS ALL SIDES... YOUR CHEERFUL AS WELL AS YOUR USUAL GLUM LOOK.
GLUM?
6-13
THRU THE FINDER YOU LOOK LIKE A PIECE OF BOLOGNA.... THERE! THAT'S IT! GET DOWN AND LOOK INTERESTED IN YOUR WORK...
YOU'LL BURN MY NOSE.
YOU GOT A DROOPY CAMERA... THAT'S WHY YOU KEEP GITTIN' A PICTURE OF A HOT DOG.
THAT'S TRUE... ...IF ONLY YOU COULD GET A MORE CHEERFUL LOOKING FRANKFURTER IT MIGHT HELP.
ALL THESE SHOTS SO FAR SHOW ONLY MY FEET.
AND THEY LOOK SAD TOO... YOU'RE JUST GOIN' TO HAVE TO GET MORE PERSONALITY INTO YOUR TOES. NEWS-LIFE WANTS A HAPPY STORY.

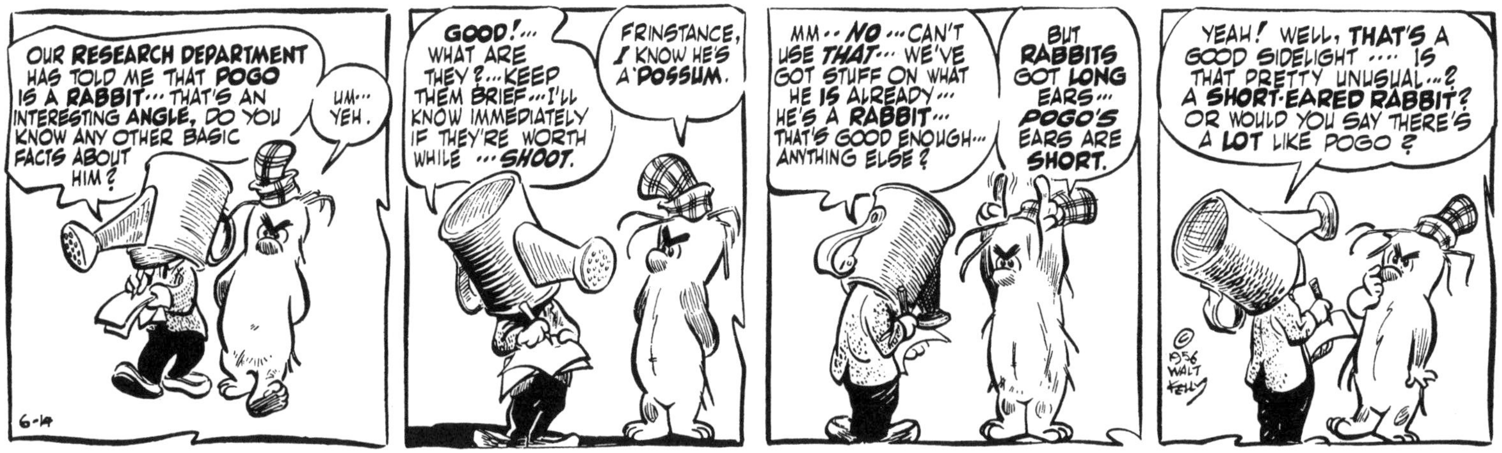
OUR RESEARCH DEPARTMENT HAS TOLD ME THAT POGO IS A RABBIT... THAT'S AN INTERESTING ANGLE, DO YOU KNOW ANY OTHER BASIC FACTS ABOUT HIM?
UM... YEH.
6-14
GOOD!... WHAT ARE THEY?... KEEP THEM BRIEF... I'LL KNOW IMMEDIATELY IF THEY'RE WORTH WHILE ... SHOOT.
FRINSTANCE, I KNOW HE'S A'POSSUM.
MM.. NO ... CAN'T USE THAT... WE'VE GOT STUFF ON WHAT HE IS ALREADY... HE'S A RABBIT... THAT'S GOOD ENOUGH... ANYTHING ELSE?
BUT RABBITS GOT LONG EARS... POGO'S EARS ARE SHORT.
YEAH! WELL, THAT'S A GOOD SIDELIGHT .... IS THAT PRETTY UNUSUAL...? A SHORT-EARED RABBIT? OR WOULD YOU SAY THERE'S A LOT LIKE POGO?
© 1956 WALT KELLY

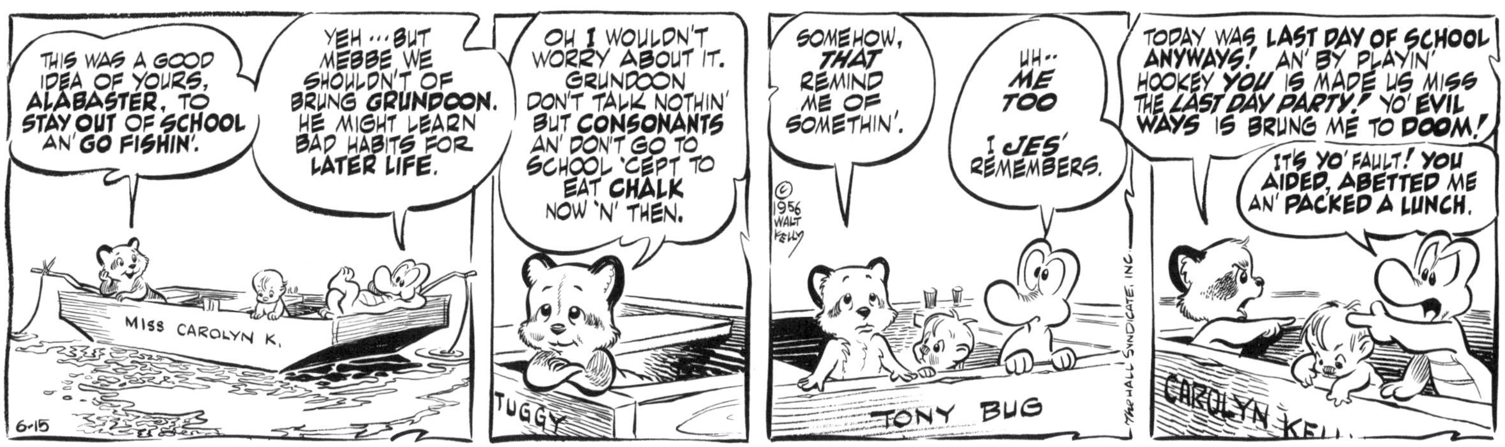
THIS WAS A GOOD IDEA OF YOURS, ALABASTER, TO STAY OUT OF SCHOOL AN' GO FISHIN'.
YEH ... BUT MEBBE WE SHOULDN'T OF BRUNG GRUNDOON. HE MIGHT LEARN BAD HABITS FOR LATER LIFE.
MISS CAROLYN K.
6-15
OH I WOULDN'T WORRY ABOUT IT. GRUNDOON DON'T TALK NOTHIN' BUT CONSONANTS AN' DON'T GO TO SCHOOL 'CEPT TO EAT CHALK NOW 'N' THEN.
TUGGY
SOMEHOW, THAT REMIND ME OF SOMETHIN'.
UH.. ME TOO
I JES' REMEMBERS.
© 1956 WALT KELLY
TONY BUG
The Hall Syndicate, Inc.
TODAY WAS LAST DAY OF SCHOOL ANYWAYS! AN' BY PLAYIN' HOOKEY YOU IS MADE US MISS THE LAST DAY PARTY! YO' EVIL WAYS IS BRUNG ME TO DOOM!
IT'S YO' FAULT! YOU AIDED, ABETTED ME AN' PACKED A LUNCH.
CAROLYN

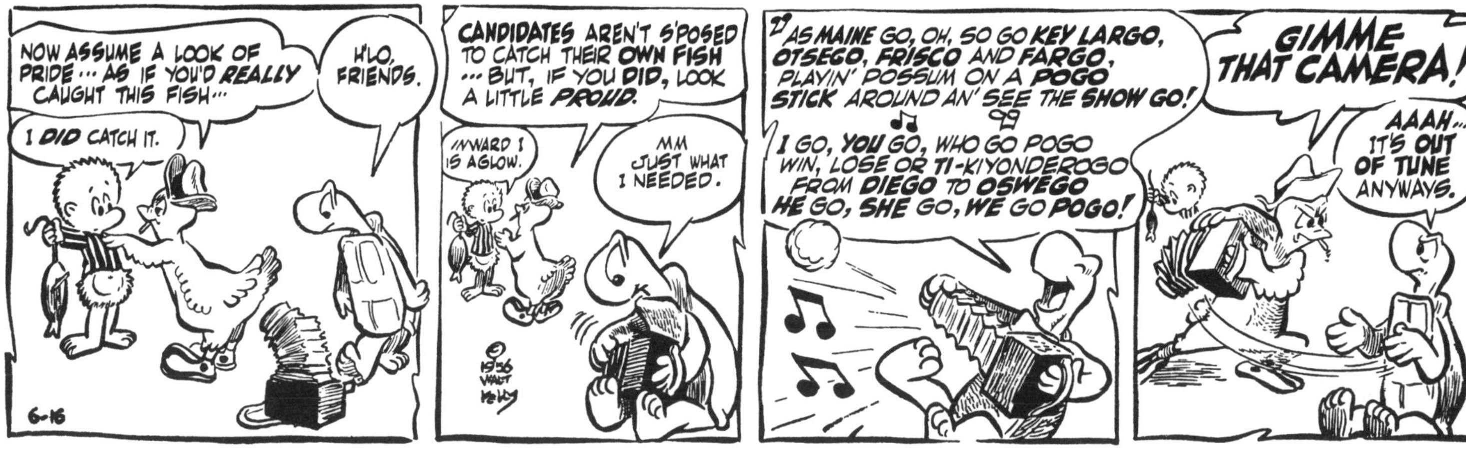
NOW ASSUME A LOOK OF PRIDE ... AS IF YOU'D REALLY CAUGHT THIS FISH...
H'LO, FRIENDS.
I DID CATCH IT.
6-16
CANDIDATES AREN'T S'POSED TO CATCH THEIR OWN FISH ... BUT, IF YOU DID, LOOK A LITTLE PROUD.
INWARD I IS AGLOW.
MM JUST WHAT I NEEDED.
© 1956 WALT KELLY
AS MAINE GO, OH, SO GO KEY LARGO, OTSEGO, FRISCO AND FARGO, PLAYIN' POSSUM ON A POGO STICK AROUND AN' SEE THE SHOW GO!
I GO, YOU GO, WHO GO POGO WIN, LOSE OR TI-KIYONDEROGO FROM DIEGO TO OSWEGO HE GO, SHE GO, WE GO POGO!
GIMME THAT CAMERA!
AAAH... IT'S OUT OF TUNE ANYWAYS.

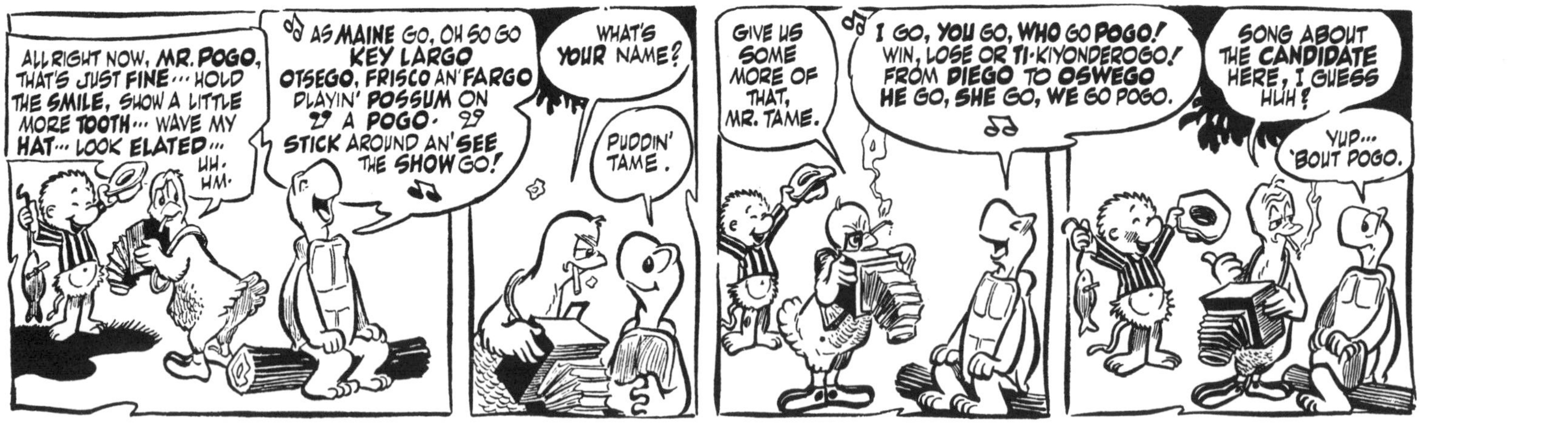
ALL RIGHT NOW, MR. POGO, THAT'S JUST FINE··· HOLD THE SMILE, SHOW A LITTLE MORE TOOTH··· WAVE MY HAT··· LOOK ELATED···
UH. HM.
AS MAINE GO, OH SO GO KEY LARGO OTSEGO, FRISCO AN' FARGO PLAYIN' POSSUM ON "A POGO" STICK AROUND AN' SEE THE SHOW GO!
WHAT'S YOUR NAME?
PUDDIN' TAME.
GIVE US SOME MORE OF THAT, MR. TAME.
I GO, YOU GO, WHO GO POGO! WIN, LOSE OR TI-KIYONDEROGO! FROM DIEGO TO OSWEGO HE GO, SHE GO, WE GO POGO.
SONG ABOUT THE CANDIDATE HERE, I GUESS HUH?
YUP... 'BOUT POGO.

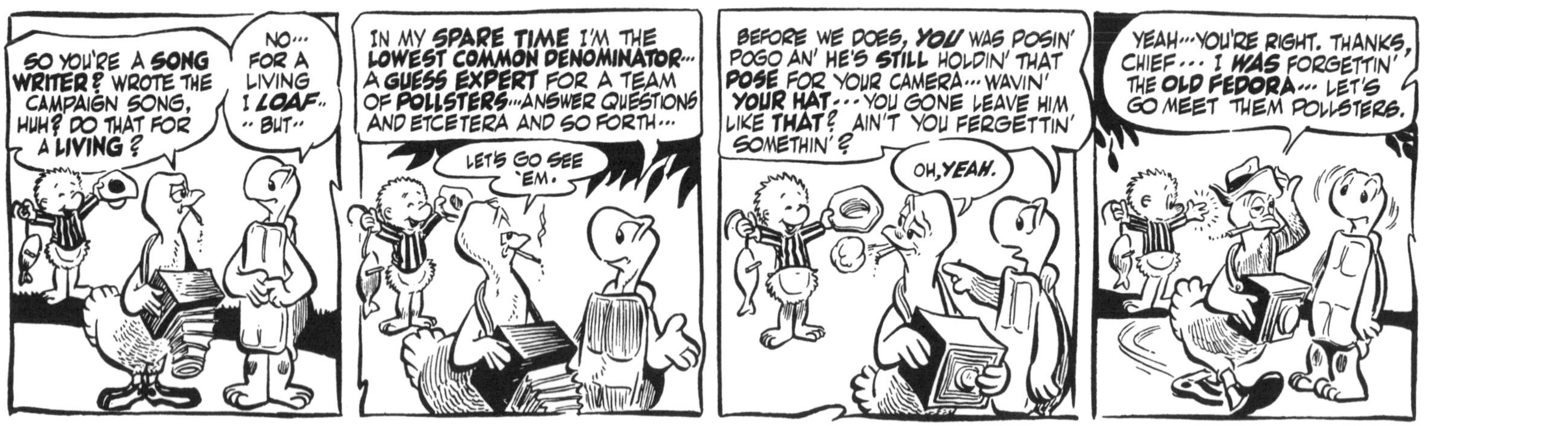
SO YOU'RE A SONG WRITER? WROTE THE CAMPAIGN SONG, HUH? DO THAT FOR A LIVING?
NO··· FOR A LIVING I LOAF.. ·· BUT··
IN MY SPARE TIME I'M THE LOWEST COMMON DENOMINATOR··· A GUESS EXPERT FOR A TEAM OF POLLSTERS···ANSWER QUESTIONS AND ETCETERA AND SO FORTH···
LET'S GO SEE 'EM.
BEFORE WE DOES, YOU WAS POSIN' POGO AN' HE'S STILL HOLDIN' THAT POSE FOR YOUR CAMERA··· WAVIN' YOUR HAT··· YOU GONE LEAVE HIM LIKE THAT? AIN'T YOU FERGETTIN' SOMETHIN'?
OH, YEAH.
YEAH···YOU'RE RIGHT. THANKS, CHIEF··· I WAS FORGETTIN' THE OLD FEDORA··· LET'S GO MEET THEM POLLSTERS.

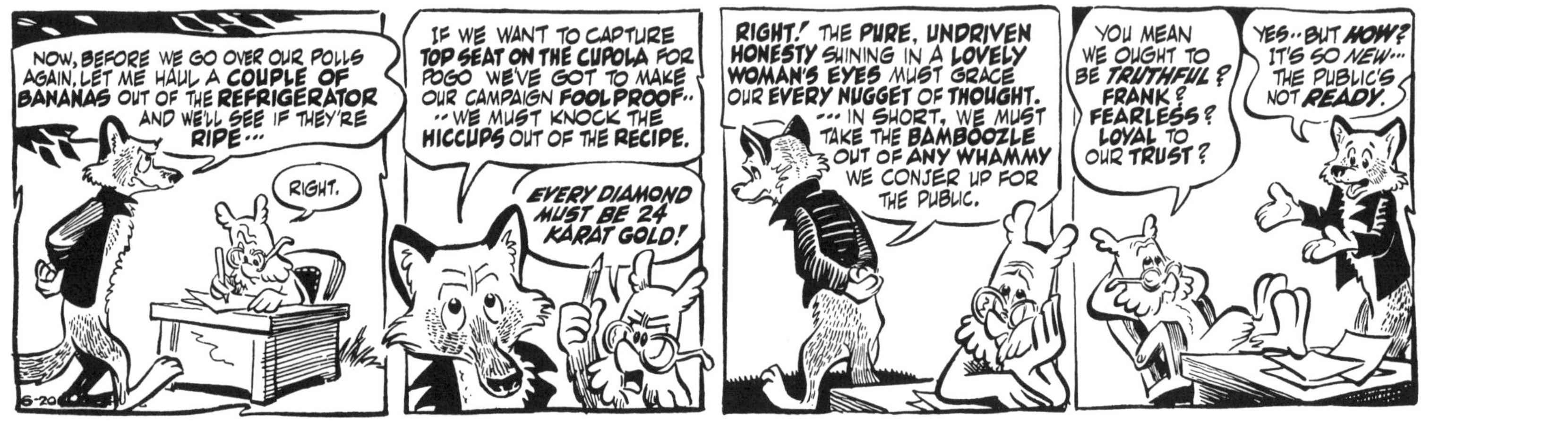
NOW, BEFORE WE GO OVER OUR POLLS AGAIN, LET ME HAUL A COUPLE OF BANANAS OUT OF THE REFRIGERATOR AND WE'LL SEE IF THEY'RE RIPE···
RIGHT.
IF WE WANT TO CAPTURE TOP SEAT ON THE CUPOLA FOR POGO WE'VE GOT TO MAKE OUR CAMPAIGN FOOLPROOF.. ·· WE MUST KNOCK THE HICCUPS OUT OF THE RECIPE.
EVERY DIAMOND MUST BE 24 KARAT GOLD!
RIGHT! THE PURE, UNDRIVEN HONESTY SHINING IN A LOVELY WOMAN'S EYES MUST GRACE OUR EVERY NUGGET OF THOUGHT. ··· IN SHORT, WE MUST TAKE THE BAMBOOZLE OUT OF ANY WHAMMY WE CONJER UP FOR THE PUBLIC.
YOU MEAN WE OUGHT TO BE TRUTHFUL? FRANK? FEARLESS? LOYAL TO OUR TRUST?
YES·· BUT HOW? IT'S SO NEW··· THE PUBLIC'S NOT READY.

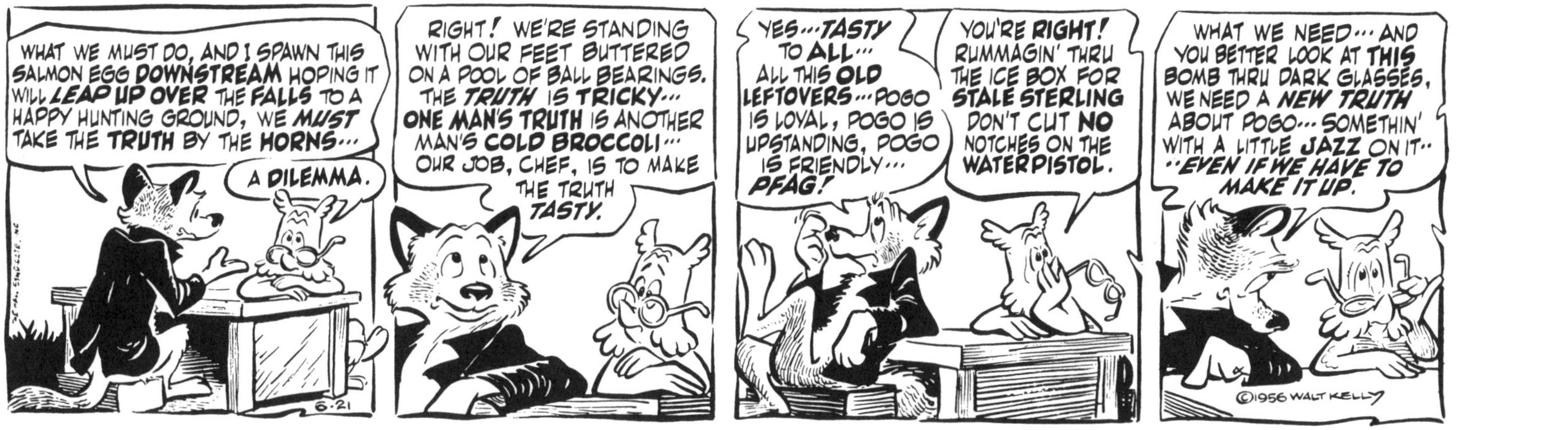
WHAT WE MUST DO, AND I SPAWN THIS SALMON EGG DOWNSTREAM HOPING IT WILL LEAP UP OVER THE FALLS TO A HAPPY HUNTING GROUND, WE MUST TAKE THE TRUTH BY THE HORNS...
A DILEMMA.
6-21
RIGHT! WE'RE STANDING WITH OUR FEET BUTTERED ON A POOL OF BALL BEARINGS. THE TRUTH IS TRICKY... ONE MAN'S TRUTH IS ANOTHER MAN'S COLD BROCCOLI... OUR JOB, CHEF, IS TO MAKE THE TRUTH TASTY.
YES... TASTY TO ALL... ALL THIS OLD LEFTOVERS... POGO IS LOYAL, POGO IS UPSTANDING, POGO IS FRIENDLY... PFAG!
YOU'RE RIGHT! RUMMAGIN' THRU THE ICE BOX FOR STALE STERLING DON'T CUT NO NOTCHES ON THE WATERPISTOL.
WHAT WE NEED... AND YOU BETTER LOOK AT THIS BOMB THRU DARK GLASSES, WE NEED A NEW TRUTH ABOUT POGO... SOMETHIN' WITH A LITTLE JAZZ ON IT... ...EVEN IF WE HAVE TO MAKE IT UP.
©1956 WALT KELLY

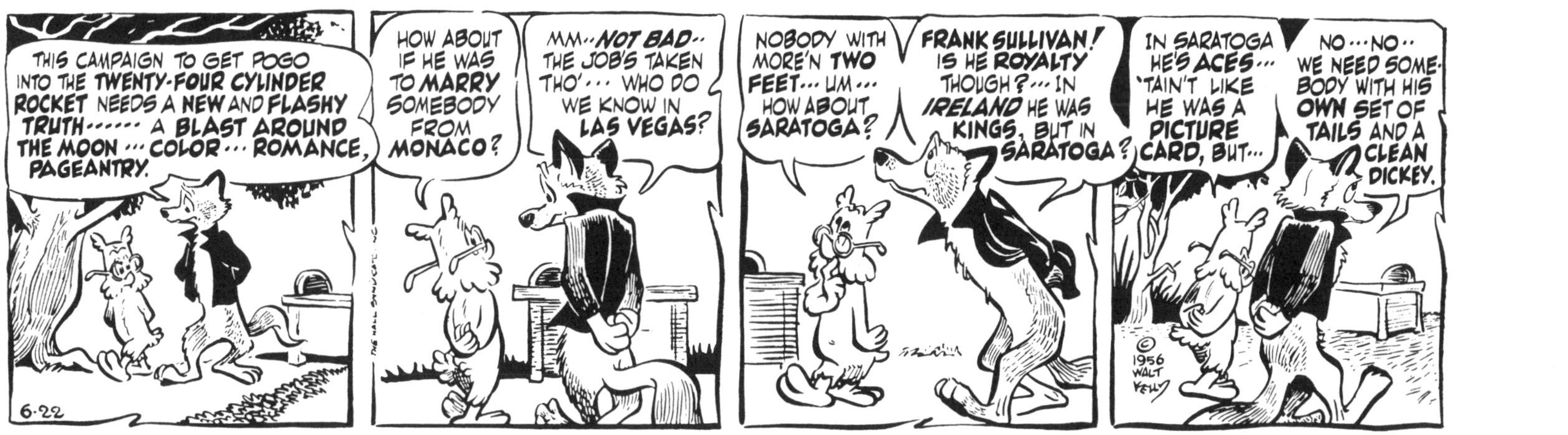
THIS CAMPAIGN TO GET POGO INTO THE TWENTY-FOUR CYLINDER ROCKET NEEDS A NEW AND FLASHY TRUTH...... A BLAST AROUND THE MOON... COLOR... ROMANCE, PAGEANTRY.
6-22
HOW ABOUT IF HE WAS TO MARRY SOMEBODY FROM MONACO?
MM... NOT BAD... THE JOB'S TAKEN THO'... WHO DO WE KNOW IN LAS VEGAS?
NOBODY WITH MORE'N TWO FEET... UM... HOW ABOUT SARATOGA?
FRANK SULLIVAN! IS HE ROYALTY THOUGH?... IN IRELAND HE WAS KINGS, BUT IN SARATOGA?
IN SARATOGA HE'S ACES... 'TAIN'T LIKE HE WAS A PICTURE CARD, BUT...
NO... NO... WE NEED SOMEBODY WITH HIS OWN SET OF TAILS AND A CLEAN DICKEY.
© 1956 WALT KELLY

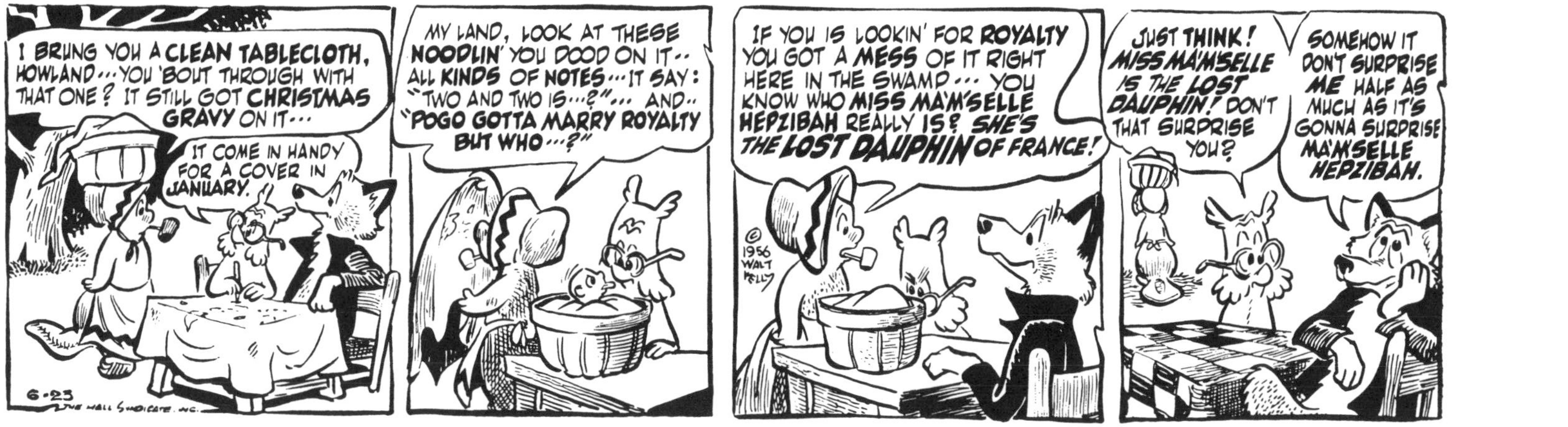
I BRUNG YOU A CLEAN TABLECLOTH, HOWLAND... YOU 'BOUT THROUGH WITH THAT ONE? IT STILL GOT CHRISTMAS GRAVY ON IT...
IT COME IN HANDY FOR A COVER IN JANUARY.
6-23
MY LAND, LOOK AT THESE NOODLIN' YOU DOOD ON IT... ALL KINDS OF NOTES... IT SAY: "TWO AND TWO IS...?"... AND... "POGO GOTTA MARRY ROYALTY BUT WHO...?"
IF YOU IS LOOKIN' FOR ROYALTY YOU GOT A MESS OF IT RIGHT HERE IN THE SWAMP... YOU KNOW WHO MISS MA'M'SELLE HEPZIBAH REALLY IS? SHE'S THE LOST DAUPHIN OF FRANCE!
© 1956 WALT KELLY
JUST THINK! MISS MA'M'SELLE IS THE LOST DAUPHIN! DON'T THAT SURPRISE YOU?
SOMEHOW IT DON'T SURPRISE ME HALF AS MUCH AS IT'S GONNA SURPRISE MA'M'SELLE HEPZIBAH.

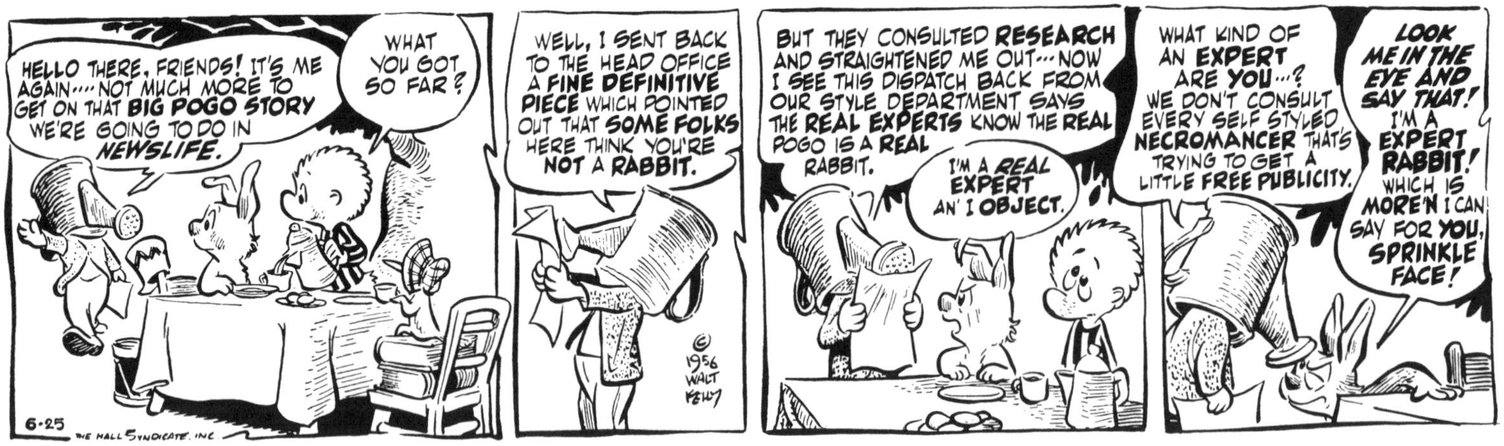
HELLO THERE, FRIENDS! IT'S ME AGAIN.... NOT MUCH MORE TO GET ON THAT BIG POGO STORY WE'RE GOING TO DO IN NEWSLIFE.
WHAT YOU GOT SO FAR?
WELL, I SENT BACK TO THE HEAD OFFICE A FINE DEFINITIVE PIECE WHICH POINTED OUT THAT SOME FOLKS HERE THINK YOU'RE NOT A RABBIT.
BUT THEY CONSULTED RESEARCH AND STRAIGHTENED ME OUT... NOW I SEE THIS DISPATCH BACK FROM OUR STYLE DEPARTMENT SAYS THE REAL EXPERTS KNOW THE REAL POGO IS A REAL RABBIT.
I'M A REAL EXPERT AN' I OBJECT.
WHAT KIND OF AN EXPERT ARE YOU...? WE DON'T CONSULT EVERY SELF STYLED NECROMANCER THAT'S TRYING TO GET A LITTLE FREE PUBLICITY.
LOOK ME IN THE EYE AND SAY THAT! I'M A EXPERT RABBIT! WHICH IS MORE'N I CAN SAY FOR YOU, SPRINKLE FACE!
© 1956 WALT KELLY
6-25 THE HALL SYNDICATE, INC.

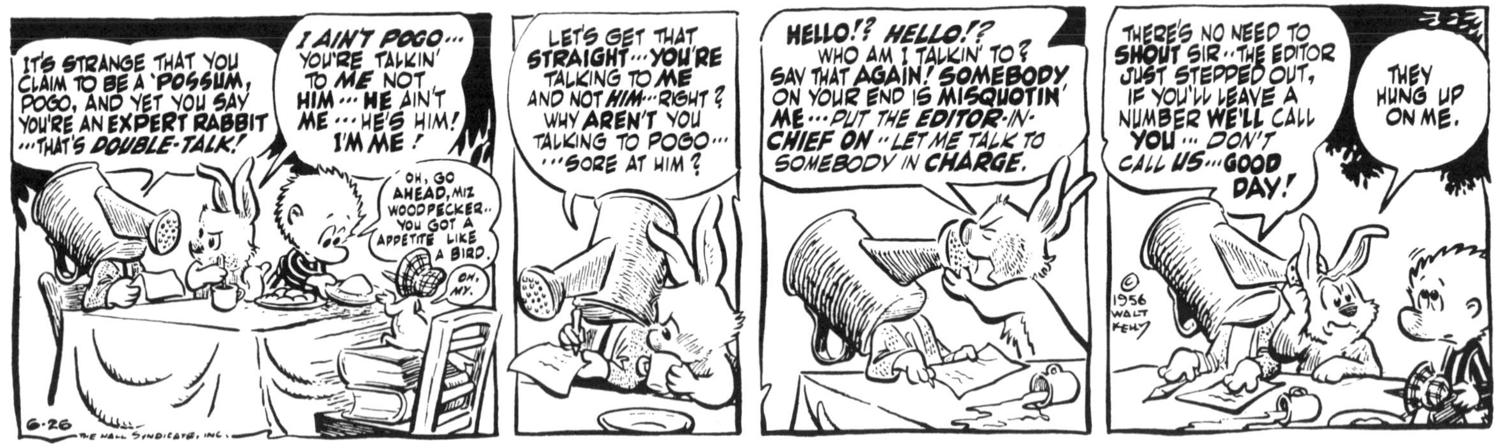
IT'S STRANGE THAT YOU CLAIM TO BE A 'POSSUM, POGO, AND YET YOU SAY YOU'RE AN EXPERT RABBIT ...THAT'S DOUBLE-TALK!
I AIN'T POGO... YOU'RE TALKIN' TO ME NOT HIM... HE AIN'T ME... HE'S HIM! I'M ME!
OH, GO AHEAD, MIZ WOODPECKER.. YOU GOT A APPETITE LIKE A BIRD.
OH, MY.
LET'S GET THAT STRAIGHT... YOU'RE TALKING TO ME AND NOT HIM... RIGHT? WHY AREN'T YOU TALKING TO POGO... ...SORE AT HIM?
HELLO!? HELLO!? WHO AM I TALKIN' TO? SAY THAT AGAIN! SOMEBODY ON YOUR END IS MISQUOTIN' ME... PUT THE EDITOR-IN-CHIEF ON .. LET ME TALK TO SOMEBODY IN CHARGE.
THERE'S NO NEED TO SHOUT SIR.. THE EDITOR JUST STEPPED OUT, IF YOU'LL LEAVE A NUMBER WE'LL CALL YOU... DON'T CALL US... GOOD DAY!
THEY HUNG UP ON ME.
© 1956 WALT KELLY
6-26 THE HALL SYNDICATE, INC.

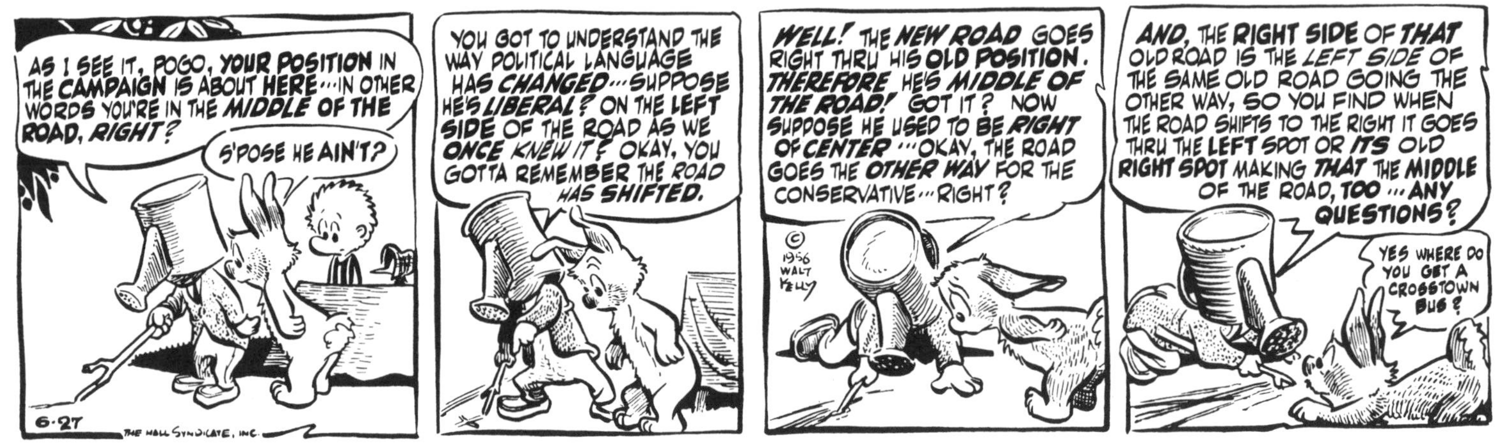
AS I SEE IT, POGO, YOUR POSITION IN THE CAMPAIGN IS ABOUT HERE... IN OTHER WORDS YOU'RE IN THE MIDDLE OF THE ROAD, RIGHT?
S'POSE HE AIN'T?
YOU GOT TO UNDERSTAND THE WAY POLITICAL LANGUAGE HAS CHANGED... SUPPOSE HE'S LIBERAL? ON THE LEFT SIDE OF THE ROAD AS WE ONCE KNEW IT? OKAY, YOU GOTTA REMEMBER THE ROAD HAS SHIFTED.
WELL! THE NEW ROAD GOES RIGHT THRU HIS OLD POSITION. THEREFORE HE'S MIDDLE OF THE ROAD! GOT IT? NOW SUPPOSE HE USED TO BE RIGHT OF CENTER ...OKAY, THE ROAD GOES THE OTHER WAY FOR THE CONSERVATIVE... RIGHT?
AND, THE RIGHT SIDE OF THAT OLD ROAD IS THE LEFT SIDE OF THE SAME OLD ROAD GOING THE OTHER WAY, SO YOU FIND WHEN THE ROAD SHIFTS TO THE RIGHT IT GOES THRU THE LEFT SPOT OR ITS OLD RIGHT SPOT MAKING THAT THE MIDDLE OF THE ROAD, TOO ... ANY QUESTIONS?
YES WHERE DO YOU GET A CROSSTOWN BUS?
© 1956 WALT KELLY
6-27 THE HALL SYNDICATE, INC.

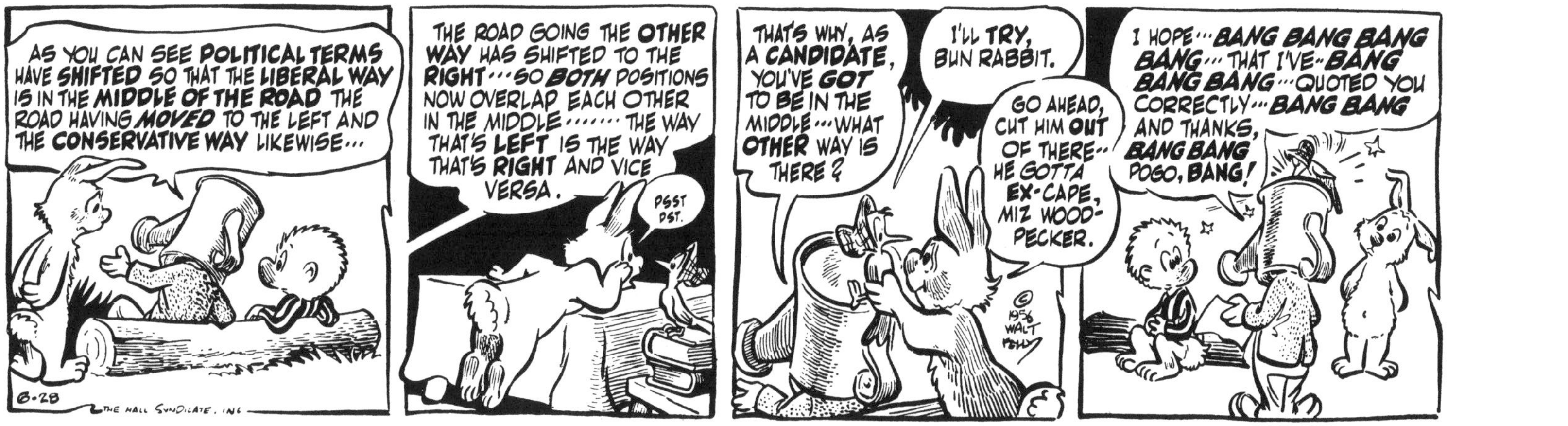
AS YOU CAN SEE POLITICAL TERMS HAVE SHIFTED SO THAT THE LIBERAL WAY IS IN THE MIDDLE OF THE ROAD THE ROAD HAVING MOVED TO THE LEFT AND THE CONSERVATIVE WAY LIKEWISE...
THE ROAD GOING THE OTHER WAY HAS SHIFTED TO THE RIGHT···SO BOTH POSITIONS NOW OVERLAP EACH OTHER IN THE MIDDLE······ THE WAY THAT'S LEFT IS THE WAY THAT'S RIGHT AND VICE VERSA.
PSST PST.
THAT'S WHY, AS A CANDIDATE, YOU'VE GOT TO BE IN THE MIDDLE···WHAT OTHER WAY IS THERE?
I'LL TRY, BUN RABBIT.
GO AHEAD, CUT HIM OUT OF THERE·· HE GOTTA EX-CAPE, MIZ WOOD-PECKER.
© 1956 WALT KELLY
I HOPE···BANG BANG BANG BANG···THAT I'VE··BANG BANG BANG···QUOTED YOU CORRECTLY···BANG BANG AND THANKS, BANG BANG POGO, BANG!
6-28
THE HALL SYNDICATE, INC

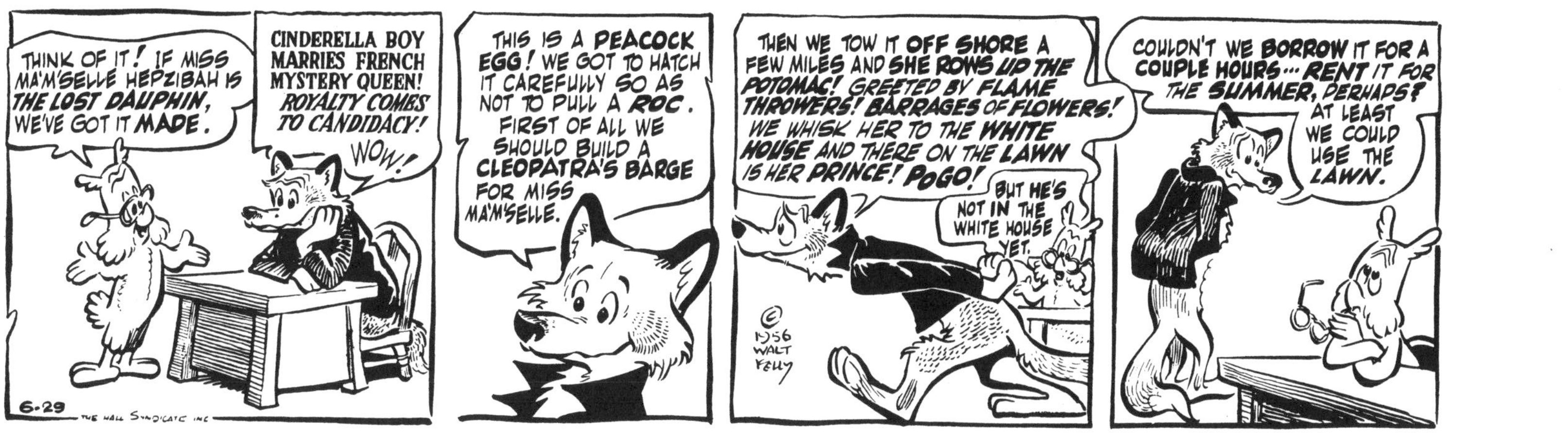
THINK OF IT! IF MISS MA'M'SELLE HEPZIBAH IS THE LOST DAUPHIN, WE'VE GOT IT MADE.
CINDERELLA BOY MARRIES FRENCH MYSTERY QUEEN! ROYALTY COMES TO CANDIDACY!
WOW!
THIS IS A PEACOCK EGG! WE GOT TO HATCH IT CAREFULLY SO AS NOT TO PULL A ROC. FIRST OF ALL WE SHOULD BUILD A CLEOPATRA'S BARGE FOR MISS MA'M'SELLE.
THEN WE TOW IT OFF SHORE A FEW MILES AND SHE ROWS UP THE POTOMAC! GREETED BY FLAME THROWERS! BARRAGES OF FLOWERS! WE WHISK HER TO THE WHITE HOUSE AND THERE ON THE LAWN IS HER PRINCE! POGO!
BUT HE'S NOT IN THE WHITE HOUSE YET.
© 1956 WALT KELLY
COULDN'T WE BORROW IT FOR A COUPLE HOURS···RENT IT FOR THE SUMMER, PERHAPS?
AT LEAST WE COULD USE THE LAWN.
6-29
THE HALL SYNDICATE INC

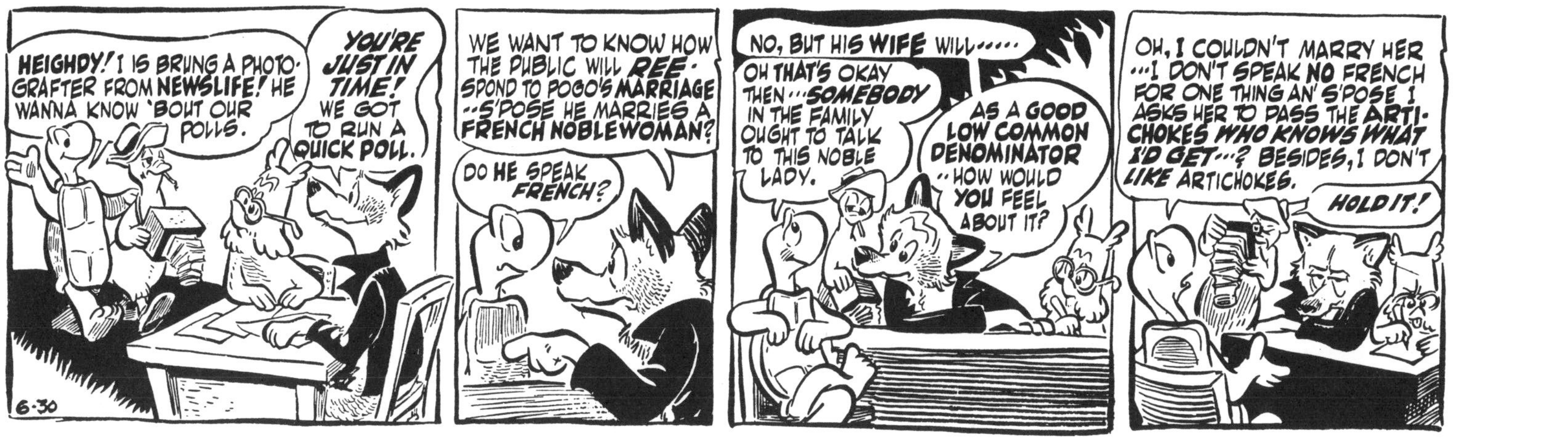
HEIGHDY! I IS BRUNG A PHOTO-GRAFTER FROM NEWSLIFE! HE WANNA KNOW 'BOUT OUR POLLS.
YOU'RE JUST IN TIME! WE GOT TO RUN A QUICK POLL.
WE WANT TO KNOW HOW THE PUBLIC WILL REE-SPOND TO POGO'S MARRIAGE ··S'POSE HE MARRIES A FRENCH NOBLEWOMAN?
DO HE SPEAK FRENCH?
NO, BUT HIS WIFE WILL·····
OH THAT'S OKAY THEN···SOMEBODY IN THE FAMILY OUGHT TO TALK TO THIS NOBLE LADY.
AS A GOOD LOW COMMON DENOMINATOR ··HOW WOULD YOU FEEL ABOUT IT?
OH, I COULDN'T MARRY HER ···I DON'T SPEAK NO FRENCH FOR ONE THING AN' S'POSE I ASKS HER TO PASS THE ARTI-CHOKES WHO KNOWS WHAT I'D GET···? BESIDES, I DON'T LIKE ARTICHOKES.
HOLD IT!
6-30

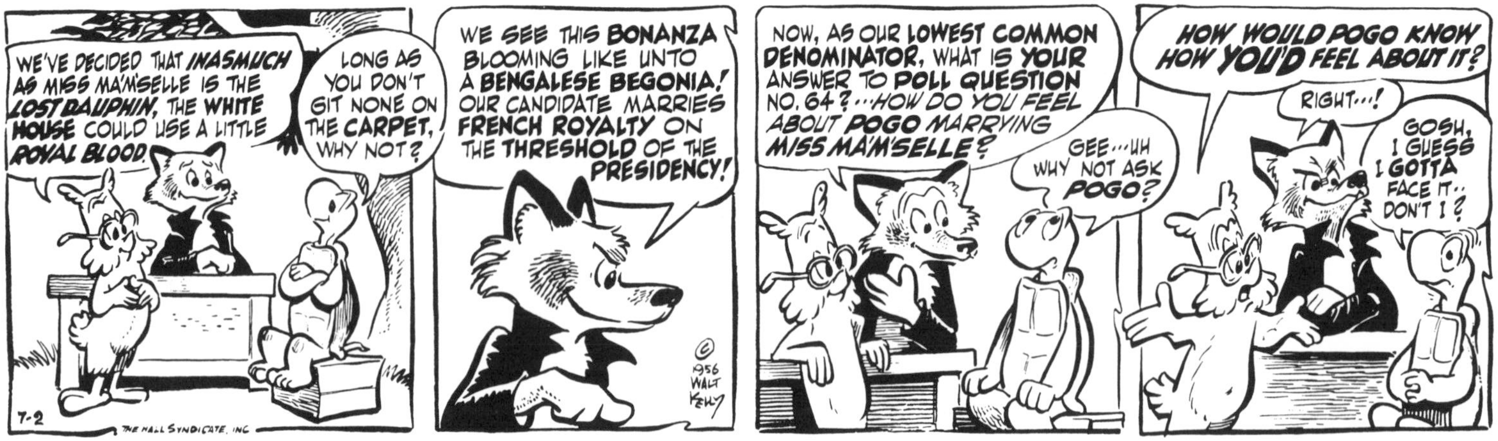
WE'VE DECIDED THAT INASMUCH AS MISS MA'MSELLE IS THE LOST DAUPHIN, THE WHITE HOUSE COULD USE A LITTLE ROYAL BLOOD.
LONG AS YOU DON'T GIT NONE ON THE CARPET, WHY NOT?
7-2
THE HALL SYNDICATE, INC
WE SEE THIS BONANZA BLOOMING LIKE UNTO A BENGALESE BEGONIA! OUR CANDIDATE MARRIES FRENCH ROYALTY ON THE THRESHOLD OF THE PRESIDENCY!
© 1956 WALT KELLY
NOW, AS OUR LOWEST COMMON DENOMINATOR, WHAT IS YOUR ANSWER TO POLL QUESTION NO. 64? .. HOW DO YOU FEEL ABOUT POGO MARRYING MISS MA'MSELLE?
GEE...UH WHY NOT ASK POGO?
HOW WOULD POGO KNOW HOW YOU'D FEEL ABOUT IT?
RIGHT...!
GOSH, I GUESS I GOTTA FACE IT.. DON'T I?

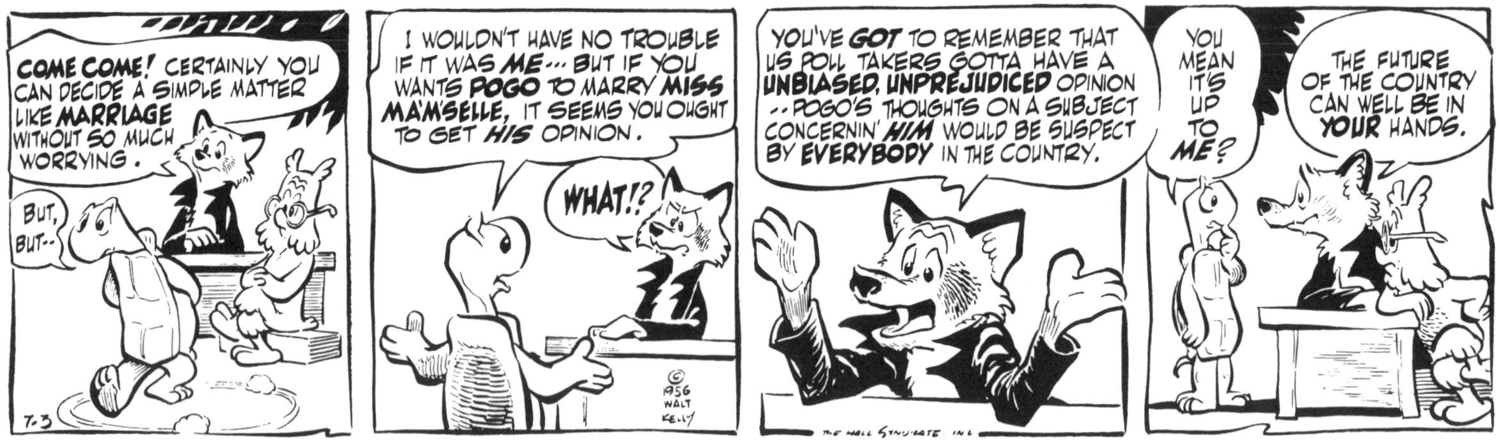
COME COME! CERTAINLY YOU CAN DECIDE A SIMPLE MATTER LIKE MARRIAGE WITHOUT SO MUCH WORRYING.
BUT, BUT--
7-3
I WOULDN'T HAVE NO TROUBLE IF IT WAS ME... BUT IF YOU WANTS POGO TO MARRY MISS MA'MSELLE, IT SEEMS YOU OUGHT TO GET HIS OPINION.
WHAT!?
© 1956 WALT KELLY
YOU'VE GOT TO REMEMBER THAT US POLL TAKERS GOTTA HAVE A UNBIASED, UNPREJUDICED OPINION -- POGO'S THOUGHTS ON A SUBJECT CONCERNIN' HIM WOULD BE SUSPECT BY EVERYBODY IN THE COUNTRY.
THE HALL SYNDICATE, INC
YOU MEAN IT'S UP TO ME?
THE FUTURE OF THE COUNTRY CAN WELL BE IN YOUR HANDS.

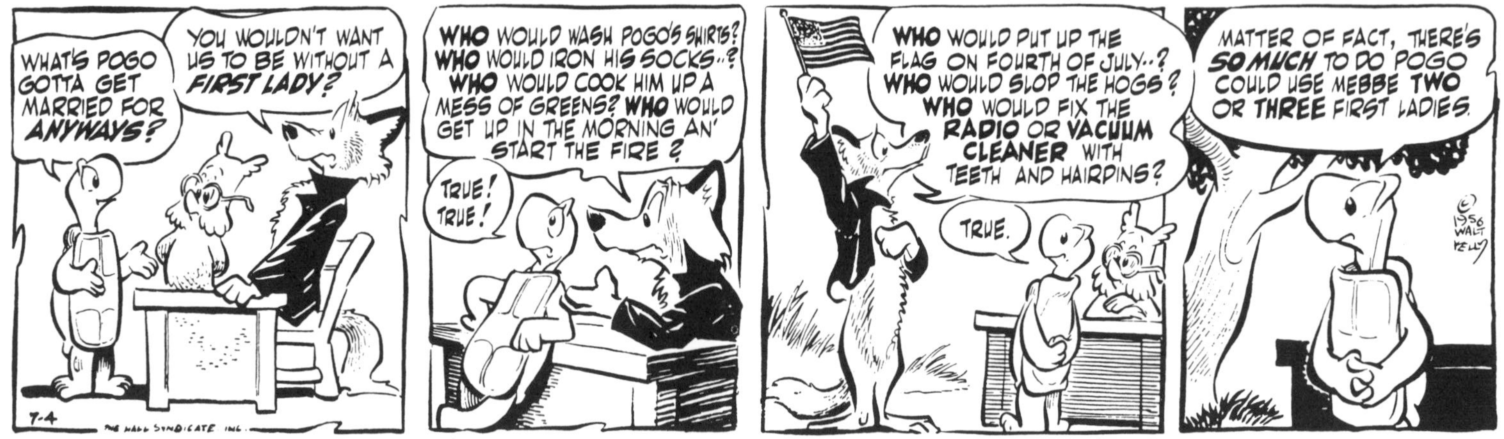
WHAT'S POGO GOTTA GET MARRIED FOR ANYWAYS?
YOU WOULDN'T WANT US TO BE WITHOUT A FIRST LADY?
7-4
THE HALL SYNDICATE, INC.
WHO WOULD WASH POGO'S SHIRTS? WHO WOULD IRON HIS SOCKS..? WHO WOULD COOK HIM UP A MESS OF GREENS? WHO WOULD GET UP IN THE MORNING AN' START THE FIRE?
TRUE! TRUE!
WHO WOULD PUT UP THE FLAG ON FOURTH OF JULY..? WHO WOULD SLOP THE HOGS? WHO WOULD FIX THE RADIO OR VACUUM CLEANER WITH TEETH AND HAIRPINS?
TRUE.
MATTER OF FACT, THERE'S SO MUCH TO DO POGO COULD USE MEBBE TWO OR THREE FIRST LADIES.
© 1956 WALT KELLY

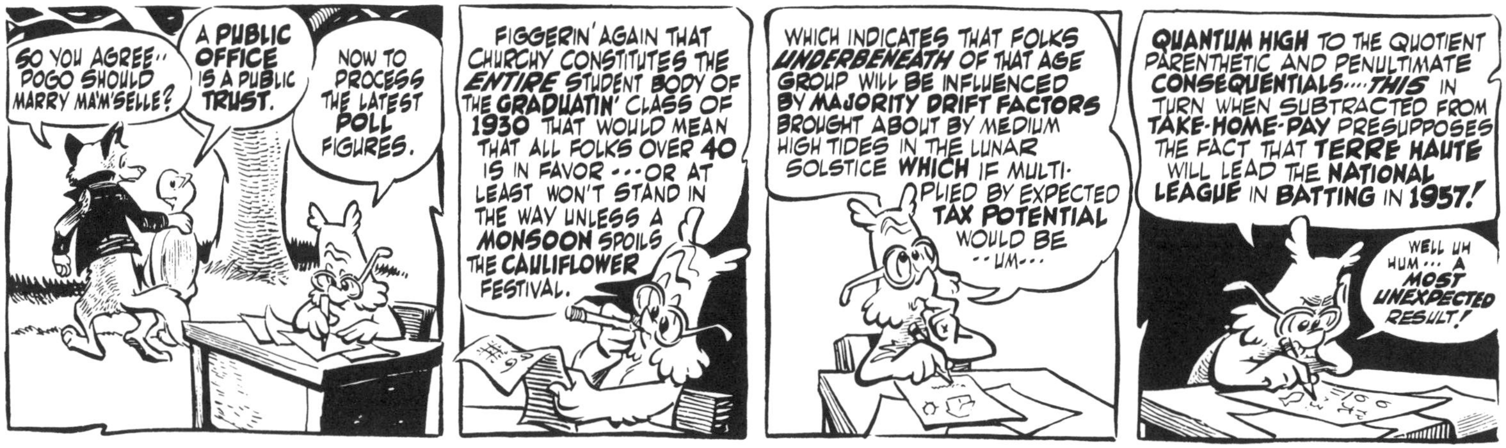
SO YOU AGREE.. POGO SHOULD MARRY MA'M'SELLE?
A PUBLIC OFFICE IS A PUBLIC TRUST.
NOW TO PROCESS THE LATEST POLL FIGURES.
FIGGERIN' AGAIN THAT CHURCHY CONSTITUTES THE ENTIRE STUDENT BODY OF THE GRADUATIN' CLASS OF 1930 THAT WOULD MEAN THAT ALL FOLKS OVER 40 IS IN FAVOR ···OR AT LEAST WON'T STAND IN THE WAY UNLESS A MONSOON SPOILS THE CAULIFLOWER FESTIVAL.
WHICH INDICATES THAT FOLKS UNDERBENEATH OF THAT AGE GROUP WILL BE INFLUENCED BY MAJORITY DRIFT FACTORS BROUGHT ABOUT BY MEDIUM HIGH TIDES IN THE LUNAR SOLSTICE WHICH IF MULTI-PLIED BY EXPECTED TAX POTENTIAL WOULD BE ··UM···
QUANTUM HIGH TO THE QUOTIENT PARENTHETIC AND PENULTIMATE CONSEQUENTIALS····THIS IN TURN WHEN SUBTRACTED FROM TAKE-HOME-PAY PRESUPPOSES THE FACT THAT TERRE HAUTE WILL LEAD THE NATIONAL LEAGUE IN BATTING IN 1957!
WELL UH HUM··· A MOST UNEXPECTED RESULT!

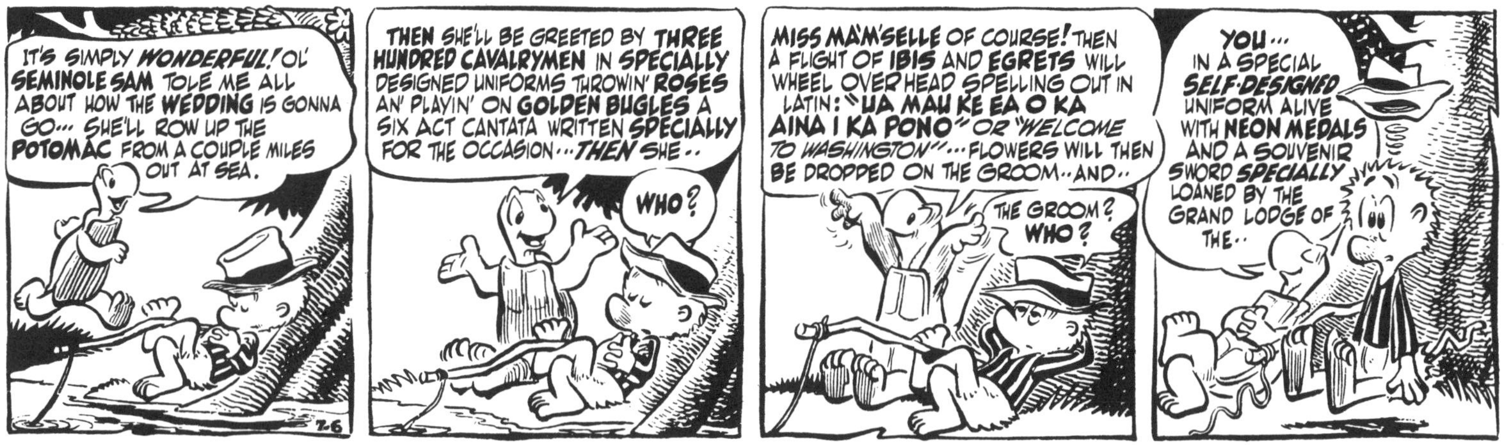
IT'S SIMPLY WONDERFUL! OL' SEMINOLE SAM TOLE ME ALL ABOUT HOW THE WEDDING IS GONNA GO··· SHE'LL ROW UP THE POTOMAC FROM A COUPLE MILES OUT AT SEA.
7-6
THEN SHE'LL BE GREETED BY THREE HUNDRED CAVALRYMEN IN SPECIALLY DESIGNED UNIFORMS THROWIN' ROSES AN' PLAYIN' ON GOLDEN BUGLES A SIX ACT CANTATA WRITTEN SPECIALLY FOR THE OCCASION···THEN SHE··
WHO?
MISS MA'M'SELLE OF COURSE! THEN A FLIGHT OF IBIS AND EGRETS WILL WHEEL OVERHEAD SPELLING OUT IN LATIN: "UA MAU KE EA O KA AINA I KA PONO" OR "WELCOME TO WASHINGTON"···FLOWERS WILL THEN BE DROPPED ON THE GROOM··AND··
THE GROOM? WHO?
YOU··· IN A SPECIAL SELF-DESIGNED UNIFORM ALIVE WITH NEON MEDALS AND A SOUVENIR SWORD SPECIALLY LOANED BY THE GRAND LODGE OF THE··

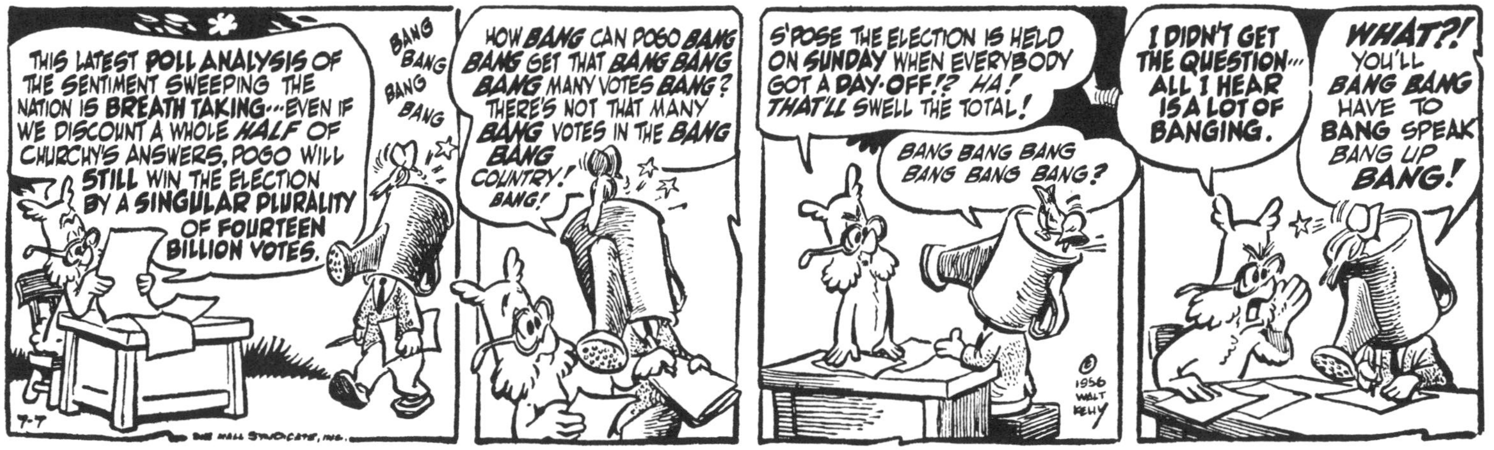
THIS LATEST POLL ANALYSIS OF THE SENTIMENT SWEEPING THE NATION IS BREATH TAKING···EVEN IF WE DISCOUNT A WHOLE HALF OF CHURCHY'S ANSWERS, POGO WILL STILL WIN THE ELECTION BY A SINGULAR PLURALITY OF FOURTEEN BILLION VOTES.
BANG BANG BANG BANG
7-7
HOW BANG CAN POGO BANG BANG GET THAT BANG BANG BANG MANY VOTES BANG? THERE'S NOT THAT MANY BANG VOTES IN THE BANG BANG COUNTRY! BANG!
S'POSE THE ELECTION IS HELD ON SUNDAY WHEN EVERYBODY GOT A DAY-OFF!? HA! THAT'LL SWELL THE TOTAL!
BANG BANG BANG BANG BANG BANG?
© 1956 WALT KELLY
I DIDN'T GET THE QUESTION··· ALL I HEAR IS A LOT OF BANGING.
WHAT?! YOU'LL BANG BANG HAVE TO BANG SPEAK BANG UP BANG!

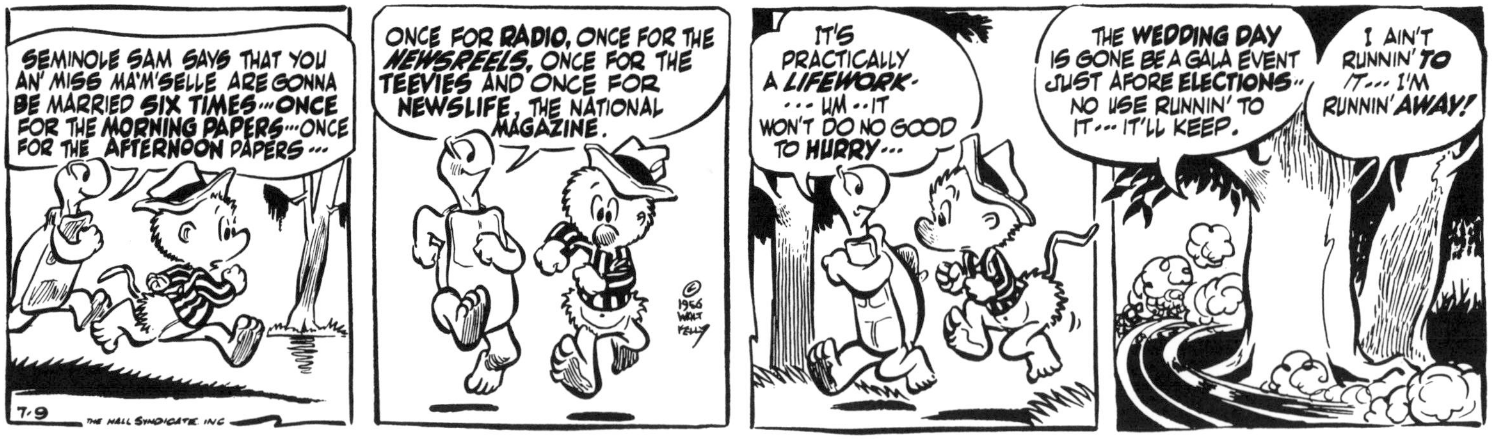
SEMINOLE SAM SAYS THAT YOU AN' MISS MA'M'SELLE ARE GONNA BE MARRIED SIX TIMES...ONCE FOR THE MORNING PAPERS...ONCE FOR THE AFTERNOON PAPERS...
ONCE FOR RADIO, ONCE FOR THE NEWSREELS, ONCE FOR THE TEEVIES AND ONCE FOR NEWSLIFE, THE NATIONAL MAGAZINE.
© 1956 WALT KELLY
IT'S PRACTICALLY A LIFEWORK---UM--IT WON'T DO NO GOOD TO HURRY...
THE WEDDING DAY IS GONE BE A GALA EVENT JUST AFORE ELECTIONS.. NO USE RUNNIN' TO IT--- IT'LL KEEP.
I AIN'T RUNNIN' TO IT... I'M RUNNIN' AWAY!
7-9
THE HALL SYNDICATE INC

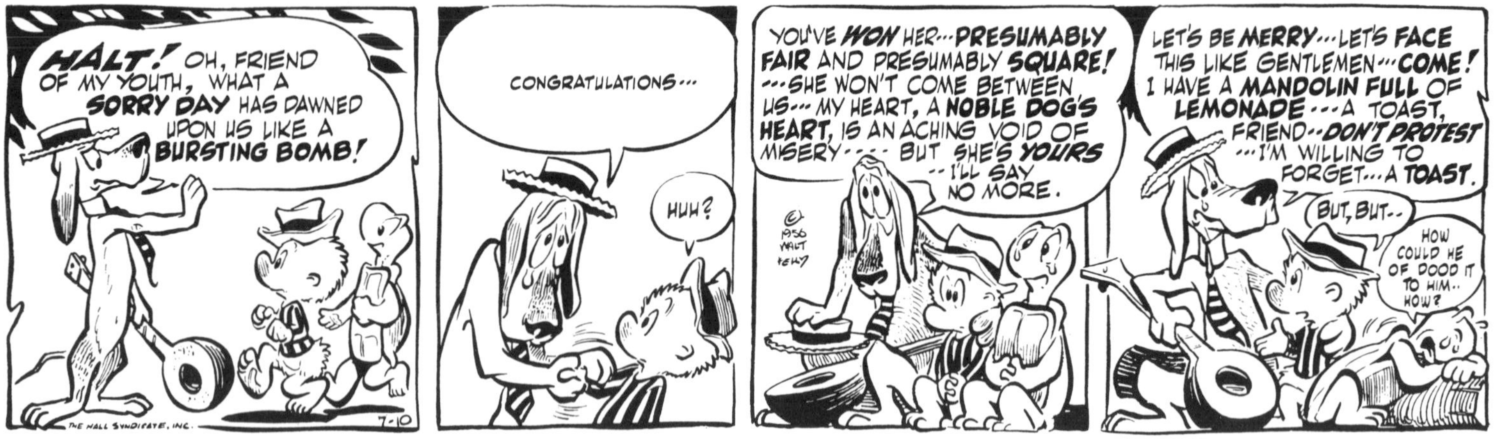
HALT! OH, FRIEND OF MY YOUTH, WHAT A SORRY DAY HAS DAWNED UPON US LIKE A BURSTING BOMB!
THE HALL SYNDICATE, INC.
7-10
CONGRATULATIONS...
HUH?
YOU'VE WON HER...PRESUMABLY FAIR AND PRESUMABLY SQUARE! ---SHE WON'T COME BETWEEN US... MY HEART, A NOBLE DOG'S HEART, IS AN ACHING VOID OF MISERY---- BUT SHE'S YOURS --I'LL SAY NO MORE.
© 1956 WALT KELLY
LET'S BE MERRY...LET'S FACE THIS LIKE GENTLEMEN...COME! I HAVE A MANDOLIN FULL OF LEMONADE---A TOAST, FRIEND--DON'T PROTEST ...I'M WILLING TO FORGET...A TOAST.
BUT, BUT--
HOW COULD HE OF DOOD IT TO HIM.. HOW?

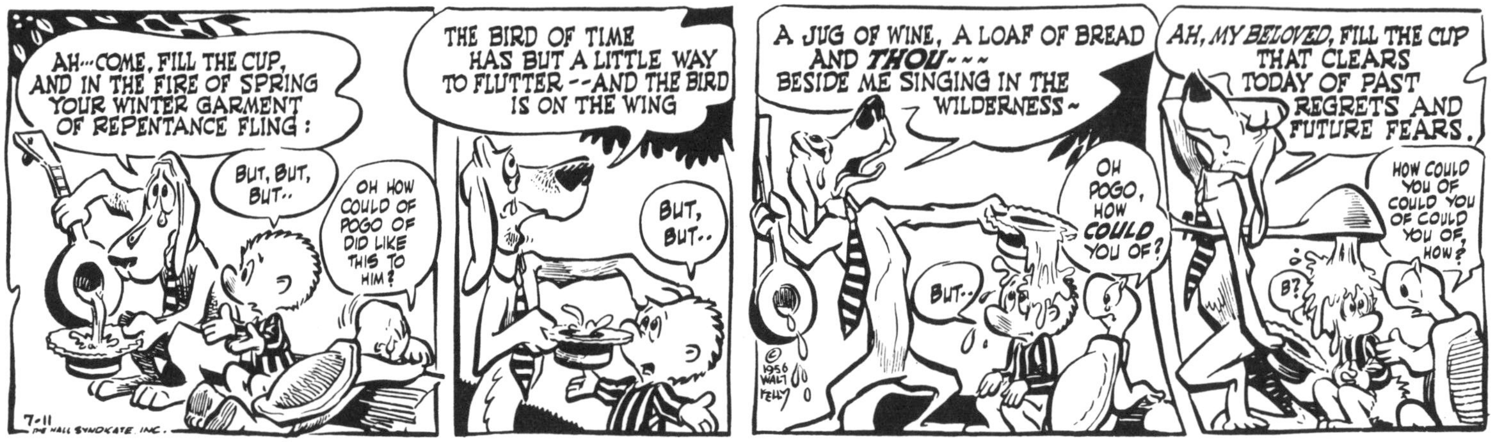
AH...COME, FILL THE CUP, AND IN THE FIRE OF SPRING YOUR WINTER GARMENT OF REPENTANCE FLING:
BUT, BUT, BUT..
OH HOW COULD OF POGO OF DID LIKE THIS TO HIM?
7-11
THE HALL SYNDICATE, INC.
THE BIRD OF TIME HAS BUT A LITTLE WAY TO FLUTTER--AND THE BIRD IS ON THE WING
BUT, BUT..
A JUG OF WINE, A LOAF OF BREAD AND THOU--- BESIDE ME SINGING IN THE WILDERNESS~
OH POGO, HOW COULD YOU OF?
BUT..
© 1956 WALT KELLY
AH, MY BELOVED, FILL THE CUP THAT CLEARS TODAY OF PAST REGRETS AND FUTURE FEARS.
HOW COULD YOU OF COULD YOU OF COULD YOU OF, HOW?
B?

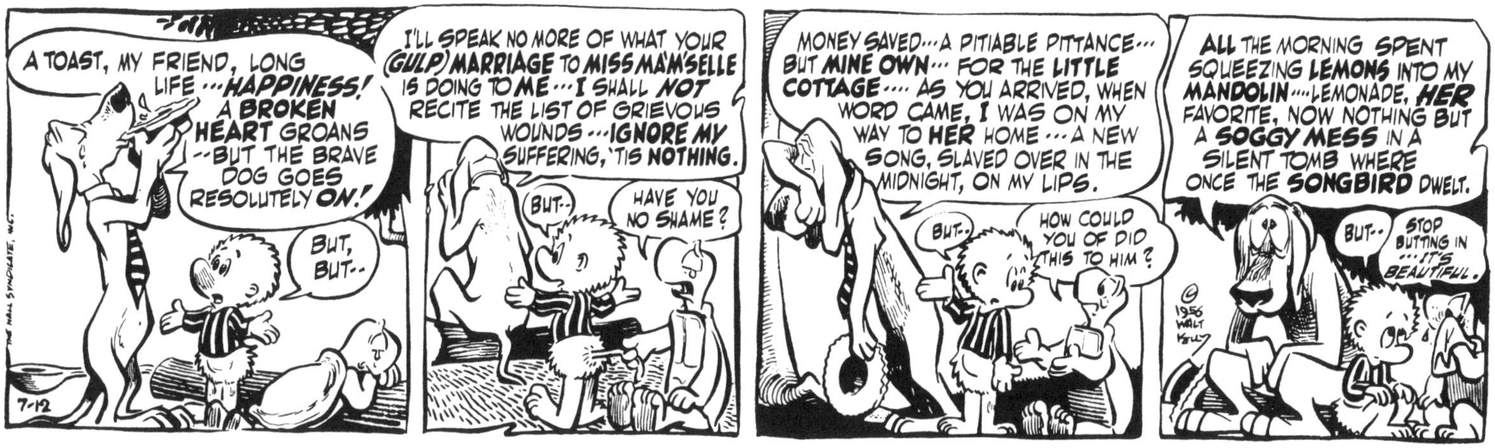
A TOAST, MY FRIEND, LONG LIFE ··· HAPPINESS! A BROKEN HEART GROANS --BUT THE BRAVE DOG GOES RESOLUTELY ON!
BUT, BUT--
I'LL SPEAK NO MORE OF WHAT YOUR (GULP) MARRIAGE TO MISS MAM'SELLE IS DOING TO ME ··· I SHALL NOT RECITE THE LIST OF GRIEVOUS WOUNDS ··· IGNORE MY SUFFERING, 'TIS NOTHING.
BUT--
HAVE YOU NO SHAME?
MONEY SAVED··· A PITIABLE PITTANCE··· BUT MINE OWN ··· FOR THE LITTLE COTTAGE ···· AS YOU ARRIVED, WHEN WORD CAME, I WAS ON MY WAY TO HER HOME ··· A NEW SONG, SLAVED OVER IN THE MIDNIGHT, ON MY LIPS.
BUT--
HOW COULD YOU OF DID THIS TO HIM?
ALL THE MORNING SPENT SQUEEZING LEMONS INTO MY MANDOLIN ···· LEMONADE, HER FAVORITE, NOW NOTHING BUT A SOGGY MESS IN A SILENT TOMB WHERE ONCE THE SONGBIRD DWELT.
BUT--
STOP BUTTING IN ··· IT'S BEAUTIFUL.
7-12
© 1956 WALT KELLY

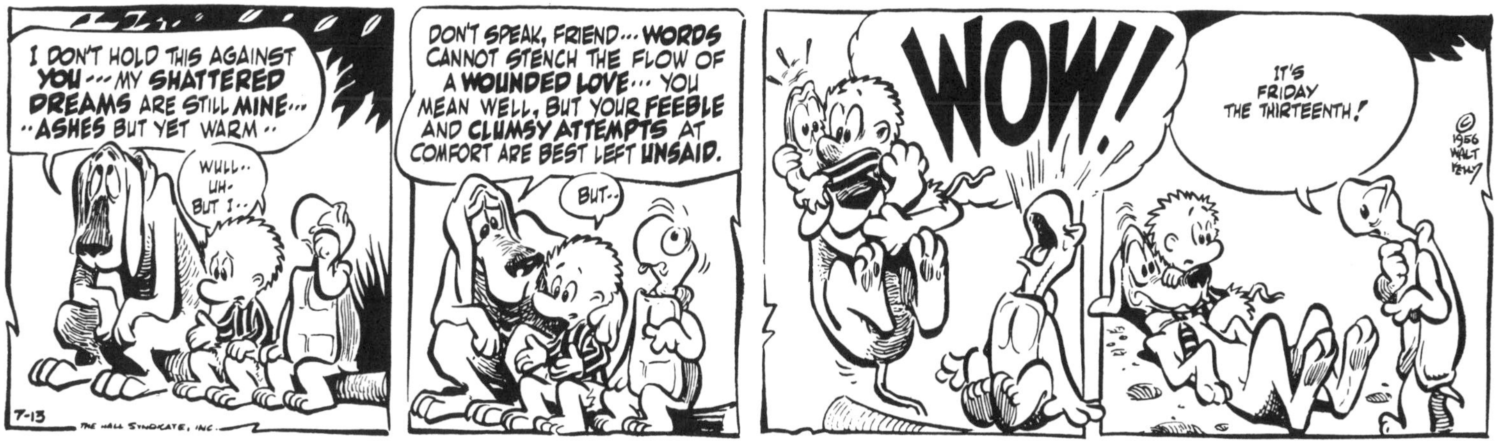
I DON'T HOLD THIS AGAINST YOU ··· MY SHATTERED DREAMS ARE STILL MINE ··· ·· ASHES BUT YET WARM ··
WULL.. UH- BUT I--
DON'T SPEAK, FRIEND··· WORDS CANNOT STENCH THE FLOW OF A WOUNDED LOVE··· YOU MEAN WELL, BUT YOUR FEEBLE AND CLUMSY ATTEMPTS AT COMFORT ARE BEST LEFT UNSAID.
BUT--
WOW!
IT'S FRIDAY THE THIRTEENTH!
7-13
THE HALL SYNDICATE, INC.
© 1956 WALT KELLY

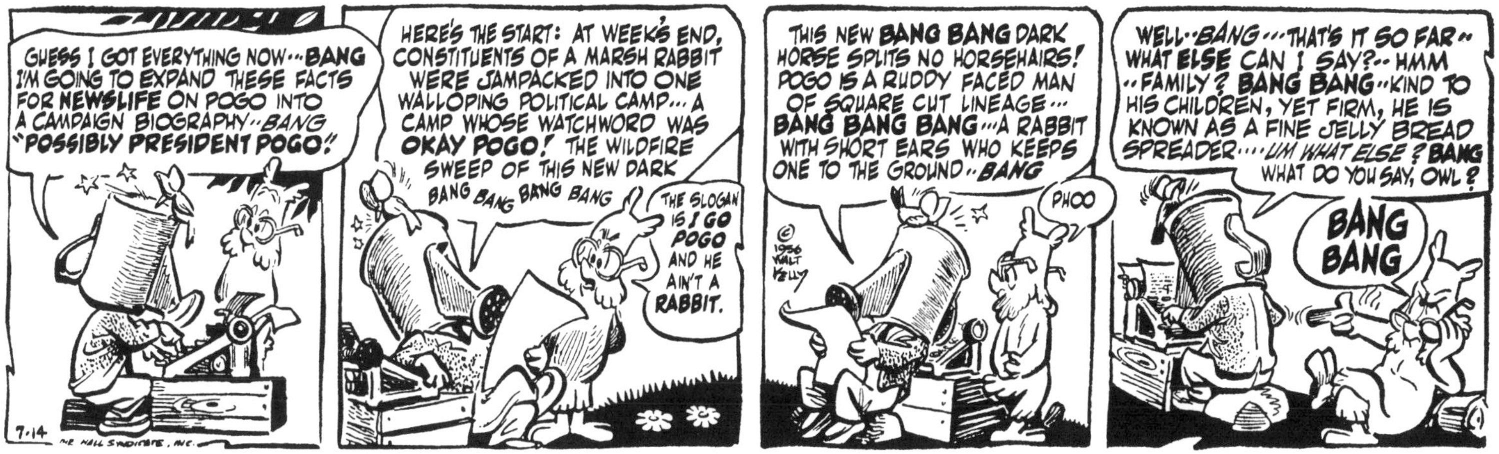
GUESS I GOT EVERYTHING NOW··· BANG I'M GOING TO EXPAND THESE FACTS FOR NEWSLIFE ON POGO INTO A CAMPAIGN BIOGRAPHY·· BANG "POSSIBLY PRESIDENT POGO."
HERE'S THE START: AT WEEK'S END, CONSTITUENTS OF A MARSH RABBIT WERE JAMPACKED INTO ONE WALLOPING POLITICAL CAMP··· A CAMP WHOSE WATCHWORD WAS OKAY POGO! THE WILDFIRE SWEEP OF THIS NEW DARK
BANG BANG BANG BANG
THE SLOGAN IS I GO POGO AND HE AIN'T A RABBIT.
THIS NEW BANG BANG DARK HORSE SPLITS NO HORSEHAIRS! POGO IS A RUDDY FACED MAN OF SQUARE CUT LINEAGE ··· BANG BANG BANG ··· A RABBIT WITH SHORT EARS WHO KEEPS ONE TO THE GROUND·· BANG
PHOO
WELL·· BANG ··· THAT'S IT SO FAR·· WHAT ELSE CAN I SAY?-- HMM ·· FAMILY? BANG BANG ·· KIND TO HIS CHILDREN, YET FIRM, HE IS KNOWN AS A FINE JELLY BREAD SPREADER ···· UM WHAT ELSE? BANG WHAT DO YOU SAY, OWL?
BANG BANG
7-14
THE HALL SYNDICATE, INC.
© 1956 WALT KELLY

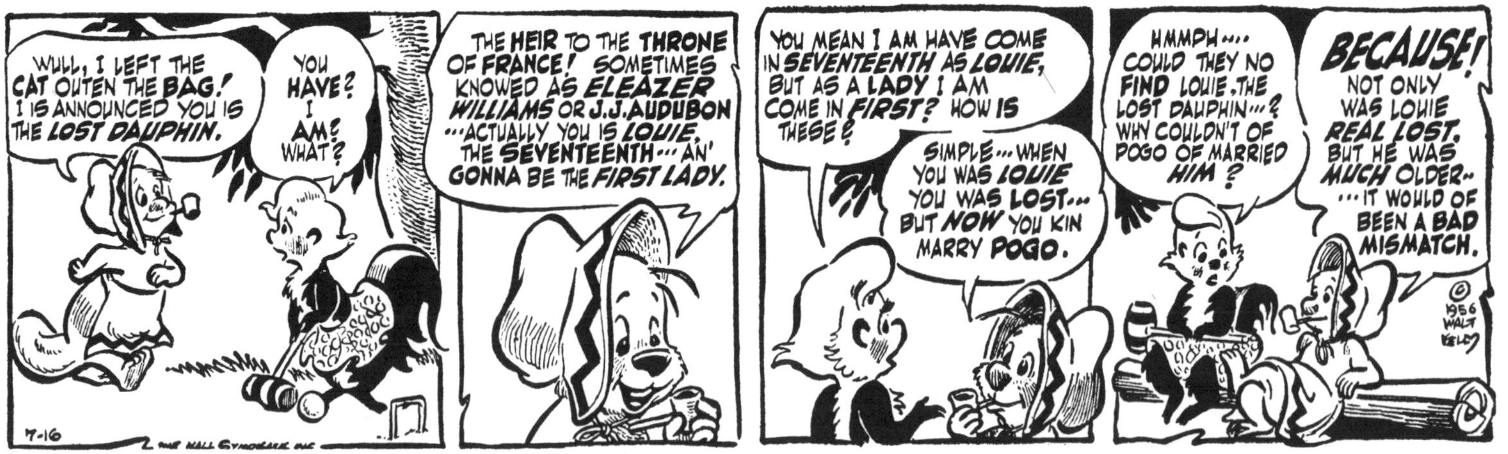
WULL, I LEFT THE CAT OUTEN THE BAG! I IS ANNOUNCED YOU IS THE LOST DAUPHIN.
YOU HAVE? I AM? WHAT?
THE HEIR TO THE THRONE OF FRANCE! SOMETIMES KNOWED AS ELEAZER WILLIAMS OR J.J. AUDUBON ... ACTUALLY YOU IS LOUIE, THE SEVENTEENTH ... AN' GONNA BE THE FIRST LADY.
YOU MEAN I AM HAVE COME IN SEVENTEENTH AS LOUIE, BUT AS A LADY I AM COME IN FIRST? HOW IS THESE?
SIMPLE ... WHEN YOU WAS LOUIE YOU WAS LOST ... BUT NOW YOU KIN MARRY POGO.
HMMPH ... COULD THEY NO FIND LOUIE, THE LOST DAUPHIN ...? WHY COULDN'T OF POGO OF MARRIED HIM?
BECAUSE! NOT ONLY WAS LOUIE REAL LOST, BUT HE WAS MUCH OLDER ... IT WOULD OF BEEN A BAD MISMATCH.
© 1956 WALT KELLY
7-16

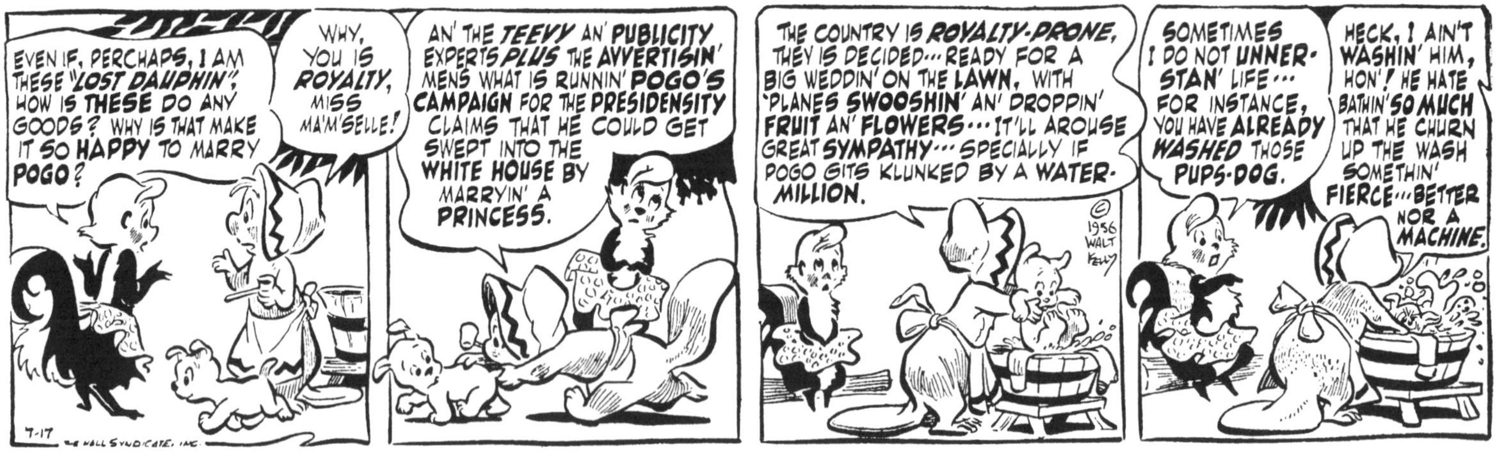
EVEN IF, PERCHAPS, I AM THESE "LOST DAUPHIN", HOW IS THESE DO ANY GOODS? WHY IS THAT MAKE IT SO HAPPY TO MARRY POGO?
WHY, YOU IS ROYALTY, MISS MA'M'SELLE!
AN' THE TEEVY AN' PUBLICITY EXPERTS PLUS THE AVVERTISIN' MENS WHAT IS RUNNIN' POGO'S CAMPAIGN FOR THE PRESIDENSITY CLAIMS THAT HE COULD GET SWEPT INTO THE WHITE HOUSE BY MARRYIN' A PRINCESS.
THE COUNTRY IS ROYALTY-PRONE, THEY IS DECIDED ... READY FOR A BIG WEDDIN' ON THE LAWN, WITH 'PLANES SWOOSHIN' AN' DROPPIN' FRUIT AN' FLOWERS ... IT'LL AROUSE GREAT SYMPATHY ... SPECIALLY IF POGO GITS KLUNKED BY A WATER-MILLION.
© 1956 WALT KELLY
SOMETIMES I DO NOT UNNER-STAN' LIFE ... FOR INSTANCE, YOU HAVE ALREADY WASHED THOSE PUPS-DOG.
HECK, I AIN'T WASHIN' HIM, HON'! HE HATE BATHIN' SO MUCH THAT HE CHURN UP THE WASH SOMETHIN' FIERCE ... BETTER NOR A MACHINE.
7-17

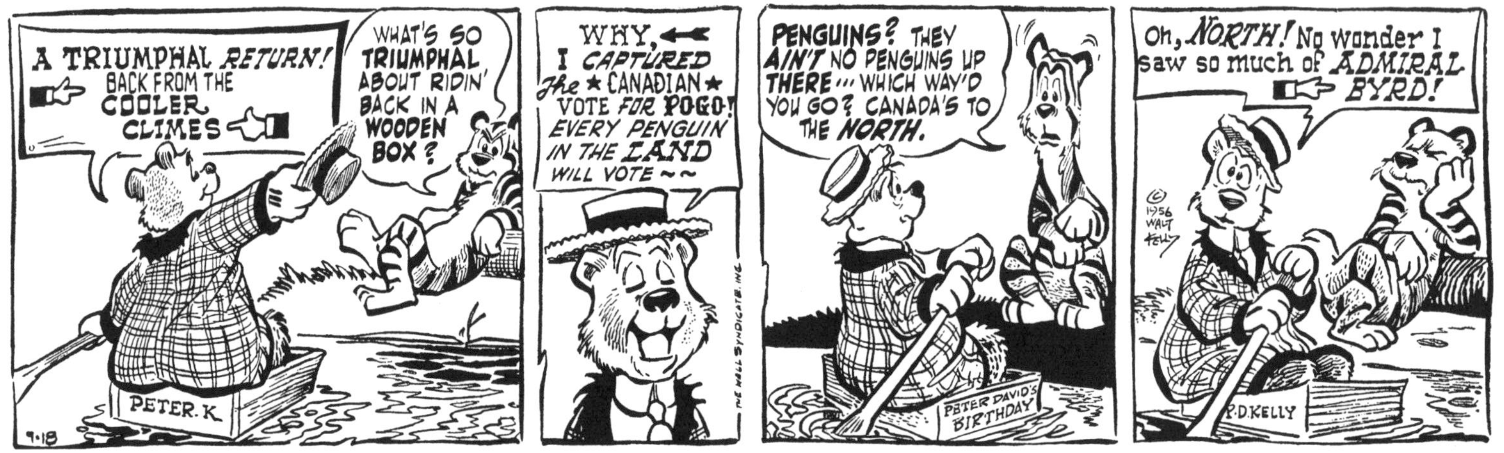
A TRIUMPHAL RETURN! BACK FROM THE COOLER CLIMES
WHAT'S SO TRIUMPHAL ABOUT RIDIN' BACK IN A WOODEN BOX?
PETER.K.
WHY, I CAPTURED the ★ CANADIAN ★ VOTE FOR POGO! EVERY PENGUIN IN THE LAND WILL VOTE ~~
PENGUINS? THEY AIN'T NO PENGUINS UP THERE ... WHICH WAY'D YOU GO? CANADA'S TO THE NORTH.
PETER DAVID'S BIRTHDAY
Oh, NORTH! No wonder I saw so much of ADMIRAL BYRD!
© 1956 WALT KELLY
P.D.KELLY
7-18

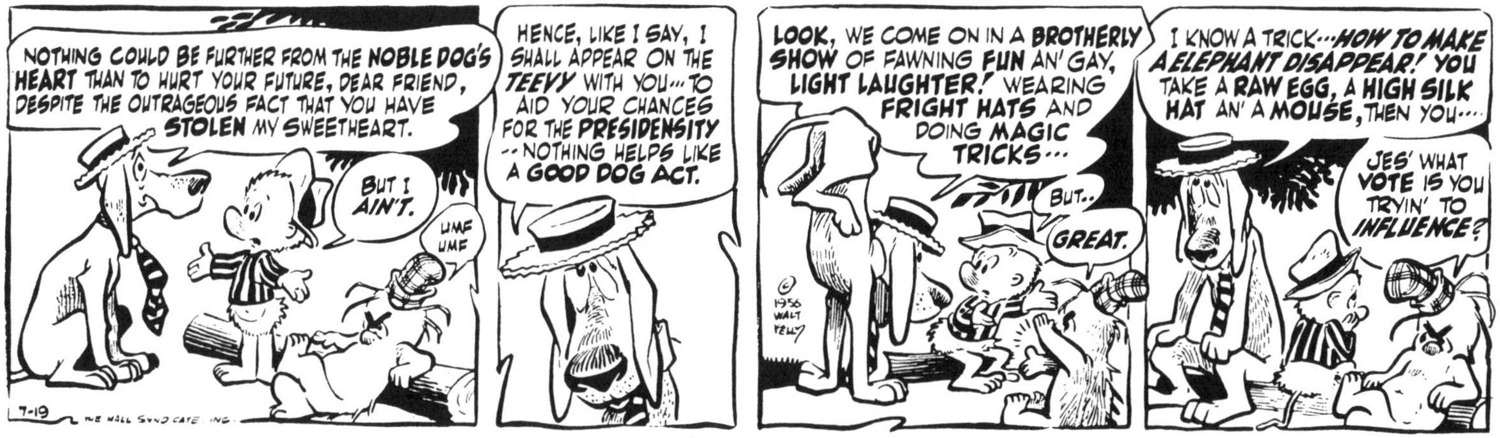
NOTHING COULD BE FURTHER FROM THE NOBLE DOG'S HEART THAN TO HURT YOUR FUTURE, DEAR FRIEND, DESPITE THE OUTRAGEOUS FACT THAT YOU HAVE STOLEN MY SWEETHEART.
BUT I AIN'T.
UMF UMF
HENCE, LIKE I SAY, I SHALL APPEAR ON THE TEEVY WITH YOU... TO AID YOUR CHANCES FOR THE PRESIDENSITY -- NOTHING HELPS LIKE A GOOD DOG ACT.
LOOK, WE COME ON IN A BROTHERLY SHOW OF FAWNING FUN AN' GAY, LIGHT LAUGHTER! WEARING FRIGHT HATS AND DOING MAGIC TRICKS...
BUT..
GREAT.
I KNOW A TRICK...HOW TO MAKE A ELEPHANT DISAPPEAR! YOU TAKE A RAW EGG, A HIGH SILK HAT AN' A MOUSE, THEN YOU....
JES' WHAT VOTE IS YOU TRYIN' TO INFLUENCE?
7-19
©1956 WALT KELLY

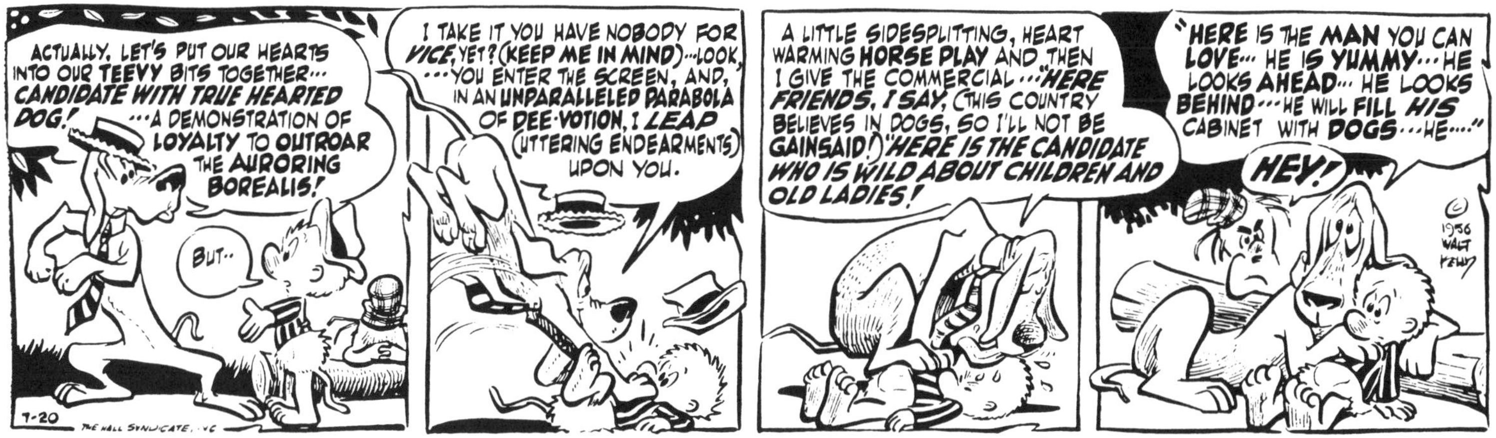
ACTUALLY, LET'S PUT OUR HEARTS INTO OUR TEEVY BITS TOGETHER... CANDIDATE WITH TRUE HEARTED DOG! ...A DEMONSTRATION OF LOYALTY TO OUTROAR THE AURORING BOREALIS!
BUT..
I TAKE IT YOU HAVE NOBODY FOR VICE, YET? (KEEP ME IN MIND)...LOOK, ...YOU ENTER THE SCREEN, AND, IN AN UNPARALLELED PARABOLA OF DEE-VOTION, I LEAP (UTTERING ENDEARMENTS) UPON YOU.
A LITTLE SIDESPLITTING, HEART WARMING HORSE PLAY AND THEN I GIVE THE COMMERCIAL ..."HERE FRIENDS, I SAY, (THIS COUNTRY BELIEVES IN DOGS, SO I'LL NOT BE GAINSAID!) "HERE IS THE CANDIDATE WHO IS WILD ABOUT CHILDREN AND OLD LADIES!
"HERE IS THE MAN YOU CAN LOVE... HE IS YUMMY... HE LOOKS AHEAD... HE LOOKS BEHIND... HE WILL FILL HIS CABINET WITH DOGS...HE...."
HEY!
7-20
©1956 WALT KELLY

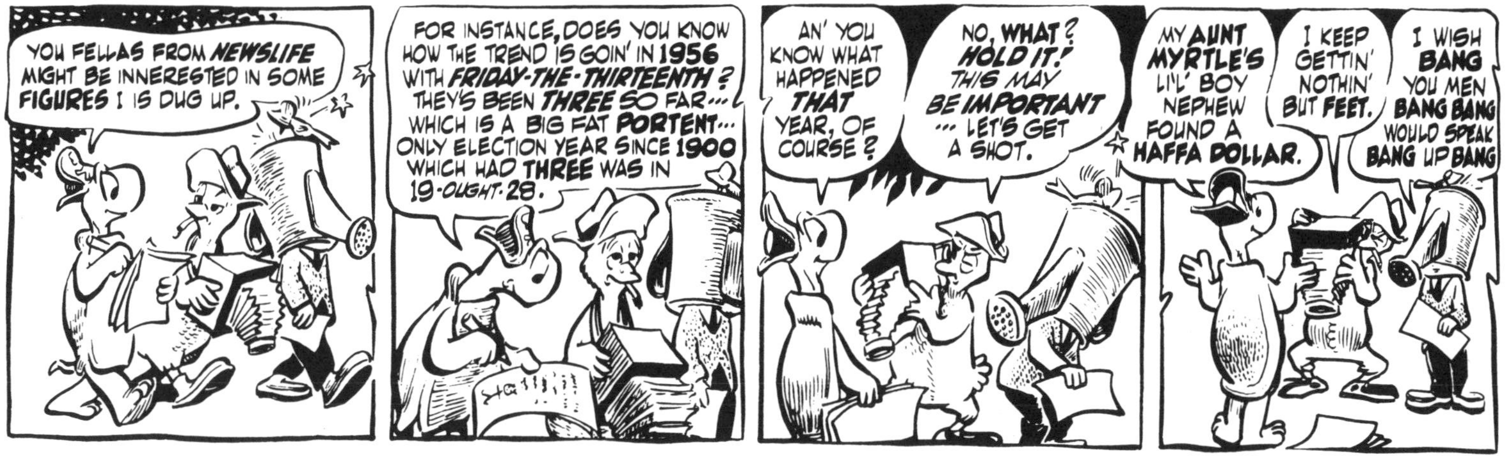
YOU FELLAS FROM NEWSLIFE MIGHT BE INNERESTED IN SOME FIGURES I IS DUG UP.
FOR INSTANCE, DOES YOU KNOW HOW THE TREND IS GOIN' IN 1956 WITH FRIDAY-THE-THIRTEENTH? THEY'S BEEN THREE SO FAR... WHICH IS A BIG FAT PORTENT... ONLY ELECTION YEAR SINCE 1900 WHICH HAD THREE WAS IN 19-OUGHT-28.
AN' YOU KNOW WHAT HAPPENED THAT YEAR, OF COURSE?
NO, WHAT? HOLD IT! THIS MAY BE IMPORTANT ... LET'S GET A SHOT.
MY AUNT MYRTLE'S LI'L' BOY NEPHEW FOUND A HAFFA DOLLAR.
I KEEP GETTIN' NOTHIN' BUT FEET.
I WISH BANG YOU MEN BANG BANG WOULD SPEAK BANG UP BANG

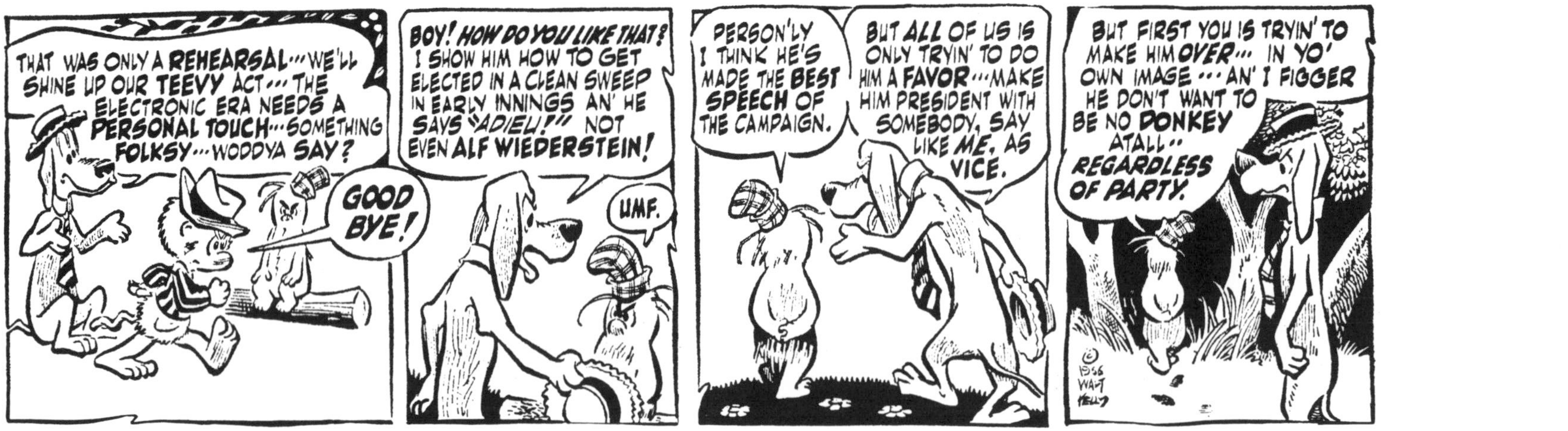
THAT WAS ONLY A REHEARSAL··· WE'LL SHINE UP OUR TEEVY ACT··· THE ELECTRONIC ERA NEEDS A PERSONAL TOUCH··· SOMETHING FOLKSY··· WODDYA SAY?
GOOD BYE!
BOY! HOW DO YOU LIKE THAT? I SHOW HIM HOW TO GET ELECTED IN A CLEAN SWEEP IN EARLY INNINGS AN' HE SAYS "ADIEU!" NOT EVEN ALF WIEDERSTEIN!
UMF.
PERSON'LY I THINK HE'S MADE THE BEST SPEECH OF THE CAMPAIGN.
BUT ALL OF US IS ONLY TRYIN' TO DO HIM A FAVOR··· MAKE HIM PRESIDENT WITH SOMEBODY, SAY LIKE ME, AS VICE.
BUT FIRST YOU IS TRYIN' TO MAKE HIM OVER··· IN YO' OWN IMAGE··· AN' I FIGGER HE DON'T WANT TO BE NO DONKEY ATALL·· REGARDLESS OF PARTY.
© 1956 WALT KELLY

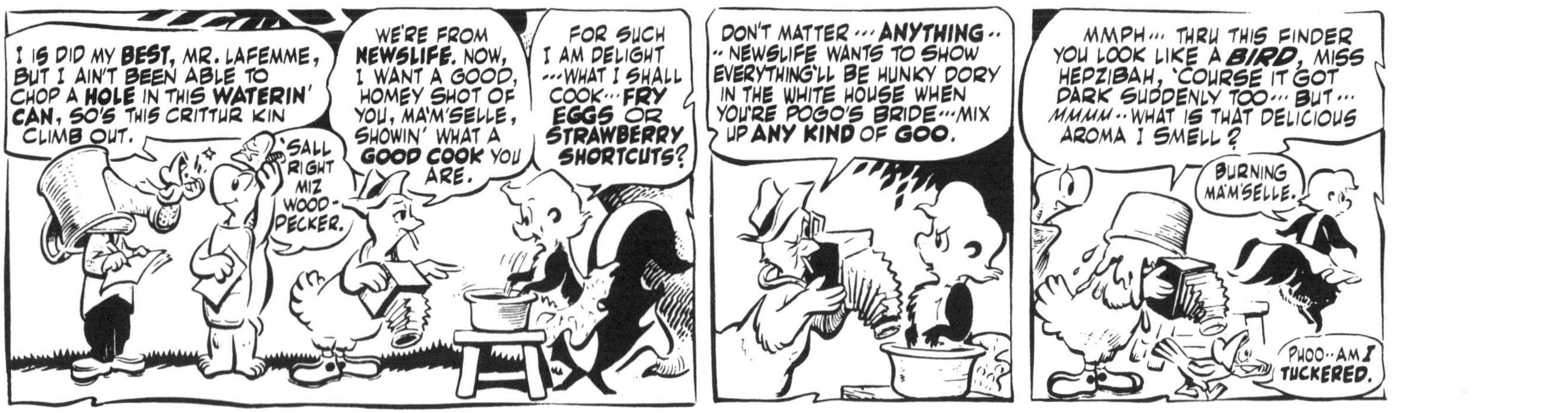
I IS DID MY BEST, MR. LAFEMME, BUT I AIN'T BEEN ABLE TO CHOP A HOLE IN THIS WATERIN' CAN, SO'S THIS CRITTUR KIN CLIMB OUT.
'SALL RIGHT MIZ WOOD-PECKER.
WE'RE FROM NEWSLIFE. NOW, I WANT A GOOD, HOMEY SHOT OF YOU, MA'M'SELLE, SHOWIN' WHAT A GOOD COOK YOU ARE.
FOR SUCH I AM DELIGHT ···WHAT I SHALL COOK··· FRY EGGS OR STRAWBERRY SHORTCUTS?
DON'T MATTER··· ANYTHING·· ·· NEWSLIFE WANTS TO SHOW EVERYTHING'LL BE HUNKY DORY IN THE WHITE HOUSE WHEN YOU'RE POGO'S BRIDE··· MIX UP ANY KIND OF GOO.
MMPH··· THRU THIS FINDER YOU LOOK LIKE A BIRD, MISS HEPZIBAH, 'COURSE IT GOT DARK SUDDENLY TOO··· BUT··· MMMM·· WHAT IS THAT DELICIOUS AROMA I SMELL?
BURNING MA'M'SELLE.
PHOO·· AM I TUCKERED.

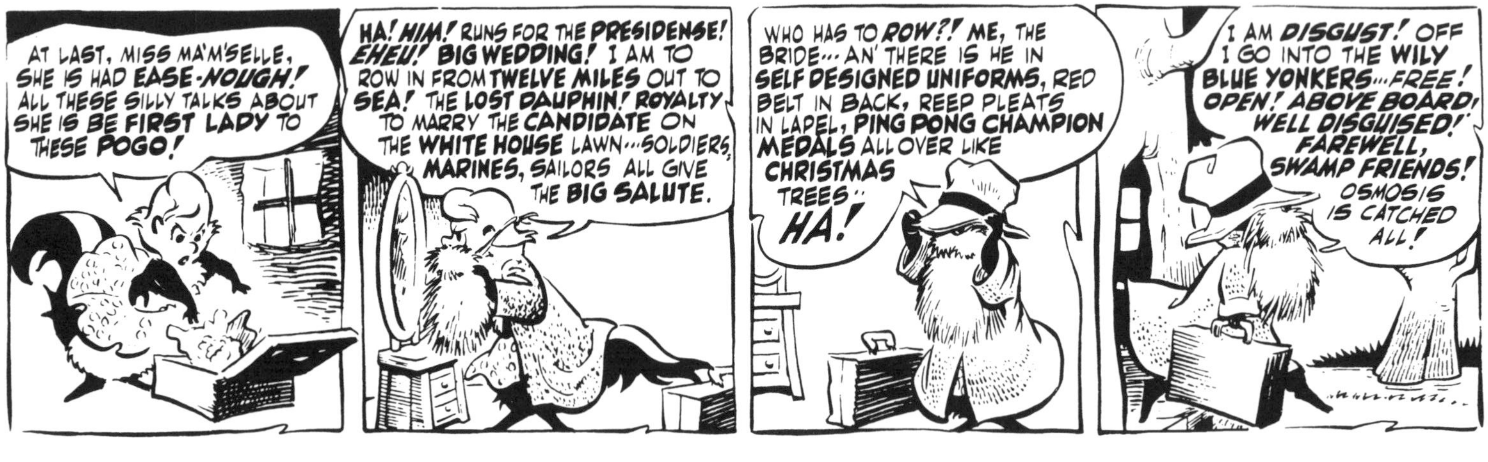
AT LAST, MISS MA'M'SELLE, SHE IS HAD EASE-NOUGH! ALL THESE SILLY TALKS ABOUT SHE IS BE FIRST LADY TO THESE POGO!
HA! HIM! RUNS FOR THE PRESIDENSE! EHEU! BIG WEDDING! I AM TO ROW IN FROM TWELVE MILES OUT TO SEA! THE LOST DAUPHIN! ROYALTY TO MARRY THE CANDIDATE ON THE WHITE HOUSE LAWN··· SOLDIERS, MARINES, SAILORS ALL GIVE THE BIG SALUTE.
WHO HAS TO ROW?! ME, THE BRIDE··· AN' THERE IS HE IN SELF DESIGNED UNIFORMS, RED BELT IN BACK, REEP PLEATS IN LAPEL, PING PONG CHAMPION MEDALS ALL OVER LIKE CHRISTMAS TREES·· HA!
I AM DISGUST! OFF I GO INTO THE WILY BLUE YONKERS··· FREE! OPEN! ABOVE BOARD! WELL DISGUISED! FAREWELL, SWAMP FRIENDS! OSMOSIS IS CATCHED ALL!

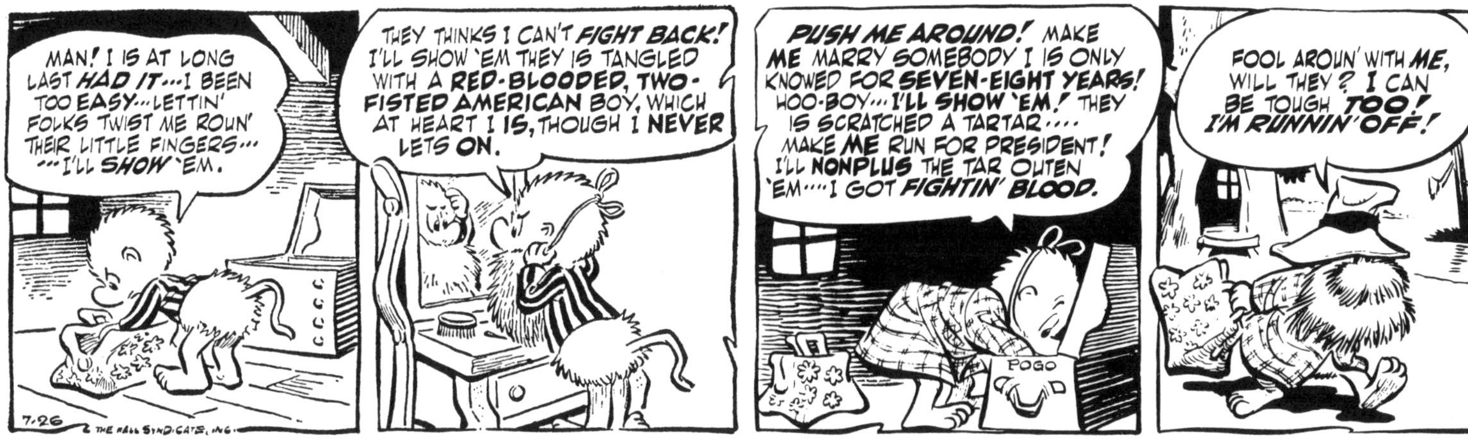
MAN! I IS AT LONG LAST HAD IT... I BEEN TOO EASY... LETTIN' FOLKS TWIST ME ROUN' THEIR LITTLE FINGERS... ...I'LL SHOW 'EM.
THEY THINKS I CAN'T FIGHT BACK! I'LL SHOW 'EM THEY IS TANGLED WITH A RED-BLOODED, TWO-FISTED AMERICAN BOY, WHICH AT HEART I IS, THOUGH I NEVER LETS ON.
PUSH ME AROUND! MAKE ME MARRY SOMEBODY I IS ONLY KNOWED FOR SEVEN-EIGHT YEARS! HOO-BOY... I'LL SHOW 'EM! THEY IS SCRATCHED A TARTAR.... MAKE ME RUN FOR PRESIDENT! I'LL NONPLUS THE TAR OUTEN 'EM.... I GOT FIGHTIN' BLOOD.
POGO
FOOL AROUN' WITH ME, WILL THEY? I CAN BE TOUGH TOO! I'M RUNNIN' OFF!
7-26
© THE HALL SYNDICATE, INC.

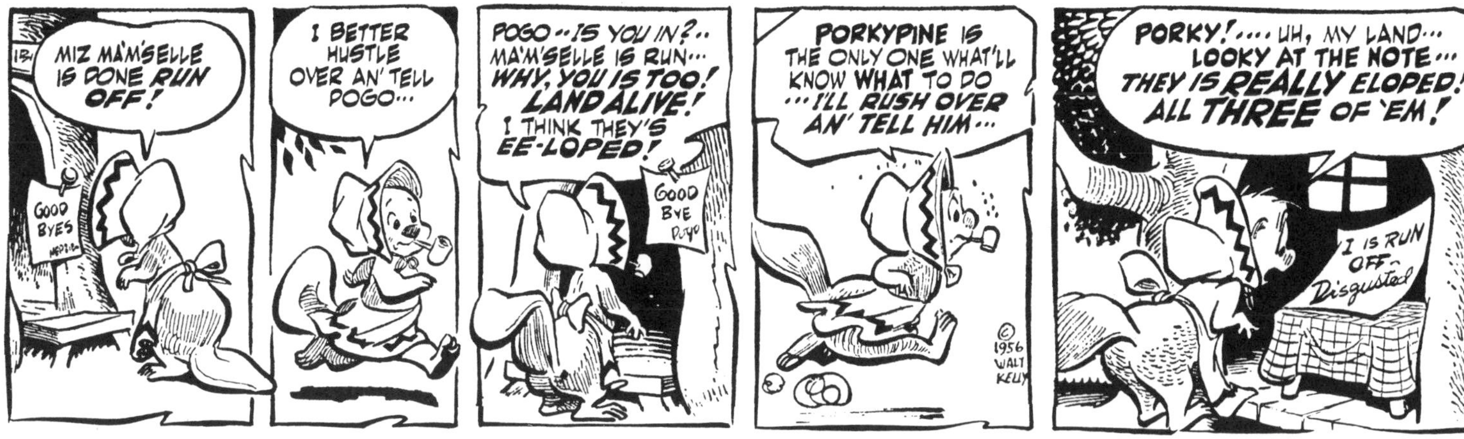
MIZ MA'M'SELLE IS DONE RUN OFF!
GOOD BYES
I BETTER HUSTLE OVER AN' TELL POGO...
POGO.. IS YOU IN?.. MA'M'SELLE IS RUN... WHY, YOU IS TOO! LAND ALIVE! I THINK THEY'S EE-LOPED!
GOOD BYE Pogo
PORKYPINE IS THE ONLY ONE WHAT'LL KNOW WHAT TO DO ...I'LL RUSH OVER AN' TELL HIM...
© 1956 WALT KELLY
PORKY!.... UH, MY LAND... LOOKY AT THE NOTE... THEY IS REALLY ELOPED! ALL THREE OF 'EM!
I IS RUN OFF. Disgusted

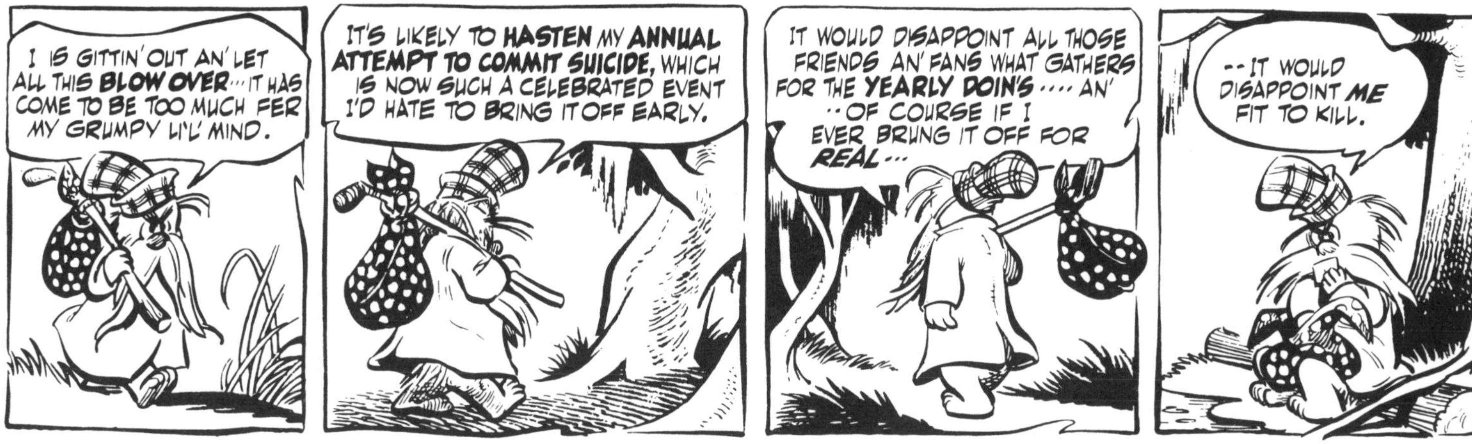
I IS GITTIN' OUT AN' LET ALL THIS BLOW OVER... IT HAS COME TO BE TOO MUCH FER MY GRUMPY LI'L' MIND.
IT'S LIKELY TO HASTEN MY ANNUAL ATTEMPT TO COMMIT SUICIDE, WHICH IS NOW SUCH A CELEBRATED EVENT I'D HATE TO BRING IT OFF EARLY.
IT WOULD DISAPPOINT ALL THOSE FRIENDS AN' FANS WHAT GATHERS FOR THE YEARLY DOIN'S.... AN' ..OF COURSE IF I EVER BRUNG IT OFF FOR REAL...
--IT WOULD DISAPPOINT ME FIT TO KILL.

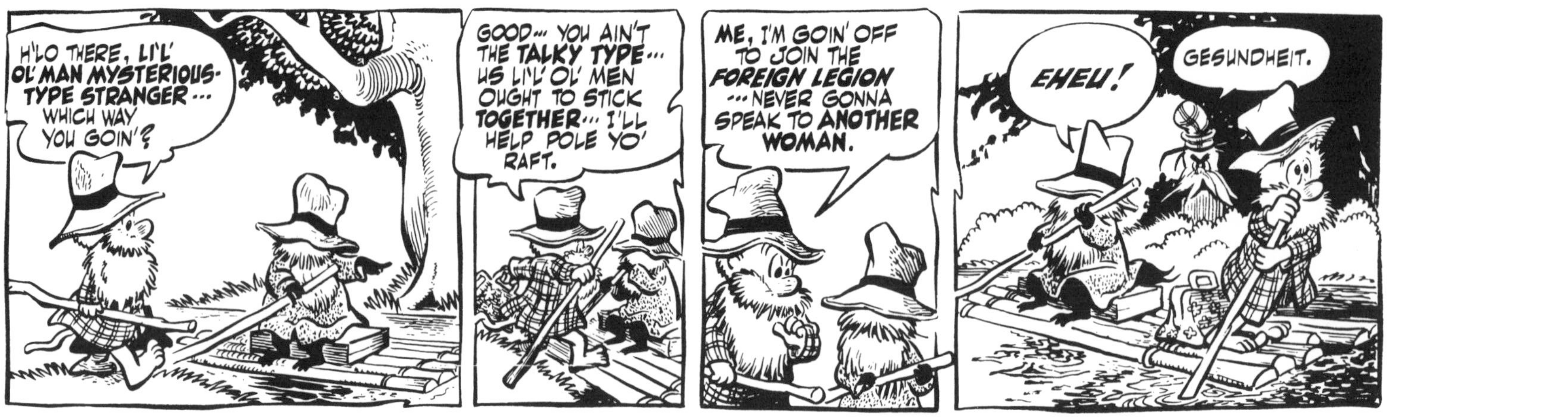
H'LO THERE, LI'L' OL' MAN MYSTERIOUS-TYPE STRANGER ... WHICH WAY YOU GOIN'?
GOOD... YOU AIN'T THE TALKY TYPE... US LI'L' OL' MEN OUGHT TO STICK TOGETHER... I'LL HELP POLE YO' RAFT.
ME, I'M GOIN' OFF TO JOIN THE FOREIGN LEGION ... NEVER GONNA SPEAK TO ANOTHER WOMAN.
EHEU!
GESUNDHEIT.

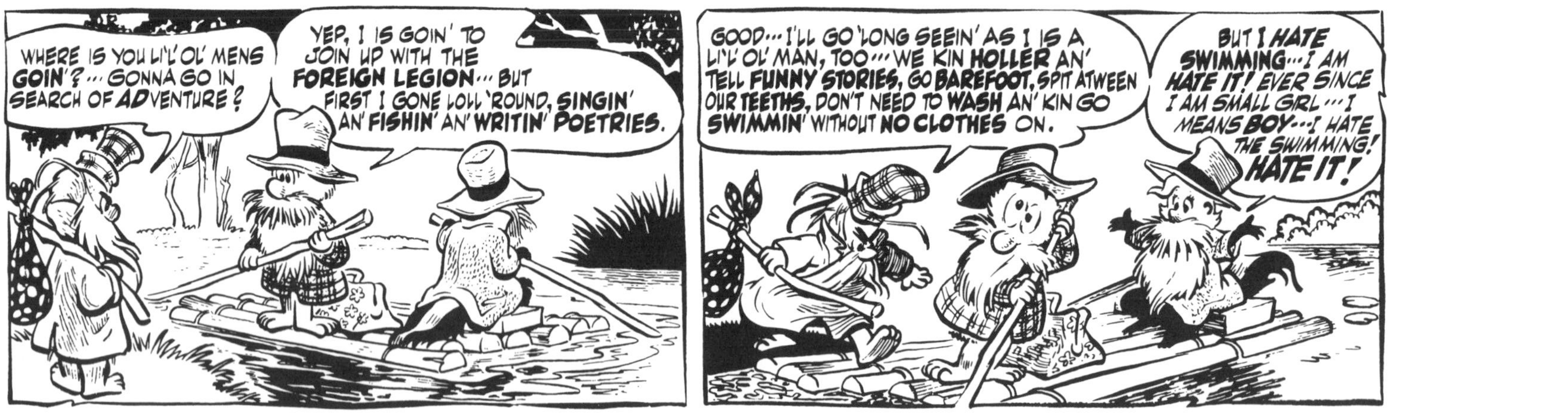
WHERE IS YOU LI'L' OL' MENS GOIN'? ... GONNA GO IN SEARCH OF ADVENTURE?
YEP, I IS GOIN' TO JOIN UP WITH THE FOREIGN LEGION ... BUT FIRST I GONE LOLL 'ROUND, SINGIN' AN' FISHIN' AN' WRITIN' POETRIES.
GOOD... I'LL GO 'LONG SEEIN' AS I IS A LI'L' OL' MAN, TOO ... WE KIN HOLLER AN' TELL FUNNY STORIES, GO BAREFOOT, SPIT ATWEEN OUR TEETHS, DON'T NEED TO WASH AN' KIN GO SWIMMIN' WITHOUT NO CLOTHES ON.
BUT I HATE SWIMMING... I AM HATE IT! EVER SINCE I AM SMALL GIRL ... I MEANS BOY... I HATE THE SWIMMING! HATE IT!

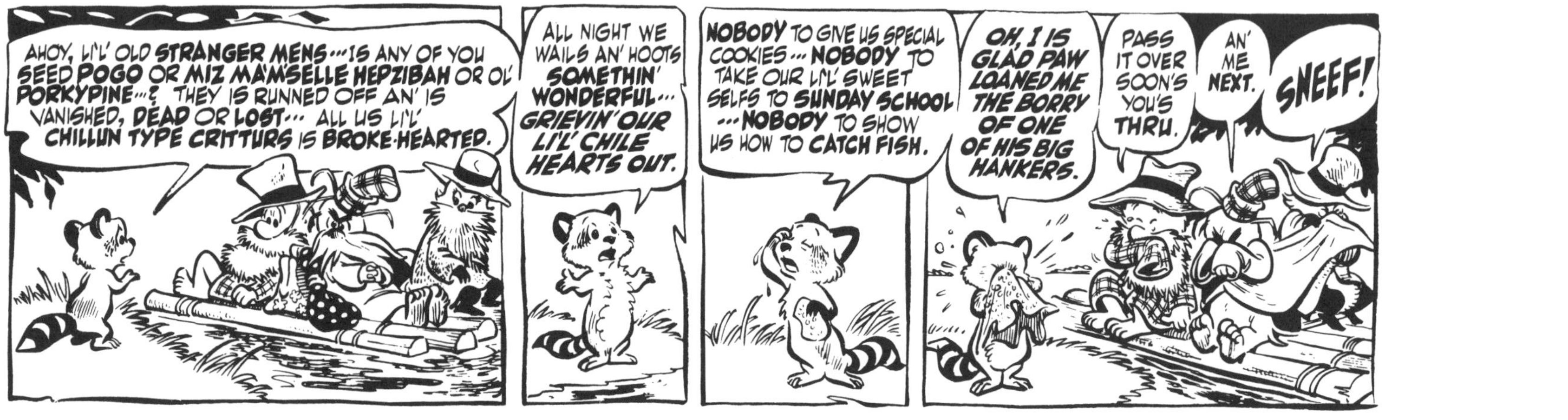
AHOY, LI'L' OLD STRANGER MENS ... IS ANY OF YOU SEED POGO OR MIZ MAM'SELLE HEPZIBAH OR OL' PORKYPINE...? THEY IS RUNNED OFF AN' IS VANISHED, DEAD OR LOST ... ALL US LI'L' CHILLUN TYPE CRITTURS IS BROKE-HEARTED.
ALL NIGHT WE WAILS AN' HOOTS SOMETHIN' WONDERFUL... GRIEVIN' OUR LI'L' CHILE HEARTS OUT.
NOBODY TO GIVE US SPECIAL COOKIES ... NOBODY TO TAKE OUR LI'L' SWEET SELFS TO SUNDAY SCHOOL ... NOBODY TO SHOW US HOW TO CATCH FISH.
OH, I IS GLAD PAW LOANED ME THE BORRY OF ONE OF HIS BIG HANKERS.
PASS IT OVER SOON'S YOU'S THRU.
AN' ME NEXT.
SNEEF!

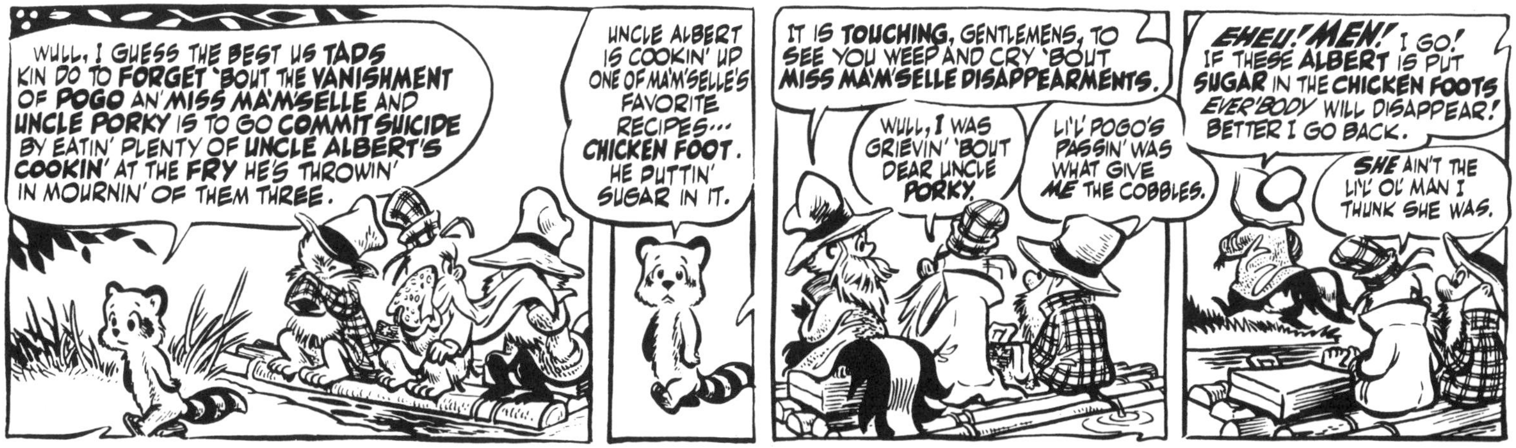
WULL, I GUESS THE BEST US TADS KIN DO TO FORGET 'BOUT THE VANISHMENT OF POGO AN' MISS MA'M'SELLE AND UNCLE PORKY IS TO GO COMMIT SUICIDE BY EATIN' PLENTY OF UNCLE ALBERT'S COOKIN' AT THE FRY HE'S THROWIN' IN MOURNIN' OF THEM THREE.
UNCLE ALBERT IS COOKIN' UP ONE OF MA'M'SELLE'S FAVORITE RECIPES... CHICKEN FOOT. HE PUTTIN' SUGAR IN IT.
IT IS TOUCHING, GENTLEMENS, TO SEE YOU WEEP AND CRY 'BOUT MISS MA'M'SELLE DISAPPEARMENTS.
WULL, I WAS GRIEVIN' 'BOUT DEAR UNCLE PORKY.
LI'L' POGO'S PASSIN' WAS WHAT GIVE ME THE COBBLES.
EHEU! MEN! I GO! IF THESE ALBERT IS PUT SUGAR IN THE CHICKEN FOOTS EVER'BODY WILL DISAPPEAR! BETTER I GO BACK.
SHE AIN'T THE LI'L' OL' MAN I THUNK SHE WAS.

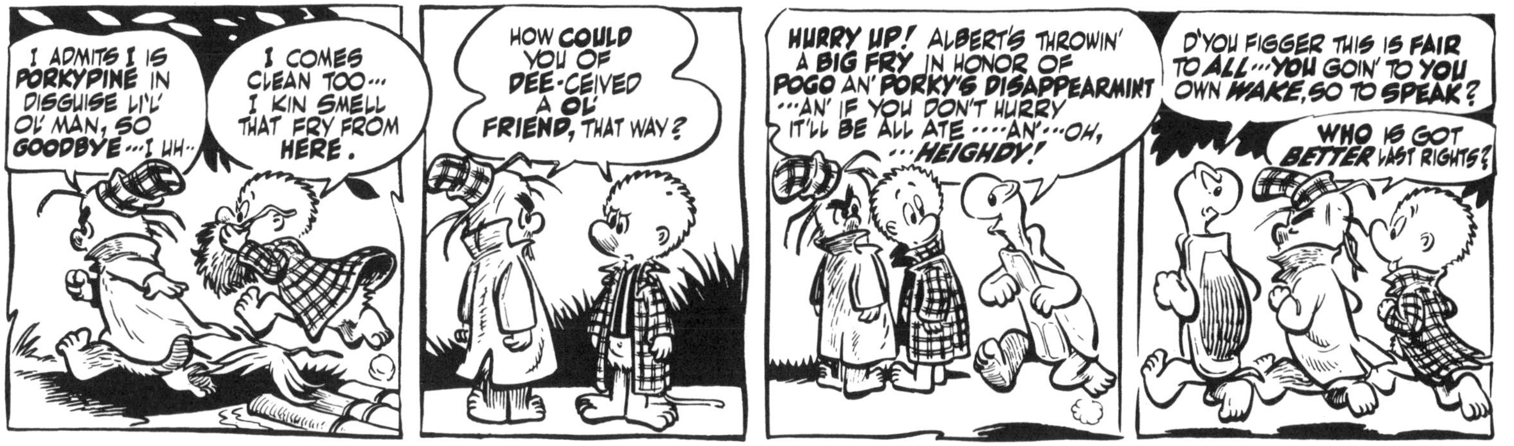
I ADMITS I IS PORKYPINE IN DISGUISE LI'L' OL' MAN, SO GOODBYE... I UH...
I COMES CLEAN TOO... I KIN SMELL THAT FRY FROM HERE.
HOW COULD YOU OF DEE-CEIVED A OL' FRIEND, THAT WAY?
HURRY UP! ALBERT'S THROWIN' A BIG FRY IN HONOR OF POGO AN' PORKY'S DISAPPEARMINT ...AN' IF YOU DON'T HURRY IT'LL BE ALL ATE....AN'...OH, ...HEIGHDY!
D'YOU FIGGER THIS IS FAIR TO ALL... YOU GOIN' TO YOU OWN WAKE, SO TO SPEAK?
WHO IS GOT BETTER LAST RIGHTS?

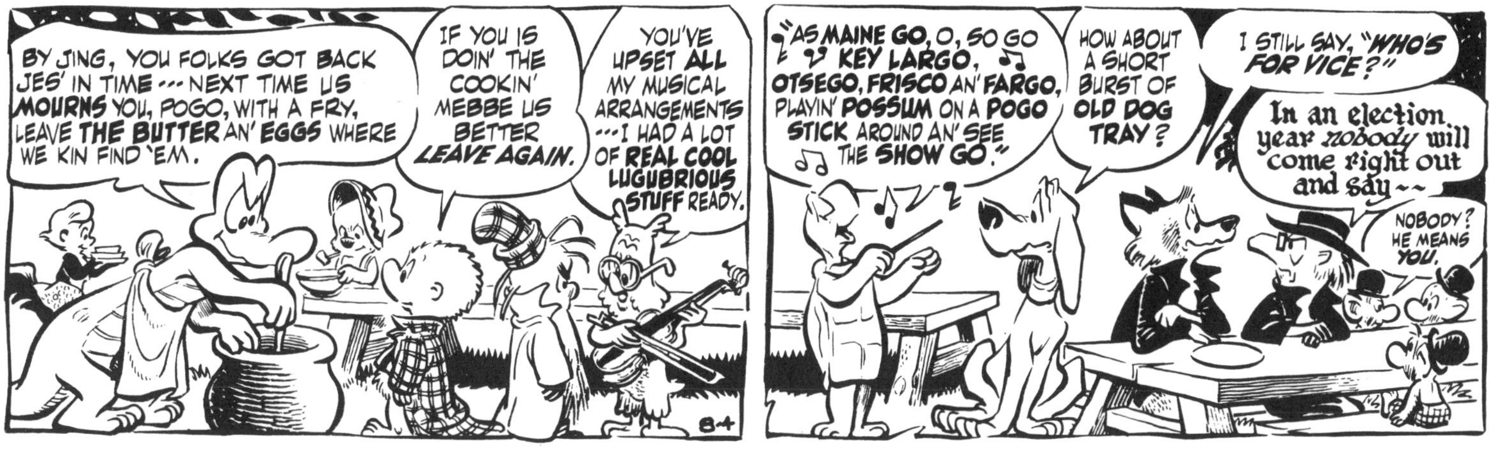
BY JING, YOU FOLKS GOT BACK JES' IN TIME --- NEXT TIME US MOURNS YOU, POGO, WITH A FRY, LEAVE THE BUTTER AN' EGGS WHERE WE KIN FIND 'EM.
IF YOU IS DOIN' THE COOKIN' MEBBE US BETTER LEAVE AGAIN.
YOU'VE UPSET ALL MY MUSICAL ARRANGEMENTS ---I HAD A LOT OF REAL COOL LUGUBRIOUS STUFF READY.
8-4
"AS MAINE GO, O, SO GO KEY LARGO, OTSEGO, FRISCO AN' FARGO, PLAYIN' POSSUM ON A POGO STICK AROUND AN' SEE THE SHOW GO."
HOW ABOUT A SHORT BURST OF OLD DOG TRAY?
I STILL SAY, "WHO'S FOR VICE?"
In an election year nobody will come right out and say ~~
NOBODY? HE MEANS YOU.

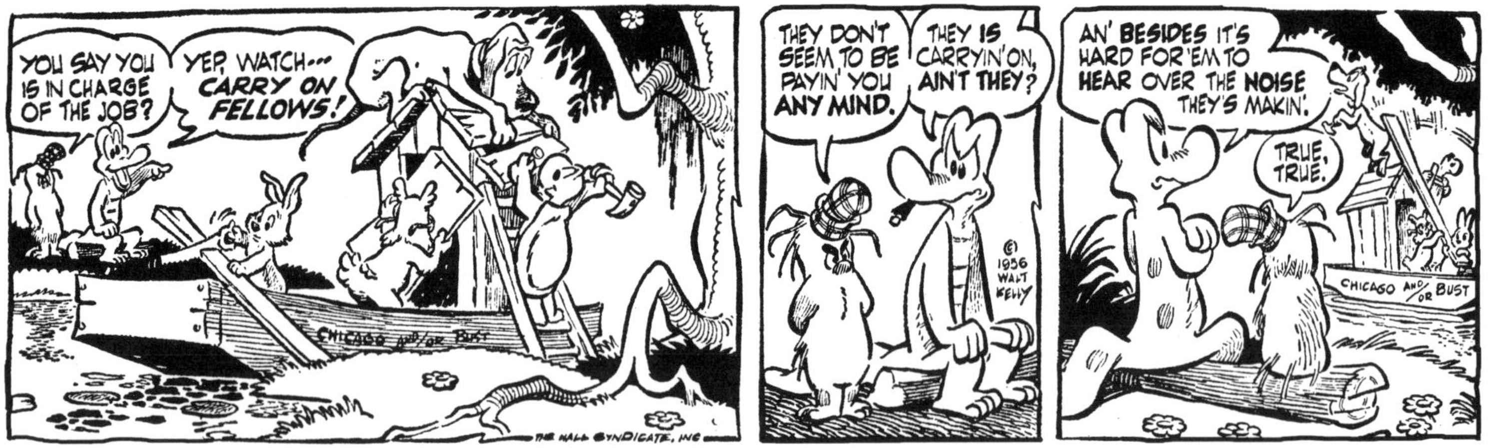
YOU SAY YOU IS IN CHARGE OF THE JOB?
YEP, WATCH--- CARRY ON FELLOWS!
CHICAGO AND/OR BUST
THE HALL SYNDICATE, INC
THEY DON'T SEEM TO BE PAYIN' YOU ANY MIND.
THEY IS CARRYIN'ON, AIN'T THEY?
© 1956 WALT KELLY
AN' BESIDES IT'S HARD FOR 'EM TO HEAR OVER THE NOISE THEY'S MAKIN'.
TRUE, TRUE.
CHICAGO AND/OR BUST

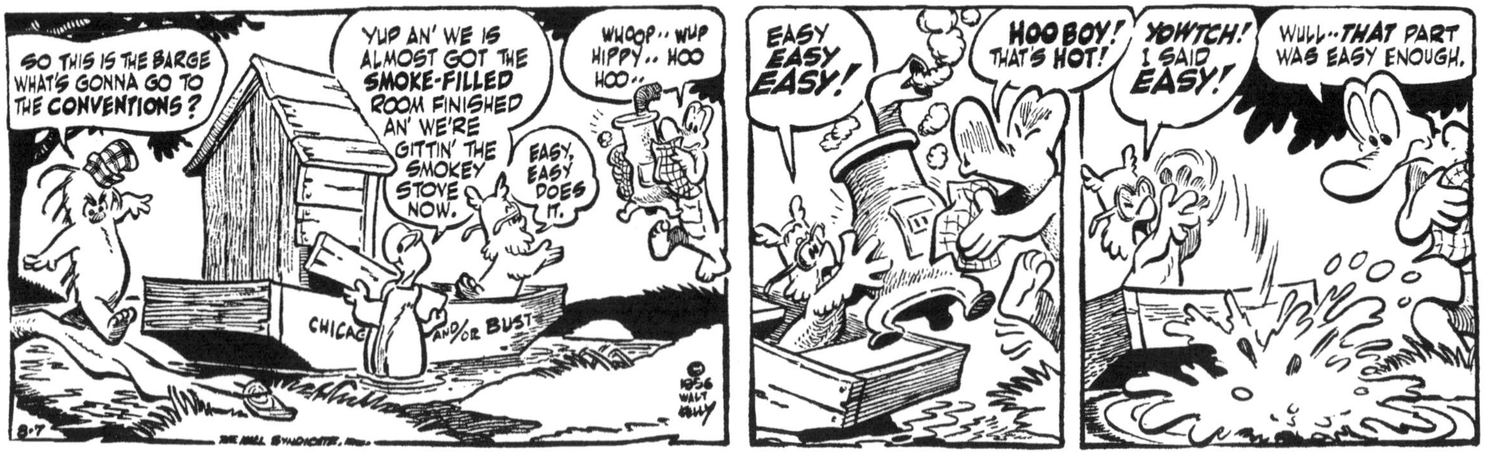
SO THIS IS THE BARGE WHAT'S GONNA GO TO THE CONVENTIONS?
YUP AN' WE IS ALMOST GOT THE SMOKE-FILLED ROOM FINISHED AN' WE'RE GITTIN' THE SMOKEY STOVE NOW.
WHOOP.. WUP HIPPY.. HOO HOO..
EASY, EASY DOES IT.
CHICAG AND/OR BUST
© 1956 WALT KELLY
8-7
THE HALL SYNDICATE, INC.
EASY EASY EASY!
HOO BOY! THAT'S HOT!
YOWTCH! I SAID EASY!
WULL..THAT PART WAS EASY ENOUGH.

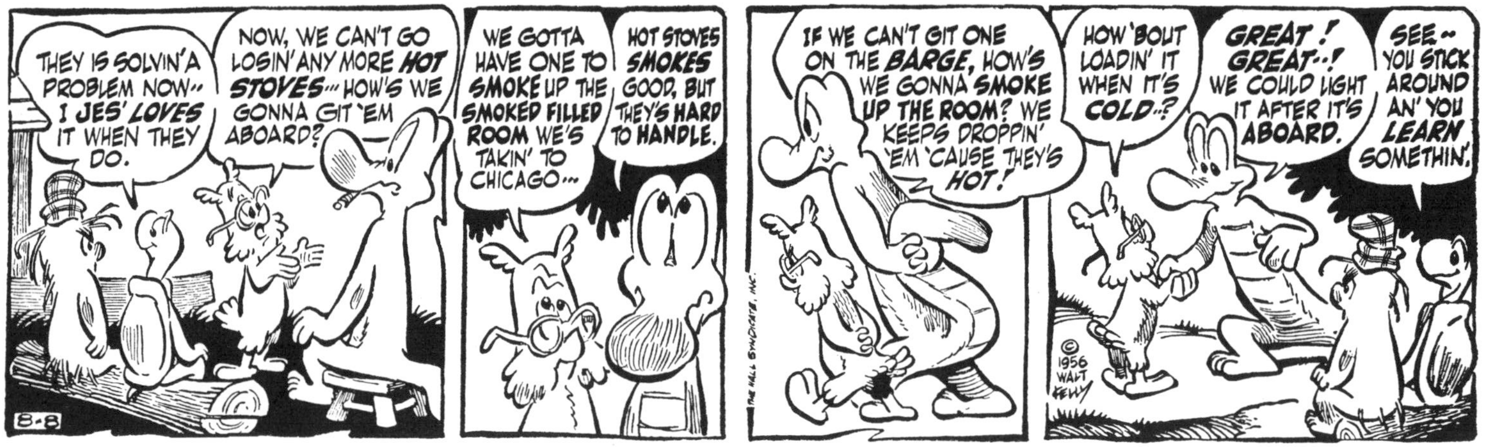
THEY IS SOLVIN' A PROBLEM NOW.. I JES' LOVES IT WHEN THEY DO.
NOW, WE CAN'T GO LOSIN' ANY MORE HOT STOVES... HOW'S WE GONNA GIT 'EM ABOARD?
WE GOTTA HAVE ONE TO SMOKE UP THE SMOKED FILLED ROOM WE'S TAKIN' TO CHICAGO...
HOT STOVES SMOKES GOOD, BUT THEY'S HARD TO HANDLE.
8-8
THE HALL SYNDICATE, INC.
IF WE CAN'T GIT ONE ON THE BARGE, HOW'S WE GONNA SMOKE UP THE ROOM? WE KEEPS DROPPIN' 'EM 'CAUSE THEY'S HOT!
HOW 'BOUT LOADIN' IT WHEN IT'S COLD..?
GREAT! GREAT..! WE COULD LIGHT IT AFTER IT'S ABOARD.
SEE.. YOU STICK AROUND AN' YOU LEARN SOMETHIN'.
© 1956 WALT KELLY

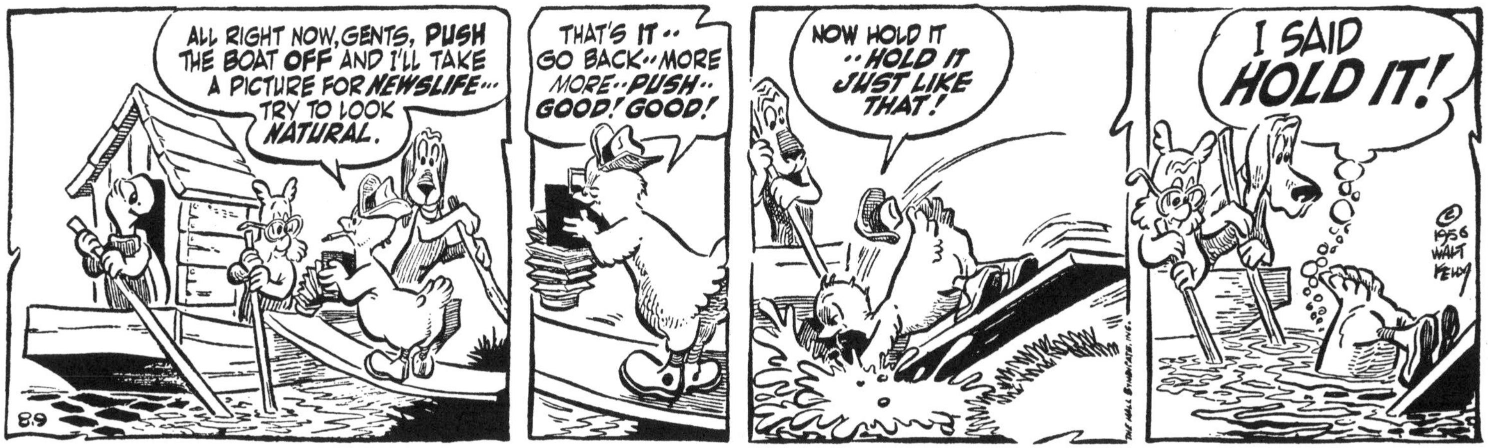
ALL RIGHT NOW, GENTS, PUSH THE BOAT OFF AND I'LL TAKE A PICTURE FOR NEWSLIFE... TRY TO LOOK NATURAL.
8-9
THAT'S IT.. GO BACK.. MORE MORE.. PUSH.. GOOD! GOOD!
NOW HOLD IT ..HOLD IT JUST LIKE THAT!
THE HALL SYNDICATE, INC.
I SAID HOLD IT!
© 1956 WALT KELLY

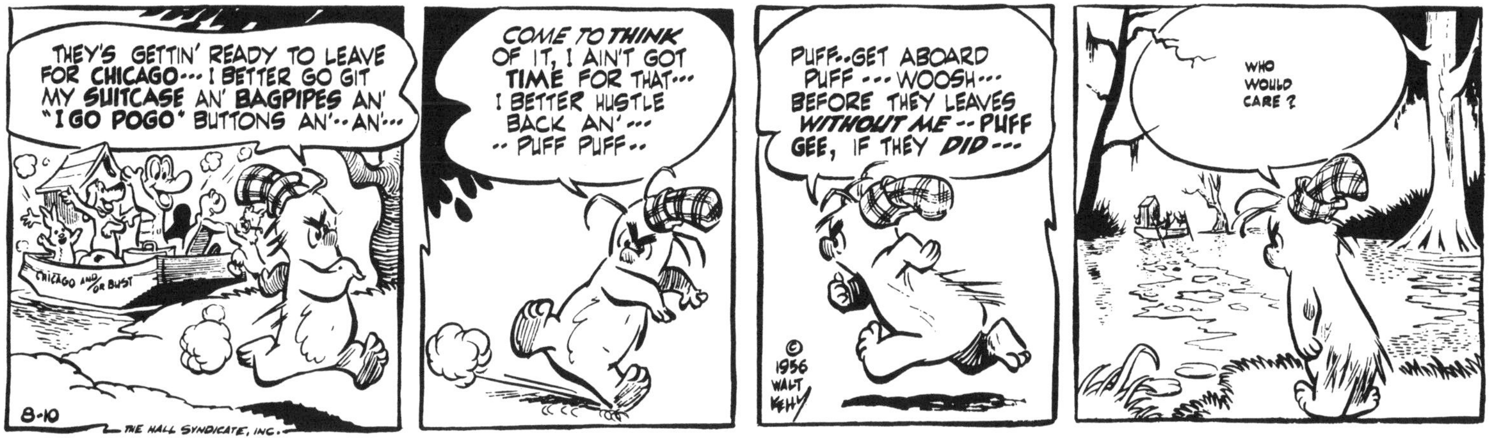
THEY'S GETTIN' READY TO LEAVE FOR CHICAGO... I BETTER GO GIT MY SUITCASE AN' BAGPIPES AN' "I GO POGO" BUTTONS AN'.. AN'...
CHICAGO AND/OR BUST
8-10
THE HALL SYNDICATE, INC.
COME TO THINK OF IT, I AIN'T GOT TIME FOR THAT... I BETTER HUSTLE BACK AN'... .. PUFF PUFF..
PUFF..GET ABOARD PUFF ... WOOSH... BEFORE THEY LEAVES WITHOUT ME -- PUFF GEE, IF THEY DID ---
© 1956 WALT KELLY
WHO WOULD CARE ?

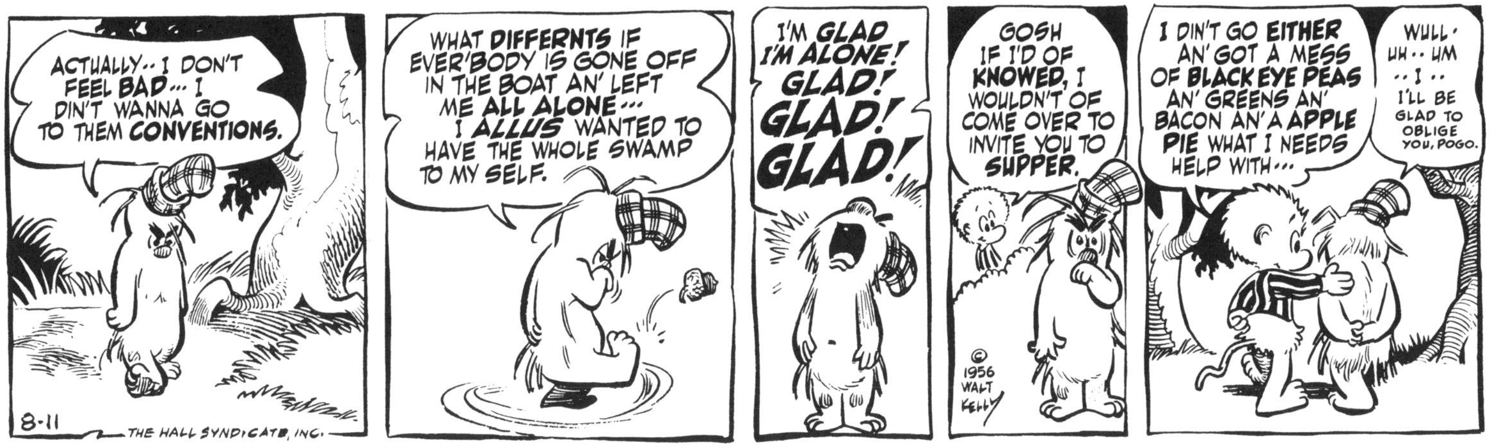
ACTUALLY.. I DON'T FEEL BAD... I DIN'T WANNA GO TO THEM CONVENTIONS.
8-11
THE HALL SYNDICATE, INC.
WHAT DIFFERNTS IF EVER'BODY IS GONE OFF IN THE BOAT AN' LEFT ME ALL ALONE... I ALLUS WANTED TO HAVE THE WHOLE SWAMP TO MY SELF.
I'M GLAD I'M ALONE! GLAD! GLAD! GLAD!
GOSH IF I'D OF KNOWED, I WOULDN'T OF COME OVER TO INVITE YOU TO SUPPER.
© 1956 WALT KELLY
I DIN'T GO EITHER AN' GOT A MESS OF BLACK EYE PEAS AN' GREENS AN' BACON AN' A APPLE PIE WHAT I NEEDS HELP WITH...
WULL. UH.. UM ..I.. I'LL BE GLAD TO OBLIGE YOU, POGO.

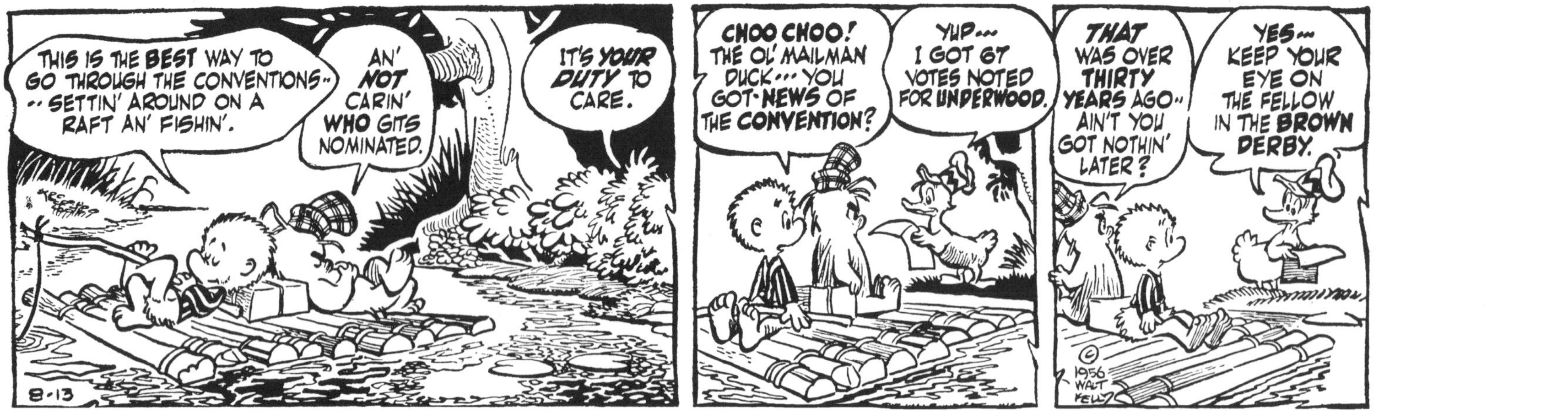
THIS IS THE BEST WAY TO GO THROUGH THE CONVENTIONS-- SETTIN' AROUND ON A RAFT AN' FISHIN'.
AN' NOT CARIN' WHO GITS NOMINATED.
IT'S YOUR DUTY TO CARE.
8-13
CHOO CHOO! THE OL' MAILMAN DUCK... YOU GOT NEWS OF THE CONVENTION?
YUP... I GOT 67 VOTES NOTED FOR UNDERWOOD.
THAT WAS OVER THIRTY YEARS AGO.. AIN'T YOU GOT NOTHIN' LATER?
YES... KEEP YOUR EYE ON THE FELLOW IN THE BROWN DERBY.
© 1956 WALT KELLY

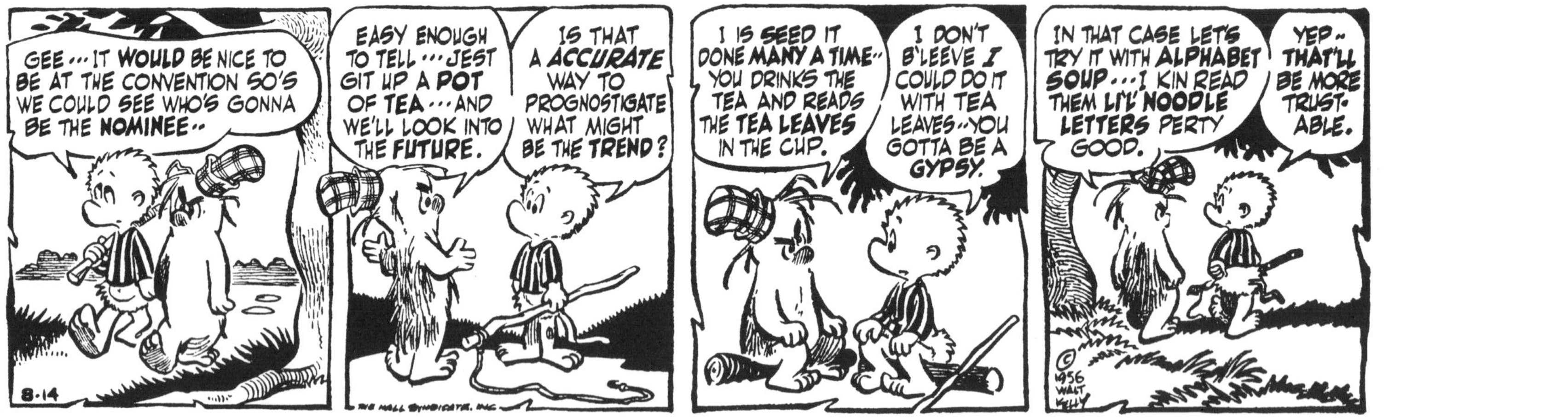
GEE... IT WOULD BE NICE TO BE AT THE CONVENTION SO'S WE COULD SEE WHO'S GONNA BE THE NOMINEE..
8-14
EASY ENOUGH TO TELL... JEST GIT UP A POT OF TEA... AND WE'LL LOOK INTO THE FUTURE.
IS THAT A ACCURATE WAY TO PROGNOSTIGATE WHAT MIGHT BE THE TREND?
THE HALL SYNDICATE, INC.
I IS SEED IT DONE MANY A TIME.. YOU DRINKS THE TEA AND READS THE TEA LEAVES IN THE CUP.
I DON'T B'LEEVE I COULD DO IT WITH TEA LEAVES..YOU GOTTA BE A GYPSY.
IN THAT CASE LET'S TRY IT WITH ALPHABET SOUP... I KIN READ THEM LI'L NOODLE LETTERS PERTY GOOD.
YEP.. THAT'LL BE MORE TRUST-ABLE.
© 1956 WALT KELLY

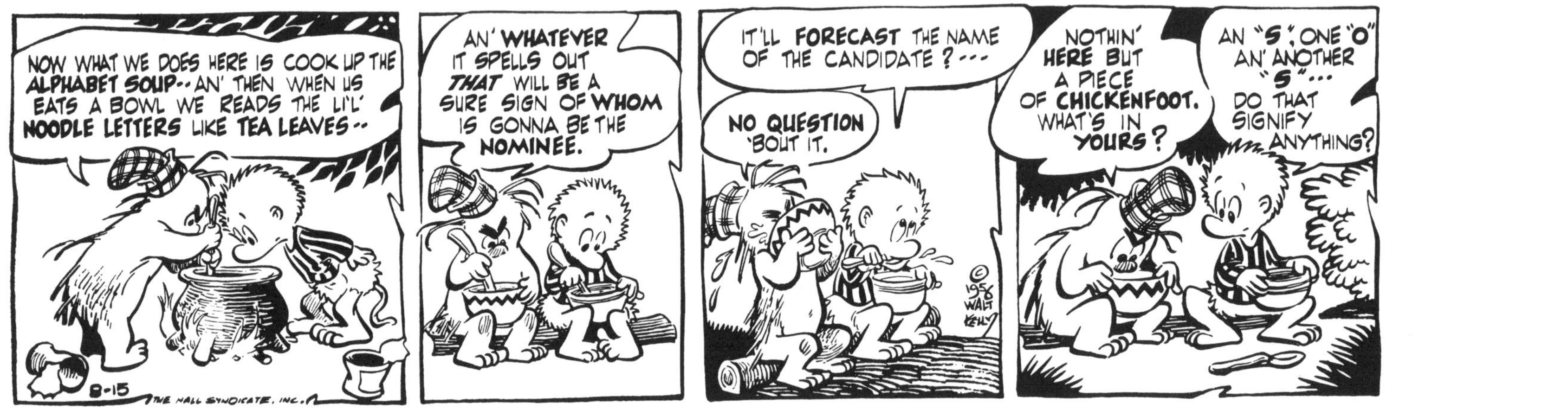
NOW WHAT WE DOES HERE IS COOK UP THE ALPHABET SOUP.. AN' THEN WHEN US EATS A BOWL WE READS THE LI'L' NOODLE LETTERS LIKE TEA LEAVES..
8-15
THE HALL SYNDICATE, INC.
AN' WHATEVER IT SPELLS OUT THAT WILL BE A SURE SIGN OF WHOM IS GONNA BE THE NOMINEE.
IT'LL FORECAST THE NAME OF THE CANDIDATE?--
NO QUESTION 'BOUT IT.
© 1956 WALT KELLY
NOTHIN' HERE BUT A PIECE OF CHICKENFOOT. WHAT'S IN YOURS?
AN "S", ONE "O" AN' ANOTHER "S"... DO THAT SIGNIFY ANYTHING?

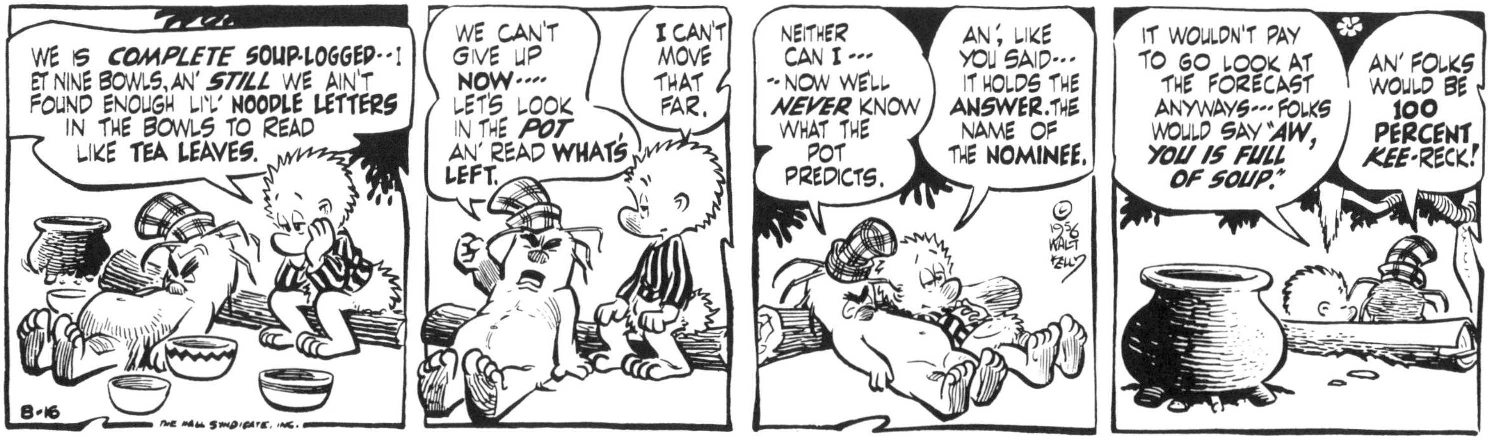
WE IS COMPLETE SOUP-LOGGED--I ET NINE BOWLS, AN' STILL WE AIN'T FOUND ENOUGH LI'L' NOODLE LETTERS IN THE BOWLS TO READ LIKE TEA LEAVES.
WE CAN'T GIVE UP NOW.... LET'S LOOK IN THE POT AN' READ WHAT'S LEFT.
I CAN'T MOVE THAT FAR.
NEITHER CAN I --- -- NOW WE'LL NEVER KNOW WHAT THE POT PREDICTS.
AN', LIKE YOU SAID--- IT HOLDS THE ANSWER. THE NAME OF THE NOMINEE.
IT WOULDN'T PAY TO GO LOOK AT THE FORECAST ANYWAYS--- FOLKS WOULD SAY "AW, YOU IS FULL OF SOUP."
AN' FOLKS WOULD BE 100 PERCENT KEE-RECK!
8-16
THE HALL SYNDICATE, INC.
© 1956 WALT KELLY

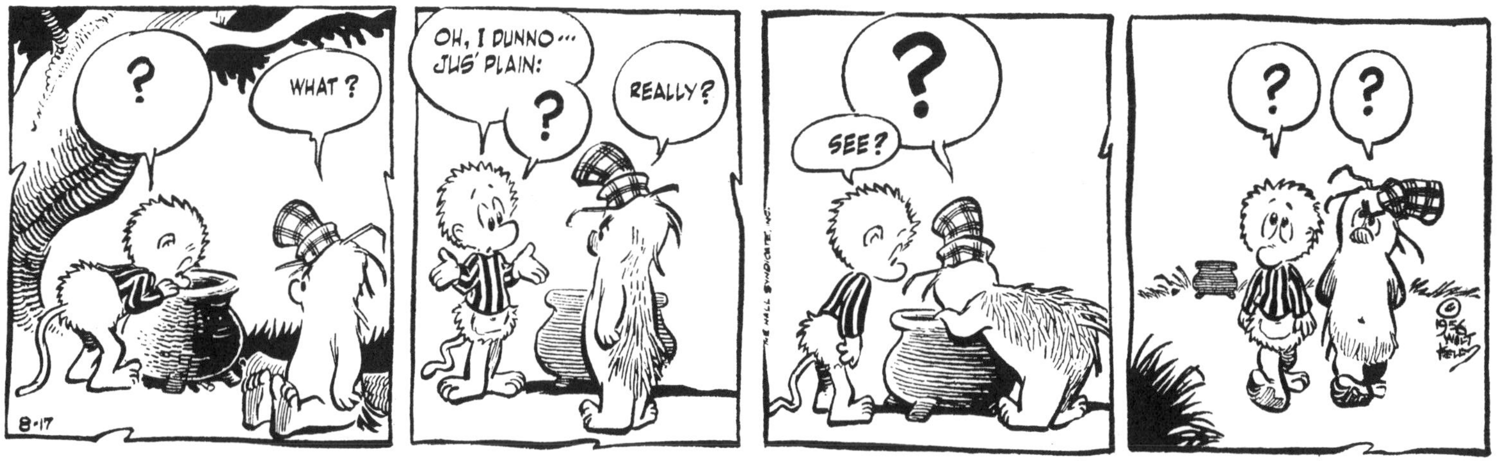
?
WHAT ?
OH, I DUNNO... JUS' PLAIN:
?
REALLY?
SEE?
?
?
?
8-17
© 1956 WALT KELLY

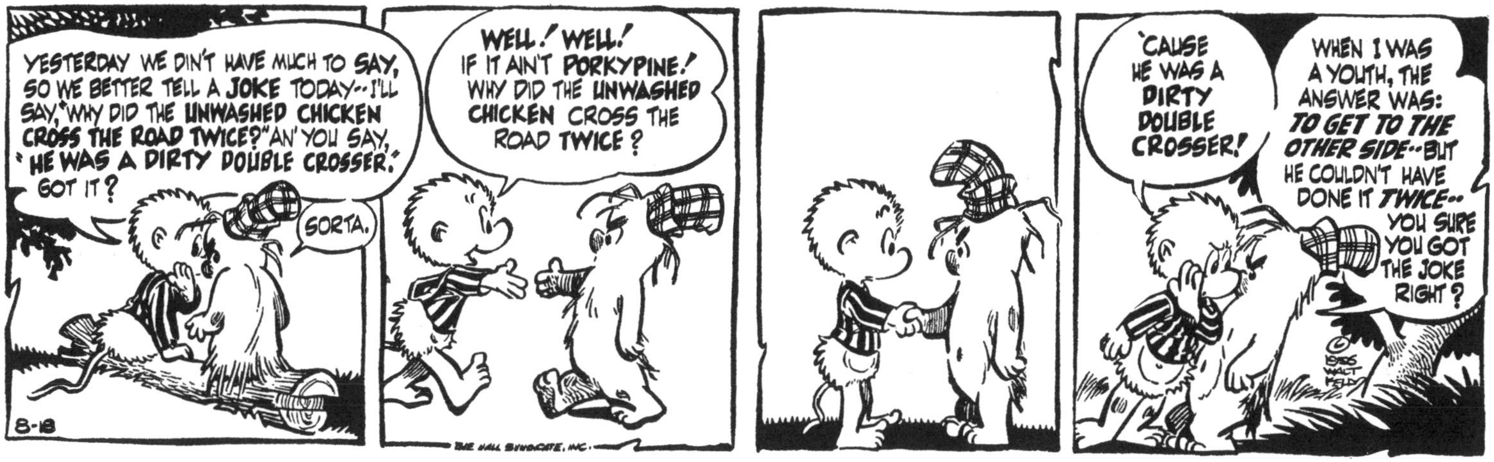
YESTERDAY WE DIN'T HAVE MUCH TO SAY, SO WE BETTER TELL A JOKE TODAY--I'LL SAY, "WHY DID THE UNWASHED CHICKEN CROSS THE ROAD TWICE?" AN' YOU SAY, "HE WAS A DIRTY DOUBLE CROSSER." GOT IT ?
SORTA.
WELL! WELL! IF IT AIN'T PORKYPINE! WHY DID THE UNWASHED CHICKEN CROSS THE ROAD TWICE ?
'CAUSE HE WAS A DIRTY DOUBLE CROSSER!
WHEN I WAS A YOUTH, THE ANSWER WAS: TO GET TO THE OTHER SIDE--BUT HE COULDN'T HAVE DONE IT TWICE--
YOU SURE YOU GOT THE JOKE RIGHT ?
8-18
THE HALL SYNDICATE, INC.

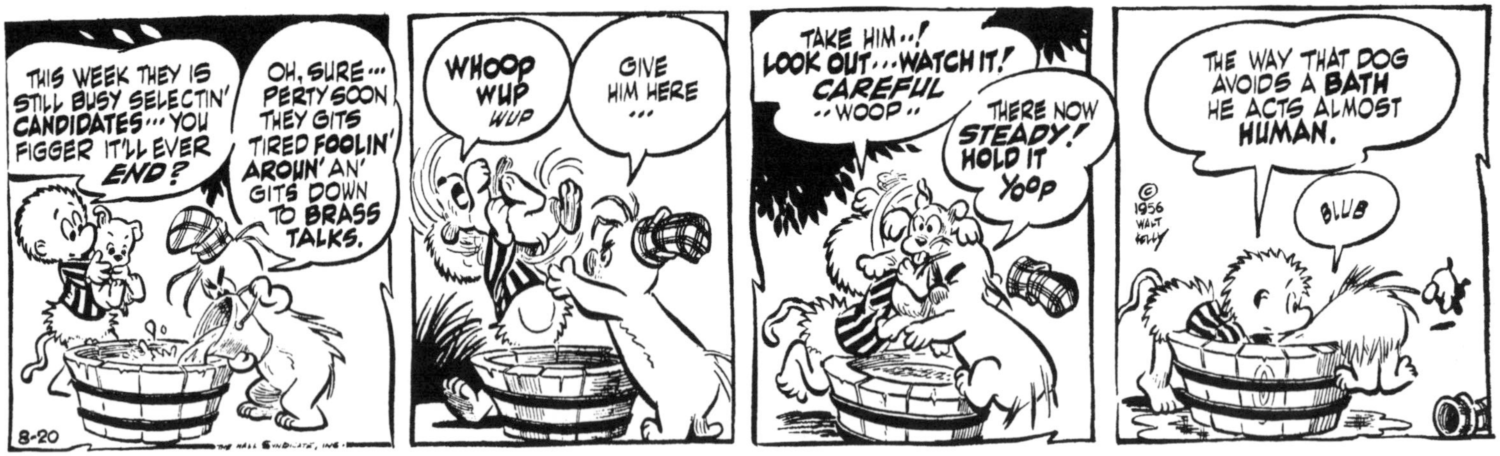
THIS WEEK THEY IS STILL BUSY SELECTIN' **CANDIDATES**... YOU FIGGER IT'LL EVER ***END?***
OH, SURE... PERTY SOON THEY GITS TIRED **FOOLIN' AROUN'** AN' GITS DOWN TO **BRASS TALKS.**
8-20
WHOOP WUP *WUP*
GIVE HIM HERE ...
TAKE HIM..! **LOOK OUT... WATCH IT!** ***CAREFUL*** ..WOOP..
THERE NOW ***STEADY!*** **HOLD IT** YOOP
THE WAY THAT DOG AVOIDS A **BATH** HE ACTS ALMOST **HUMAN.**
© 1956 WALT KELLY
BLUB

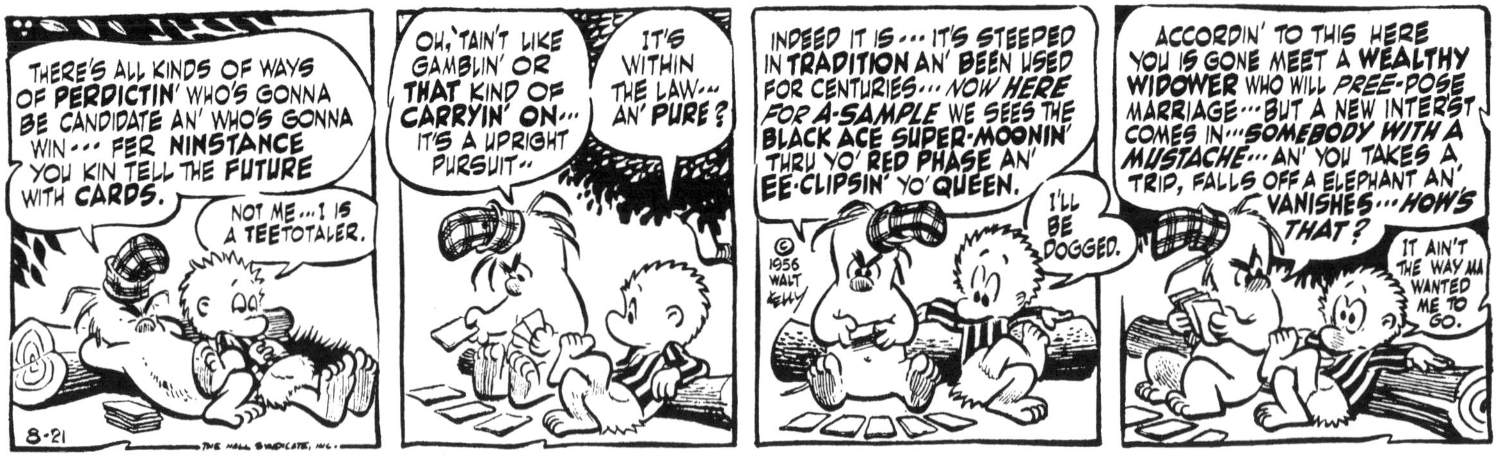
THERE'S ALL KINDS OF WAYS OF **PERDICTIN'** WHO'S GONNA BE CANDIDATE AN' WHO'S GONNA WIN... FER **NINSTANCE** YOU KIN TELL THE **FUTURE** WITH **CARDS.**
NOT ME... I IS A **TEETOTALER.**
8-21
OH, 'TAIN'T LIKE GAMBLIN' OR **THAT** KIND OF **CARRYIN' ON**... IT'S A UPRIGHT PURSUIT..
IT'S WITHIN THE LAW... AN' **PURE**?
INDEED IT IS... IT'S STEEPED IN **TRADITION AN' BEEN** USED FOR CENTURIES... ***NOW HERE FOR A-SAMPLE*** WE SEES THE **BLACK ACE SUPER-MOONIN'** THRU YO' **RED PHASE** AN' **EE-CLIPSIN'** YO' **QUEEN.**
© 1956 WALT KELLY
I'LL BE DOGGED.
ACCORDIN' TO THIS HERE YOU IS GONE MEET A **WEALTHY WIDOWER** WHO WILL *PREE-POSE* MARRIAGE... BUT A NEW INTER'ST COMES IN... ***SOMEBODY WITH A MUSTACHE***... AN' YOU TAKES A TRIP, FALLS OFF A ELEPHANT AN' **VANISHES**... ***HOW'S THAT?***
IT AIN'T THE WAY MA WANTED ME TO GO.

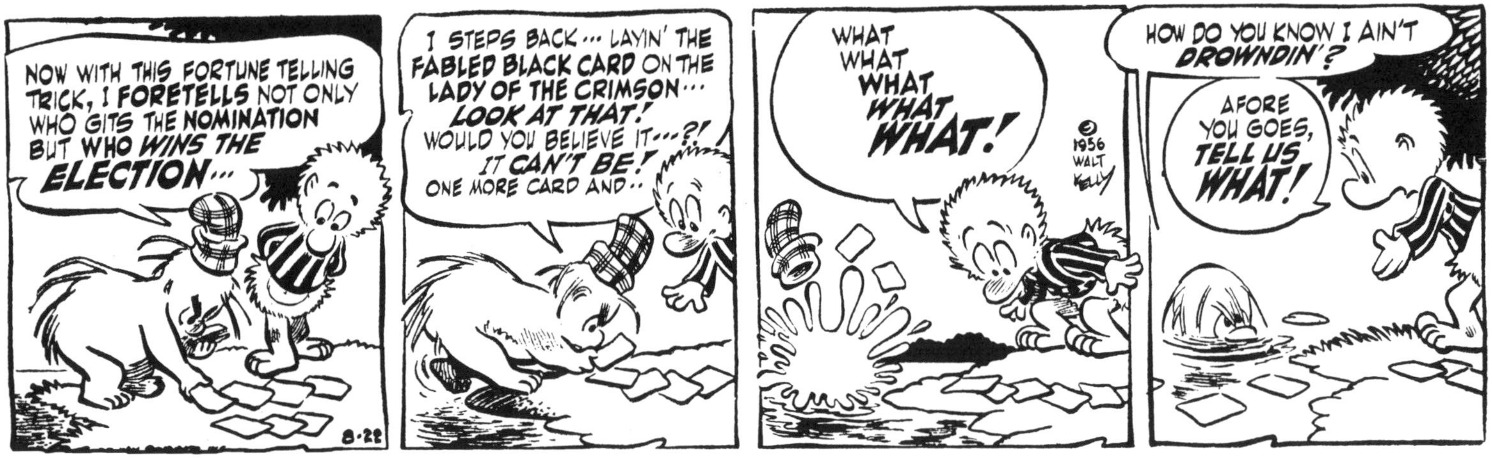
NOW WITH THIS FORTUNE TELLING TRICK, I **FORETELLS** NOT ONLY WHO GITS THE **NOMINATION** BUT **WHO *WINS THE ELECTION***...
8-22
I STEPS BACK... LAYIN' THE **FABLED BLACK CARD** ON THE **LADY OF THE CRIMSON**... ***LOOK AT THAT!*** WOULD YOU BELIEVE IT...?! ***IT CAN'T BE!*** ONE MORE CARD AND..
WHAT WHAT WHAT ***WHAT WHAT!***
© 1956 WALT KELLY
HOW DO YOU KNOW I AIN'T ***DROWNDIN'?***
AFORE YOU GOES, ***TELL US WHAT!***

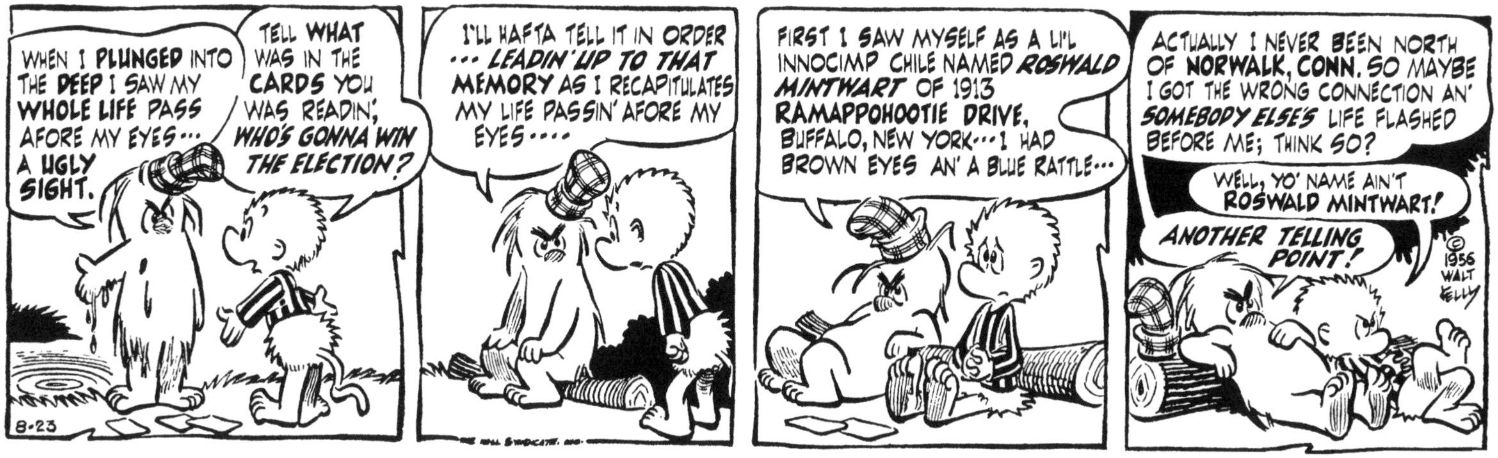
WHEN I PLUNGED INTO THE DEEP I SAW MY WHOLE LIFE PASS AFORE MY EYES... A UGLY SIGHT.
TELL WHAT WAS IN THE CARDS YOU WAS READIN', WHO'S GONNA WIN THE ELECTION?
I'LL HAFTA TELL IT IN ORDER ... LEADIN' UP TO THAT MEMORY AS I RECAPITULATES MY LIFE PASSIN' AFORE MY EYES....
FIRST I SAW MYSELF AS A LI'L INNOCIMP CHILE NAMED ROSWALD MINTWART OF 1913 RAMAPPOHOOTIE DRIVE, BUFFALO, NEW YORK... I HAD BROWN EYES AN' A BLUE RATTLE...
ACTUALLY I NEVER BEEN NORTH OF NORWALK, CONN. SO MAYBE I GOT THE WRONG CONNECTION AN' SOMEBODY ELSE'S LIFE FLASHED BEFORE ME; THINK SO?
WELL, YO' NAME AIN'T ROSWALD MINTWART!
ANOTHER TELLING POINT!
© 1956 WALT KELLY
8-23

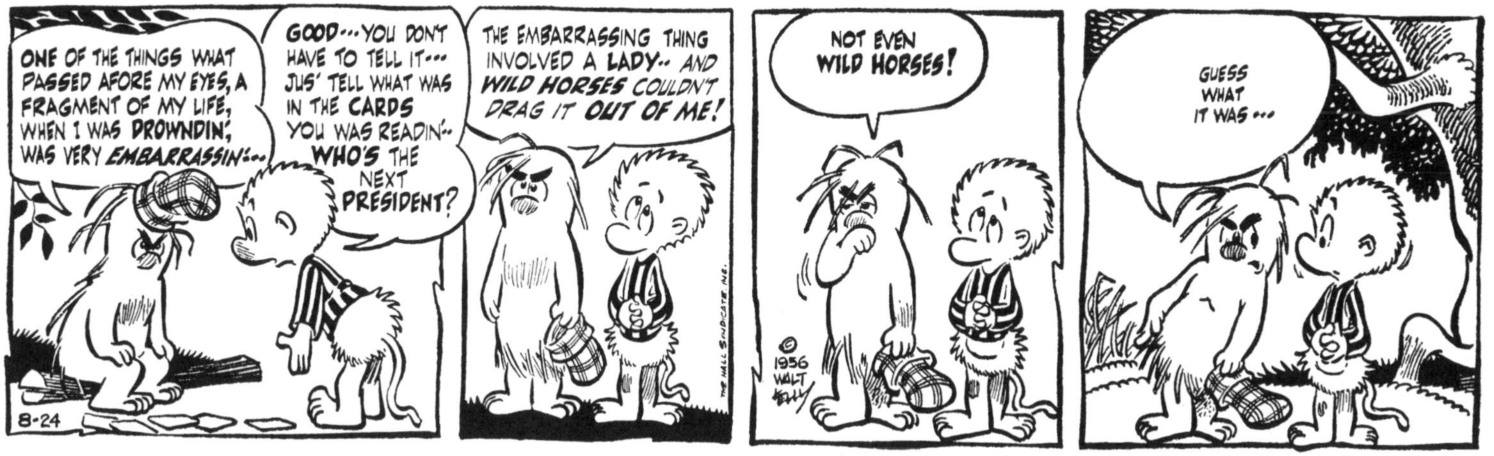
ONE OF THE THINGS WHAT PASSED AFORE MY EYES, A FRAGMENT OF MY LIFE, WHEN I WAS DROWNDIN', WAS VERY EMBARRASSIN'...
GOOD... YOU DON'T HAVE TO TELL IT... JUS' TELL WHAT WAS IN THE CARDS YOU WAS READIN'.. WHO'S THE NEXT PRESIDENT?
THE EMBARRASSING THING INVOLVED A LADY.. AND WILD HORSES COULDN'T DRAG IT OUT OF ME!
NOT EVEN WILD HORSES!
GUESS WHAT IT WAS...
© 1956 WALT KELLY
8-24

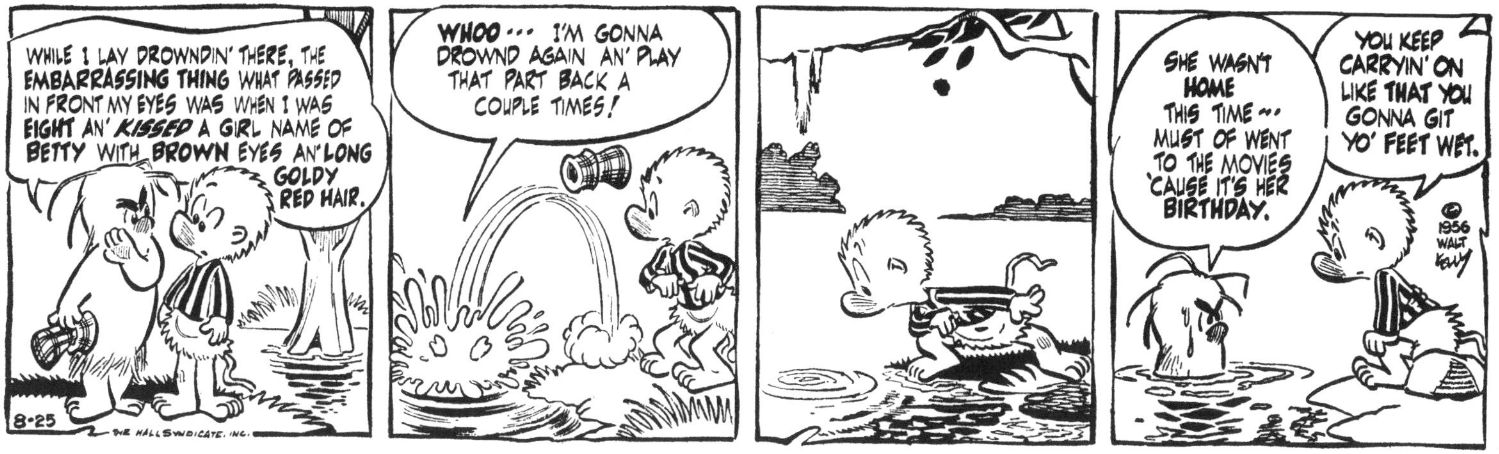
WHILE I LAY DROWNDIN' THERE, THE EMBARRASSING THING WHAT PASSED IN FRONT MY EYES WAS WHEN I WAS EIGHT AN' KISSED A GIRL NAME OF BETTY WITH BROWN EYES AN' LONG GOLDY RED HAIR.
WHOO... I'M GONNA DROWND AGAIN AN' PLAY THAT PART BACK A COUPLE TIMES!
SHE WASN'T HOME THIS TIME -- MUST OF WENT TO THE MOVIES 'CAUSE IT'S HER BIRTHDAY.
YOU KEEP CARRYIN' ON LIKE THAT YOU GONNA GIT YO' FEET WET.
© 1956 WALT KELLY
8-25

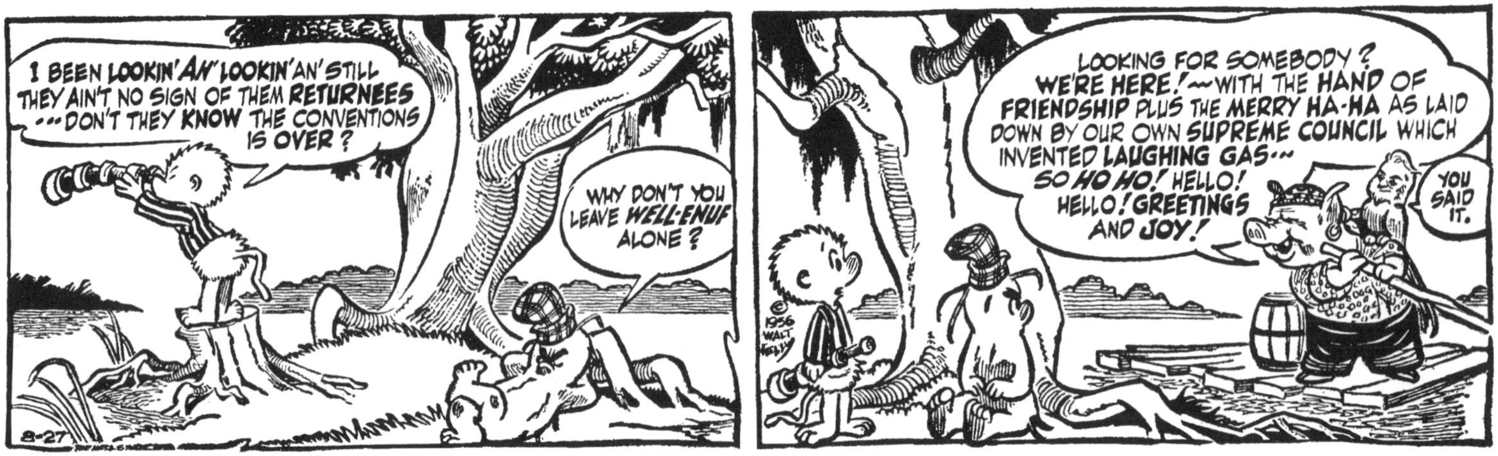
I BEEN LOOKIN' AN' LOOKIN' AN' STILL THEY AIN'T NO SIGN OF THEM RETURNEES ··· DON'T THEY KNOW THE CONVENTIONS IS OVER ?
WHY DON'T YOU LEAVE WELL-ENUF ALONE ?
8-27
LOOKING FOR SOMEBODY ? WE'RE HERE! — WITH THE HAND OF FRIENDSHIP PLUS THE MERRY HA-HA AS LAID DOWN BY OUR OWN SUPREME COUNCIL WHICH INVENTED LAUGHING GAS··· SO HO HO! HELLO! HELLO! GREETINGS AND JOY!
YOU SAID IT.
© 1956 WALT KELLY

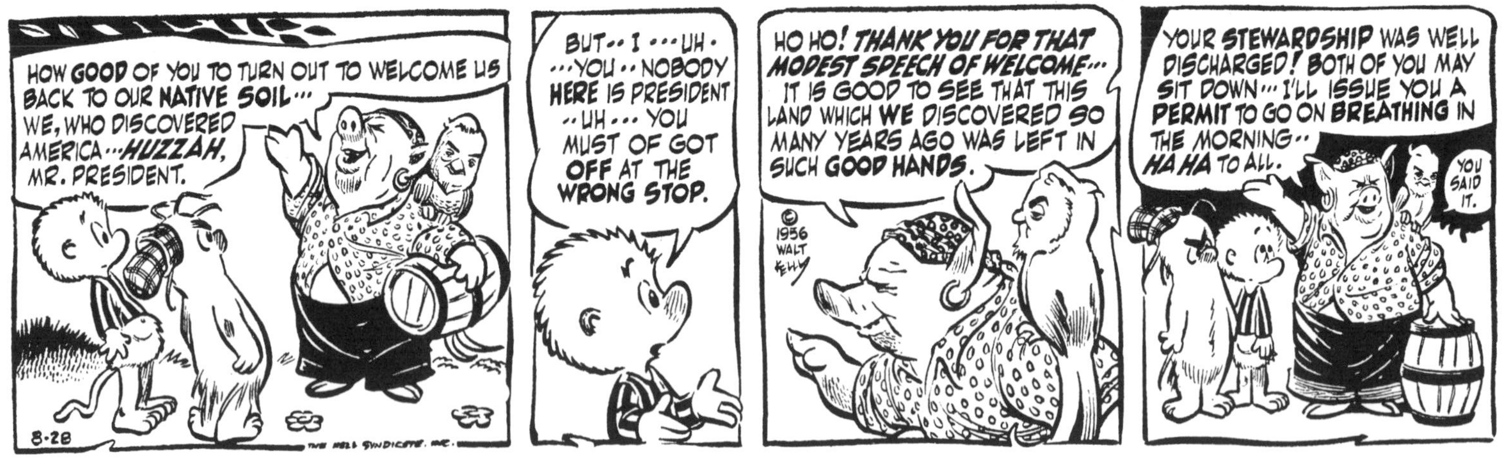
HOW GOOD OF YOU TO TURN OUT TO WELCOME US BACK TO OUR NATIVE SOIL··· WE, WHO DISCOVERED AMERICA···HUZZAH, MR. PRESIDENT.
8-28
THE HALL SYNDICATE, INC.
BUT·· I ···UH· ···YOU·· NOBODY HERE IS PRESIDENT ··UH··· YOU MUST OF GOT OFF AT THE WRONG STOP.
HO HO! THANK YOU FOR THAT MODEST SPEECH OF WELCOME··· IT IS GOOD TO SEE THAT THIS LAND WHICH WE DISCOVERED SO MANY YEARS AGO WAS LEFT IN SUCH GOOD HANDS.
© 1956 WALT KELLY
YOUR STEWARDSHIP WAS WELL DISCHARGED! BOTH OF YOU MAY SIT DOWN··· I'LL ISSUE YOU A PERMIT TO GO ON BREATHING IN THE MORNING·· HA HA TO ALL.
YOU SAID IT.

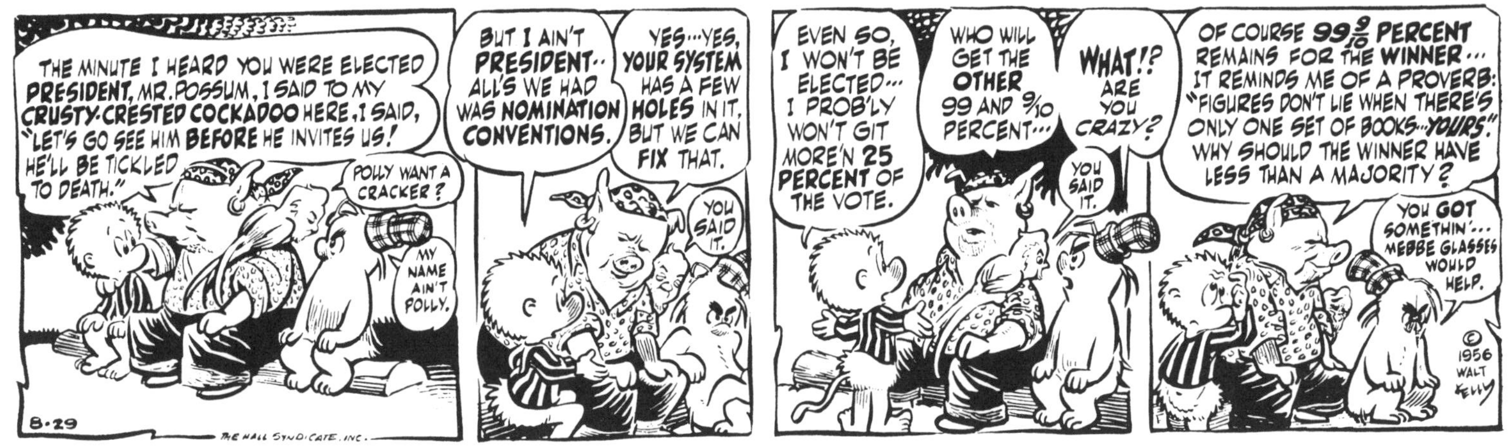
THE MINUTE I HEARD YOU WERE ELECTED PRESIDENT, MR. POSSUM, I SAID TO MY CRUSTY-CRESTED COCKADOO HERE, I SAID, "LET'S GO SEE HIM BEFORE HE INVITES US!' HE'LL BE TICKLED TO DEATH."
POLLY WANT A CRACKER ?
MY NAME AIN'T POLLY.
8-29
THE HALL SYNDICATE, INC.
BUT I AIN'T PRESIDENT·· ALL'S WE HAD WAS NOMINATION CONVENTIONS.
YES···YES, YOUR SYSTEM HAS A FEW HOLES IN IT, BUT WE CAN FIX THAT.
YOU SAID IT.
EVEN SO, I WON'T BE ELECTED··· I PROB'LY WON'T GIT MORE'N 25 PERCENT OF THE VOTE.
WHO WILL GET THE OTHER 99 AND 9/10 PERCENT···
WHAT!? ARE YOU CRAZY?
YOU SAID IT.
OF COURSE 99 9/10 PERCENT REMAINS FOR THE WINNER··· IT REMINDS ME OF A PROVERB: "FIGURES DON'T LIE WHEN THERE'S ONLY ONE SET OF BOOKS···YOURS." WHY SHOULD THE WINNER HAVE LESS THAN A MAJORITY ?
YOU GOT SOMETHIN'··· MEBBE GLASSES WOULD HELP.
© 1956 WALT KELLY

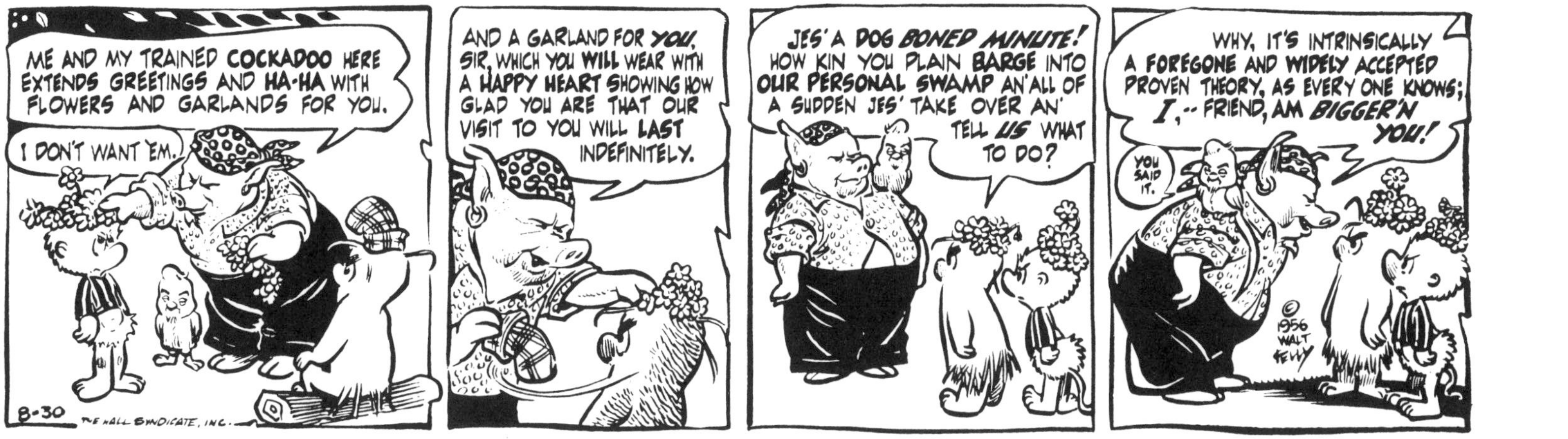
ME AND MY TRAINED COCKADOO HERE EXTENDS GREETINGS AND HA-HA WITH FLOWERS AND GARLANDS FOR YOU.
I DON'T WANT 'EM.
AND A GARLAND FOR YOU, SIR, WHICH YOU WILL WEAR WITH A HAPPY HEART SHOWING HOW GLAD YOU ARE THAT OUR VISIT TO YOU WILL LAST INDEFINITELY.
JES' A DOG BONED MINUTE! HOW KIN YOU PLAIN BARGE INTO OUR PERSONAL SWAMP AN' ALL OF A SUDDEN JES' TAKE OVER AN' TELL US WHAT TO DO?
WHY, IT'S INTRINSICALLY A FOREGONE AND WIDELY ACCEPTED PROVEN THEORY, AS EVERY ONE KNOWS; I,-- FRIEND, AM BIGGER'N YOU!
YOU SAID IT.
8-30
THE HALL SYNDICATE, INC.
© 1956 WALT KELLY

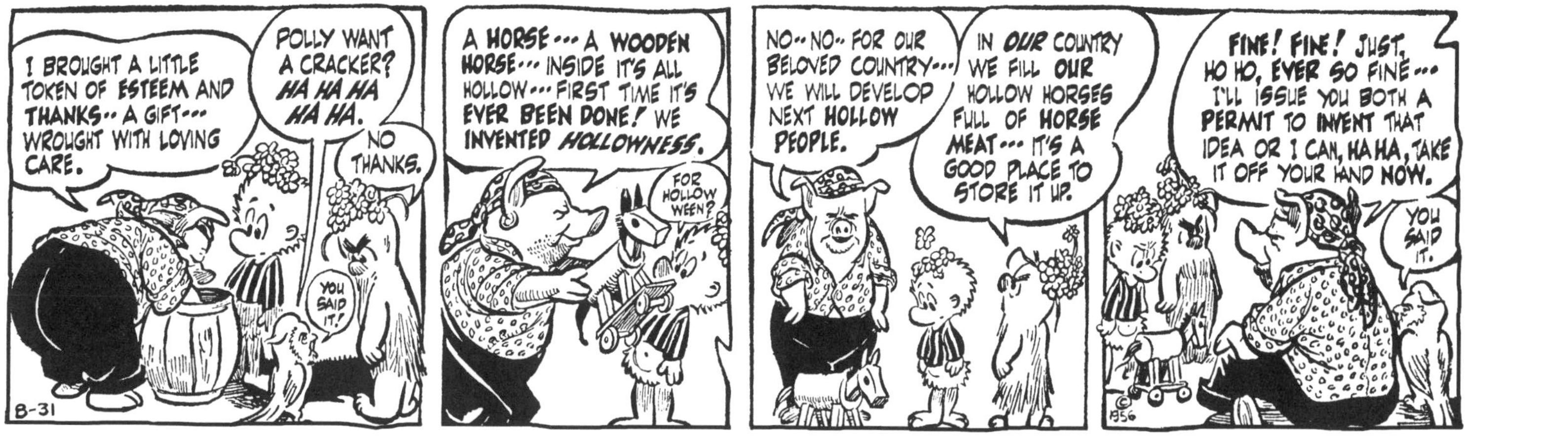
I BROUGHT A LITTLE TOKEN OF ESTEEM AND THANKS.. A GIFT... WROUGHT WITH LOVING CARE.
POLLY WANT A CRACKER? HA HA HA HA HA.
NO THANKS.
YOU SAID IT.
A HORSE... A WOODEN HORSE... INSIDE IT'S ALL HOLLOW... FIRST TIME IT'S EVER BEEN DONE! WE INVENTED HOLLOWNESS.
FOR HOLLOW WEEN?
NO.. NO.. FOR OUR BELOVED COUNTRY... WE WILL DEVELOP NEXT HOLLOW PEOPLE.
IN OUR COUNTRY WE FILL OUR HOLLOW HORSES FULL OF HORSE MEAT... IT'S A GOOD PLACE TO STORE IT UP.
FINE! FINE! JUST, HO HO, EVER SO FINE... I'LL ISSUE YOU BOTH A PERMIT TO INVENT THAT IDEA OR I CAN, HA HA, TAKE IT OFF YOUR HAND NOW.
YOU SAID IT.
8-31
© 1956

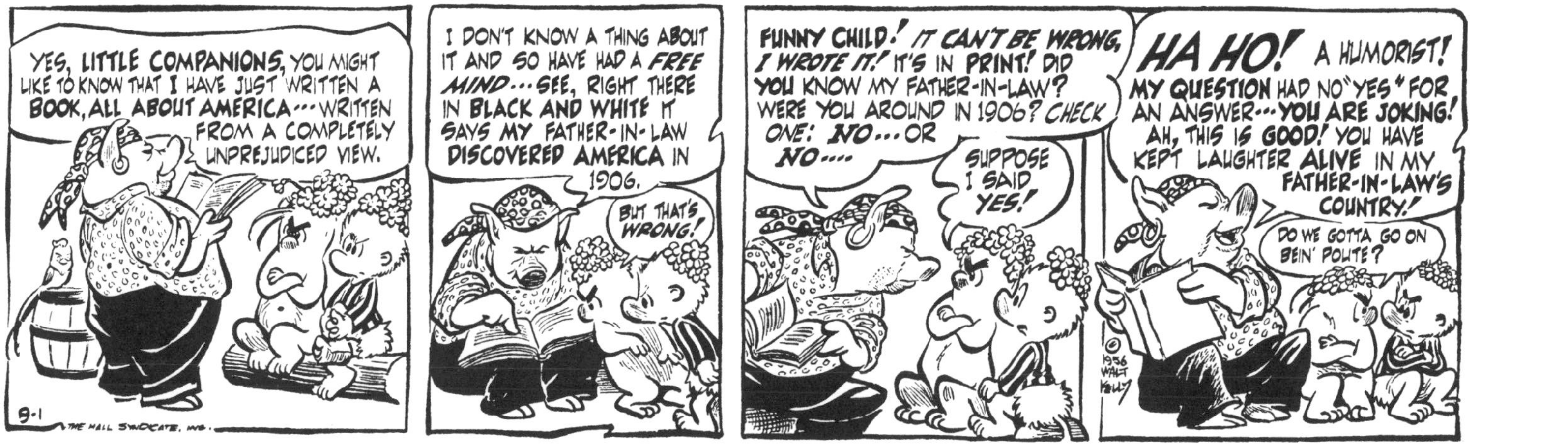
YES, LITTLE COMPANIONS, YOU MIGHT LIKE TO KNOW THAT I HAVE JUST WRITTEN A BOOK, ALL ABOUT AMERICA... WRITTEN FROM A COMPLETELY UNPREJUDICED VIEW.
I DON'T KNOW A THING ABOUT IT AND SO HAVE HAD A FREE MIND... SEE, RIGHT THERE IN BLACK AND WHITE IT SAYS MY FATHER-IN-LAW DISCOVERED AMERICA IN 1906.
BUT THAT'S WRONG!
FUNNY CHILD! IT CAN'T BE WRONG, I WROTE IT! IT'S IN PRINT! DID YOU KNOW MY FATHER-IN-LAW? WERE YOU AROUND IN 1906? CHECK ONE: NO... OR NO....
SUPPOSE I SAID YES!
HA HO! A HUMORIST! MY QUESTION HAD NO "YES" FOR AN ANSWER... YOU ARE JOKING! AH, THIS IS GOOD! YOU HAVE KEPT LAUGHTER ALIVE IN MY FATHER-IN-LAW'S COUNTRY!
DO WE GOTTA GO ON BEIN' POLITE?
9-1
THE HALL SYNDICATE, INC.
© 1956 WALT KELLY

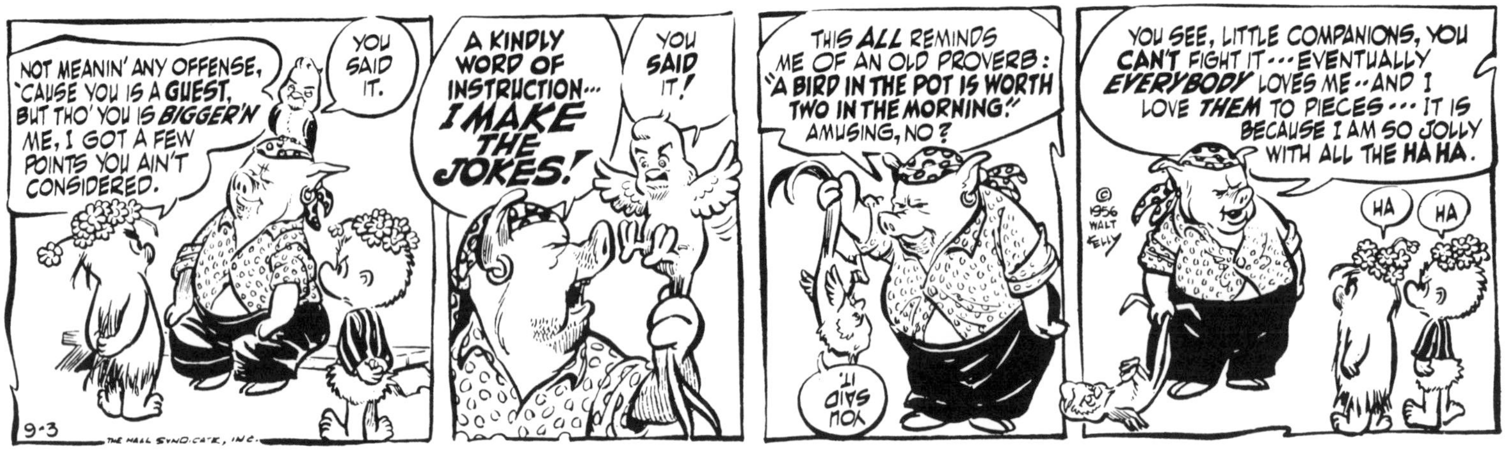
NOT MEANIN' ANY OFFENSE, 'CAUSE YOU IS A **GUEST**, BUT THO' YOU IS ***BIGGER'N*** ME, I GOT A FEW POINTS YOU AIN'T CONSIDERED.
YOU SAID IT.
9-3
THE HALL SYNDICATE, INC.
A KINDLY WORD OF INSTRUCTION... ***I MAKE THE JOKES!***
YOU **SAID** IT!
THIS ***ALL*** REMINDS ME OF AN OLD PROVERB: **"A BIRD IN THE POT IS WORTH TWO IN THE MORNING."** AMUSING, NO?
YOU SAID IT.
YOU SEE, LITTLE COMPANIONS, YOU **CAN'T** FIGHT IT... EVENTUALLY ***EVERYBODY*** LOVES ME.. AND I LOVE ***THEM*** TO PIECES... IT IS BECAUSE I AM SO JOLLY WITH ALL THE **HA HA**.
© 1956 WALT KELLY
HA
HA

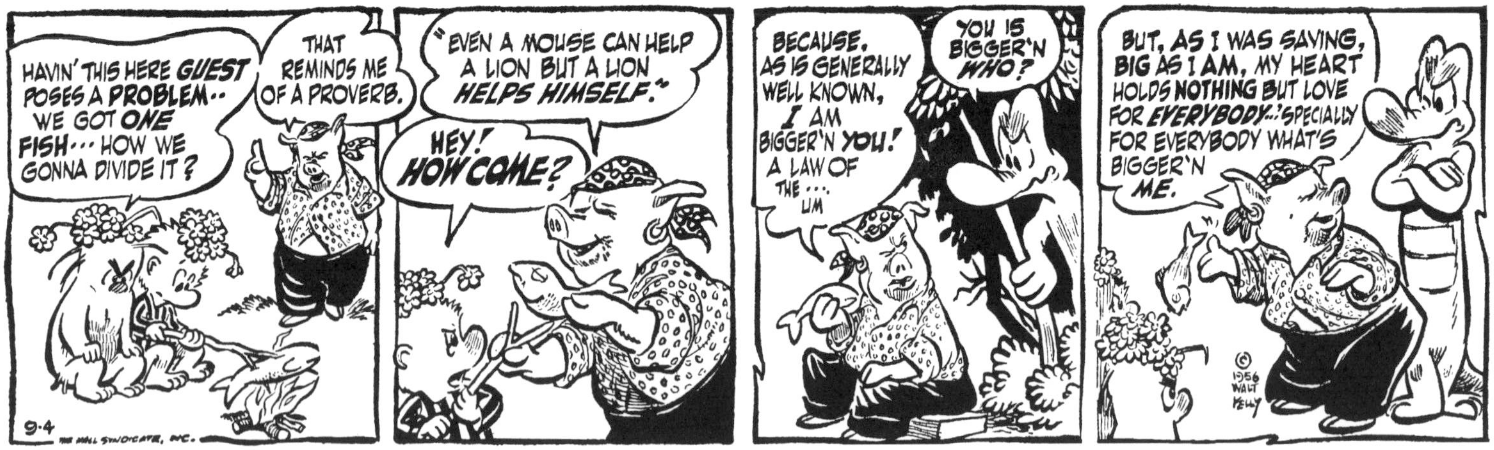
HAVIN' THIS HERE ***GUEST*** POSES A **PROBLEM**.. WE GOT ***ONE FISH***... HOW WE GONNA DIVIDE IT?
THAT REMINDS ME OF A PROVERB.
9-4
THE HALL SYNDICATE, INC.
"EVEN A MOUSE CAN HELP A LION BUT A LION ***HELPS HIMSELF***."
HEY! HOW COME?
BECAUSE, AS IS GENERALLY WELL KNOWN, ***I*** AM BIGGER'N **YOU!** A LAW OF THE.... UM
YOU IS BIGGER'N ***WHO?***
BUT, **AS** I WAS SAYING, **BIG AS I AM,** MY HEART HOLDS **NOTHING** BUT LOVE FOR ***EVERYBODY***..'SPECIALLY FOR EVERYBODY WHAT'S BIGGER'N ***ME.***
© 1956 WALT KELLY

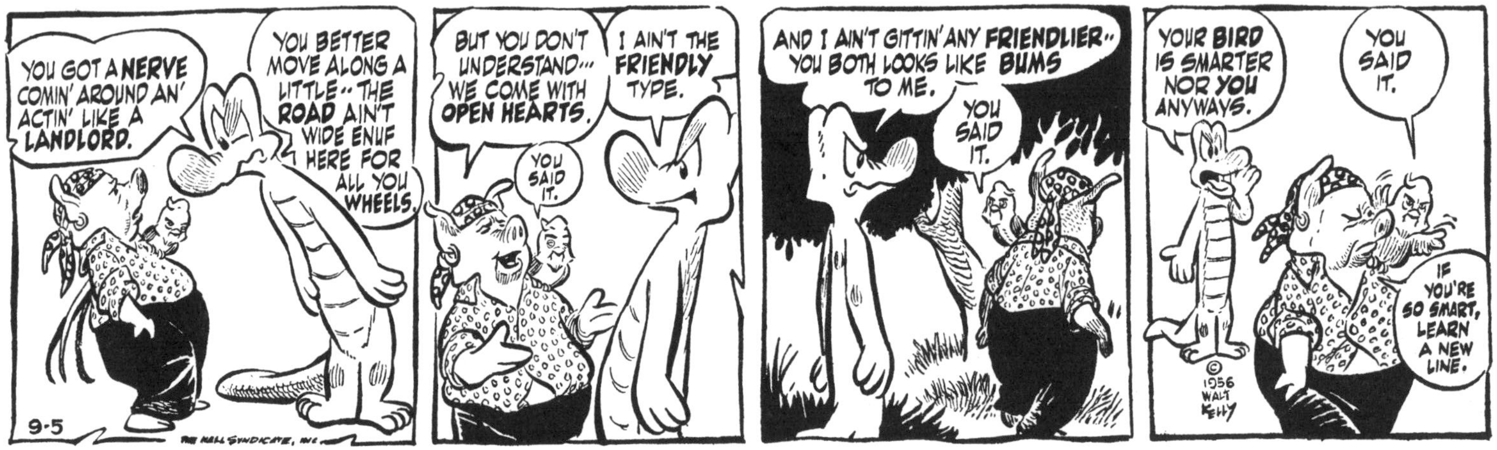
YOU GOT A **NERVE** COMIN' AROUND AN' ACTIN' LIKE A **LANDLORD.**
YOU BETTER MOVE ALONG A LITTLE.. THE **ROAD** AIN'T WIDE ENUF HERE FOR ALL YOU **WHEELS.**
9-5
THE HALL SYNDICATE, INC.
BUT YOU DON'T UNDERSTAND... WE COME WITH **OPEN HEARTS.**
YOU SAID IT.
I AIN'T THE **FRIENDLY** TYPE.
AND I AIN'T GITTIN' ANY **FRIENDLIER**.. YOU BOTH LOOKS LIKE **BUMS** TO ME.
YOU SAID IT.
YOUR **BIRD** IS SMARTER NOR **YOU** ANYWAYS.
YOU SAID IT.
IF YOU'RE SO SMART, LEARN A NEW LINE.
© 1956 WALT KELLY

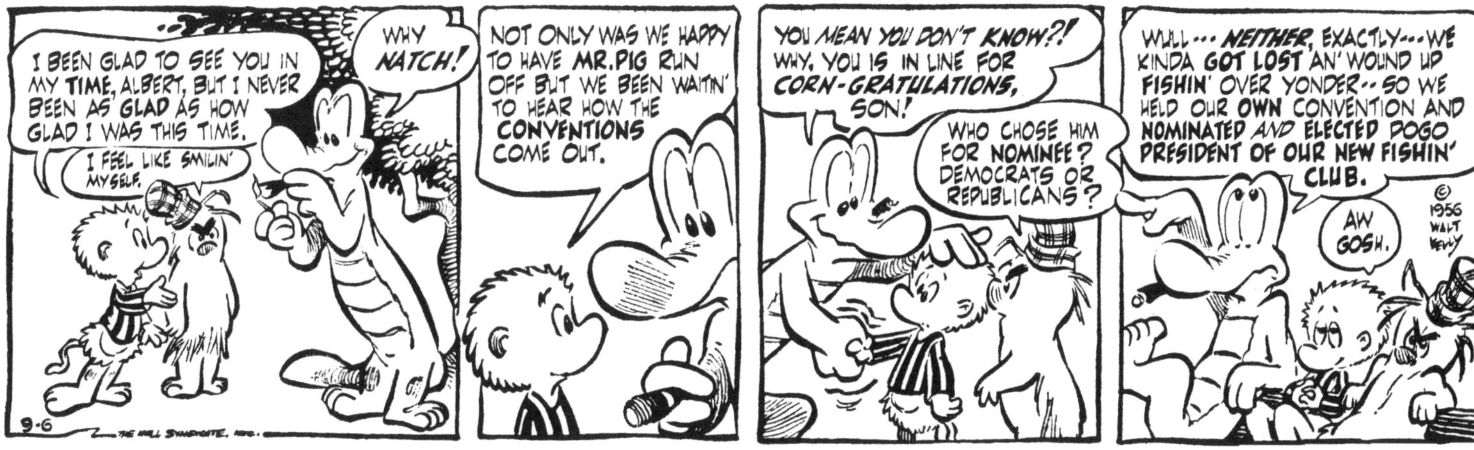
I BEEN GLAD TO SEE YOU IN MY TIME, ALBERT, BUT I NEVER BEEN AS GLAD AS HOW GLAD I WAS THIS TIME.
I FEEL LIKE SMILIN' MYSELF.
WHY NATCH!
NOT ONLY WAS WE HAPPY TO HAVE MR. PIG RUN OFF BUT WE BEEN WAITIN' TO HEAR HOW THE CONVENTIONS COME OUT.
YOU MEAN YOU DON'T KNOW?! WHY, YOU IS IN LINE FOR CORN-GRATULATIONS, SON!
WHO CHOSE HIM FOR NOMINEE? DEMOCRATS OR REPUBLICANS?
WULL ··· NEITHER, EXACTLY··· WE KINDA GOT LOST AN' WOUND UP FISHIN' OVER YONDER·· SO WE HELD OUR OWN CONVENTION AND NOMINATED AND ELECTED POGO PRESIDENT OF OUR NEW FISHIN' CLUB.
AW GOSH.
© 1956 WALT KELLY
9-6

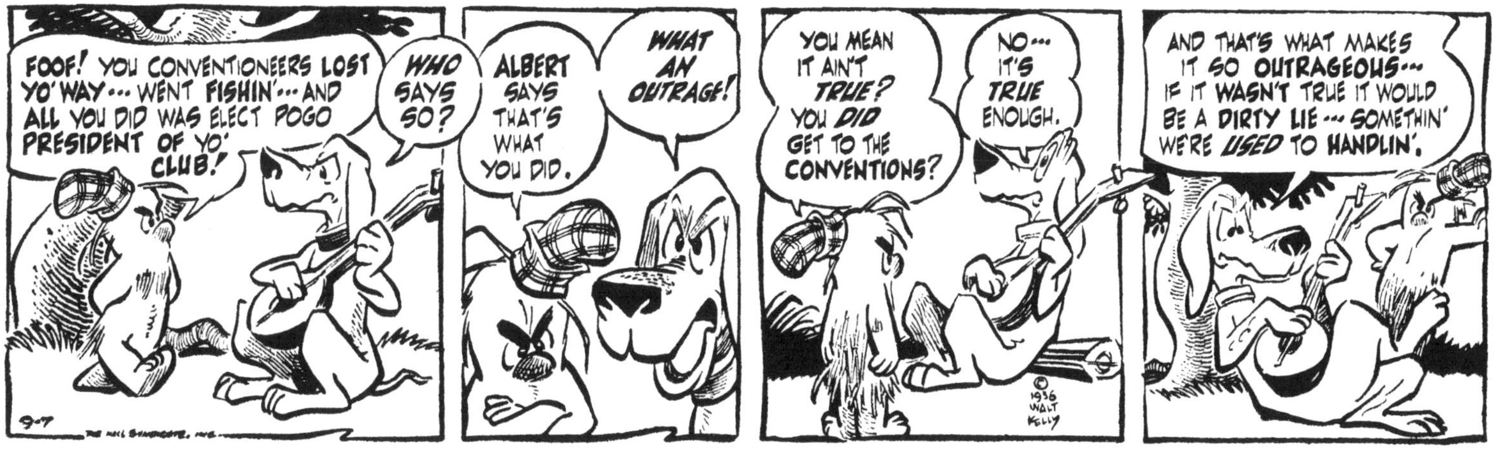
FOOF! YOU CONVENTIONEERS LOST YO' WAY··· WENT FISHIN'··· AND ALL YOU DID WAS ELECT POGO PRESIDENT OF YO' CLUB!
WHO SAYS SO?
ALBERT SAYS THAT'S WHAT YOU DID.
WHAT AN OUTRAGE!
YOU MEAN IT AIN'T TRUE? YOU DID GET TO THE CONVENTIONS?
NO··· IT'S TRUE ENOUGH.
© 1956 WALT KELLY
AND THAT'S WHAT MAKES IT SO OUTRAGEOUS··· IF IT WASN'T TRUE IT WOULD BE A DIRTY LIE··· SOMETHIN' WE'RE USED TO HANDLIN'.
9-7

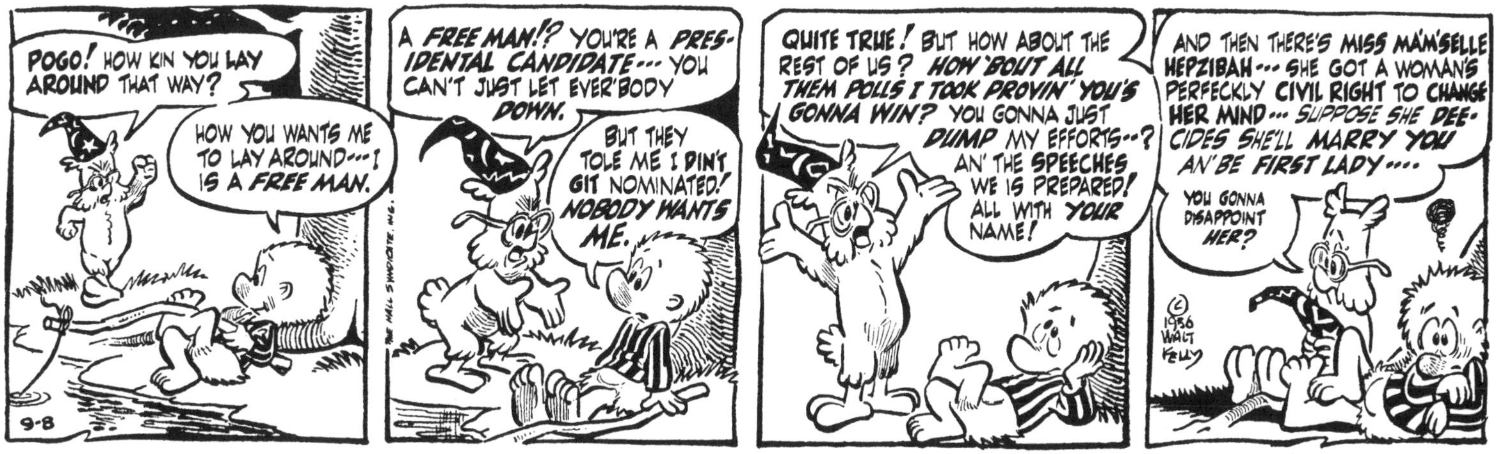
POGO! HOW KIN YOU LAY AROUND THAT WAY?
HOW YOU WANTS ME TO LAY AROUND··· I IS A FREE MAN.
A FREE MAN!? YOU'RE A PRESIDENTAL CANDIDATE··· YOU CAN'T JUST LET EVER'BODY DOWN.
BUT THEY TOLE ME I DIN'T GIT NOMINATED! NOBODY WANTS ME.
QUITE TRUE! BUT HOW ABOUT THE REST OF US? HOW 'BOUT ALL THEM POLLS I TOOK PROVIN' YOU'S GONNA WIN? YOU GONNA JUST DUMP MY EFFORTS··? AN' THE SPEECHES WE IS PREPARED! ALL WITH YOUR NAME!
AND THEN THERE'S MISS MAM'SELLE HEPZIBAH··· SHE GOT A WOMAN'S PERFECKLY CIVIL RIGHT TO CHANGE HER MIND··· SUPPOSE SHE DEECIDES SHE'LL MARRY YOU AN' BE FIRST LADY····
YOU GONNA DISAPPOINT HER?
© 1956 WALT KELLY
9-8

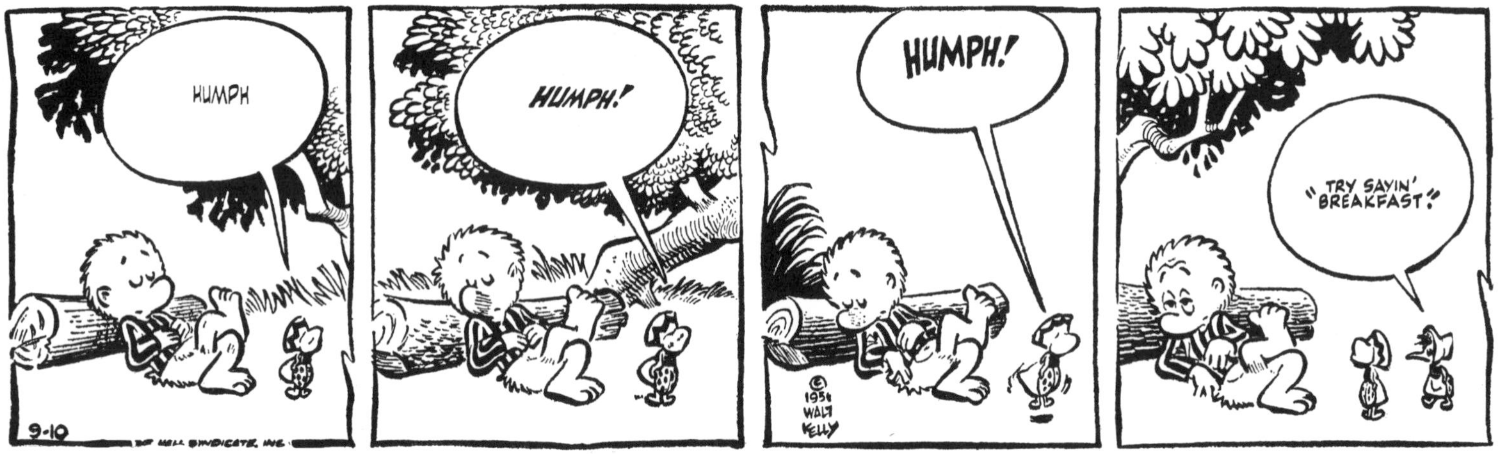
HUMPH
HUMPH!
HUMPH!
"TRY SAYIN' "BREAKFAST."
9-10
© 1956 WALT KELLY

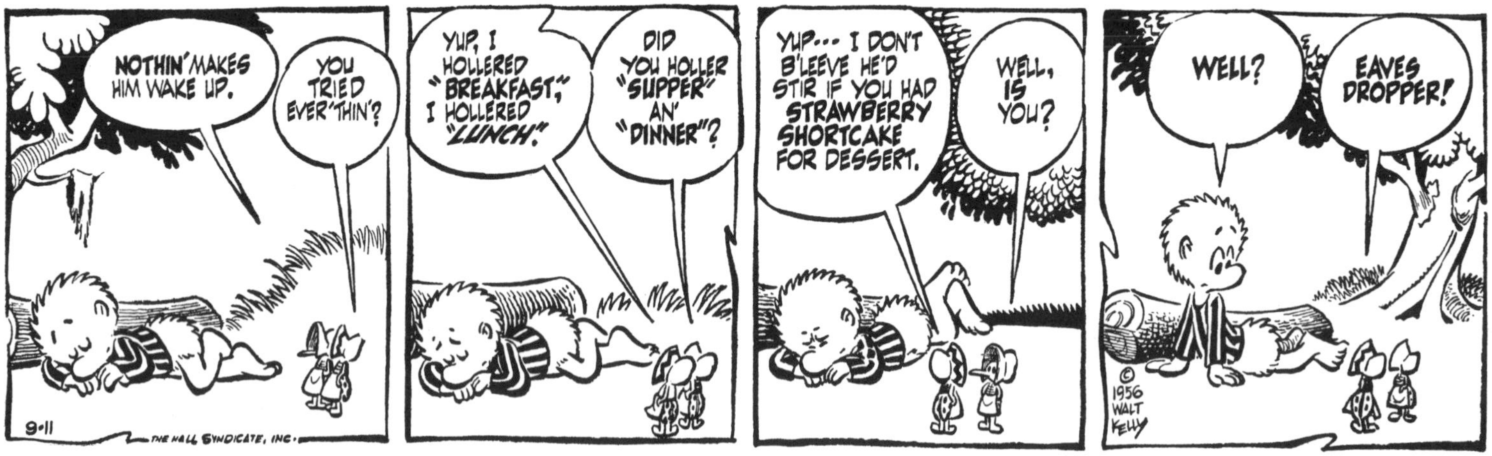
NOTHIN' MAKES HIM WAKE UP.
YOU TRIED EVER'THIN'?
YUP, I HOLLERED "BREAKFAST," I HOLLERED "LUNCH."
DID YOU HOLLER "SUPPER" AN' "DINNER"?
YUP... I DON'T B'LEEVE HE'D STIR IF YOU HAD STRAWBERRY SHORTCAKE FOR DESSERT.
WELL, IS YOU?
WELL?
EAVES DROPPER!
9-11
THE HALL SYNDICATE, INC.
© 1956 WALT KELLY

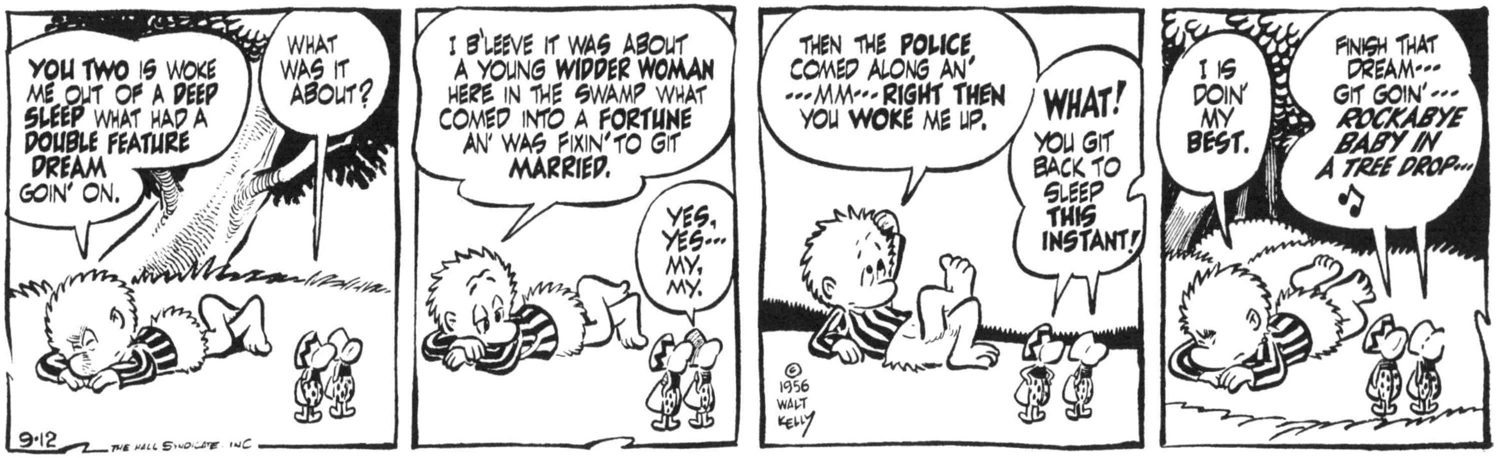
YOU TWO IS WOKE ME OUT OF A DEEP SLEEP WHAT HAD A DOUBLE FEATURE DREAM GOIN' ON.
WHAT WAS IT ABOUT?
I B'LEEVE IT WAS ABOUT A YOUNG WIDDER WOMAN HERE IN THE SWAMP WHAT COMED INTO A FORTUNE AN' WAS FIXIN' TO GIT MARRIED.
YES, YES... MY, MY.
THEN THE POLICE COMED ALONG AN' ---MM--- RIGHT THEN YOU WOKE ME UP.
WHAT! YOU GIT BACK TO SLEEP THIS INSTANT!
I IS DOIN' MY BEST.
FINISH THAT DREAM--- GIT GOIN'--- ROCKABYE BABY IN A TREE DROP...
9-12
THE HALL SYNDICATE INC
© 1956 WALT KELLY

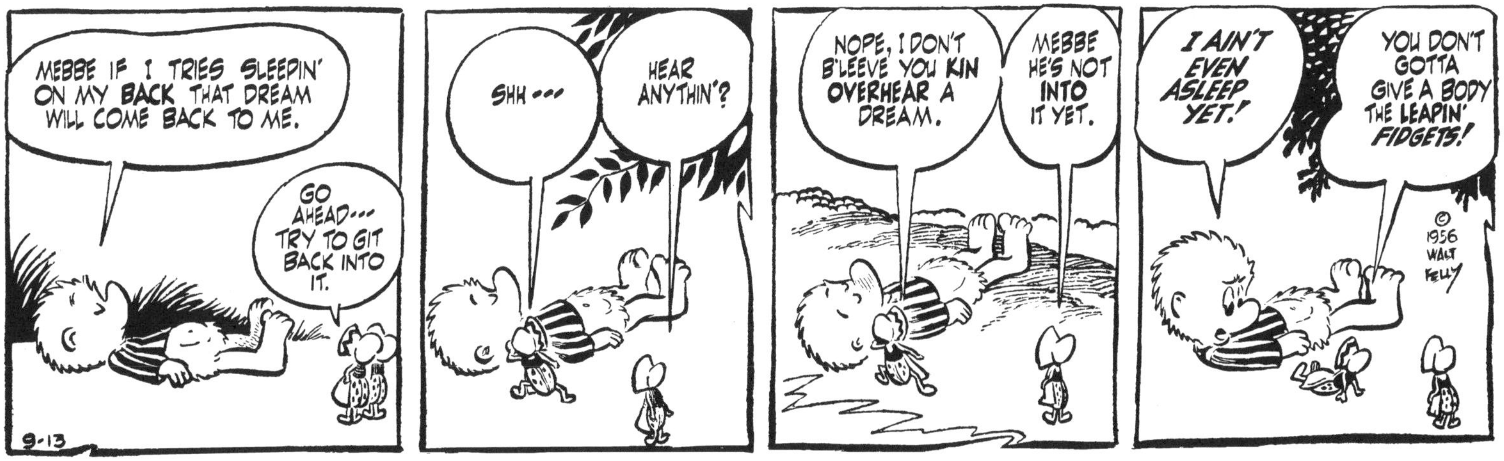
MEBBE IF I TRIES SLEEPIN' ON MY BACK THAT DREAM WILL COME BACK TO ME.
GO AHEAD... TRY TO GIT BACK INTO IT.
9-13
SHH...
HEAR ANYTHIN'?
NOPE, I DON'T B'LEEVE YOU KIN OVERHEAR A DREAM.
MEBBE HE'S NOT INTO IT YET.
I AIN'T EVEN ASLEEP YET!
YOU DON'T GOTTA GIVE A BODY THE LEAPIN' FIDGETS!
© 1956 WALT KELLY

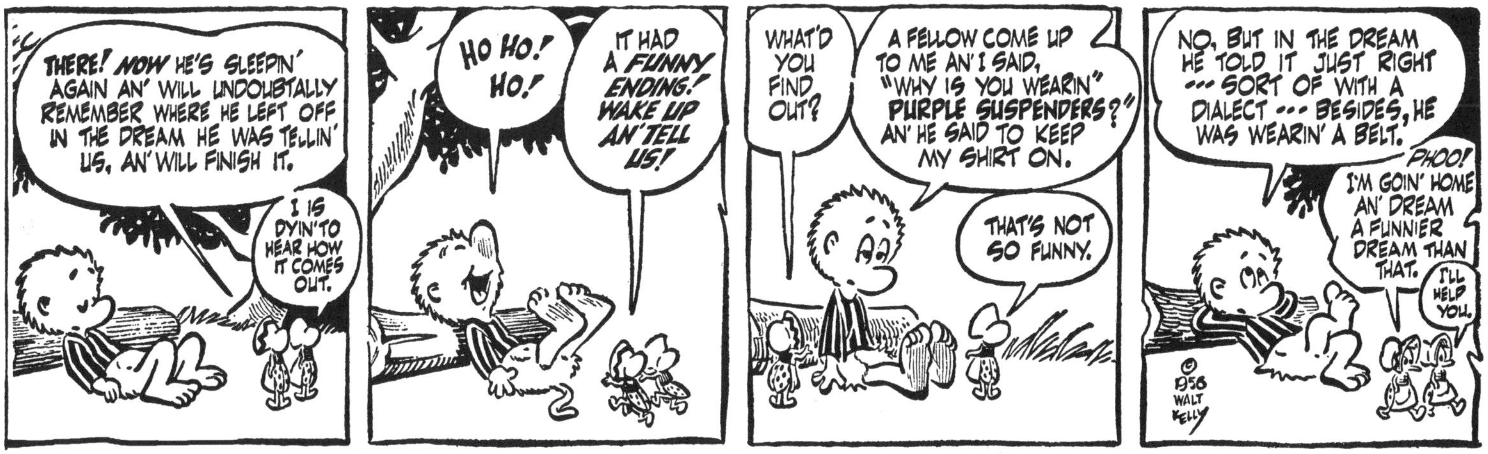
THERE! NOW HE'S SLEEPIN' AGAIN AN' WILL UNDOUBTALLY REMEMBER WHERE HE LEFT OFF IN THE DREAM HE WAS TELLIN' US, AN' WILL FINISH IT.
I IS DYIN' TO HEAR HOW IT COMES OUT.
HO HO! HO!
IT HAD A FUNNY ENDING! WAKE UP AN' TELL US!
WHAT'D YOU FIND OUT?
A FELLOW COME UP TO ME AN' I SAID, "WHY IS YOU WEARIN' PURPLE SUSPENDERS?" AN' HE SAID TO KEEP MY SHIRT ON.
THAT'S NOT SO FUNNY.
NO, BUT IN THE DREAM HE TOLD IT JUST RIGHT ... SORT OF WITH A DIALECT ... BESIDES, HE WAS WEARIN' A BELT.
PHOO! I'M GOIN' HOME AN' DREAM A FUNNIER DREAM THAN THAT.
I'LL HELP YOU.
© 1956 WALT KELLY

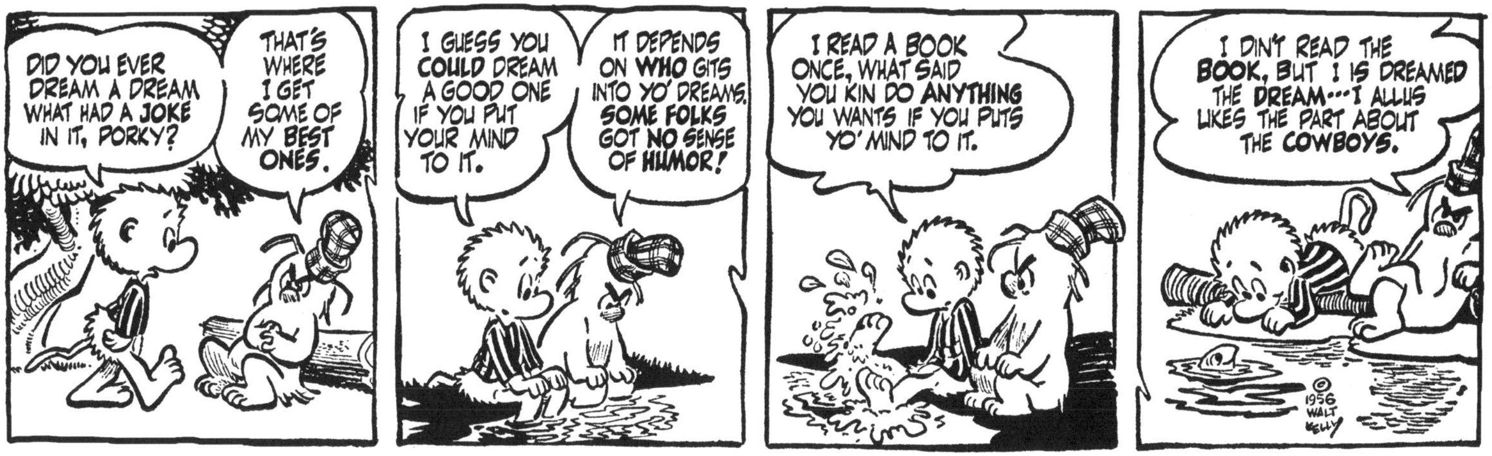
DID YOU EVER DREAM A DREAM WHAT HAD A JOKE IN IT, PORKY?
THAT'S WHERE I GET SOME OF MY BEST ONES.
I GUESS YOU COULD DREAM A GOOD ONE IF YOU PUT YOUR MIND TO IT.
IT DEPENDS ON WHO GITS INTO YO' DREAMS. SOME FOLKS GOT NO SENSE OF HUMOR!
I READ A BOOK ONCE, WHAT SAID YOU KIN DO ANYTHING YOU WANTS IF YOU PUTS YO' MIND TO IT.
I DIN'T READ THE BOOK, BUT I IS DREAMED THE DREAM... I ALLUS LIKES THE PART ABOUT THE COWBOYS.
© 1956 WALT KELLY

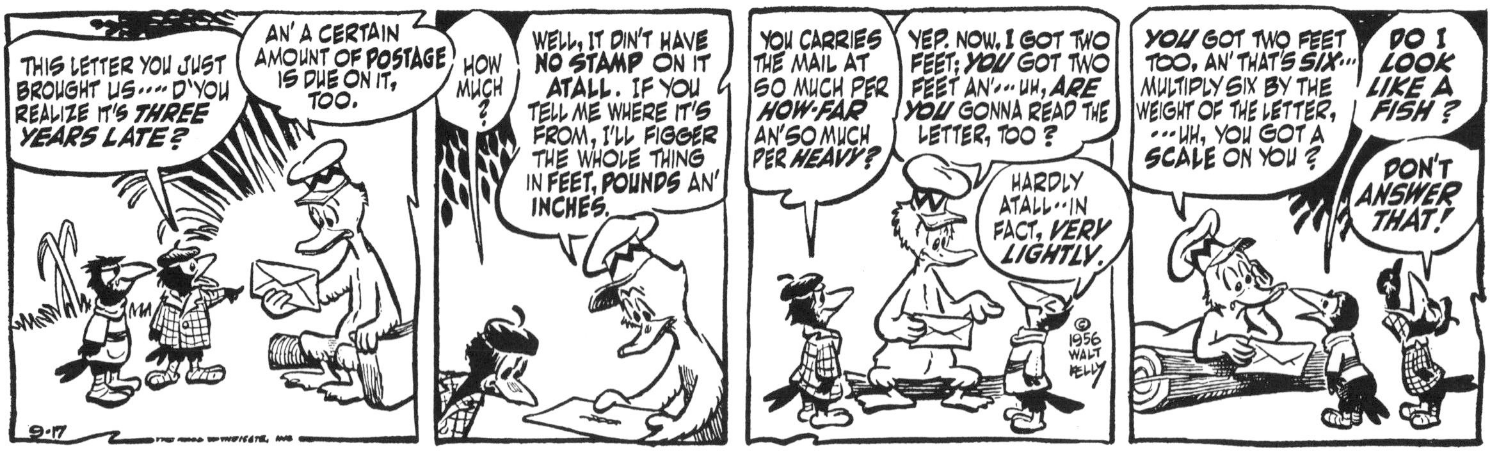
THIS LETTER YOU JUST BROUGHT US.... D'YOU REALIZE IT'S THREE YEARS LATE?
AN' A CERTAIN AMOUNT OF POSTAGE IS DUE ON IT, TOO.
HOW MUCH?
WELL, IT DIN'T HAVE NO STAMP ON IT ATALL. IF YOU TELL ME WHERE IT'S FROM, I'LL FIGGER THE WHOLE THING IN FEET, POUNDS AN' INCHES.
YOU CARRIES THE MAIL AT SO MUCH PER HOW-FAR AN' SO MUCH PER HEAVY?
YEP. NOW, I GOT TWO FEET; YOU GOT TWO FEET AN'... UH, ARE YOU GONNA READ THE LETTER, TOO?
HARDLY ATALL.. IN FACT, VERY LIGHTLY.
© 1956 WALT KELLY
YOU GOT TWO FEET TOO, AN' THAT'S SIX... MULTIPLY SIX BY THE WEIGHT OF THE LETTER, ...UH, YOU GOT A SCALE ON YOU?
DO I LOOK LIKE A FISH?
DON'T ANSWER THAT!
9-17

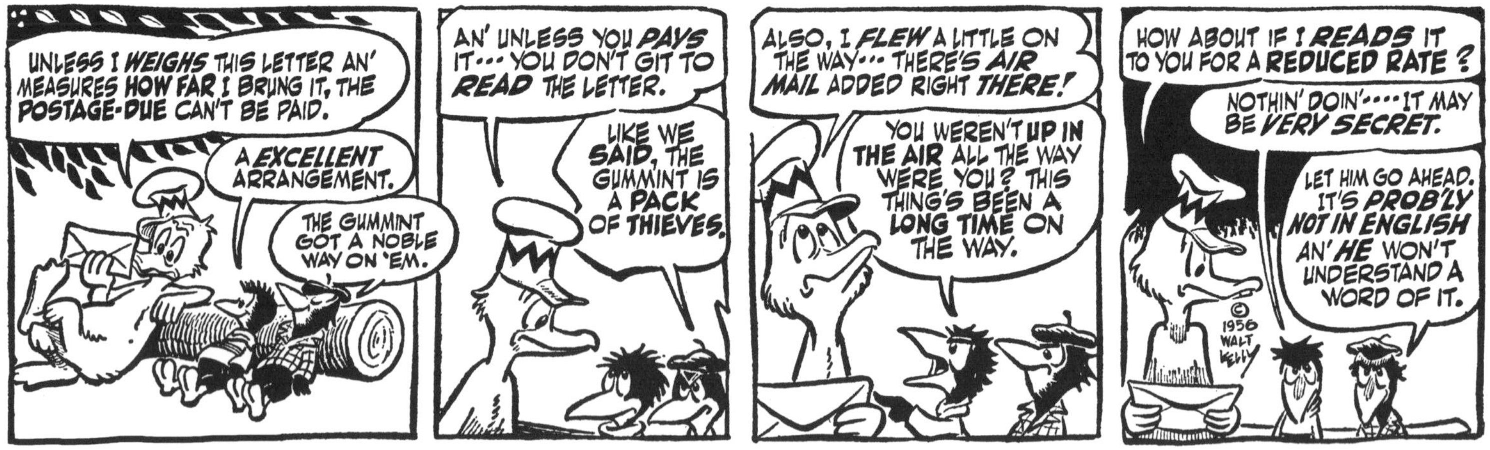
UNLESS I WEIGHS THIS LETTER AN' MEASURES HOW FAR I BRUNG IT, THE POSTAGE-DUE CAN'T BE PAID.
A EXCELLENT ARRANGEMENT.
THE GUMMINT GOT A NOBLE WAY ON 'EM.
AN' UNLESS YOU PAYS IT... YOU DON'T GIT TO READ THE LETTER.
LIKE WE SAID, THE GUMMINT IS A PACK OF THIEVES.
ALSO, I FLEW A LITTLE ON THE WAY... THERE'S AIR MAIL ADDED RIGHT THERE!
YOU WEREN'T UP IN THE AIR ALL THE WAY WERE YOU? THIS THING'S BEEN A LONG TIME ON THE WAY.
HOW ABOUT IF I READS IT TO YOU FOR A REDUCED RATE?
NOTHIN' DOIN'.... IT MAY BE VERY SECRET.
LET HIM GO AHEAD. IT'S PROB'LY NOT IN ENGLISH AN' HE WON'T UNDERSTAND A WORD OF IT.
© 1956 WALT KELLY

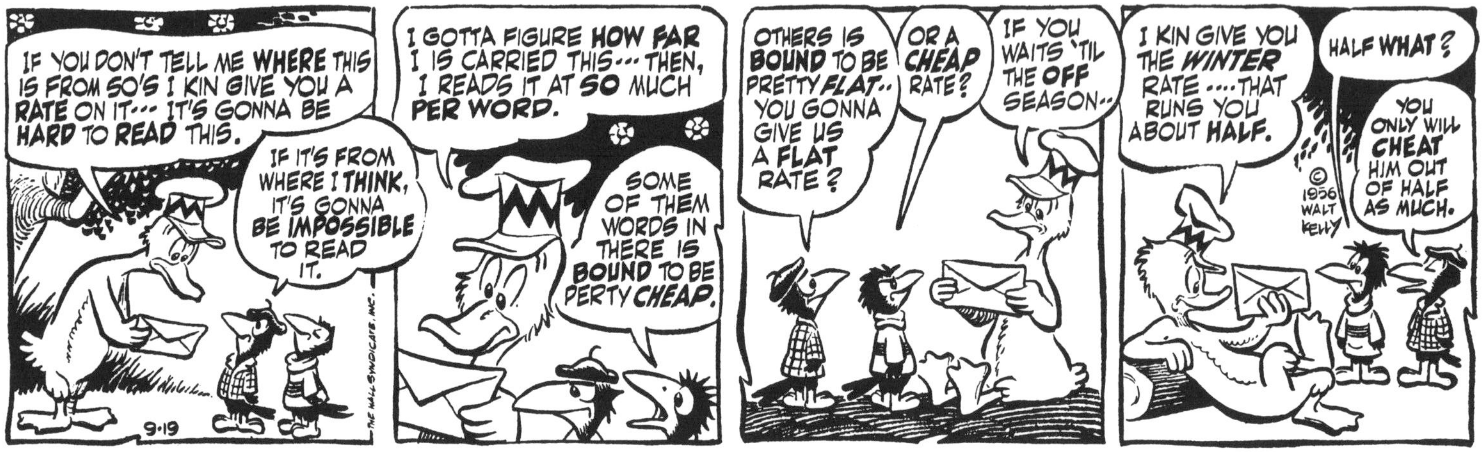
IF YOU DON'T TELL ME WHERE THIS IS FROM SO'S I KIN GIVE YOU A RATE ON IT... IT'S GONNA BE HARD TO READ THIS.
IF IT'S FROM WHERE I THINK, IT'S GONNA BE IMPOSSIBLE TO READ IT.
9-19
I GOTTA FIGURE HOW FAR I IS CARRIED THIS... THEN, I READS IT AT SO MUCH PER WORD.
SOME OF THEM WORDS IN THERE IS BOUND TO BE PERTY CHEAP.
OTHERS IS BOUND TO BE PRETTY FLAT.. YOU GONNA GIVE US A FLAT RATE?
OR A CHEAP RATE?
IF YOU WAITS 'TIL THE OFF SEASON..
I KIN GIVE YOU THE WINTER RATE ....THAT RUNS YOU ABOUT HALF.
HALF WHAT?
YOU ONLY WILL CHEAT HIM OUT OF HALF AS MUCH.
© 1956 WALT KELLY

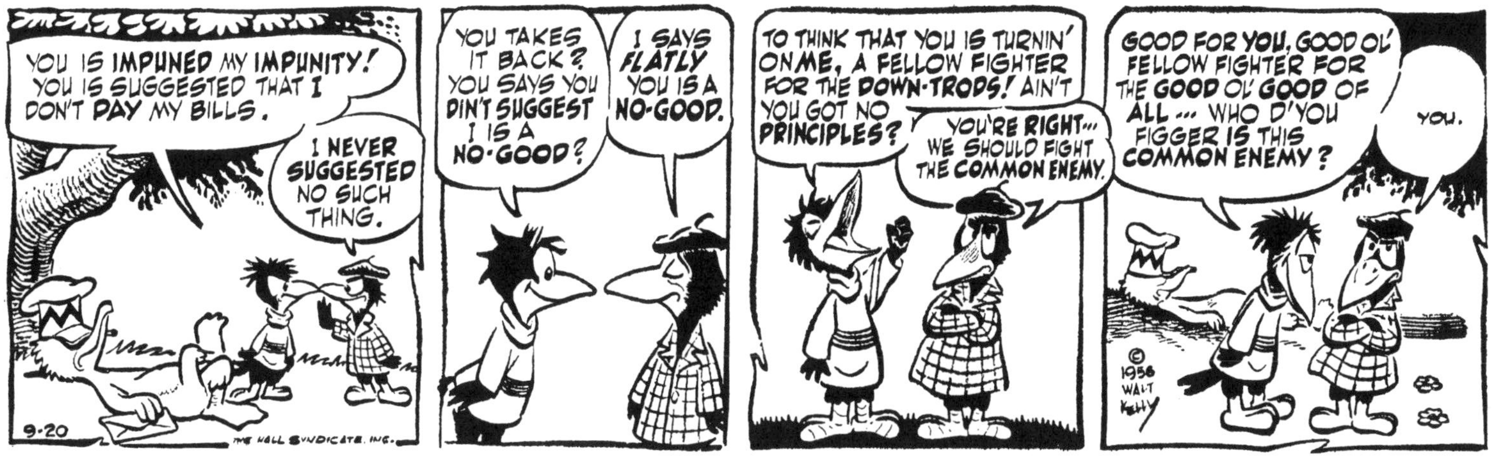
YOU IS IMPUNED MY IMPUNITY! YOU IS SUGGESTED THAT I DON'T PAY MY BILLS.
I NEVER SUGGESTED NO SUCH THING.
9-20
THE HALL SYNDICATE, INC.
YOU TAKES IT BACK? YOU SAYS YOU DIN'T SUGGEST I IS A NO-GOOD?
I SAYS FLATLY YOU IS A NO-GOOD.
TO THINK THAT YOU IS TURNIN' ON ME, A FELLOW FIGHTER FOR THE DOWN-TRODS! AIN'T YOU GOT NO PRINCIPLES?
YOU'RE RIGHT... WE SHOULD FIGHT THE COMMON ENEMY.
GOOD FOR YOU, GOOD OL' FELLOW FIGHTER FOR THE GOOD OL' GOOD OF ALL ... WHO D'YOU FIGGER IS THIS COMMON ENEMY?
YOU.
© 1956 WALT KELLY

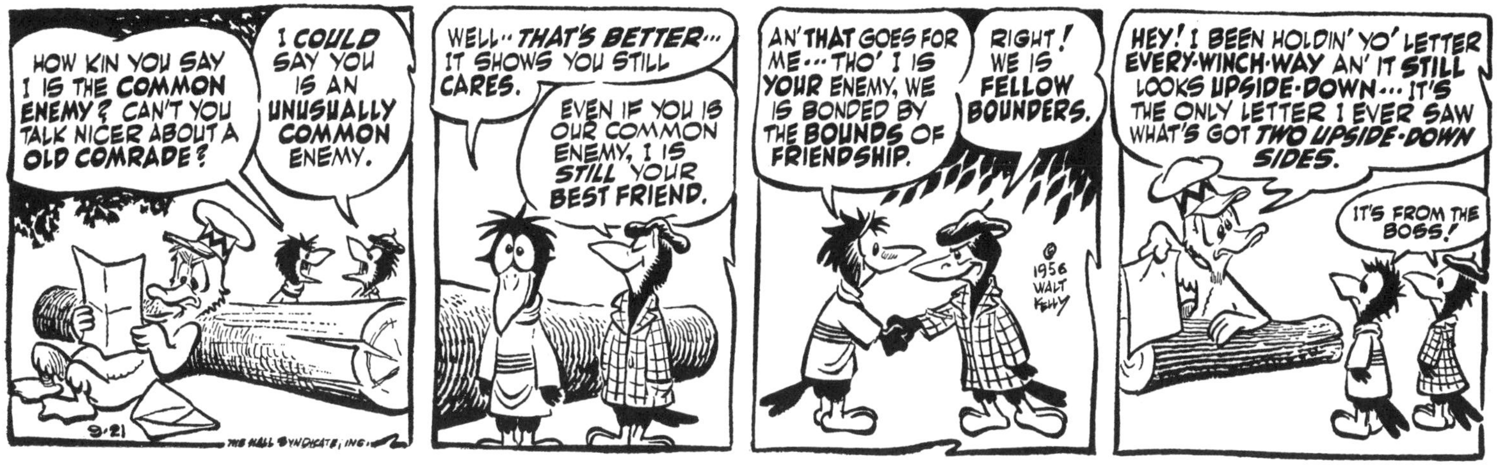
HOW KIN YOU SAY I IS THE COMMON ENEMY? CAN'T YOU TALK NICER ABOUT A OLD COMRADE?
I COULD SAY YOU IS AN UNUSUALLY COMMON ENEMY.
9-21
THE HALL SYNDICATE, INC.
WELL.. THAT'S BETTER... IT SHOWS YOU STILL CARES.
EVEN IF YOU IS OUR COMMON ENEMY, I IS STILL YOUR BEST FRIEND.
AN' THAT GOES FOR ME... THO' I IS YOUR ENEMY, WE IS BONDED BY THE BOUNDS OF FRIENDSHIP.
RIGHT! WE IS FELLOW BOUNDERS.
© 1956 WALT KELLY
HEY! I BEEN HOLDIN' YO' LETTER EVERY-WINCH-WAY AN' IT STILL LOOKS UPSIDE-DOWN... IT'S THE ONLY LETTER I EVER SAW WHAT'S GOT TWO UPSIDE-DOWN SIDES.
IT'S FROM THE BOSS!

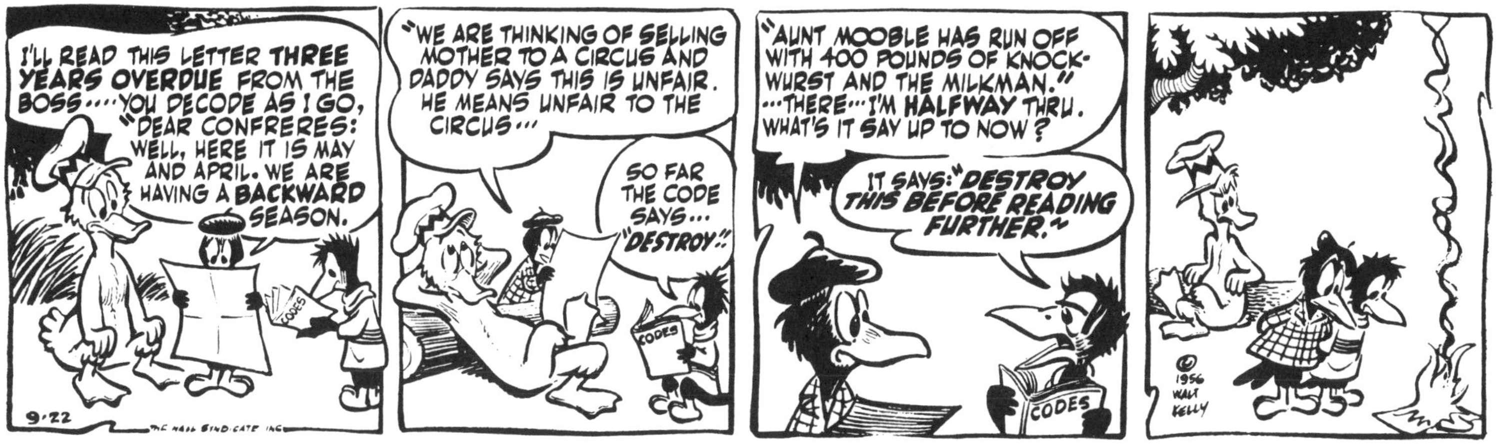
I'LL READ THIS LETTER THREE YEARS OVERDUE FROM THE BOSS.... YOU DECODE AS I GO, "DEAR CONFRERES: WELL, HERE IT IS MAY AND APRIL. WE ARE HAVING A BACKWARD SEASON.
CODES
9-22
THE HALL SYNDICATE INC.
"WE ARE THINKING OF SELLING MOTHER TO A CIRCUS AND DADDY SAYS THIS IS UNFAIR. HE MEANS UNFAIR TO THE CIRCUS...
SO FAR THE CODE SAYS... "DESTROY"!
CODES
"AUNT MOOBLE HAS RUN OFF WITH 400 POUNDS OF KNOCKWURST AND THE MILKMAN." ...THERE... I'M HALFWAY THRU. WHAT'S IT SAY UP TO NOW?
IT SAYS: "DESTROY THIS BEFORE READING FURTHER."
CODES
© 1956 WALT KELLY

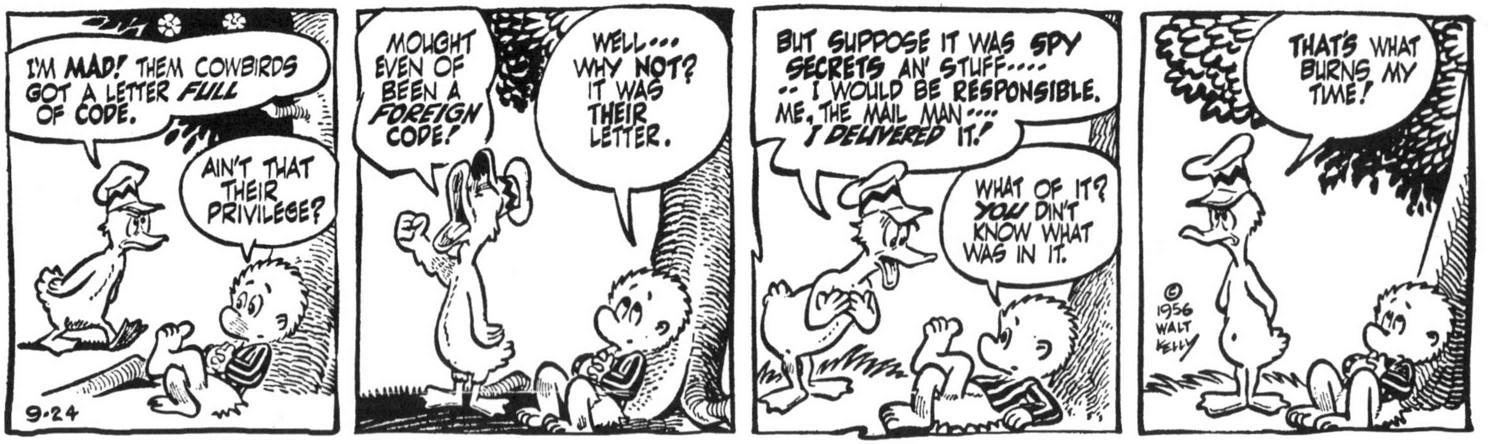
I'M MAD! THEM COWBIRDS GOT A LETTER FULL OF CODE.
AIN'T THAT THEIR PRIVILEGE?
9-24
MOUGHT EVEN OF BEEN A FOREIGN CODE!
WELL... WHY NOT? IT WAS THEIR LETTER.
BUT SUPPOSE IT WAS SPY SECRETS AN' STUFF.... -- I WOULD BE RESPONSIBLE. ME, THE MAIL MAN.... I DELIVERED IT!
WHAT OF IT? YOU DIN'T KNOW WHAT WAS IN IT.
THAT'S WHAT BURNS MY TIME!
© 1956 WALT KELLY

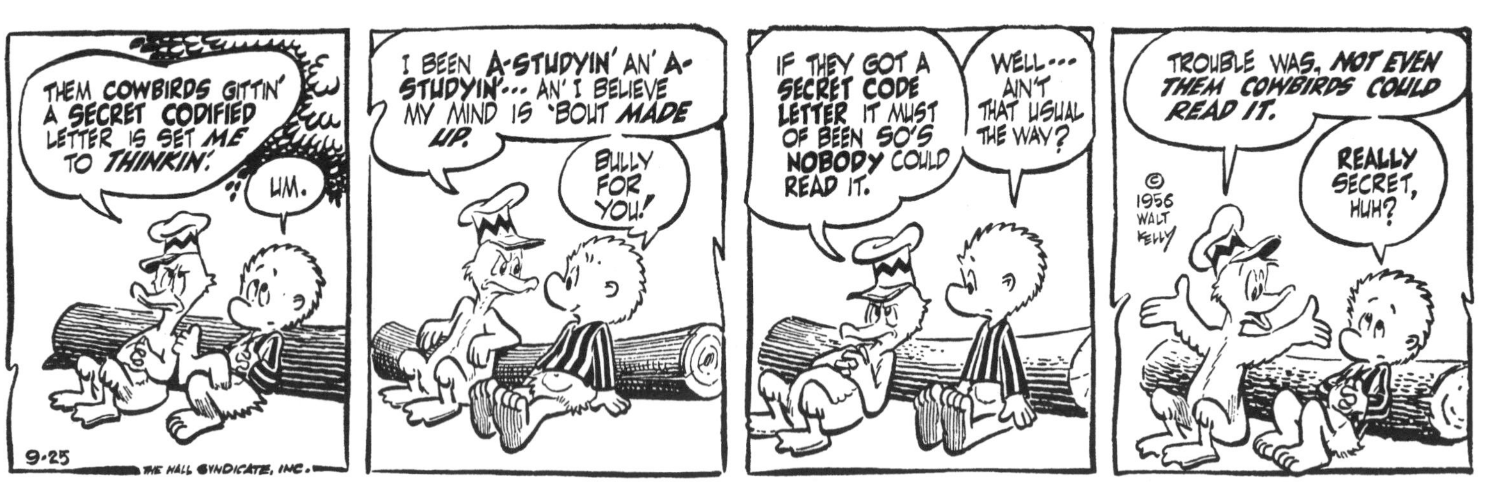
THEM COWBIRDS GITTIN' A SECRET CODIFIED LETTER IS SET ME TO THINKIN'.
UM.
9-25
THE HALL SYNDICATE, INC.
I BEEN A-STUDYIN' AN' A-STUDYIN'... AN' I BELIEVE MY MIND IS 'BOUT MADE UP.
BULLY FOR YOU!
IF THEY GOT A SECRET CODE LETTER IT MUST OF BEEN SO'S NOBODY COULD READ IT.
WELL... AIN'T THAT USUAL THE WAY?
TROUBLE WAS, NOT EVEN THEM COWBIRDS COULD READ IT.
REALLY SECRET, HUH?
© 1956 WALT KELLY

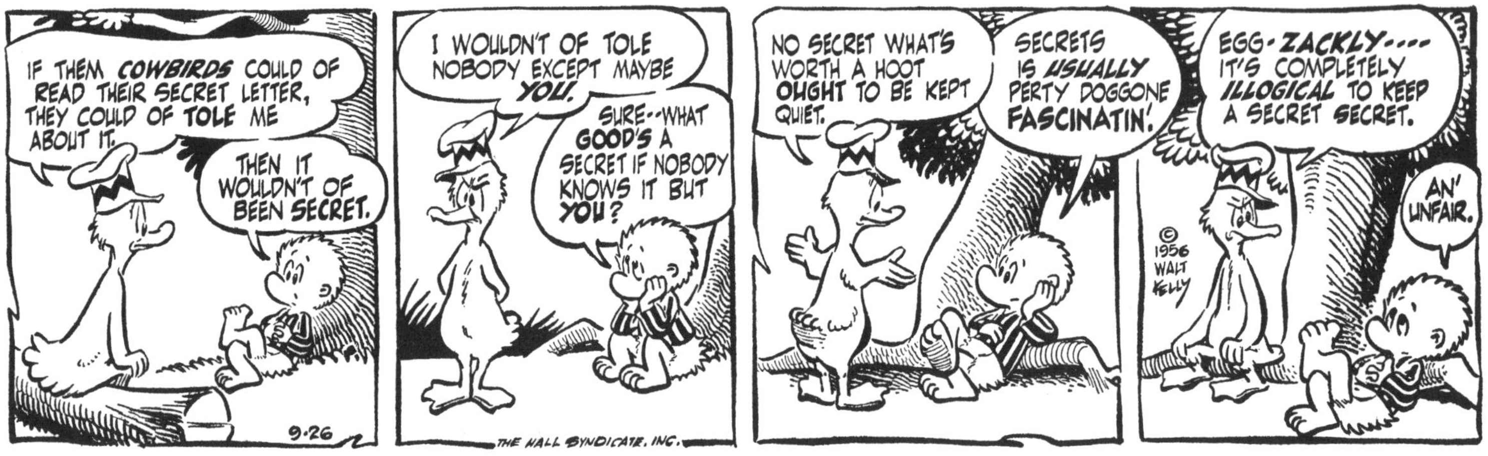
IF THEM COWBIRDS COULD OF READ THEIR SECRET LETTER, THEY COULD OF TOLE ME ABOUT IT.
THEN IT WOULDN'T OF BEEN SECRET.
9-26
I WOULDN'T OF TOLE NOBODY EXCEPT MAYBE YOU.
SURE--WHAT GOOD'S A SECRET IF NOBODY KNOWS IT BUT YOU?
THE HALL SYNDICATE, INC.
NO SECRET WHAT'S WORTH A HOOT OUGHT TO BE KEPT QUIET.
SECRETS IS USUALLY PERTY DOGGONE FASCINATIN'.
EGG-ZACKLY.... IT'S COMPLETELY ILLOGICAL TO KEEP A SECRET SECRET.
AN' UNFAIR.
© 1956 WALT KELLY

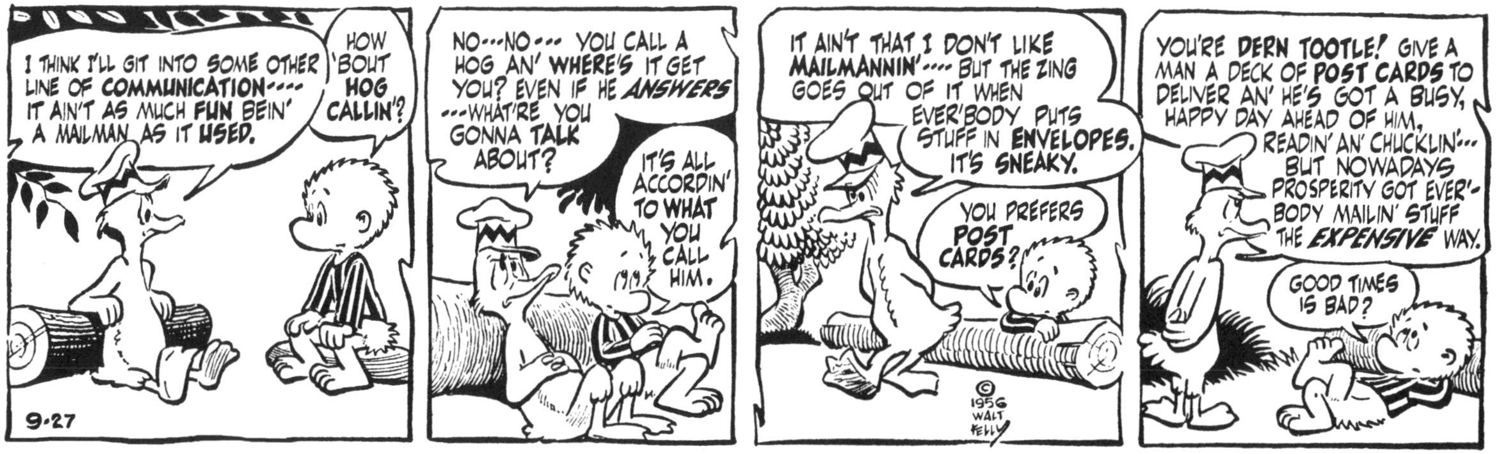
I THINK I'LL GIT INTO SOME OTHER LINE OF COMMUNICATION---- IT AIN'T AS MUCH FUN BEIN' A MAILMAN AS IT USED.
HOW 'BOUT HOG CALLIN'?
NO---NO--- YOU CALL A HOG AN' WHERE'S IT GET YOU? EVEN IF HE ANSWERS ---WHAT'RE YOU GONNA TALK ABOUT?
IT'S ALL ACCORDIN' TO WHAT YOU CALL HIM.
IT AIN'T THAT I DON'T LIKE MAILMANNIN'---- BUT THE ZING GOES OUT OF IT WHEN EVER'BODY PUTS STUFF IN ENVELOPES. IT'S SNEAKY.
YOU PREFERS POST CARDS?
YOU'RE DERN TOOTLE! GIVE A MAN A DECK OF POST CARDS TO DELIVER AN' HE'S GOT A BUSY, HAPPY DAY AHEAD OF HIM, READIN' AN' CHUCKLIN'--- BUT NOWADAYS PROSPERITY GOT EVER'-BODY MAILIN' STUFF THE EXPENSIVE WAY.
GOOD TIMES IS BAD?
9-27
© 1956 WALT KELLY

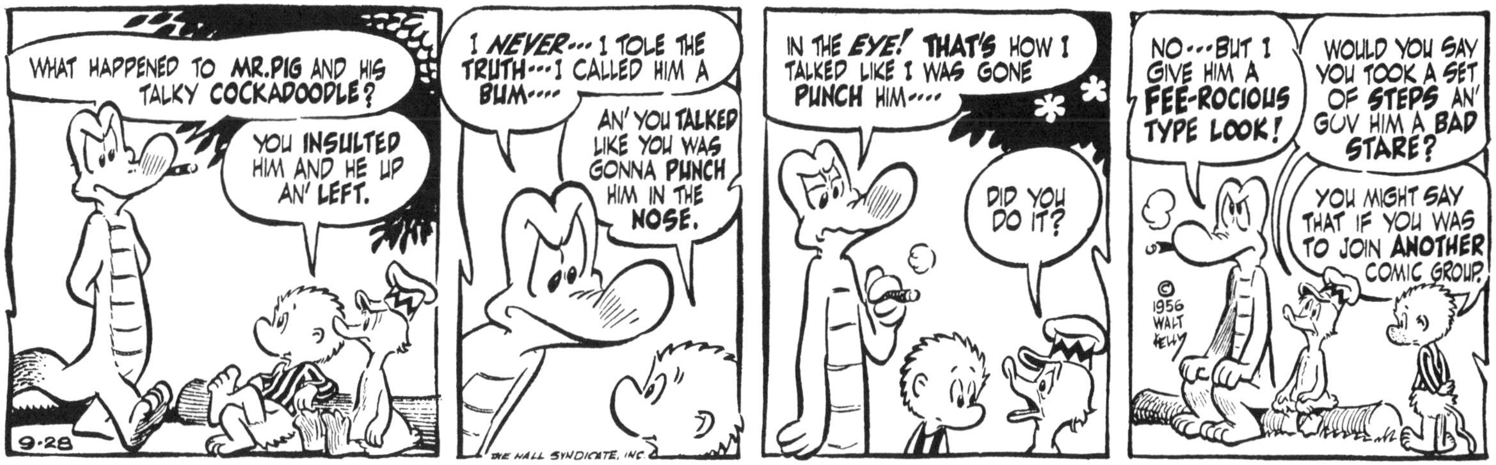
WHAT HAPPENED TO MR. PIG AND HIS TALKY COCKADOODLE?
YOU INSULTED HIM AND HE UP AN' LEFT.
I NEVER--- I TOLE THE TRUTH---I CALLED HIM A BUM----
AN' YOU TALKED LIKE YOU WAS GONNA PUNCH HIM IN THE NOSE.
IN THE EYE! THAT'S HOW I TALKED LIKE I WAS GONE PUNCH HIM----
DID YOU DO IT?
NO---BUT I GIVE HIM A FEE-ROCIOUS TYPE LOOK!
WOULD YOU SAY YOU TOOK A SET OF STEPS AN' GUV HIM A BAD STARE?
YOU MIGHT SAY THAT IF YOU WAS TO JOIN ANOTHER COMIC GROUP.
9-28
THE HALL SYNDICATE, INC.
© 1956 WALT KELLY

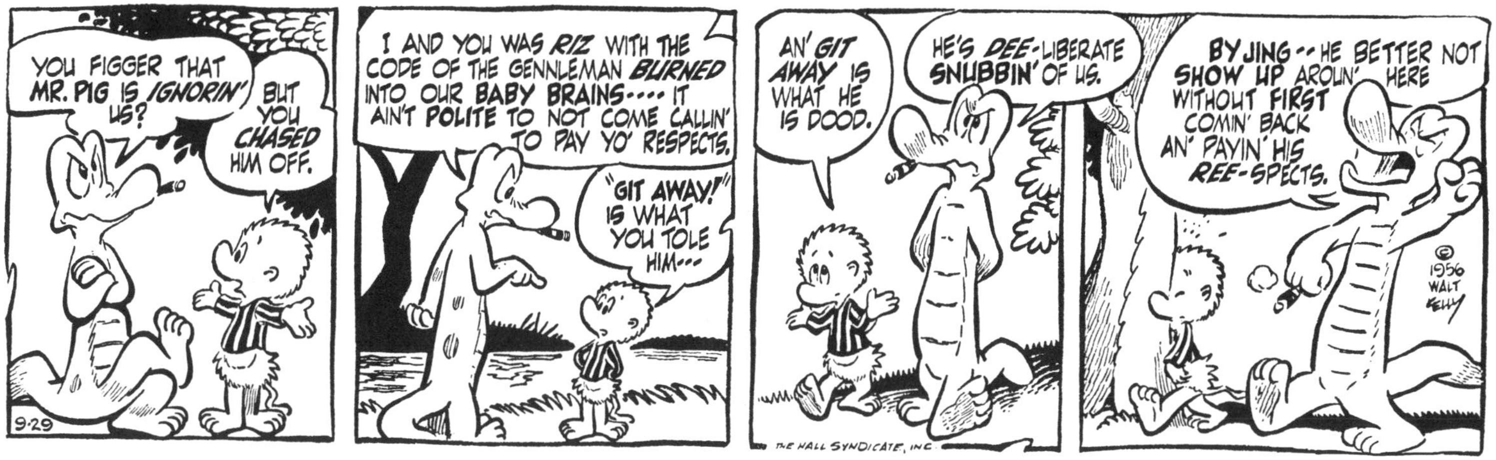
YOU FIGGER THAT MR. PIG IS IGNORIN' US?
BUT YOU CHASED HIM OFF.
I AND YOU WAS RIZ WITH THE CODE OF THE GENNLEMAN BURNED INTO OUR BABY BRAINS---- IT AIN'T POLITE TO NOT COME CALLIN' TO PAY YO' RESPECTS.
"GIT AWAY!" IS WHAT YOU TOLE HIM---
AN' GIT AWAY IS WHAT HE IS DOOD.
HE'S DEE-LIBERATE SNUBBIN' OF US.
BY JING -- HE BETTER NOT SHOW UP AROUN' HERE WITHOUT FIRST COMIN' BACK AN' PAYIN' HIS REE-SPECTS.
9-29
THE HALL SYNDICATE, INC.
© 1956 WALT KELLY

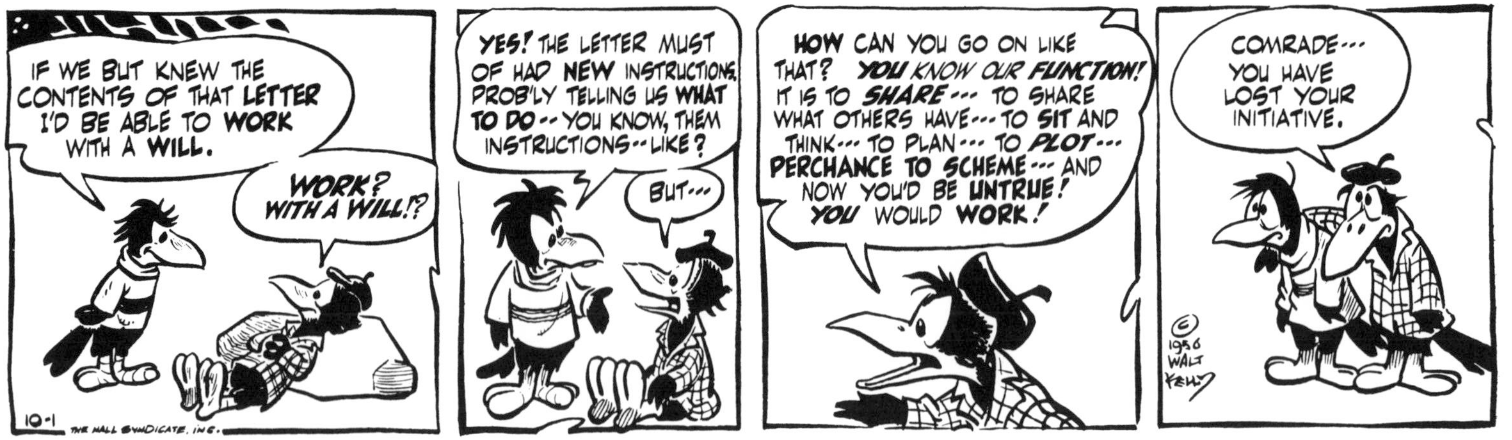
IF WE BUT KNEW THE CONTENTS OF THAT LETTER I'D BE ABLE TO WORK WITH A WILL.
WORK? WITH A WILL!?
10-1
THE HALL SYNDICATE, INC.
YES! THE LETTER MUST OF HAD NEW INSTRUCTIONS, PROB'LY TELLING US WHAT TO DO -- YOU KNOW, THEM INSTRUCTIONS -- LIKE?
BUT ...
HOW CAN YOU GO ON LIKE THAT? YOU KNOW OUR FUNCTION! IT IS TO SHARE --- TO SHARE WHAT OTHERS HAVE --- TO SIT AND THINK --- TO PLAN --- TO PLOT --- PERCHANCE TO SCHEME --- AND NOW YOU'D BE UNTRUE! YOU WOULD WORK!
COMRADE --- YOU HAVE LOST YOUR INITIATIVE.
© 1956 WALT KELLY

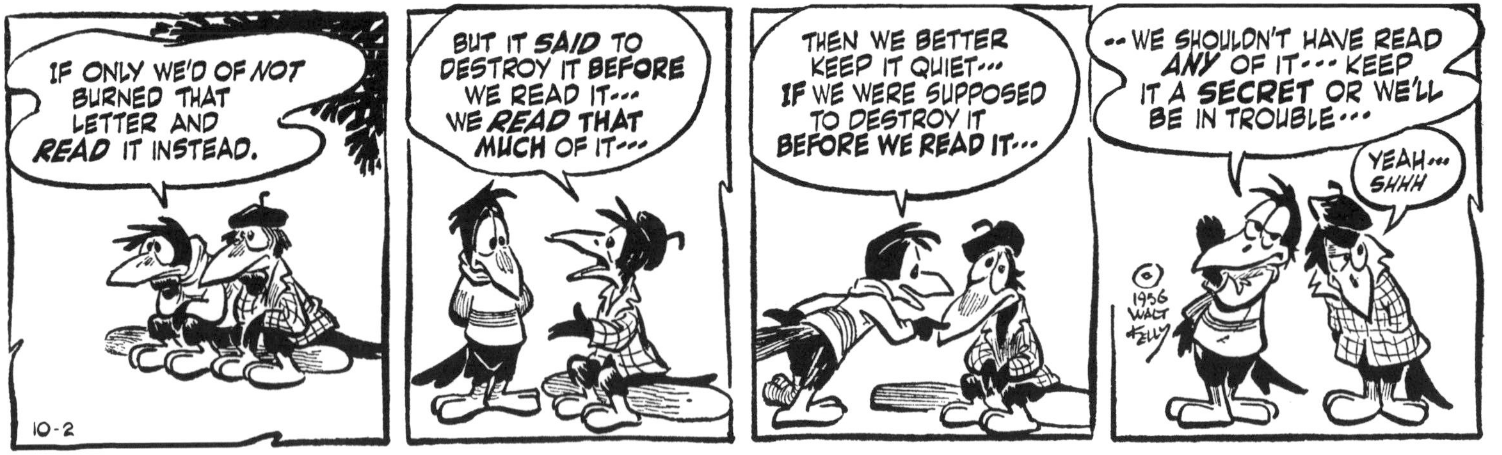
IF ONLY WE'D OF NOT BURNED THAT LETTER AND READ IT INSTEAD.
10-2
BUT IT SAID TO DESTROY IT BEFORE WE READ IT --- WE READ THAT MUCH OF IT ---
THEN WE BETTER KEEP IT QUIET --- IF WE WERE SUPPOSED TO DESTROY IT BEFORE WE READ IT ---
-- WE SHOULDN'T HAVE READ ANY OF IT --- KEEP IT A SECRET OR WE'LL BE IN TROUBLE ---
YEAH --- SHHH
© 1956 WALT KELLY

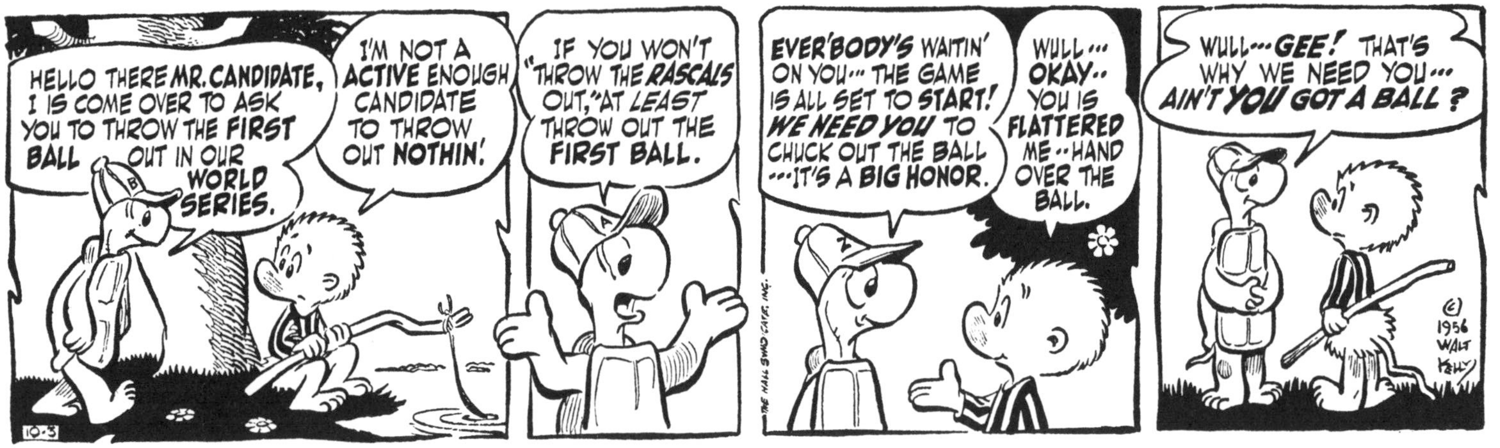
HELLO THERE MR. CANDIDATE, I IS COME OVER TO ASK YOU TO THROW THE FIRST BALL OUT IN OUR WORLD SERIES.
I'M NOT A ACTIVE ENOUGH CANDIDATE TO THROW OUT NOTHIN'.
10-3
"IF YOU WON'T THROW THE RASCALS OUT," AT LEAST THROW OUT THE FIRST BALL.
THE HALL SYND CATE, INC.
EVER'BODY'S WAITIN' ON YOU --- THE GAME IS ALL SET TO START! WE NEED YOU TO CHUCK OUT THE BALL --- IT'S A BIG HONOR.
WULL --- OKAY -- YOU IS FLATTERED ME -- HAND OVER THE BALL.
WULL --- GEE! THAT'S WHY WE NEED YOU --- AIN'T YOU GOT A BALL?
© 1956 WALT KELLY

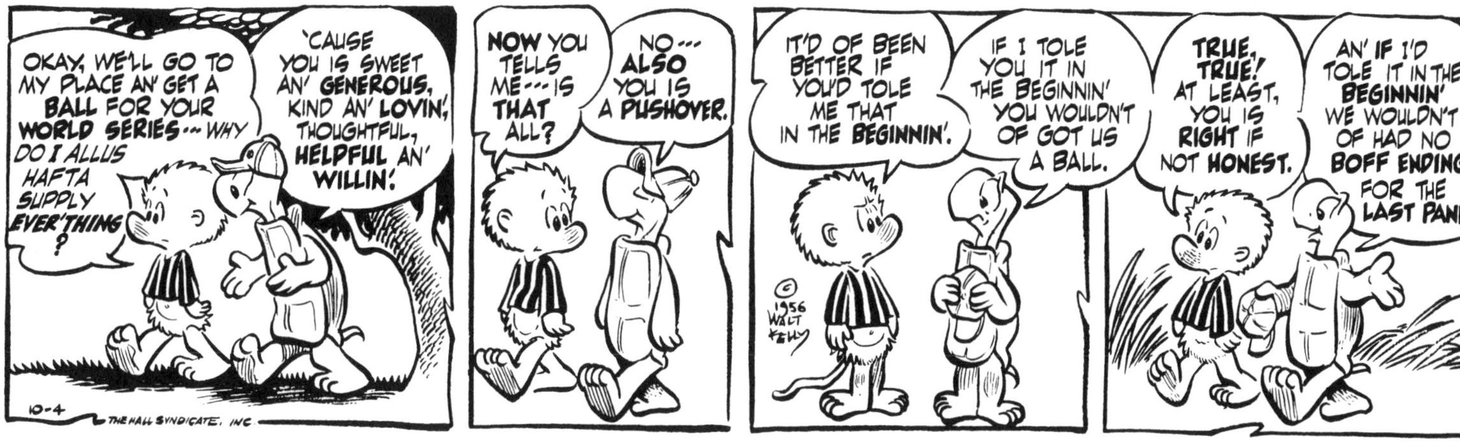
OKAY, WE'LL GO TO MY PLACE AN' GET A BALL FOR YOUR WORLD SERIES... WHY DO I ALLUS HAFTA SUPPLY EVER'THING?
'CAUSE YOU IS SWEET AN' GENEROUS, KIND AN' LOVIN', THOUGHTFUL, HELPFUL AN' WILLIN'.
10-4
THE HALL SYNDICATE, INC
NOW YOU TELLS ME... IS THAT ALL?
NO... ALSO YOU IS A PUSHOVER.
IT'D OF BEEN BETTER IF YOU'D TOLE ME THAT IN THE BEGINNIN'.
IF I TOLE YOU IT IN THE BEGINNIN' YOU WOULDN'T OF GOT US A BALL.
© 1956 WALT KELLY
TRUE, TRUE! AT LEAST, YOU IS RIGHT IF NOT HONEST.
AN' IF I'D TOLE IT IN THE BEGINNIN' WE WOULDN'T OF HAD NO BOFF ENDING FOR THE LAST PANEL.

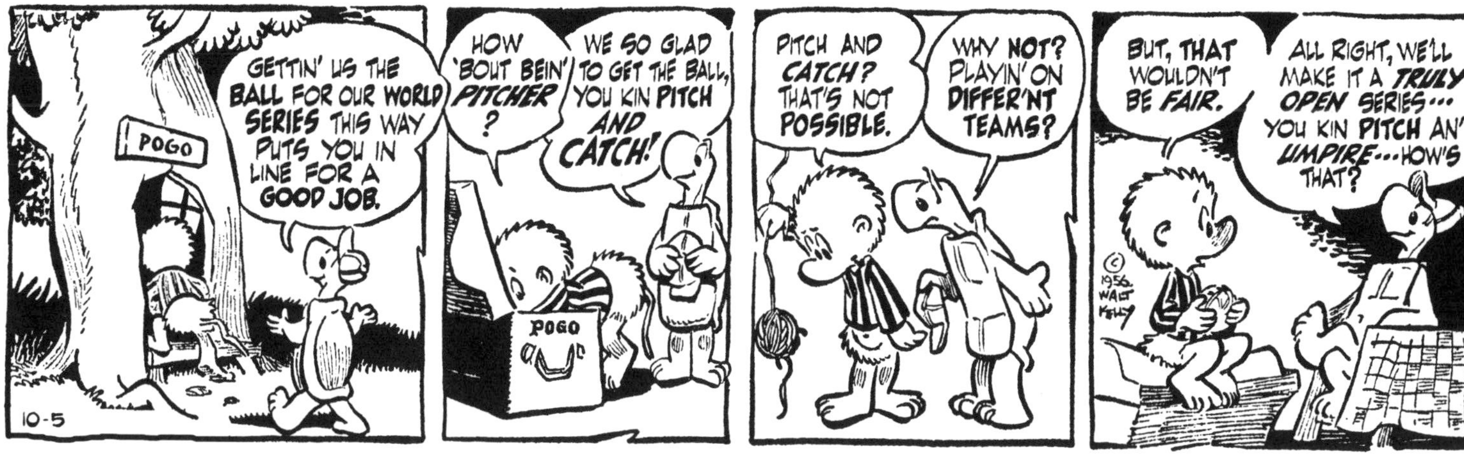
POGO
GETTIN' US THE BALL FOR OUR WORLD SERIES THIS WAY PUTS YOU IN LINE FOR A GOOD JOB.
10-5
HOW 'BOUT BEIN' PITCHER?
WE SO GLAD TO GET THE BALL, YOU KIN PITCH AND CATCH!
POGO
PITCH AND CATCH? THAT'S NOT POSSIBLE.
WHY NOT? PLAYIN' ON DIFFER'NT TEAMS?
BUT, THAT WOULDN'T BE FAIR.
ALL RIGHT, WE'LL MAKE IT A TRULY OPEN SERIES... YOU KIN PITCH AN' UMPIRE... HOW'S THAT?
© 1956 WALT KELLY

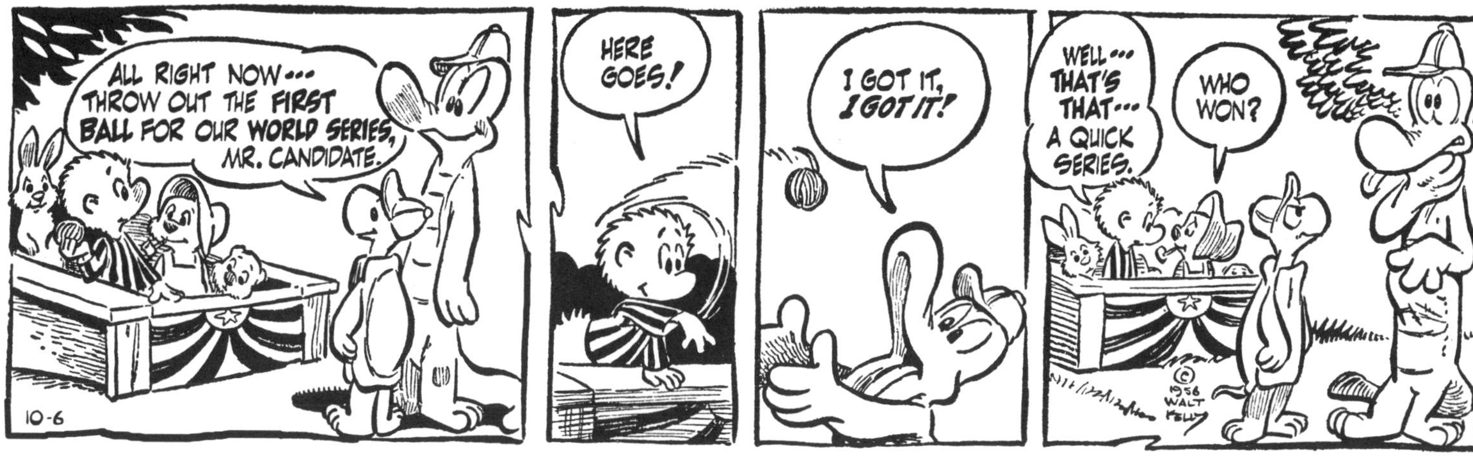
ALL RIGHT NOW... THROW OUT THE FIRST BALL FOR OUR WORLD SERIES, MR. CANDIDATE.
10-6
HERE GOES!
I GOT IT, I GOT IT!
WELL... THAT'S THAT... A QUICK SERIES.
WHO WON?
© 1956 WALT KELLY

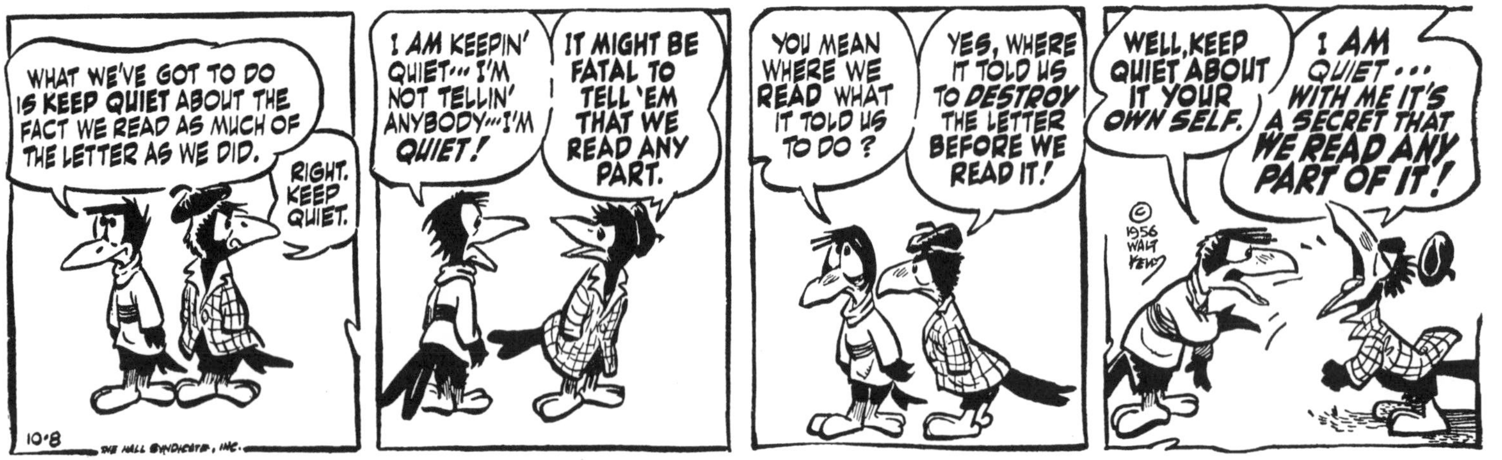
WHAT WE'VE GOT TO DO IS KEEP QUIET ABOUT THE FACT WE READ AS MUCH OF THE LETTER AS WE DID.
RIGHT. KEEP QUIET.
10-8
THE HALL SYNDICATE, INC.
I AM KEEPIN' QUIET... I'M NOT TELLIN' ANYBODY... I'M QUIET!
IT MIGHT BE FATAL TO TELL 'EM THAT WE READ ANY PART.
YOU MEAN WHERE WE READ WHAT IT TOLD US TO DO?
YES, WHERE IT TOLD US TO DESTROY THE LETTER BEFORE WE READ IT!
WELL, KEEP QUIET ABOUT IT YOUR OWN SELF.
I AM QUIET... WITH ME IT'S A SECRET THAT WE READ ANY PART OF IT!
© 1956 WALT KELLY

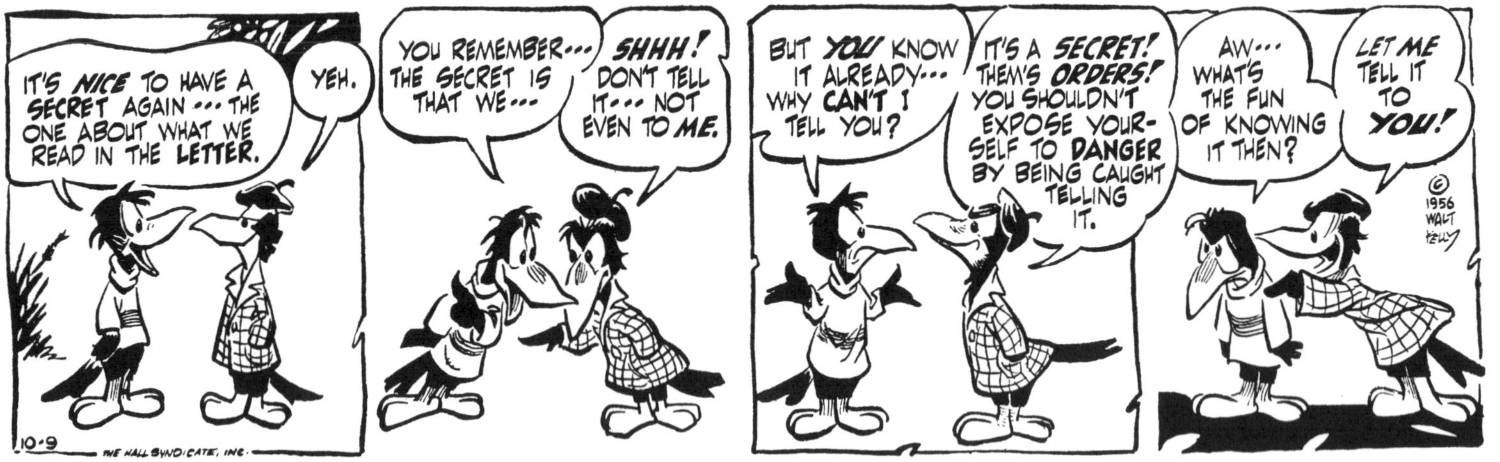
IT'S NICE TO HAVE A SECRET AGAIN... THE ONE ABOUT WHAT WE READ IN THE LETTER.
YEH.
10-9
THE HALL SYNDICATE, INC.
YOU REMEMBER... THE SECRET IS THAT WE...
SHHH! DON'T TELL IT... NOT EVEN TO ME.
BUT YOU KNOW IT ALREADY... WHY CAN'T I TELL YOU?
IT'S A SECRET! THEM'S ORDERS! YOU SHOULDN'T EXPOSE YOUR-SELF TO DANGER BY BEING CAUGHT TELLING IT.
AW... WHAT'S THE FUN OF KNOWING IT THEN?
LET ME TELL IT TO YOU!
© 1956 WALT KELLY

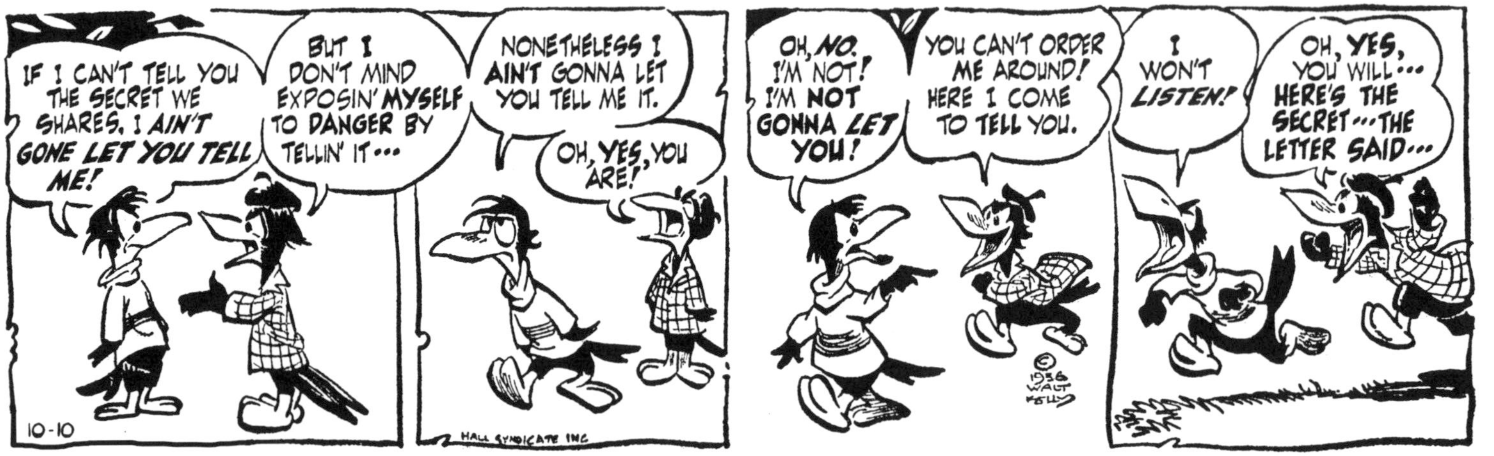
IF I CAN'T TELL YOU THE SECRET WE SHARES, I AIN'T GONE LET YOU TELL ME!
BUT I DON'T MIND EXPOSIN' MYSELF TO DANGER BY TELLIN' IT...
10-10
NONETHELESS I AIN'T GONNA LET YOU TELL ME IT.
OH, YES, YOU ARE!
HALL SYNDICATE INC
OH, NO, I'M NOT! I'M NOT GONNA LET YOU!
YOU CAN'T ORDER ME AROUND! HERE I COME TO TELL YOU.
© 1956 WALT KELLY
I WON'T LISTEN!
OH, YES, YOU WILL... HERE'S THE SECRET... THE LETTER SAID...

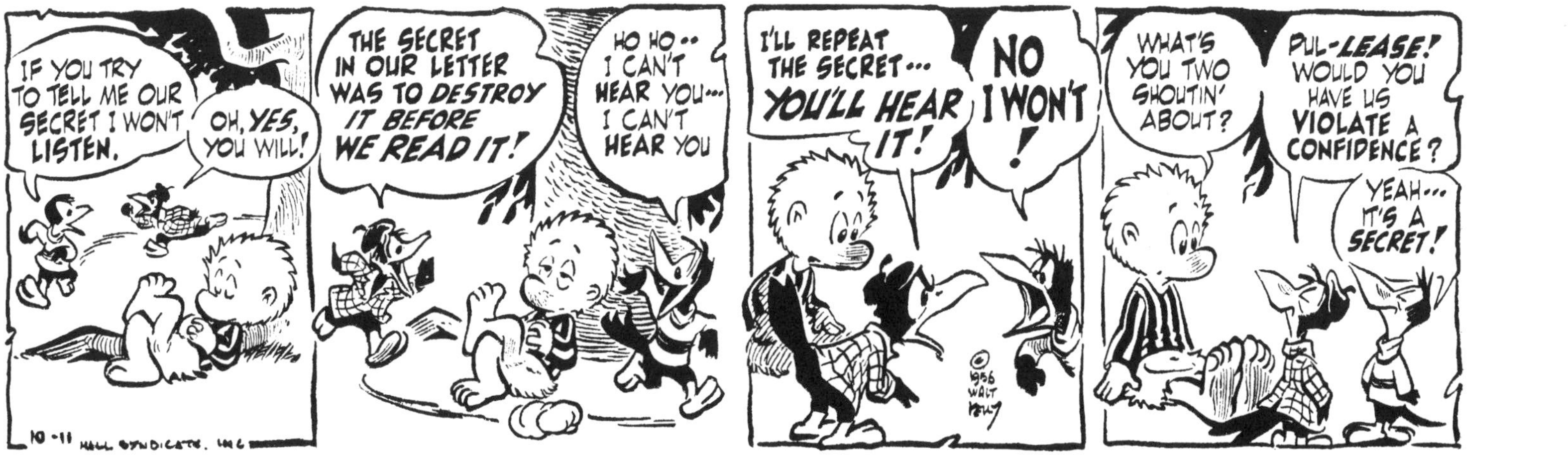
IF YOU TRY TO TELL ME OUR SECRET I WON'T LISTEN.
OH, YES, YOU WILL!
THE SECRET IN OUR LETTER WAS TO DESTROY IT BEFORE WE READ IT!
HO HO.. I CAN'T HEAR YOU... I CAN'T HEAR YOU
I'LL REPEAT THE SECRET... YOU'LL HEAR IT!
NO I WON'T!
WHAT'S YOU TWO SHOUTIN' ABOUT?
PUL-LEASE! WOULD YOU HAVE US VIOLATE A CONFIDENCE?
YEAH... IT'S A SECRET!
10-11 HALL SYNDICATE, INC
© 1956 WALT KELLY

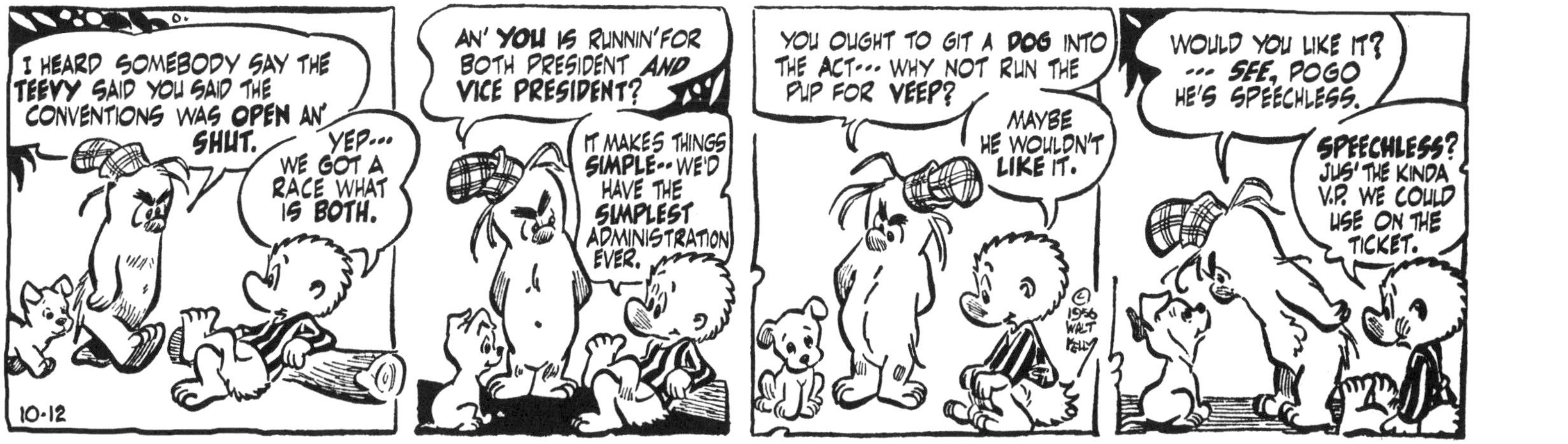
I HEARD SOMEBODY SAY THE TEEVY SAID YOU SAID THE CONVENTIONS WAS OPEN AN' SHUT.
YEP... WE GOT A RACE WHAT IS BOTH.
AN' YOU IS RUNNIN' FOR BOTH PRESIDENT AND VICE PRESIDENT?
IT MAKES THINGS SIMPLE.. WE'D HAVE THE SIMPLEST ADMINISTRATION EVER.
YOU OUGHT TO GIT A DOG INTO THE ACT... WHY NOT RUN THE PUP FOR VEEP?
MAYBE HE WOULDN'T LIKE IT.
WOULD YOU LIKE IT? ... SEE, POGO HE'S SPEECHLESS.
SPEECHLESS? JUS' THE KINDA V.P. WE COULD USE ON THE TICKET.
10-12
© 1956 WALT KELLY

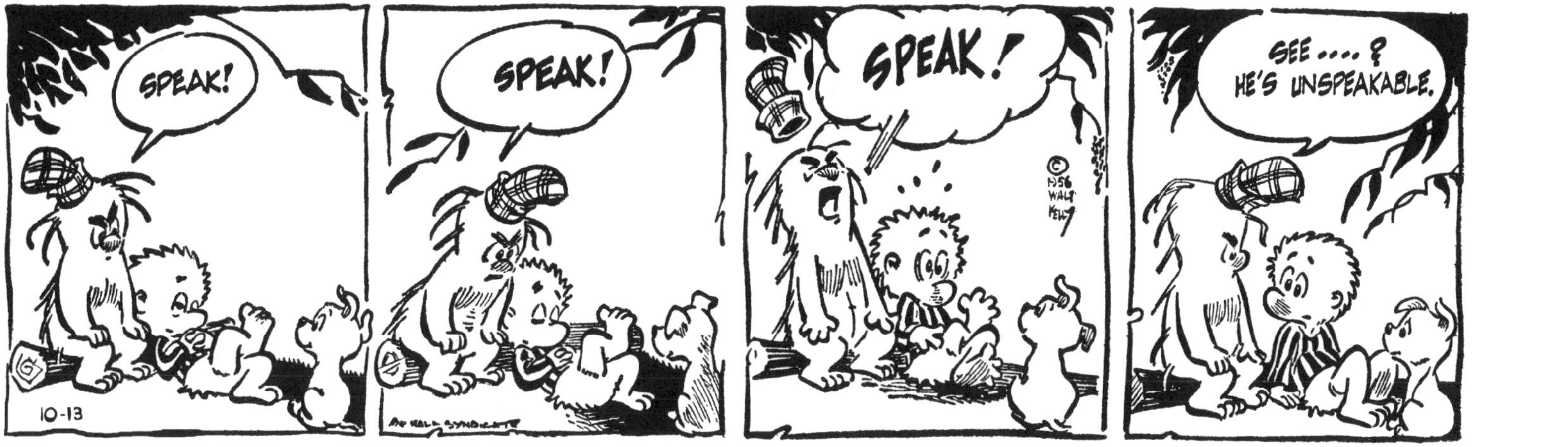
SPEAK!
SPEAK!
SPEAK!
SEE....? HE'S UNSPEAKABLE.
10-13
© 1956 WALT KELLY

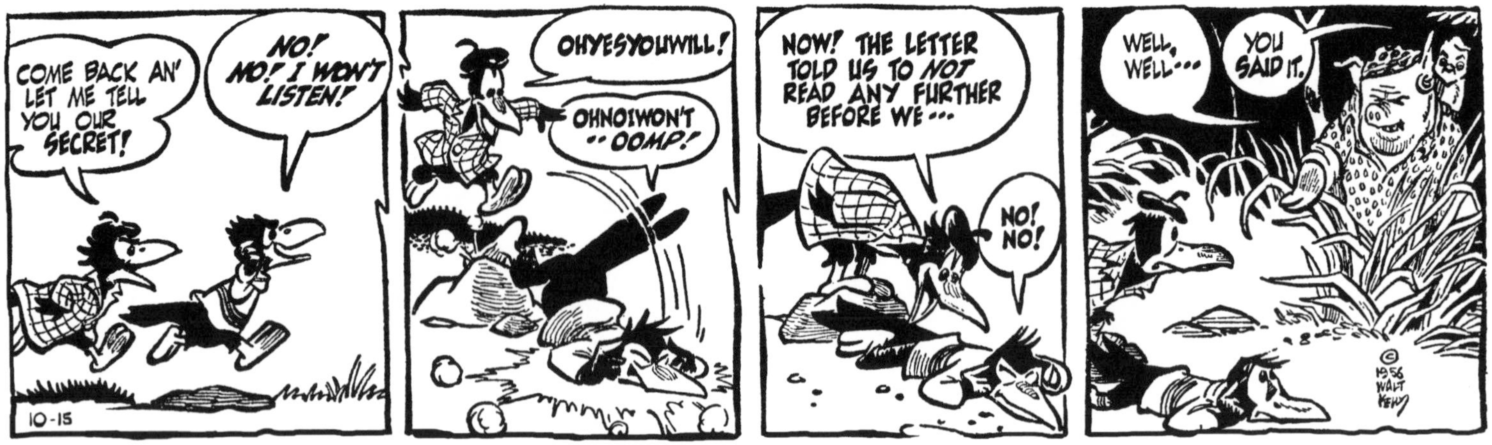
COME BACK AN' LET ME TELL YOU OUR SECRET!
NO! NO! I WON'T LISTEN!
10-15
OHYESYOUWILL!
OHNOIWON'T --OOMP!
NOW! THE LETTER TOLD US TO NOT READ ANY FURTHER BEFORE WE---
NO! NO!
WELL, WELL---
YOU SAID IT.
© 1956 WALT KELLY

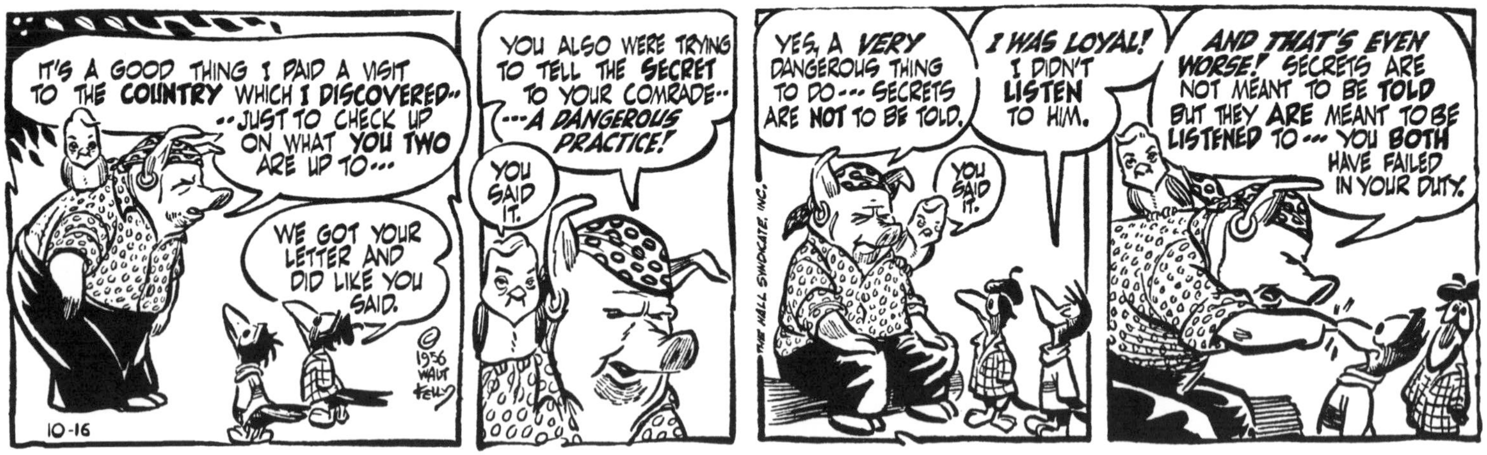
IT'S A GOOD THING I PAID A VISIT TO THE COUNTRY WHICH I DISCOVERED-- --JUST TO CHECK UP ON WHAT YOU TWO ARE UP TO---
WE GOT YOUR LETTER AND DID LIKE YOU SAID.
© 1956 WALT KELLY
10-16
YOU ALSO WERE TRYING TO TELL THE SECRET TO YOUR COMRADE-- ---A DANGEROUS PRACTICE!
YOU SAID IT.
THE HALL SYNDICATE, INC.
YES, A VERY DANGEROUS THING TO DO--- SECRETS ARE NOT TO BE TOLD.
YOU SAID IT.
I WAS LOYAL! I DIDN'T LISTEN TO HIM.
AND THAT'S EVEN WORSE! SECRETS ARE NOT MEANT TO BE TOLD BUT THEY ARE MEANT TO BE LISTENED TO--- YOU BOTH HAVE FAILED IN YOUR DUTY.

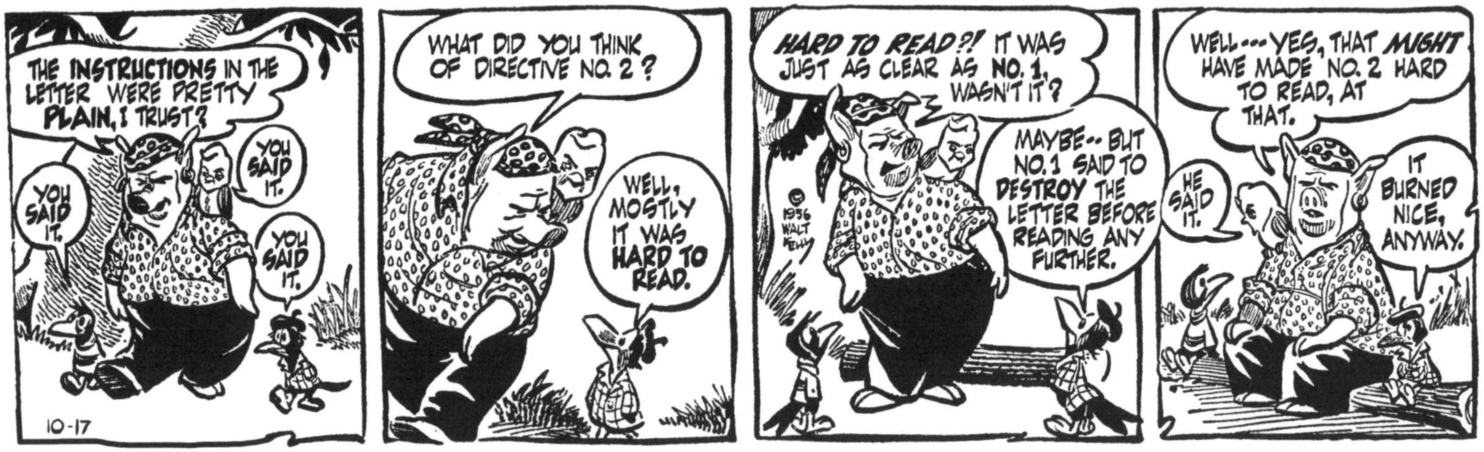
THE INSTRUCTIONS IN THE LETTER WERE PRETTY PLAIN, I TRUST?
YOU SAID IT.
YOU SAID IT.
YOU SAID IT.
10-17
WHAT DID YOU THINK OF DIRECTIVE NO. 2?
WELL, MOSTLY IT WAS HARD TO READ.
HARD TO READ?! IT WAS JUST AS CLEAR AS NO. 1, WASN'T IT?
MAYBE-- BUT NO. 1 SAID TO DESTROY THE LETTER BEFORE READING ANY FURTHER.
© 1956 WALT KELLY
WELL---YES, THAT MIGHT HAVE MADE NO. 2 HARD TO READ, AT THAT.
HE SAID IT.
IT BURNED NICE, ANYWAY.

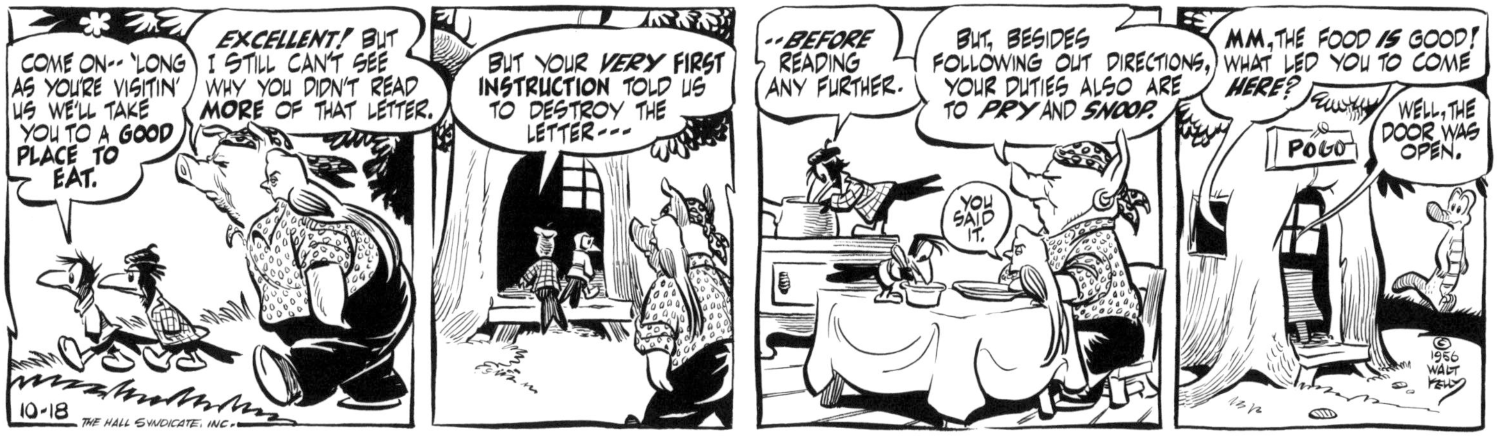
COME ON-- 'LONG AS YOU'RE VISITIN' US WE'LL TAKE YOU TO A GOOD PLACE TO EAT.
EXCELLENT! BUT I STILL CAN'T SEE WHY YOU DIDN'T READ MORE OF THAT LETTER.
BUT YOUR VERY FIRST INSTRUCTION TOLD US TO DESTROY THE LETTER---
--BEFORE READING ANY FURTHER.
BUT, BESIDES FOLLOWING OUT DIRECTIONS, YOUR DUTIES ALSO ARE TO PRY AND SNOOP.
YOU SAID IT.
MM, THE FOOD IS GOOD! WHAT LED YOU TO COME HERE?
POGO
WELL, THE DOOR WAS OPEN.
10-18
THE HALL SYNDICATE, INC.
© 1956 WALT KELLY

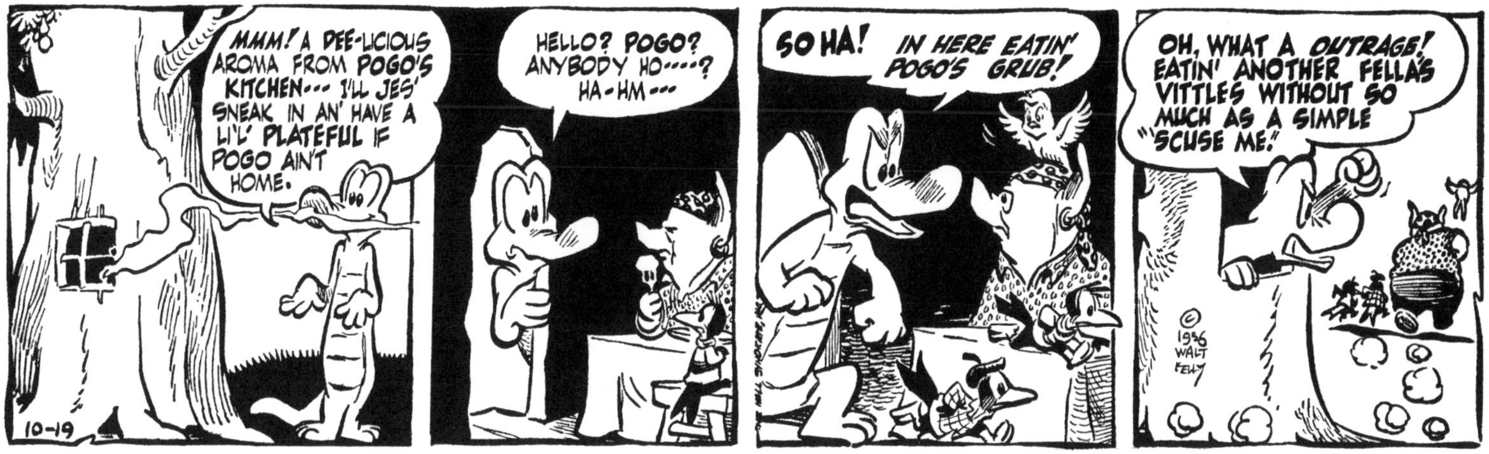
MMM! A DEE-LICIOUS AROMA FROM POGO'S KITCHEN--- I'LL JES' SNEAK IN AN' HAVE A LI'L' PLATEFUL IF POGO AIN'T HOME.
10-19
HELLO? POGO? ANYBODY HO----? HA-HM---
SO HA!
IN HERE EATIN' POGO'S GRUB!
OH, WHAT A OUTRAGE! EATIN' ANOTHER FELLA'S VITTLES WITHOUT SO MUCH AS A SIMPLE "SCUSE ME."
© 1956 WALT KELLY

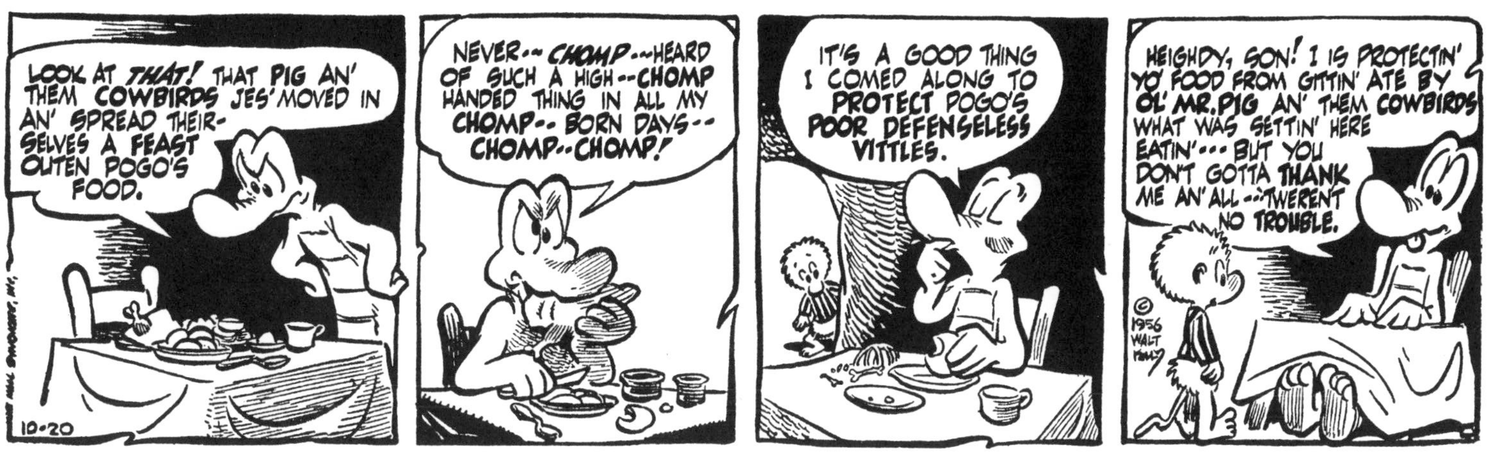
LOOK AT THAT! THAT PIG AN' THEM COWBIRDS JES' MOVED IN AN' SPREAD THEIR-SELVES A FEAST OUTEN POGO'S FOOD.
10-20
NEVER--CHOMP--HEARD OF SUCH A HIGH--CHOMP HANDED THING IN ALL MY CHOMP-- BORN DAYS-- CHOMP--CHOMP!
IT'S A GOOD THING I COMED ALONG TO PROTECT POGO'S POOR DEFENSELESS VITTLES.
HEIGHDY, SON! I IS PROTECTIN' YO' FOOD FROM GITTIN' ATE BY OL' MR. PIG AN' THEM COWBIRDS WHAT WAS GETTIN' HERE EATIN'--- BUT YOU DON'T GOTTA THANK ME AN' ALL--'TWERENT NO TROUBLE.
© 1956 WALT KELLY

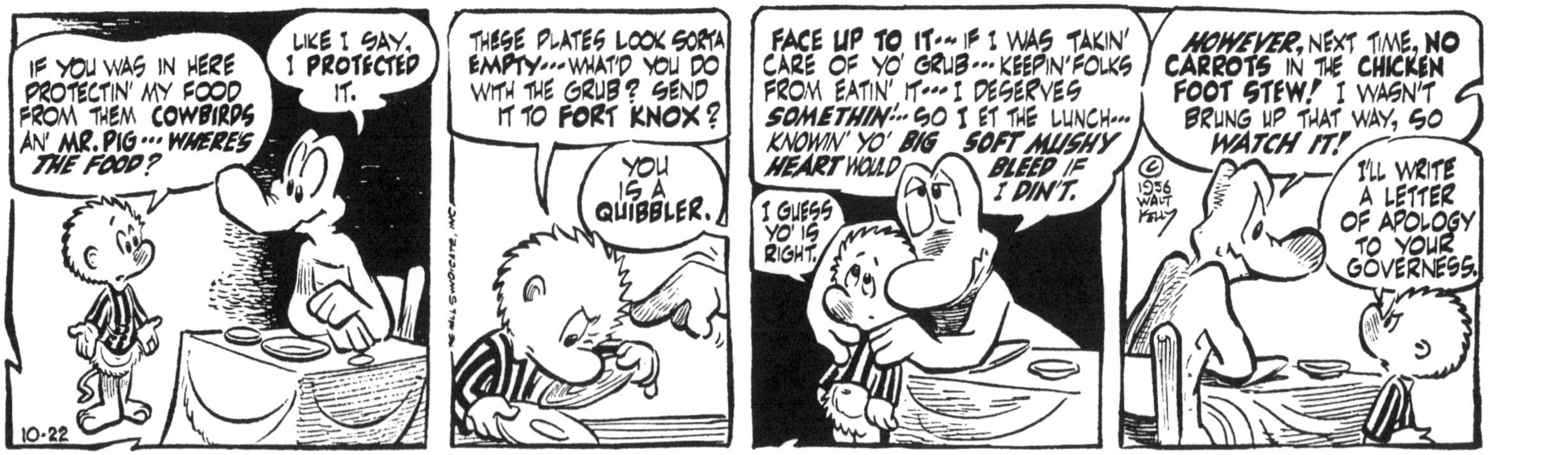
IF YOU WAS IN HERE PROTECTIN' MY FOOD FROM THEM COWBIRDS AN' MR. PIG··· WHERE'S THE FOOD?
LIKE I SAY, I PROTECTED IT.
10-22
THESE PLATES LOOK SORTA EMPTY··· WHAT'D YOU DO WITH THE GRUB? SEND IT TO FORT KNOX?
YOU IS A QUIBBLER.
FACE UP TO IT··· IF I WAS TAKIN' CARE OF YO' GRUB··· KEEPIN' FOLKS FROM EATIN' IT··· I DESERVES SOMETHIN'··· SO I ET THE LUNCH··· KNOWIN' YO' BIG SOFT MUSHY HEART WOULD BLEED IF I DIN'T.
I GUESS YO' IS RIGHT.
HOWEVER, NEXT TIME, NO CARROTS IN THE CHICKEN FOOT STEW! I WASN'T BRUNG UP THAT WAY, SO WATCH IT!
I'LL WRITE A LETTER OF APOLOGY TO YOUR GOVERNESS.
© 1956 WALT KELLY

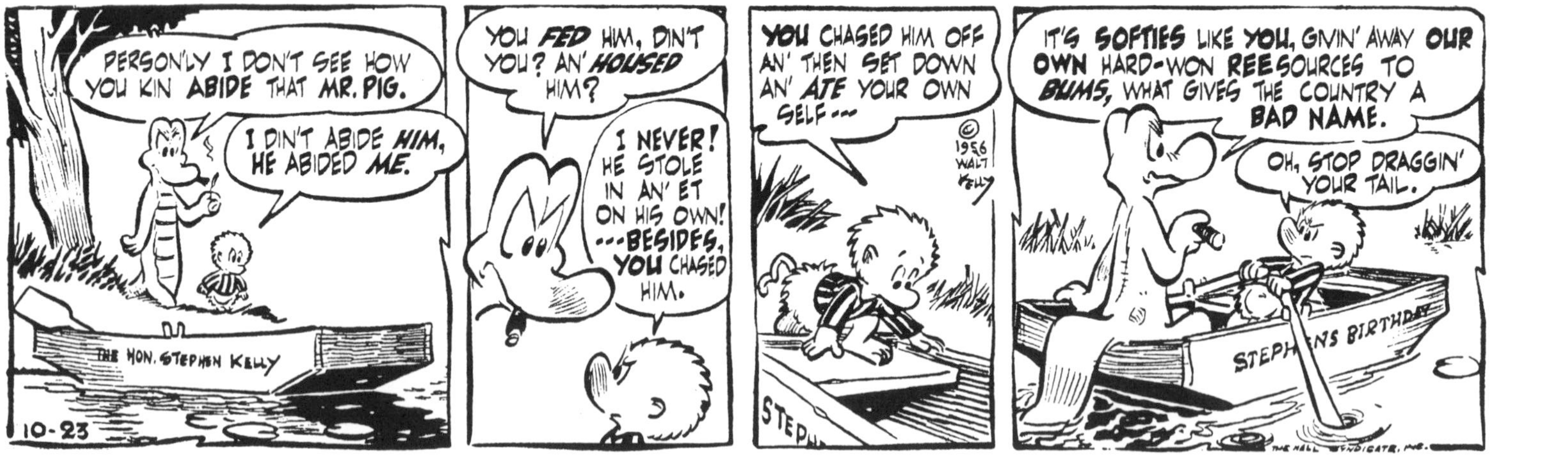
PERSON'LY I DON'T SEE HOW YOU KIN ABIDE THAT MR. PIG.
I DIN'T ABIDE HIM, HE ABIDED ME.
THE HON. STEPHEN KELLY
10-23
YOU FED HIM, DIN'T YOU? AN' HOUSED HIM?
I NEVER! HE STOLE IN AN' ET ON HIS OWN! ···BESIDES, YOU CHASED HIM.
YOU CHASED HIM OFF AN' THEN SET DOWN AN' ATE YOUR OWN SELF···
© 1956 WALT KELLY
IT'S SOFTIES LIKE YOU, GIVIN' AWAY OUR OWN HARD-WON REESOURCES TO BUMS, WHAT GIVES THE COUNTRY A BAD NAME.
OH, STOP DRAGGIN' YOUR TAIL.
STEPHENS BIRTHDAY

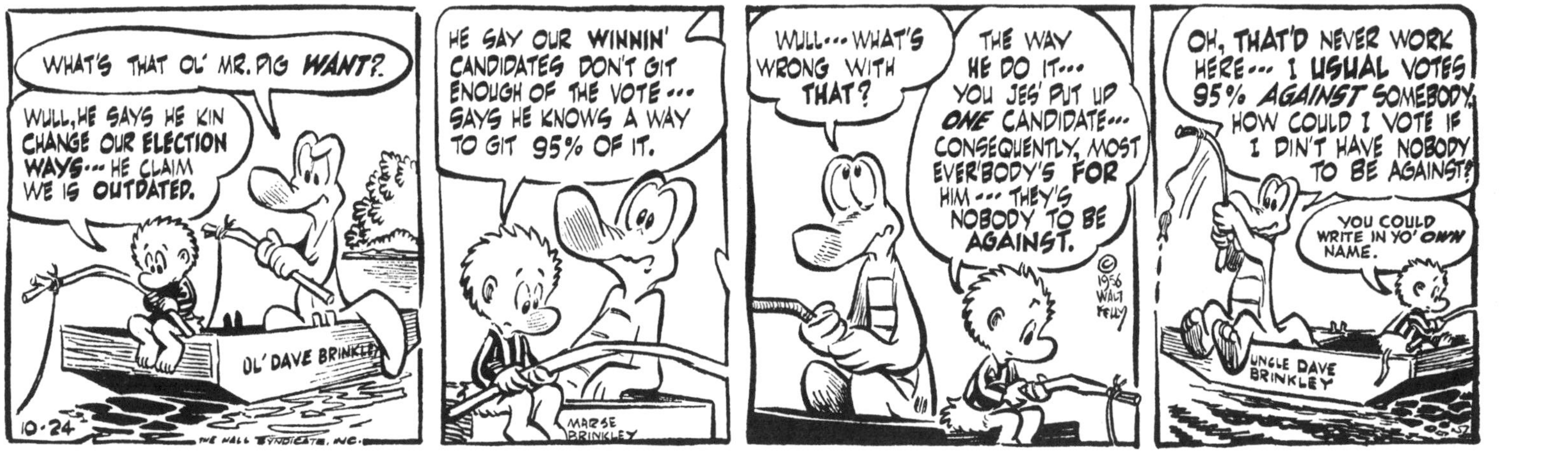
WHAT'S THAT OL' MR. PIG WANT?
WULL, HE SAYS HE KIN CHANGE OUR ELECTION WAYS··· HE CLAIM WE IS OUTDATED.
OL' DAVE BRINKLEY
10-24
HE SAY OUR WINNIN' CANDIDATES DON'T GIT ENOUGH OF THE VOTE··· SAYS HE KNOWS A WAY TO GIT 95% OF IT.
MARSE BRINKLEY
WULL··· WHAT'S WRONG WITH THAT?
THE WAY HE DO IT··· YOU JES' PUT UP ONE CANDIDATE··· CONSEQUENTLY, MOST EVER'BODY'S FOR HIM··· THEY'S NOBODY TO BE AGAINST.
© 1956 WALT KELLY
OH, THAT'D NEVER WORK HERE··· I USUAL VOTES 95% AGAINST SOMEBODY. HOW COULD I VOTE IF I DIN'T HAVE NOBODY TO BE AGAINST?
YOU COULD WRITE IN YO' OWN NAME.
UNCLE DAVE BRINKLEY

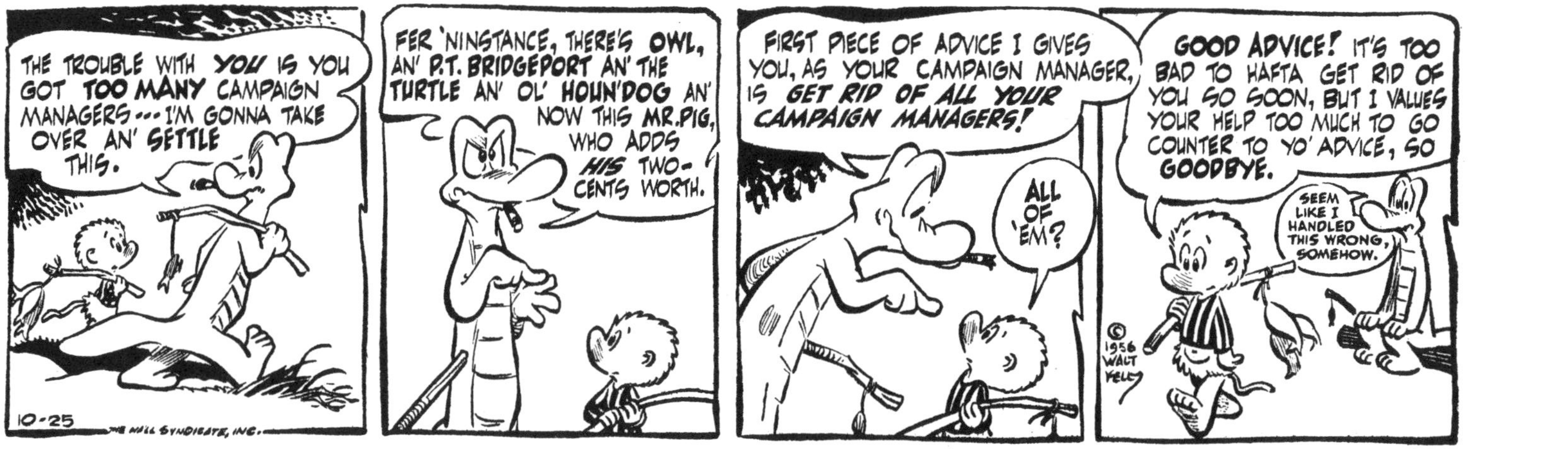
THE TROUBLE WITH YOU IS YOU GOT TOO MANY CAMPAIGN MANAGERS --- I'M GONNA TAKE OVER AN' SETTLE THIS.
10-25
THE HALL SYNDICATE, INC.
FER 'NINSTANCE, THERE'S OWL, AN' P.T. BRIDGEPORT AN' THE TURTLE AN' OL' HOUN'DOG AN' NOW THIS MR. PIG, WHO ADDS HIS TWO-CENTS WORTH.
FIRST PIECE OF ADVICE I GIVES YOU, AS YOUR CAMPAIGN MANAGER, IS GET RID OF ALL YOUR CAMPAIGN MANAGERS!
ALL OF 'EM?
GOOD ADVICE! IT'S TOO BAD TO HAFTA GET RID OF YOU SO SOON, BUT I VALUES YOUR HELP TOO MUCH TO GO COUNTER TO YO' ADVICE, SO GOODBYE.
SEEM LIKE I HANDLED THIS WRONG, SOMEHOW.
© 1956 WALT KELLY

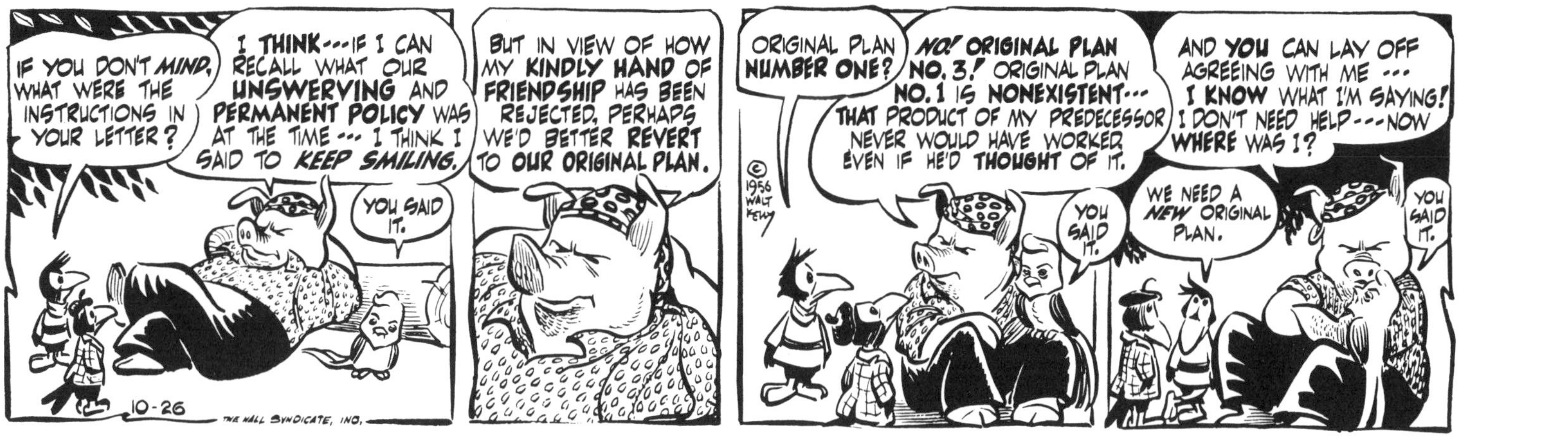
IF YOU DON'T MIND, WHAT WERE THE INSTRUCTIONS IN YOUR LETTER?
I THINK --- IF I CAN RECALL WHAT OUR UNSWERVING AND PERMANENT POLICY WAS AT THE TIME --- I THINK I SAID TO KEEP SMILING.
YOU SAID IT.
10-26
THE HALL SYNDICATE, INC.
BUT IN VIEW OF HOW MY KINDLY HAND OF FRIENDSHIP HAS BEEN REJECTED, PERHAPS WE'D BETTER REVERT TO OUR ORIGINAL PLAN.
ORIGINAL PLAN NUMBER ONE?
NO! ORIGINAL PLAN NO. 3! ORIGINAL PLAN NO. 1 IS NONEXISTENT --- THAT PRODUCT OF MY PREDECESSOR NEVER WOULD HAVE WORKED EVEN IF HE'D THOUGHT OF IT.
YOU SAID IT.
© 1956 WALT KELLY
AND YOU CAN LAY OFF AGREEING WITH ME --- I KNOW WHAT I'M SAYING! I DON'T NEED HELP --- NOW WHERE WAS I?
WE NEED A NEW ORIGINAL PLAN.
YOU SAID IT.

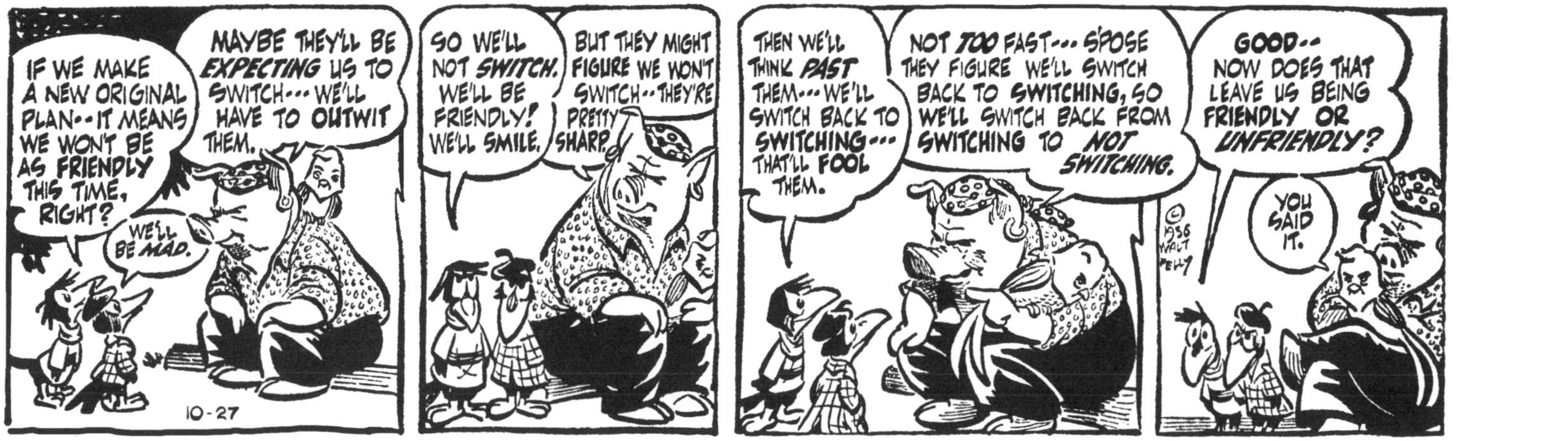
IF WE MAKE A NEW ORIGINAL PLAN -- IT MEANS WE WON'T BE AS FRIENDLY THIS TIME, RIGHT?
MAYBE THEY'LL BE EXPECTING US TO SWITCH --- WE'LL HAVE TO OUTWIT THEM.
WE'LL BE MAD.
10-27
SO WE'LL NOT SWITCH. WE'LL BE FRIENDLY! WE'LL SMILE.
BUT THEY MIGHT FIGURE WE WON'T SWITCH -- THEY'RE PRETTY SHARP.
THEN WE'LL THINK PAST THEM --- WE'LL SWITCH BACK TO SWITCHING --- THAT'LL FOOL THEM.
NOT TOO FAST --- S'POSE THEY FIGURE WE'LL SWITCH BACK TO SWITCHING, SO WE'LL SWITCH BACK FROM SWITCHING TO NOT SWITCHING.
© 1956 WALT KELLY
GOOD -- NOW DOES THAT LEAVE US BEING FRIENDLY OR UNFRIENDLY?
YOU SAID IT.

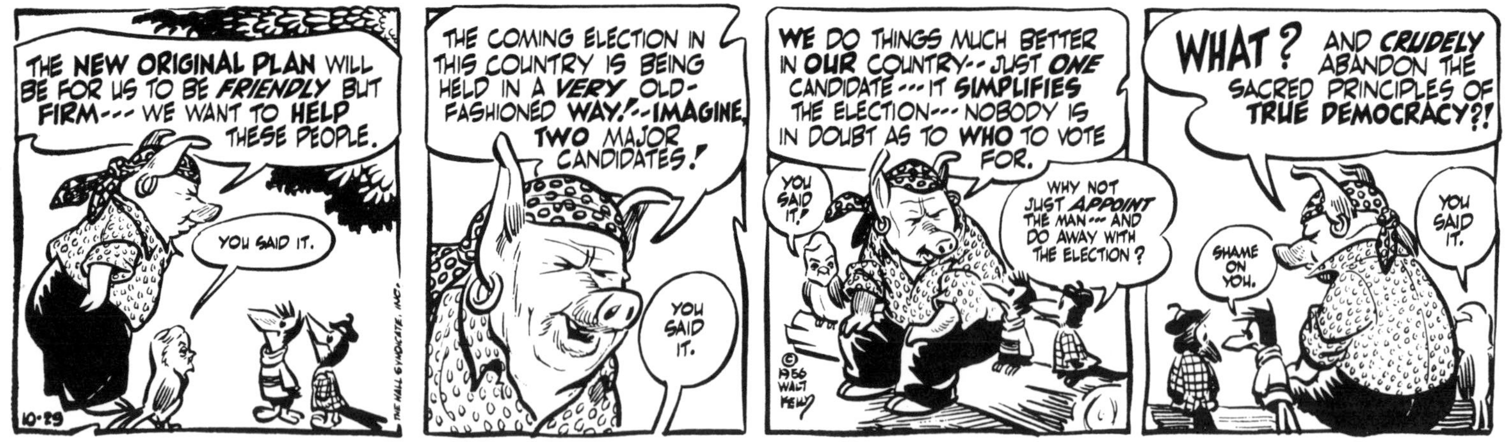
THE NEW ORIGINAL PLAN WILL BE FOR US TO BE FRIENDLY BUT FIRM--- WE WANT TO HELP THESE PEOPLE.
YOU SAID IT.
10-29
THE HALL SYNDICATE, INC.
THE COMING ELECTION IN THIS COUNTRY IS BEING HELD IN A VERY OLD-FASHIONED WAY!--IMAGINE, TWO MAJOR CANDIDATES!
YOU SAID IT.
WE DO THINGS MUCH BETTER IN OUR COUNTRY-- JUST ONE CANDIDATE--- IT SIMPLIFIES THE ELECTION--- NOBODY IS IN DOUBT AS TO WHO TO VOTE FOR.
YOU SAID IT.
WHY NOT JUST APPOINT THE MAN--- AND DO AWAY WITH THE ELECTION?
© 1956 WALT KELLY
WHAT? AND CRUDELY ABANDON THE SACRED PRINCIPLES OF TRUE DEMOCRACY?!
SHAME ON YOU.
YOU SAID IT.

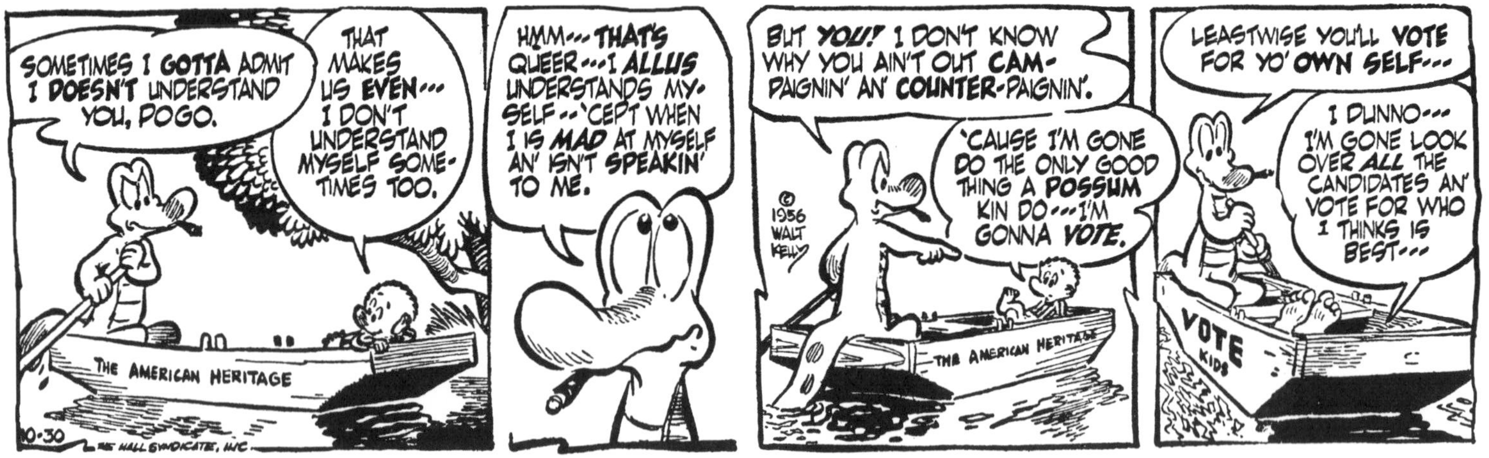
SOMETIMES I GOTTA ADMIT I DOESN'T UNDERSTAND YOU, POGO.
THAT MAKES US EVEN--- I DON'T UNDERSTAND MYSELF SOMETIMES TOO.
THE AMERICAN HERITAGE
10-30
THE HALL SYNDICATE, INC.
HMM--- THAT'S QUEER---I ALLUS UNDERSTANDS MYSELF--'CEPT WHEN I IS MAD AT MYSELF AN' ISN'T SPEAKIN' TO ME.
BUT YOU! I DON'T KNOW WHY YOU AIN'T OUT CAMPAIGNIN' AN' COUNTER-PAIGNIN'.
'CAUSE I'M GONE DO THE ONLY GOOD THING A POSSUM KIN DO---I'M GONNA VOTE.
© 1956 WALT KELLY
THE AMERICAN HERITAGE
LEASTWISE YOU'LL VOTE FOR YO' OWN SELF---
I DUNNO--- I'M GONE LOOK OVER ALL THE CANDIDATES AN' VOTE FOR WHO I THINKS IS BEST---
VOTE KIDS

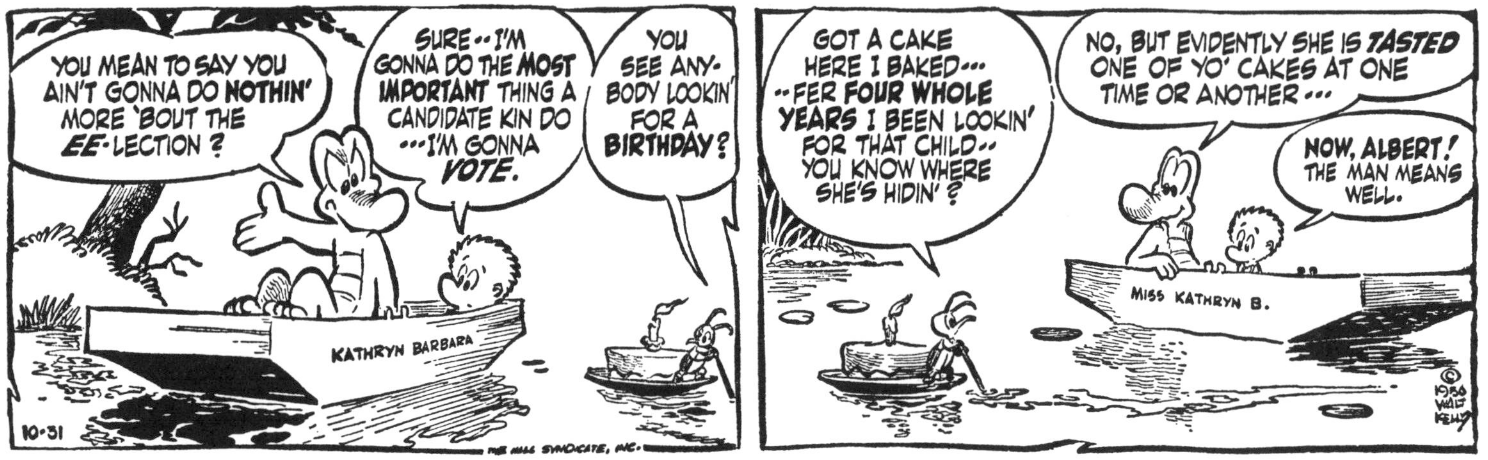
YOU MEAN TO SAY YOU AIN'T GONNA DO NOTHIN' MORE 'BOUT THE EE-LECTION?
SURE--I'M GONNA DO THE MOST IMPORTANT THING A CANDIDATE KIN DO ---I'M GONNA VOTE.
YOU SEE ANYBODY LOOKIN' FOR A BIRTHDAY?
KATHRYN BARBARA
10-31
THE HALL SYNDICATE, INC.
GOT A CAKE HERE I BAKED--- --FER FOUR WHOLE YEARS I BEEN LOOKIN' FOR THAT CHILD-- YOU KNOW WHERE SHE'S HIDIN'?
NO, BUT EVIDENTLY SHE IS TASTED ONE OF YO' CAKES AT ONE TIME OR ANOTHER ---
NOW, ALBERT! THE MAN MEANS WELL.
MISS KATHRYN B.
© 1956 WALT KELLY

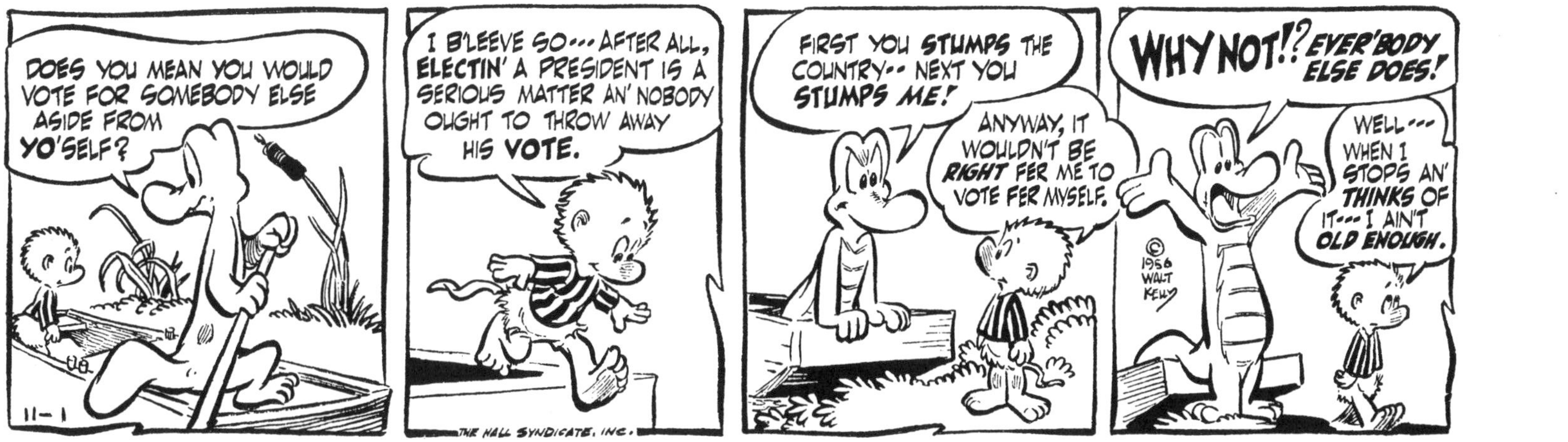
DOES YOU MEAN YOU WOULD VOTE FOR SOMEBODY ELSE ASIDE FROM YO'SELF?
11-1
I B'LEEVE SO... AFTER ALL, ELECTIN' A PRESIDENT IS A SERIOUS MATTER AN' NOBODY OUGHT TO THROW AWAY HIS VOTE.
THE HALL SYNDICATE, INC.
FIRST YOU STUMPS THE COUNTRY-- NEXT YOU STUMPS ME!
ANYWAY, IT WOULDN'T BE RIGHT FER ME TO VOTE FER MYSELF.
WHY NOT!? EVER'BODY ELSE DOES!
WELL--- WHEN I STOPS AN' THINKS OF IT--- I AIN'T OLD ENOUGH.
© 1956 WALT KELLY

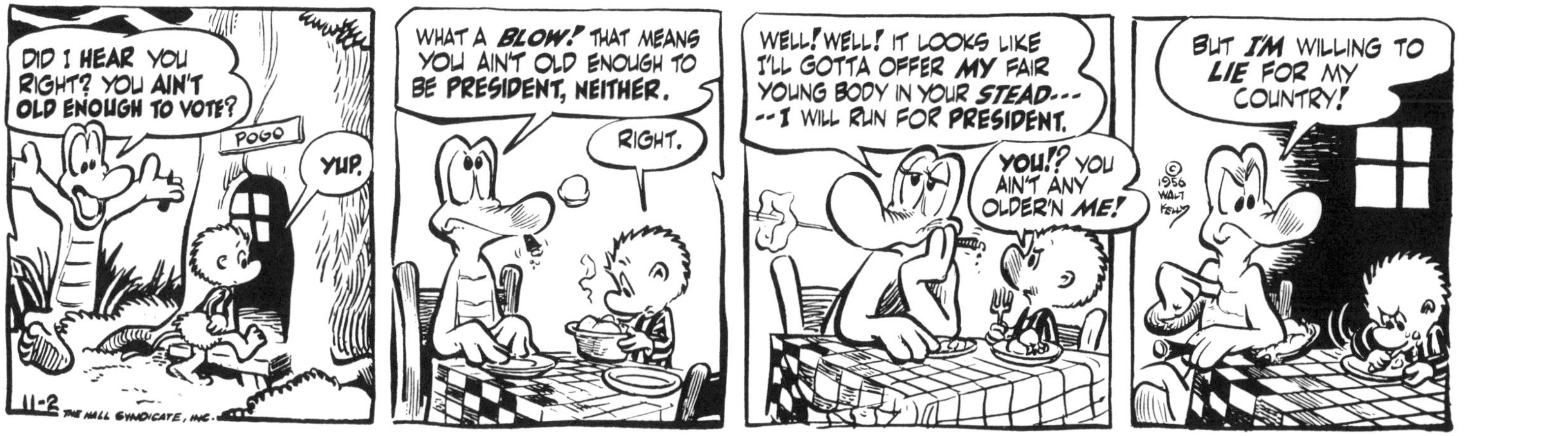
DID I HEAR YOU RIGHT? YOU AIN'T OLD ENOUGH TO VOTE?
POGO
YUP.
11-2 THE HALL SYNDICATE, INC.
WHAT A BLOW! THAT MEANS YOU AIN'T OLD ENOUGH TO BE PRESIDENT, NEITHER.
RIGHT.
WELL! WELL! IT LOOKS LIKE I'LL GOTTA OFFER MY FAIR YOUNG BODY IN YOUR STEAD--- --I WILL RUN FOR PRESIDENT.
YOU!? YOU AIN'T ANY OLDER'N ME!
© 1956 WALT KELLY
BUT I'M WILLING TO LIE FOR MY COUNTRY!

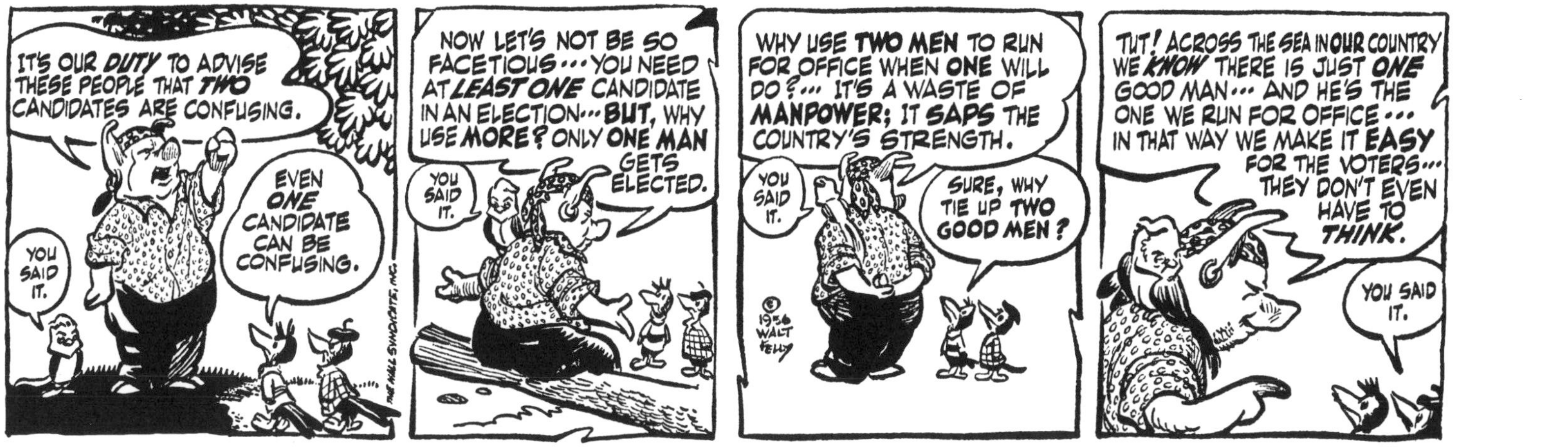
IT'S OUR DUTY TO ADVISE THESE PEOPLE THAT TWO CANDIDATES ARE CONFUSING.
YOU SAID IT.
EVEN ONE CANDIDATE CAN BE CONFUSING.
THE HALL SYNDICATE, INC.
NOW LET'S NOT BE SO FACETIOUS... YOU NEED AT LEAST ONE CANDIDATE IN AN ELECTION... BUT, WHY USE MORE? ONLY ONE MAN GETS ELECTED.
YOU SAID IT.
WHY USE TWO MEN TO RUN FOR OFFICE WHEN ONE WILL DO?... IT'S A WASTE OF MANPOWER; IT SAPS THE COUNTRY'S STRENGTH.
YOU SAID IT.
SURE, WHY TIE UP TWO GOOD MEN?
© 1956 WALT KELLY
TUT! ACROSS THE SEA IN OUR COUNTRY WE KNOW THERE IS JUST ONE GOOD MAN... AND HE'S THE ONE WE RUN FOR OFFICE... IN THAT WAY WE MAKE IT EASY FOR THE VOTERS... THEY DON'T EVEN HAVE TO THINK.
YOU SAID IT.

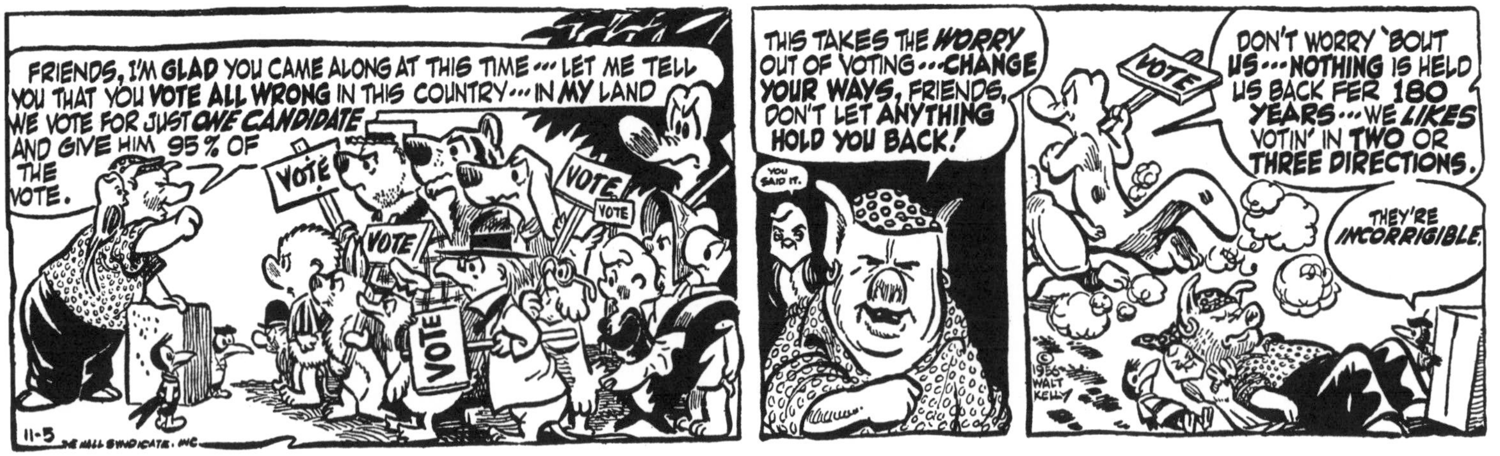
FRIENDS, I'M GLAD YOU CAME ALONG AT THIS TIME ··· LET ME TELL YOU THAT YOU VOTE ALL WRONG IN THIS COUNTRY ··· IN MY LAND WE VOTE FOR JUST ONE CANDIDATE AND GIVE HIM 95% OF THE VOTE.
VOTE
THIS TAKES THE WORRY OUT OF VOTING ··· CHANGE YOUR WAYS, FRIENDS, DON'T LET ANYTHING HOLD YOU BACK!
YOU SAID IT.
DON'T WORRY 'BOUT US ··· NOTHING IS HELD US BACK FER 180 YEARS ··· WE LIKES VOTIN' IN TWO OR THREE DIRECTIONS.
THEY'RE INCORRIGIBLE.
© 1956 WALT KELLY
11-5

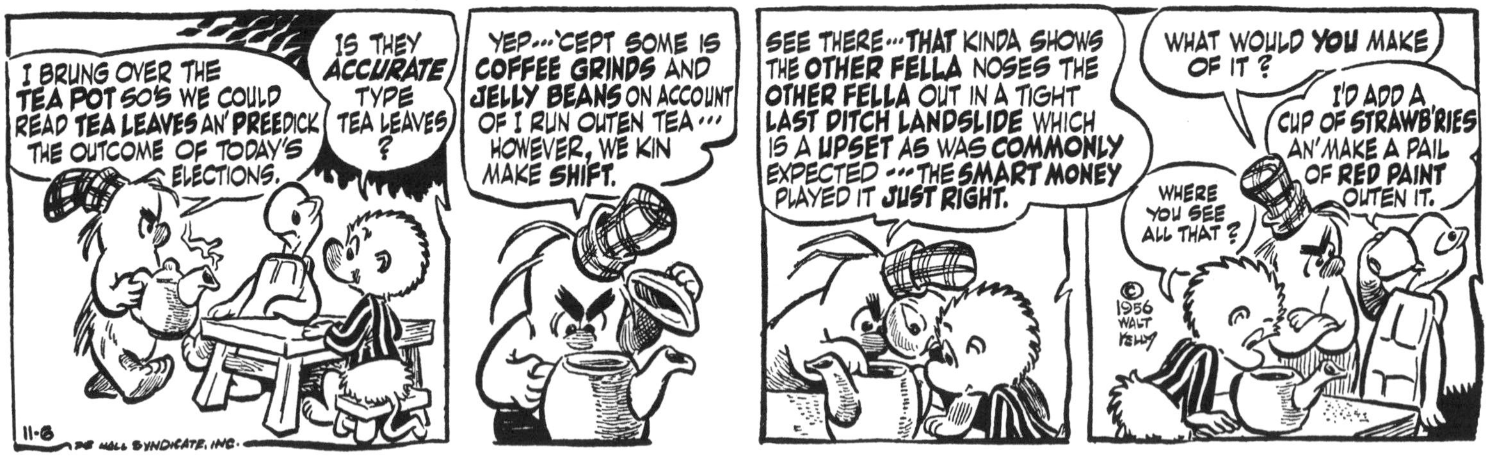
I BRUNG OVER THE TEA POT SO'S WE COULD READ TEA LEAVES AN' PREEDICK THE OUTCOME OF TODAY'S ELECTIONS.
IS THEY ACCURATE TYPE TEA LEAVES?
YEP··· 'CEPT SOME IS COFFEE GRINDS AND JELLY BEANS ON ACCOUNT OF I RUN OUTEN TEA··· HOWEVER, WE KIN MAKE SHIFT.
SEE THERE··· THAT KINDA SHOWS THE OTHER FELLA NOSES THE OTHER FELLA OUT IN A TIGHT LAST DITCH LANDSLIDE WHICH IS A UPSET AS WAS COMMONLY EXPECTED ··· THE SMART MONEY PLAYED IT JUST RIGHT.
WHAT WOULD YOU MAKE OF IT?
I'D ADD A CUP OF STRAWB'RIES AN' MAKE A PAIL OF RED PAINT OUTEN IT.
WHERE YOU SEE ALL THAT?
© 1956 WALT KELLY
11-6

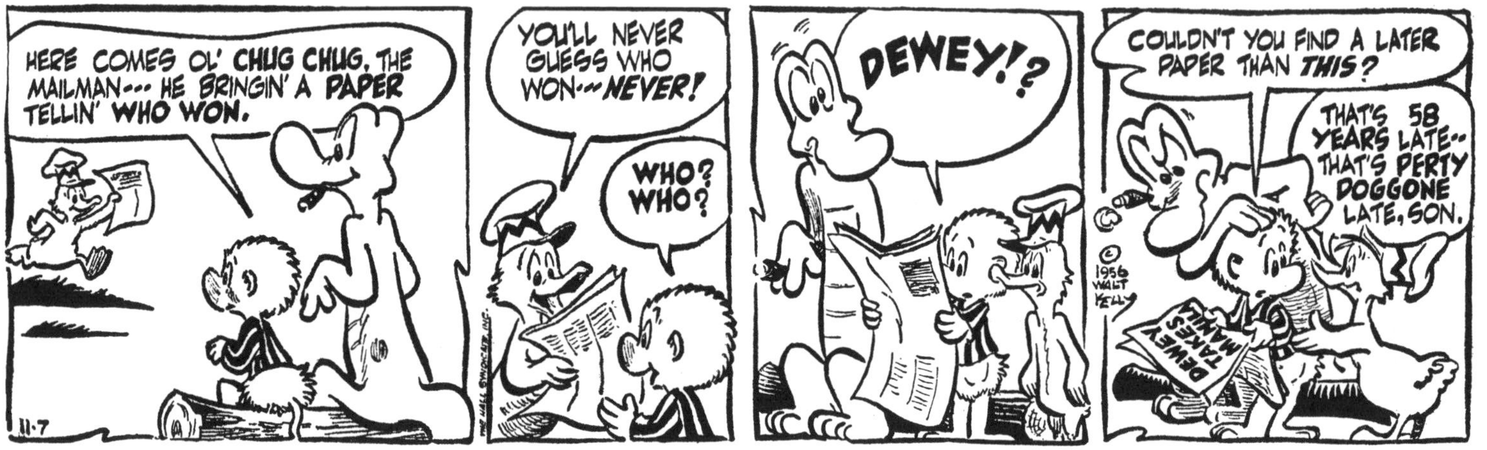
HERE COMES OL' CHUG CHUG, THE MAILMAN··· HE BRINGIN' A PAPER TELLIN' WHO WON.
YOU'LL NEVER GUESS WHO WON··· NEVER!
WHO? WHO?
DEWEY!?
COULDN'T YOU FIND A LATER PAPER THAN THIS?
THAT'S 58 YEARS LATE·· THAT'S PERTY DOGGONE LATE, SON.
DEWEY TAKES MANILA
© 1956 WALT KELLY
11-7

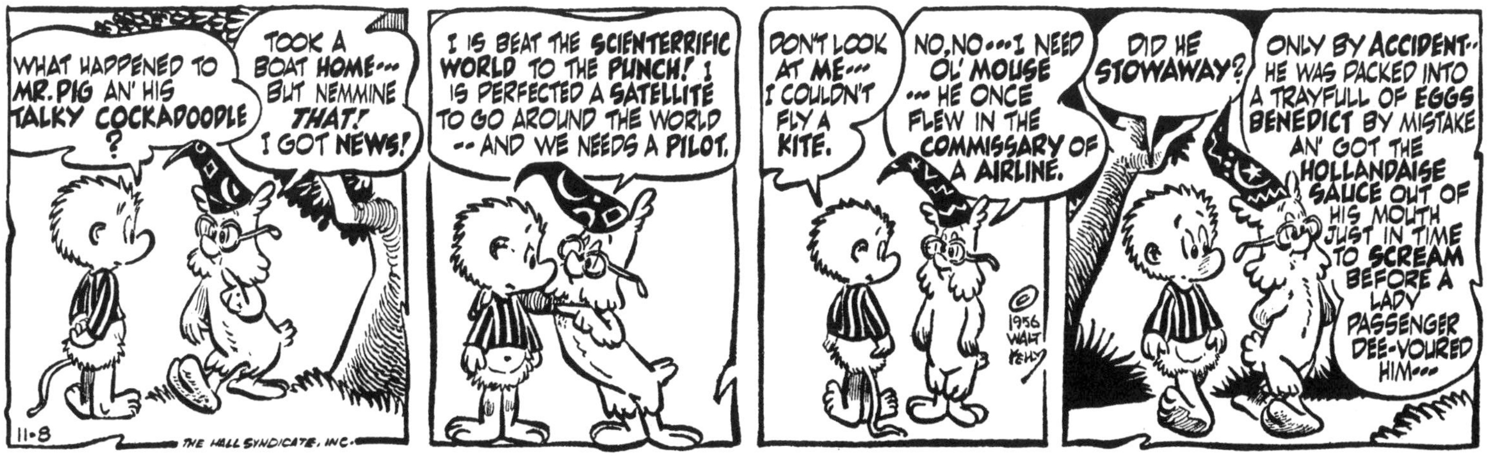
WHAT HAPPENED TO MR. PIG AN' HIS TALKY COCKADOODLE ?
TOOK A BOAT HOME... BUT NEMMINE THAT! I GOT NEWS!
I IS BEAT THE SCIENTERRIFIC WORLD TO THE PUNCH! I IS PERFECTED A SATELLITE TO GO AROUND THE WORLD --AND WE NEEDS A PILOT.
DON'T LOOK AT ME... I COULDN'T FLY A KITE.
NO, NO...I NEED OL' MOUSE ...HE ONCE FLEW IN THE COMMISSARY OF A AIRLINE.
DID HE STOWAWAY?
ONLY BY ACCIDENT.. HE WAS PACKED INTO A TRAYFULL OF EGGS BENEDICT BY MISTAKE AN' GOT THE HOLLANDAISE SAUCE OUT OF HIS MOUTH JUST IN TIME TO SCREAM BEFORE A LADY PASSENGER DEE-VOURED HIM...
© 1956 WALT KELLY
11-8
THE HALL SYNDICATE, INC.

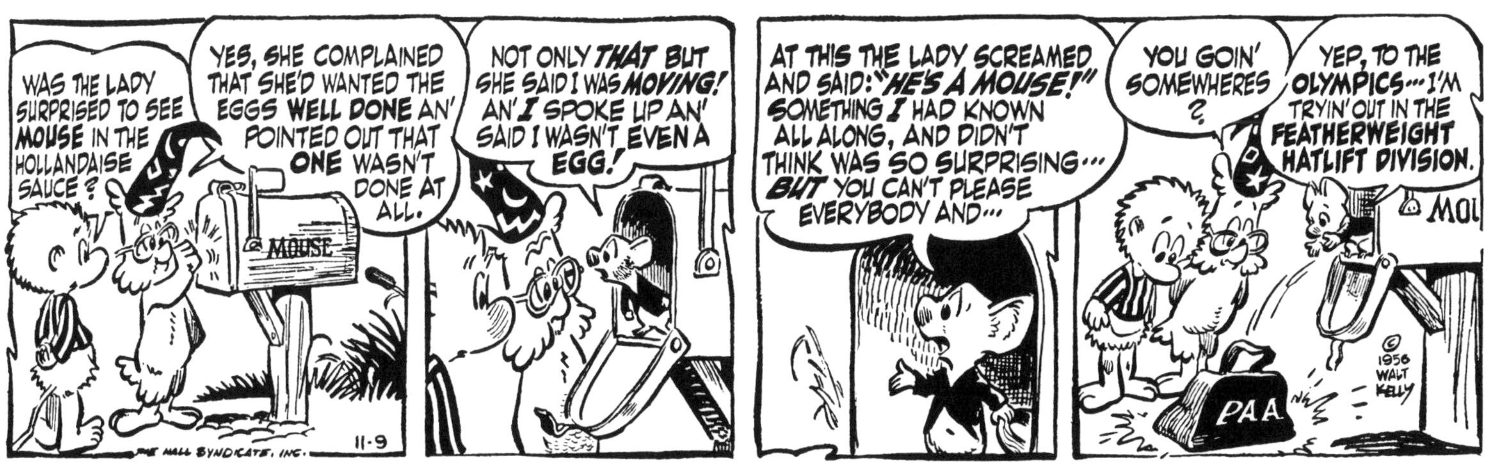
WAS THE LADY SURPRISED TO SEE MOUSE IN THE HOLLANDAISE SAUCE ?
YES, SHE COMPLAINED THAT SHE'D WANTED THE EGGS WELL DONE AN' POINTED OUT THAT ONE WASN'T DONE AT ALL.
MOUSE
NOT ONLY THAT BUT SHE SAID I WAS MOVING! AN' I SPOKE UP AN' SAID I WASN'T EVEN A EGG!
AT THIS THE LADY SCREAMED AND SAID: "HE'S A MOUSE!" SOMETHING I HAD KNOWN ALL ALONG, AND DIDN'T THINK WAS SO SURPRISING... BUT YOU CAN'T PLEASE EVERYBODY AND...
YOU GOIN' SOMEWHERES ?
YEP, TO THE OLYMPICS...I'M TRYIN' OUT IN THE FEATHERWEIGHT HATLIFT DIVISION.
MOU
PAA
© 1956 WALT KELLY
THE HALL SYNDICATE, INC.
11-9

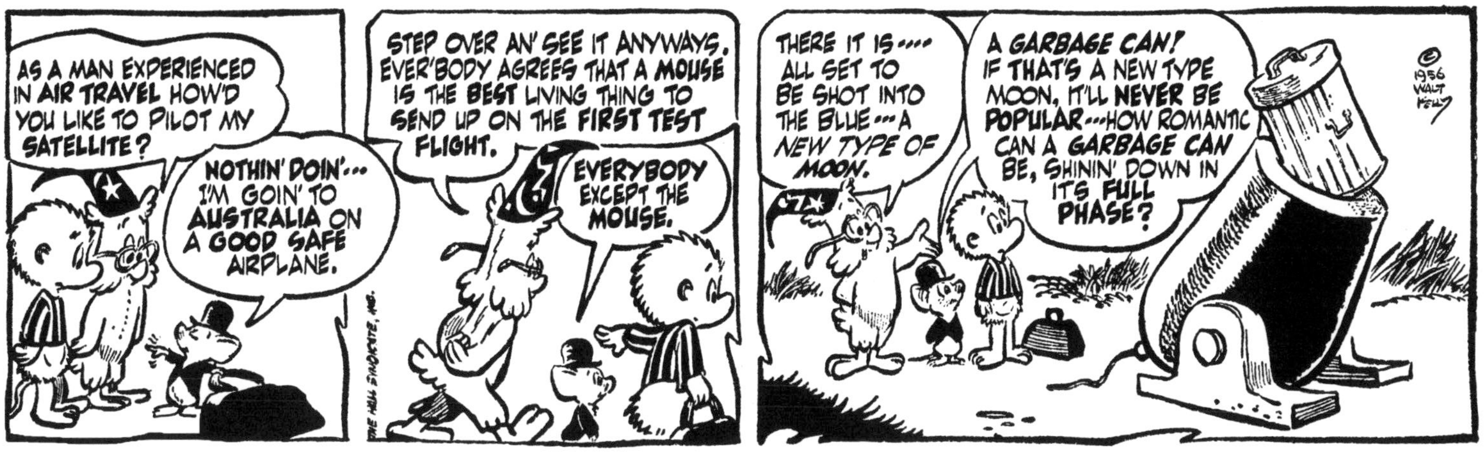
AS A MAN EXPERIENCED IN AIR TRAVEL HOW'D YOU LIKE TO PILOT MY SATELLITE ?
NOTHIN' DOIN'... I'M GOIN' TO AUSTRALIA ON A GOOD SAFE AIRPLANE.
STEP OVER AN' SEE IT ANYWAYS. EVER'BODY AGREES THAT A MOUSE IS THE BEST LIVING THING TO SEND UP ON THE FIRST TEST FLIGHT.
EVERYBODY EXCEPT THE MOUSE.
THE HALL SYNDICATE, INC.
THERE IT IS.... ALL SET TO BE SHOT INTO THE BLUE...A NEW TYPE OF MOON.
A GARBAGE CAN! IF THAT'S A NEW TYPE MOON, IT'LL NEVER BE POPULAR...HOW ROMANTIC CAN A GARBAGE CAN BE, SHININ' DOWN IN IT'S FULL PHASE?
© 1956 WALT KELLY

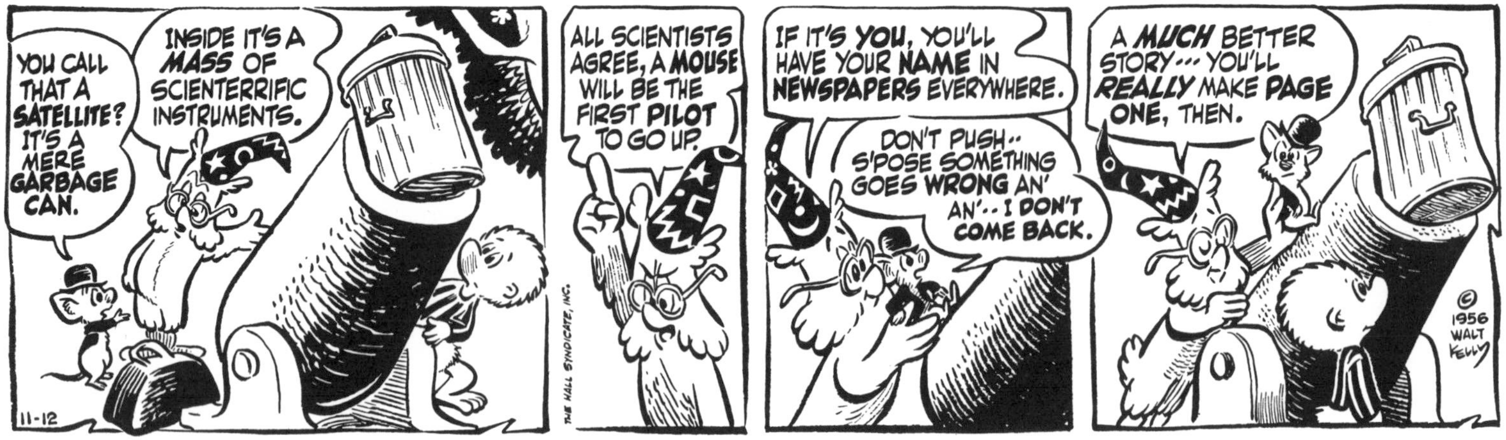
YOU CALL THAT A SATELLITE? IT'S A MERE GARBAGE CAN.
INSIDE IT'S A MASS OF SCIENTERRIFIC INSTRUMENTS.
11-12
ALL SCIENTISTS AGREE, A MOUSE WILL BE THE FIRST PILOT TO GO UP.
THE HALL SYNDICATE, INC.
IF IT'S YOU, YOU'LL HAVE YOUR NAME IN NEWSPAPERS EVERYWHERE.
DON'T PUSH.. S'POSE SOMETHING GOES WRONG AN' AN'.. I DON'T COME BACK.
A MUCH BETTER STORY... YOU'LL REALLY MAKE PAGE ONE, THEN.
© 1956 WALT KELLY

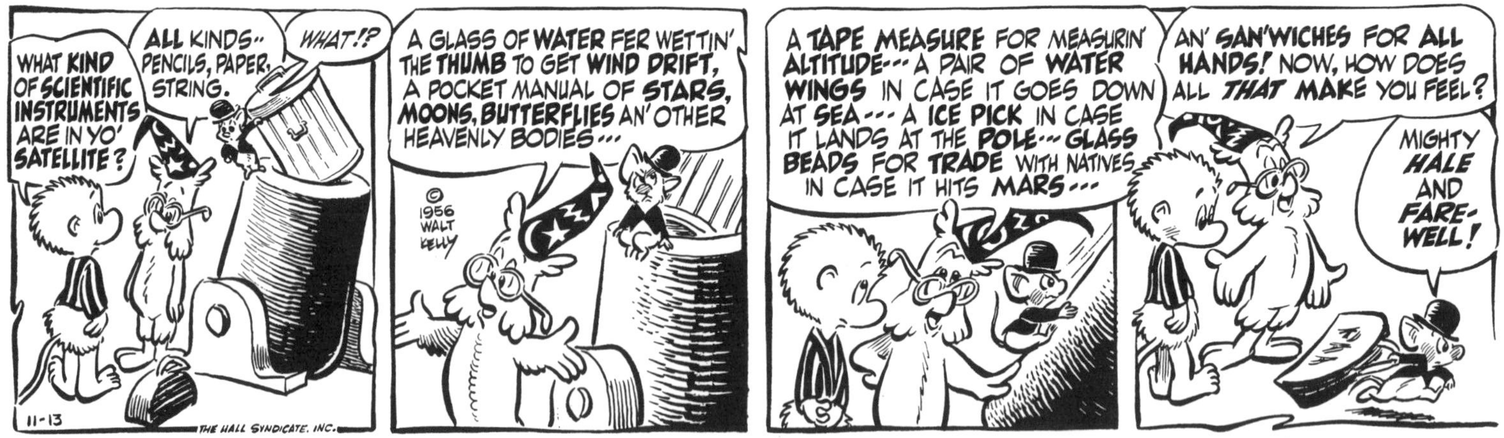
WHAT KIND OF SCIENTIFIC INSTRUMENTS ARE IN YO' SATELLITE?
ALL KINDS.. PENCILS, PAPER, STRING.
WHAT!?
11-13
THE HALL SYNDICATE, INC.
A GLASS OF WATER FER WETTIN' THE THUMB TO GET WIND DRIFT, A POCKET MANUAL OF STARS, MOONS, BUTTERFLIES AN' OTHER HEAVENLY BODIES...
© 1956 WALT KELLY
A TAPE MEASURE FOR MEASURIN' ALTITUDE... A PAIR OF WATER WINGS IN CASE IT GOES DOWN AT SEA... A ICE PICK IN CASE IT LANDS AT THE POLE... GLASS BEADS FOR TRADE WITH NATIVES IN CASE IT HITS MARS...
AN' SAN'WICHES FOR ALL HANDS! NOW, HOW DOES ALL THAT MAKE YOU FEEL?
MIGHTY HALE AND FARE-WELL!

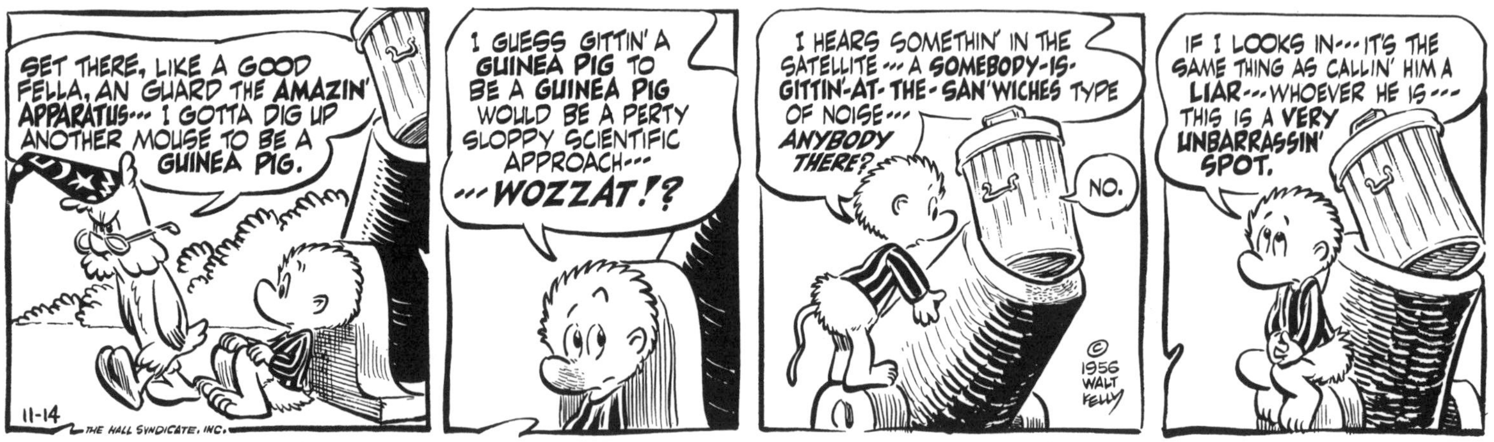
SET THERE, LIKE A GOOD FELLA, AN' GUARD THE AMAZIN' APPARATUS... I GOTTA DIG UP ANOTHER MOUSE TO BE A GUINEA PIG.
11-14
THE HALL SYNDICATE, INC.
I GUESS GITTIN' A GUINEA PIG TO BE A GUINEA PIG WOULD BE A PERTY SLOPPY SCIENTIFIC APPROACH---
...WOZZAT!?
I HEARS SOMETHIN' IN THE SATELLITE... A SOMEBODY-IS-GITTIN'-AT-THE-SAN'WICHES TYPE OF NOISE... ANYBODY THERE?
NO.
© 1956 WALT KELLY
IF I LOOKS IN... IT'S THE SAME THING AS CALLIN' HIM A LIAR... WHOEVER HE IS... THIS IS A VERY UNBARRASSIN' SPOT.

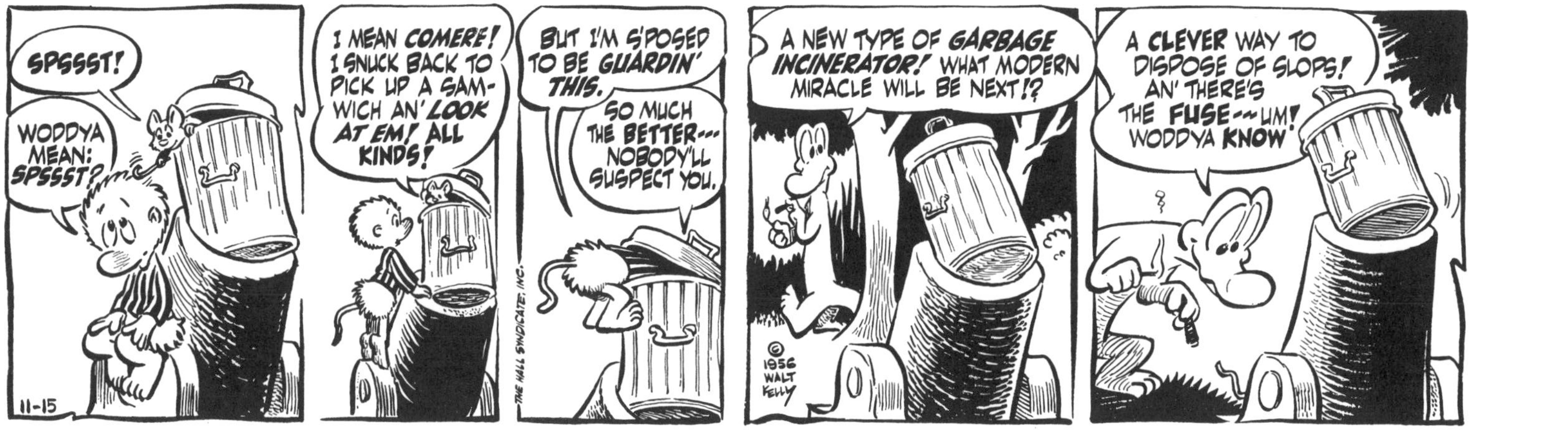
SPSSST!
WODDYA MEAN: SPSSST?
I MEAN COMERE! I SNUCK BACK TO PICK UP A SAM-WICH AN' LOOK AT EM! ALL KINDS!
BUT I'M S'POSED TO BE GUARDIN' THIS.
SO MUCH THE BETTER--- NOBODY'LL SUSPECT YOU.
A NEW TYPE OF GARBAGE INCINERATOR! WHAT MODERN MIRACLE WILL BE NEXT!?
A CLEVER WAY TO DISPOSE OF SLOPS! AN' THERE'S THE FUSE--UM! WODDYA KNOW
11-15
THE HALL SYNDICATE, INC.
© 1956 WALT KELLY

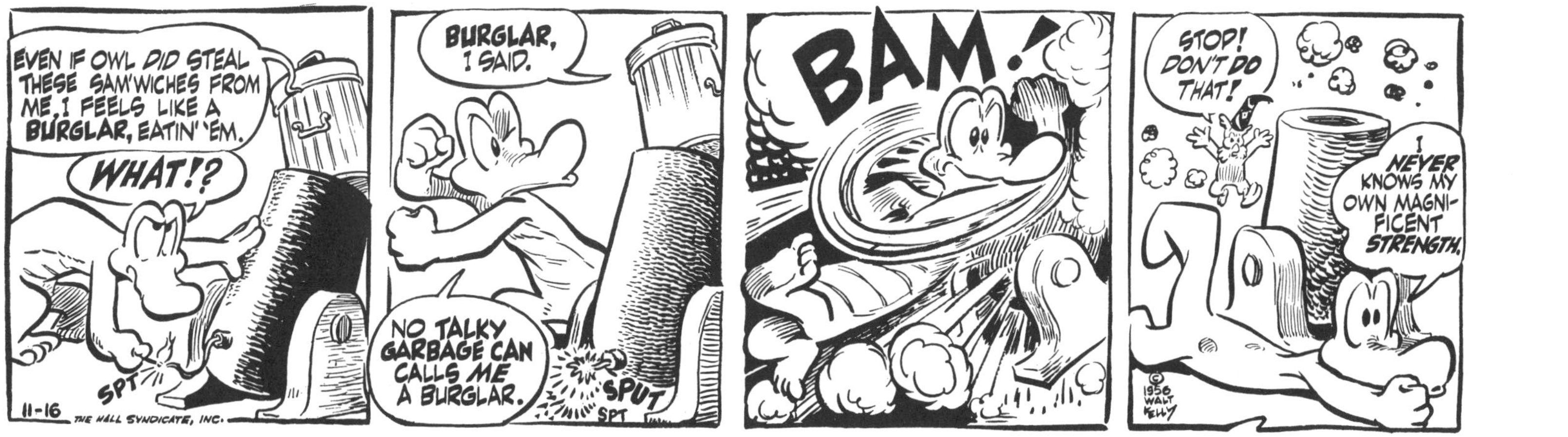
EVEN IF OWL DID STEAL THESE SAM'WICHES FROM ME, I FEELS LIKE A BURGLAR, EATIN' 'EM.
WHAT!?
SPT
BURGLAR, I SAID.
NO TALKY GARBAGE CAN CALLS ME A BURGLAR.
SPUT
SPT
BAM!
STOP! DON'T DO THAT!
I NEVER KNOWS MY OWN MAGNI-FICENT STRENGTH.
11-16
THE HALL SYNDICATE, INC.
© 1956 WALT KELLY

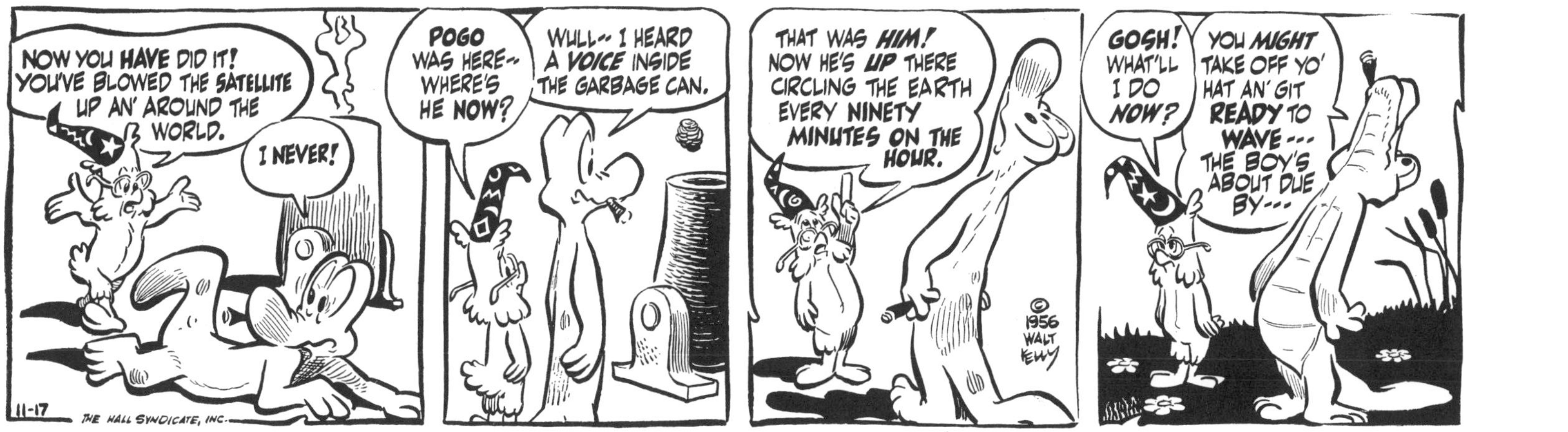
NOW YOU HAVE DID IT! YOU'VE BLOWED THE SATELLITE UP AN' AROUND THE WORLD.
I NEVER!
POGO WAS HERE-- WHERE'S HE NOW?
WULL-- I HEARD A VOICE INSIDE THE GARBAGE CAN.
THAT WAS HIM! NOW HE'S UP THERE CIRCLING THE EARTH EVERY NINETY MINUTES ON THE HOUR.
GOSH! WHAT'LL I DO NOW?
YOU MIGHT TAKE OFF YO' HAT AN' GIT READY TO WAVE--- THE BOY'S ABOUT DUE BY---
11-17
THE HALL SYNDICATE, INC.
© 1956 WALT KELLY

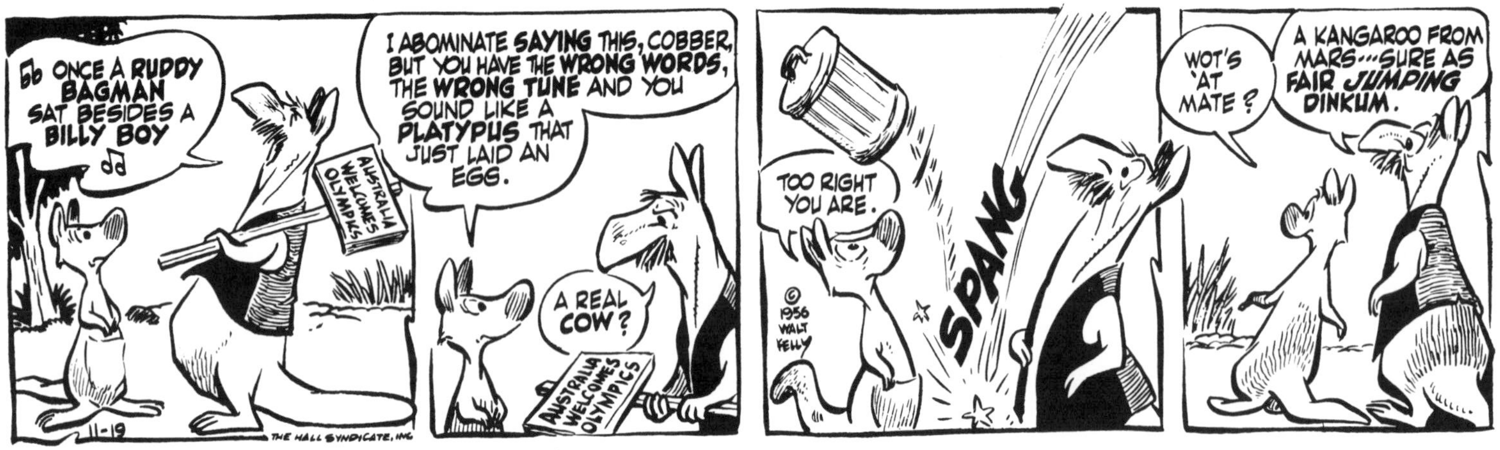
ONCE A RUDDY BAGMAN SAT BESIDES A BILLY BOY
AUSTRALIA WELCOMES OLYMPICS
11-19
THE HALL SYNDICATE, INC
I ABOMINATE SAYING THIS, COBBER, BUT YOU HAVE THE WRONG WORDS, THE WRONG TUNE AND YOU SOUND LIKE A PLATYPUS THAT JUST LAID AN EGG.
A REAL COW?
AUSTRALIA WELCOMES OLYMPICS
TOO RIGHT YOU ARE.
© 1956 WALT KELLY
SPANG
WOT'S 'AT MATE?
A KANGAROO FROM MARS---SURE AS FAIR JUMPING DINKUM.

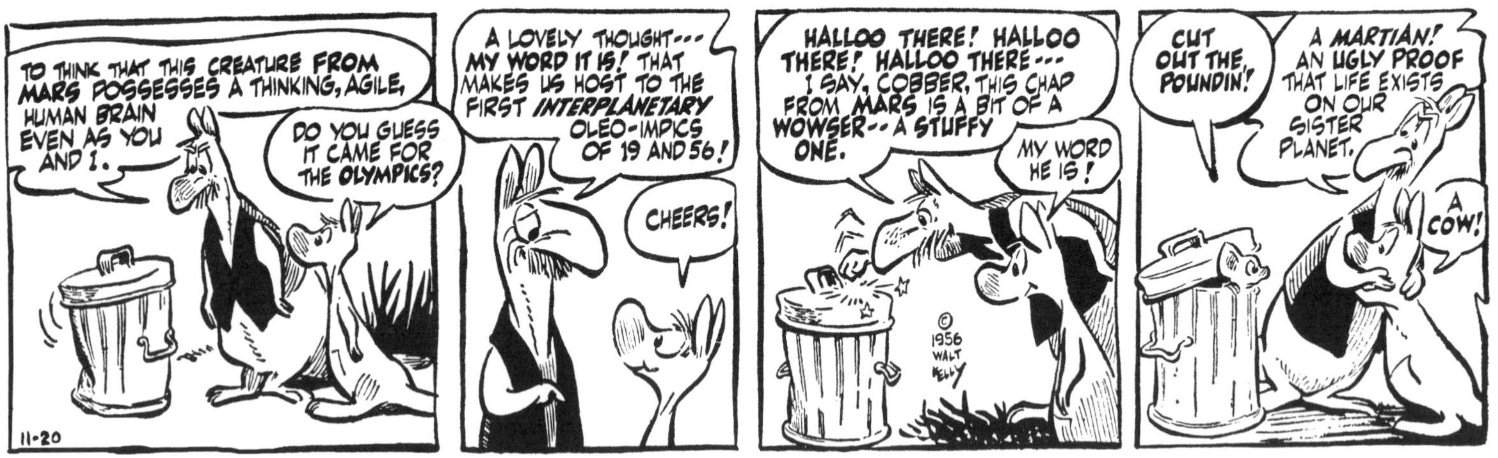
TO THINK THAT THIS CREATURE FROM MARS POSSESSES A THINKING, AGILE, HUMAN BRAIN EVEN AS YOU AND I.
DO YOU GUESS IT CAME FOR THE OLYMPICS?
11-20
A LOVELY THOUGHT--- MY WORD IT IS! THAT MAKES US HOST TO THE FIRST INTERPLANETARY OLEO-IMPICS OF 19 AND 56!
CHEERS!
HALLOO THERE! HALLOO THERE! HALLOO THERE--- I SAY, COBBER, THIS CHAP FROM MARS IS A BIT OF A WOWSER-- A STUFFY ONE.
MY WORD HE IS!
© 1956 WALT KELLY
CUT OUT THE POUNDIN'!
A MARTIAN! AN UGLY PROOF THAT LIFE EXISTS ON OUR SISTER PLANET.
A COW!

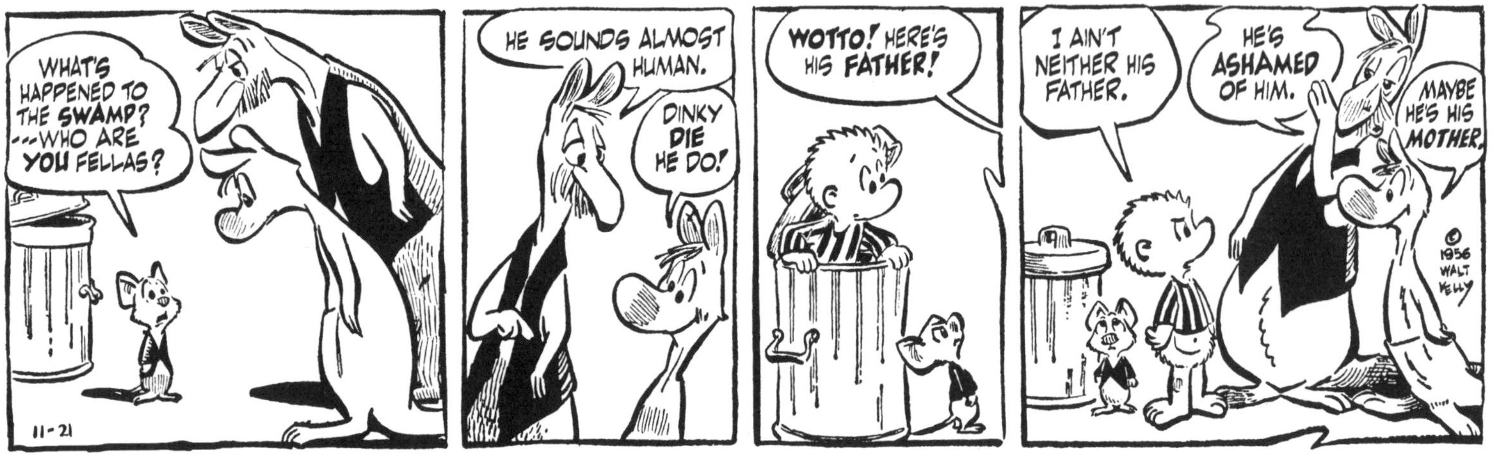
WHAT'S HAPPENED TO THE SWAMP? --WHO ARE YOU FELLAS?
11-21
HE SOUNDS ALMOST HUMAN.
DINKY DIE HE DO!
WOTTO! HERE'S HIS FATHER!
I AIN'T NEITHER HIS FATHER.
HE'S ASHAMED OF HIM.
MAYBE HE'S HIS MOTHER.
© 1956 WALT KELLY

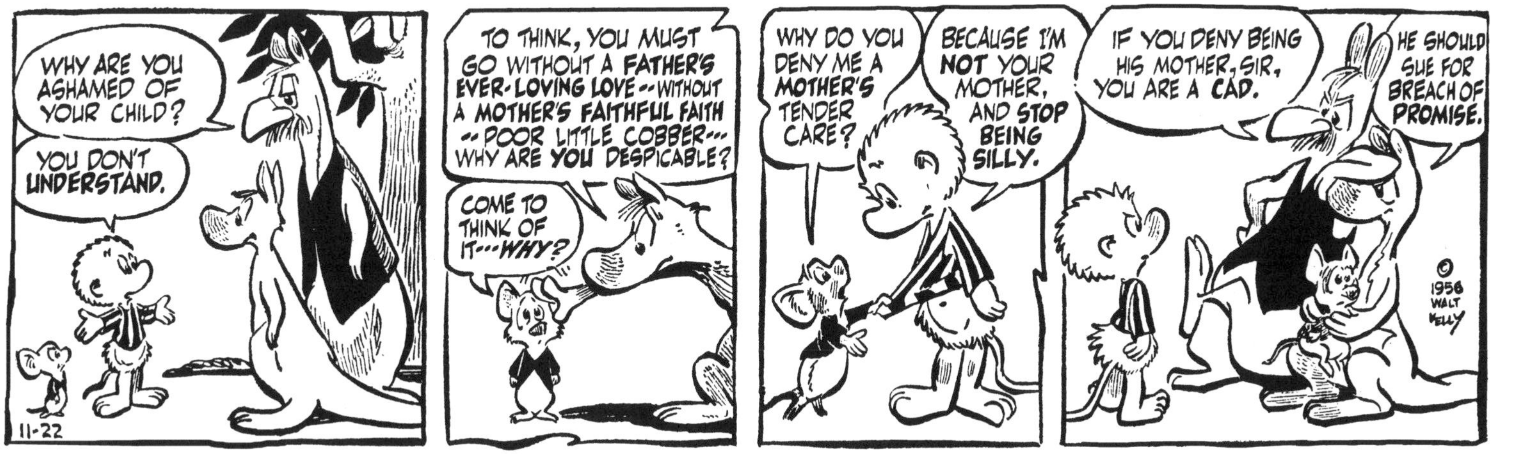
WHY ARE YOU ASHAMED OF YOUR CHILD?
YOU DON'T UNDERSTAND.
11-22
TO THINK, YOU MUST GO WITHOUT A FATHER'S EVER-LOVING LOVE--WITHOUT A MOTHER'S FAITHFUL FAITH --POOR LITTLE COBBER--- WHY ARE YOU DESPICABLE?
COME TO THINK OF IT---WHY?
WHY DO YOU DENY ME A MOTHER'S TENDER CARE?
BECAUSE I'M NOT YOUR MOTHER, AND STOP BEING SILLY.
IF YOU DENY BEING HIS MOTHER, SIR, YOU ARE A CAD.
HE SHOULD SUE FOR BREACH OF PROMISE.
© 1956 WALT KELLY

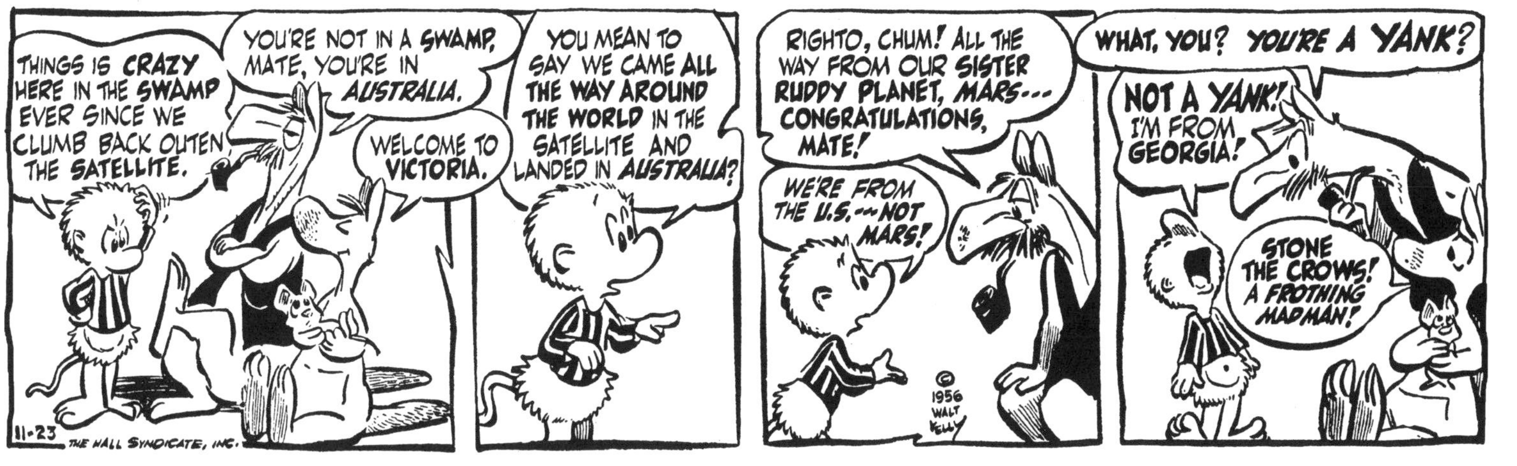
THINGS IS CRAZY HERE IN THE SWAMP EVER SINCE WE CLUMB BACK OUTEN THE SATELLITE.
YOU'RE NOT IN A SWAMP, MATE, YOU'RE IN AUSTRALIA.
WELCOME TO VICTORIA.
11-23
THE HALL SYNDICATE, INC.
YOU MEAN TO SAY WE CAME ALL THE WAY AROUND THE WORLD IN THE SATELLITE AND LANDED IN AUSTRALIA?
RIGHTO, CHUM! ALL THE WAY FROM OUR SISTER RUDDY PLANET, MARS--- CONGRATULATIONS, MATE!
WE'RE FROM THE U.S.--NOT MARS!
© 1956 WALT KELLY
WHAT, YOU? YOU'RE A YANK?
NOT A YANK! I'M FROM GEORGIA!
STONE THE CROWS! A FROTHING MADMAN!

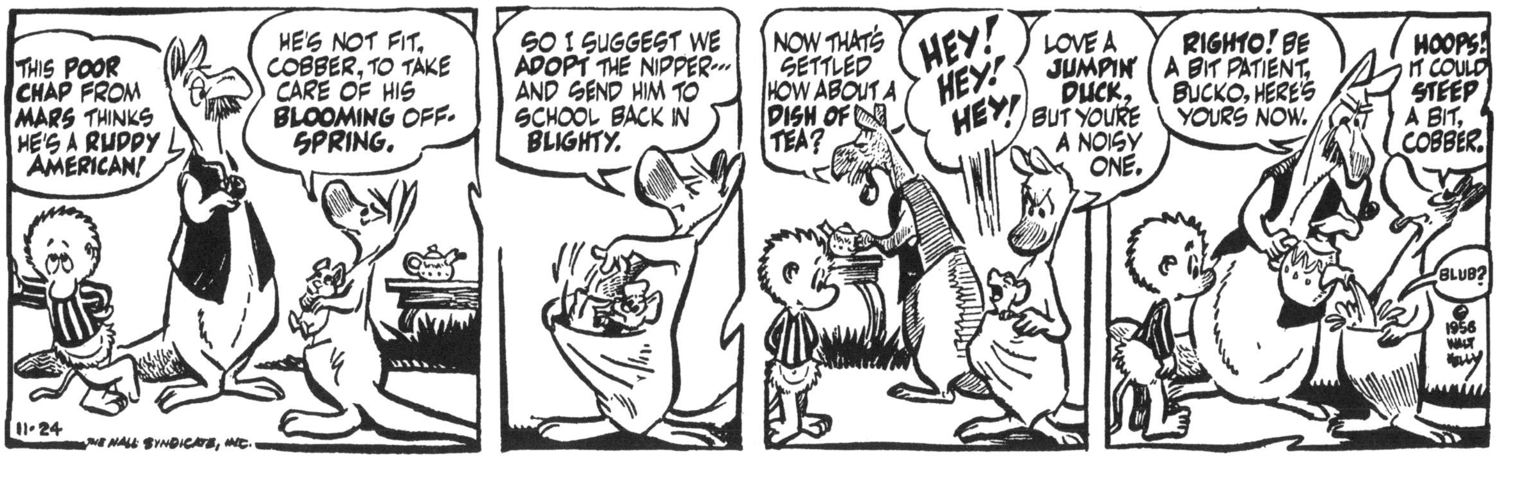
THIS POOR CHAP FROM MARS THINKS HE'S A RUDDY AMERICAN!
HE'S NOT FIT, COBBER, TO TAKE CARE OF HIS BLOOMING OFF-SPRING.
11-24
THE HALL SYNDICATE, INC.
SO I SUGGEST WE ADOPT THE NIPPER--- AND SEND HIM TO SCHOOL BACK IN BLIGHTY.
NOW THAT'S SETTLED HOW ABOUT A DISH OF TEA?
HEY! HEY! HEY!
LOVE A JUMPIN' DUCK, BUT YOU'RE A NOISY ONE.
RIGHTO! BE A BIT PATIENT, BUCKO, HERE'S YOURS NOW.
HOOPS! IT COULD STEEP A BIT, COBBER.
BLUB?
© 1956 WALT KELLY

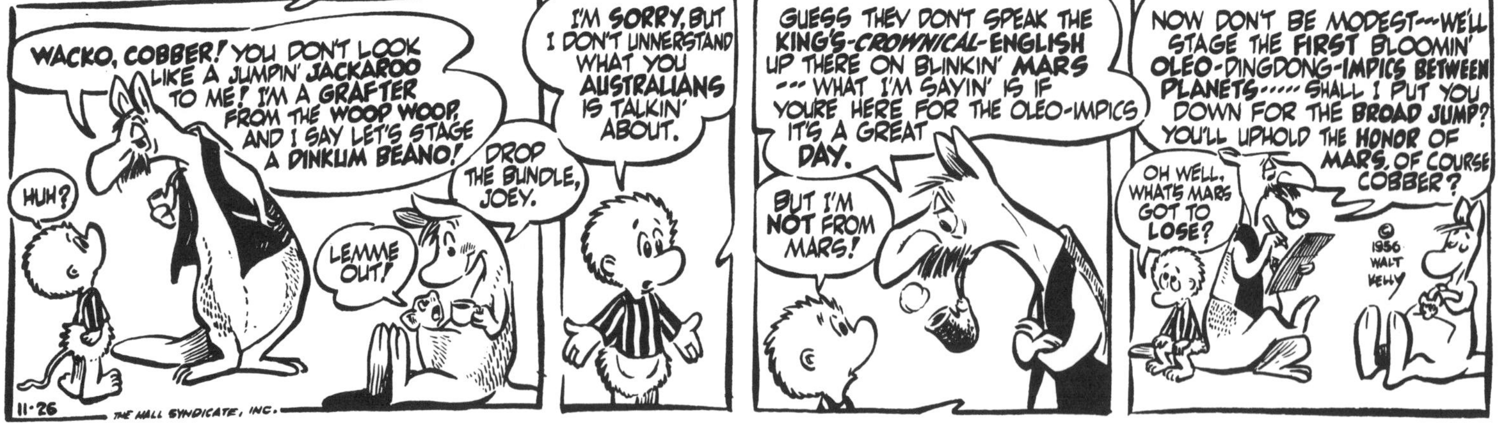
WACKO, COBBER! YOU DON'T LOOK LIKE A JUMPIN' JACKAROO TO ME! I'M A GRAFTER FROM THE WOOP WOOP, AND I SAY LET'S STAGE A DINKUM BEANO!
HUH?
DROP THE BUNDLE, JOEY.
LEMME OUT!
I'M SORRY, BUT I DON'T UNNERSTAND WHAT YOU AUSTRALIANS IS TALKIN' ABOUT.
GUESS THEY DON'T SPEAK THE KING'S-CROWNICAL-ENGLISH UP THERE ON BLINKIN' MARS --- WHAT I'M SAYIN' IS IF YOU'RE HERE FOR THE OLEO-IMPICS IT'S A GREAT DAY.
BUT I'M NOT FROM MARS!
NOW DON'T BE MODEST---WE'LL STAGE THE FIRST BLOOMIN' OLEO-DINGDONG-IMPICS BETWEEN PLANETS..... SHALL I PUT YOU DOWN FOR THE BROAD JUMP? YOU'LL UPHOLD THE HONOR OF MARS, OF COURSE COBBER?
OH WELL. WHAT'S MARS GOT TO LOSE?
© 1956 WALT KELLY
11-26
THE HALL SYNDICATE, INC.

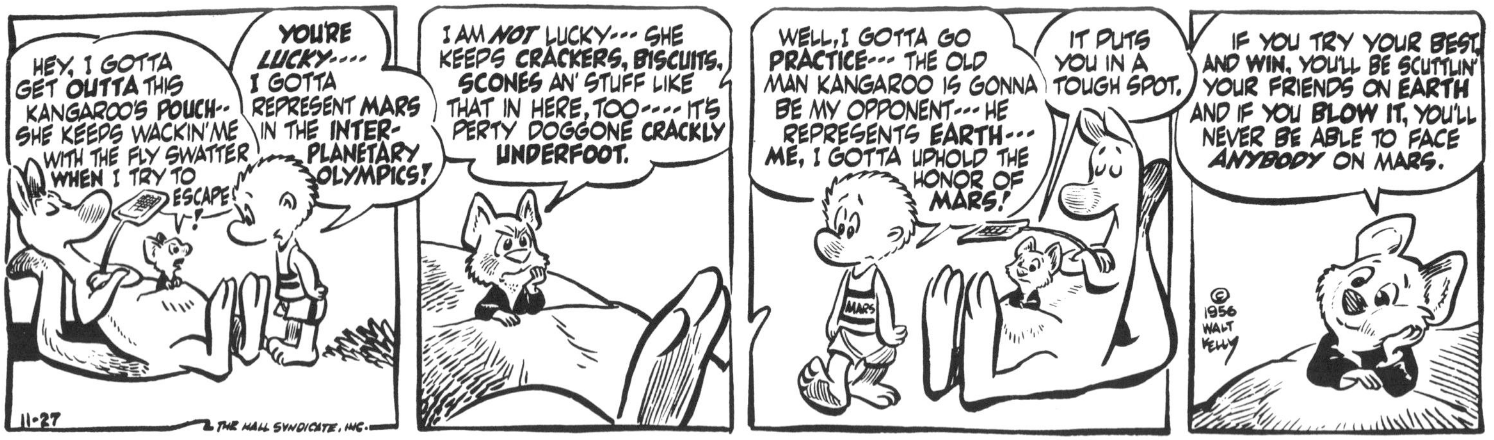
HEY, I GOTTA GET OUTTA THIS KANGAROO'S POUCH-- SHE KEEPS WACKIN' ME WITH THE FLY SWATTER WHEN I TRY TO ESCAPE!
YOU'RE LUCKY.... I GOTTA REPRESENT MARS IN THE INTER-PLANETARY OLYMPICS!
I AM NOT LUCKY--- SHE KEEPS CRACKERS, BISCUITS, SCONES AN' STUFF LIKE THAT IN HERE, TOO---- IT'S PERTY DOGGONE CRACKLY UNDERFOOT.
WELL, I GOTTA GO PRACTICE--- THE OLD MAN KANGAROO IS GONNA BE MY OPPONENT--- HE REPRESENTS EARTH--- ME, I GOTTA UPHOLD THE HONOR OF MARS!
IT PUTS YOU IN A TOUGH SPOT.
MARS
IF YOU TRY YOUR BEST, AND WIN, YOU'LL BE SCUTTLIN' YOUR FRIENDS ON EARTH AND IF YOU BLOW IT, YOU'LL NEVER BE ABLE TO FACE ANYBODY ON MARS.
© 1956 WALT KELLY
11-27
THE HALL SYNDICATE, INC.

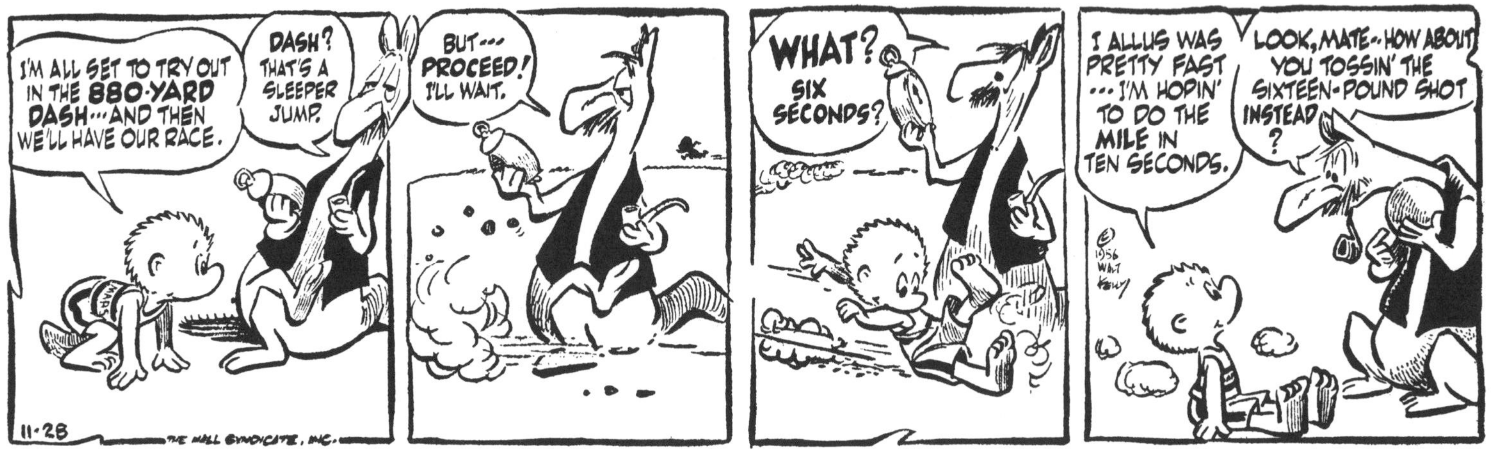
I'M ALL SET TO TRY OUT IN THE 880-YARD DASH...AND THEN WE'LL HAVE OUR RACE.
DASH? THAT'S A SLEEPER JUMP.
BUT--- PROCEED! I'LL WAIT.
WHAT? SIX SECONDS?
I ALLUS WAS PRETTY FAST ...I'M HOPIN' TO DO THE MILE IN TEN SECONDS.
LOOK, MATE-- HOW ABOUT YOU TOSSIN' THE SIXTEEN-POUND SHOT INSTEAD?
© 1956 WALT KELLY
11-28
THE HALL SYNDICATE, INC.

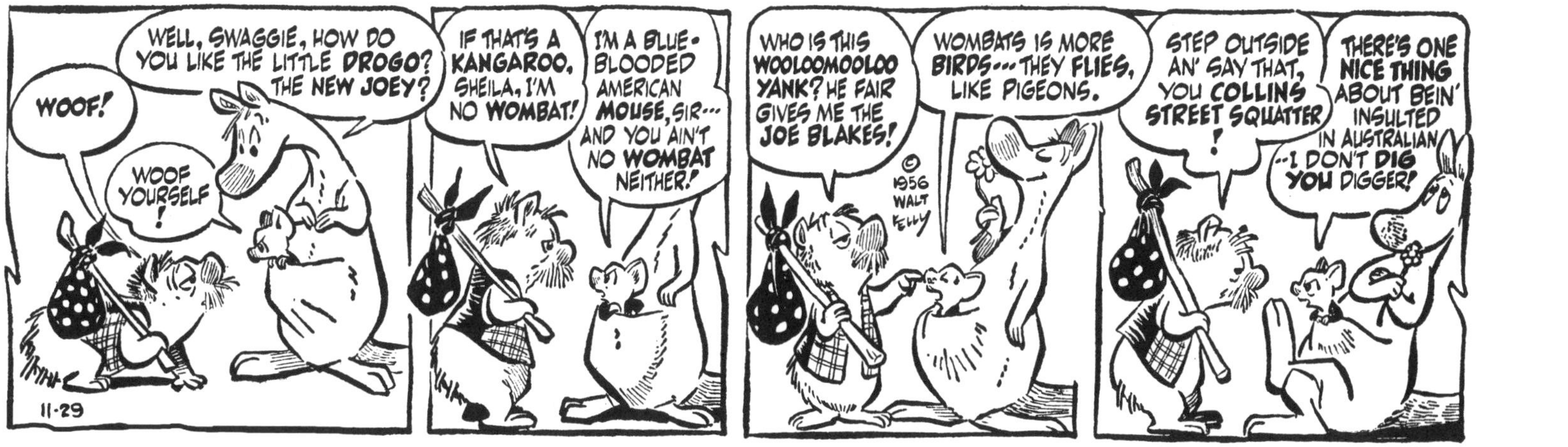
WELL, SWAGGIE, HOW DO YOU LIKE THE LITTLE DROGO? THE NEW JOEY?
WOOF!
WOOF YOURSELF!
11-29
IF THAT'S A KANGAROO, SHEILA, I'M NO WOMBAT!
I'M A BLUE-BLOODED AMERICAN MOUSE, SIR... AND YOU AIN'T NO WOMBAT NEITHER!
WHO IS THIS WOOLOOMOOLOO YANK? HE FAIR GIVES ME THE JOE BLAKES!
WOMBATS IS MORE BIRDS... THEY FLIES, LIKE PIGEONS.
© 1956 WALT KELLY
STEP OUTSIDE AN' SAY THAT, YOU COLLINS STREET SQUATTER!
THERE'S ONE NICE THING ABOUT BEIN' INSULTED IN AUSTRALIAN --I DON'T DIG YOU DIGGER!

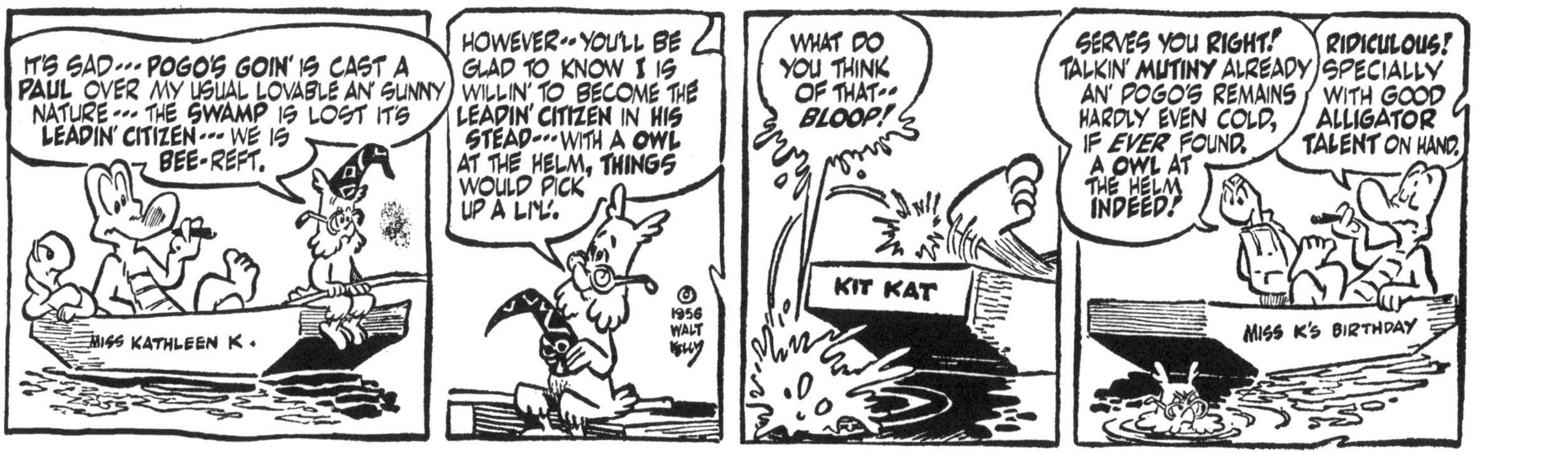
IT'S SAD... POGO'S GOIN' IS CAST A PAUL OVER MY USUAL LOVABLE AN' SUNNY NATURE... THE SWAMP IS LOST IT'S LEADIN' CITIZEN... WE IS BEE-REFT.
MISS KATHLEEN K.
HOWEVER-- YOU'LL BE GLAD TO KNOW I IS WILLIN' TO BECOME THE LEADIN' CITIZEN IN HIS STEAD... WITH A OWL AT THE HELM, THINGS WOULD PICK UP A LI'L'.
© 1956 WALT KELLY
WHAT DO YOU THINK OF THAT-- BLOOP!
KIT KAT
SERVES YOU RIGHT! TALKIN' MUTINY ALREADY AN' POGO'S REMAINS HARDLY EVEN COLD, IF EVER FOUND. A OWL AT THE HELM INDEED!
RIDICULOUS! SPECIALLY WITH GOOD ALLIGATOR TALENT ON HAND.
MISS K'S BIRTHDAY

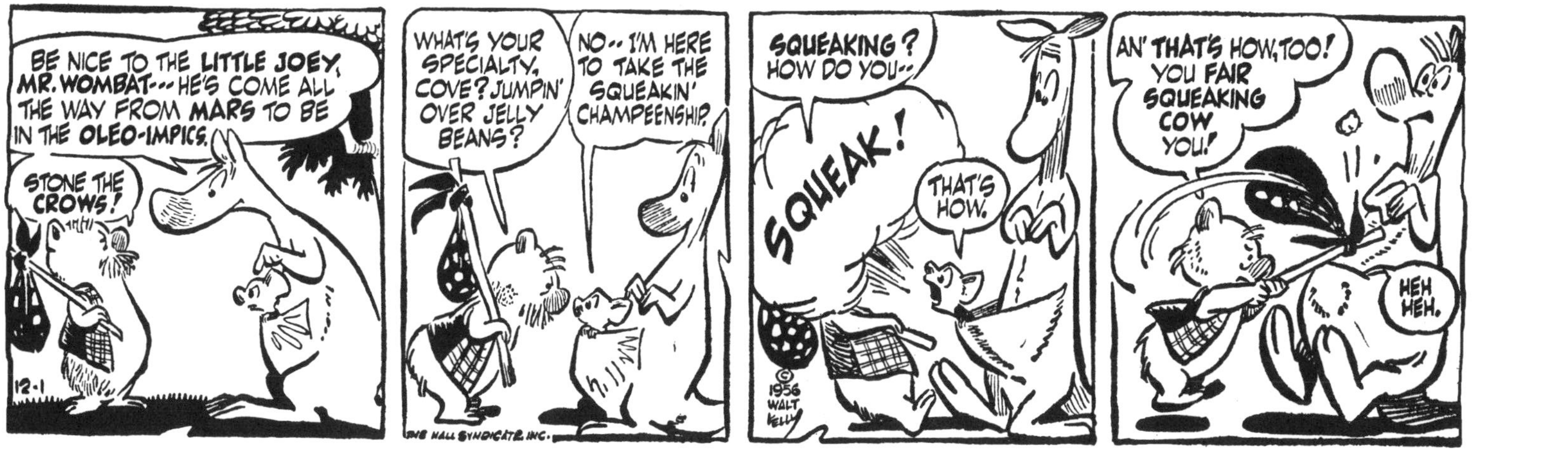
BE NICE TO THE LITTLE JOEY, MR. WOMBAT-- HE'S COME ALL THE WAY FROM MARS TO BE IN THE OLEO-IMPICS.
STONE THE CROWS!
12-1
WHAT'S YOUR SPECIALTY, COVE? JUMPIN' OVER JELLY BEANS?
NO-- I'M HERE TO TAKE THE SQUEAKIN' CHAMPEENSHIP.
THE HALL SYNDICATE, INC.
SQUEAKING? HOW DO YOU--
SQUEAK!
THAT'S HOW.
© 1956 WALT KELLY
AN' THAT'S HOW, TOO! YOU FAIR SQUEAKING COW YOU!
HEH HEH.

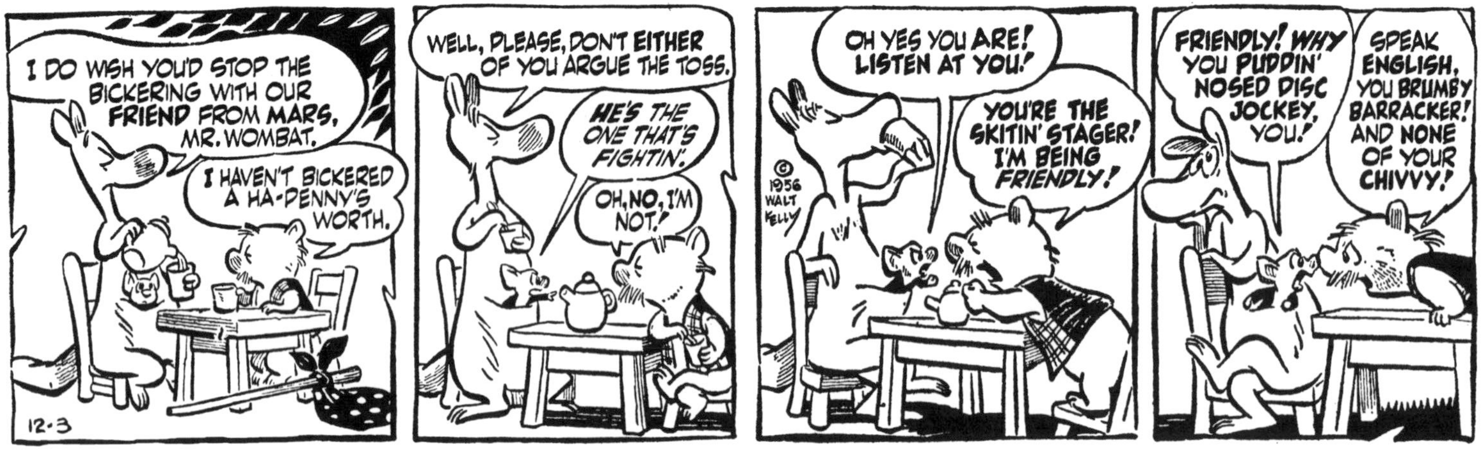
I DO WISH YOU'D STOP THE BICKERING WITH OUR FRIEND FROM MARS, MR. WOMBAT.
I HAVEN'T BICKERED A HA-PENNY'S WORTH.
12-3
WELL, PLEASE, DON'T EITHER OF YOU ARGUE THE TOSS.
HE'S THE ONE THAT'S FIGHTIN'.
OH, NO, I'M NOT!
OH YES YOU ARE! LISTEN AT YOU!
YOU'RE THE SKITIN' STAGER! I'M BEING FRIENDLY!
© 1956 WALT KELLY
FRIENDLY! WHY YOU PUDDIN' NOSED DISC JOCKEY, YOU!
SPEAK ENGLISH, YOU BRUMBY BARRACKER! AND NONE OF YOUR CHIVVY!

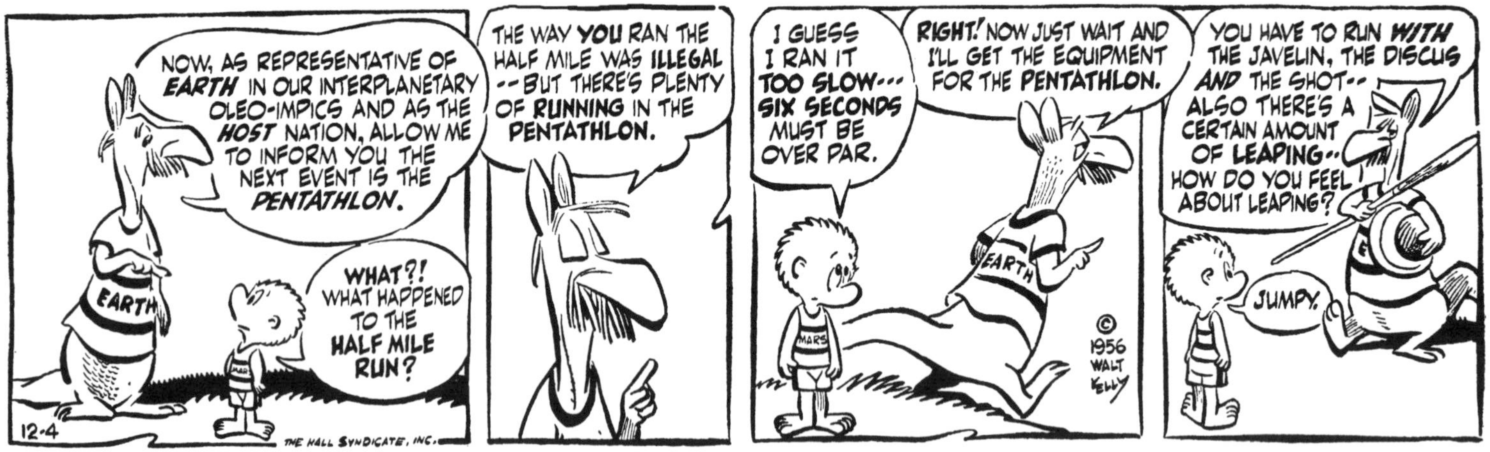
NOW, AS REPRESENTATIVE OF EARTH IN OUR INTERPLANETARY OLEO-IMPICS AND AS THE HOST NATION, ALLOW ME TO INFORM YOU THE NEXT EVENT IS THE PENTATHLON.
WHAT?! WHAT HAPPENED TO THE HALF MILE RUN?
EARTH
12-4
THE HALL SYNDICATE, INC.
THE WAY YOU RAN THE HALF MILE WAS ILLEGAL --BUT THERE'S PLENTY OF RUNNING IN THE PENTATHLON.
I GUESS I RAN IT TOO SLOW... SIX SECONDS MUST BE OVER PAR.
RIGHT! NOW JUST WAIT AND I'LL GET THE EQUIPMENT FOR THE PENTATHLON.
MARS
EARTH
© 1956 WALT KELLY
YOU HAVE TO RUN WITH THE JAVELIN, THE DISCUS AND THE SHOT-- ALSO THERE'S A CERTAIN AMOUNT OF LEAPING-- HOW DO YOU FEEL ABOUT LEAPING?
JUMPY.

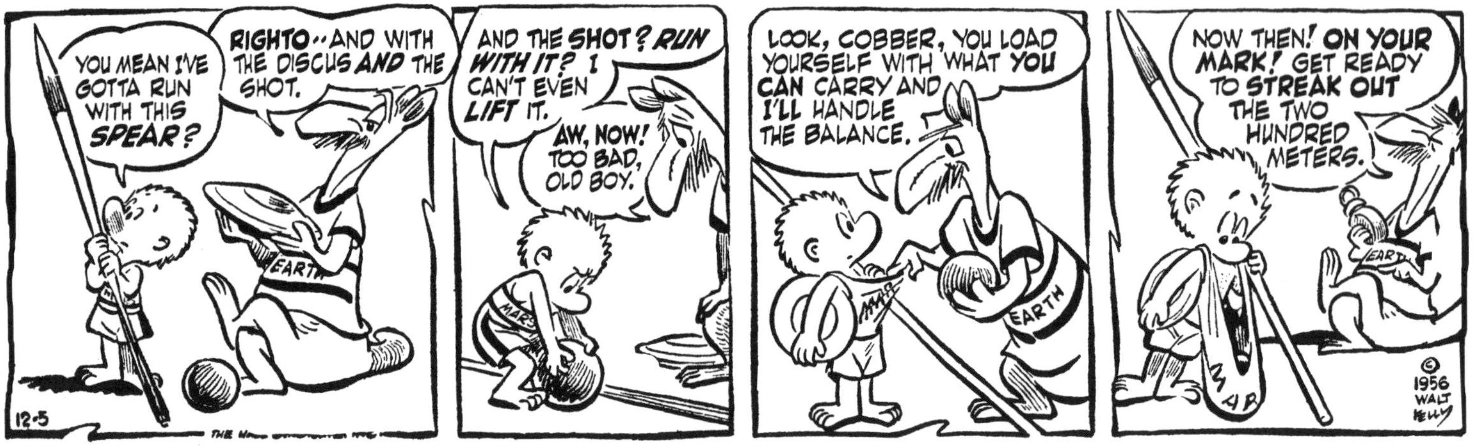
YOU MEAN I'VE GOTTA RUN WITH THIS SPEAR?
RIGHTO--AND WITH THE DISCUS AND THE SHOT.
EARTH
12-5
AND THE SHOT? RUN WITH IT? I CAN'T EVEN LIFT IT.
AW, NOW! TOO BAD, OLD BOY.
MARS
LOOK, COBBER, YOU LOAD YOURSELF WITH WHAT YOU CAN CARRY AND I'LL HANDLE THE BALANCE.
EARTH
NOW THEN! ON YOUR MARK! GET READY TO STREAK OUT THE TWO HUNDRED METERS.
© 1956 WALT KELLY

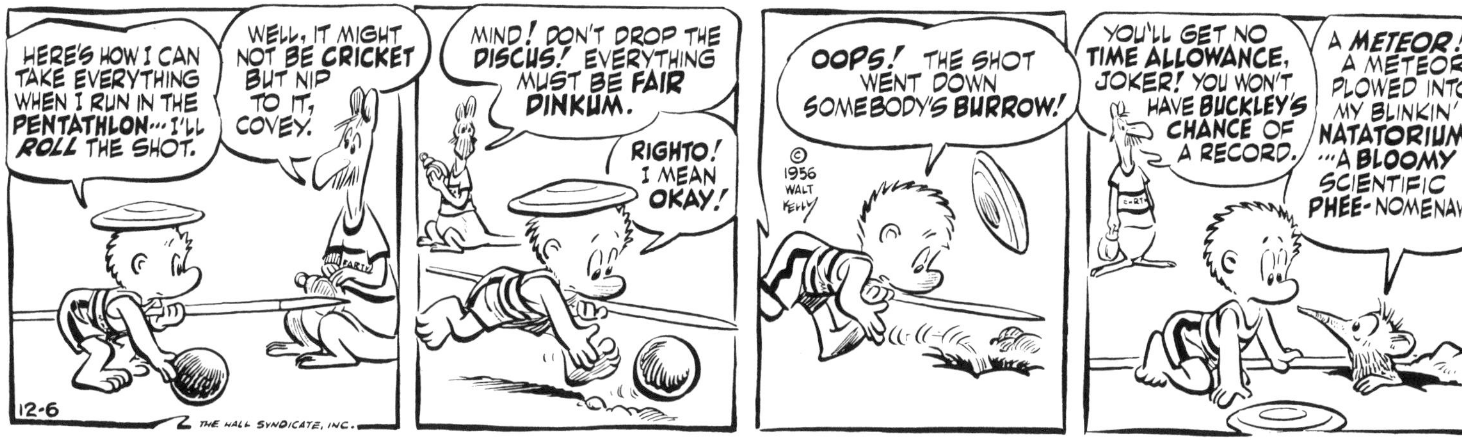
HERE'S HOW I CAN TAKE EVERYTHING WHEN I RUN IN THE PENTATHLON... I'LL ROLL THE SHOT.
WELL, IT MIGHT NOT BE CRICKET BUT NIP TO IT, COVEY.
PARTY
12-6
THE HALL SYNDICATE, INC.
MIND! DON'T DROP THE DISCUS! EVERYTHING MUST BE FAIR DINKUM.
RIGHTO! I MEAN OKAY!
OOPS! THE SHOT WENT DOWN SOMEBODY'S BURROW!
© 1956 WALT KELLY
YOU'LL GET NO TIME ALLOWANCE, JOKER! YOU WON'T HAVE BUCKLEY'S CHANCE OF A RECORD.
A METEOR! A METEOR PLOWED INTO MY BLINKIN' NATATORIUM! ...A BLOOMY SCIENTIFIC PHEE-NOMENAW!

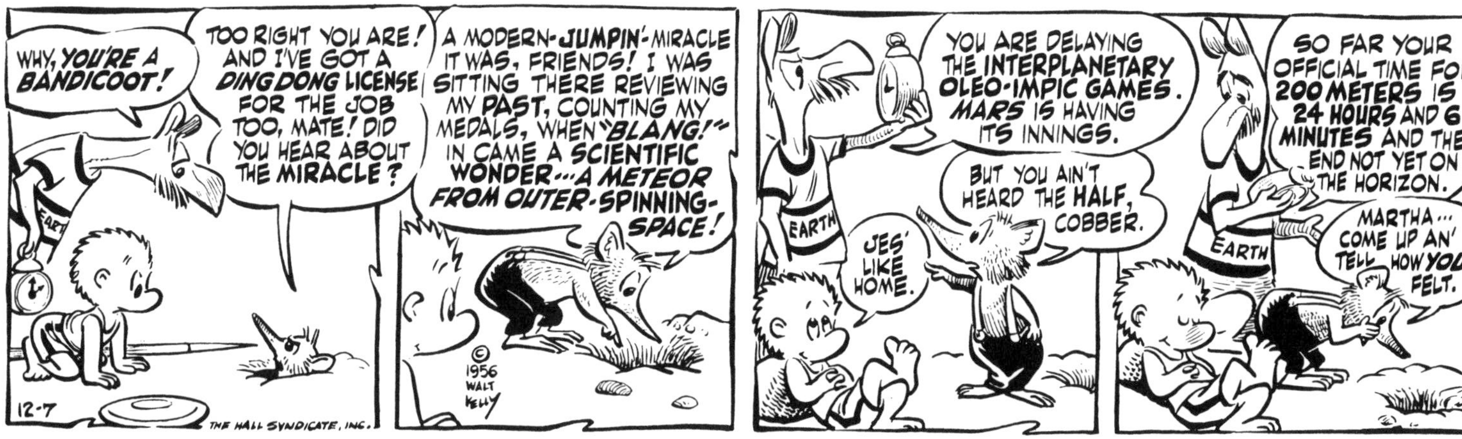
WHY, YOU'RE A BANDICOOT!
TOO RIGHT YOU ARE! AND I'VE GOT A DING DONG LICENSE FOR THE JOB TOO, MATE! DID YOU HEAR ABOUT THE MIRACLE?
EARTH
12-7
THE HALL SYNDICATE, INC.
A MODERN-JUMPIN'-MIRACLE IT WAS, FRIENDS! I WAS SITTING THERE REVIEWING MY PAST, COUNTING MY MEDALS, WHEN "BLANG!" IN CAME A SCIENTIFIC WONDER... A METEOR FROM OUTER-SPINNING-SPACE!
© 1956 WALT KELLY
YOU ARE DELAYING THE INTERPLANETARY OLEO-IMPIC GAMES. MARS IS HAVING ITS INNINGS.
BUT YOU AIN'T HEARD THE HALF, COBBER.
JES' LIKE HOME.
EARTH
SO FAR YOUR OFFICIAL TIME FOR 200 METERS IS 24 HOURS AND 6 MINUTES AND THE END NOT YET ON THE HORIZON.
MARTHA... COME UP AN' TELL HOW YOU FELT.
EARTH

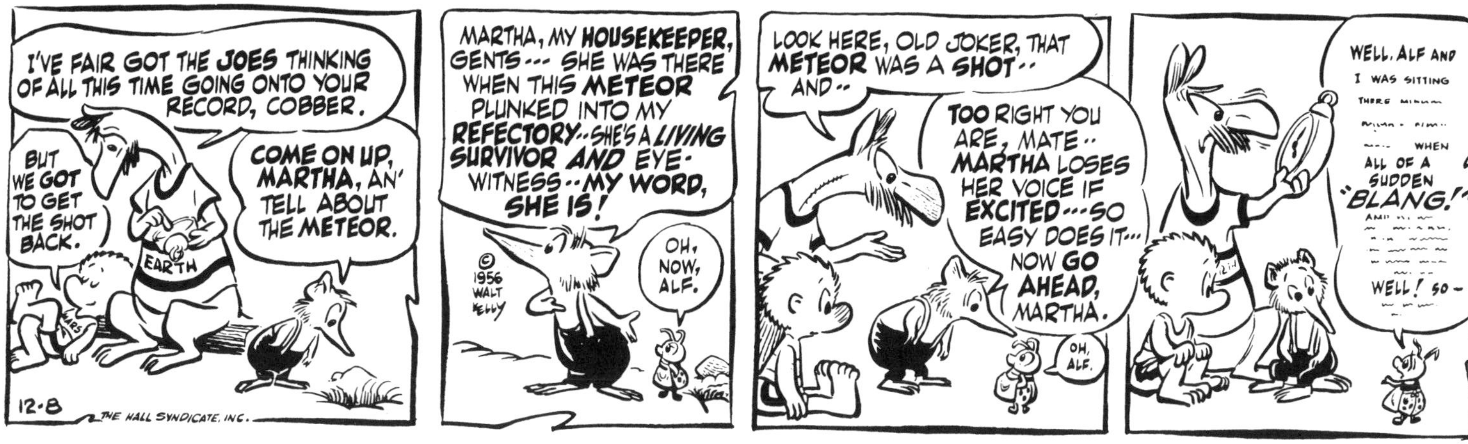
I'VE FAIR GOT THE JOES THINKING OF ALL THIS TIME GOING ONTO YOUR RECORD, COBBER.
BUT WE GOT TO GET THE SHOT BACK.
COME ON UP, MARTHA, AN' TELL ABOUT THE METEOR.
EARTH
12-8
THE HALL SYNDICATE, INC.
MARTHA, MY HOUSEKEEPER, GENTS... SHE WAS THERE WHEN THIS METEOR PLUNKED INTO MY REFECTORY.. SHE'S A LIVING SURVIVOR AND EYE-WITNESS.. MY WORD, SHE IS!
© 1956 WALT KELLY
OH, NOW, ALF.
LOOK HERE, OLD JOKER, THAT METEOR WAS A SHOT.. AND..
TOO RIGHT YOU ARE, MATE.. MARTHA LOSES HER VOICE IF EXCITED... SO EASY DOES IT... NOW GO AHEAD, MARTHA.
OH, ALF.
WELL, ALF AND I WAS SITTING
WHEN ALL OF A SUDDEN "BLANG!"
WELL! SO –

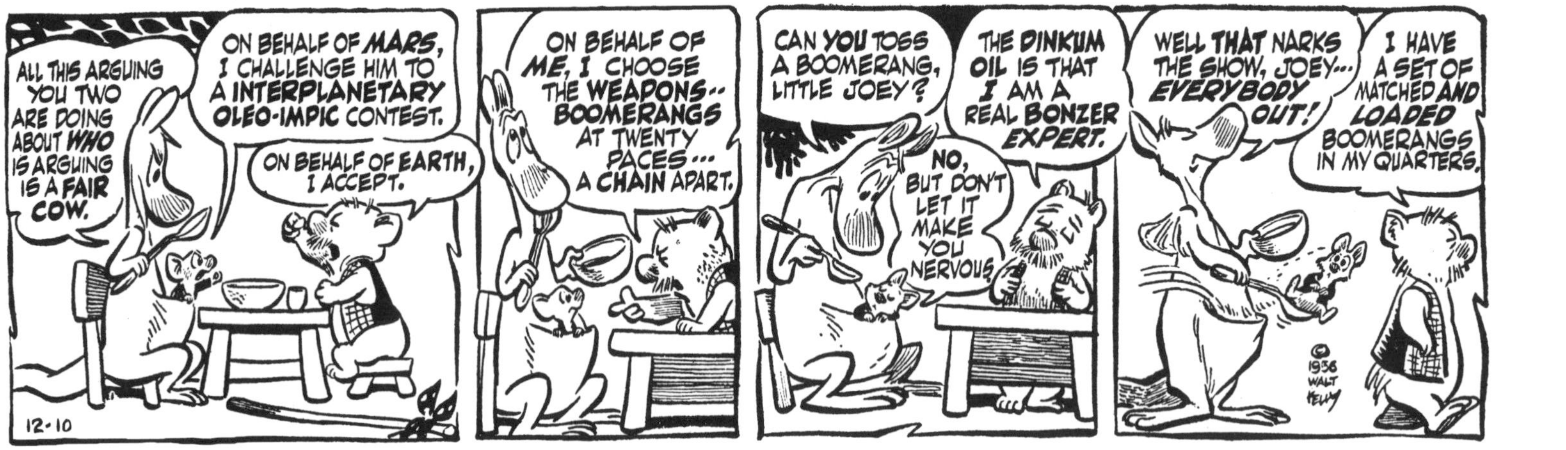
ALL THIS ARGUING YOU TWO ARE DOING ABOUT WHO IS ARGUING IS A FAIR COW.
ON BEHALF OF MARS, I CHALLENGE HIM TO A INTERPLANETARY OLEO-IMPIC CONTEST.
ON BEHALF OF EARTH, I ACCEPT.
12-10
ON BEHALF OF ME, I CHOOSE THE WEAPONS.. BOOMERANGS AT TWENTY PACES... A CHAIN APART.
CAN YOU TOSS A BOOMERANG, LITTLE JOEY?
THE DINKUM OIL IS THAT I AM A REAL BONZER EXPERT.
NO, BUT DON'T LET IT MAKE YOU NERVOUS.
WELL THAT NARKS THE SHOW, JOEY... EVERYBODY OUT!
I HAVE A SET OF MATCHED AND LOADED BOOMERANGS IN MY QUARTERS.
© 1956 WALT KELLY

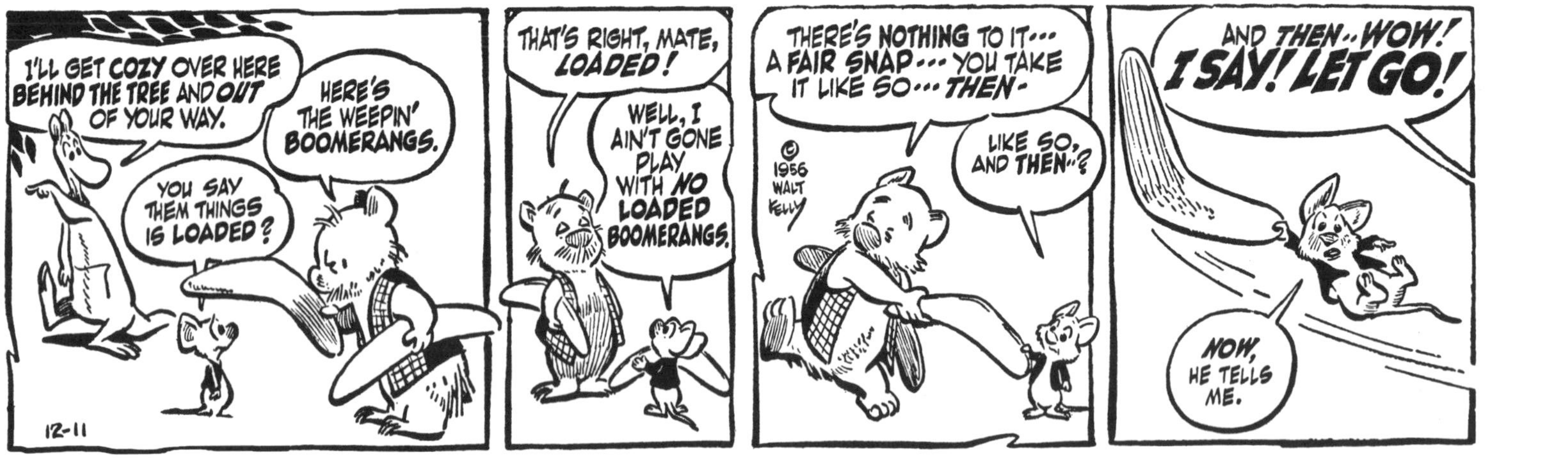
I'LL GET COZY OVER HERE BEHIND THE TREE AND OUT OF YOUR WAY.
HERE'S THE WEEPIN' BOOMERANGS.
YOU SAY THEM THINGS IS LOADED?
12-11
THAT'S RIGHT, MATE, LOADED!
WELL, I AIN'T GONE PLAY WITH NO LOADED BOOMERANGS.
THERE'S NOTHING TO IT... A FAIR SNAP... YOU TAKE IT LIKE SO... THEN-
© 1956 WALT KELLY
LIKE SO, AND THEN..?
AND THEN..WOW! I SAY! LET GO!
NOW, HE TELLS ME.

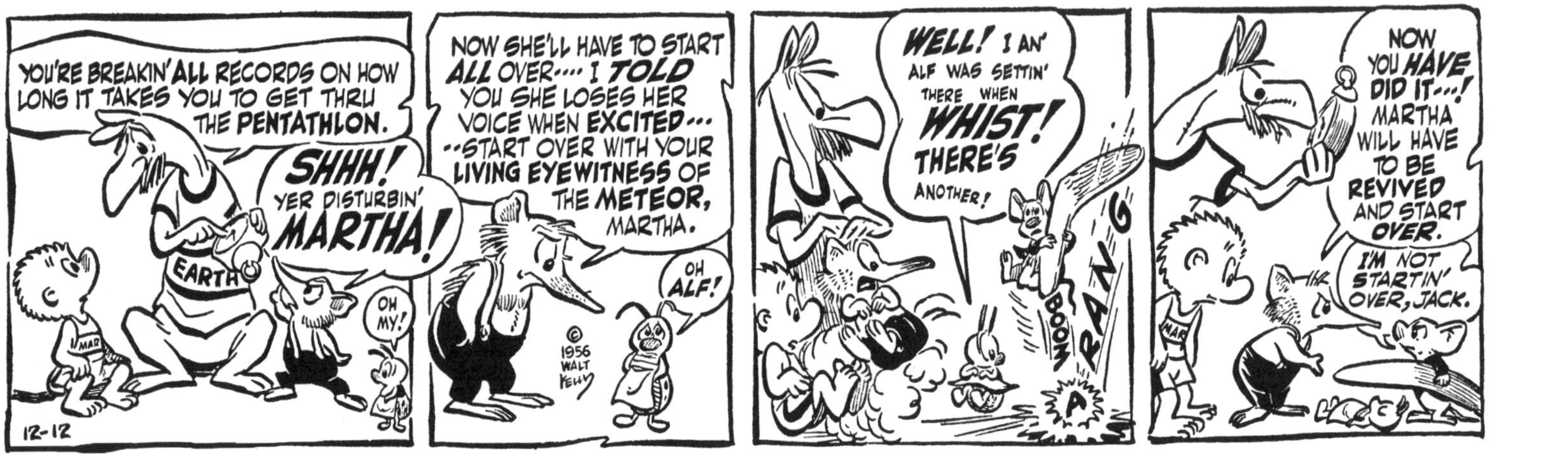
YOU'RE BREAKIN' ALL RECORDS ON HOW LONG IT TAKES YOU TO GET THRU THE PENTATHLON.
SHHH! YER DISTURBIN' MARTHA!
EARTH
MAR
OH MY!
12-12
NOW SHE'LL HAVE TO START ALL OVER.... I TOLD YOU SHE LOSES HER VOICE WHEN EXCITED... ..START OVER WITH YOUR LIVING EYEWITNESS OF THE METEOR, MARTHA.
OH ALF!
© 1956 WALT KELLY
WELL! I AN' ALF WAS SETTIN' THERE WHEN WHIST! THERE'S ANOTHER!
BOOM
RANG
NOW YOU HAVE DID IT...! MARTHA WILL HAVE TO BE REVIVED AND START OVER.
I'M NOT STARTIN' OVER, JACK.
MAR

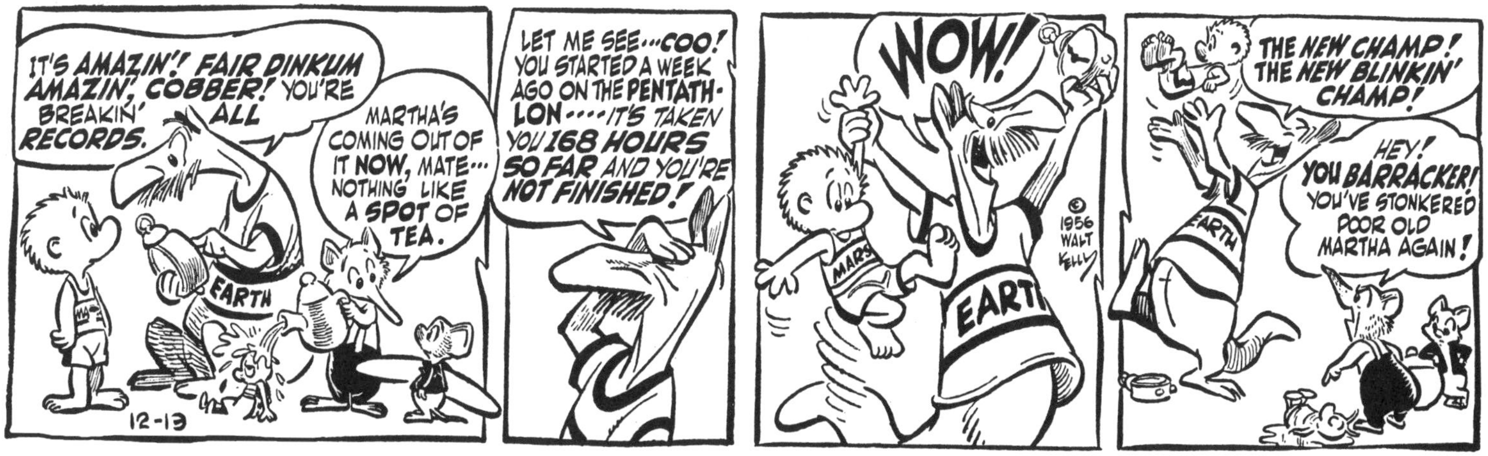
IT'S AMAZIN'! FAIR DINKUM AMAZIN', COBBER! YOU'RE BREAKIN' ALL RECORDS.
MARTHA'S COMING OUT OF IT NOW, MATE... NOTHING LIKE A SPOT OF TEA.
EARTH
12-13
LET ME SEE...COO! YOU STARTED A WEEK AGO ON THE PENTATHLON.... IT'S TAKEN YOU 168 HOURS SO FAR AND YOU'RE NOT FINISHED!
WOW!
MARS
EARTH
© 1956 WALT KELLY
THE NEW CHAMP! THE NEW BLINKIN' CHAMP!
HEY! YOU BARRACKER! YOU'VE STONKERED POOR OLD MARTHA AGAIN!
EARTH

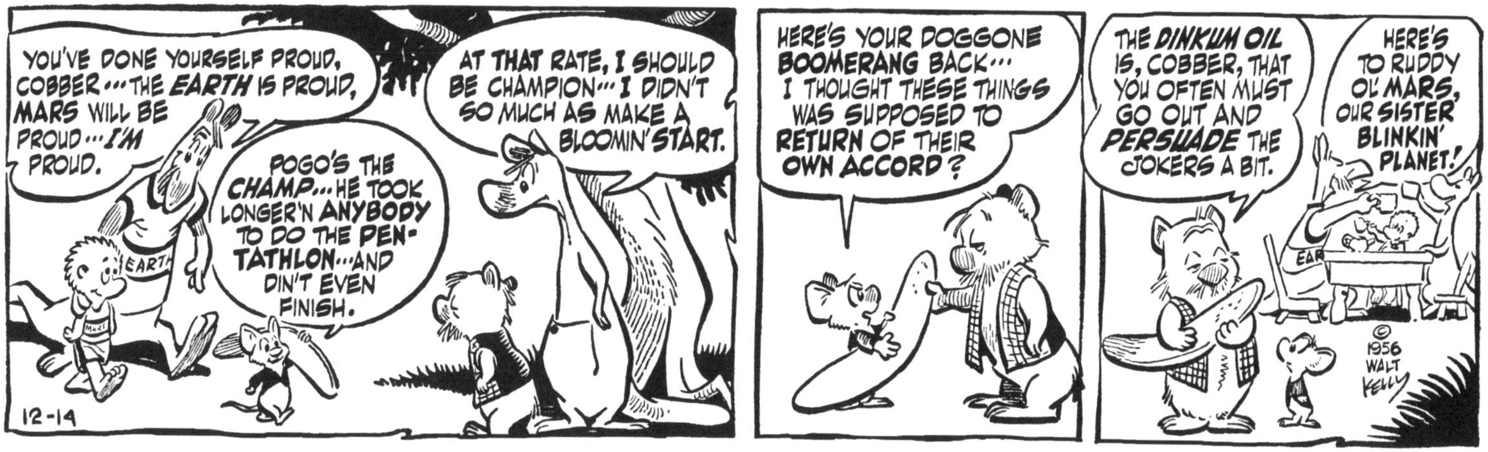
YOU'VE DONE YOURSELF PROUD, COBBER... THE EARTH IS PROUD, MARS WILL BE PROUD... I'M PROUD.
POGO'S THE CHAMP... HE TOOK LONGER'N ANYBODY TO DO THE PENTATHLON... AND DIN'T EVEN FINISH.
AT THAT RATE, I SHOULD BE CHAMPION... I DIDN'T SO MUCH AS MAKE A BLOOMIN' START.
EARTH
12-14
HERE'S YOUR DOGGONE BOOMERANG BACK... I THOUGHT THESE THINGS WAS SUPPOSED TO RETURN OF THEIR OWN ACCORD?
THE DINKUM OIL IS, COBBER, THAT YOU OFTEN MUST GO OUT AND PERSUADE THE JOKERS A BIT.
HERE'S TO RUDDY OL' MARS, OUR SISTER BLINKIN' PLANET!
© 1956 WALT KELLY

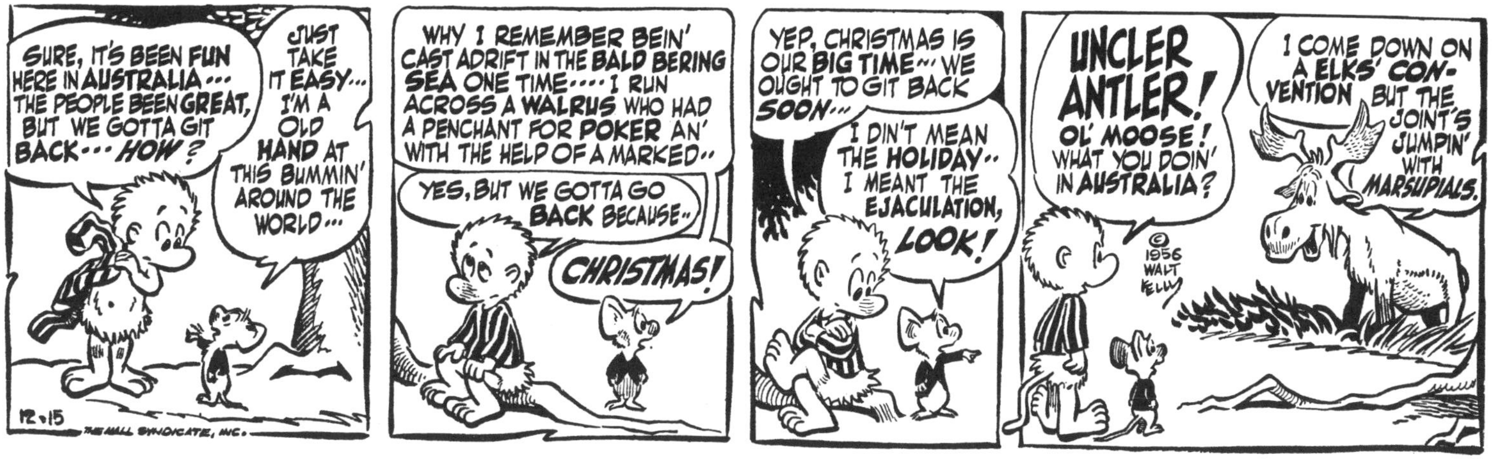
SURE, IT'S BEEN FUN HERE IN AUSTRALIA... THE PEOPLE BEEN GREAT, BUT WE GOTTA GIT BACK... HOW?
JUST TAKE IT EASY... I'M A OLD HAND AT THIS BUMMIN' AROUND THE WORLD...
12-15
THE HALL SYNDICATE, INC.
WHY I REMEMBER BEIN' CAST ADRIFT IN THE BALD BERING SEA ONE TIME.... I RUN ACROSS A WALRUS WHO HAD A PENCHANT FOR POKER AN' WITH THE HELP OF A MARKED..
YES, BUT WE GOTTA GO BACK BECAUSE..
CHRISTMAS!
YEP, CHRISTMAS IS OUR BIG TIME.. WE OUGHT TO GIT BACK SOON...
I DIN'T MEAN THE HOLIDAY.. I MEANT THE EJACULATION, LOOK!
UNCLER ANTLER! OL' MOOSE! WHAT YOU DOIN' IN AUSTRALIA?
I COME DOWN ON A ELKS' CONVENTION BUT THE JOINT'S JUMPIN' WITH MARSUPIALS.
© 1956 WALT KELLY

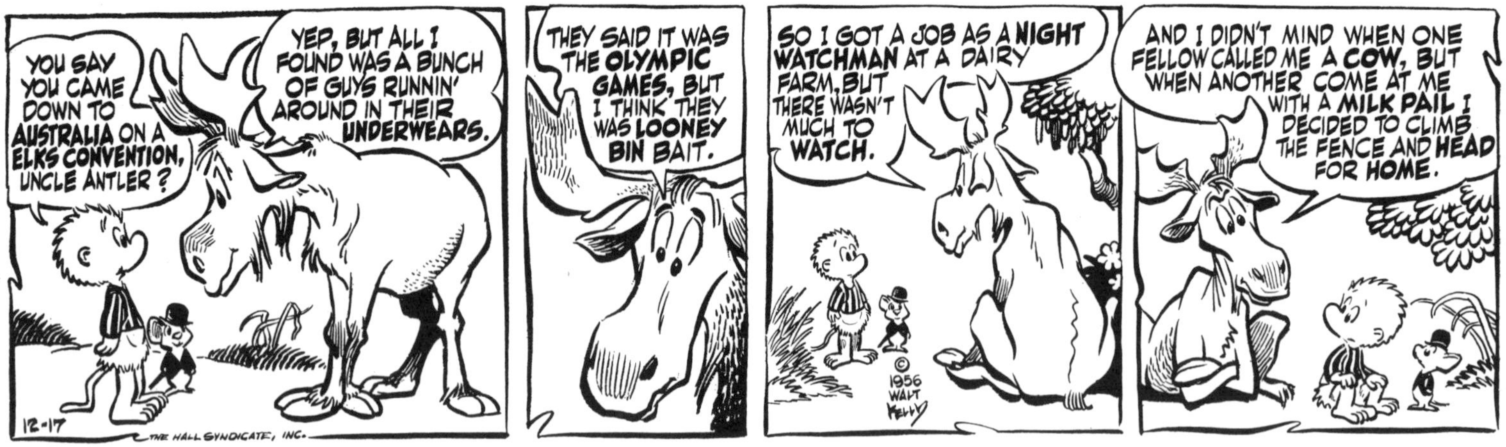
YOU SAY YOU CAME DOWN TO AUSTRALIA ON A ELKS CONVENTION, UNCLE ANTLER?
YEP, BUT ALL I FOUND WAS A BUNCH OF GUYS RUNNIN' AROUND IN THEIR UNDERWEARS.
THEY SAID IT WAS THE OLYMPIC GAMES, BUT I THINK THEY WAS LOONEY BIN BAIT.
SO I GOT A JOB AS A NIGHT WATCHMAN AT A DAIRY FARM, BUT THERE WASN'T MUCH TO WATCH.
AND I DIDN'T MIND WHEN ONE FELLOW CALLED ME A COW, BUT WHEN ANOTHER COME AT ME WITH A MILK PAIL I DECIDED TO CLIMB THE FENCE AND HEAD FOR HOME.
12-17
THE HALL SYNDICATE, INC.
© 1956 WALT KELLY

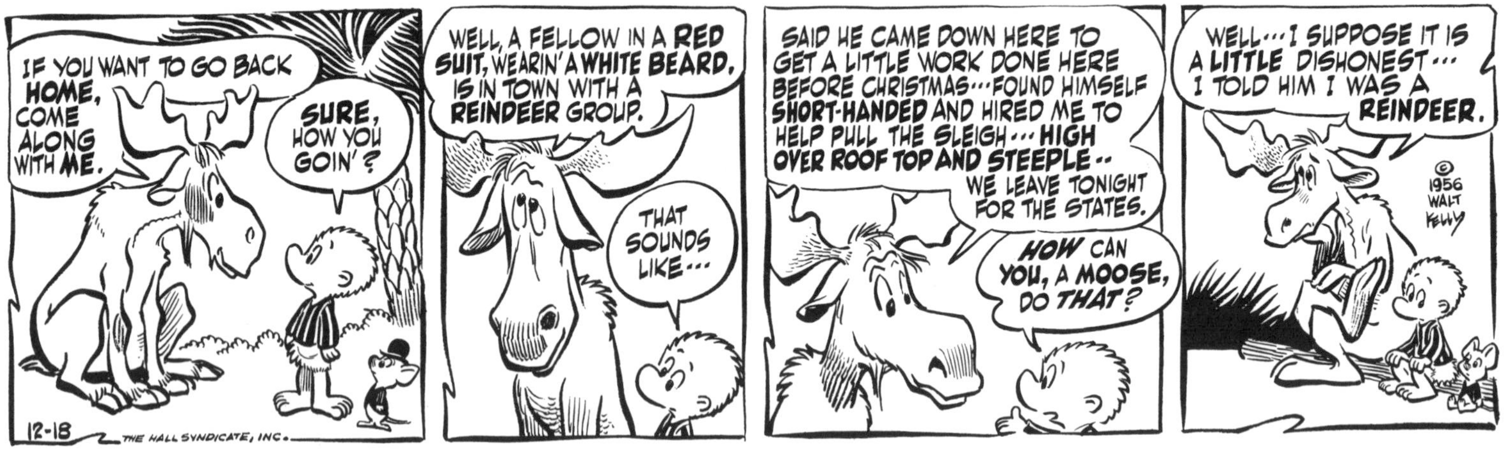
IF YOU WANT TO GO BACK HOME, COME ALONG WITH ME.
SURE, HOW YOU GOIN'?
WELL, A FELLOW IN A RED SUIT, WEARIN' A WHITE BEARD, IS IN TOWN WITH A REINDEER GROUP.
THAT SOUNDS LIKE...
SAID HE CAME DOWN HERE TO GET A LITTLE WORK DONE HERE BEFORE CHRISTMAS... FOUND HIMSELF SHORT-HANDED AND HIRED ME TO HELP PULL THE SLEIGH... HIGH OVER ROOF TOP AND STEEPLE.. WE LEAVE TONIGHT FOR THE STATES.
HOW CAN YOU, A MOOSE, DO THAT?
WELL... I SUPPOSE IT IS A LITTLE DISHONEST... I TOLD HIM I WAS A REINDEER.
12-18
THE HALL SYNDICATE, INC.
© 1956 WALT KELLY

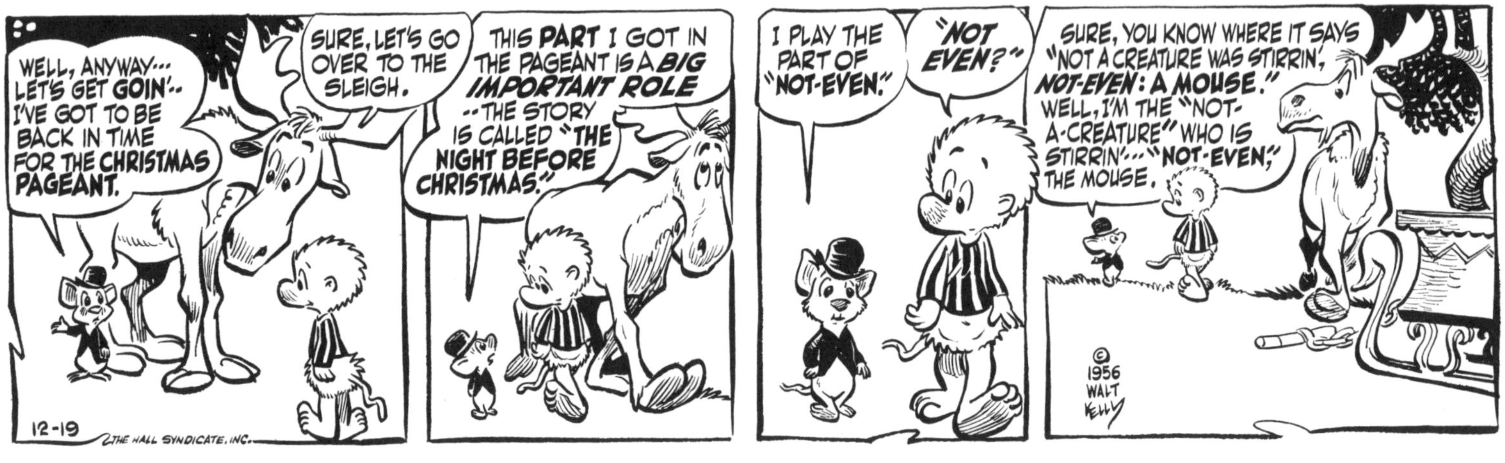
WELL, ANYWAY... LET'S GET GOIN'.. I'VE GOT TO BE BACK IN TIME FOR THE CHRISTMAS PAGEANT.
SURE, LET'S GO OVER TO THE SLEIGH.
THIS PART I GOT IN THE PAGEANT IS A BIG IMPORTANT ROLE --THE STORY IS CALLED "THE NIGHT BEFORE CHRISTMAS."
I PLAY THE PART OF "NOT-EVEN."
"NOT EVEN?"
SURE, YOU KNOW WHERE IT SAYS "NOT A CREATURE WAS STIRRIN', NOT-EVEN: A MOUSE." WELL, I'M THE "NOT-A-CREATURE" WHO IS STIRRIN'... "NOT-EVEN," THE MOUSE.
12-19
THE HALL SYNDICATE, INC.
© 1956 WALT KELLY

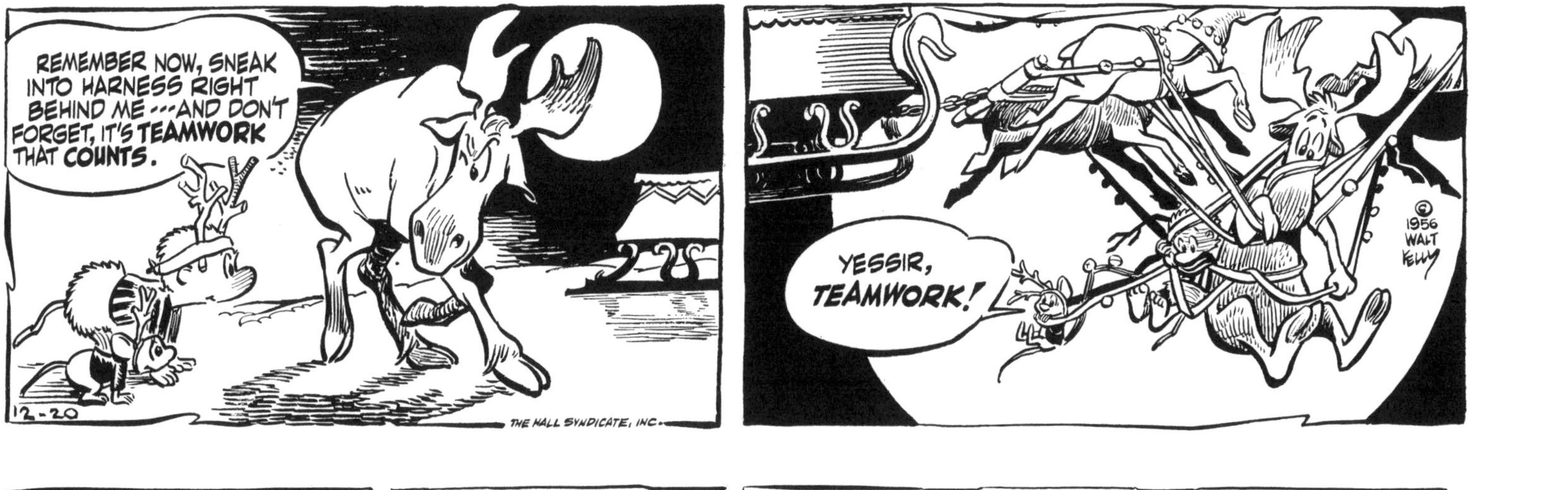
REMEMBER NOW, SNEAK INTO HARNESS RIGHT BEHIND ME --- AND DON'T FORGET, IT'S TEAMWORK THAT COUNTS.
12-20
THE HALL SYNDICATE, INC.
YESSIR, TEAMWORK!
© 1956 WALT KELLY

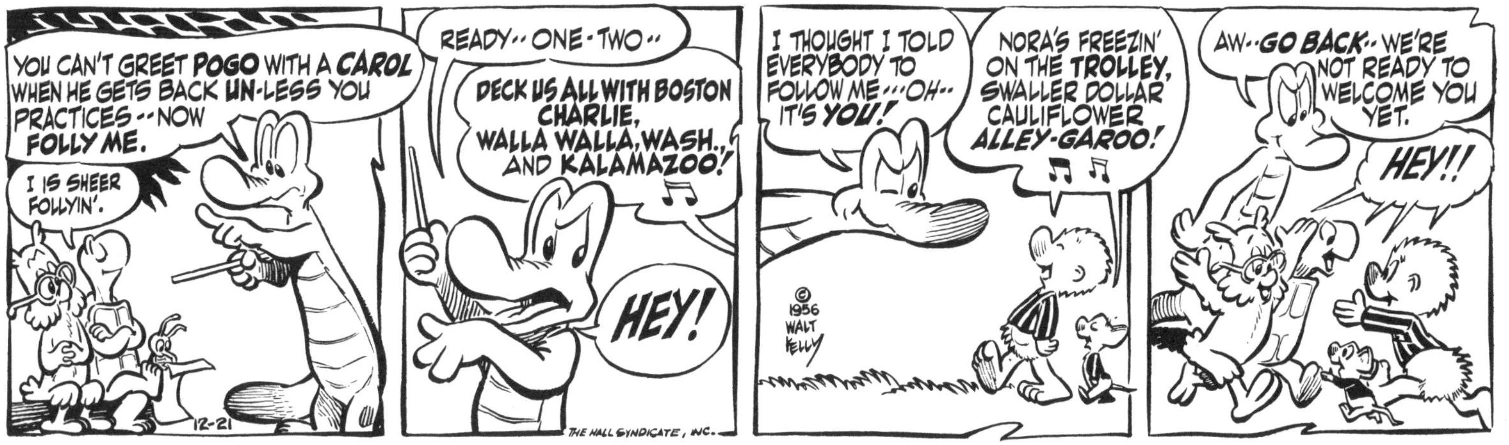
YOU CAN'T GREET POGO WITH A CAROL WHEN HE GETS BACK UN-LESS YOU PRACTICES -- NOW FOLLY ME.
I IS SHEER FOLLYIN'.
12-21
READY -- ONE - TWO --
DECK US ALL WITH BOSTON CHARLIE, WALLA WALLA, WASH., AND KALAMAZOO!
HEY!
THE HALL SYNDICATE, INC.
I THOUGHT I TOLD EVERYBODY TO FOLLOW ME --- OH -- IT'S YOU!
NORA'S FREEZIN' ON THE TROLLEY, SWALLER DOLLAR CAULIFLOWER ALLEY-GAROO!
© 1956 WALT KELLY
AW -- GO BACK -- WE'RE NOT READY TO WELCOME YOU YET.
HEY!!

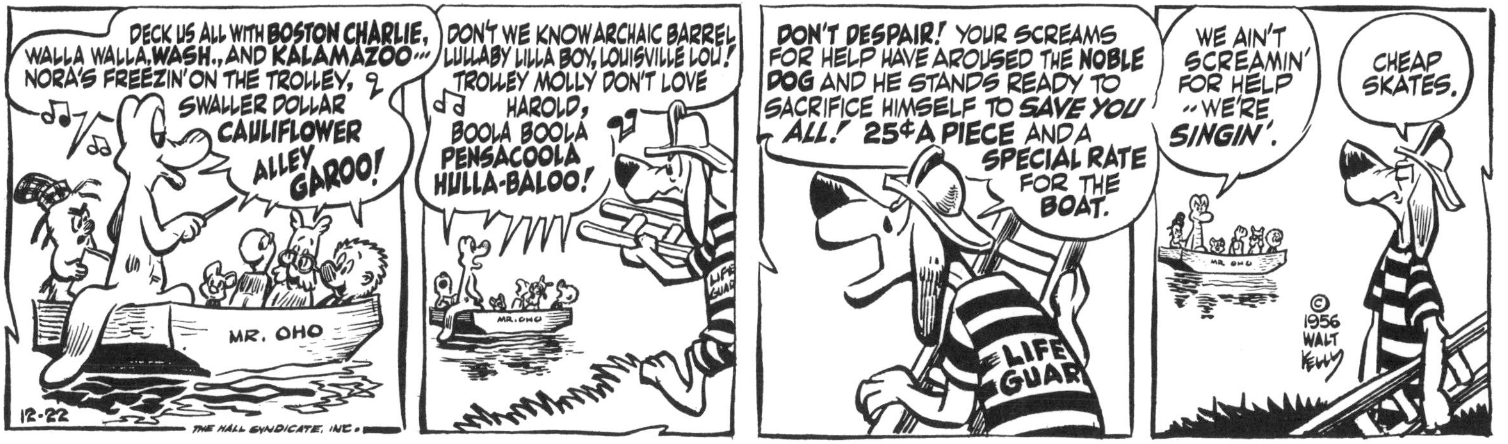
DECK US ALL WITH BOSTON CHARLIE, WALLA WALLA, WASH., AND KALAMAZOO --- NORA'S FREEZIN' ON THE TROLLEY, SWALLER DOLLAR CAULIFLOWER ALLEY GAROO!
MR. OHO
12-22
THE HALL SYNDICATE, INC.
DON'T WE KNOW ARCHAIC BARREL LULLABY LILLA BOY, LOUISVILLE LOU! TROLLEY MOLLY DON'T LOVE HAROLD, BOOLA BOOLA PENSACOOLA HULLA-BALOO!
MR. OHO
LIFE GUAR
DON'T DESPAIR! YOUR SCREAMS FOR HELP HAVE AROUSED THE NOBLE DOG AND HE STANDS READY TO SACRIFICE HIMSELF TO SAVE YOU ALL! 25¢ A PIECE AND A SPECIAL RATE FOR THE BOAT.
LIFE GUAR
WE AIN'T SCREAMIN' FOR HELP -- WE'RE SINGIN'.
CHEAP SKATES.
MR. OHO
© 1956 WALT KELLY

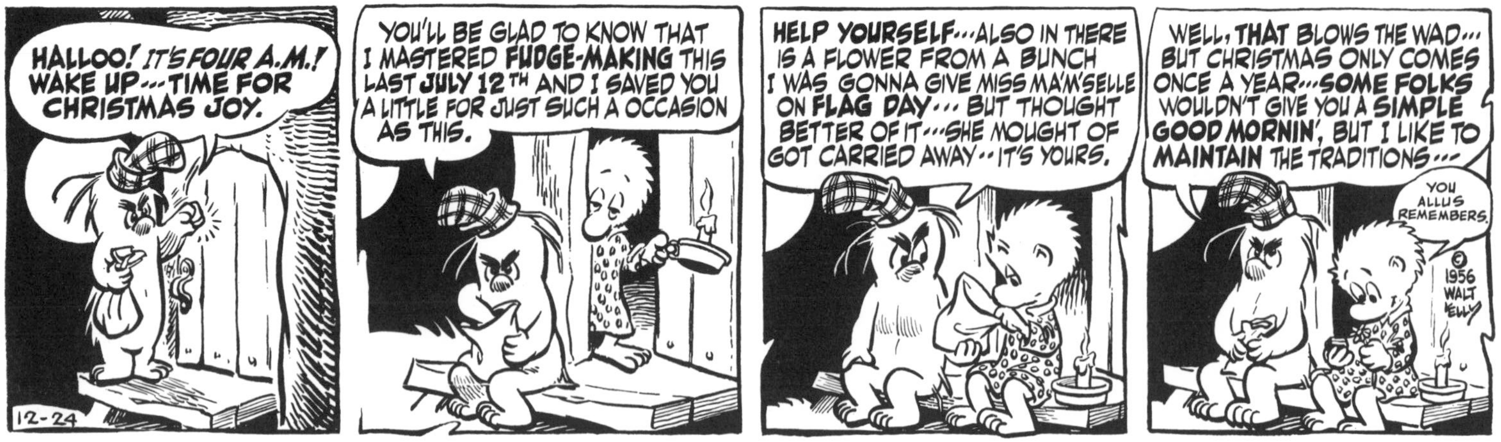
HALLOO! IT'S FOUR A.M.! WAKE UP... TIME FOR CHRISTMAS JOY.
YOU'LL BE GLAD TO KNOW THAT I MASTERED FUDGE-MAKING THIS LAST JULY 12TH AND I SAVED YOU A LITTLE FOR JUST SUCH A OCCASION AS THIS.
HELP YOURSELF... ALSO IN THERE IS A FLOWER FROM A BUNCH I WAS GONNA GIVE MISS MA'M'SELLE ON FLAG DAY... BUT THOUGHT BETTER OF IT... SHE MOUGHT OF GOT CARRIED AWAY.. IT'S YOURS.
WELL, THAT BLOWS THE WAD... BUT CHRISTMAS ONLY COMES ONCE A YEAR... SOME FOLKS WOULDN'T GIVE YOU A SIMPLE GOOD MORNIN', BUT I LIKE TO MAINTAIN THE TRADITIONS...
YOU ALLUS REMEMBERS.
© 1956 WALT KELLY
12-24

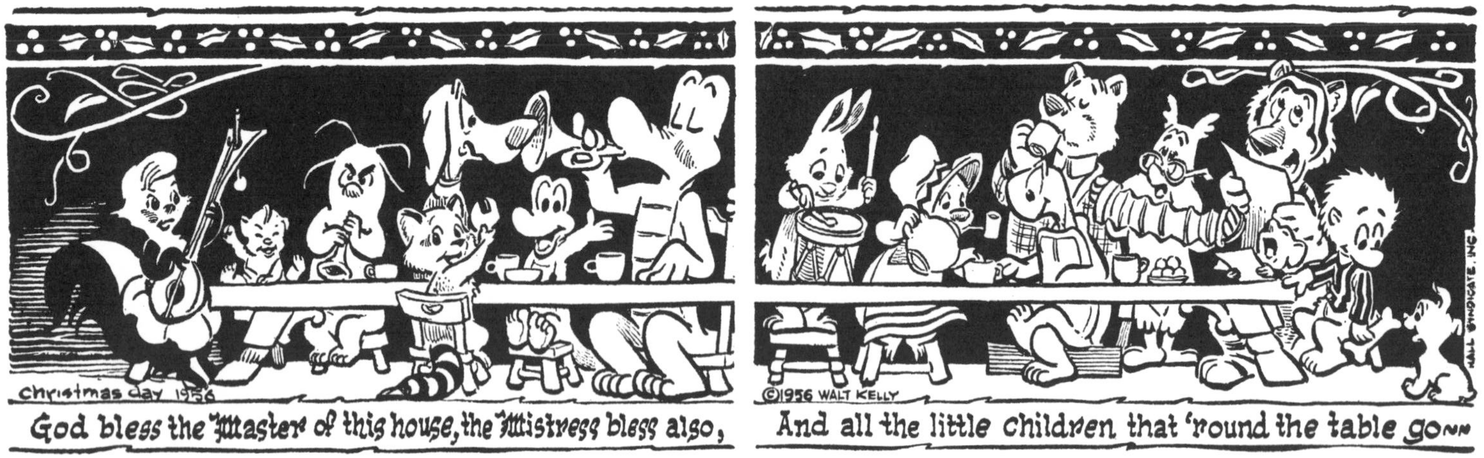
Christmas Day 1956
©1956 WALT KELLY
HALL SYNDICATE, INC.
God bless the Master of this house, the Mistress bless also,
And all the little children that 'round the table go~~

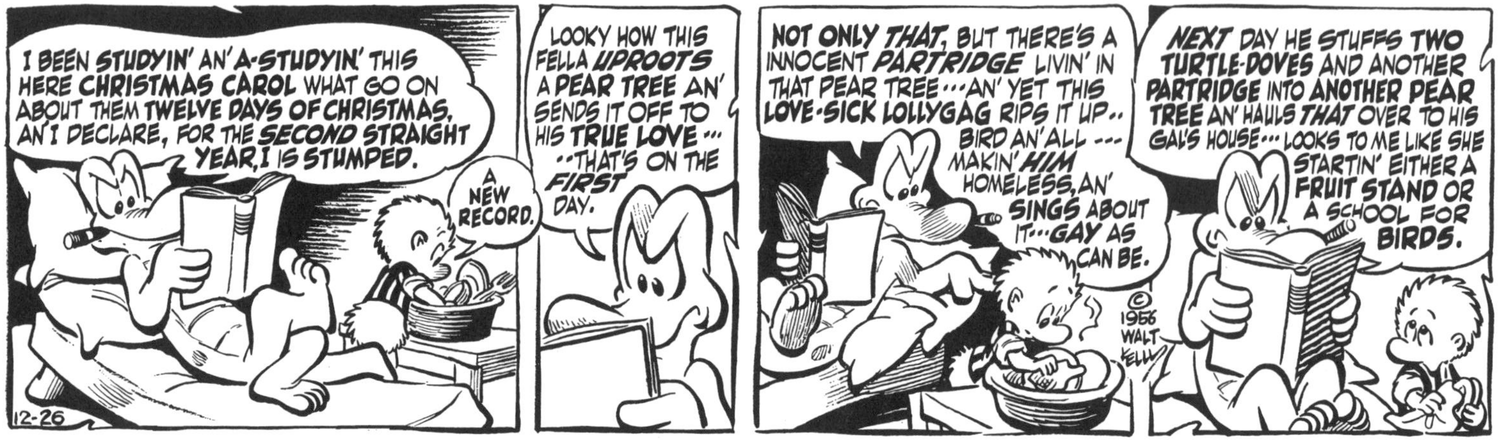
I BEEN STUDYIN' AN' A-STUDYIN' THIS HERE CHRISTMAS CAROL WHAT GO ON ABOUT THEM TWELVE DAYS OF CHRISTMAS, AN' I DECLARE, FOR THE SECOND STRAIGHT YEAR, I IS STUMPED.
A NEW RECORD.
LOOKY HOW THIS FELLA UPROOTS A PEAR TREE AN' SENDS IT OFF TO HIS TRUE LOVE... ...THAT'S ON THE FIRST DAY.
NOT ONLY THAT, BUT THERE'S A INNOCENT PARTRIDGE LIVIN' IN THAT PEAR TREE... AN' YET THIS LOVE-SICK LOLLYGAG RIPS IT UP.. BIRD AN' ALL --- MAKIN' HIM HOMELESS, AN' SINGS ABOUT IT... GAY AS CAN BE.
NEXT DAY HE STUFFS TWO TURTLE-DOVES AND ANOTHER PARTRIDGE INTO ANOTHER PEAR TREE AN' HAULS THAT OVER TO HIS GAL'S HOUSE... LOOKS TO ME LIKE SHE STARTIN' EITHER A FRUIT STAND OR A SCHOOL FOR BIRDS.
© 1956 WALT KELLY
12-26

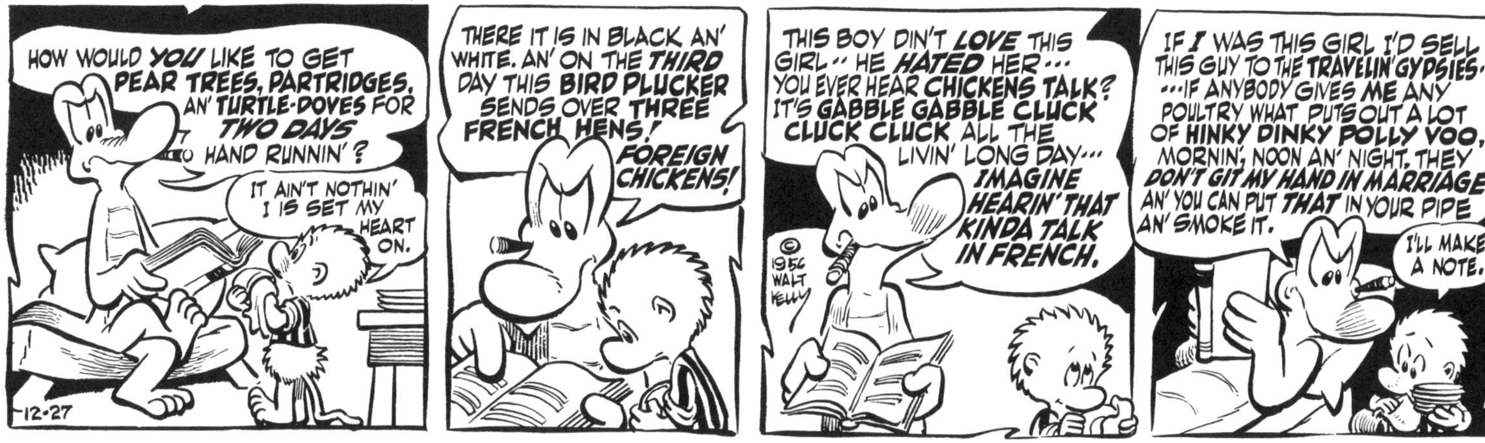
HOW WOULD YOU LIKE TO GET PEAR TREES, PARTRIDGES, AN' TURTLE-DOVES FOR TWO DAYS HAND RUNNIN'?
IT AIN'T NOTHIN' I IS SET MY HEART ON.
12-27
THERE IT IS IN BLACK AN' WHITE. AN' ON THE THIRD DAY THIS BIRD PLUCKER SENDS OVER THREE FRENCH HENS!
FOREIGN CHICKENS!
THIS BOY DIN'T LOVE THIS GIRL.. HE HATED HER... YOU EVER HEAR CHICKENS TALK? IT'S GABBLE GABBLE CLUCK CLUCK CLUCK ALL THE LIVIN' LONG DAY...
IMAGINE HEARIN' THAT KINDA TALK IN FRENCH.
© 1956 WALT KELLY
IF I WAS THIS GIRL I'D SELL THIS GUY TO THE TRAVELIN' GYPSIES.. ...IF ANYBODY GIVES ME ANY POULTRY WHAT PUTS OUT A LOT OF HINKY DINKY POLLY VOO, MORNIN', NOON AN' NIGHT, THEY DON'T GIT MY HAND IN MARRIAGE. AN' YOU CAN PUT THAT IN YOUR PIPE AN' SMOKE IT.
I'LL MAKE A NOTE.

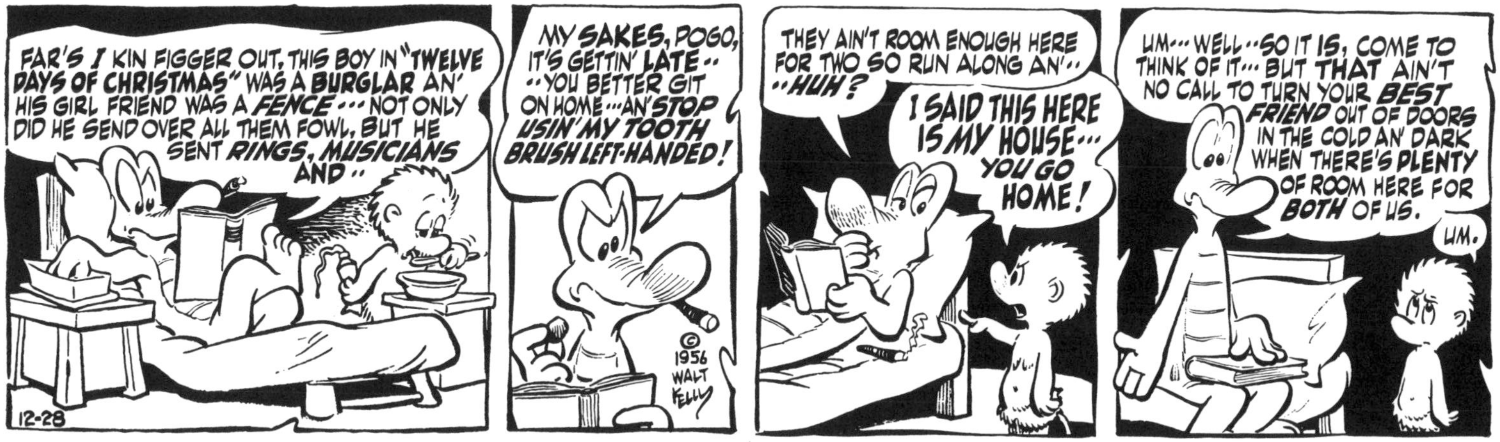
FAR'S I KIN FIGGER OUT, THIS BOY IN "TWELVE DAYS OF CHRISTMAS" WAS A BURGLAR AN' HIS GIRL FRIEND WAS A FENCE... NOT ONLY DID HE SEND OVER ALL THEM FOWL, BUT HE SENT RINGS, MUSICIANS AND..
12-28
MY SAKES, POGO, IT'S GETTIN' LATE.. ..YOU BETTER GIT ON HOME...AN' STOP USIN' MY TOOTH BRUSH LEFT-HANDED!
© 1956 WALT KELLY
THEY AIN'T ROOM ENOUGH HERE FOR TWO SO RUN ALONG AN'.. ..HUH?
I SAID THIS HERE IS MY HOUSE... YOU GO HOME!
UM... WELL..SO IT IS, COME TO THINK OF IT... BUT THAT AIN'T NO CALL TO TURN YOUR BEST FRIEND OUT OF DOORS IN THE COLD AN' DARK WHEN THERE'S PLENTY OF ROOM HERE FOR BOTH OF US.
UM.

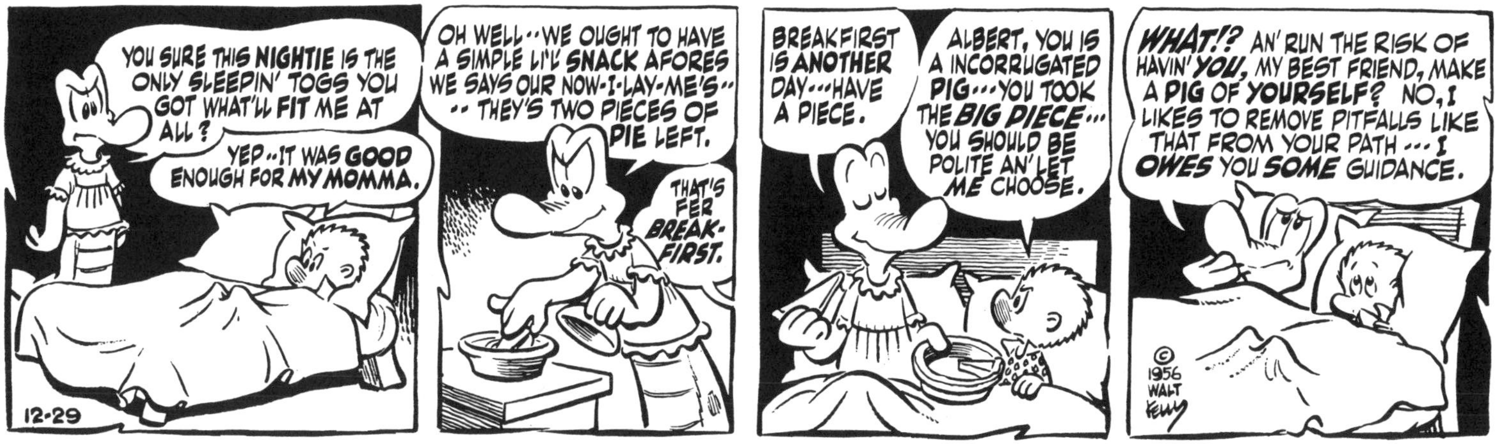
YOU SURE THIS NIGHTIE IS THE ONLY SLEEPIN' TOGS YOU GOT WHAT'LL FIT ME AT ALL?
YEP..IT WAS GOOD ENOUGH FOR MY MOMMA.
12-29
OH WELL..WE OUGHT TO HAVE A SIMPLE LI'L SNACK AFORES WE SAYS OUR NOW-I-LAY-ME'S.. .. THEY'S TWO PIECES OF PIE LEFT.
THAT'S FER BREAK-FIRST.
BREAKFIRST IS ANOTHER DAY...HAVE A PIECE.
ALBERT, YOU IS A INCORRUGATED PIG...YOU TOOK THE BIG PIECE... YOU SHOULD BE POLITE AN' LET ME CHOOSE.
© 1956 WALT KELLY
WHAT!? AN' RUN THE RISK OF HAVIN' YOU, MY BEST FRIEND, MAKE A PIG OF YOURSELF? NO, I LIKES TO REMOVE PITFALLS LIKE THAT FROM YOUR PATH ... I OWES YOU SOME GUIDANCE.

I'D LIKE TO TAKE THIS OPPORTUNITY TO WISH ONE AND ALL A MERRY CHRISTMAS.
THAT WAS LAST WEEK.
WHAT'S THIS WEEK?
HAPPY NEW YEAR!
WELL, IN THAT CASE I APOLOGIZES! I TAKES BACK THE MERRY CHRISTMAS AND WISHES YOU A HAPPY NEW YEAR!
IT AIN'T VERY COMFORTIN' TAKIN' A HAPPY NEW YEAR FROM A MAN WHAT HAS TO BE REMINDED OF WHAT HE MEANS...
IT DON'T MAKE NO DIFFERMINTS --I DIN'T MEAN NO HARM BY EITHER ONE.
© 1956 WALT KELLY
12-31

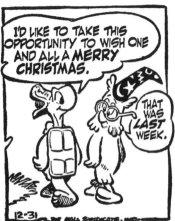

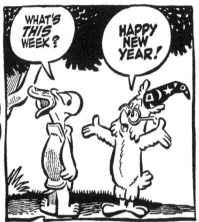

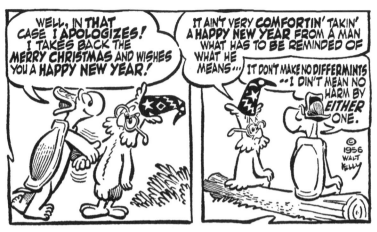

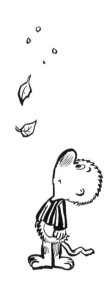

SUNDAY FUNNIES

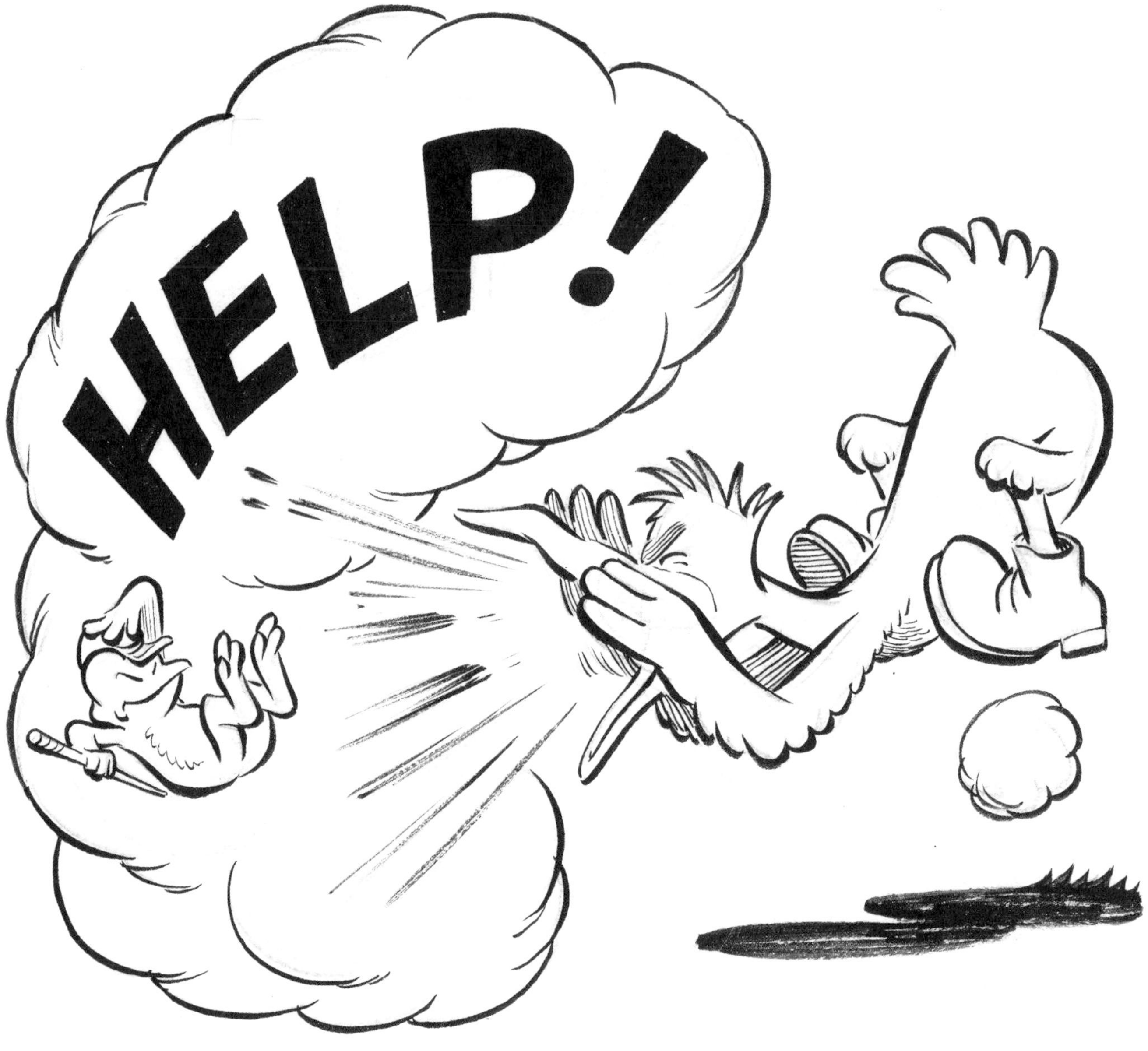
HELP!

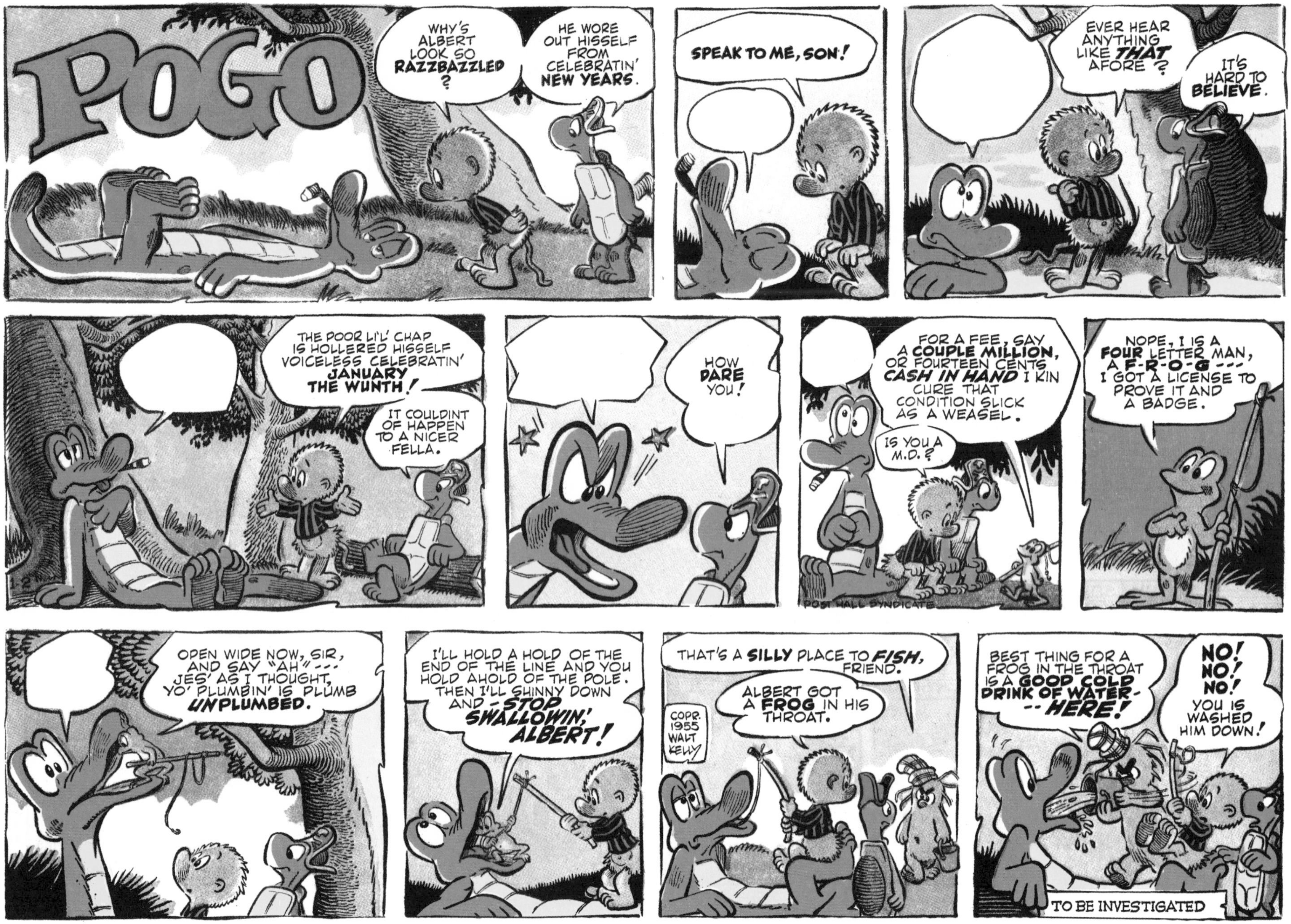
POGO
WHY'S ALBERT LOOK SO RAZZBAZZLED ?
HE WORE OUT HISSELF FROM CELEBRATIN' NEW YEARS.
SPEAK TO ME, SON!
EVER HEAR ANYTHING LIKE THAT AFORE ?
IT'S HARD TO BELIEVE.
THE POOR LI'L' CHAP IS HOLLERED HISSELF VOICELESS CELEBRATIN' JANUARY THE WUNTH!
IT COULDINT OF HAPPEN TO A NICER FELLA.
HOW DARE YOU!
FOR A FEE, SAY A COUPLE MILLION, OR FOURTEEN CENTS CASH IN HAND I KIN CURE THAT CONDITION SLICK AS A WEASEL.
IS YOU A M.D.?
POST HALL SYNDICATE
NOPE, I IS A FOUR LETTER MAN, A F-R-O-G --- I GOT A LICENSE TO PROVE IT AND A BADGE.
OPEN WIDE NOW, SIR, AND SAY "AH" --- JES' AS I THOUGHT, YO' PLUMBIN' IS PLUMB UNPLUMBED.
I'LL HOLD A HOLD OF THE END OF THE LINE AND YOU HOLD AHOLD OF THE POLE. THEN I'LL SHINNY DOWN AND - STOP SWALLOWIN', ALBERT!
THAT'S A SILLY PLACE TO FISH, FRIEND.
ALBERT GOT A FROG IN HIS THROAT.
COPR. 1955 WALT KELLY
BEST THING FOR A FROG IN THE THROAT IS A GOOD COLD DRINK OF WATER- -- HERE!
NO! NO! NO! YOU IS WASHED HIM DOWN!
TO BE INVESTIGATED

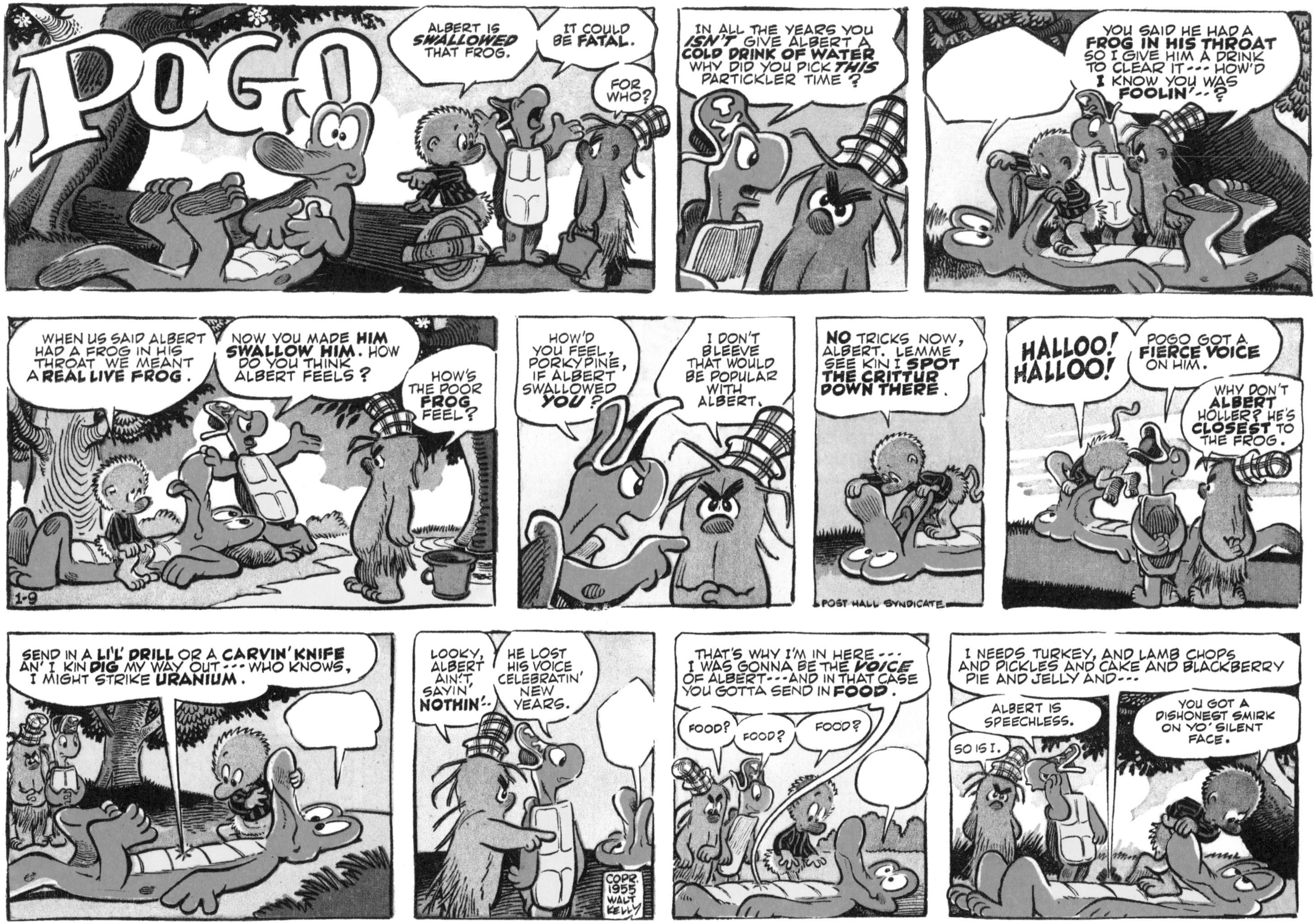
POGO
ALBERT IS SWALLOWED THAT FROG.
IT COULD BE FATAL.
FOR WHO?
IN ALL THE YEARS YOU ISN'T GIVE ALBERT A COLD DRINK OF WATER WHY DID YOU PICK THIS PARTICKLER TIME ?
YOU SAID HE HAD A FROG IN HIS THROAT SO I GIVE HIM A DRINK TO CLEAR IT --- HOW'D I KNOW YOU WAS FOOLIN'--?
WHEN US SAID ALBERT HAD A FROG IN HIS THROAT WE MEANT A REAL LIVE FROG.
NOW YOU MADE HIM SWALLOW HIM. HOW DO YOU THINK ALBERT FEELS ?
HOW'S THE POOR FROG FEEL?
1-9
HOW'D YOU FEEL, PORKYPINE, IF ALBERT SWALLOWED YOU ?
I DON'T BLEEVE THAT WOULD BE POPULAR WITH ALBERT.
NO TRICKS NOW, ALBERT. LEMME SEE KIN I SPOT THE CRITTUR DOWN THERE.
POST HALL SYNDICATE
HALLOO! HALLOO!
POGO GOT A FIERCE VOICE ON HIM.
WHY DON'T ALBERT HOLLER? HE'S CLOSEST TO THE FROG.
SEND IN A LI'L' DRILL OR A CARVIN' KNIFE AN' I KIN DIG MY WAY OUT --- WHO KNOWS, I MIGHT STRIKE URANIUM.
LOOKY, ALBERT AIN'T SAYIN' NOTHIN'.
HE LOST HIS VOICE CELEBRATIN' NEW YEARS.
COPR. 1955 WALT KELLY
THAT'S WHY I'M IN HERE --- I WAS GONNA BE THE VOICE OF ALBERT---AND IN THAT CASE YOU GOTTA SEND IN FOOD.
FOOD?
FOOD?
FOOD?
I NEEDS TURKEY, AND LAMB CHOPS AND PICKLES AND CAKE AND BLACKBERRY PIE AND JELLY AND---
ALBERT IS SPEECHLESS.
SO IS I.
YOU GOT A DISHONEST SMIRK ON YO' SILENT FACE.

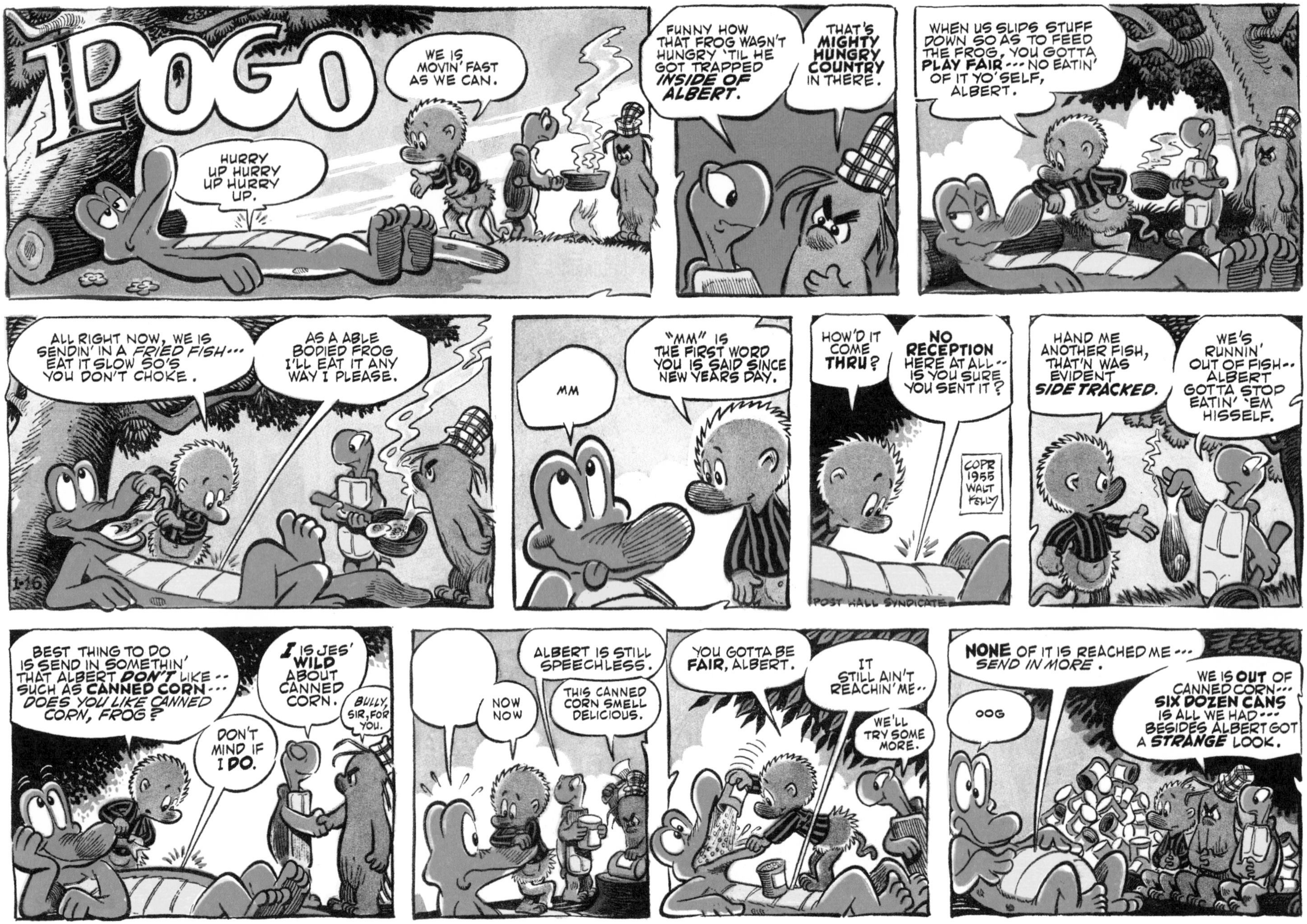
POGO
WE IS MOVIN' FAST AS WE CAN.
HURRY UP HURRY UP HURRY UP.
FUNNY HOW THAT FROG WASN'T HUNGRY 'TIL HE GOT TRAPPED INSIDE OF ALBERT.
THAT'S MIGHTY HUNGRY COUNTRY IN THERE.
WHEN US SLIPS STUFF DOWN SO AS TO FEED THE FROG, YOU GOTTA PLAY FAIR --- NO EATIN' OF IT YO'SELF, ALBERT.
ALL RIGHT NOW, WE IS SENDIN' IN A FRIED FISH --- EAT IT SLOW SO'S YOU DON'T CHOKE.
AS A ABLE BODIED FROG I'LL EAT IT ANY WAY I PLEASE.
1-16
MM
"MM" IS THE FIRST WORD YOU IS SAID SINCE NEW YEARS DAY.
HOW'D IT COME THRU?
NO RECEPTION HERE AT ALL -- IS YOU SURE YOU SENT IT?
COPR 1955 WALT KELLY
POST HALL SYNDICATE
HAND ME ANOTHER FISH, THAT'N WAS EVIDENT SIDE TRACKED.
WE'S RUNNIN' OUT OF FISH -- ALBERT GOTTA STOP EATIN' 'EM HISSELF.
BEST THING TO DO IS SEND IN SOMETHIN' THAT ALBERT DON'T LIKE -- SUCH AS CANNED CORN --- DOES YOU LIKE CANNED CORN, FROG?
I IS JES' WILD ABOUT CANNED CORN.
BULLY, SIR, FOR YOU.
DON'T MIND IF I DO.
ALBERT IS STILL SPEECHLESS.
NOW NOW
THIS CANNED CORN SMELL DELICIOUS.
YOU GOTTA BE FAIR, ALBERT.
IT STILL AIN'T REACHIN' ME --
WE'LL TRY SOME MORE.
NONE OF IT IS REACHED ME --- SEND IN MORE.
OOG
WE IS OUT OF CANNED CORN --- SIX DOZEN CANS IS ALL WE HAD --- BESIDES ALBERT GOT A STRANGE LOOK.

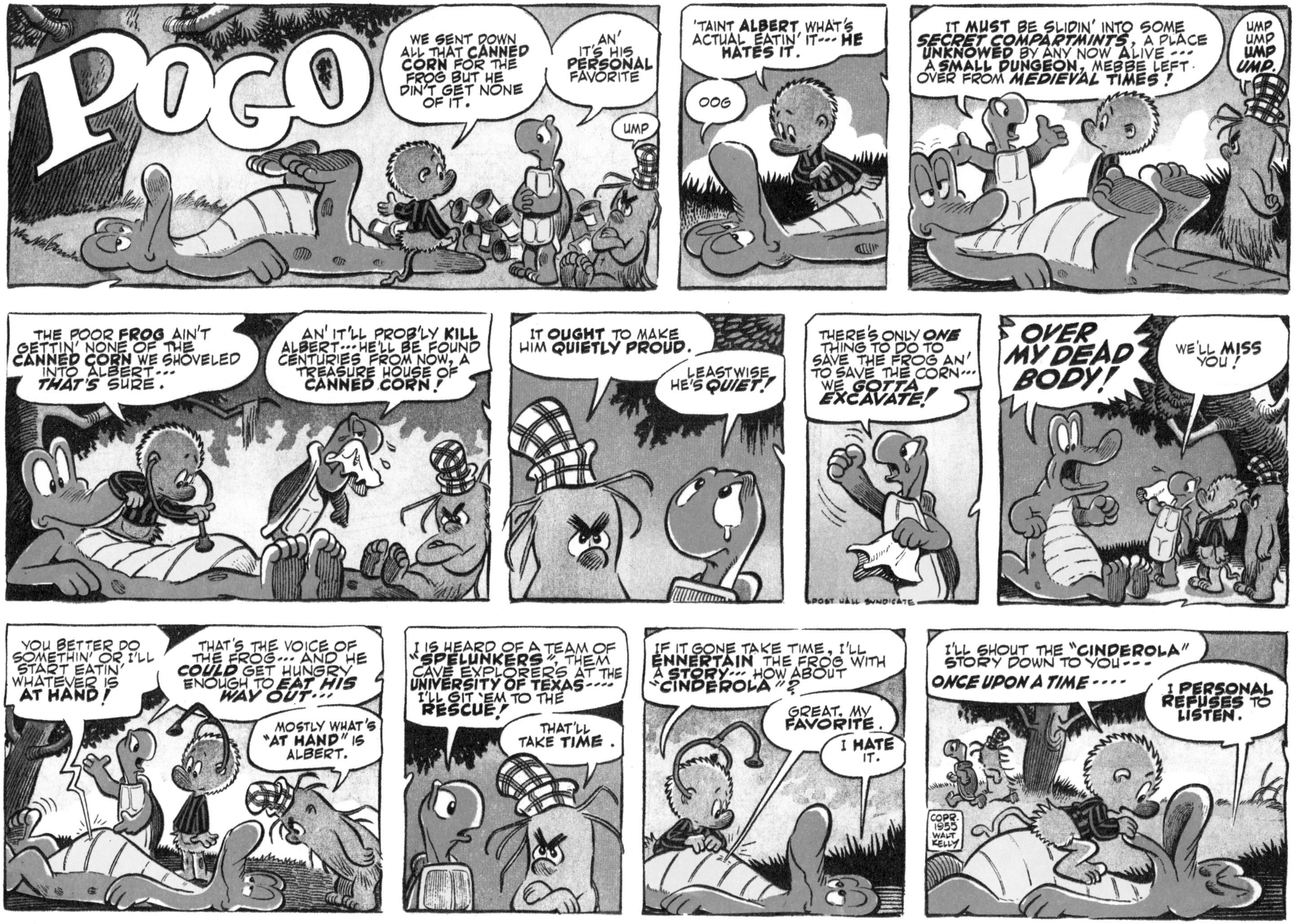
POGO
WE SENT DOWN ALL THAT CANNED CORN FOR THE FROG BUT HE DIN'T GET NONE OF IT.
AN' IT'S HIS PERSONAL FAVORITE
UMP
'TAINT ALBERT WHAT'S ACTUAL EATIN' IT--- HE HATES IT.
OOG
IT MUST BE SLIDIN' INTO SOME SECRET COMPARTMINTS, A PLACE UNKNOWED BY ANY NOW ALIVE --- A SMALL DUNGEON, MEBBE LEFT OVER FROM MEDIEVAL TIMES!
UMP UMP UMP UMP.
THE POOR FROG AIN'T GETTIN' NONE OF THE CANNED CORN WE SHOVELED INTO ALBERT--- THAT'S SURE.
AN' IT'LL PROB'LY KILL ALBERT--- HE'LL BE FOUND CENTURIES FROM NOW, A TREASURE HOUSE OF CANNED CORN!
IT OUGHT TO MAKE HIM QUIETLY PROUD.
LEASTWISE HE'S QUIET!
THERE'S ONLY ONE THING TO DO TO SAVE THE FROG AN' TO SAVE THE CORN--- WE GOTTA EXCAVATE!
POST HALL SYNDICATE
OVER MY DEAD BODY!
WE'LL MISS YOU!
YOU BETTER DO SOMETHIN' OR I'LL START EATIN' WHATEVER IS AT HAND!
THAT'S THE VOICE OF THE FROG--- AND HE COULD GET HUNGRY ENOUGH TO EAT HIS WAY OUT---
MOSTLY WHAT'S "AT HAND" IS ALBERT.
I IS HEARD OF A TEAM OF "SPELUNKERS", THEM CAVE EXPLORERS AT THE UNIVERSITY OF TEXAS---- I'LL GIT 'EM TO THE RESCUE!
THAT'LL TAKE TIME.
IF IT GONE TAKE TIME, I'LL ENNERTAIN THE FROG WITH A STORY--- HOW ABOUT "CINDEROLA"?
GREAT, MY FAVORITE.
I HATE IT.
COPR. 1955 WALT KELLY
I'LL SHOUT THE "CINDEROLA" STORY DOWN TO YOU--- ONCE UPON A TIME----
I PERSONAL REFUSES TO LISTEN.

SUNDAY, JANUARY 30, 1955

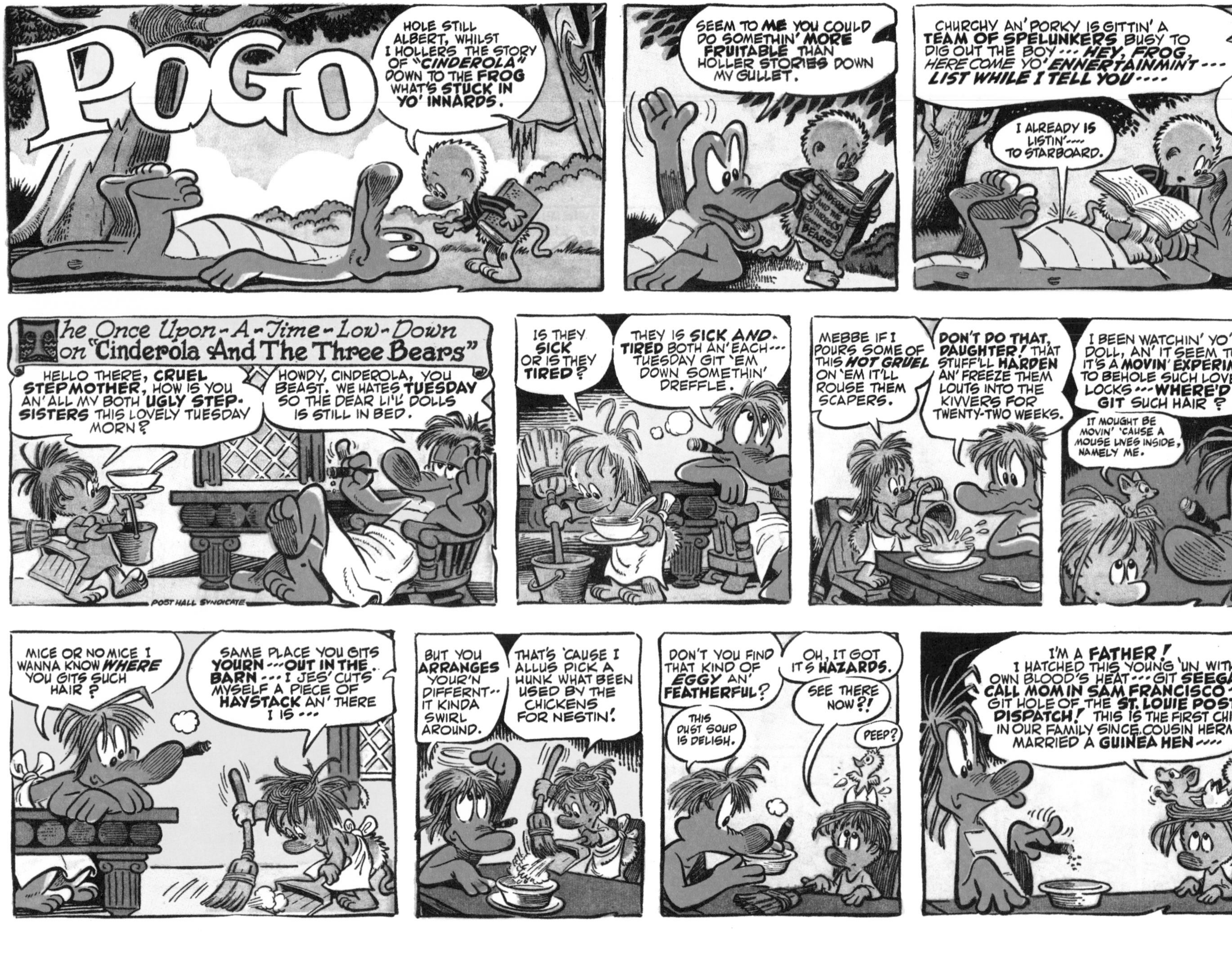
POGO
HOLE STILL ALBERT, WHILST I HOLLERS THE STORY OF "CINDEROLA" DOWN TO THE FROG WHAT'S STUCK IN YO' INNARDS.
SEEM TO ME YOU COULD DO SOMETHIN' MORE FRUITABLE THAN HOLLER STORIES DOWN MY GULLET.
CINDEROLA AND THE THREE(3) COUNT THREE BEARS
CHURCHY AN' PORKY IS GITTIN' A TEAM OF SPELUNKERS BUSY TO DIG OUT THE BOY --- HEY, FROG, HERE COME YO' ENNERTAINMINT --- LIST WHILE I TELL YOU ----
I ALREADY IS LISTIN' ---- TO STARBOARD.
I WON'T GIVE IT A SINGLE EAR.
The Once Upon-A-Time-Low-Down on "Cinderola And The Three Bears"
HELLO THERE, CRUEL STEPMOTHER, HOW IS YOU AN' ALL MY BOTH UGLY STEP-SISTERS THIS LOVELY TUESDAY MORN?
HOWDY, CINDEROLA, YOU BEAST. WE HATES TUESDAY SO THE DEAR LI'L DOLLS IS STILL IN BED.
POST HALL SYNDICATE
IS THEY SICK OR IS THEY TIRED?
THEY IS SICK AND TIRED BOTH AN' EACH --- TUESDAY GIT 'EM DOWN SOMETHIN' DREFFLE.
MEBBE IF I POURS SOME OF THIS HOT GRUEL ON 'EM IT'LL ROUSE THEM SCAPERS.
DON'T DO THAT, DAUGHTER! THAT STUFF'LL HARDEN AN' FREEZE THEM LOUTS INTO THE KIVVERS FOR TWENTY-TWO WEEKS.
I BEEN WATCHIN' YO' HAIR, DOLL, AN' IT SEEM TO ME IT'S A MOVIN' EXPERIMINTS TO BEHOLE SUCH LOVELY LOCKS --- WHERE'D YOU GIT SUCH HAIR?
IT MOUGHT BE MOVIN' 'CAUSE A MOUSE LIVES INSIDE, NAMELY ME.
MICE OR NO MICE I WANNA KNOW WHERE YOU GITS SUCH HAIR?
SAME PLACE YOU GITS YOURN --- OUT IN THE BARN --- I JES' CUTS MYSELF A PIECE OF HAYSTACK AN' THERE I IS ---
BUT YOU ARRANGES YOUR'N DIFFERNT -- IT KINDA SWIRL AROUND.
THAT'S 'CAUSE I ALLUS PICK A HUNK WHAT BEEN USED BY THE CHICKENS FOR NESTIN'.
DON'T YOU FIND THAT KIND OF EGGY AN' FEATHERFUL?
OH, IT GOT IT'S HAZARDS.
SEE THERE NOW?!
THIS DUST SOUP IS DELISH.
PEEP?
I'M A FATHER! I HATCHED THIS YOUNG 'UN WITH MY OWN BLOOD'S HEAT --- GIT SEEGARS --- CALL MOM IN SAM FRANCISCO --- GIT HOLE OF THE ST. LOUIE POST DISPATCH! THIS IS THE FIRST CHICKEN IN OUR FAMILY SINCE COUSIN HERM MARRIED A GUINEA HEN ----
OH PEEP!
COPR 1955 WALT KELLY

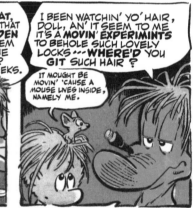

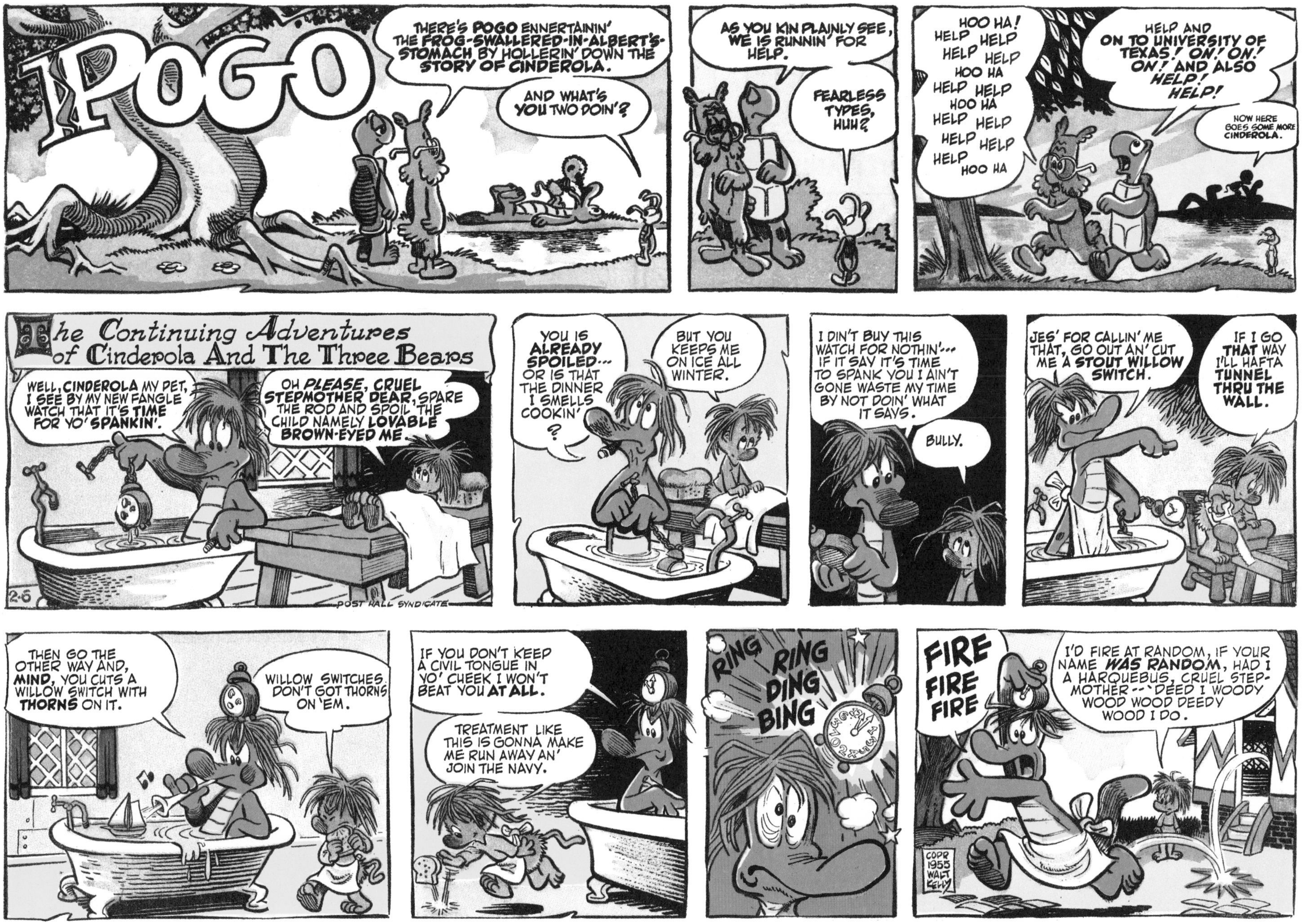
POGO
THERE'S POGO ENNERTAININ' THE FROG-SWALLERED-IN-ALBERT'S-STOMACH BY HOLLERIN' DOWN THE STORY OF CINDEROLA.
AND WHAT'S YOU TWO DOIN'?
AS YOU KIN PLAINLY SEE, WE IS RUNNIN' FOR HELP.
FEARLESS TYPES, HUH?
HOO HA! HELP HELP HELP HELP HOO HA HELP HELP HOO HA HELP HELP HELP HELP HELP HOO HA
HELP AND ON TO UNIVERSITY OF TEXAS! ON! ON! ON! AND ALSO HELP! HELP!
NOW HERE GOES SOME MORE CINDEROLA.
The Continuing Adventures of Cinderola And The Three Bears
WELL, CINDEROLA MY PET, I SEE BY MY NEW FANGLE WATCH THAT IT'S TIME FOR YO' SPANKIN'.
OH PLEASE, CRUEL STEPMOTHER DEAR, SPARE THE ROD AND SPOIL THE CHILD NAMELY LOVABLE BROWN-EYED ME.
2-6
POST HALL SYNDICATE
YOU IS ALREADY SPOILED... OR IS THAT THE DINNER I SMELLS COOKIN'?
BUT YOU KEEPS ME ON ICE ALL WINTER.
I DIN'T BUY THIS WATCH FOR NOTHIN'... IF IT SAY IT'S TIME TO SPANK YOU I AIN'T GONE WASTE MY TIME BY NOT DOIN' WHAT IT SAYS.
BULLY.
JES' FOR CALLIN' ME THAT, GO OUT AN' CUT ME A STOUT WILLOW SWITCH.
IF I GO THAT WAY I'LL HAFTA TUNNEL THRU THE WALL.
THEN GO THE OTHER WAY AND, MIND, YOU CUTS A WILLOW SWITCH WITH THORNS ON IT.
WILLOW SWITCHES DON'T GOT THORNS ON 'EM.
IF YOU DON'T KEEP A CIVIL TONGUE IN YO' CHEEK I WON'T BEAT YOU AT ALL.
TREATMENT LIKE THIS IS GONNA MAKE ME RUN AWAY AN' JOIN THE NAVY.
RING RING DING BING
FIRE FIRE FIRE
I'D FIRE AT RANDOM, IF YOUR NAME WAS RANDOM, HAD I A HARQUEBUS, CRUEL STEP-MOTHER--'DEED I WOODY WOOD WOOD DEEDY WOOD I DO.
COPR 1955 WALT KELLY

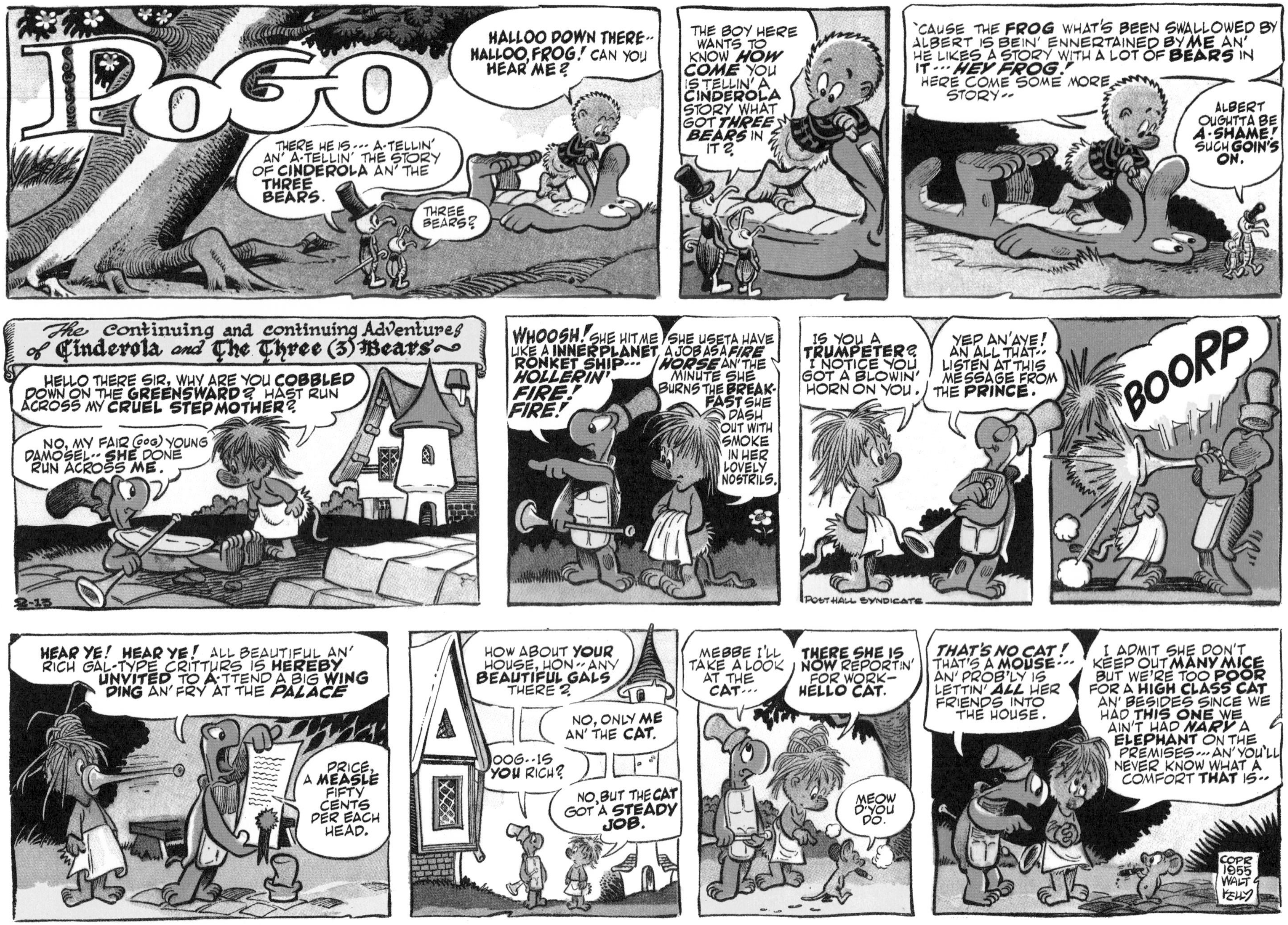
POGO
HALLOO DOWN THERE.. HALLOO, FROG! CAN YOU HEAR ME?
THERE HE IS... A-TELLIN' AN' A-TELLIN' THE STORY OF CINDEROLA AN' THE THREE BEARS.
THREE BEARS?
THE BOY HERE WANTS TO KNOW HOW COME YOU IS TELLIN' A CINDEROLA STORY WHAT GOT THREE BEARS IN IT?
'CAUSE THE FROG WHAT'S BEEN SWALLOWED BY ALBERT IS BEIN' ENNERTAINED BY ME AN' HE LIKES A STORY WITH A LOT OF BEARS IN IT... HEY FROG! HERE COME SOME MORE STORY--
ALBERT OUGHTTA BE A-SHAME! SUCH GOIN'S ON.
The continuing and continuing Adventures of Cinderola and The Three (3) Bears
HELLO THERE SIR, WHY ARE YOU COBBLED DOWN ON THE GREENSWARD? HAST RUN ACROSS MY CRUEL STEPMOTHER?
NO, MY FAIR (GOG) YOUNG DAMOSEL.. SHE DONE RUN ACROSS ME.
2-13
WHOOSH! SHE HIT ME LIKE A INNERPLANET RONKET SHIP... HOLLERIN' FIRE! FIRE!
SHE USETA HAVE A JOB AS A FIRE HORSE AN' THE MINUTE SHE BURNS THE BREAKFAST SHE DASH OUT WITH SMOKE IN HER LOVELY NOSTRILS.
IS YOU A TRUMPETER? I NOTICE YOU GOT A BLOWIN' HORN ON YOU.
YEP AN' AYE! AN' ALL THAT.. LISTEN AT THIS MESSAGE FROM THE PRINCE.
POST-HALL SYNDICATE
BOORP
HEAR YE! HEAR YE! ALL BEAUTIFUL AN' RICH GAL-TYPE CRITTURS IS HEREBY UNVITED TO A-TTEND A BIG WING DING AN' FRY AT THE PALACE
PRICE, A MEASLE FIFTY CENTS PER EACH HEAD.
HOW ABOUT YOUR HOUSE, HON.. ANY BEAUTIFUL GALS THERE?
NO, ONLY ME AN' THE CAT.
OOG..IS YOU RICH?
NO, BUT THE CAT GOT A STEADY JOB.
MEBBE I'LL TAKE A LOOK AT THE CAT...
THERE SHE IS NOW REPORTIN' FOR WORK-- HELLO CAT.
MEOW D'YOU DO.
THAT'S NO CAT! THAT'S A MOUSE... AN' PROB'LY IS LETTIN' ALL HER FRIENDS INTO THE HOUSE.
I ADMIT SHE DON'T KEEP OUT MANY MICE BUT WE'RE TOO POOR FOR A HIGH CLASS CAT AN' BESIDES SINCE WE HAD THIS ONE WE AIN'T HAD NARY A ELEPHANT ON THE PREMISES... AN' YOU'LL NEVER KNOW WHAT A COMFORT THAT IS..
COPR 1955 WALT KELLY

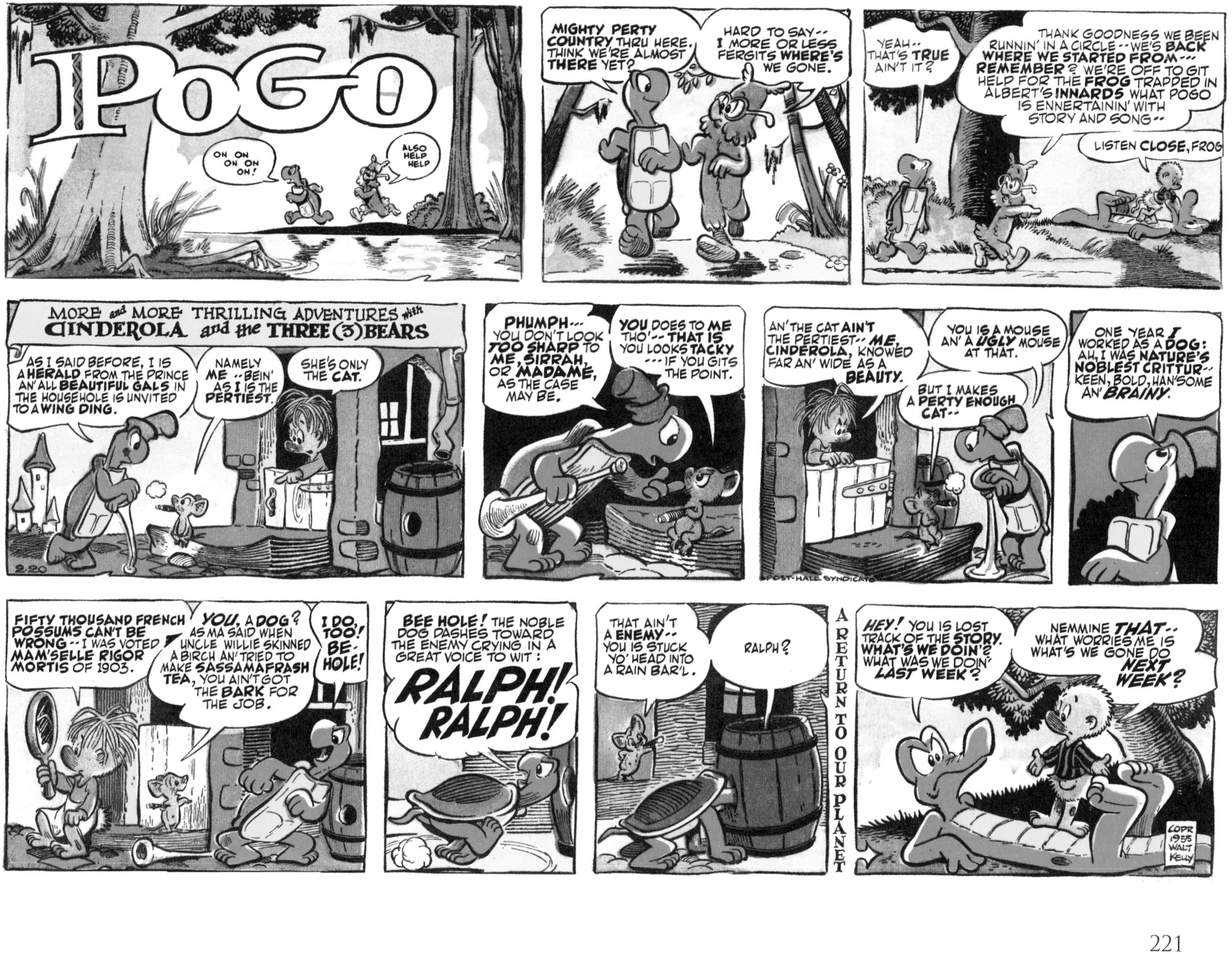
POGO
ON ON ON ON ON!
ALSO HELP HELP
MIGHTY PERTY COUNTRY THRU HERE. THINK WE'RE ALMOST THERE YET?
HARD TO SAY-- I MORE OR LESS FERGITS WHERE'S WE GONE.
YEAH.. THAT'S TRUE AIN'T IT?
THANK GOODNESS WE BEEN RUNNIN' IN A CIRCLE--WE'S BACK WHERE WE STARTED FROM--- REMEMBER? WE'RE OFF TO GIT HELP FOR THE FROG TRAPPED IN ALBERT'S INNARDS WHAT POGO IS ENNERTAININ' WITH STORY AND SONG--
LISTEN CLOSE, FROG
MORE and MORE THRILLING ADVENTURES with CINDEROLA and the THREE (3) BEARS
AS I SAID BEFORE, I IS A HERALD FROM THE PRINCE AN' ALL BEAUTIFUL GALS IN THE HOUSEHOLE IS UNVITED TO A WING DING.
NAMELY ME --BEIN' AS I IS THE PERTIEST.
SHE'S ONLY THE CAT.
2-20
PHUMPH--- YOU DON'T LOOK TOO SHARP TO ME, SIRRAH, OR MADAME, AS THE CASE MAY BE.
YOU DOES TO ME THO'--THAT IS YOU LOOKS TACKY ---IF YOU GITS THE POINT.
AN' THE CAT AIN'T THE PERTIEST-- ME, CINDEROLA, KNOWED FAR AN' WIDE AS A BEAUTY.
YOU IS A MOUSE AN' A UGLY MOUSE AT THAT.
BUT I MAKES A PERTY ENOUGH CAT--
POST-HALL SYNDICATE
ONE YEAR I WORKED AS A DOG: AH, I WAS NATURE'S NOBLEST CRITTUR-- KEEN, BOLD, HAN'SOME AN' BRAINY.
FIFTY THOUSAND FRENCH POSSUMS CAN'T BE WRONG--I WAS VOTED MAM'SELLE RIGOR MORTIS OF 1903.
YOU, A DOG? AS MA SAID WHEN UNCLE WILLIE SKINNED A BIRCH AN' TRIED TO MAKE SASSAMAFRASH TEA, YOU AIN'T GOT THE BARK FOR THE JOB.
I DO, TOO! BE-HOLE!
BEE HOLE! THE NOBLE DOG DASHES TOWARD THE ENEMY CRYING IN A GREAT VOICE TO WIT:
RALPH! RALPH!
THAT AIN'T A ENEMY-- YOU IS STUCK YO' HEAD INTO A RAIN BAR'L.
RALPH?
A RETURN TO OUR PLANET
HEY! YOU IS LOST TRACK OF THE STORY. WHAT'S WE DOIN'? WHAT WAS WE DOIN' LAST WEEK?
NEMMINE THAT-- WHAT WORRIES ME IS WHAT'S WE GONE DO NEXT WEEK?
COPR 1955 WALT KELLY

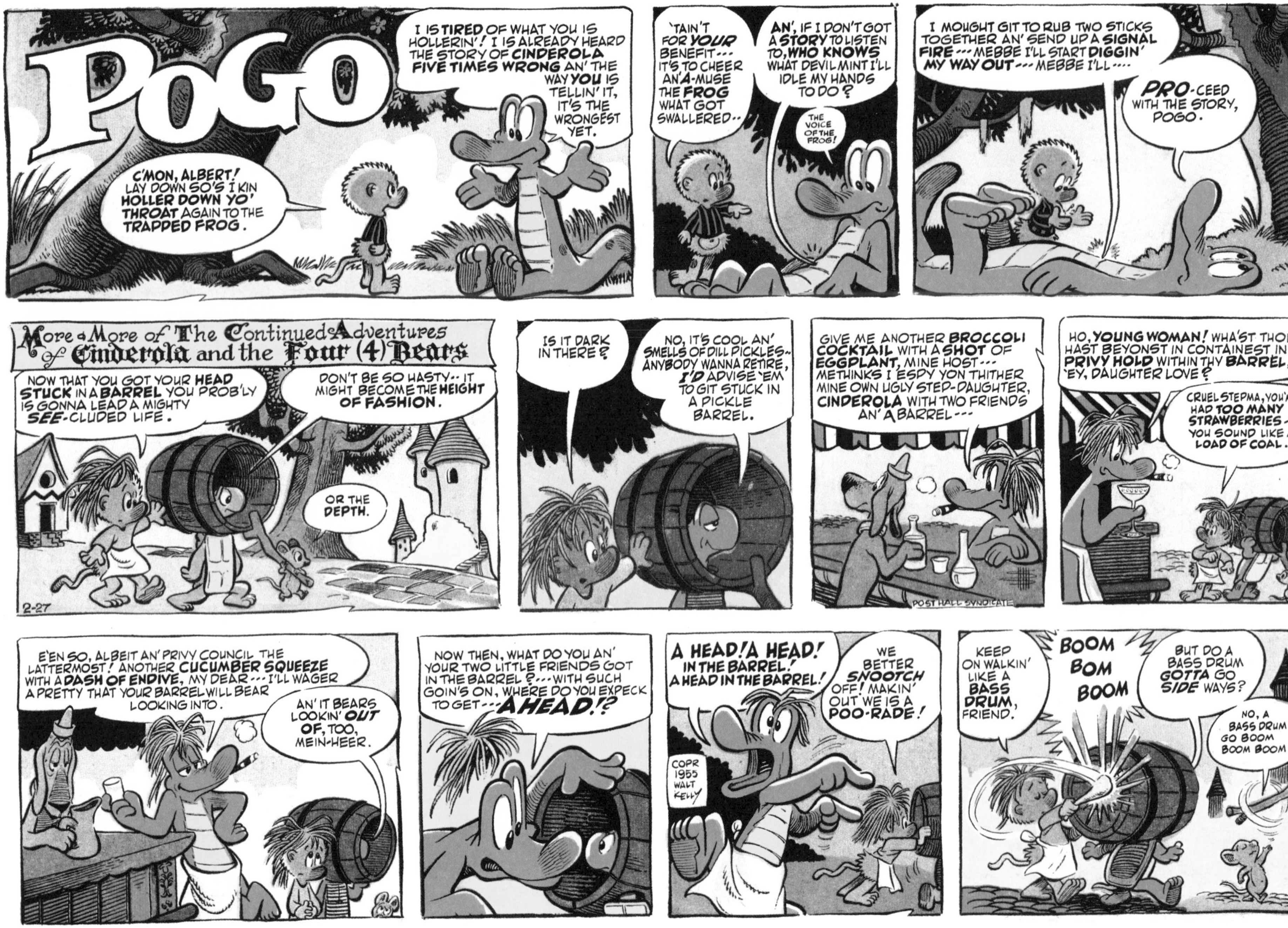
POGO
C'MON, ALBERT! LAY DOWN SO'S I KIN HOLLER DOWN YO' THROAT AGAIN TO THE TRAPPED FROG.
I IS TIRED OF WHAT YOU IS HOLLERIN'! I IS ALREADY HEARD THE STORY OF CINDEROLA FIVE TIMES WRONG AN' THE WAY YOU IS TELLIN' IT, IT'S THE WRONGEST YET.
'TAIN'T FOR YOUR BENEFIT--- IT'S TO CHEER AN' A-MUSE THE FROG WHAT GOT SWALLERED..
AN', IF I DON'T GOT A STORY TO LISTEN TO, WHO KNOWS WHAT DEVIL MINT I'LL IDLE MY HANDS TO DO?
THE VOICE OF THE FROG!
I MOUGHT GIT TO RUB TWO STICKS TOGETHER AN' SEND UP A SIGNAL FIRE --- MEBBE I'LL START DIGGIN' MY WAY OUT --- MEBBE I'LL ----
PRO-CEED WITH THE STORY, POGO.
More & More of The Continued Adventures of Cinderola and the Four (4) Bears
NOW THAT YOU GOT YOUR HEAD STUCK IN A BARREL YOU PROB'LY IS GONNA LEAD A MIGHTY SEE-CLUDED LIFE.
DON'T BE SO HASTY-- IT MIGHT BECOME THE HEIGHT OF FASHION.
OR THE DEPTH.
2-27
IS IT DARK IN THERE?
NO, IT'S COOL AN' SMELLS OF DILL PICKLES-- ANYBODY WANNA RETIRE, I'D ADVISE 'EM TO GIT STUCK IN A PICKLE BARREL.
GIVE ME ANOTHER BROCCOLI COCKTAIL WITH A SHOT OF EGGPLANT, MINE HOST--- METHINKS I ESPY YON THITHER MINE OWN UGLY STEP-DAUGHTER, CINDEROLA WITH TWO FRIENDS AN' A BARREL---
POST HALL SYNDICATE
HO, YOUNG WOMAN! WHA'ST THOU HAST BEYONST IN CONTAINEST IN PRIVY HOLD WITHIN THY BARREL, 'EY, DAUGHTER LOVE?
CRUEL STEPMA, YOU'M HAD TOO MANY STRAWBERRIES-- YOU SOUND LIKE A LOAD OF COAL.
E'EN SO, ALBEIT AN' PRIVY COUNCIL THE LATTERMOST! ANOTHER CUCUMBER SQUEEZE WITH A DASH OF ENDIVE, MY DEAR --- I'LL WAGER A PRETTY THAT YOUR BARREL WILL BEAR LOOKING INTO.
AN' IT BEARS LOOKIN' OUT OF, TOO, MEIN-HEER.
NOW THEN, WHAT DO YOU AN' YOUR TWO LITTLE FRIENDS GOT IN THE BARREL? --- WITH SUCH GOIN'S ON, WHERE DO YOU EXPECK TO GET --- A HEAD!?
A HEAD! A HEAD! IN THE BARREL! A HEAD IN THE BARREL!
WE BETTER SNOOTCH OFF! MAKIN' OUT WE IS A POO-RADE!
COPR 1955 WALT KELLY
KEEP ON WALKIN' LIKE A BASS DRUM, FRIEND.
BOOM BOM BOOM
BUT DO A BASS DRUM GOTTA GO SIDE WAYS?
NO, A BASS DRUM GO BOOM BOOM BOOM.

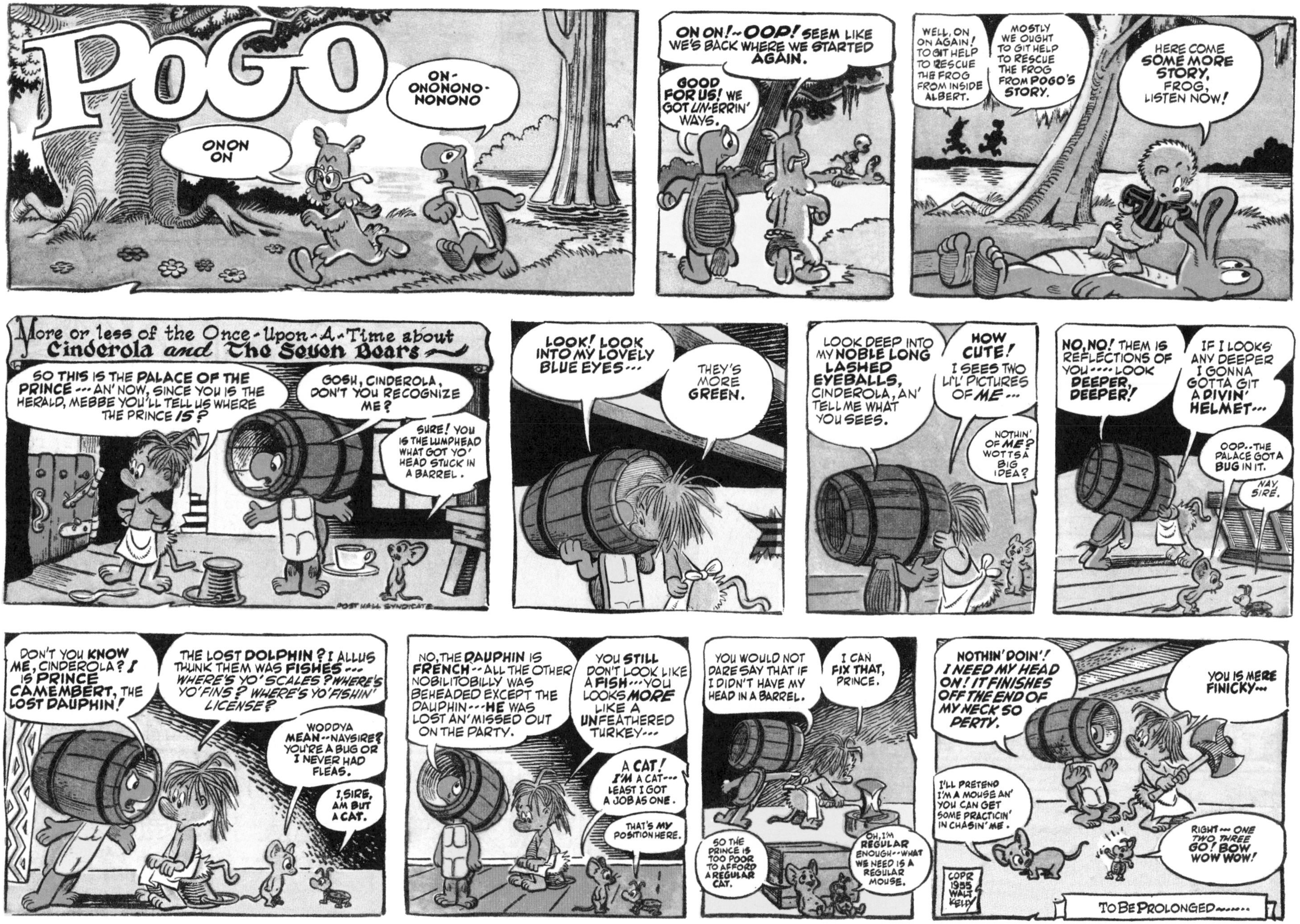
POGO
ON-ONONONO-NONONO
ONON ON
ON ON!--OOP! SEEM LIKE WE'S BACK WHERE WE STARTED AGAIN.
GOOD FOR US! WE GOT UN-ERRIN' WAYS.
WELL, ON ON AGAIN! TO GIT HELP TO RESCUE THE FROG FROM INSIDE ALBERT.
MOSTLY WE OUGHT TO GIT HELP TO RESCUE THE FROG FROM POGO'S STORY.
HERE COME SOME MORE STORY, FROG, LISTEN NOW!
More or less of the Once-Upon-A-Time about Cinderola and The Seven Bears
SO THIS IS THE PALACE OF THE PRINCE --- AN' NOW, SINCE YOU IS THE HERALD, MEBBE YOU'LL TELL US WHERE THE PRINCE IS?
GOSH, CINDEROLA, DON'T YOU RECOGNIZE ME?
SURE! YOU IS THE LUMPHEAD WHAT GOT YO' HEAD STUCK IN A BARREL.
POST HALL SYNDICATE
LOOK! LOOK INTO MY LOVELY BLUE EYES---
THEY'S MORE GREEN.
LOOK DEEP INTO MY NOBLE LONG LASHED EYEBALLS, CINDEROLA, AN' TELL ME WHAT YOU SEES.
HOW CUTE! I SEES TWO LI'L' PICTURES OF ME---
NOTHIN' OF ME? WOTTS A BIG IDEA?
NO, NO! THEM IS REFLECTIONS OF YOU---- LOOK DEEPER, DEEPER!
IF I LOOKS ANY DEEPER I GONNA GOTTA GIT A DIVIN' HELMET---
OOP.-THE PALACE GOTA BUG IN IT.
NAY, SIRE.
DON'T YOU KNOW ME, CINDEROLA? I IS PRINCE CAMEMBERT, THE LOST DAUPHIN!
THE LOST DOLPHIN? I ALLUS THUNK THEM WAS FISHES --- WHERE'S YO' SCALES? WHERE'S YO' FINS? WHERE'S YO' FISHIN' LICENSE?
WODDYA MEAN--NAYSIRE? YOU'RE A BUG OR I NEVER HAD FLEAS.
I, SIRE, AM BUT A CAT.
NO, THE DAUPHIN IS FRENCH -- ALL THE OTHER NOBILITOBILLY WAS BEHEADED EXCEPT THE DAUPHIN --- HE WAS LOST AN' MISSED OUT ON THE PARTY.
YOU STILL DON'T LOOK LIKE A FISH --- YOU LOOKS MORE LIKE A UNFEATHERED TURKEY---
A CAT! I'M A CAT--- LEAST I GOT A JOB AS ONE.
THAT'S MY POSITION HERE.
YOU WOULD NOT DARE SAY THAT IF I DIDN'T HAVE MY HEAD IN A BARREL.
I CAN FIX THAT, PRINCE.
SO THE PRINCE IS TOO POOR TO AFFORD A REGULAR CAT.
OH, I'M REGULAR ENOUGH -- WHAT WE NEED IS A REGULAR MOUSE.
NOTHIN' DOIN'! I NEED MY HEAD ON! IT FINISHES OFF THE END OF MY NECK SO PERTY.
YOU IS MERE FINICKY---
I'LL PRETEND I'M A MOUSE AN' YOU CAN GET SOME PRACTICIN' IN CHASIN' ME.
RIGHT --- ONE TWO, THREE GO! BOW WOW WOW!
COPR 1955 WALT KELLY
TO BE PROLONGED.......

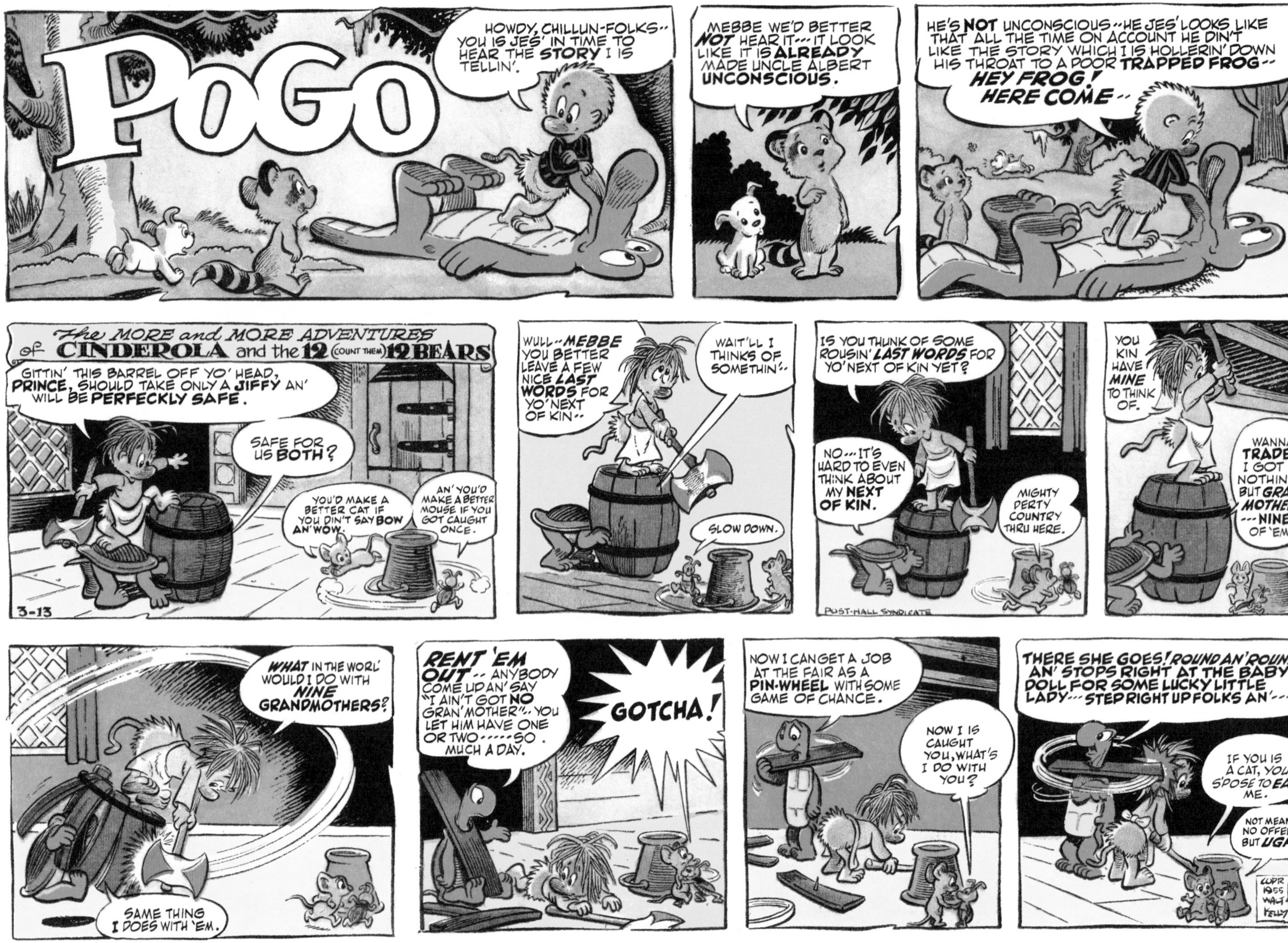
POGO
HOWDY, CHILLUN-FOLKS.. YOU IS JES' IN TIME TO HEAR THE STORY I IS TELLIN'.
MEBBE WE'D BETTER NOT HEAR IT--- IT LOOK LIKE IT IS ALREADY MADE UNCLE ALBERT UNCONSCIOUS.
HE'S NOT UNCONSCIOUS--HE JES' LOOKS LIKE THAT ALL THE TIME ON ACCOUNT HE DIN'T LIKE THE STORY WHICH I IS HOLLERIN' DOWN HIS THROAT TO A POOR TRAPPED FROG-- HEY FROG! HERE COME--
The MORE and MORE ADVENTURES of CINDEROLA and the 12 (COUNT THEM) 12 BEARS
GITTIN' THIS BARREL OFF YO' HEAD, PRINCE, SHOULD TAKE ONLY A JIFFY AN' WILL BE PERFECKLY SAFE.
SAFE FOR US BOTH?
YOU'D MAKE A BETTER CAT IF YOU DIN'T SAY BOW AN' WOW.
AN' YOU'D MAKE A BETTER MOUSE IF YOU GOT CAUGHT ONCE.
3-13
WULL--MEBBE YOU BETTER LEAVE A FEW NICE LAST WORDS FOR YO' NEXT OF KIN--
WAIT'LL I THINKS OF SOMETHIN'.
SLOW DOWN.
IS YOU THUNK OF SOME ROUSIN' LAST WORDS FOR YO' NEXT OF KIN YET?
NO--- IT'S HARD TO EVEN THINK ABOUT MY NEXT OF KIN.
MIGHTY DERTY COUNTRY THRU HERE.
POST-HALL SYNDICATE
YOU KIN HAVE MINE TO THINK OF.
WANNA TRADE? I GOT NOTHIN BUT GRAN-MOTHERS.. ---NINE OF 'EM--
WHAT IN THE WORL' WOULD I DO WITH NINE GRANDMOTHERS?
SAME THING I DOES WITH 'EM.
RENT 'EM OUT-- ANYBODY COME UP AN' SAY "I AIN'T GOT NO GRAN'MOTHER"-- YOU LET HIM HAVE ONE OR TWO----- SO. MUCH A DAY.
GOTCHA!
NOW I CAN GET A JOB AT THE FAIR AS A PIN-WHEEL WITH SOME GAME OF CHANCE.
NOW I IS CAUGHT YOU, WHAT'S I DO WITH YOU?
THERE SHE GOES! ROUND AN' ROUND AN' STOPS RIGHT AT THE BABY DOLL FOR SOME LUCKY LITTLE LADY--- STEP RIGHT UP FOLKS AN'---
IF YOU IS A CAT, YOU S'POSE TO EAT ME.
NOT MEANIN' NO OFFENSE, BUT UGH!
COPR 1955 WALT KELLY

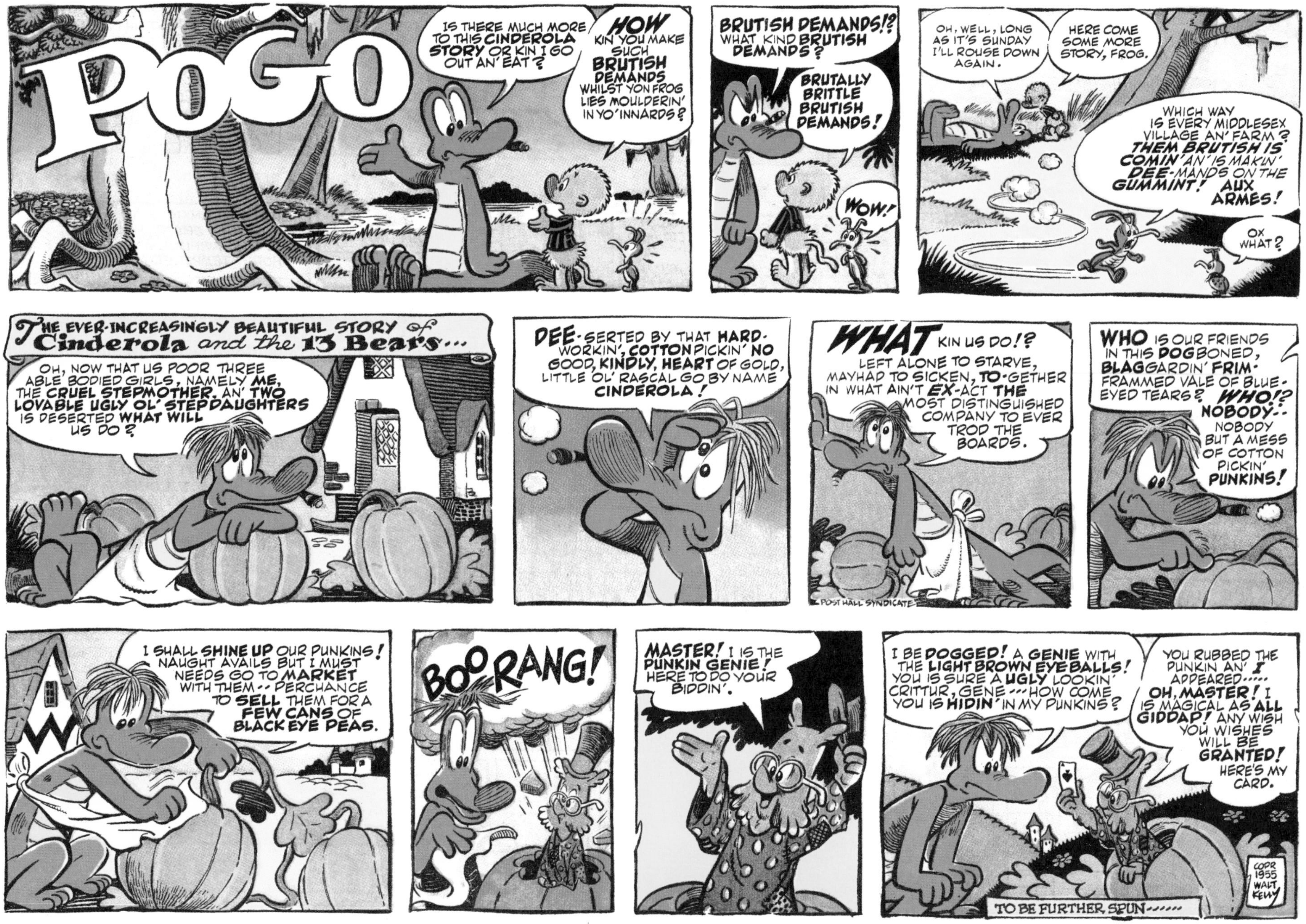
POGO
IS THERE MUCH MORE TO THIS CINDEROLA STORY OR KIN I GO OUT AN' EAT?
HOW KIN YOU MAKE SUCH BRUTISH DEMANDS WHILST YON FROG LIES MOULDERIN' IN YO' INNARDS?
BRUTISH DEMANDS!? WHAT KIND BRUTISH DEMANDS?
BRUTALLY BRITTLE BRUTISH DEMANDS!
WOW!
OH, WELL, LONG AS IT'S SUNDAY I'LL ROUSE DOWN AGAIN.
HERE COME SOME MORE STORY, FROG.
WHICH WAY IS EVERY MIDDLESEX VILLAGE AN' FARM? THEM BRUTISH IS COMIN' AN' IS MAKIN' DEE-MANDS ON THE GUMMINT! AUX ARMES!
OX WHAT?
THE EVER-INCREASINGLY BEAUTIFUL STORY of Cinderola and the 13 Bears...
OH, NOW THAT US POOR THREE ABLE BODIED GIRLS, NAMELY ME, THE CRUEL STEPMOTHER, AN' TWO LOVABLE UGLY OL' STEPDAUGHTERS IS DESERTED WHAT WILL US DO?
DEE-SERTED BY THAT HARD-WORKIN', COTTON PICKIN' NO GOOD, KINDLY, HEART OF GOLD, LITTLE OL' RASCAL GO BY NAME CINDEROLA!
WHAT KIN US DO!? LEFT ALONE TO STARVE, MAYHAD TO SICKEN, TO-GETHER IN WHAT AIN'T EX-ACT THE MOST DISTINGUISHED COMPANY TO EVER TROD THE BOARDS.
POST HALL SYNDICATE
WHO IS OUR FRIENDS IN THIS DOG BONED, BLAGGARDIN' FRIM-FRAMMED VALE OF BLUE-EYED TEARS? WHO!? NOBODY-- NOBODY BUT A MESS OF COTTON PICKIN' PUNKINS!
I SHALL SHINE UP OUR PUNKINS! NAUGHT AVAILS BUT I MUST NEEDS GO TO MARKET WITH THEM -- PERCHANCE TO SELL THEM FOR A FEW CANS OF BLACK EYE PEAS.
BOO RANG!
MASTER! I IS THE PUNKIN GENIE! HERE TO DO YOUR BIDDIN'.
I BE DOGGED! A GENIE WITH THE LIGHT BROWN EYE BALLS! YOU IS SURE A UGLY LOOKIN' CRITTUR, GENE--- HOW COME YOU IS HIDIN' IN MY PUNKINS?
YOU RUBBED THE PUNKIN AN' I APPEARED..... OH, MASTER! I IS MAGICAL AS ALL GIDDAP! ANY WISH YOU WISHES WILL BE GRANTED! HERE'S MY CARD.
COPR 1955 WALT KELLY
TO BE FURTHER SPUN......

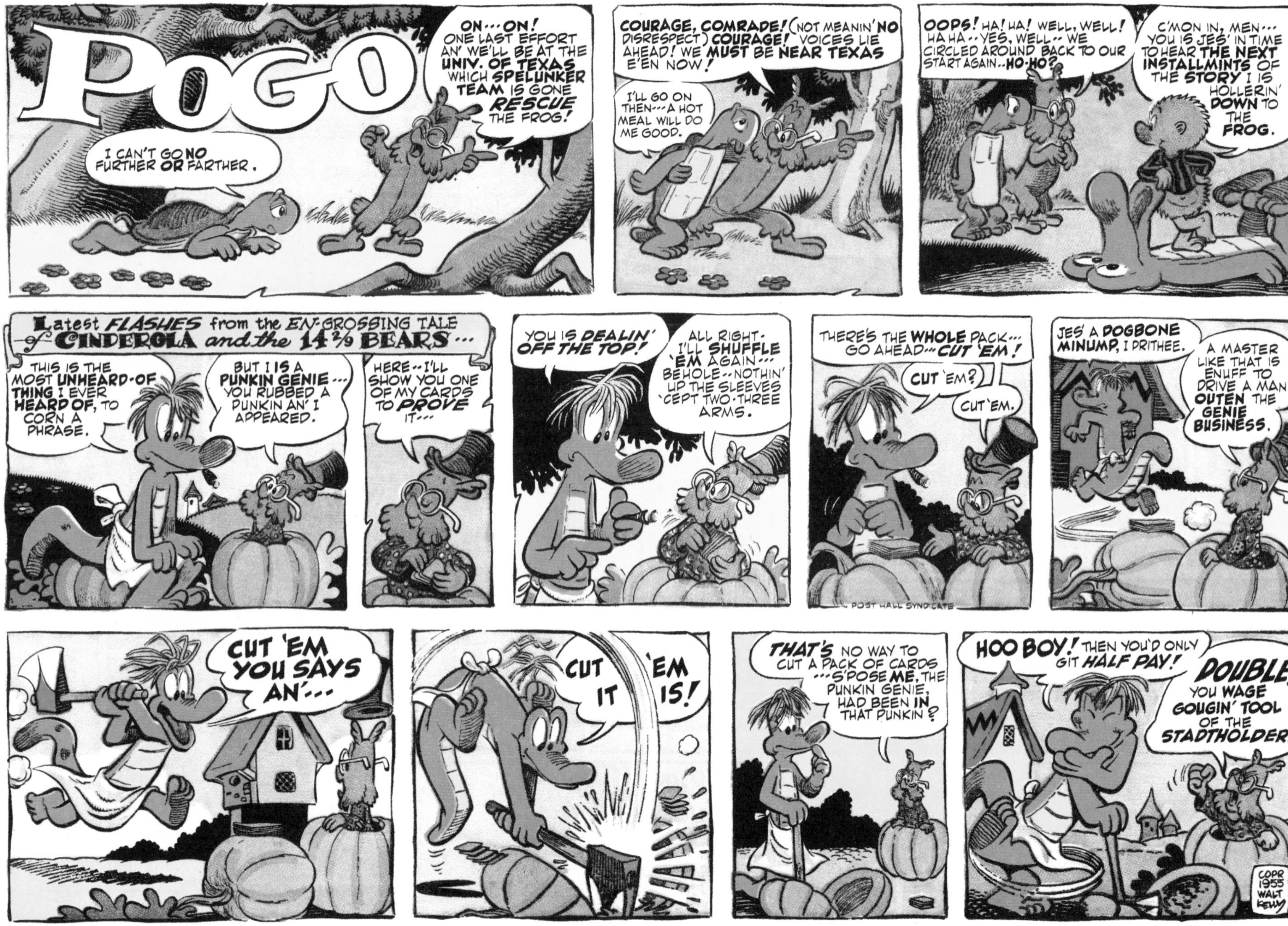
POGO
I CAN'T GO NO FURTHER OR FARTHER.
ON...ON! ONE LAST EFFORT AN' WE'LL BE AT THE UNIV. OF TEXAS WHICH SPELUNKER TEAM IS GONE RESCUE THE FROG!
COURAGE, COMRADE! (NOT MEANIN' NO DISRESPECT) COURAGE! VOICES LIE AHEAD! WE MUST BE NEAR TEXAS E'EN NOW!
I'LL GO ON THEN... A HOT MEAL WILL DO ME GOOD.
OOPS! HA! HA! WELL, WELL! HA HA.. YES, WELL.. WE CIRCLED AROUND BACK TO OUR START AGAIN.. HO-HO?
C'MON IN, MEN... YOU IS JES' IN TIME TO HEAR THE NEXT INSTALLMINTS OF THE STORY I IS HOLLERIN' DOWN TO THE FROG.
Latest FLASHES from the EN-GROSSING TALE of CINDEROLA and the 14 2/9 BEARS...
THIS IS THE MOST UNHEARD-OF THING I EVER HEARD OF, TO CORN A PHRASE.
BUT I IS A PUNKIN GENIE... YOU RUBBED A PUNKIN AN' I APPEARED.
HERE.. I'LL SHOW YOU ONE OF MY CARDS TO PROVE IT...
YOU IS DEALIN' OFF THE TOP!
ALL RIGHT. I'LL SHUFFLE 'EM AGAIN... BEHOLE.. NOTHIN' UP THE SLEEVES 'CEPT TWO-THREE ARMS.
THERE'S THE WHOLE PACK... GO AHEAD... CUT 'EM!
CUT 'EM?
CUT 'EM.
POST HALL SYNDICATE
JES' A DOGBONE MINUMP, I PRITHEE.
A MASTER LIKE THAT IS ENUFF TO DRIVE A MAN OUTEN THE GENIE BUSINESS.
CUT 'EM YOU SAYS AN'...
CUT IT 'EM IS!
THAT'S NO WAY TO CUT A PACK OF CARDS ... S'POSE ME, THE PUNKIN GENIE, HAD BEEN IN THAT PUNKIN?
HOO BOY! THEN YOU'D ONLY GIT HALF PAY!
DOUBLE! YOU WAGE GOUGIN' TOOL OF THE STADTHOLDER!
COPR 1955 WALT KELLY

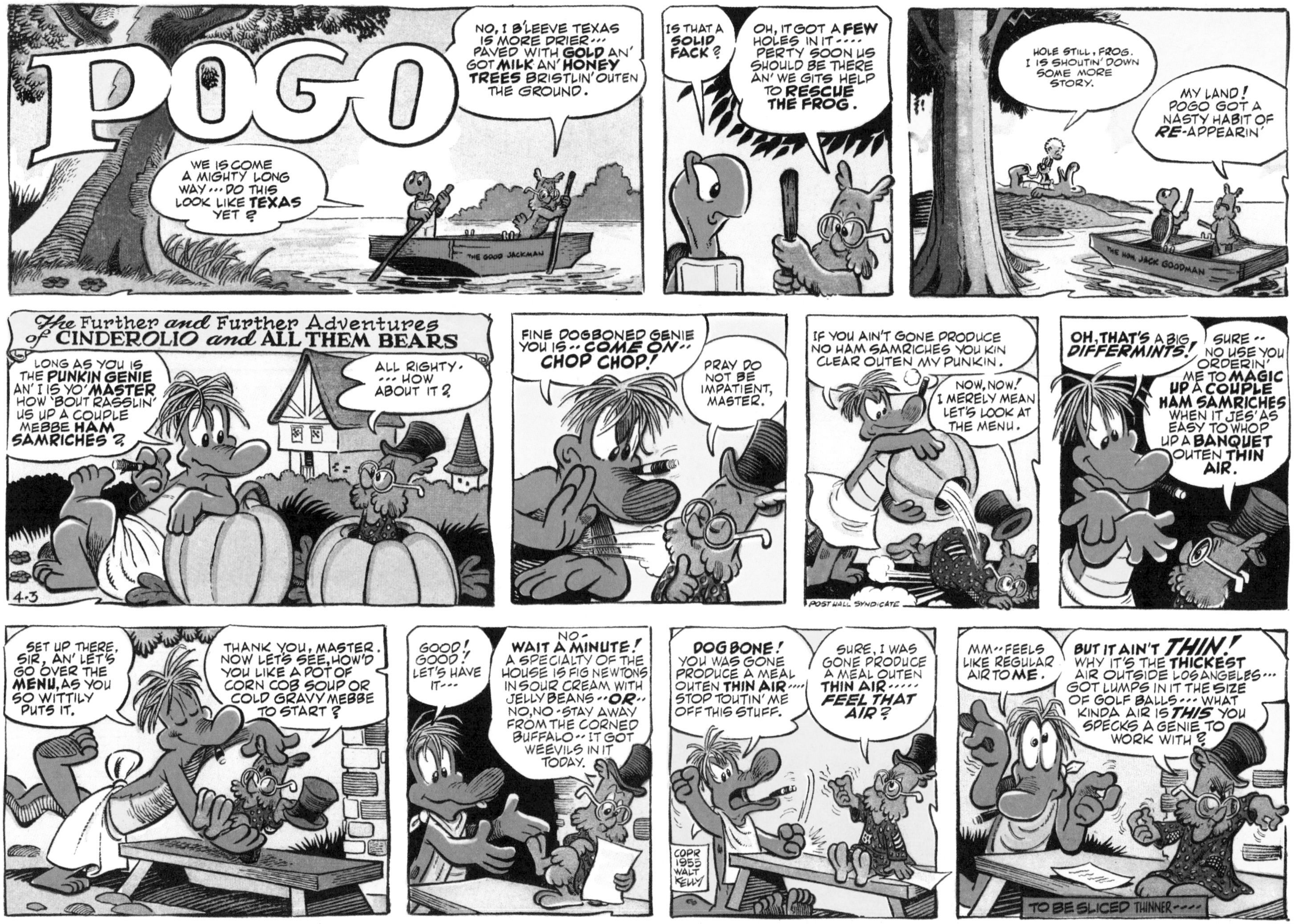
POGO
WE IS COME A MIGHTY LONG WAY... DO THIS LOOK LIKE TEXAS YET ?
NO, I B'LEEVE TEXAS IS MORE DRIER... PAVED WITH GOLD AN' GOT MILK AN' HONEY TREES BRISTLIN' OUTEN THE GROUND.
THE GOOD JACKMAN
IS THAT A SOLID FACK ?
OH, IT GOT A FEW HOLES IN IT.... PERTY SOON US SHOULD BE THERE AN' WE GITS HELP TO RESCUE THE FROG.
HOLE STILL, FROG. I IS SHOUTIN' DOWN SOME MORE STORY.
MY LAND ! POGO GOT A NASTY HABIT OF RE-APPEARIN'
THE HON. JACK GOODMAN
The Further and Further Adventures of CINDEROLIO and ALL THEM BEARS
LONG AS YOU IS THE PUNKIN GENIE AN' I IS YO' MASTER HOW 'BOUT RASSLIN' US UP A COUPLE MEBBE HAM SAMRICHES ?
ALL RIGHTY. ... HOW ABOUT IT ?
4-3
FINE DOGBONED GENIE YOU IS -- COME ON -- CHOP CHOP!
PRAY DO NOT BE IMPATIENT, MASTER.
IF YOU AIN'T GONE PRODUCE NO HAM SAMRICHES YOU KIN CLEAR OUTEN MY PUNKIN.
NOW, NOW! I MERELY MEAN LET'S LOOK AT THE MENU.
POST HALL SYNDICATE
OH, THAT'S A BIG DIFFERMINTS!
SURE -- NO USE YOU ORDERIN' ME TO MAGIC UP A COUPLE HAM SAMRICHES WHEN IT JES' AS EASY TO WHOP UP A BANQUET OUTEN THIN AIR.
SET UP THERE, SIR, AN' LET'S GO OVER THE MENU, AS YOU SO WITTILY PUTS IT.
THANK YOU, MASTER. NOW LET'S SEE, HOW'D YOU LIKE A POT OF CORN COB SOUP OR COLD GRAVY MEBBE TO START ?
GOOD! GOOD! LET'S HAVE IT---
NO- WAIT A MINUTE! A SPECIALTY OF THE HOUSE IS FIG NEWTONS IN SOUR CREAM WITH JELLY BEANS -- OR -- NO, NO - STAY AWAY FROM THE CORNED BUFFALO -- IT GOT WEEVILS IN IT TODAY.
DOG BONE! YOU WAS GONE PRODUCE A MEAL OUTEN THIN AIR.... STOP TOUTIN' ME OFF THIS STUFF.
SURE, I WAS GONE PRODUCE A MEAL OUTEN THIN AIR..... FEEL THAT AIR ?
COPR 1955 WALT KELLY
MM -- FEELS LIKE REGULAR AIR TO ME.
BUT IT AIN'T THIN! WHY IT'S THE THICKEST AIR OUTSIDE LOS ANGELES... GOT LUMPS IN IT THE SIZE OF GOLF BALLS --- WHAT KINDA AIR IS THIS YOU SPECKS A GENIE TO WORK WITH ?
TO BE SLICED THINNER ----

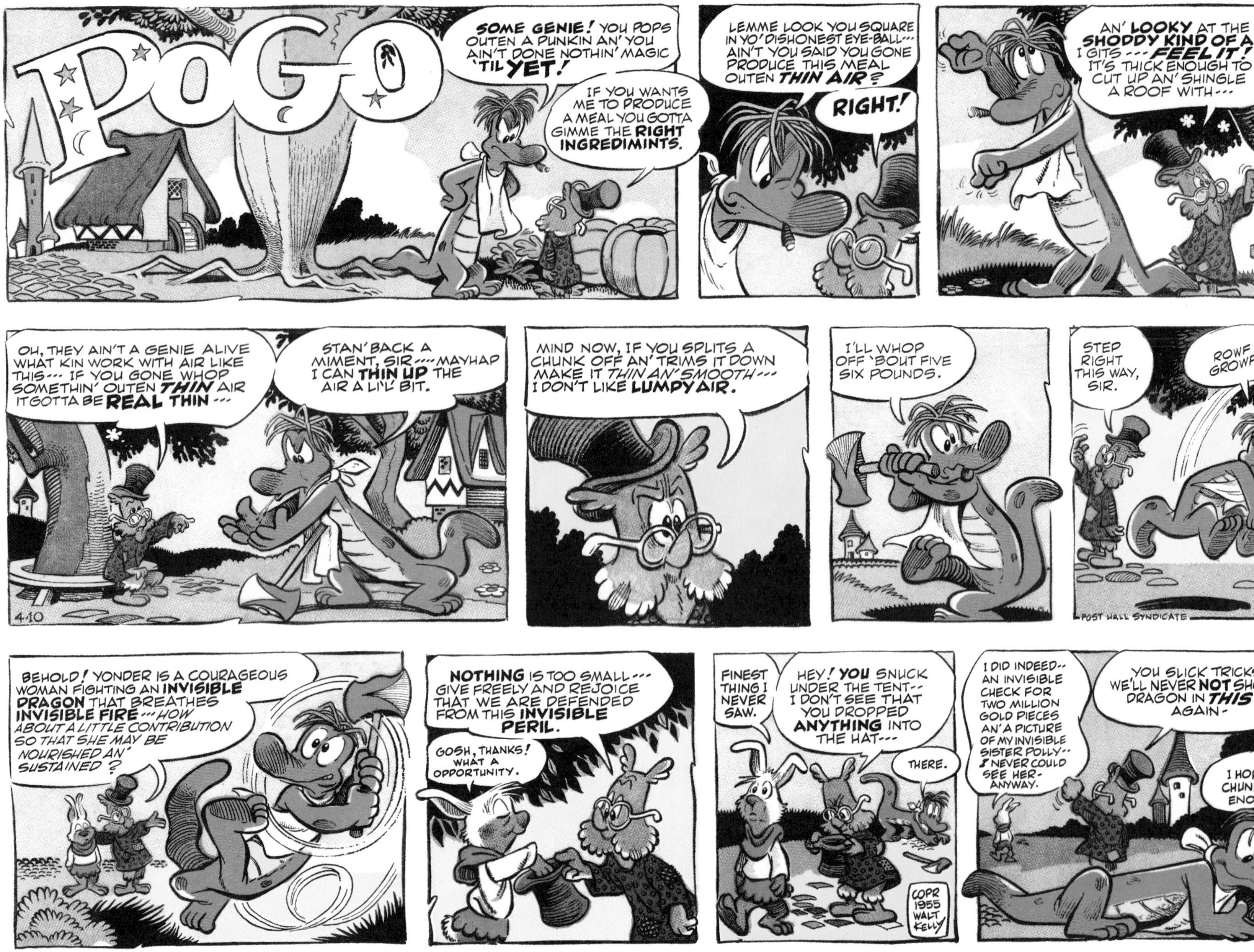
POGO
SOME GENIE! YOU POPS OUTEN A PUNKIN AN' YOU AIN'T DONE NOTHIN' MAGIC 'TIL YET!
IF YOU WANTS ME TO PRODUCE A MEAL YOU GOTTA GIMME THE RIGHT INGREDIMINTS.
LEMME LOOK YOU SQUARE IN YO' DISHONEST EYE-BALL--- AIN'T YOU SAID YOU GONE PRODUCE THIS MEAL OUTEN THIN AIR?
RIGHT!
AN' LOOKY AT THE SHODDY KIND OF AIR I GITS --- FEEL IT! --- IT'S THICK ENOUGH TO CUT UP AN' SHINGLE A ROOF WITH ---
OH, THEY AIN'T A GENIE ALIVE WHAT KIN WORK WITH AIR LIKE THIS --- IF YOU GONE WHOP SOMETHIN' OUTEN THIN AIR IT GOTTA BE REAL THIN ---
STAN' BACK A MIMENT, SIR ---- MAYHAP I CAN THIN UP THE AIR A LI'L' BIT.
4-10
MIND NOW, IF YOU SPLITS A CHUNK OFF AN' TRIMS IT DOWN MAKE IT THIN AN' SMOOTH --- I DON'T LIKE LUMPY AIR.
I'LL WHOP OFF 'BOUT FIVE SIX POUNDS.
STEP RIGHT THIS WAY, SIR.
ROWF GROWF
POST HALL SYNDICATE
BEHOLD! YONDER IS A COURAGEOUS WOMAN FIGHTING AN INVISIBLE DRAGON THAT BREATHES INVISIBLE FIRE --- HOW ABOUT A LITTLE CONTRIBUTION SO THAT SHE MAY BE NOURISHED AN' SUSTAINED?
NOTHING IS TOO SMALL --- GIVE FREELY AND REJOICE THAT WE ARE DEFENDED FROM THIS INVISIBLE PERIL.
GOSH, THANKS! WHAT A OPPORTUNITY.
FINEST THING I NEVER SAW.
HEY! YOU SNUCK UNDER THE TENT-- I DON'T SEE THAT YOU DROPPED ANYTHING INTO THE HAT---
THERE.
COPR 1955 WALT KELLY
I DID INDEED-- AN INVISIBLE CHECK FOR TWO MILLION GOLD PIECES AN' A PICTURE OF MY INVISIBLE SISTER POLLY-- I NEVER COULD SEE HER- ANYWAY.
YOU SLICK TRICKSTER --- WE'LL NEVER NOT SHOW OUR DRAGON IN THIS TOWN AGAIN-
I HOPE THIS CHUNK IS BIG ENOUGH--

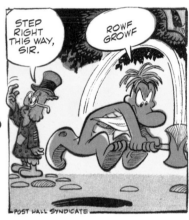

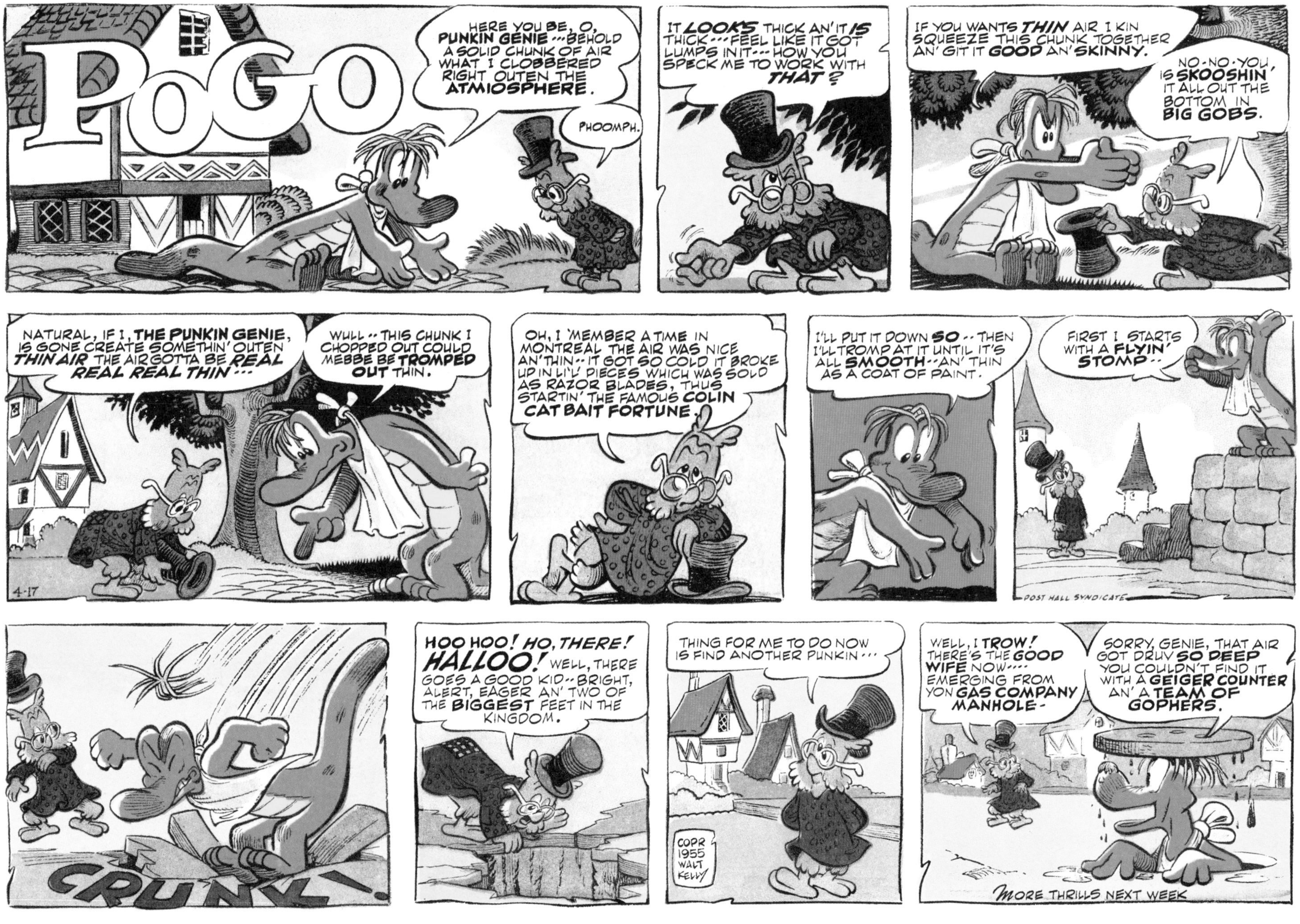
POGO
HERE YOU BE, O, PUNKIN GENIE ··· BEHOLD A SOLID CHUNK OF AIR WHAT I CLOBBERED RIGHT OUTEN THE ATMIOSPHERE.
PHOOMPH.
IT LOOKS THICK AN' IT IS THICK ··· FEEL LIKE IT GOT LUMPS IN IT ··· HOW YOU SPECK ME TO WORK WITH THAT?
IF YOU WANTS THIN AIR I KIN SQUEEZE THIS CHUNK TOGETHER AN' GIT IT GOOD AN' SKINNY.
NO-NO-YOU, IS SKOOSHIN' IT ALL OUT THE BOTTOM IN BIG GOBS.
NATURAL, IF I, THE PUNKIN GENIE, IS GONE CREATE SOMETHIN' OUTEN THIN AIR THE AIR GOTTA BE REAL REAL REAL THIN ···
WULL ·· THIS CHUNK I CHOPPED OUT COULD MEBBE BE TROMPED OUT THIN.
4-17
OH, I 'MEMBER A TIME IN MONTREAL THE AIR WAS NICE AN' THIN ·· IT GOT SO COLD IT BROKE UP IN LI'L PIECES WHICH WAS SOLD AS RAZOR BLADES, THUS STARTIN' THE FAMOUS COLIN CAT BAIT FORTUNE.
I'LL PUT IT DOWN SO ·· THEN I'LL TROMP AT IT UNTIL IT'S ALL SMOOTH ·· AN' THIN AS A COAT OF PAINT.
FIRST I STARTS WITH A FLYIN' STOMP ··
POST HALL SYNDICATE
CRUNK!
HOO HOO! HO, THERE! HALLOO! WELL, THERE GOES A GOOD KID ·· BRIGHT, ALERT, EAGER AN' TWO OF THE BIGGEST FEET IN THE KINGDOM.
THING FOR ME TO DO NOW IS FIND ANOTHER PUNKIN ···
COPR 1955 WALT KELLY
WELL, I TROW! THERE'S THE GOOD WIFE NOW ···· EMERGING FROM YON GAS COMPANY MANHOLE -
SORRY, GENIE, THAT AIR GOT DRUV SO DEEP YOU COULDN'T FIND IT WITH A GEIGER COUNTER AN' A TEAM OF GOPHERS.
MORE THRILLS NEXT WEEK

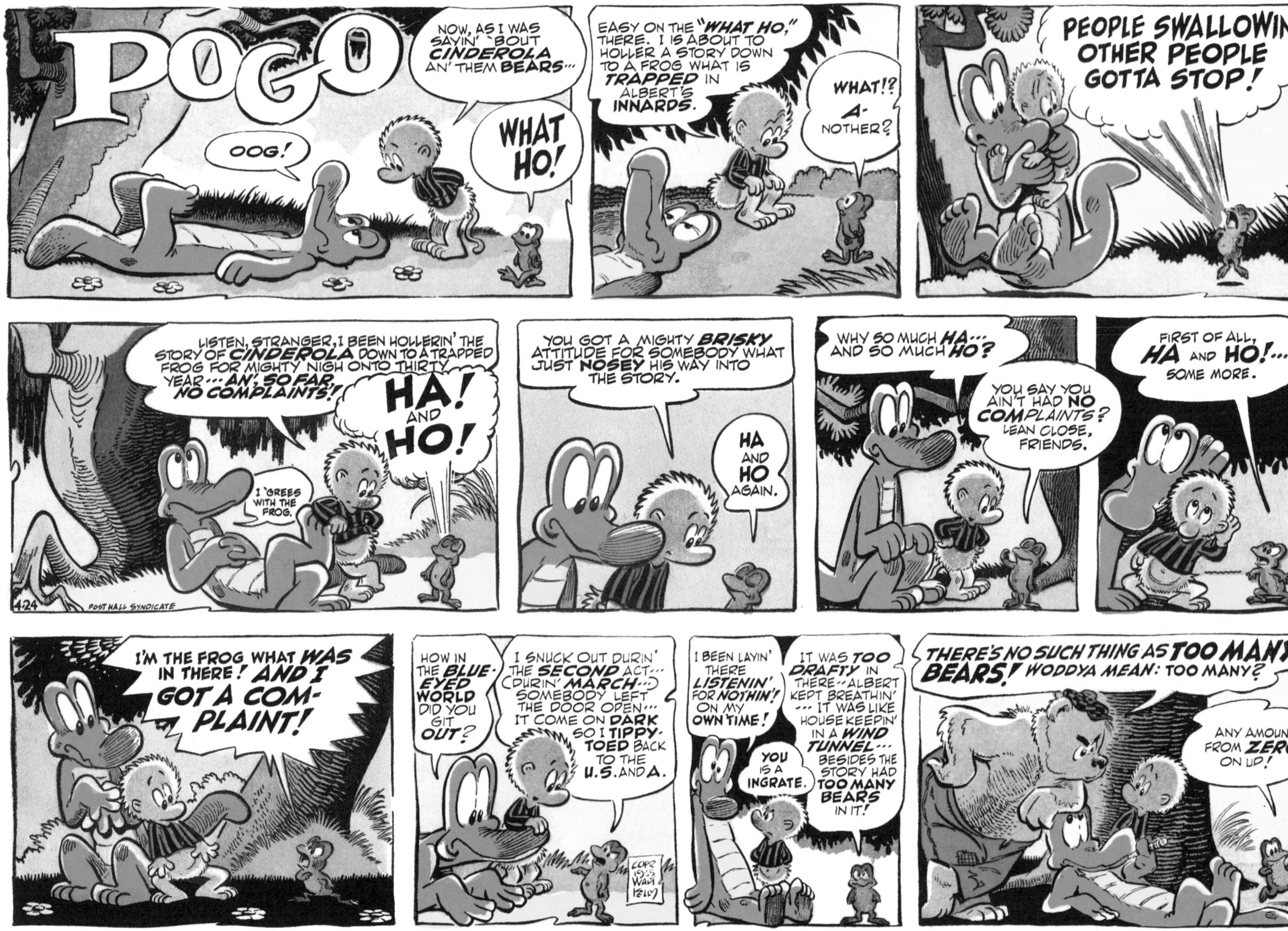
POGO
NOW, AS I WAS SAYIN' 'BOUT CINDEROLA AN' THEM BEARS...
OOG!
WHAT HO!
EASY ON THE "WHAT HO," THERE. I IS ABOUT TO HOLLER A STORY DOWN TO A FROG WHAT IS TRAPPED IN ALBERT'S INNARDS.
WHAT!? A-NOTHER?
PEOPLE SWALLOWIN' OTHER PEOPLE GOTTA STOP!
LISTEN, STRANGER, I BEEN HOLLERIN' THE STORY OF CINDEROLA DOWN TO A TRAPPED FROG FOR MIGHTY NIGH ONTO THIRTY YEAR... AN', SO FAR, NO COMPLAINTS!
HA! AND HO!
I 'GREES WITH THE FROG.
4-24
POST HALL SYNDICATE
YOU GOT A MIGHTY BRISKY ATTITUDE FOR SOMEBODY WHAT JUST NOSEY HIS WAY INTO THE STORY.
HA AND HO AGAIN.
WHY SO MUCH HA... AND SO MUCH HO?
YOU SAY YOU AIN'T HAD NO COMPLAINTS? LEAN CLOSE, FRIENDS.
FIRST OF ALL, HA AND HO!... SOME MORE.
I'M THE FROG WHAT WAS IN THERE! AND I GOT A COM-PLAINT!
HOW IN THE BLUE-EYED WORLD DID YOU GIT OUT?
I SNUCK OUT DURIN' THE SECOND ACT... (DURIN' MARCH...) SOMEBODY LEFT THE DOOR OPEN... IT COME ON DARK SO I TIPPY-TOED BACK TO THE U.S. AND A.
COPR 1955 WALT KELLY
I BEEN LAYIN' THERE LISTENIN' FOR NOTHIN'! ON MY OWN TIME!
YOU IS A INGRATE.
IT WAS TOO DRAFTY IN THERE... ALBERT KEPT BREATHIN' ... IT WAS LIKE HOUSE KEEPIN' IN A WIND TUNNEL... BESIDES THE STORY HAD TOO MANY BEARS IN IT!
THERE'S NO SUCH THING AS TOO MANY BEARS! WODDYA MEAN: TOO MANY?
ANY AMOUNT FROM ZERO ON UP!

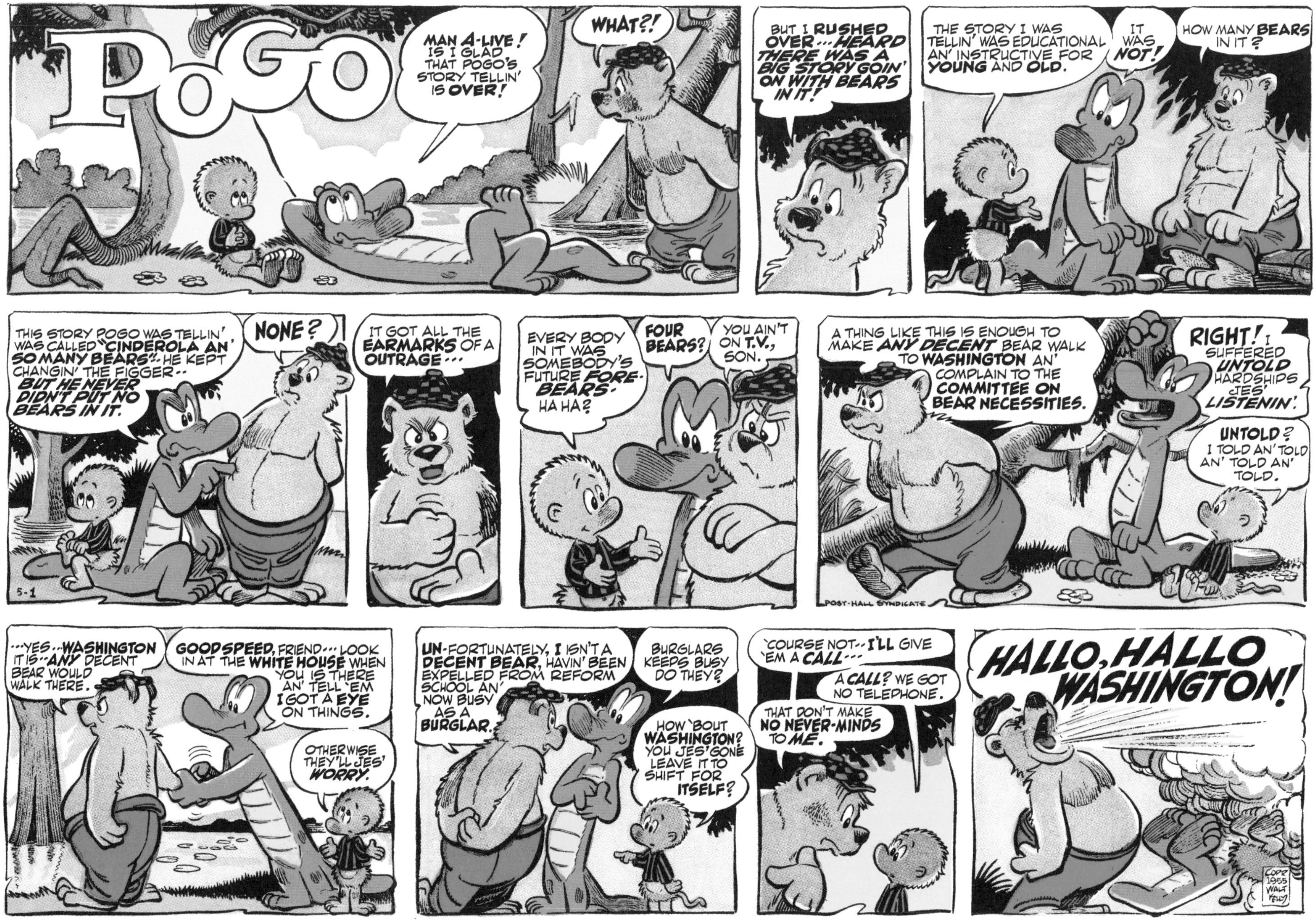
POGO
MAN A-LIVE! IS I GLAD THAT POGO'S STORY TELLIN' IS OVER!
WHAT?!
BUT I RUSHED OVER... HEARD THERE WAS A BIG STORY GOIN' ON WITH BEARS IN IT!
THE STORY I WAS TELLIN' WAS EDUCATIONAL AN' INSTRUCTIVE FOR YOUNG AND OLD.
IT WAS NOT!
HOW MANY BEARS IN IT?
THIS STORY POGO WAS TELLIN' WAS CALLED "CINDEROLA AN' SO MANY BEARS"-- HE KEPT CHANGIN' THE FIGGER-- BUT HE NEVER DIDN'T PUT NO BEARS IN IT.
NONE?
5-1
IT GOT ALL THE EARMARKS OF A OUTRAGE...
EVERY BODY IN IT WAS SOMEBODY'S FUTURE FORE-BEARS- HA HA?
FOUR BEARS?
YOU AIN'T ON T.V., SON.
A THING LIKE THIS IS ENOUGH TO MAKE ANY DECENT BEAR WALK TO WASHINGTON AN' COMPLAIN TO THE COMMITTEE ON BEAR NECESSITIES.
RIGHT! I SUFFERED UNTOLD HARDSHIPS JES' LISTENIN'.
UNTOLD? I TOLD AN' TOLD AN' TOLD AN' TOLD.
POST-HALL SYNDICATE
...YES...WASHINGTON IT IS--ANY DECENT BEAR WOULD WALK THERE.
GOODSPEED, FRIEND... LOOK IN AT THE WHITE HOUSE WHEN YOU IS THERE AN' TELL 'EM I GOT A EYE ON THINGS.
OTHERWISE THEY'LL JES' WORRY.
UN-FORTUNATELY, I ISN'T A DECENT BEAR, HAVIN' BEEN EXPELLED FROM REFORM SCHOOL AN' NOW BUSY AS A BURGLAR.
BURGLARS KEEPS BUSY DO THEY?
HOW 'BOUT WASHINGTON? YOU JES' GONE LEAVE IT TO SHIFT FOR ITSELF?
'COURSE NOT-- I'LL GIVE 'EM A CALL---
A CALL? WE GOT NO TELEPHONE.
THAT DON'T MAKE NO NEVER-MINDS TO ME.
HALLO, HALLO WASHINGTON!
COPR 1955 WALT KELLY

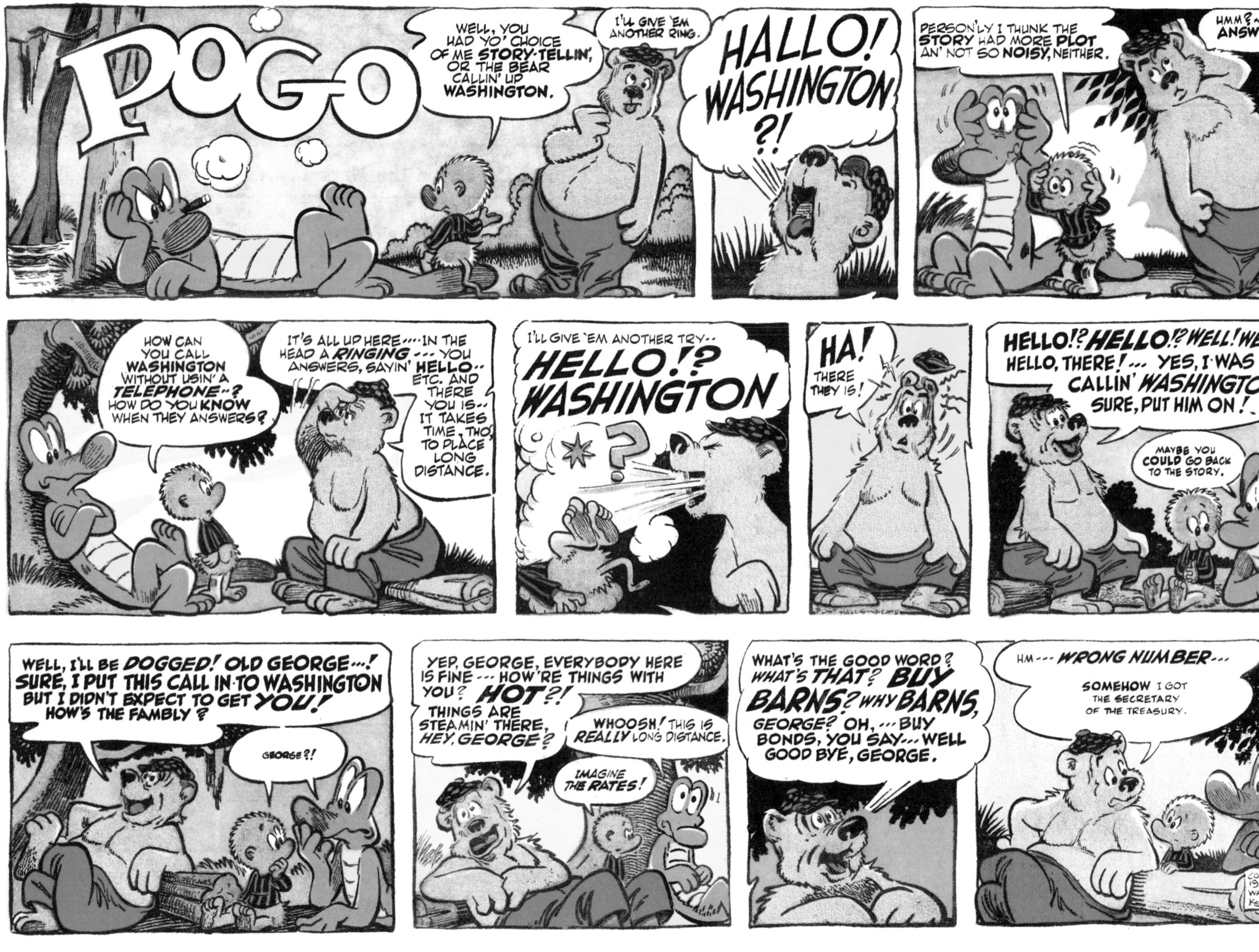
POGO
WELL, YOU HAD YO' CHOICE OF ME STORY-TELLIN', OR THE BEAR CALLIN' UP WASHINGTON.
I'LL GIVE 'EM ANOTHER RING.
HALLO! WASHINGTON ?!
PERSON'LY I THUNK THE STORY HAD MORE PLOT AN' NOT SO NOISY, NEITHER.
UMM? ~ NO ANSWER!
HOW CAN YOU CALL WASHINGTON WITHOUT USIN' A TELEPHONE--? HOW DO YOU KNOW WHEN THEY ANSWERS?
IT'S ALL UP HERE---- IN THE HEAD A RINGING --- YOU ANSWERS, SAYIN' HELLO.. ETC. AND THERE YOU IS.. IT TAKES TIME, THO', TO PLACE LONG DISTANCE.
I'LL GIVE 'EM ANOTHER TRY..
HELLO!? WASHINGTON
HA! THERE THEY IS!
HELLO!? HELLO!? WELL! WELL! HELLO, THERE! ... YES, I WAS CALLIN' WASHINGTON... SURE, PUT HIM ON!
MAYBE YOU COULD GO BACK TO THE STORY.
WELL, I'LL BE DOGGED! OLD GEORGE ...! SURE, I PUT THIS CALL IN TO WASHINGTON BUT I DIDN'T EXPECT TO GET YOU! HOW'S THE FAMBLY?
GEORGE?!
YEP, GEORGE, EVERYBODY HERE IS FINE --- HOW'RE THINGS WITH YOU? HOT?! THINGS ARE STEAMIN' THERE, HEY, GEORGE?
WHOOSH! THIS IS REALLY LONG DISTANCE.
IMAGINE THE RATES!
WHAT'S THE GOOD WORD? WHAT'S THAT? BUY BARNS? WHY BARNS, GEORGE? OH, ... BUY BONDS, YOU SAY... WELL GOOD BYE, GEORGE.
HM --- WRONG NUMBER ---
SOMEHOW I GOT THE SECRETARY OF THE TREASURY.
COPR 1955 WALT KELLY

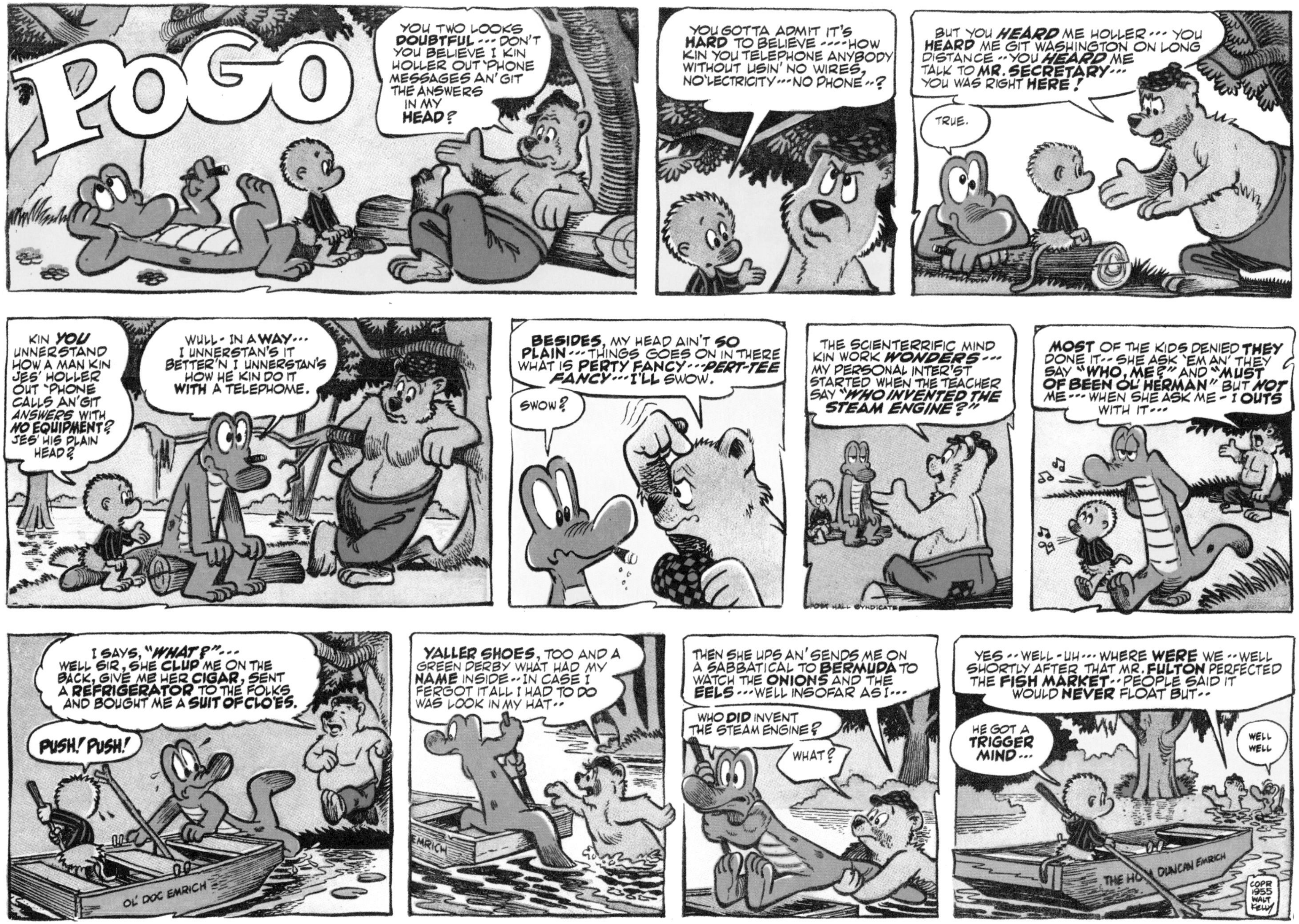
POGO
YOU TWO LOOKS DOUBTFUL --- DON'T YOU BELIEVE I KIN HOLLER OUT 'PHONE MESSAGES AN' GIT THE ANSWERS IN MY HEAD?
YOU GOTTA ADMIT IT'S HARD TO BELIEVE ----HOW KIN YOU TELEPHONE ANYBODY WITHOUT USIN' NO WIRES, NO'LECTRICITY --- NO PHONE --?
BUT YOU HEARD ME HOLLER --- YOU HEARD ME GIT WASHINGTON ON LONG DISTANCE -- YOU HEARD ME TALK TO MR. SECRETARY --- YOU WAS RIGHT HERE!
TRUE.
KIN YOU UNNERSTAND HOW A MAN KIN JES' HOLLER OUT 'PHONE CALLS AN' GIT ANSWERS WITH NO EQUIPMENT? JES' HIS PLAIN HEAD?
WULL- IN A WAY--- I UNNERSTAN'S IT BETTER'N I UNNERSTAN'S HOW HE KIN DO IT WITH A TELEPHOME.
BESIDES, MY HEAD AIN'T SO PLAIN --- THINGS GOES ON IN THERE WHAT IS PERTY FANCY --- PERT-TEE FANCY --- I'LL SWOW.
SWOW?
THE SCIENTERRIFIC MIND KIN WORK WONDERS --- MY PERSONAL INTER'ST STARTED WHEN THE TEACHER SAY "WHO INVENTED THE STEAM ENGINE?"
MOST OF THE KIDS DENIED THEY DONE IT -- SHE ASK 'EM AN' THEY SAY "WHO, ME?" AND "MUST OF BEEN OL' HERMAN" BUT NOT ME --- WHEN SHE ASK ME - I OUTS WITH IT ---
I SAYS, "WHAT?" --- WELL SIR, SHE CLUP ME ON THE BACK, GIVE ME HER CIGAR, SENT A REFRIGERATOR TO THE FOLKS AND BOUGHT ME A SUIT OF CLO'ES.
PUSH! PUSH!
OL' DOC EMRICH
YALLER SHOES, TOO AND A GREEN DERBY WHAT HAD MY NAME INSIDE -- IN CASE I FERGOT IT ALL I HAD TO DO WAS LOOK IN MY HAT --
EMRICH
THEN SHE UPS AN' SENDS ME ON A SABBATICAL TO BERMUDA TO WATCH THE ONIONS AND THE EELS --- WELL INSOFAR AS I ---
WHO DID INVENT THE STEAM ENGINE?
WHAT?
YES -- WELL - UH --- WHERE WERE WE -- WELL SHORTLY AFTER THAT MR. FULTON PERFECTED THE FISH MARKET -- PEOPLE SAID IT WOULD NEVER FLOAT BUT --
HE GOT A TRIGGER MIND ---
WELL WELL
COPR 1955 WALT KELLY

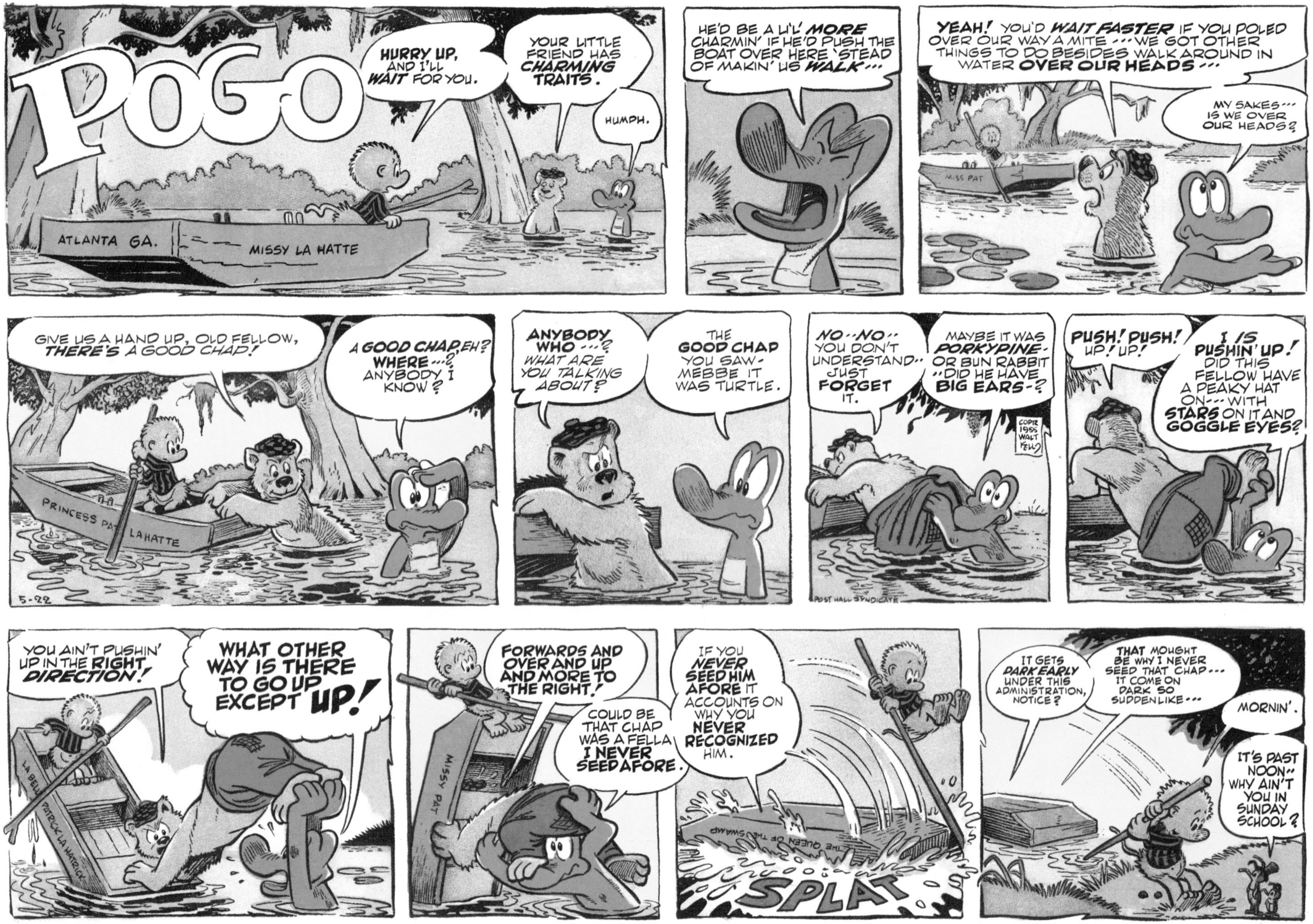
POGO
HURRY UP, AND I'LL WAIT FOR YOU.
YOUR LITTLE FRIEND HAS CHARMING TRAITS.
HUMPH.
ATLANTA GA.
MISSY LA HATTE
HE'D BE A LI'L' MORE CHARMIN' IF HE'D PUSH THE BOAT OVER HERE 'STEAD OF MAKIN' US WALK...
YEAH! YOU'D WAIT FASTER IF YOU POLED OVER OUR WAY A MITE ... WE GOT OTHER THINGS TO DO BESIDES WALK AROUND IN WATER OVER OUR HEADS...
MY SAKES... IS WE OVER OUR HEADS?
MISS PAT
GIVE US A HAND UP, OLD FELLOW, THERE'S A GOOD CHAP!
A GOOD CHAP, EH? WHERE...? ANYBODY I KNOW?
PRINCESS PAT LAHATTE
5-22
ANYBODY WHO...? WHAT ARE YOU TALKING ABOUT?
THE GOOD CHAP YOU SAW- MEBBE IT WAS TURTLE.
NO..NO.. YOU DON'T UNDERSTAND.. JUST FORGET IT.
MAYBE IT WAS PORKYPINE- OR BUN RABBIT ..DID HE HAVE BIG EARS-?
COPR 1955 WALT KELLY
POST HALL SYNDICATE
PUSH! PUSH! UP! UP!
I IS PUSHIN' UP! DID THIS FELLOW HAVE A PEAKY HAT ON... WITH STARS ON IT AND GOGGLE EYES?
YOU AIN'T PUSHIN' UP IN THE RIGHT DIRECTION!
WHAT OTHER WAY IS THERE TO GO UP EXCEPT UP!
FORWARDS AND OVER AND UP AND MORE TO THE RIGHT!
COULD BE THAT CHAP WAS A FELLA I NEVER SEED AFORE.
MISSY PAT
IF YOU NEVER SEED HIM AFORE IT ACCOUNTS ON WHY YOU NEVER RECOGNIZED HIM.
SPLAT
IT GETS DARK EARLY UNDER THIS ADMINISTRATION, NOTICE?
THAT MOUGHT BE WHY I NEVER SEED THAT CHAP... IT COME ON DARK SO SUDDENLIKE...
MORNIN'.
IT'S PAST NOON.. WHY AIN'T YOU IN SUNDAY SCHOOL?

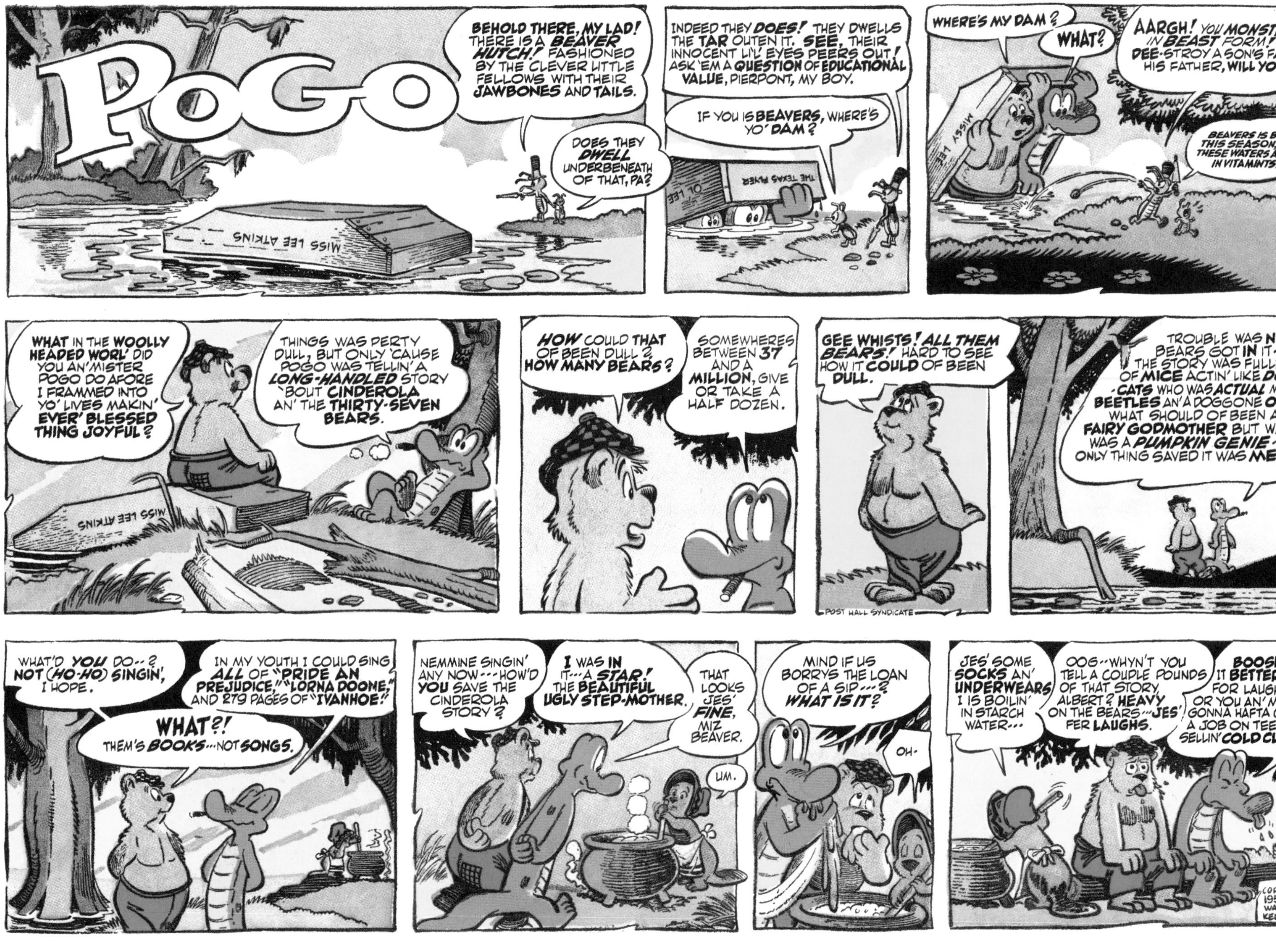
POGO
BEHOLD THERE, MY LAD! THERE IS A BEAVER HUTCH! FASHIONED BY THE CLEVER LITTLE FELLOWS WITH THEIR JAWBONES AND TAILS.
DOES THEY DWELL UNDERBENEATH OF THAT, PA?
MISS LEE ATKINS
INDEED THEY DOES! THEY DWELLS THE TAR OUTEN IT. SEE, THEIR INNOCENT LI'L' EYES PEERS OUT! ASK 'EM A QUESTION OF EDUCATIONAL VALUE, PIERPONT, MY BOY.
IF YOU IS BEAVERS, WHERE'S YO' DAM?
WHERE'S MY DAM?
WHAT?
AARGH! YOU MONSTERS, IN BEAST FORM! DEE-STROY A SON'S FAITH IN HIS FATHER, WILL YOU!?
BEAVERS IS BIG THIS SEASON, MERVIN. THESE WATERS A-BOUND IN VITAMINTS.
WHAT IN THE WOOLLY HEADED WORL' DID YOU AN' MISTER POGO DO AFORE I FRAMMED INTO YO' LIVES MAKIN' EVER' BLESSED THING JOYFUL?
THINGS WAS PERTY DULL, BUT ONLY 'CAUSE POGO WAS TELLIN' A LONG-HANDLED STORY 'BOUT CINDEROLA AN' THE THIRTY-SEVEN BEARS.
MISS LEE ATKINS
HOW COULD THAT OF BEEN DULL? HOW MANY BEARS?
SOMEWHERES BETWEEN 37 AND A MILLION, GIVE OR TAKE A HALF DOZEN.
GEE WHISTS! ALL THEM BEARS! HARD TO SEE HOW IT COULD OF BEEN DULL.
POST HALL SYNDICATE
TROUBLE WAS NO BEARS GOT IN IT.. THE STORY WAS FULLED OF MICE ACTIN' LIKE DOGS -CATS WHO WAS ACTUAL MERE BEETLES AN' A DOGGONE OWL WHAT SHOULD OF BEEN A FAIRY GODMOTHER BUT WHO WAS A PUMPKIN GENIE.... ONLY THING SAVED IT WAS ME!
WHAT'D YOU DO..? NOT (HO-HO) SINGIN', I HOPE.
IN MY YOUTH I COULD SING ALL OF "PRIDE AN PREJUDICE," "LORNA DOONE," AND 279 PAGES OF "IVANHOE!"
WHAT?! THEM'S BOOKS...NOT SONGS.
NEMMINE SINGIN' ANY NOW---HOW'D YOU SAVE THE CINDEROLA STORY?
I WAS IN IT...A STAR! THE BEAUTIFUL UGLY STEP-MOTHER.
THAT LOOKS JES' FINE, MIZ BEAVER.
UM.
MIND IF US BORRYS THE LOAN OF A SIP...? WHAT IS IT?
OH-
JES' SOME SOCKS AN' UNDERWEARS I IS BOILIN' IN STARCH WATER...
OOG..WHYN'T YOU TELL A COUPLE POUNDS OF THAT STORY, ALBERT? HEAVY ON THE BEARS...JES' FER LAUGHS.
BOOSH... IT BETTER BE FOR LAUGHS OR YOU AN' ME'S GONNA HAFTA GIT A JOB ON TEEVY SELLIN' COLD CUTS.
COPR 1955 WALT KELLY

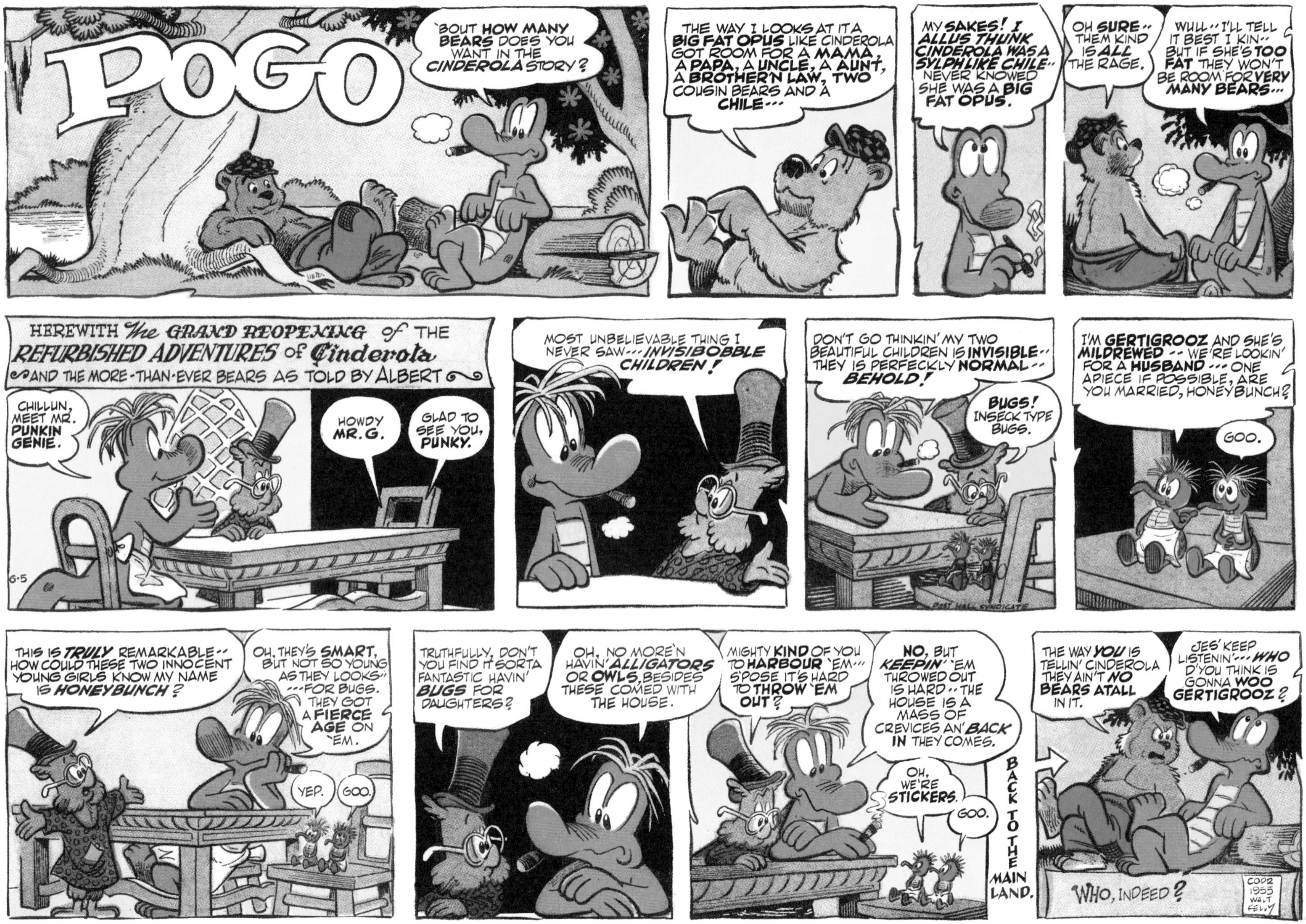
POGO
`BOUT HOW MANY BEARS DOES YOU WANT IN THE CINDEROLA STORY?
THE WAY I LOOKS AT IT A BIG FAT OPUS LIKE CINDEROLA GOT ROOM FOR A MAMA, A PAPA, A UNCLE, A AUNT, A BROTHER'N LAW, TWO COUSIN BEARS AND A CHILE---
MY SAKES! I ALLUS THUNK CINDEROLA WAS A SYLPHLIKE CHILE.. NEVER KNOWED SHE WAS A BIG FAT OPUS.
OH SURE.. THEM KIND IS ALL THE RAGE.
WULL..I'LL TELL IT BEST I KIN.. BUT IF SHE'S TOO FAT THEY WON'T BE ROOM FOR VERY MANY BEARS...
HEREWITH The GRAND REOPENING of THE REFURBISHED ADVENTURES of Cinderola AND THE MORE-THAN-EVER BEARS AS TOLD BY ALBERT
CHILLUN, MEET MR. PUNKIN GENIE.
HOWDY MR. G.
GLAD TO SEE YOU, PUNKY.
6-5
MOST UNBELIEVABLE THING I NEVER SAW--- INVISIBOBBLE CHILDREN!
DON'T GO THINKIN' MY TWO BEAUTIFUL CHILDREN IS INVISIBLE.. THEY IS PERFECKLY NORMAL -- BEHOLD!
BUGS! INSECK TYPE BUGS.
POST HALL SYNDICATE
I'M GERTIGROOZ AND SHE'S MILDREWED -- WE'RE LOOKIN' FOR A HUSBAND --- ONE APIECE IF POSSIBLE, ARE YOU MARRIED, HONEYBUNCH?
GOO.
THIS IS TRULY REMARKABLE-- HOW COULD THESE TWO INNOCENT YOUNG GIRLS KNOW MY NAME IS HONEYBUNCH?
OH, THEY'S SMART, BUT NOT SO YOUNG AS THEY LOOKS.. ---FOR BUGS. THEY GOT A FIERCE AGE ON `EM.
YEP.
GOO.
TRUTHFULLY, DON'T YOU FIND IT SORTA FANTASTIC HAVIN' BUGS FOR DAUGHTERS?
OH, NO MORE'N HAVIN' ALLIGATORS OR OWLS, BESIDES THESE COMED WITH THE HOUSE.
MIGHTY KIND OF YOU TO HARBOUR `EM-- S'POSE IT'S HARD TO THROW `EM OUT?
NO, BUT KEEPIN' `EM THROWED OUT IS HARD.. THE HOUSE IS A MASS OF CREVICES AN' BACK IN THEY COMES.
OH, WE'RE STICKERS.
GOO.
BACK TO THE MAIN LAND.
THE WAY YOU IS TELLIN' CINDEROLA THEY AIN'T NO BEARS ATALL IN IT.
JES' KEEP LISTENIN'--- WHO D'YOU THINK IS GONNA WOO GERTIGROOZ?
WHO, INDEED?
COPR 1955 WALT KELLY

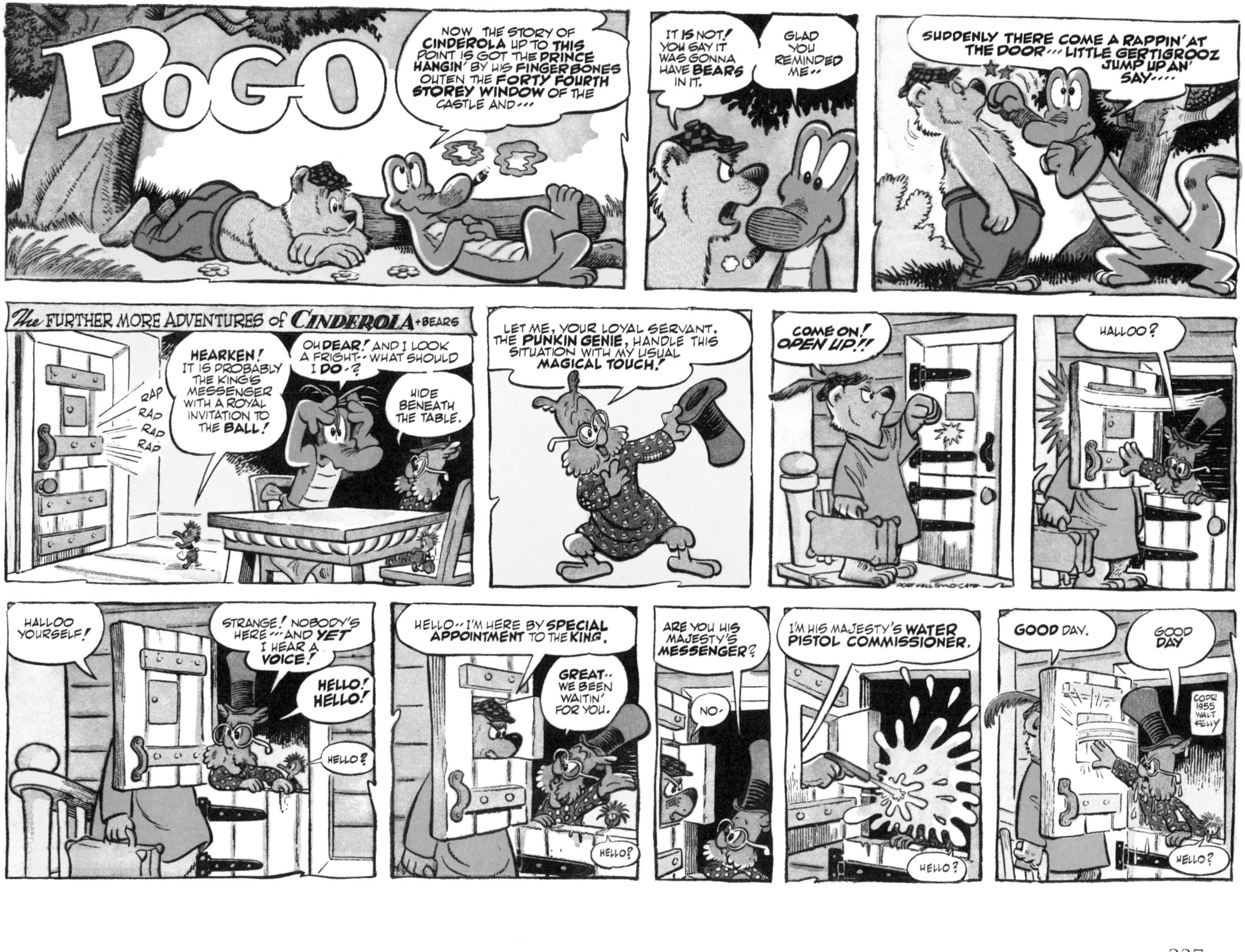
POGO
NOW THE STORY OF CINDEROLA UP TO THIS POINT IS GOT THE PRINCE HANGIN' BY HIS FINGERBONES OUTEN THE FORTY FOURTH STOREY WINDOW OF THE CASTLE AND...
IT IS NOT! YOU SAY IT WAS GONNA HAVE BEARS IN IT.
GLAD YOU REMINDED ME..
SUDDENLY THERE COME A RAPPIN' AT THE DOOR... LITTLE GERTIGROOZ JUMP UP AN' SAY....
The FURTHER MORE ADVENTURES of CINDEROLA + BEARS
RAP RAP RAP RAP
HEARKEN! IT IS PROBABLY THE KING'S MESSENGER WITH A ROYAL INVITATION TO THE BALL!
OH DEAR! AND I LOOK A FRIGHT-- WHAT SHOULD I DO-?
HIDE BENEATH THE TABLE.
LET ME, YOUR LOYAL SERVANT, THE PUNKIN GENIE, HANDLE THIS SITUATION WITH MY USUAL MAGICAL TOUCH!
COME ON! OPEN UP!!
HALLOO?
HALLOO YOURSELF!
STRANGE! NOBODY'S HERE... AND YET I HEAR A VOICE!
HELLO! HELLO!
HELLO?
HELLO.. I'M HERE BY SPECIAL APPOINTMENT TO THE KING.
GREAT.. WE BEEN WAITIN' FOR YOU.
HELLO?
ARE YOU HIS MAJESTY'S MESSENGER?
NO.
I'M HIS MAJESTY'S WATER PISTOL COMMISSIONER.
HELLO?
GOOD DAY.
GOOD DAY
COPR 1955 WALT KELLY
HELLO?

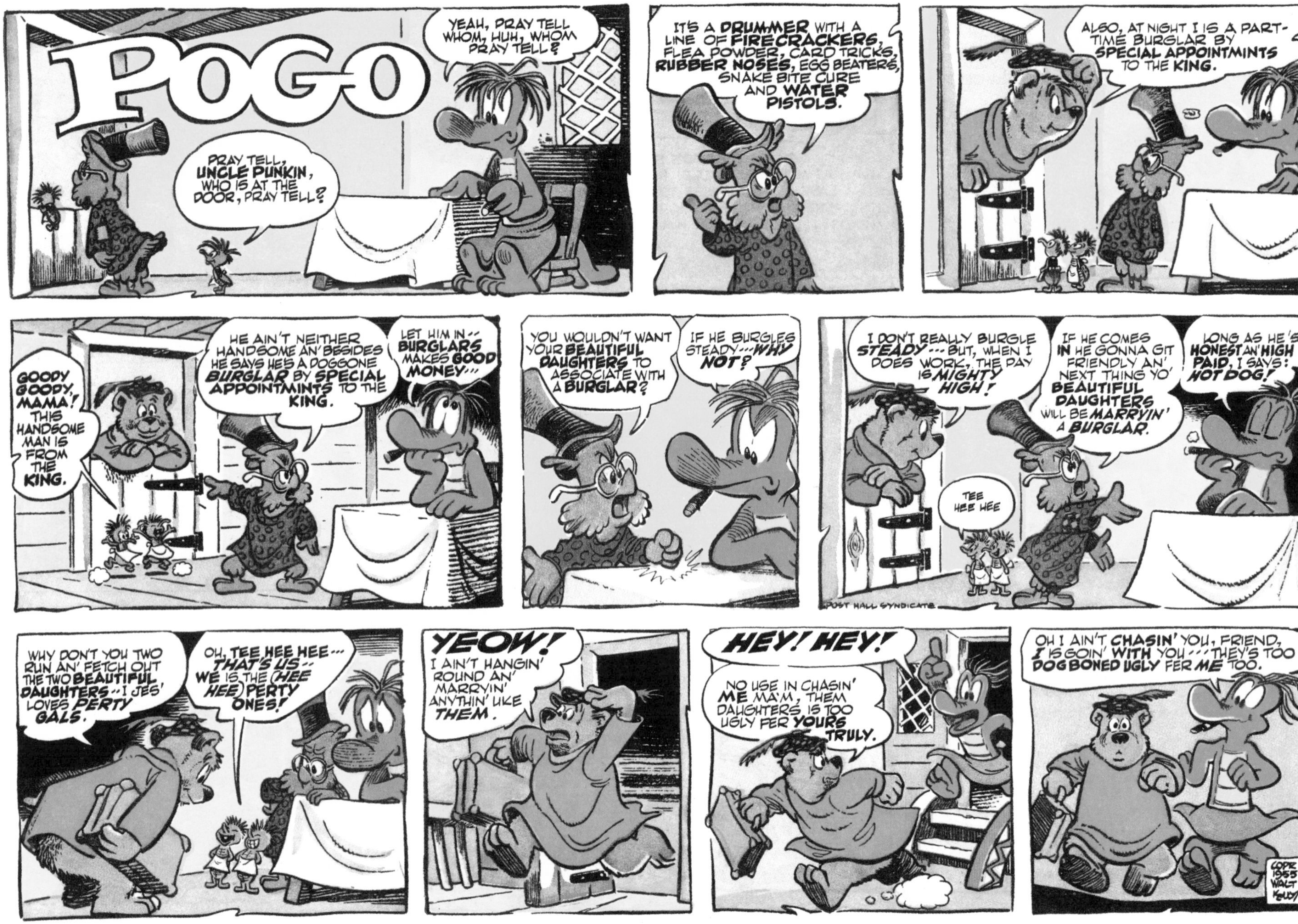
POGO
PRAY TELL, UNCLE PUNKIN, WHO IS AT THE DOOR, PRAY TELL?
YEAH, PRAY TELL WHOM, HUH, WHOM PRAY TELL?
IT'S A DRUMMER WITH A LINE OF FIRECRACKERS, FLEA POWDER, CARD TRICKS, RUBBER NOSES, EGG BEATERS, SNAKE BITE CURE AND WATER PISTOLS.
ALSO, AT NIGHT I IS A PART-TIME BURGLAR BY SPECIAL APPOINTMINTS TO THE KING.
GOODY GOODY, MAMA! THIS HANDSOME MAN IS FROM THE KING.
HE AIN'T NEITHER HANDSOME AN' BESIDES HE SAYS HE'S A DOGGONE BURGLAR BY SPECIAL APPOINTMINTS TO THE KING.
LET HIM IN -- BURGLARS MAKES GOOD MONEY...
YOU WOULDN'T WANT YOUR BEAUTIFUL DAUGHTERS TO ASSOCIATE WITH A BURGLAR?
IF HE BURGLES STEADY --- WHY NOT?
I DON'T REALLY BURGLE STEADY --- BUT, WHEN I DOES WORK, THE PAY IS MIGHTY HIGH!
TEE HEE HEE
IF HE COMES IN HE GONNA GIT FRIENDLY AN' NEXT THING YO' BEAUTIFUL DAUGHTERS WILL BE MARRYIN' A BURGLAR.
LONG AS HE'S HONEST AN' HIGH PAID, I SAYS: HOT DOG!
POST HALL SYNDICATE
WHY DON'T YOU TWO RUN AN' FETCH OUT THE TWO BEAUTIFUL DAUGHTERS -- I JES' LOVES PERTY GALS.
OH, TEE HEE HEE... THAT'S US -- WE IS THE (HEE HEE) PERTY ONES!
YEOW!
I AIN'T HANGIN' ROUND AN' MARRYIN' ANYTHIN' LIKE THEM.
HEY! HEY!
NO USE IN CHASIN' ME MA'M, THEM DAUGHTERS IS TOO UGLY FER YOURS TRULY.
OH I AIN'T CHASIN' YOU, FRIEND, I IS GOIN' WITH YOU ... THEY'S TOO DOG BONED UGLY FER ME TOO.
COPR 1955 WALT KELLY

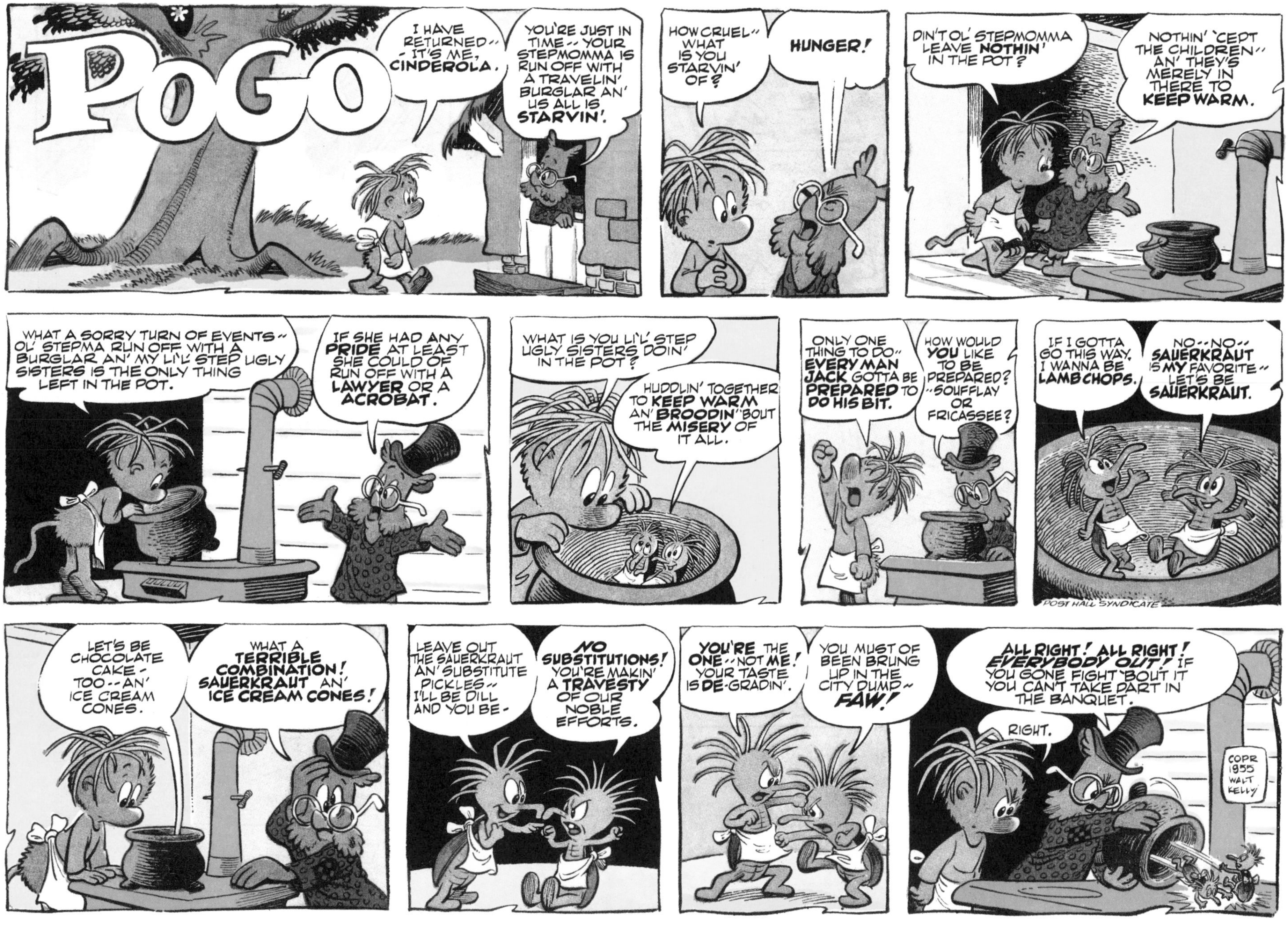
POGO
I HAVE RETURNED-- - IT'S ME, CINDEROLA.
YOU'RE JUST IN TIME -- YOUR STEPMOMMA IS RUN OFF WITH A TRAVELIN' BURGLAR AN' US ALL IS STARVIN'.
HOW CRUEL-- WHAT IS YOU STARVIN' OF?
HUNGER!
DIN'T OL' STEPMOMMA LEAVE NOTHIN' IN THE POT?
NOTHIN' 'CEPT THE CHILDREN-- AN' THEY'S MERELY IN THERE TO KEEP WARM.
WHAT A SORRY TURN OF EVENTS-- OL' STEPMA RUN OFF WITH A BURGLAR AN' MY LI'L' STEP UGLY SISTERS IS THE ONLY THING LEFT IN THE POT.
IF SHE HAD ANY PRIDE AT LEAST SHE COULD OF RUN OFF WITH A LAWYER OR A ACROBAT.
WHAT IS YOU LI'L' STEP UGLY SISTERS DOIN' IN THE POT?
HUDDLIN' TOGETHER TO KEEP WARM AN' BROODIN' 'BOUT THE MISERY OF IT ALL.
ONLY ONE THING TO DO-- EVERY MAN JACK GOTTA BE PREPARED TO DO HIS BIT.
HOW WOULD YOU LIKE TO BE PREPARED? --SOUFFLAY OR FRICASSEE?
IF I GOTTA GO THIS WAY, I WANNA BE LAMB CHOPS.
NO--NO-- SAUERKRAUT IS MY FAVORITE-- LET'S BE SAUERKRAUT.
POST HALL SYNDICATE
LET'S BE CHOCOLATE CAKE - TOO--AN' ICE CREAM CONES.
WHAT A TERRIBLE COMBINATION! SAUERKRAUT AN' ICE CREAM CONES!
LEAVE OUT THE SAUERKRAUT AN' SUBSTITUTE PICKLES-- I'LL BE DILL AND YOU BE-
NO SUBSTITUTIONS! YOU'RE MAKIN' A TRAVESTY OF OUR NOBLE EFFORTS.
YOU'RE THE ONE--NOT ME! YOUR TASTE IS DE-GRADIN'.
YOU MUST OF BEEN BRUNG UP IN THE CITY DUMP-- FAW!
ALL RIGHT! ALL RIGHT! EVERYBODY OUT! IF YOU GONE FIGHT 'BOUT IT YOU CAN'T TAKE PART IN THE BANQUET.
RIGHT.
COPR 1955 WALT KELLY

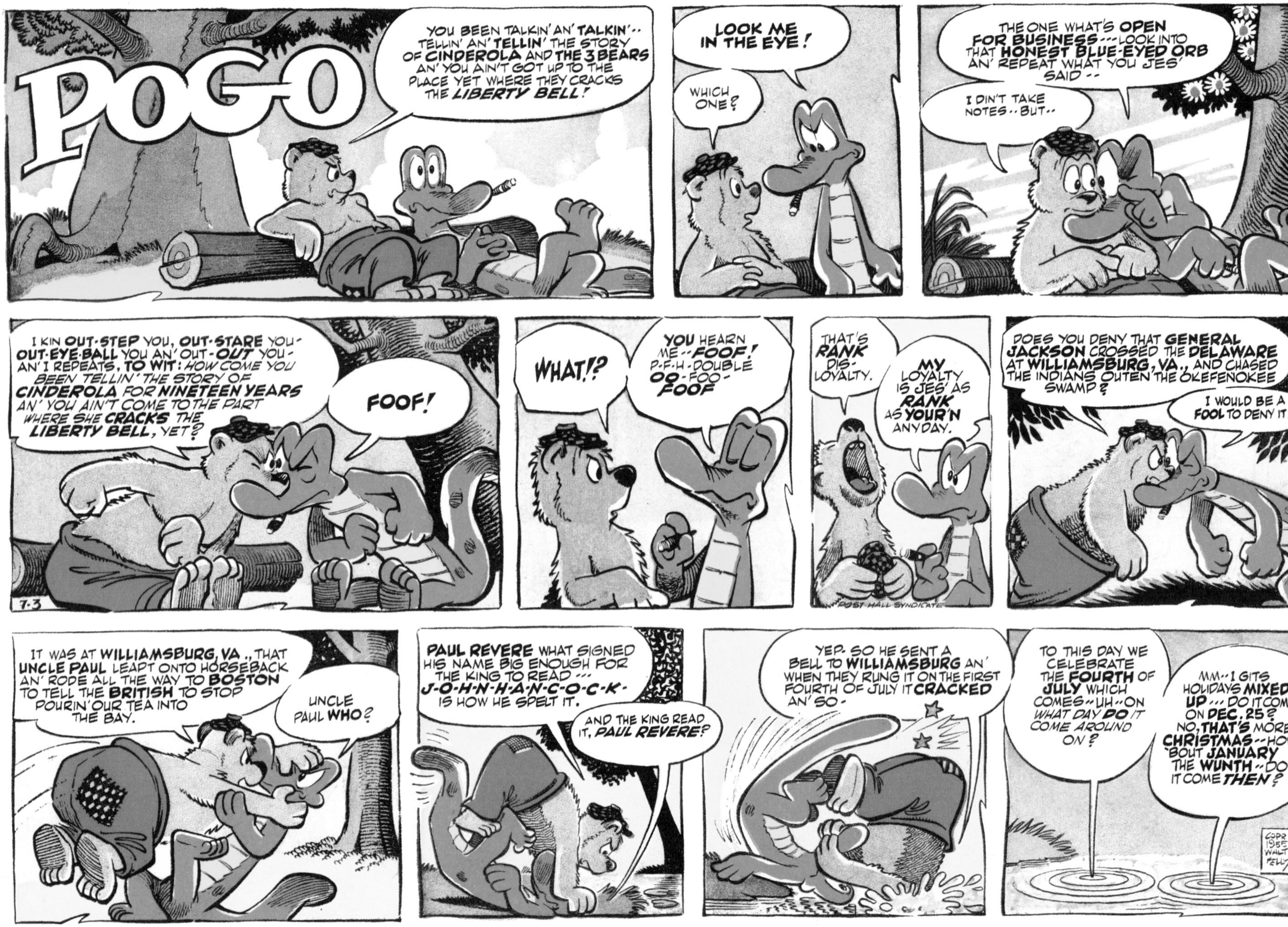
POGO
YOU BEEN TALKIN' AN' TALKIN'.. TELLIN' AN' TELLIN' THE STORY OF CINDEROLA AND THE 3 BEARS AN' YOU AIN'T GOT UP TO THE PLACE YET WHERE THEY CRACKS THE LIBERTY BELL!
LOOK ME IN THE EYE!
WHICH ONE?
THE ONE WHAT'S OPEN FOR BUSINESS--- LOOK INTO THAT HONEST BLUE-EYED ORB AN' REPEAT WHAT YOU JES' SAID --
I DIN'T TAKE NOTES.. BUT..
I KIN OUT-STEP YOU, OUT-STARE YOU- OUT-EYE-BALL YOU AN' OUT-OUT YOU- AN' I REPEATS, TO WIT: HOW COME YOU BEEN TELLIN' THE STORY OF CINDEROLA FOR NINETEEN YEARS AN' YOU AIN'T COME TO THE PART WHERE SHE CRACKS THE LIBERTY BELL, YET?
FOOF!
7-3
WHAT!?
YOU HEARN ME--FOOF! P-F-H-DOUBLE OO-FOO-FOOF
THAT'S RANK DIS-LOYALTY.
MY LOYALTY IS JES' AS RANK AS YOUR'N ANYDAY.
POST-HALL SYNDICATE
DOES YOU DENY THAT GENERAL JACKSON CROSSED THE DELAWARE AT WILLIAMSBURG, VA., AND CHASED THE INDIANS OUTEN THE OKEFENOKEE SWAMP?
I WOULD BE A FOOL TO DENY IT.
IT WAS AT WILLIAMSBURG, VA., THAT UNCLE PAUL LEAPT ONTO HORSEBACK AN' RODE ALL THE WAY TO BOSTON TO TELL THE BRITISH TO STOP POURIN' OUR TEA INTO THE BAY.
UNCLE PAUL WHO?
PAUL REVERE WHAT SIGNED HIS NAME BIG ENOUGH FOR THE KING TO READ --- J-O-H-N-H-A-N-C-O-C-K- IS HOW HE SPELT IT.
AND THE KING READ IT, PAUL REVERE?
YEP. SO HE SENT A BELL TO WILLIAMSBURG AN' WHEN THEY RUNG IT ON THE FIRST FOURTH OF JULY IT CRACKED AN' SO-
TO THIS DAY WE CELEBRATE THE FOURTH OF JULY WHICH COMES--UH--ON WHAT DAY DO IT COME AROUND ON?
MM--I GITS HOLIDAYS MIXED UP... DO IT COME ON DEC. 25? NO, THAT'S MORE CHRISTMAS--HOW 'BOUT JANUARY THE WUNTH--DO IT COME THEN?
COPR 1955 WALT KELLY

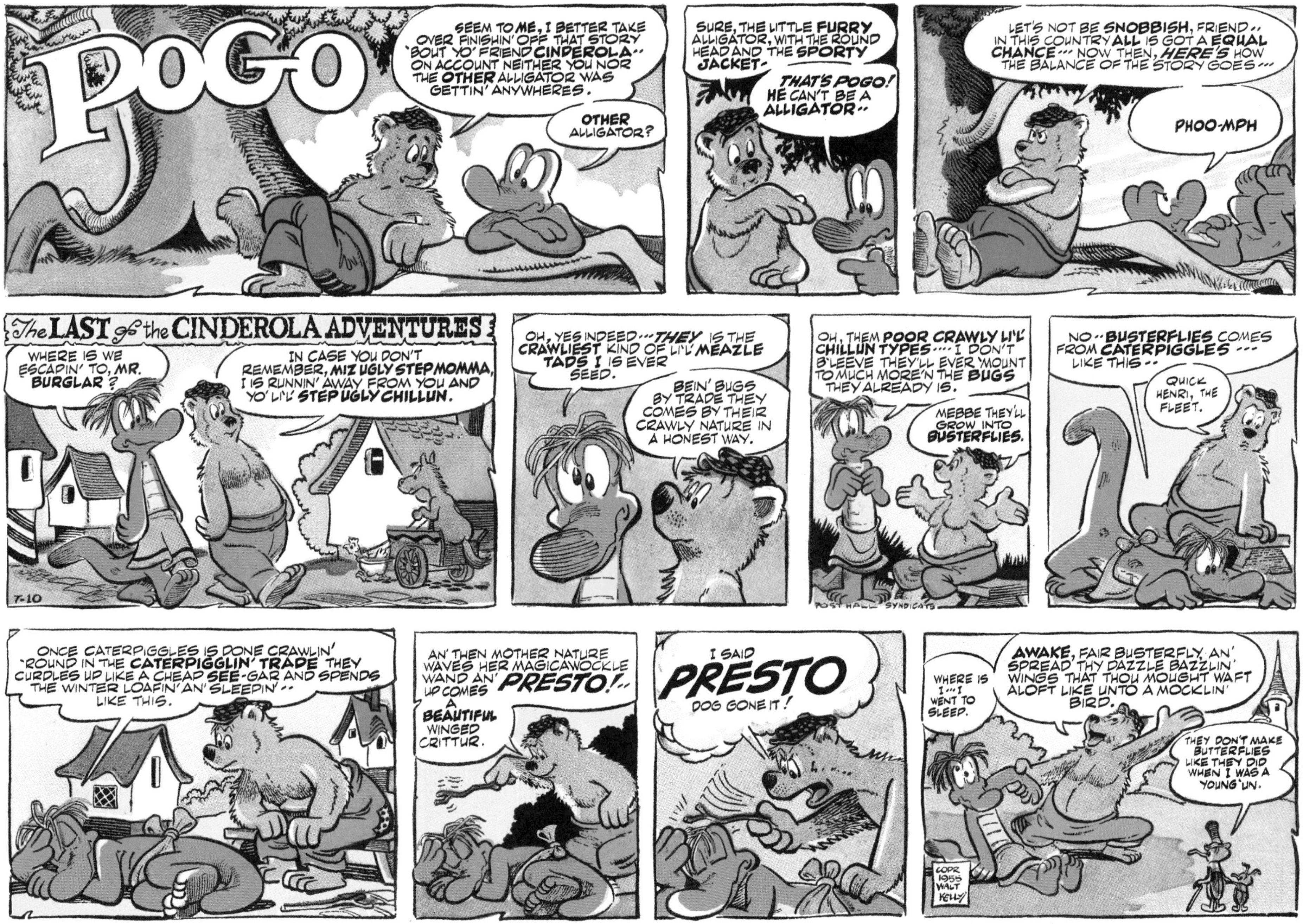
POGO
SEEM TO ME, I BETTER TAKE OVER FINISHIN' OFF THAT STORY 'BOUT YO' FRIEND CINDEROLA -- ON ACCOUNT NEITHER YOU NOR THE OTHER ALLIGATOR WAS GETTIN' ANYWHERES.
OTHER ALLIGATOR?
SURE, THE LITTLE FURRY ALLIGATOR, WITH THE ROUND HEAD AND THE SPORTY JACKET -
THAT'S POGO! HE CAN'T BE A ALLIGATOR --
LET'S NOT BE SNOBBISH, FRIEND -- IN THIS COUNTRY ALL IS GOT A EQUAL CHANCE --- NOW THEN, HERE'S HOW THE BALANCE OF THE STORY GOES ---
PHOO-MPH
The LAST of the CINDEROLA ADVENTURES
WHERE IS WE ESCAPIN' TO, MR. BURGLAR?
IN CASE YOU DON'T REMEMBER, MIZ UGLY STEPMOMMA, I IS RUNNIN' AWAY FROM YOU AND YO' LI'L' STEP UGLY CHILLUN.
7-10
OH, YES INDEED --- THEY IS THE CRAWLIEST KIND OF LI'L' MEAZLE TADS I IS EVER SEED.
BEIN' BUGS BY TRADE THEY COMES BY THEIR CRAWLY NATURE IN A HONEST WAY.
OH, THEM POOR CRAWLY LI'L' CHILLUN TYPES ---- I DON'T B'LEEVE THEY'LL EVER 'MOUNT TO MUCH MORE'N THE BUGS THEY ALREADY IS.
MEBBE THEY'LL GROW INTO BUSTERFLIES.
POST HALL SYNDICATE
NO -- BUSTERFLIES COMES FROM CATERPIGGLES --- LIKE THIS --
QUICK HENRI, THE FLEET.
ONCE CATERPIGGLES IS DONE CRAWLIN' 'ROUND IN THE CATERPIGGLIN' TRADE THEY CURDLES UP LIKE A CHEAP SEE-GAR AND SPENDS THE WINTER LOAFIN' AN' SLEEPIN' -- LIKE THIS.
AN' THEN MOTHER NATURE WAVES HER MAGICAWOCKLE WAND AN' UP COMES PRESTO! - A BEAUTIFUL WINGED CRITTUR.
I SAID PRESTO DOG GONE IT!
WHERE IS I --- I WENT TO SLEEP.
AWAKE, FAIR BUSTERFLY, AN' SPREAD THY DAZZLE BAZZLIN' WINGS THAT THOU MOUGHT WAFT ALOFT LIKE UNTO A MOCKLIN' BIRD.
THEY DON'T MAKE BUTTERFLIES LIKE THEY DID WHEN I WAS A YOUNG'UN.
COPR 1955 WALT KELLY

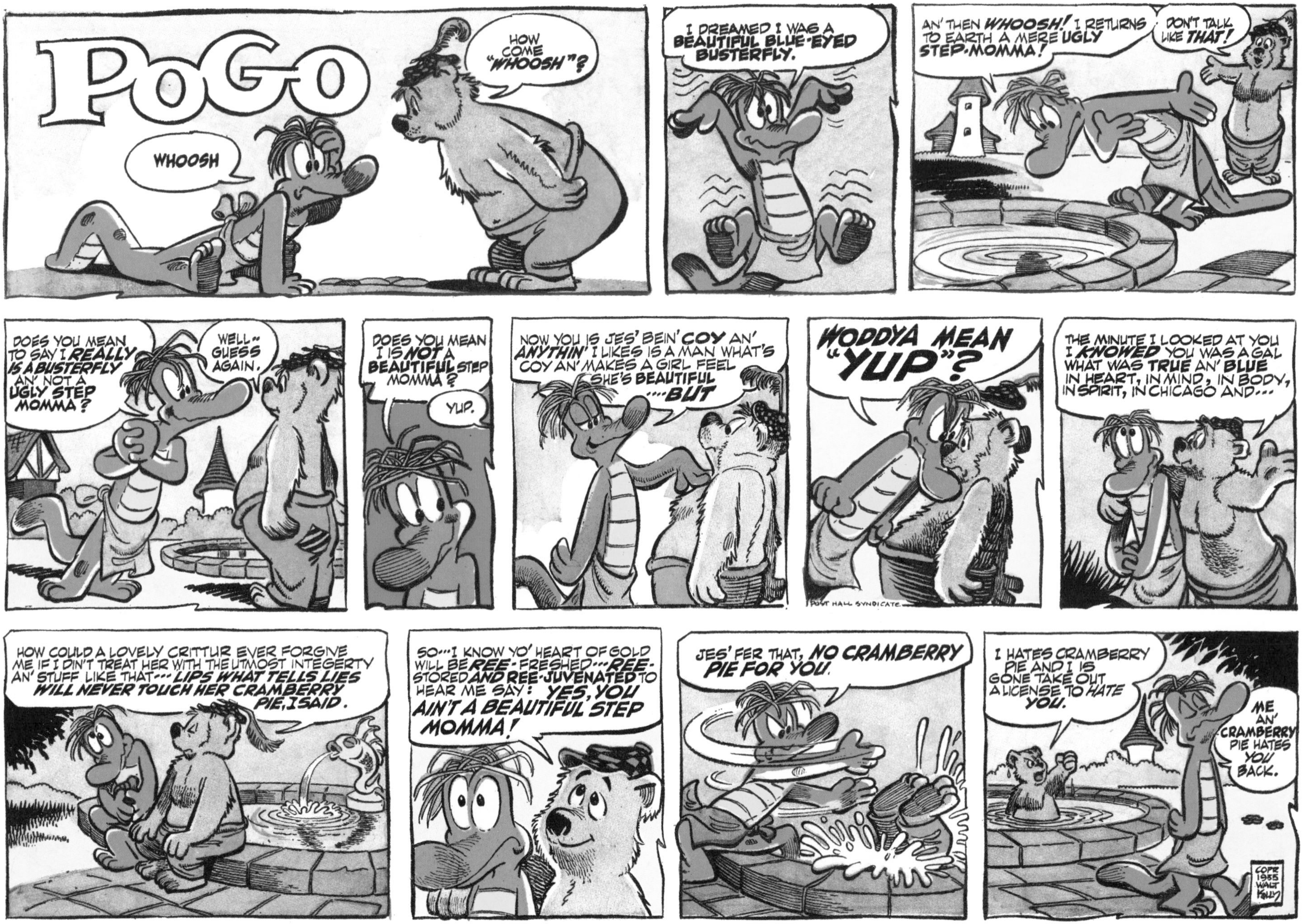
POGO
WHOOSH
HOW COME "WHOOSH"?
I DREAMED I WAS A BEAUTIFUL BLUE-EYED BUSTERFLY.
AN' THEN WHOOSH! I RETURNS TO EARTH A MERE UGLY STEP-MOMMA!
DON'T TALK LIKE THAT!
DOES YOU MEAN TO SAY I REALLY IS A BUSTERFLY AN' NOT A UGLY STEP MOMMA?
WELL.. GUESS AGAIN.
DOES YOU MEAN I IS NOT A BEAUTIFUL STEP MOMMA?
YUP.
NOW YOU IS JES' BEIN' COY AN' ANYTHIN' I LIKES IS A MAN WHAT'S COY AN' MAKES A GIRL FEEL SHE'S BEAUTIFUL ....BUT
WODDYA MEAN "YUP"?
THE MINUTE I LOOKED AT YOU I KNOWED YOU WAS A GAL WHAT WAS TRUE AN' BLUE IN HEART, IN MIND, IN BODY, IN SPIRIT, IN CHICAGO AND...
POST HALL SYNDICATE
HOW COULD A LOVELY CRITTUR EVER FORGIVE ME IF I DIN'T TREAT HER WITH THE UTMOST INTEGERTY AN' STUFF LIKE THAT--- LIPS WHAT TELLS LIES WILL NEVER TOUCH HER CRAMBERRY PIE, I SAID.
SO... I KNOW YO' HEART OF GOLD WILL BE REE-FRESHED... REE-STORED AND REE-JUVENATED TO HEAR ME SAY: YES, YOU AIN'T A BEAUTIFUL STEP MOMMA!
JES' FER THAT, NO CRAMBERRY PIE FOR YOU.
I HATES CRAMBERRY PIE AND I IS GONE TAKE OUT A LICENSE TO HATE YOU.
ME AN' CRAMBERRY PIE HATES YOU BACK.
COPR 1955 WALT KELLY

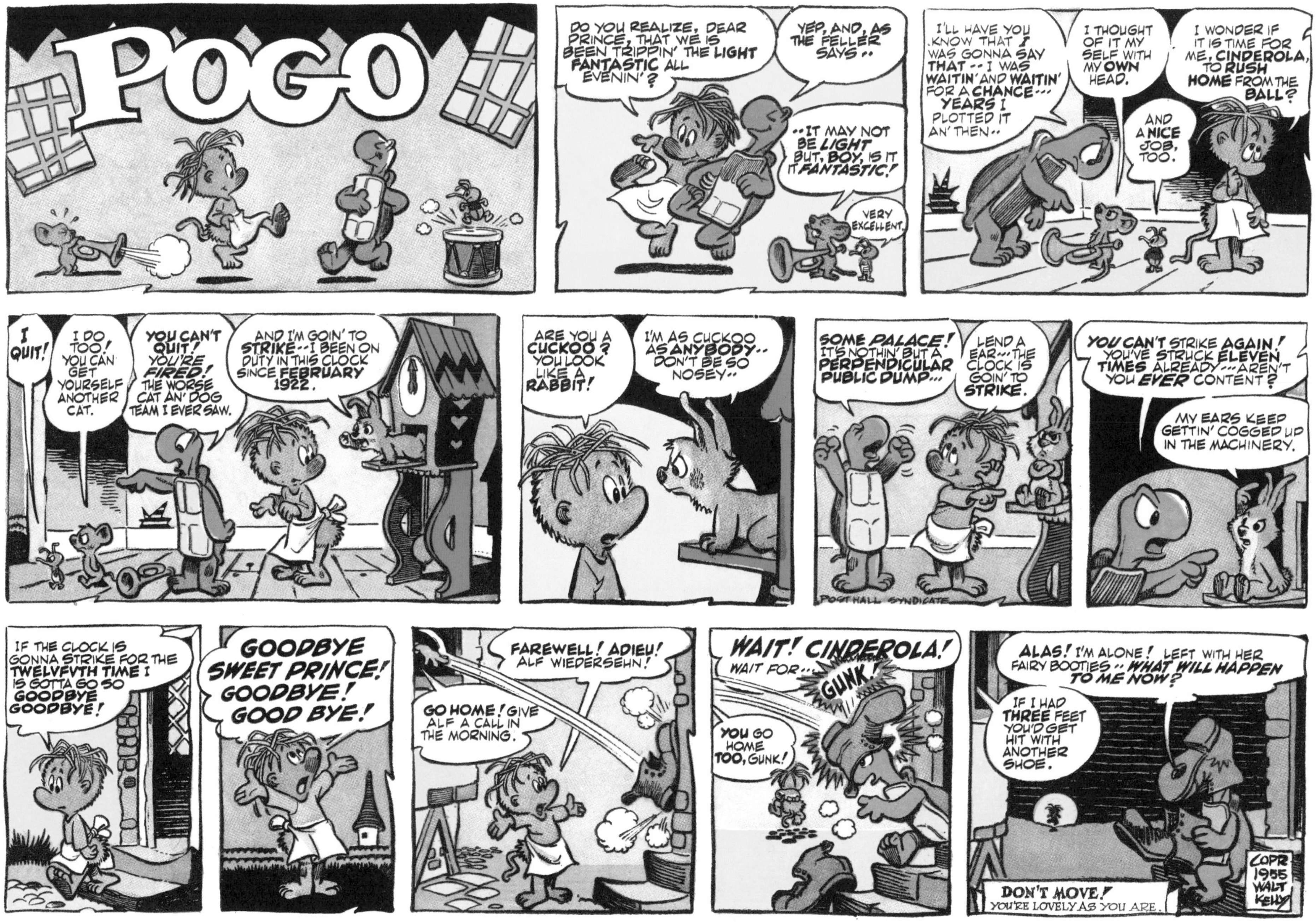
POGO
DO YOU REALIZE, DEAR PRINCE, THAT WE IS BEEN TRIPPIN' THE LIGHT FANTASTIC ALL EVENIN'?
YEP, AND, AS THE FELLER SAYS..
..IT MAY NOT BE LIGHT BUT, BOY, IS IT IT FANTASTIC!
VERY EXCELLENT.
I'LL HAVE YOU KNOW THAT I WAS GONNA SAY THAT -- I WAS WAITIN' AND WAITIN' FOR A CHANCE... YEARS I PLOTTED IT AN' THEN..
I THOUGHT OF IT MY SELF WITH MY OWN HEAD.
AND A NICE JOB, TOO.
I WONDER IF IT IS TIME FOR ME, CINDEROLA, TO RUSH HOME FROM THE BALL?
I QUIT!
I DO, TOO! YOU CAN GET YOURSELF ANOTHER CAT.
YOU CAN'T QUIT! YOU'RE FIRED! THE WORSE CAT AN' DOG TEAM I EVER SAW.
AND I'M GOIN' TO STRIKE -- I BEEN ON DUTY IN THIS CLOCK SINCE FEBRUARY 1922.
ARE YOU A CUCKOO? YOU LOOK LIKE A RABBIT!
I'M AS CUCKOO AS ANYBODY.. DON'T BE SO NOSEY..
SOME PALACE! IT'S NOTHIN' BUT A PERPENDICULAR PUBLIC DUMP...
LEND A EAR... THE CLOCK IS GOIN' TO STRIKE.
POST HALL SYNDICATE
YOU CAN'T STRIKE AGAIN! YOU'VE STRUCK ELEVEN TIMES ALREADY... AREN'T YOU EVER CONTENT?
MY EARS KEEP GETTIN' COGGED UP IN THE MACHINERY.
IF THE CLOCK IS GONNA STRIKE FOR THE TWELVFVTH TIME I IS GOTTA GO SO GOODBYE GOODBYE!
GOODBYE SWEET PRINCE! GOODBYE! GOOD BYE!
FAREWELL! ADIEU! ALF WIEDERSEHN!
GO HOME! GIVE ALF A CALL IN THE MORNING.
WAIT! CINDEROLA! WAIT FOR...
GUNK!
YOU GO HOME TOO, GUNK!
ALAS! I'M ALONE! LEFT WITH HER FAIRY BOOTIES .. WHAT WILL HAPPEN TO ME NOW?
IF I HAD THREE FEET YOU'D GET HIT WITH ANOTHER SHOE.
DON'T MOVE! YOU'RE LOVELY AS YOU ARE.
COPR 1955 WALT KELLY

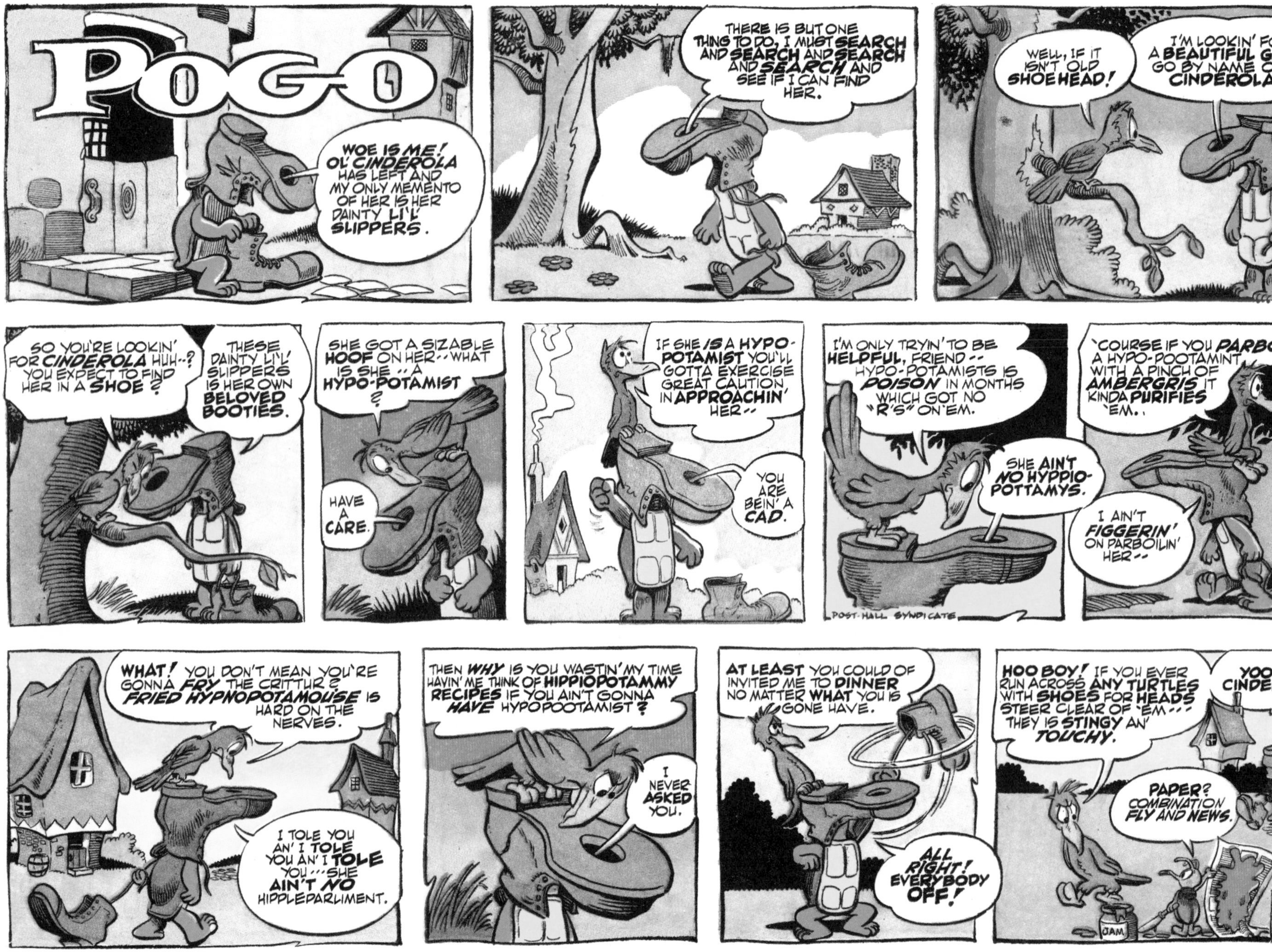
POGO
WOE IS ME! OL' CINDEROLA HAS LEFT AND MY ONLY MEMENTO OF HER IS HER DAINTY LI'L SLIPPERS.
THERE IS BUT ONE THING TO DO, I MUST SEARCH AND SEARCH AND SEARCH AND SEARCH AND SEE IF I CAN FIND HER.
WELL, IF IT ISN'T OLD SHOEHEAD!
I'M LOOKIN' FOR A BEAUTIFUL GAL GO BY NAME OF CINDEROLA.
SO YOU'RE LOOKIN' FOR CINDEROLA HUH--? YOU EXPECT TO FIND HER IN A SHOE?
THESE DAINTY LI'L SLIPPERS IS HER OWN BELOVED BOOTIES.
SHE GOT A SIZABLE HOOF ON HER--WHAT IS SHE--A HYPO-POTAMIST?
HAVE A CARE.
IF SHE IS A HYPO-POTAMIST YOU'LL GOTTA EXERCISE GREAT CAUTION IN APPROACHIN' HER--
YOU ARE BEIN' A CAD.
I'M ONLY TRYIN' TO BE HELPFUL, FRIEND-- HYPO-POTAMISTS IS POISON IN MONTHS WHICH GOT NO "R'S" ON 'EM.
SHE AIN'T NO HYPPIO-POTTAMYS.
POST-HALL SYNDICATE
'COURSE IF YOU PARBOILS A HYPO-POOTAMINT WITH A PINCH OF AMBERGRIS IT KINDA PURIFIES 'EM.
I AIN'T FIGGERIN' ON PARBOILIN' HER--
WHAT! YOU DON'T MEAN YOU'RE GONNA FRY THE CRITTUR? FRIED HYPNOPOTAMOUSE IS HARD ON THE NERVES.
I TOLE YOU AN' I TOLE YOU AN' I TOLE YOU---SHE AIN'T NO HIPPLEPARLIMENT.
THEN WHY IS YOU WASTIN' MY TIME HAVIN' ME THINK OF HIPPIOPOTAMMY RECIPES IF YOU AIN'T GONNA HAVE HYPOPOOTAMIST?
I NEVER ASKED YOU.
AT LEAST YOU COULD OF INVITED ME TO DINNER NO MATTER WHAT YOU IS GONE HAVE.
ALL RIGHT! EVERYBODY OFF!
HOO BOY! IF YOU EVER RUN ACROSS ANY TURTLES WITH SHOES FOR HEADS STEER CLEAR OF 'EM--- THEY IS STINGY AN' TOUCHY.
YOO HOO CINDEROLA!
PAPER? COMBINATION FLY AND NEWS.
JAM
COPR 1955 WALT KELLY

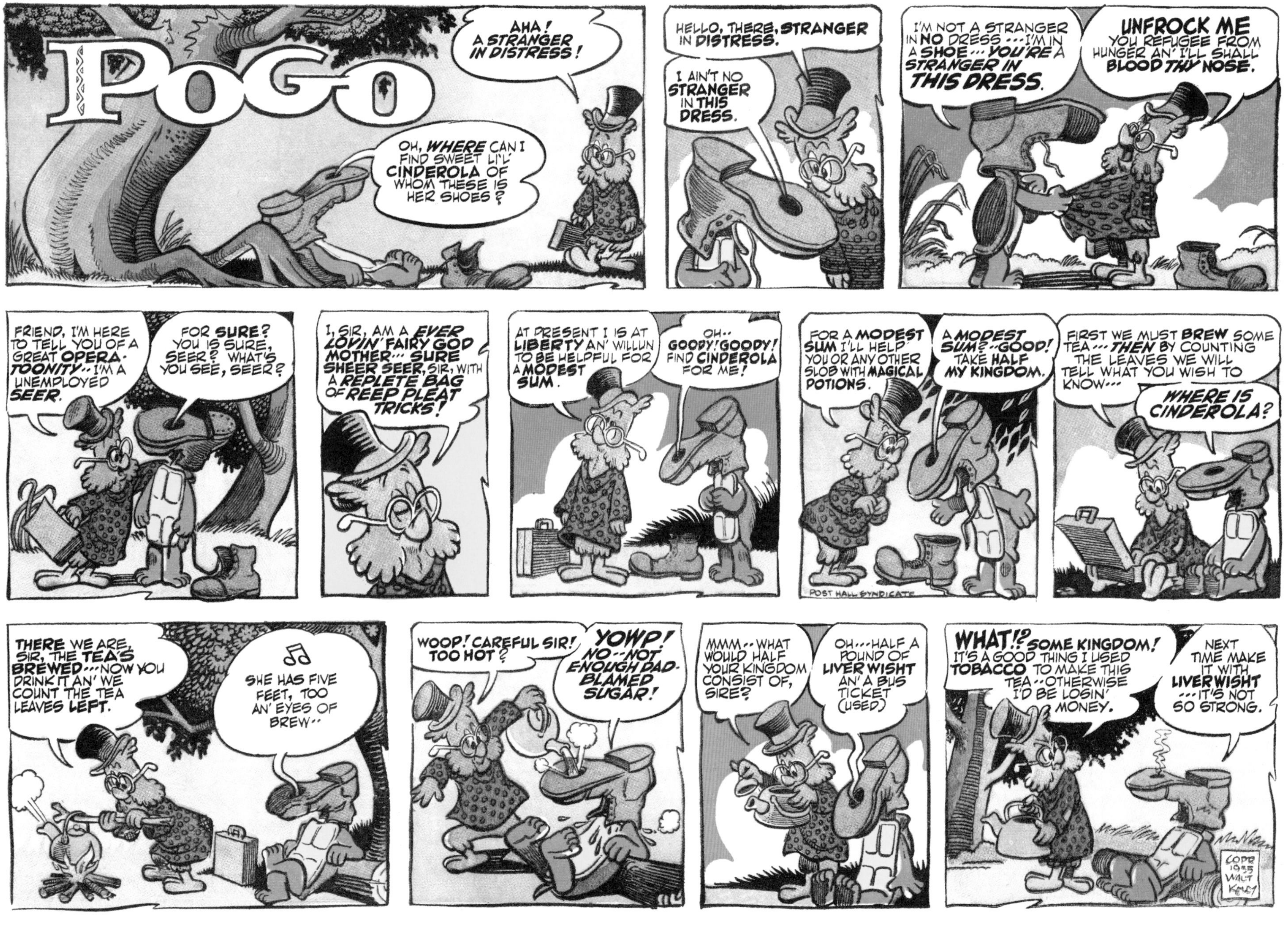
POGO
AHA! A STRANGER IN DISTRESS!
OH, WHERE CAN I FIND SWEET LI'L' CINDEROLA OF WHOM THESE IS HER SHOES?
HELLO, THERE, STRANGER IN DISTRESS.
I AIN'T NO STRANGER IN THIS DRESS.
I'M NOT A STRANGER IN NO DRESS ... I'M IN A SHOE ... YOU'RE A STRANGER IN THIS DRESS.
UNFROCK ME YOU REFUGEE FROM HUNGER AN' I'LL SHALL BLOOD THY NOSE.
FRIEND, I'M HERE TO TELL YOU OF A GREAT OPERA-TOONITY ... I'M A UNEMPLOYED SEER.
FOR SURE? YOU IS SURE, SEER? WHAT'S YOU SEE, SEER?
I, SIR, AM A EVER LOVIN' FAIRY GOD MOTHER ... SURE SHEER SEER, SIR, WITH A REPLETE BAG OF REEP PLEAT TRICKS!
AT PRESENT I IS AT LIBERTY AN' WILLUN TO BE HELPFUL FOR A MODEST SUM.
OH .. GOODY! GOODY! FIND CINDEROLA FOR ME!
FOR A MODEST SUM I'LL HELP YOU OR ANY OTHER SLOB WITH MAGICAL POTIONS.
A MODEST SUM? .. GOOD! TAKE HALF MY KINGDOM.
POST HALL SYNDICATE
FIRST WE MUST BREW SOME TEA ... THEN BY COUNTING THE LEAVES WE WILL TELL WHAT YOU WISH TO KNOW ...
WHERE IS CINDEROLA?
THERE WE ARE, SIR, THE TEA'S BREWED ... NOW YOU DRINK IT AN' WE COUNT THE TEA LEAVES LEFT.
SHE HAS FIVE FEET, TOO AN' EYES OF BREW ..
WOOP! CAREFUL SIR! TOO HOT?
YOWP! NO .. NOT ENOUGH DAD-BLAMED SUGAR!
MMM .. WHAT WOULD HALF YOUR KINGDOM CONSIST OF, SIRE?
OH ... HALF A POUND OF LIVER WISHT AN' A BUS TICKET (USED)
WHAT!? SOME KINGDOM! IT'S A GOOD THING I USED TOBACCO TO MAKE THIS TEA .. OTHERWISE I'D BE LOSIN' MONEY.
NEXT TIME MAKE IT WITH LIVER WISHT ... IT'S NOT SO STRONG.
COPR 1955 WALT KELLY

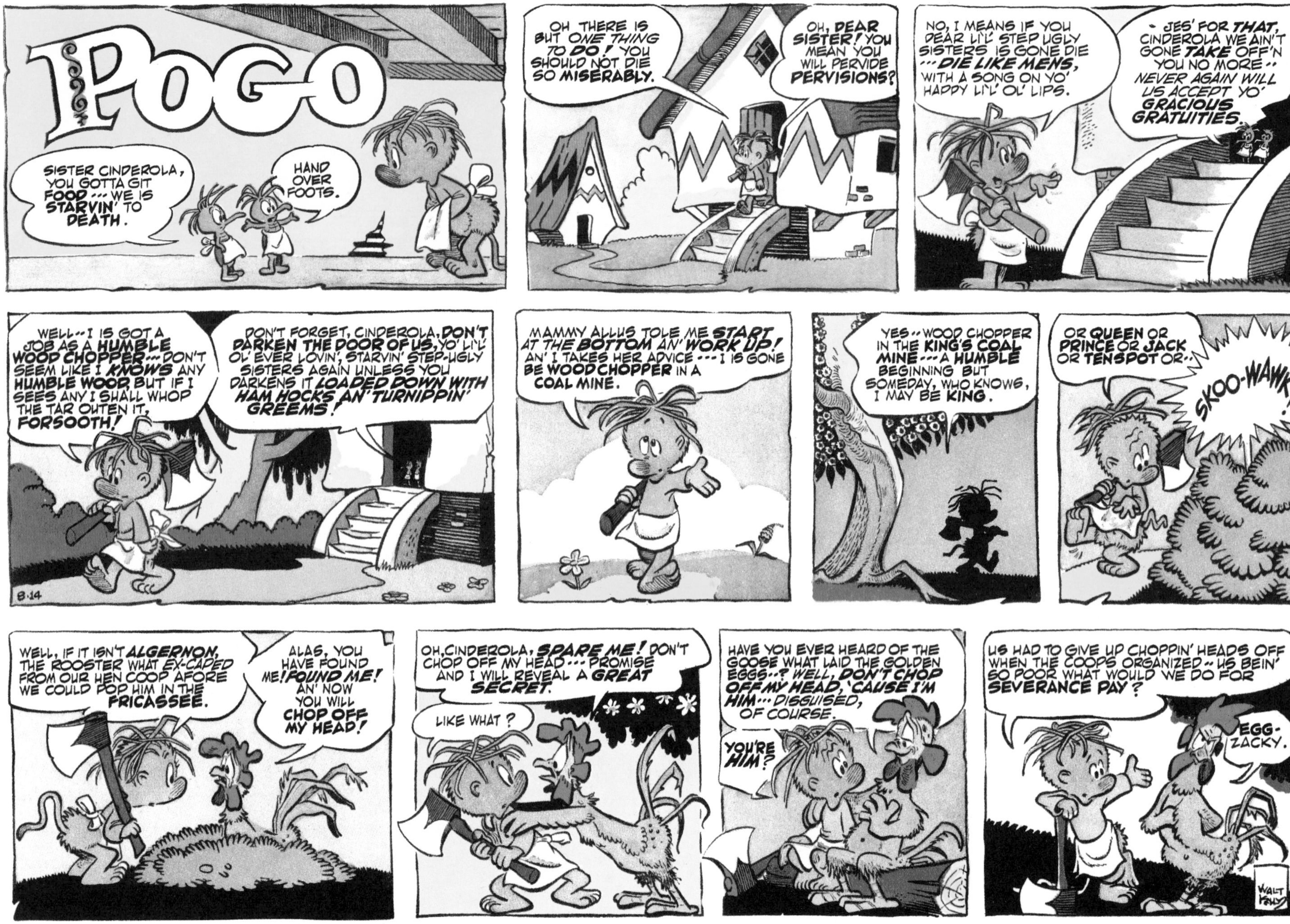
POGO
SISTER CINDEROLA, YOU GOTTA GIT FOOD ··· WE IS STARVIN' TO DEATH.
HAND OVER FOOTS.
OH THERE IS BUT ONE THING TO DO! YOU SHOULD NOT DIE SO MISERABLY.
OH, DEAR SISTER! YOU MEAN YOU WILL PERVIDE PERVISIONS?
NO, I MEANS IF YOU DEAR LI'L' STEP UGLY SISTERS IS GONE DIE ··· DIE LIKE MENS, WITH A SONG ON YO' HAPPY LI'L' OL' LIPS.
- JES' FOR THAT, CINDEROLA WE AIN'T GONE TAKE OFF'N YOU NO MORE ·· NEVER AGAIN WILL US ACCEPT YO' GRACIOUS GRATUITIES.
WELL ·· I IS GOT A JOB AS A HUMBLE WOOD CHOPPER ··· DON'T SEEM LIKE I KNOWS ANY HUMBLE WOOD, BUT IF I SEES ANY I SHALL WHOP THE TAR OUTEN IT, FORSOOTH!
DON'T FORGET, CINDEROLA, DON'T DARKEN THE DOOR OF US, YO' LI'L' OL' EVER LOVIN', STARVIN' STEP-UGLY SISTERS AGAIN UNLESS YOU DARKENS IT LOADED DOWN WITH HAM HOCKS AN' TURNIPPIN' GREEMS!
8·14
MAMMY ALLUS TOLE ME START AT THE BOTTOM AN' WORK UP! AN' I TAKES HER ADVICE ··· I IS GONE BE WOODCHOPPER IN A COAL MINE.
YES ·· WOOD CHOPPER IN THE KING'S COAL MINE ··· A HUMBLE BEGINNING BUT SOMEDAY, WHO KNOWS, I MAY BE KING.
OR QUEEN OR PRINCE OR JACK OR TENSPOT OR ··
SKOO-WAWK!
WELL, IF IT ISN'T ALGERNON, THE ROOSTER WHAT EX-CAPED FROM OUR HEN COOP AFORE WE COULD POP HIM IN THE FRICASSEE.
ALAS, YOU HAVE FOUND ME! FOUND ME! AN' NOW YOU WILL CHOP OFF MY HEAD!
OH, CINDEROLA, SPARE ME! DON'T CHOP OFF MY HEAD ··· PROMISE AND I WILL REVEAL A GREAT SECRET.
LIKE WHAT?
HAVE YOU EVER HEARD OF THE GOOSE WHAT LAID THE GOLDEN EGGS ··? WELL, DON'T CHOP OFF MY HEAD, 'CAUSE I'M HIM ··· DISGUISED, OF COURSE.
YOU'RE HIM?
US HAD TO GIVE UP CHOPPIN' HEADS OFF WHEN THE COOPS ORGANIZED ·· US BEIN' SO POOR WHAT WOULD WE DO FOR SEVERANCE PAY?
EGG-ZACKY.
WALT KELLY

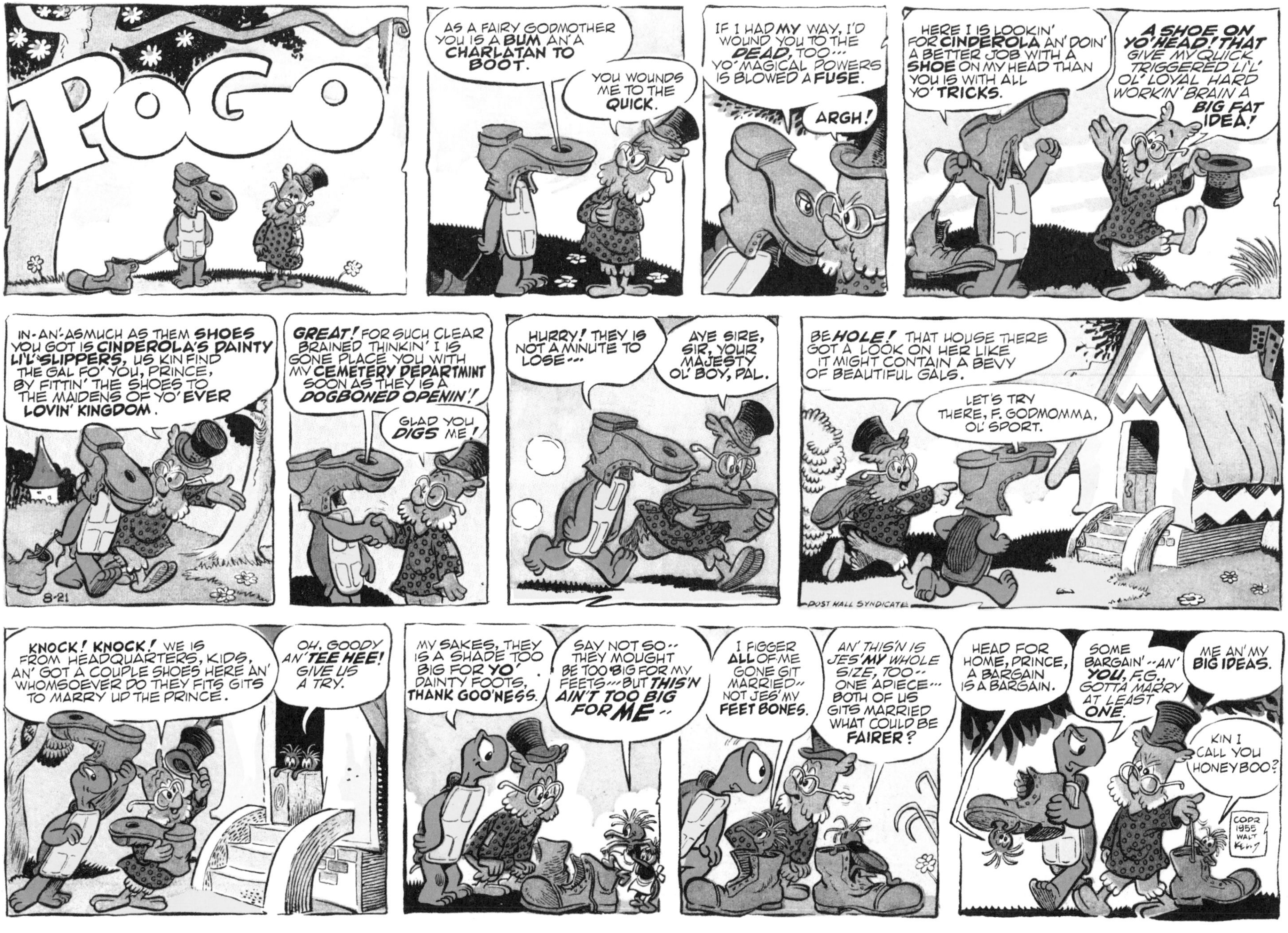
POGO
AS A FAIRY GODMOTHER YOU IS A BUM AN'A CHARLATAN TO BOOT.
YOU WOUNDS ME TO THE QUICK.
IF I HAD MY WAY, I'D WOUND YOU TO THE DEAD, TOO... YO' MAGICAL POWERS IS BLOWED A FUSE.
ARGH!
HERE I IS LOOKIN' FOR CINDEROLA AN' DOIN' A BETTER JOB WITH A SHOE ON MY HEAD THAN YOU IS WITH ALL YO' TRICKS.
A SHOE ON YO' HEAD! THAT GIVE MY QUICK TRIGGERED LI'L' OL' LOYAL HARD WORKIN' BRAIN A BIG FAT IDEA!
IN-AN'-ASMUCH AS THEM SHOES YOU GOT IS CINDEROLA'S DAINTY LI'L' SLIPPERS, US KIN FIND THE GAL FO' YOU, PRINCE, BY FITTIN' THE SHOES TO THE MAIDENS OF YO' EVER LOVIN' KINGDOM.
8-21
GREAT! FOR SUCH CLEAR BRAINED THINKIN' I IS GONE PLACE YOU WITH MY CEMETERY DEPARTMINT SOON AS THEY IS A DOGBONED OPENIN'!
GLAD YOU DIGS ME!
HURRY! THEY IS NOT A MINUTE TO LOSE...
AYE SIRE, SIR, YOUR MAJESTY OL' BOY, PAL.
BE HOLE! THAT HOUSE THERE GOT A LOOK ON HER LIKE IT MIGHT CONTAIN A BEVY OF BEAUTIFUL GALS.
LET'S TRY THERE, F. GODMOMMA, OL' SPORT.
POST HALL SYNDICATE
KNOCK! KNOCK! WE IS FROM HEADQUARTERS, KIDS, AN' GOT A COUPLE SHOES HERE AN' WHOMSOEVER DO THEY FITS GITS TO MARRY UP THE PRINCE.
OH, GOODY AN' TEE HEE! GIVE US A TRY.
MY SAKES, THEY IS A SHADE TOO BIG FOR YO' DAINTY FOOTS, THANK GOO'NESS.
SAY NOT SO-- THEY MOUGHT BE TOO BIG FOR MY FEETS... BUT THIS'N AIN'T TOO BIG FOR ME--
I FIGGER ALL OF ME GONE GIT MARRIED.. NOT JES' MY FEET BONES.
AN' THIS'N IS JES' MY WHOLE SIZE, TOO-- ONE APIECE... BOTH OF US GITS MARRIED WHAT COULD BE FAIRER?
HEAD FOR HOME, PRINCE, A BARGAIN IS A BARGAIN.
SOME BARGAIN'--AN' YOU, F.G., GOTTA MARRY AT LEAST ONE.
ME AN' MY BIG IDEAS.
KIN I CALL YOU HONEYBOO?
COPR 1955 WALT KELLY

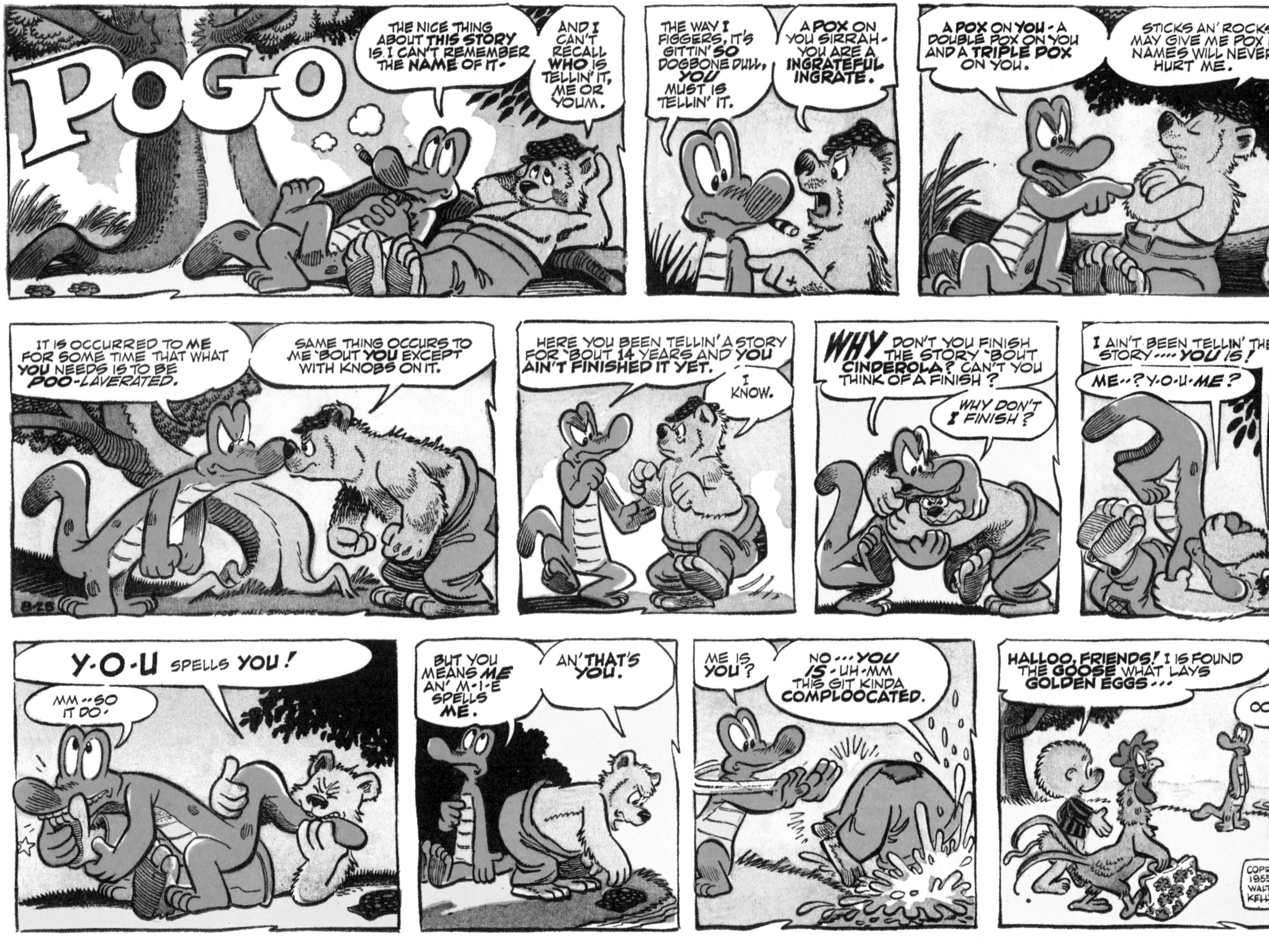
POGO
THE NICE THING ABOUT THIS STORY IS, I CAN'T REMEMBER THE NAME OF IT.
AND I CAN'T RECALL WHO IS TELLIN' IT, ME OR YOUM.
THE WAY I FIGGERS, IT'S GITTIN' SO DOGBONE DULL, YOU MUST IS TELLIN' IT.
A POX ON YOU SIRRAH - YOU ARE A INGRATEFUL INGRATE.
A POX ON YOU - A DOUBLE POX ON YOU AND A TRIPLE POX ON YOU.
STICKS AN' ROCKS MAY GIVE ME POX BUT NAMES WILL NEVER HURT ME.
IT IS OCCURRED TO ME FOR SOME TIME THAT WHAT YOU NEEDS IS TO BE POO-LAVERATED.
SAME THING OCCURS TO ME 'BOUT YOU EXCEPT WITH KNOBS ON IT.
HERE YOU BEEN TELLIN' A STORY FOR 'BOUT 14 YEARS AND YOU AIN'T FINISHED IT YET.
I KNOW.
WHY DON'T YOU FINISH THE STORY 'BOUT CINDEROLA? CAN'T YOU THINK OF A FINISH?
WHY DON'T I FINISH?
I AIN'T BEEN TELLIN' THE STORY .... YOU IS!
ME..? Y-O-U-ME?
Y-O-U SPELLS YOU!
MM .. SO IT DO.
BUT YOU MEANS ME AN' M-I-E SPELLS ME.
AN' THAT'S YOU.
ME IS YOU?
NO ... YOU IS - UH-MM THIS GIT KINDA COMPLOOCATED.
HALLOO, FRIENDS! I IS FOUND THE GOOSE WHAT LAYS GOLDEN EGGS ...
OOP.
COPR 1955 WALT KELLY

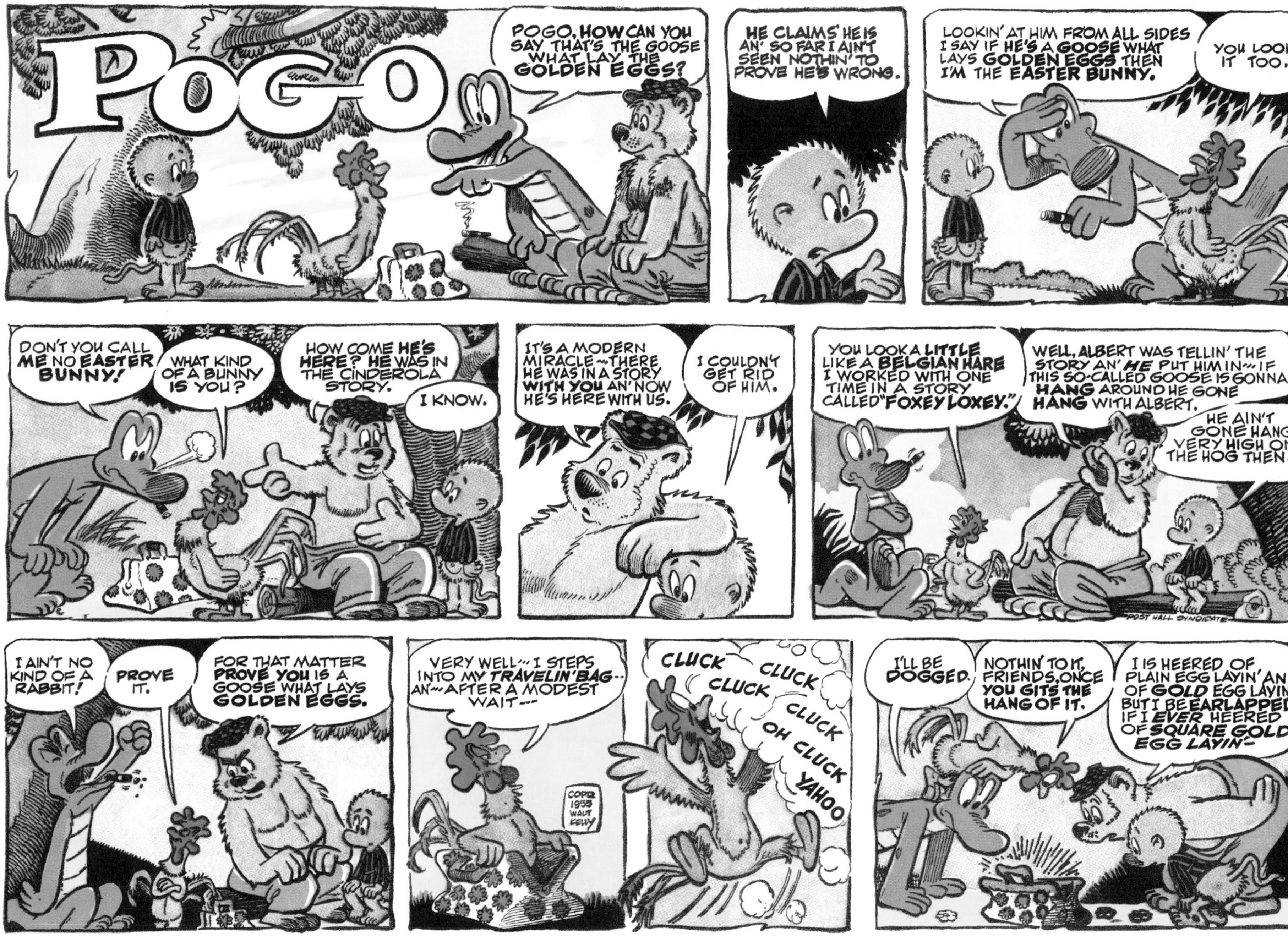
POGO
POGO, HOW CAN YOU SAY THAT'S THE GOOSE WHAT LAY THE GOLDEN EGGS?
HE CLAIMS HE IS AN' SO FAR I AIN'T SEEN NOTHIN' TO PROVE HE'S WRONG.
LOOKIN' AT HIM FROM ALL SIDES I SAY IF HE'S A GOOSE WHAT LAYS GOLDEN EGGS THEN I'M THE EASTER BUNNY.
YOU LOOK IT TOO.
DON'T YOU CALL ME NO EASTER BUNNY!
WHAT KIND OF A BUNNY IS YOU?
HOW COME HE'S HERE? HE WAS IN THE CINDEROLA STORY.
I KNOW.
IT'S A MODERN MIRACLE—THERE HE WAS IN A STORY WITH YOU AN' NOW HE'S HERE WITH US.
I COULDN'T GET RID OF HIM.
YOU LOOK A LITTLE LIKE A BELGIAN HARE I WORKED WITH ONE TIME IN A STORY CALLED "FOXEY LOXEY."
WELL, ALBERT WAS TELLIN' THE STORY AN' HE PUT HIM IN— IF THIS SO-CALLED GOOSE IS GONNA HANG AROUND HE GONE HANG WITH ALBERT.
HE AIN'T GONE HANG VERY HIGH ON THE HOG THEN.
POST HALL SYNDICATE
I AIN'T NO KIND OF A RABBIT!
PROVE IT.
FOR THAT MATTER PROVE YOU IS A GOOSE WHAT LAYS GOLDEN EGGS.
VERY WELL— I STEPS INTO MY TRAVELIN' BAG— AN'— AFTER A MODEST WAIT—
COPR 1955 WALT KELLY
CLUCK CLUCK
CLUCK
CLUCK
OH CLUCK
YAHOO
I'LL BE DOGGED.
NOTHIN' TO IT, FRIENDS, ONCE YOU GITS THE HANG OF IT.
I IS HEERED OF PLAIN EGG LAYIN' AN' OF GOLD EGG LAYIN'— BUT I BE EARLAPPED IF I EVER HEERED OF SQUARE GOLD EGG LAYIN'—

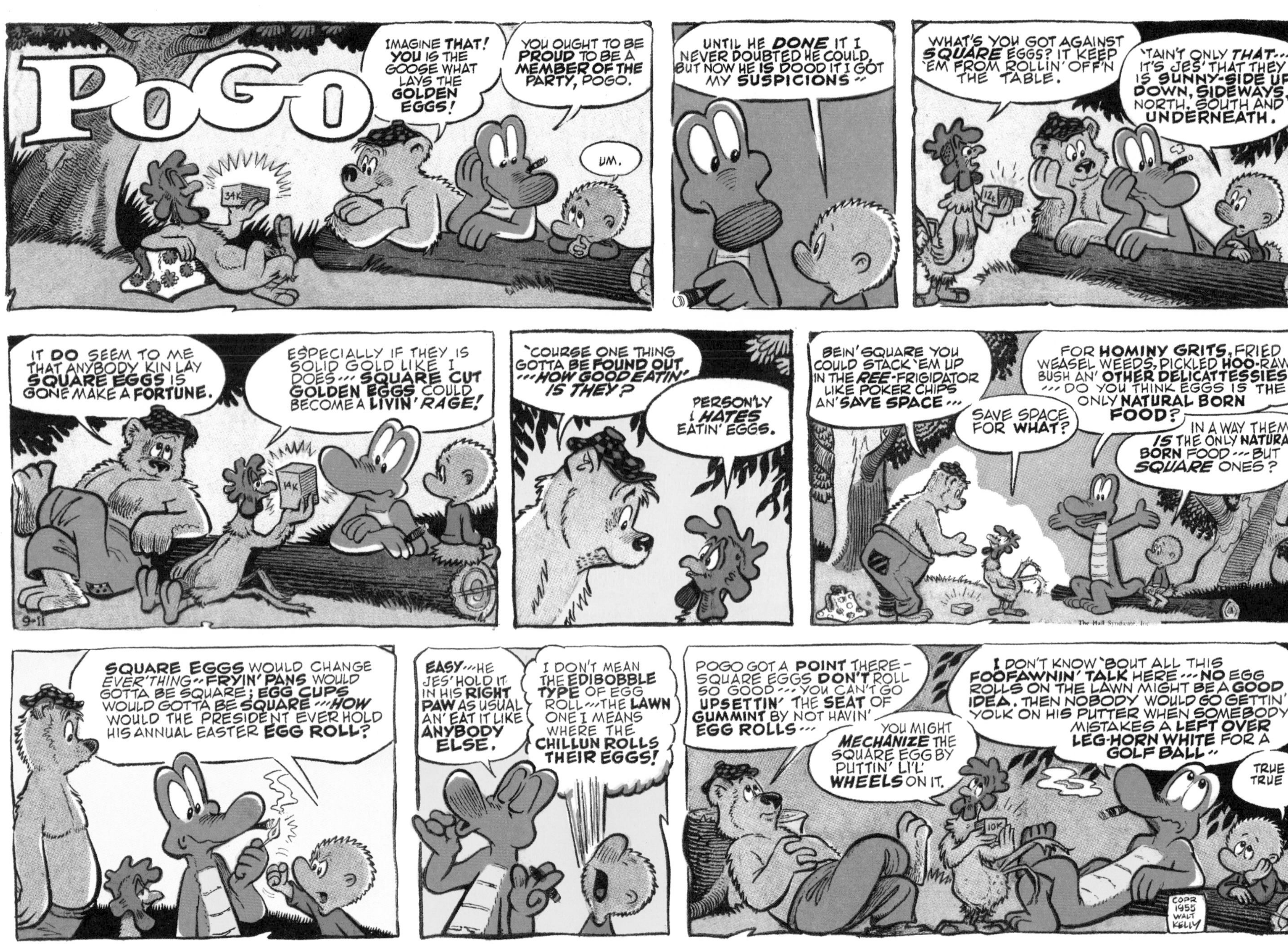
POGO
IMAGINE THAT! YOU IS THE GOOGE WHAT LAYS THE GOLDEN EGGS!
YOU OUGHT TO BE PROUD TO BE A MEMBER OF THE PARTY, POGO.
UM.
34K
UNTIL HE DONE IT I NEVER DOUBTED HE COULD, BUT NOW HE IS DOOD IT I GOT MY SUSPICIONS --
WHAT'S YOU GOT AGAINST SQUARE EGGS? IT KEEP 'EM FROM ROLLIN' OFF'N THE TABLE.
'TAIN'T ONLY THAT--- IT'S JES' THAT THEY IS SUNNY-SIDE UP, DOWN, SIDEWAYS, NORTH, SOUTH AND UNDERNEATH.
12K
IT DO SEEM TO ME THAT ANYBODY KIN LAY SQUARE EGGS IS GONE MAKE A FORTUNE.
ESPECIALLY IF THEY IS SOLID GOLD LIKE I DOES--- SQUARE CUT GOLDEN EGGS COULD BECOME A LIVIN' RAGE!
14K
9-11
'COURSE ONE THING GOTTA BE FOUND OUT --- HOW GOOD EATIN' IS THEY?
PERSON'LY I HATES EATIN' EGGS.
BEIN' SQUARE YOU COULD STACK 'EM UP IN THE REE-FRIGIDATOR LIKE POKER CHIPS AN' SAVE SPACE---
SAVE SPACE FOR WHAT?
FOR HOMINY GRITS, FRIED WEASEL WEEDS, PICKLED HOO-RAW BUSH AN' OTHER DELICATTESSIES --- DO YOU THINK EGGS IS THE ONLY NATURAL BORN FOOD?
IN A WAY THEM IS THE ONLY NATURAL BORN FOOD --- BUT SQUARE ONES?
The Hall Syndicate, Inc.
SQUARE EGGS WOULD CHANGE EVER'THING -- FRYIN' PANS WOULD GOTTA BE SQUARE; EGG CUPS WOULD GOTTA BE SQUARE --- HOW WOULD THE PRESIDENT EVER HOLD HIS ANNUAL EASTER EGG ROLL?
EASY--- HE JES' HOLD IT IN HIS RIGHT PAW AS USUAL AN' EAT IT LIKE ANYBODY ELSE.
I DON'T MEAN THE EDIBOBBLE TYPE OF EGG ROLL--- THE LAWN ONE I MEANS WHERE THE CHILLUN ROLLS THEIR EGGS!
POGO GOT A POINT THERE— SQUARE EGGS DON'T ROLL SO GOOD--- YOU CAN'T GO UPSETTIN' THE SEAT OF GUMMINT BY NOT HAVIN' EGG ROLLS---
YOU MIGHT MECHANIZE THE SQUARE EGG BY PUTTIN' LI'L' WHEELS ON IT.
I DON'T KNOW 'BOUT ALL THIS FOOFAWNIN' TALK HERE --- NO EGG ROLLS ON THE LAWN MIGHT BE A GOOD IDEA. THEN NOBODY WOULD GO GETTIN' YOLK ON HIS PUTTER WHEN SOMEBODY MISTAKES A LEFT OVER LEG-HORN WHITE FOR A GOLF BALL--
TRUE TRUE
10K
COPR 1955 WALT KELLY

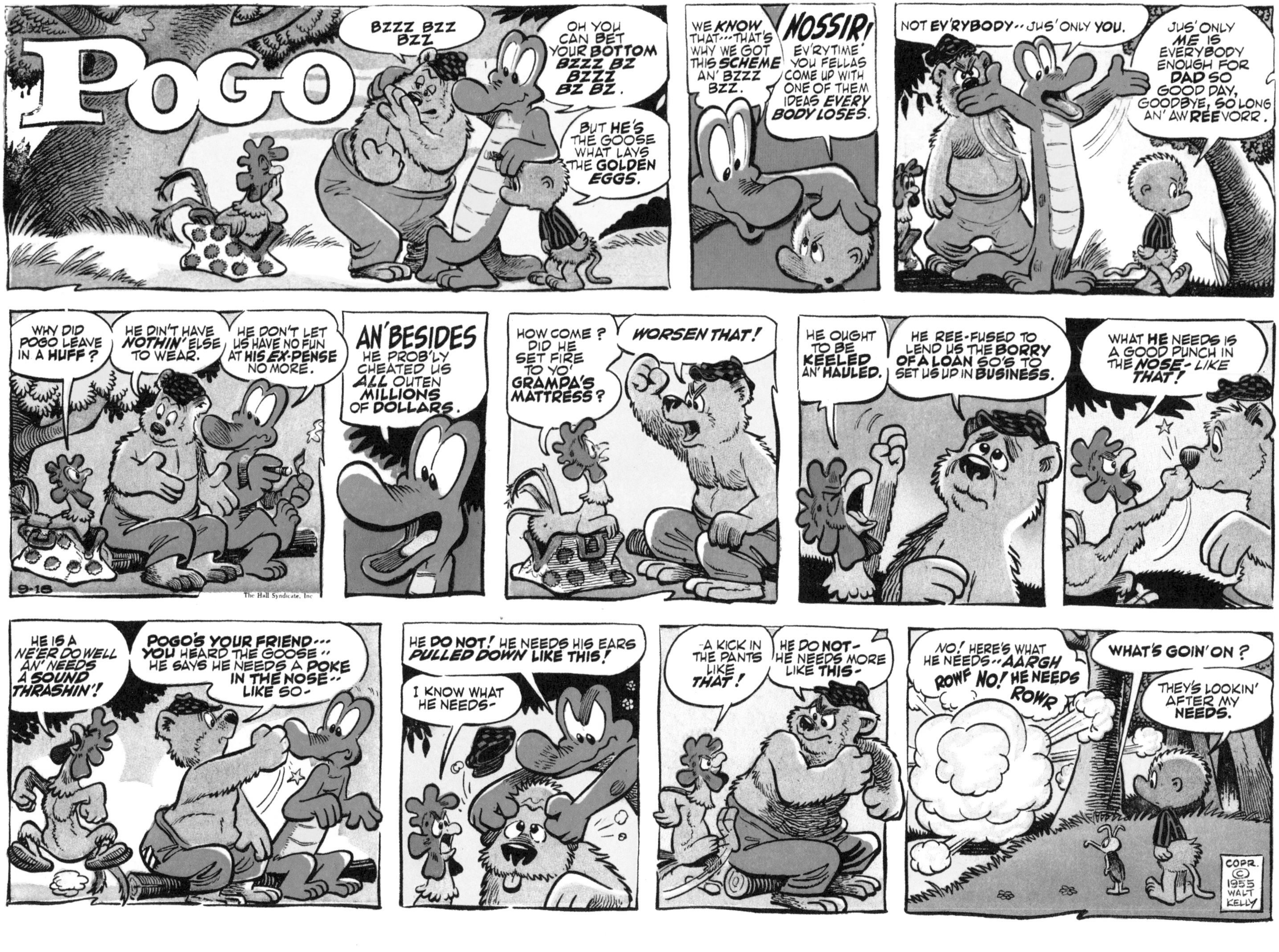
POGO
BZZZ BZZ BZZ
OH YOU CAN BET YOUR BOTTOM BZZZ BZ BZZZ BZ BZ.
BUT HE'S THE GOOSE WHAT LAYS THE GOLDEN EGGS.
WE KNOW THAT··· THAT'S WHY WE GOT THIS SCHEME AN' BZZZ BZZ.
NOSSIR! EV'RYTIME' YOU FELLAS COME UP WITH ONE OF THEM IDEAS EVERY BODY LOSES.
NOT EV'RYBODY·· JUS' ONLY YOU.
JUS' ONLY ME IS EVERYBODY ENOUGH FOR DAD SO GOOD DAY, GOODBYE, SO LONG AN' AW REE VORR.
WHY DID POGO LEAVE IN A HUFF?
HE DIN'T HAVE NOTHIN' ELSE TO WEAR.
HE DON'T LET US HAVE NO FUN AT HIS EX-PENSE NO MORE.
9-18
The Hall Syndicate, Inc
AN' BESIDES HE PROB'LY CHEATED US ALL OUTEN MILLIONS OF DOLLARS.
HOW COME? DID HE SET FIRE TO YO' GRAMPA'S MATTRESS?
WORSEN THAT!
HE OUGHT TO BE KEELED AN' HAULED.
HE REE-FUSED TO LEND US THE BORRY OF A LOAN SO'S TO SET US UP IN BUSINESS.
WHAT HE NEEDS IS A GOOD PUNCH IN THE NOSE- LIKE THAT!
HE IS A NE'ER DO WELL AN' NEEDS A SOUND THRASHIN'!
POGO'S YOUR FRIEND··· YOU HEARD THE GOOSE·· HE SAYS HE NEEDS A POKE IN THE NOSE·· LIKE SO-
HE DO NOT! HE NEEDS HIS EARS PULLED DOWN LIKE THIS!
I KNOW WHAT HE NEEDS-
-A KICK IN THE PANTS LIKE THAT!
HE DO NOT- HE NEEDS MORE LIKE THIS-
NO! HERE'S WHAT HE NEEDS·· AARGH
ROWF
NO! HE NEEDS
ROWR
WHAT'S GOIN' ON?
THEY'S LOOKIN' AFTER MY NEEDS.
COPR. © 1955 WALT KELLY

SUNDAY, SEPTEMBER 25, 1955

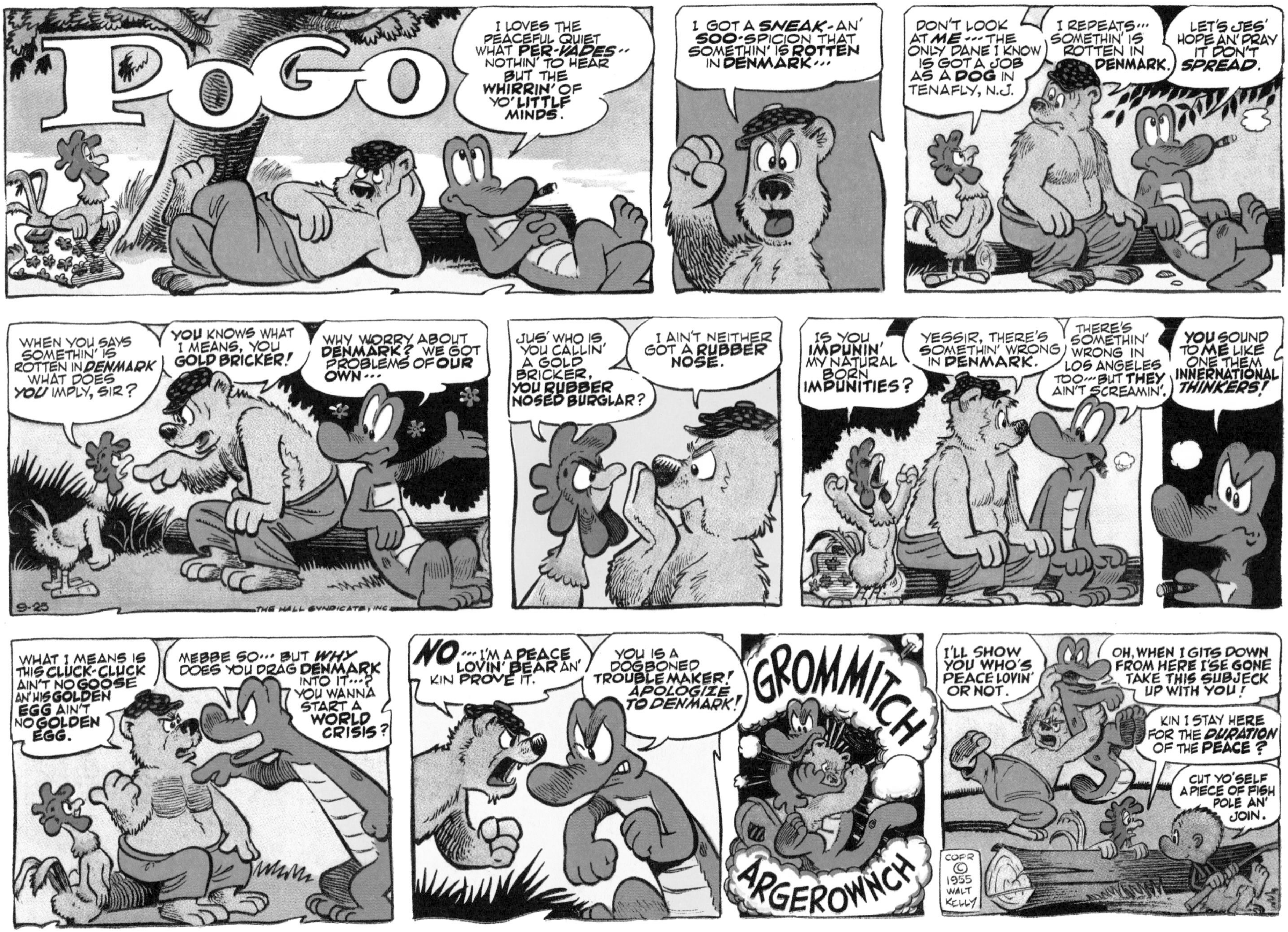
POGO
I LOVES THE PEACEFUL QUIET WHAT PER-VADES.. NOTHIN' TO HEAR BUT THE WHIRRIN' OF YO' LITTLE MINDS.
I GOT A SNEAK-AN' SOO-SPICION THAT SOMETHIN' IS ROTTEN IN DENMARK...
DON'T LOOK AT ME --- THE ONLY DANE I KNOW IS GOT A JOB AS A DOG IN TENAFLY, N.J.
I REPEATS... SOMETHIN' IS ROTTEN IN DENMARK.
LET'S JES' HOPE AN' PRAY IT DON'T SPREAD.
WHEN YOU SAYS SOMETHIN' IS ROTTEN IN DENMARK WHAT DOES YOU IMPLY, SIR?
YOU KNOWS WHAT I MEANS, YOU GOLD BRICKER!
WHY WORRY ABOUT DENMARK? WE GOT PROBLEMS OF OUR OWN...
9-25
THE HALL SYNDICATE, INC.
JUS' WHO IS, YOU CALLIN' A GOLD BRICKER, YOU RUBBER NOSED BURGLAR?
I AIN'T NEITHER GOT A RUBBER NOSE.
IS YOU IMPUNIN' MY NATURAL BORN IMPUNITIES?
YESSIR, THERE'S SOMETHIN' WRONG IN DENMARK.
THERE'S SOMETHIN' WRONG IN LOS ANGELES TOO... BUT THEY AIN'T SCREAMIN'.
YOU SOUND TO ME LIKE ONE THEM INNERNATIONAL THINKERS!
WHAT I MEANS IS THIS CLUCK-CLUCK AIN'T NO GOOSE AN' HIS GOLDEN EGG AIN'T NO GOLDEN EGG.
MEBBE SO... BUT WHY DOES YOU DRAG DENMARK INTO IT...? YOU WANNA START A WORLD CRISIS?
NO... I'M A PEACE LOVIN' BEAR AN' KIN PROVE IT.
YOU IS A DOGBONED TROUBLEMAKER! APOLOGIZE TO DENMARK!
GROMMITCH
ARGEROWNCH
I'LL SHOW YOU WHO'S PEACE LOVIN' OR NOT.
OH, WHEN I GITS DOWN FROM HERE I'SE GONE TAKE THIS SUBJECK UP WITH YOU!
KIN I STAY HERE FOR THE DURATION OF THE PEACE?
CUT YO'SELF A PIECE OF FISH POLE AN' JOIN.
COP'R © 1955 WALT KELLY

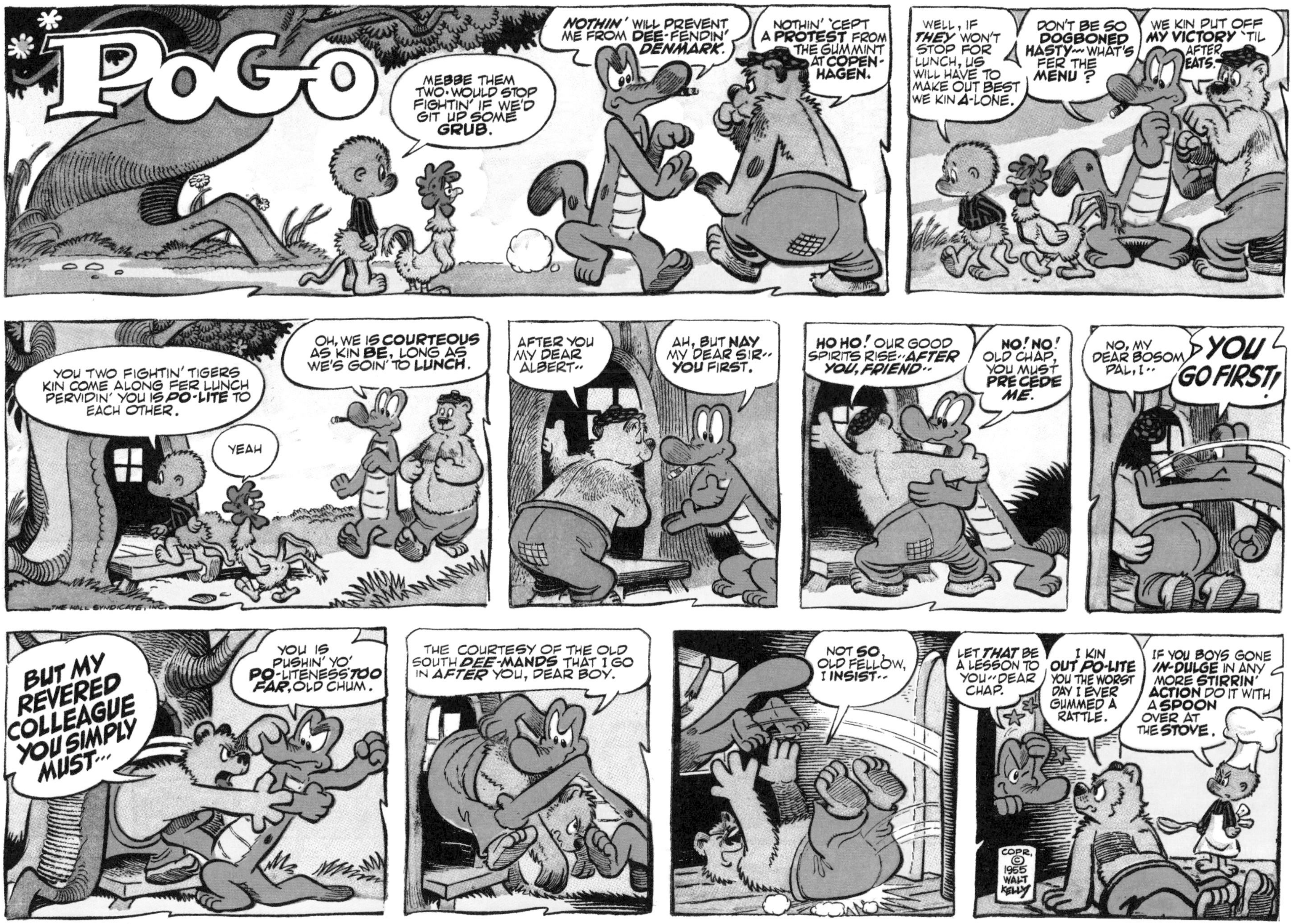
POGO
MEBBE THEM TWO·WOULD STOP FIGHTIN' IF WE'D GIT UP SOME GRUB.
NOTHIN' WILL PREVENT ME FROM DEE-FENDIN' DENMARK.
NOTHIN' 'CEPT A PROTEST FROM THE GUMMINT AT COPEN-HAGEN.
WELL, IF THEY WON'T STOP FOR LUNCH, US WILL HAVE TO MAKE OUT BEST WE KIN A-LONE.
DON'T BE SO DOGBONED HASTY— WHAT'S FER THE MENU ?
WE KIN PUT OFF MY VICTORY 'TIL AFTER EATS.
YOU TWO FIGHTIN' TIGERS KIN COME ALONG FER LUNCH PERVIDIN' YOU IS PO-LITE TO EACH OTHER.
YEAH
OH, WE IS COURTEOUS AS KIN BE, LONG AS WE'S GOIN' TO LUNCH.
THE HALL SYNDICATE, INC.
AFTER YOU MY DEAR ALBERT..
AH, BUT NAY MY DEAR SIR.. YOU FIRST.
HO HO! OUR GOOD SPIRITS RISE..AFTER YOU, FRIEND..
NO! NO! OLD CHAP, YOU MUST PRECEDE ME.
NO, MY DEAR BOSOM PAL, I..
YOU GO FIRST!
BUT MY REVERED COLLEAGUE YOU SIMPLY MUST...
YOU IS PUSHIN' YO' PO-LITENESS TOO FAR, OLD CHUM.
THE COURTESY OF THE OLD SOUTH DEE-MANDS THAT I GO IN AFTER YOU, DEAR BOY.
NOT SO, OLD FELLOW, I INSIST..
LET THAT BE A LESSON TO YOU..DEAR CHAP.
I KIN OUT PO-LITE YOU THE WORST DAY I EVER GUMMED A RATTLE.
IF YOU BOYS GONE IN-DULGE IN ANY MORE STIRRIN' ACTION DO IT WITH A SPOON OVER AT THE STOVE.
COPR. © 1955 WALT KELLY

SUNDAY, OCTOBER 9, 1955

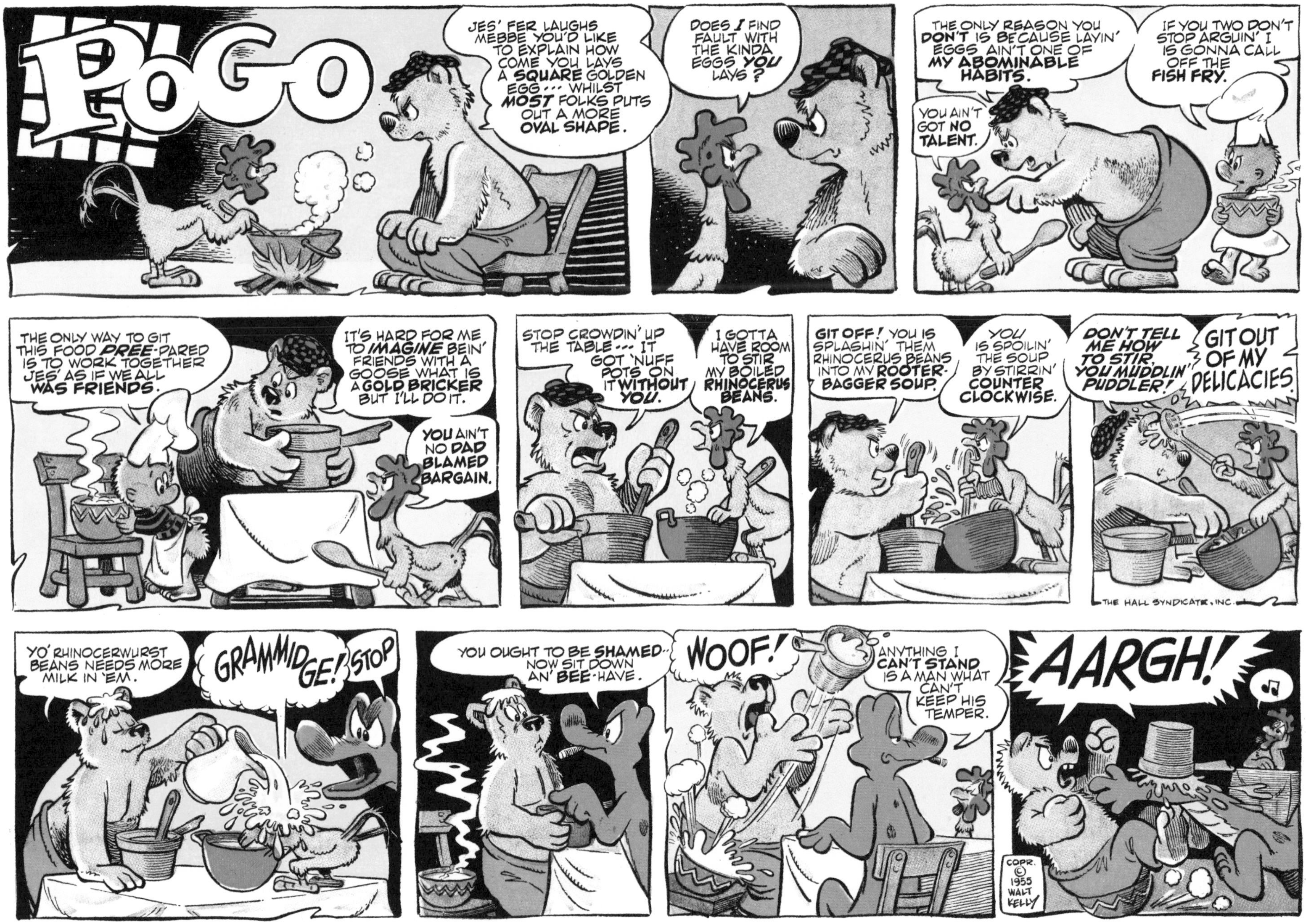
POGO
JES' FER LAUGHS MEBBE YOU'D LIKE TO EXPLAIN HOW COME YOU LAYS A **SQUARE** GOLDEN EGG --- WHILST ***MOST*** FOLKS PUTS OUT A MORE **OVAL SHAPE**.
DOES ***I*** FIND FAULT WITH THE KINDA EGGS ***YOU*** LAYS ?
THE ONLY REASON YOU **DON'T** IS BECAUSE LAYIN' EGGS AIN'T ONE OF **MY ABOMINABLE HABITS**.
IF YOU TWO **DON'T** STOP ARGUIN' I IS GONNA CALL OFF THE **FISH FRY**.
YOU AIN'T GOT **NO TALENT**.
THE ONLY WAY TO GIT THIS FOOD ***PREE***-PARED IS TO WORK TOGETHER JES' AS IF WE ALL **WAS FRIENDS**.
IT'S HARD FOR ME TO ***IMAGINE*** BEIN' FRIENDS WITH A GOOSE WHAT IS A **GOLD BRICKER** BUT I'LL DO IT.
YOU AIN'T NO **DAD BLAMED BARGAIN**.
STOP CROWDIN' UP THE TABLE --- IT GOT 'NUFF POTS ON IT ***WITHOUT YOU***.
I GOTTA HAVE ROOM TO STIR MY BOILED **RHINOCERUS BEANS**.
GIT OFF! YOU IS SPLASHIN' THEM RHINOCERUS BEANS INTO MY **ROOTER-BAGGER SOUP**.
YOU IS SPOILIN' THE SOUP BY STIRRIN' **COUNTER CLOCKWISE**.
DON'T TELL ME HOW TO STIR, YOU MUDDLIN' PUDDLER!
GIT OUT OF MY DELICACIES.
THE HALL SYNDICATE, INC.
YO' RHINOCERWURST BEANS NEEDS MORE MILK IN 'EM.
GRAMMIDGE!
STOP
YOU OUGHT TO BE **SHAMED**... NOW SIT DOWN AN' **BEE**-HAVE.
WOOF!
ANYTHING I **CAN'T STAND** IS A MAN WHAT CAN'T KEEP HIS TEMPER.
AARGH!
COPR. © 1955 WALT KELLY

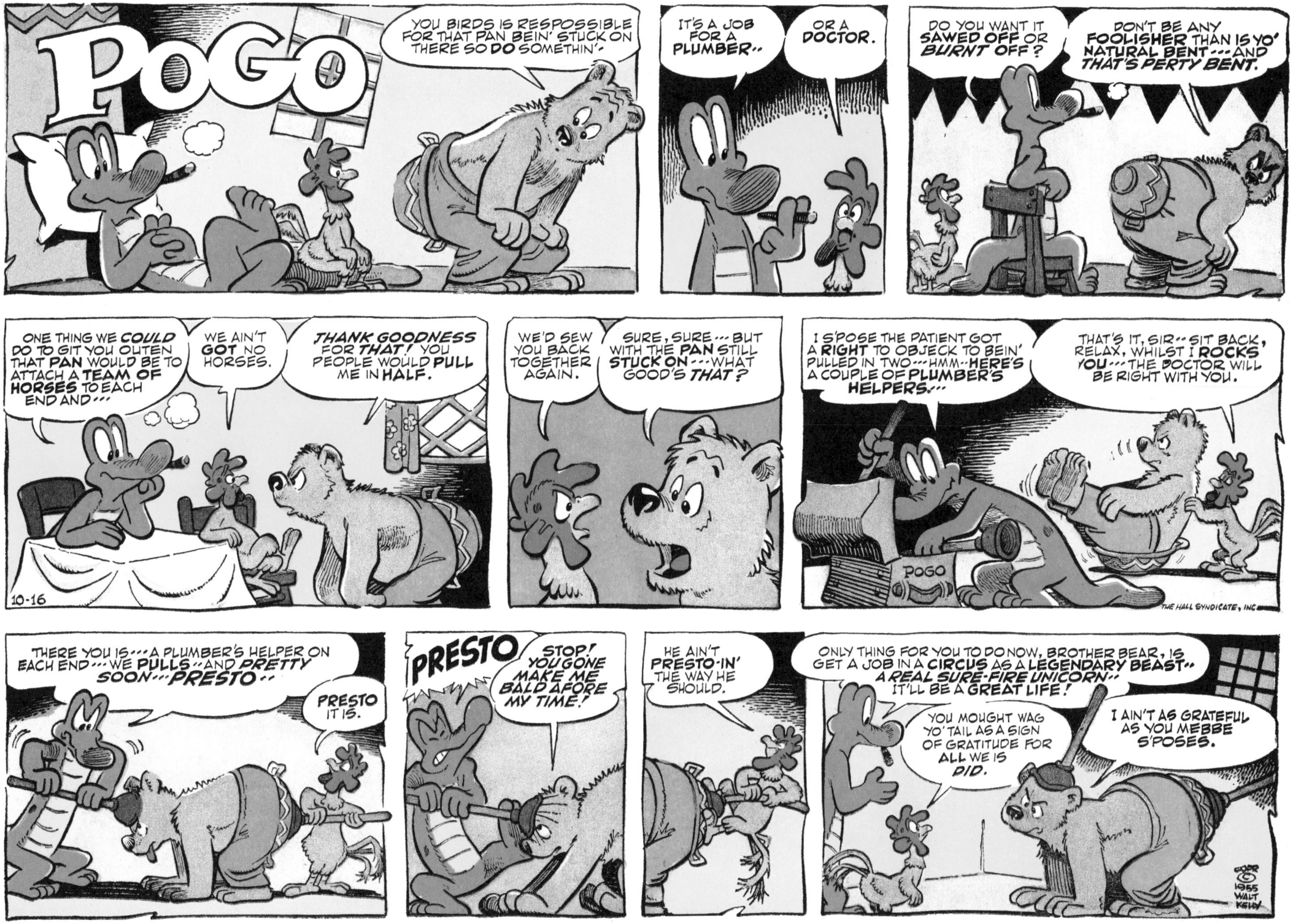
POGO
YOU BIRDS IS RESPOSSIBLE FOR THAT PAN BEIN' STUCK ON THERE SO DO SOMETHIN'-
IT'S A JOB FOR A PLUMBER..
OR A DOCTOR.
DO YOU WANT IT SAWED OFF OR BURNT OFF?
DON'T BE ANY FOOLISHER THAN IS YO' NATURAL BENT--- AND THAT'S PERTY BENT.
ONE THING WE COULD DO TO GIT YOU OUTEN THAT PAN WOULD BE TO ATTACH A TEAM OF HORSES TO EACH END AND---
WE AIN'T GOT NO HORSES.
THANK GOODNESS FOR THAT! YOU PEOPLE WOULD PULL ME IN HALF.
10-16
WE'D SEW YOU BACK TOGETHER AGAIN.
SURE, SURE--- BUT WITH THE PAN STILL STUCK ON --- WHAT GOOD'S THAT?
I S'POSE THE PATIENT GOT A RIGHT TO OBJECK TO BEIN' PULLED IN TWO---HMM--HERE'S A COUPLE OF PLUMBER'S HELPERS---
THAT'S IT, SIR-- SIT BACK, RELAX, WHILST I ROCKS' YOU--- THE DOCTOR WILL BE RIGHT WITH YOU.
POGO
THE HALL SYNDICATE, INC.
THERE YOU IS---A PLUMBER'S HELPER ON EACH END--- WE PULLS--AND PRETTY SOON---PRESTO--
PRESTO IT IS.
PRESTO
STOP! YOU GONE MAKE ME BALD AFORE MY TIME!
HE AIN'T PRESTO-IN' THE WAY HE SHOULD.
ONLY THING FOR YOU TO DO NOW, BROTHER BEAR, IS GET A JOB IN A CIRCUS AS A LEGENDARY BEAST-- A REAL SURE-FIRE UNICORN-- IT'LL BE A GREAT LIFE!
YOU MOUGHT WAG YO' TAIL AS A SIGN OF GRATITUDE FOR ALL WE IS DID.
I AIN'T AS GRATEFUL AS YOU MEBBE S'POSES.
COPR © 1955 WALT KELLY

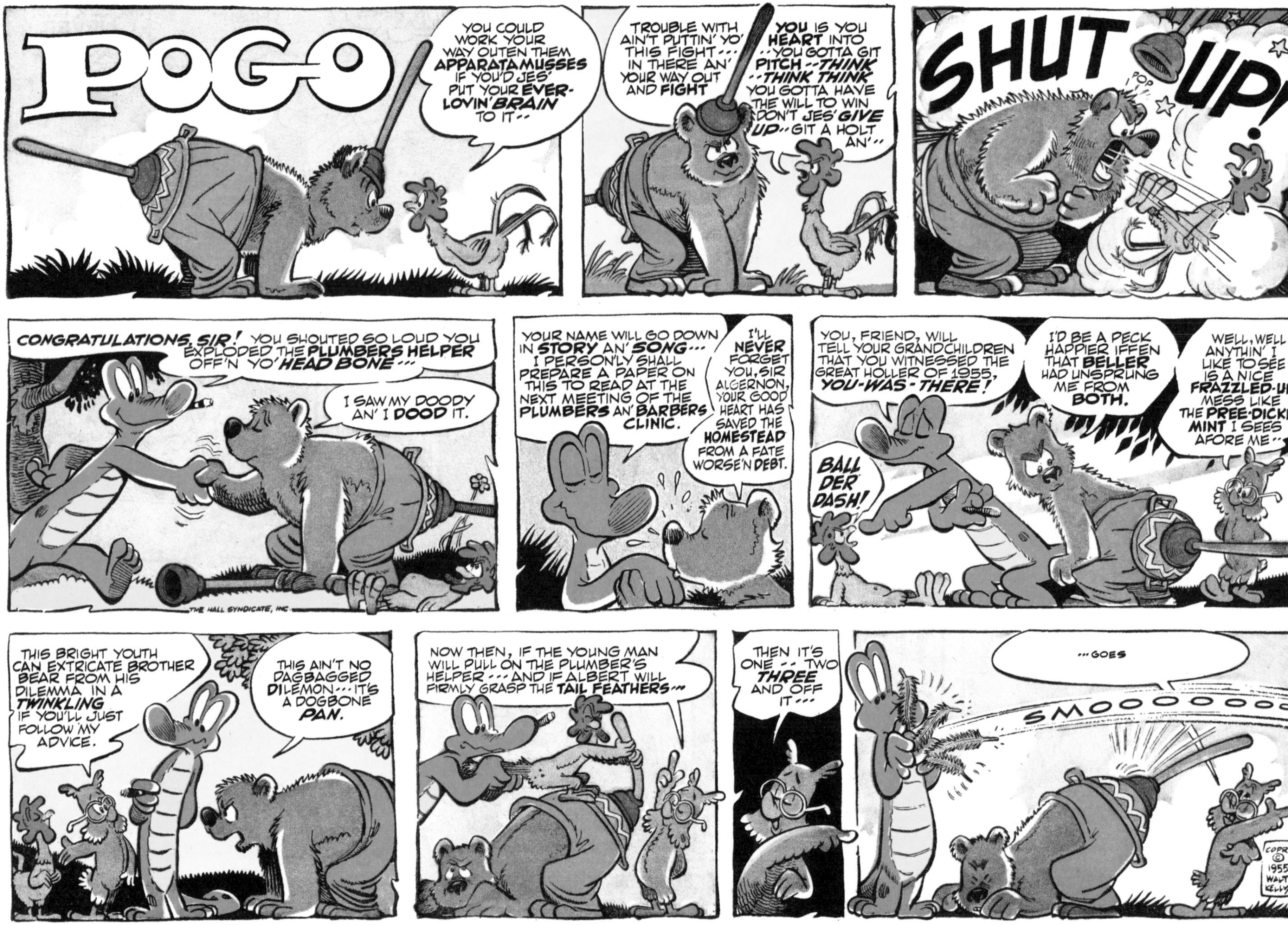
POGO
YOU COULD WORK YOUR WAY OUTEN THEM APPARATAMUSSES IF YOU'D JES' PUT YOUR EVER-LOVIN' BRAIN TO IT--
TROUBLE WITH YOU IS YOU AIN'T PUTTIN' YO' HEART INTO THIS FIGHT--- YOU GOTTA GIT IN THERE AN' PITCH--THINK YOUR WAY OUT --THINK THINK AND FIGHT YOU GOTTA HAVE THE WILL TO WIN DON'T JES' GIVE UP--GIT A HOLT AN'--
SHUT UP!
POP
CONGRATULATIONS, SIR! YOU SHOUTED SO LOUD YOU EXPLODED THE PLUMBERS HELPER OFF'N YO' HEAD BONE---
I SAW MY DOODY AN' I DOOD IT.
THE HALL SYNDICATE, INC
YOUR NAME WILL GO DOWN IN STORY AN' SONG--- I PERSON'LY SHALL PREPARE A PAPER ON THIS TO READ AT THE NEXT MEETING OF THE PLUMBERS AN' BARBERS CLINIC.
I'LL NEVER FORGET YOU, SIR ALGERNON, YOUR GOOD HEART HAS SAVED THE HOMESTEAD FROM A FATE WORSE'N DEBT.
YOU, FRIEND, WILL TELL YOUR GRANDCHILDREN THAT YOU WITNESSED THE GREAT HOLLER OF 1955, YOU-WAS-THERE!
BALL DER DASH!
I'D BE A PECK HAPPIER IFFEN THAT BELLER HAD UNSPRUNG ME FROM BOTH.
WELL, WELL-- ANYTHIN' I LIKE TO SEE IS A NICE FRAZZLED-UP MESS LIKE THE PREE-DICKLE-MINT I SEES AFORE ME--
THIS BRIGHT YOUTH CAN EXTRICATE BROTHER BEAR FROM HIS DILEMMA IN A TWINKLING IF YOU'LL JUST FOLLOW MY ADVICE.
THIS AIN'T NO DAGBAGGED DILEMON--- IT'S A DOGBONE PAN.
NOW THEN, IF THE YOUNG MAN WILL PULL ON THE PLUMBER'S HELPER --- AND IF ALBERT WILL FIRMLY GRASP THE TAIL FEATHERS---
THEN IT'S ONE -- TWO THREE AND OFF IT---
---GOES
SMOOOOOOO...
COPR © 1955 WALT KELLY

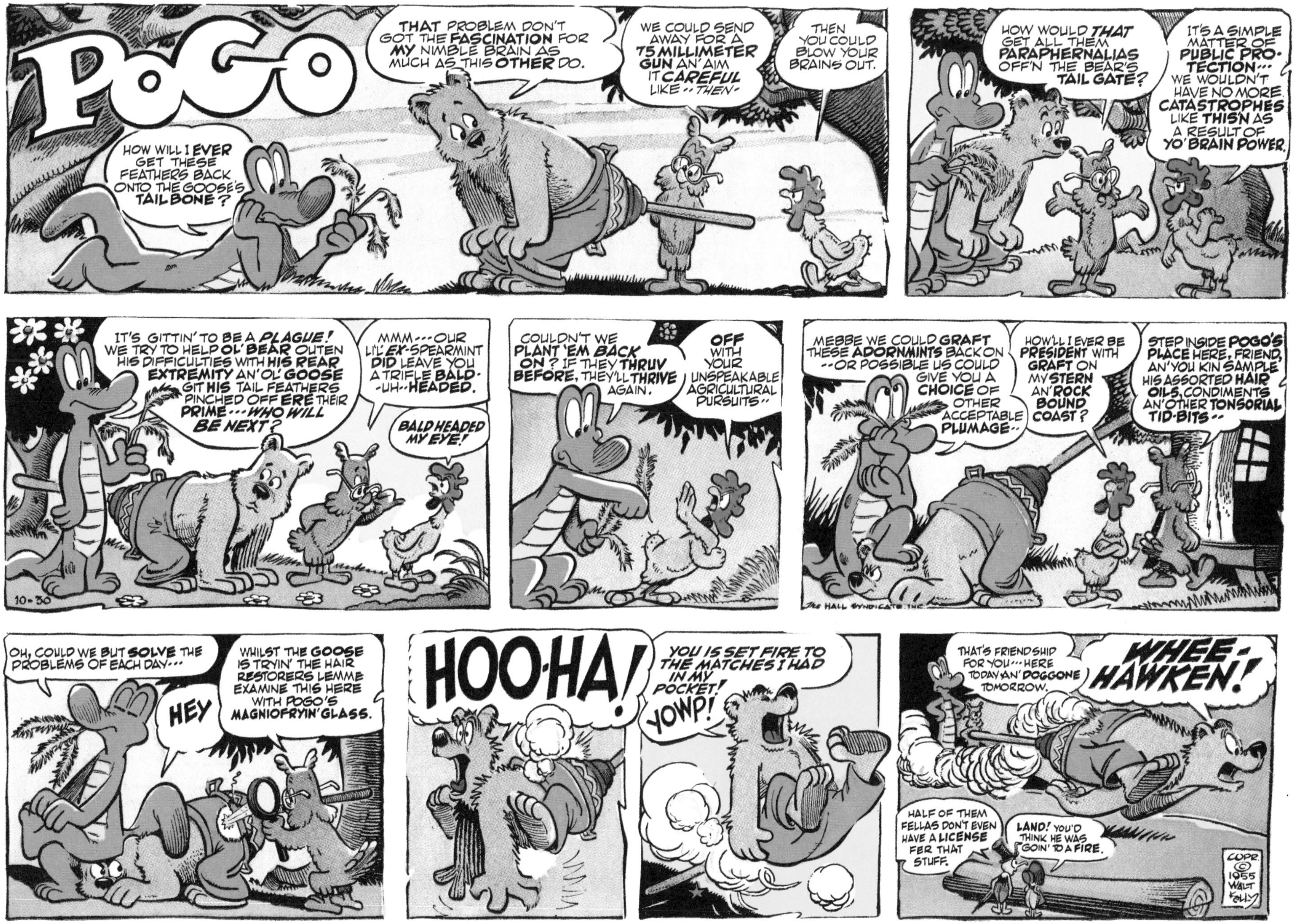
POGO
HOW WILL I EVER GET THESE FEATHERS BACK ONTO THE GOOSE'S TAILBONE?
THAT PROBLEM DON'T GOT THE FASCINATION FOR MY NIMBLE BRAIN AS MUCH AS THIS OTHER DO.
WE COULD SEND AWAY FOR A 75 MILLIMETER GUN AN' AIM IT CAREFUL LIKE -- THEN-
THEN YOU COULD BLOW YOUR BRAINS OUT.
HOW WOULD THAT GET ALL THEM PARAPHERNALIAS OFF'N THE BEAR'S TAIL GATE?
IT'S A SIMPLE MATTER OF PUBLIC PRO-TECTION... WE WOULDN'T HAVE NO MORE CATASTROPHES LIKE THIS'N AS A RESULT OF YO' BRAIN POWER.
IT'S GITTIN' TO BE A PLAGUE! WE TRY TO HELP OL' BEAR OUTEN HIS DIFFICULTIES WITH HIS REAR EXTREMITY AN' OL' GOOSE GIT HIS TAIL FEATHERS PINCHED OFF ERE THEIR PRIME --- WHO WILL BE NEXT?
MMM --- OUR LI'L EX-SPEARMINT DID LEAVE YOU A TRIFLE BALD--UH--HEADED.
BALD HEADED MY EYE!
10-30
COULDN'T WE PLANT 'EM BACK ON? IF THEY THRUV BEFORE, THEY'LL THRIVE AGAIN.
OFF WITH YOUR UNSPEAKABLE AGRICULTURAL PURSUITS--
MEBBE WE COULD GRAFT THESE ADORNMINTS BACK ON --OR POSSIBLE US COULD GIVE YOU A CHOICE OF OTHER ACCEPTABLE PLUMAGE--
HOW'LL I EVER BE PRESIDENT WITH GRAFT ON MY STERN AN' ROCK BOUND COAST?
STEP INSIDE POGO'S PLACE HERE, FRIEND, AN' YOU KIN SAMPLE HIS ASSORTED HAIR OILS, CONDIMENTS AN' OTHER TONSORIAL TID-BITS--
THE HALL SYNDICATE, INC.
OH, COULD WE BUT SOLVE THE PROBLEMS OF EACH DAY---
HEY
WHILST THE GOOSE IS TRYIN' THE HAIR RESTORERS LEMME EXAMINE THIS HERE WITH POGO'S MAGNIOFRYIN' GLASS.
HOO-HA!
YOU IS SET FIRE TO THE MATCHES I HAD IN MY POCKET!
YOWP!
THAT'S FRIENDSHIP FOR YOU--- HERE TODAY AN' DOGGONE TOMORROW.
WHEE-HAWKEN!
HALF OF THEM FELLAS DON'T EVEN HAVE A LICENSE FER THAT STUFF.
LAND! YOU'D THINK HE WAS GOIN' TO A FIRE.
COPR. © 1955 WALT KELLY

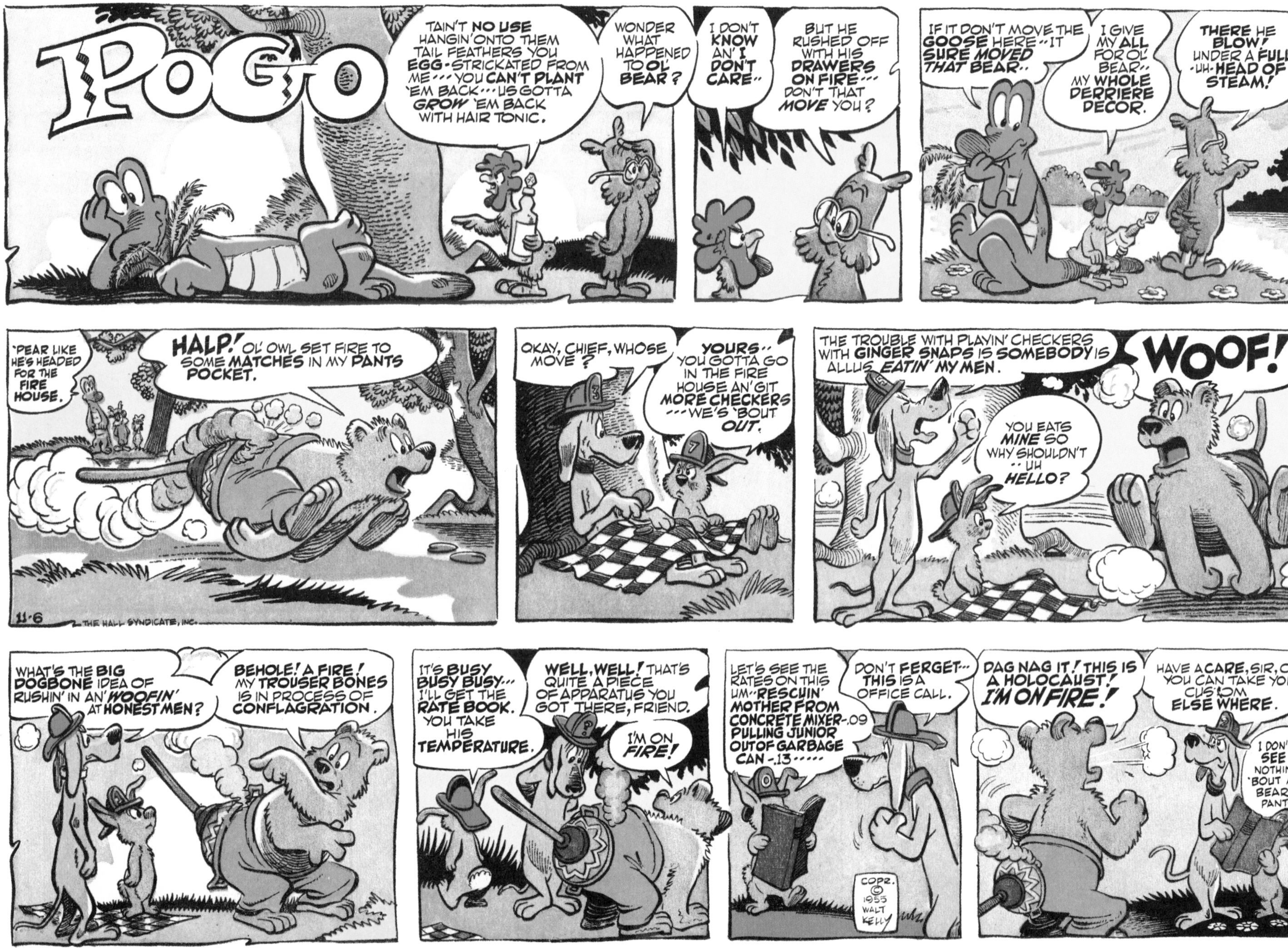
POGO
TAIN'T NO USE HANGIN'ONTO THEM TAIL FEATHERS YOU EGG-STRICKATED FROM ME··· YOU CAN'T PLANT 'EM BACK··· US GOTTA GROW 'EM BACK WITH HAIR TONIC.
WONDER WHAT HAPPENED TO OL' BEAR?
I DON'T KNOW AN' I DON'T CARE..
BUT HE RUSHED OFF WITH HIS DRAWERS ON FIRE··· DON'T THAT MOVE YOU?
IF IT DON'T MOVE THE GOOSE HERE··IT SURE MOVED THAT BEAR..
I GIVE MY ALL FOR OL' BEAR.. MY WHOLE DERRIERE DECOR.
THERE HE BLOW! UNDER A FULL ·UH· HEAD OF STEAM!
'PEAR LIKE HE'S HEADED FOR THE FIRE HOUSE.
HALP! OL' OWL SET FIRE TO SOME MATCHES IN MY PANTS POCKET.
11·6
THE HALL SYNDICATE, INC.
OKAY, CHIEF, WHOSE MOVE?
YOURS.. YOU GOTTA GO IN THE FIRE HOUSE AN' GIT MORE CHECKERS ···WE'S 'BOUT OUT.
THE TROUBLE WITH PLAYIN' CHECKERS WITH GINGER SNAPS IS SOMEBODY IS ALLUS EATIN' MY MEN.
WOOF!
YOU EATS MINE SO WHY SHOULDN'T ··UH HELLO?
WHAT'S THE BIG DOGBONE IDEA OF RUSHIN' IN AN' WOOFIN' AT HONEST MEN?
BEHOLE! A FIRE! MY TROUSER BONES IS IN PROCESS OF CONFLAGRATION.
IT'S BUSY BUSY BUSY... I'LL GET THE RATE BOOK. YOU TAKE HIS TEMPERATURE.
WELL, WELL! THAT'S QUITE A PIECE OF APPARATUS YOU GOT THERE, FRIEND.
I'M ON FIRE!
LET'S SEE THE RATES ON THIS UM·· RESCUIN' MOTHER FROM CONCRETE MIXER-.09 PULLING JUNIOR OUT OF GARBAGE CAN -.13 ·····
DON'T FERGET··· THIS IS A OFFICE CALL.
COPR. © 1955 WALT KELLY
DAG NAG IT! THIS IS A HOLOCAUST! I'M ON FIRE!
HAVE A CARE, SIR, OR YOU CAN TAKE YOUR CUSTOM ELSE WHERE.
I DON'T SEE NOTHIN' 'BOUT A BEAR'S PANTS.

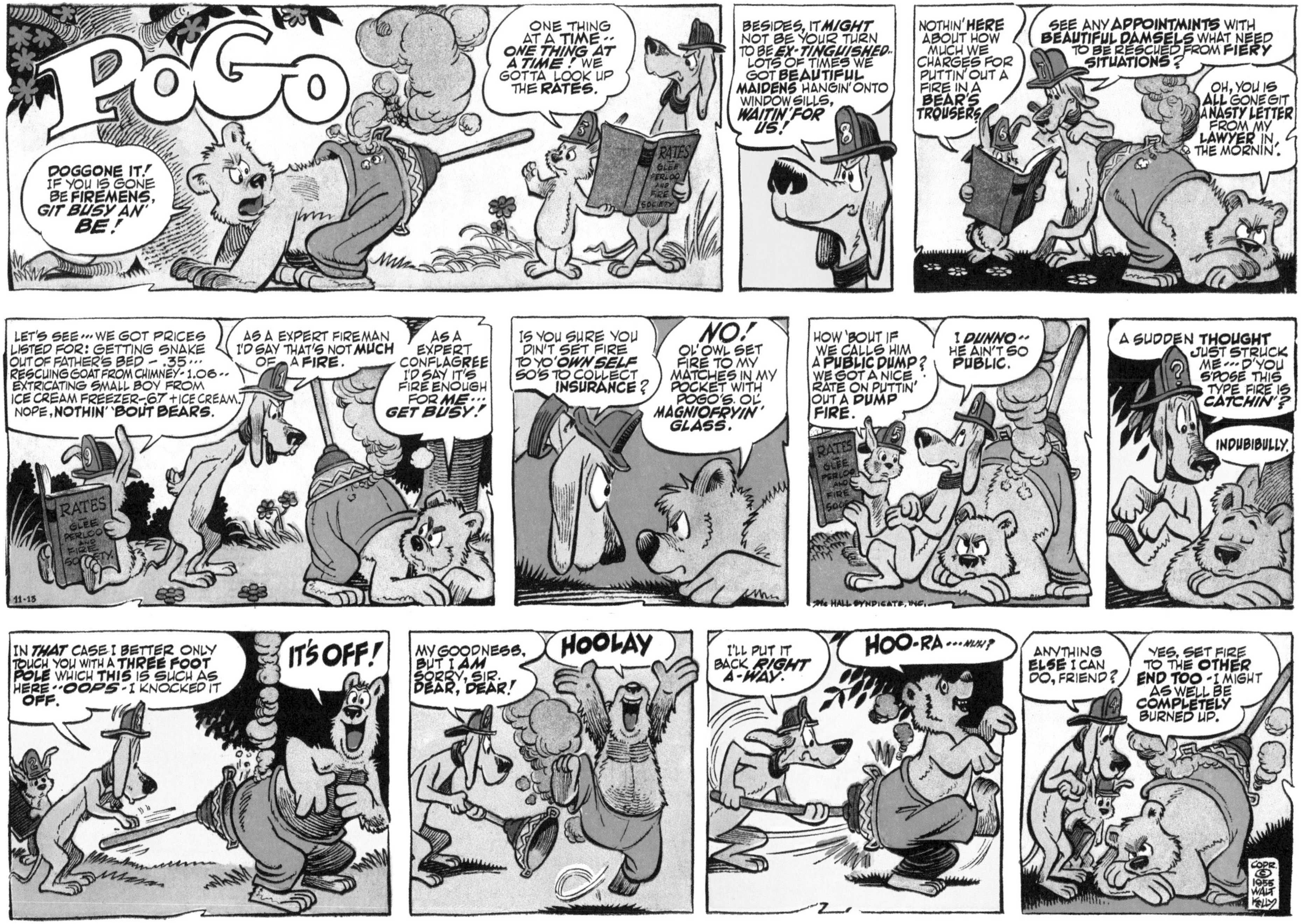
POGO
DOGGONE IT! IF YOU IS GONE BE FIREMENS, GIT BUSY AN' BE!
ONE THING AT A TIME -- ONE THING AT A TIME! WE GOTTA LOOK UP THE RATES.
RATES GLEE PERLOO AND FIRE SOCIETY
BESIDES, IT MIGHT NOT BE YOUR TURN TO BE EX-TINGUISHED.. LOTS OF TIMES WE GOT BEAUTIFUL MAIDENS HANGIN' ONTO WINDOW SILLS, WAITIN' FOR US!
NOTHIN' HERE ABOUT HOW MUCH WE CHARGES FOR PUTTIN' OUT A FIRE IN A BEAR'S TROUSERS
SEE ANY APPOINTMINTS WITH BEAUTIFUL DAMSELS WHAT NEED TO BE RESCUED FROM FIERY SITUATIONS?
OH, YOU IS ALL GONE GIT A NASTY LETTER FROM MY LAWYER IN THE MORNIN'.
LET'S SEE ... WE GOT PRICES LISTED FOR: GETTING SNAKE OUT OF FATHER'S BED - .35 ... RESCUING GOAT FROM CHIMNEY - 1.06 -- EXTRICATING SMALL BOY FROM ICE CREAM FREEZER - 67 + ICE CREAM. NOPE, NOTHIN' 'BOUT BEARS.
AS A EXPERT FIREMAN I'D SAY THAT'S NOT MUCH OF A FIRE.
AS A EXPERT CONFLAGREE I'D SAY IT'S FIRE ENOUGH FOR ME ... GET BUSY!
RATES GLEE PERLOO AND FIRE SOCIETY
11-13
IS YOU SURE YOU DIN'T SET FIRE TO YO' OWN SELF SO'S TO COLLECT INSURANCE?
NO! OL' OWL SET FIRE TO MY MATCHES IN MY POCKET WITH POGO'S. OL' MAGNIOFRYIN' GLASS.
HOW 'BOUT IF WE CALLS HIM A PUBLIC DUMP? WE GOT A NICE RATE ON PUTTIN' OUT A DUMP FIRE.
I DUNNO -- HE AIN'T SO PUBLIC.
HALL SYNDICATE, INC.
A SUDDEN THOUGHT JUST STRUCK ME --- D'YOU S'POSE THIS TYPE FIRE IS CATCHIN'?
INDUBIBULLY.
IN THAT CASE I BETTER ONLY TOUCH YOU WITH A THREE FOOT POLE WHICH THIS IS SUCH AS HERE -- OOPS - I KNOCKED IT OFF.
IT'S OFF!
MY GOODNESS, BUT I AM SORRY, SIR. DEAR, DEAR!
HOOLAY
I'LL PUT IT BACK RIGHT A-WAY.
HOO-RA ... HUH?
ANYTHING ELSE I CAN DO, FRIEND?
YES, SET FIRE TO THE OTHER END TOO - I MIGHT AS WELL BE COMPLETELY BURNED UP.
COPR. © 1955 WALT KELLY

SUNDAY, NOVEMBER 20, 1955

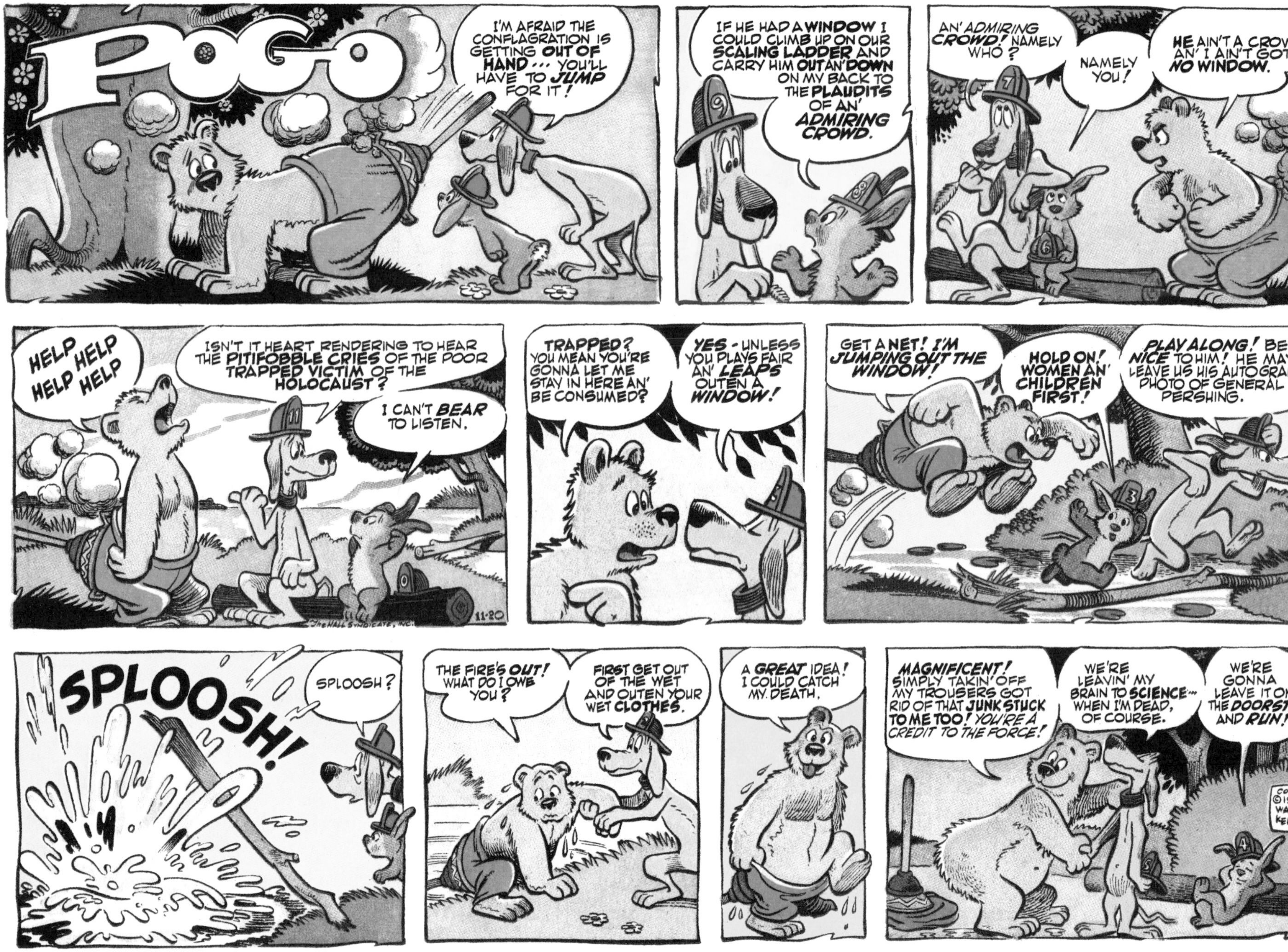
POGO
I'M AFRAID THE CONFLAGRATION IS GETTING OUT OF HAND... YOU'LL HAVE TO JUMP FOR IT!
IF HE HAD A WINDOW I COULD CLIMB UP ON OUR SCALING LADDER AND CARRY HIM OUT AN' DOWN ON MY BACK TO THE PLAUDITS OF AN' ADMIRING CROWD.
AN' ADMIRING CROWD! NAMELY WHO?
NAMELY YOU!
HE AIN'T A CROWD AN' I AIN'T GOT NO WINDOW.
HELP HELP HELP HELP HELP
ISN'T IT HEART RENDERING TO HEAR THE PITIFOBBLE CRIES OF THE POOR TRAPPED VICTIM OF THE HOLOCAUST?
I CAN'T BEAR TO LISTEN.
11-20
TRAPPED? YOU MEAN YOU'RE GONNA LET ME STAY IN HERE AN' BE CONSUMED?
YES - UNLESS YOU PLAYS FAIR AN' LEAPS OUTEN A WINDOW!
GET A NET! I'M JUMPING OUT THE WINDOW!
HOLD ON! WOMEN AN' CHILDREN FIRST!
PLAY ALONG! BE NICE TO HIM! HE MAY LEAVE US HIS AUTOGRAPHED PHOTO OF GENERAL PERSHING.
SPLOOSH!
SPLOOSH?
THE FIRE'S OUT! WHAT DO I OWE YOU?
FIRST GET OUT OF THE WET AND OUTEN YOUR WET CLOTHES.
A GREAT IDEA! I COULD CATCH MY DEATH.
MAGNIFICENT! SIMPLY TAKIN' OFF MY TROUSERS GOT RID OF THAT JUNK STUCK TO ME TOO! YOU'RE A CREDIT TO THE FORCE!
WE'RE LEAVIN' MY BRAIN TO SCIENCE... WHEN I'M DEAD, OF COURSE.
WE'RE GONNA LEAVE IT ON THE DOORSTEP AND RUN!
COPR ©1955 WALT KELLY

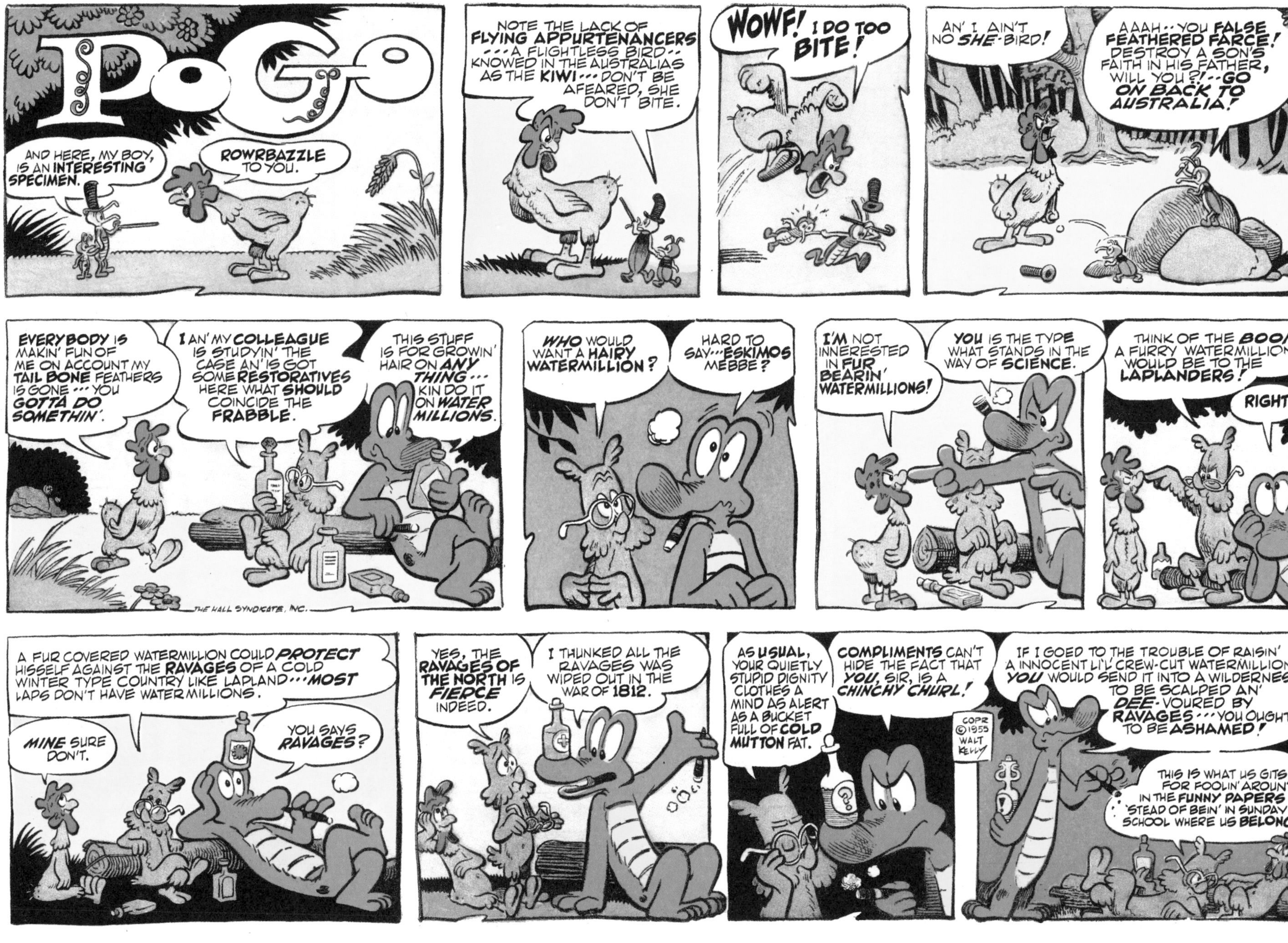
POGO
AND HERE, MY BOY, IS AN INTERESTING SPECIMEN.
ROWRBAZZLE TO YOU.
NOTE THE LACK OF FLYING APPURTENANCERS --- A FLIGHTLESS BIRD -- KNOWED IN THE AUSTRALIAS AS THE KIWI --- DON'T BE AFEARED, SHE DON'T BITE.
WOWF! I DO TOO BITE!
AN' I AIN'T NO SHE-BIRD!
AAAH -- YOU FALSE FEATHERED FARCE! DESTROY A SON'S FAITH IN HIS FATHER, WILL YOU?! -- GO ON BACK TO AUSTRALIA!
EVERYBODY IS MAKIN' FUN OF ME ON ACCOUNT MY TAIL BONE FEATHERS IS GONE --- YOU GOTTA DO SOMETHIN'.
I AN' MY COLLEAGUE IS STUDYIN' THE CASE AN' IS GOT SOME RESTORATIVES HERE WHAT SHOULD COINCIDE THE FRABBLE.
THIS STUFF IS FOR GROWIN' HAIR ON ANY THING --- KIN DO IT ON WATER MILLIONS.
THE HALL SYNDICATE, INC.
WHO WOULD WANT A HAIRY WATERMILLION?
HARD TO SAY --- ESKIMOS MEBBE?
I'M NOT INNERESTED IN FUR BEARIN' WATERMILLIONS!
YOU IS THE TYPE WHAT STANDS IN THE WAY OF SCIENCE.
THINK OF THE BOON A FURRY WATERMILLION WOULD BE TO THE LAPLANDERS!
RIGHT.
A FUR COVERED WATERMILLION COULD PROTECT HISSELF AGAINST THE RAVAGES OF A COLD WINTER TYPE COUNTRY LIKE LAPLAND --- MOST LAPS DON'T HAVE WATERMILLIONS.
MINE SURE DON'T.
YOU SAYS RAVAGES?
YES, THE RAVAGES OF THE NORTH IS FIERCE INDEED.
I THUNKED ALL THE RAVAGES WAS WIPED OUT IN THE WAR OF 1812.
AS USUAL, YOUR QUIETLY STUPID DIGNITY CLOTHES A MIND AS ALERT AS A BUCKET FULL OF COLD MUTTON FAT.
COMPLIMENTS CAN'T HIDE THE FACT THAT YOU, SIR, IS A CHINCHY CHURL!
COPR ©1955 WALT KELLY
IF I GOED TO THE TROUBLE OF RAISIN' A INNOCENT LI'L CREW-CUT WATERMILLION YOU WOULD SEND IT INTO A WILDERNESS TO BE SCALPED AN' DEE-VOURED BY RAVAGES --- YOU OUGHT TO BE ASHAMED!
THIS IS WHAT US GITS FOR FOOLIN' AROUN' IN THE FUNNY PAPERS 'STEAD OF BEIN' IN SUNDAY SCHOOL WHERE US BELONGS.

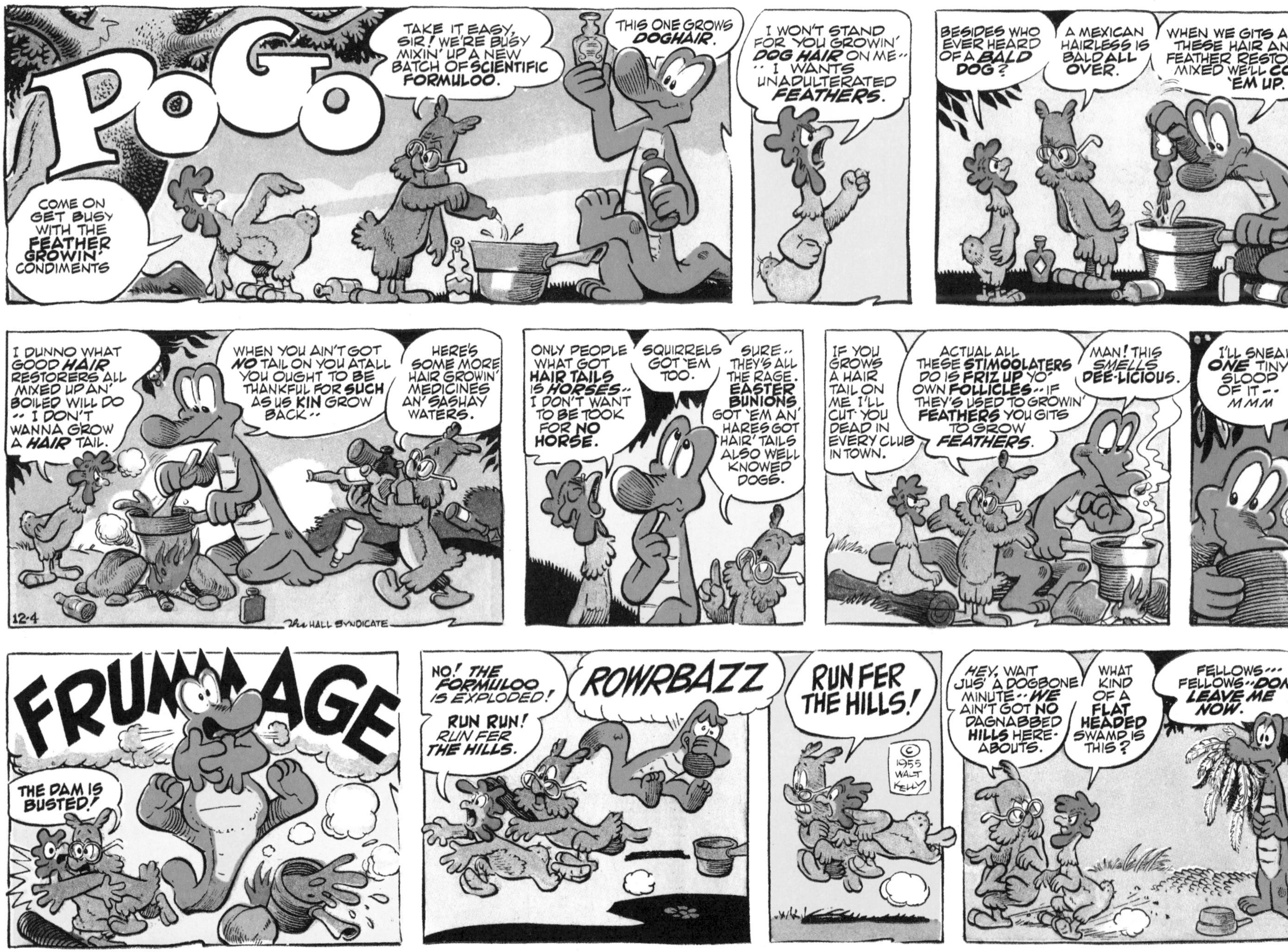
POGO
COME ON GET BUSY WITH THE FEATHER GROWIN' CONDIMENTS
TAKE IT EASY, SIR! WE'RE BUSY MIXIN' UP A NEW BATCH OF SCIENTIFIC FORMULOO.
THIS ONE GROWS DOGHAIR.
I WON'T STAND FOR YOU GROWIN' DOG HAIR ON ME.. .. I WANTS UNADULTERATED FEATHERS.
BESIDES WHO EVER HEARD OF A BALD DOG?
A MEXICAN HAIRLESS IS BALD ALL OVER.
WHEN WE GITS ALL THESE HAIR AN' FEATHER RESTORERS MIXED WE'LL COOK 'EM UP.
I DUNNO WHAT GOOD HAIR RESTORERS ALL MIXED UP AN' BOILED WILL DO -- I DON'T WANNA GROW A HAIR TAIL.
WHEN YOU AIN'T GOT NO TAIL ON YOU ATALL YOU OUGHT TO BE THANKFUL FOR SUCH AS US KIN GROW BACK --
HERE'S SOME MORE HAIR GROWIN' MEDICINES AN' SASHAY WATERS.
12-4
The HALL SYNDICATE
ONLY PEOPLE WHAT GOT HAIR TAILS IS HORSES.. I DON'T WANT TO BE TOOK FOR NO HORSE.
SQUIRRELS GOT 'EM TOO.
SURE.. THEY'S ALL THE RAGE. EASTER BUNIONS GOT 'EM AN' HARES GOT HAIR' TAILS ALSO WELL KNOWED DOGS.
IF YOU GROWS A HAIR TAIL ON ME, I'LL CUT YOU DEAD IN EVERY CLUB IN TOWN.
ACTUAL ALL THESE STIMOOLATERS DO IS FRIZ UP YO' OWN FOLLICLES -- IF THEY'S USED TO GROWIN' FEATHERS YOU GITS TO GROW FEATHERS.
MAN! THIS SMELLS DEE-LICIOUS.
I'LL SNEAK ONE TINY SLOOP OF IT -- MMM
FRUMMAGE
THE DAM IS BUSTED!
NO! THE FORMULOO IS EXPLODED!
ROWRBAZZ
RUN RUN! RUN FER THE HILLS.
RUN FER THE HILLS!
© 1955 WALT KELLY
HEY, WAIT JUS' A DOGBONE MINUTE.. WE AIN'T GOT NO DAGNABBED HILLS HERE-ABOUTS.
WHAT KIND OF A FLAT HEADED SWAMP IS THIS?
FELLOWS... FELLOWS.. DON'T LEAVE ME NOW.

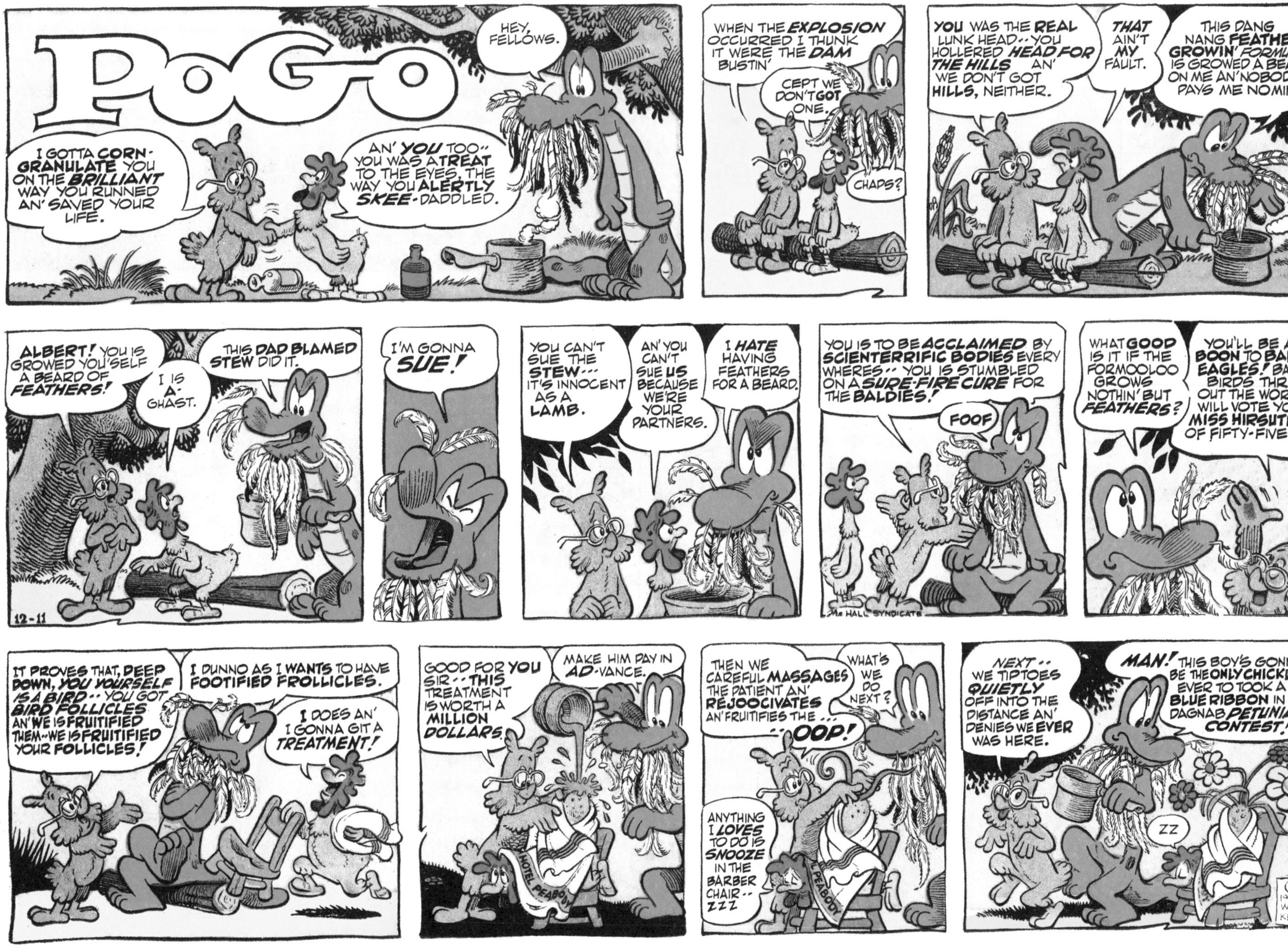
POGO
I GOTTA CORN-GRANULATE YOU ON THE BRILLIANT WAY YOU RUNNED AN' SAVED YOUR LIFE.
AN' YOU TOO-- YOU WAS A TREAT TO THE EYES, THE WAY YOU ALERTLY SKEE-DADDLED.
HEY, FELLOWS.
WHEN THE EXPLOSION OCCURRED I THUNK IT WERE THE DAM BUSTIN'
CEPT WE DON'T GOT ONE.
CHAPS?
YOU WAS THE REAL LUNK HEAD-- YOU HOLLERED HEAD FOR THE HILLS AN' WE DON'T GOT HILLS, NEITHER.
THAT AIN'T MY FAULT.
THIS DANG NANG FEATHER GROWIN' FORMULOO IS GROWED A BEARD ON ME AN' NOBODY PAYS ME NO MIND.
ALBERT! YOU IS GROWED YOU'SELF A BEARD OF FEATHERS!
I IS A-GHAST.
THIS DAD BLAMED STEW DID IT.
12-11
I'M GONNA SUE!
YOU CAN'T SUE THE STEW--- IT'S INNOCENT AS A LAMB.
AN' YOU CAN'T SUE US BECAUSE WE'RE YOUR PARTNERS.
I HATE HAVING FEATHERS FOR A BEARD.
YOU IS TO BE ACCLAIMED BY SCIENTERRIFIC BODIES EVERY WHERES-- YOU IS STUMBLED ON A SURE-FIRE CURE FOR THE BALDIES!
FOOF
WHAT GOOD IS IT IF THE FORMOOLOO GROWS NOTHIN' BUT FEATHERS?
YOU'LL BE A BOON TO BALD EAGLES! BALD BIRDS THRU-OUT THE WORL' WILL VOTE YOU MISS HIRSUTE OF FIFTY-FIVE.
IT PROVES THAT, DEEP DOWN, YOU YOURSELF IS A BIRD-- YOU GOT BIRD FOLLICLES AN' WE IS FRUITIFIED THEM--WE IS FRUITIFIED YOUR FOLLICLES!
I DUNNO AS I WANTS TO HAVE FOOTIFIED FROLLICLES.
I DOES AN' I GONNA GIT A TREATMENT!
GOOD FOR YOU SIR-- THIS TREATMENT IS WORTH A MILLION DOLLARS.
MAKE HIM PAY IN AD-VANCE.
HOTEL PEABODY
THEN WE CAREFUL MASSAGES THE PATIENT AN' REJOOCIVATES AN' FRUITIFIES THE...
WHAT'S WE DO NEXT?
..OOP!
ANYTHING I LOVES TO DO IS SNOOZE IN THE BARBER CHAIR-- ZZZ
NEXT-- WE TIPTOES QUIETLY OFF INTO THE DISTANCE AN' DENIES WE EVER WAS HERE.
MAN! THIS BOY'S GONNA BE THE ONLY CHICKEN EVER TO TOOK A BLUE RIBBON IN A DAGNAB PETUNIA CONTEST!
ZZ
© 1955 WALT KELLY

SUNDAY, DECEMBER 18, 1955

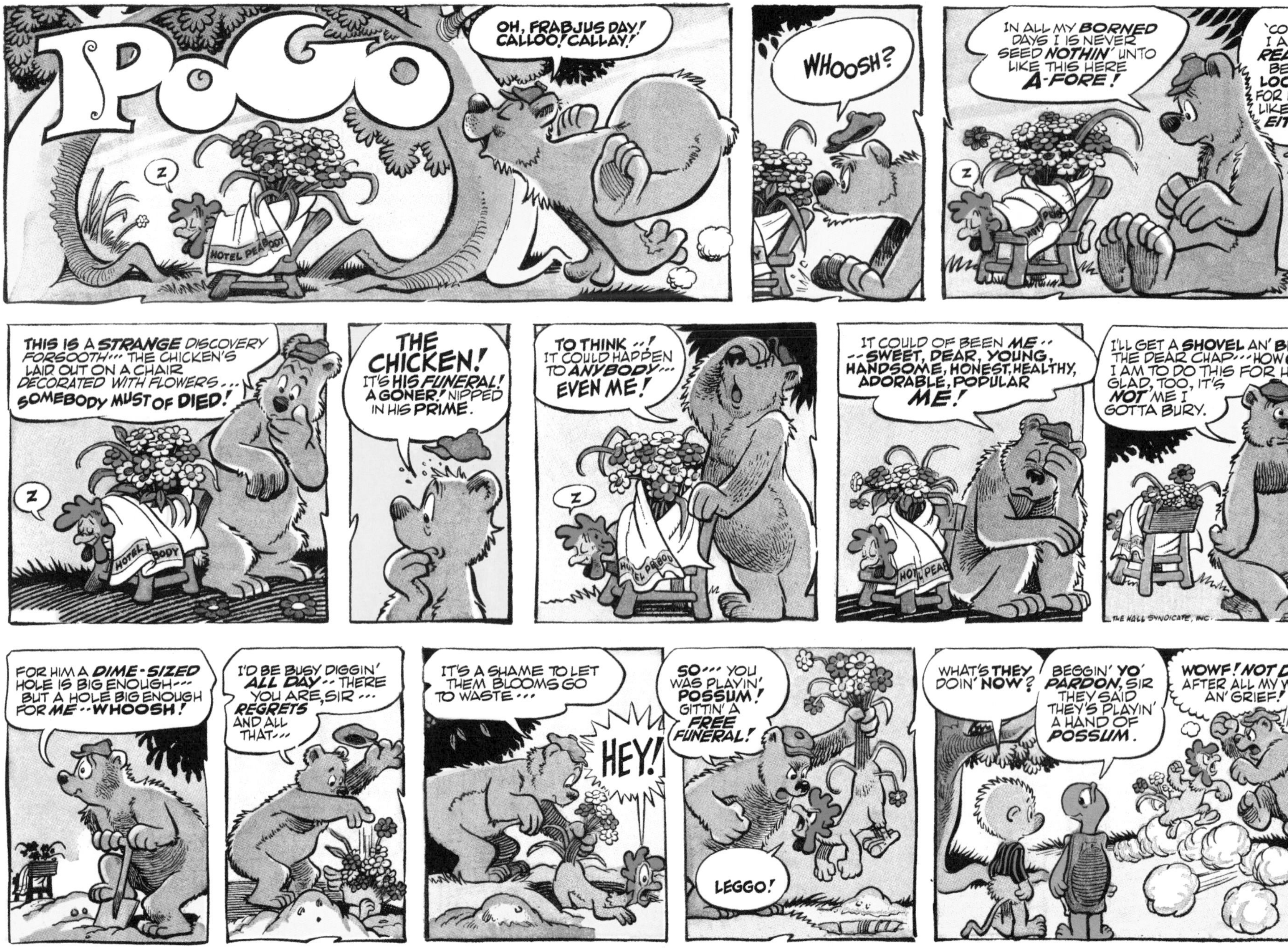
POGO
OH, FRABJUS DAY! CALLOO! CALLAY!
Z
HOTEL PEABODY
WHOOSH?
IN ALL MY BORNED DAYS I IS NEVER SEED NOTHIN' UNTO LIKE THIS HERE A-FORE!
'COURSE I AIN'T REALLY BEEN LOOKIN' FOR NOTHIN' LIKE THIS EITHER.
Z
THIS IS A STRANGE DISCOVERY FORSOOTH··· THE CHICKEN'S LAID OUT ON A CHAIR DECORATED WITH FLOWERS... SOMEBODY MUST OF DIED!
Z
THE CHICKEN! IT'S HIS FUNERAL! A GONER! NIPPED IN HIS PRIME.
TO THINK--! IT COULD HAPPEN TO ANYBODY--- EVEN ME!
Z
IT COULD OF BEEN ME-- --SWEET, DEAR, YOUNG, HANDSOME, HONEST, HEALTHY, ADORABLE, POPULAR ME!
I'LL GET A SHOVEL AN' BURY THE DEAR CHAP--- HOW GLAD I AM TO DO THIS FOR HIM--- GLAD, TOO, IT'S NOT ME I GOTTA BURY.
THE HALL SYNDICATE, INC.
FOR HIM A DIME-SIZED HOLE IS BIG ENOUGH--- BUT A HOLE BIG ENOUGH FOR ME--WHOOSH!
I'D BE BUSY DIGGIN' ALL DAY-- THERE YOU ARE, SIR--- REGRETS AND ALL THAT---
IT'S A SHAME TO LET THEM BLOOMS GO TO WASTE---
HEY!
SO--- YOU WAS PLAYIN' POSSUM! GITTIN' A FREE FUNERAL!
LEGGO!
WHAT'S THEY DOIN' NOW?
BEGGIN' YO' PARDON, SIR THEY SAID THEY'S PLAYIN' A HAND OF POSSUM.
WOWF! NOT DEAD! AFTER ALL MY WORK AN' GRIEF!
© 1955 WALT KELLY

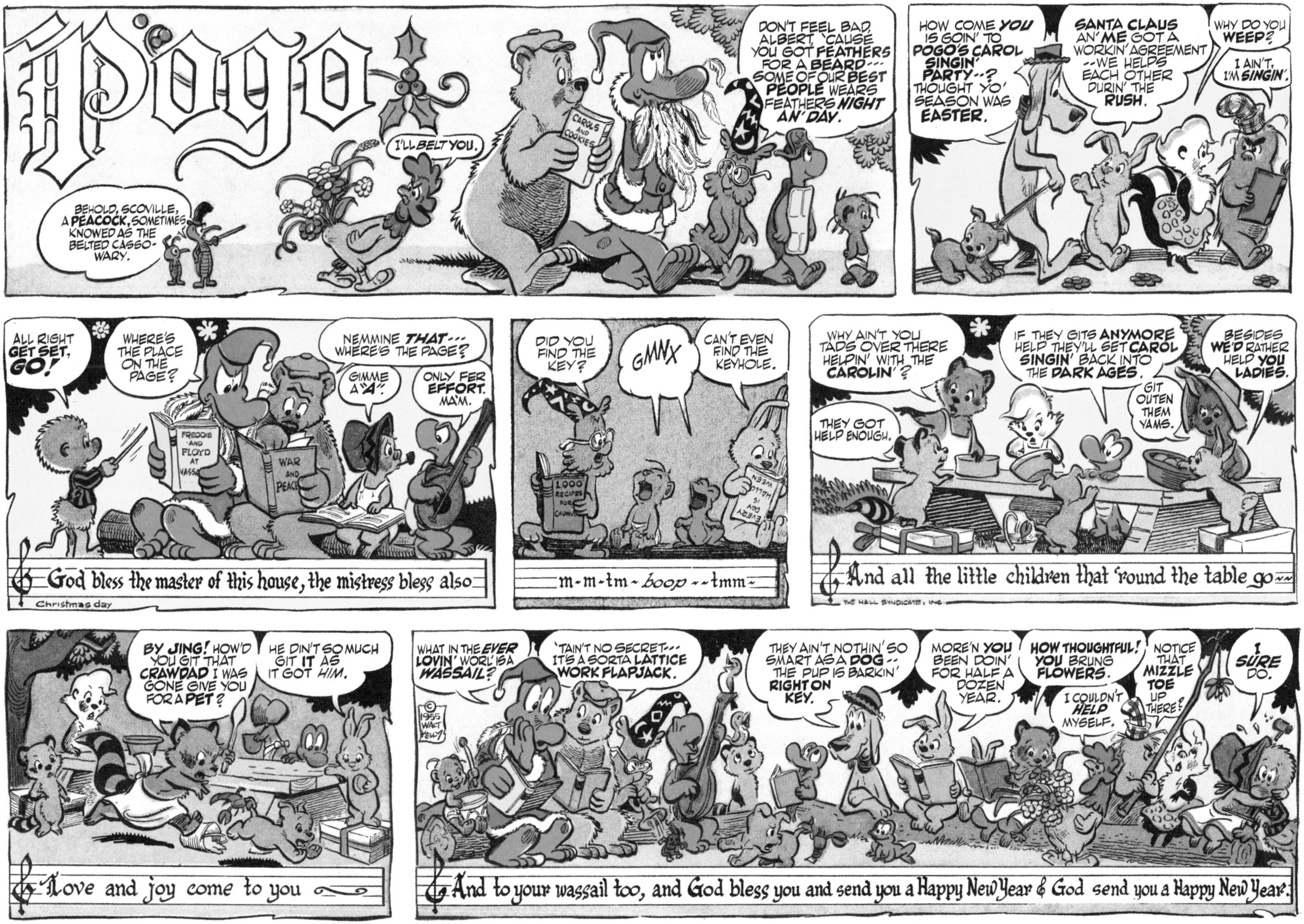
Pogo
BEHOLD, SCOVILLE, A PEACOCK, SOMETIMES KNOWED AS THE BELTED CASSOWARY.
I'LL BELT YOU.
CAROLS AND COOKIES
DON'T FEEL BAD, ALBERT, 'CAUSE YOU GOT FEATHERS FOR A BEARD--- SOME OF OUR BEST PEOPLE WEARS FEATHERS NIGHT AN' DAY.
HOW COME YOU IS GOIN' TO POGO'S CAROL SINGIN' PARTY--? THOUGHT YO' SEASON WAS EASTER.
SANTA CLAUS AN' ME GOT A WORKIN' AGREEMENT --WE HELPS EACH OTHER DURIN' THE RUSH.
WHY DO YOU WEEP?
I AIN'T, I'M SINGIN'.
ALL RIGHT GET SET, GO!
WHERE'S THE PLACE ON THE PAGE?
NEMMINE THAT--- WHERE'S THE PAGE?
GIMME A "A".
ONLY FER EFFORT, MA'M.
FREDDIE AND FLOYD AT VASSAR
WAR AND PEACE
God bless the master of this house, the mistress bless also
Christmas day
DID YOU FIND THE KEY?
GMNX
CAN'T EVEN FIND THE KEYHOLE.
m-m-tm-boop--tmm-
WHY AIN'T YOU TADS OVER THERE HELPIN' WITH THE CAROLIN'?
THEY GOT HELP ENOUGH.
IF THEY GITS ANYMORE HELP THEY'LL SET CAROL SINGIN' BACK INTO THE DARK AGES.
GIT OUTEN THEM YAMS.
BESIDES WE'D RATHER HELP YOU LADIES.
And all the little children that 'round the table go
THE HALL SYNDICATE, INC.
BY JING! HOW'D YOU GIT THAT CRAWDAD I WAS GONE GIVE YOU FOR A PET?
HE DIN'T SO MUCH GIT IT AS IT GOT HIM.
Love and joy come to you
WHAT IN THE EVER LOVIN' WORL' IS A WASSAIL?
'TAIN'T NO SECRET--- IT'S A SORTA LATTICE WORK FLAPJACK.
© 1955 WALT KELLY
THEY AIN'T NOTHIN' SO SMART AS A DOG-- THE PUP IS BARKIN' RIGHT ON KEY.
MORE'N YOU BEEN DOIN' FOR HALF A DOZEN YEAR.
HOW THOUGHTFUL! YOU BRUNG FLOWERS.
I COULDN'T HELP MYSELF.
NOTICE THAT MIZZLE TOE UP THERE?
I SURE DO.
And to your wassail too, and God bless you and send you a Happy New Year & God send you a Happy New Year.

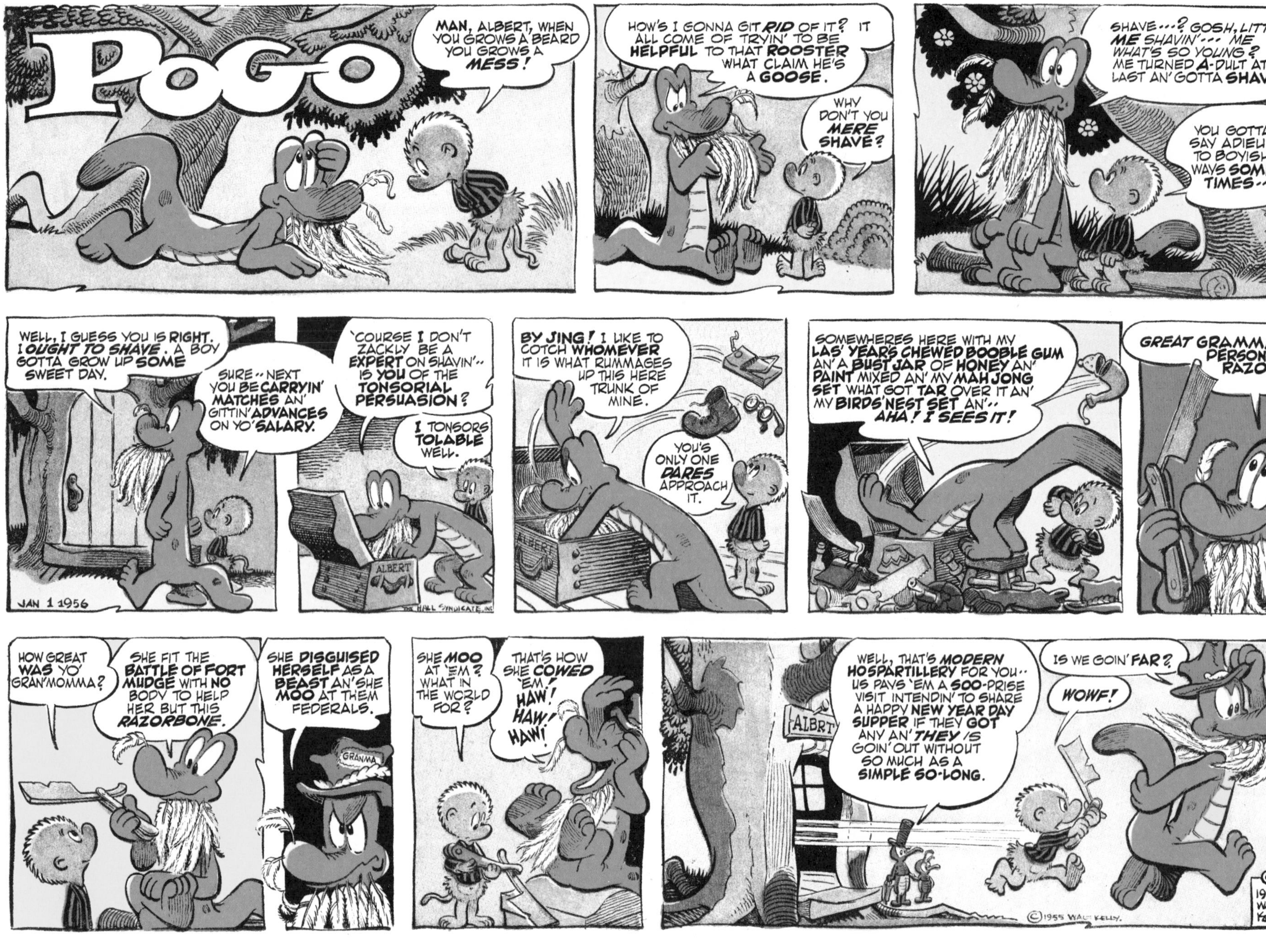
POGO
MAN, ALBERT, WHEN YOU GROWS A BEARD YOU GROWS A MESS!
HOW'S I GONNA GIT RID OF IT? IT ALL COME OF TRYIN' TO BE HELPFUL TO THAT ROOSTER WHAT CLAIM HE'S A GOOSE.
WHY DON'T YOU MERE SHAVE?
SHAVE...? GOSH, LITTLE ME SHAVIN'... ME WHAT'S SO YOUNG? ME TURNED A-DULT AT LAST AN' GOTTA SHAVE.
YOU GOTTA SAY ADIEU TO BOYISH WAYS SOME-TIMES..
WELL, I GUESS YOU IS RIGHT. I OUGHT TO SHAVE. A BOY GOTTA GROW UP SOME SWEET DAY.
SURE.. NEXT YOU BE CARRYIN' MATCHES AN' GITTIN' ADVANCES ON YO' SALARY.
JAN 1 1956
'COURSE I DON'T ZACKLY BE A EXPERT ON SHAVIN'.. IS YOU OF THE TONSORIAL PERSUASION?
I TONSORS TOLABLE WELL.
ALBERT
THE HALL SYNDICATE, INC
BY JING! I LIKE TO COTCH WHOMEVER IT IS WHAT RUMMAGES UP THIS HERE TRUNK OF MINE.
YOU'S ONLY ONE DARES APPROACH IT.
ALBERT
SOMEWHERES HERE WITH MY LAS' YEARS CHEWED BOOBLE GUM AN' A BUST JAR OF HONEY AN' PAINT MIXED AN' MY MAH JONG SET WHAT GOT TAR OVER IT AN' MY BIRDS'NEST SET AN'.. AHA! I SEES IT!
GREAT GRAMMA'S PERSONIAL RAZOR.
HOW GREAT WAS YO' GRAN'MOMMA?
SHE FIT THE BATTLE OF FORT MUDGE WITH NO BODY TO HELP HER BUT THIS RAZORBONE.
SHE DISGUISED HERSELF AS A BEAST AN' SHE MOO AT THEM FEDERALS.
GRANMA
SHE MOO AT 'EM? WHAT IN THE WORLD FOR?
THAT'S HOW SHE COWED 'EM! HAW! HAW! HAW!
ALBRT
WELL, THAT'S MODERN HOSPARTILLERY FOR YOU.. US PAYS 'EM A SOO-PRISE VISIT INTENDIN' TO SHARE A HAPPY NEW YEAR DAY SUPPER IF THEY GOT ANY AN' THEY IS GOIN' OUT WITHOUT SO MUCH AS A SIMPLE SO-LONG.
IS WE GOIN' FAR?
WOWF!
©1955 WALT KELLY.
© 1956 WALT KELLY

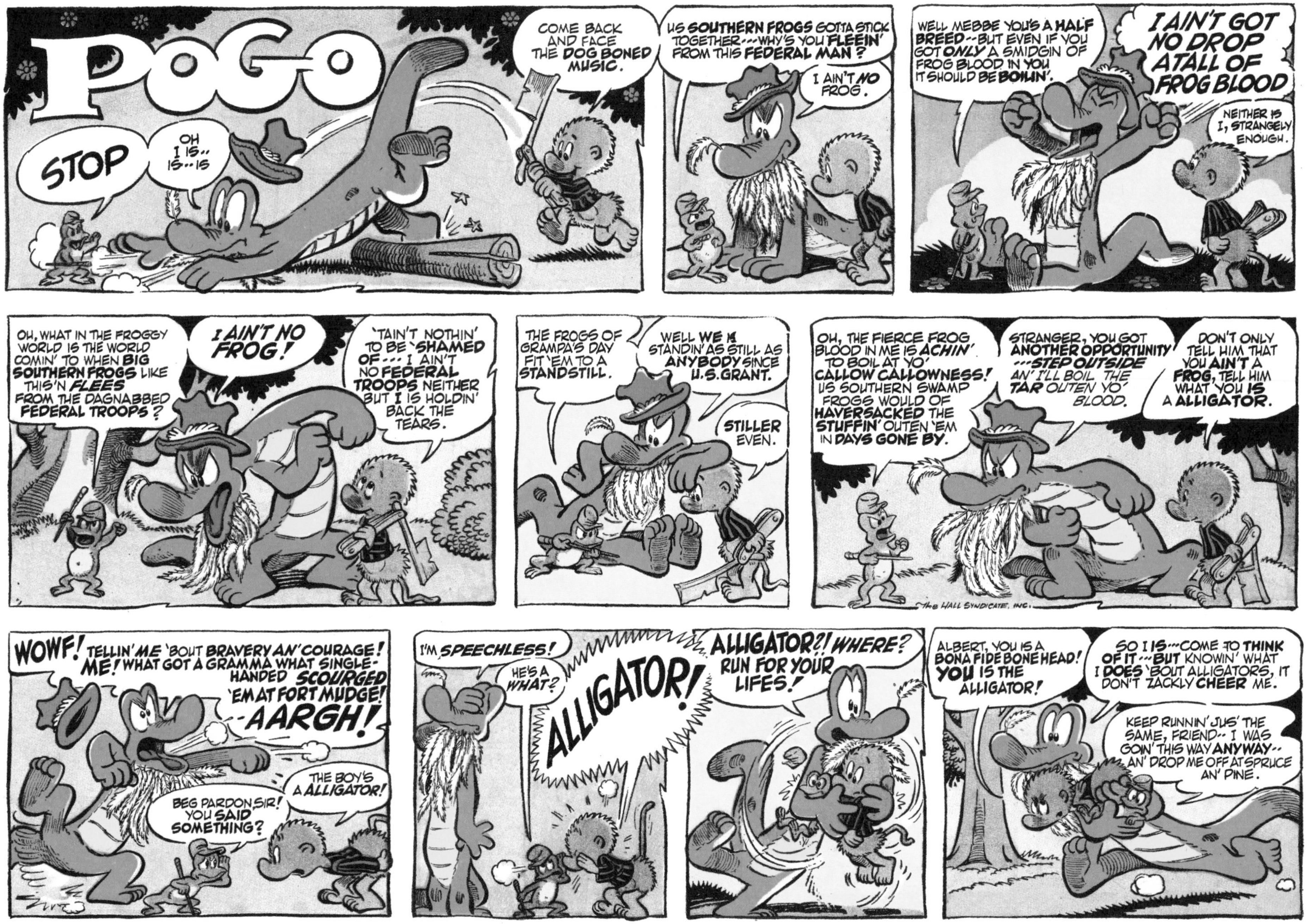
POGO
STOP
OH I IS.. IS--IS
COME BACK AND FACE THE DOG BONED MUSIC.
US SOUTHERN FROGS GOTTA STICK TOGETHER---WHY'S YOU 'FLEEIN' FROM THIS FEDERAL MAN?
I AIN'T NO FROG.
WELL MEBBE YOU'S A HALF BREED--BUT EVEN IF YOU GOT ONLY A SMIDGIN OF FROG BLOOD IN YOU IT SHOULD BE BOILIN'.
I AIN'T GOT NO DROP ATALL OF FROG BLOOD
NEITHER IS I, STRANGELY ENOUGH.
OH, WHAT IN THE FROGGY WORLD IS THE WORLD COMIN' TO WHEN BIG SOUTHERN FROGS LIKE THIS'N FLEES FROM THE DAGNABBED FEDERAL TROOPS?
I AIN'T NO FROG!
'TAIN'T NOTHIN' TO BE 'SHAMED OF--- I AIN'T NO FEDERAL TROOPS NEITHER BUT I IS HOLDIN' BACK THE TEARS.
THE FROGS OF GRAMPA'S DAY FIT 'EM TO A STANDSTILL.
WELL WE IS STANDIN' AS STILL AS ANYBODY SINCE U.S. GRANT.
STILLER EVEN.
OH, THE FIERCE FROG BLOOD IN ME IS ACHIN' TO BOIL AT YO' CALLOW CALLOWNESS! US SOUTHERN SWAMP FROGS WOULD OF HAVERSACKED THE STUFFIN' OUTEN 'EM IN DAYS GONE BY.
STRANGER, YOU GOT ANOTHER OPPORTUNITY ---STEP OUTSIDE AN' I'LL BOIL THE TAR OUTEN YO' BLOOD.
DON'T ONLY TELL HIM THAT YOU AIN'T A FROG, TELL HIM WHAT YOU IS A ALLIGATOR.
© THE HALL SYNDICATE, INC.
WOWF! TELLIN' ME 'BOUT BRAVERY AN' COURAGE! ME! WHAT GOT A GRAMMA WHAT SINGLE-HANDED SCOURGED 'EM AT FORT MUDGE! --AARGH!
BEG PARDON SIR! YOU SAID SOMETHING?
THE BOY'S A ALLIGATOR!
I'M SPEECHLESS!
HE'S A WHAT?
ALLIGATOR!
ALLIGATOR?! WHERE? RUN FOR YOUR LIFES!
ALBERT, YOU IS A BONA FIDE BONE HEAD! YOU IS THE ALLIGATOR!
SO I IS---COME TO THINK OF IT---BUT KNOWIN' WHAT I DOES 'BOUT ALLIGATORS, IT DON'T ZACKLY CHEER ME.
KEEP RUNNIN' JUS' THE SAME, FRIEND-- I WAS GOIN' THIS WAY ANYWAY-- AN' DROP ME OFF AT SPRUCE AN' PINE.

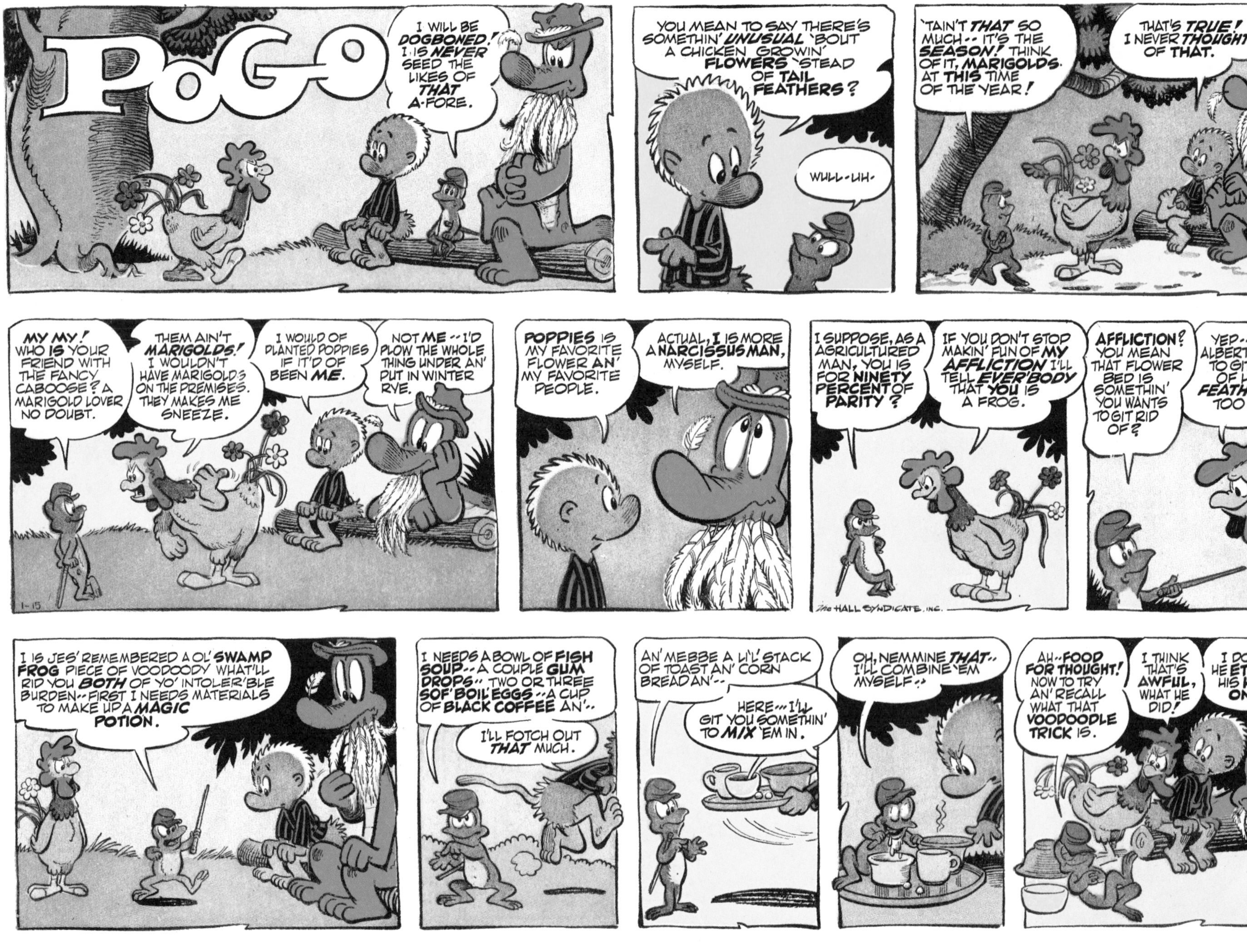
POGO
I WILL BE DOGBONED! I IS NEVER SEED THE LIKES OF THAT A-FORE.
YOU MEAN TO SAY THERE'S SOMETHIN' UNUSUAL 'BOUT A CHICKEN GROWIN' FLOWERS 'STEAD OF TAIL FEATHERS?
WULL-UH-
'TAIN'T THAT SO MUCH-- IT'S THE SEASON! THINK OF IT, MARIGOLDS AT THIS TIME OF THE YEAR!
THAT'S TRUE! I NEVER THOUGHT OF THAT.
MY MY! WHO IS YOUR FRIEND WITH THE FANCY CABOOSE? A MARIGOLD LOVER NO DOUBT.
THEM AIN'T MARIGOLDS! I WOULDN'T HAVE MARIGOLDS ON THE PREMISES. THEY MAKES ME SNEEZE.
I WOULD OF PLANTED POPPIES IF IT'D OF BEEN ME.
NOT ME-- I'D PLOW THE WHOLE THING UNDER AN' PUT IN WINTER RYE.
1-15
POPPIES IS MY FAVORITE FLOWER AN' MY FAVORITE PEOPLE.
ACTUAL, I IS MORE A NARCISSUS MAN, MYSELF.
I SUPPOSE, AS A AGRICULTURED MAN, YOU IS FOR NINETY PERCENT OF PARITY?
IF YOU DON'T STOP MAKIN' FUN OF MY AFFLICTION I'LL TELL EVER'BODY THAT YOU IS A FROG.
The HALL SYNDICATE, INC.
AFFLICTION? YOU MEAN THAT FLOWER BED IS SOMETHIN' YOU WANTS TO GIT RID OF?
YEP-- AN' ALBERT WANTS TO GIT RID OF HIS FEATHERS TOO.
I IS JES' REMEMBERED A OL' SWAMP FROG PIECE OF VOODOODY WHAT'LL RID YOU BOTH OF YO' INTOLER'BLE BURDEN-- FIRST I NEEDS MATERIALS TO MAKE UP A MAGIC POTION.
I NEEDS A BOWL OF FISH SOUP-- A COUPLE GUM DROPS-- TWO OR THREE SOF' BOIL' EGGS-- A CUP OF BLACK COFFEE AN'--
I'LL FOTCH OUT THAT MUCH.
AN' MEBBE A LI'L' STACK OF TOAST AN' CORN BREAD AN'--
HERE-- I'LL GIT YOU SOMETHIN' TO MIX 'EM IN.
OH, NEMMINE THAT-- I'LL COMBINE 'EM MYSELF--
AH-- FOOD FOR THOUGHT! NOW TO TRY AN' RECALL WHAT THAT VOODOODLE TRICK IS.
I THINK THAT'S AWFUL, WHAT HE DID!
I DO TOO-- HE ET WITH HIS HAT ON.
© 1956 WALT KELLY

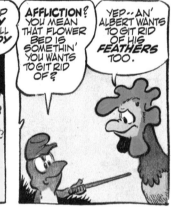

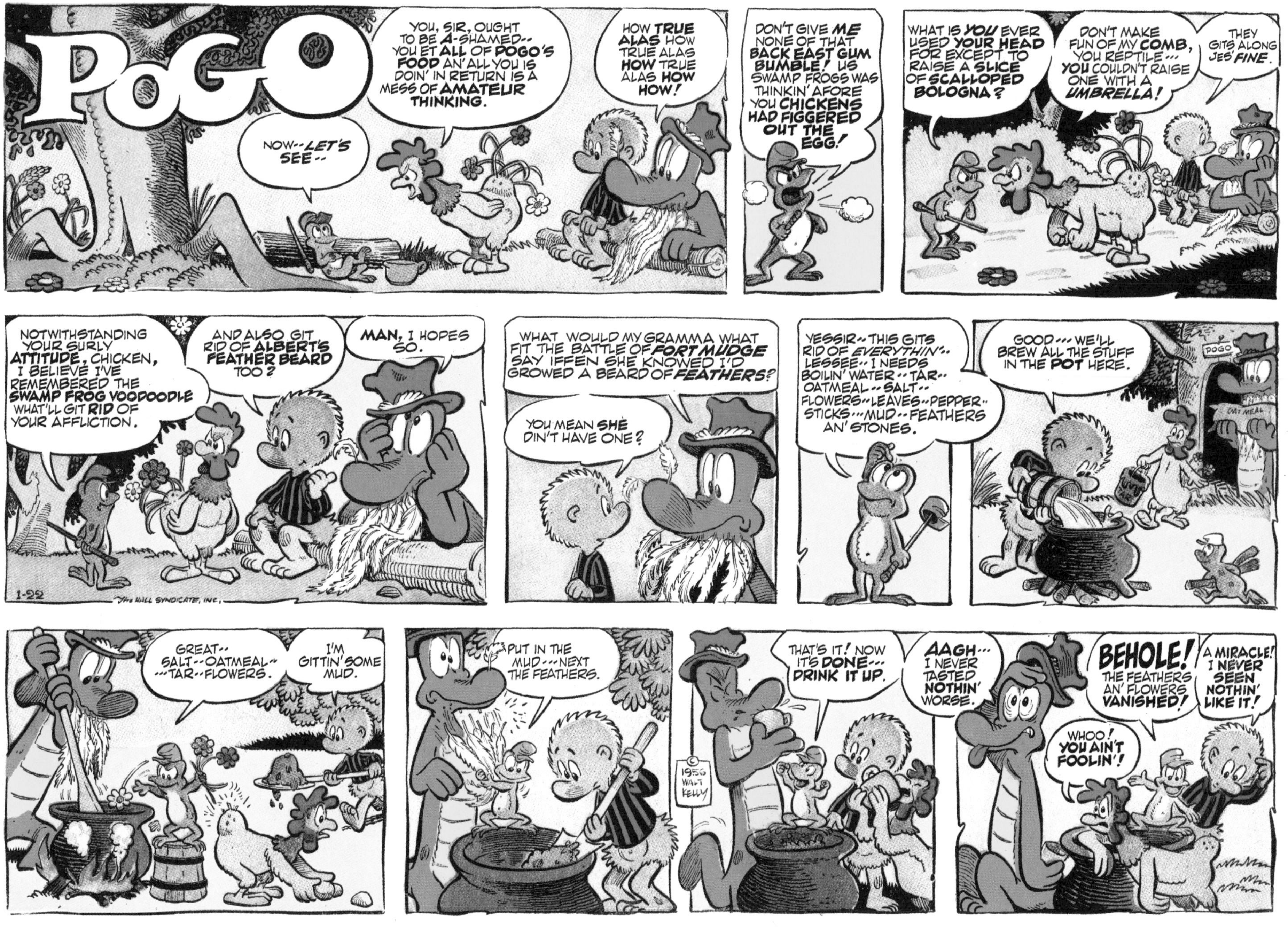
POGO
YOU, SIR, OUGHT TO BE A-SHAMED-- YOU ET ALL OF POGO'S FOOD AN' ALL YOU IS DOIN' IN RETURN IS A MESS OF AMATEUR THINKING.
NOW--LET'S SEE--
HOW TRUE ALAS HOW TRUE ALAS HOW TRUE ALAS HOW HOW!
DON'T GIVE ME NONE OF THAT BACK EAST GUM BUMBLE! US SWAMP FROGS WAS THINKIN' AFORE YOU CHICKENS HAD FIGGERED OUT THE EGG!
WHAT IS YOU EVER USED YOUR HEAD FOR EXCEPT TO RAISE A SLICE OF SCALLOPED BOLOGNA?
DON'T MAKE FUN OF MY COMB, YOU REPTILE--- YOU COULDN'T RAISE ONE WITH A UMBRELLA!
THEY GITS ALONG JES' FINE.
NOTWITHSTANDING YOUR SURLY ATTITUDE, CHICKEN, I BELIEVE I'VE REMEMBERED THE SWAMP FROG VOODOODLE WHAT'LL GIT RID OF YOUR AFFLICTION.
AND ALSO GIT RID OF ALBERT'S FEATHER BEARD TOO?
MAN, I HOPES SO.
1-22
The Hall Syndicate, Inc.
WHAT WOULD MY GRAMMA WHAT FIT THE BATTLE OF FORT MUDGE SAY IFFEN SHE KNOWED I'D GROWED A BEARD OF FEATHERS?
YOU MEAN SHE DIN'T HAVE ONE?
YESSIR-- THIS GITS RID OF EVERYTHIN'-- LESSEE-- I NEEDS BOILIN' WATER -- TAR-- OATMEAL -- SALT-- FLOWERS-- LEAVES-- PEPPER-- STICKS --- MUD -- FEATHERS AN' STONES.
GOOD --- WE'LL BREW ALL THE STUFF IN THE POT HERE.
POGO
OAT MEAL
GREAT-- SALT--OATMEAL-- --TAR--FLOWERS.
I'M GITTIN' SOME MUD.
PUT IN THE MUD---NEXT THE FEATHERS.
© 1956 WALT KELLY
THAT'S IT! NOW IT'S DONE--- DRINK IT UP.
AAGH--- I NEVER TASTED NOTHIN' WORSE.
BEHOLE! THE FEATHERS AN' FLOWERS VANISHED!
A MIRACLE! I NEVER SEEN NOTHIN' LIKE IT!
WHOO! YOU AIN'T FOOLIN'!

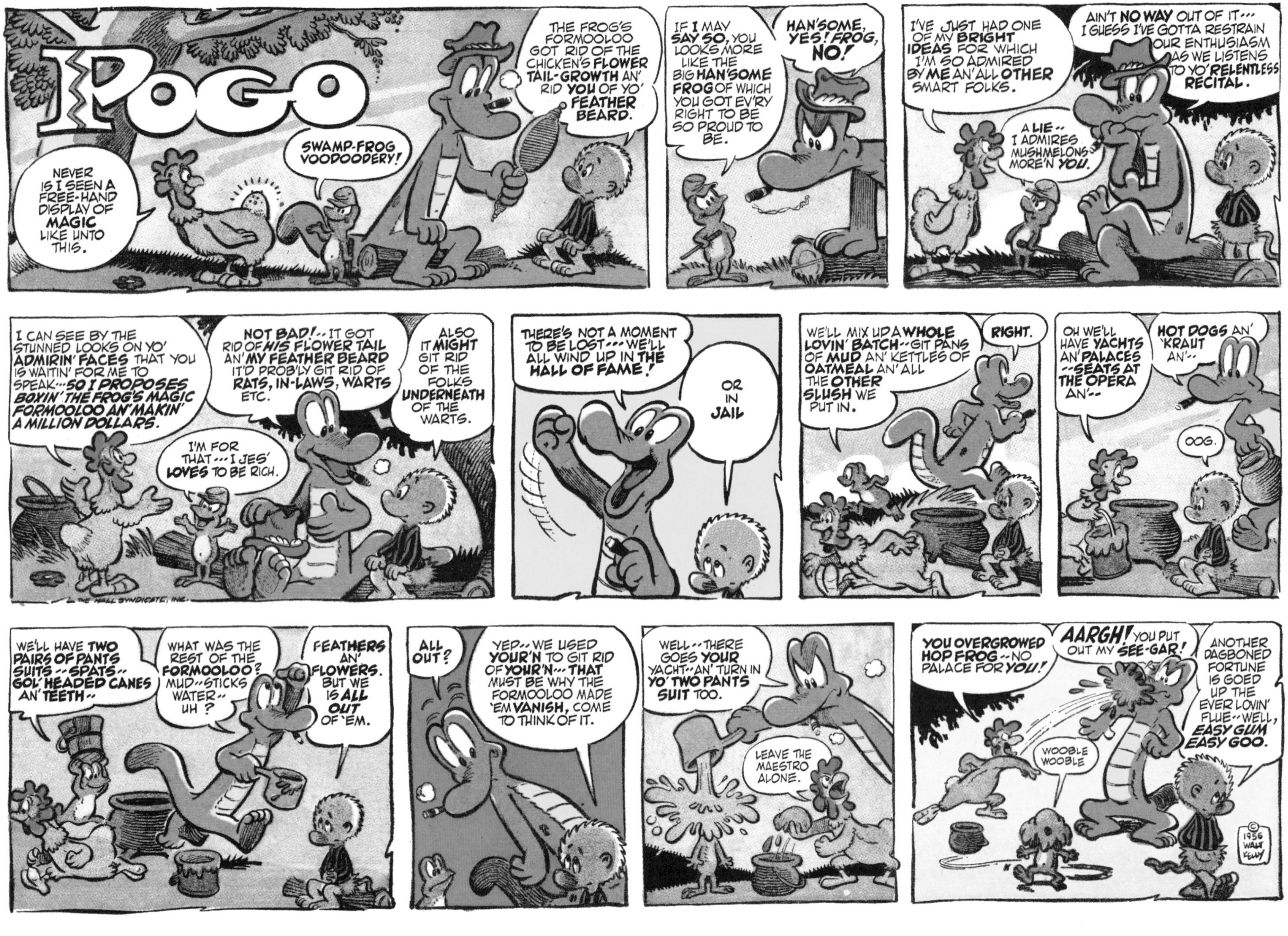
POGO
NEVER IS I SEEN A FREE-HAND DISPLAY OF MAGIC LIKE UNTO THIS.
SWAMP-FROG VOODOODERY!
THE FROG'S FORMOOLOO GOT RID OF THE CHICKEN'S FLOWER TAIL-GROWTH AN' RID YOU OF YO' FEATHER BEARD.
IF I MAY SAY SO, YOU LOOKS MORE LIKE THE BIG HAN'SOME FROG OF WHICH YOU GOT EV'RY RIGHT TO BE SO PROUD TO BE.
HAN'SOME, YES! FROG, NO!
I'VE JUST HAD ONE OF MY BRIGHT IDEAS FOR WHICH I'M SO ADMIRED BY ME AN' ALL OTHER SMART FOLKS.
A LIE -- I ADMIRES MUSHMELONS MORE'N YOU.
AIN'T NO WAY OUT OF IT --- I GUESS I'VE GOTTA RESTRAIN OUR ENTHUSIASM AS WE LISTENS TO YO' RELENTLESS RECITAL.
I CAN SEE BY THE STUNNED LOOKS ON YO' ADMIRIN' FACES THAT YOU IS WAITIN' FOR ME TO SPEAK --- SO I PROPOSES BOYIN' THE FROG'S MAGIC FORMOOLOO AN' MAKIN' A MILLION DOLLARS.
I'M FOR THAT --- I JES' LOVES TO BE RICH.
NOT BAD! -- IT GOT RID OF HIS FLOWER TAIL AN' MY FEATHER BEARD IT'D PROB'LY GIT RID OF RATS, IN-LAWS, WARTS ETC.
ALSO IT MIGHT GIT RID OF THE FOLKS UNDERNEATH OF THE WARTS.
© THE HALL SYNDICATE, INC.
THERE'S NOT A MOMENT TO BE LOST --- WE'LL ALL WIND UP IN THE HALL OF FAME!
OR IN JAIL
WE'LL MIX UP A WHOLE LOVIN' BATCH -- GIT PANS OF MUD AN' KETTLES OF OATMEAL AN' ALL THE OTHER SLUSH WE PUT IN.
RIGHT.
OH WE'LL HAVE YACHTS AN' PALACES -- SEATS AT THE OPERA AN' --
HOT DOGS AN' 'KRAUT AN' --
OOG.
WE'LL HAVE TWO PAIRS OF PANTS SUITS -- SPATS -- GOL' HEADED CANES AN' TEETH --
WHAT WAS THE REST OF THE FORMOOLOO? MUD -- STICKS WATER -- UH ?
FEATHERS AN' FLOWERS. BUT WE IS ALL OUT OF 'EM.
ALL OUT?
YEP -- WE USED YOUR'N TO GIT RID OF YOUR'N --- THAT MUST BE WHY THE FORMOOLOO MADE 'EM VANISH, COME TO THINK OF IT.
WELL -- THERE GOES YOUR YACHT -- AN' TURN IN YO' TWO PANTS SUIT TOO.
LEAVE THE MAESTRO ALONE.
YOU OVERGROWED HOP FROG -- NO PALACE FOR YOU!
AARGH! YOU PUT OUT MY SEE-GAR!
WOOBLE WOOBLE
ANOTHER DAGBONED FORTUNE IS GOED UP THE EVER LOVIN' FLUE -- WELL, EASY GUM EASY GOO.
© 1956 WALT KELLY

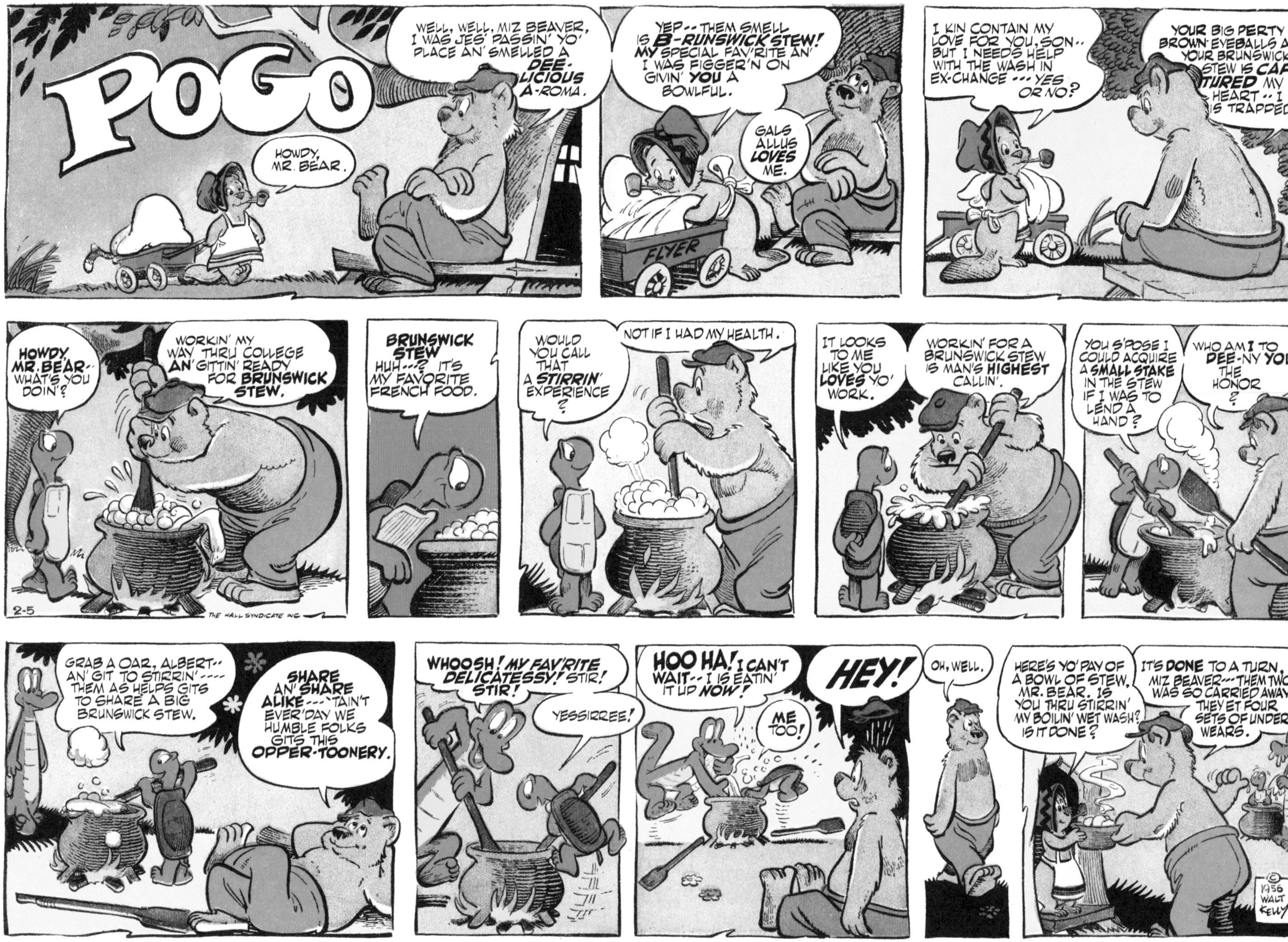
POGO
HOWDY, MR. BEAR.
WELL, WELL, MIZ BEAVER, I WAS JES' PASSIN' YO' PLACE AN' SMELLED A DEE-LICIOUS A-ROMA.
YEP-- THEM SMELL IS B-RUNSWICK STEW! MY SPECIAL FAV'RITE AN' I WAS FIGGER'N ON GIVIN' YOU A BOWLFUL.
GALS ALLUS LOVES ME.
FLYER
I KIN CONTAIN MY LOVE FOR YOU, SON.. BUT I NEEDS HELP WITH THE WASH IN EX-CHANGE --- YES OR NO?
YOUR BIG PERTY BROWN EYEBALLS AN' YOUR BRUNSWICK STEW IS CAP-TURED MY HEART -- I IS TRAPPED.
HOWDY MR. BEAR.. WHAT'S YOU DOIN'?
WORKIN' MY WAY THRU COLLEGE AN' GITTIN' READY FOR BRUNSWICK STEW.
2-5
THE HALL SYNDICATE INC
BRUNSWICK STEW HUH--? IT'S MY FAVORITE FRENCH FOOD.
WOULD YOU CALL THAT A STIRRIN' EXPERIENCE?
NOT IF I HAD MY HEALTH.
IT LOOKS TO ME LIKE YOU LOVES YO' WORK.
WORKIN' FOR A BRUNSWICK STEW IS MAN'S HIGHEST CALLIN'.
YOU S'POSE I COULD ACQUIRE A SMALL STAKE IN THE STEW IF I WAS TO LEND A HAND?
WHO AM I TO DEE-NY YOU THE HONOR?
GRAB A OAR, ALBERT-- AN' GIT TO STIRRIN' ---- THEM AS HELPS GITS TO SHARE A BIG BRUNSWICK STEW.
SHARE AN' SHARE ALIKE--- 'TAIN'T EVER'DAY WE HUMBLE FOLKS GITS THIS OPPER-TOONERY.
WHOOSH! MY FAV'RITE DELICATESSY! STIR! STIR!
YESSIRREE!
HOO HA! I CAN'T WAIT-- I IS EATIN' IT UP NOW!
ME TOO!
HEY!
OH, WELL.
HERE'S YO' PAY OF A BOWL OF STEW, MR. BEAR. IS YOU THRU STIRRIN' MY BOILIN' WET WASH? IS IT DONE?
IT'S DONE TO A TURN, MIZ BEAVER--- THEM TWO WAS SO CARRIED AWAY THEY ET FOUR SETS OF UNDER-WEARS.
© 1956 WALT KELLY

SUNDAY, FEBRUARY 12, 1956

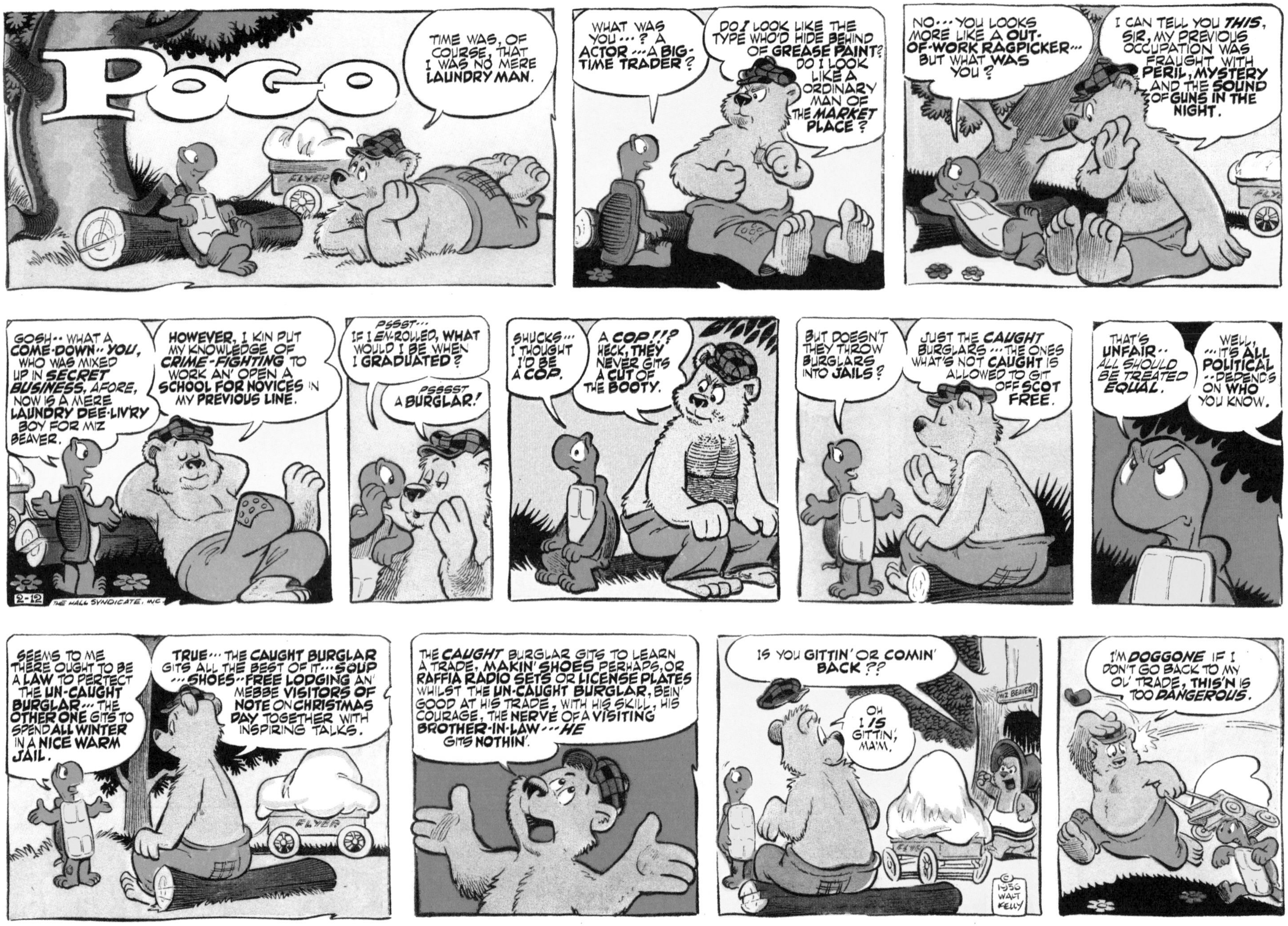
POGO
TIME WAS, OF COURSE, THAT I WAS NO MERE LAUNDRY MAN.
FLYER
WHAT WAS YOU...? A ACTOR...A BIG-TIME TRADER?
DO I LOOK LIKE THE TYPE WHO'D HIDE BEHIND OF GREASE PAINT? DO I LOOK LIKE A ORDINARY MAN OF THE MARKET PLACE?
NO... YOU LOOKS MORE LIKE A OUT-OF-WORK RAGPICKER... BUT WHAT WAS YOU?
I CAN TELL YOU THIS, SIR, MY PREVIOUS OCCUPATION WAS FRAUGHT WITH PERIL, MYSTERY AND THE SOUND OF GUNS IN THE NIGHT.
GOSH.. WHAT A COME-DOWN.. YOU, WHO WAS MIXED UP IN SECRET BUSINESS, AFORE, NOW IS A MERE LAUNDRY DEE-LIV'RY BOY FOR MIZ BEAVER.
HOWEVER, I KIN PUT MY KNOWLEDGE OF CRIME-FIGHTING TO WORK AN' OPEN A SCHOOL FOR NOVICES IN MY PREVIOUS LINE.
2-12
THE HALL SYNDICATE, INC.
PSSST... IF I EN-ROLLED, WHAT WOULD I BE WHEN I GRADUATED?
PSSSST A BURGLAR!
SHUCKS... I THOUGHT I'D BE A COP.
A COP!!? HECK, THEY NEVER GITS A CUT OF THE BOOTY.
BUT DOESN'T THEY THROW BURGLARS INTO JAILS?
JUST THE CAUGHT BURGLARS... THE ONES WHAT'S NOT CAUGHT IS ALLOWED TO GIT OFF SCOT FREE.
THAT'S UNFAIR.. ALL SHOULD BE TREATED EQUAL.
WELL, ...IT'S ALL POLITICAL ..DEPENDS ON WHO YOU KNOW.
SEEMS TO ME THERE OUGHT TO BE A LAW TO PERTECT THE UN-CAUGHT BURGLAR... THE OTHER ONE GITS TO SPEND ALL WINTER IN A NICE WARM JAIL.
TRUE... THE CAUGHT BURGLAR GITS ALL THE BEST OF IT... SOUP ...SHOES.. FREE LODGING AN' MEBBE VISITORS OF NOTE ON CHRISTMAS DAY TOGETHER WITH INSPIRING TALKS.
FLYER
THE CAUGHT BURGLAR GITS TO LEARN A TRADE, MAKIN' SHOES PERHAPS, OR RAFFIA RADIO SETS OR LICENSE PLATES WHILST THE UN-CAUGHT BURGLAR, BEIN' GOOD AT HIS TRADE, WITH HIS SKILL, HIS COURAGE, THE NERVE OF A VISITING BROTHER-IN-LAW... HE GITS NOTHIN'.
IS YOU GITTIN' OR COMIN' BACK??
MIZ BEAVER
OH I IS GITTIN', MA'M.
© 1956 WALT KELLY
I'M DOGGONE IF I DON'T GO BACK TO MY OL' TRADE, THIS'N IS TOO DANGEROUS.

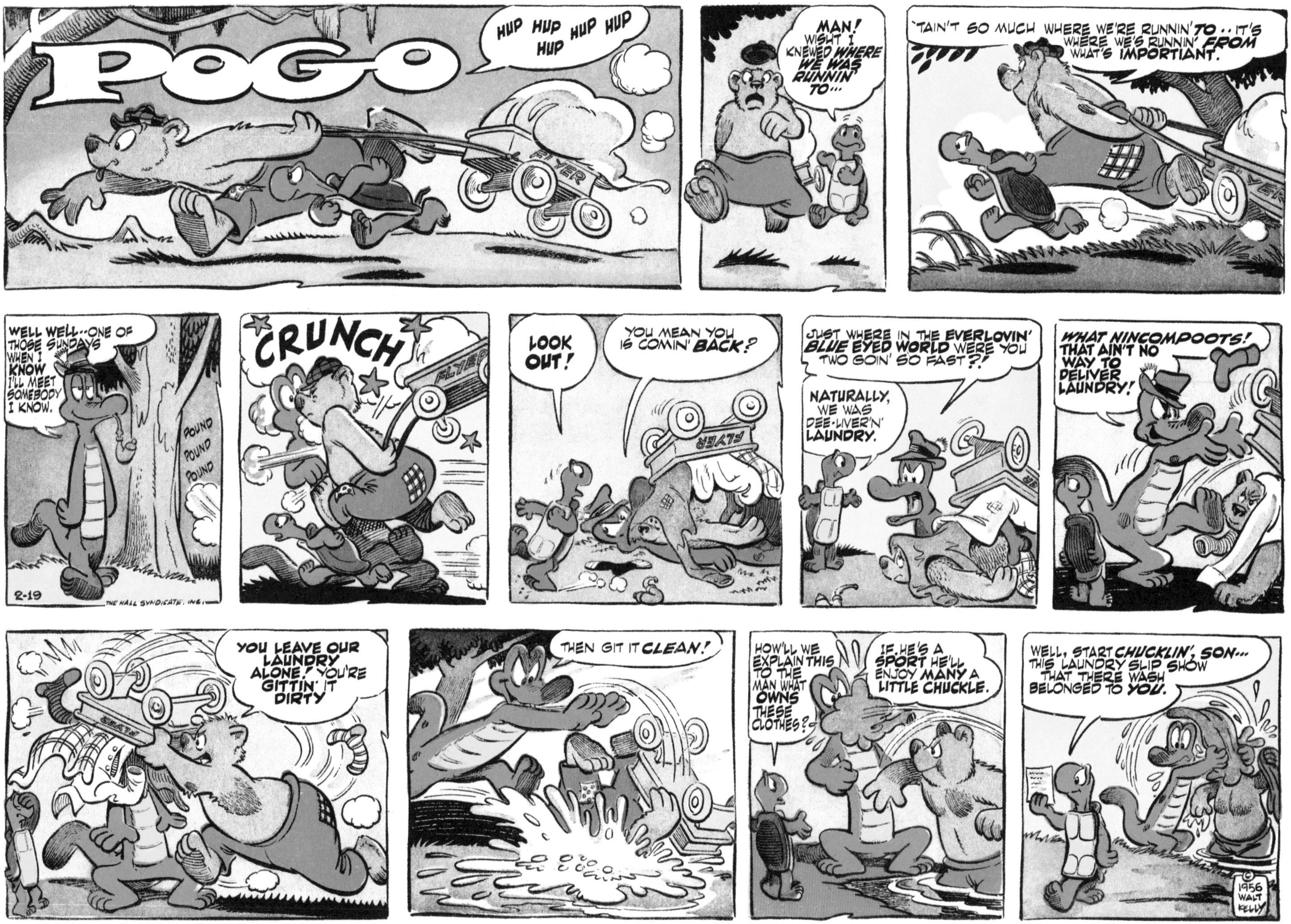
POGO
HUP HUP HUP HUP HUP HUP
MAN! WISHT I KNEWED WHERE WE WAS RUNNIN' TO...
'TAIN'T SO MUCH WHERE WE'RE RUNNIN' TO.. IT'S WHERE WE'S RUNNIN' FROM WHAT'S IMPORTIANT.
WELL WELL..ONE OF THOSE SUNDAYS WHEN I KNOW I'LL MEET SOMEBODY I KNOW.
POUND POUND POUND
2-19
THE HALL SYNDICATE, INC.
CRUNCH
FLYER
LOOK OUT!
YOU MEAN YOU IS COMIN' BACK?
JUST WHERE IN THE EVERLOVIN' BLUE EYED WORLD WERE YOU TWO GOIN' SO FAST?!
NATURALLY, WE WAS DEE-LIVER'N' LAUNDRY.
WHAT NINCOMPOOTS! THAT AIN'T NO WAY TO DELIVER LAUNDRY!
YOU LEAVE OUR LAUNDRY ALONE! YOU'RE GITTIN' IT DIRTY
THEN GIT IT CLEAN!
HOW'LL WE EXPLAIN THIS TO THE MAN WHAT OWNS THESE CLOTHES?
IF HE'S A SPORT HE'LL ENJOY MANY A LITTLE CHUCKLE.
WELL, START CHUCKLIN', SON... THIS LAUNDRY SLIP SHOW THAT THERE WASH BELONGED TO YOU.
© 1956 WALT KELLY

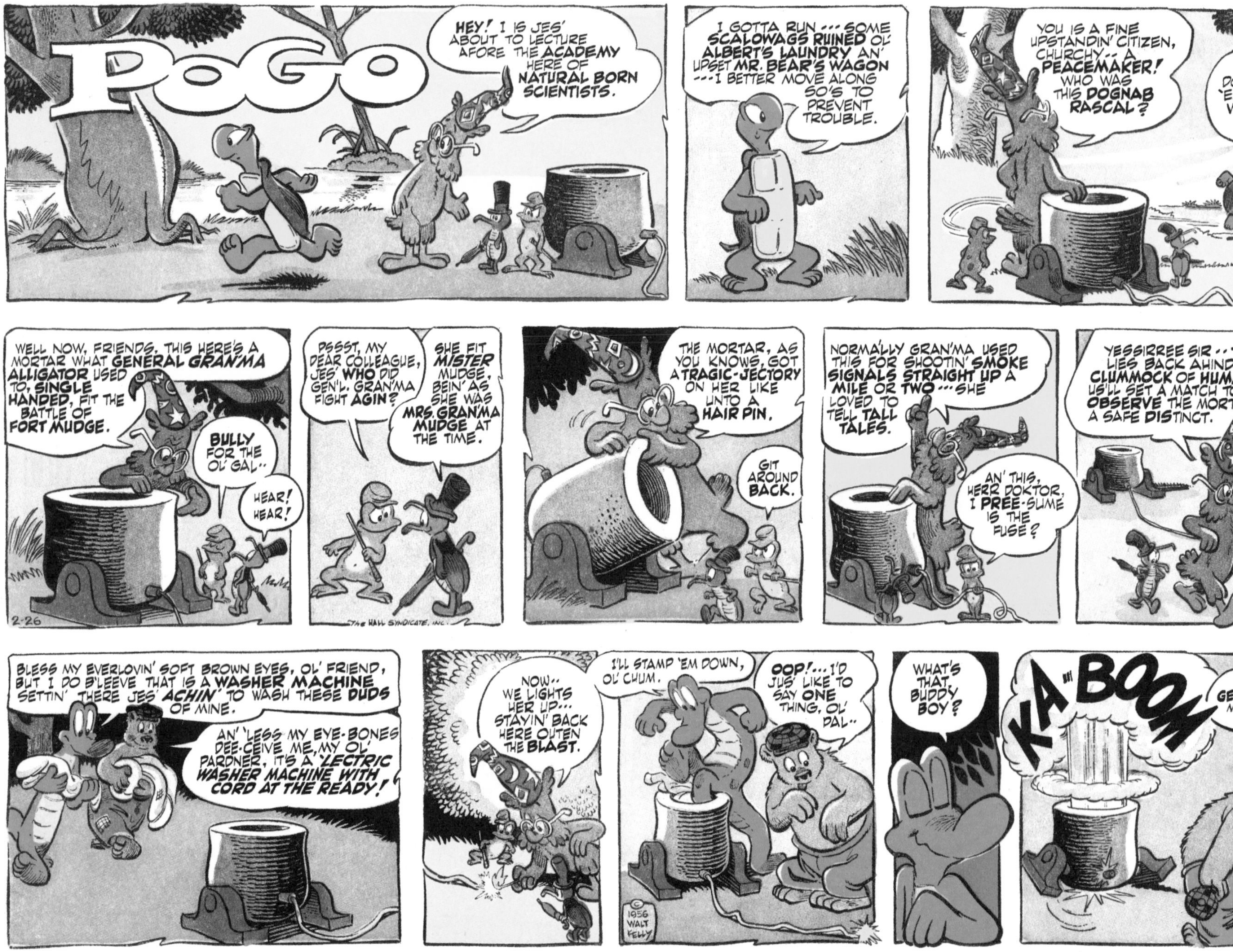
POGO
HEY! I IS JES' ABOUT TO LECTURE AFORE THE ACADEMY HERE OF NATURAL BORN SCIENTISTS.
I GOTTA RUN --- SOME SCALOWAGS RUINED OL' ALBERT'S LAUNDRY AN' UPSET MR. BEAR'S WAGON --- I BETTER MOVE ALONG SO'S TO PREVENT TROUBLE.
YOU IS A FINE UPSTANDIN' CITIZEN, CHURCHY -- A PEACEMAKER! WHO WAS THIS DOGNAB RASCAL?
ME.. DON'T TELL 'EM WHICH WAY I IS WENT.
WELL NOW, FRIENDS, THIS HERE'S A MORTAR WHAT GENERAL GRAN'MA ALLIGATOR USED TO, SINGLE HANDED, FIT THE BATTLE OF FORT MUDGE.
BULLY FOR THE OL' GAL..
HEAR! HEAR!
2-26
PSSST, MY DEAR COLLEAGUE, JES' WHO DID GEN'L. GRAN'MA FIGHT AGIN?
SHE FIT MISTER MUDGE, BEIN' AS SHE WAS MRS. GRAN'MA MUDGE AT THE TIME.
THE HALL SYNDICATE, INC.
THE MORTAR, AS YOU KNOWS, GOT A TRAGIC-JECTORY ON HER LIKE UNTO A HAIR PIN.
GIT AROUND BACK.
NORMALLY GRAN'MA USED THIS FOR SHOOTIN' SMOKE SIGNALS STRAIGHT UP A MILE OR TWO --- SHE LOVED TO TELL TALL TALES.
AN' THIS, HERR DOKTOR, I PREE-SUME IS THE FUSE?
YESSIRREE SIR .. THAT FUSE LIES BACK AHIND THIS CLUMMOCK OF HUMMOCK AN' US'LL SET A MATCH TO IT AN' OBSERVE THE MORTAR FROM A SAFE DISTINCT.
BLESS MY EVERLOVIN' SOFT BROWN EYES, OL' FRIEND, BUT I DO B'LEEVE THAT IS A WASHER MACHINE SETTIN' THERE JES' ACHIN' TO WASH THESE DUDS OF MINE.
AN' 'LESS MY EYE-BONES DEE-CEIVE ME, MY OL' PARDNER, IT'S A 'LECTRIC WASHER MACHINE WITH CORD AT THE READY!
NOW.. WE LIGHTS HER UP... STAYIN' BACK HERE OUTEN THE BLAST.
I'LL STAMP 'EM DOWN, OL' CHUM.
OOP!... I'D JUS' LIKE TO SAY ONE THING, OL' PAL..
© 1956 WALT KELLY
WHAT'S THAT, BUDDY BOY?
KA-BOOM
GESUNDHEIT! MATEY MINE!

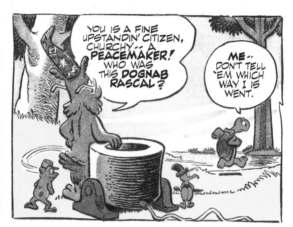

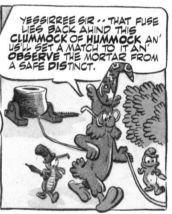

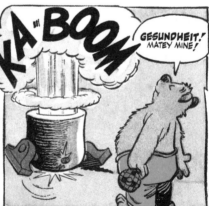

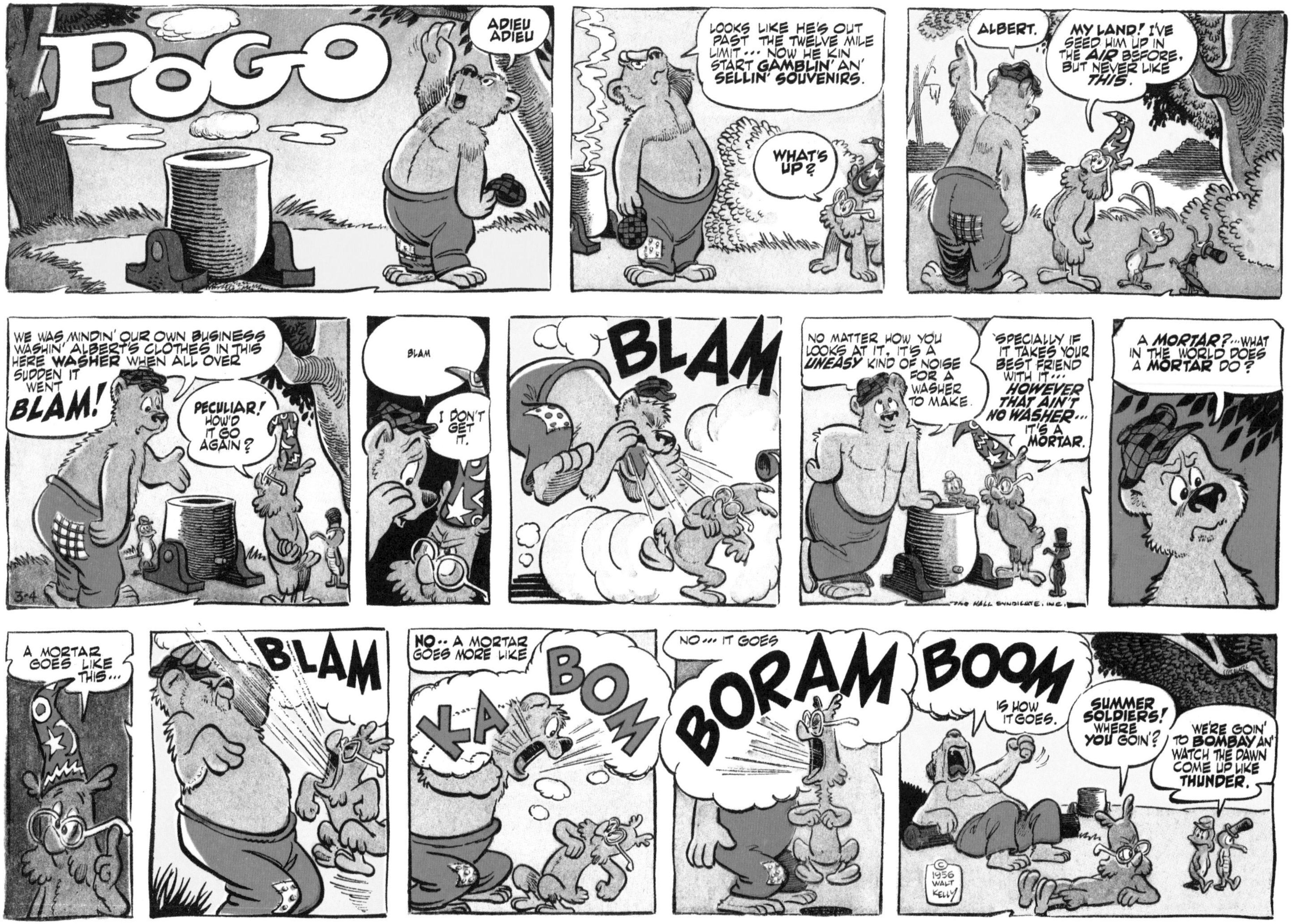
POGO
ADIEU ADIEU
LOOKS LIKE HE'S OUT PAST THE TWELVE MILE LIMIT... NOW HE KIN START GAMBLIN' AN' SELLIN' SOUVENIRS.
WHAT'S UP?
ALBERT.
MY LAND! I'VE SEED HIM UP IN THE AIR BEFORE, BUT NEVER LIKE THIS.
WE WAS MINDIN' OUR OWN BUSINESS WASHIN' ALBERT'S CLOTHES IN THIS HERE WASHER WHEN ALL OVER SUDDEN IT WENT BLAM!
PECULIAR! HOW'D IT GO AGAIN?
3-4
BLAM
I DON'T GET IT.
BLAM
NO MATTER HOW YOU LOOKS AT IT, IT'S A UNEASY KIND OF NOISE FOR A WASHER TO MAKE.
'SPECIALLY IF IT TAKES YOUR BEST FRIEND WITH IT... HOWEVER THAT AIN'T NO WASHER... IT'S A MORTAR.
A MORTAR?... WHAT IN THE WORLD DOES A MORTAR DO?
A MORTAR GOES LIKE THIS...
BLAM
NO.. A MORTAR GOES MORE LIKE
KA BOM
NO... IT GOES
BORAM
BOOM
IS HOW IT GOES.
SUMMER SOLDIERS! WHERE YOU GOIN'?
WE'RE GOIN' TO BOMBAY AN' WATCH THE DAWN COME UP LIKE THUNDER.
© 1956 WALT KELLY

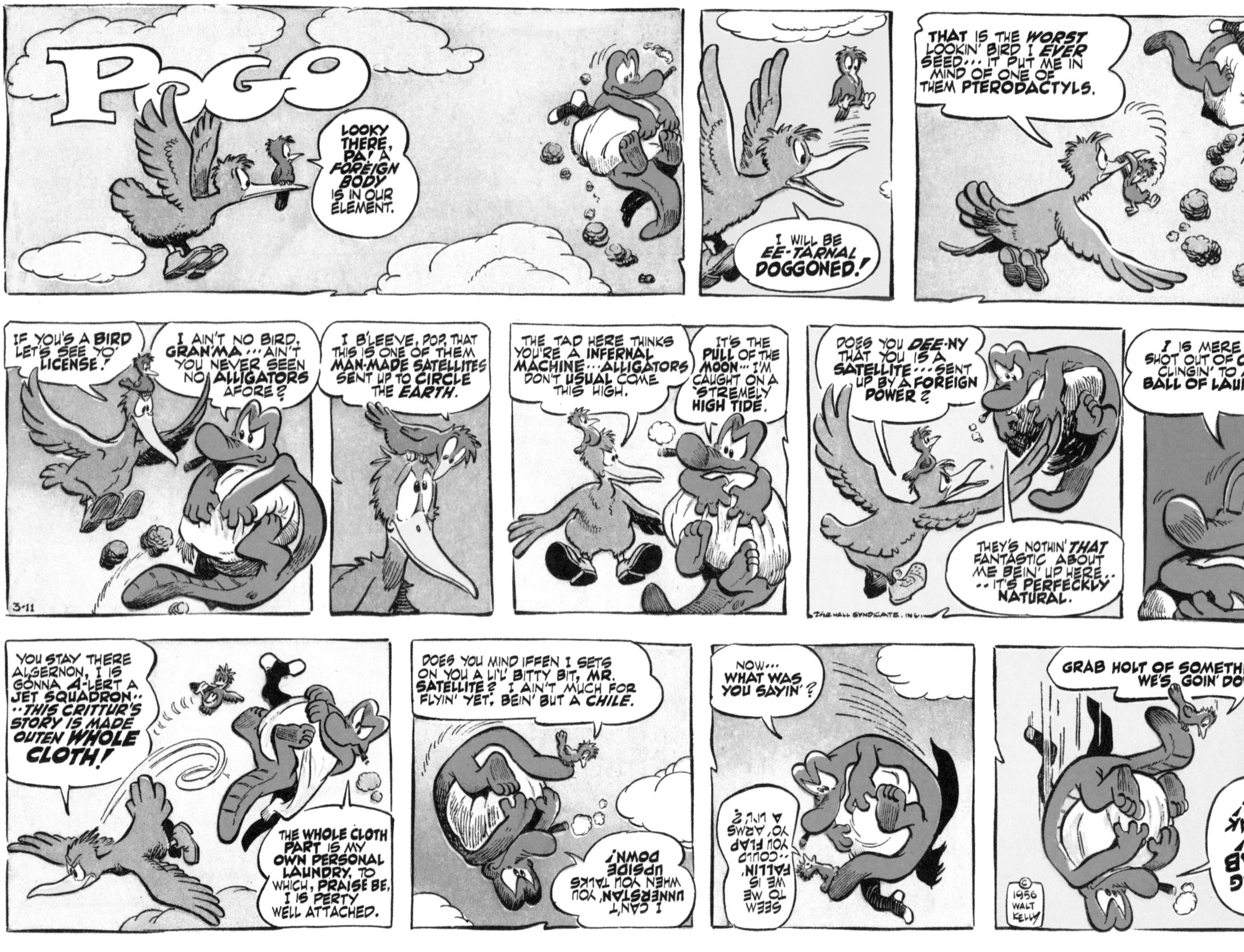
POGO
LOOKY THERE, PA! A FOREIGN BODY IS IN OUR ELEMENT.
I WILL BE EE-TARNAL DOGGONED!
THAT IS THE WORST LOOKIN' BIRD I EVER SEED... IT PUT ME IN MIND OF ONE OF THEM PTERODACTYLS.
IF YOU'S A BIRD LET'S SEE YO' LICENSE!
I AIN'T NO BIRD, GRAN'MA... AIN'T YOU NEVER SEEN NO ALLIGATORS AFORE?
3-11
I B'LEEVE, POP, THAT THIS IS ONE OF THEM MAN-MADE SATELLITES SENT UP TO CIRCLE THE EARTH.
THE TAD HERE THINKS YOU'RE A INFERNAL MACHINE... ALLIGATORS DON'T USUAL COME THIS HIGH.
IT'S THE PULL OF THE MOON... I'M CAUGHT ON A 'STREMELY HIGH TIDE.
DOES YOU DEE-NY THAT YOU IS A SATELLITE... SENT UP BY A FOREIGN POWER?
THEY'S NOTHIN' THAT FANTASTIC ABOUT ME BEIN' UP HERE... IT'S PERFECKLY NATURAL.
THE HALL SYNDICATE, INC.
I IS MERE BEEN SHOT OUT OF CANNON CLINGIN' TO A BALL OF LAUNDRY.
YOU STAY THERE ALGERNON, I IS GONNA A-LERT A JET SQUADRON... THIS CRITTUR'S STORY IS MADE OUTEN WHOLE CLOTH!
THE WHOLE CLOTH PART IS MY OWN PERSONAL LAUNDRY, TO WHICH, PRAISE BE, I IS PERTY WELL ATTACHED.
DOES YOU MIND IFFEN I SETS ON YOU A LI'L BITTY BIT, MR. SATELLITE? I AIN'T MUCH FOR FLYIN' YET, BEIN' BUT A CHILE.
I CAN'T UNNERSTAN' YOU WHEN YOU TALKS UPSIDE DOWN!
NOW... WHAT WAS YOU SAYIN'?
SEEM TO ME WE IS FALLIN'... COULD YOU FLAP YO' ARMS A LI'L?
GRAB HOLT OF SOMETHIN'! WE'S GOIN' DOWN!
DAG NAB IT! SPEAK UP!
© 1956 WALT KELLY

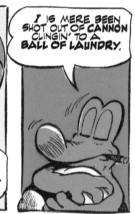

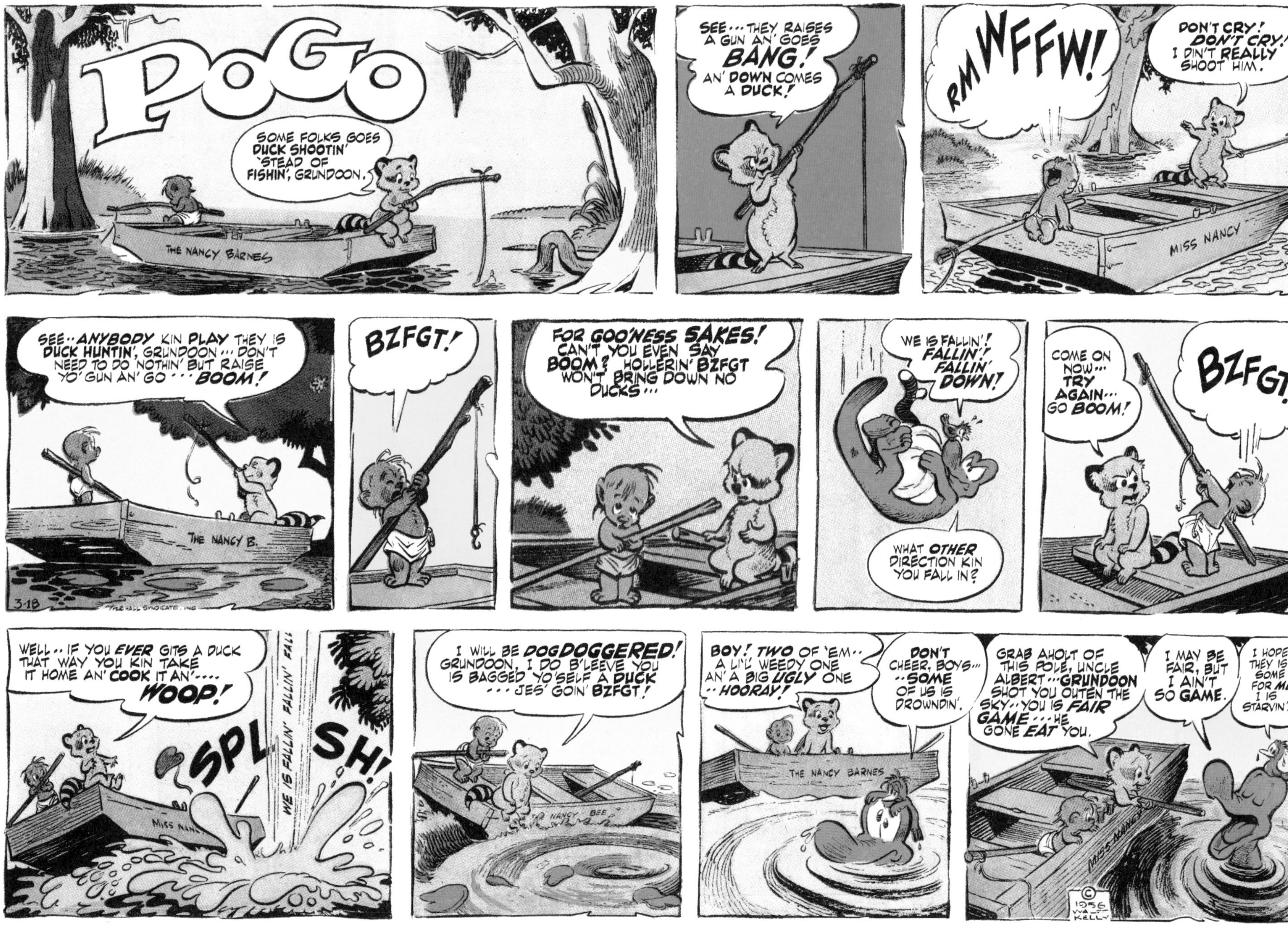
POGO
SOME FOLKS GOES DUCK SHOOTIN' 'STEAD OF FISHIN', GRUNDOON.
THE NANCY BARNES
SEE... THEY RAISES A GUN AN' GOES BANG! AN' DOWN COMES A DUCK!
RMWFFW!
DON'T CRY! DON'T CRY! I DIN'T REALLY SHOOT HIM.
MISS NANCY
SEE.. ANYBODY KIN PLAY THEY IS DUCK HUNTIN', GRUNDOON... DON'T NEED TO DO 'NOTHIN' BUT RAISE YO' GUN AN' GO ... BOOM!
THE NANCY B.
3-18
BZFGT!
FOR GOO'NESS SAKES! CAN'T YOU EVEN SAY BOOM? HOLLERIN' BZFGT WON'T BRING DOWN NO DUCKS...
WE IS FALLIN'! FALLIN'! FALLIN' DOWN!
WHAT OTHER DIRECTION KIN YOU FALL IN?
COME ON NOW... TRY AGAIN... GO BOOM!
BZFGT!
WELL.. IF YOU EVER GITS A DUCK THAT WAY YOU KIN TAKE IT HOME AN' COOK IT AN'.... WOOP!
SPLSH!
WE IS FALLIN' FALLIN' FALL
I WILL BE DOGDOGGERED! GRUNDOON, I DO B'LEEVE YOU IS BAGGED YO'SELF A DUCK ... JES' GOIN' BZFGT!
THE NANCY BEE
BOY! TWO OF 'EM.. A LI'L WEEDY ONE AN' A BIG UGLY ONE .. HOORAY!
DON'T CHEER, BOYS... ..SOME OF US IS DROWNDIN'.
THE NANCY BARNES
GRAB AHOLT OF THIS POLE, UNCLE ALBERT... GRUNDOON SHOT YOU OUTEN THE SKY.. YOU IS FAIR GAME... HE GONE EAT YOU.
I MAY BE FAIR, BUT I AIN'T SO GAME.
I HOPE THEY IS SOME FOR ME I IS STARVIN'.
©1956 WALT KELLY

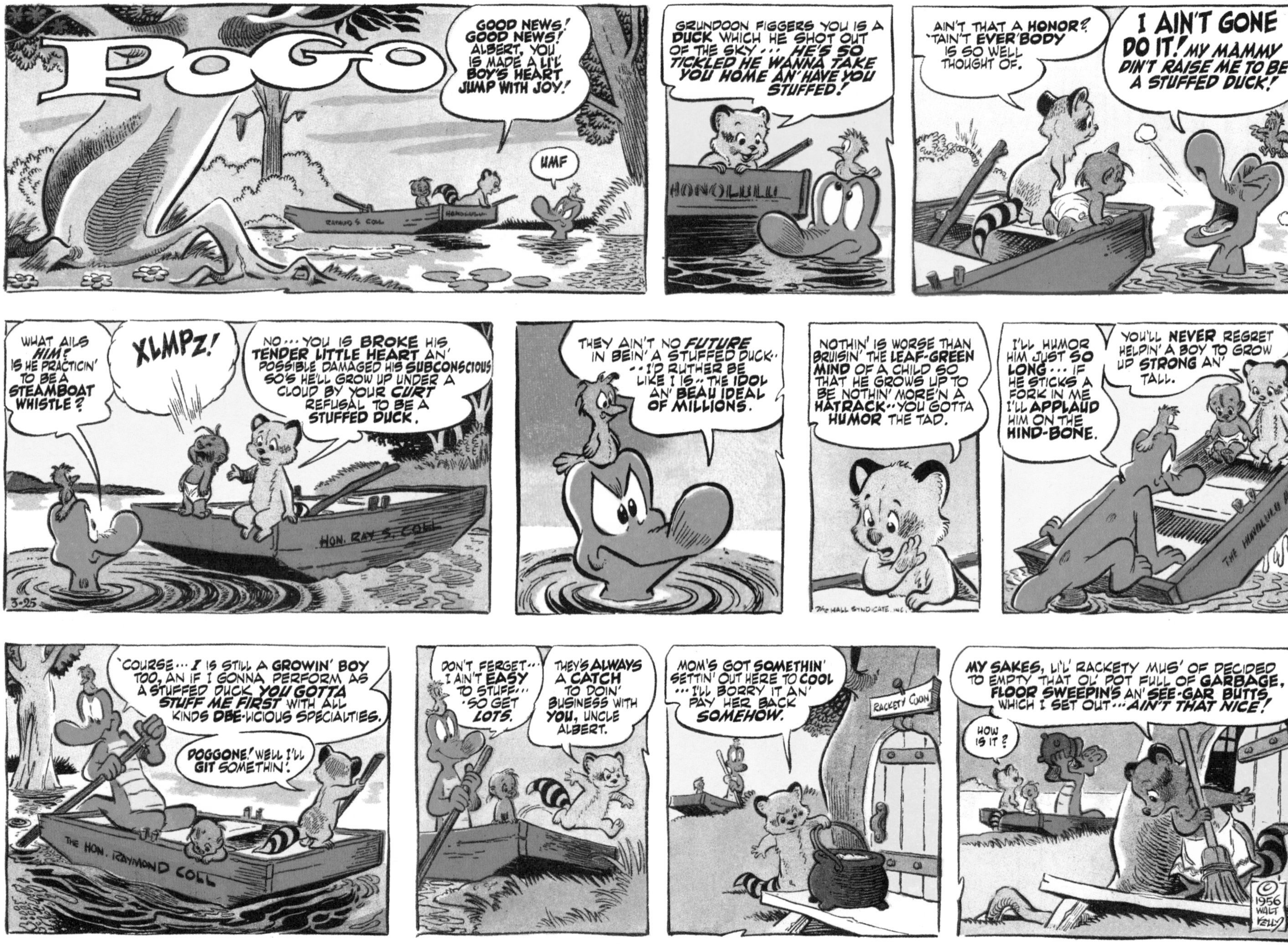
POGO
GOOD NEWS! GOOD NEWS! ALBERT, YOU IS MADE A LI'L BOY'S HEART JUMP WITH JOY!
UMF
GRUNDOON FIGGERS YOU IS A DUCK WHICH HE SHOT OUT OF THE SKY... HE'S SO TICKLED HE WANNA TAKE YOU HOME AN' HAVE YOU STUFFED!
HONOLULU
AIN'T THAT A HONOR? 'TAIN'T EVER'BODY IS SO WELL THOUGHT OF.
I AIN'T GONE DO IT! MY MAMMY DIN'T RAISE ME TO BE A STUFFED DUCK!
WHAT AILS HIM? IS HE PRACTICIN' TO BE A STEAMBOAT WHISTLE?
XLMPZ!
NO... YOU IS BROKE HIS TENDER LITTLE HEART AN' POSSIBLE DAMAGED HIS SUBCONSCIOUS SO'S HE'LL GROW UP UNDER A CLOUD BY YOUR CURT REFUSAL TO BE A STUFFED DUCK.
HON. RAY S. COLL
3-25
THEY AIN'T NO FUTURE IN BEIN' A STUFFED DUCK.. ..I'D RUTHER BE LIKE I IS.. THE IDOL AN' BEAU IDEAL OF MILLIONS.
NOTHIN' IS WORSE THAN BRUISIN' THE LEAF-GREEN MIND OF A CHILD SO THAT HE GROWS UP TO BE NOTHIN' MORE'N A HATRACK.. YOU GOTTA HUMOR THE TAD.
The Hall Syndicate, Inc.
I'LL HUMOR HIM JUST SO LONG... IF HE STICKS A FORK IN ME I'LL APPLAUD HIM ON THE HIND-BONE.
YOU'LL NEVER REGRET HELPIN' A BOY TO GROW UP STRONG AN' TALL.
'COURSE... I IS STILL A GROWIN' BOY TOO, AN IF I GONNA PERFORM AS A STUFFED DUCK YOU GOTTA STUFF ME FIRST WITH ALL KINDS DBE-LICIOUS SPECIALTIES.
DOGGONE! WELL I'LL GIT SOMETHIN'.
THE HON. RAYMOND COLL
DON'T FERGET... I AIN'T EASY TO STUFF... 'SO GET LOTS.
THEY'S ALWAYS A CATCH TO DOIN' BUSINESS WITH YOU, UNCLE ALBERT.
MOM'S GOT SOMETHIN' SETTIN' OUT HERE TO COOL ... I'LL BORRY IT AN' PAY HER BACK SOMEHOW.
RACKETY COON
MY SAKES, LI'L RACKETY MUS' OF DECIDED TO EMPTY THAT OL' POT FULL OF GARBAGE, FLOOR SWEEPIN'S AN' SEE-GAR BUTTS WHICH I SET OUT... AIN'T THAT NICE!
HOW IS IT?
© 1956 WALT KELLY

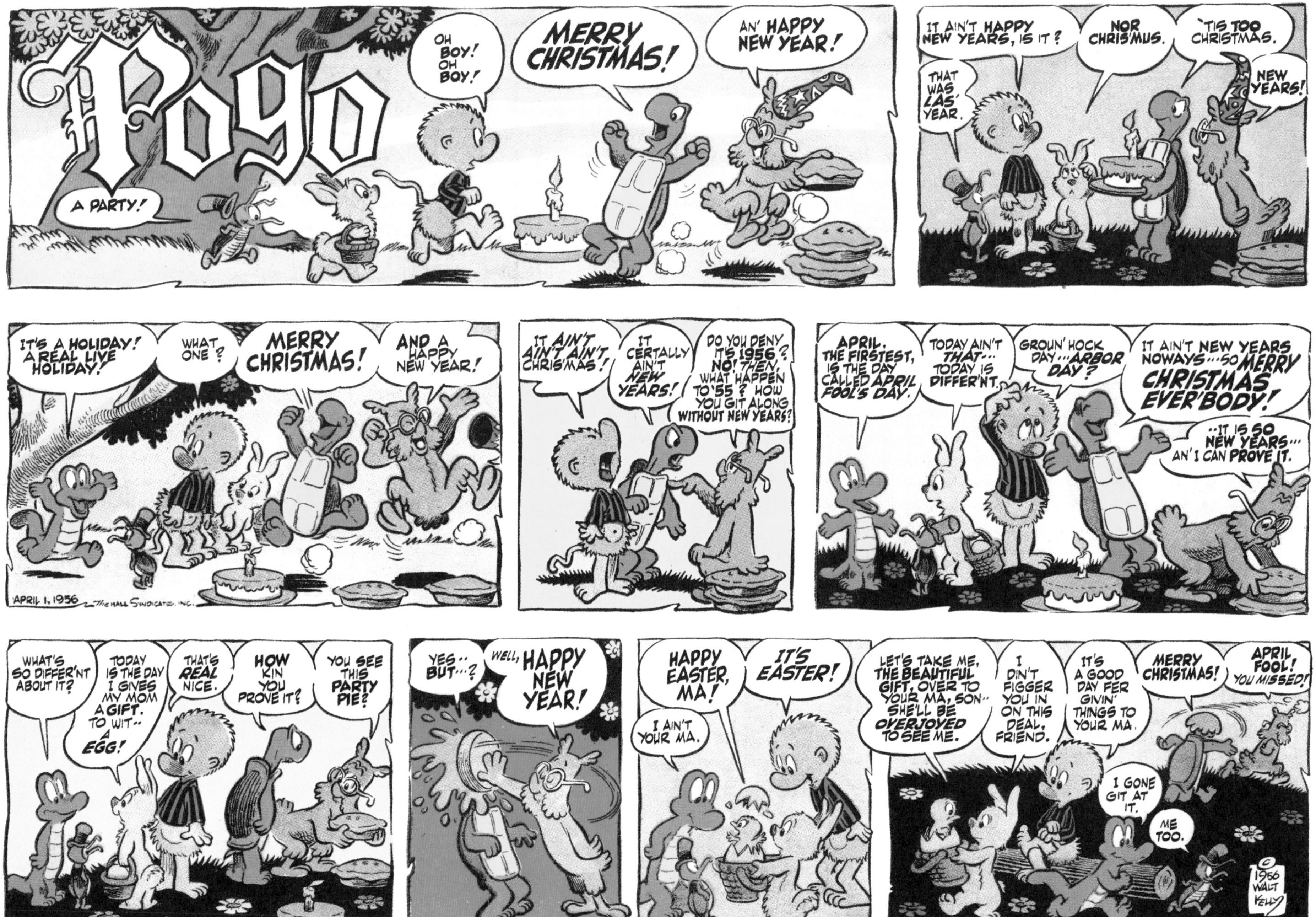
Pogo
A PARTY!
OH BOY! OH BOY!
MERRY CHRISTMAS!
AN' HAPPY NEW YEAR!
IT AIN'T HAPPY NEW YEARS, IS IT?
THAT WAS LAS' YEAR.
NOR CHRIS'MUS.
'TIS TOO CHRISTMAS.
NEW YEARS!
IT'S A HOLIDAY! A REAL LIVE HOLIDAY!
WHAT ONE?
MERRY CHRISTMAS!
AND A HAPPY NEW YEAR!
APRIL 1, 1956 The HALL SYNDICATE, INC.
IT AIN'T AIN'T AIN'T CHRIS'MAS!
IT CERTALLY AIN'T NEW YEARS!
DO YOU DENY IT'S 1956? NO! THEN, WHAT HAPPEN TO '55? HOW YOU GIT ALONG WITHOUT NEW YEARS?
APRIL, THE FIRSTEST, IS THE DAY CALLED APRIL FOOL'S DAY.
TODAY AIN'T THAT... TODAY IS DIFFER'NT.
GROUN' HOCK DAY... ARBOR DAY?
IT AIN'T NEW YEARS NOWAYS... SO MERRY CHRISTMAS EVER'BODY!
..IT IS SO NEW YEARS... AN' I CAN PROVE IT.
WHAT'S SO DIFFER'NT ABOUT IT?
TODAY IS THE DAY I GIVES MY MOM A GIFT. TO WIT... A EGG!
THAT'S REAL NICE.
HOW KIN YOU PROVE IT?
YOU SEE THIS PARTY PIE?
YES.. BUT..?
WELL, HAPPY NEW YEAR!
HAPPY EASTER, MA!
I AIN'T YOUR MA.
IT'S EASTER!
LET'S TAKE ME, THE BEAUTIFUL GIFT, OVER TO YOUR MA, SON.. SHE'LL BE OVERJOYED TO SEE ME.
I DIN'T FIGGER YOU IN ON THIS DEAL, FRIEND.
IT'S A GOOD DAY FER GIVIN' THINGS TO YOUR MA.
MERRY CHRISTMAS!
APRIL FOOL! YOU MISSED!
I GONE GIT AT IT.
ME TOO.
© 1956 WALT KELLY

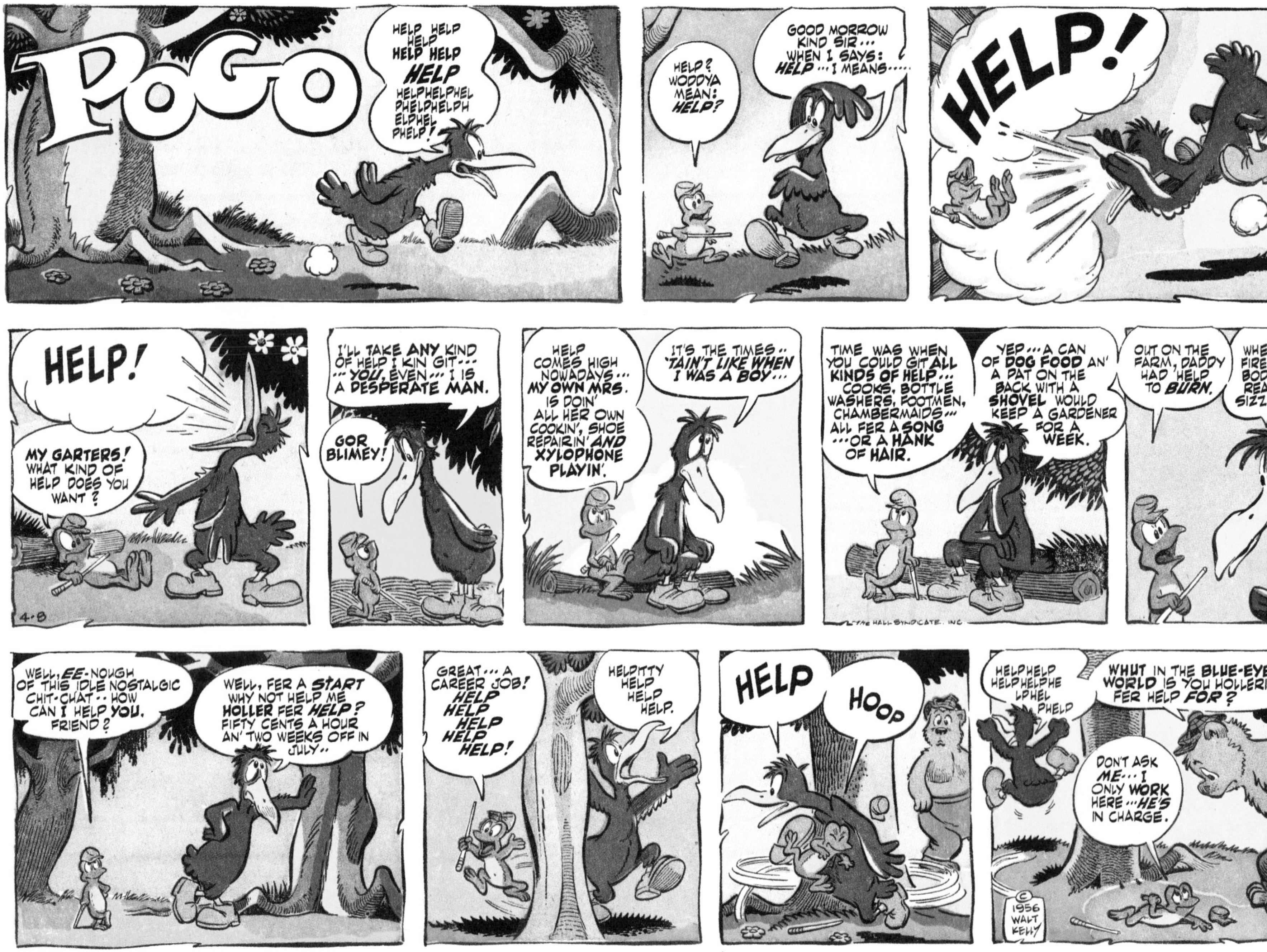
POGO
HELP HELP HELP HELP HELP HELP HELPHELPHEL PHELPHELPH ELPHEL PHELP!
HELP? WODDYA MEAN: HELP?
GOOD MORROW KIND SIR... WHEN I SAYS: HELP ... I MEANS.....
HELP!
HELP!
MY GARTERS! WHAT KIND OF HELP DOES YOU WANT?
4-8
I'LL TAKE ANY KIND OF HELP I KIN GIT--- ... YOU, EVEN ... I IS A DESPERATE MAN.
GOR BLIMEY!
HELP COMES HIGH NOWADAYS... MY OWN MRS. IS DOIN' ALL HER OWN COOKIN', SHOE REPAIRIN' AND XYLOPHONE PLAYIN'.
IT'S THE TIMES.. 'TAIN'T LIKE WHEN I WAS A BOY...
TIME WAS WHEN YOU COULD GIT ALL KINDS OF HELP... COOKS, BOTTLE WASHERS, FOOTMEN, CHAMBERMAIDS... ALL FER A SONG ...OR A HANK OF HAIR.
YEP... A CAN OF DOG FOOD AN' A PAT ON THE BACK WITH A SHOVEL WOULD KEEP A GARDENER FOR A WEEK.
OUT ON THE FARM, DADDY HAD 'HELP' TO BURN.
WHEN HE FIRED ANY-BODY THEY REALLY SIZZLED.
WELL, EE-NOUGH OF THIS IDLE NOSTALGIC CHIT-CHAT.. HOW CAN I HELP YOU, FRIEND?
WELL, FER A START WHY NOT HELP ME HOLLER FER HELP? FIFTY CENTS A HOUR AN' TWO WEEKS OFF IN JULY..
GREAT... A CAREER JOB! HELP HELP HELP HELP HELP!
HELPITTY HELP HELP HELP.
HELP
HOOP
HELPHELP HELPHELPHE LPHEL PHELP
WHUT IN THE BLUE-EYED WORLD IS YOU HOLLERIN' FER HELP FOR?
DON'T ASK ME... I ONLY WORK HERE... HE'S IN CHARGE.
© 1956 WALT KELLY

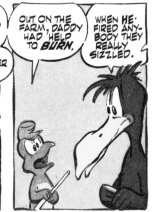

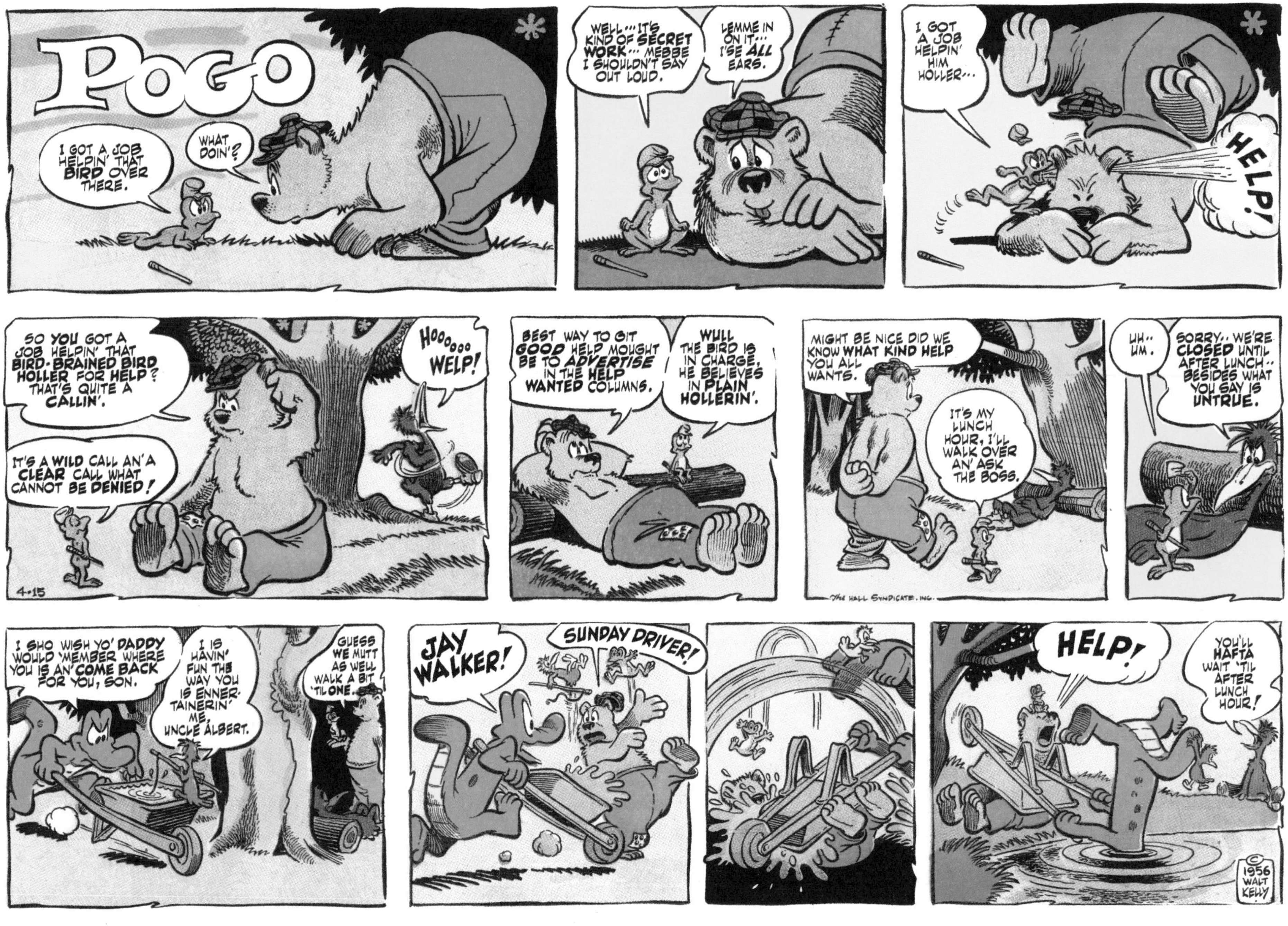
POGO
I GOT A JOB HELPIN' THAT BIRD OVER THERE.
WHAT DOIN'?
WELL... IT'S KIND OF SECRET WORK... MEBBE I SHOULDN'T SAY OUT LOUD.
LEMME IN ON IT... I'SE ALL EARS.
I GOT A JOB HELPIN' HIM HOLLER...
HELP!
SO YOU GOT A JOB HELPIN' THAT BIRD-BRAINED BIRD HOLLER FOR HELP? THAT'S QUITE A CALLIN'.
HOOOOOOO WELP!
IT'S A WILD CALL AN' A CLEAR CALL WHAT CANNOT BE DENIED!
4-15
BEST WAY TO GIT GOOD HELP MOUGHT BE TO ADVERTISE IN THE HELP WANTED COLUMNS.
WULL THE BIRD IS IN CHARGE, HE BELIEVES IN PLAIN HOLLERIN'.
MIGHT BE NICE DID WE KNOW WHAT KIND HELP YOU ALL WANTS.
IT'S MY LUNCH HOUR, I'LL WALK OVER AN' ASK THE BOSS.
THE HALL SYNDICATE, INC.
UH.. UM.
SORRY.. WE'RE CLOSED UNTIL AFTER LUNCH.. BESIDES WHAT YOU SAY IS UNTRUE.
I SHO WISH YO' DADDY WOULD 'MEMBER WHERE YOU IS AN' COME BACK FOR YOU, SON.
I IS HAVIN' FUN THE WAY YOU IS ENNER-TAINERIN' ME, UNCLE ALBERT.
GUESS WE MUTT AS WELL WALK A BIT 'TIL ONE.
JAY WALKER!
SUNDAY DRIVER!
HELP!
YOU'LL HAFTA WAIT 'TIL AFTER LUNCH HOUR!
© 1956 WALT KELLY

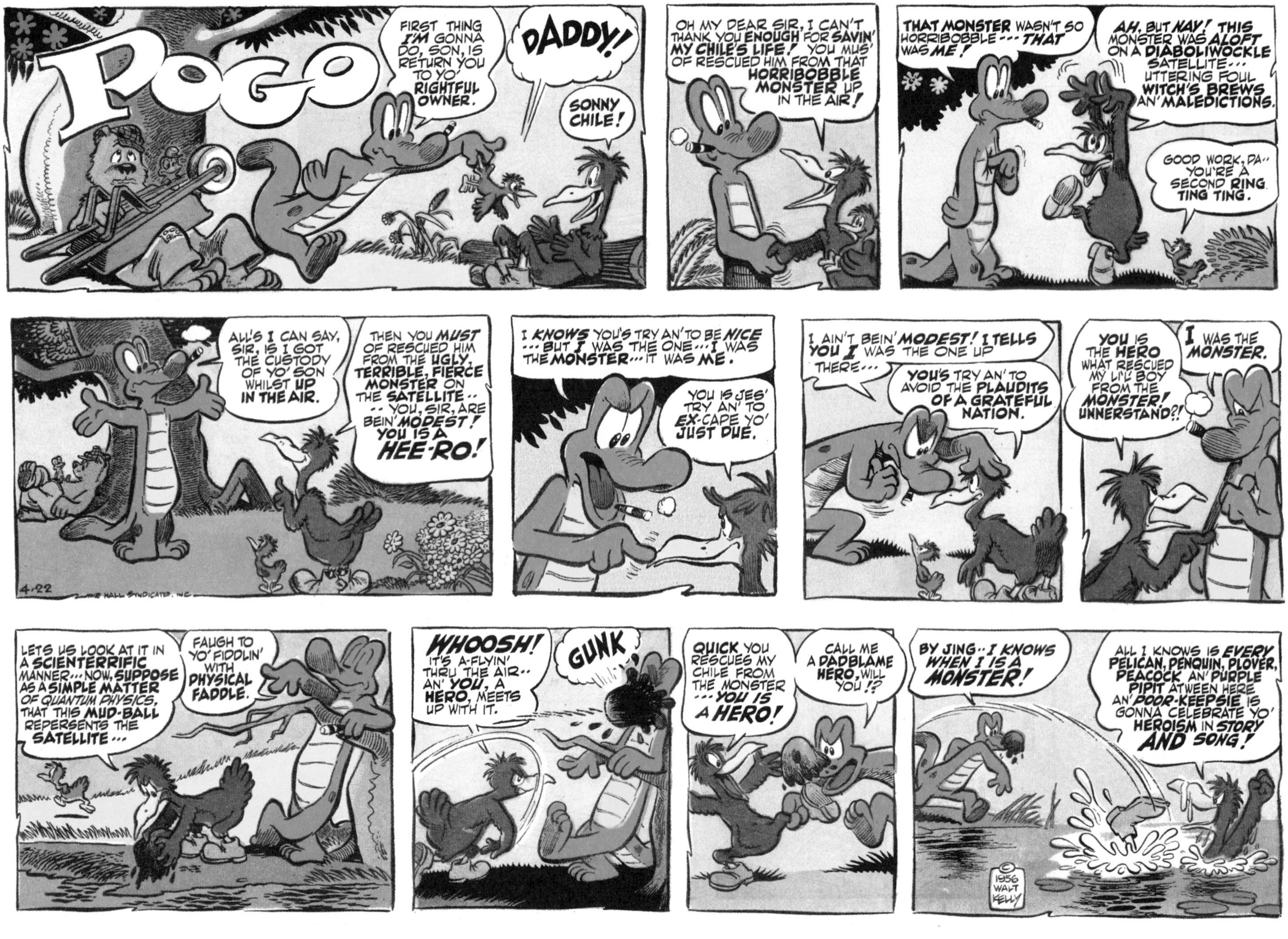
POGO
FIRST THING I'M GONNA DO, SON, IS RETURN YOU TO YO' RIGHTFUL OWNER.
DADDY!
SONNY CHILE!
OH MY DEAR SIR, I CAN'T THANK YOU ENOUGH FOR SAVIN' MY CHILE'S LIFE! YOU MUS' OF RESCUED HIM FROM THAT HORRIBOBBLE MONSTER UP IN THE AIR!
THAT MONSTER WASN'T SO HORRIBOBBLE --- THAT WAS ME!
AH, BUT NAY! THIS MONSTER WAS ALOFT ON A DIABOLIWOCKLE SATELLITE... UTTERING FOUL WITCH'S BREWS AN' MALEDICTIONS.
GOOD WORK, PA.. YOU'RE A SECOND RING TING TING.
ALL'S I CAN SAY, SIR, IS I GOT THE CUSTODY OF YO' SON WHILST UP IN THE AIR.
THEN YOU MUST OF RESCUED HIM FROM THE UGLY, TERRIBLE, FIERCE MONSTER ON THE SATELLITE.. .. YOU, SIR, ARE BEIN' MODEST! YOU IS A HEE-RO!
4-22
THE HALL SYNDICATE, INC.
I KNOWS YOU'S TRY AN' TO BE NICE --- BUT I WAS THE ONE... I WAS THE MONSTER... IT WAS ME.
YOU IS JES' TRY AN' TO EX-CAPE YO' JUST DUE.
I AIN'T BEIN' MODEST! I TELLS YOU I WAS THE ONE UP THERE...
YOU'S TRY AN' TO AVOID THE PLAUDITS OF A GRATEFUL NATION.
YOU IS THE HERO WHAT RESCUED MY LI'L BOY FROM THE MONSTER! UNNERSTAND?!
I WAS THE MONSTER.
LETS US LOOK AT IT IN A SCIENTERRIFIC MANNER... NOW, SUPPOSE AS A SIMPLE MATTER OF QUANTUM PHYSICS, THAT THIS MUD-BALL REPERSENTS THE SATELLITE...
FAUGH TO YO' FIDDLIN' WITH PHYSICAL FADDLE.
WHOOSH! IT'S A-FLYIN' THRU THE AIR.. AN' YOU, A HERO, MEETS UP WITH IT.
GUNK
QUICK YOU RESCUES MY CHILE FROM THE MONSTER --- YOU IS A HERO!
CALL ME A DADBLAME HERO, WILL YOU !?
BY JING.. I KNOWS WHEN I IS A MONSTER!
ALL I KNOWS IS EVERY PELICAN, PENQUIN, PLOVER, PEACOCK AN' PURPLE PIPIT ATWEEN HERE AN' POOR-KEEPSIE IS GONNA CELEBRATE YO' HEROISM IN STORY AND SONG!
© 1956 WALT KELLY

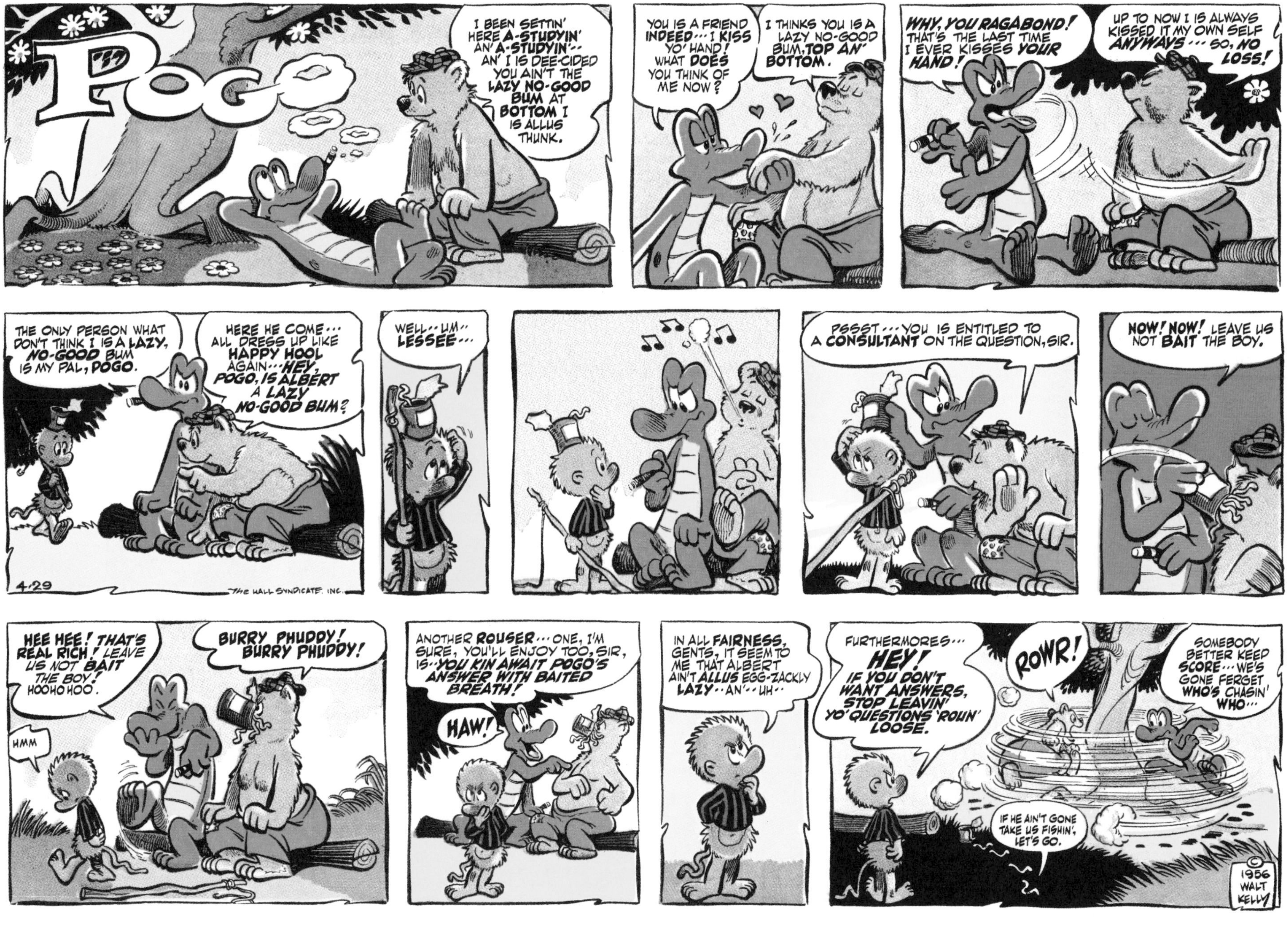
POGO
I BEEN SETTIN' HERE A-STUDYIN' AN' A-STUDYIN'-- AN' I IS DEE-CIDED YOU AIN'T THE LAZY NO-GOOD BUM AT BOTTOM I IS ALLUS THUNK.
YOU IS A FRIEND INDEED... I KISS YO' HAND! WHAT DOES YOU THINK OF ME NOW?
I THINKS YOU IS A LAZY NO-GOOD BUM, TOP AN' BOTTOM.
WHY, YOU RAGABOND! THAT'S THE LAST TIME I EVER KISSES YOUR HAND!
UP TO NOW I IS ALWAYS KISSED IT MY OWN SELF ANYWAYS... SO, NO LOSS!
THE ONLY PERSON WHAT DON'T THINK I IS A LAZY, NO-GOOD BUM IS MY PAL, POGO.
HERE HE COME... ALL DRESS UP LIKE HAPPY HOOL AGAIN... HEY, POGO, IS ALBERT A LAZY NO-GOOD BUM?
4·29
THE HALL SYNDICATE, INC.
WELL.. UM.. LESSEE...
PSSST... YOU IS ENTITLED TO A CONSULTANT ON THE QUESTION, SIR.
NOW! NOW! LEAVE US NOT BAIT THE BOY.
HEE HEE! THAT'S REAL RICH! LEAVE US NOT BAIT THE BOY! HOOHO HOO.
BURRY PHUDDY! BURRY PHUDDY!
HMM
ANOTHER ROUSER... ONE, I'M SURE, YOU'LL ENJOY TOO, SIR, IS.. YOU KIN AWAIT POGO'S ANSWER WITH BAITED BREATH!
HAW!
IN ALL FAIRNESS, GENTS, IT SEEM TO ME THAT ALBERT AIN'T ALLUS EGG-ZACKLY LAZY.. AN'.. UH..
FURTHERMORES... HEY! IF YOU DON'T WANT ANSWERS, STOP LEAVIN' YO' QUESTIONS 'ROUN' LOOSE.
ROWR!
SOMEBODY BETTER KEEP SCORE... WE'S GONE FERGET WHO'S CHASIN' WHO...
IF HE AIN'T GONE TAKE US FISHIN', LET'S GO.
© 1956 WALT KELLY

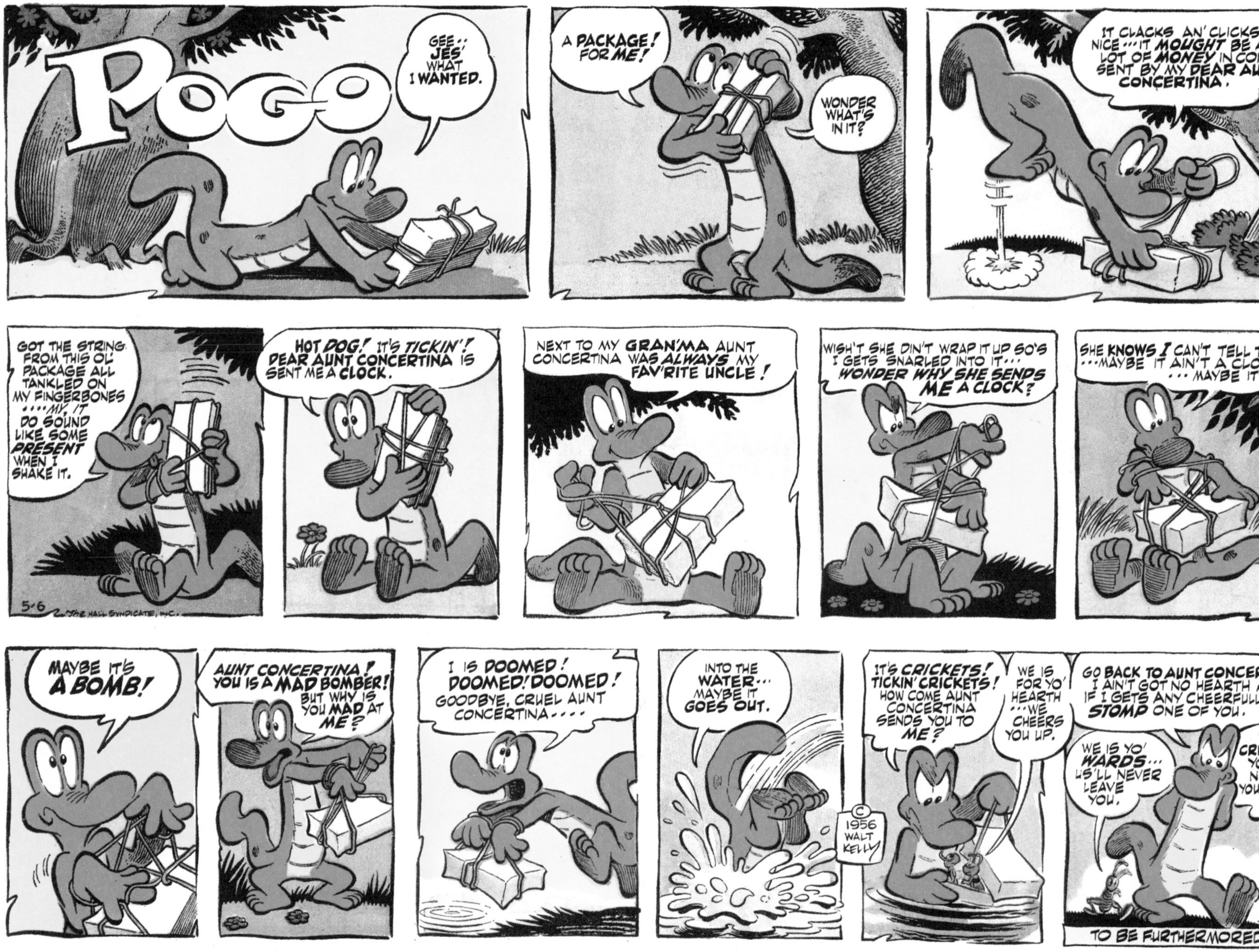
POGO
GEE.. JES' WHAT I WANTED.
A PACKAGE! FOR ME!
WONDER WHAT'S IN IT?
IT CLACKS AN' CLICKS NICE ··· IT MOUGHT BE A LOT OF MONEY IN COINS SENT BY MY DEAR AUNT CONCERTINA.
GOT THE STRING FROM THIS OL' PACKAGE ALL TANKLED ON MY FINGERBONES ···· MY, IT DO SOUND LIKE SOME PRESENT WHEN I SHAKE IT.
5-6
HOT DOG! IT'S TICKIN'! DEAR AUNT CONCERTINA IS SENT ME A CLOCK.
NEXT TO MY GRAN'MA AUNT CONCERTINA WAS ALWAYS MY FAV'RITE UNCLE!
WISH'T SHE DIN'T WRAP IT UP SO'S I GETS SNARLED INTO IT··· WONDER WHY SHE SENDS ME A CLOCK?
SHE KNOWS I CAN'T TELL TIME ··· MAYBE IT AIN'T A CLOCK ··· ··· MAYBE IT'S··
MAYBE IT'S A BOMB!
AUNT CONCERTINA! YOU IS A MAD BOMBER! BUT WHY IS YOU MAD AT ME?
I IS DOOMED! DOOMED! DOOMED! GOODBYE, CRUEL AUNT CONCERTINA····
INTO THE WATER... MAYBE IT GOES OUT.
© 1956 WALT KELLY
IT'S CRICKETS! TICKIN' CRICKETS! HOW COME AUNT CONCERTINA SENDS YOU TO ME?
WE IS FOR YO' HEARTH ··· WE CHEERS YOU UP.
GO BACK TO AUNT CONCERTINA.. I AIN'T GOT NO HEARTH AN' IF I GETS ANY CHEERFULLER, I'LL STOMP ONE OF YOU.
WE IS YO' WARDS... US'LL NEVER LEAVE YOU.
WE'LL CRICK AT YOU ALL NIGHT··· YOU'LL LOVE IT.
TO BE FURTHERMORED ---

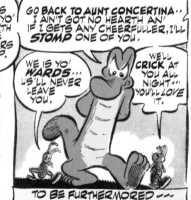

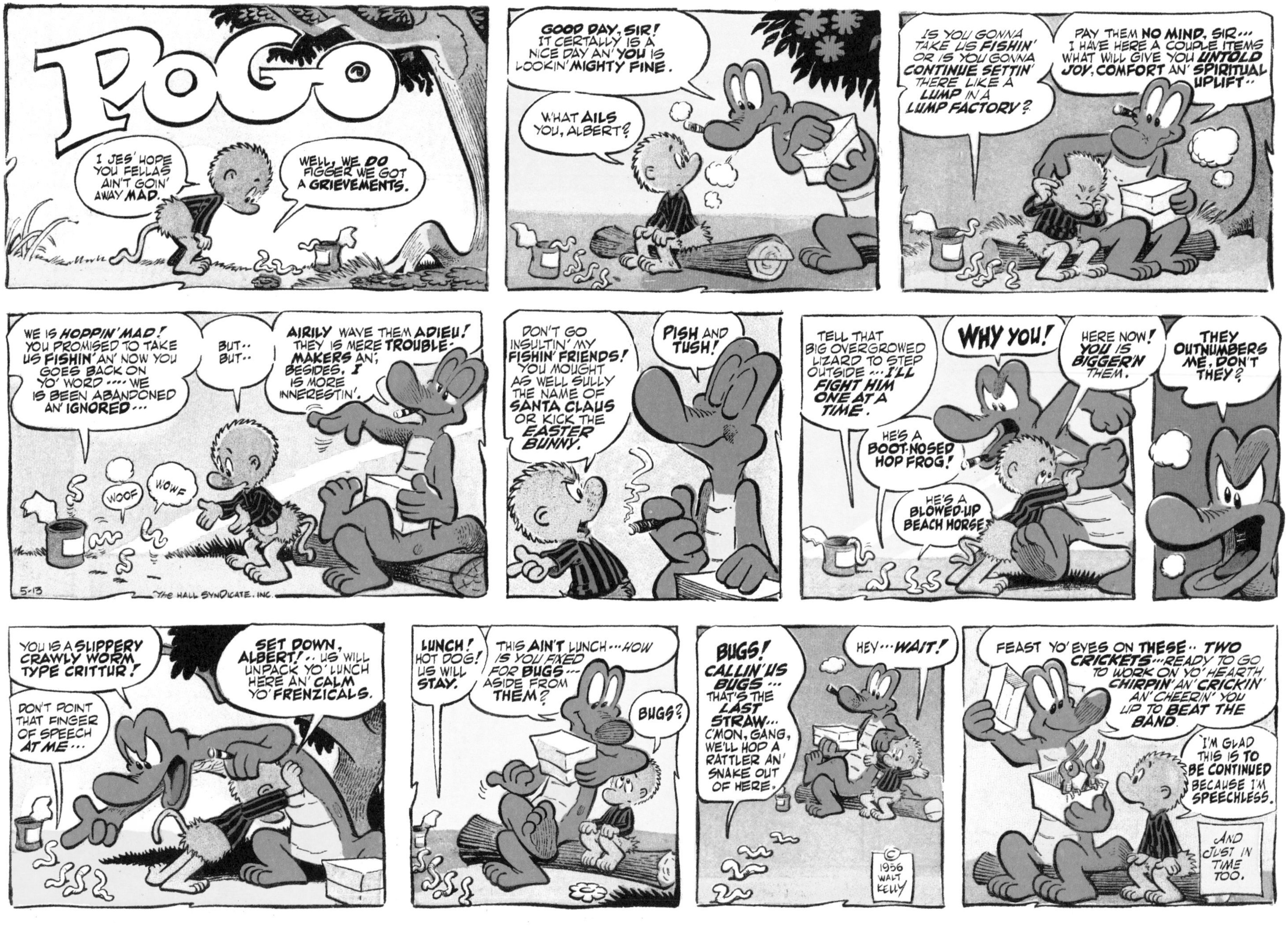
POGO
I JES' HOPE YOU FELLAS AIN'T GOIN' AWAY MAD.
WELL, WE DO FIGGER WE GOT A GRIEVEMENTS.
GOOD DAY, SIR! IT CERTAILY IS A NICE DAY AN' YOU IS LOOKIN' MIGHTY FINE.
WHAT AILS YOU, ALBERT?
IS YOU GONNA TAKE US FISHIN' OR IS YOU GONNA CONTINUE SETTIN' THERE LIKE A LUMP IN A LUMP FACTORY?
PAY THEM NO MIND, SIR... I HAVE HERE A COUPLE ITEMS WHAT WILL GIVE YOU UNTOLD JOY, COMFORT AN' SPIRITUAL UPLIFT..
WE IS HOPPIN' MAD! YOU PROMISED TO TAKE US FISHIN' AN' NOW YOU GOES BACK ON YO' WORD .... WE IS BEEN ABANDONED AN' IGNORED...
BUT.. BUT..
AIRILY WAVE THEM ADIEU! THEY IS MERE TROUBLE-MAKERS AN; BESIDES, I IS MORE INNERESTIN'.
WOOF
WOWF
5-13
THE HALL SYNDICATE, INC.
DON'T GO INSULTIN' MY FISHIN' FRIENDS! YOU MOUGHT AS WELL SULLY THE NAME OF SANTA CLAUS OR KICK THE EASTER BUNNY.
PISH AND TUSH!
TELL THAT BIG OVERGROWED LIZARD TO STEP OUTSIDE ... I'LL FIGHT HIM ONE AT A TIME.
WHY YOU!
HERE NOW! YOU IS BIGGER'N THEM.
HE'S A BOOT-NOSED HOP FROG!
HE'S A BLOWED-UP BEACH HORSE
THEY OUTNUMBERS ME, DON'T THEY?
YOU IS A SLIPPERY CRAWLY WORM TYPE CRITTUR!
SET DOWN, ALBERT! .. US WILL UNPACK YO' LUNCH HERE AN' CALM YO' FRENZICALS.
DON'T POINT THAT FINGER OF SPEECH AT ME...
LUNCH! HOT DOG! US WILL STAY.
THIS AIN'T LUNCH... HOW IS YOU FIXED FOR BUGS... ASIDE FROM THEM?
BUGS?
BUGS! CALLIN' US BUGS... THAT'S THE LAST STRAW... C'MON, GANG, WE'LL HOP A RATTLER AN' SNAKE OUT OF HERE.
HEY... WAIT!
© 1956 WALT KELLY
FEAST YO' EYES ON THESE.. TWO CRICKETS... READY TO GO TO WORK ON YO' HEARTH CHIRPIN' AN' CRICKIN' AN' CHEERIN' YOU UP TO BEAT THE BAND.
I'M GLAD THIS IS TO BE CONTINUED BECAUSE I'M SPEECHLESS.
AND JUST IN TIME TOO.

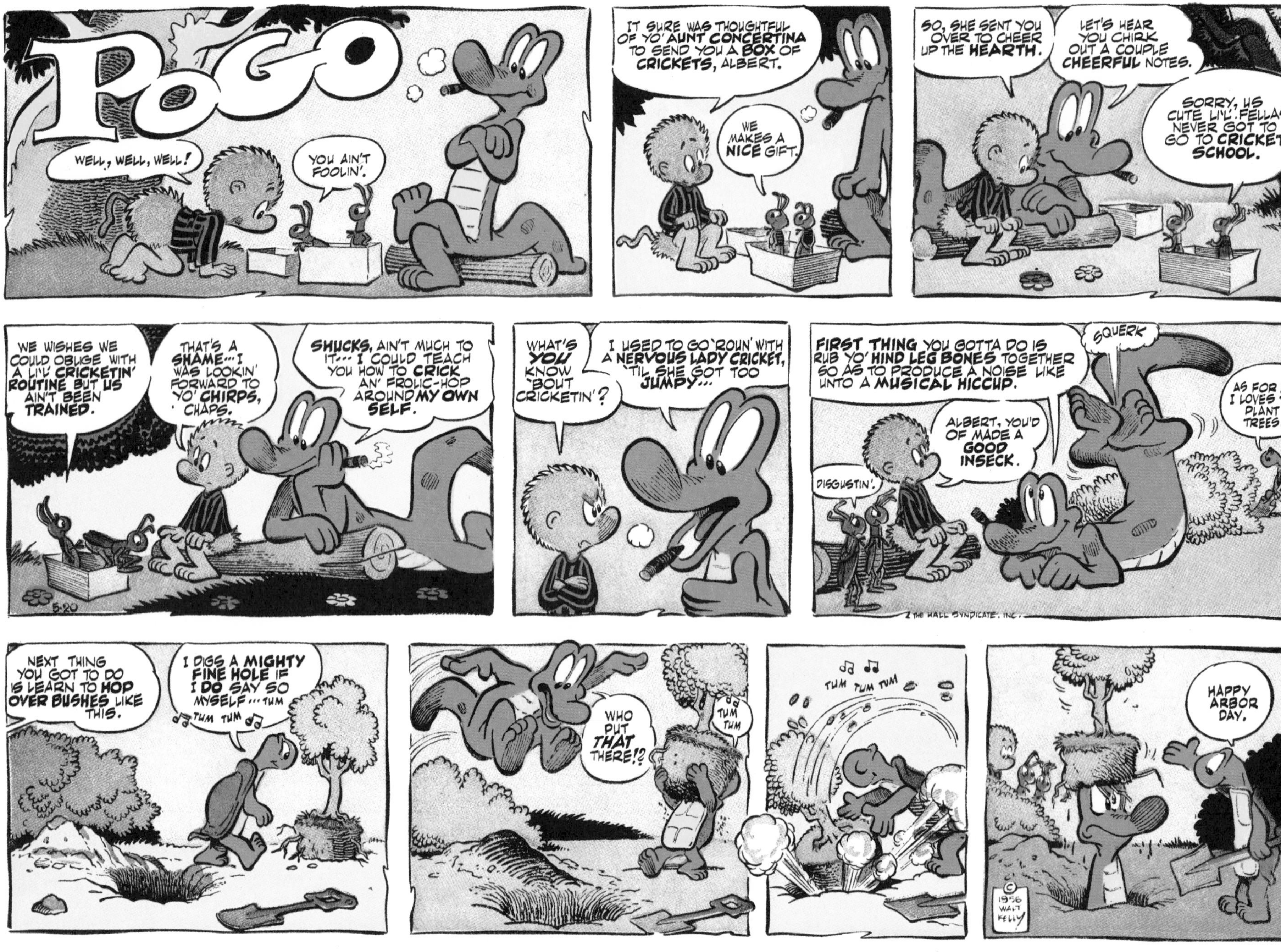
POGO
WELL, WELL, WELL!
YOU AIN'T FOOLIN'.
IT SURE WAS THOUGHTFUL OF YO' AUNT CONCERTINA TO SEND YOU A BOX OF CRICKETS, ALBERT.
WE MAKES A NICE GIFT.
SO, SHE SENT YOU OVER TO CHEER UP THE HEARTH.
LET'S HEAR YOU CHIRK OUT A COUPLE CHEERFUL NOTES.
SORRY, US CUTE LI'L' FELLAS NEVER GOT TO GO TO CRICKET SCHOOL.
WE WISHES WE COULD OBLIGE WITH A LI'L' CRICKETIN' ROUTINE BUT US AIN'T BEEN TRAINED.
THAT'S A SHAME... I WAS LOOKIN' FORWARD TO YO' CHIRPS, CHAPS.
SHUCKS, AIN'T MUCH TO IT... I COULD TEACH YOU HOW TO CRICK AN' FROLIC-HOP AROUND MY OWN SELF.
5-20
WHAT'S YOU KNOW 'BOUT CRICKETIN'?
I USED TO GO 'ROUN' WITH A NERVOUS LADY CRICKET, 'TIL SHE GOT TOO JUMPY...
FIRST THING YOU GOTTA DO IS RUB YO' HIND LEG BONES TOGETHER SO AS TO PRODUCE A NOISE LIKE UNTO A MUSICAL HICCUP.
SQUERK
AS FOR ME I LOVES TO PLANT TREES.
ALBERT, YOU'D OF MADE A GOOD INSECK.
DISGUSTIN'.
© THE HALL SYNDICATE, INC.
NEXT THING YOU GOT TO DO IS LEARN TO HOP OVER BUSHES LIKE THIS.
I DIGS A MIGHTY FINE HOLE IF I DO SAY SO MYSELF... TUM TUM TUM
WHO PUT THAT THERE!?
TUM TUM
TUM TUM TUM
HAPPY ARBOR DAY.
© 1956 WALT KELLY

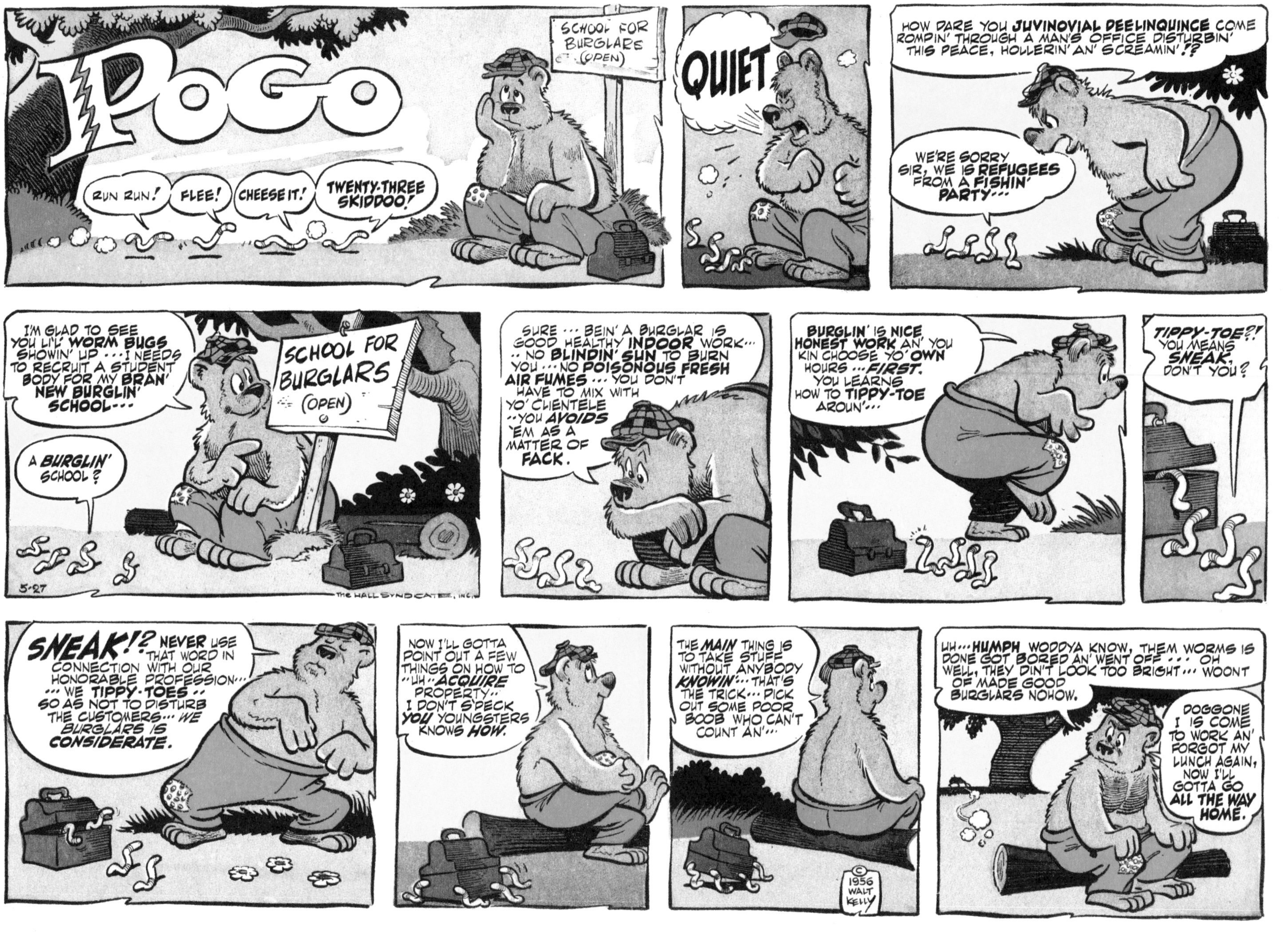
POGO
SCHOOL FOR BURGLARS (OPEN)
RUN RUN!
FLEE!
CHEESE IT!
TWENTY-THREE SKIDDOO!
QUIET
HOW DARE YOU JUVINOVIAL DEELINQUINCE COME ROMPIN' THROUGH A MAN'S OFFICE DISTURBIN' THIS PEACE, HOLLERIN' AN' SCREAMIN'!?
WE'RE SORRY SIR, WE IS REFUGEES FROM A FISHIN' PARTY...
I'M GLAD TO SEE YOU LI'L' WORM BUGS SHOWIN' UP... I NEEDS TO RECRUIT A STUDENT BODY FOR MY BRAN' NEW BURGLIN' SCHOOL...
SCHOOL FOR BURGLARS (OPEN)
A BURGLIN' SCHOOL?
5-27
THE HALL SYNDICATE, INC.
SURE... BEIN' A BURGLAR IS GOOD HEALTHY INDOOR WORK... NO BLINDIN' SUN TO BURN YOU... NO POISONOUS FRESH AIR FUMES... YOU DON'T HAVE TO MIX WITH YO' CLIENTELE... YOU AVOIDS 'EM AS A MATTER OF FACK.
BURGLIN' IS NICE HONEST WORK AN' YOU KIN CHOOSE YO' OWN HOURS... FIRST. YOU LEARNS HOW TO TIPPY-TOE AROUN'...
TIPPY-TOE?! YOU MEANS SNEAK, DON'T YOU?
SNEAK!? NEVER USE THAT WORD IN CONNECTION WITH OUR HONORABLE PROFESSION... WE TIPPY-TOES... SO AS NOT TO DISTURB THE CUSTOMERS... WE BURGLARS IS CONSIDERATE.
NOW I'LL GOTTA POINT OUT A FEW THINGS ON HOW TO "UH... ACQUIRE PROPERTY... I DON'T S'PECK YOU YOUNGSTERS KNOWS HOW.
THE MAIN THING IS TO TAKE STUFF WITHOUT ANYBODY KNOWIN'... THAT'S THE TRICK... PICK OUT SOME POOR BOOB WHO CAN'T COUNT AN'...
© 1956 WALT KELLY
UH... HUMPH WODDYA KNOW, THEM WORMS IS DONE GOT BORED AN' WENT OFF... OH WELL, THEY DIN'T LOOK TOO BRIGHT... WOONT OF MADE GOOD BURGLARS NOHOW.
DOGGONE I IS COME TO WORK AN' FORGOT MY LUNCH AGAIN, NOW I'LL GOTTA GO ALL THE WAY HOME.

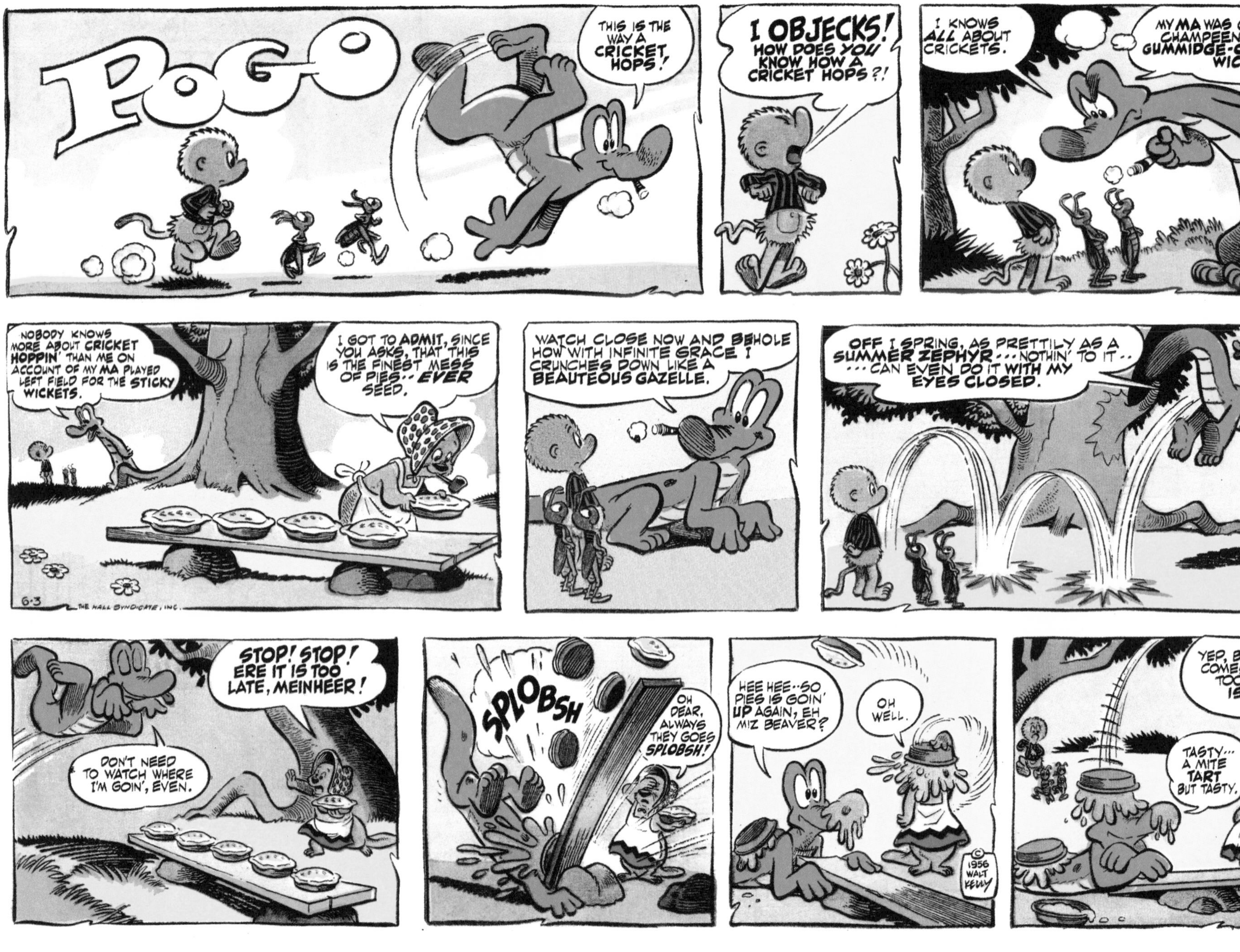
POGO
THIS IS THE WAY A CRICKET HOPS!
I OBJECKS! HOW DOES YOU KNOW HOW A CRICKET HOPS?!
I KNOWS ALL ABOUT CRICKETS.
MY MA WAS CRICKET CHAMPEEN OF OL' GUMMIDGE-ON-THE-WICKET.
NOBODY KNOWS MORE ABOUT CRICKET HOPPIN' THAN ME ON ACCOUNT OF MY MA PLAYED LEFT FIELD FOR THE STICKY WICKETS.
I GOT TO ADMIT, SINCE YOU ASKS, THAT THIS IS THE FINEST MESS OF PIES -- EVER SEED.
6-3
THE HALL SYNDICATE, INC.
WATCH CLOSE NOW AND BEHOLE HOW WITH INFINITE GRACE I CRUNCHES DOWN LIKE A BEAUTEOUS GAZELLE.
OFF I SPRING, AS PRETTILY AS A SUMMER ZEPHYR... NOTHIN' TO IT... ...CAN EVEN DO IT WITH MY EYES CLOSED.
STOP! STOP! ERE IT IS TOO LATE, MEINHEER!
DON'T NEED TO WATCH WHERE I'M GOIN', EVEN.
SPLOBSH
OH DEAR, ALWAYS THEY GOES SPLOBSH!
HEE HEE.. SO PIES IS GOIN' UP AGAIN, EH MIZ BEAVER?
OH WELL.
© 1956 WALT KELLY
YEP, BUT THEY COMES DOWN TOO... HOW IS THEY?
TASTY... A MITE TART BUT TASTY.

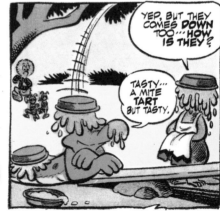

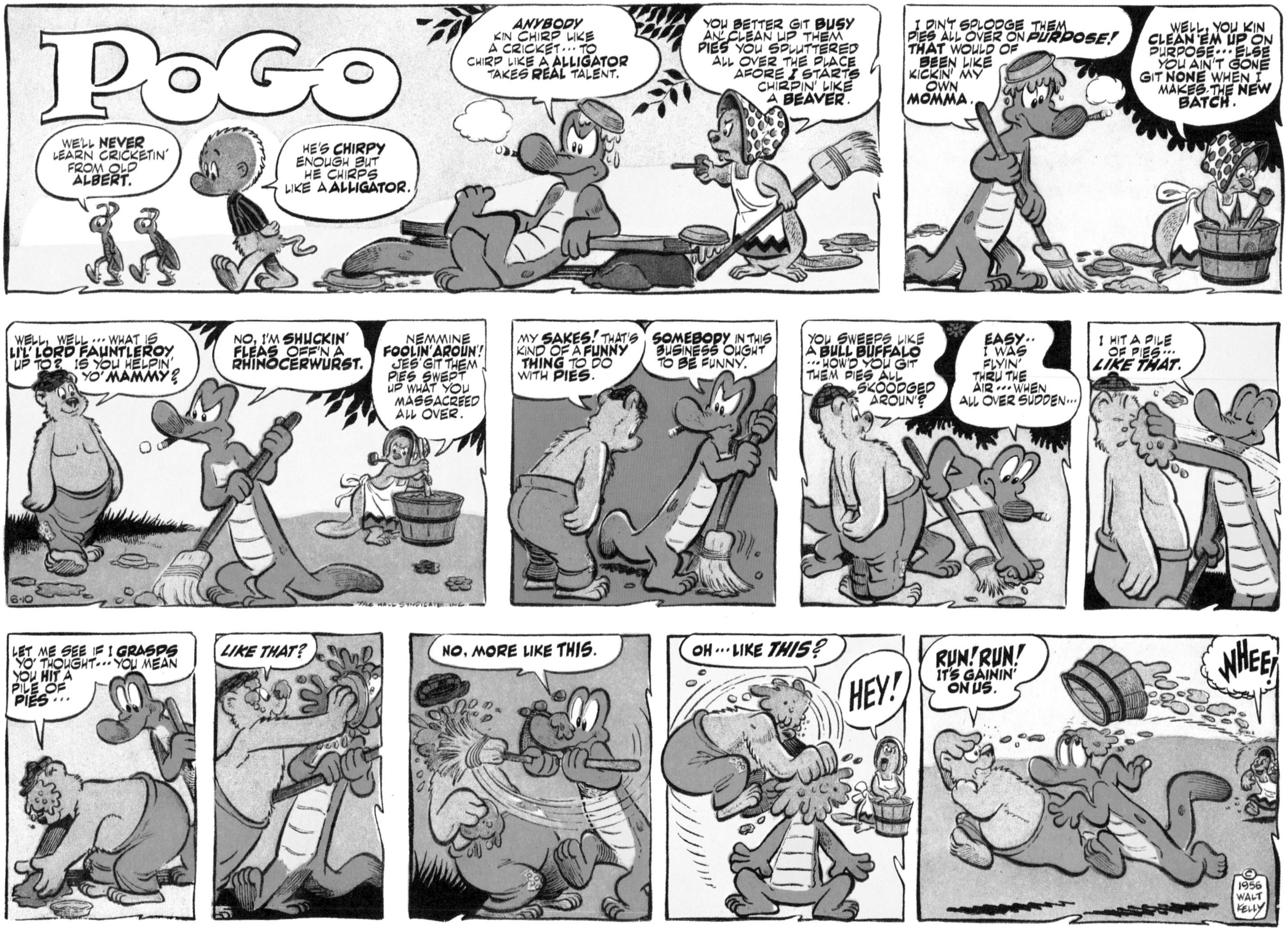
POGO
WE'LL NEVER LEARN CRICKETIN' FROM OLD ALBERT.
HE'S CHIRPY ENOUGH BUT HE CHIRPS LIKE A ALLIGATOR.
ANYBODY KIN CHIRP LIKE A CRICKET... TO CHIRP LIKE A ALLIGATOR TAKES REAL TALENT.
YOU BETTER GIT BUSY AN' CLEAN UP THEM PIES YOU SPLUTTERED ALL OVER THE PLACE AFORE I STARTS CHIRPIN' LIKE A BEAVER.
I DIN'T SPLODGE THEM PIES ALL OVER ON PURPOSE! THAT WOULD OF BEEN LIKE KICKIN' MY OWN MOMMA.
WELL, YOU KIN CLEAN 'EM UP ON PURPOSE... ELSE YOU AIN'T GONE GIT NONE WHEN I MAKES THE NEW BATCH.
WELL, WELL... WHAT IS LI'L LORD FAUNTLEROY UP TO? IS YOU HELPIN' YO' MAMMY?
NO, I'M SHUCKIN' FLEAS OFF'N A RHINOCERWURST.
NEMMINE FOOLIN' AROUN'! JES' GIT THEM PIES SWEPT UP WHAT YOU MASSACREED ALL OVER.
6·10
MY SAKES! THAT'S KIND OF A FUNNY THING TO DO WITH PIES.
SOMEBODY IN THIS BUSINESS OUGHT TO BE FUNNY.
YOU SWEEPS LIKE A BULL BUFFALO... HOW'D YOU GIT THEM PIES ALL SKOODGED AROUN'?
EASY.. I WAS FLYIN' THRU THE AIR... WHEN ALL OVER SUDDEN...
I HIT A PILE OF PIES... LIKE THAT.
LET ME SEE IF I GRASPS YO' THOUGHT... YOU MEAN YOU HIT A PILE OF PIES...
LIKE THAT?
NO, MORE LIKE THIS.
OH... LIKE THIS?
HEY!
RUN! RUN! IT'S GAININ' ON US.
WHEE!
© 1956 WALT KELLY

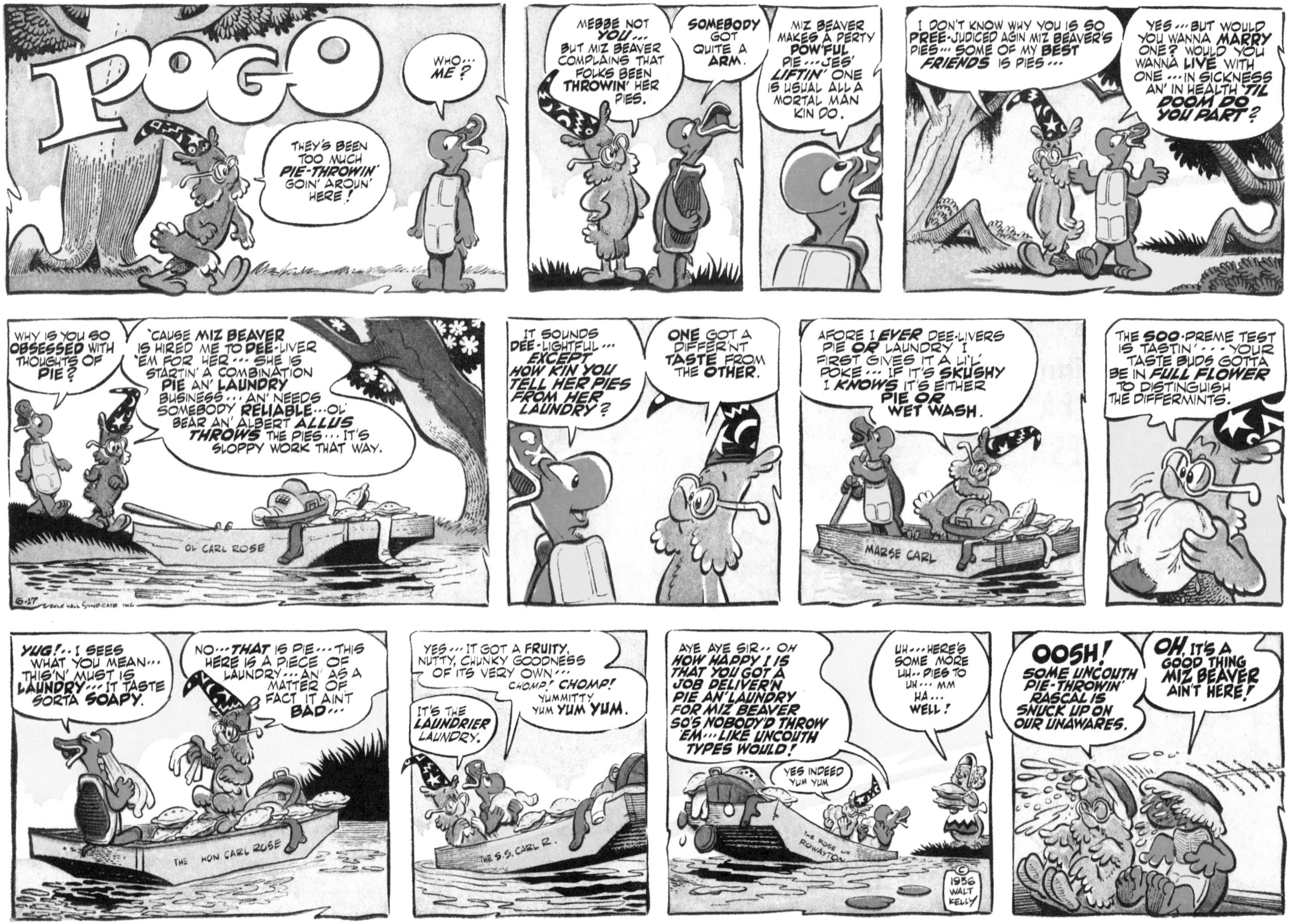
POGO
THEY'S BEEN TOO MUCH PIE-THROWIN' GOIN' AROUN' HERE!
WHO... ME?
MEBBE NOT YOU... BUT MIZ BEAVER COMPLAINS THAT FOLKS BEEN THROWIN' HER PIES.
SOMEBODY GOT QUITE A ARM.
MIZ BEAVER MAKES A PERTY POW'FUL PIE... JES' LIFTIN' ONE IS USUAL ALL A MORTAL MAN KIN DO.
I DON'T KNOW WHY YOU IS SO PREE-JUDICED AGIN MIZ BEAVER'S PIES... SOME OF MY BEST FRIENDS IS PIES...
YES... BUT WOULD YOU WANNA MARRY ONE? WOULD YOU WANNA LIVE WITH ONE... IN SICKNESS AN' IN HEALTH 'TIL DOOM DO YOU PART?
WHY IS YOU SO OBSESSED WITH THOUGHTS OF PIE?
'CAUSE MIZ BEAVER IS HIRED ME TO DEE-LIVER 'EM FOR HER... SHE IS STARTIN' A COMBINATION PIE AN' LAUNDRY BUSINESS... AN' NEEDS SOMEBODY RELIABLE... OL' BEAR AN' ALBERT ALLUS THROWS THE PIES... IT'S SLOPPY WORK THAT WAY.
OL' CARL ROSE
6-17
IT SOUNDS DEE-LIGHTFUL... EXCEPT HOW KIN YOU TELL HER PIES FROM HER LAUNDRY?
ONE GOT A DIFFER'NT TASTE FROM THE OTHER.
AFORE I EVER DEE-LIVERS PIE OR LAUNDRY I FIRST GIVES IT A LI'L POKE... IF IT'S SKUSHY I KNOWS IT'S EITHER PIE OR WET WASH.
MARSE CARL
THE SOO-PREME TEST IS TASTIN'... YOUR TASTE BUDS GOTTA BE IN FULL FLOWER TO DISTINGUISH THE DIFFERMINTS.
YUG!.. I SEES WHAT YOU MEAN... THIS'N' MUST IS LAUNDRY... IT TASTE SORTA SOAPY.
NO... THAT IS PIE... THIS HERE IS A PIECE OF LAUNDRY... AN' AS A MATTER OF FACT IT AINT BAD...
THE HON CARL ROSE
YES... IT GOT A FRUITY, NUTTY, CHUNKY GOODNESS OF ITS VERY OWN...
CHOMP! CHOMP! YUMMITTY YUM YUM YUM.
IT'S THE LAUNDRIER LAUNDRY.
THE S.S. CARL R.
AYE AYE SIR.. OH HOW HAPPY I IS THAT YOU GOT A JOB DELIVER'N PIE AN' LAUNDRY FOR MIZ BEAVER SO'S NOBODY'D THROW 'EM... LIKE UNCOUTH TYPES WOULD!
YES INDEED YUM YUM
UH... HERE'S SOME MORE UH.. PIES TO UH... MM HA... WELL!
ROWAYTON
© 1956 WALT KELLY
OOSH! SOME UNCOUTH PIE-THROWIN' RASCAL IS SNUCK UP ON OUR UNAWARES.
OH, IT'S A GOOD THING MIZ BEAVER AIN'T HERE!

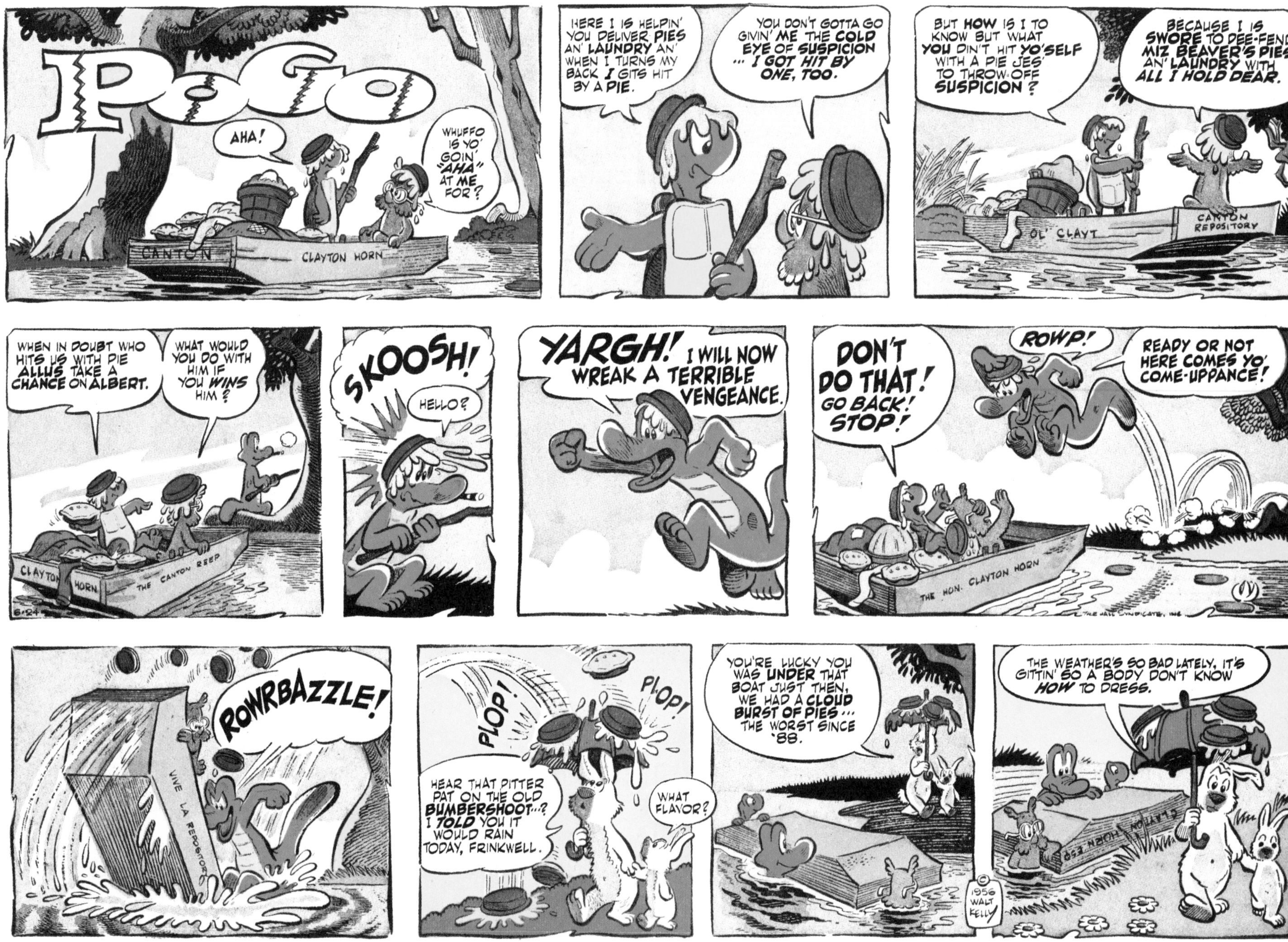
POGO
AHA!
WHUFFO IS YO' GOIN' "AHA" AT ME FOR?
CANTON
CLAYTON HORN
HERE I IS HELPIN' YOU DELIVER PIES AN' LAUNDRY AN' WHEN I TURNS MY BACK I GITS HIT BY A PIE.
YOU DON'T GOTTA GO GIVIN' ME THE COLD EYE OF SUSPICION ... I GOT HIT BY ONE, TOO.
BUT HOW IS I TO KNOW BUT WHAT YOU DIN'T HIT YO'SELF WITH A PIE JES' TO THROW-OFF SUSPICION?
BECAUSE I IS SWORE TO DEE-FEND MIZ BEAVER'S PIES AN' LAUNDRY WITH ALL I HOLD DEAR.
OL' CLAYT
CANTON REPOSITORY
WHEN IN DOUBT WHO HITS US WITH PIE ALLUS TAKE A CHANCE ON ALBERT.
WHAT WOULD YOU DO WITH HIM IF YOU WINS HIM?
CLAYTON HORN
SKOOSH!
HELLO?
YARGH! I WILL NOW WREAK A TERRIBLE VENGEANCE.
DON'T DO THAT! GO BACK! STOP!
ROWP!
READY OR NOT HERE COMES YO' COME-UPPANCE!
THE HON. CLAYTON HORN
ROWRBAZZLE!
PLOP!
PLOP!
HEAR THAT PITTER PAT ON THE OLD BUMBERSHOOT...? I TOLD YOU IT WOULD RAIN TODAY, FRINKWELL.
WHAT FLAVOR?
YOU'RE LUCKY YOU WAS UNDER THAT BOAT JUST THEN, WE HAD A CLOUD BURST OF PIES... THE WORST SINCE '88.
© 1956 WALT KELLY
THE WEATHER'S SO BAD LATELY, IT'S GITTIN' SO A BODY DON'T KNOW HOW TO DRESS.

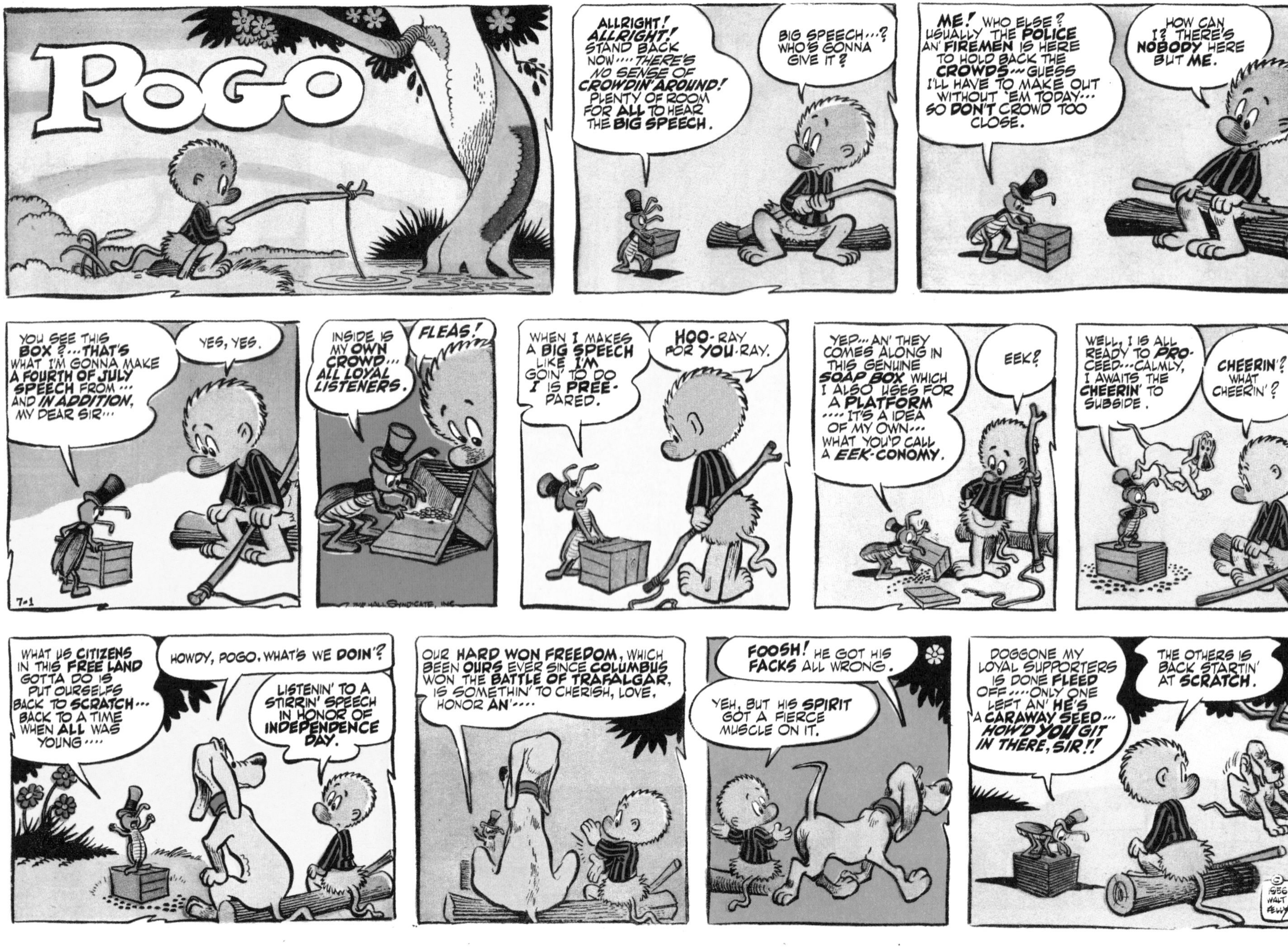
POGO
ALLRIGHT! ALLRIGHT! STAND BACK NOW.... THERE'S NO SENSE OF CROWDIN' AROUND! PLENTY OF ROOM FOR ALL TO HEAR THE BIG SPEECH.
BIG SPEECH...? WHO'S GONNA GIVE IT?
ME! WHO ELSE? USUALLY THE POLICE AN' FIREMEN IS HERE TO HOLD BACK THE CROWDS... GUESS I'LL HAVE TO MAKE OUT WITHOUT 'EM TODAY... SO DON'T CROWD TOO CLOSE.
HOW CAN I? THERE'S NOBODY HERE BUT ME.
YOU SEE THIS BOX?...THAT'S WHAT I'M GONNA MAKE A FOURTH OF JULY SPEECH FROM... AND IN ADDITION, MY DEAR SIR...
YES, YES.
7-1
INSIDE IS MY OWN CROWD... ALL LOYAL LISTENERS.
FLEAS!
WHEN I MAKES A BIG SPEECH LIKE I'M GOIN' TO DO I IS PREE-PARED.
HOO-RAY FOR YOU-RAY.
YEP... AN' THEY COMES ALONG IN THIS GENUINE SOAP BOX WHICH I ALSO USES FOR A PLATFORM.... IT'S A IDEA OF MY OWN... WHAT YOU'D CALL A EEK-CONOMY.
EEK?
WELL, I IS ALL READY TO PRO-CEED... CALMLY, I AWAITS THE CHEERIN' TO SUBSIDE.
CHEERIN'? WHAT CHEERIN'?
WHAT US CITIZENS IN THIS FREE LAND GOTTA DO IS PUT OURSELFS BACK TO SCRATCH... BACK TO A TIME WHEN ALL WAS YOUNG....
HOWDY, POGO. WHAT'S WE DOIN'?
LISTENIN' TO A STIRRIN' SPEECH IN HONOR OF INDEPENDENCE DAY.
OUR HARD WON FREEDOM, WHICH BEEN OURS EVER SINCE COLUMBUS WON THE BATTLE OF TRAFALGAR, IS SOMETHIN' TO CHERISH, LOVE, HONOR AN'....
FOOSH! HE GOT HIS FACKS ALL WRONG.
YEH, BUT HIS SPIRIT GOT A FIERCE MUSCLE ON IT.
DOGGONE MY LOYAL SUPPORTERS IS DONE FLEED OFF.... ONLY ONE LEFT AN' HE'S A CARAWAY SEED... HOW'D YOU GIT IN THERE, SIR!!
THE OTHERS IS BACK STARTIN' AT SCRATCH.
© 1956 WALT KELLY

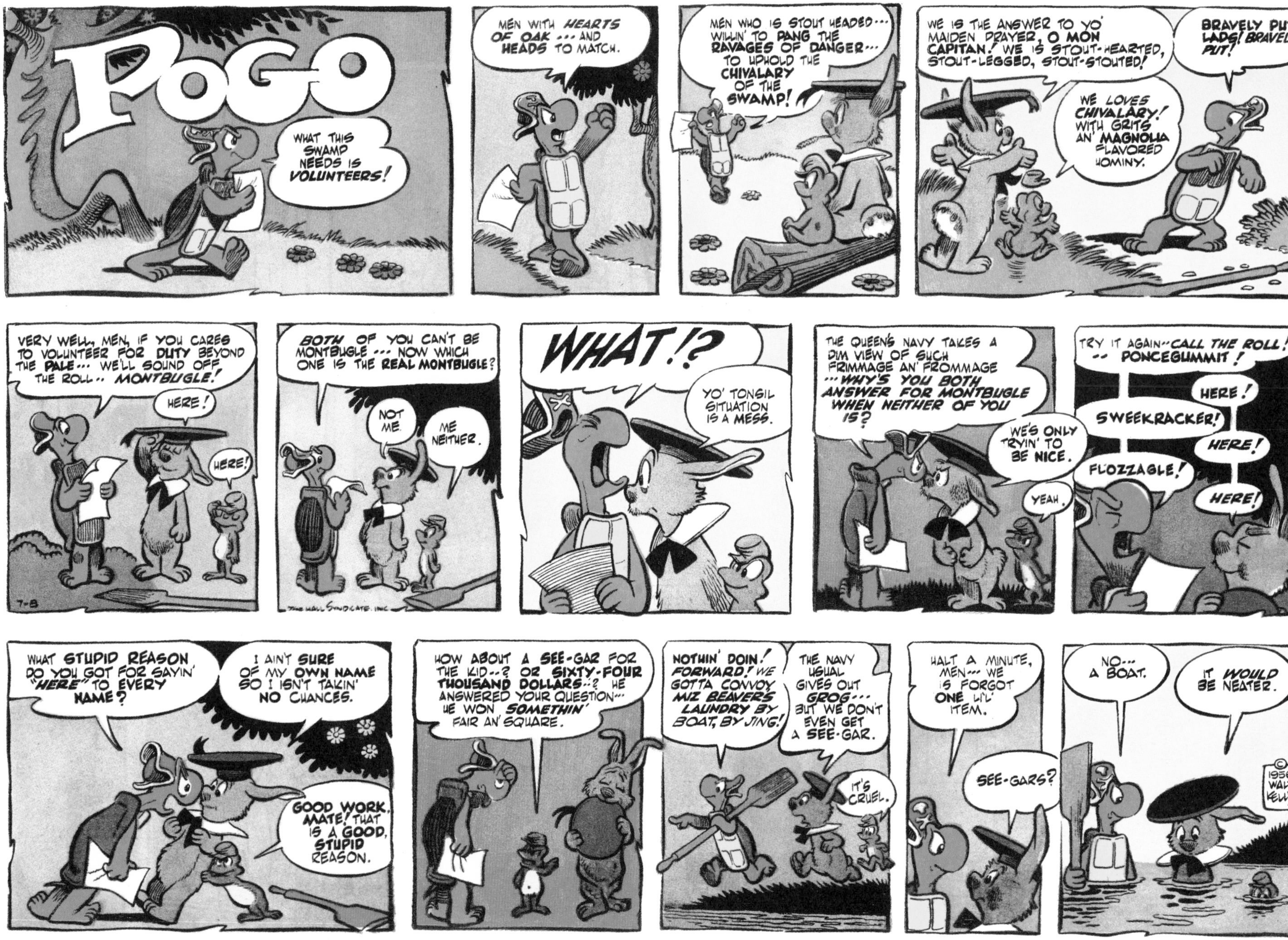
POGO
WHAT THIS SWAMP NEEDS IS VOLUNTEERS!
MEN WITH HEARTS OF OAK... AND HEADS TO MATCH.
MEN WHO IS STOUT HEADED... WILLIN' TO PANG THE RAVAGES OF DANGER... TO UPHOLD THE CHIVALARY OF THE SWAMP!
WE IS THE ANSWER TO YO' MAIDEN PRAYER, O MON CAPITAN! WE IS STOUT-HEARTED, STOUT-LEGGED, STOUT-STOUTED!
WE LOVES CHIVALARY! WITH GRITS AN' MAGNOLIA FLAVORED HOMINY.
BRAVELY PUT, LADS! BRAVELY PUT!
VERY WELL, MEN, IF YOU CARES TO VOLUNTEER FOR DUTY BEYOND THE PALE... WE'LL SOUND OFF THE ROLL.. MONTBUGLE!
HERE!
HERE!
7-8
BOTH OF YOU CAN'T BE MONTBUGLE... NOW WHICH ONE IS THE REAL MONTBUGLE?
NOT ME.
ME NEITHER.
WHAT!?
YO' TONSIL SITUATION IS A MESS.
THE QUEEN'S NAVY TAKES A DIM VIEW OF SUCH FRIMMAGE AN' FROMMAGE ...WHY'S YOU BOTH ANSWER FOR MONTBUGLE WHEN NEITHER OF YOU IS?
WE'S ONLY TRYIN' TO BE NICE.
YEAH.
TRY IT AGAIN-- CALL THE ROLL! -- PONCEGUMMIT!
HERE!
SWEEKRACKER!
HERE!
FLOZZAGLE!
HERE!
WHAT STUPID REASON DO YOU GOT FOR SAYIN' "HERE" TO EVERY NAME?
I AIN'T SURE OF MY OWN NAME SO I ISN'T TAKIN' NO CHANCES.
GOOD WORK, MATE! THAT IS A GOOD, STUPID REASON.
HOW ABOUT A SEE-GAR FOR THE KID--? OR SIXTY-FOUR THOUSAND DOLLARS--? HE ANSWERED YOUR QUESTION-- HE WON SOMETHIN' FAIR AN' SQUARE.
NOTHIN' DOIN'! FORWARD! WE GOTTA CONVOY MIZ BEAVERS LAUNDRY BY BOAT, BY JING!
THE NAVY USUAL GIVES OUT GROG... BUT WE DON'T EVEN GET A SEE-GAR.
IT'S CRUEL.
HALT A MINUTE, MEN... WE IS FORGOT ONE LI'L' ITEM.
SEE-GARS?
NO... A BOAT.
IT WOULD BE NEATER.
© 1956 WALT KELLY

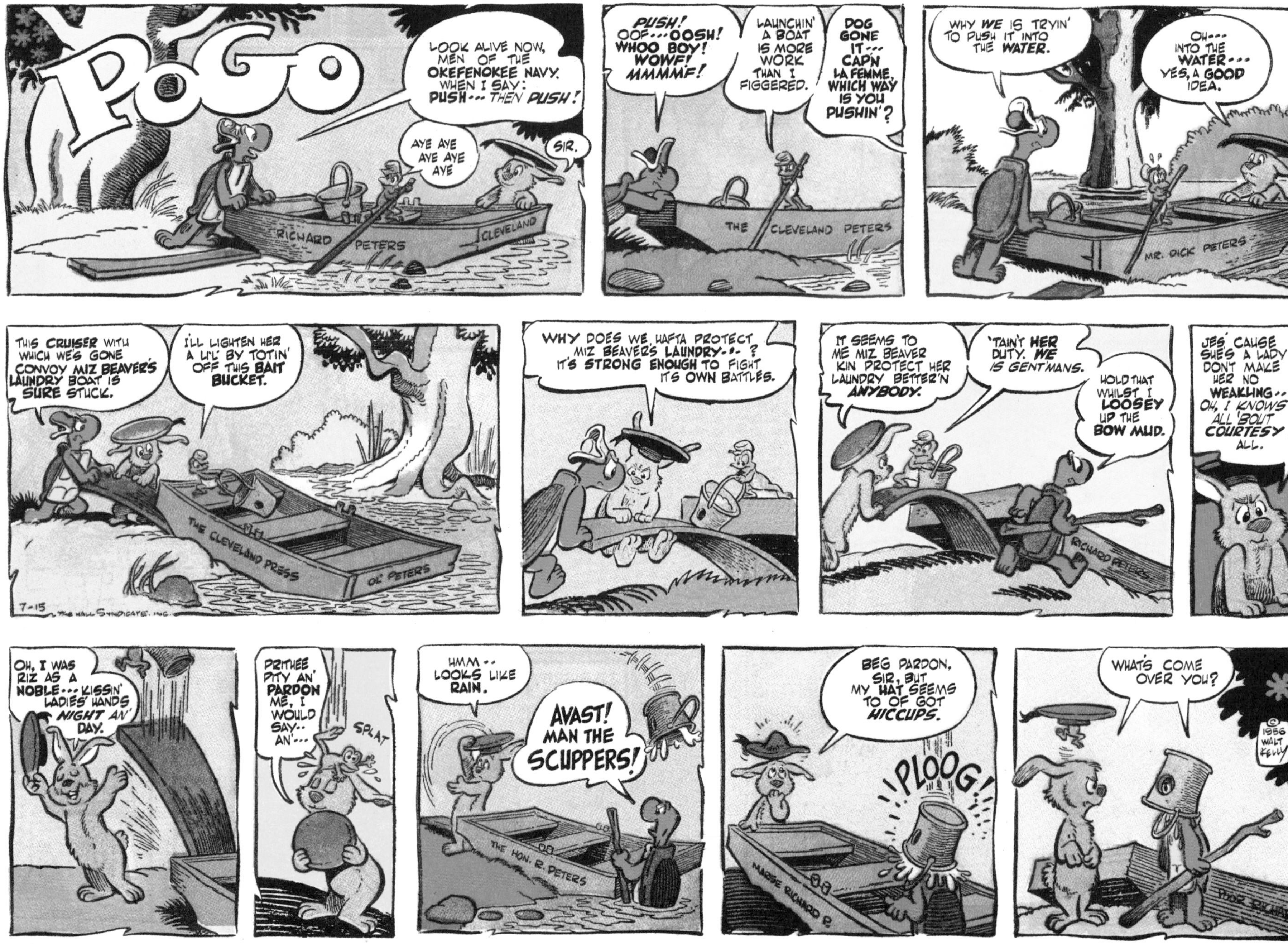
POGO
LOOK ALIVE NOW, MEN OF THE OKEFENOKEE NAVY. WHEN I SAY: PUSH... THEN PUSH!
AYE AYE AYE AYE AYE
SIR.
RICHARD PETERS
CLEVELAND
PUSH! OOF... OOSH! WHOO BOY! WOWF! MMMMF!
LAUNCHIN' A BOAT IS MORE WORK THAN I FIGGERED.
DOG GONE IT... CAP'N LA FEMME, WHICH WAY IS YOU PUSHIN'?
THE CLEVELAND PETERS
WHY WE IS TRYIN' TO PUSH IT INTO THE WATER.
OH... INTO THE WATER... YES, A GOOD IDEA.
MR. DICK PETERS
THIS CRUISER WITH WHICH WE'S GONE CONVOY MIZ BEAVER'S LAUNDRY BOAT IS SURE STUCK.
I'LL LIGHTEN HER A LI'L BY TOTIN' OFF THIS BAIT BUCKET.
THE CLEVELAND PRESS
OL' PETERS
7-15
WHY DOES WE HAFTA PROTECT MIZ BEAVER'S LAUNDRY...? IT'S STRONG ENOUGH TO FIGHT IT'S OWN BATTLES.
IT SEEMS TO ME MIZ BEAVER KIN PROTECT HER LAUNDRY BETTER'N ANYBODY.
'TAIN'T HER DUTY. WE IS GENT'MANS.
HOLD THAT WHILST I LOOSEY UP THE BOW MUD.
RICHARD PETERS
JES' CAUSE SHE'S A LADY DON'T MAKE HER NO WEAKLING.... OH, I KNOWS ALL 'BOUT COURTESY AN' ALL.
OH, I WAS RIZ AS A NOBLE... KISSIN' LADIES' HANDS NIGHT AN' DAY.
PRITHEE PITY AN' PARDON ME, I WOULD SAY.. AN'...
SPLAT
HMM.. LOOKS LIKE RAIN.
AVAST! MAN THE SCUPPERS!
THE HON. R. PETERS
BEG PARDON, SIR, BUT MY HAT SEEMS TO OF GOT HICCUPS.
PLOOG!
MADGE RICHARD P.
WHAT'S COME OVER YOU?
© 1956 WALT KELLY
POOR RICHARD

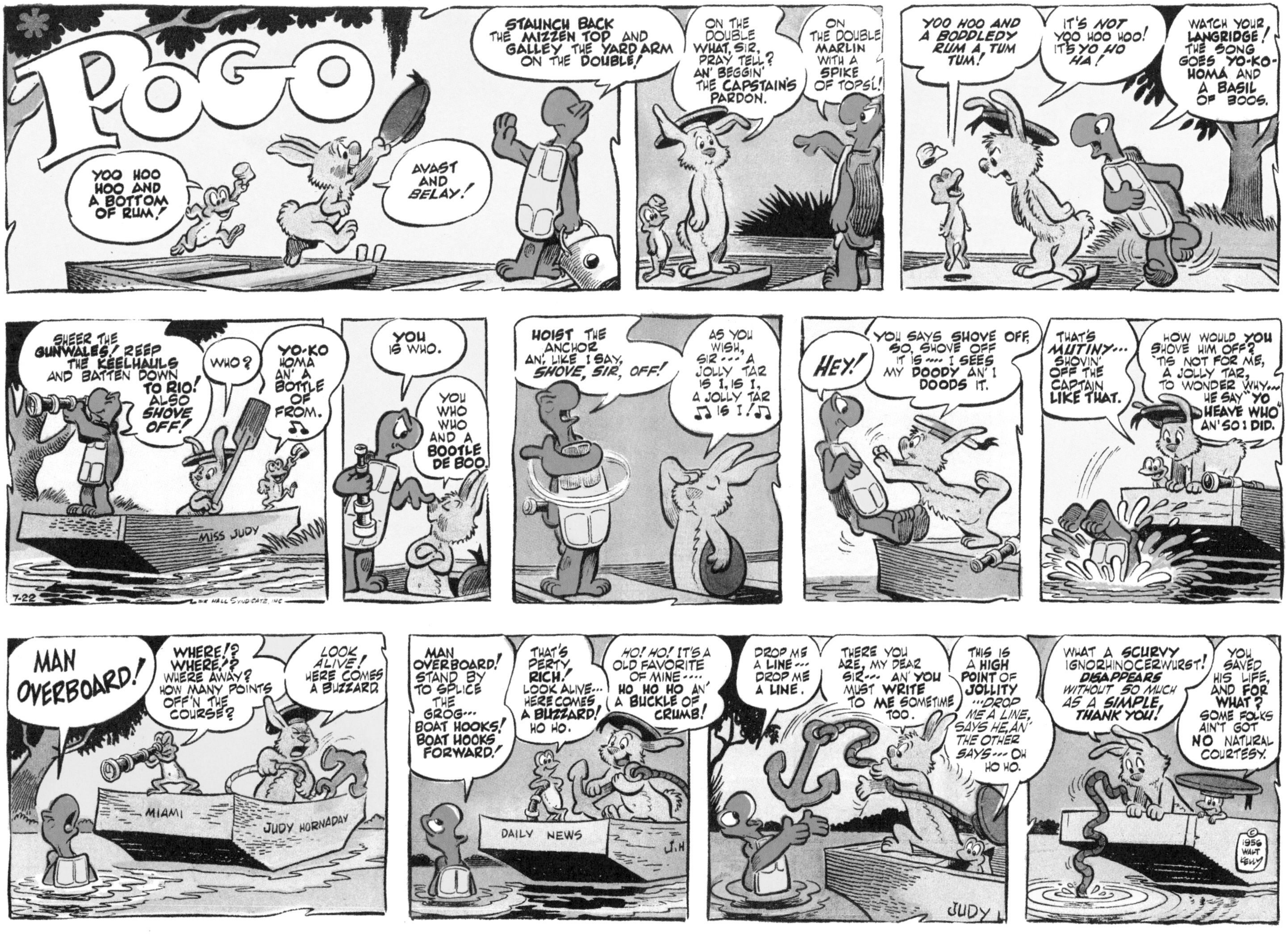
POGO
YOO HOO HOO AND A BOTTOM OF RUM!
AVAST AND BELAY!
STAUNCH BACK THE MIZZEN TOP AND GALLEY THE YARD ARM ON THE DOUBLE!
ON THE DOUBLE WHAT, SIR, PRAY TELL? AN' BEGGIN' THE CAPSTAIN'S PARDON.
ON THE DOUBLE MARLIN WITH A SPIKE OF TOPS'L!
YOO HOO AND A BODDLEDY RUM A TUM TUM!
IT'S NOT YOO HOO HOO! IT'S YO HO HA!
WATCH YOUR LANGRIDGE! THE SONG GOES YO-KO-HOMA AND A BASIL OF BOOS.
SHEER THE GUNWALES! REEP THE KEELHAULS AND BATTEN DOWN TO RIO! ALSO SHOVE OFF!
WHO?
YO-KO HOMA AN' A BOTTLE OF FROM.
MISS JUDY
7-22
YOU IS WHO.
YOU WHO WHO AND A BOOTLE DE BOO.
HOIST THE ANCHOR AN', LIKE I SAY, SHOVE, SIR, OFF!
AS YOU WISH, SIR --- A JOLLY TAR IS I, IS I, A JOLLY TAR IS I!
HEY!
YOU SAYS SHOVE OFF, SO, SHOVE OFF IT IS --- I SEES MY DOODY AN' I DOODS IT.
THAT'S MUTINY... SHOVIN' OFF THE CAPTAIN LIKE THAT.
HOW WOULD YOU SHOVE HIM OFF? 'TIS NOT FOR ME, A JOLLY TAR, TO WONDER WHY... HE SAY "YO HEAVE WHO" AN' SO I DID.
MAN OVERBOARD!
WHERE!? WHERE!? WHERE AWAY? HOW MANY POINTS OFF'N THE COURSE?
LOOK ALIVE! HERE COMES A BUZZARD.
MIAMI
JUDY HORNADAY
MAN OVERBOARD! STAND BY TO SPLICE THE GROG... BOAT HOOKS! BOAT HOOKS FORWARD!
THAT'S PERTY RICH! LOOK ALIVE... HERE COMES A BUZZARD! HO HO.
HO! HO! IT'S A OLD FAVORITE OF MINE.... HO HO HO AN' A BUCKLE OF CRUMB!
DAILY NEWS
J.H
DROP ME A LINE... DROP ME A LINE.
THERE YOU ARE, MY DEAR SIR--- AN' YOU MUST WRITE TO ME SOMETIME TOO.
THIS IS A HIGH POINT OF JOLLITY ...DROP ME A LINE, SAYS HE, AN' THE OTHER SAYS--- OH HO HO.
JUDY
WHAT A SCURVY IGNORHINOCERWURST! DISAPPEARS WITHOUT SO MUCH AS A SIMPLE THANK YOU!
YOU SAVED HIS LIFE, AND FOR WHAT? SOME FOLKS AIN'T GOT NO NATURAL COURTESY.
© 1956 WALT KELLY

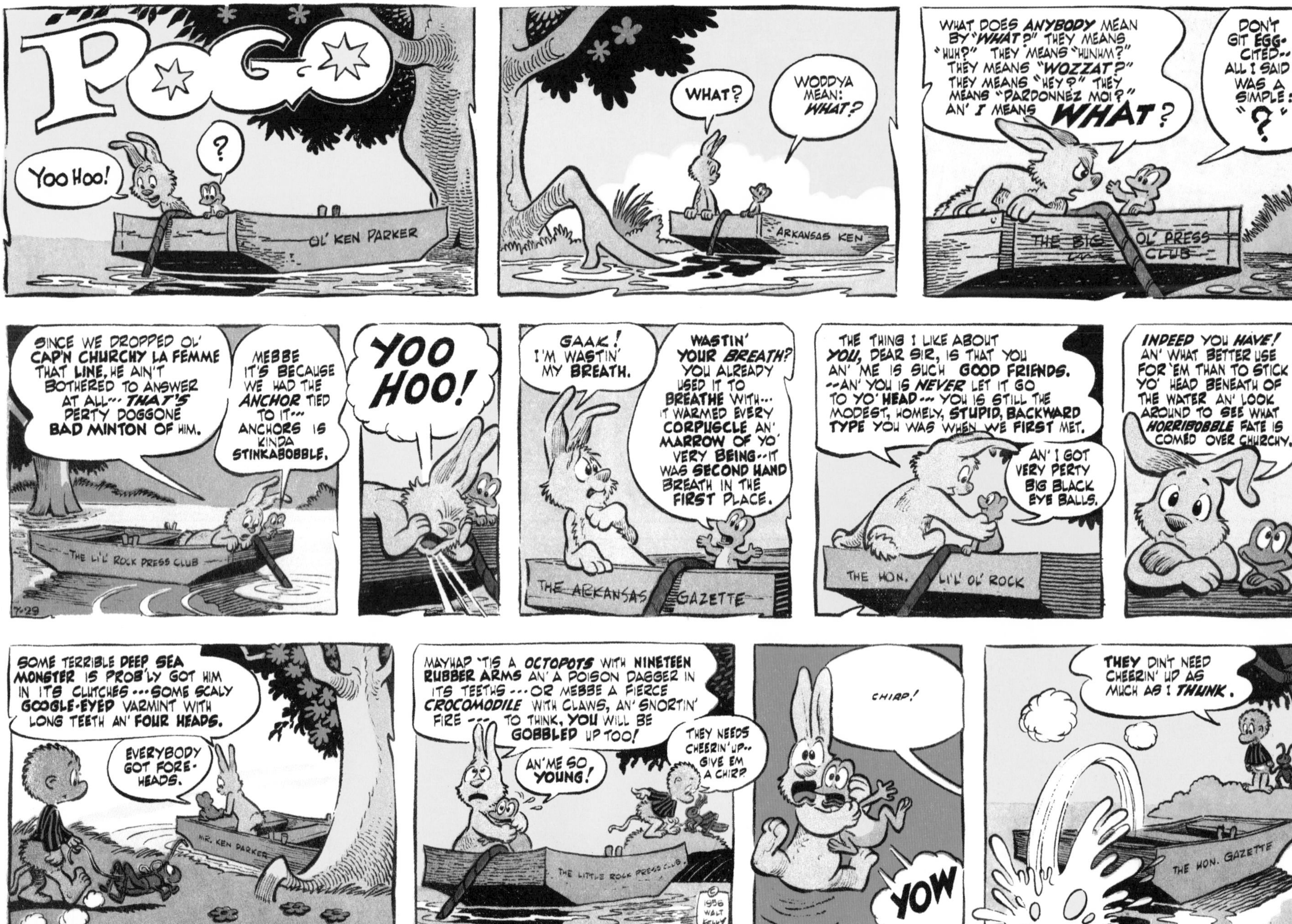
POGO
YOO HOO!
?
OL' KEN PARKER
WHAT?
WOODYA MEAN: WHAT?
ARKANSAS KEN
WHAT DOES ANYBODY MEAN BY "WHAT?" THEY MEANS "HUH?" THEY MEANS "HUNHM?" THEY MEANS "WOZZAT?" THEY MEANS "HEY?" THEY MEANS "PARDONNEZ MOI?" AN' I MEANS WHAT?
DON'T GIT EGG-CITED-- ALL I SAID WAS A SIMPLE: "?"
THE BIG OL' PRESS CLUB
SINCE WE DROPPED OL' CAP'N CHURCHY LA FEMME THAT LINE, HE AIN'T BOTHERED TO ANSWER AT ALL--- THAT'S PERTY DOGGONE BAD MINTON OF HIM.
MEBBE IT'S BECAUSE WE HAD THE ANCHOR TIED TO IT--- ANCHORS IS KINDA STINKABOBBLE.
THE LI'L ROCK PRESS CLUB
7-29
YOO HOO!
GAAK! I'M WASTIN' MY BREATH.
WASTIN' YOUR BREATH? YOU ALREADY USED IT TO BREATHE WITH--- IT WARMED EVERY CORPUSCLE AN' MARROW OF YO' VERY BEING--IT WAS SECOND HAND BREATH IN THE FIRST PLACE.
THE ARKANSAS GAZETTE
THE THING I LIKE ABOUT YOU, DEAR SIR, IS THAT YOU AN' ME IS SUCH GOOD FRIENDS. --AN' YOU IS NEVER LET IT GO TO YO' HEAD--- YOU IS STILL THE MODEST, HOMELY, STUPID, BACKWARD TYPE YOU WAS WHEN WE FIRST MET.
AN' I GOT VERY PERTY BIG BLACK EYE BALLS.
THE HON. LI'L OL' ROCK
INDEED YOU HAVE! AN' WHAT BETTER USE FOR 'EM THAN TO STICK YO' HEAD BENEATH OF THE WATER AN' LOOK AROUND TO SEE WHAT HORRIBOBBLE FATE IS COMED OVER CHURCHY.
SOME TERRIBLE DEEP SEA MONSTER IS PROB'LY GOT HIM IN ITS CLUTCHES --- SOME SCALY GOOGLE-EYED VARMINT WITH LONG TEETH AN' FOUR HEADS.
EVERYBODY GOT FORE-HEADS.
MR. KEN PARKER
MAYHAP 'TIS A OCTOPOTS WITH NINETEEN RUBBER ARMS AN' A POISON DAGGER IN ITS TEETHS --- OR MEBBE A FIERCE CROCOMODILE WITH CLAWS, AN' SNORTIN' FIRE --- TO THINK, YOU WILL BE GOBBLED UP TOO!
AN' ME SO YOUNG!
THEY NEEDS CHEERIN' UP-- GIVE EM A CHIRP.
THE LITTLE ROCK PRESS CLUB
© 1956 WALT KELLY
CHIRP!
YOW
THEY DIN'T NEED CHEERIN' UP AS MUCH AS I THUNK.
THE HON. GAZETTE

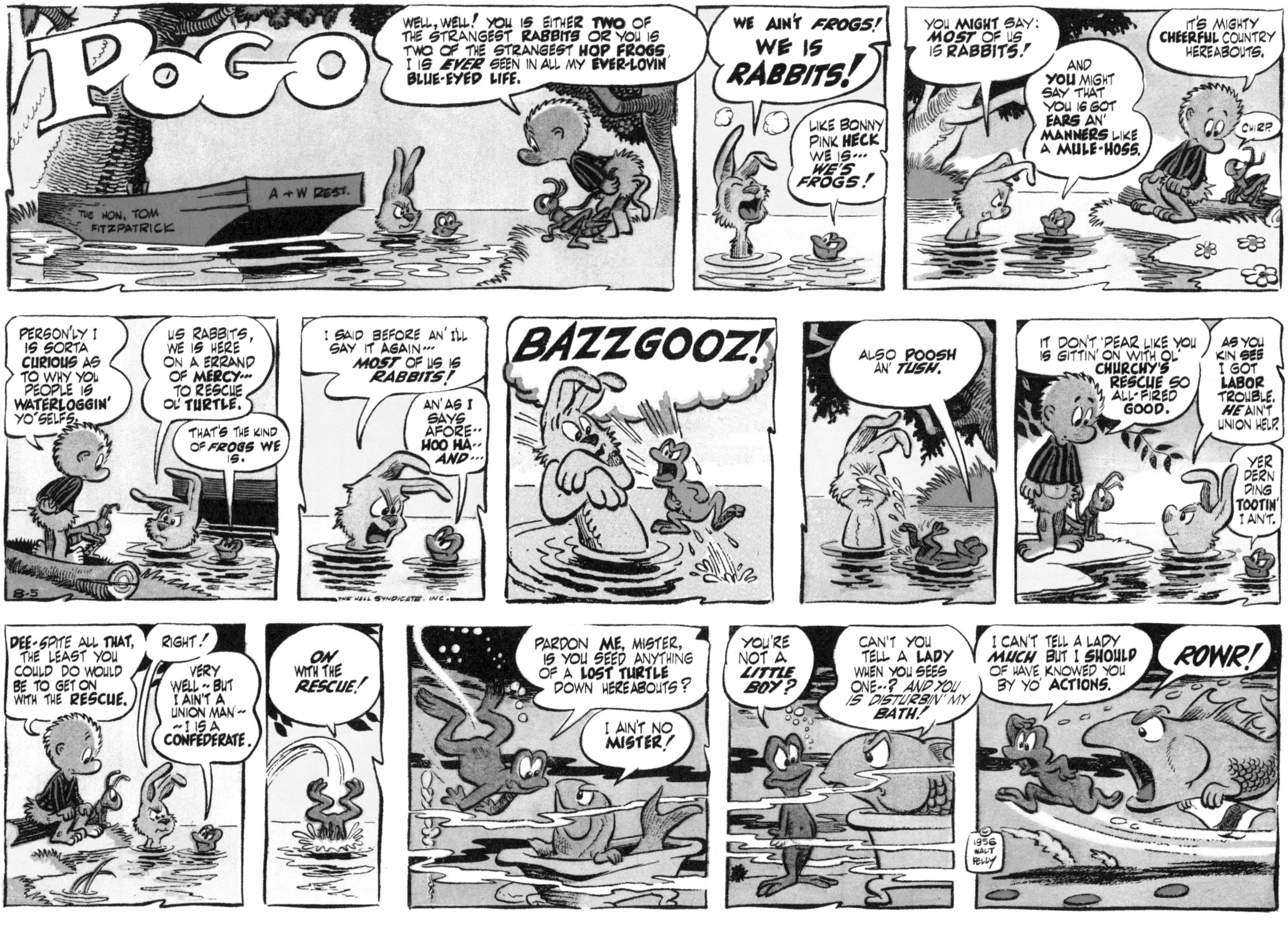
POGO
WELL, WELL! YOU IS EITHER TWO OF THE STRANGEST RABBITS OR YOU IS TWO OF THE STRANGEST HOP FROGS I IS EVER SEEN IN ALL MY EVER-LOVIN' BLUE-EYED LIFE.
THE HON. TOM FITZPATRICK
A + W REST.
WE AIN'T FROGS! WE IS RABBITS!
LIKE BONNY PINK HECK WE IS... WE'S FROGS!
YOU MIGHT SAY: MOST OF US IS RABBITS!
AND YOU MIGHT SAY THAT YOU IS GOT EARS AN' MANNERS LIKE A MULE-HOSS.
IT'S MIGHTY CHEERFUL COUNTRY HEREABOUTS.
CHIRP.
PERSON'LY I IS SORTA CURIOUS AS TO WHY YOU PEOPLE IS WATERLOGGIN' YO'SELFS.
US RABBITS, WE IS HERE ON A ERRAND OF MERCY... TO RESCUE OL' TURTLE.
THAT'S THE KIND OF FROGS WE IS.
8-5
I SAID BEFORE AN' I'LL SAY IT AGAIN... MOST OF US IS RABBITS!
AN' AS I SAYS AFORE.. HOO HA.. AND...
THE HALL SYNDICATE, INC.
BAZZGOOZ!
ALSO POOSH AN' TUSH.
IT DON'T 'PEAR LIKE YOU IS GITTIN' ON WITH OL' CHURCHY'S RESCUE SO ALL-FIRED GOOD.
AS YOU KIN SEE I GOT LABOR TROUBLE. HE AIN'T UNION HELP.
YER DERN DING TOOTIN' I AIN'T.
DEE-SPITE ALL THAT, THE LEAST YOU COULD DO WOULD BE TO GET ON WITH THE RESCUE.
RIGHT!
VERY WELL -- BUT I AIN'T A UNION MAN -- -- I IS A CONFEDERATE.
ON WITH THE RESCUE!
PARDON ME, MISTER, IS YOU SEED ANYTHING OF A LOST TURTLE DOWN HEREABOUTS?
I AIN'T NO MISTER!
YOU'RE NOT A LITTLE BOY?
CAN'T YOU TELL A LADY WHEN YOU SEES ONE--? AND YOU IS DISTURBIN' MY BATH!
©1956 WALT KELLY
I CAN'T TELL A LADY MUCH BUT I SHOULD OF HAVE KNOWED YOU BY YO' ACTIONS.
ROWR!

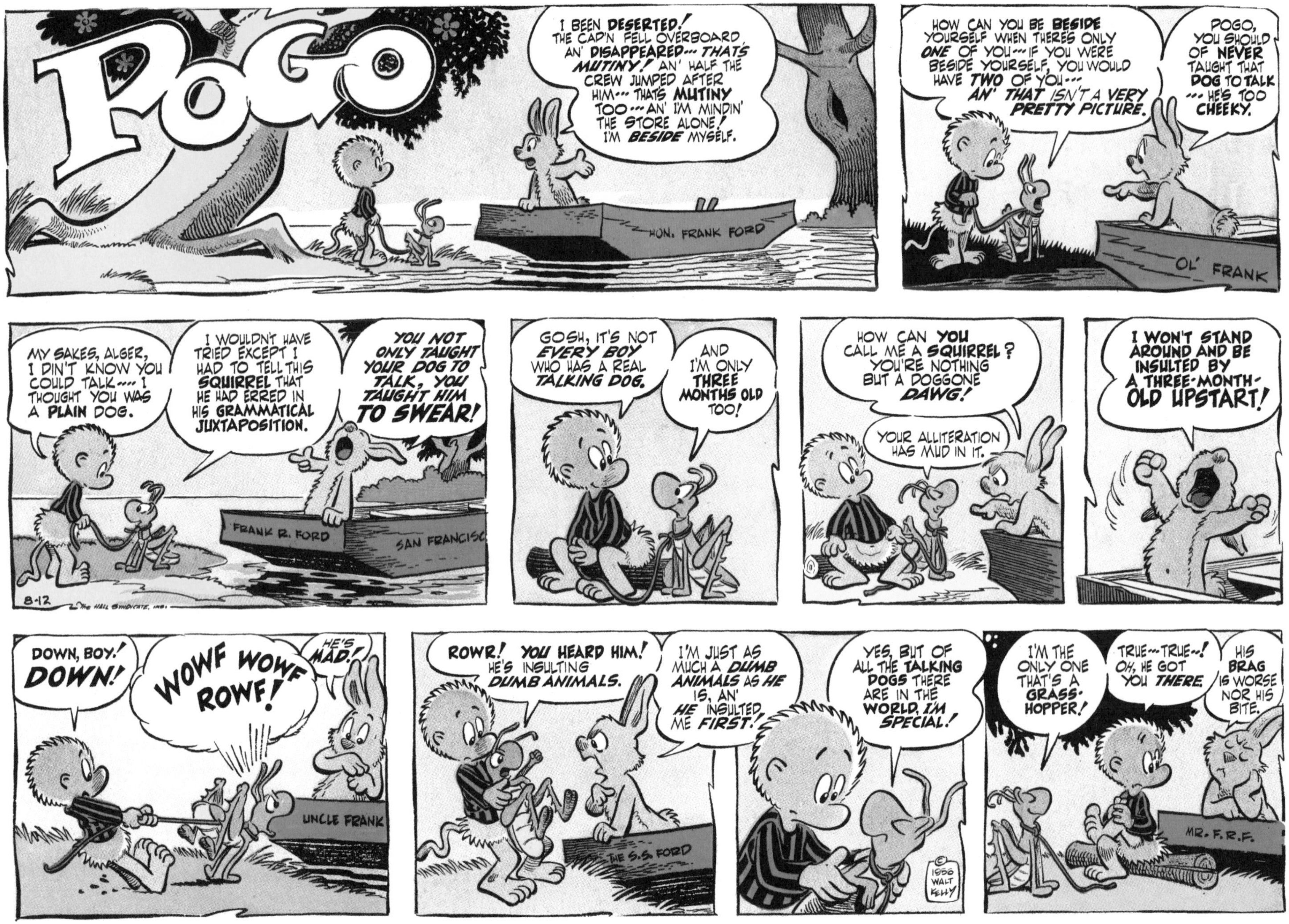
POGO
I BEEN DESERTED! THE CAP'N FELL OVERBOARD AN' DISAPPEARED... THAT'S MUTINY! AN' HALF THE CREW JUMPED AFTER HIM... THAT'S MUTINY TOO... AN' I'M MINDIN' THE STORE ALONE! I'M BESIDE MYSELF.
HON. FRANK FORD
HOW CAN YOU BE BESIDE YOURSELF WHEN THERE'S ONLY ONE OF YOU... IF YOU WERE BESIDE YOURSELF, YOU WOULD HAVE TWO OF YOU... AN' THAT ISN'T A VERY PRETTY PICTURE.
POGO, YOU SHOULD OF NEVER TAUGHT THAT DOG TO TALK ... HE'S TOO CHEEKY.
OL' FRANK
MY SAKES, ALGER, I DIN'T KNOW YOU COULD TALK.... I THOUGHT YOU WAS A PLAIN DOG.
I WOULDN'T HAVE TRIED EXCEPT I HAD TO TELL THIS SQUIRREL THAT HE HAD ERRED IN HIS GRAMMATICAL JUXTAPOSITION.
YOU NOT ONLY TAUGHT YOUR DOG TO TALK, YOU TAUGHT HIM TO SWEAR!
FRANK R. FORD
SAN FRANCISC
8-12
GOSH, IT'S NOT EVERY BOY WHO HAS A REAL TALKING DOG.
AND I'M ONLY THREE MONTHS OLD TOO!
HOW CAN YOU CALL ME A SQUIRREL? YOU'RE NOTHING BUT A DOGGONE DAWG!
YOUR ALLITERATION HAS MUD IN IT.
I WON'T STAND AROUND AND BE INSULTED BY A THREE-MONTH-OLD UPSTART!
DOWN, BOY! DOWN!
WOWF WOWF ROWF!
HE'S MAD!
UNCLE FRANK
ROWR! YOU HEARD HIM! HE'S INSULTING DUMB ANIMALS.
I'M JUST AS MUCH A DUMB ANIMALS AS HE IS, AN' HE INSULTED ME FIRST!
THE S.S. FORD
YES, BUT OF ALL THE TALKING DOGS THERE ARE IN THE WORLD, I'M SPECIAL!
© 1956 WALT KELLY
I'M THE ONLY ONE THAT'S A GRASS-HOPPER!
TRUE... TRUE..! OH, HE GOT YOU THERE.
HIS BRAG IS WORSE NOR HIS BITE.
MR. F.R.F.

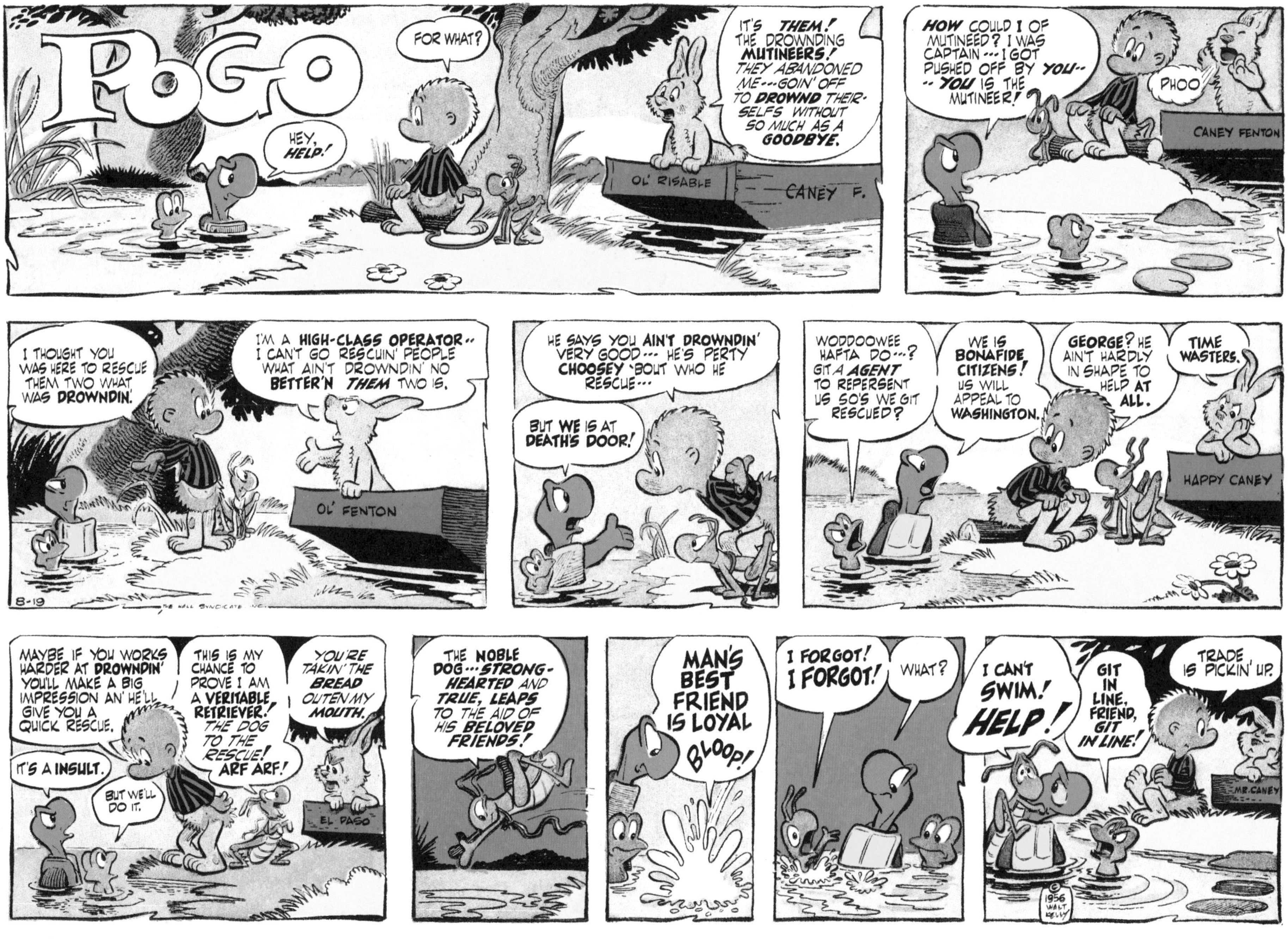
POGO
HEY, HELP!
FOR WHAT?
IT'S THEM! THE DROWNDING MUTINEERS! THEY ABANDONED ME---GOIN' OFF TO DROWND THEIR-SELFS WITHOUT SO MUCH AS A GOODBYE.
OL' RISABLE
CANEY F.
HOW COULD I OF MUTINEED? I WAS CAPTAIN---I GOT PUSHED OFF BY YOU-- --YOU IS THE MUTINEER!
PHOO
CANEY FENTON
I THOUGHT YOU WAS HERE TO RESCUE THEM TWO WHAT WAS DROWNDIN'.
I'M A HIGH-CLASS OPERATOR.. I CAN'T GO RESCUIN' PEOPLE WHAT AIN'T DROWNDIN' NO BETTER'N THEM TWO IS.
OL' FENTON
8-19
HE SAYS YOU AIN'T DROWNDIN' VERY GOOD--- HE'S PERTY CHOOSEY 'BOUT WHO HE RESCUE---
BUT WE IS AT DEATH'S DOOR!
WODDOOWEE HAFTA DO---? GIT A AGENT TO REPERSENT US SO'S WE GIT RESCUED?
WE IS BONAFIDE CITIZENS! US WILL APPEAL TO WASHINGTON.
GEORGE? HE AIN'T HARDLY IN SHAPE TO HELP AT ALL.
TIME WASTERS.
HAPPY CANEY
MAYBE IF YOU WORKS HARDER AT DROWNDIN' YOU'LL MAKE A BIG IMPRESSION AN' HE'LL GIVE YOU A QUICK RESCUE.
IT'S A INSULT.
BUT WE'LL DO IT.
THIS IS MY CHANCE TO PROVE I AM A VERITABLE RETRIEVER! THE DOG TO THE RESCUE! ARF ARF!
YOU'RE TAKIN' THE BREAD OUTEN MY MOUTH.
EL PASO
THE NOBLE DOG---STRONG-HEARTED AND TRUE, LEAPS TO THE AID OF HIS BELOVED FRIENDS!
MAN'S BEST FRIEND IS LOYAL
BLOOP!
I FORGOT! I FORGOT!
WHAT?
I CAN'T SWIM! HELP!
GIT IN LINE, FRIEND, GIT IN LINE!
TRADE IS PICKIN' UP.
MR. CANEY
© 1956 WALT KELLY

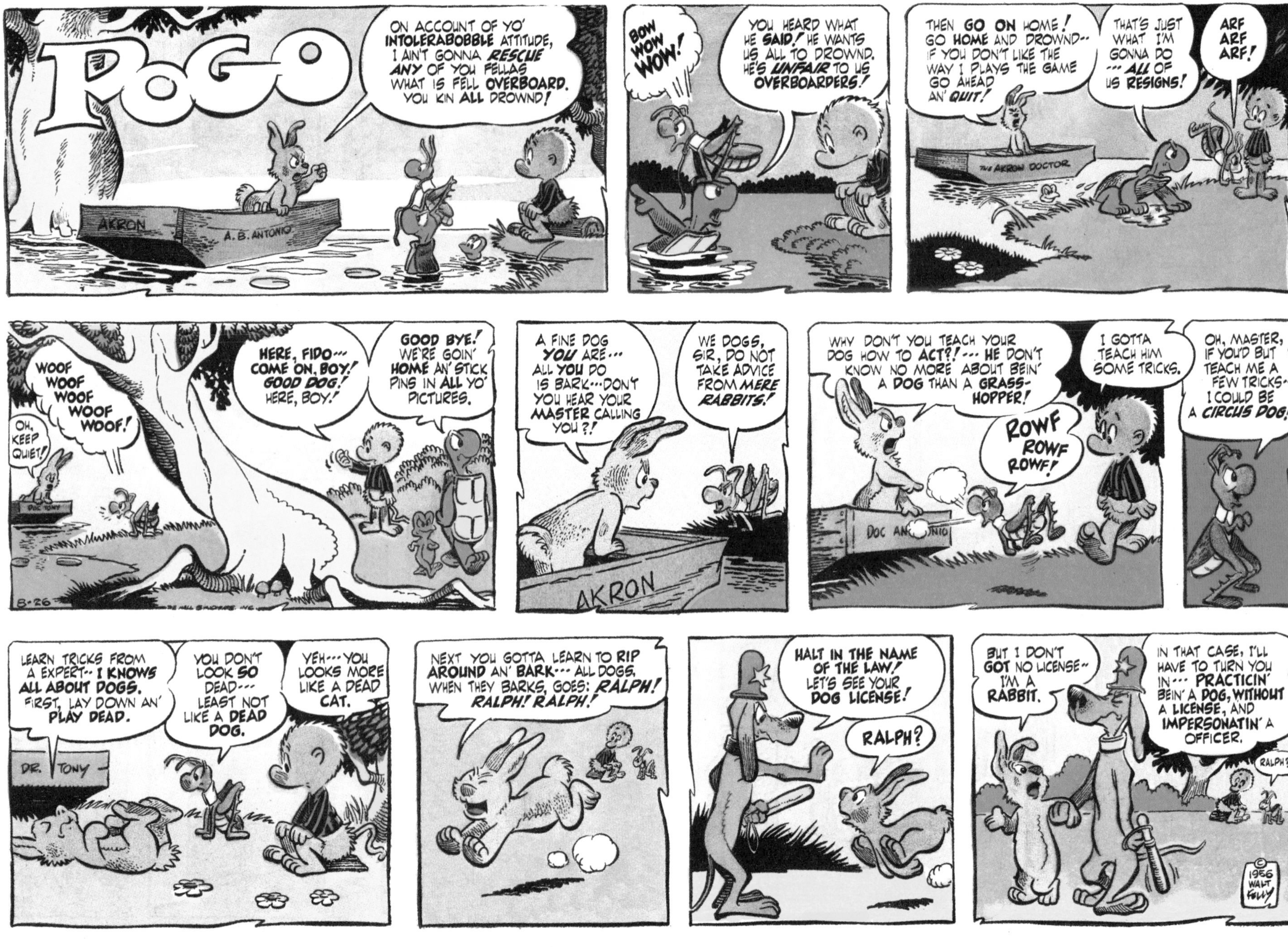
POGO
ON ACCOUNT OF YO' INTOLERABOBBLE ATTITUDE, I AIN'T GONNA RESCUE ANY OF YOU FELLAS WHAT IS FELL OVERBOARD. YOU KIN ALL DROWND!
AKRON
A. B. ANTONIO
BOW WOW WOW!
YOU HEARD WHAT HE SAID! HE WANTS US ALL TO DROWND. HE'S UNFAIR TO US OVERBOARDERS!
THEN GO ON HOME! GO HOME AND DROWND-- IF YOU DON'T LIKE THE WAY I PLAYS THE GAME GO AHEAD AN' QUIT!
THAT'S JUST WHAT I'M GONNA DO --- ALL OF US RESIGNS!
ARF ARF ARF!
THE AKRON DOCTOR
WOOF WOOF WOOF WOOF WOOF!
OH, KEEP QUIET!
DOC TONY
HERE, FIDO--- COME ON, BOY! GOOD DOG! HERE, BOY!
GOOD BYE! WE'RE GOIN' HOME AN' STICK PINS IN ALL YO' PICTURES.
8-26
A FINE DOG YOU ARE--- ALL YOU DO IS BARK---DON'T YOU HEAR YOUR MASTER CALLING YOU?!
WE DOGS, SIR, DO NOT TAKE ADVICE FROM MERE RABBITS!
AKRON
WHY DON'T YOU TEACH YOUR DOG HOW TO ACT?!--- HE DON'T KNOW NO MORE ABOUT BEIN' A DOG THAN A GRASS-HOPPER!
ROWF ROWF ROWF!
DOC ANTONIO
I GOTTA TEACH HIM SOME TRICKS.
OH, MASTER, IF YOU'D BUT TEACH ME A FEW TRICKS-- I COULD BE A CIRCUS DOG!
LEARN TRICKS FROM A EXPERT-- I KNOWS ALL ABOUT DOGS. FIRST, LAY DOWN AN' PLAY DEAD.
YOU DON'T LOOK SO DEAD--- LEAST NOT LIKE A DEAD DOG.
YEH--- YOU LOOKS MORE LIKE A DEAD CAT.
DR. TONY
NEXT YOU GOTTA LEARN TO RIP AROUND AN' BARK--- ALL DOGS, WHEN THEY BARKS, GOES: RALPH! RALPH! RALPH!
HALT IN THE NAME OF THE LAW! LET'S SEE YOUR DOG LICENSE!
RALPH?
BUT I DON'T GOT NO LICENSE-- I'M A RABBIT.
IN THAT CASE, I'LL HAVE TO TURN YOU IN--- PRACTICIN' BEIN' A DOG, WITHOUT A LICENSE, AND IMPERSONATIN' A OFFICER.
RALPH?
© 1956 WALT KELLY

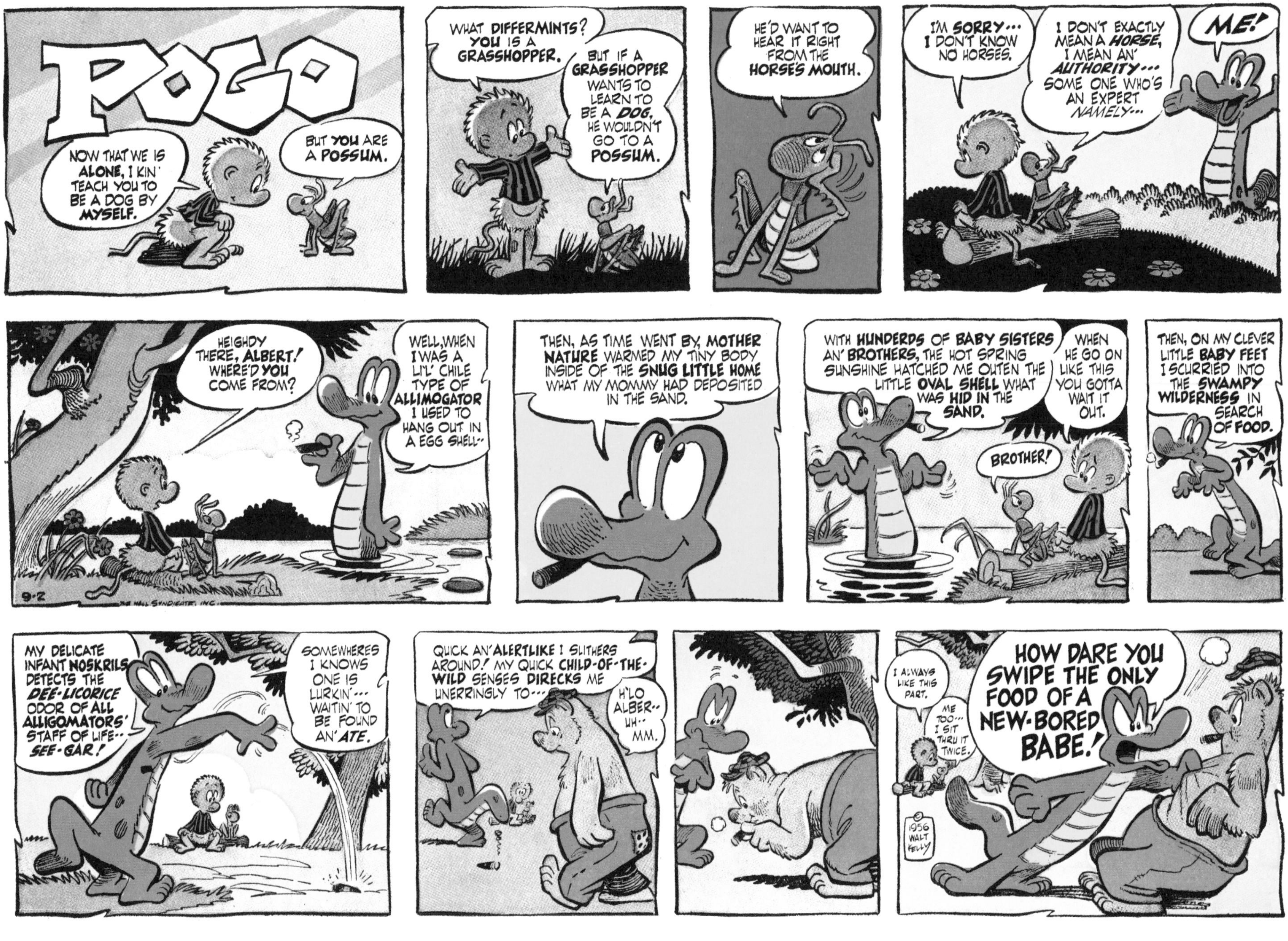
POGO
NOW THAT WE IS ALONE, I KIN' TEACH YOU TO BE A DOG BY MYSELF.
BUT YOU ARE A POSSUM.
WHAT DIFFERMINTS? YOU IS A GRASSHOPPER.
BUT IF A GRASSHOPPER WANTS TO LEARN TO BE A DOG, HE WOULDN'T GO TO A POSSUM.
HE'D WANT TO HEAR IT RIGHT FROM THE HORSE'S MOUTH.
I'M SORRY... I DON'T KNOW NO HORSES.
I DON'T EXACTLY MEAN A HORSE, I MEAN AN' AUTHORITY... SOME ONE WHO'S AN EXPERT NAMELY...
ME!
HEIGHDY THERE, ALBERT! WHERE'D YOU COME FROM?
WELL, WHEN I WAS A LI'L' CHILE TYPE OF ALLIMOGATOR I USED TO HANG OUT IN A EGG SHELL...
9-2
THEN, AS TIME WENT BY, MOTHER NATURE WARMED MY TINY BODY INSIDE OF THE SNUG LITTLE HOME WHAT MY MOMMY HAD DEPOSITED IN THE SAND.
WITH HUNDERDS OF BABY SISTERS AN' BROTHERS, THE HOT SPRING SUNSHINE HATCHED ME OUTEN THE LITTLE OVAL SHELL WHAT WAS HID IN THE SAND.
WHEN HE GO ON LIKE THIS YOU GOTTA WAIT IT OUT.
BROTHER!
THEN, ON MY CLEVER LITTLE BABY FEET I SCURRIED INTO THE SWAMPY WILDERNESS IN SEARCH OF FOOD.
MY DELICATE INFANT NOSKRILS DETECTS THE DEE-LICORICE ODOR OF ALL ALLIGOMATORS' STAFF OF LIFE... SEE-GAR!
SOMEWHERES I KNOWS ONE IS LURKIN'... WAITIN' TO BE FOUND AN' ATE.
QUICK AN' ALERTLIKE I SLITHERS AROUND! MY QUICK CHILD-OF-THE-WILD SENSES DIRECKS ME UNERRINGLY TO...
H'LO ALBER... UH... MM.
I ALWAYS LIKE THIS PART.
ME TOO... I SIT THRU IT TWICE.
HOW DARE YOU SWIPE THE ONLY FOOD OF A NEW-BORED BABE!
©1956 WALT KELLY

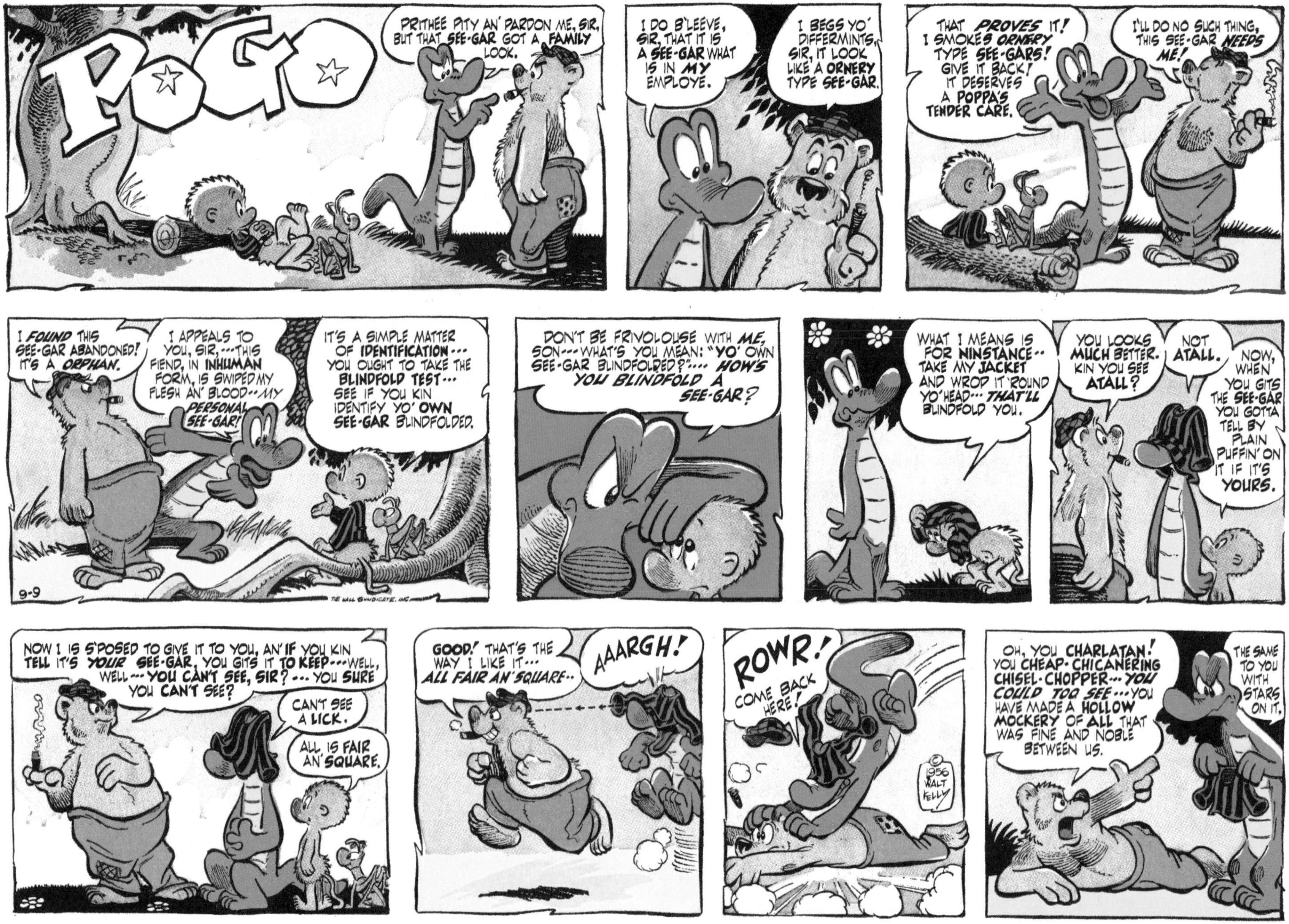
POGO
PRITHEE PITY AN' PARDON ME, SIR, BUT THAT SEE-GAR GOT A FAMILY LOOK.
I DO B'LEEVE, SIR, THAT IT IS A SEE-GAR WHAT IS IN MY EMPLOYE.
I BEGS YO' DIFFERMINTS, SIR, IT LOOK LIKE A ORNERY TYPE SEE-GAR.
THAT PROVES IT! I SMOKES ORNERY TYPE SEE-GARS! GIVE IT BACK! IT DESERVES A POPPA'S TENDER CARE.
I'LL DO NO SUCH THING, THIS SEE-GAR NEEDS ME!
I FOUND THIS SEE-GAR ABANDONED! IT'S A ORPHAN.
I APPEALS TO YOU, SIR,---THIS FIEND, IN INHUMAN FORM, IS SWIPED MY FLESH AN' BLOOD--MY PERSONAL SEE-GAR!
IT'S A SIMPLE MATTER OF IDENTIFICATION--- YOU OUGHT TO TAKE THE BLINDFOLD TEST--- SEE IF YOU KIN IDENTIFY YO' OWN SEE-GAR BLINDFOLDED.
9-9
THE HALL SYNDICATE, INC.
DON'T BE FRIVOLOUSE WITH ME, SON---WHAT'S YOU MEAN: "YO' OWN SEE-GAR BLINDFOLDED?"--- HOW'S YOU BLINDFOLD A SEE-GAR?
WHAT I MEANS IS FOR NINSTANCE-- TAKE MY JACKET AND WROP IT 'ROUND YO' HEAD--- THAT'LL BLINDFOLD YOU.
YOU LOOKS MUCH BETTER. KIN YOU SEE ATALL?
NOT ATALL.
NOW, WHEN YOU GITS THE SEE-GAR YOU GOTTA TELL BY PLAIN PUFFIN' ON IT IF IT'S YOURS.
NOW I IS S'POSED TO GIVE IT TO YOU, AN' IF YOU KIN TELL IT'S YOUR SEE-GAR, YOU GITS IT TO KEEP---WELL, WELL--- YOU CAN'T SEE, SIR? --- YOU SURE YOU CAN'T SEE?
CAN'T SEE A LICK.
ALL IS FAIR AN' SQUARE.
GOOD! THAT'S THE WAY I LIKE IT--- ALL FAIR AN' SQUARE--
AAARGH!
ROWR!
COME BACK HERE!
©1956 WALT KELLY
OH, YOU CHARLATAN! YOU CHEAP-CHICANERING CHISEL-CHOPPER--- YOU COULD TOO SEE---YOU HAVE MADE A HOLLOW MOCKERY OF ALL THAT WAS FINE AND NOBLE BETWEEN US.
THE SAME TO YOU WITH STARS ON IT.

SUNDAY, SEPTEMBER 16, 1956

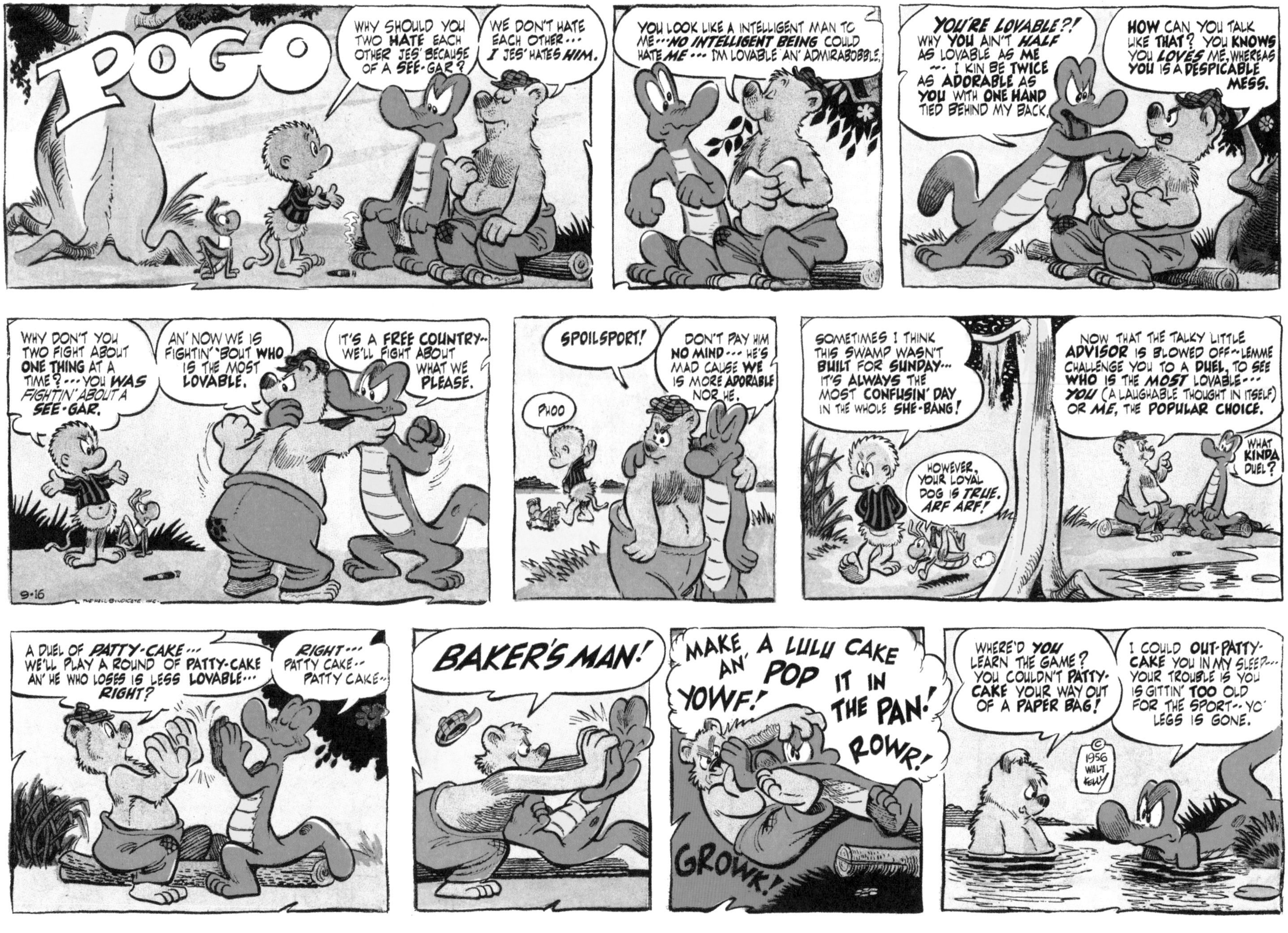
POGO
WHY SHOULD YOU TWO HATE EACH OTHER JES' BECAUSE OF A SEE-GAR?
WE DON'T HATE EACH OTHER··· I JES' HATES HIM.
YOU LOOK LIKE A INTELLIGENT MAN TO ME···NO INTELLIGENT BEING COULD HATE ME··· I'M LOVABLE AN' ADMIRABOBBLE.
YOU'RE LOVABLE?! WHY YOU AIN'T HALF AS LOVABLE AS ME ··· I KIN BE TWICE AS ADORABLE AS YOU WITH ONE HAND TIED BEHIND MY BACK.
HOW CAN YOU TALK LIKE THAT? YOU KNOWS YOU LOVES ME, WHEREAS YOU IS A DESPICABLE MESS.
WHY DON'T YOU TWO FIGHT ABOUT ONE THING AT A TIME?···YOU WAS FIGHTIN' ABOUT A SEE-GAR.
AN' NOW WE IS FIGHTIN' 'BOUT WHO IS THE MOST LOVABLE.
IT'S A FREE COUNTRY-- WE'LL FIGHT ABOUT WHAT WE PLEASE.
9-16
SPOILSPORT!
PHOO
DON'T PAY HIM NO MIND··· HE'S MAD CAUSE WE IS MORE ADORABLE NOR HE.
SOMETIMES I THINK THIS SWAMP WASN'T BUILT FOR SUNDAY··· IT'S ALWAYS THE MOST CONFUSIN' DAY IN THE WHOLE SHE-BANG!
HOWEVER, YOUR LOYAL DOG IS TRUE. ARF ARF!
NOW THAT THE TALKY LITTLE ADVISOR IS BLOWED OFF-- LEMME CHALLENGE YOU TO A DUEL, TO SEE WHO IS THE MOST LOVABLE··· YOU (A LAUGHABLE THOUGHT IN ITSELF) OR ME, THE POPULAR CHOICE.
WHAT KINDA DUEL?
A DUEL OF PATTY-CAKE··· WE'LL PLAY A ROUND OF PATTY-CAKE AN' HE WHO LOSES IS LESS LOVABLE··· RIGHT?
RIGHT··· PATTY CAKE-- PATTY CAKE--
BAKER'S MAN!
MAKE A LULU CAKE AN' POP IT IN THE PAN!
YOWF!
ROWR!
GROWK!
WHERE'D YOU LEARN THE GAME? YOU COULDN'T PATTY-CAKE YOUR WAY OUT OF A PAPER BAG!
© 1956 WALT KELLY
I COULD OUT-PATTY-CAKE YOU IN MY SLEEP··· YOUR TROUBLE IS YOU IS GITTIN' TOO OLD FOR THE SPORT-- YO' LEGS IS GONE.

SUNDAY, SEPTEMBER 23, 1956

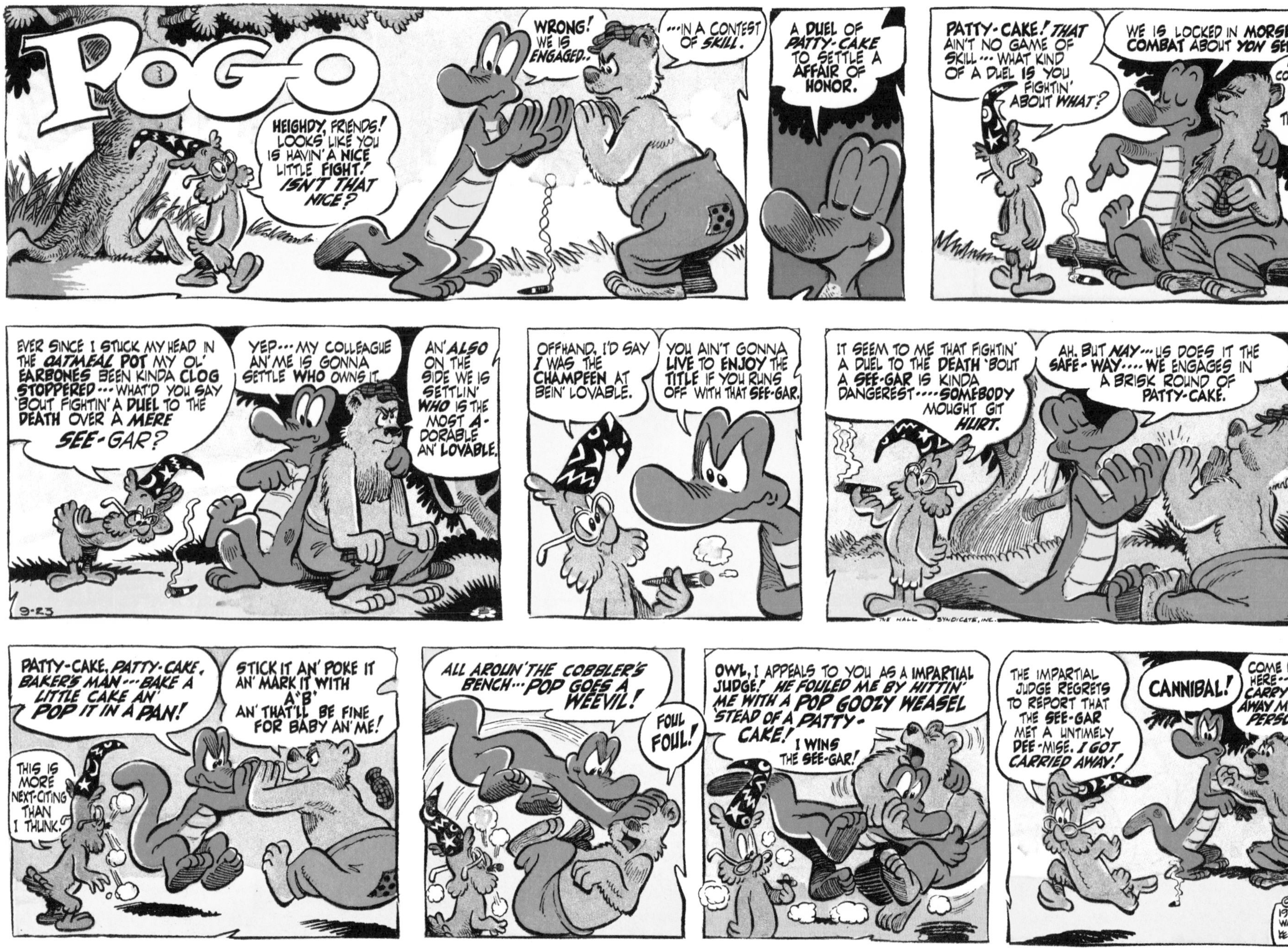
POGO
HEIGHDY, FRIENDS! LOOKS LIKE YOU IS HAVIN' A NICE LITTLE FIGHT! ISN'T THAT NICE?
WRONG! WE IS ENGAGED..
...IN A CONTEST OF SKILL.
A DUEL OF PATTY-CAKE TO SETTLE A AFFAIR OF HONOR.
PATTY-CAKE! THAT AIN'T NO GAME OF SKILL... WHAT KIND OF A DUEL IS YOU FIGHTIN' ABOUT WHAT?
WE IS LOCKED IN MORSEL COMBAT ABOUT YON SEE-GAR.
MY COLLEAGUE AN' I, THAT IS.
EVER SINCE I STUCK MY HEAD IN THE OATMEAL POT MY OL' EARBONES BEEN KINDA CLOG STOPPERED... WHAT'D YOU SAY 'BOUT FIGHTIN' A DUEL TO THE DEATH OVER A MERE SEE-GAR?
YEP... MY COLLEAGUE AN' ME IS GONNA SETTLE WHO OWNS IT.
AN' ALSO ON THE SIDE WE IS SETTLIN' WHO IS THE MOST A-DORABLE AN' LOVABLE.
9-23
OFFHAND, I'D SAY I WAS THE CHAMPEEN AT BEIN' LOVABLE.
YOU AIN'T GONNA LIVE TO ENJOY THE TITLE IF YOU RUNS OFF WITH THAT SEE-GAR.
IT SEEM TO ME THAT FIGHTIN' A DUEL TO THE DEATH 'BOUT A SEE-GAR IS KINDA DANGEREST.... SOMEBODY MOUGHT GIT HURT.
AH, BUT NAY... US DOES IT THE SAFE-WAY.... WE ENGAGES IN A BRISK ROUND OF PATTY-CAKE.
THE HALL SYNDICATE, INC.
PATTY-CAKE, PATTY-CAKE, BAKER'S MAN... BAKE A LITTLE CAKE AN' POP IT IN A PAN!
STICK IT AN' POKE IT AN' MARK IT WITH A 'B' AN' THAT'LL BE FINE FOR BABY AN' ME!
THIS IS MORE NEXT-CITING THAN I THUNK.
ALL AROUN' THE COBBLER'S BENCH... POP GOES A WEEVIL!
FOUL FOUL!
OWL, I APPEALS TO YOU AS A IMPARTIAL JUDGE! HE FOULED ME BY HITTIN' ME WITH A POP GOOZY WEASEL 'STEAD OF A PATTY-CAKE!
I WINS THE SEE-GAR!
THE IMPARTIAL JUDGE REGRETS TO REPORT THAT THE SEE-GAR MET A UNTIMELY DEE-MISE. I GOT CARRIED AWAY!
CANNIBAL!
COME BACK HERE... I'LL CARRY YOU AWAY MYSELF PERSONAL!
© 1956 WALT KELLY

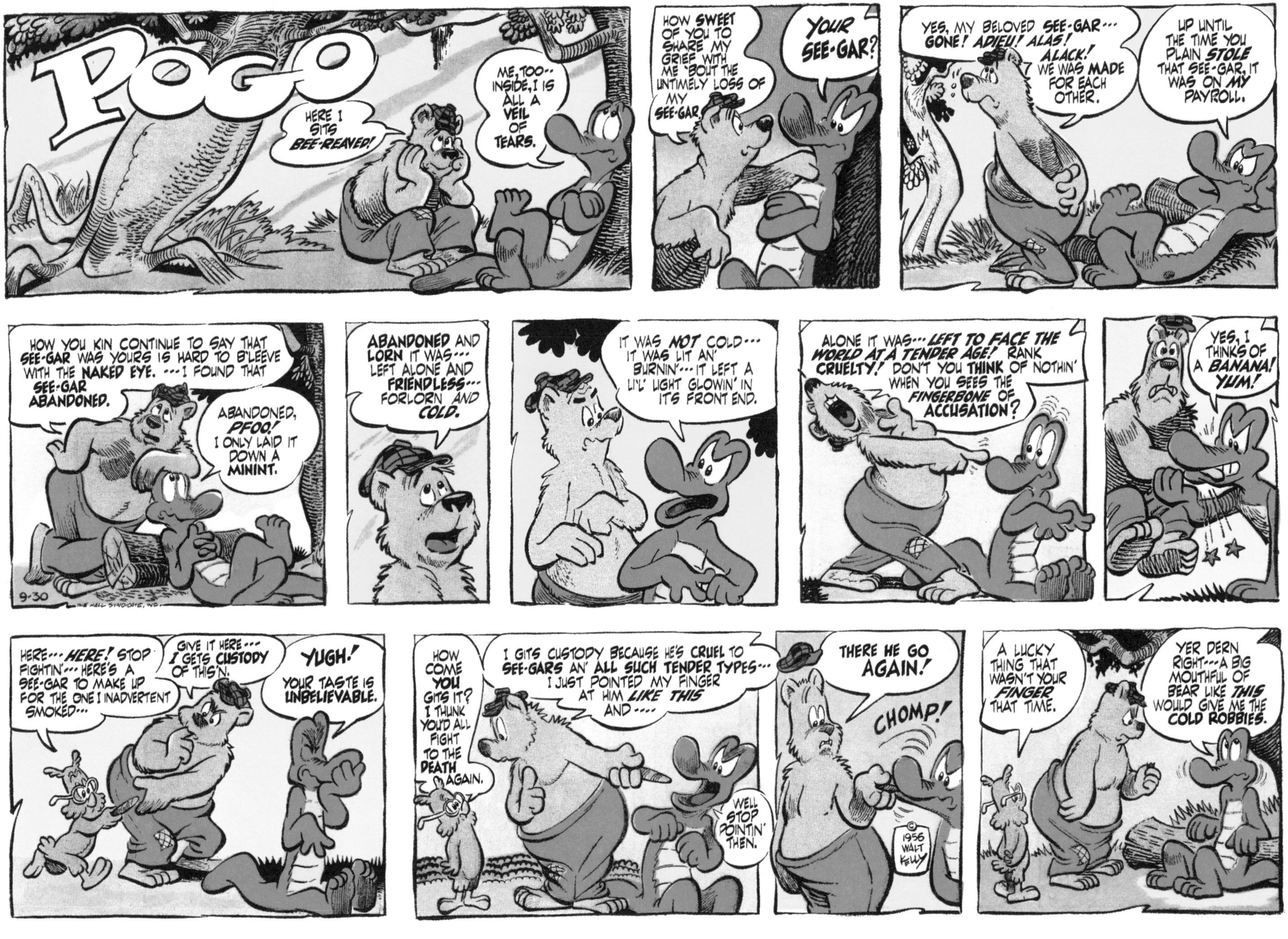
POGO
HERE I SITS BEE-REAVED!
ME, TOO-- INSIDE, I IS ALL A VEIL OF TEARS.
HOW SWEET OF YOU TO SHARE MY GRIEF WITH ME 'BOUT THE UNTIMELY LOSS OF MY SEE-GAR
YOUR SEE-GAR?
YES, MY BELOVED SEE-GAR... GONE! ADIEU! ALAS! ALACK! WE WAS MADE FOR EACH OTHER.
UP UNTIL THE TIME YOU PLAIN STOLE THAT SEE-GAR, IT WAS ON MY PAYROLL.
HOW YOU KIN CONTINUE TO SAY THAT SEE-GAR WAS YOURS IS HARD TO B'LEEVE WITH THE NAKED EYE. ...I FOUND THAT SEE-GAR ABANDONED.
ABANDONED, PFOO! I ONLY LAID IT DOWN A MININT.
9-30
ABANDONED AND LORN IT WAS... LEFT ALONE AND FRIENDLESS... FORLORN AND COLD.
IT WAS NOT COLD... IT WAS LIT AN' BURNIN'... IT LEFT A LI'L' LIGHT GLOWIN' IN ITS FRONT END.
ALONE IT WAS... LEFT TO FACE THE WORLD AT A TENDER AGE! RANK CRUELTY! DON'T YOU THINK OF NOTHIN' WHEN YOU SEES THE FINGERBONE OF ACCUSATION?
YES, I THINKS OF A BANANA! YUM!
HERE... HERE! STOP FIGHTIN'... HERE'S A SEE-GAR TO MAKE UP FOR THE ONE I INADVERTENT SMOKED...
GIVE IT HERE... I GETS CUSTODY OF THIS'N.
YUGH! YOUR TASTE IS UNBELIEVABLE.
HOW COME YOU GITS IT? I THUNK YOU'D ALL FIGHT TO THE DEATH AGAIN.
I GITS CUSTODY BECAUSE HE'S CRUEL TO SEE-GARS AN' ALL SUCH TENDER TYPES... I JUST POINTED MY FINGER AT HIM LIKE THIS AND....
WELL STOP POINTIN' THEN.
THERE HE GO AGAIN!
CHOMP!
© 1956 WALT KELLY
A LUCKY THING THAT WASN'T YOUR FINGER THAT TIME.
YER DERN RIGHT... A BIG MOUTHFUL OF BEAR LIKE THIS WOULD GIVE ME THE COLD ROBBIES.

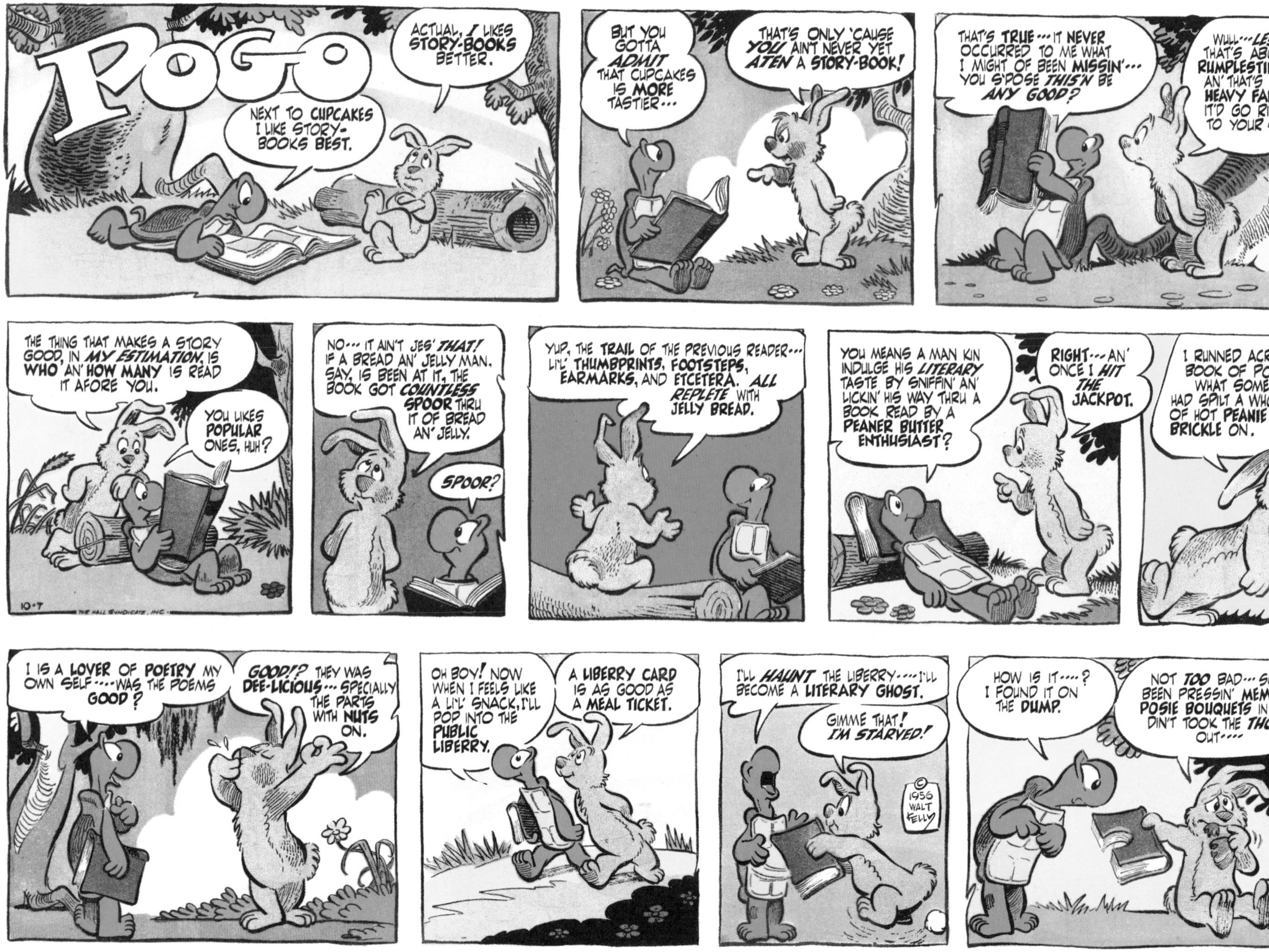
POGO
NEXT TO CUPCAKES I LIKE STORY-BOOKS BEST.
ACTUAL, I LIKES STORY-BOOKS BETTER.
BUT YOU GOTTA ADMIT THAT CUPCAKES IS MORE TASTIER...
THAT'S ONLY 'CAUSE YOU AIN'T NEVER YET ATEN A STORY-BOOK!
THAT'S TRUE... IT NEVER OCCURRED TO ME WHAT I MIGHT OF BEEN MISSIN'... YOU S'POSE THIS'N BE ANY GOOD?
WULL... LESSEE... THAT'S ABOUT RUMPLESTILTSKIN AN' THAT'S PERTY HEAVY FARE.... IT'D GO RIGHT TO YOUR STOMACH!
THE THING THAT MAKES A STORY GOOD, IN MY ESTIMATION, IS WHO AN' HOW MANY IS READ IT AFORE YOU.
YOU LIKES POPULAR ONES, HUH?
NO... IT AIN'T JES' THAT! IF A BREAD AN' JELLY MAN, SAY, IS BEEN AT IT, THE BOOK GOT COUNTLESS SPOOR THRU IT OF BREAD AN' JELLY.
SPOOR?
YUP, THE TRAIL OF THE PREVIOUS READER... LI'L' THUMBPRINTS, FOOTSTEPS, EARMARKS, AND ETCETERA. ALL REPLETE WITH JELLY BREAD.
YOU MEANS A MAN KIN INDULGE HIS LITERARY TASTE BY SNIFFIN' AN' LICKIN' HIS WAY THRU A BOOK READ BY A PEANER BUTTER ENTHUSIAST?
RIGHT... AN' ONCE I HIT THE JACKPOT.
I RUNNED ACROSS A BOOK OF POETRIES WHAT SOMEBODY HAD SPILT A WHOLE PAN OF HOT PEANIE BRICKLE ON.
10-7
I IS A LOVER OF POETRY MY OWN SELF.... WAS THE POEMS GOOD?
GOOD!? THEY WAS DEE-LICIOUS... SPECIALLY THE PARTS WITH NUTS ON.
OH BOY! NOW WHEN I FEELS LIKE A LI'L' SNACK, I'LL POP INTO THE PUBLIC LIBERRY.
A LIBERRY CARD IS AS GOOD AS A MEAL TICKET.
I'LL HAUNT THE LIBERRY.... I'LL BECOME A LITERARY GHOST.
GIMME THAT! I'M STARVED!
© 1956 WALT KELLY
HOW IS IT....? I FOUND IT ON THE DUMP.
NOT TOO BAD... SOMEBODY BEEN PRESSIN' MEMENTO POSIE BOUQUETS IN HER AN' DIN'T TOOK THE THORNS OUT....

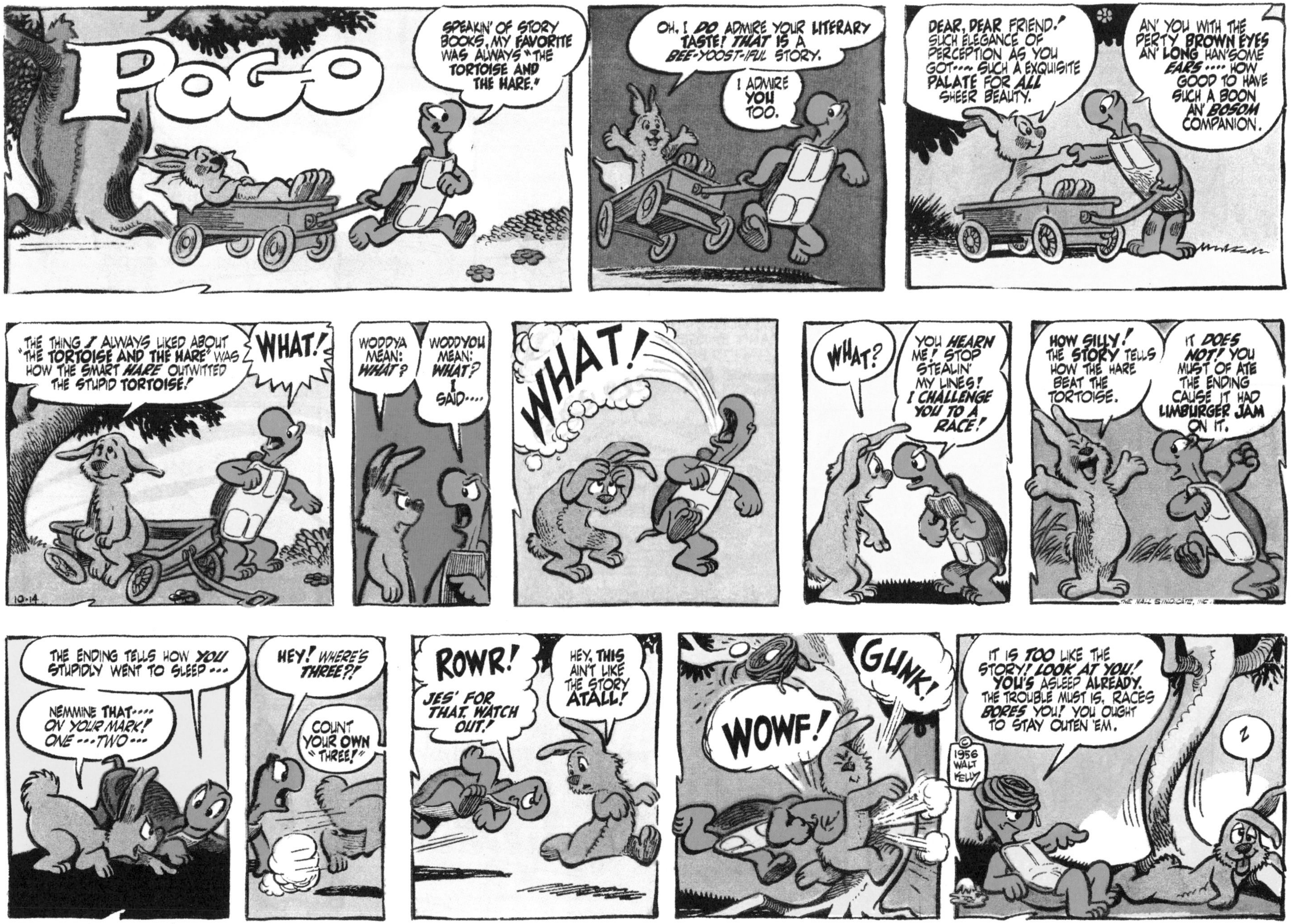
POGO
SPEAKIN' OF STORY BOOKS, MY FAVORITE WAS ALWAYS "THE TORTOISE AND THE HARE."
OH, I DO ADMIRE YOUR LITERARY TASTE! THAT IS A BEE-YOOST-IFUL STORY.
I ADMIRE YOU TOO.
DEAR, DEAR FRIEND! SUCH ELEGANCE OF PERCEPTION AS YOU GOT.... SUCH A EXQUISITE PALATE FOR ALL SHEER BEAUTY.
AN' YOU WITH THE PERTY BROWN EYES AN' LONG HAN'SOME EARS.... HOW GOOD TO HAVE SUCH A BOON AN' BOSOM COMPANION.
"THE THING I ALWAYS LIKED ABOUT "THE TORTOISE AND THE HARE" WAS HOW THE SMART HARE OUTWITTED THE STUPID TORTOISE!
WHAT!
10-14
WODDYA MEAN: WHAT?
WODDYOU MEAN: WHAT? I SAID....
WHAT!
WHAT?
YOU HEARN ME! STOP STEALIN' MY LINES! I CHALLENGE YOU TO A RACE!
HOW SILLY! THE STORY TELLS HOW THE HARE BEAT THE TORTOISE.
IT DOES NOT! YOU MUST OF ATE THE ENDING CAUSE IT HAD LIMBURGER JAM ON IT.
THE HALL SYNDICATE, INC.
THE ENDING TELLS HOW YOU STUPIDLY WENT TO SLEEP...
NEMMINE THAT.... ON YOUR MARK! ONE ... TWO ...
HEY! WHERE'S THREE?!
COUNT YOUR OWN "THREE!"
ROWR!
JES' FOR THAT, WATCH OUT!
HEY, THIS AIN'T LIKE THE STORY ATALL!
GUNK!
WOWF!
© 1956 WALT KELLY
IT IS TOO LIKE THE STORY! LOOK AT YOU! YOU'S ASLEEP ALREADY. THE TROUBLE MUST IS, RACES BORES YOU! YOU OUGHT TO STAY OUTEN 'EM.
Z

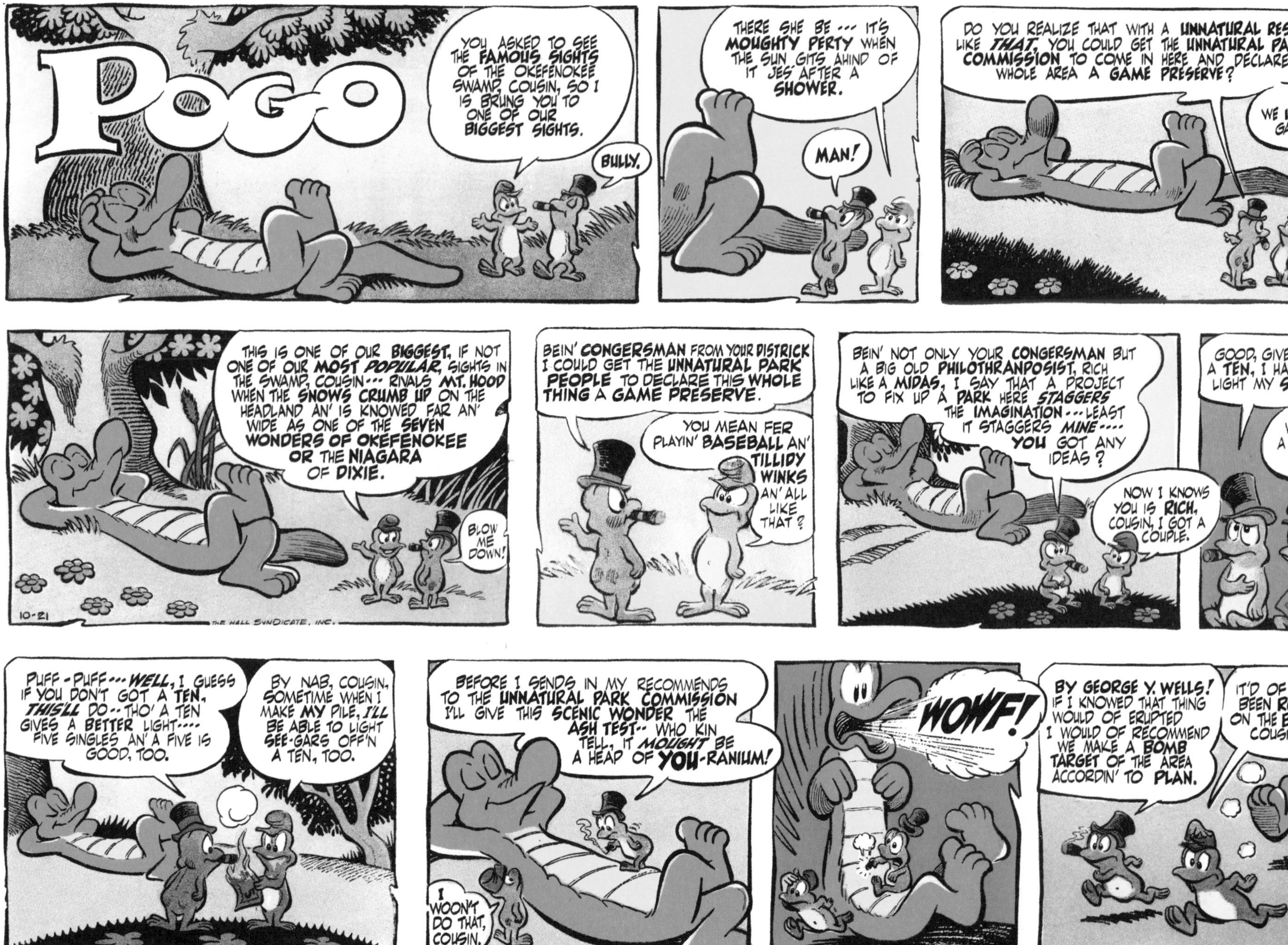
POGO
YOU ASKED TO SEE THE FAMOUS SIGHTS OF THE OKEFENOKEE SWAMP, COUSIN, SO I IS BRUNG YOU TO ONE OF OUR BIGGEST SIGHTS.
BULLY.
THERE SHE BE --- IT'S MOUGHTY PERTY WHEN THE SUN GITS AHIND OF IT JES' AFTER A SHOWER.
MAN!
DO YOU REALIZE THAT WITH A UNNATURAL RESOURCE LIKE THAT, YOU COULD GET THE UNNATURAL PARK COMMISSION TO COME IN HERE AND DECLARE THIS WHOLE AREA A GAME PRESERVE?
WE IS PERTY GAMEY.
THIS IS ONE OF OUR BIGGEST, IF NOT ONE OF OUR MOST POPULAR, SIGHTS IN THE SWAMP, COUSIN--- RIVALS MT. HOOD WHEN THE SNOWS CRUMB UP ON THE HEADLAND AN' IS KNOWED FAR AN' WIDE AS ONE OF THE SEVEN WONDERS OF OKEFENOKEE OR THE NIAGARA OF DIXIE.
BLOW ME DOWN!
10-21
THE HALL SYNDICATE, INC.
BEIN' CONGERSMAN FROM YOUR DISTRICK I COULD GET THE UNNATURAL PARK PEOPLE TO DECLARE THIS WHOLE THING A GAME PRESERVE.
YOU MEAN FER PLAYIN' BASEBALL AN' TILLIDY WINKS AN' ALL LIKE THAT?
BEIN' NOT ONLY YOUR CONGERSMAN BUT A BIG OLD PHILOTHRANPOSIST, RICH LIKE A MIDAS, I SAY THAT A PROJECT TO FIX UP A PARK HERE STAGGERS THE IMAGINATION --- LEAST IT STAGGERS MINE ---- YOU GOT ANY IDEAS?
NOW I KNOWS YOU IS RICH, COUSIN, I GOT A COUPLE.
GOOD, GIVE ME A TEN. I HAVE TO LIGHT MY SEE-GAR.
WOULD A FIVE DO?
PUFF-PUFF--- WELL, I GUESS IF YOU DON'T GOT A TEN, THIS'LL DO -- THO' A TEN GIVES A BETTER LIGHT---- FIVE SINGLES AN' A FIVE IS GOOD, TOO.
BY NAB, COUSIN, SOMETIME WHEN I MAKE MY PILE, I'LL BE ABLE TO LIGHT SEE-GARS OFF'N A TEN, TOO.
BEFORE I SENDS IN MY RECOMMENDS TO THE UNNATURAL PARK COMMISSION I'LL GIVE THIS SCENIC WONDER THE ASH TEST -- WHO KIN TELL, IT MOUGHT BE A HEAP OF YOU-RANIUM!
I WOON'T DO THAT, COUSIN.
WOWF!
BY GEORGE Y. WELLS! IF I KNOWED THAT THING WOULD OF ERUPTED I WOULD OF RECOMMEND WE MAKE A BOMB TARGET OF THE AREA ACCORDIN' TO PLAN.
IT'D OF ONLY BEEN ROUGH ON THE BOMBS, COUSIN!
© 1956 WALT KELLY

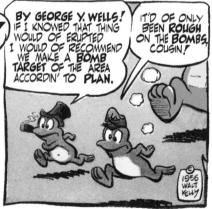

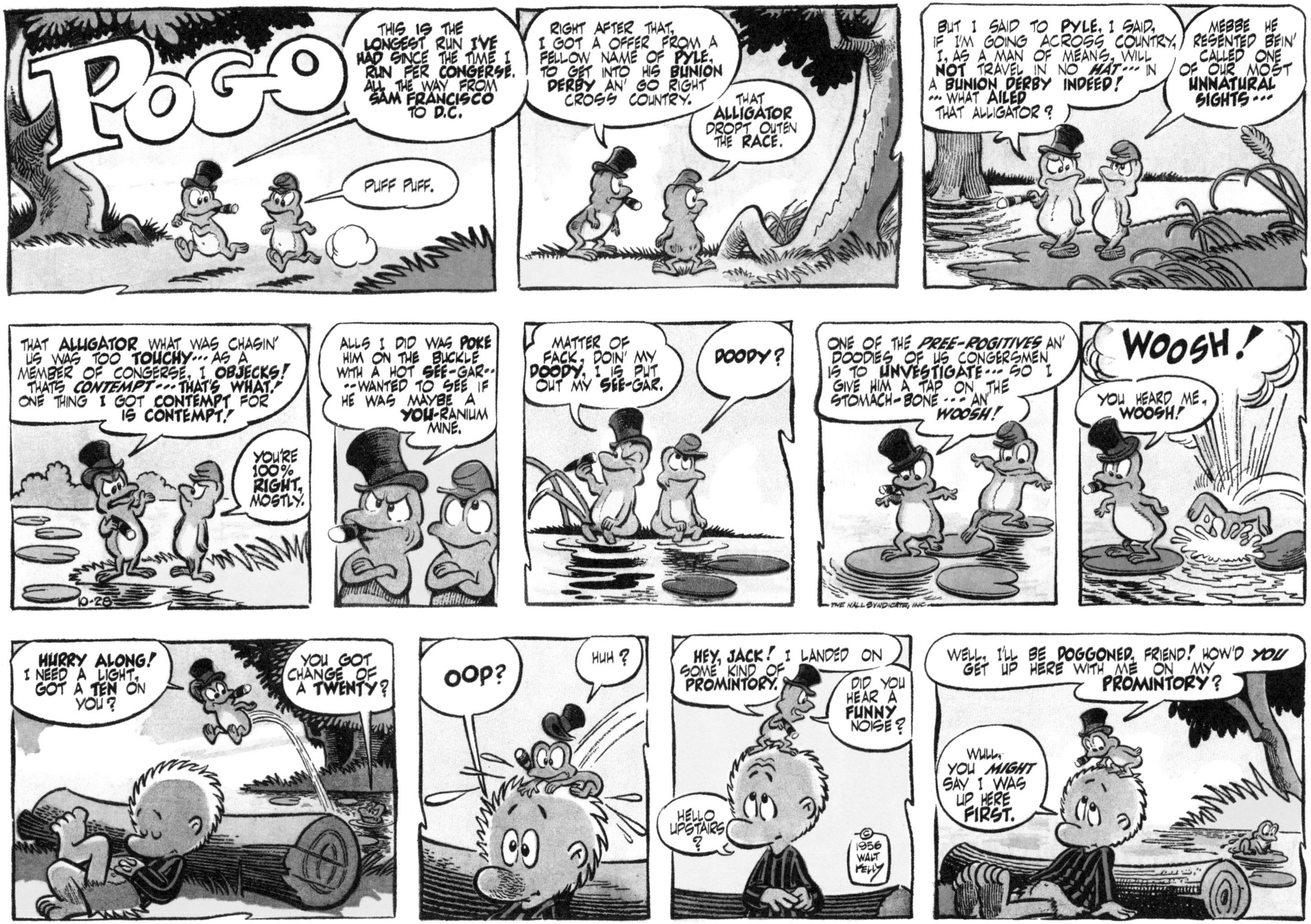
POGO
THIS IS THE LONGEST RUN I'VE HAD SINCE THE TIME I RUN FER CONGERSE. ALL THE WAY FROM SAM FRANCISCO TO D.C.
PUFF PUFF.
RIGHT AFTER THAT, I GOT A OFFER FROM A FELLOW NAME OF PYLE, TO GET INTO HIS BUNION DERBY AN' GO RIGHT CROSS COUNTRY.
THAT ALLIGATOR DROPT OUTEN THE RACE.
BUT I SAID TO PYLE, I SAID, IF I'M GOING ACROSS COUNTRY, I, AS A MAN OF MEANS, WILL NOT TRAVEL IN NO HAT... IN A BUNION DERBY INDEED! ... WHAT AILED THAT ALLIGATOR?
MEBBE HE RESENTED BEIN' CALLED ONE OF OUR MOST UNNATURAL SIGHTS...
THAT ALLIGATOR WHAT WAS CHASIN' US WAS TOO TOUCHY... AS A MEMBER OF CONGERSE, I OBJECKS! THATS CONTEMPT... THAT'S WHAT! ONE THING I GOT CONTEMPT FOR IS CONTEMPT!
YOU'RE 100% RIGHT, MOSTLY.
10-28
ALLS I DID WAS POKE HIM ON THE BUCKLE WITH A HOT SEE-GAR-- --WANTED TO SEE IF HE WAS MAYBE A YOU-RANIUM MINE.
MATTER OF FACK, DOIN' MY DOODY, I IS PUT OUT MY SEE-GAR.
DOODY?
ONE OF THE PREE-ROGITIVES AN' DOODIES OF US CONGERSMEN IS TO UNVESTIGATE... SO I GIVE HIM A TAP ON THE STOMACH-BONE... AN' WOOSH!
WOOSH!
YOU HEARD ME, WOOSH!
THE HALL SYNDICATE, INC.
HURRY ALONG! I NEED A LIGHT, GOT A TEN ON YOU?
YOU GOT CHANGE OF A TWENTY?
OOP?
HUH?
HEY, JACK! I LANDED ON SOME KIND OF PROMINTORY.
DID YOU HEAR A FUNNY NOISE?
HELLO UPSTAIRS?
©1956 WALT KELLY
WELL, I'LL BE DOGGONED, FRIEND! HOW'D YOU GET UP HERE WITH ME ON MY PROMINTORY?
WULL, YOU MIGHT SAY I WAS UP HERE FIRST.

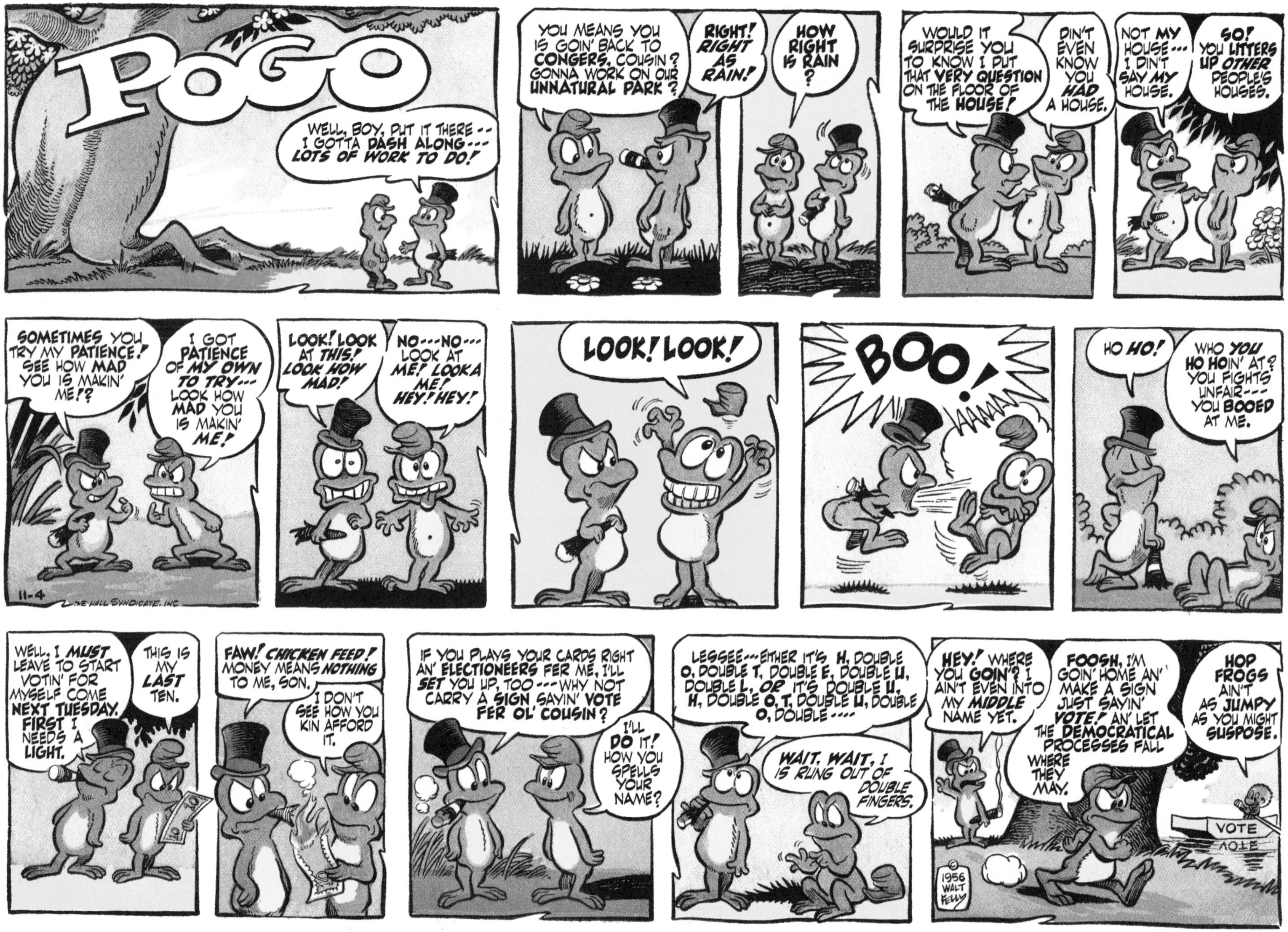
POGO
WELL, BOY, PUT IT THERE -- I GOTTA DASH ALONG --- LOTS OF WORK TO DO!
YOU MEANS YOU IS GOIN' BACK TO CONGERS, COUSIN? GONNA WORK ON OUR UNNATURAL PARK?
RIGHT! RIGHT AS RAIN!
HOW RIGHT IS RAIN?
WOULD IT SURPRISE YOU TO KNOW I PUT THAT VERY QUESTION ON THE FLOOR OF THE HOUSE!
DIN'T EVEN KNOW YOU HAD A HOUSE.
NOT MY HOUSE... I DIN'T SAY MY HOUSE.
SO! YOU LITTERS UP OTHER PEOPLE'S HOUSES.
SOMETIMES YOU TRY MY PATIENCE! SEE HOW MAD YOU IS MAKIN' ME!?
I GOT PATIENCE OF MY OWN TO TRY--- LOOK HOW MAD YOU IS MAKIN' ME!
11-4
THE HALL SYNDICATE, INC
LOOK! LOOK AT THIS! LOOK HOW MAD!
NO---NO--- LOOK AT ME! LOOKA ME! HEY! HEY!
LOOK! LOOK!
BOO!
HO HO!
WHO YOU HO HOIN' AT? YOU FIGHTS UNFAIR--- YOU BOOED AT ME.
WELL, I MUST LEAVE TO START VOTIN' FOR MYSELF COME NEXT TUESDAY. FIRST I NEEDS A LIGHT.
THIS IS MY LAST TEN.
FAW! CHICKEN FEED! MONEY MEANS NOTHING TO ME, SON.
I DON'T SEE HOW YOU KIN AFFORD IT.
IF YOU PLAYS YOUR CARDS RIGHT AN' ELECTIONEERS FER ME, I'LL SET YOU UP, TOO --- WHY NOT CARRY A SIGN SAYIN' VOTE FER OL' COUSIN?
I'LL DO IT! HOW YOU SPELLS YOUR NAME?
LESSEE--- EITHER IT'S H, DOUBLE O, DOUBLE T, DOUBLE E, DOUBLE U, DOUBLE L, OR IT'S DOUBLE U, H, DOUBLE O, T, DOUBLE U, DOUBLE O, DOUBLE ----
WAIT, WAIT, I IS RUNG OUT OF DOUBLE FINGERS.
HEY! WHERE YOU GOIN'? I AIN'T EVEN INTO MY MIDDLE NAME YET.
FOOSH, I'M GOIN' HOME AN' MAKE A SIGN JUST SAYIN' VOTE! AN' LET THE DEMOCRATICAL PROCESSES FALL WHERE THEY MAY.
HOP FROGS AIN'T AS JUMPY AS YOU MIGHT SUSPOSE.
VOTE
© 1956 WALT KELLY

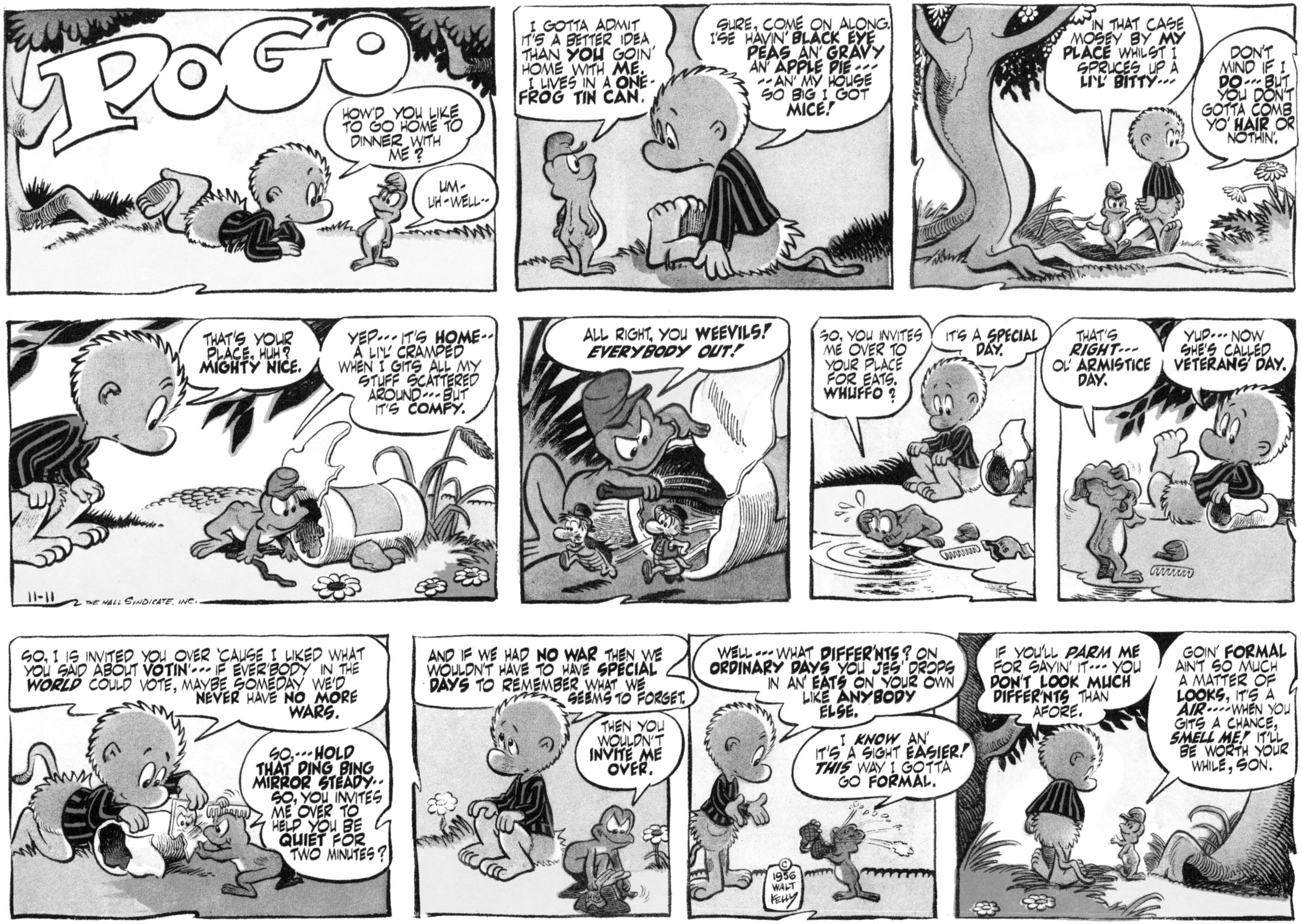
POGO
HOW'D YOU LIKE TO GO HOME TO DINNER WITH ME?
UM-UH-WELL--
I GOTTA ADMIT IT'S A BETTER IDEA THAN YOU GOIN' HOME WITH ME. I LIVES IN A ONE-FROG TIN CAN.
SURE, COME ON ALONG. I'SE HAVIN' BLACK EYE PEAS AN' GRAVY AN' APPLE PIE--- --AN' MY HOUSE SO BIG I GOT MICE!
IN THAT CASE MOSEY BY MY PLACE WHILST I SPRUCES UP A LI'L' BITTY---
DON'T MIND IF I DO---BUT YOU DON'T GOTTA COMB YO' HAIR OR NOTHIN'.
THAT'S YOUR PLACE, HUH? MIGHTY NICE.
YEP--- IT'S HOME-- A LI'L' CRAMPED WHEN I GITS ALL MY STUFF SCATTERED AROUND---BUT IT'S COMFY.
11-11
THE HALL SYNDICATE, INC.
ALL RIGHT, YOU WEEVILS! EVERYBODY OUT!
SO, YOU INVITES ME OVER TO YOUR PLACE FOR EATS. WHUFFO?
IT'S A SPECIAL DAY.
THAT'S RIGHT--- OL' ARMISTICE DAY.
YUP--- NOW SHE'S CALLED VETERANS' DAY.
SO, I IS INVITED YOU OVER 'CAUSE I LIKED WHAT YOU SAID ABOUT VOTIN'--- IF EVER'BODY IN THE WORLD COULD VOTE, MAYBE SOMEDAY WE'D NEVER HAVE NO MORE WARS.
SO,---HOLD THAT DING BING MIRROR STEADY.. SO, YOU INVITES ME OVER TO HELP YOU BE QUIET FOR TWO MINUTES?
AND IF WE HAD NO WAR THEN WE WOULDN'T HAVE TO HAVE SPECIAL DAYS TO REMEMBER WHAT WE SEEMS TO FORGET.
THEN YOU WOULDN'T INVITE ME OVER.
WELL--- WHAT DIFFER'NTS? ON ORDINARY DAYS YOU JES' DROPS IN AN' EATS ON YOUR OWN LIKE ANYBODY ELSE.
I KNOW AN' IT'S A SIGHT EASIER! THIS WAY I GOTTA GO FORMAL.
© 1956 WALT KELLY
IF YOU'LL PARM ME FOR SAYIN' IT--- YOU DON'T LOOK MUCH DIFFER'NTS THAN AFORE.
GOIN' FORMAL AIN'T SO MUCH A MATTER OF LOOKS, IT'S A AIR----WHEN YOU GITS A CHANCE, SMELL ME! IT'LL BE WORTH YOUR WHILE, SON.

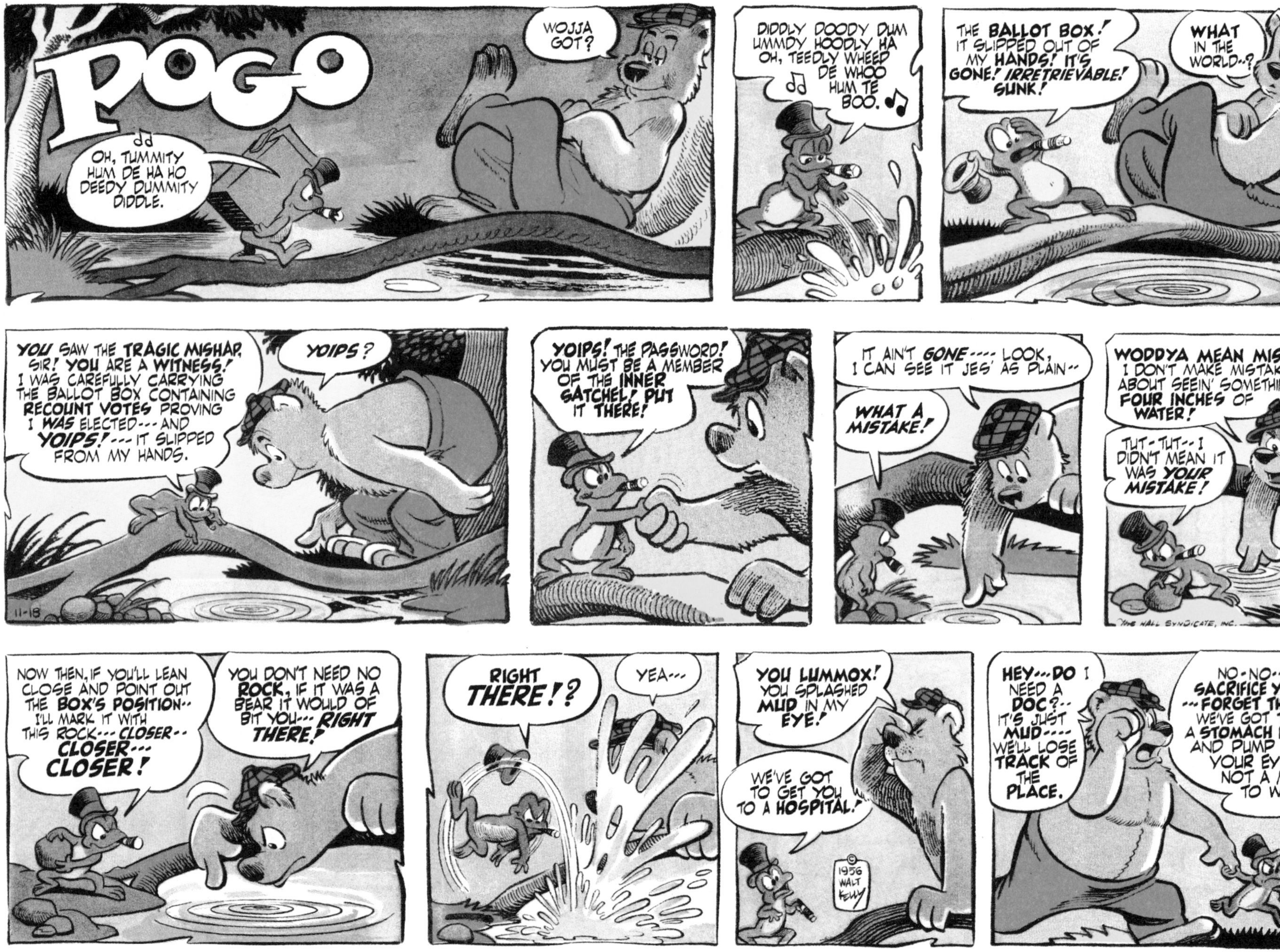
POGO
OH, TUMMITY HUM DE HA HO DEEDY DUMMITY DIDDLE.
WOJJA GOT?
DIDDLY DOODY DUM UMMDY HOODLY HA OH, TEEDLY WHEED DE WHOO HUM TE BOO.
THE BALLOT BOX! IT SLIPPED OUT OF MY HANDS! IT'S GONE! IRRETRIEVABLE! SUNK!
WHAT IN THE WORLD..?
YOU SAW THE TRAGIC MISHAP, SIR! YOU ARE A WITNESS! I WAS CAREFULLY CARRYING THE BALLOT BOX CONTAINING RECOUNT VOTES PROVING I WAS ELECTED--- AND YOIPS!--- IT SLIPPED FROM MY HANDS.
YOIPS?
11-18
YOIPS! THE PASSWORD! YOU MUST BE A MEMBER OF THE INNER SATCHEL! PUT IT THERE!
IT AIN'T GONE---- LOOK, I CAN SEE IT JES' AS PLAIN--
WHAT A MISTAKE!
WODDYA MEAN MISTAKE!? I DON'T MAKE MISTAKES ABOUT SEEIN' SOMETHIN' IN FOUR INCHES OF WATER!
TUT-TUT-- I DIDN'T MEAN IT WAS YOUR MISTAKE!
THE HALL SYNDICATE, INC.
NOW THEN, IF YOU'LL LEAN CLOSE AND POINT OUT THE BOX'S POSITION-- I'LL MARK IT WITH THIS ROCK--- CLOSER-- CLOSER--- CLOSER!
YOU DON'T NEED NO ROCK, IF IT WAS A BEAR IT WOULD OF BIT YOU--- RIGHT THERE!
RIGHT THERE!?
YEA---
YOU LUMMOX! YOU SPLASHED MUD IN MY EYE!
WE'VE GOT TO GET YOU TO A HOSPITAL!
© 1956 WALT KELLY
HEY---DO I NEED A DOC?-- IT'S JUST MUD---- WE'LL LOSE TRACK OF THE PLACE.
NO-NO---DON'T SACRIFICE YOURSELF ---FORGET THE BOX! WE'VE GOT TO GET A STOMACH PUMP AND PUMP OUT YOUR EYE---- NOT A MINUTE TO WASTE!

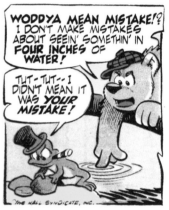

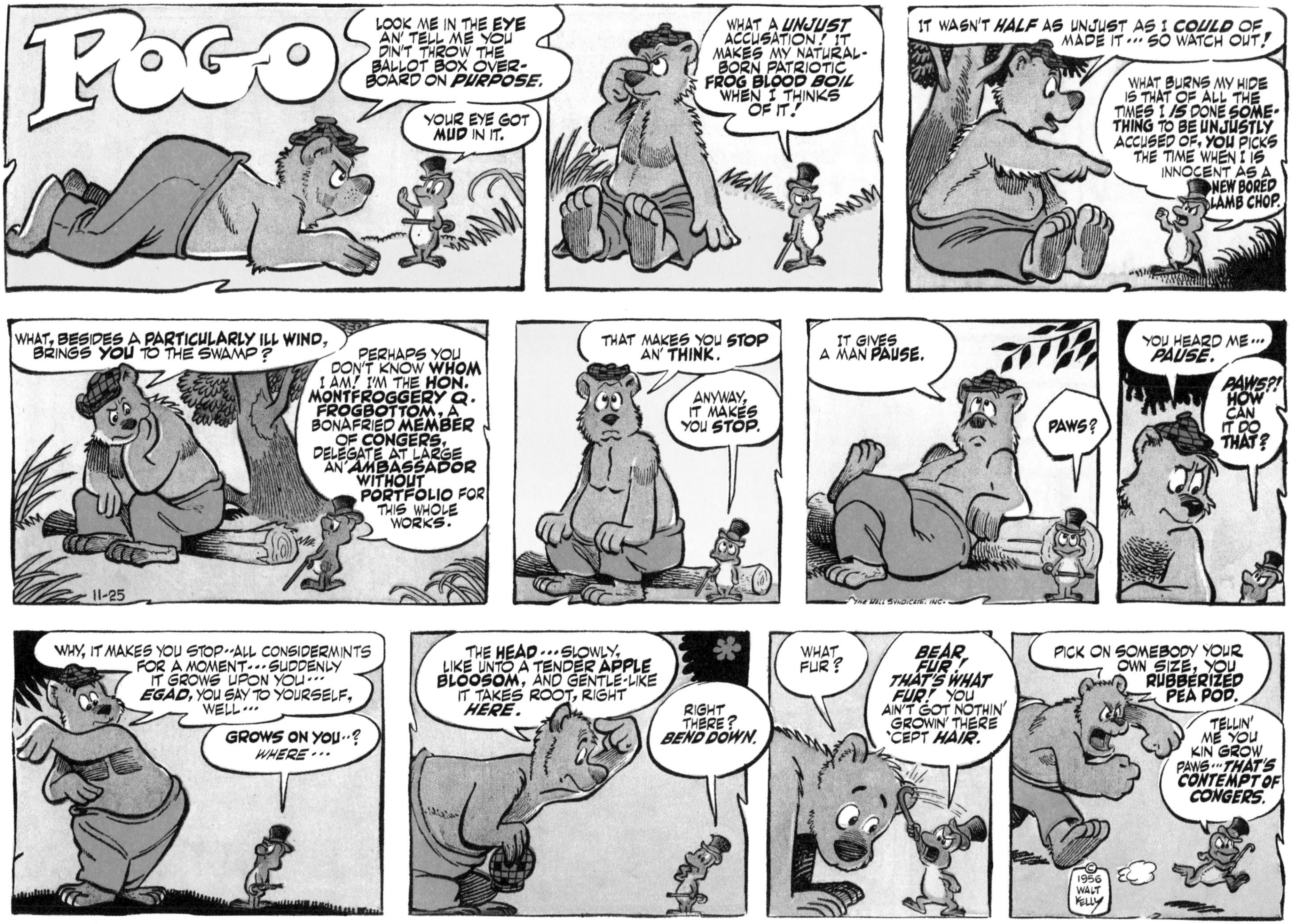
POGO
LOOK ME IN THE EYE AN' TELL ME YOU DIN'T THROW THE BALLOT BOX OVER-BOARD ON PURPOSE.
YOUR EYE GOT MUD IN IT.
WHAT A UNJUST ACCUSATION! IT MAKES MY NATURAL-BORN PATRIOTIC FROG BLOOD BOIL WHEN I THINKS OF IT!
IT WASN'T HALF AS UNJUST AS I COULD OF MADE IT ... SO WATCH OUT!
WHAT BURNS MY HIDE IS THAT OF ALL THE TIMES I IS DONE SOME-THING TO BE UNJUSTLY ACCUSED OF, YOU PICKS THE TIME WHEN I IS INNOCENT AS A NEW BORED LAMB CHOP.
WHAT, BESIDES A PARTICULARLY ILL WIND, BRINGS YOU TO THE SWAMP?
PERHAPS YOU DON'T KNOW WHOM I AM! I'M THE HON. MONTFROGGERY Q. FROGBOTTOM, A BONAFRIED MEMBER OF CONGERS, DELEGATE AT LARGE AN' AMBASSADOR WITHOUT PORTFOLIO FOR THIS WHOLE WORKS.
11-25
THAT MAKES YOU STOP AN' THINK.
ANYWAY, IT MAKES YOU STOP.
IT GIVES A MAN PAUSE.
PAWS?
THE HALL SYNDICATE, INC.
YOU HEARD ME... PAUSE.
PAWS?! HOW CAN IT DO THAT?
WHY, IT MAKES YOU STOP--ALL CONSIDERMINTS FOR A MOMENT--- SUDDENLY IT GROWS UPON YOU--- EGAD, YOU SAY TO YOURSELF, WELL---
GROWS ON YOU--? WHERE---
THE HEAD --- SLOWLY, LIKE UNTO A TENDER APPLE BLOOSOM, AND GENTLE-LIKE IT TAKES ROOT, RIGHT HERE.
RIGHT THERE? BEND DOWN.
WHAT FUR?
BEAR FUR! THAT'S WHAT FUR! YOU AIN'T GOT NOTHIN' GROWIN' THERE 'CEPT HAIR.
PICK ON SOMEBODY YOUR OWN SIZE, YOU RUBBERIZED PEA POD.
TELLIN' ME YOU KIN GROW PAWS--- THAT'S CONTEMPT OF CONGERS.
© 1956 WALT KELLY

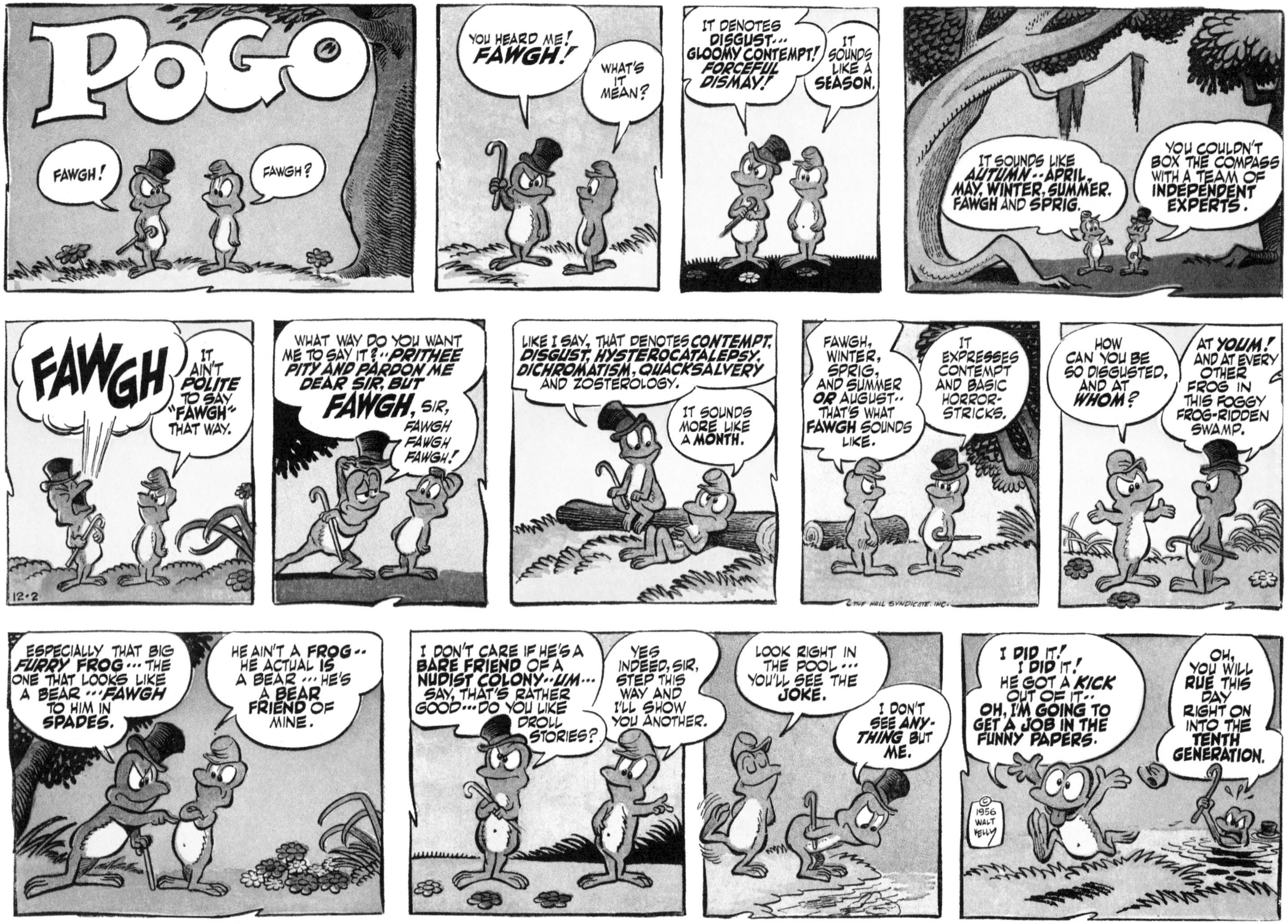
POGO
FAWGH!
FAWGH?
YOU HEARD ME! FAWGH!
WHAT'S IT MEAN?
IT DENOTES DISGUST... GLOOMY CONTEMPT! FORCEFUL DISMAY!
IT SOUNDS LIKE A SEASON.
IT SOUNDS LIKE AUTUMN--APRIL, MAY, WINTER, SUMMER, FAWGH AND SPRIG.
YOU COULDN'T BOX THE COMPASS WITH A TEAM OF INDEPENDENT EXPERTS.
FAWGH
IT AIN'T POLITE TO SAY "FAWGH" THAT WAY.
12-2
WHAT WAY DO YOU WANT ME TO SAY IT?..PRITHEE PITY AND PARDON ME DEAR SIR, BUT FAWGH, SIR, FAWGH FAWGH FAWGH!
LIKE I SAY, THAT DENOTES CONTEMPT, DISGUST, HYSTEROCATALEPSY, DICHROMATISM, QUACKSALVERY AND ZOSTEROLOGY.
IT SOUNDS MORE LIKE A MONTH.
FAWGH, WINTER, SPRIG, AND SUMMER OR AUGUST.. THAT'S WHAT FAWGH SOUNDS LIKE.
IT EXPRESSES CONTEMPT AND BASIC HORROR-STRICKS.
©THE HALL SYNDICATE, INC.
HOW CAN YOU BE SO DISGUSTED, AND AT WHOM?
AT YOUM! AND AT EVERY OTHER FROG IN THIS FOGGY FROG-RIDDEN SWAMP.
ESPECIALLY THAT BIG FURRY FROG... THE ONE THAT LOOKS LIKE A BEAR...FAWGH TO HIM IN SPADES.
HE AIN'T A FROG-- HE ACTUAL IS A BEAR...HE'S A BEAR FRIEND OF MINE.
I DON'T CARE IF HE'S A BARE FRIEND OF A NUDIST COLONY--UM... SAY, THAT'S RATHER GOOD...DO YOU LIKE DROLL STORIES?
YES INDEED, SIR, STEP THIS WAY AND I'LL SHOW YOU ANOTHER.
LOOK RIGHT IN THE POOL... YOU'LL SEE THE JOKE.
I DON'T SEE ANY-THING BUT ME.
© 1956 WALT KELLY
I DID IT! I DID IT! HE GOT A KICK OUT OF IT.. OH, I'M GOING TO GET A JOB IN THE FUNNY PAPERS.
OH, YOU WILL RUE THIS DAY RIGHT ON INTO THE TENTH GENERATION.

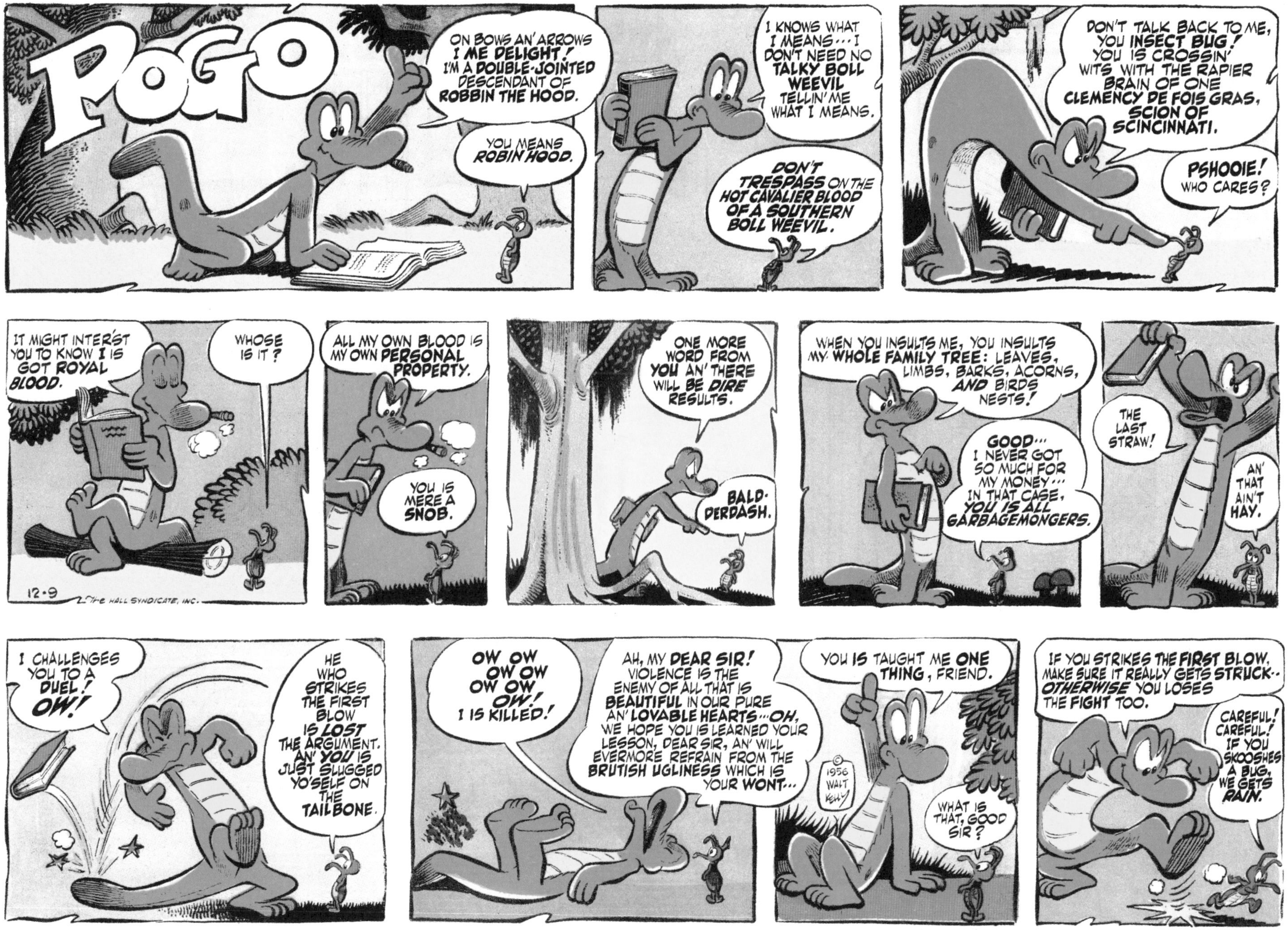
POGO
ON BOWS AN' ARROWS I ME DELIGHT! I'M A DOUBLE-JOINTED DESCENDANT OF ROBBIN THE HOOD.
YOU MEANS ROBIN HOOD.
I KNOWS WHAT I MEANS... I DON'T NEED NO TALKY BOLL WEEVIL TELLIN' ME WHAT I MEANS.
DON'T TRESPASS ON THE HOT CAVALIER BLOOD OF A SOUTHERN BOLL WEEVIL.
DON'T TALK BACK TO ME, YOU INSECT BUG! YOU IS CROSSIN' WITS WITH THE RAPIER BRAIN OF ONE CLEMENCY DE FOIS GRAS, SCION OF SCINCINNATI.
PSHOOIE! WHO CARES?
IT MIGHT INTER'ST YOU TO KNOW I IS GOT ROYAL BLOOD.
WHOSE IS IT?
12-9
© THE HALL SYNDICATE, INC.
ALL MY OWN BLOOD IS MY OWN PERSONAL PROPERTY.
YOU IS MERE A SNOB.
ONE MORE WORD FROM YOU AN' THERE WILL BE DIRE RESULTS.
BALD-DERDASH.
WHEN YOU INSULTS ME, YOU INSULTS MY WHOLE FAMILY TREE: LEAVES, LIMBS, BARKS, ACORNS, AND BIRDS NESTS!
GOOD... I NEVER GOT SO MUCH FOR MY MONEY... IN THAT CASE, YOU IS ALL GARBAGEMONGERS.
THE LAST STRAW!
AN' THAT AIN'T HAY.
I CHALLENGES YOU TO A DUEL! OW!
HE WHO STRIKES THE FIRST BLOW IS LOST THE ARGUMENT. AN' YOU IS JUST SLUGGED YO'SELF ON THE TAILBONE.
OW OW OW OW OW OW OW! I IS KILLED!
AH, MY DEAR SIR! VIOLENCE IS THE ENEMY OF ALL THAT IS BEAUTIFUL IN OUR PURE AN' LOVABLE HEARTS...OH, WE HOPE YOU IS LEARNED YOUR LESSON, DEAR SIR, AN' WILL EVERMORE REFRAIN FROM THE BRUTISH UGLINESS WHICH IS YOUR WONT...
YOU IS TAUGHT ME ONE THING, FRIEND.
© 1956 WALT KELLY
WHAT IS THAT, GOOD SIR?
IF YOU STRIKES THE FIRST BLOW, MAKE SURE IT REALLY GETS STRUCK.. OTHERWISE YOU LOSES THE FIGHT TOO.
CAREFUL! CAREFUL! IF YOU SKOOSHES A BUG, WE GETS RAIN.

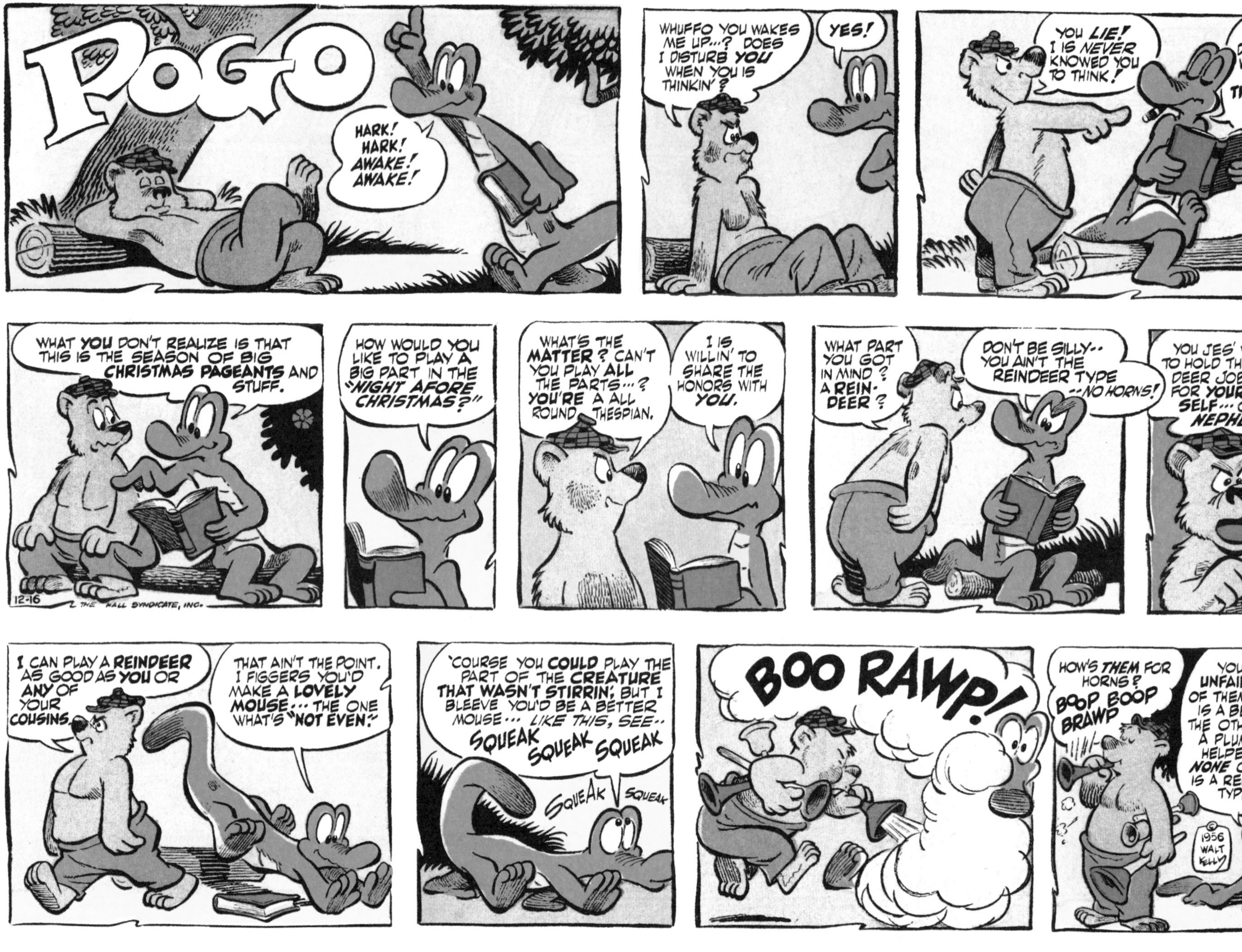
POGO
HARK! HARK! AWAKE! AWAKE!
WHUFFO YOU WAKES ME UP...? DOES I DISTURB YOU WHEN YOU IS THINKIN'?
YES!
YOU LIE! I IS NEVER KNOWED YOU TO THINK!
YOU DISTURB ME WHETHER I IS THINKIN' OR NOT.
WHAT YOU DON'T REALIZE IS THAT THIS IS THE SEASON OF BIG CHRISTMAS PAGEANTS AND STUFF.
12-16
© THE HALL SYNDICATE, INC.
HOW WOULD YOU LIKE TO PLAY A BIG PART IN THE "NIGHT AFORE CHRISTMAS?"
WHAT'S THE MATTER? CAN'T YOU PLAY ALL THE PARTS...? YOU'RE A ALL ROUND THESPIAN.
I IS WILLIN' TO SHARE THE HONORS WITH YOU.
WHAT PART YOU GOT IN MIND? A REIN-DEER?
DON'T BE SILLY.. YOU AIN'T THE REINDEER TYPE --NO HORNS!
YOU JES' WANTS TO HOLD THE REIN-DEER JOBS OPEN FOR YOUR OWN SELF... OR A NEPHEW.
I CAN PLAY A REINDEER AS GOOD AS YOU OR ANY OF YOUR COUSINS.
THAT AIN'T THE POINT. I FIGGERS YOU'D MAKE A LOVELY MOUSE... THE ONE WHAT'S "NOT EVEN."
'COURSE YOU COULD PLAY THE PART OF THE CREATURE THAT WASN'T STIRRIN', BUT I BLEEVE YOU'D BE A BETTER MOUSE... LIKE THIS, SEE..
SQUEAK SQUEAK SQUEAK
SQUEAK SQUEAK
BOO RAWP!
HOW'S THEM FOR HORNS?
BOOP BOOP BRAWP
YOU PLAYS UNFAIR! ONE OF THEM HORNS IS A BELL AN' THE OTHER IS A PLUMBER'S HELPER AN' NONE OF 'EM IS A REINDEER TYPE.
© 1956 WALT KELLY

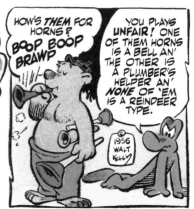

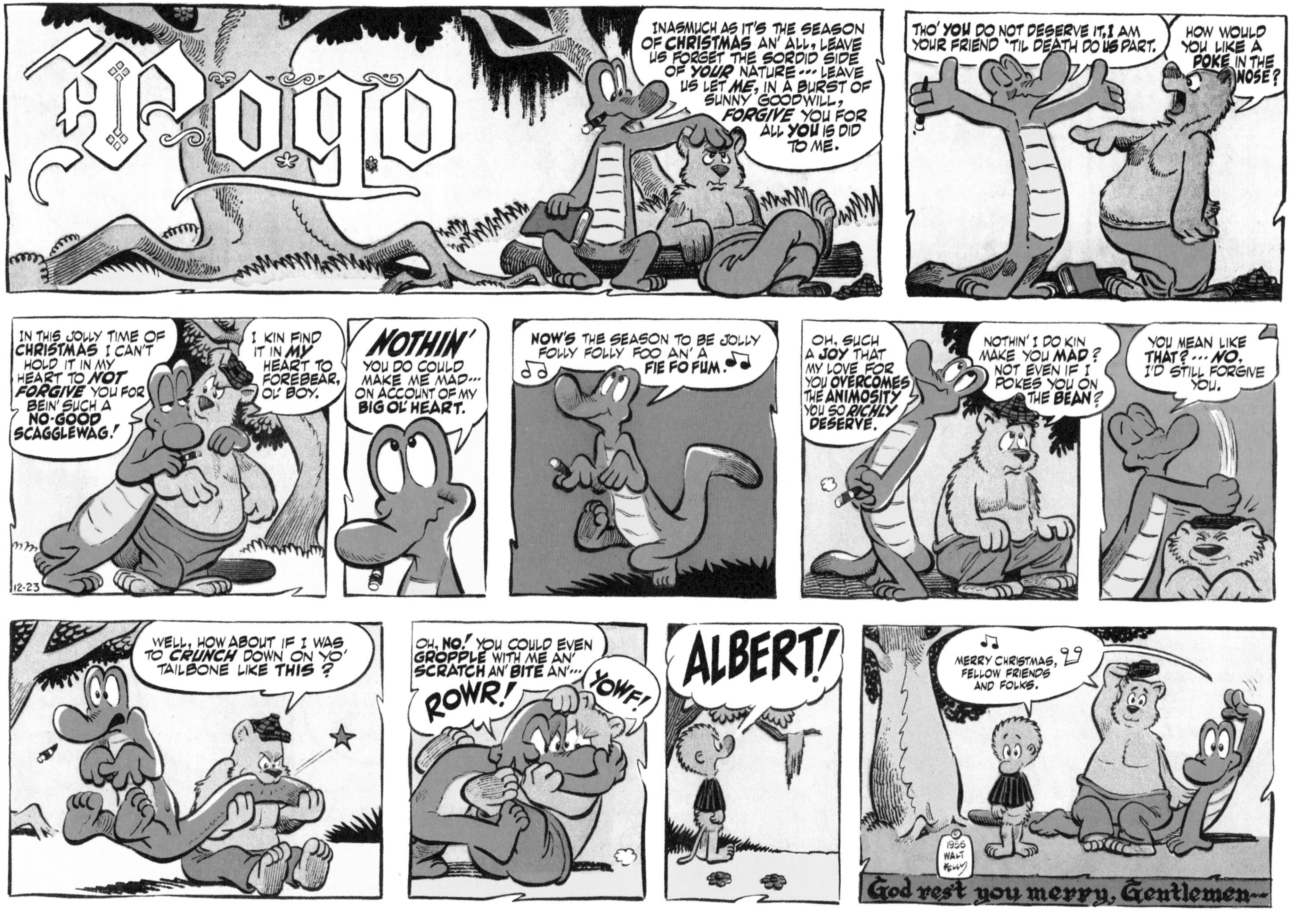
Pogo
INASMUCH AS IT'S THE SEASON OF CHRISTMAS AN' ALL, LEAVE US FORGET THE SORDID SIDE OF YOUR NATURE--- LEAVE US LET ME, IN A BURST OF SUNNY GOODWILL, FORGIVE YOU FOR ALL YOU IS DID TO ME.
THO' YOU DO NOT DESERVE IT, I AM YOUR FRIEND 'TIL DEATH DO US PART.
HOW WOULD YOU LIKE A POKE IN THE NOSE?
IN THIS JOLLY TIME OF CHRISTMAS I CAN'T HOLD IT IN MY HEART TO NOT FORGIVE YOU FOR BEIN' SUCH A NO-GOOD SCAGGLEWAG!
I KIN FIND IT IN MY HEART TO FOREBEAR, OL' BOY.
12-23
NOTHIN' YOU DO COULD MAKE ME MAD... ON ACCOUNT OF MY BIG OL' HEART.
NOW'S THE SEASON TO BE JOLLY FOLLY FOLLY FOO AN' A FIE FO FUM.
OH, SUCH A JOY THAT MY LOVE FOR YOU OVERCOMES THE ANIMOSITY YOU SO RICHLY DESERVE.
NOTHIN' I DO KIN MAKE YOU MAD? NOT EVEN IF I POKES YOU ON THE BEAN?
YOU MEAN LIKE THAT?... NO. I'D STILL FORGIVE YOU.
WELL, HOW ABOUT IF I WAS TO CRUNCH DOWN ON YO' TAILBONE LIKE THIS?
OH, NO! YOU COULD EVEN GROPPLE WITH ME AN' SCRATCH AN' BITE AN'...
ROWR!
YOWF!
ALBERT!
MERRY CHRISTMAS, FELLOW FRIENDS AND FOLKS.
© 1956 WALT KELLY
God rest you merry, Gentlemen--

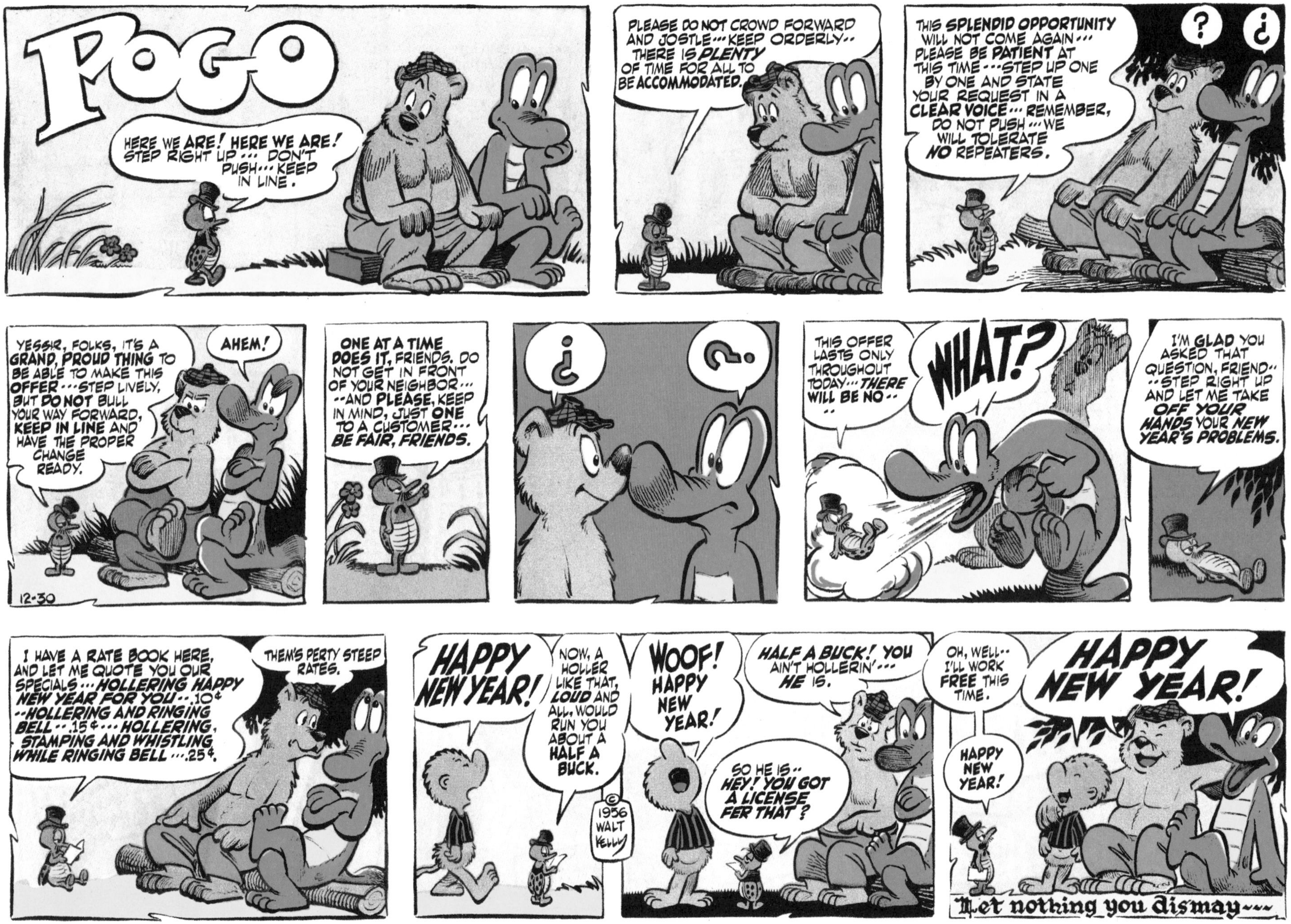
POGO
HERE WE ARE! HERE WE ARE! STEP RIGHT UP ... DON'T PUSH... KEEP IN LINE.
PLEASE DO NOT CROWD FORWARD AND JOSTLE... KEEP ORDERLY.. THERE IS PLENTY OF TIME FOR ALL TO BE ACCOMMODATED.
THIS SPLENDID OPPORTUNITY WILL NOT COME AGAIN... PLEASE BE PATIENT AT THIS TIME... STEP UP ONE BY ONE AND STATE YOUR REQUEST IN A CLEAR VOICE... REMEMBER, DO NOT PUSH... WE WILL TOLERATE NO REPEATERS.
?
¿
YESSIR, FOLKS, IT'S A GRAND, PROUD THING TO BE ABLE TO MAKE THIS OFFER... STEP LIVELY, BUT DO NOT BULL YOUR WAY FORWARD, KEEP IN LINE AND HAVE THE PROPER CHANGE READY.
AHEM!
12-30
ONE AT A TIME DOES IT, FRIENDS. DO NOT GET IN FRONT OF YOUR NEIGHBOR... ..AND PLEASE, KEEP IN MIND, JUST ONE TO A CUSTOMER... BE FAIR, FRIENDS.
¿
?
THIS OFFER LASTS ONLY THROUGHOUT TODAY... THERE WILL BE NO-- ..
WHAT?
I'M GLAD YOU ASKED THAT QUESTION, FRIEND.. ..STEP RIGHT UP AND LET ME TAKE OFF YOUR HANDS YOUR NEW YEAR'S PROBLEMS.
I HAVE A RATE BOOK HERE, AND LET ME QUOTE YOU OUR SPECIALS... HOLLERING HAPPY NEW YEAR FOR YOU.. .10¢ ..HOLLERING AND RINGING BELL.. .15¢... HOLLERING, STAMPING AND WHISTLING WHILE RINGING BELL ... .25¢.
THEM'S PERTY STEEP RATES.
HAPPY NEW YEAR!
NOW, A HOLLER LIKE THAT, LOUD AND ALL, WOULD RUN YOU ABOUT A HALF A BUCK.
© 1956 WALT KELLY
WOOF! HAPPY NEW YEAR!
HALF A BUCK! YOU AIN'T HOLLERIN'... HE IS.
SO HE IS.. HEY! YOU GOT A LICENSE FER THAT?
OH, WELL.. I'LL WORK FREE THIS TIME.
HAPPY NEW YEAR!
HAPPY NEW YEAR!
Let nothing you dismay---

SWAMP TALK
ANNOTATIONS AND HISTORICAL DATA
BY R.C. HARVEY

In the unlikely event that you've picked up this, the fourth volume reprinting Walt Kelly's celebrated comic strip *Pogo*, without owning the three predecessors, I'll repeat here some of what I've said in the appenda to those by way of orienting you to what you might expect herein.

Walt Kelly is admired—and revered in some quarters (this one, for instance)—for his deft blending of the verbal and visual resources of the comic strip medium for the purposes of nonsense slapstick and other irreverences, chiefly political satire. The period embraced by this volume includes a presidential election year, so it offers ample opportunities for the hilarities of ridicule. Republicans re-nominated incumbents Dwight Eisenhower and Richard Nixon, and the Democrats nominated Adlai Stevenson again, adding Estes Kefauver to the ticket. The GOP won again.

In the spring of 1953—reprinted in the previous volume of this series—Kelly had committed as neat a sustained piece of political satire as had ever been attempted on the funnies pages of American newspapers. In a long and elaborately devised sequence, he exposed and ridiculed Joseph R. McCarthy, the demagogic Commie-hunting senator from Wisconsin. Caricaturing McCarthy as a rogue wild cat named Simple J. Malarkey, Kelly

ended the sequence by having his satiric target fall into a kettle of tar that was warming up so Malarkey could tar and feather his foes. Allegorical translation: those who seek to smear others are likely to be tarred with their own brush. The satiric success of the sequence depended upon Kelly's yoking word and picture in perfect concert: neither meant much when taken by itself, but when taken in tandem, the verbal and the visual achieved allegorical impact and a powerful satiric thrust. It was a cartooning *tour de force*.

But, by 1955, the first of the two years in this volume, Kelly opted for comedy in another vein. Said he: "The fact that the Dog and Albert got themselves entangled in a thinking contest in the opening innings of the year should have been a tip-off that the serious side of life was going to take a rest for a while. Malarkey, for all practical purposes, was out of business and normal lunacy burst once more upon us."

The ultimate lunatic nonsense may be Albert's run-in with an inflated toy horse, November 1955.

Kelly customarily littered the panels of his strip with puns and linguistic whimsy as well as historical and literary and topical allusions that render aspects of the comedy too obscure for understanding—and appreciating—in the twenty-first century, hence the reason for this annotative apostrophe. Into which we now plunge, giggling and grinning all the way.

1955 DAILIES

1/4 – Howland is presumably not drilling for "swamp gas" (also known as "wetlands flatulence").

1/28 – Albert and Beauregard Bugleboy (aka Hound Dog) have managed to confuse baseball with the Civil War and other aspects of American history. "The general" could be Dwight Eisenhower, who was elected in 1952, or Ulysses S. Grant, who belongs in the same Civil War era as General George B. McClellan, the notoriously hesitant commander of the Union forces in 1861.

2/14 – Even if you miss the date at the lower left of the first panel, you can't miss the Valentine's Day occasion that prompts the third panel's affectionate demonstration.

2/23 – Reggie and Alf are fugitives from Cockney London. The *pinnae* is the external part of the ear, which, among professional boxers, is sometimes mauled into the shape of a cauliflower.

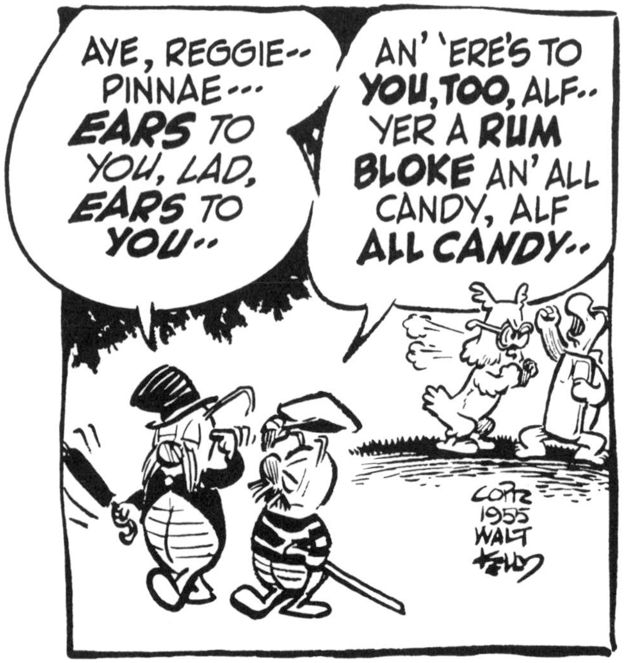
AYE, REGGIE-- PINNAE--- EARS TO YOU, LAD, EARS TO YOU--
AN' 'ERE'S TO YOU, TOO, ALF-- YER A RUM BLOKE AN' ALL CANDY, ALF ALL CANDY--
COPR 1955 WALT KELLY

2/24 – *Briny* is British slang for the ocean; *dustbin*, for garbage can.

2/26 – The "Firehouse Five plus Two" was the name of a dixieland band formed by Kelly's friend and erstwhile cohort Ward Kimball, along with other Disney animators, in the late 1940s.

3/1 – About this sequence, Kelly wrote (in *Ten Ever-lovin' Blue-eyed Years of Pogo)*: "The Bats have always seemed to have trouble with their trousers. This is something that I cannot explain. The loss of a pair of pants does not seem as funny to me as you might think. And to be aloft in a March wind without benefit of pantaloons is something that I would not wish on my best friend. I don't know what came over me this day."

3/4 – *Cap'n Wimby's Bird Atlas* exists, as far as I can determine, only in *Pogo.*

3/5 – According to Wikipedia, a *fossa*, akin to a mongoose, is native to Madagascar. *Douroucouli* are night monkeys, sometimes called "owl monkeys." *Umbles* are the edible viscera of deer or hogs. "A *hemicellulose* (also known as polyose) is any of several heteropolymers (matrix polysaccharides), such as arabinoxylans, present along with cellulose in almost all plant cell walls.

3/12 – Kelly lettered the sides of the skiff with the names of friends and newspaper editors whose papers printed *Pogo.* Few, if any, of the persons named were famous or well-known. John Keasler was undoubtedly one of the newspapermen, probably at the *St. Louis Post Dispatch*, whose name appears on the other end of the boat. Most of the subsequent names on the skiff we must pass by without comment because they were known only to Kelly. A few, whose names appear with that of a newspaper, I have been able to find and have annotated in the same manner as I do here with Keasler.

3/19 – In Greek mythology, Psyche is the name of a mortal woman who becomes the wife of Eros and divine. In Latin mythology, the story is much more prolonged: Psyche is pursued by Cupid and, after numerous trials and tribulations (imposed by a jealous Venus), marries him.

3/21 – Anyone struck by Cupid's arrow will fall in love with the first being he/she sees thereafter. Miz Beaver has confused

and confounded this story with the first lines of a poem by Henry Wadsworth Longfellow: "I shot an arrow into the air, it fell to earth I know not where."

4/5 – The tiger, Tammanany, is Kelly's allusion to (and deliberate misspelling of) the Tammany Society of nineteenth century New York, a social and patriotic club that eventually became a notorious instrument of political patronage. In the strip, Tammanany usually accompanies P.T. Bridgeport on whatever political intrigue is in the offing—mostly, running Pogo for president. For more about the origins of the Tammany Society see Volume 2 note for 7/13/51.

5/2 – Bob Hall is the president of the Post Hall Syndicate, which distributes *Pogo.*

5/6 – *Raffia* is a fiber widely used on twine, rope, baskets, placemats and textiles.

5/17 – A *dugong* is a medium-sized marine mammal in the same family as the manatee.

5/20 – *Ipso facto*, Latin, means "by that very fact"; *ipse dixit,* "he himself said it," an arbitrary dogmatic statement the speaker of which expects his listener to accept as valid without further proofs or demonstrations. *Buncombe* or *bunkum* eventually

degenerated into "bunk," referring to inconsequential speech (full of balderdash, gobbledegook, and the like) of the kind a congressman from Buncombe County, North Carolina, once made solely to please his constituents.

5/24 – Tammanany's piano, with "a mass of flickering candles" and his toothy grin, allude to the flamboyant and popular pianist of fifties and sixties television, Liberace, on whose piano always perched an ornate candelabra.

5/25 – As early as May 1955, Kelly was preparing to have Pogo make another run at the White House in 1956. Pogo's opponents will reprise the 1952 contest: Republican incumbent Dwight Eisenhower and Democrat Adlai Stevenson. Pogo is quoting what Civil War General William Tecumseh Sherman said in 1884 when approached by the Republican Party. Others since then have invoked the "Sherman Pledge."

5/30 – In those days, Memorial Day was celebrated on the last Monday in May.

7/1 – Two popular TV shows starring dogs—*Lassie* (1954) and *The Adventures of Rin Tin Tin* (1953) had debuted in the previous year.

7/6 – Beauregard has the dog genealogy about right.

7/11 – *The First Folio* is the name given to the first publication of Shakespeare's plays in 1623, seven years after the playwright died.

7/13 – Albert is right: the bark of the cinchona bush (or tree) is a source of quinine and other medicinal extracts.

7/21 – In the Low Countries, a *stadtholder* was a government functionary, evolving in the sixteenth, seventeenth, and eighteenth centuries into a sort of head of state. Rawson's Own is a mysterious concoction.

7/28 – From context, we may assume that *ripjack*, like *cutpurse*, refers to a petty criminal, a thief.

8/9 – The mouse is conflating two Latin expressions: *de rigueur*, meaning "required by etiquette or custom," and *rigor mortis*, literally "stiffness" and "death," which is usually cited as an indication of death.

8/15 – Cal Alley, whose name appears on the skiff, was the editorial cartoonist at the *Commercial Appeal* in Memphis from 1945 until he retired in 1965. He also produced a syndicated comic strip, *The Ryatts*, which he launched October 11, 1954.

8/17 – The inscription on the skiff mocks a popular advertising slogan of the day, "Pepsi Cola Hits the Spot."

9/26 – The celebrated band leader Fred Waring ("the man who taught America to sing") had a passion for cartoons and comics that was second only to his devotion to the vocal orchestrations of his fellow Pennsylvanians, and when he learned that cartoonists had formed a club, the National Cartoonists Society (of which Kelly was president at this time, 1954–56), he invited the entire membership to be his guests at the Shawnee Inn, a resort in the Poconos. The group returned every summer for several years thereafter.

9/27 – Bryant Park is a leafy oasis in the asphalt desert on Manhattan's 42nd Street, just behind the Public Library.

9/28 – The Browns was the name of St. Louis' second major league baseball team.

"McGraw" no doubt is the legendary scrapper John McGraw, longtime manager of the New York Giants. McGraw finished his career holding the sport's record for the most ejections from the field during play, 132.

10/11 – The character whose face is obscured with a speech balloon is Kelly's stand-in for the rabble-rousing Commie hunter Senator Joseph R. McCarthy—Simple J. Malarkey (whose name echoes in its rhythms that of his namesake and whose face is McCarthy's spitting image). This three-strip sequence marked Malarkey's final appearance in the strip, and Kelly covered his face because one of the strip's subscribing newspapers, the Providence (R.I.) *Bulletin* had threatened to drop the strip if Malarkey ever showed his face again.

Malarkey had made one other encore appearance in October 1954. For that, Kelly had put a pillowcase over Malarkey's head, preventing his face from showing up (and creating the visual suggestion of the KKK, "which identified his kind a little more," as Kelly explained; see Volume 3, page 189 and page 339 for more explanation).

In *Ten Ever-lovin' Blue-eyed Years with Pogo,* Kelly offers the following comment on Malarkey's last appearance, which came a year after the last time his presence graced the strip: "I was annoyed by the dictum that he should never show his face around the

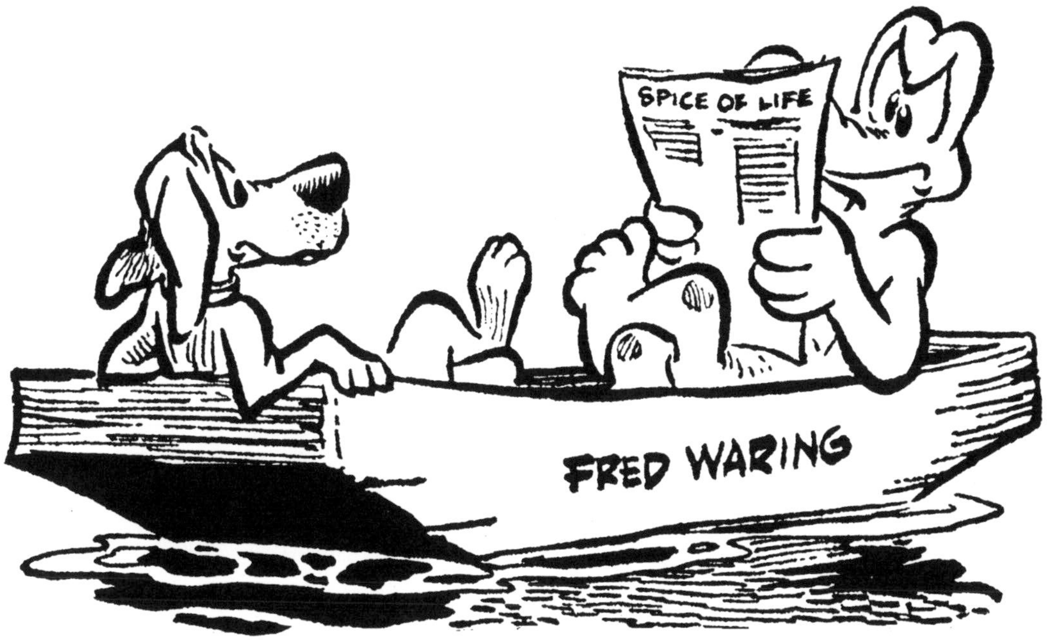
SPICE OF LIFE
FRED WARING

place again and would have defied the edict, except that a happier thought occurred. I covered his face with the balloon to see how many would recognize him from his conversational style alone. As a result I got a number of letters from people who told me it was shameful to kick a man when he was down. Well, they identified him, I didn't."

"Kick a man when he is down" was the advice Senator McCarthy said he'd received from a childhood mentor called Indian Charlie, which accounts for Malarkey's badger sidekick in 1954; see page 175 of Volume 3. And McCarthy was indeed "down": on December 2, 1954, the Senate voted 67–22 to condemn McCarthy for conduct "contrary to senatorial traditions ... [tending] to bring the Senate into disrepute."

Upon his arrival in Albert's house, Malarkey cautions Albert against interrupting him, a rhetorical mannerism that McCarthy deployed to silence his opposition during the Army-McCarthy hearings in May–June 1954; see pages 179 and 338 of Volume 3.

10/20 – George Y. Wells was editor of the short-lived *New York Star* in 1948 and invited Kelly to join the staff as art director. Wells remained a lifelong friend, and Kelly often affectionately deployed his name as an oath in the strip.

10/22 – *Bermoothes* is a name fabricated for an enchanted island by Shakespeare in his play *The Tempest*. Kelly is using it here to refer to Bermuda shorts, the plaid knee-length garments which were fashionable in the mid-1950s, but there's probably also a nod to a poem by American poetess Lucy Larcom (1826–1893). She penned a paean to Shakespeare's Bermoothes/ Bermuda that cites characters in the play and extolls extravagantly the flora and fauna of the place (the onion and the eel perhaps). Onions and eels had been united before in *Pogo*.

10/31 – Kathryn Barbara was Kelly's daughter, who died in infancy before reaching her first birthday. Biographer Steve Thompson explains this poignant reference in his Introduction

to Volume 1: "For many years in late October, Kelly would draw a bug floating through the swamp with a birthday cake, trying to find someone looking for a birthday."

11/1 – *Neddy* is Australian slang for horse; a *dingo* is an Australian wild dog.

11/11 – Two minutes of silence to reflect on the meaning of Armistice Day.

11/18 – Lochinvar is the hero, "faithful in love ... dauntless in war" who rode "all unarm'd ... all alone ... out of the west" in an eponymous poem by Walter Scott. Here, his name becomes part of a parody lyric to the Hoagy Carmichael song, "Rockin' Chair."

11/19 – Waycross is the nearest town in Georgia to Okefenokee Swamp, the presumed habitat of Pogo, *et al.*

11/23 – The Suwannee River is a major river in southern Georgia, nowhere near Jersey City. Continuing to conflate two unrelated facts in his typically grandiose effort to cloak reality in high-sounding terms, P.T. connects Jersey City to the Jersey Lily, Lillie Langtry, a woman noted for beauty and for being the mis-

tress of Queen Victoria's oldest son, Albert Edward, the Prince of Wales. Langtry was born on the island of Jersey off the coast of England, hence the cognomen. Tammanany perpetuates P.T.'s error-prone proclivity by changing "crystal ball" into Cristobal, the name of a city in Panama.

12/14 – *The $64,000 Question* was a popular prime time TV quiz show of the day.

12/22 – A drummer is a salesman, usually of the traveling sort.

12/24 – Porky is quoting from the *Rubaiyat of Omar Khayyam.*

12/26 – Christmas fell on Sunday this year, hence the dailies' celebration was a day late.

12/28 – George Ward, Kelly's assistant and friend, was in the art department of the *New York Star* when Kelly asked him to help out on the *Pogo* daily strips and comic books, which he did for many years.

1956 DAILIES

1/13 – This is a Friday. Churchy, who always notices Friday the Thirteenth, is unusually derelict. He catches himself the next day. Labrador is the largest and most northern area in Canada's Atlantic region, known for its remoteness.

1/21 – The Mouse refers to the remodeling of the White House during the administration of Harry S. Truman. The "change" alludes to the arrival of the Republican president, Dwight Eisenhower. The elephant has been a symbol for the GOP since editorial cartoonist Thomas Nast first used the beast to represent the party in or around 1874.

2/9 – "Cold robbies" is apparently how Albert refers to the kohlrabi, a kind of cabbage.

2/13 – It's entirely possible that Kelly did not have Rosa Parks in mind when he has Bun Rab insist that "I ain't gone move—I got my rights." But just two months before this strip saw publication, Ms. Parks, on December 1, 1955, had refused to give up her seat in the front (white section) of the bus so a white person could sit there. When this strip ran, a bus boycott was in progress in Montgomery, the scene of the original confrontation.

2/16 – Jefferson Davis was president of the Confederate States of America. Pogo, unlike his creator, pretends the Confederacy is still alive and well in the swamp.

2/18 – Captain William Kidd was either a pirate or a privateer. According to the mythology that has grown up around his name, Kidd buried some of his ill-gotten gains along the coast of the southern United States. Clearly, Albert and Porky have discovered Kidd's cache.

2/21 – Adlai Stevenson, who was again running for the Democrat's presidential nomination, was a bachelor, divorced from his first (and only) wife in 1949 after twenty-one years of

LESSEE, CHURCHY FIGGERS HE LIKES OUR MAN... CHURCHY REPERSENTS HALF THE POPULATION OF FORT MUDGE, A TYPICALLY TYPICAL TYPE OF A TOWN... ...NOW THE REST OF FORT MUDGE MIGHT NOT VOTE... LEAST NOT ALL OF IT.
THE HALL SYNDICATE, INC.
5-29
WE CAN SAFELY PRESUME THAT A GOOD THIRD OF THE BALANCE, OR A SIXTH OF THE TOTAL IS UNDERAGE, NOT INTERESTED OR UNDETERMINED... ...FIGURES WILL PROVE THAT OF THE REMAINING TWO SIXTHS AT LEAST ONE QUARTER WILL BE INFIRM AND UNABLE TO REACH POLLS OR OUT OF TOWN BUYING PEACHES.
ANOTHER QUARTER, CONSTITUTING THE NOW ONE HALF, (OR ANOTHER SIXTH IN ALL) WILL REACH THE VOTING BOOTHS TOO LATE OR TOO EMPTY, BECOME DISCOURAGED, INASMUCH AS RAIN IS ONE THIRD LIKELY TO OCCUR...

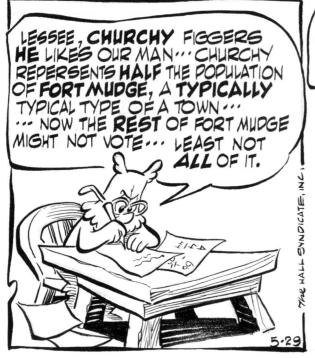

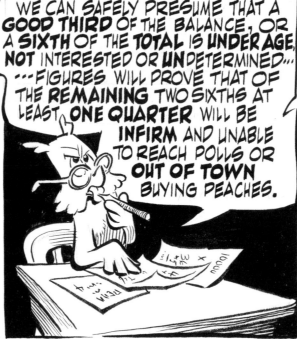

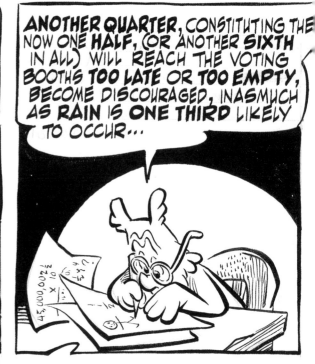

marriage. Not very much was made of his being single during either of his runs for the White House, but there were a few mutterings, enough, no doubt, to prompt Kelly into introducing a marital theme in Pogo's candidacy.

3/17 – Costello's was a bar and restaurant in midtown Manhattan at Third and 44th, opened by Tim Costello. There, writers were known to gather, their ranks including James Thurber, Joe Liebling, John McNulty, Dorothy Parker, Edmund Wilson, John O'Hara, Ernest Hemingway and Walt Kelly. It was torn down in the early seventies, about the same time Kelly left us.

3/26 – John "Jack" Kramer was an American tennis player, ranked No. 1 in the world for a number of years in the 1950s and 1960s.

3/27 – In Henry Wadsworth Longellow's poem "The Courtship of Miles Standish," John Alden is Miles's best friend. They are both in love with the same woman, Priscilla Mullins, and Miles, pleading overwhelming shyness, persuades John to propose marriage to her on his, Miles's, behalf. As soon as he does so, Priscilla says, "Why don't you speak for yourself, John?" He did, and they married and had eleven children. Miz Beaver has a somewhat different version of the story.

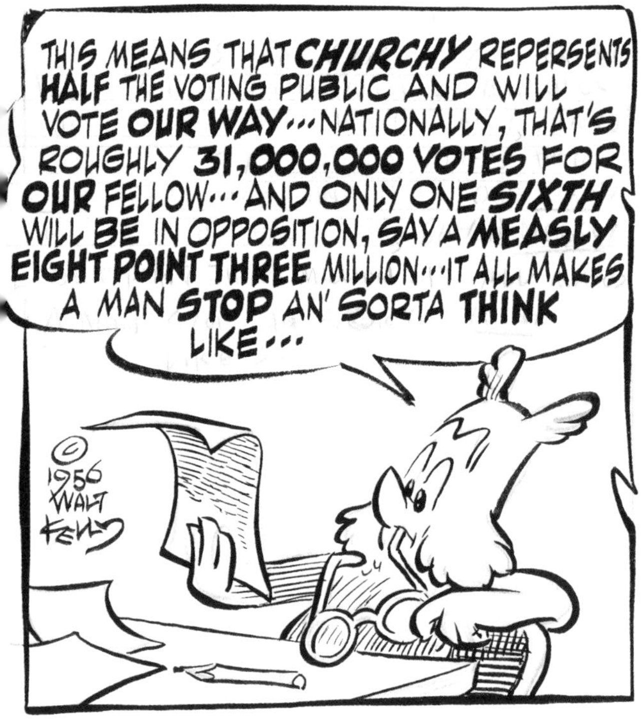
THIS MEANS THAT CHURCHY REPERSENTS HALF THE VOTING PUBLIC AND WILL VOTE OUR WAY... NATIONALLY, THAT'S ROUGHLY 31,000,000 VOTES FOR OUR FELLOW... AND ONLY ONE SIXTH WILL BE IN OPPOSITION, SAY A MEASLY EIGHT POINT THREE MILLION... IT ALL MAKES A MAN STOP AN' SORTA THINK LIKE...
© 1956 WALT KELLY

5/8 – *Ars est celare artem* is a Latin phrase meaning "it is art to conceal art; true art conceals the means by which it is achieved."

5/16 – The discussion here no doubt alludes to President Eisenhower's press conferences. Ike was noted for giving garbled, circular non-answers to reporters' questions.

5/29 – Kelly was not keen on polls—particularly the polls newspapers ran to see which comic strips were highest in their readers' esteem, and which were lowest, dropping the latter. Such polls, he maintained, were responded to by people other than the ones reading the comics and so were invalid. In *Blue-eyed Years*, he repeated a common comic strip cartoonist observation: "All that a newspaper has to do is drop a strip ... and it soon discovers who answers polls. Hundreds of letters have flooded into editorial offices and switchboards have literally been plugged up with incoming calls of protest. In almost every case that I know of, the strip has been restored, usually with a front-page apology to the readers" for dropping the strip to begin with. The strip at hand was published as an advertisement in trade journals by Kelly's syndicate, hoping to discourage papers from dropping a strip after conducting the sort of imperfect survey that most newspapers indulged in.

6/4 – In *Blue-Eyed Years*, Kelly wrote: "The continued flourishing rise of publications that breathe, think, and regurgitate pre-digested wisdom and knowledge for the reader in 1956 made it imperative that Pogo be interviewed by representatives of a news magazine just as a sign of recognition. To be a candidate without making the cover of at least one of such major omniscient weeklies is like entering a freckle contest without your skin. The paternal, godlike blessing is needed for mere identification."

The reporter and the photographer were later named Typo and Hypo, and, in 1964, when Barry Goldwater ran for president, Typo looked remarkably like Goldwater. Here, however, I suspect Typo is a generic brand of newsmagazine factotum just as the name of the magazine for which he works, *Newslife*, is.

6/5 – *Au naturel* means "in a natural state"—sometimes, "nude."

6/15 – Once more, Kelly labels the boat with the name (and childhood nicknames) of one of his children, in this case the co-editor and designer of this series. And it wasn't even her birthday!

6/16 – "I Like Ike" was Eisenhower's slogan in both 1952 and 1956. It was, as some commentators have proclaimed, "the best-known slogan in the entire history of American presidential campaigns." Its virtues were unequivocal affectionate support and punchy brevity. Pogo's slogan in both years was "I Go Pogo."

A version of the song joyously performed by Churchy was heard on the record album, "Songs of the Pogo," issued that same year as was a book of the same title. The book offered the sheet music, magnificently illustrated, to all the songs which had been written by Kelly and his friend, Norman Monath. Monath was the music and chess editor for Simon & Schuster Publishing and a successful composer on his own. Kelly also performed several of the numbers on the album including "Go-Go Pogo," which is the song with which Churchy favors us here.

6/22 – The much-admired Grace Kelly married Prince Rainier III of Monaco on April 19, just two months before this strip appeared.

Frank Sullivan was a newspaper humorist and magazine writer (most conspicously, for *The New Yorker*) who had been born in Saratoga Springs, New York. He was a marginal member of the famed Algonquin Roundtable and probably a friend of Kelly's.

A *dickey* is a detachable false shirt front usually worn with a tuxedo. To the cynical, it looks like it might be a kind of bib, hence Seminole Sam's final comment.

6/25 – Sometimes those sitting on the fence watching the political shenanigans of the Election Year wondered if Eisenhower

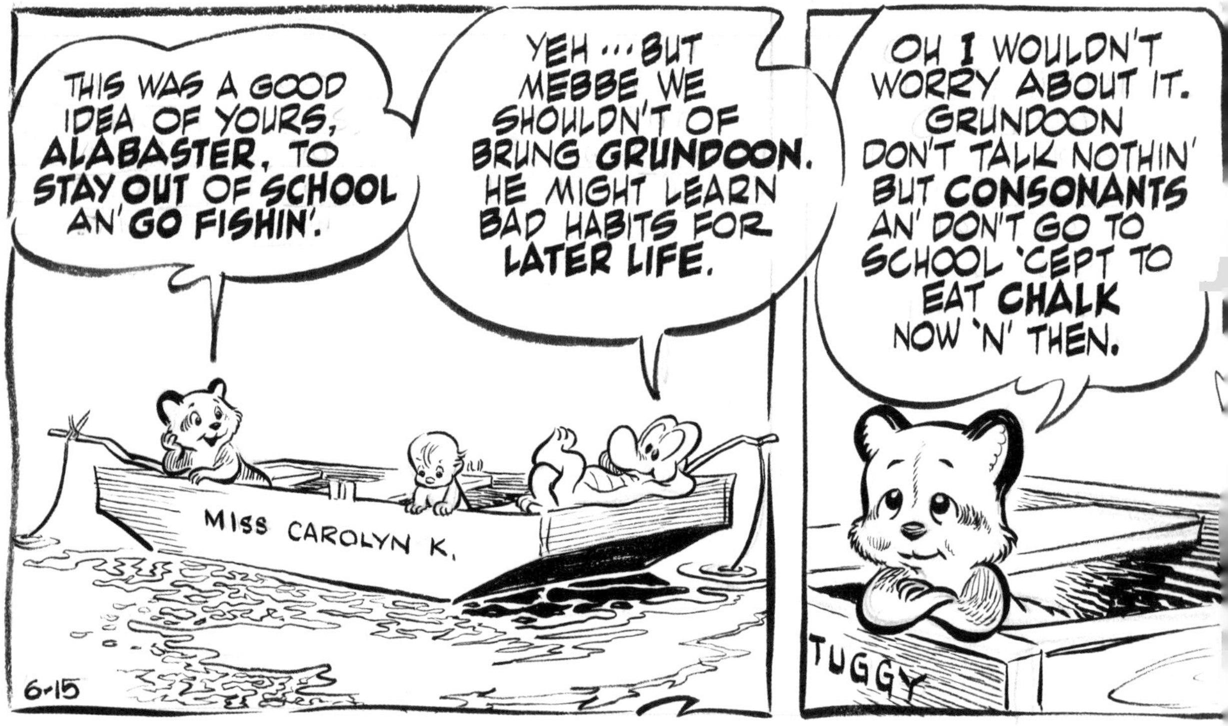
THIS WAS A GOOD IDEA OF YOURS, ALABASTER, TO STAY OUT OF SCHOOL AN' GO FISHIN'.
YEH ... BUT MEBBE WE SHOULDN'T OF BRUNG GRUNDOON. HE MIGHT LEARN BAD HABITS FOR LATER LIFE.
MISS CAROLYN K.
6-15
OH I WOULDN'T WORRY ABOUT IT. GRUNDOON DON'T TALK NOTHIN' BUT CONSONANTS AN' DON'T GO TO SCHOOL 'CEPT TO EAT CHALK NOW 'N' THEN.
TUGGY

was a true Republican, his career in the military having been conspicuously apolitical. That was the question most asked when he was sought out to run in 1952; and some still thought he was not a rabbit—er, Republican.

7/11 – Beauregard is quoting Omar Khayyam.

7/13 – Kelly got in trouble with this one, as he tells the story in *Blue-Eyed Years*: "He who runs with the language must expect to be taken into custody by the authorities every once in a while. I had a lot of trouble convincing the several brains in charge of the hands through which [this strip] flowed that I meant what I said. 'Stench' did not seem to them to be the word I wanted. This was like having them decide which way they wanted my hair cut. Humpty Dumpty had similar trouble in *Alice in Wonderland* with the word 'Glory.' It happens all the time, and as H.D. said, 'Who's to be the master? You, or the word?' Carroll had all his buttons."

But Kelly, in this isolated case, did not. The word he hoped he'd found is spelled "stanch," sometimes "staunch," but not "stench," which offends the nostrils. But Kelly, with the unquestioned authority of Humpty Dumpty, was boss, and so "stench" prevailed.

7/18 – Peter Kelly is one of the cartoonist's sons and this strip ran on his ninth birthday.

8/6 – Judging from the name on the skiff, the nominating convention toward which Pogo's supporters are wending their way is the one meeting in Chicago, that of the Democrat Party, August 13–17. The meeting site of the Republicans the following week, August 20–23, San Francisco, never got a notice on the skiff.

8/7 – The expression "a smoke-filled room" in political jargon refers to a convening of political power brokers who meet secretly away from the convention in a private room where they decide the issues being endlessly debated on the convention

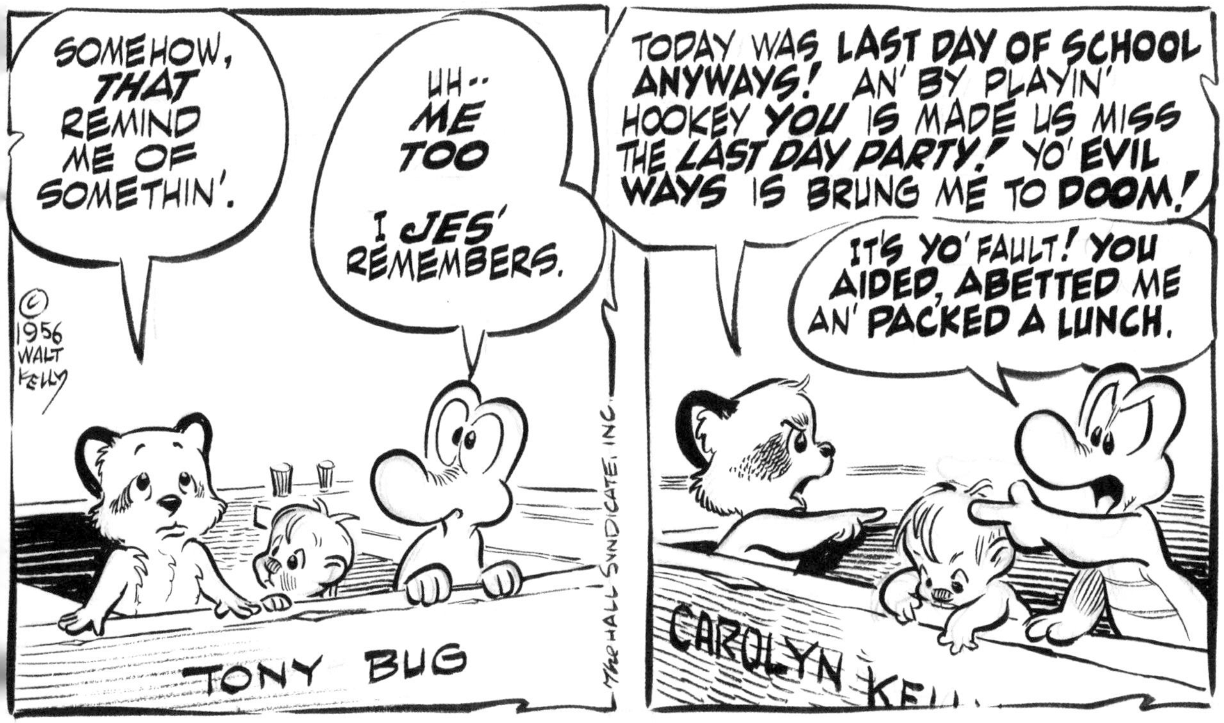
SOMEHOW, THAT REMIND ME OF SOMETHIN'.
UH.. ME TOO
I JES' REMEMBERS.
© 1956 WALT KELLY
TONY BUG
POST-HALL SYNDICATE, INC.
TODAY WAS LAST DAY OF SCHOOL ANYWAYS! AN' BY PLAYIN' HOOKEY YOU IS MADE US MISS THE LAST DAY PARTY! YO' EVIL WAYS IS BRUNG ME TO DOOM!
IT'S YO' FAULT! YOU AIDED, ABETTED ME AN' PACKED A LUNCH.
CAROLYN KE

floor. The original smoke-filled room—the one that inspired the expression—was Room 404 of the Blackstone Hotel in Chicago: it was there in 1920 that the Republican elite resolved a deadlocked convention by settling the party's nomination on Warren G. Harding, at the time a relatively unknown politician but handsome and dignified-looking, just as a president ought to be.

8/13 – The fellow in the brown derby was Al Smith, erstwhile governor of New York who the Democrats ran unsuccessfully against Herbert Hoover in 1928.

8/17 – The Democrats convention ended on this date, but since Kelly produced the strip 4–5 weeks prior to publication, he couldn't know the outcome. And so neither could Pogo or Porky. As noted earlier, Stevenson was re-nominated by the Democrats, but in an unprecedented move, Stevenson did not pick his running mate but let the convention delegates make the choice; they chose Estes Kefauver, who had achieved national prominence by investigating "organized crime" a few years before, investigating comic books as part of the process. In 1954, one of those who testified before the committee and was interrogated by Senator Kefauver was Walt Kelly.

8/27 – When Joseph Stalin died March 5, 1953, he was replaced as head of the Russian state by Georgy Malenkov, but Malenkov's reign was short: he was forced to resign on February 8, 1955 and was replaced as Premier by Nikolai Bulganin, who was the choice of Nikita Khrushchev, First Secretary of the Communist Party, who, with the support of the army, was effectively the strongman ruler of the Soviet Union. The relationship between the First Secretary and the Premier is accurately depicted in Kelly's conception of Khrushchev as a pirate with Bulganin as a cockatoo (taking the customary role assigned to a parrot) on his shoulder, endorsing his every utterance with an approving "You said it."

Khrushchev appears as a pig partly because the pudgy balding leader looked somewhat like a pig, but Kelly's choice of animal may have been influenced by George Orwell's bitting satirical allegory, *Animal Farm.* Published in the summer of 1945, the book tells the story of how the animals on Mr. Jones's farm took over and banished him. The leader of the revolt was a pig, Old Major. When he dies, his place is taken by a pair of younger pigs, who effectively subjugate the rest of the animals and subvert the principles of the revolution. Their original motto, "All animals are equal," is eventually expanded to accommodate the new ruling pigs—"All animals are equal but some animals are more equal than others." As an attack on post-revolutionary Russia, the book offered pigs as political opponents of democracy, the villains of the modern age in America.

A prevailing joke of the fifties alleged that communists were always claiming to have invented everything from rockets to radios, not to mention the light bulb, television, and various social/political practices, all of which are blatantly the innovations of Western culture. Hence, the Pig here claims "we" invented laughing gas and, in the next strip, discovered America and, later yet, invented "hollowness." The joke continues with the Pig's return in October.

9/17 – The return of the Cowbirds, who, in the strip, represent Communists, "fellow travelers."

10/1 – An echo of Shakespeare's *Hamlet* in "to plan ... to plot ... perchance to scheme."

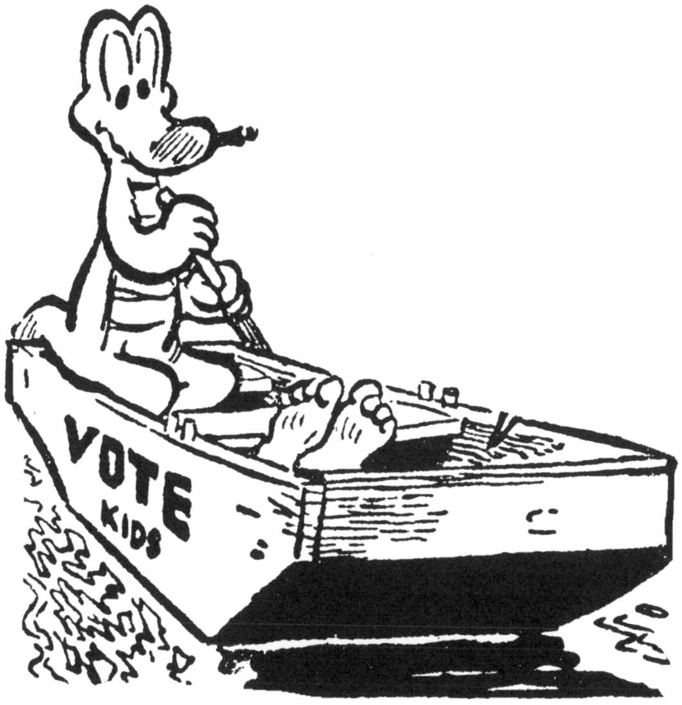
VOTE
KIDS

10/23 – Stephen Kelly is one of the cartoonist's sons.

10/24 – Chet Huntley and David Brinkley had teamed up to cover the nominating conventions in August, and they had generated such favorable viewer response that NBC paired them for its evening news program. *The Huntley-Brinkley Report* debuted on October 29 (the week after this strip ran) with Huntley reporting from New York and Brinkley from Washington. When Huntley retired in February 1970, the program was renamed *The NBC Evening News*.

10/26 – The now nonexistent original plan was probably Stalin's; de-Stalinization continued.

10/30 – In anticipation of Election Day, Kelly does his patriotic duty to get out the vote.

11/7 – The Dewey in Chug Chug's paper is not, as one might assume, Thomas Dewey, the Republican candidate for president who lost a close election in 1948 to incumbent Democrat Harry Truman.

The Dewey in Chug Chug's paper is Admiral George Dewey, a hero of the Spanish-American War who attacked and defeated the Spanish fleet at Manila Bay in the Phillippines on May 1, 1898. It was this Dewey who issued the memorable order that launched the battle of Manila Bay almost as it was being won: "You may fire when you are ready," he told his next in command, Captain Charles Gridley. The Spanish were so surprised that the battle was over in six hours; only one American life was lost.

11/9 – The PAA on the Mouse's luggage recalls that Kelly sometimes drew an elaborate, full-page illustration for the Pan American Airlines ad in the annual convention program of the National Cartoonists Society.

11/17 – When Russia launched Sputnik 1, it was the first artificial satellite to go into orbit. But that didn't happen until next year, October 4, 1957, so maybe Kelly's swampland was first.

11/19 – The XVI summer Olympics were held in Australia, beginning November 22, their summer being our winter. The taller kangaroo is singing a makeshift verse of "Waltzing Matilda," which, if not officially the Australian national anthem, ought to be. "Once a jolly swagman camped by a billabong / Under the

shade of a Coolibah tree / And he sang as he watched and waited til his billy boiled—You'll come a waltzing Matilda with me." In Australian slang (the most extreme instance of which is called "strine," as indecipherable as rhyming cockney), a *swagman* is a hobo; his bedroll or satchel holding his belongings is his *matilda.* A *billabong* is a waterhole; *fair dinkum* means "true, genuine." *Cobber* is not a name but slang for "friend or pal."

A platypus, native only to Australia, is one of the world's oddest creatures—duck-billed, beaver-tailed, otter-footed, it is the only mammal that lays eggs instead of giving birth.

The ensuing sequence regales us with a lot of Australian slang, the meanings of which are doubtless apparent, in a general way, from context. We'll explain only a few of the more fortified of them.

11/23 – *Stone the crows;* an exclamation of shock.

11/24 – *Blighty,* England.

11/26 – *Jackaroo,* a male ranch hand, probably young; *grafter,* a person, perhaps an operator or conman, fellow hobo; *woop woop,* a small undistinguished town or place a long way from civilization; *joey,* a baby kangaroo.

11/29 – *Swaggie,* familiar form of swagman; *digger,* a miner or a soldier; *wombat,* a burrowing marsupial with short legs and a rudimentary tail (also, a simpleminded person who eats roots and leaves).

12/1 – *Cove,* an individual (like cobber except not usually used in direct address).

12/6 – The bandicoot exaggerates: a *natatorium* is a building with a built-in swimming pool.

12/7 – *Bandicoot,* another variety of marsupial.

12/10 – *Bonzer,* the best.

12/13 – *Stonkered,* drunk (or killed in action).

1955 SUNDAYS

1/2 – Like all Sunday comic strips, *Pogo* was laid out in a way that permitted newspapers to drop portions of the strip in order to reduce the space the feature took, thereby permitting the paper to cram more comic strips onto a single page of the Sunday funnies. In *Pogo's* case, the first tier of panels was the portion that could be discarded, and many newspapers published only the remaining panels, beginning with the one that carried the day's date in the lower left-hand corner. From the writer's perspective, that meant delaying the official "start" of the strip until, in the strip at hand, the fourth panel, while also devising something stand-alone humorous for the first three panels, something also related, however vaguely, to the rest of the day's installment. The fifth panel in many *Pogo* strips of this design was also a "throwaway" panel and could be discarded without damage to the internal continuity of the day's strip.

5/8 – The Secretary of Treasury at the time was George M. Humphrey.

5/15 – The Fulton Fish Market was on South Street near

the Brooklyn Bridge in New York. For "onions and eels," see the preceding note for the daily 10/22/55.

5/22 – Patricia LaHatte was a writer, artist, and newspaper executive, beginning in 1939 as art editor of the *Atlanta Journal's* Sunday magazine. In 1954, she became promotion manager of both the *Journal* and the *Constitution* (now, one paper, the *Journal-Consitution)* and the first female member of the paper's executive committee.

7/17 – The Bear is misquoting the title of a famous Temperance song, "Lips That Touch Liquor Shall Never Touch Mine."

7/24 – "Trippin' the light fantastic" is a fragment of the lyric of the popular song "The Sidewalks of New York." "Goodbye sweet prince" is taken, perhaps, from Shakespeare's *Hamlet.* "Farewell, adieu, auf wiedersehen" is from the chorus of a song in *The Sound of Music.*

7/31 – Ambergris, which comes from some species of sperm whale, is a valuable raw material in the manufacture of perfume.

8/7 – With "five feet too," Churchy is singing and slightly mangling the lyric of the popular song "Has Anybody Seen My Girl" (or "Gal").

9/11 – Eisenhower played golf, thereby encouraging others to do the same.

9/25 – "Something's rotten in Denmark" is barely misquoted from Shakepeare's *Hamlet.*

12/4 – "Frummage" looks a lot like "fromage," French for "cheese."

12/25 – A cassowary is a large, flightless bird related to the emu (and, even, the ostrich), native to the rain forests of northern Australia and New Guinea.

1956 SUNDAYS

1/8 – "Haversack," appearances here to the contrary notwithstanding, is not a verb: it is a noun, the name of a smallish backpack.

3/25 – Raymond S. Coll was the editor of the *Honolulu Advertiser* from 1922 until he retired in 1959.

6/3 – A wicket is the playing surface for the sport of cricket. When the ground is wet, the wicket is sticky.

6/17 – Carl Rose was a prolific magazine cartoonist, a contributor to *The New Yorker* since its first issue in 1925. He lived in Rowayton, Connecticut, which is the only clue we have for connecting the name on the boat to the cartoonist in *The New Yorker.*

7/1 – The Battle of Trafalgar (October 21, 1805) in the Napoleonic Wars was one of the most celebrated naval engagements in history. Under the command of Admiral Lord Nelson, the outnumbered British fleet of twenty-seven ships of the line defeated the French and Spanish fleet, destroying twenty-two of its thirty-three ships without losing one of its own.

7/15 – Richard D. Peters was the chief editorial writer for the *Cleveland Press* from 1947 until 1957, when the Scripps-Howard chain made him its public service director. *Scuppers* are to boats and ships what roof gutters are to houses: located at

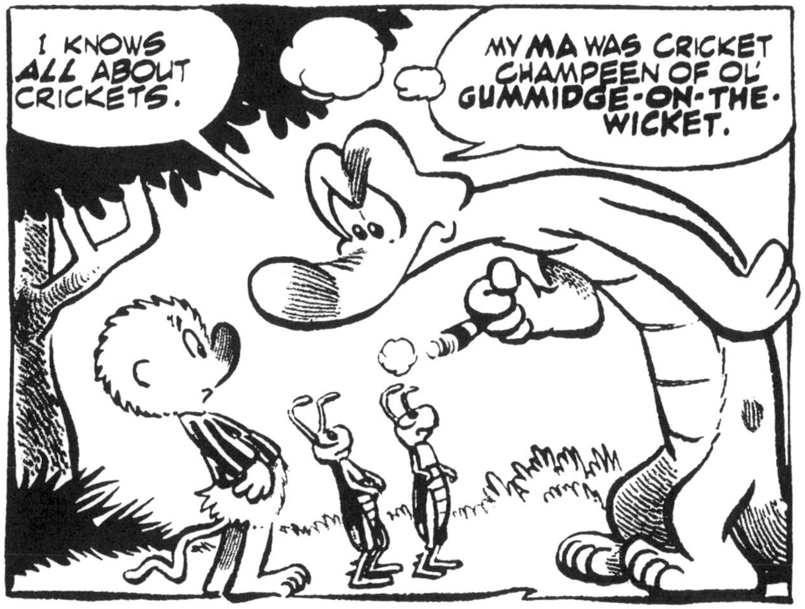
I KNOWS ALL ABOUT CRICKETS.
MY MA WAS CRICKET CHAMPEEN OF OL' GUMMIDGE-ON-THE-WICKET.

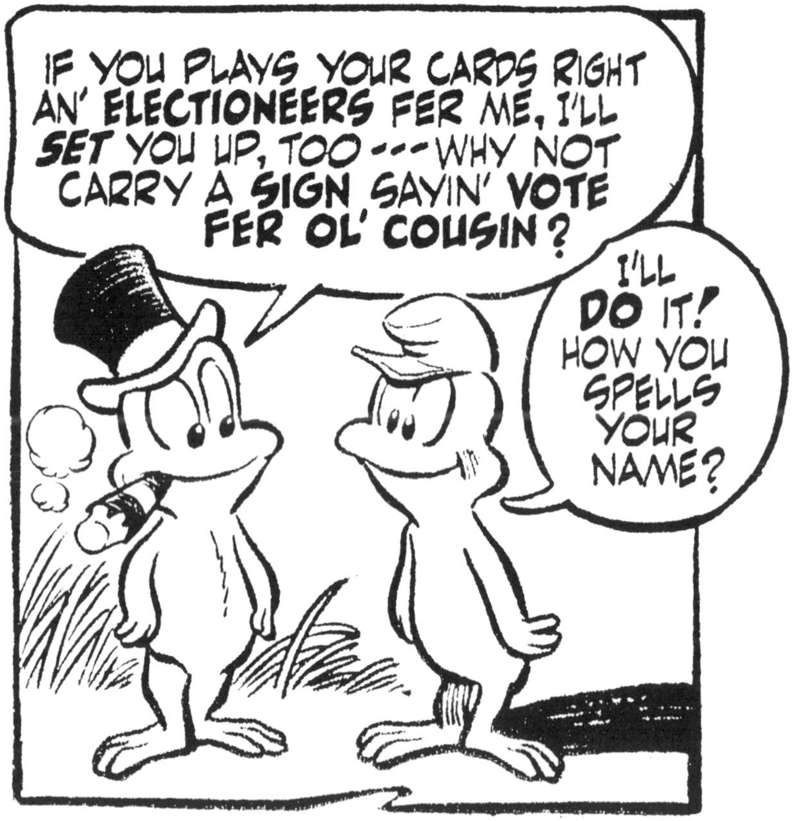
IF YOU PLAYS YOUR CARDS RIGHT AN' ELECTIONEERS FER ME, I'LL SET YOU UP, TOO---WHY NOT CARRY A SIGN SAYIN' VOTE FER OL' COUSIN?
I'LL DO IT! HOW YOU SPELLS YOUR NAME?

deck level, scuppers permit rainwater to drain away without waterlogging the vessel.

7/22 – Kelly's troubles with the proper use of the word *staunch* may ante-date the daily strip published 7/13. This Sunday strip would have been sent to the syndicate before the daily strip; perhaps Churchy's mangling of nautical terms here led Kelly astray when he next used the word—in the 7/13 daily. Neither use—in the daily or here in the Sunday—had anything to do with nautical matters.

A ship's *mizzen mast* is the shorter mast aft of the main mast; mizzen top would refer to a second sail, one located on the mizzen mast above the main sail. The Rabbit confuses *captain* with *capstan*, a vertical axeled device for tightening ropes; similar to a windlass, the axle of which is horizontal. *Marlin spikes* are tapered wooden or metal rods used with rope work aboard ship, splicing or knotting. The *gunwhales* of a ship are the top edges of the vessel's sides, originally strengthened to serve as platforms for guns. *Keelhauling* was a form of punishment: the miscreant was tied to a rope that looped beneath the ship, then he was dropped overboard and pulled under the ship—under the keel—to the opposite side of the boat. *Sheer, reep,* and *batten* are not terms used as Church is using them: sheering keeps the ship clear of its anchor; reeving (not reeping) involves passing a rope through a hole, ring, pulley or block; and a batten is a strip of wood used to fasten down the edges of coverings of hatches during bad weather. A *boat hook* is a long pole with a hook at the end, used for reaching out from a dock to the edge of a boat or vice versa to bring the boat alongside.

7/29 – Kenneth W. Parker began working as a general assignment reporter at the *Arkansas Gazette* in Little Rock in 1950 and was state news editor 1952–1960.

10/28 – Charles C. Pyle (1882–1939) was also known as "Cash and Carry" Pyle. He was a promoter and sports agent, and a generally colorful figure.

11/4 – Kelly does his patriotic duty for Sunday readers, urging them to vote on Tuesday.

12/2 – *Zoster* is another word for shingles; *zosterology*, therefore, must be the science of shingles, one of those sciences associated with the other disciplines Congersman Frog mentions.

12/9 – Clemency de Fois Gras, Scion of Scincinnati, is all nonsense, which the word-play sounds of the last two words ought to hint at. And do.

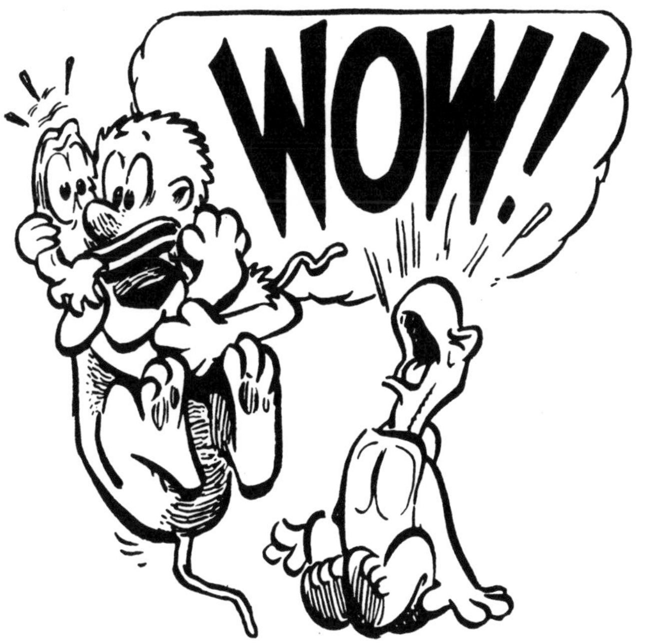
WOW!

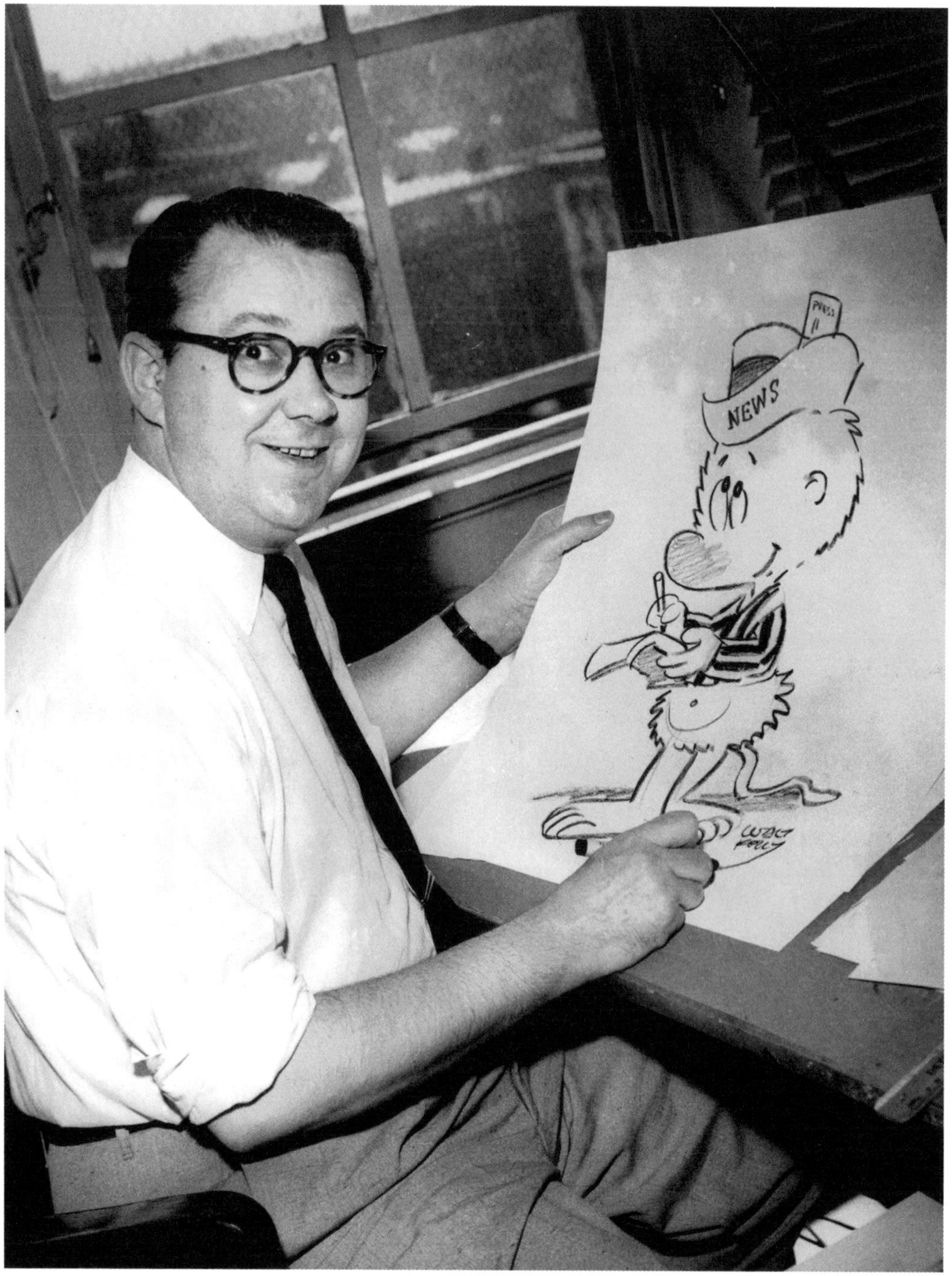
PRESS
NEWS

ABOUT WALT KELLY

By Mark Evanier

At some early age, this person named Walter Crawford Kelly Jr. became a kid with a flair for drawing and a good sense of humor. He stayed pretty much that way all his life, even as the drawing got better and the humor reached an ever-widening audience.

Birth? August 25, 1913 in Philadelphia. And then the family hurriedly relocated to Bridgeport, Connecticut. As early as high school, cartooning was one interest; journalism, another. Seemed pretty obvious that he should combine the two and become a newspaper strip cartoonist. The *Bridgeport Post* got the first salvos and then it was on to other cartooning jobs in other markets, some in New York City.

Another Walt, this one named Disney, was on a talent search to which Kelly applied. Accepted, it was off to Hollywood he went. There, he learned to animate as he applied his skills new and old to, among other films, *Dumbo*, *Pinocchio*, and *Fantasia*. When a strike divided the studio in 1941, Kelly decided it was a good time to get out of animation and Southern California—in that order. But he didn't leave behind Disney characters altogether. He began drawing stories and covers for Western Printing and Lithography, the firm responsible for *Walt Disney's Comics and Stories* and other best-selling four-color ephemera published and distributed by Dell Comics.

This led to other, non-Disney funnybooks that Dell/Western issued ... like *Animal Comics*, an anthology whose first issue (December 1942) introduced Pogo, Albert, and others. Crude by later Walt Kelly standards, the first stories nonetheless had life and energy and they were also wildly funny. It was all there in the drawing, which was fluid with recognizable human attitudes grafted expertly onto animal forms. It was also all there in the dialogue, where characters spoke in dialects not quite Southern but not quite Anywhere Else. It was kind of a Walt Kelly accent, infectious if not irresistible. Anyway, it sure went well with the pictures.

In 1948, he went to work doing art and political cartoons for *The New York Star*. Pogo and his friends, by now somewhat matured in design and purpose, tagged along. He put them to work in a six-day-a-week strip and when the *Star* celebrated its first anniversary by going out of business, Walt's swampland band endured. Soon, the Hall Syndicate began to do what it did, which was to syndicate.

More and more papers snatched it up. A Sunday page was added. Western/Dell contracted for a new comic book—all *Pogo*, all the time. Soon, Simon and Schuster contracted for paperbacks reprinting the newspaper strips ... but Kelly didn't just hand them proof sheets to print from. He jigsawed them, repasting horizontal strips into vertical pages, cutting a little of this, adding a little of that. New material plus effort created books that really worked in book form. In cities where *Pogo* ran, avid fans pounced on them. In cities where *Pogo* didn't yet run, curious readers bought, read, fell in love, and demanded their local paper pick up the possum.

Kelly won acclaim and also awards. He got the National Cartoonists Society's Reuben Award in '51 and was its President from '54 to '56. Pogo, meanwhile, was being promoted for a less important presidency, that of the U.S. of A. Admirers in the strip and the real world nominated him every four years and sometimes if the mood struck them, more often. He occasionally got more votes than real people who thought they were actually running.

Not everyone understood *Pogo* but *Pogo* understood everyone. New characters arrived weekly. They all seemed instantly familiar to us because they were all beings we'd met and knew or followed in our world. They just weren't literally animals before. At times, they resembled prominent names in the news and what Kelly did with them caused some editors to moan, "Too political," and drop the feature. If it bothered Kelly, it didn't stop him. He kept on producing the strip he wanted to do, the way he wanted to do it.

Only failing health stopped him, which it did in 1972 and then he died in '73. Friends and family still miss him in all the expected ways. He was by all accounts as funny and lovable a character as any he drew ... and the sum and total of them all. Readers who were just readers miss him their own way. When they get to the end of this multi-volume reprint set, they'll have read all twenty-six years of *Pogo* and they'll all ask aloud, "What? Is that all?" Too much Walt Kelly is never enough.

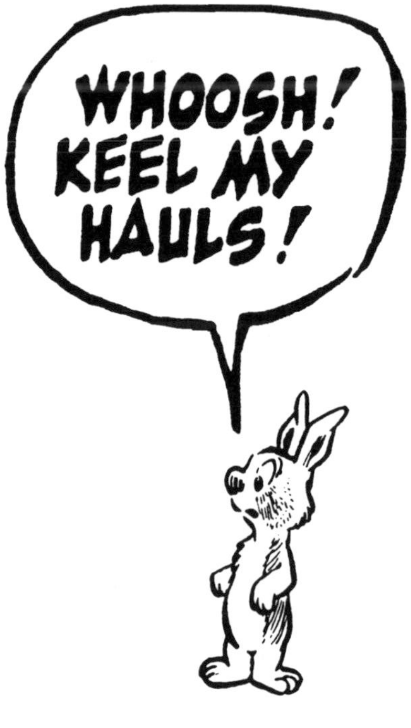
WHOOSH! KEEL MY HAULS!

NOTEWORTHY QUOTES

"The place to settle a argumints is at the end! Not at the start ... You go stoppin' fights afore they gits goin' an' you gone have nothin' but dull quiet ..."

—Grackle, March 8, 1955

"Six jacks beats five kings any day."

—Bats, March 12, 1955

"If you can't lick them—enjoin them!"

—P.T. Bridgeport, May 24, 1955

"A man can't help his own natural beauty, son."

—Albert Alligator, June 20, 1955

"You can believe in some of the people most of the time and in most of the people some of the time—but you'll never believe all of the people you can believe in all of the time."

—Porky Pine, June 29, 1955

"They is inseparable—always fightin' together like the good friends they is ..."
"Yup, only yestiddy the frog says 'They is two sides to every argument an' both of 'em's mine!'"

—Pogo Possum and Porky Pine exchange, July 9, 1955

"Mebbe you got a point there, Owl—an' if you combs yo' hair jes' right nobody'll notice."

—Porky Pine, July 16, 1955

"I challenge you to a dagger duel at 100 paces."

—Churchy La Femme, August 19, 1955

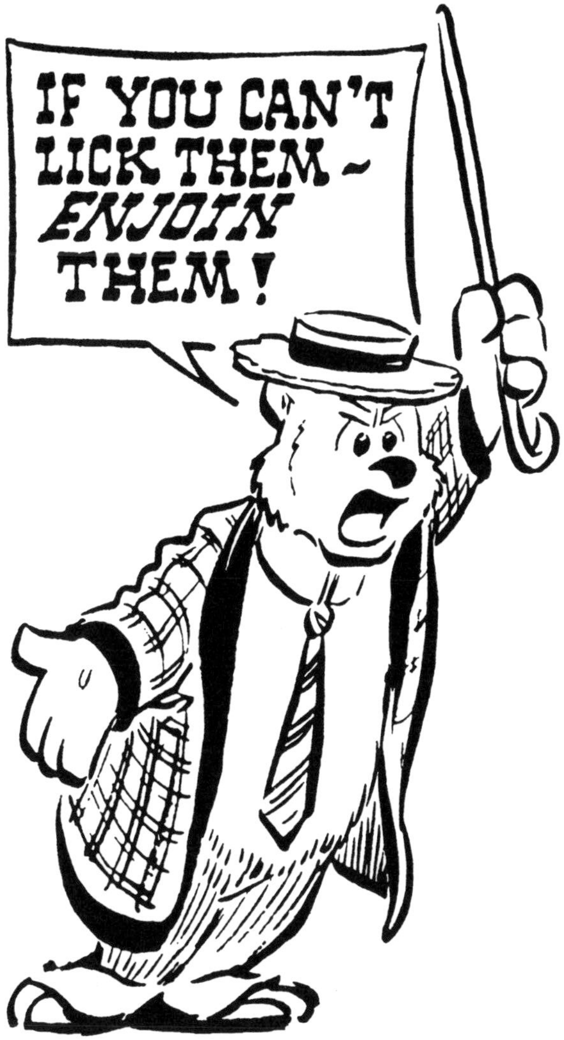
IF YOU CAN'T LICK THEM – ENJOIN THEM!

"You is a leaky bag of doughnut holes."
—Albert Alligator, September 1, 1955

"The best break anybody ever gets is in bein' alive in the first place ... An' you don't unnerstan' what a perfect deal it is until you realizes that you ain't gone be stuck with it forever, either."
—Porky Pine, September 15, 1955

"I saw my doody an' I dood it."
—Grizzle Bear, October 23, 1955

"Dee-stroy a son's faith in his father will you—?! What queasy quackery!"
—bug, November 1, 1955

"I swear that turtle gets brainlesser and brainlesser every day."
—Howland Owl, November 8, 1955

"Oh, you is all gone git a nasty letter from my lawyer in the mornin'."
—Grizzle Bear, November 13, 1955

"As usual, your quietly stupid dignity clothes a mind as alert as a bucket full of cold mutton fat."
—Howland Owl, November 27, 1955

"You looks puzzled—mebbe my fresh young brain kin help on account I ain't used it today."
—Churchy La Femme, December 3, 1955

"It's a hard s'pose but I'll do it."
—Churchy La Femme, December 21, 1955

"When she learn to talk she kin tell us what her name is—no sense in guessin' this way."
—Churchy La Femme, February 10, 1956

"You is caught yo'self a case of the uglies what's fit to curdle a whole herd of cattle."
—Miz Beaver, March 1, 1956

"Yo' mammy is prouder'n' a purple pig."
—Miz Woodpecker, March 12, 1956

"Whoosh! Keel my hauls!"
—Bun Rabbit, March 29, 1956

"I asks my pop—He knows perty near everything—an' what he don't know he kin make up—Someways he's better at that last part."
—Rackety Coon child, April 26, 1956

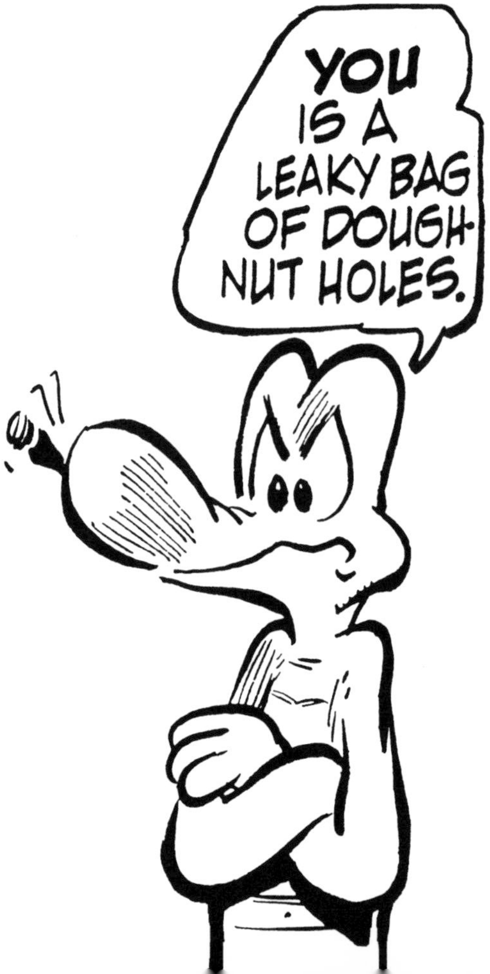
YOU IS A LEAKY BAG OF DOUGH-NUT HOLES.

"We're for vice! What a slogan! Why didn't I think of that?"

—Seminole Sam, May 2, 1956

"You makes me come all over gulpy."

—Churchy La Femme, May 12, 1956

"Is you gonna take us fishin' or is you gonna continue settin' there like a lump in a lump factory?"

—worms, May 13, 1956

"We figger you is about as common as the common man kin git ..."

—Howland Owl, May 14, 1956

"Figures don't lie when there's only one set of books—yours."

—Pig, August 29, 1956

"What good's a secret if nobody knows it but you?"

—Pogo Possum, September 26, 1956

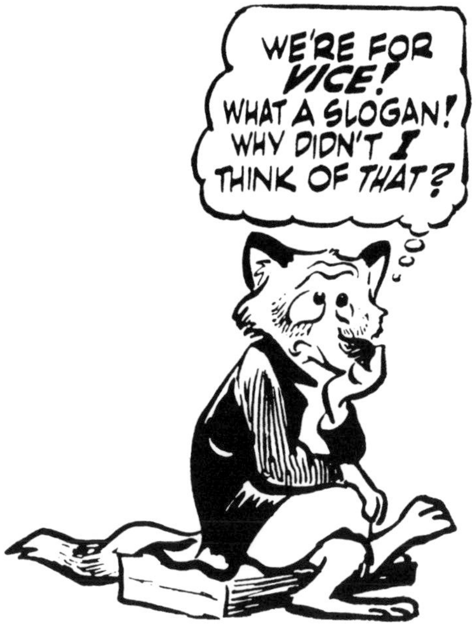
WE'RE FOR VICE! WHAT A SLOGAN! WHY DIDN'T I THINK OF THAT?

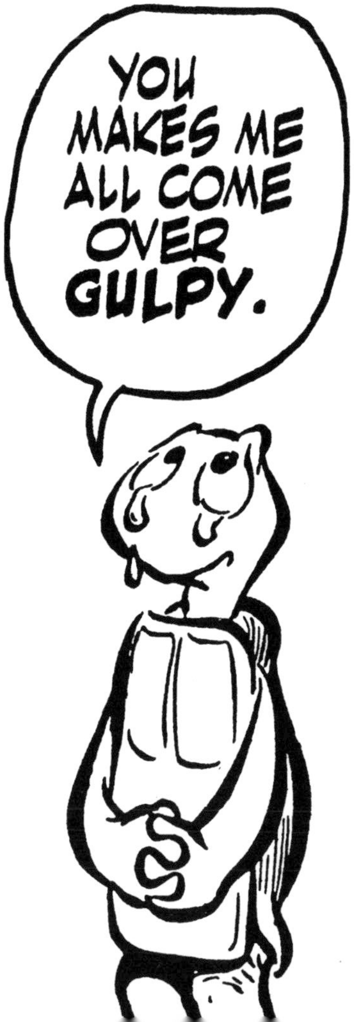
YOU MAKES ME ALL COME OVER GULPY.

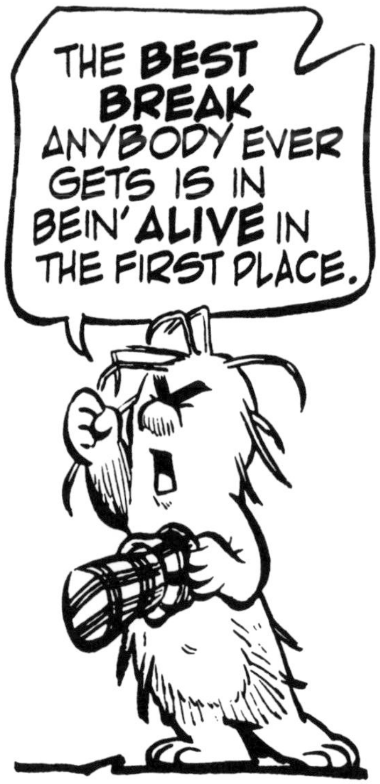
THE BEST BREAK ANYBODY EVER GETS IS IN BEIN' ALIVE IN THE FIRST PLACE.

INDEX OF THE STRIPS

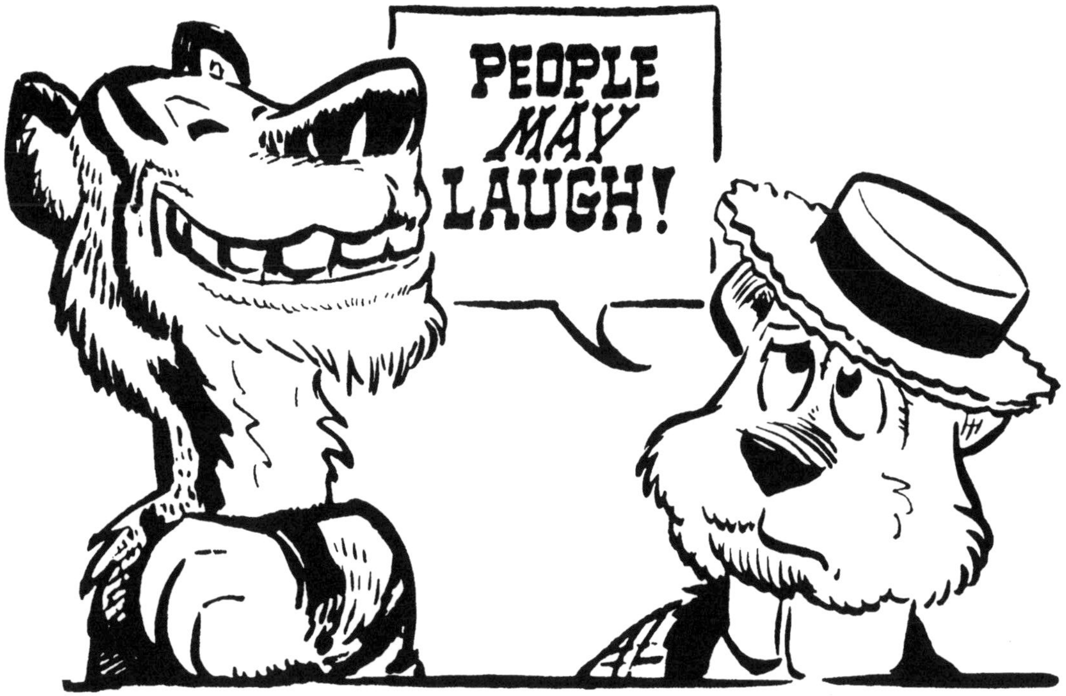
PEOPLE MAY LAUGH!

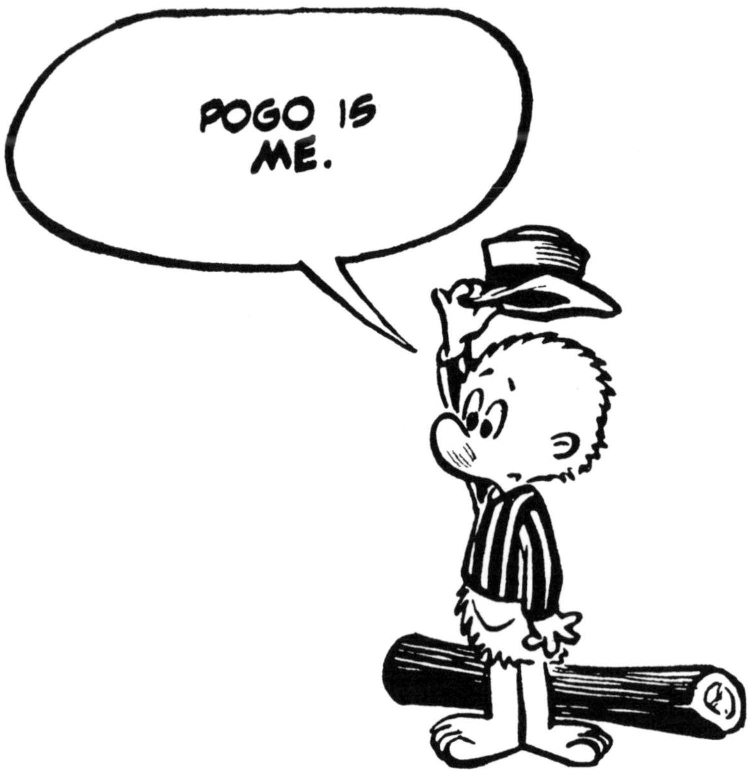
POGO IS ME.

ACKNOWLEDGMENTS

As always, we have folks to thank for making this book happen...

For finding and loaning high quality copies of Walt Kelly's high quality strips, we thank Rick Norwood, Pogo Fan Club President Steve Thompson, and the folks at Ohio State University's Billy Ireland Cartoon Library & Museum.

For supplying images of the Walt Kelly original art used in this volume, we thank Mark Burstein, as well as Jim Halperin and Margaret Croft of Heritage Auctions.

The Newsweek *cover painting seen on page ix and the* Pogo *strip seen on page xi and again on pages 330 and 331 were pieces that Walt Kelly gave to his daughter Carolyn. She gave the painting to Mark Evanier as a Christmas present in December of 2015, and Mark found the rough sketch (seen on page vii) among her personal papers after her death in April of 2017, as well as the drawing on page 319 and the photo of Walt Kelly on page 338.*

Special thanks and a tip of the Pogo Porkpie to Maggie Thompson for impressive indexing and uncanny consultation; to John Plunkett for assistance with the Kelly Archives; to R.C. Harvey for his expert annotating; to Kristy Valenti for expert proofreading; and to all of you Pogo fans for sticking with us.

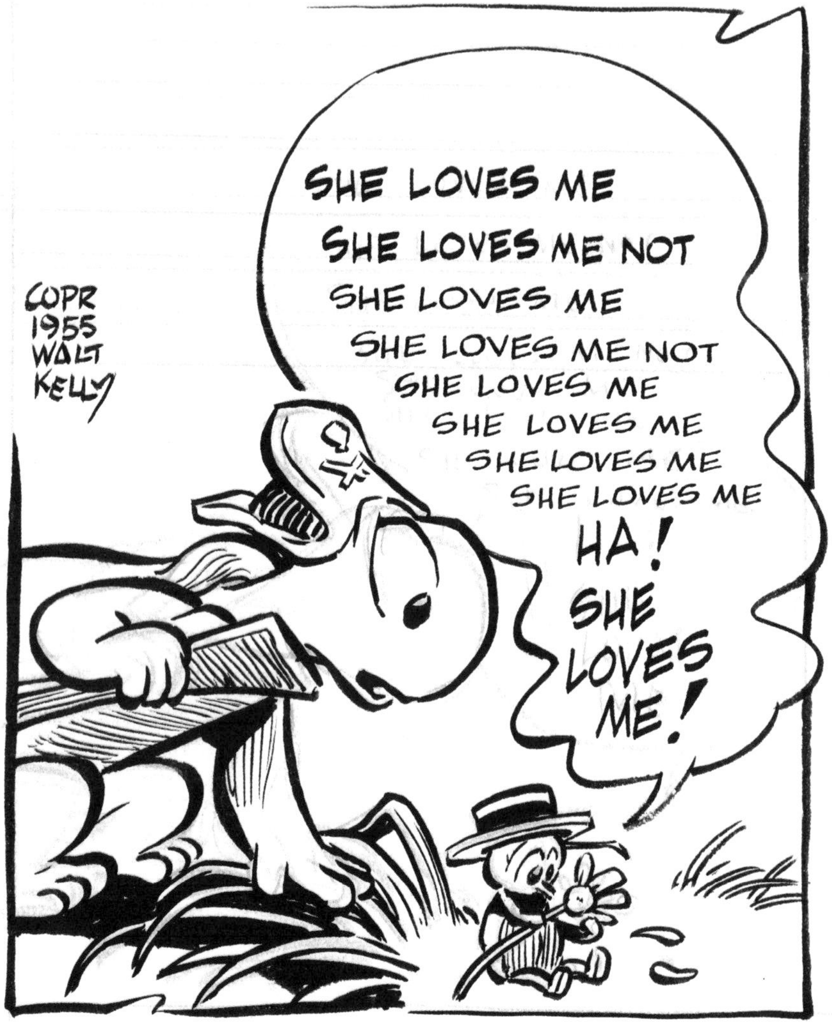
SHE LOVES ME
SHE LOVES ME NOT
SHE LOVES ME
SHE LOVES ME NOT
SHE LOVES ME
SHE LOVES ME
SHE LOVES ME
SHE LOVES ME
HA! SHE LOVES ME!
COPR 1955 WALT KELLY